广东统计年鉴

GUANGDONG STATISTICAL YEARBOOK

2024

（总第40期　No.40）

广　东　省　统　计　局
国家统计局广东调查总队　编

Compiled by
Statistics Bureau of Guangdong Province
Survey Office Of National Bureau of Statistics In Guangdong

中国统计出版社
China Statistics Press

图书在版编目（CIP）数据

广东统计年鉴. 2024 = Guangdong Statistical Yearbook 2024 : 汉、英 / 广东省统计局，国家统计局广东调查总队编. -- 北京 : 中国统计出版社，2024. 9.
ISBN 978-7-5230-0461-6

Ⅰ. ①广… Ⅱ. ①广… ②国… Ⅲ. ①统计资料一广东一2024一年鉴一汉、英 Ⅳ. ①C832.65-54

中国国家版本馆 CIP 数据核字第 20247PP505 号

广东统计年鉴 2024

作　　者/ 广东省统计局　国家统计局广东调查总队
责任编辑/ 高媛媛
装帧设计/ 广州睡一觉文化艺术发展有限责任公司
出版发行/ 中国统计出版社有限公司
地　　址/ 北京市丰台区西三环南路甲 6 号
邮政编码/ 100073
电　　话/ 邮购（010）63376909　书店（010）68783171
网　　址/ http://www.zgtjcbs.com
印　　刷/ 广州星河印刷有限公司
经　　销/ 新华书店
开　　本/ 890mm×1240mm　1/16
字　　数/ 1450 千字
印　　张/ 43.75
版　　别/ 2024 年 9 月第 1 版
版　　次/ 2024 年 9 月第 1 次印刷
定　　价/ 460.00 元　Price: 460.00yuan(RMB)

本书附同版本 CD-ROM 一张，光盘内容以书面文字为准。
如有印装差错，由本社发行部调换。

《广东统计年鉴2024》
编委会和编辑出版人员

Guangdong Statistical Yearbook 2024
EDITORIAL BOARD AND STAFF

2024

编者说明

一、《广东统计年鉴2024》系统收录了全省及各市、县（区）2023年经济、社会各方面的统计数据，以及1978年以来各个主要时期全省主要统计数据，是一部全面反映广东国民经济和社会发展情况的资料性年刊。

二、本年鉴正文内容分为23个篇章，即：1.综合；2.国民经济核算；3.人口；4.就业和工资；5.固定资产投资；6.对外经济；7.能源、资源和环境；8.财政、银行和保险；9.价格；10.人民生活；11.农业；12.工业；13.建筑业；14.规模以上服务业；15.运输和邮电；16.批发零售业；17.住宿餐饮业和旅游；18.房地产业；19.教育和科技；20.文化和体育；21.卫生、社会福利、社会保障和其他；22.区域经济主要指标；23.县（市、区）主要经济指标。同时，附录有4个篇章：1.全国31个省（市）主要统计指标；2.中国香港特别行政区和中国澳门特别行政区主要统计资料；3.中国台湾省主要统计指标；4.部分国家和地区主要统计资料。

为方便读者使用，各篇章前设有《简要说明》，对本篇章的主要内容、资料来源、统计范围、统计方法以及历史变动情况予以简要概述，篇末附有《主要统计指标解释》。

三、本年鉴资料主要来自政府各级统计局、国家统计局调查总队的各种统计报表和抽样调查资料；部分资料来自中央部属单位和省直有关部门。附录资料根据国家统计局有关资料整理。

四、本年鉴涉及珠三角、粤东、粤西和粤北的具体划分为：

珠三角包括：广州、深圳、珠海、佛山、惠州、东莞、中山、江门和肇庆。

粤东指汕头、汕尾、潮州和揭阳。

粤西指阳江、湛江和茂名。

粤北指韶关、河源、梅州、清远和云浮。

五、资料中所使用的度量衡单位，除灌溉、播种面积照顾我国使用习惯继续用“亩”为单位外，其余均采用国际统一标准计量单位。

六、本年鉴中涉及到的历史数据，均以最新出版的本年鉴数据为准；年鉴中部分数据合计数或相对数由于单位取舍不同而产生的计算误差，均未做机械调整。

七、本年鉴统计表中的符号使用说明：

“…”表示数据不足本表最小单位数；

“#”表示其中主要项；

“空格”表示该项统计指标数据不详或无该项数据；

“①”表示本表下有注解。

八、与《广东统计年鉴2023》相比较，本年鉴根据现行统计调查制度和统计工作开展情况，主要作如下修订：

为了满足统计调查划分经济类型需要，国家统计局会同市场监管总局对《关于划分企业登记注册类型的规定》（国统字〔2011〕86号）（以下简称“原标准”）进行修订，联合印发《关于市场主体统计分类的划分规定》（国统字〔2023〕14号）（以下简称“新标准”），本年鉴对相关分组按“新标准”作出相应调整。

1.修订工作背景

原标准是由国家统计局和原国家工商总局于1998年共同制定印发，并于2011年进行修订。实施以来，该标准为开展统计调查、统计分析和市场监管等工作提供了重要支撑。近年来,《中华人民共和国外商投资法》《中华人民共和国市场主体登记管理条例》等新法律法规陆续出台实施，原《中华人民共和国公司登记管理条例》《中华人民共和国企业法人登记管理条例》《中华人民共和国私营企业暂行条例》等法规已被废止，原标准所依据相关法律法规发生重大变化。为适应市场监管部门登记注册管理范围从“企业”扩大为“市场主体”的新变化，确保依法依规开展统计工作，国家统计局会同市场监管总局于2022年起开展该项标准修订工作，在广泛征求各专业各地方和相关部门意见建议的基础上，于2023年1月联合印发《关于市场主体统计分类的划分规定》（“新标准”)。

2. 修订主要内容

（1）拓展适用范围

为了更全面覆盖统计调查对象，新标准按照市场主体登记注册管理实际对分类范围作相应调整，从“企业”扩大至所有“市场主体”，增加了“农民专业合作社（联合社)”和“个体工商户”等类别。

（2）取消相关类别

由于《中华人民共和国私营企业暂行条例》已被废止，根据《中华人民共和国公司法》《中华人民共和国个人独资企业法》《中华人民共和国合作企业法》，将相关“私营有限责任公司”“私营股份有限公司”分别列入“有限责任公司”“股份有限公司”类别范围，“私营独资企业”调整为“个人独资企业”，“私营合伙企业”调整为“合伙企业”。

（3）调整分类结构

一是关于“内资企业”。根据《中华人民共和国市场主体登记管理条例》规定，将原内资企业分类“国有企业”“集体企业”“股份合作企业”“联营企业”“有限责任公司”“股份有限公司”“私营企业”“其他企业”等8个类别调整为“有限责任公司”“股份有限公司”“非公司企业法人”“个人独资企业”“合伙企业”“其他内资企业”等6个类别。其中，原“国有企业”“集体企业”“股份合作企业”“联营企业”纳入新类别“非公司企业法人”下；原“私营企业”类别取消（上段已述)。二是关于“外商投资企业”和“港澳台投资企业”。根据《中华人民共和国外商投资法》规定，将原外商投资企业分类“中外合资经营企业”“中外合作经营企业”“外资企业”“外商投资股份有限公司”“其他外商投资企业”等5个类别调整为“外商投资有限责任公司”“外商投资股份有限公司”“外商投资合伙企业”“其他外商投资企业”等4个类别。港澳台投资企业参照外商投资企业分类方法调整。

（4）规范类别名称

根据市场监管部门对登记注册管理的规范名称，分别将原“国有企业”“集体企业”更名为“全民所有制企业（国有企业)”“集体所有制企业（集体企业)”。

（5）统一内资范围

根据《中华人民共和国外商投资法》和相关部门规定，将登记注册为内资公司的有限责任公司（外商投资企业投资)、登记注册为内资公司的股份有限公司（上市、外商投资企业投资）等市场主体，即外商投资企业市场主体在中国境内的再投资市场主体，由原标准中的“外商投资企业”调整为新标准中的“内资企业”相关类别。

此外，“对外经济”部分完善进出口商品分类名称，取消天然气、液化天然气指标，增加塑料制品指标。“价格”部分取消商品零售价格分类指数、各市工业生产者出厂价格指数等指标。“批发零售业”部分取消批发零售业商品销售总额、批发业销售额、零售业销售额、限额以下销售额、限额以下企业和个体户等指标，增加限额以上批发业销售额、限额以上零售业销售额等指标。“房地产业”部分取消土地开发购置指标。“教育和科技”部分取消研究机构数、研究与试验发展（R&D）活动课题（项目）数等指标，增加按活动类型分组的R&D活动情况。“县市区主要经济指标”部分增加农林牧渔业总产值指数、商品房销售面积等指标。

九、由于第五次全国经济普查数据尚未发布，本年鉴部分与经济普查有关的专业如国民经济核算、规模以上服务业等2023年数据均采用年快报数，部分数据暂时无法提供，上述专业2023年年报数据将在2025年出版的统计年鉴反映。

本年鉴在整理编辑过程中，得到省直有关部门和单位的大力支持，在此表示感谢!

EDITOR'S NOTES

Ⅰ. *Guangdong Statistical Yearbook 2024* is an annual statistical publication, which reflects comprehensively the economic and social development of Guangdong Province. It covers data for 2023 and key statistical data in some historically important years since 1978 at the provincial level and the local levels of city, county and district.

Ⅱ. The yearbook contains twenty-three chapters: 1. General Survey; 2. National Accounts; 3. Population; 4. Employment and Wages; 5. Investment in Fixed Assets; 6. Foreign Trade and Economic Cooperation ; 7. Energy, Resources and Environment ; 8. Government Finance, Banking and Insurance; 9. Prices; 10. People's Living Conditions; 11. Agriculture; 12. Industry; 13. Service Enterprises Above Designated Size;14.Construction; 15. Transport, Postal and Telecommunication Services; 16. Wholesale , Retail Trades and Tourism; 17. Hotels, Catering Services and Tourism; 18. Real Estate 19. Education, Science and Technology; 20. Culture and Sports. 21.Public Health, Social Welfare, Social Insurance and Others; 22. Main Economic Indicators of Economic Regions; 23. Main Economic Indicators of Counties (County-level Cities) and Districts. Meanwhile, four chapters are listed as appendices: 1. Main Statistical Indicators of 31 Provinces and Municipalities; 2. Main Statistics of Hong Kong and Macao Special Administrative Regions; 3. Main Statistical Indicators of Taiwan Province; 4. Main Statistics of Some Countries and Territories. To facilitate readers, the Brief Introduction at the beginning of each chapter provides a summary of the main contents of the chapter, data sources, statistical scope, statistical methods and historical changes. At the end of each chapter, Explanatory Notes on Main Statistical Indicators are included.

Ⅲ. The data in this yearbook are mainly obtained from regular statistical reports and sample surveys conducted by the Statistical Bureaus at all levels of government and Survey Office of the National Bureau of Statistics. Some data are collected from the departments of the central government and the provincial government. Data in the appendices are compiled from statistical publications published by the National Bureau of Statistics and other sources.

Ⅳ. The pearl river delta, east wing, west wing and mountainous areas in the yearbook are divided as following:

The pearl river delta include Guangzhou, Shenzhen, Zhuhai, Foshan, Jiangmen, Dongguan, Zhongshan, Huizhou and Zhaoqing.

The eastern region includes Shantou, Shanwei, Chaozhou and Jieyang.

The western region includes Zhanjiang, Maoming and Yangjiang.

The northern region include Shaoguan, Heyuan, Meizhou, Qingyuan and Yunfu.

Ⅴ. The units of measurement used in the yearbook are internationally standard measurement units, except that the unit of cultivated land and sown areas uses"mu" with regard to the Chinese tradition.

Ⅵ. Please refer to the newly published version of the yearbook for updated historical data. Statistical discrepancies on totals and relative figures due to rounding are not adjusted in the yearbook.

Ⅶ. Notations used in the yearbook:

" … " indicates that the figure is not large enough to be measured with the smallest unit in the table;

" # " indicates a major breakdown of the total;

" blank space " indicates that the data are unknown or are not available;

" ① " indicates footnotes at the end of the table.

Ⅷ. In comparison with Guangdong Statistical Yearbook 2023,following revisions have been made in this new version in terms of the current statistical survey system and the progress of statistical work.

In order to meet the needs of economic classification in statistical surveys, the National Bureau of Statistics together with the State Administration for Market Regulation revised the Regulations on the Classification of Enterprises by Registration Status (Guotongzi [2011] No. 86) (hereinafter referred to as the original standard) and then jointly issued the Regulations on the Classification of Market Entity Statistics (Guotongzi [2023] No. 14) (hereinafter referred to as the new standard). The yearbook has made corresponding adjustments to the relevant groups according to the "new standard".

1. Revision work background

The original standard was jointly formulated and issued by the National Bureau of Statistics and the former State Administration for Industry and Commerce in 1998, and revised in 2011. Since its implementation, this standard has provided important support for conducting statistical surveys, statistical analysis, and market supervision. In recent years, new laws and regulations such as the Foreign Investment Law of the People's Republic of China and the Regulations on the Administration of Market Entity Registration of the People's Republic of China have been successively introduced and implemented. The original Regulations on the Administration of Company Registration of the People's Republic of China, the Regulations on the Administration of Enterprise Legal Person Registration of the People's Republic of China, and the Interim Regulations on Private Enterprises of the People's Republic of China have been abolished, and significant changes have occurred in the relevant laws and regulations on which the original standards were based. In order to adapt to the new changes in the registration and management scope of the market supervision department from "enterprises" to "market entities", and to ensure that statistical work is carried out in accordance with laws and regulations, the National Bureau of Statistics, together with the State Administration for Market Regulation, will carry out the revision of this standard from 2022. Based on extensive solicitation of opinions and suggestions from various professions, localities, and relevant departments, the Regulations on the Classification of Market Entity Statistics (the new standard) will be jointly issued in January 2023.

2. Revision of the main contents

(1) Expand the scope of application

In order to comprehensively cover the statistical survey objects, the new standard adjusts the classification scope according to the actual registration and management of market entities, expanding from enterprises to all market entities, and adding categories such as professional farmers cooperatives and individual businesses and other categories.

(2) Cancel related categories

Due to the abolition of the Provisional Regulations of the People´s Republic of China on Private Enterprises, according to the Company Law of the People´s Republic of China, the Law of the People´s Republic of China on Sole Proprietorship Enterprises, and the Law of the People´s Republic of China on Cooperative Enterprises, the private limited liability corporations and private share-holding limited corporations are respectively included in the categories of limited liability corporations and share-holding limited corporations. The private sole-proprietorship enterprises are adjusted to the sole proprietorship enterprises and the private partnership enterprises are adjusted to partnership enterprises.

(3) Adjust the classification structure

The first is about domestic invested enterprises. According to the Regulations on the Administration of Market Entity Registration of the People´s Republic of China, the original classification of domestic invested enterprises, including "state-owned enterprises", "collective-owned enterprises", "share-holding cooperative enterprises", "joint ownership enterprises", "limited liability corporations", " share-holding limited corporations", "private enterprises" and "other enterprises" have been adjusted to six categories, including "limited liability corporations", "share-holding limited corporations", "non corporate legal entity", " sole proprietorship enterprises", "partnership enterprises" and "other domestic invested enterprises" with which the original " state-owned enterprises", "collective-owned enterprises", "share-holding cooperative enterprises," and "joint ownership enterprises" are included in the new category of "non corporate legal entity"; The original category of "private enterprises" has been cancelled (as mentioned in the previous paragraph). The second is about foreign invested enterprises and enterprises with investment from Hong Kong, Macao, and Taiwan. According to the Foreign Investment Law of the People´s Republic of China, the original classification of foreign invested enterprises, including "Sino foreign joint ventures", "Sino foreign cooperative enterprises", "foreign funded enterprises", "foreign invested share-holding companies", and "other foreign-invested enterprises" are adjusted to four categories: "foreign invested limited liability corporations", "foreign-invested share-holding corporations", "foreign invested partnership enterprises", and "other foreign invested enterprises". Enterprises with investment from Hong Kong, Macao, and Taiwan are adjusted according to the classification method for foreign invested enterprises.

(4) Standardize names of categories

According to the standardized names for registration management by the market supervision department, the original " state-owned enterprises" and "collective-owned enterprises" will be renamed as "state-owned enterprises" and "collective-owned enterprises" respectively.

(5) Unify domestic invested scope

According to the Foreign Investment Law of the People´s Republic of China and relevant departmental regulations, market entities such as limited liability companies registered as domestic invested companies (foreign-invested enterprises investment) and share-holding limited companies registered as domestic companies (listed and foreign-invested enterprises investment), namely the reinvestment market entities of foreign-invested enterprises in China, have been adjusted from the original category of "foreign-invested enterprises" to the relevant category of "domestic enterprises" in the new standard.

In addition, the "Foreign Economy" section has improved the classification names of import and export commodities, cancelled the indicators for natural gas and liquefied natural gas, and added indicators for plastic products. The "Price" section cancels indicators such as the commodity retail price classification index and the factory price index of industrial producers in various cities. The "Wholesale and Retail Industry" has partially cancelled indicators such as total sales of wholesale and retail goods, wholesale sales revenue, retail sales revenue, sales revenue below quota, and sales revenue of enterprises and individual businesses below quota, and increased indicators such as sales revenue of wholesale industry above quota and sales revenue of retail industry above quota. The "Real Estate" has partially cancelled the land development and purchase indicators. The "Education and Technology" section has removed indicators such as the number of research institutions and the number of research and experimental development (R&D) projects, and added R&D activities grouped by activity type. Add indicators such as the total output value index of agriculture, forestry, animal husbandry, and fishery, and the sales area of commercial housing to the "Counties and Districts under City Administration" section.

Ⅸ.Because the result of the Fifth National Economic Census have not yet been released, data of 2023 in this Yearbook related to the census such as national economic account, service above designated size adopt the result of flash annual report. Some data are not offered for the present. The data based on the annual report of these industries will be reflected in the Yearbook 2025.

Acknowledgements: our gratitude goes to relevant departments and units under the provincial government, from which we have received tremendous support when compiling the yearbook.

目　　录

CONTENTS

一、综合

General Survey

五、固定资产投资

Investment in Fixed Assets

六、对外经济

Foreign Economy

七、能源、资源和环境

Energy, Resources and Environment

八、财政、银行和保险

Government Finance，Banking and Insurance

十一、农业

Agriculture

十二、工业
Industry

十三、建筑业

Construction

十四、规模以上服务业

Service Enterprises Above Designated Size

十五、运输和邮电

Transportation，Postal and Telecommunication Services

十七、住宿餐饮业和旅游

Hotels, Catering Services and Tourism

十八、房地产业
Real Estate

十九、教育和科技
Education and Technology

二十、文化与体育

Culture and Sports

二十二、区域主要经济指标

Major Economic Regions

二十三、县（市、区）主要经济指标
Counties and Districts Under City Administration

附录

Appendix

一、综合

GENERAL SURVEY

一 综合

简要说明

一、本篇资料反映广东行政区划、国民经济和社会发展综合资料，并收录了基本单位统计情况。

二、本篇资料分别由广东省民政厅，广东省统计局各专业处、综合统计处、普查中心和国家统计局广东调查总队整理提供。

三、综合统计资料是根据广东省统计局各专业统计年报资料以及国家统计局、广东省有关部门提供的统计资料加工整理而成。

四、基本单位资料中的产业活动单位按“在地”原则，国民经济行业分类标准（GB/T 4754-2017)汇总。

1 General Survey

Brief Introduction

Ⅰ.The summary data in this chapter reflect the divisions of administrative areas, summary data on the national economy and social development, and related indications on.

Ⅱ.The data are prepared and provided by the Civil Affairs Department of Guangdong Province., the Division of Professional Statistics, the Division of Comprehensive Statistics, the Census Center of Statistics Bureau of Guangdong Province, and the Survey Office in Guangdong of National Bureau of Statistics respectively.

Ⅲ.The summary data are processed and prepared on the basis of the annual reports of various specialized fields provided by Statistics Bureau of Guangdong Province and the statistics provided by the National Bureau of Statistics and some related departments of Guangdong Province.

Ⅳ. The data on “Units of Industrial Establishments” of the basic industrial units are prepared on the principle of location and the standard of Industrial Classification of the National Economy(GB/T 4754-2017).

1-1 行政区划（2023年）

Divisions of Administrative Areas (2023)

单位：个 (unit)

市别	City	地级市 Number of Cities at Prefecture Level	县级市 Number of Cities at County Level	县 Number of Counties	自治县 Number of Autonomous Counties	市辖区 Number of Districts under the Jurisdiction of Cities	镇 Number of Towns	乡 Number of Townships	民族乡 Ethnic Townships	街道 Number of Street Communities
全省	**Provincial Total**	**21**	**20**	**34**	**3**	**65**	**1112**	**4**	**7**	**490**
广州	Guangzhou	1				11	34			143
深圳	Shenzhen	1				9				74
珠海	Zhuhai	1				3	15			10
汕头	Shantou	1		1		6	30			37
佛山	Foshan	1				5	21			11
韶关	Shaoguan	1	2	4	1	3	94		1	10
河源	Heyuan	1		5		1	94		1	6
梅州	Meizhou	1	1	5		2	104			6
惠州	Huizhou	1		3		2	48		1	22
汕尾	Shanwei	1	1	2		1	40			14
东莞	Dongguan	1					28			4
中山	Zhongshan	1					15			8
江门	Jiangmen	1	4			3	61			12
阳江	Yangjiang	1	1	1		2	38			10
湛江	Zhanjiang	1	3	2		4	82	2		38
茂名	Maoming	1	3			2	86			26
肇庆	Zhaoqing	1	1	4		3	87		1	17
清远	Qingyuan	1	2	2	2	2	77		3	5
潮州	Chaozhou	1		1		2	41			5
揭阳	Jieyang	1	1	2		2	62	2		24
云浮	Yunfu	1	1	2		2	55			8

注：本行政区划截至2023年底。
Note: The divisions of administrative areas reflect the status at the end of 2023.

1-2 国民经济和社会发展总量与速度指标

指　　标	Item	1978	1990	2000
人口与就业	**Population and Employment**			
人口　　（万人）	**Population　　(10000 persons)**			
年末户籍总人口	Population with Residence Registration at the Year-end	5064.15	6246.32	7498.54
年末常住人口	Permanent Population at the Year-end	5064.15	6347.19	8650.03
男性人口	Male	2586.68	3249.76	4402.87
女性人口	Female	2477.47	3097.43	4247.16
城镇人口	Urban Population		2335.77	4757.52
乡村人口	Rural Population		4011.42	3892.51
就业　　（万人）	**Employment　　(10000 persons)**			
年末就业人员人数	Employed Persons at the Year-end	2275.95	3118.10	3989.32
宏观经济	**Macro Economy**			
国民经济核算　　（亿元）	**National Accounting　　(100 million yuan)**			
地区生产总值	Gross Domestic Product	185.85	1559.03	10810.21
第一产业	Primary Industry	55.31	384.59	986.32
第二产业	Secondary Industry	86.62	615.86	5042.75
第三产业	Tertiary Industry	43.92	558.58	4781.15
人均地区生产总值　　（元）	Per Capita Gross Domestic Product　　(yuan)	370	2484	12817
支出法地区生产总值（亿元）	Gross Domestic Product by Expenditure Approach (100 million yuan)	194.14	1541.99	10810.21
最终消费支出	Final Consumption Expenditures	130.02	938.48	5717.11
居民消费	Household Consumption Expenditures	111.46	807.84	4474.11
政府消费	Government Consumption Expenditures	18.56	130.64	1243.00
资本形成总额	Gross Capital Formation	54.79	502.90	3917.11
固定资本形成总额	Gross Fixed Capital Formation	37.93	336.61	3160.12
存货增加	Changes in Inventories	16.86	166.29	756.99
货物和服务净流出	Net Exports of Goods and Services	9.33	100.61	1175.99
固定资产投资　　（亿元）	**Investment in Fixed Assets　　(100 million yuan)**			
房地产开发投资额	Real Estate Development		32.70	858.61
消费　　（亿元）	**Domestic Trade　　(100 million yuan)**			
社会消费品零售总额	Total Retail Sales of Consumer Goods	79.86	667.36	4320.73
对外贸易　　（亿美元）	**Foreign Trade　　(USD 100 million)**			
货物进出口总额	Total Exports and Imports		418.98	1700.42
出口额	Exports		222.21	918.49
进口额	Imports		196.77	781.94
利用外资	**Foreign Capital Utilized**			
实际使用外资金额（亿美元）	Amount of Foreign Capital Actually Utilized　　(USD 100 million)		14.60	122.37
实际使用外资金额　　（亿元）	Amount of Foreign Capital Actually Utilized　　(RMB 100 million)			
财政　　（亿元）	**Government Finance　　(100 million yuan)**			
地方一般公共预算收入	Local Public Budgetary Revenue	41.82	131.02	910.56
地方一般公共预算支出	Local Public Budgetary Expenditure	28.70	150.69	1069.86
价格指数　　（上年=100）	**Price Indices　　(preceding year=100)**			
居民消费价格指数	Consumer Price Index		97.5	101.4
工业生产者出厂价格指数	Producer Price Index for Manufactured Goods			103.4
工业生产者购进价格指数	Producer Price Index for Purchased Goods			110.9
能源生产与消费（万吨标准煤）	**Production and Consumption of Energy　　(10000 tons of SCE)**			
能源生产总量	Total Energy Production		1006.24	3711.69
能源消费总量	Total Energy Consumption		4044.28	9447.70

Principal Aggregate Indicators on National Economic and Social Development and Growth Rates

2010	2022	2023	速度指标(%) Indices and Growth Rates (%)								
			指数(2023为以下各年) Index (2023 as percentage of the following years)					平均增长速度 Average Annual Growth Rate			
			1978	1990	2000	2010	2022	1979–2023	1991–2023	2001–2023	2011–2023
8521.55	10049.72	10146.21	200.4	162.4	135.3	119.1	101.0	1.6	1.5	1.3	1.4
10440.94	12656.80	12706.00	250.9	200.2	146.9	121.7	100.4	2.1	2.1	1.7	1.5
5444.95	6673.80	6689.00	258.6	205.8	151.9	122.8	100.2	2.1	2.2	1.8	1.6
4995.99	5983.00	6017.00	242.9	194.3	141.7	120.4	100.6	2.0	2.0	1.5	1.4
6909.85	9465.40	9583.00		410.3	201.4	138.7	101.2		4.4	3.1	2.5
3531.09	3191.40	3123.00		77.9	80.2	88.4	97.9		-0.8	-1.0	-0.9
6051.00	6904.00	7057.00	310.1	226.3	176.9	116.6	102.2	2.5	2.5	2.5	1.2
45944.62	129513.55	135673.16	13552.0	3214.5	776.4	233.6	104.8	11.5	11.1	9.3	6.7
2199.60	5350.09	5540.70	878.8	368.2	244.3	168.6	104.8	4.9	4.0	4.0	4.1
22917.43	52620.72	54437.26	25113.1	5110.5	849.5	217.6	104.8	13.1	12.7	9.7	6.2
20827.59	71542.74	75695.21	17717.9	3112.2	800.5	256.8	104.7	12.2	11.0	9.5	7.5
44669	102217	106985	5372.1	1590.9	516.4	189.5	104.7	9.3	8.7	7.4	5.0
45944.62	129513.55										
22501.78	65167.52										
17702.35	48484.05										
4799.43	16683.47										
18226.60	54600.37										
17035.10	48448.61										
1191.50	6151.76										
5216.24	9745.65										
3659.69	15096.93	13693.33		41875.6	1594.8	374.2	90.7		20.0	12.7	10.5
16991.39	44882.92	47494.86	59472.7	7116.8	1099.2	279.5	105.8	15.3	13.8	11.0	7.8
7851.13	12423.95	11799.20		2816.2	693.9	150.3	95.0		10.6	8.8	3.2
4531.91	7961.30	7729.29		3478.4	841.5	170.6	97.1		11.4	9.7	4.2
3319.22	4462.65	4069.91		2068.4	520.5	122.6	91.2		9.6	7.4	1.6
202.61											
	1819.02	1591.64					87.5				
4517.04	13260.88	13850.78	33120.0	10571.5	1521.1	306.6	104.4	13.8	15.2	12.6	9.0
5421.54	18533.08	18527.03	64554.1	12294.8	1731.7	341.7	100.0	15.5	15.7	13.2	9.9
103.1	102.2	100.4									
103.2	103.0	98.5									
107.3	104.1	97.6									
4858.07	9647.31										
25445.22	36519.05										

1-2 续表 1

指　　标	Item	1978	1990	2000
产业	**Industry**			
农业	**Agriculture**			
农林牧渔业总产值 (亿元)	Gross Output Value of Farming, Forestry, Animal Husbandry and Fishery (100 million yuan)	85.94	600.71	1701.18
主要农产品产量 (万吨)	Output of Major Farm Products (10000 tons)			
粮食	Grain	1509.51	1896.29	1822.33
油料	Oil-bearing Crops	36.04	58.93	78.78
糖蔗	Sugarcane	835.42	2093.46	1137.59
茶叶	Tea	0.92	2.59	4.21
园林水果	Fruits	29.40	328.58	643.52
肉类	Meat	48.45	202.45	324.48
水产品	Aquatic Products	65.50	207.66	593.19
工业	**Industry**			
主要工业产品产量	Output of Major Industrial Products			
布 (亿米)	Cloth (100 million m)	2.27	4.59	16.99
机制纸及纸板 (万吨)	Machine-made Paper and Paperboard (10000 tons)	27.47	104.13	260.30
成品糖 (万吨)	Sugar (10000 tons)	96.15	184.50	91.30
家用电冰箱 (万台)	Household Refrigerators (10000 sets)		105.75	320.70
家用洗衣机 (万台)	Household Washing Machines (10000 sets)		143.01	244.18
彩色电视机 (万台)	Color Television Sets (10000 sets)		262.37	1531.53
照相机 (万架)	Cameras (10000 sets)		99.30	3545.88
原油 (万吨)	Crude Oil (10000 tons)	10.22	49.05	1393.17
发电量 (亿千瓦时)	Electricity (100 million kwh)	92.32	343.98	1292.69
粗钢 (万吨)	Raw Steel (10000 tons)	35.84	116.96	286.99
钢材 (万吨)	Steel Products (10000 tons)	43.67	133.74	406.28
水泥 (万吨)	Cement (10000 tons)	369.08	2070.91	5872.00
汽车 (万辆)	Motor Vehicles (10000 units)			3.94
规模以上工业企业主要指标	Main Indicators of Industrial Enterprises above Designated Size			
资产总计 (亿元)	Total Assets (100 million yuan)	104.06	546.72	14370.57
营业收入 (亿元)	Business Revenue (100 million yuan)	168.91	689.83	12480.93
利税总额 (亿元)	Pre-tax Profits (100 million yuan)	32.91	121.50	1042.77
建筑业	**Construction**			
建筑业总产值(当年价) (亿元)	Gross Output Value (at current prices) (100 million yuan)	5.47	113.40	944.61
交通运输业	**Transportation**			
客运量 (万人)	Passenger Traffic (10000 persons)	15906	78046	164791
铁路	Railways	2410	4467	12165
公路	Highways	10897	70681	148945
水运	Waterways	2546	2428	2363
民航	Civil Aviation	53	470	1318
货运量 (万吨)	Freight Traffic (10000 tons)	15204	85809	119216
铁路	Railways	3206	4803	15172
公路	Highways	3967	63709	75365
水运	Waterways	7887	16198	25696
民航	Civil Aviation	1	8	31
管道	Pipelines	143	1091	2952
港口货物吞吐量 (万吨)	Volume of Freight Handled at Ports (10000 tons)	7133	11904	31649

1-2 1 continued

2010	2022	2023	速度指标(%) Indices and Growth Rates (%)								
			指数(2023为以下各年) Index (2023 as percentage of the following years)					平均增长速度 Average Annual Growth Rate			
			1978	1990	2000	2010	2022	1979–2023	1991–2023	2001–2023	2011–2023
3697.18	8892.29	9202.09	966.8	422.3	248.3	164.7	105.1	5.2	4.5	4.0	3.9
1249.15	1291.54	1285.19	85.1	67.8	70.5	102.9	99.5	-0.4	-1.2	-1.5	0.2
83.34	117.43	121.01	335.8	205.4	153.6	145.2	103.1	2.7	2.2	1.9	2.9
1064.09	1107.76	1087.43	130.2	51.9	95.6	102.2	98.2	0.6	-2.0	-0.2	0.2
5.38	16.08	17.89	1944.3	690.6	424.9	332.2	111.2	6.8	6.0	6.5	9.7
1049.21	1895.18	1991.87	6775.1	606.2	309.5	189.8	105.1	9.8	5.6	5.0	5.1
454.86	481.01	507.46	1047.4	250.7	156.4	111.6	105.5	5.4	2.8	2.0	0.8
729.03	894.03	924.02	1410.7	445.0	155.8	126.7	103.4	6.1	4.6	1.9	1.8
28.27	20.17	16.30	718.2	355.2	96.0	57.7	79.3	4.5	3.9	-0.2	-4.1
1434.68	2374.14	2509.21	9134.4	2409.7	964.0	174.9	103.4	10.6	10.1	10.4	4.4
91.66	119.16	103.40	107.5	56.0	113.3	112.8	69.4	0.2	-1.7	0.5	0.9
1457.76	1773.35	2195.00		2075.7	684.4	150.6	121.0		9.6	8.7	3.2
467.83	686.72	785.56		549.3	321.7	167.9	116.3		5.3	5.2	4.1
4494.78	10792.02	11211.09		4273.0	732.0	249.4	101.2		12.1	9.0	7.3
3798.93	444.43	792.51		798.1	22.4	20.9	92.8		6.5	-6.3	-11.4
1287.15	1884.62										
3101.28	6093.81										
1239.34	3571.77	4448.54	12412.2	3803.5	1550.1	358.9	103.4	11.3	11.7	12.7	10.3
2918.89	5627.44	6192.39	14180.0	4630.2	1524.2	212.1	112.3	11.6	12.3	12.6	6.0
11536.67	15131.17	14251.58	3861.4	688.2	242.7	123.5	94.2	8.5	6.0	3.9	1.6
156.29	415.37	518.30			13154.9	331.6	116.9			23.6	9.7
62626.90	196419.19	211484.21			1412.8	324.2	107.2			12.2	9.5
85824.64	183027.35	185496.87			1437.7	209.1	101.5			12.3	5.8
9418.42	15857.14	17448.34			1539.7	170.5	108.8			12.5	4.1
4742.09	22956.50	25399.21	464336.5	22397.9	2688.9	535.6	110.6	20.6	17.8	15.3	13.7
467049	47632	82680	516.8	384.7	186.4	99.3	173.6	3.7	4.2	2.7	-0.1
14956	17526	36351	1616.8	896.0	473.7	277.0	207.4	6.4	6.9	7.0	8.2
442224	23730	30583	327.3	199.9	94.9	50.0	128.9	2.7	2.1	-0.2	-5.2
2241	884	2774	31.3	142.4	146.3	127.7	313.8	-2.5	1.1	1.7	1.9
7628	5492	12972	23916.1	2688.2	958.6	165.7	236.2	12.9	10.5	10.3	4.0
205034	364199	382401	1633.9	698.6	532.0	220.6	105.0	6.4	6.1	7.5	6.3
12170	9374	9633	402.5	236.0	131.3	112.1	102.8	3.1	2.6	1.2	0.9
142389	242474	252809	1507.7	812.3	686.7	235.0	104.3	6.2	6.6	8.7	6.8
43092	97628	105880	944.1	645.7	407.0	223.1	108.5	5.1	5.8	6.3	6.4
116	221	246	19849.2	2408.9	621.6	166.6	111.6	12.5	10.1	8.3	4.0
7267	14503	13831	6842.1	896.8	331.4	140.2	95.4	9.8	6.9	5.3	2.6
122258	204802	221462	3803.7	2279.2	857.3	221.9	108.1	8.4	9.9	9.8	6.3

1-2 续表 2

指　　标	Item	1978	1990	2000
邮政、电信	**Postal，Telecommunication**			
邮政业务总量 (亿元)	Business Volume of Postal Services (100 million yuan)		3.91	50.40
电信业务总量 (亿元)	Business Volume of Telecommunications Services (100 million pieces)		22.39	706.82
固定电话用户 (万户)	Number of Subscribers of Local Telephones (10000 accounts)		113.00	1414.94
移动电话用户 (万户)	Number of Subscribers of Mobile Telephones (10000 accounts)		1.11	1357.26
固定互联网宽带接入用户(万户)	Broadband Subscribers of Internet (10000 accounts)			216.41
国际旅游	**International Tourism**			
国际旅游外汇收入 (亿美元)	Foreign Exchange Earnings from International Tourism (USD 100 million)		7.17	41.12
金融保险	**Banking and Insurance**			
金融机构存款余额 (亿元)	Deposits of Financial Institutions (100 million yuan)			19083.64
金融机构贷款余额 (亿元)	Loans in in Financial Institutions (100 million yuan)			13227.62
保费收入 (亿元)	Premium Income (100 million yuan)		18.05	191.88
教育、科技、文化	**Education, Science and Technology and Culture**			
教育	**Education**			
专任教师数 (万人)	Full-time Teachers (10000 persons)			
普通高等学校	Institutions of Higher Education	0.90	1.57	2.04
中等学校	Secondary Schools	15.93	16.33	27.24
小学	Primary Schools	26.09	27.73	36.41
在校学生数 (万人)	Students Enrollment (10000 persons)			
普通高等学校	Institutions of Higher Education	3.07	9.59	29.95
中等学校	Secondary Schools	316.96	284.52	541.72
小学	Primary Schools	743.02	747.29	929.93
财政教育支出 (亿元)	Government Expenditures on Education (100 million yuan)		21.34	144.39
科技	**Science and Technology**			
研究与试验发展(R&D)活动人员 (万人)	Number of R&D Personnel (10000 persons)			
研究与试验发展(R&D)经费内部支出 (亿元)	Internal Expenditure on R&D (100 million yuan)			107.12
文化	**Culture**			
出版数量	Number of Publications			
图书 (亿册)	Number of Books Published (100 million copies)	1.72	2.81	2.70
杂志 (万册)	Number of Magazines Issued (10000 copies)	1519	11325	26299
报纸 (亿份)	Number of Newspapers Issued (100 million copies)	3.19	13.81	34.63

1-2 2 continued

2010	2022	2023	速度指标(%) Indices and Growth Rates (%)								
			指数(2023为以下各年) Index (2023 as percentage of the following years)					平均增长速度 Average Annual Growth Rate			
			1978	1990	2000	2010	2022	1979–2023	1991–2023	2001–2023	2011–2023
118.57	3112.87	3645.36		160263.2	12432.9	3934.2	117.1		25.1	23.3	32.6
4714.37	1950.26	2024.09		952958.4	30187.0	3605.2	103.8		32.0	28.2	31.8
3169.14	1944.08	1783.72		1578.5	126.1	56.3	91.8		8.7	1.0	-4.3
9710.09	16650.76	17048.20		1535873.6	1256.1	175.6	102.4		33.9	11.6	4.4
1523.22	4628.72	4824.35			2229.3	316.7	104.2			14.4	9.3
124.32	17.37	110.19					634.4				
82019.40	322357.66	350887.61			1838.7	427.8	108.9			13.5	11.8
51799.30	245722.94	271561.63			2053.0	524.3	110.5			14.0	13.6
1421.68	5894.16	6556.04		36321.6	3416.7	461.1	111.2		19.6	16.6	12.5
7.86	13.59	14.35	1594.4	914.0	703.4	182.6	105.6	6.3	6.9	8.9	4.7
45.48	56.48	58.77	368.9	359.9	215.7	129.2	104.1	2.9	4.0	3.4	2.0
43.07	60.20	61.34	235.1	221.2	168.5	142.4	101.9	1.9	2.4	2.3	2.8
142.66	267.09	260.14	8473.6	2712.6	868.6	182.3	97.4	10.4	10.5	9.9	4.7
939.39	824.62	861.91	271.9	302.9	159.1	91.8	104.5	2.2	3.4	2.0	-0.7
848.55	1084.05	1110.52	149.5	148.6	119.4	130.9	102.4	0.9	1.2	0.8	2.1
921.48	3871.14	4004.45		18765.0	2773.4	434.6	103.4		17.2	15.5	12.0
44.66	133.98	158.27				354.4	118.1				10.2
808.75	4411.90	4802.62			4483.4	593.8	108.9			18.0	14.7
2.31	5.06	5.53	312.8	196.9	205.0	239.6	109.4	2.6	2.1	3.2	7.0
21201	9113	7992	526.1	70.6	30.4	37.7	87.7	3.8	-1.1	-5.0	-7.2
45.59	13.19	12.74	399.4	92.3	36.8	27.9	96.6	3.1	-0.2	-4.3	-9.3

1-2 续表 3

指　标	Item	1978	1990	2000
家庭、生活、环境	**Family, People's Livelihood and Environment**			
家庭	**Family**			
城镇居民平均每户家庭人口 (人)	Average Permanent Household Size in Urban Areas (person)	4.84	3.85	3.57
农村居民平均每户家庭人口 (人)	Average Permanent Household Size in Rural Areas (person)	5.99	5.65	5.15
婚姻	**Marriages and Divorces**			
结婚登记总数 (万对)	Registered Number of Marriages (10000 couples)		50.66	56.21
离婚数 (万对)	Number of Divorces (10000 couples)		2.58	4.75
生活	**People's Livelihood**			
全体居民人均可支配收入 (元)	Per Capita Disposable Income of Residents (yuan)			
城镇居民人均可支配收入 (元)	Per Capita Disposable Income of Urban Residents (yuan)	412	2303	9762
农村居民人均可支配收入 (元)	Per Capita Disposable Income of Rural Residents (yuan)	193	1043	3654
人民币住户存款 (亿元)	Savings Deposits by Households in Renminbi (100 million yuan)	17.56	752.16	8667.29
工资	**Wages**			
城镇单位就业人员工资总额 (亿元)	Earnings of Employed Persons in Urban Areas (100 million yuan)	30.59	223.29	1057.57
城镇单位就业人员平均工资 (元)	Average Earnings of Employed Persons in Urban Areas (yuan)	615	2929	13859
卫生	**Health Care**			
医院、卫生院 (个)	Number of Hospitals (unit)	1968	1885	2426
执业(助理)医师 (万人)	Number of Doctors (10000 persons)	4.79	8.11	11.12
医院、卫生院床位数 (万张)	Number of Hospital Beds (10000 units)	8.41	11.41	15.72
环境、灾害	**Environment and Disaster**			
火灾发生数 (起)	Number of Fire Disasters (time)		1725	8622
火灾损失 (万元)	Fire Loss (10000 yuan)		9102	10065
交通事故发生数 (起)	Number of Traffic Accidents (time)		25909	66072
交通事故损失 (万元)	Loss of Traffic Accidents (10000 yuan)		5044	27526

注：1.2011—2020年年末常住人口根据2020年第七次全国人口普查数据进行平滑修正。

2.2003年起，职工改为单位从业人员，2000年数据作了相应调整。2006—2009年就业人员人数,根据第六次全国人口普查资料作了相应调整。从2020年起，国家统计局对各省、自治区、直辖市就业人数及其产业构成以常住人口口径统一测算，同时对2010—2019年就业人数及其产业结构进行平滑修正。

3.农业总产值、工业增加值绝对数按当年价格计算，增长速度按可比价计算。

4.工业指标统计范围为规模以上工业企业(即年主营业务收入2000万元以上的法人工业企业，2000—2006年为全部国有工业企业及年主营业务收入500万元以上的非国有工业企业，2011年起，调整为年主营业务收入2000万元及以上的法人工业企业)。

5.2000年起，粮食产量为抽样调查数据。

6.邮电业务总量2000年以前按1990年不变价计算，2000—2010年按2000年不变价计算,2011年起按2010年不变价计算,2017年起电信业务总量按2015年不变价格计算，邮政业务总量仍按2010年不变价计算，2021年起均按2020年不变价计算。2022年，电信业务总量按上年不变价计算。

7.1986年以前中等学校不含成人中专数据。

8.2011年起，固定资产投资项目统计起点由50万元提高至500万元，且不包含农村农户投资；2010年以前为全社会固定资产投资。

9.2015年起，地方公共财政预算收入和地方公共财政预算支出统一更名为地方一般公共预算收入和地方一般公共预算支出。

10.2013年起，居民人均可支配收入为城乡一体化住户收支与生活状况调查数据，与此前分城镇和农村住户调查的统计口径不可比，2013年以前农村居民收入为纯收入。

11.2018年起，实际使用外资金额使用商务部反馈人民币数据。

12.2023年能源相关数据未经国家统计局核定，原油产量、发电量数据暂缺。

1-2 3 continued

2010	2022	2023	速度指标(%) Indices and Growth Rates (%)								
			指数(2023为以下各年) Index (2023 as percentage of the following years)					平均增长速度 Average Annual Growth Rate			
			1978	1990	2000	2010	2022	1979–2023	1991–2023	2001–2023	2011–2023
3.21	3.37	2.98	61.6	77.4	83.5	92.8	88.4	-1.1	-0.8	-0.8	-0.6
4.95	3.72	3.57	59.6	63.2	69.3	72.1	96.0	-1.1	-1.4	-1.6	-2.5
85.71	57.31	63.22		124.8	112.5	73.8	110.3		0.7	0.5	-2.3
12.70	18.45	22.61		876.3	476.0	177.9	122.5		6.8	7.0	4.5
	47065	49327					104.8				
23898	56905	59307					104.2				
7890	23598	25142					106.5				
36318.66	112555.17	125616.81	715357.7	16700.8	1449.3	345.9	111.6	21.8	16.8	12.3	10.0
4484.29	26200.89	26266.90	85867.6	11763.6	2483.7	585.8	100.3	16.2	15.5	15.0	14.6
40432	124916	131418	21368.8	4486.8	948.2	325.0	105.2	12.7	12.2	10.3	9.5
2444	2981	3044	154.7	161.5	125.5	124.5	102.1	1.0	1.5	1.0	1.7
17.51	33.52	35.95	750.5	443.3	323.3	205.3	107.2	4.6	4.6	5.2	5.7
27.71	56.41	58.34	693.5	511.5	371.2	210.5	103.4	4.4	5.1	5.9	5.9
6065	55629	57785		3349.9	670.2	952.8	103.9		11.2	8.6	18.9
17500	70995	71742		788.2	712.8	410.0	101.1		6.5	8.9	11.5
30480	38782	44104		170.2	66.8	144.7	113.7		1.6	-1.7	2.9
8051	8649	11220		222.4	40.8	139.4	129.7		2.5	-3.8	2.6

Notes: a)Figures of permanent population at the year-end from 2011 to 2020 have been adjusted in accordance with the flash sums of the 7th National Population Census in 2020.

b)The number of staff and workers has been recoded as employed persons in units since 2003.The data of 2000 have been adjusted accordingly. The number of employed persons from 2006 to 2009 have been adjusted in accordance with the data of the 6th National Census. Since 2020, the NBS is uniformly calculated the number of employed persons and industrial composition by permanent resident method in all Provinces, Autonomous Regions and Municipalities, the number of employed persons and industrial compositon from 2010 to 2019 have been adjusted at the same time.

c)Figures in value terms on gross output value of agriculture and industry are calculated at current prices , whereas their growth rates are calculated at constant prices.

d)The statistical coverage of the industrial indicators refers to the industrial enterprises above designated size, i.e.legal person industrial enterprises with annual main business revenue over 5 million yuan.The industrial indicators from 2000 to 2006 covered all state-owned industrial enterprises and non-state-owned industrial enterprises with annual main business revenue over 5 million yuan. Since 2011, it refers to legal person industrial enterprises with annual principal business revenue of over 20 million yuan.

e) Figures of output of grain have been obtained from sample surveys since 2000.

f)The total business volume of postal and telecommunication services are at 1990 constant prices before 2000 and at 2000 constant prices from 2000 to 2010,and at 2010 constant price since 2011. The total bussiness volume of telecommunication services are at 2015 constant price since 2017, and the total bussiness volume of postal services are still at 2010 constant price, and since 2021 both at 2020 constant price. In 2022, the total business volume of postal and telecommunication services are at last year's constant prices.

g) Before 1986, the figures of secondary schools excluded those of specialized secondary schools for adults.

h) Since 2011, the cut-off point of investment statistics is changed from a minimum of 500,000 yuan to a minimum of 5,000,000 yuan, and the data do not include the investment made by rural households. Data before 2010 refer to total investment in fixed assets.

i) From 2015, the name of local government budgetary revenue and local government budgetary expenditure have been changed to local public budgetary revenue and local public budgetary expenditure.

j) Since 2013, Per Capita Disposable Income of Residents are the data of investigation on income and expenditure and living conditions of urban and rural integrated households, it is not comparable with the statistical caliber of previous urban and rural househlods survey. Before 2013, the income of rural residents is net income.

k) Since 2018, the actual amount of foreign investment used has been reported in RMB by the Ministry of Commerce.

l)The energy related data for 2023 has not been approved by the National Bureau of Statistics, and the data on crude oil production and power generation are currently missing.

1-3 国民经济和社会发展结构指标

Composition Indicators of National Economic and Social Development

单位：% (%)

指 标	Item	2000	2010	2015	2022	2023
人口与就业	**Population and Employment**					
人口	**Population**					
城乡结构(常住人口)	Urban and Rural Composition(by permanent population)					
城镇	Urban	55.0	66.2	69.5	74.8	75.4
乡村	Rural	45.0	33.8	30.5	25.2	24.6
性别结构(户籍人口)	Sexual Composition(by residential population)					
男	Male	51.6	51.5	51.5	51.1	51.1
女	Female	48.4	48.5	48.5	48.9	48.9
就业	**Employment**					
产业结构	Industrial Structure					
第一产业	Primary Industry	40.0	24.4	15.9	10.5	9.7
第二产业	Secondary Industry	27.9	42.4	40.0	36.6	36.6
第三产业	Tertiary Industry	32.1	33.2	44.1	53.0	53.6
宏观经济	**Macro Economy**					
国民经济核算	**National Accounts**					
地区生产总值产业结构	Industrial Structure of Gross Domestic Product					
第一产业	Primary Industry	9.1	4.8	4.3	4.1	4.1
第二产业	Secondary Industry	46.7	49.9	45.4	40.6	40.1
第三产业	Tertiary Industry	44.2	45.3	50.3	55.3	55.8
支出法地区生产总值结构	Domestic Expenditure Structure					
最终消费	Final Consumption	52.9	49.0	51.0	50.3	
居民消费	Household Consumption	41.4	38.5	39.3	37.4	
城镇居民	Urban Households	28.9	33.6	33.1	31.5	
农村居民	Rural Households	12.5	4.9	6.2	6.0	
政府消费	Government Consumption	11.5	10.4	11.7	12.9	
资本形成总额	Gross Capital Formation	36.2	39.7	42.3	42.2	
固定资本形成总额	Gross Fixed Capital Formation	29.2	37.1	40.8	37.4	
存货增加	Changes in Inventories	7.0	2.6	1.5	4.7	
净流出	Net Exports	10.9	11.4	6.7	7.5	
固定资产投资	**Investment**					
按登记注册统计类别分投资额结构	Investment amount structure by Registered Statistical Categories					
内资	Domestic Invested	82.8	85.4	88.4	91.0	91.7
港澳台商投资	Investment from Hong Kong, Macao & Taiwan	12.9	9.2	6.9	5.0	4.7
外商投资	Foreign Invested	4.3	5.4	4.7	4.0	3.6

注：本表登记注册统计类别按《关于市场主体统计分类的划分规定》(国统字〔2023〕14号)执行。

Ntote: The registered statistical categories of this table is implemented in accordance with the Regulations onStatistics the Classification of Market Entity (Guotongzi [2023] No. 14).

1-3 续表 1 continued

单位：% (%)

指 标	Item	2000	2010	2015	2022	2023
资金来源结构	Structure of Sources of Funds					
国家预算资金	State Budgetary Appropriation	1.7	2.2	4.9	14.2	14.3
国内贷款	Domestic Loans	17.2	16.8	12.5	15.9	16.9
利用外资	Foreign Investment	10.5	3.3	0.6	0.4	0.3
自筹投资	Fundraising	42.9	56.6	57.9	46.6	46.6
其他投资	Others	27.7	21.1	24.2	22.9	21.9
对外贸易(美元计价)	**Foreign Trade (USD)**					
按贸易方式分出口额结构	Export Volume Grouped by Trade Mode					
一般贸易	Ordinary Trade	18.9	22.4	42.9	57.6	62.4
加工贸易	Processing Trade	78.1	73.5	43.7	26.5	23.6
其他	Others	3.0	4.1	13.4	15.8	14.0
按贸易方式分进口额结构	Import Volume Grouped by Trade Mode					
一般贸易	Ordinary Trade	26.6	25.5	40.9	49.4	48.5
加工贸易	Processing Trade	63.1	61.6	41.9	25.0	22.9
其他	Others	10.3	12.8	17.2	25.5	28.6
国内贸易	**Domestic Trade**					
社会消费品零售总额结构	Structure of Total Retail Sales of Consumer Goods					
城镇	Urban Areas	76.2	86.9	89.3	87.5	87.1
乡村	Rural Areas	23.8	13.1	10.7	12.5	12.9
能源生产与消费	**Production and Consumption of Energy**					
能源生产总量结构	Structure of Total Energy Production					
原煤	Coal	8.0				
原油	Crude Oil	53.6	37.8	32.8	27.9	
电力	Electricity	27.1	40.7	48.5	56.4	
天然气	Natural Gas	11.3	21.5	18.7	15.6	
一次能源消费总量结构	Structure of Total Primary Energy Consumption					
原煤	Coal	52.2	45.2	40.2	32.6	
原油	Crude Oil	35.0	29.0	25.9	25.5	
电力	Electricity	12.6	20.1	26.8	30.9	
天然气	Natural Gas	0.2	5.7	7.1	11.0	
其他	Others					
农业	**Agriculture**					
农林牧渔业产值结构	Structure of Gross Output Value of Farming, Forestry, Animal Husbandry and Fishery					
农业	Farming	47.5	45.1	47.0	48.4	48.2
林业	Forestry	3.5	4.9	5.8	6.2	6.1
牧业	Animal Husbandry	26.5	26.5	22.6	18.9	18.4
渔业	Fishery	22.5	19.9	20.8	21.3	21.8
农林牧渔专业及辅助性活动	Services for Farming, Forestry, Animal Husbandry and Fishery		3.6	3.9	5.1	5.5
工业(规模以上)	**Industry(above designated size)**					
工业企业资产	Assets of Industrial Enterprises					
按工业门类分	Grouped by Industries					
采矿业	Mining	1.5	1.3	1.5	1.1	1.1
制造业	Manufacturing	80.2	84.2	85.6	85.2	85.1
电力、热力、燃气及水生产和供应业	Production and Supply of Electricity, Heat, Gas and Water	18.3	14.5	12.9	13.7	13.8
按企业规模分	Grouped by Size of Enterprises					
大型企业	Large Enterprises	44.1	37.0	45.2	50.7	51.3
中型企业	Medium-sized Enterprises	13.4	36.0	27.6	20.8	20.3
小微型企业	Small and Micro Enterprises	42.4	27.0	27.2	28.5	28.3
按登记注册统计类别分	By Registered Statistical Categories					
#内资企业	Domestic Invested Enterprises	50.3	47.0	59.0	69.6	71.7
港澳台投资企业	Enterprises with Investment from Hong Kong, Macao and Taiwan	35.2	25.8	22.8	17.1	14.2
外商投资企业	Foreign Invested Enterprises	14.5	27.2	18.2	13.4	14.1

注：2018—2020年，资金来源中不含5000万元以下项目。
Note: Source of funds exclude projects below 50 million yuan between 2018 and 2020.

1-3 续表 2 continued

单位：% (%)

指　　标	Item	2000	2010	2015	2022	2023
建筑业	**Construction**					
按登记注册统计类别分总产值结构	Total Output Value Structure by Registration Statistical Categories					
内资	Domestic Invested Enterprises	97.6	96.5	97.4	98.3	98.6
港澳台商投资	Enterprises with Investment from Hong Kong, Macao & Taiwan	1.6	1.5	0.8	0.9	0.8
外商投资	Foreign Invested Enterprises	0.8	2.0	1.7	0.8	0.6
交通运输和旅游	**Transportation and Tourism**					
客运量结构	Structure of Passenger Traffic					
铁路	Railways	7.4	3.2	12.8	36.8	44.0
公路	Highways	90.4	94.6	81.0	49.8	37.0
水运	Waterways	1.4	0.5	1.3	1.9	3.4
民用航空	Civil Aviation	0.8	1.6	4.8	11.5	15.7
货运量结构	Structure of Freight Traffic					
铁路	Railways	12.7	5.9	2.7	2.6	2.5
公路	Highways	63.2	69.4	74.4	66.6	66.0
水运	Waterways	21.6	21.0	20.7	26.8	27.7
民用航空	Civil Aviation	...	0.1	...	0.1	0.1
管道输油(气)	Pipelines	2.5	3.5	2.2	4.0	3.7
接待过夜旅游者人数	Composition of Tourists Staying Overnight					
入境旅游者	Overseas Visitor Arrivals Inbound Tourists	15.6	14.8	9.5	0.9	4.8
国内旅游者	Domestic Tourists	84.4	85.2	90.5	99.1	95.2
教育与科技	**Education and Technology**					
教育	**Education**					
在校学生结构	Structure of Enrolled Students					
大学生	Colleges and Universities	2.1	8.4	11.5	12.3	11.7
中学生	Regular Secondary Schools	32.4	41.7	34.7	37.9	38.6
小学生	Primary Schools	65.5	49.9	53.8	49.8	49.7
专任教师结构	Structure of Full-time Teachers					
大学	Colleges and Universities	3.3	8.7	10.0	10.4	10.7
中学	Secondary Schools	37.3	43.5	42.9	43.4	43.7
小学	Primary Schools	59.4	47.8	47.1	46.2	45.6
科技	**Science and Technology**					
研究与试验发展(R&D)经费内部支出结构	Internal Expenditure Structure of Funds of Research and Experimental Development (R&D)					
按活动主体分组	By Activity Subject					
政府属科研机构	Basic Statistics on Research and Development Institutions under Government Departments		2.6	3.6	4.7	4.2
高等学校	Higher Education		3.5	3.5	5.4	5.4
企业	Enterprises		87.0	84.6	87.1	87.1
其他	Others		6.8	8.4	2.8	3.3
按活动类型分组	By Activity Type					
基础研究	Basic Research		2.1	3.0	5.4	5.6
应用研究	Applied Research		4.6	9.2	9.4	7.5
试验发展	Experimental Development		93.3	87.8	85.2	87.0

1-3 续表 3 continued

单位：% (%)

指 标	Item	2000	2010	2015	2022	2023
生活、卫生、环境	**People's Livelihood，Health Care and Environment**					
生活	**People's Livelihood**					
全体居民消费结构	Composition of Consumption Expenditure Province Wide					
食品烟酒	Food,Tobacco and Liquor			34.5	34.3	32.4
衣着	Clothing			5.3	3.7	3.8
居住	Living			22.3	26.1	25.8
生活用品及服务	Daily Necessities and Services			5.9	5.1	4.9
交通通信	Transportation and Telecommunication			14.4	13.0	14.2
教育文化娱乐	Education,Culture and Entertainment			10.1	9.9	10.3
医疗保健	Health Service			4.7	5.5	6.2
其他用品和服务	Other Necessities and Services			2.8	2.4	2.4
城镇居民消费结构	Composition of Consumption Expenditure of Urban Households					
食品烟酒	Food,Tobacco and Liquor	38.6	36.5	33.2	32.8	31.2
衣着	Clothing	4.6	6.7	5.7	3.7	4.0
居住	Living	13.7	10.4	22.3	26.9	26.2
生活用品及服务	Daily Necessities and Services	7.5	6.5	5.9	5.2	5.1
交通通信	Transportation and Telecommunication	13.4	18.5	15.2	13.2	14.4
教育文化娱乐	Education,Culture and Entertainment	11.5	12.9	10.4	10.2	10.5
医疗保健	Health Service	4.3	5.0	4.3	5.5	6.0
其他用品和服务	Other Necessities and Services	6.4	3.5	3.0	2.5	2.6
农村居民消费结构	Composition of Consumption Expenditure of Rural Households					
食品烟酒	Food,Tobacco and Liquor	49.8	47.7	40.6	40.3	37.6
衣着	Clothing	3.9	3.9	3.3	3.3	2.9
居住	Living	14.3	17.9	22.5	23.0	23.7
生活用品及服务	Daily Necessities and Services	4.7	4.3	5.9	4.8	4.2
交通通信	Transportation and Telecommunication	7.8	11.6	10.5	11.9	13.2
教育文化娱乐	Education,Culture and Entertainment	11.8	5.9	8.6	9.0	9.6
医疗保健	Health Service	3.9	5.6	6.5	5.9	7.0
其他用品和服务	Other Necessities and Services	3.8	3.1	2.2	1.8	1.8
卫生	**Health Care**					
卫生技术人员结构	Structure of Medical Technical Personnel					
#执业(助理)医生	Doctors	42.0	37.7	36.4	36.5	36.7
注册护士	Nurses	31.4	37.1	41.3	45.8	46.0
床位结构	Structure of Hospital Beds					
#医院	Hospitals	71.4	74.7	79.2	81.7	82.0
事故、灾害	**Cash and Disaster**					
火灾事故损失额结构	Structure of Fire Losses Converted into Cash					
特大或重大	Extraordinarily Serious Fires					
较大	Serious Fires		0.2	0.8	0.6	0.2
一般	Ordinary Fires		99.8	99.2	99.4	99.8
交通事故损失额结构	Structure of Losses from Traffic Accidents Converted into Cash					
机动车道	Roads for Motored Vehicles		81.5	83.9	81.5	80.3
非机动车道	Roads for Nonmotored Vehicles		1.4	1.4	2.4	2.6
混合道	Mixed Roads		12.8	11.8	12.0	11.8
其他道	Others		4.3	3.0	4.1	5.3

注：1.由于数据计算进位的原因，部分结构总和不等于100。
2.按照国家统计局统一部署，广东省从2013年开始正式对外发布全省居民调查数据。

Note: a) Owing to the rounding-off of figures, some totals in this table are not equal to 100.
b) Under the unified deployment by NBS, Since 2013, Guangdong Province has officially released the provincial residents survey data.

1-4 国民经济和社会发展比例和效益指标
Indicators on National Economic and Social Development

指 标	Item	2000	2015	2022	2023
人口	**Population and Employment**				
总抚养比 (%)	Gross Dependency Ratio (%)	43.31	34.86	39.01	38.78
少儿抚养比 (%)	Children Dependency Ratio (%)	34.64	23.43	25.67	24.95
老年抚养比 (%)	Old Dependency Ratio (%)	8.67	11.44	13.34	13.83
国民经济核算	**National Accounts**				
第一产业增加值占地区生产总值比重 (%)	Percentage of Value-added of Primary Industry in Gross Domestic Product (%)	9.1	4.3	4.1	4.1
第二产业增加值占地区生产总值比重 (%)	Percentage of Value-added of Secondary Industry in Gross Domestic Product (%)	46.7	45.4	40.6	40.1
第三产业增加值占地区生产总值比重 (%)	Percentage of Value-added of Tertiary Industry in Gross Domestic Product (%)	44.2	50.3	55.3	55.8
文化产业增加值占地区生产总值比重 (%)	Percentage of Value-added of Cultural Industry in Gross Domestic Product (%)		5.2	5.4	
新经济增加值占地区生产总值比重 (%)	Percentage of Value-added of New Economy in Gross Domestic Product (%)			25.9	25.6
全社会劳动生产率 (万元/人)	Gross labour productivity (million yuan/person)	2.78	11.50	18.53	19.44
人民生活	**People's Living Conditions**				
全省居民恩格尔系数 (%)	Engel coefficient for all permanent residents (%)		34.5	34.3	32.4
城镇居民恩格尔系数 (%)	Engel coefficient of permanent urban residents (%)	38.6	33.2	32.8	31.2
农村居民恩格尔系数 (%)	Engel coefficient of permanent rural residents (%)	49.8	40.6	40.3	37.6
城乡收入比 (农村居民收入为1)	Urban and Rural Income ratio (Rural Income as 1)	2.67	2.60	2.41	2.36
财政	**Government Finance**				
一般公共预算收入与地区生产总值之比(%)	Proportion of Government Revenue to GDP (%)	8.4	12.5	10.2	10.2
一般公共预算支出与地区生产总值之比(%)	Proportion of Government Expenditure to GDP (%)	9.9	17.2	14.3	13.7
能源	**Energy**				
能源生产弹性系数	Elasticity Ratio of Energy Production	0.50	2.84	4.47	
电力生产弹性系数	Elasticity Ratio of Electricity Production	1.63	0.06	0.50	
能源消费弹性系数	Elasticity Ratio of Energy Consumption	0.71	0.24	0.00	
电力消费弹性系数	Elasticity Ratio of Electricity Consumption	1.99	0.18	0.02	
能源加工转换总效率 (%)	Total Efficiency of Energy Conversion (%)	66.63	69.07	69.99	
资源环境	**Resources and Environment**				
万元地区生产总值用水量 (立方米)	Water Use Per 10000 Yuan GDP (cu.m)		61	31	30
万元工业增加值用水量 (立方米)	Water Use Per 10000 Yuan of Industrial Added Value (cu.m)		37	15	15
固定资产投资	**Investment in Fixed Assets**				
项目建成投产率 (%)	Rate of Projects Completed and Put into Use (%)	49.3	70.8	33.8	33.9
对外贸易	**Foreign Trade**				
进出口总额相当于地区生产总值比重 (%)	Proportion of Total Value of Imports & Exports to GDP (%)	130.3	85.0	63.9	61.2
高新技术产品出口额占出口总额的比重(%)	Proportion of High and New-tech Products to Total Exports (%)	18.5	36.1	31.4	30.6
一般贸易进出口总额占进出口总额的比重	Proportion of Ordinary Trade to Total Value of	22.5	42.1	54.7	57.6
加工贸易进出口总额占进出口总额的比重	Proportion of Processing Trade to Total Value of	71.2	43.1	26.0	23.4

1-4 续表 continued

指 标	Item	2000	2015	2022	2023
农业	**Agriculture**				
每公顷播种面积农产品产量 （公斤）	Output of Farm Crops per Hectare of Sown Area (kg)				
粮食	Grain	5879	5524	5791	5764
糖料	Sugar Crops	70380	77619	87778	89176
油料	Oil-bearing Crops	2295	2963	3306	3342
工业	**Industry**				
总资产贡献率 (%)	Ratio of Total Assets to Industrial Output Value (%)	8.86	13.58	8.47	8.57
资产负债率 (%)	Assets-Liability Ratio (%)	57.56	57.38	58.39	58.75
成本费用利润率 (%)	Ratio of Profits to Industrial Costs (%)	4.82	6.85	5.98	6.63
产品销售率 (%)	Proportion of Products Sold (%)	97.40	97.11	96.40	96.24
每百元营业收入的成本 （元）	Cost per Every 100 Yuan Revenue in Businesses (yuan)		84.40	83.72	83.15
建筑业	**Construction**				
建筑业劳动生产率 （元／人）（按增加值计算）	Overall Labor Productivity (yuan/person) (in terms of value-added per employee)	39831	103972	131746	130177
交通运输业	**Transport**				
铁路网密度 （公里／万平方公里）	Railway Density (km/10000sq.km)	108	215	287	289
公路网密度 （公里／万平方公里）	Highway Density (km/10000sq.km)	5710	12021	12414	12424
邮电通信业	**Postal and Telecommunication Services**				
电话普及率(含移动电话) (部/百人)	Popularization Rate of Telephone (set/100 persons)	39.5	164.2	146.9	148.8
移动电话普及率 (部/百人)	Popularization Rate of Mobile Telephone (set/100 persons)	15.7	138.4	131.6	134.7
金融业	**Financial Intermediation**				
金融机构存款与地区生产总值之比 (%)	Proportion of Deposits of Financial Institutions to GDP (%)	176.5	217.1	248.9	258.6
金融机构贷款与地区生产总值之比 (%)	Proportion of Loans of Financial Institutions to GDP (%)	122.4	129.5	189.7	200.2
金融机构人民币贷、存款余额比例 (%)	Proportion of Loans to Deposits of Financial Institutions in RMB (%)	69.7	58.1	76.7	77.7
科技	**Science and Technology**				
研究与试验发展经费内部支出占地区生产总值比重 (%)	Porportion of R&D Expenditure to GDP (%)	0.99	2.43	3.42	3.54
每万人口发明专利拥有量 (件/万人)	Number of patents per 10 000 persons (patents/10 000 persons)		12.80	42.51	52.59
教育	**Education**				
学龄儿童入学率 (%)	Percentage of School-age Children Enrolled (%)	99.70	99.98	99.93	100.00
高中毛入学率 (%)	Gross Enrollment Rate of Senior Secondary Schools (%)	38.70	95.70	97.58	97.17
高等教育毛入学率 (%)	Gross Enrollment Rate of High Education (%)	11.35	33.00	60.07	63.10
卫生	**Public Health**				
每千人口执业(助理)医师数 (人)	Number of Licensed(Assistant) Doctors per 10000 Population (person)	1.29	1.96	2.65	2.83
每千人口医疗卫生机构床位数 (张)	Number of Beds of Hospitals and Health Centers per 1000 Population (bed)	1.94	3.73	4.81	4.95
医院病床使用率 (%)	Beds Utilization Rate of Medical Organizations (%)	68.1	83.5	72.2	78.8
城市市政建设	**Municipal Works**				
人均公园绿地面积 （平方米）	Per Capita Public Green Area (Sq.m)		17.40	17.68	17.95

1-5 国民经济和社会发展主要指标占全国比重
Percentage of National Total of Main Indicators of Economic and Social Development of Guangdong

指标	Item	2022 广东 Guang-dong	2022 全国 National Total	2022 广东占全国(%) As Percentage of National Total	2023 广东 Guang-dong	2023 全国 National Total	2023 广东占全国(%) As Percentage of National Total
人口	**Population**						
年末常住人口数 (万人)	Permanent Population at the Year-end (10000 persons)	12656.8	141175.0	9.0	12706.0	140967.0	9.0
土地面积 (万平方公里)	**Land Area (10000 sp.km)**	**17.98**	**960**	**1.9**	**17.98**	**960**	**1.9**
国内(地区)生产总值(亿元)	**Gross Domestic Product (100 million yuan)**	**129513.6**	**1204724.0**	**10.8**	**135673.2**	**1260582.1**	**10.8**
第一产业	Primary Industry	5350.1	88207.0	6.1	5540.7	89755.2	6.2
第二产业	Secondary Industry	52620.7	473789.9	11.1	54437.3	482588.5	11.3
第三产业	Tertiary Industry	71542.7	642727.1	11.1	75695.2	688238.4	11.0
人均国内(地区)生产总值 (元)	**Per Capita Gross Domestic Product (yuan)**	**102217**	**85310**		**106985**	**89358**	
主要工农业产品产量	**Output of Major Farm Products and Industrial Products**						
粮食 (万吨)	Grain (10000 tons)	1291.5	68652.8	1.9	1285.2	69541.0	1.8
油料 (万吨)	Oil-bearing Crops (10000 tons)	117.4	3654.2	3.2	121.0	3863.7	3.1
肉类 (万吨)	Meat (10000 tons)	481.0	9328.4	5.2	507.5	9748.2	5.2
水产品 (万吨)	Aquatic Products (10000 tons)	894.0	6865.9	13.0	924.0	7116.2	13.0
甘蔗 (万吨)	sugarcane (10000 tons)	1292.1	10338.1	12.5	1271.1	10456.6	12.2
水果 (万吨)	Fruits (10000 tons)	2028.4	31296.2	6.5	2127.8	32744.3	6.5
茶叶 (万吨)	Tea (10000 tons)	16.1	334.2	4.8	17.9	354.1	5.1
农用化肥 (万吨)	Chemical Fertilizer (10000 tons)	5.5	5573.4	0.1	12.8	5683.8	0.2
发电量 (亿千瓦时)	Electricity (100 million kwh)	6093.8	88487.1	6.9		94564.4	
水泥 (亿吨)	Cement (100 million tons)	1.5	21.3	7.0	1.4	20.2	7.1
布 (亿米)	Cloth (100 million m)	20.2	467.7	4.3	16.3	318.9	5.1
机制纸及纸板 (万吨)	Machine-made Paper and Paperboard (10000 tons)	2374.1	13691.4	17.3	2509.2	15129.4	16.6
钢材 (万吨)	Steel (10000 tons)	5627.4	134033.5	4.2	6192.4	138378.7	4.5
成品糖 (万吨)	Sugar (10000 tons)	119.2	1486.8	8.0	103.4	1291.5	8.0
平板玻璃 (万重量箱)	Flat Glass (10000 wt.cases)	10336.0	101668.7	10.2	8931.6	98752.8	9.0
家用电冰箱 (万台)	Household Refrigerators (10000 units)	1773.3	8664.4	20.5	2195.0	9942.3	22.1
家用洗衣机 (万台)	Household Washing Machines (10000 units)	686.7	9106.3	7.5	785.6	10529.4	7.5
彩色电视机 (万台)	Color Television Sets (10000 sets)	10792.0	19578.3	55.1	11211.1	19807.8	56.6
房间空气调节器 (万台)	Air Conditioners (10000 sets)	6637.7	22247.3	29.8	7438.5	25088.7	29.6
汽车 (万辆)	Vehicles	415.4	2713.6	15.3	518.3	3009.9	17.2
微型计算机设备 (万台)	Microcomputers (10000 units)	6948.8	43418.2	16.0	7458.1	32855.1	22.7
房地产开发投资 (亿元)	**Real Estate Development (100 million yuan)**	**15096.9**	**123847.8**	**12.2**	**13693.3**	**112142.3**	**12.2**

1－5 续表 continued

指 标	Item	2022 广东 Guang-dong	2022 全国 National Total	2022 广东占全国(%) As Percentage of National Total	2023 广东 Guang-dong	2023 全国 National Total	2023 广东占全国(%) As Percentage of National Total
运输、邮电	**Transport, Postal and Telecommunication Services**						
货物周转量 (亿吨公里)	Freight Traffic (100 million ton-kilometers)	28438.6	231782.7	12.3	29668.1	247745.3	12.0
旅客周转量 (亿人公里)	Passenger Traffic (100 million person-kilometers)	1621.4	12921.5	12.5	3530.7	29832.2	11.8
港口货物吞吐量 (万吨)	Volume of Freight Handled at Major Coastal Ports (10000 tons)	204801.6	1568452.7	13.1	221462.1	1697326.4	13.0
邮电业务总量 (亿元)	Total Business Volume of Postal and Telecommunication Services (100 million yuan)	5063.1	31814.3	15.9	5669.5		
财政金融	**Government Finance and Banking**						
地方一般公共预算收入 (亿元)	Local Public Budgetary Revenue (100 million yuan)	13260.9	108762.2	12.2	13850.8	117228.7	11.8
地方一般公共预算支出 (亿元)	Local Public Budgetary Expenditure (100 million yuan)	18533.1	224981.3	8.2	18527.0	236403.5	7.8
人民币住户存款 (亿元)	Savings Deposits by Residents in Renminbi (100 million yuan)	112555.2	1203386.8	9.4	125616.8	1369894.6	9.2
外经	**Foreign Trade**						
出口总额 (亿元)	Total Exports (RMB 100 million)	53070.3	236336.8	22.5	54374.3	237656.4	22.9
进口总额 (亿元)	Total Imports (RMB 100 million)	29722.9	180391.0	16.5	28642.9	179853.7	15.9
实际外商直接投资 (亿元)	Foreign Direct Investment(RMB 100 million)	1819.0	12326.8	14.8	1591.6	11339.1	14.0
国内贸易和物价	**Domestic Trade and Prices**						
社会消费品零售总额 (亿元)	Total Amount of Retail Sales of Consumer Goods (100 million yuan)	44882.9	439732.5	10.2	47494.9	471495.2	10.1
居民消费价格指数	General Consumer Price Index	102.2	102.0		100.4	100.2	
人民生活	**People's Livelihood**						
城镇非私营单位就业人员工资总额 (亿元)	Total Wage Bill of Employed Persons in Urban Non-Private Units and Indices (100 million yuan)	26200.9	190820.2	13.7	26266.9	197416.7	13.3
全体居民人均可支配收入 (元)	Per Capita Disposable Income of Residents (yuan)	47064.6	36883.3		49327.4	39218.0	
城镇居民人均可支配收入 (元)	Per Capita Disposable Income of Urban Residents (yuan)	56905.3	49282.9		59306.6	51820.7	
农村居民人均可支配收入 (元)	Per Capita Disposable Income of Rural Residents (yuan)	23597.8	20132.8		25141.8	21690.9	
教育、科技、卫生	**Education, Science and Technology and Health Care**						
普通本专科学校在校学生数 (万人)	Students Enrolled in Colleges and Universities (10000 persons)	267.1	3659.4	7.3	260.1	3775.0	6.9
研究与试验发展(R&D)经费内部支出 (亿元)	Internal Expenditure on R&D (100 million yuan)	4411.9	30782.9	14.3	4802.6	33357.1	14.4
医疗卫生机构床位数(万张)	Number of Hospital Beds (10000 units)	60.8	975.0	6.2	62.9	1017.4	6.2
专业卫生技术人员 (万人)	Number of Medical Technical Personnel (10000 persons)	91.8	1165.8	7.9	97.9	1248.8	7.8

注：1.全国数据来自《中国统计年鉴2024》。
2.本表水果产量含瓜果产量。

Note: a) The data of the whole nation comes from the China Statistical Yearbook 2024.
b) Data of output of fruits in this table include melons.

1–6 各部门机构数
Grassroots Units in Various Sectors

部 门	Sector	2010	2015	2022	2023
农村基层组织 （个）	**Rural Grassroots Units (unit)**				
村民委员会	Villagers' Committees	22140	19632	19431	19436
工业企业 （个）	**Industrial Enterprises (unit)**	**250853**	**379804**	**732757**	
规模以上工业	Industrial Enterprises above Designated Size	53418	42134	70725	71996
#国有控股工业企业	State-holding Industrial Enterprises	1279	1035	1573	1646
建筑业企业 （个）	**Construction Enterprises (unit)**	**20195**	**36124**	**186025**	
#国有企业	State-owned	648	482	760	
批发零售和住宿餐饮企业法人单位数 （万个）	**Number of Corporate Units in Wholesale and Retail Trades, Accommodations and Catering Services (10000 units)**	**22.18**	**41.58**	**126.74**	
医疗卫生机构数 （个）	**Health Care (unit)**	**16541**	**21189**	**59531**	**62862**
#医院、卫生院	Hospitals and Health Centers	2444	2539	2981	3044
提供住宿的社会服务机构（个）	**Social Welfare Institutions (unit)**	**2514**	**1588**	**2058**	**2076**
教育事业	**Education**				
普通高等学校 （所）	Regular Institutions of Higher Education (unit)	131	143	161	162
中等学校 （所）	Secondary Schools (unit)	5146	5078	5544	5630
#普通中学	Regular Secondary Schools	4334	4434	5024	5110
小学 （万所）	Primary Schools (10000 units)	1.68	1.01	1.06	1.07
幼儿园 （所）	Kindergartens (unit)	11161	16368	21566	21662
文化和旅游部门所属艺术表演团体 （个）	**Art Performance Groups Affiliated with the Cultural and Tourism Sector (unit)**	**133**	**72**	**76**	**74**
文化事业 （个）	**Cultural Institutions (unit)**	**2384**	**2275**	**2308**	**2275**
文物事业 （个）	**Cultural Relic Establishments (unit)**	**208**	**260**	**227**	**231**
广播电视 （座）	**Radio and Television (unit)**				
广播电台	Radio Stations	22	22	2	2
电视台	Television Stations	24	24	3	3
广播电视台	Radio and Television Stations	79		95	95

注：2023年起，艺术表演团体统计口径调整为文化和旅游部门所属艺术表演团体(事业)和文化和旅游部门所属艺术表演团体(企业)。

Note: Starting from 2023, it will become an art performance group (business) under the Ministry of Culture and Tourism and an art performance group (enterprise) under the Ministry of Culture and Tourism.

1-7 法人和产业活动单位数

Number of Legal Entities and Industrial Establishments

单位：个 (unit)

项 目	Item	2021 法人单位数 Corporate Units	2021 产业单位数 Industrial Establishments	2022 法人单位数 Corporate Units	2022 产业单位数 Industrial Establishments
全 省	**Provincial Total**	**3634403**	**3894498**	**3838318**	**4085262**
按行业分	By Sector				
农、林、牧、渔业	Farming,Forestry,Animal Husbandry and Fishery	49050	49823	53402	54131
采矿业	Mining	2757	2944	2832	3029
制造业	Manufacture	661042	669491	708572	716790
电力、燃气及水的生产和供应业	Production and Supply of Electric Power, Gas and Water	10723	13015	11300	13385
建筑业	Construction	155020	165561	175128	186025
批发和零售业	Wholesale and Retail Trades	1135371	1217915	1201165	1280584
交通运输、仓储和邮政业	Transport, Storage and Postal Services	87925	102669	96391	110297
住宿和餐饮业	Hotels and Catering Services	63852	77765	70299	83847
信息传输、软件和信息技术服务业	Information Transmission, Computer Services and Software	185523	195172	192060	201347
金融业	Finance	31248	55016	32283	55552
房地产业	Real Estate	139385	160615	147384	167771
租赁和商务服务业	Leasing and Business Services	560720	587115	572160	596173
科学研究和技术服务业	Scientific Research, Technical Services	218335	229418	236298	247680
水利、环境和公共设施管理业	Management of Water Conservancy, Environment and Public Facilities	14912	16206	16521	17780
居民服务、修理和其他服务业	Services to Households,Repair and Other Services	70170	75253	74396	79181
教育	Education	78297	86210	77691	84698
卫生和社会工作	Health and Social Service	19346	24173	19072	22218
文化、体育和娱乐业	Culture, Sports and Entertainment	68047	71407	71134	74169
公共管理、社会保障和社会组织	Public Administration,Social Security and Social Organizations	82280	94730	80230	90605
按登记注册类型分	By Status of Registration				
内资	Domestic-funded	3548646	3790872	3750591	3979474
国有	State-owned	65282	94121	65876	90991
集体	Collective-owned	135573	143793	133542	140750
股份合作企业	Share-holding Cooperative Enterprises	5250	7430	5795	7740
联营企业	Joint-operation Enterprises	2177	2788	2358	2938
有限责任公司	Limited Liability Corporations	356709	407066	408707	457730
股份有限公司	Share-holding Corporations Ltd.	19418	42574	23635	46464
私营企业	Private Enterprises	2834689	2958964	2983063	3102555
其他	Other	129548	134136	127615	130306
港、澳、台商投资企业	Enterprises with Investment from Hong Kong,Macao and Taiwan	64722	72001	66052	73186
合资经营企业(港或澳、台资)	Joint Ventures	6430	7848	7414	8821
合作经营企业(港或澳、台资)	Cooperative Enterprises	1483	1657	1477	1652
港、澳、台商独资经营企业	Sole Investment Enterprises	54839	59795	54792	59610
港、澳、台商投资股份有限公司	Share-holding Corporations Ltd.	870	1169	1008	1303
其他港、澳、台商投资	Other Enterprises	1100	1532	1361	1800
外商投资企业	Enterprises with Foreign Investment	20635	31625	21675	32602
中外合资经营企业	Sino-foreign Joint Ventures	3862	5833	3865	5784
中外合作经营企业	Sino-foreign Cooperative Enterprises	347	453	345	444
外资企业	Foreign-funded Enterprises	14516	22075	15366	22964
外商投资股份有限公司	Share-holding Corporations Ltd.	738	1334	816	1393
其他外商投资	Other Enterprises	1172	1930	1283	2017

注：产业单位数包含法人单位数。
Note: The number of the industrial establishments include the number of the corporate units.

1-8　各市法人和产业活动单位数
Number of Corporate Units and Industrial Establishments by City

单位：个　　(unit)

市　别	City	2021 法人单位数 Corporate Units	2021 产业单位数 Industrial Establishments	2022 法人单位数 Corporate Units	2022 产业单位数 Industrial Establishments
全　省	**Provincial Total**	**3634003**	**3894498**	**3838318**	**4085262**
广　州	Guangzhou	837112	886204	876356	925731
深　圳	Shenzhen	939274	993874	942370	989981
珠　海	Zhuhai	128544	137029	136027	143651
汕　头	Shantou	66828	74016	84484	91973
佛　山	Foshan	277608	297191	297263	316834
韶　关	Shaoguan	49366	55014	53629	59155
河　源	Heyuan	35086	40733	40038	45778
梅　州	Meizhou	39986	46849	41108	46671
惠　州	Huizhou	185855	199090	208055	221079
汕　尾	Shanwei	19013	22254	20192	23537
东　莞	Dongguan	441075	463145	456383	477379
中　山	Zhongshan	136885	146284	184345	194391
江　门	Jiangmen	83222	90653	87954	95421
阳　江	Yangjiang	38812	42770	55031	59015
湛　江	Zhanjiang	80191	92215	73003	83598
茂　名	Maoming	80149	88061	77817	83943
肇　庆	Zhaoqing	42712	48537	45076	50994
清　远	Qingyuan	59523	66483	62428	68734
潮　州	Chaozhou	26211	28868	28887	31510
揭　阳	Jieyang	44705	49247	43820	47545
云　浮	Yunfu	21846	25981	24052	28342
按经济区域分	By Region				
珠三角	Pearl River Delta	3072287	3262007	3233829	3415461
粤　东	Eastern Region	156757	174385	177383	194565
粤　西	Western Region	199152	223046	205851	226556
粤　北	Northern Region	205807	235060	221255	248680

1−9　按行业和登记注册类型分组的法人单位数（2022年）

Number of Corporate Units by Sector and by Status of Registration (2022)

单位：个　　(unit)

项　目	Item	总 计 Total	内资 Domestic-funded	国有 State-owned	集体 Collective-owned	股份合作企业 Share-holding Cooperative Enterprises
全　省	**Provincial Total**	**3838318**	**3750591**	**65876**	**133542**	**5795**
农、林、牧、渔业	Farming,Forestry,Animal Husbandry and Fishery	53402	52703	447	957	68
采矿业	Mining	2832	2793	27	31	3
制造业	Manufacture	708572	679470	958	1523	1237
电力、燃气及水的生产和供应业	Production and Supply of Electric Power, Gas and Water	11300	10923	459	935	40
建筑业	Construction	175128	174045	427	539	228
批发和零售业	Wholesale and Retail Trades	1201165	1178585	2052	3329	1498
交通运输、仓储和邮政业	Transport, Storage and Postal Services	96391	94310	926	377	124
住宿和餐饮业	Hotels and Catering Services	70299	68871	253	203	238
信息传输、软件和信息技术服务业	Information Transmission, Computer Services and Software	192060	185725	459	83	95
金融业	Finance	32283	30853	390	40	101
房地产业	Real Estate	147384	143271	1356	3062	671
租赁和商务服务业	Leasing and Business Services	572160	560921	3360	116934	765
科学研究和技术服务业	Scientific Research, Technical Services	236298	230850	3617	497	222
水利、环境和公共设施管理业	Management of Water Conservancy, Environment and Public Facilities	16521	16341	2016	198	20
居民服务、修理和其他服务业	Services to Households,Repair and Other Services	74396	73825	451	349	200
教育	Education	77691	77450	16790	1777	139
卫生和社会工作	Health and Social Service	19072	18977	4301	709	40
文化、体育和娱乐业	Culture, Sports and Entertainment	71134	70455	1897	197	90
公共管理、社会保障和社会组织	Public Administration,Social Security and Social Organizations	80230	80223	25690	1802	16

1-9 续表 1 continued

单位：个 (unit)

项　目	Item	联营企业 Joint-operation Enterprises	有限责任公司 Limited Liability Corporations	股份有限公司 Share-holding Corporations Ltd.	私营企业 Private Enterprises	其他 Other
全　省	**Provincial Total**	**2358**	**408707**	**23635**	**2983063**	**127615**
农、林、牧、渔业	Farming,Forestry,Animal Husbandry and Fishery	37	2989	319	21278	26608
采矿业	Mining	4	447	42	2215	24
制造业	Manufacture	256	89538	5092	576605	4261
电力、燃气及水的生产和供应业	Production and Supply of Electric Power, Gas and Water	83	2081	186	7062	77
建筑业	Construction	56	23249	1105	147456	985
批发和零售业	Wholesale and Retail Trades	431	116480	5820	1039533	9442
交通运输、仓储和邮政业	Transport, Storage and Postal Services	41	10917	646	80842	437
住宿和餐饮业	Hotels and Catering Services	37	8627	490	58466	557
信息传输、软件和信息技术服务业	Information Transmission, Computer Services and Software	24	20595	1401	162369	699
金融业	Finance	15	5601	1341	23177	188
房地产业	Real Estate	122	25439	1296	110713	612
租赁和商务服务业	Leasing and Business Services	448	52829	2749	373642	10194
科学研究和技术服务业	Scientific Research, Technical Services	75	26943	1666	194709	3121
水利、环境和公共设施管理业	Management of Water Conservancy, Environment and Public Facilities	17	2714	164	11025	187
居民服务、修理和其他服务业	Services to Households,Repair and Other Services	38	6875	438	63946	1528
教育	Education	171	4132	273	41267	12901
卫生和社会工作	Health and Social Service	63	1699	103	9472	2590
文化、体育和娱乐业	Culture, Sports and Entertainment	41	7415	486	58080	2249
公共管理、社会保障和社会组织	Public Administration,Social Security and Social Organizations	399	137	18	1206	50955

1-9 续表 2 continued

单位：个 (unit)

项目	Item	港、澳、台商投资企业 Enterprises with Investment from Hong Kong, Macao and Taiwan	合资经营企业(港或澳、台资) Joint Ventures	合作经营企业(港或澳、台资) Cooperative Enterprises	港、澳、台商独资经营企业 Sole Investment Enterprises	港、澳、台商投资股份有限公司 Shareholding Corporations Ltd.	其他港、澳、台商投资 Other Enterprises
全 省	**Provincial Total**	**66052**	**7414**	**1477**	**54792**	**1008**	**1361**
农、林、牧、渔业	Farming,Forestry,Animal Husbandry and Fishery	624	60	12	535	4	13
采矿业	Mining	30	9	2	19		
制造业	Manufacture	21630	2377	445	18054	437	317
电力、燃气及水的生产和供应业	Production and Supply of Electric Power,Gas and Water	243	104	13	116	7	3
建筑业	Construction	973	121	19	791	20	22
批发和零售业	Wholesale and Retail Trades	16002	1246	101	14175	184	296
交通运输、仓储和邮政业	Transport, Storage and Postal Services	1587	212	408	916	27	24
住宿和餐饮业	Hotels and Catering Services	991	251	53	623	25	39
信息传输、软件和信息技术服务业	Information Transmission, Computer Services and Software	5358	389	34	4768	71	96
金融业	Finance	1001	372	10	565	13	41
房地产业	Real Estate	3178	597	242	2205	55	79
租赁和商务服务业	Leasing and Business Services	8816	896	49	7526	91	254
科学研究和技术服务业	Scientific Research, Technical Services	4272	487	30	3587	42	126
水利、环境和公共设施管理业	Management of Water Conservancy, Environment and Public Facilities	140	32	7	96	4	1
居民服务、修理和其他服务业	Services to Households,Repair and Other Services	425	72	10	315	11	17
教育	Education	167	35	6	119	4	3
卫生和社会工作	Health and Social Service	72	22	4	40		6
文化、体育和娱乐业	Culture, Sports and Entertainment	541	131	32	341	13	24
公共管理、社会保障和社会组织	Public Administration,Social Security and Social Organizations	2	1		1		

1-9 续表 3 continued

单位：个 (unit)

项　目	Item	外商投资企业 Enterprises with Foreign Investment	中外合资经营企业 Sino-foreign Joint Ventures	中外合作经营企业 Sino-foreign Cooperative Enterprises	外资企业 Foreign-funded Enterprises	外商投资股份有限公司 Share-holding Corporations Ltd.	其他外商投资 Other Enter-prises
全　省	**Provincial Total**	**21675**	**3865**	**345**	**15366**	**816**	**1283**
农、林、牧、渔业	Farming,Forestry,Animal Husbandry and Fishery	75	15	6	46	3	5
采矿业	Mining	9	5	1	3		
制造业	Manufacture	7472	1385	118	5515	221	233
电力、燃气及水的生产和供应业	Production and Supply of Electric Power,Gas and Water	134	52	9	59	8	6
建筑业	Construction	110	30	3	58	4	15
批发和零售业	Wholesale and Retail Trades	6578	705	28	5215	275	355
交通运输、仓储和邮政业	Transport, Storage and Postal Services	494	130	56	261	22	25
住宿和餐饮业	Hotels and Catering Services	437	92	11	256	44	34
信息传输、软件和信息技术服务业	Information Transmission, Computer Services and Software	977	222	6	652	22	75
金融业	Finance	429	184	3	167	40	35
房地产业	Real Estate	935	267	46	503	55	64
租赁和商务服务业	Leasing and Business Services	2423	330	24	1716	77	276
科学研究和技术服务业	Scientific Research, Technical Services	1176	346	17	687	32	94
水利、环境和公共设施管理业	Management of Water Conservancy, Environment and Public Facilities	40	8		22	2	8
居民服务、修理和其他服务业	Services to Households,Repair and Other Services	146	25	6	88	6	21
教育	Education	74	18	4	34	1	17
卫生和社会工作	Health and Social Service	23	12	1	7		3
文化、体育和娱乐业	Culture, Sports and Entertainment	138	39	6	75	4	14
公共管理、社会保障和社会组织	Public Administration,Social Security and Social Organizations	5			2		3

1-10 各市按机构类型分法人单位数（2022年）

Number of Corporate Units by Type by City (2022)

单位：个 (unit)

市别	city	法人单位 Corporate Units	企业 Enterprises	事业单位 Institutions	机关 Government Agencies	社会团体 Social Organizations	民办非企业 Non-enterprise Units Run by l NGO	其他组织机构 Other Organizations
全 省	**Provincial Total**	**3838318**	**3531854**	**43856**	**12467**	**27571**	**35321**	**187249**
广 州	Guangzhou	876356	844211	5515	1172	4752	4655	16051
深 圳	Shenzhen	942370	929977	2316	876	3369	4042	1790
珠 海	Zhuhai	136027	131053	956	514	1239	1359	906
汕 头	Shantou	84484	75527	2101	511	1170	1629	3546
佛 山	Foshan	297263	283370	1913	830	2485	2517	6148
韶 关	Shaoguan	53629	35807	2024	686	1166	710	13236
河 源	Heyuan	40038	30175	1260	492	625	934	6552
梅 州	Meizhou	41108	30567	1957	630	1080	1014	5860
惠 州	Huizhou	208055	189577	2202	585	1270	1853	12568
汕 尾	Shanwei	20192	13167	1230	424	623	688	4060
东 莞	Dongguan	456383	446132	1671	745	1211	3460	3164
中 山	Zhongshan	184345	178561	1137	196	713	1533	2205
江 门	Jiangmen	87954	72974	1944	547	1625	1026	9838
阳 江	Yangjiang	55031	40215	1025	422	737	927	11705
湛 江	Zhanjiang	73003	50084	3868	758	892	2227	15174
茂 名	Maoming	77817	38283	3352	491	843	1383	33465
肇 庆	Zhaoqing	45076	32639	1984	766	1019	1297	7371
清 远	Qingyuan	62428	33831	1672	532	853	1364	24176
潮 州	Chaozhou	28887	23464	1565	315	621	883	2039
揭 阳	Jieyang	43820	34625	2254	471	672	1366	4432
云 浮	Yunfu	24052	17615	1910	504	606	454	2963
按经济区域分	By Region							
珠 三 角	Pearl River Delta	3233829	3108494	19638	6231	17683	21742	60041
粤 东	Eastern Region	177383	146783	7150	1721	3086	4566	14077
粤 西	Western Region	205851	128582	8245	1671	2472	4537	60344
粤 北	Northern Region	221255	147995	8823	2844	4330	4476	52787

1-11 各市按行业分法人单位数（2022年）
Number of Corporate Units by Sector by City (2022)

单位：个 (unit)

市别	city	总计 Total	农、林、牧、渔业 Farming, Forestry, Animal Husbandry and Fishery	采矿业 Mining	制造业 Manufacture	电力、燃气及水的生产和供应业 Production and Supply of Electric Power, Gas and Water
全省	**Provincial Total**	**3838318**	**53402**	**2832**	**708572**	**11300**
广州	Guangzhou	876356	3290	73	89455	823
深圳	Shenzhen	942370	453	58	128604	472
珠海	Zhuhai	136027	709	54	11615	214
汕头	Shantou	84484	1555	26	19562	204
佛山	Foshan	297263	1367	27	81341	351
韶关	Shaoguan	53629	5002	232	3559	1290
河源	Heyuan	40038	6748	321	3734	646
梅州	Meizhou	41108	4526	287	3641	830
惠州	Huizhou	208055	3421	234	35816	699
汕尾	Shanwei	20192	1787	22	2103	227
东莞	Dongguan	456383	642	29	176567	389
中山	Zhongshan	184345	1087	10	72730	203
江门	Jiangmen	87954	2022	107	25998	360
阳江	Yangjiang	55031	2991	138	8149	572
湛江	Zhanjiang	73003	4077	156	5617	289
茂名	Maoming	77817	2689	236	4496	780
肇庆	Zhaoqing	45076	2330	231	7172	706
清远	Qingyuan	62428	4286	423	4799	1251
潮州	Chaozhou	28887	1188	23	10458	253
揭阳	Jieyang	43820	1905	35	8736	320
云浮	Yunfu	24052	1327	110	4420	421
按经济区域分	By Region					
珠三角	Pearl River Delta	3233829	15321	823	629298	4217
粤东	Eastern Region	177383	6435	106	40859	1004
粤西	Western Region	205851	9757	530	18262	1641
粤北	Northern Region	221255	21889	1373	20153	4438

1-11 续表 1 continued

单位：个 (unit)

市别	city	建筑业 Construction	批发和零售业 Wholesale and Retail Trades	交通运输、仓储和邮政业 Transport, Storage and Postal Services	住宿和餐饮业 Hotels and Catering Services	信息传输、软件和信息技术服务业 Information Transmission, Computer Services and Software
全 省	**Provincial Total**	**175128**	**1201165**	**96391**	**70299**	**192060**
广 州	Guangzhou	36041	305254	25262	20456	66635
深 圳	Shenzhen	26726	375832	29896	13902	67402
珠 海	Zhuhai	12140	32859	3229	3123	9370
汕 头	Shantou	2982	25104	2059	2230	2718
佛 山	Foshan	10435	99463	7069	6535	8976
韶 关	Shaoguan	3677	9883	1072	842	1512
河 源	Heyuan	3891	7766	783	703	1108
梅 州	Meizhou	3912	8500	815	495	1686
惠 州	Huizhou	21049	53445	3694	4558	6457
汕 尾	Shanwei	889	3489	340	611	424
东 莞	Dongguan	19804	130454	8379	6637	10235
中 山	Zhongshan	10544	42239	3822	3233	4735
江 门	Jiangmen	4993	17673	1940	1630	1814
阳 江	Yangjiang	2761	13652	1069	757	1319
湛 江	Zhanjiang	3742	18239	1771	1345	1810
茂 名	Maoming	2753	16403	1014	646	1393
肇 庆	Zhaoqing	2203	8454	1003	583	1328
清 远	Qingyuan	2709	7954	1340	679	1052
潮 州	Chaozhou	893	6096	464	414	455
揭 阳	Jieyang	1644	13116	823	643	1192
云 浮	Yunfu	1340	5290	547	277	439
按经济区域分	By Region					
珠三角	Pearl River Delta	143935	1065673	84294	60657	176952
粤 东	Eastern Region	6408	47805	3686	3898	4789
粤 西	Western Region	9256	48294	3854	2748	4522
粤 北	Northern Region	15529	39393	4557	2996	5797

1-11 续表 2 continued

单位：个 (unit)

市别	city	金融业 Finance	房地产业 Real Estate	租赁和商务服务业 Leasing and Business Services	科学研究和技术服务业 Scientific Research, Technical Services and Geological Prospecting	水利、环境和公共设施管理业 Management of Water Conservancy, Environment and Public Facilities
全省	**Provincial Total**	**32283**	**147384**	**572160**	**236298**	**16521**
广州	Guangzhou	6999	36773	139586	74352	3136
深圳	Shenzhen	13920	27282	136808	60048	2538
珠海	Zhuhai	6207	7813	23760	11499	703
汕头	Shantou	294	2732	7957	4959	480
佛山	Foshan	985	11544	28434	16709	1105
韶关	Shaoguan	183	1998	13131	2743	535
河源	Heyuan	136	1965	3689	1767	407
梅州	Meizhou	160	1338	4522	1660	571
惠州	Huizhou	430	16195	30294	13766	1530
汕尾	Shanwei	53	1149	3630	609	143
东莞	Dongguan	1150	11467	46522	19313	1296
中山	Zhongshan	353	7446	16443	9155	771
江门	Jiangmen	246	4022	14614	2979	514
阳江	Yangjiang	90	2157	13207	2401	391
湛江	Zhanjiang	193	3331	16167	3044	400
茂名	Maoming	134	2083	32810	2423	378
肇庆	Zhaoqing	226	2345	7756	2546	382
清远	Qingyuan	139	3215	24403	2552	486
潮州	Chaozhou	97	494	1437	1227	186
揭阳	Jieyang	155	1003	4573	1327	321
云浮	Yunfu	133	1032	2417	1219	248
按经济区域分	By Region					
珠三角	Pearl River Delta	30516	124887	444217	210367	11975
粤东	Eastern Region	599	5378	17597	8122	1130
粤西	Western Region	417	7571	62184	7868	1169
粤北	Northern Region	751	9548	48162	9941	2247

1-11 续表 3 continued

单位：个 (unit)

市 别	city	居民服务、修理和其他服务业 Services to Households and Other Services	教育 Education	卫生和社会工作 Health Care, Social Security and Social Welfare	文化、体育和娱乐业 Culture, Sports and Recreation	公共管理、社会保障和社会组织 Public Administration and Social Organizations
全 省	**Provincial Total**	**74396**	**77691**	**19072**	**71134**	**80230**
广 州	Guangzhou	18982	14091	4124	20549	10475
深 圳	Shenzhen	18445	15098	3475	15229	6182
珠 海	Zhuhai	3329	2368	811	3643	2581
汕 头	Shantou	1954	2837	885	2400	3546
佛 山	Foshan	6352	4455	1241	6062	4812
韶 关	Shaoguan	905	1528	484	923	4130
河 源	Heyuan	804	1499	442	633	2996
梅 州	Meizhou	620	1626	498	671	4750
惠 州	Huizhou	4036	3607	984	3967	3873
汕 尾	Shanwei	432	1373	214	408	2289
东 莞	Dongguan	7520	5356	1094	6422	3107
中 山	Zhongshan	3816	2972	804	2521	1461
江 门	Jiangmen	1483	1772	563	1118	4106
阳 江	Yangjiang	692	1354	339	751	2241
湛 江	Zhanjiang	1341	4950	785	1282	4464
茂 名	Maoming	745	3768	513	949	3604
肇 庆	Zhaoqing	718	1850	457	829	3957
清 远	Qingyuan	901	1740	485	892	3122
潮 州	Chaozhou	352	1578	195	627	2450
揭 阳	Jieyang	661	2794	348	830	3394
云 浮	Yunfu	308	1075	331	428	2690
按经济区域分	By Region					
珠 三 角	Pearl River Delta	64681	51569	13553	60340	40554
粤 东	Eastern Region	3399	8582	1642	4265	11679
粤 西	Western Region	2778	10072	1637	2982	10309
粤 北	Northern Region	3538	7468	2240	3547	17688

1-12 各市按登记注册类型分法人单位数（2022年）

Number of Corporate Units by Status of Registration by City (2022)

单位：个 (unit)

市 别	city	总 计 Total	内资 Domestic-funded	国有 State-owned	集体 Collective-owned	股份合作企业 Share-holding Cooperative Enterprises
全 省	**Provincial Total**	**3838318**	**3750591**	**65876**	**133542**	**5795**
广 州	Guangzhou	876356	858467	8788	14486	1891
深 圳	Shenzhen	942370	918070	4254	586	902
珠 海	Zhuhai	136027	126387	1947	649	112
汕 头	Shantou	84484	83726	3434	2314	268
佛 山	Foshan	297263	293234	2886	5717	365
韶 关	Shaoguan	53629	52991	3177	8886	217
河 源	Heyuan	40038	38940	2118	387	106
梅 州	Meizhou	41108	38797	2897	939	87
惠 州	Huizhou	208055	203531	3299	9508	181
汕 尾	Shanwei	20192	19785	1984	2281	19
东 莞	Dongguan	456383	444222	2518	3836	827
中 山	Zhongshan	184345	180871	1155	2524	107
江 门	Jiangmen	87954	85325	2861	8145	157
阳 江	Yangjiang	55031	54653	1673	6951	19
湛 江	Zhanjiang	73003	72722	5182	9921	125
茂 名	Maoming	77817	77213	4357	29018	70
肇 庆	Zhaoqing	45076	44312	3142	4160	33
清 远	Qingyuan	62428	61471	2451	19498	85
潮 州	Chaozhou	28887	28594	2089	498	97
揭 阳	Jieyang	43820	43489	3039	1962	82
云 浮	Yunfu	24052	23791	2625	1276	45
按经济区域分	By Region					
珠 三 角	Pearl River Delta	3233829	3154419	30850	49611	4575
粤 东	Eastern Region	177383	175594	10546	7055	466
粤 西	Western Region	205851	204588	11212	45890	214
粤 北	Northern Region	221255	215990	13268	30986	540

1-12 续表 1 continued

单位：个 (unit)

市 别	city	联营企业 Joint-operation Enterprises	有限责任公司 Limited Liability Corporations	股份有限公司 Share-holding Corporations Ltd.	私营企业 Private Enterprises	其他 Other
全 省	**Provincial Total**	**2358**	**408707**	**23635**	**2983063**	**127615**
广 州	Guangzhou	318	61977	4502	753106	13399
深 圳	Shenzhen	207	51300	4136	848029	8656
珠 海	Zhuhai	46	37396	615	82355	3267
汕 头	Shantou	85	12791	2681	56990	5163
佛 山	Foshan	115	15929	1091	261227	5904
韶 关	Shaoguan	56	4161	390	29766	6338
河 源	Heyuan	83	5215	401	22892	7738
梅 州	Meizhou	75	2940	391	24739	6729
惠 州	Huizhou	135	36615	1636	143916	8241
汕 尾	Shanwei	34	1222	127	11165	2953
东 莞	Dongguan	280	109143	3660	314184	9774
中 山	Zhongshan	83	24866	516	149185	2435
江 门	Jiangmen	205	13247	712	54653	5345
阳 江	Yangjiang	18	2650	223	36770	6349
湛 江	Zhanjiang	112	3125	480	45945	7832
茂 名	Maoming	207	9280	601	28065	5615
肇 庆	Zhaoqing	66	3581	305	27918	5107
清 远	Qingyuan	58	3157	296	29483	6443
潮 州	Chaozhou	46	2513	226	19987	3138
揭 阳	Jieyang	97	4924	461	28457	4467
云 浮	Yunfu	32	2675	185	14231	2722
按经济区域分	By Region					
珠 三 角	Pearl River Delta	1455	354054	17173	2634573	62128
粤 东	Eastern Region	262	21450	3495	116599	15721
粤 西	Western Region	337	15055	1304	110780	19796
粤 北	Northern Region	304	18148	1663	121111	29970

1-12 续表 2 continued

单位：个 (unit)

市别	city	港、澳、台商投资企业 Enterprises with Investment from Hong Kong, Macao and Taiwan	合资经营企业（港或澳、台资） Joint Ventures	合作经营企业（港或澳、台资） Cooperative Enterprises	港、澳、台商独资经营企业 Sole Investment Enterprises	港、澳、台商投资股份有限公司 Share-holding Corporations Ltd.	其他港、澳、台商投资 Other Enterprises
全省	**Provincial Total**	**66052**	**7414**	**1477**	**54792**	**1008**	**1361**
广州	Guangzhou	10175	1567	391	7764	176	277
深圳	Shenzhen	19995	1465	183	17805	207	335
珠海	Zhuhai	8405	1574	105	6409	91	226
汕头	Shantou	558	103	59	362	16	18
佛山	Foshan	2477	640	55	1684	49	49
韶关	Shaoguan	550	58	34	437	13	8
河源	Heyuan	1022	49	27	907	23	16
梅州	Meizhou	2253	91	29	2103	12	18
惠州	Huizhou	3822	298	80	3286	91	67
汕尾	Shanwei	378	26	16	324	5	7
东莞	Dongguan	8706	509	131	7704	157	205
中山	Zhongshan	2489	309	36	2027	68	49
江门	Jiangmen	2105	341	68	1606	53	37
阳江	Yangjiang	315	43	27	239	2	4
湛江	Zhanjiang	174	51	28	85	4	6
茂名	Maoming	558	50	14	478	9	7
肇庆	Zhaoqing	591	83	23	457	16	12
清远	Qingyuan	767	75	65	615	4	8
潮州	Chaozhou	240	33	55	145	4	3
揭阳	Jieyang	267	21	37	203	4	2
云浮	Yunfu	205	28	14	152	4	7
按经济区域分	By Region						
珠三角	Pearl River Delta	58765	6786	1072	48742	908	1257
粤东	Eastern Region	1443	183	167	1034	29	30
粤西	Western Region	1047	144	69	802	15	17
粤北	Northern Region	4797	301	169	4214	56	57

1-12 续表 3 continued

单位：个 (unit)

市 别	city	外商投资企业 Enterprises with Foreign Investment	中外合资经营企业 Sino-foreign Joint Ventures	中外合作经营企业 Sino-foreign Cooperative Enterprises	外资企业 Foreign-funded Enterprises	外商投资股份有限公司 Share-holding Corporations Ltd.	其他外商投资 Other Enterprises
全 省	**Provincial Total**	**21675**	**3865**	**345**	**15366**	**816**	**1283**
广 州	Guangzhou	7714	1242	89	5758	204	421
深 圳	Shenzhen	4305	970	47	2911	106	271
珠 海	Zhuhai	1235	272	33	766	39	125
汕 头	Shantou	200	38	11	125	12	14
佛 山	Foshan	1552	342	28	1056	66	60
韶 关	Shaoguan	88	26	1	54	3	4
河 源	Heyuan	76	12	3	53	5	3
梅 州	Meizhou	58	14	6	28	5	5
惠 州	Huizhou	702	114	15	499	31	43
汕 尾	Shanwei	29	6	2	17	2	2
东 莞	Dongguan	3455	355	34	2655	231	180
中 山	Zhongshan	985	152	6	701	66	60
江 门	Jiangmen	524	140	7	327	14	36
阳 江	Yangjiang	63	7	4	48	1	3
湛 江	Zhanjiang	107	43	3	52	3	6
茂 名	Maoming	46	12	2	25	4	3
肇 庆	Zhaoqing	173	49	11	102	3	8
清 远	Qingyuan	190	37	14	108	6	25
潮 州	Chaozhou	53	10	19	22	1	1
揭 阳	Jieyang	64	15	5	27	8	9
云 浮	Yunfu	56	9	5	32	6	4
按经济区域分	By Region						
珠 三 角	Pearl River Delta	20645	3636	270	14775	760	1204
粤 东	Eastern Region	346	69	37	191	23	26
粤 西	Western Region	216	62	9	125	8	12
粤 北	Northern Region	468	98	29	275	25	41

1—13　全省商品、服务类电子商务交易情况(2023年)

E-commerce Transactions in Commodities and Services of Guangdong(2023)

单位：亿元　　(100 million yuan)

指　　标	Item	总量 Total	2023年比2022年增长(%) Growth Rate in 2023 over 2022(%)
广东商品、服务类电子商务交易额	E-commerce transactions in commodities and services of Guangdong	81157.73	5.4
按交易平台分	According to the Transaction Platform		
广东在本地平台实现的电子商务交易额	E-commerce Transaction Volume of Guangdong on the Local Platform	30967.12	-0.2
广东在省外平台实现的电子商务交易额	E-commerce Transaction Volume of Guangdong not on the Local Platform	50190.62	9.2
按交易对象分	According to the Transaction Object		
B2B+B2G	B2B+B2G	41276.51	1.0
B2C+C2C	B2C+C2C	39881.22	10.4
按交易内容分	According to the Transaction Content		
商品	Commodity	59444.81	4.7
服务	Service	21712.92	7.2

注：1.统计范围：辖区内规模以上工业、有资质的建筑业、限额以上批发和零售业、限额以上住宿和餐饮业、房地产开发经营业、规模以上服务业法人单位拥有的商品、服务类电子商务交易平台，辖区内规模以下法人单位拥有的且电子商务年交易额1000万元以上的商品、服务类电子商务交易平台。

2.电子商务交易额=在本地平台实现的电子商务交易额+在省外平台实现的电子商务交易额。

3.2016年起国家统计局仅反馈商品、服务类电子商务交易分地区数据，合约类电子商务交易数据不分地区反馈，增速按可比口径计算。

Note: a)Statistical scope: within the jurisdiction of the industrial enterprises above Designated Size, qualified construction enterprises, the enterprises above designated size in wholesale and retail industry, enterprises above designated size of hotels and catering services,real estate enterprises, the services enterprises above designated size have e-commerce trading platform,within the jurisdiction of the enterprises below the designated size have e-commerce trading platform with e-commerce transaction volume of more than 10 million yuan.

b)E-commerce transaction volume=E-commerce transaction volume of Guangdong on the local platform+E-commerce transaction volume not on the local platform.

c)since 2016, the National Bureau of statistics only feedback the data of commodity and service e-commerce transactions regard of region, but the data of contract e-commerce transaction data regardless of region.And the growth rates are calculated at constant prices.

1-14 粤港澳大湾区主要经济指标（2023年）

Main Indicators of Guangdong-Hong Kong-Macao Greater Bay Area (2023)

地区	Region	土地面积（平方公里） Land Area (sq.m)	地区生产总值 Gross Domestic Product			人均地区生产总值 Per Capita GDP		
			绝对值（亿元） Absolute (100 million yuan)	指数（上年=100） Index (preceding year =100)	绝对值（亿美元） Absolute (USD 100 million)	绝对值（元） Absolute (yuan)	指数（上年=100） Index (preceding year =100)	绝对值（美元） Absolute (USD)
广州	Guangzhou	7238.46	30355.73	104.6	4307.79	161634	104.5	22938
深圳	Shenzhen	1987.01	34606.40	106.0	4911.01	195230	105.6	27705
珠海	Zhuhai	1725.07	4233.22	103.8	600.74	170306	103.2	24168
佛山	Foshan	3797.79	13276.14	105.0	1884.02	138526	104.9	19658
惠州	Huizhou	11350.36	5639.68	105.6	800.33	93036	105.5	13203
东莞	Dongguan	2460.38	11438.13	102.6	1623.19	109339	102.8	15516
中山	Zhongshan	1780.99	3850.65	105.6	546.45	86636	105.7	12295
江门	Jiangmen	9535.19	4022.25	105.5	570.80	83409	105.6	11837
肇庆	Zhaoqing	14891.43	2792.51	103.7	396.29	67614	103.6	9595
香港特别行政区	Hong Kong Special Administrative Region	1114.60	26840.37	103.2	3808.41	356157	102.2	50535
澳门特别行政区	Macao Special Administrative Region	33.30	3334.47	180.5	470.58	491628	180.5	69382

1-14 续表 continued

地区	Region	年末人口（万人） Population at the Year-end (10000 persons)	港口集装箱吞吐量（万标准集装箱） Container Throughput (10000 TEUs)	进出口总额（亿美元） Total Exports and Imports (USD 100 million)	出口总额（亿美元） Total Exports (USD 100 million)	进口总额（亿美元） Total Imports (USD 100 million)
广州	Guangzhou	1882.70	2541.44	1552.87	925.38	627.49
深圳	Shenzhen	1779.01	2988.00	5492.98	3482.67	2010.31
珠海	Zhuhai	249.41	122.52	421.10	287.32	133.78
佛山	Foshan	961.54	347.13	851.93	697.00	154.93
惠州	Huizhou	607.34	54.58	484.09	289.48	194.61
东莞	Dongguan	1048.53	390.15	1822.75	1203.64	619.11
中山	Zhongshan	445.82	129.66	366.34	314.43	51.92
江门	Jiangmen	482.24	160.85	246.32	200.18	46.15
肇庆	Zhaoqing	413.17	61.14	52.86	39.18	13.68
香港特别行政区	Hong Kong Special Administrative Region	753.61	1440.10	11268.87	5335.80	5933.07
澳门特别行政区	Macao Special Administrative Region	67.90	14.43	191.94	16.54	175.40

注：1.本表香港、澳门统计数据来自《中国统计摘要》、香港特别行政区政府统计处以及澳门特别行政区统计暨普查局。
2.香港特别行政区和澳门特别行政区地区生产总值为“本地生产总值 ”,年末人口为“年中人口 ”。
3.本表汇率按照100港币=90.02人民币元，100澳门元=87.87人民币元，100美元=704.67人民币元,100美元=782.9港币,100美元=806.4澳门元计算。
4.本表中，广州、深圳、珠海、佛山、惠州、东莞、中山、江门、肇庆九市土地面积为2022年数据。

Note:a) Data in this chart regarding Hong Kong and Macao come from the Hong Kong Special Administrative Region Census and Statistics Department, and the Macao Special Administrative Region Statistics and Census Service.
b)The regional GDP of the Hong Kong Special Administrative Region and the Macao Special Administrative Region are labeled as “Regional GDP.”
c)This chart is calculated using currency conversion rates of 100HKD=90.02RMB,100MOP=83.41RMB, 100USD=704.67RMB, 100USD=782.9HKD,100USD=806.4MOP.
d) In this table, the land area data of Guangzhou, Shenzhen, Zhuhai, Foshan, Huizhou, Dongguan, Zhongshan, Jiangmen and Zhaoqing are the data of 2022.

主要统计指标解释

行政区划 指国家对行政区域的划分。根据有关法规规定，我国的行政区域划分如下：(1)全国分为省、自治区、直辖市；(2)省、自治区分为自治州、县、自治县、市；(3)自治州分为县、自治县、市；(4)县、自治县分为乡、民族乡、镇；(5)直辖市和较大的市分为区、县；(6)国家在必要时设立的特别行政区。

发展速度 用以反映社会经济发展程度的相对指标，根据两个不同时期发展水平的对比而得。由于比较的标准时期不同，发展速度可分为定期发展速度和环比发展速度两种。

增长速度 发展速度－1（或100%）就是增长速度。即增长速度＝发展速度－1（或100%）。

平均每年增长速度 我国计算平均增长速度有两种方法，一种是习惯上经常使用的“水平法”，又称几何平均法，是以间隔最后一年的水平同基期水平对比来计算平均每年增长（或下降）的速度；另一种是“累计法”又称代数平均法或方程法，是以间隔年内各年水平的总和同基期水平对比来计算平均每年增长（或下降）的速度。具体计算方法，可参照中国财经出版社出版的《平均增长速度查对表》。

在一般正常情况下，两种方法计算的平均每年增长速度比较接近，但在经济发展不平衡出现大起大落时，两种方法计算的结果差别较大。

本《年鉴》内所列的平均每年增长速度都是用水平法计算的。从某年到某年平均增长速度的年份，均不包基期年在内。如1979－2023年平均每年增长速度，是以1978年为基期，2023年为报告期，年份从1979年算起，共45年。

当年价格 是报告期的实际价格，如工厂的出厂价格、农产品的收购价格、商品的零售价格等。按当年价格计算，是指一些以货币表现的物量指标，如工业总产值、国内生产总值等，按照当年的实际价格来计算总量。按当年价格计算的价值指标，在不同年份之间进行对比时，因为包含有各年间价格变动的因素，不能确切地反映实物量的增减变动。因此，在计算增长速度时都使用按可比价格计算的数字。

国民经济行业分类 自2017年统计年报和2018年定期统计报表开始使用新的《国民经济行业分类》（GB/T 4754-2017）。该分类是由国家统计局组织修订，国家质量监督检验检疫总局和中国国家标准化管理委员会于2017年6月30日发布。这次修订是在2011年分类标准的基础上，参照联合国《所有经济活动的国际标准产业分类》（2006年，修订第四版，简称ISIC/Rev.4）进行的。修订后的《国民经济行业分类》（GB/T 4754-2017）共有门类20个，大类97个，中类473个，小类1382个。

企业(单位)登记注册类型 是以在工商行政管理机关登记注册的各类企业为划分对象，以工商行政管理部门对企业登记注册的类型为依据，将企业登记注册类型分为内资企业、港澳台商投资企业和外商投资企业三大类。内资企业包括国有企业、集体企业、股份合作企业、联营企业、有限责任公司、股份有限公司、私营企业和其他企业；港澳台商投资企业和外商投资企业分别包括合资经营企业、合作经营企业、独资经营企业和股份有限公司等。对不在工商行政管理部门进行登记注册的行政机关、事业单位和社会团体，主要按其经费来源和管理方式进行划分。

国有企业 指企业全部资产归国家所有，并按《中华人民共和国企业法人登记管理条例》规定登记注册的非公司制的经济组织。不包括有限责任公司中的国有独资公司。

集体企业 指企业资产归集体所有，并按《中华人民共和国企业法人登记管理条例》规定登记注册的经济组织。

股份合作企业 指以合作制为基础，由企业职工共同出资入股，吸收一定比例的社会资产投资组建，实行自主经营，自负盈亏，共同劳动，民主管理，按劳分配与按股分红相结合的一种集体经济组织。

联营企业 指两个及两个以上相同或不同所有制性质的企业法人或事业单位法人，按自愿、平等、互利的原则，共同投资组成的经济组织。联营企业包括国有联营企业、集体联营企业、国有与集体联营企业和其他联营企业。

有限责任公司 指根据《中华人民共和国公司登记管理条例》规定登记注册，由两个以上、五十个以下的股东共同出资，每个股东以其所认缴的出资额对公司承担有限责任，公司以其全部资产对其债务承担责任的经济组织。有限责任公司包括国有独资公司以及其他有限责任公司。

股份有限公司 指根据《中华人民共和国公司登记管理条例》规定登记注册，其全部注册资本由等额股份构成并通过发行股票筹集资本，股东以其认购的股份对公司承担有限责任，公司以其全部资产对其债务承担责任的经济组织。

私营企业 指由自然人投资设立或由自然人控股，以雇佣劳动为基础的营利性经济组织。包括按照《公司法》《合伙企业法》《私营企业暂行条例》规定登记注册的私营有限责任公司、私营股份有限公司、私营合伙企业和私营独资企业。

其他企业 指上述企业之外的其他内资经济组织。

合资经营企业（港或澳、台资） 指港澳台地区投资者与内地企业依照《中华人民共和国中外合资经营企业法》及有关法律的规定，按合同规定的比例投资设立、分享利润和分担风险的企业。

合作经营企业（港或澳、台资） 指港澳台地区投资者与内地企业依照《中华人民共和国中外合作经营企业法》及有关法律的规定，依照合作合同的约定进行投资或提供条件设立、分配利润和分担风险的企业。

港澳台商独资经营企业 指依照《中华人民共和国外资企业法》及有关法律的规定，在内地由港澳台地区投资者全额投资设立的企业。

港澳台商投资股份有限公司 指根据国家有关规定，经原外经贸部依法批准设立，其中港、澳、台商的股本占公司注册资本的比例达25%以上的股份有限公司。凡其中港、澳、台商的股本占公司注册资本的比例小于25%的，属于内资企业中的股份有限公司。

其他港澳台商投资企业 指在中国境内参照《外国企业或个人在中国境内设立合伙企业管理办法》和《外商投资合伙企业登记管理规定》，依法设立的港、澳、台商投资合伙企业等。

中外合资经营企业 指外国企业或外国人与中国内地企业依照《中华人民共和国中外合资经营企业法》及有关法律的规定，按合同规定的比例投资设立、分享利润和分担风险的企业。

中外合作经营企业 指外国企业或外国人与中国内地企业依照《中华人民共和国中外合作经营企业法》及有关法律的规定，依照合作合同的约定进行投资或提供条件设立、分配利润和分担风险的企业。

外资企业 指依照《中华人民共和国外资企业法》及有关法律的规定，在中国内地由外国投资者全额投资设立的企业。

外商投资股份有限公司 指根据国家有关规定，经原外经贸部依法批准设立，其中外资的股本占公司注册资本的比例达25% 以上的股份有限公司。凡其中外资股本占公司注册资本的比例小于25%的，属于内资企业中的股份有限公司。

其他外商投资企业 指在中国境内依照《外国企业或个人在中国境内设立合伙企业管理办法》和《外商投资合伙企业登记管理规定》，依法设立的外商投资合伙企业等。

行政机关、事业单位和社会团体 参照企业登记注册类型，主要按其经费来源和管理方式划分。具体规定如下：

⑴行政机关：包括国家机关和政党机关，原则上均列为“国有”。但有特殊规定的，如供销社等，则列为“集体”。

⑵事业单位：包括经国家机构编制部门和有关业务主管部门批准成立的各类事业单位，不包括实行企业化管理的事业单位。事业单位的划分办法如下：

①由国家财政预算拨款或列入财政预算外资金管理以及经费主要来源于国有主管部门或国有上级单位的事业单位，列为“国有”。

②经费主要来源于集体单位的事业单位，列为“集体”。

③公民个人(或个人合伙)开办的事业单位，列为“私营”。

④上述以外的其他事业单位，如果其经费来源不明确，按管理方式进行归类。

⑶社会团体：包括经民政部门批准成立以及未纳入社会团体管理条例范围的工会、妇联等各类社会团体。社会团体的划分办法如下：

①未纳入民政部社会团体管理条例范围的工会、妇联、共青团、青联、工商联、科协、侨联等社会团体，国家拨款设立的基金会或基金管理组织以及经费主要来源于国有业务主管部门或国有上级单位的社会团体，列为“国有”。

②经费主要来源于集体单位的社会团体，列为“集体”。

③公民个人(或个人合伙)开办的社会团体，划为“私营”。

④上述以外的其他社会团体，如果其经费来源不明确，改按管理方式进行归类。

电子商务交易平台　指在电子商务活动中为交易双方或多方提供交易撮合及相关服务的信息网络系统总合。

Explanatory Notes on Main Statistical Indicators

Divisions of Administrative Areas refer to the divisions of administrative areas by the state. Relevant laws of the People’s Republic of China stipulate the following principles for the divisions of administrative areas: 1)The whole country is divided into provinces, autonomous regions and municipalities directly under the central government; 2) Provinces and autonomous regions are divided into autonomous prefectures, counties, autonomous counties and cities; 3) Autonomous prefectures are divided into counties, autonomous counties and cities; 4) Counties and autonomous counties are divided into townships, ethnic townships and towns, 5) Municipalities under the central government and large cities are divided into districts and counties; 6) The state will, when necessary, establish special administrative regions.

Development Rate is a relative indicator of the degree of social and economic development calculated through the comparison of two different periods in the degree of development. Development rate can take the form of either fixed-base development rate or chain base development rate.

Growth Rate is equal to development rate minus one (or 100%), i.e. growth rate = development rate －1 (or 100%)

Average Annual Growth Rate Two methods for calculating average annual growth rate are applied in China, one is the more commonly-used “level approach” or the method of calculating geometric average, which is derived by comparing the level of the last year of the interval to that of the base year; the other is called “accumulative approach” or algebraic average or equation method, which is derived by comparing the summation of the actual figure of each year in the interval to the figure in the base year. The detailed calculating methods can be found by reference to the Check Table of Average Growth Rate published by China Financial Publishing House.

Under normal conditions the results calculated by the two methods are fairly close, but they differed sharply when uneven economic development occurred with striking fluctuations in growth.

The average annual growth rates listed in this statistical yearbook are calculated by level approach. The base years are not included when the years are listed for average annual growth rates. For instance, the average annual growth rate of 45 years since 1979 is listed as average annual growth rate of 1979-2010, among which 1978 is the base year and 2023 is the reference year.

Current Price refers to the actual price in the reference period, such as ex-factory price, purchasing price of agricultural products, retail price of commodities, etc. Total values of some quantum indicators in value terms at current prices, such as gross industrial output value and gross domestic product, are calculated in accordance with actual prices of the current year. When comparing indicators of value over time at current prices, they cannot accurately reflect the changes in real term due to price fluctuations of each year. That is why growth rates are calculated at constant prices.

Industrial Classification of the National Economy The new Industrial Classification of the National Economy (GB/T 4754-2017) is introduced starting from the compilation of 2017 annual statistics and 2018 regular statistics. The revision, based on the 2011 classification, was organized by the National Bureau of Statistics taking into consideration of the International Standards of the Industrial Classification of All Economic Activities (2006, Revised Fourth Edition, ISIC/Rev.4) of the United Nations. The new Classification was promulgated by the National Administration of Quality Supervision, Inspection and Quarantine and the Standardization Administration of the People's Republic of China on June 30, 2017. The revised version of the Industrial Classification of the National Economy (GB/T 4754-2017) is composed of 20 sections, 97divisions, 473 groups and 1382 classes.

Registration Status of Enterprises (Units) Enterprises are classified into 3 categories, namely domestic-funded enterprises, enterprises with investment from Hong Kong, Macao and Taiwan, and enterprises with foreign investment, according to the registration status of an enterprise in industrial and commercial administration agencies. Domestic-funded enterprises include State-owned enterprises, collective-owned enterprises, cooperative enterprises, joint ownership enterprises, limited liability corporations, share-holding corporations Ltd., private enterprises and other enterprises. Included in the enterprises with investment from Hong Kong, Macao and Taiwan and enterprises with foreign investment are joint-venture enterprises, cooperative enterprises, sole investment enterprises and share-holding corporations Ltd. For government agencies, institutions and social organizations which are not registered in industrial and commercial administration agencies, they are classified mainly by their sources of funding and manner of management.

State-owned Enterprises refer to non-corporation economic units where the entire assets are owned by the State and which have been registered in accordance with the Regulation of the People's Republic of China on the Management of Registration of Corporate Enterprises. Not included from this category are solely State-funded corporations in the limited liability corporations.

Collective-owned Enterprises refer to economic units where the assets are owned collectively and which have been registered in accordance with the Regulation of the People's Republic of China on the Management of Registration of Corporate Enterprises.

Cooperative Enterprises refer to a form of collective economic units (enterprises) where capitals come mainly from employees as their shares, with certain proportion of capital from the outside, where production is organized on the basis of independent operation, independent accounting for profits and losses, joint work, democratic management, and a distribution system that integrates remuneration according to work with dividend according to capital share.

Joint Ownership Enterprises refer to economic units established by two or more corporate enterprises or corporate institutions of the same or different ownership, through joint investment on the basis of voluntary participation, equality, and mutual benefits. They include State joint ownership enterprises; collective joint ownership enterprises; joint State-collective enterprises; and other joint ownership enterprises.

Limited Liability Corporations refer to economic units established with investment from 2-50 investors and registered in accordance with the Regulation of the People's Republic of China on the Management of Registration of Corporations, each investor bearing limited liability to the corporation depending on its share of investment, and the corporation bearing liability to its debt to the maximum of its total assets. Limited liability corporations include solely State-funded limited liability corporations and other limited liability corporations.

Share-holding Corporations Ltd. refer to economic units registered in accordance with the Regulation of the People's Republic of China on the Management of Registration of Corporations, with total registered capital divided into equal shares and raised through issuing stocks. Each investor bears limited liability to the corporation depending on the holding of shares, and the corporation bears liability to its debt to the maximum of its total assets.

Private Enterprises refer to profit-making economic units invested and established by natural persons, or controlled by natural persons using employed labour. Included in this category are private limited liability corporations, private share-holding corporations Ltd., private partnership enterprises and private-funded enterprises registered in accordance with the Company Law, the Law on Partnership Business and Interim Regulations on Private Enterprises.

Other Domestic-funded Enterprises refer to domestic-funded economic units other than those mentioned above.

Joint Venture Enterprises(Funds are from Hong Kong, Macao or Taiwan.) are enterprises established by investors from Hong Kong, Macao and Taiwan with enterprises in the mainland of China in accordance with the Law of the People's Republic of China on Sino-foreign Equity Joint Ventures and other relevant laws, where the establishment of the investment and the sharing of profits and risks are stipulated under joint venture contracts.

Cooperative Enterprises(Funds are from Hong Kong, Macao or Taiwan.) established by investors from Hong Kong, Macao and Taiwan with enterprises in the mainland of China in accordance with the Law of the People's Republic of China on Sino-foreign Contractual Joint Venture and other relevant laws, where the investment or provision of facilities and the sharing of profits and risks are stipulated under cooperative contracts.

Enterprises with Sole (exclusive) Investment from Hong Kong, Macao and Taiwan refer to enterprises established in the mainland of China with exclusive investment from investors from Hong Kong, Macao and Taiwan in accordance with the Law of the People's Republic of China on Wholly Foreign-owned Enterprises and other relevant laws.

Share-holding Corporations Ltd. with Investment from Hong Kong, Macao and Taiwan refer to share-holding corporations Ltd. established with the approval from the former Ministry of Foreign Trade and Economic Relations in line with relevant State regulations, where the share of investment from Hong Kong, Macao or Taiwan businessmen exceeds 25% of the total registered capital of the corporation. In case the share of investment from Hong Kong, Macao or Taiwan is less than 25% of the total registered capital, the enterprise is to be classified as domestic-funded share-holding corporation Ltd.

Other Enterprises with Funds From Hong Kong, Macao and Taiwan refer to partnership enterprises with investments from Hong Kong, Macao and Taiwan established within the territory of China in accordance With Administrative Measures on the Establishment of Partnership Enterprises in China by Foreign Enterprises or Foreign Individuals and Regulations for the Administration of the Registration of Foreign-invested Partnership Enterprises.

Joint Venture Enterprises with Foreign Investment refer to enterprises jointly established by foreign enterprises or foreigners with enterprises in the mainland of China in accordance with the Law of the People's Republic of China on Sino-foreign Equity Joint Ventures and other relevant laws, where the sharing of investment, profits and risks is stipulated under contract.

Cooperative Enterprises with Foreign Investment refer to enterprises jointly established by foreign enterprises or foreigners with enterprises in the mainland of China in accordance with the Law of the People's Republic of China on Sino-foreign Contractual Joint Venture and other relevant laws, where the investment or provision of facilities and the sharing of profits and risks are stipulated under cooperative contracts.

Enterprises with Sole (exclusive) Foreign Investment refer to enterprises established in the mainland of China with exclusive investment from foreign investors in accordance with the Law of the People's Republic of China on Wholly Foreign-owned Enterprises and other relevant laws.

Share-holding Corporations Ltd. with Foreign Investment refer to share-holding corporations Ltd. established with the approval from the former Ministry of Foreign Trade and Economic Relations in line with relevant State regulations, where the share of investment from foreign investors exceeds 25% of the total registered capital of the corporation. In case the share of foreign investment is less than 25% of the total registered capital, the enterprise is to be classified as domestic-funded share-holding corporation Ltd.

Other Enterprises with Foreign Funds refer to partnership enterprises established within the territory of China in accordance with Administrative Measures on the Establishment of Partnership Enterprises in China by Foreign Enterprises or Foreign Individuals and Regulations for the Administration of the Registration of Foreign-invested Partnership Enterprises.

Government Agencies, Institutions and Social Organizations are classified into the following categories by source of funds and manner of management taking reference of the registration status of enterprises:

(1) Government agencies: include State and party agencies, classified in principle as State-owned. There are exceptions, such as supply and marketing cooperatives which are classified as collective-owned.

(2) Institutions: include institutions of various types established with the approval by organization and staffing departments of the government, but exclude institutions where enterprise management system is introduced. Institutions are further classified as follows:

(a) Institutions for which their main budgets are from government budget appropriations or extra-budget funds, or allocated from the budget of their competent government agencies. Such institutions are classified as state-owned.

(b) Institutions for which their budget mainly come from collective units. Such institutions are classified as collective-owned.

(c) Social institutions established by individual or a group of citizens, which are classified as private.

(d) Institutions other than those mentioned above for which their sources of budget are not clear. Such institutions are classified by the manner of management.

(3) Social organizations: include social organizations established with the approval from the Ministry of Civil Affairs, and organizations that are not covered by social organization management regulations such as trade unions, women's federations etc.. Social organizations are further classified as follows:

(a) Social organizations that are not covered by social organization management regulations of the Ministry of Civil Affairs such as trade unions, women federations, communist youth leagues, youth associations, industrial and commerce associations, scientist associations, overseas Chinese associations, etc., foundations and fund management organizations established with funds from the state, and social organizations whose funds mainly come from the budget of their competent government agencies. Such institutions are classified as State-owned.

(b) Social organizations for which their budget mainly come from collective units. Such institutions are classified as collective-owned.

(c) Social organizations established by individual or a group of citizens, which are classified as private.

(d) Social organizations other than those mentioned above for which their sources of budget are not clear. Such organizations are classified by the manner of management.

E-commerce Trading Platform refers to the total information network system which provide the deal making and related service for the transaction parties in e-commerce activities.

二、国民经济核算

NATIONAL ECONOMIC ACCOUNTS

二 国民经济核算

简要说明

一、本篇资料反映广东国民经济核算情况。

二、国民经济核算资料主要包括地区生产总值及其有关资料。地区生产总值是根据不同产业部门、不同支出构成的特点和资料来源情况而采用不同方法计算的。

三、本年鉴公布的地区生产总值以及与之有关的指标数据，最后一年数据不是最终数，还会在获得更多的财务和行政记录等资料后发生变动。如果遇到普查或者重大核算方法改革，在能够获得更详细的基础资料的情况下，地区生产总值的历史数据还会发生变动。2018 年，根据全国第四次经济普查结果和国家统计局地区生产总值统一核算要求，对历史年份全省生产总值进行了修订。2020 年，根据全国第七次人口普查结果，对 2010 年后的人均生产总值及支出法地区生产总值有关数据进行了修订。本年鉴中的数据是修订后的数据。

四、国民经济核算数据绝对数按当年价格计算，速度和指数按不变价格计算。

五、分市的国民经济核算历史数据在 2018 年以前采取分级核算，2018 年及以后采取统一核算方式核算。

六、本篇资料由广东省统计局国民经济核算处整理提供。

2 National Economic Accounts

Brief Introduction

Ⅰ.The data in this chapter reflect the national accounts of Guangdong Province.

II. The data on national accounts mainly include gross domestic product (GDP) and related data. Data on GDP are calculated with various approaches in accordance with the features of various industrial sectors, various expenditure structures and the data resources.

Ⅲ. The data on gross domestic product (GDP) and related measures publicized in this statistical yearbook for the latest year is not final and may be altered when more financial and administrative information is available. Major changes to census and accounting policies will lead to changes to GDP and historical data, if more detailed basic information is obtainable. In 2018, provincial GDP data in previous statistical yearbooks was edited according to the results of the 4th National Economic Census and requirements for the unified calculation of national GDP. In 2020, according to the results of the 7th National census, the relevant data of GDP per capita and GDP by expenditure method after 2010 have been revised. Data in this statistical yearbook contains the edited data.

Ⅳ. The data on national accounts are calculated at current prices, and the growth rates and the index are calculated at constant prices.

Ⅴ. Historical data on the economies of sub-cities was calculated with separate hierarchies prior to 2018. Starting in 2018, data was calculated in a unified manner.

Ⅵ. The data in this chapter are prepared and provided by the Division of National Accounts of Statistics Bureau of Guangdong Province.

2-1 国民经济核算主要指标

Main Indicators of Gross Domestic Product

指　　标	Item	2000	2020	2022	2023
地区生产总值 (亿元)	Gross Domestic Product (100 million yuan)	10810.21	111151.63	129513.55	135673.16
第一产业	Primary Industry	986.32	4732.74	5350.09	5540.70
第二产业	Secondary Industry	5042.75	43868.05	52620.72	54437.26
第三产业	Tertiary Industry	4781.15	62550.84	71542.74	75695.21
地区生产总值指数 (上年=100)	Indices of Gross Domestic Product (preceding year=100)	111.7	102.3	102.0	104.8
第一产业	Primary Industry	102.3	103.7	104.9	104.8
第二产业	Secondary Industry	112.3	101.9	101.3	104.8
第三产业	Tertiary Industry	113.5	102.5	102.3	104.7
地区生产总值构成 (%)	Composition of Gross Domestic Product (%)				
第一产业	Primary Industry	9.1	4.2	4.1	4.1
第二产业	Secondary Industry	46.7	39.5	40.6	40.1
第三产业	Tertiary Industry	44.2	56.3	55.3	55.8
地区生产总值贡献率 (%)	Share of the Contribution of the Three Strata of Industry (%)				
第一产业	Primary Industry	1.9	6.1	10.2	4.4
第二产业	Secondary Industry	59.7	36.1	25.8	40.0
第三产业	Tertiary Industry	38.4	57.8	64.0	55.7
三次产业对地区生产总值增长的拉动 (百分点)	Contribution of the Three Strata of Industry to Gross Domestic Product Growth (percentage points)				
第一产业	Primary Industry	0.2	0.2	0.2	0.2
第二产业	Secondary Industry	7.0	0.8	0.5	1.9
第三产业	Tertiary Industry	4.5	1.3	1.3	2.6
人均地区生产总值 (元)	Per Capita Gross Gross Domestic Product Product (yuan)	12817	88521	102217	106985
人均地区生产总值指数 (上年=100)	Indices of Per Capita Gross Domestic Product (preceding year=100)	107.3	101.1	101.9	104.7
支出法地区生产总值 (亿元)	Gross Domestic Product by Expenditure Approach (100 million yuan)	10810.21	111151.63	129513.55	
最终消费支出	Final Consumption Expenditures	5717.11	56585.06	65167.52	
资本形成总额	Gross Capital Formation	3917.11	49319.71	54600.37	
货物和服务净流出	Net Exports of Goods and Services	1175.99	5246.86	9745.65	
支出法地区生产总值构成 (%)	Composition of Gross Domestic Product by Expenditure Approach (%)				
最终消费支出	Final Consumption Expenditures	52.9	50.9	50.3	
资本形成总额	Gross Capital Formation	36.2	44.4	42.2	
货物和服务净流出	Net Exports of Goods and Services	10.9	4.7	7.5	
支出法地区生产总值贡献率(%)	Share of the Contribution of Gross Domestic Product by Expenditure Approach (%)				
最终消费支出	Final Consumption Expenditures	32.9	-17.5	46.8	
资本形成总额	Gross Capital Formation	27.2	61.6	-16.5	
货物和服务净流出	Net Exports of Goods and Services	39.9	55.9	69.7	
文化及相关产业增加值 (亿元)	Value-added of Culture and Related Industries (100 million yuan)		6210.60	6986.67	
新经济增加值 (亿元)	Value-added of New Economy (100 million yuan)		28199.82	33484.50	34736.46
占地区生产总值比重 (%)	Percentage of Value-added of New Economy in Gross (%)		25.4	25.9	25.6

2-2 地区生产总值
Gross Domestic Product

单位：亿元 (100 million yuan)

年份 Year	地区生产总值 Gross Domestic Product	第一产业 Primary Industry	第二产业 Secondary Industry	第三产业 Tertiary Industry	#工业 Industry	#建筑业 Construction	#批发和零售业 Wholesale and Retail Trades	#交通运输、仓储和邮政业 Transport, Storage, and Post	#金融业 Financial Interme-diation	#房地产业 Real Estate
1978	185.85	55.31	86.62	43.92	76.12	10.49	19.39	10.05	4.53	1.42
1979	209.34	66.62	91.65	51.06	82.36	9.29	23.52	11.26	4.74	1.62
1980	249.65	82.97	102.53	64.14	89.87	12.66	29.53	13.72	6.10	2.13
1981	290.36	94.30	120.34	75.71	103.60	16.74	33.57	16.71	6.76	2.79
1982	339.92	118.17	135.37	86.39	113.13	22.24	38.07	18.34	7.98	3.39
1983	368.75	121.24	152.27	95.24	125.82	26.45	41.42	19.47	8.94	4.09
1984	458.74	145.25	187.55	125.93	154.33	33.22	54.41	25.68	11.76	5.09
1985	577.38	171.87	229.82	175.69	185.81	44.01	79.86	35.91	12.74	6.16
1986	667.53	188.37	255.88	223.28	208.46	47.42	89.78	40.18	20.84	11.69
1987	846.69	232.14	330.35	284.20	273.77	56.58	104.17	53.20	34.25	16.44
1988	1155.37	306.50	460.17	388.70	386.35	73.82	145.89	65.22	46.80	22.84
1989	1381.39	351.73	554.13	475.53	464.06	90.07	136.65	79.02	72.70	41.36
1990	1559.03	384.59	615.86	558.58	523.42	92.45	152.90	101.61	82.46	42.87
1991	1893.30	416.00	782.67	694.63	675.55	107.12	185.77	138.54	94.83	54.09
1992	2447.54	465.83	1098.75	882.96	899.28	201.04	202.75	96.40	122.79	81.74
1993	3469.28	558.70	1702.46	1208.12	1386.83	318.05	291.79	127.20	149.29	126.09
1994	4619.02	692.25	2249.99	1676.77	1865.44	387.80	416.88	183.19	199.84	170.68
1995	5940.34	864.49	2901.99	2173.86	2454.87	451.40	555.12	238.66	229.27	229.89
1996	6848.22	935.23	3313.55	2599.44	2853.85	464.66	684.33	277.41	264.86	282.32
1997	7792.97	978.32	3713.92	3100.73	3250.72	468.97	809.50	354.11	302.87	339.57
1998	8555.33	994.55	4080.96	3479.82	3584.54	502.87	919.83	388.75	306.39	415.38
1999	9289.64	1009.01	4384.22	3896.41	3864.77	526.56	1006.73	427.02	331.10	500.21
2000	10810.21	986.32	5042.75	4781.15	4518.65	537.06	1175.32	536.54	443.69	616.25
2001	12126.59	988.84	5564.66	5573.09	5012.16	565.75	1323.01	657.08	450.81	682.89
2002	13601.89	1015.08	6209.06	6377.76	5628.70	596.03	1509.35	725.85	454.65	788.40
2003	15979.77	1072.92	7684.41	7222.44	6991.52	710.77	1729.08	747.89	539.41	930.80
2004	18658.34	1219.83	9191.71	8246.80	8433.23	780.81	1950.55	840.80	614.36	1039.13
2005	21962.99	1395.23	11049.21	9518.55	10231.13	847.44	2175.03	1000.38	681.73	1274.31
2006	25961.24	1494.69	13158.01	11308.54	12259.42	934.97	2529.92	1164.22	923.73	1564.13
2007	31742.61	1663.49	16022.56	14056.56	14990.77	1073.17	2957.99	1351.81	1716.57	1969.26
2008	36704.16	1920.80	18519.40	16263.96	17356.70	1208.40	3524.94	1541.26	2019.35	1999.67
2009	39464.69	1945.95	19439.71	18079.03	18128.48	1350.61	4024.32	1486.63	2372.87	2374.45
2010	45944.62	2199.60	22917.43	20827.59	21387.71	1574.96	4825.08	1670.49	2890.11	2672.34
2011	53072.79	2553.17	26161.08	24358.54	24460.73	1755.04	5935.31	1889.87	3326.82	3084.98
2012	57007.74	2711.32	27346.12	26950.30	25526.22	1876.07	6670.82	2100.81	3757.12	3378.45
2013	62503.41	2876.42	29342.97	30284.02	27142.10	2260.48	7404.60	2237.30	4498.84	3956.04
2014	68173.03	3038.71	31930.37	33203.95	29497.80	2496.15	7946.25	2490.13	4872.81	4309.34
2015	74732.44	3189.76	33913.76	37628.92	31315.46	2684.40	8030.87	2662.73	6119.66	5280.52
2016	82163.22	3500.49	35499.24	43163.49	32677.94	2909.50	8924.66	2877.45	6570.01	6615.72
2017	91648.73	3611.44	38536.61	49500.68	35343.97	3289.32	9642.05	3166.69	7311.19	8178.60
2018	99945.22	3836.40	41398.45	54710.37	37651.05	3849.75	10476.03	3363.48	7962.26	8533.74
2019	107986.92	4350.61	43368.21	60268.10	39141.79	4333.96	11000.23	3657.96	8764.09	9543.22
2020	111151.63	4732.74	43868.05	62550.84	39353.92	4616.38	10728.95	3370.13	10016.11	10377.02
2021	124719.53	4984.70	50555.79	69179.04	45510.34	5167.75	12102.12	4054.91	10937.34	11042.82
2022	129513.55	5350.09	52620.72	71542.74	47356.89	5405.88	12498.16	4246.41	11557.10	10710.74
2023	135673.16	5540.70	54437.26	75695.21	48712.94	5892.49	13174.53	4847.71	12418.82	10545.72

注：1.1991年以前第一产业不包括农林牧渔服务业，交通运输仓储和邮政业包括电信业，但不包括城市公共交通业，批发与零售业包括餐饮业（以下相关表同）。

2.三次产业分类执行国家统计局2018年修订的《三次产业划分规定》，全省数据修订至1992年(以下相关表同)。

Notes: a)In 1991 and prior to it, the primary industry did not include service activities for farming, forestry, animal husbandry and fishery; transport, storage,and postal services included telecommunication services,but excluded urban public transport;and wholesale and retail trades included catering services. The same applies to the following tables.

b)The classification of the three strata of industry shall comply with the "Regulations on the Classification of the Three Strata of Industries" revised by the National Bureau of Statistics in 2018, and the data for the whole province shall be revised to 1992 (the same as the relevant table

2-3 地区生产总值指数
Indices of Gross Domestic Product

上年=100 (preceding year=100)

年份 Year	地区生产总值 Gross Domestic Product	第一产业 Primary Industry	第二产业 Secondary Industry	第三产业 Tertiary Industry	#工业 Industry	#建筑业 Construction	#批发和零售业 Wholesale and Retail Trades	#交通运输、仓储和邮政业 Transport, Storage, and Post	#金融业 Financial Intermediation	#房地产业 Real Estate
1978	101.0	105.2	98.0	102.1	102.8	70.8	107.4	104.8	93.1	97.5
1979	108.5	106.6	104.7	118.1	106.7	88.7	123.8	113.2	103.7	115.4
1980	116.6	112.4	116.6	121.7	114.4	138.0	119.5	119.4	126.1	136.3
1981	109.0	104.6	112.3	109.4	110.9	122.2	106.4	107.2	106.1	129.1
1982	112.0	112.0	111.5	112.6	109.2	126.3	108.0	117.5	110.0	121.1
1983	107.3	103.2	109.6	108.5	109.3	111.3	106.7	104.8	109.7	117.4
1984	115.6	112.0	118.3	115.2	119.5	112.0	116.6	105.7	116.8	109.5
1985	118.0	105.7	120.2	128.1	120.3	119.5	127.1	122.6	129.5	147.7
1986	112.7	106.2	108.6	125.4	109.1	105.7	118.6	121.6	130.9	161.9
1987	119.6	108.6	126.2	119.4	128.9	109.8	115.0	120.7	138.6	130.7
1988	115.8	105.3	123.4	112.4	125.4	109.1	106.7	120.0	113.3	125.7
1989	107.2	107.0	108.3	105.5	109.8	96.2	79.6	117.4	132.2	140.5
1990	111.6	107.1	112.5	113.2	113.6	102.0	112.7	107.3	117.8	98.1
1991	117.7	105.5	123.7	119.4	123.1	127.5	119.6	128.3	107.2	114.3
1992	122.1	105.6	133.6	119.0	130.6	149.6	119.4	119.6	121.2	146.2
1993	123.0	102.6	136.4	116.8	140.4	117.5	122.0	122.6	102.5	128.8
1994	119.7	103.2	125.8	118.5	127.4	116.5	119.4	127.4	107.4	127.3
1995	115.7	105.4	119.0	114.7	119.9	112.9	115.9	118.0	101.8	122.0
1996	111.3	104.9	112.7	111.5	114.2	102.8	114.2	109.2	107.5	115.6
1997	111.2	104.7	113.0	110.7	114.7	100.2	113.6	108.5	109.6	111.2
1998	110.9	103.8	112.5	110.4	113.1	107.7	115.0	105.6	103.1	110.4
1999	110.3	103.9	110.8	111.3	111.2	107.5	110.4	105.6	110.8	119.3
2000	111.7	102.3	112.3	113.5	113.8	99.4	109.4	118.4	122.7	114.8
2001	110.5	102.2	110.8	112.0	111.3	106.1	111.6	117.7	101.7	108.3
2002	112.4	104.3	113.7	112.5	114.8	103.5	113.3	108.0	100.6	111.3
2003	114.8	102.2	120.2	111.3	120.9	113.2	111.6	105.6	110.7	115.0
2004	113.2	103.8	116.8	110.5	118.4	101.1	108.0	113.0	107.6	105.3
2005	114.2	104.8	115.3	114.3	116.0	106.6	111.1	118.8	107.7	122.1
2006	114.9	103.9	117.2	113.8	117.8	109.0	113.1	116.1	124.1	113.6
2007	115.0	103.1	117.3	113.9	118.0	107.6	108.0	111.1	140.6	114.0
2008	110.5	103.8	111.6	110.0	112.3	100.6	112.6	108.1	109.5	94.2
2009	109.9	105.1	109.1	111.4	108.6	116.0	117.2	104.9	117.7	120.5
2010	112.5	104.5	114.5	110.9	114.7	112.0	114.8	111.3	114.2	104.2
2011	110.2	104.3	110.4	110.7	110.7	105.3	113.9	111.9	107.6	105.7
2012	108.3	103.9	107.3	109.8	107.5	103.5	110.1	112.5	110.7	108.6
2013	108.5	102.4	108.0	109.7	107.9	109.1	110.6	107.5	114.7	111.4
2014	107.8	103.3	108.0	108.0	108.1	106.3	107.3	110.8	108.1	103.0
2015	108.0	103.4	107.0	109.6	107.1	105.6	106.7	106.1	117.6	109.2
2016	107.5	103.1	106.1	109.2	106.3	104.3	107.1	108.2	106.4	110.9
2017	107.5	103.6	106.5	108.6	106.8	103.0	105.4	108.8	107.4	107.4
2018	106.8	104.4	105.9	107.8	105.9	105.5	104.7	106.3	107.9	103.1
2019	106.2	103.8	104.2	107.9	104.0	107.9	103.9	106.7	109.1	108.1
2020	102.3	103.7	101.9	102.5	101.4	107.3	95.7	96.6	109.0	104.2
2021	108.1	107.8	109.2	107.4	109.9	104.1	110.8	114.7	104.8	103.7
2022	102.0	104.9	101.3	102.3	101.2	102.7	101.9	97.1	106.2	97.1
2023	104.8	104.8	104.8	104.7	104.4	108.4	104.9	109.9	107.1	98.4

2–4 地区生产总值指数
Indices of Gross Domestic Product

1978年=100 (year of 1978=100)

年份 Year	地区生产总值 Gross Domestic Product	第一产业 Primary Industry	第二产业 Secondary Industry	第三产业 Tertiary Industry	#工业 Industry	#建筑业 Construction	#批发和零售业 Wholesale and Retail Trades	#交通运输、仓储和邮政业 Transport, Storage, and Post	#金融业 Financial Intermediation	#房地产业 Real Estate
1978	100.0	100.0	100.0	100.0	100.0	100.0	100.0	100.0	100.0	100.0
1979	108.5	106.6	104.7	118.1	106.7	88.7	123.8	113.2	103.7	115.4
1980	126.5	119.8	122.1	143.7	122.0	122.4	147.9	135.2	130.8	157.3
1981	137.9	125.3	137.1	157.2	135.4	149.6	157.4	144.9	138.7	203.1
1982	154.4	140.4	152.9	177.0	147.9	188.9	169.9	170.2	152.7	245.9
1983	165.6	144.9	167.7	192.0	161.7	210.3	181.4	178.4	167.5	288.7
1984	191.4	162.3	198.4	221.2	193.2	235.5	211.5	188.6	195.6	316.1
1985	225.7	171.5	238.4	283.5	232.3	281.6	268.8	231.3	253.2	466.7
1986	254.5	182.2	259.0	355.4	253.6	297.6	318.6	281.1	331.5	755.4
1987	304.5	197.8	326.9	424.5	326.9	326.9	366.6	339.4	459.3	987.3
1988	352.5	208.2	403.3	477.0	409.9	356.8	391.0	407.1	520.4	1240.6
1989	377.9	222.9	437.0	503.1	450.1	343.3	311.3	478.2	687.9	1743.5
1990	421.6	238.7	491.4	569.3	511.3	350.0	351.0	512.9	810.3	1709.5
1991	496.1	251.8	608.0	679.7	629.2	446.4	419.8	658.1	868.6	1953.5
1992	605.8	266.0	812.3	809.2	822.1	667.9	501.3	787.0	1053.0	2856.3
1993	745.1	272.9	1108.1	945.0	1154.2	784.8	611.5	965.2	1079.1	3678.7
1994	891.9	281.5	1393.9	1119.5	1470.7	914.1	730.2	1229.7	1158.6	4682.6
1995	1031.9	296.8	1658.4	1284.3	1764.1	1032.0	846.3	1451.5	1178.9	5713.4
1996	1148.9	311.3	1869.5	1432.3	2015.2	1060.5	966.8	1585.5	1267.3	6605.0
1997	1278.1	325.9	2111.8	1585.8	2311.5	1062.7	1098.0	1720.9	1388.4	7345.6
1998	1416.9	338.3	2376.1	1751.2	2613.9	1144.7	1262.6	1818.2	1431.8	8111.2
1999	1562.4	351.5	2633.4	1949.3	2906.9	1230.9	1394.4	1920.5	1587.0	9674.1
2000	1745.4	359.7	2956.2	2213.4	3307.7	1223.3	1526.1	2273.9	1946.4	11110.7
2001	1929.2	367.7	3274.5	2478.9	3681.4	1297.8	1703.4	2676.0	1980.2	12036.3
2002	2167.8	383.5	3722.3	2789.5	4227.9	1343.4	1930.1	2891.0	1992.8	13396.0
2003	2488.6	392.1	4474.4	3104.6	5111.6	1520.2	2154.9	3052.3	2206.2	15408.0
2004	2816.2	407.1	5227.8	3429.6	6049.8	1537.2	2326.4	3449.8	2374.2	16219.1
2005	3215.4	426.5	6026.3	3919.2	7017.0	1638.6	2584.7	4098.3	2557.0	19811.1
2006	3693.6	443.2	7060.6	4460.8	8268.1	1786.6	2923.8	4760.0	3173.2	22502.1
2007	4247.7	456.9	8280.0	5080.1	9756.0	1922.4	3158.1	5289.0	4462.7	25655.5
2008	4693.4	474.2	9238.0	5587.0	10958.6	1933.7	3554.7	5719.9	4885.9	24165.1
2009	5156.0	498.6	10077.6	6221.5	11902.6	2242.5	4166.4	5998.2	5748.8	29112.8
2010	5800.4	521.2	11541.2	6898.3	13651.0	2511.1	4783.8	6676.1	6563.5	30332.9
2011	6392.9	543.8	12736.5	7635.2	15117.7	2644.1	5447.7	7471.7	7061.2	32051.5
2012	6920.7	564.8	13661.5	8382.1	16253.0	2737.2	5997.5	8407.9	7817.8	34808.3
2013	7511.9	578.5	14750.3	9197.8	17537.7	2985.0	6635.9	9035.2	8964.4	38783.5
2014	8098.3	597.6	15924.1	9937.5	18953.0	3172.3	7121.9	10009.3	9686.2	39940.8
2015	8749.5	617.8	17033.6	10888.2	20296.3	3349.7	7601.3	10621.5	11390.8	43622.1
2016	9407.4	637.2	18073.6	11885.9	21566.3	3493.0	8140.2	11489.8	12118.9	48381.0
2017	10112.3	660.0	19254.1	12914.0	23039.1	3599.4	8581.1	12505.1	13015.9	51984.1
2018	10801.1	688.9	20383.9	13922.2	24397.5	3797.4	8981.1	13288.9	14040.4	53616.6
2019	11465.5	715.4	21249.5	15025.9	25361.3	4098.7	9331.0	14184.0	15316.1	57968.9
2020	11723.4	741.6	21648.6	15394.4	25715.3	4399.3	8927.8	13698.7	16699.1	60396.3
2021	12677.6	799.3	23650.8	16531.7	28249.8	4580.9	9893.7	15717.8	17495.0	62604.8
2022	12937.3	838.8	23963.9	16919.7	28588.7	4702.6	10082.7	15265.3	18580.4	60771.9
2023	13552.0	878.8	25113.1	17717.9	29849.8	5099.8	10577.2	16777.9	19893.8	59786.6

2–5 地区生产总值产业构成

Composition of Gross Domestic Product

单位：%　　　　(%)

年份 Year	地区生产总值 Gross Domestic Product	第一产业 Primary Industry	第二产业 Secondary Industry	第三产业 Tertiary Industry	#工业 Industry
1978	100.0	29.8	46.6	23.6	41.0
1979	100.0	31.8	43.8	24.4	39.3
1980	100.0	33.2	41.1	25.7	36.0
1981	100.0	32.5	41.4	26.1	35.7
1982	100.0	34.8	39.8	25.4	33.3
1983	100.0	32.9	41.3	25.8	34.1
1984	100.0	31.7	40.9	27.4	33.6
1985	100.0	29.8	39.8	30.4	32.2
1986	100.0	28.2	38.3	33.5	31.2
1987	100.0	27.4	39.0	33.6	32.3
1988	100.0	26.5	39.8	33.7	33.4
1989	100.0	25.5	40.1	34.4	33.6
1990	100.0	24.7	39.5	35.8	33.6
1991	100.0	22.0	41.3	36.7	35.7
1992	100.0	19.0	44.9	36.1	36.7
1993	100.0	16.1	49.1	34.8	40.0
1994	100.0	15.0	48.7	36.3	40.4
1995	100.0	14.6	48.8	36.6	41.3
1996	100.0	13.6	48.4	38.0	41.7
1997	100.0	12.5	47.7	39.8	41.7
1998	100.0	11.6	47.7	40.7	41.9
1999	100.0	10.9	47.2	41.9	41.6
2000	100.0	9.1	46.7	44.2	41.8
2001	100.0	8.1	45.9	46.0	41.3
2002	100.0	7.5	45.6	46.9	41.4
2003	100.0	6.7	48.1	45.2	43.8
2004	100.0	6.5	49.3	44.2	45.2
2005	100.0	6.4	50.3	43.3	46.6
2006	100.0	5.7	50.7	43.6	47.2
2007	100.0	5.2	50.5	44.3	47.2
2008	100.0	5.2	50.5	44.3	47.3
2009	100.0	4.9	49.3	45.8	45.9
2010	100.0	4.8	49.9	45.3	46.6
2011	100.0	4.8	49.3	45.9	46.1
2012	100.0	4.7	48.0	47.3	44.8
2013	100.0	4.6	46.9	48.5	43.4
2014	100.0	4.5	46.8	48.7	43.3
2015	100.0	4.3	45.4	50.3	41.9
2016	100.0	4.3	43.2	52.5	39.8
2017	100.0	3.9	42.1	54.0	38.6
2018	100.0	3.8	41.4	54.8	37.7
2019	100.0	4.0	40.2	55.8	36.2
2020	100.0	4.2	39.5	56.3	35.4
2021	100.0	4.0	40.5	55.5	36.5
2022	100.0	4.1	40.6	55.3	36.6
2023	100.0	4.1	40.1	55.8	35.9

2-6 三次产业贡献率

Contribution Rate of Three Industries

单位：%　　　　　　　　　　　　　　　　　　　　　　(%)

年份 Year	地区生产总值 Gross Domestic Product	第一产业 Primary Industry	第二产业 Secondary Industry	第三产业 Tertiary Industry	#工 业 Industry
1979	100.0	23.9	25.7	50.4	32.4
1980	100.0	22.4	44.2	33.5	34.8
1981	100.0	17.0	56.2	26.8	43.7
1982	100.0	32.1	40.8	27.1	28.3
1983	100.0	14.1	55.7	30.2	45.8
1984	100.0	23.7	50.7	25.6	45.6
1985	100.0	9.5	49.6	41.0	42.6
1986	100.0	13.0	30.4	56.6	27.5
1987	100.0	11.0	57.8	31.2	54.7
1988	100.0	7.6	67.7	24.7	64.4
1989	100.0	20.3	56.5	23.3	59.3
1990	100.0	12.7	53.0	34.3	52.2
1991	100.0	7.6	53.0	39.3	43.8
1992	100.0	5.6	63.0	31.4	48.7
1993	100.0	2.2	71.9	25.9	66.0
1994	100.0	2.6	65.9	31.6	59.7
1995	100.0	4.8	63.9	31.3	58.0
1996	100.0	5.4	61.0	33.6	59.4
1997	100.0	4.9	63.5	31.6	63.5
1998	100.0	3.9	64.4	31.7	60.3
1999	100.0	4.0	59.8	36.2	55.7
2000	100.0	1.9	59.7	38.4	60.6
2001	100.0	1.9	47.7	50.4	44.9
2002	100.0	2.9	51.7	45.4	50.5
2003	100.0	1.2	64.6	34.3	60.8
2004	100.0	2.0	63.4	34.6	63.2
2005	100.0	2.1	55.1	42.8	53.4
2006	100.0	1.7	58.1	40.3	55.9
2007	100.0	1.2	59.1	39.7	57.3
2008	100.0	1.9	57.7	40.4	57.6
2009	100.0	2.5	48.7	48.8	43.6
2010	100.0	1.7	61.0	37.3	57.9
2011	100.0	2.0	50.6	47.4	49.0
2012	100.0	2.1	43.9	53.9	42.5
2013	100.0	1.2	46.2	52.6	43.0
2014	100.0	1.7	50.2	48.1	47.7
2015	100.0	1.7	42.7	55.6	40.8
2016	100.0	1.8	36.8	61.4	34.9
2017	100.0	2.0	39.0	59.0	37.7
2018	100.0	2.5	38.2	59.2	35.6
2019	100.0	2.4	30.4	67.2	26.2
2020	100.0	6.1	36.1	57.8	24.8
2021	100.0	4.1	44.8	51.1	42.9
2022	100.0	10.2	25.8	64.0	21.1
2023	100.0	4.4	40.0	55.7	33.1

注：三次产业贡献率指各产业增加值增量与GDP增量之比。
Notes: The contribution rate of three industries refers to the ratio of the value-added increment of each industry to the GDP increment.

2-7 三次产业对地区生产总值增长的拉动

Contribution of the Three Strata of Industry to GDP Growth

单位：百分点 (percentage points)

年份 Year	地区生产总值 Gross Domestic Product	第一产业 Primary Industry	第二产业 Secondary Industry	第三产业 Tertiary Industry	#工 业 Industry
1979	8.5	2.0	2.2	4.3	2.7
1980	16.6	3.7	7.3	5.6	5.8
1981	9.0	1.5	5.1	2.4	3.9
1982	12.0	3.8	4.9	3.2	3.4
1983	7.3	1.0	4.1	2.2	3.3
1984	15.6	3.7	7.9	4.0	7.1
1985	18.0	1.7	8.9	7.4	7.6
1986	12.7	1.7	3.9	7.2	3.5
1987	19.6	2.2	11.4	6.1	10.7
1988	15.8	1.2	10.7	3.9	10.2
1989	7.2	1.5	4.1	1.7	4.3
1990	11.6	1.5	6.1	4.0	6.0
1991	17.7	1.4	9.4	7.0	7.7
1992	22.1	1.2	13.9	6.9	10.8
1993	23.0	0.5	16.5	6.0	15.2
1994	19.7	0.5	13.0	6.2	11.8
1995	15.7	0.7	10.0	4.9	9.1
1996	11.3	0.6	6.9	3.8	6.7
1997	11.2	0.6	7.1	3.5	7.1
1998	10.9	0.4	7.0	3.4	6.6
1999	10.3	0.4	6.1	3.7	5.7
2000	11.7	0.2	7.0	4.5	7.1
2001	10.5	0.2	5.0	5.3	4.7
2002	12.4	0.4	6.4	5.6	6.2
2003	14.8	0.2	9.6	5.1	9.0
2004	13.2	0.3	8.3	4.6	8.3
2005	14.2	0.3	7.8	6.1	7.6
2006	14.9	0.2	8.6	6.0	8.3
2007	15.0	0.2	8.9	6.0	8.6
2008	10.5	0.2	6.1	4.2	6.0
2009	9.9	0.2	4.8	4.8	4.3
2010	12.5	0.2	7.6	4.7	7.2
2011	10.2	0.2	5.2	4.8	5.0
2012	8.3	0.2	3.6	4.5	3.5
2013	8.5	0.1	3.9	4.5	3.7
2014	7.8	0.1	3.9	3.8	3.7
2015	8.0	0.1	3.4	4.5	3.3
2016	7.5	0.1	2.8	4.6	2.6
2017	7.5	0.1	2.9	4.4	2.8
2018	6.8	0.2	2.6	4.0	2.4
2019	6.2	0.1	1.9	4.1	1.6
2020	2.3	0.2	0.8	1.3	0.6
2021	8.1	0.3	3.7	4.2	3.5
2022	2.0	0.2	0.5	1.3	0.4
2023	4.8	0.2	1.9	2.6	1.6

注：三次产业拉动指GDP增长速度与各产业贡献率之乘积。
Notes: The Three Industries pulling rate is the growth rate of GDP multiplying industrial contribution rate.

2-8 支出法地区生产总值

Gross Domestic Product by Expenditure Approach

年份 Year	支出法地区生产总值(亿元) Gross Domestic Product by Expenditure Approach (100 million yuan)	最终消费支出 Final Consumption Expenditure	资本形成总额 Gross Capital Formation	货物和服务净流出 Net Exports of Goods and Services	最终消费率(消费率)(%) Final Consumption Rate (Consumption Rate) (%)	资本形成率(投资率)(%) Capital Formation Rate (Investment Rate) (%)
1978	194.14	130.02	54.79	9.33	67.0	28.2
1979	215.43	147.11	55.86	12.46	68.3	25.9
1980	259.32	180.93	71.37	7.02	69.8	27.5
1981	305.22	201.43	96.74	7.05	66.0	31.7
1982	349.13	233.21	112.35	3.57	66.8	32.2
1983	367.36	252.07	113.49	1.80	68.6	30.9
1984	446.06	288.26	150.07	7.72	64.6	33.6
1985	568.98	347.18	238.58	-16.78	61.0	41.9
1986	650.99	415.91	256.75	-21.67	63.9	39.4
1987	815.05	516.02	312.33	-13.29	63.3	38.3
1988	1129.64	667.03	462.07	0.54	59.0	40.9
1989	1348.54	857.33	472.75	18.46	63.6	35.1
1990	1541.99	938.48	502.90	100.61	60.9	32.6
1991	1847.99	1081.39	610.18	156.42	58.5	33.0
1992	2440.58	1359.08	987.96	93.54	55.7	40.5
1993	3465.31	1852.06	1554.46	58.79	53.4	44.9
1994	4618.25	2598.57	1930.86	88.82	56.3	41.8
1995	5940.34	3363.65	2401.80	174.89	56.6	40.4
1996	6848.22	3859.84	2795.64	192.74	56.4	40.8
1997	7792.97	4245.89	2992.18	554.90	54.5	38.4
1998	8555.33	4583.10	3354.63	617.60	53.6	39.2
1999	9289.64	5085.11	3548.75	655.78	54.7	38.2
2000	10810.21	5717.11	3917.11	1175.99	52.9	36.2
2001	12126.59	6259.29	4476.48	1390.82	51.6	36.9
2002	13601.89	7290.47	4858.53	1452.89	53.6	35.7
2003	15979.77	8647.86	6022.16	1309.75	54.1	37.7
2004	18658.34	10167.48	7350.24	1140.62	54.5	39.4
2005	21962.99	11457.36	8399.25	2106.38	52.2	38.2
2006	25961.24	12643.78	9512.26	3805.20	48.7	36.6
2007	31742.61	14853.52	10967.58	5921.51	46.8	34.6
2008	36704.16	17215.48	12590.33	6898.35	46.9	34.3
2009	39464.69	19196.56	15378.86	4889.27	48.6	39.0
2010	45944.62	22501.78	18226.60	5216.24	49.0	39.7
2011	53072.79	26235.01	21689.40	5148.38	49.4	40.9
2012	57007.74	29581.98	23699.14	3726.62	51.9	41.6
2013	62503.41	30900.24	27020.20	4582.97	49.4	43.2
2014	68173.03	34595.53	29850.24	3727.26	50.7	43.8
2015	74732.44	38116.43	31602.04	5013.97	51.0	42.3
2016	82163.22	42095.22	34647.12	5420.89	51.2	42.2
2017	91648.73	46682.78	39657.57	5308.39	50.9	43.3
2018	99945.22	51531.96	44379.92	4033.34	51.6	44.4
2019	107986.92	55827.36	48076.62	4082.94	51.7	44.5
2020	111151.63	56585.06	49319.71	5246.86	50.9	44.4
2021	124719.53	62237.05	56914.11	5568.37	49.9	45.6
2022	129513.55	65167.52	54600.37	9745.65	50.3	42.2

注：2013年起，国家统计局推行城乡住户调查一体化改革，支出法地区生产总值数据与以前年份不可比(以下相关表同)。

Notes: The data of gross domestic product by expenditure approach are not comparable to the previous years due to the integrated household reform conducted by the NBS(the same applied to the related table) since 2013.

2–9 资本形成总额及构成

Gross Capital Formation and Composition

年份 Year	资本形成总额 (亿元) Gross Capital Formation (100 million yuan)	固定资本形成总额 Gross Fixed Capital Formation	存货变动 Change in Inventories	比重(资本形成总额=100) Proportion (gross capital formation=100) 固定资本形成总额 Gross Fixed Capital Formation	存货变动 Change in Inventories
1978	54.79	37.93	16.86	69.2	30.8
1979	55.86	41.81	14.05	74.8	25.2
1980	71.37	57.15	14.23	80.1	19.9
1981	96.74	73.39	23.34	75.9	24.1
1982	112.35	94.64	17.71	84.2	15.8
1983	113.49	96.80	16.69	85.3	14.7
1984	150.07	133.04	17.03	88.7	11.3
1985	238.58	163.84	74.74	68.7	31.3
1986	256.75	182.15	74.59	70.9	29.1
1987	312.33	197.01	115.32	63.1	36.9
1988	462.07	286.00	176.07	61.9	38.1
1989	472.75	266.68	206.07	56.4	43.6
1990	502.90	336.61	166.29	66.9	33.1
1991	610.18	396.49	213.70	65.0	35.0
1992	987.96	683.66	304.30	69.2	30.8
1993	1554.46	1110.69	443.77	71.5	28.5
1994	1930.86	1375.09	555.76	71.2	28.8
1995	2401.80	1826.18	575.62	76.0	24.0
1996	2795.64	1932.16	863.48	69.1	30.9
1997	2992.18	2096.88	895.30	70.1	29.9
1998	3354.63	2497.33	857.30	74.4	25.6
1999	3548.75	2907.86	640.89	81.9	18.1
2000	3917.11	3160.12	756.99	80.7	19.3
2001	4476.48	3531.49	944.99	78.9	21.1
2002	4858.53	4119.36	739.17	84.8	15.2
2003	6022.16	5096.72	925.44	84.6	15.4
2004	7350.24	6093.41	1256.83	82.9	17.1
2005	8399.25	7577.75	821.50	90.2	9.8
2006	9512.26	8694.07	818.19	91.4	8.6
2007	10967.58	10230.11	737.47	93.3	6.7
2008	12590.33	11803.75	786.58	93.8	6.2
2009	15378.86	14452.53	926.33	94.0	6.0
2010	18226.60	17035.10	1191.50	93.5	6.5
2011	21689.40	20118.29	1571.11	92.8	7.2
2012	23699.14	22860.84	838.30	96.5	3.5
2013	27020.20	25966.92	1053.28	96.1	3.9
2014	29850.24	29021.09	829.15	97.2	2.8
2015	31602.04	30478.30	1123.74	96.4	3.6
2016	34647.12	33279.65	1367.47	96.1	3.9
2017	39657.57	38390.85	1266.72	96.8	3.2
2018	44379.92	42319.88	2060.04	95.4	4.6
2019	48076.62	45950.04	2126.58	95.6	4.4
2020	49319.71	46332.16	2987.55	93.9	6.1
2021	56914.11	50735.78	6178.33	89.1	10.9
2022	54600.37	48448.61	6151.76	88.7	11.3

2-10 最终消费及构成

Final Consumption Expenditure and Composition

年份 Year	最终消费支出(亿元) Final Consumption Expenditure (100 million yuan)	居民消费支出 Household Consumption	城镇居民 Urban Households	农村居民 Rural Households	政府消费支出 Government Consumption	比重 Proportion: 最终消费支出=100 Final Consumption Expenditure=100: 居民消费支出 Household Consumption	政府消费支出 Government Consumption	居民消费支出=100 Household Consumption=100: 城镇居民 Urban Households	农村居民 Rural Households
1978	130.02	111.46	40.12	71.34	18.56	85.7	14.3	36.0	64.0
1979	147.11	128.48	46.57	81.91	18.63	87.3	12.7	36.2	63.8
1980	180.93	156.51	60.55	95.95	24.42	86.5	13.5	38.7	61.3
1981	201.43	175.12	64.50	110.62	26.31	86.9	13.1	36.8	63.2
1982	233.21	202.70	74.76	127.93	30.51	86.9	13.1	36.9	63.1
1983	252.07	220.14	85.69	134.45	31.93	87.3	12.7	38.9	61.1
1984	288.26	250.92	105.87	145.05	37.34	87.0	13.0	42.2	57.8
1985	347.18	298.00	137.84	160.16	49.17	85.8	14.2	46.3	53.7
1986	415.91	349.52	164.49	185.03	66.39	84.0	16.0	47.1	52.9
1987	516.02	442.20	223.51	218.69	73.82	85.7	14.3	50.5	49.5
1988	667.03	566.25	283.39	282.86	100.77	84.9	15.1	50.0	50.0
1989	857.33	743.90	377.08	366.82	113.42	86.8	13.2	50.7	49.3
1990	938.48	807.84	406.22	401.62	130.64	86.1	13.9	50.3	49.7
1991	1081.39	923.37	511.00	412.36	158.02	85.4	14.6	55.3	44.7
1992	1359.08	1118.52	648.51	470.01	240.55	82.3	17.7	58.0	42.0
1993	1852.06	1574.61	957.16	617.45	277.45	85.0	15.0	60.8	39.2
1994	2598.57	2287.69	1442.66	845.03	310.88	88.0	12.0	63.1	36.9
1995	3363.65	2912.58	1890.75	1021.83	451.07	86.6	13.4	64.9	35.1
1996	3859.84	3343.00	2154.56	1188.44	516.84	86.6	13.4	64.4	35.6
1997	4245.89	3539.63	2317.15	1222.48	706.26	83.4	16.6	65.5	34.5
1998	4583.10	3781.21	2499.29	1281.92	801.89	82.5	17.5	66.1	33.9
1999	5085.11	4072.05	2774.14	1297.91	1013.06	80.1	19.9	68.1	31.9
2000	5717.11	4474.11	3125.44	1348.67	1243.00	78.3	21.7	69.9	30.1
2001	6259.29	4733.53	3318.28	1415.25	1525.76	75.6	24.4	70.1	29.9
2002	7290.47	5449.58	4025.54	1424.04	1840.89	74.7	25.3	73.9	26.1
2003	8647.86	6537.53	5273.69	1263.84	2110.33	75.6	24.4	80.7	19.3
2004	10167.48	7953.60	6729.38	1224.22	2213.88	78.2	21.8	84.6	15.4
2005	11457.36	8968.54	7560.24	1408.30	2488.82	78.3	21.7	84.3	15.7
2006	12643.78	9895.13	8470.02	1425.11	2748.65	78.3	21.7	85.6	14.4
2007	14853.52	11781.66	10229.41	1552.25	3071.86	79.3	20.7	86.8	13.2
2008	17215.48	13599.73	11812.60	1787.13	3615.75	79.0	21.0	86.9	13.1
2009	19196.56	15261.29	13233.01	2028.28	3935.27	79.5	20.5	86.7	13.3
2010	22501.78	17702.35	15438.42	2263.93	4799.43	78.7	21.3	87.2	12.8
2011	26235.01	20636.84	17860.12	2776.72	5598.17	78.7	21.3	86.5	13.5
2012	29581.98	23321.42	20179.53	3141.89	6260.56	78.8	21.2	86.5	13.5
2013	30900.24	23901.02	20109.64	3791.38	6999.22	77.3	22.7	84.1	15.9
2014	34595.53	26936.81	22536.12	4400.69	7658.72	77.9	22.1	83.7	16.3
2015	38116.43	29356.72	24734.89	4621.84	8759.71	77.0	23.0	84.3	15.7
2016	42095.22	32336.89	27234.11	5102.78	9758.33	76.8	23.2	84.2	15.8
2017	46682.78	35650.88	30154.13	5496.75	11031.90	76.4	23.6	84.6	15.4
2018	51531.96	39312.83	32963.41	6349.42	12219.13	76.3	23.7	83.8	16.2
2019	55827.36	42318.90	35556.70	6762.19	13508.47	75.8	24.2	84.0	16.0
2020	56585.06	42098.56	35482.91	6615.65	14486.50	74.4	25.6	84.3	15.7
2021	62237.05	46666.46	39322.44	7344.02	15570.60	75.0	25.0	84.3	15.7
2022	65167.52	48484.05	40737.19	7746.86	16683.47	74.4	25.6	84.0	16.0

2-11 三大需求对地区生产总值增长的贡献率和拉动

Contribution Share and Contribution of the Three Major Demands to GDP Growth

年份 Year	最终消费支出 Final Consumption Expenditure		资本形成总额 Gross Capital Formation		货物和服务净流出 Net Exports of Goods and Services	
	贡献率(%) Contribution Share (%)	拉动(百分点) Contribution (percentage points)	贡献率(%) Contribution Rate (%)	拉动(百分点) Contribution (percentage points)	贡献率(%) Contribution Rate (%)	拉动(百分点) Contribution (percentage points)
1979	95.7	5.3	-13.8	-0.8	18.2	1.0
1980	71.3	13.0	33.5	6.1	-4.8	-0.9
1981	50.5	6.3	56.4	7.1	-6.9	-0.9
1982	72.7	8.3	40.6	4.6	-13.2	-1.5
1983	124.4	5.6	-12.9	-0.6	-11.5	-0.5
1984	56.5	8.5	42.2	6.3	1.3	0.2
1985	32.0	6.9	80.6	17.4	-12.6	-2.7
1986	83.6	8.8	15.5	1.6	0.8	0.1
1987	38.6	4.9	34.9	4.4	26.4	3.3
1988	-2.8	-0.3	60.1	7.4	42.8	5.2
1989	110.8	9.4	-35.6	-3.0	24.8	2.1
1990	60.9	7.2	9.5	1.1	29.6	3.5
1991	39.9	7.1	35.1	6.3	25.0	4.5
1992	56.0	12.4	65.2	14.5	-21.1	-4.7
1993	50.2	11.6	60.1	13.9	-10.3	-2.4
1994	53.8	10.4	36.1	7.0	10.1	1.9
1995	48.5	8.0	39.6	6.5	11.9	2.0
1996	44.8	5.1	52.1	5.9	3.1	0.3
1997	21.6	2.4	7.5	0.8	71.0	8.0
1998	39.4	4.3	43.9	4.8	16.7	1.8
1999	54.5	5.6	22.5	2.3	23.1	2.4
2000	32.9	3.9	27.2	3.2	39.9	4.7
2001	45.8	4.8	49.0	5.2	5.3	0.6
2002	68.0	8.4	23.3	2.9	8.7	1.1
2003	63.4	9.4	50.4	7.5	-13.8	-2.0
2004	56.4	7.4	41.8	5.5	1.8	0.2
2005	43.3	6.1	31.2	4.4	25.6	3.6
2006	32.3	4.8	30.3	4.5	37.4	5.6
2007	46.3	7.0	24.7	3.7	28.9	4.3
2008	46.9	4.9	36.3	3.8	16.8	1.8
2009	65.2	6.4	83.4	8.2	-48.5	-4.8
2010	54.6	6.8	48.7	6.1	-3.3	-0.4
2011	51.0	5.2	50.5	5.2	-1.5	-0.1
2012	57.1	4.7	45.8	3.8	-2.9	-0.2
2013	46.1	0.3	43.5	6.2	10.3	2.0
2014	53.7	4.2	50.7	4.0	-4.4	-0.3
2015	51.9	4.2	49.1	3.9	-1.0	-0.1
2016	53.7	4.0	48.2	3.6	-1.9	-0.1
2017	53.3	4.0	44.7	3.3	2.0	0.2
2018	56.4	3.8	54.8	3.7	-11.1	-0.8
2019	55.1	3.4	49.5	3.0	-4.6	-0.3
2020	-17.5	-0.4	61.6	1.4	55.9	1.3
2021	56.4	4.6	41.7	3.4	1.9	0.2
2022	46.8	1.0	-16.5	-0.3	69.7	1.4

注：1.三大需求指支出法地区生产总值的三大构成项目，即最终消费支出、资本形成总额、货物和服务净流出。
2.贡献率指三大需求增量与支出法地区生产总值增量之比。
3.拉动指地区生产总值增长速度与三大需求贡献率的乘积。

Notes: a) Three major demands refer to three major components of gross domestic product by expenditure approach,i.e.final consumption expenditure, gross capital formation, and net exports of goods and services.
b) Contribution rate refers to the proportion of the increment of three major demands to the increment of gross domestic product by expenditure approach.
c) Pulling rate refers to the growth rate of gross regional product multiplying the contribution rates of three major demands.

2-12 人均地区生产总值及人均消费水平指数

Indices of Per Capita Gross Domestic Product and Consumption

年份 Year	人均地区生产总值 Per Capita Gross Domestic Product		人均消费水平 Per Capita Consumption					
			全体居民 Households		城镇居民 Urban Households		农村居民 Rural Households	
	绝对数（元） Absolute Figure (yuan)	指数（上年=100） Index (preceding year=100)	绝对数（元） Absolute Figure (yuan)	指数（上年=100） Index (preceding year=100)	绝对数（元） Absolute Figure (yuan)	指数（上年=100） Index (preceding year=100)	绝对数（元） Absolute Figure (yuan)	指数（上年=100） Index (preceding year=100)
1978	370		222		466		171	
1979	410	106.9	252	108.3	507	102.6	196	109.8
1980	481	114.8	302	114.9	620	112.7	228	114.1
1981	550	107.1	332	107.9	627	98.1	260	113.3
1982	633	110.0	377	110.3	696	108.3	298	110.4
1983	675	105.6	403	107.2	764	108.5	310	105.1
1984	827	113.8	453	110.3	878	109.7	334	107.8
1985	1026	116.2	529	105.7	1038	110.2	372	97.4
1986	1164	110.6	609	109.5	1146	108.4	430	106.3
1987	1443	117.0	754	106.4	1382	101.1	515	104.9
1988	1926	113.2	944	96.5	1716	93.2	651	100.5
1989	2251	104.8	1212	119.7	2188	115.0	831	123.1
1990	2484	109.1	1287	109.3	2263	104.7	896	112.9
1991	2941	114.7	1434	108.3	2712	114.8	906	100.2
1992	3699	118.8	1690	114.7	3210	115.7	1023	109.7
1993	5085	119.3	2308	120.5	4280	117.0	1347	117.6
1994	6530	115.5	3234	117.8	5870	115.7	1831	114.3
1995	8139	112.1	3991	110.1	7091	107.6	2206	108.4
1996	9157	108.7	4470	106.9	7660	102.3	2547	111.6
1997	10154	108.4	4612	97.9	7807	95.2	2597	99.6
1998	10850	107.9	4796	104.2	8054	102.2	2681	105.8
1999	11463	107.3	5025	104.5	8598	105.9	2661	100.8
2000	12817	107.3	5305	100.2	9189	100.2	2680	98.7
2001	13952	107.3	5445	101.9	9312	100.3	2759	103.0
2002	15478	111.1	6199	113.2	10358	110.2	2904	105.7
2003	17950	113.3	7342	117.0	11136	106.4	3032	103.4
2004	20647	111.5	8800	115.9	12409	107.9	3386	108.2
2005	23997	112.7	9799	110.0	13609	108.6	3915	113.2
2006	27861	112.8	10619	107.4	14695	106.9	4010	102.2
2007	33236	112.2	12336	112.9	16982	112.6	4401	105.0
2008	37543	107.9	13911	107.1	19101	107.1	4975	105.6
2009	39418	107.3	15243	110.9	20852	111.3	5533	106.9
2010	44669	109.5	17211	109.3	23159	107.5	6255	109.4
2011	50076	107.0	19186	105.8	24943	102.9	7722	112.2
2012	52308	105.3	21123	106.9	27218	106.3	8663	106.7
2013	56029	106.0	21208	110.0	26206	109.6	10543	110.9
2014	59909	105.7	23446	107.6	28586	106.3	12206	112.3
2015	64516	106.1	25138	106.8	30472	105.6	12980	108.5
2016	69671	105.6	27156	105.6	32602	104.8	14356	106.8
2017	76218	105.4	29364	105.4	35110	104.5	15473	107.6
2018	81625	104.9	31837	105.7	37175	103.1	18241	115.2
2019	86956	104.7	33885	105.6	39188	105.1	19797	104.7
2020	88521	101.1	33348	96.1	37906	94.7	20273	98.4
2021	98561	107.3	36879	109.1	41773	107.5	22662	113.8
2022	102217	101.9	38266	101.4	43036	100.7	24174	104.4
2023	106985	104.7						

注：2006—2009年人均地区生产总值根据2010年第六次全国人口普查结果进行修订，2011—2019年人均地区生产总值根据2020年第七次全国人口普查结果进行修订。

Note: The per capita GDP in 2006-2009 is revised according to the results of the sixth national census in 2010, and the per capita GDP in 2011-2019 is revised according to the results of the seventh national census in 2020.

2-13 人均地区生产总值及人均消费水平指数

Indices of Per Capita Gross Domestic Product and Consumption

年份 Year	人均地区生产总值 Per Capita Gross Domestic Product		人均消费水平 Per Capita Consumption					
			全体居民 Households		城镇居民 Urban Households		农村居民 Rural Households	
	绝对数(元) Value (yuan)	指数(1978年=100) Index (year of 1978=100)	绝对数(元) Value (yuan)	指数(1978年=100) Index (year of 1978=100)	绝对数(元) Value (yuan)	指数(1978年=100) Index (year of 1978=100)	绝对数(元) Value (yuan)	指数(1978年=100) Index (year of 1978=100)
1978	370	100.0	222	100.0	466	100.0	171	100.0
1979	410	106.9	252	108.3	507	102.6	196	109.8
1980	481	122.6	302	124.4	620	115.6	228	125.2
1981	550	131.3	332	134.2	627	113.4	260	141.9
1982	633	144.4	377	148.1	696	122.8	298	156.7
1983	675	152.4	403	158.7	764	133.3	310	164.8
1984	827	173.5	453	175.0	878	146.3	334	177.6
1985	1026	201.6	529	184.9	1038	161.2	372	172.9
1986	1164	223.1	609	202.5	1146	174.7	430	183.7
1987	1443	260.9	754	215.6	1382	176.6	515	192.6
1988	1926	295.4	944	208.1	1716	164.6	651	193.6
1989	2251	309.6	1212	249.0	2188	189.3	831	238.2
1990	2484	337.7	1287	272.1	2263	198.2	896	269.0
1991	2941	387.4	1434	294.7	2712	227.5	906	269.5
1992	3699	460.3	1690	338.1	3210	263.2	1023	295.7
1993	5085	549.0	2308	407.5	4280	308.1	1347	347.8
1994	6530	633.9	3234	480.2	5870	356.5	1831	397.6
1995	8139	710.7	3991	528.9	7091	383.5	2206	430.8
1996	9157	772.3	4470	565.4	7660	392.3	2547	480.6
1997	10154	837.2	4612	553.4	7807	373.4	2597	478.6
1998	10850	903.3	4796	576.9	8054	381.6	2681	506.5
1999	11463	969.2	5025	602.6	8598	404.2	2661	510.6
2000	12817	1040.3	5305	603.5	9189	405.0	2680	503.8
2001	13952	1115.8	5445	615.2	9312	406.3	2759	519.0
2002	15478	1240.1	6199	696.1	10358	447.6	2904	548.8
2003	17950	1405.3	7342	814.5	11136	476.2	3032	567.2
2004	20647	1566.6	8800	944.4	12409	513.8	3386	613.6
2005	23997	1766.1	9799	1039.2	13609	557.8	3915	694.5
2006	27861	1992.7	10619	1116.5	14695	596.5	4010	709.8
2007	33236	2235.7	12336	1260.3	16982	671.5	4401	745.1
2008	37543	2413.3	13911	1350.1	19101	719.3	4975	787.1
2009	39418	2588.9	15243	1496.8	20852	800.5	5533	841.2
2010	44669	2834.9	17211	1636.4	23159	860.4	6255	920.5
2011	50076	3032.2	19186	1730.9	24943	885.0	7722	1033.1
2012	52308	3192.2	21123	1850.9	27218	940.9	8663	1101.9
2013	56029	3385.1	21208	2035.2	26206	1031.1	10543	1222.5
2014	59909	3577.5	23446	2190.0	28586	1095.8	12206	1372.6
2015	64516	3797.1	25138	2338.3	30472	1157.7	12980	1489.9
2016	69671	4010.1	27156	2469.4	32602	1213.6	14356	1591.5
2017	76218	4227.6	29364	2602.2	35110	1268.1	15473	1711.8
2018	81625	4434.4	31837	2750.1	37175	1307.9	18241	1971.7
2019	86956	4641.2	33885	2903.7	39188	1375.3	19797	2063.7
2020	88521	4693.5	33348	2790.0	37906	1302.6	20273	2029.6
2021	98561	5036.4	36879	3043.1	41773	1400.7	22662	2310.2
2022	102217	5132.9	38266	3086.2	43036	1410.1	24174	2411.0
2023	106985	5372.1						

2-14 各市地区生产总值
Gross Domestic Product by City

单位：亿元 (100 million yuan)

市别	City	2000	2005	2010	2013	2014	2015	2016
广州	Guangzhou	2505.58	5187.85	10640.67	15050.40	16135.95	17347.37	18559.73
深圳	Shenzhen	2219.20	5035.77	10069.06	15234.24	16795.35	18436.84	20685.74
珠海	Zhuhai	335.92	640.53	1241.74	1780.87	2008.86	2216.54	2452.61
汕头	Shantou	450.16	637.68	1125.75	1569.58	1710.57	1869.53	2097.48
佛山	Foshan	1050.38	2450.67	5665.45	7064.30	7509.96	8107.60	8756.31
韶关	Shaoguan	192.72	337.03	624.77	898.41	961.90	987.86	1040.69
河源	Heyuan	87.22	204.81	444.03	668.92	734.84	768.68	847.80
梅州	Meizhou	180.64	315.17	602.79	790.82	870.73	943.58	1029.74
惠州	Huizhou	439.19	805.11	1723.56	2674.50	2959.11	3090.22	3359.52
汕尾	Shanwei	128.49	205.75	455.02	678.22	729.36	766.86	843.92
东莞	Dongguan	821.14	2189.46	4339.85	5740.44	6174.83	6665.34	7260.92
中山	Zhongshan	345.44	894.59	1808.48	2470.06	2580.59	2711.36	2830.43
江门	Jiangmen	504.66	801.70	1574.73	2020.97	2099.29	2274.26	2480.94
阳江	Yangjiang	160.20	294.55	614.99	971.17	1066.82	1108.12	1117.03
湛江	Zhanjiang	373.81	682.67	1390.02	2031.80	2201.88	2319.49	2487.25
茂名	Maoming	417.36	739.13	1482.26	2186.93	2375.38	2439.73	2618.91
肇庆	Zhaoqing	249.78	420.95	965.12	1437.04	1580.50	1691.85	1810.67
清远	Qingyuan	157.92	323.60	867.13	1099.54	1194.42	1266.26	1404.30
潮州	Chaozhou	177.87	283.44	556.51	772.28	833.19	891.11	948.16
揭阳	Jieyang	311.09	414.00	969.82	1465.36	1604.73	1664.39	1804.26
云浮	Yunfu	137.70	202.46	396.21	596.67	645.74	696.60	758.68
按经济区域分	By Region							
珠三角	Pearl River Delta	8471.28	18426.64	38028.65	53472.83	57844.44	62541.37	68196.86
粤东	Eastern Region	1067.61	1540.87	3107.09	4485.43	4877.85	5191.89	5693.82
粤西	Western Region	951.37	1716.35	3487.27	5189.91	5644.08	5867.34	6223.19
粤北	Northern Region	756.20	1383.07	2934.93	4054.36	4407.64	4662.99	5081.21

2-14 续表 continued

单位：亿元 (100 million yuan)

市 别	City	2017	2018	2019	2020	2021	2022	2023
广 州	Guangzhou	19871.67	21002.44	23844.69	25068.75	28225.21	28833.06	30355.73
深 圳	Shenzhen	23280.27	25266.08	26992.33	27759.02	30820.10	32480.71	34606.40
珠 海	Zhuhai	2943.83	3216.78	3444.23	3518.26	3896.04	4070.18	4233.22
汕 头	Shantou	2368.16	2503.08	2687.28	2704.74	2949.58	3034.66	3158.32
佛 山	Foshan	9382.16	9976.72	10739.76	10758.50	12185.75	12695.00	13276.14
韶 关	Shaoguan	1133.62	1217.48	1316.35	1375.16	1550.06	1563.47	1620.83
河 源	Heyuan	968.10	1006.98	1079.75	1114.31	1273.91	1302.39	1348.22
梅 州	Meizhou	1086.59	1127.24	1187.08	1227.27	1309.39	1325.78	1408.43
惠 州	Huizhou	3745.75	4003.33	4192.93	4283.72	5033.06	5400.27	5639.68
汕 尾	Shanwei	904.57	1004.00	1076.27	1112.63	1285.41	1330.66	1430.84
东 莞	Dongguan	8079.20	8818.11	9474.43	9756.77	10931.69	11375.66	11438.13
中 山	Zhongshan	2939.52	3053.73	3123.79	3189.15	3578.88	3632.22	3850.65
江 门	Jiangmen	2745.89	3001.24	3150.22	3202.97	3598.04	3774.42	4022.25
阳 江	Yangjiang	1142.24	1167.73	1291.67	1349.53	1511.19	1541.66	1581.79
湛 江	Zhanjiang	2744.98	2944.48	3055.90	3103.32	3565.46	3710.82	3793.59
茂 名	Maoming	2881.07	3095.11	3248.11	3285.44	3695.90	3902.79	3987.22
肇 庆	Zhaoqing	1964.97	2102.29	2250.67	2313.24	2645.81	2721.57	2792.51
清 远	Qingyuan	1474.54	1575.32	1704.47	1804.36	2000.69	2050.14	2120.19
潮 州	Chaozhou	960.68	1005.30	1082.94	1102.88	1244.52	1317.73	1356.59
揭 阳	Jieyang	1842.67	2002.09	2099.91	2088.00	2280.97	2276.85	2445.03
云 浮	Yunfu	804.63	855.67	944.14	1033.62	1137.87	1173.50	1207.42
按经济区域分	By Region							
珠 三 角	Pearl River Delta	74953.26	80440.72	87213.05	89850.38	100914.59	104983.11	110214.70
粤 东	Eastern Region	6076.09	6514.48	6946.39	7008.25	7760.48	7959.90	8390.78
粤 西	Western Region	6768.29	7207.33	7595.68	7738.29	8772.55	9155.27	9362.60
粤 北	Northern Region	5467.48	5782.69	6231.80	6554.71	7271.92	7415.27	7705.08

注：2017年起，深圳市地区生产总值数据包含深汕合作区。
Notes: Since 2017, GDP of Shenshan Special Cooperation Zone is included in that of Shenzhen city.

2-15 各市地区生产总值指数
Indices of Gross Domestic Product by City

上年=100　　(preceding year=100)

市　别	City	2000	2005	2010	2013	2014	2015	2016
广　州	Guangzhou	113.4	113.0	113.0	111.5	108.5	108.3	107.6
深　圳	Shenzhen	116.3	115.3	112.3	110.6	108.9	109.0	109.3
珠　海	Zhuhai	112.0	113.2	113.3	110.9	110.4	110.0	108.1
汕　头	Shantou	107.0	111.3	110.4	110.1	108.9	108.4	108.6
佛　山	Foshan	112.5	119.3	114.3	109.8	108.2	108.2	107.9
韶　关	Shaoguan	111.3	110.1	112.5	110.7	107.6	105.9	106.1
河　源	Heyuan	110.7	122.9	112.5	112.1	108.6	106.3	106.6
梅　州	Meizhou	108.1	107.9	114.1	111.0	108.6	108.6	107.8
惠　州	Huizhou	111.3	116.1	118.2	113.7	110.0	109.3	108.1
汕　尾	Shanwei	111.5	116.0	117.0	112.3	109.0	108.1	107.0
东　莞	Dongguan	119.7	119.5	110.4	110.0	108.0	108.4	108.0
中　山	Zhongshan	112.4	121.1	113.8	109.7	107.5	108.2	104.3
江　门	Jiangmen	110.2	112.6	114.5	109.6	107.5	108.4	107.3
阳　江	Yangjiang	109.6	113.9	116.3	115.0	110.2	107.9	106.4
湛　江	Zhanjiang	107.1	113.6	114.2	111.8	109.8	108.7	106.8
茂　名	Maoming	111.2	114.1	114.0	113.6	110.1	107.6	107.4
肇　庆	Zhaoqing	110.6	115.8	115.5	109.7	109.7	107.9	105.0
清　远	Qingyuan	108.3	127.7	112.8	108.1	107.7	108.0	109.3
潮　州	Chaozhou	105.6	111.5	114.0	110.8	108.1	108.2	107.0
揭　阳	Jieyang	105.4	111.3	119.3	114.1	110.3	107.8	107.5
云　浮	Yunfu	105.3	113.3	113.9	113.5	110.3	108.6	108.0
按经济区域分	By Region							
珠三角	Pearl River Delta	113.9	115.7	113.1	110.7	108.6	108.6	108.0
粤　东	Eastern Region	106.7	112.0	114.6	111.8	109.2	108.1	107.8
粤　西	Western Region	109.4	113.8	114.5	113.2	110.0	108.1	107.0
粤　北	Northern Region	108.7	115.7	113.1	110.7	108.4	107.5	107.7

2-15 续表 continued

上年=100 (preceding year=100)

市 别	City	2017	2018	2019	2020	2021	2022	2023
广 州	Guangzhou	106.7	106.0	106.9	102.7	108.1	101.0	104.6
深 圳	Shenzhen	108.8	107.7	106.7	103.1	107.0	103.4	106.0
珠 海	Zhuhai	111.1	107.9	106.8	103.0	107.2	102.3	103.8
汕 头	Shantou	109.1	106.9	106.1	102.0	106.4	101.3	104.2
佛 山	Foshan	108.0	106.4	106.8	101.5	108.5	102.1	105.0
韶 关	Shaoguan	106.4	104.0	106.0	103.0	108.6	100.2	104.6
河 源	Heyuan	106.7	105.8	105.5	101.3	108.0	101.2	104.0
梅 州	Meizhou	106.9	102.3	103.4	101.5	105.6	100.7	106.5
惠 州	Huizhou	107.9	105.9	104.2	101.5	110.4	104.2	105.6
汕 尾	Shanwei	108.1	108.0	106.7	104.6	112.7	101.7	105.0
东 莞	Dongguan	108.8	107.5	107.4	101.1	108.5	101.7	102.6
中 山	Zhongshan	103.8	103.1	102.0	101.5	108.4	100.5	105.6
江 门	Jiangmen	108.1	107.8	104.3	102.2	108.4	103.4	105.5
阳 江	Yangjiang	105.8	103.8	108.2	104.4	108.3	100.8	103.8
湛 江	Zhanjiang	106.9	105.7	104.0	101.9	108.7	101.3	103.0
茂 名	Maoming	107.6	105.8	104.3	101.5	107.6	100.5	103.7
肇 庆	Zhaoqing	105.1	106.5	106.3	103.0	110.5	101.2	103.7
清 远	Qingyuan	104.1	104.0	106.3	103.8	108.1	101.4	104.5
潮 州	Chaozhou	106.1	104.9	105.0	101.3	109.3	102.5	103.0
揭 阳	Jieyang	105.2	105.2	103.0	100.2	106.4	98.8	107.5
云 浮	Yunfu	105.3	104.0	106.4	104.1	108.1	102.4	103.8
按经济区域分	By Region							
珠 三 角	Pearl River Delta	107.8	106.8	106.4	102.4	108.0	102.2	104.8
粤 东	Eastern Region	107.2	106.2	105.0	101.7	107.9	100.8	105.0
粤 西	Western Region	107.0	105.4	104.9	102.2	108.2	100.9	103.4
粤 北	Northern Region	105.8	103.9	105.5	102.8	107.7	101.1	104.6

2-16 各市地区生产总值指数
Indices of Gross Domestic Product by City

2000年=100 (year of 2000=100)

市 别	City	2001	2005	2010	2013	2014	2015	2016
广 州	Guangzhou	112.8	191.3	361.2	495.3	537.3	581.8	626.1
深 圳	Shenzhen	114.5	213.8	402.8	540.5	588.7	641.5	701.5
珠 海	Zhuhai	111.9	190.6	342.3	457.4	505.0	555.4	600.6
汕 头	Shantou	98.1	139.9	234.4	311.1	338.7	367.1	398.7
佛 山	Foshan	113.2	214.8	454.5	601.5	650.9	704.3	760.0
韶 关	Shaoguan	110.2	165.0	301.8	411.7	443.0	469.1	497.8
河 源	Heyuan	111.7	215.4	460.6	651.6	707.4	752.2	801.7
梅 州	Meizhou	108.6	159.1	270.8	375.0	407.1	442.0	476.4
惠 州	Huizhou	109.5	181.9	373.6	550.2	605.1	661.2	714.5
汕 尾	Shanwei	108.9	179.3	383.3	557.1	607.2	656.3	702.4
东 莞	Dongguan	120.0	252.1	473.2	599.9	648.0	702.3	758.1
中 山	Zhongshan	117.0	245.0	467.3	643.9	692.1	748.7	781.0
江 门	Jiangmen	105.3	160.2	295.2	395.6	425.2	460.8	494.7
阳 江	Yangjiang	109.7	174.4	335.0	497.1	548.0	591.2	628.9
湛 江	Zhanjiang	108.3	169.6	307.6	425.0	466.6	507.0	541.5
茂 名	Maoming	110.3	176.6	314.5	437.9	482.1	518.8	557.1
肇 庆	Zhaoqing	108.2	174.6	339.4	464.8	510.0	550.5	578.1
清 远	Qingyuan	106.5	204.6	462.3	567.9	611.4	660.0	721.2
潮 州	Chaozhou	106.9	160.4	296.2	410.5	443.7	480.1	513.9
揭 阳	Jieyang	103.5	133.0	289.2	418.3	461.3	497.4	534.8
云 浮	Yunfu	104.6	151.3	279.1	409.8	452.0	490.7	530.2
按经济区域分	By Region							
珠 三 角	Pearl River Delta	113.4	205.3	394.4	531.2	576.8	626.2	676.4
粤 东	Eastern Region	102.4	146.0	277.8	387.1	422.7	457.1	492.5
粤 西	Western Region	109.4	173.4	315.3	442.8	487.1	526.4	563.0
粤 北	Northern Region	108.2	175.2	341.5	461.0	499.6	536.9	578.1

2-16 续表 continued

2000年=100 (year of 2000=100)

市别	City	2017	2018	2019	2020	2021	2022	2023
广州	Guangzhou	668.2	708.6	757.6	778.1	841.4	849.6	888.3
深圳	Shenzhen	763.3	822.4	877.1	903.9	967.1	1000.3	1059.8
珠海	Zhuhai	667.2	720.1	769.0	792.0	849.3	869.0	901.6
汕头	Shantou	434.9	464.8	493.2	503.0	535.3	542.4	564.9
佛山	Foshan	820.6	872.8	932.0	945.7	1026.0	1047.9	1099.8
韶关	Shaoguan	529.9	551.0	584.1	601.8	653.4	654.7	684.5
河源	Heyuan	855.2	904.8	954.6	967.3	1045.1	1057.5	1099.4
梅州	Meizhou	509.3	521.0	538.8	547.1	577.8	581.9	619.5
惠州	Huizhou	771.2	816.4	850.8	863.6	953.8	994.2	1049.5
汕尾	Shanwei	759.6	820.7	875.7	916.0	1032.5	1049.6	1101.6
东莞	Dongguan	824.7	886.2	951.4	961.8	1043.5	1060.9	1087.9
中山	Zhongshan	811.1	836.3	853.3	866.4	938.9	943.9	996.4
江门	Jiangmen	534.7	576.4	601.2	614.3	665.6	688.5	726.1
阳江	Yangjiang	665.4	690.6	747.3	779.8	844.6	851.1	883.1
湛江	Zhanjiang	578.9	612.1	636.5	648.6	705.2	714.3	735.4
茂名	Maoming	599.4	633.9	661.2	670.9	722.2	726.1	752.6
肇庆	Zhaoqing	607.7	647.2	687.7	708.1	782.5	791.8	820.7
清远	Qingyuan	751.1	781.0	830.2	861.7	931.5	944.3	986.3
潮州	Chaozhou	545.4	572.2	600.7	608.2	664.8	681.6	701.8
揭阳	Jieyang	562.7	591.8	609.4	610.4	649.7	641.6	689.5
云浮	Yunfu	558.2	580.7	618.2	643.2	695.5	711.9	738.6
按经济区域分	By Region							
珠三角	Pearl River Delta	729.4	778.7	828.8	848.4	916.5	936.9	982.2
粤东	Eastern Region	528.0	560.5	588.7	598.7	645.8	651.1	684.0
粤西	Western Region	602.3	634.8	665.8	680.4	736.1	742.6	767.7
粤北	Northern Region	611.5	635.6	670.8	689.7	743.0	751.4	786.3

2-17 各市第一产业增加值
Value-added of the Primary Industry by City

单位：亿元 (100 million yuan)

市别	City	2000	2005	2010	2015	2019	2020	2021	2022	2023
广州	Guangzhou	94.37	130.22	168.62	206.52	247.13	286.27	299.75	312.42	317.78
深圳	Shenzhen	15.57	9.74	6.11	7.21	25.58	25.59	23.75	24.76	24.71
珠海	Zhuhai	15.27	22.69	30.00	48.30	58.09	51.00	54.20	66.88	69.71
汕头	Shantou	39.38	44.52	62.45	91.39	120.40	122.51	126.42	136.39	141.98
佛山	Foshan	61.74	75.76	98.74	127.29	160.40	190.05	202.68	219.56	228.78
韶关	Shaoguan	44.01	55.47	87.97	131.73	176.67	199.87	215.03	226.92	238.71
河源	Heyuan	30.36	42.42	58.69	93.34	121.07	133.52	153.21	162.66	172.63
梅州	Meizhou	56.02	72.73	118.40	172.97	223.63	238.66	241.07	256.29	266.05
惠州	Huizhou	62.23	75.10	99.89	146.13	206.73	216.98	248.39	279.05	296.06
汕尾	Shanwei	46.71	46.12	73.23	112.97	149.64	157.16	166.48	185.73	192.50
东莞	Dongguan	25.91	21.82	15.56	19.92	28.85	30.40	34.83	35.92	36.25
中山	Zhongshan	23.51	30.71	48.32	59.56	62.69	71.01	84.71	89.25	94.13
江门	Jiangmen	69.83	72.47	115.91	170.46	254.35	272.91	294.89	323.43	347.01
阳江	Yangjiang	62.95	80.38	129.98	190.04	244.42	254.74	245.58	252.93	255.85
湛江	Zhanjiang	105.06	160.50	279.81	429.39	584.25	608.53	644.41	684.11	706.91
茂名	Maoming	125.91	167.04	272.89	398.05	580.66	648.67	648.85	708.11	725.28
肇庆	Zhaoqing	91.75	120.72	189.81	288.50	386.58	431.99	462.18	487.12	498.94
清远	Qingyuan	61.43	71.54	118.22	192.30	262.16	288.85	303.81	332.08	343.05
潮州	Chaozhou	28.76	32.64	38.76	62.64	98.90	108.93	115.98	124.43	131.72
揭阳	Jieyang	71.06	65.20	100.86	141.33	186.69	203.41	208.29	223.80	230.09
云浮	Yunfu	54.81	63.42	92.46	129.44	171.74	191.70	210.20	218.27	222.55
按经济区域分	By Region									
珠三角	Pearl River Delta	460.17	559.23	772.96	1073.87	1430.38	1576.19	1705.36	1838.39	1913.38
粤东	Eastern Region	185.92	188.48	275.30	408.34	555.64	592.01	617.17	670.35	696.29
粤西	Western Region	293.92	407.92	682.67	1017.49	1409.33	1511.94	1538.85	1645.14	1688.04
粤北	Northern Region	246.64	305.58	475.73	719.77	955.27	1052.60	1123.32	1196.21	1242.99

2-18 各市第二产业增加值

Value-added of the Secondary Industry by City

单位：亿元 (100 million yuan)

市 别	City	2000	2005	2010	2015	2019	2020	2021	2022	2023
广 州	Guangzhou	1029.94	2067.00	4053.30	5777.17	6509.40	6716.16	7736.13	7727.05	7775.71
深 圳	Shenzhen	1108.76	2709.69	4727.94	7687.41	10402.00	10380.65	11607.80	12313.63	13015.32
珠 海	Zhuhai	176.30	344.14	670.63	1043.69	1519.85	1463.16	1651.11	1798.87	1872.11
汕 头	Shantou	217.39	328.07	594.67	937.58	1282.67	1322.53	1422.03	1455.88	1523.26
佛 山	Foshan	553.61	1494.20	3581.59	5003.35	6088.54	5887.79	6780.94	7148.34	7513.72
韶 关	Shaoguan	75.71	143.51	244.52	353.14	448.85	474.36	559.34	549.93	559.16
河 源	Heyuan	20.99	80.46	208.19	310.43	372.32	388.34	464.44	482.26	499.12
梅 州	Meizhou	63.30	129.80	248.19	347.19	369.04	396.35	422.62	408.37	444.11
惠 州	Huizhou	255.26	456.79	1022.99	1744.62	2158.14	2137.61	2718.75	2964.08	3070.35
汕 尾	Shanwei	37.31	83.10	199.88	321.40	390.94	411.63	491.47	511.13	563.89
东 莞	Dongguan	451.47	1232.14	2313.00	3479.05	5298.93	5534.57	6359.21	6587.22	6478.18
中 山	Zhongshan	180.83	548.21	1069.62	1516.61	1556.02	1525.97	1777.09	1835.46	1965.92
江 门	Jiangmen	235.11	425.57	868.35	1061.67	1326.60	1400.69	1623.27	1730.03	1855.14
阳 江	Yangjiang	47.03	110.83	258.10	503.26	443.23	473.81	590.12	589.00	602.01
湛 江	Zhanjiang	135.52	298.80	565.19	892.89	1045.62	1098.46	1382.26	1453.66	1454.61
茂 名	Maoming	147.72	260.23	560.77	920.24	1078.28	1060.92	1278.32	1342.11	1346.00
肇 庆	Zhaoqing	53.10	99.87	348.13	783.60	889.50	895.70	1106.37	1139.32	1154.56
清 远	Qingyuan	40.72	127.21	397.65	483.73	558.19	669.69	774.20	781.38	809.03
潮 州	Chaozhou	86.52	151.68	309.50	476.77	517.69	516.15	581.94	625.27	633.99
揭 阳	Jieyang	141.91	202.13	537.79	865.09	809.87	775.62	859.99	798.32	913.79
云 浮	Yunfu	39.98	73.69	158.18	274.79	302.54	337.90	368.41	379.41	387.29
按经济区域分	By Region									
珠三角	Pearl River Delta	4044.38	9377.60	18655.55	28097.17	35748.98	35942.30	41360.66	43244.01	44701.01
粤 东	Eastern Region	483.13	764.98	1641.84	2600.84	3001.16	3025.92	3355.43	3390.60	3634.93
粤 西	Western Region	330.27	669.87	1384.06	2316.39	2567.13	2633.18	3250.70	3384.76	3402.62
粤 北	Northern Region	240.70	554.68	1256.73	1769.29	2050.94	2266.64	2589.00	2601.35	2698.70

2-19 各市第三产业增加值

Value-added of the Tertiary Industry by City

单位：亿元 (100 million yuan)

市别	City	2000	2005	2010	2015	2019	2020	2021	2022	2023
广州	Guangzhou	1381.27	2990.63	6418.75	11363.68	17088.17	18066.32	20189.34	20793.59	22262.23
深圳	Shenzhen	1094.87	2316.34	5335.01	10742.22	16564.75	17352.77	19188.56	20142.32	21566.38
珠海	Zhuhai	144.35	273.71	541.10	1124.55	1866.29	2004.10	2190.73	2204.43	2291.39
汕头	Shantou	193.39	265.10	468.63	840.56	1284.21	1259.71	1401.12	1442.39	1493.08
佛山	Foshan	435.03	880.70	1985.13	2976.96	4490.82	4680.66	5202.13	5327.11	5533.64
韶关	Shaoguan	73.00	138.05	292.28	502.99	690.83	700.92	775.70	786.63	822.97
河源	Heyuan	35.87	81.93	177.15	364.91	586.36	592.44	656.26	657.46	676.47
梅州	Meizhou	61.32	112.64	236.20	423.42	594.41	592.26	645.70	661.12	698.27
惠州	Huizhou	121.70	273.22	600.68	1199.48	1828.06	1929.14	2065.92	2157.14	2273.27
汕尾	Shanwei	44.48	76.53	181.92	332.49	535.69	543.84	627.45	633.81	674.45
东莞	Dongguan	343.76	935.50	2011.28	3166.37	4146.65	4191.80	4537.66	4752.53	4923.71
中山	Zhongshan	141.09	315.67	690.54	1135.19	1505.07	1592.17	1717.08	1707.50	1790.59
江门	Jiangmen	199.72	303.66	590.47	1042.13	1569.27	1529.37	1679.88	1720.97	1820.10
阳江	Yangjiang	50.21	103.33	226.92	414.81	604.03	620.98	675.49	699.74	723.93
湛江	Zhanjiang	133.24	223.37	545.02	997.21	1426.03	1396.33	1538.79	1573.05	1632.06
茂名	Maoming	143.73	311.87	648.60	1121.44	1589.17	1575.86	1768.73	1852.58	1915.94
肇庆	Zhaoqing	104.93	200.37	427.18	619.76	974.60	985.55	1077.26	1095.13	1139.01
清远	Qingyuan	55.77	124.85	351.27	590.24	884.12	845.82	922.68	936.68	968.12
潮州	Chaozhou	62.59	99.12	208.25	351.69	466.35	477.80	546.60	568.03	590.88
揭阳	Jieyang	98.11	146.66	331.16	657.97	1103.35	1108.97	1212.69	1254.73	1301.14
云浮	Yunfu	42.90	65.34	145.58	292.37	469.86	504.02	559.26	575.83	597.58
按经济区域分	By Region									
珠三角	Pearl River Delta	3966.73	8489.80	18600.14	33370.33	50033.69	52331.89	57848.57	59900.71	63600.32
粤东	Eastern Region	398.57	587.41	1189.95	2182.71	3389.59	3390.31	3787.87	3898.95	4059.55
粤西	Western Region	327.18	638.56	1420.54	2533.46	3619.23	3593.17	3983.01	4125.37	4271.93
粤北	Northern Region	268.86	522.80	1202.47	2173.92	3225.59	3235.47	3559.60	3617.71	3763.40

2-20 各市第一产业增加值指数

Indices of Value-added of the Primary Industry by City

上年=100 (preceding year=100)

市别	City	2000	2005	2010	2015	2019	2020	2021	2022	2023
广州	Guangzhou	101.7	105.6	103.1	102.4	104.2	109.8	106.3	102.9	103.5
深圳	Shenzhen	103.1	79.6	88.8	104.2	105.9	96.1	101.0	100.8	102.6
珠海	Zhuhai	108.5	105.2	105.5	100.3	104.2	101.6	106.7	106.7	105.1
汕头	Shantou	105.2	104.6	105.1	103.0	102.2	100.0	102.5	104.5	103.4
佛山	Foshan	107.2	102.0	104.4	101.5	104.2	99.4	109.5	106.0	104.7
韶关	Shaoguan	103.6	102.6	105.7	103.8	104.6	104.4	113.1	104.7	106.1
河源	Heyuan	106.5	102.6	103.3	103.8	106.2	105.9	107.8	104.7	106.2
梅州	Meizhou	102.8	103.0	106.4	103.4	103.6	100.7	105.3	104.7	105.8
惠州	Huizhou	106.1	105.6	103.8	104.3	102.2	104.4	116.8	107.0	106.6
汕尾	Shanwei	106.1	102.5	106.1	104.5	104.8	103.9	109.0	106.6	103.0
东莞	Dongguan	99.8	102.3	101.5	102.6	108.3	105.9	112.3	98.0	105.0
中山	Zhongshan	101.9	101.9	103.2	99.6	96.0	117.5	113.1	105.9	105.5
江门	Jiangmen	104.9	100.9	104.9	103.2	106.6	103.3	109.8	106.2	105.9
阳江	Yangjiang	106.4	95.5	105.9	103.9	100.7	101.5	101.5	102.2	103.2
湛江	Zhanjiang	104.0	108.4	104.2	102.9	103.4	100.2	106.6	104.4	103.8
茂名	Maoming	108.5	104.0	104.1	104.0	103.8	105.4	106.8	105.6	104.6
肇庆	Zhaoqing	105.0	105.8	105.4	103.8	104.7	105.3	107.6	103.8	104.4
清远	Qingyuan	102.7	104.0	106.8	104.4	104.2	104.7	109.2	106.6	105.9
潮州	Chaozhou	101.0	102.1	104.5	102.9	103.3	104.4	109.8	105.5	104.9
揭阳	Jieyang	104.0	102.9	104.9	103.6	103.7	103.1	104.6	105.5	104.8
云浮	Yunfu	106.0	106.2	104.6	103.0	102.7	108.0	109.7	104.2	105.6
按经济区域分	By Region									
珠三角	Pearl River Delta	104.4	103.6	104.1	102.8	104.1	105.3	109.4	104.8	104.9
粤东	Eastern Region	104.3	103.0	105.2	103.6	103.6	102.8	106.3	105.6	104.0
粤西	Western Region	106.6	103.7	104.5	103.5	103.1	102.6	105.8	104.5	104.1
粤北	Northern Region	104.1	103.9	105.6	103.7	104.1	104.4	109.0	105.1	105.9

2-21 各市第二产业增加值指数

Indices of Value-added of the Secondary Industry by City

上年=100 (preceding year=100)

市 别	City	2000	2005	2010	2015	2019	2020	2021	2022	2023
广 州	Guangzhou	111.9	113.0	113.0	106.8	105.4	103.3	108.7	99.0	102.6
深 圳	Shenzhen	118.5	117.9	113.8	107.4	104.4	101.8	107.2	103.0	106.5
珠 海	Zhuhai	114.7	116.9	118.2	110.2	104.1	101.9	108.5	105.0	104.7
汕 头	Shantou	107.2	113.5	110.1	107.2	102.9	103.6	104.6	100.2	104.7
佛 山	Foshan	112.4	125.2	115.2	107.3	106.8	101.2	108.9	103.0	106.2
韶 关	Shaoguan	115.6	109.7	113.4	102.8	105.9	104.7	105.9	96.6	103.2
河 源	Heyuan	113.1	145.6	113.9	104.3	105.9	101.9	110.5	102.2	104.7
梅 州	Meizhou	109.2	108.0	118.3	108.5	103.1	101.7	102.7	95.8	109.5
惠 州	Huizhou	113.1	117.4	124.2	109.8	101.5	101.6	117.1	104.8	106.0
汕 尾	Shanwei	115.7	123.8	122.5	106.8	106.2	104.0	115.1	101.3	105.7
东 莞	Dongguan	120.7	120.0	117.5	106.3	106.5	99.2	110.9	101.0	101.4
中 山	Zhongshan	115.3	119.6	115.8	107.2	100.9	101.4	111.3	101.8	107.3
江 门	Jiangmen	111.1	122.3	116.9	108.4	100.4	102.9	110.1	104.4	107.3
阳 江	Yangjiang	111.7	125.2	121.3	110.1	113.5	109.5	113.7	97.1	103.0
湛 江	Zhanjiang	106.2	111.4	116.9	109.9	100.8	104.9	112.7	98.8	100.5
茂 名	Maoming	110.8	114.3	113.8	108.3	102.3	100.7	103.8	93.9	103.8
肇 庆	Zhaoqing	114.2	120.6	130.8	109.6	101.4	102.7	116.1	101.1	102.8
清 远	Qingyuan	104.6	162.1	111.1	106.2	104.4	106.3	108.7	100.0	105.6
潮 州	Chaozhou	105.5	115.1	115.5	106.5	101.9	101.5	107.1	101.5	102.0
揭 阳	Jieyang	104.9	114.3	125.6	106.5	100.1	97.4	106.3	90.9	114.4
云 浮	Yunfu	105.2	128.3	120.2	106.3	108.8	104.8	105.0	101.7	103.3
按经济区域分	By Region									
珠 三 角	Pearl River Delta	114.6	118.3	115.5	107.5	104.7	101.7	109.5	102.1	104.8
粤 东	Eastern Region	106.8	115.1	117.4	106.8	102.3	101.5	106.9	98.2	106.7
粤 西	Western Region	109.2	114.8	116.6	109.3	104.0	104.3	109.3	96.6	102.2
粤 北	Northern Region	109.5	125.9	114.6	105.8	105.4	104.0	106.8	99.2	105.2

2-22 各市第三产业增加值指数

Indices of Value-added of the Tertiary Industry by City

上年=100 (preceding year=100)

市别	City	2000	2005	2010	2015	2019	2020	2021	2022	2023
广州	Guangzhou	116.4	113.3	113.2	109.3	107.7	102.3	108.0	101.7	105.3
深圳	Shenzhen	113.8	112.3	110.7	110.3	108.3	103.9	106.9	103.7	105.6
珠海	Zhuhai	108.9	109.2	107.5	110.1	109.5	104.1	106.3	100.2	103.0
汕头	Shantou	106.9	109.9	111.3	110.6	110.1	100.5	108.7	102.2	103.7
佛山	Foshan	113.6	112.2	113.0	110.2	106.8	102.0	108.0	100.9	103.3
韶关	Shaoguan	110.8	114.0	113.3	108.9	106.4	101.7	109.1	101.2	104.9
河源	Heyuan	112.4	117.1	113.5	109.7	105.1	99.9	106.5	99.7	102.9
梅州	Meizhou	112.6	110.9	113.2	110.6	103.5	101.7	107.7	102.3	104.9
惠州	Huizhou	108.6	117.3	110.3	108.9	107.8	101.1	102.4	103.1	104.8
汕尾	Shanwei	112.0	119.7	114.5	111.3	107.7	105.3	112.0	100.5	104.9
东莞	Dongguan	120.0	119.4	103.3	110.9	108.4	103.4	105.3	102.7	104.1
中山	Zhongshan	110.0	126.0	111.4	110.3	103.5	101.1	105.3	99.0	103.7
江门	Jiangmen	110.2	104.0	111.9	109.1	107.9	101.3	106.5	102.0	103.6
阳江	Yangjiang	111.1	120.5	116.6	106.2	105.4	99.5	107.0	103.2	104.5
湛江	Zhanjiang	110.4	119.4	115.8	109.6	107.0	100.1	106.5	102.0	104.5
茂名	Maoming	114.4	120.5	117.5	108.0	105.9	100.8	110.6	102.7	103.2
肇庆	Zhaoqing	112.2	120.2	110.2	107.6	112.2	102.4	106.7	100.1	104.2
清远	Qingyuan	120.0	118.2	117.3	111.0	108.3	101.8	107.3	100.6	103.0
潮州	Chaozhou	107.8	109.6	113.9	111.7	109.1	100.5	111.6	102.9	103.5
揭阳	Jieyang	107.2	112.0	113.1	111.5	105.8	102.3	106.8	103.0	103.7
云浮	Yunfu	104.7	107.8	112.4	114.2	106.1	102.1	109.6	102.1	103.3
按经济区域分	By Region									
珠三角	Pearl River Delta	114.1	113.7	110.9	109.8	107.9	102.9	107.0	102.2	104.8
粤东	Eastern Region	107.7	111.6	112.7	111.1	108.2	101.8	109.0	102.3	103.9
粤西	Western Region	112.3	120.1	116.8	108.4	106.3	100.3	108.4	102.5	103.9
粤北	Northern Region	111.9	113.9	114.3	110.6	106.1	101.5	108.0	101.1	103.8

2-23 各市地区生产总值（2023年）
Gross Domestic Product by City (2023)

单位：亿元 (100 million yuan)

市别	City	地区生产总值 Gross Domestic Product	第一产业 Primary Industry	第二产业 Secondary Industry	第三产业 Tertiary Industry	#农、林、牧、渔业 Farming, Forestry, Animal Husbandry and Fishery	#工业 Industry
广州	Guangzhou	30355.73	317.78	7775.71	22262.23	357.90	6728.88
深圳	Shenzhen	34606.40	24.71	13015.32	21566.38	25.80	11818.61
珠海	Zhuhai	4233.22	69.71	1872.11	2291.39	74.62	1651.82
汕头	Shantou	3158.32	141.98	1523.26	1493.08	150.67	1284.94
佛山	Foshan	13276.14	228.78	7513.72	5533.64	244.89	7091.01
韶关	Shaoguan	1620.83	238.71	559.16	822.97	240.88	464.55
河源	Heyuan	1348.22	172.63	499.12	676.47	174.63	399.20
梅州	Meizhou	1408.43	266.05	444.11	698.27	271.14	311.64
惠州	Huizhou	5639.68	296.06	3070.35	2273.27	299.30	2725.87
汕尾	Shanwei	1430.84	192.50	563.89	674.45	200.19	476.35
东莞	Dongguan	11438.13	36.25	6478.18	4923.71	37.00	6180.17
中山	Zhongshan	3850.65	94.13	1965.92	1790.59	95.59	1817.15
江门	Jiangmen	4022.25	347.01	1855.14	1820.10	358.75	1567.58
阳江	Yangjiang	1581.79	255.85	602.01	723.93	263.04	539.67
湛江	Zhanjiang	3793.59	706.91	1454.61	1632.06	729.66	1171.43
茂名	Maoming	3987.22	725.28	1346.00	1915.94	742.28	1014.57
肇庆	Zhaoqing	2792.51	498.94	1154.56	1139.01	516.76	1009.82
清远	Qingyuan	2120.19	343.05	809.03	968.12	360.40	717.13
潮州	Chaozhou	1356.59	131.72	633.99	590.88	137.29	584.88
揭阳	Jieyang	2445.03	230.09	913.79	1301.14	241.41	842.11
云浮	Yunfu	1207.42	222.55	387.29	597.58	231.39	315.56
按经济区域分	By Region						
珠三角	Pearl River Delta	110214.70	1913.38	44701.01	63600.32	2010.61	40590.92
粤东	Eastern Region	8390.78	696.29	3634.93	4059.55	729.56	3188.27
粤西	Western Region	9362.60	1688.04	3402.62	4271.93	1734.98	2725.66
粤北	Northern Region	7705.08	1242.99	2698.70	3763.40	1278.45	2208.08

2-23 续表 continued

单位：亿元 (100 million yuan)

市 别	City	#建筑业 Construction	#批发和零售业 Wholesale and Retail Trades	#交通运输、仓储和邮政业 Transport, Storage and Post	#住宿和餐饮业 Hotels and Catering Services	#金融业 Financial Interme-diation	#房地产业 Real Estate
广 州	Guangzhou	1107.58	4248.59	2029.96	515.99	2736.74	2967.61
深 圳	Shenzhen	1239.65	2923.08	979.84	467.88	5253.48	2814.44
珠 海	Zhuhai	243.00	328.32	88.55	48.69	494.05	287.52
汕 头	Shantou	240.03	342.85	83.59	47.52	150.06	251.15
佛 山	Foshan	428.49	967.27	243.30	169.44	782.48	744.75
韶 关	Shaoguan	95.01	113.13	59.76	21.42	89.91	105.77
河 源	Heyuan	100.07	129.86	25.21	25.28	73.62	119.35
梅 州	Meizhou	132.75	100.99	38.63	22.67	101.20	104.95
惠 州	Huizhou	347.77	425.88	114.20	81.05	339.60	516.37
汕 尾	Shanwei	88.23	140.00	42.72	21.50	68.04	92.88
东 莞	Dongguan	307.56	800.99	274.24	213.87	830.43	816.86
中 山	Zhongshan	150.57	387.09	75.11	59.07	308.81	263.43
江 门	Jiangmen	290.62	205.82	112.79	71.23	312.05	226.84
阳 江	Yangjiang	62.83	158.52	72.59	24.96	83.19	92.82
湛 江	Zhanjiang	294.43	309.31	151.56	57.34	181.76	264.26
茂 名	Maoming	332.72	449.42	154.89	67.42	137.95	220.00
肇 庆	Zhaoqing	145.20	289.76	92.16	51.69	132.94	137.04
清 远	Qingyuan	92.40	129.69	47.21	32.10	136.58	160.60
潮 州	Chaozhou	49.52	141.65	39.37	18.99	66.53	78.24
揭 阳	Jieyang	72.08	465.53	74.43	35.96	80.34	192.05
云 浮	Yunfu	72.00	116.77	47.60	19.79	59.08	88.82
按经济区域分	By Region						
珠 三 角	Pearl River Delta	4260.44	10576.81	4010.15	1678.91	11190.58	8774.85
粤 东	Eastern Region	449.86	1090.03	240.11	123.96	364.96	614.31
粤 西	Western Region	689.97	917.25	379.04	149.72	402.89	577.07
粤 北	Northern Region	492.22	590.44	218.41	121.26	460.38	579.49

2-24 各市地区生产总值指数（2023年）

Growth Indices of Gross Domestic Product by City (2023)

上年=100 (preceding year=100)

市别	City	地区生产总值 Gross Domestic Product	第一产业 Primary Industry	第二产业 Secondary Industry	第三产业 Tertiary Industry	#农、林、牧、渔业 Farming, Forestry, Animal Husbandry and Fishery	#工业 Industry
广州	Guangzhou	104.6	103.5	102.6	105.3	104.2	101.6
深圳	Shenzhen	106.0	102.6	106.5	105.6	102.8	106.1
珠海	Zhuhai	103.8	105.1	104.7	103.0	105.2	105.5
汕头	Shantou	104.2	103.4	104.7	103.7	103.6	104.9
佛山	Foshan	105.0	104.7	106.2	103.3	105.3	106.1
韶关	Shaoguan	104.6	106.1	103.2	104.9	106.2	104.1
河源	Heyuan	104.0	106.2	104.7	102.9	106.3	103.4
梅州	Meizhou	106.5	105.8	109.5	104.9	105.8	107.7
惠州	Huizhou	105.6	106.6	106.0	104.8	106.7	104.8
汕尾	Shanwei	105.0	103.0	105.7	104.9	103.2	106.4
东莞	Dongguan	102.6	105.0	101.4	104.1	105.1	101.2
中山	Zhongshan	105.6	105.5	107.3	103.7	105.5	106.6
江门	Jiangmen	105.5	105.9	107.3	103.6	106.2	106.4
阳江	Yangjiang	103.8	103.2	103.0	104.5	103.4	102.7
湛江	Zhanjiang	103.0	103.8	100.5	104.5	104.0	99.4
茂名	Maoming	103.7	104.6	103.8	103.2	104.8	105.0
肇庆	Zhaoqing	103.7	104.4	102.8	104.2	104.6	103.2
清远	Qingyuan	104.5	105.9	105.6	103.0	106.0	105.8
潮州	Chaozhou	103.0	104.9	102.0	103.5	105.1	102.3
揭阳	Jieyang	107.5	104.8	114.4	103.7	105.0	116.6
云浮	Yunfu	103.8	105.6	103.3	103.3	105.8	103.2
按经济区域分	By Region						
珠三角	Pearl River Delta	104.8	104.9	104.8	104.8	105.2	104.4
粤东	Eastern Region	105.0	104.0	106.7	103.9	104.2	107.5
粤西	Western Region	103.4	104.1	102.2	103.9	104.2	102.0
粤北	Northern Region	104.6	105.9	105.2	103.8	106.0	104.9

2-24 续表 continued

单位：% (%)

市 别	City	#建筑业 Construction	#批发和零售业 Wholesale and Retail Trades	#交通运输、仓储和邮政业 Transport, Storage and Post	#住宿和餐饮业 Hotels and Catering Services	#金融业 Financial Interme-diation	#房地产业 Real Estate
广 州	Guangzhou	110.3	107.4	112.2	110.5	107.5	99.3
深 圳	Shenzhen	110.9	103.8	109.1	109.4	105.8	102.5
珠 海	Zhuhai	100.5	103.9	120.6	111.0	104.4	91.1
汕 头	Shantou	103.7	102.5	107.5	109.9	106.0	100.0
佛 山	Foshan	107.9	104.3	105.8	110.8	111.1	90.5
韶 关	Shaoguan	99.5	103.1	107.8	112.4	106.6	99.4
河 源	Heyuan	110.6	100.2	110.2	111.6	103.7	98.8
梅 州	Meizhou	114.7	106.6	108.6	110.1	107.7	101.5
惠 州	Huizhou	116.5	120.2	109.3	109.5	109.9	92.7
汕 尾	Shanwei	102.3	104.5	142.2	106.7	107.8	98.0
东 莞	Dongguan	108.3	100.8	109.0	110.4	110.9	93.7
中 山	Zhongshan	117.7	103.1	112.5	114.3	108.4	95.3
江 门	Jiangmen	113.0	98.1	106.9	109.7	107.2	99.7
阳 江	Yangjiang	106.1	101.1	113.9	112.9	110.0	98.0
湛 江	Zhanjiang	104.9	103.2	102.8	109.3	107.1	104.0
茂 名	Maoming	100.8	102.1	103.2	110.1	107.1	99.5
肇 庆	Zhaoqing	100.1	105.3	109.2	106.5	107.2	98.7
清 远	Qingyuan	103.9	100.9	109.0	112.6	107.2	97.9
潮 州	Chaozhou	98.4	104.6	111.5	111.1	106.4	100.2
揭 阳	Jieyang	93.3	103.4	105.0	108.5	104.3	102.7
云 浮	Yunfu	103.7	103.5	100.7	110.4	107.4	98.9
按经济区域分	By Region						
珠 三 角	Pearl River Delta	110.0	105.5	110.6	110.1	107.1	98.1
粤 东	Eastern Region	101.1	103.4	111.9	109.2	106.0	100.5
粤 西	Western Region	103.0	102.3	104.9	110.3	107.7	101.3
粤 北	Northern Region	106.9	102.6	106.9	111.5	106.6	99.1

2-25 各市地区生产总值产业构成（2023年）

Composition of Gross Domestic Product by Industry by City (2023)

单位：%　　　　(%)

市别	City	地区生产总值 Gross Domestic Product	第一产业 Primary Industry	第二产业 Secondary Industry	第三产业 Tertiary Industry	#工业 Industry
广州	Guangzhou	100.0	1.1	25.6	73.3	22.2
深圳	Shenzhen	100.0	0.1	37.6	62.3	34.2
珠海	Zhuhai	100.0	1.7	44.2	54.1	39.0
汕头	Shantou	100.0	4.5	48.2	47.3	40.7
佛山	Foshan	100.0	1.7	56.6	41.7	53.4
韶关	Shaoguan	100.0	14.7	34.5	50.8	28.7
河源	Heyuan	100.0	12.8	37.0	50.2	29.6
梅州	Meizhou	100.0	18.9	31.5	49.6	22.1
惠州	Huizhou	100.0	5.3	54.4	40.3	48.3
汕尾	Shanwei	100.0	13.5	39.4	47.1	33.3
东莞	Dongguan	100.0	0.3	56.6	43.1	54.0
中山	Zhongshan	100.0	2.4	51.1	46.5	47.2
江门	Jiangmen	100.0	8.6	46.1	45.3	39.0
阳江	Yangjiang	100.0	16.2	38.0	45.8	34.1
湛江	Zhanjiang	100.0	18.6	38.4	43.0	30.9
茂名	Maoming	100.0	18.2	33.8	48.0	25.4
肇庆	Zhaoqing	100.0	17.9	41.3	40.8	36.2
清远	Qingyuan	100.0	16.2	38.1	45.7	33.8
潮州	Chaozhou	100.0	9.7	46.7	43.6	43.1
揭阳	Jieyang	100.0	9.4	37.4	53.2	34.4
云浮	Yunfu	100.0	18.4	32.1	49.5	26.1
按经济区域分	By Region					
珠三角	Pearl River Delta	100.0	1.7	40.6	57.7	36.8
粤东	Eastern Region	100.0	8.3	43.3	48.4	38.0
粤西	Western Region	100.0	18.1	36.3	45.6	29.1
粤北	Northern Region	100.0	16.1	35.0	48.9	28.7

2-26 各市人均地区生产总值

Per Capita Gross Domestic Product by City

单位：元 (yuan)

市别	City	2000	2005	2010	2013	2014	2015	2016
广　州	Guangzhou	25758	54160	86582	104235	107528	111060	113400
深　圳	Shenzhen	33276	61843	99095	124208	130448	135271	142494
珠　海	Zhuhai	28068	45682	80024	100939	109846	117879	127167
汕　头	Shantou	9741	12919	21208	28985	31480	34294	38413
佛　山	Foshan	20231	42434	80511	87194	89742	94608	100699
韶　关	Shaoguan	7028	11608	21996	31726	33954	34854	36682
河　源	Heyuan	3826	7483	15234	22746	25034	26304	29216
梅　州	Meizhou	4731	7684	14315	18997	21115	23083	25402
惠　州	Huizhou	13877	21942	38507	52211	55900	56802	60361
汕　尾	Shanwei	5262	7419	15503	23527	25469	26968	29912
东　莞	Dongguan	13563	33383	53959	60843	63065	66810	72028
中　山	Zhongshan	15077	36800	59411	67973	67955	69129	70352
江　门	Jiangmen	12844	19546	35719	44718	46177	49767	53941
阳　江	Yangjiang	7377	12724	25640	39105	42717	44085	44144
湛　江	Zhanjiang	6231	10269	19945	29047	31487	33184	35602
茂　名	Maoming	7981	12743	25328	36984	40105	41171	44151
肇　庆	Zhaoqing	7422	11505	24875	36171	39625	42333	45151
清　远	Qingyuan	5003	9088	23497	29013	31247	32878	36258
潮　州	Chaozhou	7398	11256	21004	28774	31029	33738	36522
揭　阳	Jieyang	6001	7417	16585	25099	27558	28692	31239
云　浮	Yunfu	6399	8690	16871	25234	27300	29415	31943
按经济区域分	By Region							
珠三角	Pearl River Delta	20369	40661	69281	84537	88318	92510	97721
粤　东	Eastern Region	7287	9747	18561	26667	29025	31020	34190
粤　西	Western Region	7099	11626	22912	33719	36618	38027	40284
粤　北	Northern Region	5345	8847	18338	25198	27411	29028	31676

2-26 续表 continued

单位：元 (yuan)

市 别	City	2017	2018	2019	2020	2021	2022	2023
广 州	Guangzhou	116051	118511	131400	135315	150330	153593	161634
深 圳	Shenzhen	150739	155320	159883	159820	174542	183801	195230
珠 海	Zhuhai	146096	150345	151702	147164	158495	164655	170306
汕 头	Shantou	43295	45672	48953	49191	53463	54815	56910
佛 山	Foshan	105729	109272	114914	113545	127390	132482	138526
韶 关	Shaoguan	39887	42775	46200	48200	54242	54649	56677
河 源	Heyuan	33585	35131	37838	39209	44884	45838	47472
梅 州	Meizhou	27037	28339	30149	31506	33800	34280	36549
惠 州	Huizhou	66007	69206	70949	71220	83032	89141	93036
汕 尾	Shanwei	33049	36976	39910	41532	47996	49564	53252
东 莞	Dongguan	78637	84708	90696	93194	104010	108475	109339
中 山	Zhongshan	71198	72119	72014	72329	80442	81641	86636
江 门	Jiangmen	59244	64163	66622	67027	74654	78167	83409
阳 江	Yangjiang	44816	45526	50031	51937	57827	58809	60294
湛 江	Zhanjiang	39304	42169	43769	44453	50893	52762	53757
茂 名	Maoming	48330	51394	53326	53411	59613	62656	63844
肇 庆	Zhaoqing	48781	51879	55176	56357	64167	65913	67614
清 远	Qingyuan	37858	40198	43228	45514	50289	51456	53188
潮 州	Chaozhou	37053	38822	41885	42834	48414	51172	52665
揭 阳	Jieyang	32124	35235	37192	37243	40748	40474	43322
云 浮	Yunfu	33805	35941	39635	43365	47639	49000	50382
按经济区域分	By Region							
珠 三 角	Pearl River Delta	103863	108094	114532	115880	128684	133821	140408
粤 东	Eastern Region	36677	39560	42310	42842	47425	48473	50988
粤 西	Western Region	43684	46290	48520	49192	55456	57640	58790
粤 北	Northern Region	34132	36165	39033	41126	45630	46494	48350

2-27 各市人均地区生产总值指数

Indices of Per Capita Gross Domestic Product by City

上年=100 (preceding year=100)

市 别	City	2000	2005	2010	2013	2014	2015	2016
广 州	Guangzhou	108.4	114.3	105.8	106.7	104.4	104.0	102.7
深 圳	Shenzhen	105.8	111.8	107.8	104.6	103.8	102.9	102.7
珠 海	Zhuhai	104.9	110.5	111.4	106.4	106.5	107.0	105.4
汕 头	Shantou	104.5	110.4	107.8	109.8	108.5	108.1	108.4
佛 山	Foshan	106.3	117.7	109.2	105.5	104.8	105.7	106.3
韶 关	Shaoguan	111.8	108.7	113.2	110.7	107.6	105.8	106.0
河 源	Heyuan	111.9	118.3	110.5	112.2	108.8	106.8	107.3
梅 州	Meizhou	108.9	106.5	113.0	111.9	109.6	109.5	108.7
惠 州	Huizhou	107.7	113.2	112.7	109.4	106.4	106.3	105.6
汕 尾	Shanwei	110.2	113.3	116.6	113.2	109.7	108.8	107.9
东 莞	Dongguan	105.1	119.5	105.5	105.0	104.1	106.4	106.8
中 山	Zhongshan	105.4	120.7	108.2	104.2	102.9	104.7	101.7
江 门	Jiangmen	108.7	112.1	112.3	108.9	106.8	107.8	106.7
阳 江	Yangjiang	109.6	112.7	114.8	114.0	109.6	107.2	105.7
湛 江	Zhanjiang	106.0	111.6	113.5	111.9	109.8	108.7	106.9
茂 名	Maoming	110.5	111.9	115.1	113.0	109.9	107.6	107.3
肇 庆	Zhaoqing	109.9	114.1	113.8	109.1	109.3	107.7	104.7
清 远	Qingyuan	108.8	124.7	112.3	107.2	106.7	107.1	108.7
潮 州	Chaozhou	104.3	110.8	112.4	110.6	108.0	110.0	108.9
揭 阳	Jieyang	103.0	110.2	118.3	114.4	110.6	108.2	108.0
云 浮	Yunfu	105.1	111.8	113.3	113.5	110.3	108.4	107.7
按经济区域分	By Region							
珠 三 角	Pearl River Delta	106.5	114.6	108.2	106.3	104.9	105.2	104.6
粤 东	Eastern Region	105.0	111.1	113.1	112.0	109.3	108.6	108.3
粤 西	Western Region	109.0	112.1	114.3	112.8	109.9	108.0	106.8
粤 北	Northern Region	109.0	113.5	112.3	110.7	108.4	107.6	107.8

2−27 续表 continued

上年=100 (preceding year=100)

市 别	City	2017	2018	2019	2020	2021	2022	2023
广 州	Guangzhou	102.0	102.5	104.4	100.6	106.7	101.0	104.5
深 圳	Shenzhen	102.7	102.3	102.8	100.2	105.2	103.3	105.6
珠 海	Zhuhai	106.3	101.7	100.6	97.8	104.3	101.7	103.2
汕 头	Shantou	108.9	106.7	105.9	101.8	106.0	101.0	103.9
佛 山	Foshan	105.8	103.4	104.3	100.1	107.5	102.0	104.9
韶 关	Shaoguan	106.3	103.8	105.9	102.9	108.4	100.1	104.6
河 源	Heyuan	107.4	106.4	106.0	101.8	108.2	101.1	104.0
梅 州	Meizhou	107.8	103.4	104.5	102.6	106.2	100.9	106.8
惠 州	Huizhou	105.9	103.9	102.0	99.7	109.6	104.3	105.5
汕 尾	Shanwei	109.0	108.9	107.4	105.3	112.7	101.4	104.9
东 莞	Dongguan	106.7	106.1	107.0	100.9	108.1	101.9	102.8
中 山	Zhongshan	101.2	100.5	99.6	99.9	107.4	100.5	105.7
江 门	Jiangmen	107.3	106.8	103.2	101.1	107.4	103.2	105.6
阳 江	Yangjiang	105.0	103.1	107.5	103.7	107.7	100.5	103.7
湛 江	Zhanjiang	106.9	105.8	104.0	101.9	108.3	100.9	102.6
茂 名	Maoming	107.1	104.7	103.1	100.5	106.8	100.1	103.4
肇 庆	Zhaoqing	104.6	105.9	105.6	102.3	110.0	101.0	103.6
清 远	Qingyuan	103.6	103.3	105.7	103.2	107.7	101.2	104.4
潮 州	Chaozhou	106.3	105.0	105.1	101.7	109.5	102.4	102.9
揭 阳	Jieyang	105.9	106.2	103.6	100.9	106.6	98.3	107.1
云 浮	Yunfu	105.1	104.0	106.4	104.0	107.9	102.1	103.7
按经济区域分	By Region							
珠 三 角	Pearl River Delta	104.3	103.6	104.0	100.5	106.8	102.2	104.8
粤 东	Eastern Region	107.6	106.8	105.3	102.1	107.8	100.5	104.8
粤 西	Western Region	106.7	104.9	104.3	101.7	107.6	100.5	103.1
粤 北	Northern Region	105.9	104.1	105.7	103.0	107.7	101.1	104.7

2-28 各市人均地区生产总值指数

Indices of Per Capita Gross Domestic Product by City

2000年=100 (year of 2000=100)

市别	City	2001	2005	2010	2013	2014	2015	2016
广州	Guangzhou	110.2	194.3	285.9	333.7	348.3	362.3	372.1
深圳	Shenzhen	107.2	175.1	264.6	294.1	305.2	314.2	322.5
珠海	Zhuhai	106.3	162.6	263.9	310.2	330.4	353.4	372.6
汕头	Shantou	95.8	130.9	203.9	265.2	287.7	310.9	337.0
佛山	Foshan	108.6	193.1	335.3	385.5	403.9	426.7	453.8
韶关	Shaoguan	109.7	155.9	291.4	398.7	428.9	453.9	481.2
河源	Heyuan	109.3	179.3	360.2	505.1	549.4	586.8	629.8
梅州	Meizhou	107.5	148.1	245.7	344.2	377.2	413.1	449.0
惠州	Huizhou	105.6	156.9	264.3	340.1	362.0	384.9	406.5
汕尾	Shanwei	106.2	157.9	318.9	471.8	517.7	563.5	608.0
东莞	Dongguan	111.8	232.7	356.2	384.9	400.6	426.2	455.3
中山	Zhongshan	112.9	230.9	351.9	406.2	417.8	437.5	445.0
江门	Jiangmen	123.6	183.1	311.1	406.8	434.6	468.6	499.8
阳江	Yangjiang	108.4	163.6	303.7	435.2	477.1	511.4	540.4
湛江	Zhanjiang	106.0	153.1	264.8	364.5	400.3	435.2	465.0
茂名	Maoming	108.2	159.2	281.0	387.2	425.6	457.8	491.0
肇庆	Zhaoqing	106.4	160.6	294.4	393.7	430.3	463.5	485.2
清远	Qingyuan	104.7	181.4	395.5	473.1	505.0	541.1	587.9
潮州	Chaozhou	105.8	153.1	268.7	367.6	397.2	436.9	475.8
揭阳	Jieyang	101.1	123.6	256.5	371.7	411.0	444.8	480.3
云浮	Yunfu	103.0	139.7	255.8	373.0	411.3	446.0	480.5
按经济区域分	By Region							
珠三角	Pearl River Delta	109.4	186.2	294.6	344.4	361.1	379.8	397.4
粤东	Eastern Region	101.5	140.1	252.3	349.9	382.5	415.2	449.7
粤西	Western Region	107.6	158.9	283.0	392.9	431.6	466.0	497.8
粤北	Northern Region	106.8	158.7	303.2	407.1	441.5	475.0	512.2

2−28 续表 continued

2000年=100 (year of 2000=100)

市 别	City	2017	2018	2019	2020	2021	2022	2023
广 州	Guangzhou	379.6	388.9	406.1	408.6	435.9	440.3	460.1
深 圳	Shenzhen	331.3	338.9	348.3	348.8	367.1	379.4	400.8
珠 海	Zhuhai	396.1	402.7	405.2	396.4	413.4	420.6	434.0
汕 头	Shantou	367.0	391.5	414.7	422.3	447.9	452.3	469.9
佛 山	Foshan	480.1	496.3	517.8	518.2	556.8	567.7	595.8
韶 关	Shaoguan	511.3	530.9	562.2	578.4	627.0	627.6	656.4
河 源	Heyuan	676.3	719.6	762.6	776.0	839.4	848.5	882.5
梅 州	Meizhou	484.2	500.5	522.8	536.5	569.8	574.8	614.2
惠 州	Huizhou	430.4	446.9	455.9	454.7	498.3	519.7	548.3
汕 尾	Shanwei	662.8	721.9	775.6	816.7	920.8	933.7	979.2
东 莞	Dongguan	485.9	515.4	551.4	556.2	601.1	612.4	629.6
中 山	Zhongshan	450.3	452.7	450.9	450.4	483.7	486.3	513.9
江 门	Jiangmen	536.1	572.6	590.8	597.3	641.8	662.5	699.6
阳 江	Yangjiang	567.6	585.4	629.3	652.5	702.7	705.9	731.8
湛 江	Zhanjiang	497.3	525.9	547.0	557.4	603.9	609.3	625.2
茂 名	Maoming	525.7	550.4	567.6	570.3	609.1	609.5	630.1
肇 庆	Zhaoqing	507.7	537.5	567.4	580.6	638.7	645.3	668.8
清 远	Qingyuan	608.9	629.2	664.8	686.2	739.2	748.3	781.3
潮 州	Chaozhou	505.6	531.1	558.4	567.8	621.6	636.2	654.8
揭 阳	Jieyang	508.9	540.2	559.9	564.8	602.0	591.7	633.7
云 浮	Yunfu	504.8	525.0	558.6	580.9	626.7	639.8	663.4
按经济区域分	By Region							
珠 三 角	Pearl River Delta	414.6	429.3	446.5	448.9	479.4	489.9	513.3
粤 东	Eastern Region	483.7	516.6	544.2	555.4	599.0	601.8	630.8
粤 西	Western Region	531.0	556.9	580.9	590.7	635.6	638.6	658.5
粤 北	Northern Region	542.5	564.9	597.1	614.9	662.5	669.5	701.2

2-29　文化及相关产业增加值

Value-added of Culture and related Industry

单位：亿元　　(100 million yuan)

指　　标	Item	2015	2019	2020	2021	2022
文化及相关产业增加值	**Value-added of Culture and related Industry**	**3879.99**	**6227.18**	**6210.60**	**6910.06**	**6986.67**
分行业大类	Grouped by Sector					
文化制造业	Cultural Manufacturing	2101.45	2419.32	2265.07	2575.56	2616.70
文化批发和零售业	Cultural Wholesale and Retail Sale	282.13	509.38	506.48	599.55	632.34
文化服务业	Cultural Services	1496.41	3298.48	3439.05	3734.95	3737.64
分活动性质	Grouped by Nature of Activities					
文化核心领域	Core Areas of Culture	2003.64	3718.36	3855.85	4224.20	4230.93
新闻信息服务	New Information Services	341.74	1016.98	1185.11	1153.57	1365.54
内容创作生产	Content Creation and Production	815.92	1241.31	1341.66	1533.50	1323.73
创意设计服务	Creative Design Services	472.34	848.30	850.02	954.49	976.56
文化传播渠道	Cultural Transmission Channel	231.11	403.53	333.03	410.80	409.93
文化投资运营	Cultural Investment and Operation	21.08	3.94	31.30	29.87	34.63
文化娱乐休闲服务	Culture and Recreation Services	121.45	204.30	114.73	141.96	120.53
文化相关领域	Culture Related Areas	1876.35	2508.83	2354.75	2685.85	2755.75
文化辅助生产和中介服务	Cultural Auxiliary Production and Intermediary Services	644.69	982.26	935.27	1038.30	1034.21
文化装备生产	Cultural Equipment Production	449.94	576.37	496.93	543.79	578.45
文化消费终端生产	Cultural Consumer Terminal Production	781.72	950.20	922.55	1103.76	1143.09

注：若数据分项合计与总计不等，是由于数值修约误差所致。

Note: If the itemized total data is different from the total，caused by Numerical rounding error.

主要统计指标解释

国内（地区）生产总值 指一个国家（或地区）所有常住单位在一定时期内生产活动的最终成果。国内（地区）生产总值有三种表现形态，即价值形态、收入形态和产品形态。从价值形态看，它是所有常住单位在一定时期内生产的全部货物和服务价值与同期投入的全部非固定资产货物和服务价值的差额，即所有常住单位的增加值之和；从收入形态看，它是所有常住单位在一定时期内创造的各项收入之和，包括劳动者报酬、生产税净额、固定资产折旧和营业盈余；从产品形态看，它是所有常住单位在一定时期内最终使用的货物和服务价值与货物和服务净出口价值之和。在实际核算中，国内（地区）生产总值有三种计算方法，即生产法、收入法和支出法。三种方法分别从不同的方面反映国内（地区）生产总值及其构成。□

三次产业 三次产业的划分是世界上较为常用的产业结构分类，但各国的划分不尽一致。根据《国民经济行业分类》（GB/T4754—2017）和国家统计局 2018 年修订的《三次产业划分规定》，我国的三产产业划分是：

第一产业是指农、林、牧、渔业（不含农、林、牧、渔服务业）。

第二产业是指采矿业（不含开采专业及辅助性活动），制造业（不含金属制品、机械和设备修理业），电力、热力、燃气及水生产和供应业，建筑业。

第三产业即服务业，是指除第一产业、第二产业以外的其他行业。

劳动者报酬 指劳动者从事生产活动应获得的全部报酬，既包括货币形式的报酬，也包括实物形式的报酬。主要包括工资、奖金、津贴和补贴，单位为其员工交纳的社会保险费、补充社会保险费和住房公积金、行政事业单位职工的离退休金、单位为其员工提供的其他各种形式的福利和报酬等。

生产税净额 指生产税减生产补贴后的差额。其中，生产税指政府对生产单位从事生产、销售和经营活动，以及因从事生产活动使用某些生产要素（如固定资产和土地等）所征收的各种税收、附加费和其他规费。生产税分为产品税和其他生产税，产品税主要有：增值税、消费税、进口关税、出口税等；其他生产税主要有：房产税、车船使用税、城镇土地使用税等。生产补贴则相反，它是政府为影响生产单位的生产、销售及定价等生产活动而对其提供的无偿支付，包括农业生产补贴、政策亏损补贴、进口补贴等。生产补贴作为负生产税处理。

固定资产折旧 指由于自然退化、正常淘汰或损耗而导致的固定资产价值下降，用以代表固定资产通过生产过程被转移到其产出中的价值。原则上，固定资产折旧应按照固定资产的重置价值计算。

营业盈余 指常住单位创造的增加值扣除劳动者报酬、生产税净额和固定资产折旧后的余额。

支出法国内生产总值 是从最终使用的角度反映一个国家(或地区)一定时期内生产活动最终成果的一种方法，包括最终消费支出、资本形成总额及货物和服务净出口三部分。计算公式为：

支出法国内生产总值=最终消费支出+资本形成总额+货物和服务净出口

最终消费支出 指常住单位为满足物质、文化和精神生活的需要，从本国经济领土和国外购买的货物和服务的支出。它不包括非常住单位在本国经济领土内的消费支出。最终消费支出分为居民消费支出和政府消费支出。

居民消费支出 指常住住户在一定时期内对于货物和服务的全部最终消费支出。居民消费支出除了直接以货币形式购买的货物和服务的消费支出外，还包括以其他方式获得的货物和服务的消费支出，后者称为虚拟消费支出。居民虚拟消费支出主要包括：单位以实物报酬及实物转移的形式提供给劳动者的货物和服务；住户生产用于自身消费的货物（如自产自用的农产品），以及纳入生产核算范围并用于自身消费的服务（如住户的自有住房服务）；银行和保险机构提供的间接计算的金融服务。

政府消费支出 指政府部门为全社会提供的公共服务的消费支出和免费或以较低的价格向居民住户提供的货物和服务的净支出，前者等于政府服务的产出价值减去政府单位所获得的经营收入的价值，后者等于政府部门免费或以较低价格向居民住户提供的货物和服务的市场价值减去向住户收取的价值。

资本形成总额 指常住单位在一定时期内获得减去处置的固定资产和存货的净额，包括固定资本形成总额和存货变动两部分。

固定资本形成总额 指常住单位在一定时期内获得的固定资产减处置的固定资产的价值总额。固定资产是通过生产活动生产出来的，且其使用年限在一年以上、单位价值在规定标准以上的资产，不包括自然资产、耐用消费品、小型工器具。固定资本形成总额包括住宅、其他建筑和构筑物、机器和设备、培育性生物资源、知识产权产品（研发支出、矿藏的勘探、计算机软件）的价值获得减处置。

存货变动 指常住单位在一定时期内存货实物量变动的市场价值，即期末价值减期初价值的差额，再扣除当期由于价格变动而产生的持有收益。存货变动可以是正值，也可以是负值，正值表示存货上升，负值表示存货下降。存货包括生产单位购进的原材料、燃料和储备物资等存货，以及生产单位生产的产成品、在制品和半成品等存货。

货物和服务净出口 指货物和服务出口减货物和服务进口的差额。出口包括常住单位向非常住单位出售或无偿转让的各种货物和服务的价值；进口包括常住单位从非常住单位购买或无偿得到的各种货物和服务的价值。货物的出口和进口都按离岸价格计算。

新经济增加值占地区生产总值比重 是指新经济增加值占地区生产总值之比。新经济增加值是指一个国家（或地区）所有常住单位在一定时期内从事新产业、新业态、新商业模式经济生产活动的最终成果，是常住单位进行新产业、新业态、新商业模式经济生产活动的增加值之和。

Explanatory Notes on Main Statistical Indicators

Gross Domestic (Regional) Product refers to the final products produced by all resident units in a country during a certain period of time. Gross domestic (regional) product is expressed in three different perspectives, namely value, income, and products respectively. GDP in its value perspective refers to the balance of total value of all goods and services produced by all resident units during a certain period of time, minus the total value of input of goods and services of the nature of non-fixed assets; in other words, it is the sum of the value-added of all resident units. GDP from the perspective of income refers to the sum of all kinds of revenue, including Compensation of Employees, Net Taxes on Production, Depreciation of Fixed Assets, and Operating Surplus. GDP from the perspective of products refers to the value of all goods and services for final demand by all resident units plus the net exports of goods and services during a given period of time. In the practice of national accounting, gross domestic (regional) product is calculated from three approaches, namely production approach, income approach and expenditure approach, which reflect gross domestic (regional) product and its composition from different angles.

Three Strata of Industry Classification of economic activities into three strata of industry is a common practice in the world, although the grouping varies to some extent from country to country. In China, according to Industrial classification for National Economic Activities (GB/T 4754—2017) and Dividing Basis of Three Industries revised by National Bureau of Statistics in 2018, economic activities are categorized into the following three strata of industry:

Primary industry refers to agriculture, forestry, animal husbandry and fishery industries (not including services in support of agriculture, forestry, animal husbandry and fishery industries).

Secondary industry refers to mining and quarrying(not including support activities for mining), manufacturing(not including repair service of metal products, machinery and equipment), production and supply of electricity, heat, gas and water, and construction.

Tertiary industry refers to all other economic activities not included in the primary or secondary industries.

Compensation of Employees refers to the total payment of various forms to employees for the productive activities they are engaged in. It includes the employees earn in cash or in kind. It mainly include: wages, bonuses and allowances, subsidies, social insurance paid by company or unit for its staff, supplementary social insurance, housing fund, the pension for the employees of the administrative institution, other forms of welfare and remuneration provide by the units for its employees.

Net Taxes on Production refers to taxes on production less subsidies on production. The taxes on production refers to the various taxes, extra charges and fees levied on the production units on their production, sale and business activities as well as on the use of some factors of production, such as fixed assets, land etc. in the production activities they are engaged in. Taxes on production are divided into product tax and other kinds of taxes on production, product tax mainly includes: value-added tax, consumption tax, import duty, export duty; other taxes on production mainly include: House Property Tax, Tax on Vehicles and Boat Operation, Urban Land Use Tax, etc. In contrast to taxes on production, subsidies on production refer to the payment by the government for free to the production units to influence production activities of production units such as production, sales and pricing, which include agricultural production subsidies, subsidies for policy losses, import subsidies, etc. Subsidies on production are therefore regarded as negative taxes on production.

Depreciation of Fixed Assets refers to the decline of the value of fixed assets due to natural deterioration, normal elimination or loss, it reflects the value of transfer of the fixed assets in the production of the current period. In principle, the depreciation of fixed assets should be calculated on the basis of the re-purchased value of the fixed assets.

Operating Surplus refers to the balance of the value added created by the resident units after deducting the labourers remuneration, net taxes on production and the depreciation of fixed assets.

Gross Domestic (Regional) Product Calculated by Expenditure Approach refers to the method of measuring the final results of production activities of a country (region) during a given period from the perspective of final uses. It includes final consumption expenditure, gross capital formation and net export of goods and services. The formula for computation is:

GDP by expenditure approach = final consumption expenditure + gross capital formation + net export of goods and services

Final Consumption Expenditure refers to the total expenditure of resident units for purchases of goods and services from both the domestic economic territory and abroad to meet the needs of material, cultural and spiritual life. It does not include the expenditure of non-resident units on consumption in the economic territory of the country. The final consumption expenditure is broken down into household consumption expenditure and government consumption expenditure.

Household Consumption Expenditure refers to the total expenditure of resident households on the final consumption of goods and services. In addition to the consumption of goods and services bought by the households directly with money, the household consumption expenditure also includes expenditure on goods and services obtained by the households in other ways, i.e. the latter so-called imputed consumption expenditure, which mainly includes: (a) the goods and services provided to households by employers in the form of payment in kind and transfer in kind; (b) goods and services produced and consumed by the households themselves (such as self produced agricultural products); (c) financial intermediate services provided by banking and insurance institutions.

Government Consumption Expenditure refers to the consumption expenditure spent for the provision of public services provided by the government to the whole country and the net expenditure on the goods and services provided by the government to households free of charge or at reduced prices. The former equals to the output value of the government services minus the value of operating income obtained by the government departments. The latter equals to the market value of the goods and services provided by the government free of charge or at reduced prices to the households minus the value received by the government from the households.

Gross Capital Formation refers to the fixed assets acquired less disposals and the net value of inventory, thus including gross fixed capital formation and changes in inventories.

Gross Fixed Capital Formation refers to the value of acquisitions less those disposals of fixed assets during a given period. Fixed assets are the assets produced through production activities with unit value above a specified amount and which could be used for over one year. Natural assets, consumer durables, small instruments are not included. Gross Fixed Capital Formation includes the value of housing, other buildings and structure, equipment and machinery, breeding biological resources, intellectual property right product (expenditure for R&D, the prospecting of minerals and the acquisition of computer software) minus the disposal of them.

Changes in Inventories refers to the market value of the change in the physical volume of inventory of resident units during a given period, i.e. the difference between the values at the beginning and at the end of the period minus the gains due to the change in prices. The changes in inventories can have a positive or a negative value. A positive value indicates an increase in inventory while a negative value indicates a decrease in inventory. The inventory includes raw materials, fuels and reserve materials purchased by the production units as well as the inventory of finished products, semi-finished products and work-in-progress.

Net Export of Goods and Services refers to the exports of goods and services subtracting the imports of goods and services. Exports include the value of various goods and services sold or gratuitously transferred by resident units to non-resident units. Imports include the value of various goods and services purchased or gratuitously acquired resident units from non-resident units. Because the provision of services and the use of them happen simultaneously, the acquisition of services by resident units from abroad is usually treated as import while the acquisition of services by non-resident units in this country is usually treated as export. The exports and imports of goods are calculated at FOB.

Percentage of Value-added of New Economy in Gross Domestic Product refers to the percentage of value-added of new economy in GDP. The value -added of new economy refers to the final result of all resident units in a country (or a region) engaging in economic production activities of new industries, new forms of business and new business models during a certain period of time. It is the sum of the value-added of economy production activities of permanent units in new industries, new forms of business and new business models.

三、人口

POPULATION

三 人口

简要说明

一、本篇资料反映广东人口发展变化基本情况，主要内容包括：

1. 年末常住人口、年龄性别比例、城镇人口比例以及人口自然增长。数据由广东省统计局根据人口普查、1%人口抽样调查或年度人口变动情况抽样调查评估测算。

2. 1990-2019 年年末常住人口数、出生率、死亡率以及自然增长率，除人口普查和 1%人口抽样调查年份直接计算外，其余年份数据均已按人口普查和 1%人口抽样调查结果作平滑调整。

3. 年末户籍人口、分性别以及迁移变动等，数据来源于广东省公安厅人口统计年报。

二、本资料由广东省统计局人口和就业统计处整理提供。

3 Population

Brief Introduction

Ⅰ. The data in this chapter show the basic conditions of development and changes of population in Guangdong, including mainly:

（1）Permanent population at the end of the year, age and sex ratio, urban population ratio and natural population growth. The data are evaluated and calculated by Guangdong Provincial Bureau of statistics according to the population census, national one-percent sample survey or annual population change sampling survey.

（2）Permanent population at the year-end, birth rate, death rate and natural growth rate of population from 1990 to 2019 result from smooth adjustment on population census and national one-percent sample survey on population with the exceptions of 1990 and 2020 data, which are direct calculated from the result of population censuses.

（3）Registered residence population at the end of the year by gender and migration change etc, the data are obtained from the annual reports of population of Guangdong Provincial Department of Public Security.

Ⅱ. The date in this chapter are prepared and provided by the Division of Population and Employment Statistics of Statistics Bureau of Guangdong Province.

3-1 人口主要指标

Main Population Indicators

项 目	Item	2000	2010	2015	2021	2022	2023
年末常住人口 （万人）	**Permanent Population at the Year-end (10000 persons)**	**8650.03**	**10440.94**	**11678.00**	**12684.00**	**12656.80**	**12706.00**
男性比例 (%)	Proportion of Male Population (%)	50.90	52.15	52.29	52.77	52.73	52.64
女性比例 (%)	Proportion of Female Population (%)	49.10	47.85	47.71	47.23	47.27	47.36
0−14岁人口比例 (%)	Proportion of Population Aged 0-14 (%)	24.17	16.88	17.37	18.73	18.47	17.98
15−64岁人口比例 (%)	Proportion of Population Aged 15-64 (%)	69.78	76.33	74.15	72.15	71.94	72.06
65岁及以上人口比例(%)	Proportion of Population Aged 65 And Over (%)	6.05	6.79	8.48	9.12	9.59	9.96
城镇人口比例 (%)	Proportion of Urban Population (%)	55.00	66.18	69.51	74.63	74.79	75.42
人口密度（人/平方公里）	Population Density (person/sq.km.)	486	581	650	705	704	707
户籍人口	**Population with Residence Registration**						
年末总户数 (万户)	Total Households at the Year-end (10000 households)	1901.91	2296.61	2415.90	2681.91	2734.83	2757.00
年末总人口 (万人)	Total Population at the Year-end(10000 persons)	7498.54	8521.55	9008.38	9946.95	10049.72	10146.21
性别比 (女=100)	Sex Ratio (female=100)	106.70	106.20	106.08	104.75	104.57	104.37
人口变动情况 (‰)	**Status of Population Changes (‰)**						
出生率	Birth Rate	12.91	11.18	11.12	9.35	8.30	8.12
死亡率	Death Rate	4.77	4.21	4.32	4.83	4.97	5.36
自然增长率	Natural Growth Rate	8.14	6.97	6.80	4.52	3.33	2.76
迁入率	Immigration Rate	16.59	12.07	8.34	14.65	12.13	12.63
迁出率	Emigration Rate	12.94	8.35	7.45	8.43	7.27	7.22
总迁移率	Total Migration Rate	29.53	20.42	15.79	23.08	19.40	19.85
净迁移率	Net Migration Rate	3.65	3.72	0.89	6.23	4.86	5.41
跨省净迁移率	Net Cross-Provincial Migration Rate	1.01	2.52	0.80	5.87	4.68	5.12

3-2 人口自然变动情况

Status of Natural Population Changes

单位：万人、‰ (10000 persons, ‰)

年 份 Year	常住人口 Permanent Population	出生 Birth		死亡 Death		自然增长 Natural Growth		人口密度 (人/平方公里) Population Density (person/sq.km.)
		出生人数 Number of Birth	出生率 Birth Rate	死亡人数 Number of Death	死亡率 Death Rate	自然增长人数 Number of Natural Growth	自然增长率 Rate of Natural Growth	
1978	5064.15	111.23	22.14	27.35	5.44	83.88	16.70	285
1980	5230.00	118.31	22.82	28.40	5.48	89.91	17.34	294
1982	5419.35	123.98	23.09	31.79	5.92	92.19	17.17	304
1983	5501.85	114.55	21.00	34.47	6.32	80.08	14.68	309
1984	5585.61	114.86	20.75	34.37	6.21	80.49	14.54	313
1985	5670.65	115.70	20.60	35.53	6.33	80.17	14.27	318
1986	5799.75	126.23	22.15	32.48	5.70	93.75	16.45	323
1987	5931.79	128.00	22.12	32.98	5.70	95.02	16.42	328
1988	6066.84	122.90	20.90	29.81	5.07	93.09	15.83	333
1989	6204.96	121.15	20.27	34.25	5.73	86.90	14.54	338
1990	6347.19	140.11	22.26	36.25	5.76	103.86	16.50	353
1991	6527.01	131.31	20.40	38.04	5.91	93.27	14.49	363
1992	6706.45	125.17	18.92	40.00	6.05	85.17	12.87	373
1993	6936.69	120.00	17.59	38.00	5.57	82.00	12.02	386
1994	7209.58	121.00	17.11	38.00	5.37	83.00	11.74	401
1995	7387.49	123.54	16.93	38.91	5.33	84.63	11.60	411
1996	7569.78	124.80	16.69	42.11	5.63	82.69	11.06	421
1997	7779.69	118.40	15.43	37.83	4.93	80.57	10.50	433
1998	7990.03	117.00	14.84	40.00	5.07	77.00	9.77	444
1999	8217.91	110.00	13.57	39.00	4.81	71.00	8.76	457
2000	8650.03	108.85	12.91	40.21	4.77	68.64	8.14	486
2001	8733.18	107.99	12.42	39.63	4.56	68.36	7.86	486
2002	8842.08	103.94	11.82	39.73	4.52	64.21	7.30	492
2003	8962.69	108.00	12.13	41.98	4.71	66.02	7.42	499
2004	9110.66	106.73	11.81	41.62	4.60	65.11	7.21	507
2005	9194.00	107.11	11.70	42.24	4.68	64.87	7.02	511
2006	9442.07	108.96	11.69	41.53	4.46	67.43	7.24	525
2007	9659.52	112.00	11.73	44.00	4.61	68.00	7.12	537
2008	9893.48	112.00	11.46	43.00	4.40	69.00	7.06	550
2009	10130.19	113.00	11.29	43.00	4.29	70.00	6.99	563
2010	10440.94	115.00	11.18	43.27	4.21	71.73	6.97	581
2011	10756.00	109.44	10.45	45.56	4.35	63.88	6.10	598
2012	11041.00	122.37	11.60	49.06	4.65	73.31	6.95	614
2013	11270.00	113.73	10.71	49.80	4.69	63.93	6.02	627
2014	11489.00	115.39	10.80	50.21	4.70	65.18	6.10	639
2015	11678.00	119.95	11.12	46.60	4.32	73.35	6.80	650
2016	11908.00	129.45	11.85	48.17	4.41	81.28	7.44	663
2017	12141.00	151.63	13.68	50.10	4.52	101.53	9.16	676
2018	12348.00	143.98	12.79	51.22	4.55	92.76	8.24	687
2019	12489.00	143.38	12.54	50.99	4.46	92.38	8.08	695
2020	12624.00	129.08	10.28	59.02	4.70	70.06	5.58	702
2021	12684.00	118.31	9.35	61.12	4.83	57.19	4.52	705
2022	12656.80	105.20	8.30	63.00	4.97	42.20	3.33	704
2023	12706.00	103.00	8.12	68.00	5.36	35.00	2.76	707

注：2011—2019年年末常住人口根据2020年第七次全国人口普查结果平滑调整。

Note: Figures of permanent population at the year-end from 2011 to 2019 have been adjusted in accordance with the flash sums of the 7th National Population Census in 2020.

3-3 常住人口构成

Composition of Permanent Population

单位：万人、%　　　　　　　　　　(10000 persons, %)

年份 Year	按性别分 By Sex				按城乡分 By Residence			
	男 Male		女 Female		城镇 Urban		农村 Rural	
	人口数 Population	比重 Proportion	人口数 Population	比重 Proportion	人口数 Population	比重 Proportion	人口数 Population	比重 Proportion
1982	2774.17	51.19	2645.18	48.81	972.23	17.94	4447.12	82.06
1990	3249.76	51.20	3097.43	48.80	2335.77	36.80	4011.42	63.20
2000	4402.87	50.90	4247.16	49.10	4757.52	55.00	3892.51	45.00
2005	4655.84	50.64	4538.16	49.36	5578.92	60.68	3615.08	39.32
2006	4787.13	50.70	4654.94	49.30	5948.50	63.00	3493.57	37.00
2007	4926.36	51.00	4733.16	49.00	6099.02	63.14	3560.50	36.86
2008	5065.46	51.20	4828.02	48.80	6269.50	63.37	3623.98	36.63
2009	5166.40	51.00	4963.79	49.00	6422.54	63.40	3707.65	36.60
2010	5444.95	52.15	4995.99	47.85	6909.85	66.18	3531.09	33.82
2011	5689.92	52.90	5066.08	47.10	7160.27	66.57	3595.73	33.43
2012	5807.57	52.60	5233.43	47.40	7414.03	67.15	3626.97	32.85
2013	5871.67	52.10	5398.33	47.90	7673.74	68.09	3596.26	31.91
2014	6081.13	52.93	5407.87	47.07	7883.75	68.62	3605.25	31.38
2015	6106.43	52.29	5571.57	47.71	8117.38	69.51	3560.62	30.49
2016	6239.79	52.40	5668.21	47.60	8353.46	70.15	3554.54	29.85
2017	6372.81	52.49	5768.19	47.51	8588.54	70.74	3552.46	29.26
2018	6443.19	52.18	5904.81	47.82	8867.10	71.81	3480.90	28.19
2019	6528.00	52.27	5961.00	47.73	9073.26	72.65	3415.74	27.35
2020	6699.56	53.07	5924.44	46.93	9360.70	74.15	3263.30	25.85
2021	6693.00	52.77	5991.00	47.23	9466.07	74.63	3217.93	25.37
2022	6673.80	52.73	5983.00	47.27	9465.40	74.79	3191.40	25.21
2023	6689.00	52.64	6017.00	47.36	9583.00	75.42	3123.00	24.58

注：2011—2019年年末常住人口根据2020年第七次全国人口普查结果平滑调整。

Note: Figures of permanent population at the year-end from 2011 to 2019 have been adjusted in accordance with the flash sums of the 7th National Population Census in 2020.

3-4 常住人口年龄结构和抚养比
Age Composition and Dependency Ratio of Permanent Population

单位：万人、% (10000 persons, %)

年份 Year	0—14岁 Aged 0-14		15—64岁 Aged 15-64		65岁及以上 Aged 65 and Over		少年儿童抚养比 Children Dependency Ratio	老年人口抚养比 Old Dependency Ratio	总抚养比 Gross Dependency Ratio
	人数 Population	比重 Proportion	人数 Population	比重 Proportion	人数 Population	比重 Proportion			
1982	1802.68	33.61	3267.68	60.93	292.83	5.46	55.16	8.96	64.12
1990	1879.73	29.92	4030.66	64.15	372.58	5.93	46.64	9.24	55.88
2000	2088.56	24.17	6029.96	69.78	523.65	6.05	34.64	8.67	43.31
2005	1960.16	21.32	6552.56	71.27	681.28	7.41	29.91	10.40	40.31
2006	1935.62	20.50	6807.73	72.10	698.71	7.40	28.43	10.26	38.70
2007	1941.56	20.10	6983.83	72.30	734.12	7.60	27.80	10.51	38.31
2008	1949.02	19.70	7162.88	72.40	781.58	7.90	27.21	10.91	38.12
2009	1955.13	19.30	7364.65	72.70	810.42	8.00	26.55	11.00	37.55
2010	1760.40	16.88	7963.03	76.33	708.62	6.79	22.11	8.90	31.01
2011	1817.76	16.90	8206.83	76.30	731.41	6.80	22.15	8.91	31.06
2012	1766.56	16.00	8501.57	77.00	772.87	7.00	20.78	9.09	29.87
2013	1649.93	14.64	8699.31	77.19	920.76	8.17	18.97	10.58	29.55
2014	1767.01	15.38	8771.85	76.35	950.14	8.27	20.14	10.83	30.98
2015	2028.47	17.37	8659.24	74.15	990.29	8.48	23.43	11.44	34.86
2016	2051.75	17.23	8838.12	74.22	1018.13	8.55	23.21	11.52	34.73
2017	2089.47	17.21	9004.98	74.17	1046.55	8.62	23.20	11.62	34.83
2018	2121.39	17.18	9162.21	74.20	1064.40	8.62	23.15	11.62	34.77
2019	2033.21	16.28	9331.78	74.72	1124.01	9.00	21.79	12.04	33.83
2020	2374.99	18.85	9144.96	72.57	1081.30	8.58	25.97	11.82	37.79
2021	2376.00	18.73	9151.00	72.15	1157.00	9.12	25.97	12.64	38.61
2022	2337.30	18.47	9105.10	71.94	1214.40	9.59	25.67	13.34	39.01
2023	2284.00	17.98	9156.00	72.06	1266.00	9.96	24.95	13.83	38.78

注：1982、1990、2000、2010、2020年常住人口年龄结构使用普查数据，其合计数据与表3-2不一致。

Note: Age composition of permanent population for the years 1982, 1990, 2000, 2010 and 2020 are census year estimates. Therefore, the total data is inconsistent with table 3-2.

3-5 年末户籍总人口

Total Population with Residence Registration at Year-end

单位：万人、%　　(10000 persons,%)

年份 Year	总人口 Total Population	按性别分 By Sex			
		男 Male		女 Female	
		人口数 Total Population	比例 Proportion	人口数 Total Population	比例 Proportion
1978	5064.15	2586.68	51.08	2477.47	48.92
1980	5227.67	2671.28	51.10	2556.39	48.90
1982	5415.35	2771.86	51.19	2643.49	48.81
1983	5494.12	2818.92	51.31	2675.20	48.69
1984	5576.62	2865.90	51.39	2710.72	48.61
1985	5655.60	2909.52	51.44	2746.08	48.56
1986	5740.70	2955.68	51.49	2785.02	48.51
1987	5832.15	3003.09	51.49	2829.06	48.51
1988	5928.31	3053.50	51.51	2874.81	48.49
1989	6024.98	3106.37	51.56	2918.61	48.44
1990	6246.32	3213.20	51.44	3033.12	48.56
1991	6348.95	3266.26	51.45	3082.69	48.55
1992	6463.17	3327.67	51.49	3135.50	48.51
1993	6581.60	3390.37	51.51	3191.23	48.49
1994	6691.46	3450.68	51.57	3240.78	48.43
1995	6788.74	3501.19	51.57	3287.55	48.43
1996	6896.77	3559.54	51.61	3337.23	48.39
1997	7013.73	3620.32	51.62	3393.41	48.38
1998	7115.65	3676.95	51.67	3438.70	48.33
1999	7298.88	3769.70	51.65	3529.18	48.35
2000	7498.54	3871.13	51.63	3627.41	48.37
2001	7565.33	3905.28	51.62	3660.05	48.38
2002	7649.29	3948.25	51.62	3701.04	48.38
2003	7723.42	3989.24	51.65	3734.18	48.35
2004	7804.75	4025.87	51.58	3778.88	48.42
2005	7899.64	4080.74	51.66	3818.90	48.34
2006	8048.71	4154.03	51.61	3894.68	48.39
2007	8156.05	4204.47	51.55	3951.58	48.45
2008	8267.09	4263.24	51.57	4003.85	48.43
2009	8365.98	4309.11	51.51	4056.87	48.49
2010	8521.55	4388.61	51.50	4132.94	48.50
2011	8637.19	4445.48	51.47	4191.71	48.53
2012	8635.89	4448.45	51.51	4187.44	48.49
2013	8759.46	4513.51	51.53	4245.95	48.47
2014	8886.88	4577.10	51.50	4309.78	48.50
2015	9008.38	4637.13	51.48	4371.25	48.52
2016	9164.90	4717.29	51.47	4447.61	48.53
2017	9316.91	4788.55	51.40	4528.36	48.60
2018	9502.12	4877.64	51.33	4624.48	48.67
2019	9663.41	4955.32	51.28	4708.09	48.72
2020	9808.66	5023.14	51.21	4785.52	48.79
2021	9946.95	5088.93	51.16	4858.02	48.84
2022	10049.72	5137.03	51.12	4912.69	48.88
2023	10146.21	5181.48	51.07	4964.73	48.93

3–6 户籍人口迁移变动情况

Status of Migrant Changes

单位：万人、‰ (10000 persons, ‰)

年份 Year	迁入 Immigration		迁出 Emigration		总迁移 Total Migration		净迁移 Net Migration	
	迁入人数 Number of Immigration	迁入率 Immigration Rate	迁出人数 Number of Emigration	迁出率 Emigration Rate	总迁人数 Total Number of Migration	总迁移率 Total Migration Rate	净迁移人数 Net Number of Migration	净迁移率 Net Migration Rate
1978	81.83	16.29	75.58	15.04	157.41	31.33	6.25	1.25
1980	91.45	17.64	82.09	15.83	173.54	33.47	9.36	1.81
1982	71.63	13.34	65.06	12.11	136.69	25.45	6.57	1.23
1983	66.26	12.14	59.35	10.88	125.61	23.02	6.91	1.26
1984	92.30	16.67	83.31	15.05	175.61	31.72	8.99	1.62
1985	100.10	17.82	84.90	15.12	185.00	32.94	15.20	2.70
1986	85.61	15.02	70.83	12.43	156.44	27.45	14.78	2.59
1987	92.89	16.05	73.26	12.66	166.15	28.71	19.63	3.39
1988	93.82	15.96	73.46	12.49	167.28	28.45	20.36	3.47
1989	95.26	15.94	73.87	12.36	169.13	28.30	21.39	3.58
1990	94.39	15.38	77.07	12.56	171.46	27.94	17.32	2.82
1991	97.23	15.44	83.74	13.30	180.97	28.74	13.49	2.14
1992	135.89	21.21	108.39	16.92	244.28	38.13	27.50	4.29
1993	158.20	24.25	128.06	19.63	286.26	43.88	30.14	4.62
1994	140.93	21.24	115.72	17.44	256.65	38.68	25.21	3.80
1995	108.09	16.04	89.74	13.31	197.83	29.35	18.35	2.73
1996	113.47	16.58	88.88	12.99	202.35	29.57	24.59	3.59
1997	130.94	18.83	98.90	14.22	229.84	33.05	32.04	4.61
1998	117.93	16.69	94.18	13.33	212.11	30.02	23.75	3.36
1999	107.68	14.94	89.13	12.37	196.81	27.31	18.55	2.57
2000	122.72	16.59	95.76	12.94	218.48	29.53	26.96	3.65
2001	109.88	14.59	92.34	12.26	202.22	26.85	17.54	2.33
2002	102.26	13.44	81.95	10.77	184.21	24.21	20.31	2.67
2003	105.27	13.70	83.22	10.83	188.49	24.53	22.05	2.87
2004	133.91	17.25	104.26	13.43	238.17	30.68	29.65	3.82
2005	107.21	13.65	70.45	8.97	177.66	22.62	36.76	4.68
2006	145.49	18.25	80.56	10.10	226.05	28.35	64.93	8.14
2007	119.95	14.80	71.67	8.85	191.62	23.65	48.28	5.96
2008	110.56	13.46	79.47	9.68	190.03	23.14	31.09	3.79
2009	96.80	11.64	64.93	7.81	161.73	19.45	31.87	3.83
2010	101.90	12.07	70.48	8.35	172.38	20.42	31.43	3.72
2011	94.47	11.01	65.37	7.62	159.84	18.63	29.10	3.39
2012	97.91	11.34	112.62	13.04	210.53	24.38	-14.70	-1.70
2013	97.86	11.25	77.72	8.94	175.58	20.19	20.14	2.32
2014	93.48	10.60	68.29	7.74	161.78	18.34	25.19	2.85
2015	74.65	8.34	66.67	7.45	141.32	15.79	7.98	0.89
2016	88.31	9.72	73.84	8.13	162.15	17.84	14.47	1.59
2017	133.09	14.40	85.91	9.30	219.00	23.70	47.18	5.11
2018	160.20	17.02	95.20	10.12	255.40	27.14	64.99	6.91
2019	148.35	15.48	84.90	8.86	233.25	24.34	63.45	6.62
2020	142.67	14.65	84.82	8.71	227.50	23.37	57.85	5.94
2021	144.74	14.65	83.24	8.43	227.98	23.08	61.50	6.23
2022	121.27	12.13	72.68	7.27	193.94	19.40	48.59	4.86
2023	127.53	12.63	72.94	7.22	200.47	19.85	54.59	5.41

3-7 各市年末常住人口数

Permanent Population at Year-end by City

单位：万人 (10000 persons)

市别	City	2000	2005	2010	2018	2019	2020	2021	2022	2023
全省	**Provincial Total**	**8650.03**	**9194.00**	**10440.94**	**12348.00**	**12489.00**	**12624.00**	**12684.00**	**12656.80**	**12706.00**
广州	Guangzhou	994.80	949.68	1270.96	1798.13	1831.21	1874.03	1881.06	1873.41	1882.70
深圳	Shenzhen	701.24	827.75	1043.76	1666.12	1710.40	1763.38	1768.16	1766.18	1779.01
珠海	Zhuhai	123.65	141.57	156.16	220.90	233.18	244.96	246.67	247.72	249.41
汕头	Shantou	467.78	494.45	539.62	548.59	549.31	550.37	553.04	554.19	555.75
佛山	Foshan	534.05	580.03	719.91	926.04	943.14	951.88	961.26	955.23	961.54
韶关	Shaoguan	273.65	292.26	283.02	284.78	285.07	285.53	286.01	286.18	285.77
河源	Heyuan	226.78	278.24	295.82	285.89	284.83	283.56	284.09	284.17	283.83
梅州	Meizhou	380.52	411.84	424.46	395.51	391.96	387.10	387.69	385.80	384.91
惠州	Huizhou	321.80	370.69	460.11	584.72	597.23	605.72	606.60	605.02	607.34
汕尾	Shanwei	245.71	279.87	287.34	270.50	268.85	266.94	268.69	268.26	269.13
东莞	Dongguan	644.84	656.07	822.48	1043.77	1045.50	1048.36	1053.68	1043.70	1048.53
中山	Zhongshan	236.47	243.46	312.27	428.82	438.73	443.11	446.69	443.11	445.82
江门	Jiangmen	395.24	410.29	445.08	470.38	475.32	480.41	483.51	482.22	482.24
阳江	Yangjiang	217.20	232.14	242.53	257.26	259.09	260.59	262.07	262.22	262.47
湛江	Zhanjiang	603.43	668.95	700.38	698.23	698.16	698.07	703.09	703.54	707.84
茂名	Maoming	524.82	584.04	582.64	605.95	612.26	618.00	621.97	623.82	625.23
肇庆	Zhaoqing	337.69	367.60	392.22	406.58	409.24	411.69	412.97	412.84	413.17
清远	Qingyuan	314.98	359.37	370.38	393.12	395.48	397.40	398.28	398.57	398.67
潮州	Chaozhou	240.44	252.01	267.21	258.81	258.29	256.66	257.46	257.56	257.62
揭阳	Jieyang	524.61	559.69	588.30	565.81	563.42	557.87	561.68	563.41	565.36
云浮	Yunfu	215.49	233.99	236.29	238.09	238.33	238.37	239.33	239.65	239.66
按经济区域分	By Region									
珠三角	Pearl River Delta	4289.78	4547.14	5622.95	7545.46	7683.95	7823.54	7860.60	7829.43	7869.76
粤东	Eastern Region	1478.54	1586.02	1682.47	1643.71	1639.87	1631.84	1640.87	1643.42	1647.86
粤西	Western Region	1345.45	1485.13	1525.55	1561.44	1569.51	1576.66	1587.13	1589.58	1595.54
粤北	Northern Region	1411.42	1575.70	1609.97	1597.39	1595.67	1591.96	1595.40	1594.37	1592.84

注：1.2000年全省数据含根据普查误差率推算的漏登人口。
2.2006—2009年年末常住人口根据2010年第六次全国人口普查结果平滑调整。
3.2010年开始，深圳市包含深汕合作区人口。
4.2011—2019年年末常住人口根据2020年第七次全国人口普查结果平滑调整。

Note: a)Data for the permanent population of 2000 has been adjusted to account for the unregistered population,per the Population Census Error Rate.
b)Data for the permanent population from 2006 to 2009 have been adjusted with flash sums from the 6th National Population Census in 2010.
c)Data for the 2010 permanent population of Shenzhen includes the permanent population of the Shenshan Special Cooperation Zone.
d)Figures of permanent population at the year-end from 2011 to 2019 have been adjusted in accordance with the flash sums of the 7th National Population Census in 2020.

3-8 各市城镇人口占常住人口的比例

Proportion of Urban Population to Permanent Population by City

单位：% (%)

市别	City	2000	2005	2010	2018	2019	2020	2021	2022	2023
全省	**Provincial Total**	**55.00**	**60.68**	**66.18**	**71.81**	**72.65**	**74.15**	**74.63**	**74.79**	**75.42**
广州	Guangzhou	83.79	91.51	83.79	84.75	85.13	86.19	86.46	86.48	86.76
深圳	Shenzhen	92.46	100.00	99.76	99.82	99.52	99.54	99.81	99.79	99.80
珠海	Zhuhai	85.48	87.90	87.66	88.79	89.21	90.47	90.75	90.76	90.87
汕头	Shantou	67.00	72.34	68.47	69.58	69.96	70.70	70.74	70.75	71.15
佛山	Foshan	75.06	78.39	94.10	94.50	94.67	95.20	95.21	95.22	95.39
韶关	Shaoguan	51.13	49.76	52.54	55.11	55.96	57.33	58.13	58.54	59.65
河源	Heyuan	26.53	32.47	40.06	44.59	46.13	48.50	49.75	50.25	51.96
梅州	Meizhou	37.21	41.63	43.03	47.59	49.10	51.58	52.38	52.68	54.39
惠州	Huizhou	51.66	55.01	61.85	67.61	69.61	72.80	72.90	72.91	73.30
汕尾	Shanwei	52.58	51.88	54.03	55.32	56.29	57.12	57.56	57.86	59.31
东莞	Dongguan	60.04	73.02	88.47	89.93	90.31	92.15	92.24	92.25	92.83
中山	Zhongshan	60.67	74.29	87.84	87.15	87.06	86.96	87.00	87.02	87.56
江门	Jiangmen	47.08	56.78	62.31	65.12	66.04	67.63	67.84	67.85	68.66
阳江	Yangjiang	41.92	44.09	46.82	50.77	52.08	54.16	54.96	55.26	56.99
湛江	Zhanjiang	38.47	39.71	36.69	41.33	42.88	45.46	46.46	47.31	48.07
茂名	Maoming	37.45	39.30	35.08	39.58	41.09	43.56	45.06	45.84	47.32
肇庆	Zhaoqing	32.52	38.99	42.40	46.99	48.52	51.02	51.91	52.14	53.09
清远	Qingyuan	32.60	38.46	47.56	51.26	52.47	54.50	55.40	56.30	57.16
潮州	Chaozhou	43.41	53.62	62.78	63.55	63.82	64.19	64.80	64.81	65.10
揭阳	Jieyang	37.91	41.15	47.33	49.09	49.68	50.65	51.52	51.93	52.27
云浮	Yunfu	35.86	37.26	36.97	40.65	41.90	43.77	44.55	45.04	46.59
按经济区域分	By Region									
珠三角	Pearl River Delta	71.59	77.32	82.71	85.66	86.10	87.24	87.47	87.48	87.83
粤东	Eastern Region	50.45	54.75	57.71	59.23	59.78	60.60	61.07	61.26	61.79
粤西	Western Region	38.64	40.23	37.69	42.21	43.70	46.15	47.31	48.04	49.25
粤北	Northern Region	36.96	40.16	44.31	48.26	49.56	51.62	52.52	53.06	54.42

注：1.本表2000年、2005年数据按国家统计局1999年发布的《关于统计上划分城乡的规定（试行）》计算；2006年起数据按国家统计局2006年颁布的《关于统计上划分城乡的暂行规定》计算。

2.2006—2009年年末常住人口根据2010年第六次全国人口普查结果平滑调整，城镇人口比例也作相应调整。

3.2011—2019年年末常住人口根据2020年第七次全国人口普查结果平滑调整，城镇人口比例也作相应调整。

Note: a) The 2000 and 2005 data in this table are calculated according to Interim Regulations on Statistical Classification of Urban and Rural Populationissued by National Bureau of Statistics in 1999. The 2006 data are calculated according to Provisional Regulations on Statistical Classification of Urban and Rural Population issued by National Bureau of Statistics in 2006.

b) Figures of permanent population at the year-end from 2006 to 2009 have been adjusted in accordance with the flash sums of the 6th National Population Census in 2010 and the proportion of urban population to permanent population is also adjusted.

c) Figures of permanent population at the year-end from 2011 to 2019 have been adjusted in accordance with the flash sums of the 7th National Population Census in 2020. and the proportion of urban population to permanent population is also adjusted.

3-9 各市年末户籍人口数（2023年）

Total Population with Residence Registration at Year-end by City (2023)

单位：万人、% (10000 persons,%)

市别	City	总人口 Total Population	按性别分 By Sex 男 Male 人口数 Total Population	比例 Proportion	女 Female 人口数 Total Population	比例 Proportion
全 省	**Provincial Total**	**10146.21**	**5181.48**	**51.07**	**4964.73**	**48.93**
广 州	Guangzhou	1056.61	520.78	49.29	535.83	50.71
深 圳	Shenzhen	687.39	337.84	49.15	349.56	50.85
珠 海	Zhuhai	161.37	78.15	48.43	83.22	51.57
汕 头	Shantou	579.34	291.94	50.39	287.40	49.61
佛 山	Foshan	509.07	244.20	47.97	264.87	52.03
韶 关	Shaoguan	336.01	173.61	51.67	162.40	48.33
河 源	Heyuan	369.18	190.88	51.70	178.29	48.30
梅 州	Meizhou	535.08	278.14	51.98	256.94	48.02
惠 州	Huizhou	425.29	210.60	49.52	214.69	50.48
汕 尾	Shanwei	363.93	191.25	52.55	172.68	47.45
东 莞	Dongguan	307.88	148.66	48.29	159.21	51.71
中 山	Zhongshan	215.31	101.46	47.12	113.86	52.88
江 门	Jiangmen	403.48	201.44	49.93	202.04	50.07
阳 江	Yangjiang	303.31	161.10	53.11	142.21	46.89
湛 江	Zhanjiang	871.38	465.89	53.47	405.49	46.53
茂 名	Maoming	824.14	443.85	53.86	380.29	46.14
肇 庆	Zhaoqing	457.98	238.80	52.14	219.18	47.86
清 远	Qingyuan	453.35	235.61	51.97	217.74	48.03
潮 州	Chaozhou	273.67	139.25	50.88	134.43	49.12
揭 阳	Jieyang	711.88	368.78	51.80	343.10	48.20
云 浮	Yunfu	300.55	159.25	52.99	141.30	47.01
按经济区域分	By Region					
珠 三 角	Pearl River Delta	4224.39	2081.93	49.28	2142.46	50.72
粤 东	Eastern Region	1928.82	991.22	51.39	937.60	48.61
粤 西	Western Region	1998.82	1070.84	53.57	927.98	46.43
粤 北	Northern Region	1994.17	1037.48	52.03	956.68	47.97

3-10 各市年末户籍迁移人口数（2023年）
Number of Migrant Population at the Year-end by City (2023)

单位：人 (person)

市别	City	迁入 Immigration		迁出 Emigration		净迁移 Net Migration	
		省内迁入 Within Guangdong	省外迁入 Outside Guangdong	迁往省内 Within Guangdong	迁往省外 Outside Guangdong	省内 Within Guangdong	省外 Outside Guangdong
全　省	**Provincial Total**	**609874**	**665409**	**580770**	**148645**	**29104**	**516764**
广　州	Guangzhou	113178	107338	19479	23307	93699	84031
深　圳	Shenzhen	98265	182378	14081	29057	84184	153321
珠　海	Zhuhai	24979	36704	4018	5474	20961	31230
汕　头	Shantou	7846	5237	29851	4608	-22005	629
佛　山	Foshan	66773	64884	10517	5371	56256	59513
韶　关	Shaoguan	5529	5583	23288	3519	-17759	2064
河　源	Heyuan	2725	3769	29888	3425	-27163	344
梅　州	Meizhou	5479	4482	54556	5204	-49077	-722
惠　州	Huizhou	78812	57118	50415	8440	28397	48678
汕　尾	Shanwei	6032	3168	29811	8733	-23779	-5565
东　莞	Dongguan	50844	93313	6961	3841	43883	89472
中　山	Zhongshan	27540	42275	3864	2671	23676	39604
江　门	Jiangmen	11825	15798	13558	7387	-1733	8411
阳　江	Yangjiang	4643	2240	16417	1495	-11774	745
湛　江	Zhanjiang	24216	6625	61445	8255	-37229	-1630
茂　名	Maoming	28173	7478	57603	11092	-29430	-3614
肇　庆	Zhaoqing	19817	7379	31914	3061	-12097	4318
清　远	Qingyuan	14042	10596	30205	3745	-16163	6851
潮　州	Chaozhou	4117	1786	15529	1638	-11412	148
揭　阳	Jieyang	10650	5038	58242	5840	-47592	-802
云　浮	Yunfu	4389	2220	19128	2482	-14739	-262
按经济区域分	By Region						
珠三角	Pearl River Delta	492033	607187	154807	88609	337226	518578
粤　东	Eastern Region	28645	15229	133433	20819	-104788	-5590
粤　西	Western Region	57032	16343	135465	20842	-78433	-4499
粤　北	Northern Region	32164	26650	157065	18375	-124901	8275

主要统计指标解释

总人口 指一定时点、一定地区范围内有生命的个人的总和。按不同的统计范围可分为常住人口和户籍人口；统计时点通常为每年 12 月 31 日 24 时。

0-14 岁人口比例 （少年儿童人口系数或少年儿童人口比例） 指 0-14 岁的少年儿童人口与同期总人口之比，反映人口的年龄结构特征。通常以百分比表示。

15-64 岁人口比例 （成年人口系数或成年人口比例） 指 15-64 岁的成年人口与同期总人口之比，反映人口的年龄结构特征。通常以百分比表示。

65 岁及以上人口比例 （老年人口系数或老年人口比例） 指 65 岁及以上的老年人口与同期总人口之比，反映人口的老龄化程度。通常以百分比表示。

城镇人口比例 指城镇人口与同期总人口之比，反映该区域人口的城镇化水平。通常以百分比表示。

人口密度 指某一时点单位土地面积上居住的人口数。通常以每平方公里常住的人口数表示。

性别比 总人口（或分年龄人口）中男性人数与女性人数之比。通常以每 100 个女性人口相应有多少男性人口表示。

其计算公式为：性别比=男性人口数/女性人口数×100

出生率 也称粗出生率。指某一人口在一定时期（通常为一年）内活产婴儿数与同期总人口的生存人口数（或同期平均总人口、年中人口数）之比。通常以千分比表示。

死亡率 也称粗死亡率。指一定时期（通常为一年）内全部死亡人数与同期平均总人口之比，反映该时期人口的死亡强度。通常以千分比表示。

自然增长率 指一定时期（通常为一年）内人口自然增加数（出生人口减死亡人口）与同期平均总人口之比。通常以千分比表示。

迁入率（迁出率） 指一定时期（通常为一年）内迁入（迁出）人数与同期平均总人口之比。通常以千分比表示。

总迁移率 指一定时期（通常为一年）内人口迁移总量（迁入人口加迁出人口）与同期平均总人口之比。通常以千分比表示。

净迁移率 指一定时期（通常为一年）内人口迁入迁出相抵后（迁入人口减迁出人口）与同期平均总人口之比。通常以千分比表示。

跨省净迁移率 指一定时期（通常为一年）内省外迁入人口和迁往省外（含出国）人口之差与同期平均总人口之比。通常以千分比表示。

总抚养比 总抚养比也称总负担系数，是指人口总体中非劳动年龄人口数（0-14 岁人口+65 岁及以上人口）与劳动年龄人口数（15-64 岁人口）之比，通常用百分比表示。

少年儿童抚养比 少年儿童抚养比也称少年儿童抚养系数，是指某一人口中少年儿童人口数（0-14 岁人口）与劳动年龄人口数（15-64 岁人口）之比，通常用百分比表示。

老年人口抚养比 老年人口抚养比也称老年人口抚养系数，是指某一人口中老年人口数（65 岁及以上人口）与劳动年龄人口数（15-64 岁人口）之比，通常用百分比表示。

Explanatory Notes on Main Statistical Indicators

Total Population refers to the total number of people alive within a given area at a certain point of time. It can be divided into the permanent population and the population with residence registration according to different statistical coverage. The reference time of the statistics on total population is usually taken at midnight of December 31.

Proportion of Population Aged 0-14 (coefficient of child population or proportion of child population) refers to the proportion of population aged 0-14 in the total population during the same period of time. It is an indicator of age structure, usually expressed in percentage.

Proportion of Population Aged 15-64 (coefficient of adult population or proportion of adult population) refers to the proportion of population aged 15-64 in the total population during the same period of time. It is an indicator of age structure, usually expressed in percentage.

Proportion of Population Aged 65 and Over (coefficient of aged population or proportion of aged population) refers to the proportion of population aged 65 and over in the total population during the same period of time. It is an indicator of population ageing, usually expressed in percentage.

Proportion of Urban Population refers to the proportion of urban population in the total population during the same period of time. It is an indicator of population urbanization in a certain region, usually expressed in percentage.

Population Density refers to the number of people located in a given land area at a certain point of time, usually expressed in the number of permanent population per square kilometer.

Sex Ratio refers to the ratio of the male population to the female population among the total population (or population grouped by age), usually expressed in the number of males per 100 females.

The following formula is used:

Sex Ration = Number of Male Population / Number of Female Population ×100

Birth Rate (or Crude Birth Rate) refers to the ratio of live births to the total number of population alive (or average population, mid-year population) during a certain period of time (usually one year), expressed in ‰.

Death Rate (or Crude Death Rate) refers to the ratio of deaths to the average population during a certain period of time (usually one year), expressed in ‰. Death rate reflects the death intensity of the population during the same period of time.

Natural Growth Rate refers to the ratio of natural increase in population (number of births minus number of deaths) during a certain period of time (usually one year) to the average population of the same period, expressed in ‰.

Immigration Rate (Emigration Rate) refers to the ratio of the number of immigration (emigration) to the average population during a certain period of time (usually one year), expressed in ‰.

Total Migration Rate refers to the ratio of the total number of migration (number of immigration plus number of emigration) to the average population during a certain period of time (usually one year),expressed in ‰.

Net Migration Rate refers to the ratio of the net number of migration (number of immigration minus number of emigration) to the average population during a certain period of time (usually one year), expressed in ‰

Net Migration Rate across Province refers to the ratio of the number of immigration from outside the province minus the number of emigration to outside the province (including those going abroad) to the average population during a certain period of time (usually one year), expressed in ‰.

Total Dependency Ratio Total dependency ratio is also called total burden coefficient,refers to the ratio of the number of people of non working age (0-14 years old+65 years old and above) to the number of people of working age (15-64 years old) in the population, usually expressed as a percentage.

Child Dependency ratio Child dependency ratio is also called child dependency coefficient,refers to the ratio of the population of children (0-14 years old) to the population of working age (15-64 years old) in a certain population, usually expressed as a percentage.

Old Age Dependency Ratio The dependency ratio of the elderly population is also called the dependency coefficient of the elderly population,refers to the ratio of the number of middle-aged and elderly people (65 years old and above) to the number of working age people (15-64 years old), usually expressed as a percentage.

四、就业和工资

EMPLOYMENT AND WAGES

四 就业和工资

简要说明

一、本篇资料反映广东劳动就业与工资的基本情况。主要内容包括全社会就业人员数，城镇非私营单位就业人员、在岗职工人数，城镇非私营单位就业人员、在岗职工工资总额、平均工资。

二、本篇资料由广东省统计局人口和就业统计处整理提供。

三、本篇资料主要根据国家统计调查制度搜集汇总。

四、本篇资料中的城镇非私营单位（包括统计上认定的视同法人单位的产业活动单位）具体包括：除私营单位以外的内资（包括机关、事业）单位、港澳台投资和外商投资企业。劳动工资统计主要统计法人单位的就业人员和工资情况，个体就业人员、自由职业者等非单位就业人员不在统计范围内。

五、自 2023 年起，劳动工资统计按照《关于市场主体统计分类的划分规定》（国统字[2023]14 号）执行新的登记注册统计类别。

4 Employment and Wages

Brief Introduction

Ⅰ. The data in this chapter reflects the basic situation of labor employment and wages in Guangdong Province. The main content includes the number of employees in the whole society, the number of Urban Non private employees and on-the-job employees, the total wages and average wages of Urban Non private employees and on-the-job employees etc.

Ⅱ. The data in this chapter are prepared and provided by the Division of Population and Employment Statistics of Statistics Bureau of Guangdong Province.

Ⅲ. The data in this chapter are collected and tabulated mainly in accordance with the statistical survey scheme of the National Bureau of Statistics.

IV. The non private urban units mentioned in this article (including industrial activity units recognized as legal entities in statistics) specifically include domestic (including government agencies and institutions) units, Hong Kong, Macao and Taiwan invested enterprises, and foreign-invested enterprises other than private units. Labor wage statistics mainly statistics the employment and wage situation of legal entities, and non unit employment personnel such as individual employees and freelancers are not included in the scope of statistics.

V. Starting from 2023, labor wage statistics was registered and classified according to the "Classification Regulations on Market Entity Statistics" (Guotongzi [2023] No. 14).

4-1 就业基本情况
Employment

指 标	Item	2000	2010	2015	2021	2022	2023
就业人员 （万人）	**Number of Employed Persons (10000 persons)**	**3989.32**	**6051.00**	**6566.00**	**7072.00**	**6904.00**	**7057.00**
第一产业	Primary Industry	1593.68	1476.00	1046.00	753.00	722.00	688.00
第二产业	Secondary Industry	1114.86	2566.00	2627.00	2565.00	2524.00	2584.00
第三产业	Tertiary Industry	1280.78	2009.00	2893.00	3754.00	3658.00	3785.00
按城乡分就业人员 （万人）	**Number of Employed Persons by Urban and Rural Areas (10 000 persons)**						
城镇就业人员	Urban Employed Persons		4004.55	4822.00	5473.00	5389.00	5573.00
乡村就业人员	Rural Employed Persons		2046.45	1744.00	1599.00	1515.00	1484.00
#城镇非私营单位就业人员 （万人）	Urban Employed Persons (10000 persons)	759.21	1118.52	1948.04	2110.88	2066.65	1990.00
国有单位	State-owned Units	425.52	400.65	388.81	431.54	438.30	
城镇集体单位	Urban Collective-owned Units	105.97	57.66	50.34	36.32	33.06	
其他各种单位	Units of Other Types of Ownership	227.73	660.21	1508.89	1643.02	1595.29	
城镇非私营单位就业人员工资总额 （亿元）	**Earnings of Urban Employed Persons (100 million yuan)**	**1057.57**	**4484.29**	**12918.81**	**24978.70**	**26200.89**	**26266.90**
国有单位	State-owned Units	612.17	1951.16	2975.96	6855.32	7272.19	
城镇集体单位	Urban Collective-owned Units	93.04	129.01	227.71	273.36	256.00	
其他各种单位	Units of Other Types of Ownership	352.37	2404.12	9715.14	17850.02	18672.70	
城镇非私营单位就业人员年平均工资 （元）	**Average Labor Remuneration of Urban Employed Persons (yuan)**	**13859**	**40432**	**65788**	**118133**	**124916**	**131418**
国有单位	State-owned Units	14296	49027	76870	160329	167521	
城镇集体单位	Urban Collective-owned Units	8605	22453	45027	76875	78973	
其他各种单位	Units of Other Types of Ownership	15538	36779	63664	108095	114489	

注：2006—2009年就业人员人数，根据第六次全国人口普查资料作了相应调整。从2020年起，国家统计局对各省、自治区、直辖市就业人数及其产业构成以常住人口口径统一测算，同时对2010—2019年就业人数及其产业、城乡结构进行平滑修正。

Note: The number of Employed Persons from 2006 to 2009 have been adjusted in accordance with the data of the 6th National Census. Since 2020, the National Bureau of Statistics calculates the number of Employed Persons and Industrial Composition of all Province、Autonomous Region and Municipality directly under the Central Government according to the caliber of permanent population, also adjusted the number of Employed Persons and Industrial Structure from 2010 to 2019.

4-2 就业人员年末人数
Number of Employed Persons at the Year-end

单位：万人 (10000 persons)

年份 Year	就业人员年末人数 Number of Employed Persons at the Year-end	#城镇非私营单位就业人员 Urban Employed Persons	国有单位 State-owned Units	城镇集体单位 Urban Collective-owned Units	其他单位 Units of Other Types of Ownership	城镇就业人员 Urban Employed Persons	乡村就业人员 Rural Employed Persons
1978	2275.95	515.85	369.04	146.81			
1979	2304.95	535.37	378.57	156.80			
1980	2367.78	563.62	400.19	163.43			
1981	2423.79	587.34	422.03	165.31			
1982	2521.38	608.12	443.43	164.69			
1983	2569.70	612.65	446.51	166.14			
1984	2637.49	631.77	429.65	197.89	4.23		
1985	2731.11	660.82	449.40	203.32	8.10		
1986	2811.92	686.20	465.59	208.85	11.76		
1987	2910.99	720.34	485.59	216.16	18.59		
1988	2994.72	747.67	503.20	216.96	27.51		
1989	3041.27	762.61	511.88	212.50	38.23		
1990	3118.10	785.49	528.13	207.62	49.74		
1991	3259.20	827.58	544.55	216.86	66.17		
1992	3367.21	858.12	559.71	216.57	81.84		
1993	3433.91	877.16	563.63	199.99	113.54		
1994	3493.15	901.57	568.80	202.86	129.91		
1995	3551.20	931.58	565.48	204.12	161.98		
1996	3641.30	920.55	565.68	193.24	161.63		
1997	3701.90	912.74	556.56	181.44	174.74		
1998	3783.87	897.98	521.34	161.50	215.13		
1999	3796.32	793.54	449.87	122.70	220.97		
2000	3989.32	759.21	425.52	105.97	227.73		
2001	4058.63	737.12	400.12	91.33	245.67		
2002	4134.37	751.23	382.91	82.81	285.51		
2003	4395.93	781.14	376.56	78.47	326.11		
2004	4681.89	830.72	374.34	72.28	384.10		
2005	5022.97	904.27	380.19	68.70	455.38		
2006	5177.02	954.44	384.78	67.25	502.41		
2007	5341.50	1001.46	381.00	65.49	554.97		
2008	5471.72	1007.87	385.14	60.64	562.09		
2009	5688.62	1055.03	389.17	58.33	607.53		
2010	6051.00	1118.52	400.65	57.66	660.21	4004.55	2046.45
2011	6087.00	1238.22	423.88	62.83	751.51	4150.51	1936.49
2012	6171.00	1303.98	430.33	55.28	818.38	4305.70	1865.30
2013	6273.00	1966.98	402.75	58.52	1505.71	4454.56	1818.44
2014	6428.00	1973.28	396.20	56.69	1520.39	4642.00	1786.00
2015	6566.00	1948.04	388.81	50.34	1508.89	4822.00	1744.00
2016	6703.00	1957.57	387.75	47.83	1521.99	4998.00	1705.00
2017	6858.00	1963.10	384.09	45.46	1533.56	5187.00	1671.00
2018	6960.00	1994.14	375.11	42.62	1576.41	5314.00	1646.00
2019	6995.00	2064.59	385.06	37.94	1641.59	5364.00	1631.00
2020	7039.00	2085.27	423.26	36.85	1625.16	5418.00	1621.00
2021	7072.00	2110.88	431.54	36.32	1643.02	5473.00	1599.00
2022	6904.00	2066.65	438.30	33.06	1595.29	5389.00	1515.00
2023	7057.00	1990.00				5573.00	1484.00

注：2006—2009年就业人员人数，根据第六次全国人口普查资料作了相应调整。从2020年起，国家统计局对各省、自治区、直辖市就业人数及其产业构成以常住人口口径统一测算，同时对2010—2019年就业人数及其产业、城乡结构进行平滑修正。1993年及以前城镇单位就业人员为城镇单位职工人数。

Note: Figures of "Number of Employed Persons" from 2006 to 2009 have been adjusted in accordance with the results of the 6th population census. Since 2020, the National Bureau of Statistics calculates the number of Employed Persons and Industrial Composition of all Province、Autonomous Region and Municipality directly under the Central Government according to the caliber of permanent population,also adjusted the number of Employed Persons and Industrial Structure from 2010 to 2019. Employed persons of urban units are the number of staff and workers of urban units in 1993 and before.

 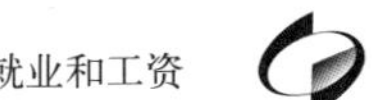

4-3 按三次产业分就业人员年末人数

Number of Employed Persons at Year-end by Three strata of Industry

年 份 Year	就业人数（万人） Total Employed Persons (10000 persons)	第一产业 Primary Industry	第二产业 Secondary Industry	第三产业 Tertiary Industry	构成（%）Composition in Percentage(%) 第一产业 Primary Industry	第二产业 Secondary Industry	第三产业 Tertiary Industry
1978	2275.95	1677.01	312.94	286.00	73.7	13.7	12.6
1979	2304.95	1659.01	381.11	264.83	72.0	16.5	11.5
1980	2367.78	1673.57	404.80	289.41	70.7	17.1	12.2
1981	2423.79	1699.85	409.93	314.01	70.1	16.9	13.0
1982	2521.38	1723.46	447.18	350.74	68.4	17.7	13.9
1983	2569.70	1729.47	458.80	381.43	67.3	17.9	14.8
1984	2637.49	1679.46	498.09	459.94	63.7	18.9	17.4
1985	2731.11	1646.82	614.52	469.77	60.3	22.5	17.2
1986	2811.92	1624.15	637.76	550.01	57.8	22.6	19.6
1987	2910.99	1605.10	704.24	601.65	55.1	24.2	20.7
1988	2994.72	1607.11	743.91	643.70	53.7	24.8	21.5
1989	3041.27	1632.36	747.78	661.13	53.7	24.6	21.7
1990	3118.10	1651.71	848.37	618.02	53.0	27.2	19.8
1991	3259.20	1645.25	932.76	681.19	50.5	28.6	20.9
1992	3367.21	1594.32	1024.98	747.91	47.3	30.5	22.2
1993	3433.91	1512.88	1115.42	805.61	44.1	32.4	23.5
1994	3493.15	1478.37	1172.84	841.94	42.3	33.6	24.1
1995	3551.20	1473.60	1199.00	878.60	41.5	33.8	24.7
1996	3641.30	1481.40	1218.00	941.90	40.7	33.4	25.9
1997	3701.90	1511.38	1217.25	973.27	40.8	32.9	26.3
1998	3783.87	1554.33	1214.96	1014.58	41.1	32.1	26.8
1999	3796.32	1574.25	1181.58	1040.49	41.5	31.1	27.4
2000	3989.32	1593.68	1114.86	1280.78	40.0	27.9	32.1
2001	4058.63	1587.48	1131.96	1339.19	39.1	27.9	33.0
2002	4134.37	1572.92	1202.92	1358.53	38.0	29.1	32.9
2003	4395.93	1617.69	1557.19	1221.05	36.8	35.4	27.8
2004	4681.89	1622.50	1727.86	1331.53	34.7	36.9	28.4
2005	5022.97	1609.89	1916.16	1496.92	32.1	38.1	29.8
2006	5177.02	1562.17	2015.88	1598.97	30.2	38.9	30.9
2007	5341.50	1562.19	2102.28	1677.04	29.2	39.4	31.4
2008	5471.72	1526.66	2172.93	1772.13	27.9	39.7	32.4
2009	5688.62	1514.04	2292.05	1882.53	26.6	40.3	33.1
2010	6051.00	1476.00	2566.00	2009.00	24.4	42.4	33.2
2011	6087.00	1340.00	2611.00	2136.00	22.0	42.9	35.1
2012	6171.00	1243.00	2628.00	2300.00	20.1	42.6	37.3
2013	6273.00	1172.00	2620.00	2481.00	18.7	41.8	39.6
2014	6428.00	1112.00	2606.00	2710.00	17.3	40.5	42.2
2015	6566.00	1046.00	2627.00	2893.00	15.9	40.0	44.1
2016	6703.00	987.00	2611.00	3105.00	14.7	39.0	46.3
2017	6858.00	933.00	2592.00	3333.00	13.6	37.8	48.6
2018	6960.00	864.00	2506.00	3590.00	12.4	36.0	51.6
2019	6995.00	823.00	2522.00	3650.00	11.8	36.1	52.2
2020	7039.00	767.00	2526.00	3746.00	10.9	35.9	53.2
2021	7072.00	753.00	2565.00	3754.00	10.6	36.3	53.1
2022	6904.00	722.00	2524.00	3658.00	10.5	36.6	53.0
2023	7057.00	688.00	2584.00	3785.00	9.7	36.6	53.6

注：2006—2009年就业人员人数，根据第六次全国人口普查资料作了相应调整。从2020年起，国家统计局对各省、自治区、直辖市就业人数及其产业构成以常住人口口径统一测算，同时对2010—2019年就业人数及其产业、城乡结构进行平滑修正。

Note: Data for the employed population from 2006 to 2009 have been adjusted from the 6th National Census.Since 2020, the National Bureau of Statistics calculates the number of Employed Persons and Industrial Composition of all Province、Autonomous Region and Municipality directly under the Central Government according to the caliber of permanent population, also adjusted the number of Employed Persons and Industrial Structure from 2010 to 2019.

4-4 各市就业人员年末人数

Number of Employed Persons at the Year-end by City

单位：万人 (10000 persons)

市别	City	2005	2010	2015	2021	2022	2023
全省	**Provincial Total**	**5022.97**	**6051.00**	**6566.00**	**7072.00**	**6904.00**	**7057.00**
广州	Guangzhou	574.46	732.93	927.91	1163.44	1119.82	1138.80
深圳	Shenzhen	576.26	781.45	1083.35	1245.42	1193.41	1228.90
珠海	Zhuhai	94.01	106.19	124.11	148.48	135.13	139.01
汕头	Shantou	179.81	245.22	243.92	247.97	252.30	255.05
佛山	Foshan	348.69	457.09	523.37	600.90	575.57	581.25
韶关	Shaoguan	138.44	146.89	137.53	125.58	120.06	121.85
河源	Heyuan	118.20	137.25	131.40	135.13	139.01	141.83
梅州	Meizhou	211.98	214.47	183.28	170.22	175.45	179.66
惠州	Huizhou	222.62	268.14	299.29	337.58	330.51	340.34
汕尾	Shanwei	117.78	122.81	122.34	125.55	128.33	132.54
东莞	Dongguan	388.13	645.51	680.09	717.94	679.31	697.46
中山	Zhongshan	188.85	213.71	241.21	275.91	262.71	268.67
江门	Jiangmen	214.53	257.22	254.36	258.01	263.04	266.70
阳江	Yangjiang	146.63	135.38	117.13	113.69	107.34	109.23
湛江	Zhanjiang	305.00	329.61	343.98	322.65	324.77	331.15
茂名	Maoming	287.36	281.58	282.89	271.99	269.70	276.27
肇庆	Zhaoqing	215.05	219.61	209.87	201.68	204.19	208.20
清远	Qingyuan	195.95	202.10	196.50	183.61	181.81	185.81
潮州	Chaozhou	129.18	142.74	116.98	109.00	112.49	113.90
揭阳	Jieyang	253.70	278.57	232.25	217.54	226.33	235.50
云浮	Yunfu	114.30	132.53	114.24	99.71	102.72	104.88
按经济区域分	By Region						
珠三角	Pearl River Delta	2822.60	3681.85	4343.56	4949.36	4763.69	4869.33
粤东	Eastern Region	680.47	789.34	715.49	700.06	719.45	736.99
粤西	Western Region	738.99	746.57	744.00	708.33	701.81	716.65
粤北	Northern Region	778.87	833.24	762.95	714.25	719.05	734.03

注：从2020年起，国家统计局对各省、自治区、直辖市就业人数及其产业构成以常住人口口径统一测算，同时对2010—2019年就业人数及其产业、城乡结构进行平滑修正。

Note: Since 2020, the National Bureau of Statistics calculates the number of Employed Persons and Industrial Composition of all Province、Autonomous Region and Municipality directly under the Central Government according to the caliber of permanent population, also adjusted the number of Employed Persons and Industrial、City-countryside Structure from 2010 to 2019.

4-5 各市按三次产业分就业人员年末人数

Number of Employed Persons at the Year-end by Strata of Industry by City

单位：万人 (10000 persons)

市别	City	2022 合计 Total	2022 第一产业 Primary Industry	2022 第二产业 Secondary Industry	2022 第三产业 Tertiary Industry	2023 合计 Total	2023 第一产业 Primary Industry	2023 第二产业 Secondary Industry	2023 第三产业 Tertiary Industry
全 省	**Provincial Total**	**6904.00**	**722.00**	**2524.00**	**3658.00**	**7057.00**	**688.00**	**2584.00**	**3785.00**
广 州	Guangzhou	1119.82	46.84	255.66	817.31	1138.80	44.64	257.09	837.07
深 圳	Shenzhen	1193.41	0.65	467.95	724.81	1228.90	0.62	479.46	748.82
珠 海	Zhuhai	135.13	2.19	58.21	74.73	139.01	2.08	59.76	77.17
汕 头	Shantou	252.30	36.72	100.76	114.82	255.05	34.99	102.36	117.70
佛 山	Foshan	575.57	14.56	295.68	265.33	581.25	13.87	298.48	268.90
韶 关	Shaoguan	120.06	30.35	25.23	64.48	121.85	28.92	25.85	67.08
河 源	Heyuan	139.01	33.17	30.57	75.27	141.83	31.60	31.76	78.47
梅 州	Meizhou	175.45	43.03	40.43	91.98	179.66	41.00	42.49	96.17
惠 州	Huizhou	330.51	33.89	151.54	145.08	340.34	32.30	156.67	151.37
汕 尾	Shanwei	128.33	31.52	31.32	65.48	132.54	30.05	32.99	69.50
东 莞	Dongguan	679.31	3.96	435.87	239.48	697.46	3.78	443.61	250.07
中 山	Zhongshan	262.71	6.76	151.34	104.62	268.67	6.44	154.84	107.39
江 门	Jiangmen	263.04	32.31	88.80	141.93	266.70	30.78	90.87	145.05
阳 江	Yangjiang	107.34	25.05	25.90	56.39	109.23	23.87	26.59	58.77
湛 江	Zhanjiang	324.77	95.33	79.16	150.28	331.15	90.85	81.61	158.69
茂 名	Maoming	269.70	75.64	62.36	131.70	276.27	72.08	65.25	138.94
肇 庆	Zhaoqing	204.19	50.48	48.03	105.68	208.20	48.10	49.53	110.57
清 远	Qingyuan	181.81	42.58	40.67	98.56	185.81	40.57	42.38	102.86
潮 州	Chaozhou	112.49	27.33	40.78	44.38	113.90	26.04	41.68	46.18
揭 阳	Jieyang	226.33	60.41	68.32	97.60	235.50	57.57	74.29	103.64
云 浮	Yunfu	102.72	29.22	25.40	48.10	104.88	27.85	26.44	50.59
按经济区域分	By Region								
珠 三 角	Pearl River Delta	4763.69	191.64	1953.09	2618.96	4869.33	182.61	1990.31	2696.41
粤 东	Eastern Region	719.45	155.98	241.19	322.28	736.99	148.65	251.32	337.02
粤 西	Western Region	701.81	196.03	167.41	338.37	716.65	186.80	173.45	356.40
粤 北	Northern Region	719.05	178.35	162.31	378.39	734.03	169.94	168.92	395.17

注：从2020年起，国家统计局对各省、自治区、直辖市就业人数及其产业构成以常住人口口径统一测算，同时对2010—2019年就业人数及其产业、城乡结构进行平滑修正。

Note: Since 2020, the National Bureau of Statistics calculates the number of Employed Persons and Industrial Composition of all Province、Autonomous Region and Municipality directly under the Central Government according to the caliber of permanent population, also adjusted the number of Employed Persons and Industrial、City-countryside Structure from 2010 to 2019.

4-6 各市按城乡分就业人员年末人数

Number of Employed Persons at the Year-end by Strata of Industry by City

单位：万人 (10000 persons)

市别	City	2010 合计 Total	2010 城镇 Urban	2010 乡村 Rural	2022 合计 Total	2022 城镇 Urban	2022 乡村 Rural	2023 合计 Total	2023 城镇 Urban	2023 乡村 Rural
全省	**Provincial Total**	**6051.00**	**4004.55**	**2046.45**	**6904.00**	**5389.00**	**1515.00**	**7057.00**	**5573.00**	**1484.00**
广州	Guangzhou	732.93	614.14	118.79	1119.82	975.42	144.40	1138.80	998.84	139.96
深圳	Shenzhen	781.45	781.04	0.41	1193.41	1190.90	2.51	1228.90	1226.45	2.45
珠海	Zhuhai	106.19	93.09	13.10	135.13	125.64	9.49	139.01	129.73	9.28
汕头	Shantou	245.22	123.76	121.46	252.30	143.00	109.30	255.05	149.62	105.43
佛山	Foshan	457.09	378.33	78.76	575.57	563.06	12.51	581.25	569.22	12.03
韶关	Shaoguan	146.89	72.77	74.12	120.06	70.28	49.78	121.85	73.30	48.55
河源	Heyuan	137.25	54.98	82.27	139.01	69.85	69.16	141.83	73.62	68.21
梅州	Meizhou	214.47	92.29	122.18	175.45	92.43	83.02	179.66	97.48	82.18
惠州	Huizhou	268.14	165.84	102.30	330.51	249.93	80.58	340.34	261.17	79.17
汕尾	Shanwei	122.81	61.44	61.37	128.33	74.25	54.08	132.54	78.68	53.86
东莞	Dongguan	645.51	534.04	111.47	679.31	631.00	48.31	697.46	650.04	47.42
中山	Zhongshan	213.71	164.32	49.39	262.71	236.61	26.10	268.67	243.16	25.51
江门	Jiangmen	257.22	160.27	96.95	263.04	185.47	77.57	266.70	191.35	75.35
阳江	Yangjiang	135.38	63.38	72.00	107.34	59.32	48.02	109.23	61.98	47.25
湛江	Zhanjiang	329.61	120.93	208.68	324.77	153.65	171.12	331.15	164.06	167.09
茂名	Maoming	281.58	98.78	182.80	269.70	123.63	146.07	276.27	131.96	144.31
肇庆	Zhaoqing	219.61	93.11	126.50	204.19	106.46	97.73	208.20	112.60	95.60
清远	Qingyuan	202.10	81.56	120.54	181.81	102.36	79.45	185.81	107.97	77.84
潮州	Chaozhou	142.74	69.63	73.11	112.49	62.90	49.59	113.90	66.05	47.85
揭阳	Jieyang	278.57	131.85	146.72	226.33	126.53	99.80	235.50	136.47	99.03
云浮	Yunfu	132.53	49.00	83.53	102.72	46.27	56.45	104.88	49.25	55.63
按经济区域分	By Region									
珠三角	Pearl River Delta	3681.85	2984.18	697.67	4763.69	4264.50	499.19	4869.33	4382.56	486.77
粤东	Eastern Region	789.34	386.68	402.66	719.45	406.69	312.76	736.99	430.82	306.17
粤西	Western Region	746.57	283.09	463.48	701.81	336.60	365.21	716.65	358.00	358.65
粤北	Northern Region	833.24	350.60	482.64	719.05	381.19	337.86	734.03	401.62	332.41

注：从2020年起，国家统计局对各省、自治区、直辖市就业人数及其产业构成以常住人口口径统一测算，同时对2010—2019年就业人数及其产业、城乡结构进行平滑修正。

Note: Since 2020, the National Bureau of Statistics calculates the number of Employed Persons and Industrial Composition of all Province、Autonomous Region and Municipality directly under the Central Government according to the caliber of permanent population, also adjusted the number of Employed Persons and Industrial、City-countryside Structure from 2010 to 2019.

4-7 城镇非私营单位就业人员和在岗职工年末人数（2023年）

Number of Employed Persons and Fully Employed Staff and Workers in Urban Non Private Units at the Year-end (2023)

单位：万人 (10000 persons)

行　业	Item	就业人员 Employed Persons	#女性 Female	#在岗职工 Fully Employed Staff and Workers
全　省	**Provincial Total**	**1990.00**	**828.71**	**1911.42**
农、林、牧、渔业	Farming, Forestry, Animal Husbandry and Fishery	1.37	0.45	1.31
采矿业	Mining and Quarrying	1.73	0.30	1.72
制造业	Manufacture	750.61	297.42	745.21
电力、热力、燃气及水生产和供应业	Production and Supply of Electric Power, Gas and Water	25.81	5.87	25.51
建筑业	Construction	124.43	19.05	104.28
批发和零售业	Wholesale and Retail Trade	102.31	51.65	99.78
交通运输、仓储和邮政业	Transport, Storage and Postal Services	74.02	19.75	72.84
住宿和餐饮业	Hotels and Catering Services	45.01	24.43	37.39
信息传输、软件和信息技术服务业	Information Transmission, Computer Services and Software	81.55	30.95	80.44
金融业	Finance	71.22	38.47	54.09
房地产业	Real Estate	89.68	35.17	88.20
租赁和商务服务业	Leasing and Business Services	125.96	48.93	117.94
科学研究和技术服务业	Scientific Research and Technical Services	48.15	17.16	46.95
水利、环境和公共设施管理业	Water Conservancy, Environment and Public Facilities Management	21.33	8.50	20.73
居民服务、修理和其他服务业	Household's Services,Repair and Other Services	13.60	7.55	12.60
教育	Education	155.14	102.05	150.42
卫生和社会工作	Health Care and Social Work	95.14	65.41	93.05
文化、体育和娱乐业	Culture, Sports and Recreation	12.08	5.87	11.25
公共管理、社会保障和社会组织	Public Administration and Social Security and Social Organizations	150.85	49.74	147.71

4-8 各市城镇非私营单位各行业在岗职工年末人数（2023年）

Number of Fully Employed Staff and Workers in Urban Non Private Units at the Year-end by Sector and by City (2023)

单位：万人 (10000 persons)

市别	City	合计 Total	农、林、牧、渔业 Farming, Forestry, Animal Husbandry and Fishery	采矿业 Mining and Quarrying	制造业 Manufacture	电力、热力、燃气及水生产和供应业 Production and Supply of Electric Power,Gas and Water	建筑业 Construction	批发和零售业 Wholesale and Retail Trade
全　省	**Provincial Total**	**1911.42**	**1.31**	**1.72**	**745.21**	**25.51**	**104.28**	**99.78**
广　州	Guangzhou	387.52	0.18	0.01	68.61	5.31	17.27	29.94
深　圳	Shenzhen	472.85	0.02	0.50	182.65	4.07	26.57	28.14
珠　海	Zhuhai	77.45	0.09	0.04	33.41	0.88	3.31	3.08
汕　头	Shantou	41.88	0.01		8.15	0.79	8.86	1.59
佛　山	Foshan	150.48	0.05	0.01	79.10	2.04	4.31	7.81
韶　关	Shaoguan	27.20	0.10	0.33	5.08	0.87	2.29	1.28
河　源	Heyuan	25.79	0.05	0.02	10.38	0.42	0.69	0.61
梅　州	Meizhou	23.57	0.04	0.08	4.68	0.79	1.84	0.67
惠　州	Huizhou	97.48	0.04	0.03	61.25	1.28	2.88	2.35
汕　尾	Shanwei	13.35	0.03	…	2.24	0.39	0.26	0.43
东　莞	Dongguan	249.97	0.02	…	174.14	2.07	7.15	8.38
中　山	Zhongshan	71.55	0.10		43.62	0.69	1.98	3.21
江　门	Jiangmen	60.29	0.09	0.01	27.68	0.87	4.67	3.37
阳　江	Yangjiang	15.70	0.04	0.03	2.00	0.51	1.16	0.64
湛　江	Zhanjiang	39.40	0.09	0.30	4.10	0.69	4.61	2.32
茂　名	Maoming	40.21	0.01	0.06	3.10	0.96	9.17	1.75
肇　庆	Zhaoqing	34.29	0.11	0.09	13.60	0.71	1.37	1.44
清　远	Qingyuan	30.61	0.02	0.03	10.20	0.73	1.72	1.08
潮　州	Chaozhou	14.48	0.01	0.01	3.54	0.45	1.13	0.35
揭　阳	Jieyang	21.14	0.09	…	2.84	0.63	1.61	0.71
云　浮	Yunfu	16.20	0.12	0.17	4.85	0.37	1.41	0.63
按经济区域分	By Region							
珠三角	Pearl River Delta	1601.89	0.69	0.70	684.05	17.92	69.52	87.72
粤　东	Eastern Region	90.85	0.14	0.01	16.77	2.25	11.87	3.07
粤　西	Western Region	95.31	0.15	0.38	9.20	2.16	14.94	4.71
粤　北	Northern Region	123.37	0.33	0.63	35.19	3.17	7.94	4.27

4-8 续表 1 continued 1

单位：万人 (10000 persons)

市别	City	交通运输、仓储和邮政业 Transport, Storage and Postal Services	住宿和餐饮业 Hotels and Catering Services	信息传输、软件和信息技术服务业 Information Transmission, Computer Services and Software	金融业 Finance	房地产业 Real Estate	租赁和商务服务业 Leasing and Business Services	科学研究和技术服务业 Scientific Research and Technical Services
全　省	**Provincial Total**	**72.84**	**37.39**	**80.44**	**54.09**	**88.20**	**117.94**	**46.95**
广　州	Guangzhou	28.27	13.47	28.02	10.43	30.42	47.21	19.03
深　圳	Shenzhen	20.68	9.72	38.39	21.36	30.24	33.46	13.99
珠　海	Zhuhai	2.72	2.27	2.85	1.98	3.50	9.18	1.57
汕　头	Shantou	1.57	0.77	0.96	1.33	1.34	0.60	0.39
佛　山	Foshan	4.03	2.24	2.50	3.83	4.98	4.67	2.58
韶　关	Shaoguan	0.69	0.28	0.23	0.81	1.40	0.48	0.19
河　源	Heyuan	0.49	0.18	0.31	0.51	0.37	0.49	0.21
梅　州	Meizhou	0.65	0.13	0.36	0.47	0.27	0.66	0.61
惠　州	Huizhou	1.81	1.17	0.60	1.15	2.77	2.09	0.49
汕　尾	Shanwei	0.36	0.12	0.24	0.62	0.19	0.59	0.09
东　莞	Dongguan	3.50	2.92	2.29	3.05	3.90	9.30	3.19
中　山	Zhongshan	1.11	0.97	0.47	1.36	3.38	1.77	1.01
江　门	Jiangmen	1.28	0.83	0.78	1.44	1.25	1.72	0.63
阳　江	Yangjiang	0.36	0.18	0.18	0.41	0.20	0.69	0.38
湛　江	Zhanjiang	1.65	0.56	0.37	0.93	0.93	0.95	0.31
茂　名	Maoming	1.29	0.26	0.47	1.01	0.82	1.57	0.66
肇　庆	Zhaoqing	0.68	0.36	0.24	0.76	0.86	0.38	0.66
清　远	Qingyuan	0.63	0.60	0.29	0.70	0.74	0.83	0.33
潮　州	Chaozhou	0.40	0.13	0.32	1.00	0.15	0.30	0.21
揭　阳	Jieyang	0.46	0.11	0.35	0.52	0.22	0.78	0.29
云　浮	Yunfu	0.21	0.12	0.20	0.43	0.25	0.25	0.12
按经济区域分	By Region							
珠三角	Pearl River Delta	64.08	33.94	76.16	45.35	81.31	109.78	43.16
粤　东	Eastern Region	2.80	1.14	1.87	3.48	1.91	2.26	0.98
粤　西	Western Region	3.31	1.00	1.02	2.34	1.95	3.21	1.36
粤　北	Northern Region	2.66	1.31	1.39	2.93	3.03	2.70	1.46

4-8 续表 2 continued 2

单位：万人 (10000 persons)

市 别	City	水利、环境和公共设施管理业 Management of Water Conservancy, Environment and Public Facilities	居民服务、修理和其他服务业 Household's Services, Repair and Other Services	教育 Education	卫生和社会工作 Health and Social Service	文化、体育和娱乐业 Culture, Sports and Entertainment	公共管理、社会保障和社会组织 Public Management, Social Security and Social Organizations
全 省	**Provincial Total**	**20.73**	**12.60**	**150.42**	**93.05**	**11.25**	**147.71**
广 州	Guangzhou	6.18	3.45	28.75	23.77	3.32	23.91
深 圳	Shenzhen	3.12	3.86	17.56	14.61	2.32	21.59
珠 海	Zhuhai	1.30	0.31	3.51	2.54	0.99	3.90
汕 头	Shantou	0.34	0.26	6.66	3.07	0.16	5.02
佛 山	Foshan	2.10	1.85	10.91	5.95	0.94	10.56
韶 关	Shaoguan	0.68	0.10	4.15	2.26	0.16	5.84
河 源	Heyuan	0.25	0.07	4.43	1.85	0.10	4.36
梅 州	Meizhou	0.29	0.05	4.48	2.38	0.14	4.99
惠 州	Huizhou	0.44	0.23	6.66	3.13	0.36	8.76
汕 尾	Shanwei	0.10	0.07	2.90	1.20	0.10	3.42
东 莞	Dongguan	1.65	0.98	9.16	6.63	0.77	10.87
中 山	Zhongshan	0.67	0.19	4.39	2.93	0.32	3.38
江 门	Jiangmen	0.74	0.30	5.13	3.40	0.30	5.82
阳 江	Yangjiang	0.39	0.05	3.27	1.96	0.12	3.13
湛 江	Zhanjiang	0.65	0.37	8.86	5.04	0.35	6.32
茂 名	Maoming	0.40	0.14	8.63	3.68	0.26	5.97
肇 庆	Zhaoqing	0.60	0.11	4.80	2.74	0.31	4.47
清 远	Qingyuan	0.20	0.03	4.53	2.20	0.09	5.67
潮 州	Chaozhou	0.34	0.04	2.89	1.16	0.07	1.98
揭 阳	Jieyang	0.18	0.11	5.77	1.53	0.03	4.90
云 浮	Yunfu	0.12	0.05	2.99	1.02	0.04	2.85
按经济区域分	By Region						
珠 三 角	Pearl River Delta	16.80	11.27	90.86	65.70	9.63	93.25
粤 东	Eastern Region	0.96	0.48	18.22	6.96	0.36	15.33
粤 西	Western Region	1.43	0.56	20.75	10.69	0.73	15.42
粤 北	Northern Region	1.54	0.28	20.58	9.71	0.53	23.72

4-9 城镇非私营单位职工工资总额与年平均工资

Total Wages Bill and Average Wage of Staff and Workers in Urban Non Private Units

年份 Year	工资总额 (亿元) Total Wages Bill (100 million yuan)	指数 (上年=100) Indices (preceding year=100)	平均工资 (元) Average Wage (yuan)	指数 (上年=100) Indices (preceding year=100)
1978	30.59	111.3	615	108.8
1979	35.56	116.2	685	111.4
1980	42.83	120.4	789	115.2
1981	49.40	115.3	873	110.6
1982	56.69	114.8	961	110.1
1983	60.85	107.3	1021	106.2
1984	72.82	119.7	1187	116.3
1985	88.91	122.1	1393	117.4
1986	102.13	114.9	1541	110.6
1987	121.10	118.6	1743	113.1
1988	162.76	134.4	2250	129.1
1989	200.39	123.1	2678	119.0
1990	223.29	111.4	2929	109.4
1991	268.19	120.1	3358	114.6
1992	334.61	124.8	4027	119.9
1993	455.33	136.1	5327	132.3
1994	612.73	134.6	7117	133.6
1995	734.14	119.8	8250	115.9
1996	803.50	109.4	9127	110.6
1997	858.35	106.8	9698	106.3
1998	899.68	104.8	10233	105.5
1999	970.70	107.9	11309	110.5
2000	1038.38	107.0	13823	122.2
2001	1146.11	110.4	15682	113.4
2002	1306.32	114.0	17814	113.6
2003	1515.58	116.0	19986	112.2
2004	1771.05	116.9	22116	110.7
2005	2085.64	117.8	23959	108.3
2006	2413.63	115.7	26186	109.3
2007	2854.99	118.3	29443	112.4
2008	3294.17	115.4	33110	112.5
2009	3698.34	112.3	36355	109.8
2010	4363.82	118.0	40358	111.0
2011	5444.34	124.8	45152	111.9
2012	6397.01	117.5	50577	112.0
2013	10213.35	159.7	53611	106.0
2014	11471.24	112.3	59827	111.6
2015	12596.61	109.8	66296	110.8
2016	13790.07	109.5	72848	109.9
2017	15110.67	109.6	80020	109.8
2018	17232.72	114.0	89826	112.3
2019	19945.83	115.7	100689	112.1
2020	21804.42	109.3	110324	109.6
2021	24346.28	111.7	120299	109.0
2022	25639.81	105.3	126925	105.5
2023	25654.23	100.1	133452	105.1

注：从2000年起统计口径为在岗职工。
Note: Since 2000, statistical coverage refers to the fully employed staff and workers.

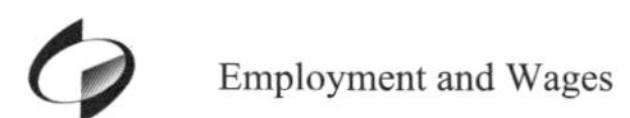

4-10 各市城镇非私营单位就业人员工资总额和在岗职工年平均工资

Total Wages of Employed Persons and Average Wages of Fully Employed Staff and Workers in Urban Non Private Units by City

市别	City	2022		2023	
		就业人员工资 Earnings of Employed Persons	在岗职工工资 Wages of Fully Employed Staff and Workers	就业人员工资 Earnings of Employed Persons	在岗职工工资 Wages of Fully Employed Staff and Workers
总额(亿元)	**Total(100 million yuan)**				
全省	**Provincial Total**	**26200.89**	**25639.81**	**26266.90**	**25654.23**
广州	Guangzhou	6325.25	6151.75	6364.99	6159.10
深圳	Shenzhen	8418.22	8285.62	8481.33	8351.06
珠海	Zhuhai	1023.68	997.81	1071.43	1044.58
汕头	Shantou	444.82	433.48	422.45	407.59
佛山	Foshan	1660.50	1613.97	1795.87	1739.71
韶关	Shaoguan	289.08	280.77	312.79	304.48
河源	Heyuan	269.79	264.90	245.73	241.64
梅州	Meizhou	245.04	240.32	231.59	226.79
惠州	Huizhou	1081.65	1061.15	1044.36	1024.45
汕尾	Shanwei	179.91	177.42	135.98	133.17
东莞	Dongguan	2627.19	2591.18	2517.83	2482.50
中山	Zhongshan	780.18	761.82	784.88	766.32
江门	Jiangmen	619.38	602.25	633.87	614.12
阳江	Yangjiang	156.99	154.46	163.31	159.42
湛江	Zhanjiang	463.35	443.81	452.17	434.49
茂名	Maoming	437.91	428.00	440.11	418.65
肇庆	Zhaoqing	348.67	342.29	351.47	346.47
清远	Qingyuan	316.15	308.73	321.53	315.44
潮州	Chaozhou	141.64	135.47	144.23	138.45
揭阳	Jieyang	198.67	195.74	183.59	180.97
云浮	Yunfu	172.81	168.84	167.35	164.84
平均工资(元)	**Average Wage (yuan)**				
全省	**Provincial Total**	**124916**	**126925**	**131418**	**133452**
广州	Guangzhou	147947	152324	154475	158318
深圳	Shenzhen	162680	164754	171854	174640
珠海	Zhuhai	124430	126132	132169	133869
汕头	Shantou	91667	92765	95982	97346
佛山	Foshan	108656	108934	114384	115084
韶关	Shaoguan	105316	107183	108567	110689
河源	Heyuan	90286	91606	92696	93592
梅州	Meizhou	90226	92567	94247	96631
惠州	Huizhou	99928	101386	103472	104326
汕尾	Shanwei	96024	97474	98697	99929
东莞	Dongguan	93299	93768	98172	98726
中山	Zhongshan	100994	101729	105974	106342
江门	Jiangmen	96927	98720	100325	101805
阳江	Yangjiang	94334	96957	99302	102011
湛江	Zhanjiang	102909	107616	107881	111895
茂名	Maoming	96425	97984	101767	104313
肇庆	Zhaoqing	95767	97317	99829	100848
清远	Qingyuan	97092	99502	100545	102113
潮州	Chaozhou	87834	90544	92622	94269
揭阳	Jieyang	79997	80562	84426	85538
云浮	Yunfu	97985	100328	100448	101608

4-11 按行业分城镇非私营单位就业人员与在岗职工工资总额（2023年）

Total Wages of Urban Employed Persons and Fully Employed Staff and Workers by Industry (2023)

单位：亿元 (100 million yuan)

行 业	Item	就业人员 Employed Persons	在岗职工 Fully Employed Staff and Workers
全 省	**Provincial Total**	**26266.90**	**25654.23**
农、林、牧、渔业	Farming, Forestry, Animal Husbandry and Fishery	11.52	11.24
采矿业	Mining and Quarrying	38.15	38.10
制造业	Manufacture	7945.37	7890.01
电力、热力、燃气及水生产和供应业	Production and Supply of Electric Power, Gas and Water	485.09	484.15
建筑业	Construction	1103.79	988.00
批发和零售业	Wholesale and Retail Trade	1225.32	1209.09
交通运输、仓储和邮政业	Transport, Storage and Postal Services	1030.00	1021.33
住宿和餐饮业	Hotels and Catering Services	256.53	242.70
信息传输、软件和信息技术服务业	Information Transmission, Computer Services and Software	2007.16	2001.83
金融业	Finance	1931.14	1711.25
房地产业	Real Estate	914.24	905.29
租赁和商务服务业	Leasing and Business Services	1339.65	1285.02
科学研究和技术服务业	Scientific Research and Technical Services	887.87	872.09
水利、环境和公共设施管理业	Management of Water Conservancy, Environment and Public Facilities	181.41	178.82
居民服务、修理和其他服务业	Household's Services,Repair and Other Services	96.35	91.98
教育	Education	2362.89	2322.15
卫生和社会工作	Health Care and Social Service	1861.88	1835.04
文化、体育和娱乐业	Culture, Sports and Entertainment	165.73	162.51
公共管理、社会保障和社会组织	Public Administration and Social Security and Social Organizations	2422.80	2403.65

4-12 按行业分城镇非私营单位就业人员与在岗职工年平均工资（2023年）

Average Annual Wages of Urban Employed Persons and Fully Employed Staff and Workers by Industry (2023)

单位：元 (yuan)

行业	Item	就业人员 Employed Persons	在岗职工 Fully Employed Staff and Workers
全 省	**Provincial Total**	**131418**	**133452**
农、林、牧、渔业	Farming, Forestry, Animal Husbandry and Fishery	83936	85493
采矿业	Mining and Quarrying	213297	213843
制造业	Manufacture	104424	104450
电力、热力、燃气及水生产和供应业	Production and Supply of Electric Power, Gas and Water	187410	189462
建筑业	Construction	92727	97537
批发和零售业	Wholesale and Retail Trade	117872	119246
交通运输、仓储和邮政业	Transport, Storage and Postal Services	137150	138191
住宿和餐饮业	Hotels and Catering Services	57881	65491
信息传输、软件和信息技术服务业	Information Transmission, Computer Services and Software	243832	246685
金融业	Finance	267444	315793
房地产业	Real Estate	99128	99943
租赁和商务服务业	Leasing and Business Services	107547	109775
科学研究和技术服务业	Scientific Research and Technical Services	181616	183672
水利、环境和公共设施管理业	Management of Water Conservancy, Environment and Public Facilities	83890	84976
居民服务、修理和其他服务业	Household's Services,Repair and Other Services	70693	72816
教育	Education	153345	155298
卫生和社会工作	Health Care and Social Service	197354	198847
文化、体育和娱乐业	Culture, Sports and Entertainment	136749	141942
公共管理、社会保障和社会组织	Public Administration and Social Security and Social Organizations	161104	163215

主要统计指标解释

就业人员 指在一定年龄以上，有劳动能力，为取得劳动报酬或经营收入而从事一定社会劳动的人员。具体指年满16周岁，为取得报酬或经营利润，在调查周内从事了1小时（含1小时）以上劳动的人员；或由于学习、休假等原因在调查周内暂时处于未工作状态，但有工作单位或场所的人员；或由于临时停工放假、单位不景气放假等原因在调查周内暂时处于未工作状态，但不满三个月的人员。

单位就业人员 指报告期末最后一日24时在本单位中工作，并取得工资或其他形式劳动报酬的人员数。该指标为时点指标，不包括最后一日当天及以前已经与单位解除劳动合同关系的人员，是在岗职工、劳务派遣人员及其他就业人员之和。就业人员不包括：

(1)离开本单位仍保留劳动关系，并定期领取生活费的人员；

(2)在本单位实习的各类在校学生；

(3)本单位因劳务外包而使用的人员。

在岗职工 指在本单位工作且与本单位签订劳动合同，并由单位支付各项工资和社会保险、住房公积金的人员，以及上述人员中由于学习、病伤、产假等原因暂未工作仍由单位支付工资的人员。在岗职工还包括：

(1)应订立劳动合同而未订立劳动合同人员(如使用的农村户籍人员)；

(2)处于试用期人员；

(3)编制外招用的人员；

(4)派往外单位工作，但工资仍由本单位发放的人员(如挂职锻炼、外派工作等情况)。

工资总额 指根据《关于工资总额组成的规定》(1990年1月1日国家统计局发布的一号令)进行修订，在报告期内(季度或年度)直接支付给本单位全部就业人员的劳动报酬总额。包括计时工资、计件工资、奖金、津贴和补贴、加班加点工资、特殊情况下支付的工资，是在岗职工工资总额、劳务派遣人员工资总额和其他就业人员工资总额之和。

工资总额是税前工资，包括单位从个人工资中直接为其代扣或代缴的房费、水费、电费、住房公积金、职工年金和社会保险基金个人缴纳部分等。

工资总额不论是计入成本的还是不计入成本的，不论是以货币形式支付的还是以实物形式支付的，均应列入工资总额的计算范围。

平均工资 是指在报告期内单位发放工资的人均水平。计算公式为：

$$\text{平均工资} = \frac{\text{报告期工资总额}}{\text{报告期平均人数}}$$

平均工资通常是以年平均工资的形式表现，月平均工资就是用年平均工资除以12求得。

Explanatory Notes on Main Statistical Indicators

Employed Persons refer to persons, aged 16 and over, who performed some work for compensation or business gains for one hour or more during the reference period; or persons who do not work for the reasons of study or on holiday, but had work units or sites during the reference period; or persons temporary absence from a job for disorganization or suspension of work, recession, etc, but not exceeding three months during the reference period.

Persons Employed in Various Units refer to the total number of employees who work at his unit and obtain wages or other forms of payment at the end of the reporting period. This indicator is a kind of time point index and it equals to the sum of the number of employed staff and workers, labor dispatch personnel and other employed persons. Employed persons do not include:

1)persons who have left their working units while keeping their labour contract (employment relation) unchanged and receiving regular alimony;

2)students who do part-time jobs in spare time and all kinds of enrolled students who do internship in various units;

3)persons employed due to labor outsourcing;

Employed Staff and Workers refer to persons who signed labor contracts with working units and working units would pay wages, social insurance and housing funds for them. Persons who have their work posts but are temporarily absent from work for reasons of study or on sick, injury or maternal leave and still receive wages from their working units are also included. Employed staff and workers also include:

1)Persons who should have signed the labor contracts but not (like people with rural household registration);

2)Employees on probation;

3)Employees beyond the staffing quota;

4)Employees who are sent to other working units but still obtain wages from their original units (situations like on-the-job placement, expatriated assignment, etc.)

Total Wage Bill It is revised according to the “Provision of Composition of Total Wages” (Order No.1 by National Bureau of Statistics on January, 1st, ,1990), total wage bill refers to the total remuneration payment to all employed persons in various units during the reporting period (by quarter or by year), including hourly-paid wages, piece-rate wages, bonuses, allowance and subsidies, overtime wages and wages paid under special circumstances. It equals to the sum of total wages of employed staff and workers, dispatch labors and other employed persons.

Total wage bill is pre-tax wages, including the room charges, utility bills, housing funds and social insurance paid or withheld by employee’s units.

Total wage bill, whether or not included in cost, whether or not paid in money or in kind, shall be included in the calculation of total wage.

Average Wage refers to the average per capita wage in money terms during a certain period of time for employed persons. It shows the general level of wage income of staff and worker during a certain period of time, one major indicator to reflect the wage level. It is calculated as follows:

$$\text{Average Wage} = \frac{\text{Total Wage Bill of Employed Persons at Reference Time}}{\text{Average Number of Persons Employed at Reference Time}}$$

Average Wage in this yearbook is the annual average wage.The average monthly wage is calculated by dividing the annual average wage by 12.

五、固定资产投资

INVESTMENT IN FIXED ASSETS

五　固定资产投资

简要说明

一、本篇资料反映广东省固定资产投资的基本情况，主要包括：固定资产投资以及各市固定资产投资的主要指标数据。

二、本篇资料由广东省统计局固定资产投资统计处整理提供。

三、固定资产投资统计的资料来源主要为全面统计报表。

四、2011 年起，固定资产投资项目统计起点由 50 万元提高到 500 万元，且不包含农户投资；2010 年以前为全社会固定资产投资。

五、2011 年定报起，原国家预算内资金改为国家预算资金。

六、2014 年定报起，固定资产投资取消城乡分组。

5　Investment in Fixed Assets

Brief Introduction

Ⅰ.The data in this chapter reflect the basic conditions of investment in fixed assets of Guangdong Province, mainly including investment in fixed assets in the whole province, and main indicators on investment in fixed assets by city.

Ⅱ.The data in this chapter are prepared and provided by the Division of Investment and Construction Statistics of Statistics Bureau of Guangdong Province.

Ⅲ.The data sources for the statistics of investment in fixed assets mainly come from complete statistical report forms.

Ⅳ.Since 2011, the cut-off point of investment statistics is changed from a minimum of 500,000 yuan to a minimum of 5,000,000 yuan, and the data do not include the investment made by rural households. Data before 2010 refer to total investment in fixed assets.

Ⅴ.Since 2011, state budget is changed to state and local budget.

VI.Since 2014, fixed asset investment grouped by urban and rural areas is canceled.

5-1 固定资产投资主要指标增长速度

Main Indicators of Investment in Fixed Assets

单位：% (%)

项　目	Item	2019	2020	2021	2022	2023
投资完成额	**Investment**	**11.1**	**7.2**	**6.3**	**-2.6**	**2.5**
#房地产开发	Real Estate Development	10.0	9.2	0.9	-13.6	-9.3
#民间投资	Non-governmental Investment	6.4	1.1	7.8	-9.4	-6.5
按登记注册统计类别分	By Registered Statistical Categories					
内资	Domestic Invested	12.6	8.8	5.3	-3.1	3.2
港澳台商投资	Investment from Hong Kong,Macao and Taiwan	-0.3	-3.6	12.6	4.3	-3.8
外商投资	Foreign Invested	-0.9	-14.3	18.3	-3.4	-8.0
按构成分	Grouped by Use of Funds					
建筑安装工程	Construction and Installation	12.0	7.3	7.9	-3.5	3.9
设备工具器具购置	Purchase of Equipments and Instruments	2.0	-11.7	6.8	-3.1	10.6
其他费用	Others	14.4	15.6	2.1	-1.1	-3.7
按三次产业分	Grouped by Three Strata of Industry					
第一产业	Primary Industry	-18.0	81.0	31.8	-21.2	-1.6
第二产业	Secondary Industry	6.3	-1.1	19.4	10.4	22.2
第三产业	Tertiary Industry	13.0	9.3	2.2	-6.9	-5.3
按财务拨贷款合计	**Grouped by Source of Funds**	**10.5**	**14.7**	**9.4**	**-11.5**	**5.3**
国家预算资金	State and Local Budget	19.5	53.5	3.4	28.1	6.0
国内贷款	Domestic Loans	1.9	9.6	4.4	-13.0	11.3
利用外资	Foreign Investment	-6.6	-14.6	37.7	26.6	-26.2
自筹资金	Self-raising Funds	12.3	18.8	13.3	-4.5	5.3
其他资金	Others	11.9	5.0	8.9	-33.7	1.2

注：1.2011年起固定资产投资项目统计起点由50万元提高至500万元，且不包含农村农户投资；2010年以前为全社会固定资产投资，下表同。
2.2011年报起，原国家预算内资金改为国家预算资金，下表同。
3.2018年-2020年，资金来源指标不包含5000万元以下项目数据，增速为可比口径，下表同。
4.本表登记注册统计类别按《关于市场主体统计分类的划分规定》(国统字〔2023〕14号)执行。

Note: a) Since 2011, the cut-off point of investment statistics is changed from a minimum of 500,000 yuan to a minimum of 5,000,000 yuan, and the data do not include the investment made by rural households. Data before 2010 refer to total investment in fixed assets. The same applies to all tables following.
b) Since 2011, state budget is changed to state and local budget.The samc applies to all tables following.
c)From 2018 to 2020,sources of funds for investment do not include projects under 50 million yuan.The growth rate is caculated by comparable coverage, and the same applies to the following table.
d)The registered statistical categories of this table is implemented in accordance with the Regulations onStatistics the Classification of Market Entity (Guotongzi [2023] No. 14).

5-2 固定资产投资增长速度
Growth Rate of Investment in Fixed Assets

单位：% (%)

年份 Year	全部投资 Total Investment	#房地产开发 Real Estate Development	按产业分 Grouped by Three Strata of Industry 第一产业 Primary Industry	第二产业 Secondary Industry	第三产业 Tertiary Industry
1978					
1979	3.9		-40.4	74.9	-33.2
1980	35.3		…	33.3	54.1
1981	57.7		11.2	21.3	136.9
1982	40.3		10.7	33.9	50.0
1983	4.7		-13.1	1.3	9.2
1984	47.0		4.5	34.8	59.5
1985	41.6		33.2	91.4	9.4
1986	17.3		-8.4	48.0	-16.5
1987	15.9	62.9	-6.7	18.4	12.3
1988	40.9	34.8	12.6	42.8	38.2
1989	-1.8	119.3	5.7	-46.8	97.6
1990	9.8	-32.1	13.4	25.1	0.6
1991	25.4	52.1	61.0	9.1	36.5
1992	92.8	152.4	-17.8	56.8	117.5
1993	76.8	152.1	25.9	91.7	71.1
1994	31.4	27.7	12.7	36.3	29.2
1995	8.7	39.5	34.2	-4.6	15.2
1996	…	-6.2	36.0	-2.5	0.7
1997	-1.3	-0.1	-15.2	-9.3	2.1
1998	16.1	14.1	18.3	9.4	18.5
1999	13.5	17.8	8.2	11.1	14.3
2000	6.8	20.9	11.2	4.7	7.4
2001	9.4	13.2	-0.1	16.0	7.4
2002	12.3	14.7	3.0	36.5	4.1
2003	26.7	10.6	-39.6	12.2	33.7
2004	19.8	9.9	68.2	57.7	5.4
2005	18.9	17.4	17.3	33.2	10.9
2006	13.5	15.8	71.3	13.2	13.3
2007	18.0	36.6	42.1	8.2	24.4
2008	16.3	16.4	56.7	12.1	18.4
2009	19.6	1.0	18.9	13.2	23.1
2010	20.7	23.6	39.6	17.6	22.0
2011	17.6	31.4	53.9	17.8	17.0
2012	14.6	11.3	28.4	17.7	12.8
2013	18.2	21.2	29.1	13.4	20.5
2014	15.9	17.7	-1.2	16.8	15.9
2015	15.8	11.8	52.5	20.8	12.8
2016	10.0	20.7	5.9	8.9	10.5
2017	13.5	17.2	-11.2	9.4	16.2
2018	10.7	19.3	-20.9	0.6	14.9
2019	11.1	10.0	-18.0	6.3	13.0
2020	7.2	9.2	81.0	-1.1	9.3
2021	6.3	0.9	31.8	19.4	2.2
2022	-2.6	-13.6	-21.2	10.4	-6.9
2023	2.5	-9.3	-1.6	22.2	-5.3

注：1993年以前房地产开发投资主要是商品房建设投资。
Notes: Prior to 1993, investment in real estate development focused mainly on the construction of commercial buildings.

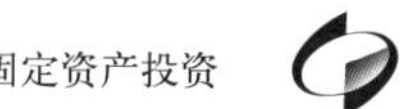

5-3 按资金来源和构成分固定资产投资增速及比重

Growth Rate and Percentage Investment in Fixed Assets by Source of Funds and Structure of Investment

单位：% (%)

年份 Year	按财务拨贷款资金来源分 By Source of Funds				按构成分 By Structure of Investment		
	国家预算资金 State Budget Funds	国内贷款 Domestic Loans	利用外资 Foreign Investment	自筹和其他资金 Fundraising and Others	建筑安装工程 Construction and Installation	设备工具器具购置 Purchase of Equipment and Instruments	其他费用 Others
增长速度 Growth Rate							
1985	1.8	45.7	73.2	43.1			
1990	7.8	32.5	15.5	-1.7			
1995	30.3	12.1	-3.0	27.1	11.1	-6.9	24.5
1996	-16.5	-7.5	6.4	-4.1	-0.1	7.3	-9.2
1997	-3.4	-14.7	-3.4	2.0	0.3	-6.9	0.1
1998	113.9	39.8	-17.4	22.8	11.7	17.5	34.8
1999	31.0	32.7	-18.0	9.9	16.1	7.7	10.4
2000	-6.8	6.2	10.3	10.7	7.3	1.5	11.2
2001	2.3	1.4	1.1	11.7	9.0	16.9	2.1
2002	26.6	26.4	21.7	13.4	11.1	12.2	17.3
2003	22.6	26.9	29.5	31.5	25.6	24.8	33.5
2004	-19.8	19.0	15.3	21.7	18.2	27.6	16.7
2005	-4.5	20.7	19.9	17.7	19.5	27.7	5.6
2006	52.7	21.5	10.1	16.3	15.5	12.7	6.2
2007	70.0	5.8	13.7	27.5	16.6	10.2	37.3
2008	41.1	7.0	-20.8	9.4	17.3	14.4	15.1
2009	50.0	43.5	-12.5	30.5	23.3	9.0	18.4
2010	8.3	17.7	-7.6	20.8	18.1	20.2	32.0
2011	3.2	-10.0	-0.8	21.9	20.2	16.1	10.2
2012	142.9	15.1	4.4	12.7	16.1	11.4	12.3
2013	17.1	27.4	14.0	21.1	19.3	18.3	13.9
2014	28.9	8.5	-37.1	11.1	16.8	14.0	20.6
2015	24.4	4.5	-49.6	24.5	14.9	25.1	10.4
2016	8.4	9.8	29.2	8.4	6.9	8.8	24.5
2017	27.3	37.3	-1.5	1.7	11.6	11.0	23.6
2018	26.3	8.3	-28.9	9.9	3.4	3.0	38.8
2019	19.5	1.9	-6.6	12.1	12.0	2.0	14.4
2020	53.5	9.6	-14.6	12.4	7.3	-11.7	15.6
2021	3.4	4.4	37.7	11.3	7.9	6.8	2.1
2022	28.1	-13.0	26.6	-16.6	-3.5	-3.1	-1.1
2023	6.0	11.3	-26.2	3.9	3.9	10.6	-3.7

5-3 续表 continued

单位：% (%)

年份 Year	按财务拨贷款资金来源分 By Source of Funds				按构成分 By Structure of Investment		
	国家预算资金 State Budget Funds	国内贷款 Domestic Loans	利用外资 Foreign Investment	自筹和其他资金 Fundraising and Others	建筑安装工程 Construction and Installation	设备工具器具购置 Purchase of Equipment and Instruments	其他费用 Others
比重 Percentage							
1985	8.1	24.8	10.3	56.8	74.9	17.7	7.4
1990	3.2	18.1	14.9	63.9	64.6	27.3	8.1
1995	1.1	15.0	18.5	65.4	64.8	20.0	15.2
1996	0.9	14.3	20.3	64.5	64.7	21.4	13.8
1997	0.9	12.3	19.9	66.9	65.8	20.2	14.0
1998	1.6	14.7	14.0	69.7	63.3	20.5	16.3
1999	2.0	17.7	10.4	69.9	64.7	19.4	15.8
2000	1.7	17.2	10.5	70.6	65.1	18.5	16.5
2001	1.6	16.1	9.8	72.6	64.9	19.8	15.4
2002	1.7	17.4	10.2	70.7	64.2	19.7	16.1
2003	1.6	17.0	10.1	71.3	63.6	19.4	16.9
2004	1.1	16.8	9.8	72.3	62.8	20.7	16.5
2005	0.9	17.2	9.9	72.1	63.1	22.2	14.7
2006	1.1	17.9	9.3	71.7	64.2	22.1	13.7
2007	1.6	15.4	8.6	74.4	63.4	20.6	15.9
2008	2.1	15.4	6.4	76.1	64.0	20.3	15.7
2009	2.4	16.9	4.3	76.4	65.9	18.5	15.6
2010	2.2	16.8	3.3	77.7	64.5	18.4	17.1
2011	2.1	14.4	2.9	80.6	65.4	17.9	16.6
2012	4.4	14.4	2.6	78.6	66.3	17.4	16.3
2013	4.3	15.0	2.5	78.2	66.9	17.4	15.7
2014	4.7	14.4	1.3	79.5	67.4	16.5	16.1
2015	4.9	12.5	0.6	82.1	66.9	17.8	15.4
2016	4.8	12.6	0.7	81.9	65.0	17.6	17.4
2017	5.7	16.1	0.6	77.5	63.9	17.2	18.9
2018	6.8	20.2	0.4	72.6	59.7	14.0	26.3
2019	7.4	18.6	0.3	73.7	60.1	12.8	27.0
2020	9.9	17.8	0.2	72.1	60.3	10.6	29.2
2021	9.8	16.2	0.3	73.7	61.3	10.7	28.1
2022	14.2	15.9	0.4	69.5	60.9	10.6	28.5
2023	14.3	16.9	0.3	68.6	61.7	11.5	26.8

注：1986年及以后的资金来源为财务拨贷款数，各项相加不等于投资总额；从2012年定报开始，资金来源中的“国家预算内资金”改为“国家预算资金”，包括中央预算资金和地方预算资金，口径有所扩大；2018年—2020年，资金来源不含计划总投资5000万元以下项目。

Note: Source of funds for investment since 1986 refers to financial appropriations, which do not add up to total investment.Since 2012,state budget is changed to state and local budget including central budget funds and local budget funds, the caliber has been expanded. From 2018 to 2020, sources of funds for Investment do not include projects with total planed investment under 50 million yuan.

5-4 按构成分固定资产投资增长速度

Growth Rate of Investment in Fixed Assets by Structure

单位：% (%)

项 目	Item	2022年 全部投资 Total	2022年 项目投资 Project	2022年 房地产开发 Real Estate Devel-opment	2023年 全部投资 Total	2023年 项目投资 Project	2023年 房地产开发 Real Estate Devel-opment
建设项目个数	**Number of Projects**	**0.8**	**0.8**		**5.3**	**5.3**	
其中：本年新开工	Newly-commenced Projects	-7.3	-7.3		4.6	4.6	
全部建成投产项目	Projects Completed and Put into Use	-8.9	-8.9		5.5	5.5	
计划总投资	**Total Planned Investment**	**11.0**	**18.9**	**3.2**	**2.8**	**3.5**	**2.2**
本年投资总额	**Total Investment in this year**	**-2.6**	**4.7**	**-13.6**	**2.5**	**9.0**	**-9.3**
#住宅	Residential Buildings	-14.3	-24.1	-12.9	-10.5	-59.8	-8.2
按构成分	Grouped by Structure						
建筑安装工程	Construction and Installation	-3.5	3.9	-16.8	3.9	9.8	-9.7
设备工具器具购置	Purchase of Equipment and Instruments	-3.1	-2.4	-27.4	10.6	10.6	11.1
其他费用	Others	-1.1	14.5	-9.3	-3.7	4.9	-9.2
财务拨贷款合计	**Total Financial Appropriations**	**-11.5**	**14.4**	**-33.0**	**5.3**	**12.5**	**-3.6**
国家预算资金	State and Local Budget	28.1	28.1		6.0	6.0	
国内贷款	Domestic Loans	-13.0	12.7	-35.9	11.3	20.7	1.8
利用外资	Foreign Investment	26.6	31.0	-13.9	-26.2	-30.7	36.8
自筹资金	Self-raising Funds	-4.5	8.3	-22.4	5.3	15.4	-15.9
其他资金	Others	-33.7	26.5	-38.8	1.2	-5.5	4.4
新增固定资产	**Newly Increased Fixed Assets**	**2.0**	**1.3**	**3.3**	**14.2**	**18.1**	**7.9**
房屋建筑面积	**Floor Space of Buildings**						
施工面积	Floor Space under Construction			-5.9			-6.5
竣工面积	Floor Space Completed			1.5			1.5
#住宅	Residential Buildings			1.0			-1.3

注：建设项目个数不含房地产开发。
Note: The total number of projects under construction excludes the projects of real estate development.

5-5 按行业分固定资产投资主要指标增长速度(2023年)
Growth Rate of Main Indicators of Investment by Sector (2023)

单位：% (%)

行业	Sector	投资额 Investment	施工项目个数 Number of Projects under Construction	全部建成投产项目个数 Number of Projects Completed and Put into Use	新增固定资产 Newly Increased Fixed Assets
全　省	**Provincial Total**	**2.5**	**5.3**	**5.5**	**14.2**
农、林、牧、渔业	**Farming, Forestry, Animal Husbandry and Fishery**	**0.2**	**19.0**	**35.7**	**10.1**
农业	Farming	8.6	17.8	31.9	22.1
林业	Forestry	307.5	88.2	90.9	161.2
畜牧业	Animal Husbandry	-21.0	0.7	21.7	-17.6
渔业	Fishery	-10.6	41.1	14.7	-24.5
农、林、牧、渔专业及辅助性活动	Service Activities for Farming, Forestry, Animal Husbandry and Fishery	8.5	28.1	62.1	53.9
采矿业	**Mining**	**64.5**	**44.8**	**48.4**	**108.3**
煤炭开采和洗选业	Mining and Washing of Coal				
石油和天然气开采业	Extraction of Petroleum and Natural Gas	15.7	50.0	100.0	64.7
黑色金属矿采选业	Mining and Dressing of Ferrous Metal Ores	183.3	400.0		
有色金属矿采选业	Mining and Dressing of Non-Ferrous Metal Ores	54.6	38.5	40.0	-68.7
非金属矿采选业	Mining and Dressing of Nonmetal Ores	144.9	42.9	43.5	713.6
开采专业及辅助性活动	Auxiliary Mining Operations				
其他采矿业	Mining of Other Ores	-86.0	50.0		799.2
制造业	**Manufacture**	**20.7**	**5.9**	**5.1**	**25.0**
农副食品加工业	Processing of Farm and Sideline Food	**37.8**	**29.4**	**47.0**	**91.3**
食品制造业	Manufacture of Food	46.3	21.1	40.0	98.5
酒、饮料和精制茶制造业	Manufacture of Wine, Beverage and Refined Tea	20.2	18.6	29.7	38.4
烟草制品业	Tobacco Products	82.1	123.1		-24.6
纺织业	Textile Industry	8.0	1.8	-10.1	13.1
纺织服装、服饰业	Manufacture of Textile Garments, Apparel	28.6	10.5	-8.6	4.0
皮革、毛皮、羽毛及其制品和制鞋业	Leather, Fur, Feather and Related Products, and Footwear	-2.2	6.2	-22.0	-2.6
木材加工及木、竹、藤、棕、草制品业	Timber Processing, Bamboo, Cane, Palm Fiber & Straw Products	62.1	11.8	-5.5	48.2
家具制造业	Manufacture of Furniture	-3.9	3.0	13.8	-11.4
造纸和纸制品业	Papermaking and Paper Products	14.1	-1.4	-1.8	99.6
印刷业和记录媒介复制业	Printing and Record Medium Reproduction	-3.8	-0.5	-10.2	-3.4
文教、工美、体育和娱乐用品制造业	Manufacture of Culture, Arts, Sports and Entertainment Articles	21.6	3.1	-12.0	6.9
石油加工、炼焦和核燃料加工业	Petroleum Refining, Coking and Nuclear Fuel Processing	-66.1	23.0	94.6	22.0
化学原料和化学制品制造业	Manufacture of Raw Chemical Materials and Chemical Products	16.9	-0.2	-5.9	1.4
医药制造业	Manufacture of Medicines	32.9	8.9	12.9	125.4
化学纤维制造业	Manufacture of Chemical Fibers	82.6	26.5	18.2	191.6
橡胶和塑料制品业	Manufacture of Rubber and Plastic Products	20.8	2.1	-2.1	27.9
非金属矿物制品业	Nonmetal Mineral Products	29.3	-3.2	-9.3	3.2
黑色金属冶炼及压延加工业	Smelting and Pressing of Ferrous Metals	14.1	17.7	21.4	-78.0
有色金属冶炼及压延加工业	Smelting and Pressing of Nonferrous Metals	-8.2	-13.0	-9.7	38.7
金属制品业	Metal Products	15.4	2.8	2.6	-1.2
通用设备制造业	Manufacture of General-purpose Machinery	40.8	7.2	12.5	25.2
专用设备制造业	Manufacture of Special-purpose Machinery	30.2	7.7	11.3	48.4
汽车制造业	Manufacture of Automobile	31.8	6.7	35.7	25.1

注：建设项目个数不含房地产开发；2018年—2020年，本年新增固定资产不含计划总投资5000万元以下项目。

Note: Projects under construction do not include real estate investment and newly increased fixed assets do not include project under 50 million from 2018 to 2020.

5-5 续表 1 continued 1

单位：% (%)

行 业	Sector	投资额 Investment	施工项目个数 Number of Projects under Construction	全部建成投产项目个数 Number of Projects Completed and Put into Use	新增固定资产 Newly Increased Fixed Assets
铁路、船舶、航空航天和其他运输设备制造业	Manufacture of Railway, Slip, Aeronautics and Other Transport Equipment	20.5		-13.1	10.0
电气机械及器材制造业	Manufacture of Electrical Machinery and Equipment	21.1	10.6	15.1	52.9
计算机、通信和其他电子设备制造业	Manufacture of Computers, Communication Equipment and Other Electronic Equipment	20.6	3.8	2.5	44.8
仪器仪表制造业	Manufacture of Instruments and Meters	14.1	-4.1	-23.8	0.3
其他制造业	Other Manufactures	94.2	36.0	21.1	68.8
废弃资源综合利用业	Comprehensive Utilization of Waste	19.0	3.0	-15.1	-25.4
金属制品、机械和设备修理业	Manufacture of Metal Products, Machinery and Equipment Maintenance	-1.0	-26.5	-53.8	-36.5
电力、热力、燃气及水生产和供应业	**Production and Supply of Electric Power, Heat Power, Gas and Water**	**21.8**	**28.0**	**42.6**	**3.3**
电力、热力生产和供应业	Production and Supply of Electric Power and Heat Power	24.3	55.2	77.6	11.9
燃气生产和供应业	Production and Supply of Gas	32.3	12.8	85.1	42.7
水的生产和供应业	Production and Supply of Water	10.3	-4.7	-20.2	-30.4
建筑业	**Construction**	**24.0**	**9.1**	**125.0**	**652.8**
房屋建筑业	Housing Construction	49.2	-33.3		-82.3
土木工程建筑业	Civil Engineering Construction	23.9		300.0	2067.0
建筑安装业	Construction and Installation				
建筑装饰和其他建筑业	Architectural Decoration and Other Construction	-48.9	200.0	100.0	-61.8
批发和零售业	**Wholesale and Retail Trades**	**-7.0**	**3.1**	**6.3**	**9.1**
批发业	Wholesale	**20.9**	**-11.3**	**-16.7**	**-33.0**
零售业	Retail Trade	-26.1	12.3	18.4	39.9
交通运输、仓储和邮政业	**Transport, Storage and Postal Services**	**-2.7**	**1.7**	**1.6**	**69.0**
铁路运输业	Railway Transport	4.8	-5.2	14.3	58.2
道路运输业	Road Transport	-4.9	4.8	0.9	115.0
水上运输业	Waterway Transport	10.1	-6.9	-17.3	45.8
航空运输业	Air Transport	6.0	-13.9	-4.8	154.5
管道运输业	Pipeline Transport	5.0		500.0	11829.7
多式联运和运输代理业	Multimodal Transportation and Transport Agency Industry	-15.4	-3.4	-33.3	-63.3
装卸搬运和仓储业	Handling, handling and storage	-8.3	2.4	17.6	-31.1
邮政业	Postal Services	-70.3	-5.9	16.7	-79.3
住宿和餐饮业	**Hotels and Catering Services**	**-19.8**	**29.7**	**21.1**	**-2.6**
住宿业	Hotels	-22.4	27.0	21.6	-6.2
餐饮业	Catering Services	13.6	47.9	19.4	37.6
信息传输、软件和信息技术服务业	**Information Transmission, Software and Information Technology Services**	**-2.4**	**18.4**	**-5.1**	**0.7**
电信、广播电视和卫星传输服务	Telecommunications, Broadcasting Television and Satellite Transmission Services	0.5	31.0	-21.4	-19.1
互联网和相关服务	Internet and Related Services	11.4	16.9	57.6	110.3
软件和信息技术服务业	Software and Information Technology Services	-13.1	4.0	-15.6	53.5
金融业	**Finance**	**-21.1**	**1.4**	**9.1**	**-73.7**
货币金融服务	Monetary and Financial Services	-39.4	13.9	42.9	-87.8

5-5 续表 2 continued 2

单位：% (%)

行业	Sector	投资额 Investment	施工项目个数 Number of Projects under Construction	全部建成投产项目个数 Number of Projects Completed and Put into Use	新增固定资产 Newly Increased Fixed Assets
资本市场服务	Capital Market Services	10.3	-9.5	-33.3	1918.6
保险业	Insurance	6.0	-11.1		-99.7
其他金融活动	Other Financial Activities	26.6	-16.7		-100.0
房地产业	**Real Estate**	**-9.6**	**10.7**	**28.3**	**7.4**
房地产业	Real Estate	-9.6	10.7	28.3	7.4
租赁和商务服务业	**Leasing and Business Services**	**19.9**	**1.8**	**13.2**	**72.5**
租赁业	Leasing	602.4	33.3	90.9	1036.0
商务服务业	Business Services	12.9	1.4	9.1	39.7
科学研究、技术服务业	**Scientific Research, Technological Services**	**-3.4**	**-2.8**	**-17.9**	**45.2**
研究与试验发展	Research and Experimental Development	-6.5	-5.0	-34.9	7.4
专业技术服务业	Professional Technical Services	-14.4	-11.7	-3.4	104.1
科技推广和应用服务业	Science and Technology Popularization and Application Services	29.1	17.2	-22.7	45.2
水利、环境和公共设施管理业	**Management of Water Conservancy, Environment and Public Facilities**	**0.1**	**-3.4**	**-8.3**	**-4.1**
水利管理业	Management of Water Conservancy	-4.1	-10.0	-10.5	-22.9
生态保护和环境治理业	Ecological Protection and Environmental Treatment	-22.4	-20.8	-12.4	-27.9
公共设施管理业	Management of Public Facilities	2.1	-1.7	-7.6	-1.3
土地管理业	Land Management	-35.8	-41.7	-75.0	-77.0
居民服务、修理和其他服务业	**Households' service, Repair and Other Services**	**1.5**	**32.0**	**4.3**	**22.4**
居民服务业	Services to Households	2.6	37.7	3.3	38.2
机动车、电子产品和日用产品修理业	Motor Vehicle, Electronic Products and Consumer Products Repair	25.1	80.0	14.3	-33.8
其他服务业	Other Services	-13.5	-9.5		-39.4
教育	**Education**	**-0.3**	**-1.9**	**-7.9**	**-16.4**
教育	Education	-0.3	-1.9	-7.9	-16.4
卫生和社会工作	**Health and Social Work**	**-6.2**	**1.7**	**25.2**	**8.0**
卫生	Health	-6.0	2.5	27.8	7.3
社会工作	Social Work	-9.3	-5.3	-3.7	23.6
文化、体育和娱乐业	**Culture, Sports and Recreation**	**16.3**	**1.9**	**8.4**	**35.5**
新闻出版业	Publication	19.5	12.5		626.5
广播、电视、电影和影视录音制作业	Production of Radio, Television, Film and Video Recording	-57.4	-45.5	-50.0	-33.1
文化艺术业	Culture and Arts	1.3	-5.9	3.2	74.7
体育	Sports	17.5	1.9	-5.4	-52.8
娱乐业	Recreation	46.7	16.9	31.0	46.3
公共管理、社会保障和社会组织	**Public Administration, Social Security and Social Organizations**	**5.8**	**-0.9**	**-8.9**	**-20.3**
中国共产党机关	Organs of Communist Party of China	-33.8	50.0	100.0	-64.5
国家机构	Government Agencies	4.3	-2.6	-16.0	-23.6
人民政协、民主党派	Chinese Peoples Political Consultative Conference, Democratic Parties				
社会保障	Social Security				
群众社团、社会团体和其他成员组织	Mass Organizations, Social Organizations and Other Member Organizations	29.0	39.1	233.3	125.3
基层群众自治组织	Self-governing Mass Organizations at the Grass-roots Level	18.9	-13.6	15.4	-0.6

5-6 各行业财务拨贷款资金来源主要指标增长速度(2023年)

Growth Rate of Main Indicators on Sources of Funds and Loans for Investment by Sector (2023)

单位：% (%)

项　目	Item	本年资金来源合计 Sources of Funds	国家预算资金 State and Local Budget	国内贷款 Domestic Loans	利用外资 Foreign Investment	自筹资金 Self-raising Fund	其他资金 Others
全　省	**Provincial Total**	**5.3**	**6.0**	**11.3**	**-26.2**	**5.3**	**1.2**
农、林、牧、渔业	**Farming, Forestry, Animal Husbandry and Fishery**	**-4.0**	**9.8**	**-52.2**	**-100.0**	**-7.1**	**19.5**
农业	Farming	8.2	27.2	-5.4	-100.0	2.4	-3.5
林业	Forestry	97.4	136.8			-38.5	168.4
畜牧业	Animal Husbandry	-24.5	-82.2	-73.2		-14.0	-80.3
渔业	Fishery	-7.6	-60.5	86.1	-100.0	4.1	226.1
农、林、牧、渔服务业	Service Activities for Farming, Forestry, Animal Husbandry and Fishery	8.1	-1.5	-76.0		-10.0	85.4
采矿业	**Mining**	**38.1**		**50.7**		**24.6**	**185.7**
煤炭开采和洗选业	Mining and Washing of Coal						
石油和天然气开采业	Extraction of Petroleum and Natural Gas	15.7				13.3	
黑色金属矿采选业	Mining and Dressing of Ferrous Metal Ores	183.3				183.3	
有色金属矿采选业	Mining and Dressing of Non-Ferrous Metal Ores	63.3				65.8	-100.0
非金属矿采选业	Mining and Dressing of Nonmetal Ores	65.0		50.7		51.9	257.1
开采辅助活动	Auxiliary Mining Operations	-100.0				-100.0	
其他采矿业	Mining of Other Ores	-86.0				-89.9	-97.7
制造业	**Manufacture**	**17.8**	**88.4**	**58.1**	**-38.4**	**12.2**	**24.3**
农副食品加工业	Processing of Farm and Sideline Food	32.4	103.5	28.1	-90.0	28.4	13.2
食品制造业	Manufacture of Food	44.4	3140.9	62.0	-14.3	31.0	571.0
酒、饮料和精制茶制造业	Manufacture of Wine,Beverage and refined tea	9.9	9.5	-37.5	-100.0	12.7	-4.3
烟草制品业	Tobacco Products	107.9		-100.0		105.6	375.5
纺织业	Textile Industry	11.0		97.5	6.0	6.9	-18.7
纺织服装、服饰业	Manufacture of Textile Garments, Apparel	27.2	1347.4	48.9	1411.3	20.0	-9.0
皮革、毛皮、羽毛及其制品和制鞋业	Leather, Fur, Feather and Related Products, and Footwear	0.1	-87.8	171.9		9.8	-92.6
木材加工及木、竹、藤、棕、草制品业	Timber Processing, Bamboo, Cane, Palm Fiber & Straw Products	60.4		212.3		20.3	679.8
家具制造业	Manufacture of Furniture	-0.3		1.8	-100.0	6.7	-93.5
造纸和纸制品业	Papermaking and Paper Products	12.5	-100.0	-18.5	143.9	22.0	-21.3
印刷业和记录媒介复制业	Printing and Record Medium Reproduction	-5.3	-100.0	63.2	-100.0	-0.7	-91.0
文教、工美、体育和娱乐用品制造业	Manufacture of Culture, Arts, Sports and Entertainment Articles	20.7		23.0	128.3	22.3	-17.2
石油加工、炼焦及核燃料加工业	Petroleum Refining, Coking and Nuclear Fuel Processing	-70.0		3576.7		-80.6	
化学原料及化学制品制造业	Manufacture of Raw Chemical Materials and Chemical Products	10.6	13.8	1.1	-41.9	27.7	23.4
医药制造业	Manufacture of Medicines	24.7	249.3	84.6	-87.3	9.2	-9.8
化学纤维制造业	Manufacture of Chemical Fibers	203.6		214.6		144.6	997.7
橡胶和塑料制品业	Manufacture of Rubber and Plastic Products	18.5	-35.7	55.9	44.2	19.8	-35.7
非金属矿物制品业	Nonmetal Mineral Products	41.4	96.2	621.2	151.5	1.5	196.5
黑色金属冶炼及压延加工业	Smelting and Pressing of Ferrous Metals	13.7	-100.0	0.8	-100.0	14.5	-21.4
有色金属冶炼及压延加工业	Smelting and Pressing of Nonferrous Metals	-5.0		11.4	-100.0	-5.2	-28.3
金属制品业	Metal Products	14.2	9286.9	29.4	58.3	11.1	16.0
通用设备制造业	Manufacture of General-purpose Machinery	40.7	31253.5	36.3	-99.1	44.1	-23.6
专用设备制造业	Manufacture of Special-purpose Machinery	29.5	194.3	32.0	-62.0	29.6	-4.2
汽车制造业	Manufacture of Automobile	34.1	1044.0	58.0	-93.5	31.3	30.3

5-6 续表 1 continued 1

单位：% (%)

项目	Item	本年资金来源合计 Sources of Funds	国家预算内资金 State Budget	国内贷款 Domestic Loans	利用外资 Foreign Inves-tment	自筹资金 Self-raising Fund	其他资金 Others
铁路、船舶、航空航天和其他运输设备制造业	Manufacture of Railway, Slip, Aeronautics and Other Transport Equipment	20.7	-88.0	188.6		1.4	54.2
电气机械及器材制造业	Manufacture of Electrical Machinery and Equipment	23.3	-41.0	114.4	-73.5	17.5	13.5
计算机、通信和其他电子设备制造业	Manufacture of Computers, Communication Equipment and Other Electronic Equipment	10.7	30.4	48.2	-53.2	1.7	40.1
仪器仪表制造业	Manufacture of Instruments and Meters	17.2	-79.1	106.4	298.6	11.7	47.4
其他制造业	Other Manufactures	117.4	249386.7	84.8		103.9	252.4
废弃资源综合利用业	Comprehensive Utilization of Waste	18.0		40.8		16.1	-26.6
金属制品、机械和设备修理业	Manufacture of Metal Products, Machinery and Equipment Maintenance	1.6		-87.8	-100.0	22.3	-100.0
电力、热力、燃气及水生产和供应业	**Production and Supply of Electric Power, Heat Power, Gas and Water**	**18.5**	**16.9**	**37.4**	**-57.2**	**7.7**	**24.1**
电力、热力生产和供应业	Production and Supply of Electric Power and Heat Power	21.4	39.7	39.8	-26.2	6.8	88.3
燃气生产和供应业	Production and Supply of Gas	20.8	50.5	27.4	-67.8	22.2	-73.5
水的生产和供应业	Production and Supply of Water	7.3	8.3	17.5		6.9	-3.1
建筑业	**Construction**	**0.5**		**108.1**		**-57.7**	**143.8**
房屋建筑业	Housing Construction	74.8		-100.0		-39.9	630.0
土木工程建筑业	Civil Engineering Construction	-2.3		125.8		-58.7	67.8
建筑安装业	Construction and Installation						
建筑装饰和其他建筑业	Architectural Decoration and Other Construction	-58.2				-63.1	
批发和零售业	**Wholesale and Retail Trades**	**-20.9**	**22.8**	**-59.6**	**51.9**	**-16.9**	**-31.3**
批发业	Wholesale	-16.1	-61.4	-51.8	2200.0	-6.5	-43.8
零售业	Retail Trade	-24.5	1593.7	-67.0	42.3	-24.0	-26.9
交通运输、仓储和邮政业	**Transport, Storage and Postal Services**	**-6.3**	**-7.9**	**-4.1**	**-80.9**	**-5.7**	**-9.7**
铁路运输业	Railway Transport	29.5	19.1	22.1		69.8	156.3
道路运输业	Road Transport	-14.7	-17.3	-9.6		-20.3	-25.0
水上运输业	Waterway Transport	-5.1	7.8	23.1	-100.0	-4.0	-68.6
航空运输业	Air Transport	-14.4	-48.5	-14.6	-100.0	-0.4	86.9
管道运输业	Pipeline Transport	-3.6	-34.4	508.4	-100.0	10.6	-100.0
多式联运和运输代理业	Multimodal Transportation and Transport Agency Industry	-14.8	46.2	-78.9	-100.0	-30.9	1374.9
装卸搬运和仓储业	Handling, handling and storage	-14.9	19.9	-29.8	-84.9	-12.7	-34.1
邮政业	Postal Services	-1.2				2.8	-39.3
住宿和餐饮业	**Hotels and Catering Services**	**-16.3**	**-90.7**	**-57.2**	**34.6**	**-4.1**	**-25.8**
住宿业	Hotels	-19.8	-92.0	-63.5	34.6	-7.5	-24.2
餐饮业	Catering Services	36.6		192.1		38.5	-54.4
信息传输、软件和信息技术服务业	**Information Transmission, Software and Information Technology Services**	**-0.8**	**0.4**	**119.4**	**-100.0**	**-3.0**	**-23.7**
电信、广播电视和卫星传输服务	Telecommunications, Broadcasting Television and Satellite Transmission Services	3.0	-45.0	-8.7		5.9	-89.5
互联网和相关服务	Internet and Related Services	16.1	-39.1	144.0	-100.0	20.3	-62.9
软件和信息技术服务业	Software and Information Technology Services	-14.3	58.2	148.5		-25.9	8.8
金融业	**Finance**	**-28.9**	**-100.0**	**-62.7**	**-100.0**	**-24.4**	**262.2**
货币金融服务	Monetary and Financial Services	-45.5				-45.6	262.2

5-6 续表 2 continued 2

单位：% (%)

项　目	Item	本年资金来源合计 Sources of Funds	国家预算内资金 State Budget	国内贷款 Domestic loans	利用外资 Foreign Inives-tment	自筹资金 Self-raising Fund	其他资金 Others
资本市场服务	Capital Market Services	-5.2			-100.0	-4.3	
保险业	Insurance	-7.2				-7.2	
其他金融活动	Other Financial Activities	27.6	-100.0	-62.7		1162.3	
房地产业	**Real Estate**	**2.5**	**41.4**	**-2.5**	**34.6**	**4.1**	**2.1**
房地产业	Real Estate	2.5	41.4	-2.5	34.6	4.1	2.1
租赁和商务服务业	**Leasing and Business Services**	**7.3**	**38.0**	**28.8**	**212.6**		**0.2**
租赁业	Leasing	553.1		16555.2	-95.8	296.9	464.4
商务服务业	Business Services	-0.1	38.0	4.7	249.4	-4.5	-14.4
科学研究、技术服务业	**Scientific Research, Technological Services**	**-5.9**	**18.8**	**18.7**	**-100.0**	**2.2**	**-70.6**
研究与试验发展	Research and Experimental Development	-15.3	9.0	-49.2	-100.0	-16.7	-75.2
专业技术服务业	Professional Technical Services	-19.9	7.7	-49.9	-100.0	14.5	-64.1
科技推广和应用服务业	Science and Technology Popularization and Application Services	68.7	635.7	1681.9	-100.0	20.3	-80.9
水利、环境和公共设施管理业	**Management of Water Conservancy, Environment and Public Facilities**	**0.8**	**10.4**	**8.4**	**-54.6**	**-22.7**	**-23.2**
水利管理业	Management of Water Conservancy	2.5	2.9	252.2		-13.3	-35.7
生态保护和环境治理业	Ecological Protection and Environmental Treatment	-19.1	-12.0	-26.8	-96.7	-39.0	-14.4
公共设施管理业	Management of Public Facilities	1.9	12.2	-10.0	-12.8	-22.6	-21.8
土地管理业	Land Management	-36.1	-31.3			-39.6	-63.3
居民服务、修理和其他服务业	**Households'service,Repair and Other Services**	**5.2**	**201.2**	**0.8**	**-62.2**	**-12.6**	**31.4**
居民服务业	Services to Households	7.1	174.9	-0.6	-62.2	-6.9	-11.3
机动车、电子产品和日用产品修理业	Motor Vehicle, Electronic Products and Consumer Products repair	19.4				10.2	
其他服务业	Other Services	-11.4	385.9			-47.0	687.6
教育	**Education**	**-0.2**	**9.7**	**1.4**		**-5.6**	**-46.3**
教育	Education	-0.2	9.7	1.4		-5.6	-46.3
卫生和社会工作	**Health and Social Work**	**-4.5**	**-11.3**	**-9.7**	**-20.8**	**19.1**	**1.1**
卫生	Health	-4.0	-11.6	-2.4	-20.8	21.5	9.2
社会工作	Social Work	-13.1	-0.8	-64.3		1.0	-68.7
文化、体育和娱乐业	**Culture, Sports and Recreation**	**12.3**	**6.1**	**-47.2**	**197.3**	**32.1**	**-7.3**
新闻出版业	Publication	35.8	284.4	285.5		-22.2	-100.0
广播、电视、电影和影视录音制作业	Production of Radio, Television, Film and Video Recording	-59.9	-43.3	-100.0		-31.3	-100.0
文化艺术业	Culture and Arts	6.6	6.4	-69.7		41.4	-51.3
体育	Sports	13.6	1.4	33.3		-10.8	3.9
娱乐业	Recreation	21.9	27.3	-57.0	-100.0	41.1	21.4
公共管理、社会保障和社会组织	**Public Administration, Social Security and Social Organizations**	**4.5**	**8.6**	**1943.8**		**-20.8**	**-0.2**
中国共产党机关	Organs of Communist Party of China	-46.3	-32.1			-100.0	
国家机构	Government Agencies	3.4	9.7	1943.8		-34.7	1.7
人民政协、民主党派	Chinese Peoples Political Consultative Conference, Democratic Parties						
社会保障	Social Security						
群众社团、社会团体和其他成员组织	Mass Organizations, Social Organizations and Other Member Organizations	16.6	-87.8			90.4	10.6
基层群众自治组织	Self-governing Mass Organizations at the Grass-roots Level	25.8	-80.4			92.2	-76.8

5-7 各市按项目和房地产开发分固定资产投资增长速度

Growth Rate of Investment in Fixed Assets By Project and Real Estate Development and by City

单位：% (%)

市别	City	2022 全部投资 Total	2022 项目投资 Project	2022 房地产开发 Real Estate Development	2023 全部投资 Total	2023 项目投资 Project	2023 房地产开发 Real Estate Development
全　省	**Provincial Total**	**-2.6**	**4.7**	**-13.6**	**2.5**	**9.0**	**-9.3**
广　州	Guangzhou	-2.1	0.3	-3.6	3.6	12.3	-5.3
深　圳	Shenzhen	8.4	5.5	15.6	11.0	11.2	9.8
珠　海	Zhuhai	-8.8	21.5	-34.8	-13.1	-1.0	-32.6
汕　头	Shantou	-14.5	-11.3	-22.0	9.2	18.4	-15.8
佛　山	Foshan	-3.6	11.8	-16.5	-9.9	12.4	-34.7
韶　关	Shaoguan	-19.7	-7.1	-48.5	2.9	5.0	-4.2
河　源	Heyuan	-29.3	-20.8	-49.1	11.0	15.6	-5.5
梅　州	Meizhou	-11.0	15.4	-49.8	7.6	13.8	-13.6
惠　州	Huizhou	8.8	30.2	-17.9	5.3	10.4	-5.7
汕　尾	Shanwei	-6.2	8.1	-49.4	-3.3	-2.3	-9.7
东　莞	Dongguan	0.8	6.0	-7.9	2.7	4.1	0.9
中　山	Zhongshan	-0.7	14.7	-23.4	1.8	14.4	-25.9
江　门	Jiangmen	-0.8	11.4	-23.4	0.1	9.6	-25.9
阳　江	Yangjiang	-32.8	-33.9	-26.2	29.5	35.0	0.1
湛　江	Zhanjiang	-9.6	2.0	-31.1	3.2	4.9	-1.8
茂　名	Maoming	6.3	24.5	-19.7	5.3	9.5	-4.2
肇　庆	Zhaoqing	-14.9	-3.9	-41.7	-4.6	2.8	-34.2
清　远	Qingyuan	-6.9	2.5	-23.6	-3.1	-0.6	-8.8
潮　州	Chaozhou	0.4	4.1	-11.6	-12.7	-4.8	-43.5
揭　阳	Jieyang	-23.5	-16.1	-44.3	-19.1	-19.0	-19.5
云　浮	Yunfu	5.3	24.7	-32.3	9.2	17.4	-20.1
按经济区域分	By Region						
珠三角	Pearl River Delta	0.4	7.9	-9.0	2.4	9.7	-9.1
粤　东	Eastern Region	-13.4	-6.2	-32.8	-3.2	0.9	-18.8
粤　西	Western Region	-10.6	-3.2	-26.4	8.6	12.6	-2.6
粤　北	Northern Region	-14.4	-1.6	-39.6	4.4	9.0	-9.6

5-8 各市按登记注册类型分固定资产投资增长速度（2023年）

Growth Rate of Investment in Fixed Assets by Status of Registration and City (2023)

单位：%　　　　(%)

市　别	City	全部投资 Total	内资 Domestic	港、澳、台商 Funds from Hong Kong Macao and Taiwan	外商 Foreign Funded
全　省	**Provincial Total**	**2.5**	**3.2**	**-3.8**	**-8.0**
广　州	Guangzhou	3.6	6.0	1.0	-24.9
深　圳	Shenzhen	11.0	13.9	-18.3	-9.5
珠　海	Zhuhai	-13.1	-12.1	-22.7	-21.5
汕　头	Shantou	9.2	9.4	-26.5	42.2
佛　山	Foshan	-9.9	-11.4	5.6	7.3
韶　关	Shaoguan	2.9	3.1	17.9	-18.9
河　源	Heyuan	11.0	11.6	7.0	-24.0
梅　州	Meizhou	7.6	7.9	-30.8	84.0
惠　州	Huizhou	5.3	5.3	-10.9	19.5
汕　尾	Shanwei	-3.3	-3.7	37.7	-29.2
东　莞	Dongguan	2.7	3.5	-0.9	-13.8
中　山	Zhongshan	1.8	2.7	16.3	-30.4
江　门	Jiangmen	0.1	1.8	-14.9	-14.4
阳　江	Yangjiang	29.5	28.9	47.2	43.2
湛　江	Zhanjiang	3.2	-7.8	74.4	69.4
茂　名	Maoming	5.3	8.2	47.3	-56.2
肇　庆	Zhaoqing	-4.6	-5.9	23.6	-9.5
清　远	Qingyuan	-3.1	-2.6	-1.1	-28.0
潮　州	Chaozhou	-12.7	-12.7	26.4	-62.9
揭　阳	Jieyang	-19.1	-18.6	-42.5	-47.2
云　浮	Yunfu	9.2	10.0	-7.1	29.0
按经济区域分	By Region				
珠 三 角	Pearl River Delta	2.4	3.7	-7.2	-11.9
粤　东	Eastern Region	-3.2	-3.2	-8.9	-1.5
粤　西	Western Region	8.6	4.9	68.6	32.6
粤　北	Northern Region	4.4	5.0	-0.7	-15.1

注：内资含个体经济，下表同。
Note: Domestic investment include individuals and the same applies to the following table.

5-9 各市按控股类型分固定资产投资增长速度（2023年）

Growth Rate of Investment in Fixed Assets Divided by Holding Type and by City

单位：% (%)

市别	City	全部投资 Total	#国有控股 State Holding	集体控股 Collective Holding	私人控股 Private Holding
全省	**Provincial Total**	**2.5**	**12.2**	**-1.9**	**5.0**
广州	Guangzhou	3.6	21.1	-26.2	2.9
深圳	Shenzhen	11.0	18.3	-3.5	15.9
珠海	Zhuhai	-13.1	-0.9	-36.0	-4.3
汕头	Shantou	9.2	8.8	27.6	29.1
佛山	Foshan	-9.9	10.9	3.6	-12.7
韶关	Shaoguan	2.9	-0.9	137.9	2.7
河源	Heyuan	11.0	9.8	-61.8	23.3
梅州	Meizhou	7.6	14.7	-26.9	6.2
惠州	Huizhou	5.3	21.6	104.8	5.1
汕尾	Shanwei	-3.3	-6.2	48.6	2.1
东莞	Dongguan	2.7	9.4	49.3	6.9
中山	Zhongshan	1.8	0.4	41.8	17.5
江门	Jiangmen	0.1	9.6	20.9	4.0
阳江	Yangjiang	29.5	19.0	-75.4	48.4
湛江	Zhanjiang	3.2	-12.2	2.7	16.5
茂名	Maoming	5.3	17.9	0.4	4.2
肇庆	Zhaoqing	-4.6	19.6	-78.1	-9.8
清远	Qingyuan	-3.1	7.6	-46.6	10.9
潮州	Chaozhou	-12.7	-10.6	-28.3	-11.6
揭阳	Jieyang	-19.1	-37.3	76.3	28.0
云浮	Yunfu	9.2	31.7	53.3	-8.3
按经济区域分	By Region				
珠三角	Pearl River Delta	2.4	16.1	-6.4	2.7
粤东	Eastern Region	-3.2	-11.2	36.3	16.0
粤西	Western Region	8.6	3.3	-3.6	17.5
粤北	Northern Region	4.4	11.0	-8.1	8.5

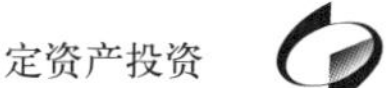

5-10 各市按行业分固定资产投资增长速度（2023年）

Growth Rate of Investment in Fixed Assets by Sector and by City (2023)

单位：% (%)

市别	City	全部投资 Total	农、林、牧、渔业 Agriculture, Forestry, Animal Husbandry and Fishery	采矿业 Mining	制造业 Manufacturing	电力、热力、燃气及水的生产和供应业 Production and Supply of Electricity, Gas and Water	建筑业 Construction	批发和零售业 Wholesale and Retail Trades
全　省	**Provincial Total**	**2.5**	**0.2**	**64.5**	**20.7**	**21.8**	**24.0**	**-7.0**
广　州	Guangzhou	3.6	-1.0	6701.2	22.9	12.0	-36.0	116.6
深　圳	Shenzhen	11.0	26000.0	6.9	53.8	18.5	380.2	-64.9
珠　海	Zhuhai	-13.1	-66.0	-58.9	4.8	-2.7		-2.0
汕　头	Shantou	9.2	14.1	809.3	64.4	-14.2	-67.7	-24.2
佛　山	Foshan	-9.9	-38.9		28.5	69.7		70.9
韶　关	Shaoguan	2.9	17.1	69.2	4.8	37.4		23.7
河　源	Heyuan	11.0	43.5	-2.6	17.8	112.2		399.2
梅　州	Meizhou	7.6	-36.3	1236.5	12.6	52.4		94.1
惠　州	Huizhou	5.3	-41.7	-30.1	5.1	63.7		146.3
汕　尾	Shanwei	-3.3	-18.5		-1.7	-9.7	82.8	682.5
东　莞	Dongguan	2.7	331.0		7.6	-1.4		-33.9
中　山	Zhongshan	1.8	-25.7		49.6	26.9	-18.5	
江　门	Jiangmen	0.1	66.9	162.2	16.6	9.7		171.8
阳　江	Yangjiang	29.5	-37.6	46885.4	32.3	60.1	253.1	81.1
湛　江	Zhanjiang	3.2	49.5	30.2	76.7	-1.9		21.1
茂　名	Maoming	5.3	-20.9	325.0	-8.2	78.9		11.5
肇　庆	Zhaoqing	-4.6	-31.6	292.4	18.5	12.6		-35.4
清　远	Qingyuan	-3.1	-44.2	-5.6	-4.8	44.0		-82.0
潮　州	Chaozhou	-12.7	-38.6	697.0	26.9	3.8		-45.7
揭　阳	Jieyang	-19.1	125.0	498.5	-60.5	-21.0	515.0	51.1
云　浮	Yunfu	9.2	27.5	270.0	4.6	13.7		16.5
按经济区域分	By Region							
珠三角	Pearl River Delta	2.4	-12.7	21.5	23.0	23.9	-21.0	-13.0
粤　东	Eastern Region	-3.2	1.2	1292.7	2.7	-12.2	164.1	1.0
粤　西	Western Region	8.6	10.6	65.3	38.8	32.5	259.4	15.6
粤　北	Northern Region	4.4	8.6	147.1	7.3	46.6		56.2

5-10 续表 1 continued 1

单位：% (%)

市别	City	交通运输、仓储和邮政业 Transport, Storage and Post	住宿和餐饮业 Hotels and Catering Services	信息传输、软件和信息技术服务业 Information Transmission, Software and Information Technology Services	金融业 Financial Intermediation	房地产业 Real Estate	租赁和商务服务业 Leasing and Business Services	科学研究和技术服务业 Scientific Research, Technical Service
全省	**Provincial Total**	**-2.7**	**-19.8**	**-2.4**	**-21.1**	**-9.6**	**19.9**	**-3.4**
广州	Guangzhou	9.3	-65.6	29.3	-3.6	-8.8	62.3	-36.2
深圳	Shenzhen	-25.1	-55.9	-8.8	-28.8	9.9	19.5	96.3
珠海	Zhuhai	-7.9	-23.1	-14.4		-29.8	0.6	-19.3
汕头	Shantou	51.6	60.6	-25.2	-75.4	-15.6	-10.0	-56.4
佛山	Foshan	-25.2	-44.3	-34.1	9.2	-34.7	3.3	-50.7
韶关	Shaoguan	9.6	23.9	66.6	-48.3	-5.6	-53.8	13.0
河源	Heyuan	-23.7	108.1	-39.7		-4.4	55.7	172.0
梅州	Meizhou	11.1		-14.0	-33.9	-14.1	141.3	140.9
惠州	Huizhou	11.9	82.8	-29.2	-99.4	-4.1	-17.5	-0.2
汕尾	Shanwei	-14.0	-27.5	-24.1		-8.7	93.6	-57.7
东莞	Dongguan	24.7	-71.5	50.4	-83.3	-1.0	-33.7	-19.1
中山	Zhongshan	-18.3	432.1	7.9	7.0	-26.3	2.4	110.2
江门	Jiangmen	-14.2	13.3	-9.7	64.6	-26.4	8.6	43.0
阳江	Yangjiang	-7.3	20.4	-6.1		-5.8	70.7	576.1
湛江	Zhanjiang	-13.1	-52.6	-29.6	171.6	-2.3	43.5	-36.4
茂名	Maoming	3.5	51.5	20.6	-33.0	-4.8	9.5	67.2
肇庆	Zhaoqing	40.7	-18.9	1.7	-97.6	-37.9	-42.1	-42.9
清远	Qingyuan	39.6	69.2	-32.4		-8.0	-15.4	-89.2
潮州	Chaozhou	11.8	114.6	1.1		-45.5	-42.7	-58.1
揭阳	Jieyang	10.6	73.9	33.6		-7.6	19.5	313.0
云浮	Yunfu	32.4	-29.4	-24.6		-20.5	-18.1	-95.5
按经济区域分	By Region							
珠三角	Pearl River Delta	-5.9	-39.9	2.4	-21.2	-9.6	24.1	4.6
粤东	Eastern Region	18.9	14.7	-13.6	-75.4	-16.2	-8.2	-54.4
粤西	Western Region	-5.1	26.8	-10.7	106.8	-3.7	27.8	56.1
粤北	Northern Region	9.3	35.5	-21.7	-36.1	-9.6	4.7	-60.3

5-10 续表 2 continued 2

单位：% (%)

市 别	City	水利、环境和公共设施管理业 Management of Water Conservancy, Environment and Public Facilities	居民、修理服务和其他服务业 Household's Services, Repair and Other Services	教育 Education	卫生和社会工作 Health and Social Service	文化、体育和娱乐业 Culture, Sports and Entertainment	公共管理、社会保障和社会组织 Public Management, Social Security and Social Organization
全 省	**Provincial Total**	**0.1**	**1.5**	**-0.3**	**-6.2**	**16.3**	**5.8**
广 州	Guangzhou	15.2	-46.9	-14.5	14.9	34.1	53.3
深 圳	Shenzhen	16.8	111.9	17.0	-10.4	29.4	27.1
珠 海	Zhuhai	-10.1	-49.1	30.7	-10.9	3.0	-21.0
汕 头	Shantou	-8.0	-32.0	18.2	-4.3	-5.5	13.2
佛 山	Foshan	5.4	187.7	-23.3	23.3	-35.4	17.1
韶 关	Shaoguan	-17.1	-52.8	25.1	-17.6	-2.3	-43.3
河 源	Heyuan	0.5	141.0	-1.5	12.0	4.6	-46.5
梅 州	Meizhou	27.8	1922.0	-25.2	-27.8	-38.1	-54.3
惠 州	Huizhou	1.9	228.9	30.0	11.4	-75.3	-10.4
汕 尾	Shanwei	-27.0	208.8	47.2	16.3	104.7	-12.6
东 莞	Dongguan	-2.1	551.6	-10.2	7.1	9.7	-19.9
中 山	Zhongshan	3.4	70.5	-29.3	11.3	37.2	89.8
江 门	Jiangmen	-2.2	394.3	-5.0	-5.5	-36.1	88.0
阳 江	Yangjiang	-20.0		20.9	-22.9	35.2	88.8
湛 江	Zhanjiang	-17.7	-32.1	-34.8	-43.8	-60.2	16.3
茂 名	Maoming	-10.2	155.4	40.1	39.0	-42.3	30.1
肇 庆	Zhaoqing	-20.1	11.0	-27.9	-10.9	37.1	-49.8
清 远	Qingyuan	-14.9		48.9	-66.7	67.8	50.1
潮 州	Chaozhou	-20.7	-62.6	-43.9	-22.2	117.0	16.3
揭 阳	Jieyang	-4.1	181.2	16.4	-27.4	-8.3	1.5
云 浮	Yunfu	-29.6	-11.3	-12.4	-25.7	293.3	-24.8
按经济区域分	By Region						
珠 三 角	Pearl River Delta	5.8	18.6	-1.1	-0.4	13.5	9.7
粤 东	Eastern Region	-14.8	-24.2	10.8	-5.7	47.1	5.3
粤 西	Western Region	-14.5	-6.6	-4.4	-17.0	-48.1	23.4
粤 北	Northern Region	-8.8	163.0	5.0	-29.6	35.0	-25.6

5-11 各市按领域分固定资产投资增长速度(2023年)

Growth Rate of Investment in Fixed Assets by Sector and City(2023)

单位：% (%)

市别	City	全部投资 Total	#基础设施 Infrastructure	制造业 Manufacture	房地产开发 Real Estate Development
全省	**Provincial Total**	**2.5**	**4.2**	**20.7**	**-9.3**
广州	Guangzhou	3.6	12.2	22.9	-5.3
深圳	Shenzhen	11.0	-5.1	53.8	9.8
珠海	Zhuhai	-13.1	-8.6	4.8	-32.6
汕头	Shantou	9.2	7.3	64.4	-15.8
佛山	Foshan	-9.9	5.4	28.5	-34.7
韶关	Shaoguan	2.9	4.4	4.8	-4.2
河源	Heyuan	11.0	7.0	17.8	-5.5
梅州	Meizhou	7.6	28.9	12.6	-13.6
惠州	Huizhou	5.3	24.7	5.1	-5.7
汕尾	Shanwei	-3.3	-15.4	-1.7	-9.7
东莞	Dongguan	2.7	6.3	7.6	0.9
中山	Zhongshan	1.8	-6.0	49.6	-25.9
江门	Jiangmen	0.1	-3.7	16.6	-25.9
阳江	Yangjiang	29.5	28.7	32.3	0.1
湛江	Zhanjiang	3.2	-10.0	76.7	-1.8
茂名	Maoming	5.3	13.9	-8.2	-4.2
肇庆	Zhaoqing	-4.6	3.6	18.5	-34.2
清远	Qingyuan	-3.1	7.5	-4.8	-8.8
潮州	Chaozhou	-12.7	-6.8	26.9	-43.5
揭阳	Jieyang	-19.1	-3.0	-60.5	-19.5
云浮	Yunfu	9.2	-0.3	4.6	-20.1
按经济区域分	By Region				
珠三角	Pearl River Delta	2.4	4.5	23.0	-9.1
粤东	Eastern Region	-3.2	-3.7	2.7	-18.8
粤西	Western Region	8.6	7.2	38.8	-2.6
粤北	Northern Region	4.4	9.6	7.3	-9.6

5-12 各市财务拨贷款资金来源主要指标增长速度（2023年）
Growth Rate of Main Indicators on Sources of Funds and Loans for Investment by City (2023)

单位：% (%)

市别	City	本年资金来源合计 Sources of Funds	国家预算资金 State and Local Budget	国内贷款 Domestic Loans	利用外资 Foreign Investment	自筹资金 Self-raising Fund	其他资金 Others
全省	**Provincial Total**	**5.3**	**6.0**	**11.3**	**-26.2**	**5.3**	**1.2**
广州	Guangzhou	8.1	14.4	1.9	174.5	11.4	4.1
深圳	Shenzhen	25.5	9.6	35.6	2.7	34.9	13.6
珠海	Zhuhai	-4.0	-10.8	11.7	-6.9	-12.1	8.5
汕头	Shantou	24.4	21.1	90.5		16.9	28.3
佛山	Foshan	-8.9	44.0	-13.0	262.7	-12.2	-16.7
韶关	Shaoguan	-0.4	-16.3	16.6	2531.8	7.0	-5.8
河源	Heyuan	2.6	8.4	24.5		1.2	-6.1
梅州	Meizhou	-2.5	-0.3	75.9	19.0	-21.3	-6.8
惠州	Huizhou	-0.9	7.3	1.1	-45.5	-5.0	7.4
汕尾	Shanwei	4.2	-39.8	74.3	-80.3	11.4	-27.2
东莞	Dongguan	-9.9	7.5	-15.2	150.4	-14.8	-3.6
中山	Zhongshan	0.7	22.1	-14.0	-67.1	-2.4	6.3
江门	Jiangmen	4.2	14.4	-6.0	-67.6	5.8	0.6
阳江	Yangjiang	-0.5	-33.2	55.0	-85.2	-19.0	-4.6
湛江	Zhanjiang	-1.7	-32.5	-26.0	-56.0	21.5	17.6
茂名	Maoming	2.0	-14.4	67.1	59.9	8.5	-12.9
肇庆	Zhaoqing	-1.9	14.9	73.1	247.8	-15.7	-5.9
清远	Qingyuan	-5.8	-10.4	7.6	-9.6	-3.2	-15.7
潮州	Chaozhou	-17.9	-15.0	12.2	-100.0	-18.3	-31.6
揭阳	Jieyang	-16.8	23.8	-28.4	-41.3	-23.2	-17.6
云浮	Yunfu	-4.8	-12.0	-12.7	-24.7	12.9	-20.1
按经济区域分	By Region						
珠三角	Pearl River Delta	6.5	12.6	8.1	-7.8	5.9	3.2
粤东	Eastern Region	4.8	-0.8	49.3	-44.2	2.5	-10.0
粤西	Western Region	-0.2	-25.6	22.9	-56.7	9.4	0.7
粤北	Northern Region	-2.4	-6.0	15.8	1.6	-0.9	-11.8

5-13 各市按构成和建设性质分固定资产投资增长速度（2023年）

Growth Rate of Investment in Fixed Assets in Urban Area by Composition of Funds, Type of Construction and City (2023)

单位：% (%)

市别	City	全部投资 Total	按构成分 By Composition of Funds			按建设性质分 By Type of Construction		
			建筑安装工程 Construction and Installation	设备、工具器具购置 Purchase of Equipment and Instruments	其他费用 Others	新建 New Construction	扩建 Expansion	改建和技术改造 Reconstruction and Technological Transformation
全　省	**Provincial Total**	**2.5**	**3.9**	**10.6**	**-3.7**	**-0.1**	**24.7**	**14.5**
广　州	Guangzhou	3.6	9.8	6.1	-3.0	-0.3	28.3	40.3
深　圳	Shenzhen	11.0	9.7	34.8	5.4	10.6	23.4	5.1
珠　海	Zhuhai	-13.1	-9.0	21.7	-34.4	-15.9	21.9	-2.2
汕　头	Shantou	9.2	12.4	0.9	-2.8	8.6	4.3	19.0
佛　山	Foshan	-9.9	2.9	3.2	-40.2	-18.7	-1.0	38.1
韶　关	Shaoguan	2.9	-2.2	16.3	16.3	-1.2	94.3	8.1
河　源	Heyuan	11.0	8.3	22.6	18.3	10.4	12.1	30.3
梅　州	Meizhou	7.6	15.8	1.9	-24.3	7.2	35.5	-7.6
惠　州	Huizhou	5.3	3.9	16.7	5.1	0.7	81.0	5.1
汕　尾	Shanwei	-3.3	-4.6	-32.7	38.1	-9.1	25.3	25.9
东　莞	Dongguan	2.7	1.1	-11.8	12.0	1.9	15.1	-1.3
中　山	Zhongshan	1.8	11.5	4.9	-20.3	-3.0	38.0	12.1
江　门	Jiangmen	0.1	4.9	-10.9	-16.4	-2.7	14.3	7.0
阳　江	Yangjiang	29.5	9.8	163.9	12.3	34.0	-6.1	-4.0
湛　江	Zhanjiang	3.2	5.5	13.7	-11.1	4.7	13.0	-11.0
茂　名	Maoming	5.3	-0.6	30.2	15.1	4.2	-11.1	20.9
肇　庆	Zhaoqing	-4.6	-7.9	-13.5	37.2	-5.5	12.6	-1.5
清　远	Qingyuan	-3.1	-4.0	-1.0	-2.4	-2.4	60.0	19.4
潮　州	Chaozhou	-12.7	-16.2	13.2	-8.2	-13.5	-11.4	-7.9
揭　阳	Jieyang	-19.1	-20.5	-37.9	8.2	-23.2	35.5	32.1
云　浮	Yunfu	9.2	1.3	-0.4	45.5	16.3	-47.5	8.1
按经济区域分	By Region							
珠三角	Pearl River Delta	2.4	4.9	11.3	-5.0	-0.7	27.6	15.2
粤　东	Eastern Region	-3.2	-3.1	-19.0	9.3	-6.3	15.4	17.5
粤　西	Western Region	8.6	4.2	47.1	2.2	9.8	-1.4	0.1
粤　北	Northern Region	4.4	3.2	7.5	7.0	4.6	20.5	12.0

5-14 各市农业、能源、原材料、运输邮电业投资比重

Proportion of Investment in Capital Construction of Agriculture, Energy, Raw Materials, Transport, Post and Telecommunications

单位：% (%)

市别	City	2022（以投资总额为100）Proportion (total investment=100)				2023（以投资总额为100）Proportion (total investment=100)			
		农、林、牧、渔业 Farming, Forestry, Animal Husbandry and Fishery	能源 Energy	原材料 Raw Materials	交通运输、仓储和邮政业 Transport, Storage and Postal Services	农、林、牧、渔业 Farming, Forestry, Animal Husbandry and Fishery	能源 Energy	原材料 Raw Materials	交通运输、仓储和邮政业 Transport, Storage and Postal Services
全省	**Provincial Total**	**0.7**	**5.9**	**3.0**	**10.7**	**0.7**	**6.7**	**4.0**	**10.1**
广州	Guangzhou	0.2	2.5	1.0	13.7	0.2	2.3	1.3	14.4
深圳	Shenzhen	…	3.9	0.3	12.9		4.1	0.2	8.7
珠海	Zhuhai	0.1	2.4	1.5	5.3		3.2	2.2	5.6
汕头	Shantou	1.0	8.2	1.9	10.5	1.1	6.5	2.4	14.6
佛山	Foshan	0.1	1.4	2.1	4.8	0.1	3.3	2.6	4.0
韶关	Shaoguan	5.0	7.0	8.1	8.8	5.7	11.1	9.6	9.4
河源	Heyuan	3.8	3.7	2.5	10.5	5.0	10.0	3.0	7.2
梅州	Meizhou	2.7	9.5	2.0	18.0	1.6	16.3	4.1	18.6
惠州	Huizhou	0.5	7.1	9.2	8.5	0.3	10.7	8.8	9.0
汕尾	Shanwei	4.3	19.0	2.8	12.3	3.6	18.0	6.4	10.9
东莞	Dongguan	…	5.0	1.7	6.2		4.0	1.9	7.5
中山	Zhongshan	0.0	1.9	1.5	20.5		2.7	2.1	16.4
江门	Jiangmen	0.8	4.4	7.2	9.6	1.4	5.1	9.5	8.3
阳江	Yangjiang	0.3	34.8	3.4	20.3	0.2	43.2	6.2	14.6
湛江	Zhanjiang	1.9	19.4	8.1	10.4	2.7	21.8	15.8	8.8
茂名	Maoming	3.0	6.9	6.0	16.5	2.2	11.1	3.1	16.2
肇庆	Zhaoqing	3.2	8.2	6.7	5.5	2.3	9.7	13.8	8.1
清远	Qingyuan	1.5	9.8	7.0	5.4	0.9	15.5	6.8	7.8
潮州	Chaozhou	1.5	8.0	1.2	9.9	1.0	10.9	2.2	12.7
揭阳	Jieyang	0.8	33.1	4.5	12.0	2.2	9.8	6.6	16.4
云浮	Yunfu	2.6	10.5	16.3	5.8	3.1	10.5	28.5	7.0
按经济区域分	By Region								
珠三角	Pearl River Delta	0.3	3.7	2.4	10.5	0.3	4.4	3.0	9.6
粤东	Eastern Region	1.9	16.8	2.6	11.2	1.9	10.6	4.2	13.8
粤西	Western Region	2.0	17.9	6.6	14.3	2.0	22.9	9.5	12.5
粤北	Northern Region	3.0	8.0	6.8	9.2	3.2	12.8	9.3	9.6

5-15 各市工业投资比重

Proportion of Industrial Investment by City

单位：% (%)

市别	City	2022（以投资总额为100）Proportion (total investment=100) 合计 Total	采矿业 Mining	制造业 Manufa-cturing	电力、燃气及水的生产和供应业 Production and Supply of Electri-city,Gas and Water	2023（以投资总额为100）Proportion (total investment=100) 合计 Total	采矿业 Mining	制造业 Manufa-cturing	电力、燃气及水的生产和供应业 Production and Supply of Electri-city,Gas and Water
全省	**Provincial Total**	**27.9**	**0.8**	**21.0**	**6.2**	**33.3**	**1.3**	**24.7**	**7.4**
广州	Guangzhou	14.9	…	11.8	3.1	17.5	0.1	14.0	3.3
深圳	Shenzhen	18.3	1.7	13.2	3.4	23.6	1.6	18.3	3.6
珠海	Zhuhai	30.1	0.3	26.5	3.4	35.8	0.1	31.9	3.8
汕头	Shantou	29.6	…	19.5	10.1	37.3		29.3	7.9
佛山	Foshan	27.6	…	25.4	2.2	40.4		36.3	4.1
韶关	Shaoguan	32.9	0.7	23.2	9.0	36.9	1.2	23.6	12.1
河源	Heyuan	33.0	0.3	27.0	5.8	39.9	0.2	28.6	11.0
梅州	Meizhou	27.4	…	14.3	13.0	34.0	0.6	14.9	18.5
惠州	Huizhou	43.2	1.6	34.1	7.4	46.7	1.1	34.0	11.6
汕尾	Shanwei	39.8		19.8	19.9	43.0	4.3	20.2	18.6
东莞	Dongguan	41.0		35.0	6.1	42.5		36.7	5.8
中山	Zhongshan	27.2		24.4	2.8	39.3		35.8	3.5
江门	Jiangmen	44.2	0.8	37.5	5.9	52.3	2.1	43.7	6.5
阳江	Yangjiang	47.1	…	11.6	35.5	59.4	3.7	11.8	43.9
湛江	Zhanjiang	35.9	5.5	11.9	18.6	44.9	6.9	20.4	17.7
茂名	Maoming	20.9	0.1	12.7	8.2	25.2	0.2	11.0	13.9
肇庆	Zhaoqing	43.3	0.5	33.2	9.7	54.6	2.0	41.2	11.4
清远	Qingyuan	27.7	1.9	14.6	11.2	32.9	1.8	14.4	16.7
潮州	Chaozhou	27.6	…	17.1	10.5	37.6	0.3	24.8	12.4
揭阳	Jieyang	45.8	0.5	33.5	11.8	31.9	4.0	16.4	11.5
云浮	Yunfu	41.7	5.5	21.7	14.4	54.5	18.7	20.8	15.0
按经济区域分	By Region								
珠三角	Pearl River Delta	26.4	0.7	21.6	4.2	31.8	0.8	25.9	5.1
粤东	Eastern Region	35.7	0.1	22.6	13.0	37.7	1.9	24.0	11.8
粤西	Western Region	32.8	2.6	12.1	18.1	41.5	4.0	15.4	22.1
粤北	Northern Region	31.8	1.5	19.8	10.4	38.6	3.7	20.4	14.6

主要统计指标解释

固定资产投资额　是以货币形式表现的在一定时期内建造和购置固定资产的工作量以及与此有关的费用的总称。它是反映固定资产投资规模、结构和发展速度的综合性指标，又是观察工程进度和考核投资效果的重要依据。

固定资产投资的资金来源　根据固定资产投资的资金来源不同，分为国家预算资金、国内贷款、利用外资、自筹资金和其他资金来源。

(1) 国家预算资金　自 2011 年起，按照全国人大和国务院的要求，各级财政的所有资金，包括税收和非税收入，均必须纳入预算管理，我国已不存在预算外资金的概念，因此各级政府用于固定资产投资的财政资金均为预算资金。由于已经没有预算外资金，因此名称改为国家预算资金，包括中央预算资金和地方预算资金，旧的国家预算内资金的内容和现中央预算资金的内容基本一致。

国家预算包括一般预算、政府性基金预算、国有资本经营预算和社保基金预算。各类预算中用于固定资产投资的资金全部作为国家预算资金填报，其中一般预算中用于固定资产投资的部分包括基建投资、车购税、灾后恢复重建基金和其他财政投资。各级政府债券也应归入国家预算资金。

(2) 国内贷款　指报告期固定资产投资单位向银行及非银行金融机构借入的用于固定资产投资的各种国内借款，包括银行利用自有资金及吸收存款发放的贷款、上级主管部门拨入的国内贷款、国家专项贷款（包括煤代油贷款、劳改煤矿专项贷款等），地方财政专项资金安排的贷款、国内储备贷款、周转贷款等。

(3) 利用外资　指报告期内收到的用于固定资产建造和购置的国外资金（包括设备、材料、技术）。包括对外借款、外商直接投资、外商其他投资。不包括我国自有外汇资金。

(4) 自筹资金　指固定资产投资单位报告期内收到的，由各地区、各部门及企事业单位筹集用于固定资产投资的预算外资金，包括中央各部门、各级地方和企事业单位的自筹资金。

(5) 其他资金来源　指报告期收到的除以上各种资金之外其他用于固定资产投资的资金。包括集资、个人资金、无偿捐赠的资金及其他单位拨入的资金。

新增固定资产　指已经完成建造和购置过程，并已交付生产或使用单位的固定资产的价值。它是表示固定资产投资成果的价值指标，也是反映建设进度，计算固定资产投资效果的重要依据。

基础设施　基础设施投资指在电力、热力的生产和供应业，燃气生产和供应业，水的生产和供应业，铁路运输业，道路运输业，水上运输业，航空运输业，管道运输业，装卸搬运和运输代理业，邮政业，电信、广播电视和卫星传输服务，互联网和相关服务，水利管理业，生态保护和环境治理业和公共设施管理业等行业方面的固定资产投资。

Explanatory Notes on Main Statistical Indicators

Amount of Investment in Fixed Assets　refers to the sum in monetary terms of the volume of activities in the construction and purchase of fixed assets as well as related expenses. It is not only a comprehensive indicator of the size, proportional relations and developmental pace of investment in fixed assets, but also an important basis to follow the progress of projects and check the result of investment on.

Sources of Funds for Investment in Fixed Assets　are categorized as funds from the State budget, domestic loans, foreign investment, self-raised funds, and others, depending on the sources of investment.

(1)State Budgetary Funds Since 2011, in accordance with the requirements of the National People's Congress and the State Council, budgetary funds at all levels, including tax and non-tax revenues, must be included into budgetary management. As a result, the concept of "extra-budgetary funds" no longer exist. Therefore, all the fiscal funds used in fixed asset investment by governments at all levels are state budgetary funds. Without extra-budgetary funds, the name is changed into State Budgetary Funds. It includes central budgetary funds and local budgetary funds. The contents of the previously named "Fund from the State budget" is basically the same as the content of the central budgetary funds.

State budget includes general budget, government fund budget, state-owned capital operation budget and social insurance fund budget. Of all the budgets, the funds used in fixed asset investment are recorded as state budgetary funds. In general budget, the funds used in fixed asset investment include investment in infrastructure, vehicle purchase tax, post-disaster reconstruction fund and other fiscal investments. Government bonds at all levels shall also be included in state budgetary funds.

(2) Domestic loans refer to loans of various forms borrowed by investing units from banks and non-bank financial institutions during the reference period for the purpose of investment in fixed assets, including loans issued by banks from their self-owned funds and deposit, loans appropriated by higher authorities, special loans by government, loans arranged by local government from special funds, domestic reserve loan, and working loan.

(3) Foreign investment refers to foreign funds received during the reference period for the purpose of construction and purchase of fixed assets (including equipment, materials and technologies). It includes foreign loans, foreign direct investment and other foreign investment, but excludes self-owned foreign exchanges of China.

(4) Fundraising refers to extra-budgetary funds received and raised by enterprises and institutions at all levels during the reference period for the purpose of investment in fixed assets, including funds raised by various departments under the central government, government departments of various levels, enterprises and institutions.

(5) Other funds refer to funds received during the reference period for the purpose of investment in fixed assets which are not included in the above-mentioned sources, including mass financing, individual funds, donations and funds from other units.

Newly Increased Fixed Assets refer to the value of fixed assets which have been completed and transferred to production units or users. It is a value indicator of the achievements of investment in fixed assets as well as an important basis to evaluate the result of investment in fixed assets on.

Infrastructure Investment Infrastructure investment refers to the fixed assets investments in the industry of electric power, hot water production and supply industry, gas production and supply industry, water production and supply industry, railway transport, road transport, water transport, air transport industry, pipeline transportation, handling and transportation agent industry, postal services, telecommunications, radio, television and satellite transmission service, Internet and related services, water management industry, ecological protection and environmental governance industry and public facilities management.

六、对外经济

FOREIGN ECONOMY

六 对外经济

简要说明

一、本篇资料综合反映广东对外贸易、利用外资、对外承包工程和劳务合作以及外商投资企业工商登记等历年概况和近年发展的详细情况。

二、本篇资料由广东省统计局贸易外经统计处负责整理、编辑。

三、资料来源和统计范围：

1. 人民币对美元、日元、港元的年平均汇价资料来源于外汇管理部门，是根据当年国家外汇管理局提供的每日汇价进行加权平均计算而得出的。

2. 进出口贸易规模、结构情况资料，来源于海关总署广东分署，统计范围为在广东境内经海关报关注册登记的经营单位（包括有进出口经营权和无进出口经营权的经营单位）。进出口商品价值，出口按离岸价（FOB）、进口按到岸价（CIF）统计；进出口商品分类按海关合作理事会制定的《商品名称及编码协调制度》（HS）目录进行分类统计。

3. 利用外资规模、结构、对外直接投资和广东对外承包工程和劳务合作状况资料来源于广东省商务厅。

4. 外商投资企业注册登记情况资料来源于广东省市场监督管理局。

5. 对外开放使用口岸分布状况资料来源于广东省商务厅。

6 Foreign Economy

Brief Introduction

Ⅰ. This data in this chapter comprehensively reflects the situation of Guangdong's foreign trade, utilization of foreign capital, foreign contracted projects and labor cooperation and the industrial and commercial registration of foreign-funded enterprises over the years and the detailed development in recent years.

Ⅱ. The data in this chapter are prepared and edited by the Division of Trade and External Economic Relations Statistics of Statistics Bureau of Guangdong Province.

Ⅲ. Data sources and statistical coverage:

(1) The data on the average exchange rates of RMB yuan to US dollar, Japanese yen and Hong Kong dollar over the years come from the State Administration of Foreign Exchange. The annual average exchange rate is calculated as the weighted mean of the daily exchange rates provided by the State Administration of Foreign Exchange in current year.

(2) The data on the size and composition of Guangdong's imports and exports come from Guangdong Customs Office. The statistics cover the operating units (with or without the right to handle imports and exports) which have a declaration and register at customs within the boundary of Guangdong. The values of export commodities are calculated on an FOB basis, while the values of import commodities are calculated on a CIF basis. The Harmonized Commodity Description and Coding System (HS) stipulated by the Customs Cooperation Council is used in the classification of import and export commodities.

(3) The data on the scale and composition of the utilization of foreign capital,overseas direct invest ment and the conditions of contracted projects and labor cooperation with foreign countries or territories in Guangdong come from the Department of Commerce of Guangdong Province.

(4) The data on registration status of enterprises with foreign investment come from Guangdong Administration for Market Regulation.

(5) The data on the distribution of ports opening to the outside world come from the Department of Commerce of Guangdong Province.

6-1 对外经济主要指标

Main Indicators of Foreign Trade and Economic Cooperation

指标	Item	2019	2020	2021	2022	2023
进出口总额 (亿元)	Total Value of Imports and Exports (RMB 100 million)	71487.70	70871.12	82489.62	82793.20	83017.23
出口总额	Total Exports	43415.38	43490.21	50348.32	53070.26	54374.31
进口总额	Total Imports	28072.32	27380.90	32141.30	29722.94	28642.93
进出口总额 (亿美元)	Total Value of Imports and Exports (USD 100 million)	10366.27	10240.24	12765.91	12423.95	11799.20
出口总额	Total Exports	6294.54	6282.57	7791.13	7961.30	7729.29
#农产品	Farm Produce	98.69	93.13	105.77	172.70	186.05
机电产品	Machanical and Electrical Products	4280.64	4300.48	5397.15	5287.69	5052.81
高新技术产品	High and New-tech Products	2193.71	2173.74	2654.52	2499.70	2361.33
进口总额	Total Imports	4071.73	3957.67	4974.78	4462.65	4069.91
#农产品	Farm Produce	214.80	244.10	292.61	321.89	315.20
机电产品	Machanical and Electrical Products	2774.89	2734.06	3313.97	2885.22	2579.87
高新技术产品	High and New-tech Products	2220.18	2214.70	2749.98	2326.81	2099.00
新设外商投资企业数量 (个)	Number of Newly Established Foreign-invested Enterprises (unit)	14350	12864	16155	13365	21685
合同外资金额 (亿元)	Amount of Contracted Foreign Direct Investment (RMB 100 million)	5523.84	5032.99	4894.14	4051.57	4516.85
实际使用外资金额 (亿元)	Amount of Foreign Capital Actually Utilized (RMB 100 million)	1522.00	1620.29	1840.02	1819.02	1591.64
外商投资企业年底工商登记数 (户)	Number of Registered Enterprises with Foreign Investment at the Year-end (unit)	179268	175378	185553	189439	199057
投资总额 (亿美元)	Total Investment (USD 100 million)	19532.52	21670.90	23284.71	24141.48	23059.11
注册资本 (亿美元)	Registered Capital (USD 100 million)	8542.58	9853.35	10723.77	11363.18	16253.07
对外承包工程合同数 (份)	Number of Contracted Projects with Foreign Countries and Territories (unit)	1030	878	787	859	961
合同金额 (亿美元)	Contracted Value (USD 100 million)	255.61	187.31	183.52	197.94	177.13
完成营业额 (亿美元)	Value of Turnover Fulfilled (USD 100 million)	167.06	156.65	156.23	162.02	144.57
对外劳务人员合同工资总额 (亿美元)	Total Wages of Contract Workers (USD 100 million)	7.36	5.59	6.37	4.40	6.32
对外劳务人员实际收入总额 (亿美元)	Actual Total Income of Contract Workers (USD 100 million)	9.29	7.92	8.74	8.82	9.80
对外直接投资企业(机构)数量 (个)	Number of Companies(Institutions) Engaged in Overseas Direct Investment (unit)	932	865	1075	1230	1690
对外直接投资额 (亿美元)	Amount of Overseas Direct Investment (USD 100 million)	102.77	158.16	169.67	220.72	238.32

6–2 人民币对主要外币中间价汇率（年平均价）

Middle Exchange Rate of RMB Against Major Foreign Currencies (Period Average)

单位：人民币，元 (RMB/yuan)

年份 Year	100美元 100 US Dollars	100日元 100 Japanese Yen	100港元 100 Hong Kong Dollars	100欧元 100 Euros
1987	372.21	2.5799	47.74	
1988	372.21	2.9082	47.70	
1989	376.51	2.7360	48.28	
1990	478.32	3.3233	61.39	
1991	532.33	3.9602	68.45	
1992	551.46	4.3608	71.24	
1993	576.20	5.2020	74.41	
1994	861.87	8.4370	111.53	
1995	835.10	8.9225	107.96	
1996	831.42	7.6352	107.51	
1997	828.98	6.8600	107.09	
1998	827.91	6.3488	106.88	
1999	827.83	7.2932	106.66	
2000	827.84	7.6864	106.18	
2001	827.70	6.8075	106.08	
2002	827.70	6.6237	106.07	800.58
2003	827.70	7.1466	106.24	936.13
2004	827.68	7.6552	106.23	1029.00
2005	819.17	7.4484	105.30	1019.53
2006	797.18	6.8570	102.62	1001.90
2007	760.40	6.4632	97.46	1041.75
2008	694.51	6.7427	89.19	1022.27
2009	683.10	7.2986	88.12	952.70
2010	676.95	7.7279	87.13	897.25
2011	645.88	8.1050	82.97	900.11
2012	631.25	7.9037	81.38	810.78
2013	619.36	6.3323	79.85	822.19
2014	614.28	5.8196	79.22	816.51
2015	622.84	5.1543	80.34	691.41
2016	664.23	6.1243	85.58	734.26
2017	675.18	6.0244	86.64	763.03
2018	661.74	5.9890	84.43	780.16
2019	689.85	6.3389	88.05	772.55
2020	689.76	6.4626	88.93	787.55
2021	645.15	5.8735	83.00	762.93
2022	669.84	5.1050	85.54	704.30
2023	704.67	5.0350	90.02	764.25

6-3 进出口总额
Total Value of Imports and Exports

年份 Year	亿元人民币 RMB 100 million				亿美元 USD 100 million			
	进出口总额 Total Imports and Exports	出口 Exports	进口 Imports	差额 Balance	进出口总额 Total Imports and Exports	出口 Exports	进口 Imports	差额 Balance
1987	782.91	377.37	405.54	-28.17	210.37	101.40	108.97	-7.57
1988	1154.40	551.43	602.97	-51.54	310.19	148.17	162.02	-13.85
1989	1324.07	674.09	649.98	24.11	355.78	181.13	174.65	6.48
1990	1994.18	1057.63	936.55	121.08	418.98	222.21	196.77	25.44
1991	2774.47	1430.16	1344.31	85.85	525.21	270.73	254.48	16.25
1992	3584.97	1824.33	1760.64	63.69	657.48	334.58	322.90	11.68
1993	4507.68	2151.54	2356.14	-204.60	783.44	373.94	409.50	-35.56
1994	8354.58	4339.74	4014.84	324.90	966.63	502.11	464.52	37.59
1995	8700.58	4735.73	3964.85	770.88	1039.72	565.92	473.80	92.12
1996	9144.27	4935.21	4209.06	726.15	1099.60	593.46	506.14	87.32
1997	10789.42	6182.77	4606.65	1576.12	1301.20	745.64	555.56	190.08
1998	10745.98	6260.41	4485.56	1774.85	1297.98	756.18	541.80	214.38
1999	11620.08	6432.65	5187.43	1245.22	1404.23	776.87	627.36	149.51
2000	14087.25	7608.93	6478.31	1130.62	1700.42	918.49	781.94	136.55
2001	14614.46	7898.16	6716.30	1181.86	1765.67	954.21	811.46	142.75
2002	18307.52	9804.73	8502.79	1301.94	2211.89	1184.63	1027.27	157.36
2003	23489.82	12656.98	10832.84	1835.34	2836.21	1528.48	1307.72	220.76
2004	29566.08	15855.58	13710.49	2145.09	3572.40	1915.71	1656.69	259.02
2005	35131.76	19542.06	15589.70	3962.32	4280.86	2381.59	1899.28	482.31
2006	42126.33	24119.13	18007.20	6111.93	5273.47	3019.46	2254.00	765.46
2007	48513.28	28257.16	20256.12	7976.50	6351.46	3699.21	2652.25	1046.97
2008	47883.10	28342.66	19540.44	8802.22	6851.80	4056.64	2795.16	1261.49
2009	41747.98	24517.40	17230.58	7286.82	6112.68	3589.55	2523.13	1066.42
2010	53217.91	30718.98	22498.93	8220.05	7851.13	4531.91	3319.22	1212.69
2011	59294.17	34519.93	24774.24	9763.71	9137.45	5319.27	3818.18	1501.08
2012	62141.48	36242.46	25899.02	10343.44	9842.98	5740.51	4102.48	1638.03
2013	67806.19	39513.95	28292.23	11221.72	10918.23	6363.64	4554.59	1809.04
2014	66128.10	39685.07	26443.03	13242.04	10765.84	6460.87	4304.97	2155.90
2015	63530.65	39958.26	23572.39	16385.87	10224.96	6431.72	3793.24	2638.48
2016	63100.52	39523.08	23577.44	15945.63	9552.98	5986.02	3566.96	2419.06
2017	68168.76	42192.52	25976.24	16216.28	10066.78	6228.68	3838.10	2390.58
2018	71602.10	42706.52	28895.58	13810.95	10844.65	6465.01	4379.64	2085.37
2019	71487.70	43415.38	28072.32	15343.06	10366.27	6294.54	4071.73	2222.82
2020	70871.12	43490.21	27380.90	16109.31	10240.24	6282.57	3957.67	2324.90
2021	82489.62	50348.32	32141.30	18369.37	12765.91	7791.13	4974.78	2816.34
2022	82793.20	53070.26	29722.94	23347.31	12423.95	7961.30	4462.65	3498.65
2023	83017.23	54374.31	28642.93	25731.38	11799.20	7729.29	4069.91	3659.37

注：进出口差额负数为入超。

Note: A negative balance indicates trade deficit. That is, imports surpassing exports.

6-4 按贸易方式和经济类型分的进出口额(人民币)

Total Value of Imports and Exports by Customs Regime and Ownership Type (RMB)

单位：亿元人民币 (RMB 100 million)

项目	Item	2021		2022		2023	
		出口 Exports	进口 Imports	出口 Exports	进口 Imports	出口 Exports	进口 Imports
全省	**Provincial Total**	**50348.32**	**32141.30**	**53070.26**	**29722.94**	**54374.31**	**28642.93**
按贸易方式分	By Customs Regime						
一般贸易	Ordinary Trade	26954.48	16135.87	30600.47	14659.41	33916.28	13894.49
来料加工	Processing and Assembling with Customer's Materials	1136.83	900.18	1092.90	824.91	1012.91	753.60
补偿贸易	Compensation Trade						
进料加工	Processing and Assembling with Import Materials	13422.88	7147.74	12985.96	6634.05	11844.33	5796.19
加工设备	Processing Equipments		14.18		11.57		5.41
外资设备	Foreign-funded Equipments		29.46		26.55		10.06
保税仓库	Bonded Warehouse	5345.84	7718.28	6276.15	7401.66	6580.54	8012.38
捐赠	Donation	0.14	0.01	0.83	0.19	0.04	0.01
其他	Others	3488.15	239.24	2113.94	164.60	1020.21	170.78
按经济类型分	By Type of Ownership						
国有经济	State-owned Economy	2544.77	1708.17	2752.78	2062.09	2646.57	1949.93
集体经济	Collective-owned Economy	1061.14	77.97	1117.18	83.28	1016.77	75.91
私营经济	Private Economy	27787.95	17510.33	30771.35	15502.37	33489.26	15705.15
外商投资经济	Foreign-funded Economy	18854.71	12726.58	18350.46	11991.48	17115.94	10847.31
其他经济	Others	99.75	118.25	78.48	83.71	105.77	64.63

6-5 按贸易方式和经济类型分的进出口额(美元)

Total Value of Imports and Exports by Customs Regime and Ownership Type(USD)

单位：亿美元 (USD 100 million)

项目	Item	2021		2022		2023	
		出口 Exports	进口 Imports	出口 Exports	进口 Imports	出口 Exports	进口 Imports
全省	**Provincial Total**	**7791.13**	**4974.78**	**7961.30**	**4462.65**	**7729.29**	**4069.91**
按贸易方式分	By Customs Regime						
一般贸易	Ordinary Trade	4170.74	2496.13	4588.41	2206.52	4820.57	1975.24
来料加工	Processing and Assembling with Customer's Materials	176.02	139.42	163.70	123.80	144.00	107.19
补偿贸易	Compensation Trade						
进料加工	Processing and Assembling with Import Materials	2078.04	1106.87	1947.99	993.62	1683.40	823.17
加工设备	Processing Equipments		2.20		1.76		0.77
外资设备	Foreign-funded Equipments		4.55		4.09		1.45
保税仓库	Bonded Warehouse	829.32	1195.46	939.06	1117.02	935.10	1137.85
捐赠	Donation	0.02		0.13	0.03	0.01	…
其他	Others	536.99	36.91	322.01	21.66	146.20	26.46
按经济类型分	By Type of Ownership						
国有经济	State-owned Economy	393.75	264.38	413.46	310.02	376.30	277.17
集体经济	Collective-owned Economy	164.19	12.05	167.75	12.51	144.84	10.84
私营经济	Private Economy	4299.39	2709.97	4612.22	2327.01	4760.14	2230.44
外商投资经济	Foreign-funded Economy	2918.51	1970.19	2756.09	1800.48	2432.97	1542.27
其他经济	Others	15.29	18.20	11.78	12.64	15.03	9.20

6-6 按产品类型分的进出口额

Total Value of Imports and Exports by Product Type

项目	Item	亿元人民币 RMB 100 million			亿美元 USD 100 million		
		2021	2022	2023	2021	2022	2023
出口总额	**Total Exports**	**50348.32**	**53070.26**	**54374.31**	**7791.13**	**7961.30**	**7729.29**
#农产品	Farm Produce	683.30	1155.94	1309.05	105.77	172.70	186.05
机电产品	Machanical and Electrical Products	34872.55	35236.28	35541.49	5397.15	5287.69	5052.81
自动数据处理设备及其零部件	Automated Data Processing Equipment and their Parts	3354.69	3557.36	3554.35	519.53	533.84	505.15
电工器材	Electrical Equipment	3108.66	3692.69	3726.94	481.18	553.15	530.51
电子元件	Electrical Components	4451.76	4433.30	4761.81	689.25	663.65	676.50
汽车零配件	Automobile Parts	551.78	567.12	608.34	85.33	85.01	86.56
液晶显示板	LCD Display Panels	722.41			111.78		
液晶平板显示模组	Liquid Crystal Display Modules		753.64	715.75		113.49	101.71
计量检测分析自控仪器及器具	Automated Measurement, Detection, Analysis Equipment and their Parts	457.97	472.95	502.52	70.88	70.85	71.46
高新技术产品	High and New-tech Products	17145.23	16669.67	16626.10	2654.52	2499.70	2361.33
生物技术	Biotechnology	13.29	2.31	3.04	2.07	0.35	0.43
生命科学技术	Life Sciences Technology	386.22	452.66	370.95	59.78	68.40	52.76
光电技术	Photoelectric Technology	897.08	928.54	917.41	138.82	139.72	130.33
计算机与通信技术	Computer and Communication Technology	11826.91	11016.08	10629.87	1831.11	1652.23	1509.49
电子技术	Electronic Technology	3503.39	3592.30	3947.98	542.53	537.42	560.88
计算机集成制造技术	Computer Integrated Manufacturing Technology	325.74	330.92	401.20	50.40	49.64	56.99
材料技术	Material Technology	102.88	113.18	128.44	15.93	16.99	18.24
航空航天技术	Aerospace Technology	66.98	213.70	212.18	10.37	31.94	30.07
其他	Others	22.74	19.97	15.04	3.52	3.01	2.14
进口总额	**Total Imports**	**32141.30**	**29722.94**	**28642.93**	**4974.78**	**4462.65**	**4069.91**
#农产品	Farm Produce	1892.15	2145.08	2213.43	292.61	321.89	315.20
机电产品	Machinery and Electrical Products	21409.31	19200.99	18168.40	3315.71	2893.43	2579.87
自动数据处理设备及其零部件	Automatic Data Processing Equipment and their Parts	1388.24	1248.24	1297.60	214.96	188.01	183.78
电工器材	Electrical Equipment	989.55	828.19	711.94	153.17	124.49	101.19
电子元件	Electrical Components	12836.78	12130.75	11244.58	1987.33	1823.72	1597.88
汽车零配件	Automobile Parts	278.76	210.06	160.26	43.05	31.72	22.73
液晶显示板	LCD Display Panels	511.57			79.19		
液晶平板显示模组	Liquid Crystal Display Modules		383.10	299.76		57.90	42.64
计量检测分析自控仪器及器具	Automated Measurement, Detection, Analysis Equipment and their Parts	372.89	368.01	385.49	57.70	55.14	54.72
高新技术产品	High and New-tech Products	17763.20	15481.74	14780.67	2749.98	2326.81	2099.00
生物技术	Biotechnology	23.73	16.70	25.42	3.66	2.49	3.62
生命科学技术	Life Sciences Technology	316.29	331.37	353.70	48.95	49.68	50.29
光电技术	Photoelectric Technology	661.47	529.23	467.96	102.38	79.78	66.46
计算机与通信技术	Computer and Communication Technology	3606.76	2061.83	2038.57	558.33	309.56	288.79
电子技术	Electronic Technology	12284.52	11731.84	10917.36	1901.92	1763.56	1551.37
计算机集成制造技术	Computer Integrated Manufacturing Technology	527.55	492.84	619.88	81.60	74.05	87.48
材料技术	Material Technology	95.52	90.50	80.47	14.79	13.62	11.42
航空航天技术	Aerospace Technology	237.38	218.16	262.37	36.77	32.62	37.46
其他	Others	9.98	9.26	14.95	1.56	1.44	2.10

注：自2022年1月起，海关删除编码“液晶显示板”，新增编码“液晶平板显示模组”。

Note: Since January 2022, the customs has deleted the item "LCD Display Panel" and added the item "Liquid Crystal Display Modules".

6-7 广东同主要国家(地区)进出口额 (2023年)

Total Value of Imports and Exports with Main Countries and Regions (2023)

国别（地区）	Country (Region)	亿元人民币 RMB 100 million			亿美元 USD 100 million		
		进出口 Total	出口 Exports	进口 Imports	进出口 Total	出口 Exports	进口 Imports
合计	**Total**	**83017.23**	**54374.31**	**28642.93**	**11799.20**	**7729.29**	**4069.91**
亚洲	**Asia**	**48852.68**	**27521.16**	**21331.53**	**6942.07**	**3911.88**	**3030.19**
#中国香港	Hong Kong, China	10361.77	10131.27	1438.37	1471.11	230.50	32.74
韩国	Republic of Korea	3543.21	1182.81	2360.40	503.67	168.30	335.37
中国台湾	Taiwan, China	6417.62	983.32	5434.29	911.64	139.59	772.05
日本	Japan	4232.28	1940.96	2291.32	601.34	276.05	325.29
越南	Vietnam	3397.99	1783.78	1614.22	482.41	253.50	228.92
马来西亚	Malaysia	2919.03	1560.48	1358.55	415.27	222.22	193.06
泰国	Thailand	2143.31	1087.94	1055.37	304.97	154.78	150.19
印度	India	2061.29	1887.73	173.57	292.83	268.16	24.67
新加坡	Singapore	1677.35	1184.54	492.82	239.03	169.04	69.99
菲律宾	Philippines	1218.20	711.18	507.02	173.17	101.16	72.01
印度尼西亚	Indonesia	1529.25	915.93	613.31	217.50	130.25	87.25
阿联酋	United Arab Emirates	929.34	755.46	173.88	132.18	107.49	24.68
沙特阿拉伯	Saudi Arabia	931.70	641.56	290.14	132.34	91.25	41.09
东盟	Association of Southeast Asian Nations	13427.21	7594.81	5832.41	1909.70	1080.74	828.96
非洲	**Africa**	**2710.29**	**2117.08**	**593.21**	**386.28**	**301.87**	**84.41**
#南非	South Africa	683.72	363.45	320.27	97.45	51.83	45.62
尼日利亚	Nigeria	272.33	251.74	20.59	38.84	35.94	2.90
欧洲	**Europe**	**13376.40**	**10331.05**	**3045.35**	**1901.20**	**1468.86**	**432.34**
#德国	Germany	2189.19	1464.97	724.22	311.06	208.28	102.77
英国	United Kingdom	1542.73	1398.96	143.77	219.19	198.78	20.41
荷兰	Netherlands	1787.28	1592.07	195.21	254.11	226.51	27.60
法国	France	1093.86	727.87	365.99	155.40	103.45	51.95
意大利	Italy	905.56	703.52	202.04	128.90	100.16	28.73
俄罗斯	Russia	1430.96	1129.43	301.53	203.16	160.25	42.91
西班牙	Spain	648.81	564.40	84.41	92.31	80.28	12.03
波兰	Poland	630.61	601.15	29.46	89.66	85.48	4.18
比利时	Belgium	469.39	324.60	144.78	66.79	46.14	20.65
瑞士	Switzerland	470.00	89.85	380.14	66.49	12.78	53.71
匈牙利	Hungary	294.64	243.62	51.02	41.96	34.71	7.26
瑞典	Sweden	183.64	143.17	40.47	26.10	20.34	5.77
捷克	Czech	238.80	205.17	33.64	33.98	29.21	4.77
欧盟	European Union	9696.42	7539.36	2157.06	1378.75	1072.40	306.34
拉丁美洲	**Latin America**	**4699.21**	**3413.93**	**1285.28**	**668.04**	**485.00**	**183.05**
#墨西哥	Mexico	1463.57	1327.63	135.94	207.97	188.66	19.31
巴西	Brazil	1256.32	708.19	548.13	178.48	100.56	77.92
智利	Chile	468.48	219.26	249.22	66.86	31.16	35.69
阿根廷	Argentina	202.35	139.57	62.79	28.84	19.89	8.95
北美洲	**North America**	**10994.17**	**9578.45**	**1415.72**	**1562.76**	**1360.98**	**201.78**
#美国	United States of America	10009.79	8805.84	1203.95	1422.65	1251.18	171.47
加拿大	Canada	978.63	770.60	208.03	139.30	109.52	29.78
大洋洲及其他	**Oceania and others**	**2384.48**	**1412.64**	**971.84**	**338.85**	**200.70**	**138.15**
#澳大利亚	Australia	2000.72	1231.34	769.38	284.22	174.95	109.27
新西兰	New Zealand	238.78	131.31	107.47	33.99	18.66	15.33

注：本表数字按产终国别原则统计。
Note: The data in the table are calculated on the basis of production and consumption countries.

6-8 按商品类章分进出口商品金额（2023年）

International Trade in Goods by HS Section and Division (2023)

商品类别		Commodity (by HS Section and Division)	万元人民币 RMB10 000		万美元 USD 10 000	
			出口 Exports	进口 Imports	出口 Exports	进口 Imports
全 省		**Provincial Total**	**543743072**	**286429276**	**77292855**	**40699122**
第一类	**活动物；动物产品**	**Live Animals; Animal Products**	**1449974**	**6554091**	**206219**	**934443**
01章	活动物	Live Animals	154051	3045	21869	437
02章	肉及食用杂碎	Meat and Edible Meat Offal	365112	3787401	51958	540213
03章	鱼、甲壳动物、软体动物及其他水生无脊椎动物	Fish and Crustaceans Molluscs and Other Aquatic Invertebrates	821929	2039140	116897	290460
04章	乳品；蛋品；天然蜂蜜；其他食用动物产品	Dairy Produce; Birds' Eggs; Natural Honey; Edible Products of Animal Origin, not Elsewhere Specified or Included	79007	606816	11240	86571
05章	其他动物产品	Products of Animal Origin, not Elsewhere Specified or Included	29874	117690	4256	16762
第二类	**植物产品**	**Vegetable Products**	**1452977**	**8786566**	**206683**	**1252702**
06章	活树及其他活植物；鳞茎、根及类似品；插花及装饰用簇叶	Live Tree and Other Plants; Bulbs, Roots and the Like; Cut Flowers and Ornamental Foliage	83077	27569	11829	3888
07章	食用蔬菜、根及块茎	Edible Vegetables and Certain Roots and Tubers	416987	119995	59334	17202
08章	食用水果及坚果；甜瓜或柑桔属水果的果皮	Edible Fruit and Nuts; Peel of Citrus Fruit or Melons	375215	4222553	53278	603034
09章	咖啡、茶、马黛茶及调味香料	Coffee, Tea, Mate and Spices	131119	177613	18630	25331
10章	谷物	Cereals	469	1869891	67	266163
11章	制粉工业产品；麦芽；淀粉；菊粉；面筋	Products of The Milling Industry；Malt；Starches；Inulin；Wheat Gluten	173770	126670	24766	17993
12章	含油子仁及果实；杂项子仁及果实；工业用或药用植物；稻草、秸秆及饲料	Oil Seeds and Oleaginous Fruits; Miscellaneous Grains, Seeds and Fruit; Industrial or Medicinal Plants; Straw and Fodder	172685	2182654	24522	310591
13章	虫胶；树胶、树脂及其他植物液、汁	Lac; Gums, Resins And Other Vegetable Saps and Extracts	61325	36937	8788	5275
14章	编结用植物材料；其他植物产品	Vegetable Plaiting Materials; Vegetable Products Not Elsewhere Specified or Included	38330	22683	5469	3224
第三类	**动、植物油、脂及其分解产品；精制的食用油脂；动、植物蜡**	**Animal or Vegetable Fats and Oils and their Cleavage Products; Prepared Edible Fats; Animal or Vegetable Waxes**	**245953**	**968873**	**34956**	**137494**
15章	动、植物油、脂及其分解产品；精制的食用油脂；动、植物蜡	Animal or Vegetable Fats and Oils and Their Cleavage Products; Prepared Edible Fats; Animal or Vegetable Waxes	245953	968873	34956	137494
第四类	**食品；饮料、酒及醋；烟草、烟草及烟草代用品的制品**	**Prepared Foodstuffs; Beverages, Spirits And Vinegar;Tobacco and Manufactured Tobacco Substitutes**	**9849883**	**5594355**	**1399539**	**794692**
16章	肉、鱼、甲壳动物、软体动物及其他水生无脊椎动物的制品	Preparations of Meat, of Fish or of Crustaceans, Molluscs or other Aquatic Invertebrates	1008986	74222	143466	10559
17章	糖及糖食	Sugars and Sugar Confectionery	668653	317346	95006	44767
18章	可可及可可制品	Cocoa and Cocoa Preparations	93567	118748	13200	16771
19章	谷物、粮食粉、淀粉或乳的制品；糕饼点心	Preparations of Cereals, Flour, Starch or Milk; Pastry-Cooks' Products	643848	1624341	91478	230740

6-8 续表 1 continued 1

商品类别	Commodity (by HS Section and Division)	万元人民币 RMB10 000		万美元 USD 10 000	
		出口 Exports	进口 Imports	出口 Exports	进口 Imports
20章 蔬菜、水果、坚果或植物其他部分的制品	Preparations of Vegetables, Fruit, Nuts or Other Parts of Plants	226222	337137	32280	47981
21章 杂项食品	Miscellaneous Edible Preparations	634337	1219746	90248	173569
22章 饮料、酒及醋	Beverages, Spirits and Vinegar	875796	1103222	124312	156279
23章 食品工业的残渣及废料；配制的动物饲料	Residues and Waste from The Food Industries; Prepared Animal Fodder	220842	618910	31490	88286
24章 烟草、烟草及烟草代用品的制品	Tobacco, Tobacco and Manufactured Tobacco Substitutes	5477632	180683	778058	25740
第五类 矿产品	**Mineral Products**	**5153596**	**23504973**	**733459**	**3339163**
25章 盐；硫磺；泥土及石料；石膏料、石灰及水泥	Salt; Sulphur; Earths and Stone; Plastering Materials, Lime and Cement	789673	396058	111870	56522
26章 矿砂、矿渣及矿灰	Ores, Slag and Ash	103010	6061247	14705	862511
27章 矿物燃料、矿物油及其蒸馏产品；沥青物质；矿物蜡	Mineral Fuels, Mineral Oils and Products of Their Distillation; Bituminous Substances; Mineral Waxes	4260913	17047668	606884	2420130
第六类 化学工业及其相关工业的产品	**Products of The Chemical or Industries Allied**	**11716021**	**12330860**	**1664024**	**1755432**
28章 无机化学品；贵金属、稀土金属、放射性元素及其同位素的有机及无机化合物	Inorganic Chemicals; Organic or Inorganic Compounds of Precious Metals, of Rare-Earth Metals, of Radioactive Elements or of Isotopes	1644861	1247937	233194	178202
29章 有机化学品	Organic Chemicals	2047167	2562073	291013	364943
30章 药品	Pharmaceutical Products	940453	3019155	133793	429608
31章 肥料	Fertilizers	119032	324780	16736	46549
32章 鞣料浸膏及染料浸膏；鞣酸及其衍生物；染料、颜料及其他着色料；油漆及清漆；油灰及其他类似胶粘剂；墨水、油墨	Tanning or Dyeing Extracts; Tannins and Their Derivatives; Dyes, Pigments and Other Colouring Matter; Paints and Varnishes; Putty and Other Mastics; Inks	905991	540550	128614	76750
33章 精油及香膏；芳香料制品及化妆盥洗品	Essential Oils and Retinoid; Perfumery, Cosmetic or Toilet Preparations	1730082	1182961	245640	168452
34章 肥皂、有机表面活性剂、洗涤剂、润滑剂、人造蜡、调制蜡、光洁剂、蜡烛及类似品、塑型用膏、“牙科用蜡”及牙科用熟石膏制剂	Soap,Organic Surface-Active Agents,Washing Preparations,Lubricating Preparations, Artificial Waxes, Prepared Waxes, Polishing or Scouring Preparations, Candles and Similar Articles, Modelling Pastes, "Dental Waxes" And Dental Preparations With a Basis of Plast	943859	529109	134054	75273
35章 蛋白类物质；改性淀粉；胶；酶	Albuminoidal Substances; Modified Starches; Glues; Enzymes	607493	520673	86350	73842
36章 炸药；烟火制品；火柴；引火合金；易燃材料制品	Explosives; Pyrotechnic Products; Matches; Pyrophoric Alloys; Certain Combustible Preparations	17919	77	2548	11
37章 照相及电影用品	Photographic or Cinematographic Goods	104025	417027	14816	59228
38章 杂项化学产品	Miscellaneous Chemical Products	2655140	1986518	377268	282574
第七类 塑料及其制品；橡胶及其制品	**Plastics and Articles Thereof Rubber and Articles Thereof**	**20926189**	**10565297**	**2978541**	**1503076**
39章 塑料及其制品	Plastics and Articles Thereof	19399890	9640673	2761323	1371593
40章 橡胶及其制品	Rubber and Articles Thereof	1526299	924623	217219	131483
第八类 生皮、皮革、毛皮及其制品；鞍具及挽具；旅行用品、手提包及类似品；动物肠线(蚕胶丝除外)制品	**Raw Hides and Skins, Leather, Fur Skins and Articles Thereof; Saddlery and Harness; Travel Goods,Handbags and Similar Containers; Articles of Animal Gut (Other Than Silk-Worm Gut)**	**7890469**	**791619**	**1122524**	**112727**
41章 生皮(毛皮除外)及皮革	Raw Hides and Skins(Other Than Fur Skins) and Leather	204034	446283	28993	63519
42章 皮革制品；鞍具及挽具；旅行用品、手提包及类似容器；动物肠线制品	Articles of Leather; Saddlery and Harness;Travel Goods, Handbags and Similar Containers; Articles of Animal Gut	7667589	325749	1090867	46428

6-8 续表 2 continued 2

商品类别		Commodity (by HS Section and Division)	万元人民币 RMB10 000		万美元 USD 10 000	
			出口 Exports	进口 Imports	出口 Exports	进口 Imports
43章	毛皮、人造毛皮及其制品	Fur Skins and Artificial Fur; Manufactures Thereof	18846	19588	2665	2780
第九类	**木及木制品；木炭；软木及软木制品；稻草，秸秆、针茅或其他编结材料制品；篮筐及柳条编结品**	**Wood and Articles of Wood; Wood Charcoal; Cork and Articles of Cork; Manufactures of Straw, of Esparto or of Other Plaiting Materials; Basket Ware and Wickerwork**	**1336507**	**1249305**	**189681**	**177624**
44章	木及木制品；木炭	Wood and Articles of Wood; Wood Charcoal	1236414	1246118	175442	177173
45章	软木及软木制品	Cork and Articles of Cork	2030	1199	288	170
46章	稻草、 秸秆、 针茅或其他编结材料制品； 篮筐及柳条编结品	Manufactures of Straw, of Esparto or of Other Plaiting Materials; Basket Ware and Wickerwork	98063	1988	13952	281
第十类	**木浆及其他纤维状纤维素浆；回收(废碎)纸或纸板；纸板及其制品**	**Pulp of Wood or of Other Fibrous Cellulosic Material; Recycled Waste and Scrap of Paper or Paperboard; Paperboard and Articles Thereof**	**5893817**	**3240012**	**837869**	**461642**
47章	木浆及其他纤维状纤维素浆；回收(废碎)纸或纸板	Pulp of Wood or of Other Fibrous Cellulosic Material;Waste and Scrap of Paper or Paperboard	14766	1893060	2096	270035
48章	纸及纸板；纸浆、纸或纸板制品	Paper and Paperboard; Articles of Paper Pulp, of Paper or Paperboard	4357420	1020212	619560	145115
49章	书籍、报纸、印刷图画及其他印制品；手稿、打字稿及设计图纸	Printed Books, Newspapers, Pictures and Other Products of The Printing Industry; Manuscripts, Typescripts and Plans	1521631	326740	216214	46493
第十一类	**纺织原料及纺织制品**	**Textiles and Textile Articles**	**24937454**	**2357384**	**3548274**	**335248**
50章	蚕丝	Silk	38651	7009	5509	990
51章	羊毛、动物细毛或粗毛；马毛纱线及其机织物	Wool, Fine or Coarse Animal Hair;Horsehair Yarn and Woven Fabric	31394	55997	4507	8022
52章	棉花	Cotton	803520	613526	114445	87212
53章	其他植物纺织纤维；纸纱线及其机织物	Other Vegetable Textile Fibres; Paper Yarn and Woven Fabrics of Paper Yarn	130418	45917	18439	6504
54章	化学纤维长丝；化学纤维纺织材料制扁条及类似品	Man-Made Filaments; Man-Made Textile Materials Making Flat Strips and Similar Products	536202	331485	76306	47127
55章	化学纤维短纤	Man-Made Short Fibres	242224	89012	34442	12657
56章	絮胎、毡呢及无纺织物；特种纱线；线、绳、索、缆及其制品	Wadding, Felt and Nonwoven; Special Yarns; Twine,Cordage, Ropes and Cables and Articles Thereof	792407	160419	112765	22835
57章	地毯及纺织材料的其他铺地制品	Carpets and Other Textile Floor Coverings	233625	5314	33279	755
58章	特种机织物；簇绒织物；花边；装饰毯；装饰带；刺绣品	Special Woven Fabrics; Tufted Textile Fabrics; Lace; Tapestries; Trimmings; Embroidery	756125	48545	107675	6898
59章	浸渍、涂布、包覆或层压的纺织物；工业用纺织制品	Impregnated, Coated, Covered or Laminated Textile Fabrics; Textile Articles of a Kind Suitable for Industrial Use	890337	177940	126799	25303
60章	针织物及钩编织物	Knitted or Crocheted Fabrics	1831374	152429	260681	21693
61章	针织或钩编的服装及衣着附件	Articles of Apparel and Clothing Accessories, Knitted or Crocheted	8230521	322075	1170195	45821
62章	非针织或非钩编的服装及衣着附件	Articles of Apparel and Clothing Accessories, not Knitted or Crocheted	7882079	302895	1122299	43057
63章	其他纺织制成品；成套物品；旧衣着及旧纺织品；碎织物	Other Made Up Textile Articles; Sets; Worn Clothing And Worn Textile Articles; Rags Articles; Rags	2538578	44822	360932	6375

6-8 续表 3 continued 3

商品类别	Commodity (by HS Section and Division)	万元人民币 RMB10 000		万美元 USD 10 000	
		出口 Exports	进口 Imports	出口 Exports	进口 Imports
第十二类 鞋、帽、伞、杖、鞭及其零件；已加工的羽毛及其制品；人造花；人发制品	**Footwear, Headgear, Umbrellas, Sun Umbrellas, Walking-Sticks, Seat-Sticks,Whips, Riding-Crops and Parts Thereof; Prepared Feathers and Articles Made Therewith; Artificial Flowers; Articles of Human Hair**	**9810515**	**452546**	**1397451**	**64351**
64章 鞋靴、护腿和类似品及其零件	Footwear, Gaiters and The Like; Parts of Such Articles	7822825	412984	1114371	58734
65章 帽类及其零件	Headgear and Parts Thereof	686034	16858	97652	2411
66章 雨伞、阳伞、手杖、鞭子、马鞭及其零件	Umbrellas, Sun Umbrellas, Walking-Sticks,Seat-Sticks, Whips, Riding-Crops And Parts Thereof	215296	5153	30669	733
67章 已加工羽毛、羽绒及其制品；人造花；人发制品	Prepared Feathers and Down and Articles Made of Feathers or of Down; Artificial Flowers; Articles of Human Hair	1086361	17552	154759	2472
第十三类 石料、石膏、水泥、石棉、云母及类似材料的制品；陶瓷产品；玻璃及其制品	**Articles of Stone, Plaster, Cement,Asbestos, Mica or Similar Materials;Ceramic Products; Glass and Glassware**	**10402791**	**1632330**	**1480857**	**232119**
68章 石料、石膏、水泥、石棉、云母及类似材料的制品	Articles of Stone, Plaster, Cement,Asbestos, Mica or Similar Materials; Ceramic Products; Glass and Glassware	1637943	203968	233486	29018
69章 陶瓷产品	Ceramic Products	5236038	104460	745766	14856
70章 玻璃及其制品	Glass and Glassware	3528810	1323902	501604	188244
第十四类 天然或养殖珍珠、宝石或半宝石、贵金属、包贵金属及其制品；仿首饰；硬币	**Natural or Cultured Pearls, Precious or Semi-Precious Stones, Precious Metals,Metals Clad With Precious Metal and Stones,Precious Metals, Metals Clad With Precious Metal and Articles Thereof; Imitation Jewellery; Coin**	**11039405**	**13724838**	**1572013**	**1953095**
71章 天然或养殖珍珠、宝石或半宝石、 贵金属、包贵金属及其制品；仿首饰；硬币	Natural or Cultured Pearls, Precious or Semi-Precious Stones, Precious Metals, Metals Clad With Precious Metal and Articles Thereof; Imitation Jewellery; Coin	11039405	13724838	1572013	1953095
第十五类 贱金属及其制品	**Base Metals and Articles of Base Metal**	**34295148**	**12528186**	**4868480**	**1780562**
72章 钢铁	Iron and Steel	6669651	2075932	939026	294890
73章 钢铁制品	Articles of Iron or Steel	11639511	635588	1655764	90230
74章 铜及其制品	Copper and Articles Thereof	1127070	6032740	160513	857194
75章 镍及其制品	Nickel and Articles Thereof	64602	522206	9295	74480
76章 铝及其制品	Aluminium and Articles Thereof	4967051	2285487	706066	324828
78章 铅及其制品	Lead and Articles Thereof	28451	16517	3991	2346
79章 锌及其制品	Zinc and Articles Thereof	36852	73066	5224	10382
80章 锡及其制品	Tin and Articles Thereof	21927	85308	3071	12151
81章 其他贱金属、金属陶瓷及其制品	Other Base Metals; Cermets; Articles Thereof	765420	359939	108816	51339
82章 贱金属工具、器具、利口器、餐匙、餐叉及其零件	Tools, Implements, Cutlery, Spoons and Forks, of Base Metal; Parts Thereof of Base Metal	3644190	266982	518074	37953
83章 贱金属杂项制品	Miscellaneous Articles of Base Metal	5330423	174422	758640	24769
第十六类 机器、机械器具、电气设备及其零件；录音机及放声机、电视图像、声音的录制和重放设备及其零件、附件	**Machinery and Mechanical Appliances;Electrical Equipment; Parts Thereof; Sound Recorders and Reproducers, Television Image and Sound Recorders and Reproducers; and Parts and Accessories of Recorders and Reproducers; and Parts and Accessories of Such Artic**	**280813835**	**168316038**	**39919813**	**23899779**

6-8 续表 4 continued 4

商品类别	Commodity (by HS Section and Division)	万元人民币 RMB10 000		万美元 USD 10 000	
		出口 Exports	进口 Imports	出口 Exports	进口 Imports
84章 核反应堆、锅炉、机器、机械器具及其零件	Nuclear Reactors, Boilers, Machinery and Mechanical Appliances; Parts Thereof	79248162	26073493	11277670	3691798
85章 电机、电气设备及其零件；录音机及放声机、电视图像、声音的录制和重放设备及其零件、附件	Electrical Machinery and Equipment and Parts Thereof; Sound Recorders and Reproducers, Television Image and Sound Recorders and Reproducers, and Parts and Accessories of Such Articles	201565673	142242545	28642142	20207982
第十七类 车辆、航空器、船舶及有关运输设备	**Vehicles, Aircraft, Vessels And Associated Transport Equipment**	**18123743**	**3314014**	**2573868**	**471338**
86章 铁道及电车道机车、车辆及其零件；铁道及电车轨道固定装置及其零件、附件；各种机械(包括电动机械)交通信号设备	Railway or Tramway Locomotives, Rolling-Stock and Parts Thereof;Railway or Tramway Track Fixtures And Fittings and Parts Thereof; Mechanical(Including Electro-Mechanical) Traffic Signalling Equipment of All Kinds	994630	6532	141533	926
87章 车辆及其零件、附件，但铁道及电车道车辆除外	Vehicles Other Than Railway or Tramway Rolling-Stock, and Parts and Accessories Thereof	13029106	2256703	1851584	319694
88章 航空器、航天器及其零件	Aircraft, Spacecraft, and Parts Thereof	1626154	1011866	230254	145119
89章 船舶及浮动结构体	Ships, Boats and Floating Structures	2473853	38913	350497	5600
第十八类 光学、照相、电影、计量、检验、医疗或外科用仪器及设备、精密仪器及设备；钟表；乐器；上述物品的零件、附件	**Optical, Photographic, Cinematographic, Measuring, Checking, Precision, Medical or Surgical Instruments and Apparatus; Clocks And Watches; Musical Instruments; Parts and Accessories Thereof**	**15710049**	**8238640**	**2233457**	**1169628**
90章 光学、照相、电影、计量、检验、医疗或外科用仪器及设备、精密仪器及设备；上述物品的零件、附件	Optical, Photographic, Cinematographic, Measuring,Checking, Precision Medical or Surgical Instruments and Apparatus; Parts and Accessories Thereof	13306437	7716373	1892137	1095528
91章 钟表及其零件	Clocks and Watches and Parts Thereof	1930750	477695	274188	67778
92章 乐器及其零件、附件	Musical Instruments; Parts and Accessories of Such Articles	472862	44572	67133	6322
第十九类 杂项制品	**Miscellaneous Manufactured Articles**	**47626754**	**1314505**	**6772410**	**186819**
94章 家具；寝具、褥垫、弹簧床垫、软坐垫及类似的填充制品；未列名灯具及照明装置；发光标志、发光名牌及类似品；活动房屋	Furniture; Bedding, Mattresses, Mattress Supports,Cushions and Similar Stuffed Furnishings; Lamps and Lighting Fittings, not Elsewhere Specified or Included; Illuminated Signs, Illuminated	25482101	242091	3626336	34396
95章 玩具、游戏品、运动用品及其零件、附件	Toys, Games and Sports Requisites; Parts and Accessories Thereof	18759936	717960	2664682	102119
96章 杂项制品	Miscellaneous Manufactured Articles	3384717	354454	481392	50304
第二十类 艺术品、收藏品及古物	**Works of Art, Collectors' Pieces and Antiques**	**71899**	**102869**	**10120**	**14678**
97章 艺术品、收藏品及古物	Works of Art, Collectors' Pieces and Antiques	71899	102869	10120	14678

6-9 出口主要商品数量和金额（2023年）

Volume and Value of Main Export Commodities (2023)

商品名称		Item		数量 Volume	金额 Value	
					万元人民币 RMB 10 000	万美元 USD 10 000
肉类(包含杂碎)	(吨)	Meat Products (Including Minced Products)	(ton)	129024	366574	52165
水产品	(吨)	Aquatic Products	(ton)	447603	1633449	232311
蔬菜及食用菌	(吨)	Vegetables and Edible Fungi	(ton)	648587	455241	64806
干鲜瓜果及坚果	(吨)	Dried and Fresh Fruits and Nuts	(ton)	360655	373106	52979
茶叶	(吨)	Tea Leaves	(ton)	4613	43390	6144
粮食	(吨)	Grain	(ton)	115937	50396	7151
罐头	(吨)	Canned Products	(ton)	42041	65995	9474
酒类及饮料	(吨)	Liquor and Drinks	(ton)	1436770	877752	124600
烟草及其制品	(吨)	Tobacco and Tobacco Products	(ton)	7674	40465	5737
制盐	(吨)	Salt	(ton)	28950	4759	676
水泥及水泥熟料	(吨)	Cement and Cement Clinker	(ton)	1907395	85961	12171
钨品	(吨)	Tungsten Products	(ton)	1746	46755	6671
煤及褐煤	(吨)	Coal and Lignite	(ton)	329180	71519	10176
焦炭及半焦炭	(吨)	Coke and Semi-coke	(ton)	509378	105673	15048
成品油	(吨)	Refined Oil	(ton)	2617576	1399586	198669
氧化铝	(吨)	Aluminum Oxide	(ton)	13055	6535	920
稀土及其制品	(吨)	Rare Earths and Rare Earth Products	(ton)	4901	137958	19660
基本有机化学品		Basic Organic Chemical Products			1494401	212436
医药材及药品	(吨)	Medicinal Materials and Drugs	(ton)	140158	1788471	254323
肥料	(吨)	Fertilizer	(ton)	693266	119362	16782
合成有机染料	(吨)	Synthetic Organic Dyes	(ton)	17359	39855	5646
美容化妆品及洗护用品	(吨)	Cosmetics and Skincare Products	(ton)	408969	1603513	227615
烟花、爆竹	(吨)	Fireworks and Firecrackers	(ton)	3639	9436	1339
塑料制品	(吨)	Plastic Products	(ton)	4790864	17599616	2504822
橡胶轮胎	(吨)	Rubber Tires	(ton)	323725	587017	83557
皮革、毛皮及其制品		Leather, Furs, and their Products			1051153	149403
箱包及类似容器	(吨)	Luggage Bags and Similar Containers	(ton)	678304	7181553	1021707
木及其制品	(吨)	Wood and Wood Products	(ton)	964452	1212940	172141
植物材料编结品	(吨)	Knitted Plant Material Products	(ton)	34979	98063	13952
纸浆、纸及其制品	(吨)	Paper Pulp, Paper, and their Products	(ton)	2475929	4372043	621635
纺织原料	(吨)	Textile Raw Materials	(ton)	32668	50727	7220
纺织纱线、织物及其制品		Textile Yarn, Fabric, and their Products			8773308	1248442
服装及衣着附件		Clothing and Clothing Accessories			16565741	2356943
鞋靴	(吨)	Footwear	(ton)	667244	7011161	998865
帽类	(千个)	Hats	(1000 units)	545674	648982	92376
伞	(吨)	Umbrellas	(ton)	25979	146445	20871
花岗岩石材及其制品	(吨)	Granite Materials and Products	(ton)	133306	87763	12604
陶瓷产品	(吨)	Pottery Products	(ton)	8719323	5236038	745766
玻璃及其制品		Glass and Glassware			3633789	516558

6-9 续表 continued

商品名称	Item	数量 Volume	金额 Value 万元人民币 RMB 10 000	金额 Value 万美元 USD 10 000
珍珠、宝石及半宝石	Pearls, Precious Stones, and Semi-Precious Stones		575991	82483
贵金属或包贵金属的首饰 (吨)	Precious Metals or Jewelry with Precious Metals (ton)	594	7184917	1022786
铁合金 (吨)	Ferroalloy (ton)	311531	386204	55177
钢材 (吨)	Steel (ton)	13893823	7490107	1053131
未锻轧铜及铜材 (吨)	Unwrought Copper and Copper Materials (ton)	144610	912984	130102
未锻轧铝及铝材 (吨)	Unwrought Aluminum and Aluminum Materials (ton)	942817	2181409	310193
家具及其零件	Furniture and Furniture Parts		11677214	1661904
玩具	Toys		11172029	1587003
体育用品及设备	Sports Equipment and Devices		2729867	388945
笔及其零件	Pens and Pen Parts		286460	40679
机械基础件	Basic Mechanical Parts		2622454	373134
手用或机用工具 (吨)	Hand or Machine Tools (ton)	238940	1935538	275120
农业机械	Agricultural Machinery		256795	36727
食品加工机械 (千台)	Food Processing Machinery (1000 sets)	4747	446488	63544
包装机械 (千台)	Packaging Machinery (1000 sets)	6536	608596	86410
印刷、装订机械及其零件	Printing and Binding Machinery and their Parts		5229001	744785
通用机械设备	General Machinery		8718059	1243415
纺织机械及其零件	Textile Machinery and their Parts		289140	41139
缝制机械及其零件	Sewing Machinery and their Parts		125227	17831
机床 (千台)	Machine Tools (1000 sets)	1649	1343998	190736
自动数据处理设备及其零部件	Automatic Data Processing Equipment and their Parts		35543492	5051500
电工器材	Electrical Equipment		37269356	5305050
手机 (千台)	Mobile Phones (1000 sets)	229867	23599347	3340616
家用电器	Household Appliances		30613913	4353741
音视频设备及其零件	Audiovisual Equipment and their Parts		11843226	1682011
电子元件	Electrical Components		47618114	6764998
集装箱 (千个)	Containers (1000 units)	331	958225	136350
摩托车 (千辆)	Motorcycles (1000 units)	7775	2239552	318122
自行车 (千辆)	Bicycles (1000 units)	2596	201322	28851
摩托车及自行车的零配件	Motorcycle and Bicycle Parts		1973262	281792
汽车 (包含底盘)	Automobiles (Including Chassis)		3631756	513460
汽车零配件	Automobile Parts		6083417	865595
婴孩车及其零件 (吨)	Baby Carriages and their Parts (ton)	69186	394561	56095
船舶	Ships		2423157	343277
眼镜及其零件	Eyeglasses and their Parts		1872811	266349
液晶平板显示模组	Liquid Crystal Display Modules		7157539	1017054
计量检测分析自控仪器及器具	Automated Measurement, Detection, Analysis Devices		5025230	714595
医疗仪器及器械	Medical Equipment and Devices		3948953	561510
钟表及其零件	Clocks and their Parts		1930750	274188
灯具、照明装置及其零件	Lamps, Lighting Devices, and their Parts		11885464	1691738
游戏机及其零附件	Gaming Consoles and their Parts		1475407	209565

6-10 进口主要商品数量和金额（2023年）
Volume and Value of Main Import Commodities (2023)

商品名称	Item	数量 Volume	金额 Value 万元人民币 RMB 10 000	万美元 USD 10 000
肉类(包含杂碎) (吨)	Meat Products (Including Minced Products) (ton)	1554521	3866785	551521
#猪肉及猪杂碎 (吨)	Pork and Minced Pork Products (ton)	551629	963501	137626
水产品 (吨)	Aquatic Products (ton)	542184	2127518	303040
乳品 (吨)	Dairy Products (ton)	308865	1551769	221215
#奶粉 (吨)	Milk Powder (ton)	166697	1322173	188512
干鲜瓜果及坚果 (吨)	Dried and Fresh Fruit and Nuts (ton)	1888723	3958273	565686
粮食 (吨)	Grain (ton)	11191076	3580712	509027
#稻谷及大米 (吨)	Unmilled and Milled Rice (ton)	1084231	432973	62045
大豆 (吨)	Soybeans (ton)	3883824	1623220	230446
食用植物油 (吨)	Edible Vegetable Oils (ton)	700018	499204	70731
#棕榈油 (吨)	Palm Oil (ton)	451615	287829	40753
食糖 (吨)	Sugar (ton)	306246	133201	18641
酒类及饮料	Liquor and Drinks		1199073	169939
#葡萄酒 (千升)	Wine (1000 liters)	40274	171144	24348
制盐 (吨)	Salt (ton)	9272	3433	488
金属矿及矿砂 (吨)	Metal Ores and Other Ores (ton)	64301569	6065779	863158
#铁矿砂及其精矿 (吨)	Iron Ore and Iron Ore Concentrate (ton)	50669838	4141362	589673
煤及褐煤 (吨)	Coal and Lignite (ton)	60755574	4188743	595944
原油 (吨)	Crude Oil (ton)	10306081	4493544	637139
成品油 (吨)	Refined Oil (ton)	3430180	1284608	181540
#航空煤油 (吨)	Aviation Kerosene (ton)			
多晶硅 (吨)	Polysilicon (ton)	171	2545	368
基本有机化学品	Basic Organic Chemicals		2607650	371547
医药材及药品 (吨)	Medicinal Materials and Drugs (ton)	67945	3297752	469268
肥料 (吨)	Fertilizer (ton)	1005103	324842	46558
美容化妆品及洗护用品 (吨)	Cosmetics and Skincare Products (ton)	48777	1110231	158120
初级形状的塑料 (吨)	Plastics in their Initial Form (ton)	6265609	7075979	1007600
塑料制品	Plastic Products		2712673	385044
天然及合成橡胶(包括胶乳)(吨)	Natural and Synthetic Rubber (Including Latex) (ton)	306440	376207	53566
皮革、毛皮及其制品	Leather, Furs, and their Products	126754	546755	77864
木及其制品 (吨)	Wood and Wood Products (ton)	4870779	1167653	166003
#锯材 (吨)	Saws (ton)	3058755	830326	118116
纸浆、纸及其制品 (吨)	Paper Pulp, Paper, and their Products (ton)	7660916	2829853	403273
#纸浆 (吨)	Paper Pulp (ton)	5039712	1809640	258158
纺织原料 (吨)	Textile Raw Materials (ton)	204623	86410	12271
纺织纱线、织物及其制品	Textile Yarn, Fabric, and their Products		1644889	233941
#纺织纱线 (吨)	Textile Yarn (ton)	308748	722203	102748

6-10 续表 continued

商品名称	Item	数量 Volume	金额 Value 万元人民币 RMB 10 000	万美元 USD 10 000
服装及衣着附件	Clothing and Clothing Accessories		684875	97433
玻璃及其制品	Glass and Glassware		1337077	190113
珍珠、宝石及半宝石	Pearls, Precious Stones, Semi-Precious Stones		3422778	490660
#钻石 (千克拉)	Diamonds (1000 carats)	4991	2711698	387150
钢材 (吨)	Steel (ton)	1718697	1480275	210482
未锻轧铜及铜材 (吨)	Unwrought Copper and Copper Materials (ton)	661646	4045285	574421
未锻轧铝及铝材 (吨)	Unwrought Aluminum and Aluminum Materials (ton)	267395	543452	77247
机械基础件	Basic Mechanical Parts		788111	112053
农业机械	Agricultural Machinery		27623	3927
食品加工机械 (千台)	Food Processing Machinery (1000 sets)	47	86942	12278
包装机械 (千台)	Packaging Machinery (1000 sets)	4	73200	10413
印刷、装订机械及其零件	Printing and Binding Machinery, and their Parts		1093814	155746
#打印机、复印机及一体机 (千台)	Printers, Copiers, and All-in-one Machines (1000 sets)	1020	296902	42338
通用机械设备	General Mechanical Equipment		1345993	190789
机床 (千台)	Machine Tools (1000 units)	13	610718	86666
自动数据处理设备及其零部件	Automatic Data Processing Equipment and their Parts		12976036	1837758
#存储部件 (千台)	Storage Components (1000 sets)	61694	2822645	400507
自动数据处理设备的零件、附件 (吨)	Parts and Accessories of Automatic Data Processing Equipment (ton)	18491	4126919	586725
半导体制造设备 (千台)	Semiconductor Manufacturing Equipment (1000 units)	9	3530680	496541
#制造平板显示器用的机器及装置	Flat Panel Display Manufacturing Machinery and Equipment	1	221497	31356
电工器材	Electrical Equipment		7119352	1011916
#电气控制装置	Electrical Control Devices	9658574	3204305	455480
电线及电缆 (吨)	Electrical Wires and Cables (ton)	33939	734667	104464
音视频设备及其零件	Audiovisual Equipment and their Parts		2265019	319469
#音视频设备的零件	Audiovisual Equipment Parts		1974471	278039
电子元件	Electrical Components		112445751	15978804
#集成电路 (千个)	Integrated Circuits (1000 units)	162520505	97853625	13904579
汽车 (包含底盘)	Automobiles (Including Chassis)		763962	107905
#乘用车 (千辆)	Passenger Automobiles (1000 units)	12	726087	102505
汽车零配件	Automobile Parts		1602554	227342
飞机及其他航空器 (千架)	Aircraft and other Aviation Vehicles (1000 units)	37	705284	101373
航空器零部件	Aircraft Parts		1590546	226695
船舶	Ships		34333	4953
液晶平板显示模组 (千个)	Liquid Crystal Display Modules (1000 units)	716993	2997589	426369
计量检测分析自控仪器及器具	Automated Measurement, Detection, Analysis Equipment and Appliances		3854909	547157
医疗仪器及器械	Medical Devices and Equipment		656299	93375
钟表及其零件	Clocks and their Parts		477695	67778
#手表 (千只)	Wristwatches (1000 units)	6165	167920	23867

6-11 各市出口总额
Total Value of Exports by City

市别	City	亿元 RMB100 million					亿美元 USD100 million				
		2019	2020	2021	2022	2023	2019	2020	2021	2022	2023
全省	**Provincial Total**	**43415.38**	**43490.21**	**50348.32**	**53070.26**	**54374.31**	**6294.54**	**6282.57**	**7791.13**	**7961.30**	**7729.29**
广州	Guangzhou	5258.42	5422.86	6299.90	6147.43	6501.57	762.24	782.11	974.42	919.02	925.38
深圳	Shenzhen	16715.37	16971.57	19250.46	21816.21	24544.53	2422.14	2452.95	2980.24	3260.49	3482.67
珠海	Zhuhai	1654.57	1608.48	1883.98	1968.68	2022.10	239.89	232.43	291.51	295.98	287.32
汕头	Shantou	464.00	542.47	591.59	634.87	513.45	67.33	78.03	91.43	95.89	73.12
佛山	Foshan	3727.61	4131.10	5007.31	5590.28	4875.13	540.87	597.85	773.59	844.74	697.00
韶关	Shaoguan	75.24	71.06	92.49	91.04	87.27	10.91	10.30	14.32	13.70	12.39
河源	Heyuan	251.20	242.05	246.64	194.09	166.49	36.27	35.05	38.17	29.18	23.64
梅州	Meizhou	100.74	86.79	97.83	91.51	79.18	14.64	12.52	15.14	13.73	11.27
惠州	Huizhou	1821.63	1687.76	2130.96	2043.16	2035.37	264.61	243.88	329.86	307.24	289.48
汕尾	Shanwei	87.56	88.88	110.96	98.39	131.85	12.70	12.80	17.18	14.76	18.65
东莞	Dongguan	8658.45	8280.95	9530.68	9286.03	8459.98	1255.07	1195.22	1475.19	1397.02	1203.64
中山	Zhongshan	1928.99	1815.00	2188.54	2268.30	2211.72	280.22	262.05	338.69	342.03	314.43
江门	Jiangmen	1136.09	1125.63	1447.57	1443.36	1408.25	164.89	162.57	224.01	217.43	200.18
阳江	Yangjiang	117.12	142.59	186.84	178.52	144.65	16.98	20.59	28.92	26.98	20.56
湛江	Zhanjiang	209.38	193.03	203.08	200.40	203.66	30.37	27.93	31.42	30.14	29.00
茂名	Maoming	170.55	169.24	129.96	66.22	48.97	24.69	24.62	20.08	9.95	6.97
肇庆	Zhaoqing	271.67	299.86	271.96	273.40	275.85	39.33	43.48	42.09	41.02	39.18
清远	Qingyuan	214.54	210.06	238.62	257.09	255.04	31.10	30.32	36.93	38.65	36.29
潮州	Chaozhou	180.75	152.52	193.02	206.91	201.04	26.23	22.05	29.87	31.13	28.54
揭阳	Jieyang	308.36	181.08	163.46	125.48	131.37	44.89	26.10	25.29	18.90	18.66
云浮	Yunfu	63.15	67.25	82.47	88.88	76.85	9.15	9.72	12.76	13.32	10.92
按经济区域分	By Region										
珠三角	Pearl River Delta	41172.79	41343.22	48011.36	50836.84	52334.49	5969.27	5972.54	7429.60	7624.97	7439.27
粤东	Eastern Region	1040.68	964.94	1059.04	1065.66	977.71	151.16	138.97	163.78	160.68	138.97
粤西	Western Region	497.05	504.86	519.88	445.15	397.29	72.04	73.15	80.42	67.07	56.53
粤北	Northern Region	704.86	677.20	758.04	722.61	664.83	102.07	97.91	117.33	108.59	94.51

6-12 各市进口总额
Total Value of Imports by City

市别	City	亿元 RMB100 million					亿美元 USD100 million				
		2019	2020	2021	2022	2023	2019	2020	2021	2022	2023
全省	**Provincial Total**	**28072.32**	**27380.90**	**32141.30**	**29722.94**	**28642.93**	**4071.73**	**3957.67**	**4974.78**	**4462.65**	**4069.91**
广州	Guangzhou	4748.61	4116.54	4512.51	4755.70	4411.53	688.82	595.07	698.15	713.02	627.49
深圳	Shenzhen	13065.18	13534.41	16170.54	14742.24	14153.08	1893.55	1955.67	2503.10	2211.79	2010.31
珠海	Zhuhai	1253.45	1124.60	1431.78	1123.37	941.49	182.18	162.57	221.48	169.02	133.78
汕头	Shantou	136.53	139.19	149.91	136.09	126.40	19.84	20.05	23.19	20.57	18.00
佛山	Foshan	1100.73	929.41	1153.93	1075.20	1090.05	159.79	134.56	178.60	161.45	154.93
韶关	Shaoguan	107.09	115.71	127.89	105.93	109.79	15.55	16.71	19.79	15.90	15.62
河源	Heyuan	51.77	51.14	60.24	49.94	42.99	7.51	7.42	9.33	7.47	6.08
梅州	Meizhou	19.88	12.20	23.94	18.52	21.74	2.90	1.76	3.71	2.78	3.10
惠州	Huizhou	887.98	800.56	922.82	1047.57	1373.41	128.99	115.92	142.89	157.04	194.61
汕尾	Shanwei	80.18	80.76	91.23	63.42	74.49	11.64	11.64	14.13	9.52	10.57
东莞	Dongguan	5175.51	5022.66	5682.02	4678.89	4353.57	751.04	725.79	879.53	704.41	619.11
中山	Zhongshan	457.96	393.95	463.34	470.76	364.79	66.50	56.95	71.71	70.86	51.92
江门	Jiangmen	289.29	303.38	323.71	327.67	324.27	42.00	43.92	50.11	49.25	46.15
阳江	Yangjiang	34.65	49.29	81.74	89.66	72.00	5.03	7.11	12.65	13.52	10.22
湛江	Zhanjiang	205.38	253.16	331.80	410.86	496.96	29.80	36.78	51.38	62.03	70.62
茂名	Maoming	25.81	30.16	58.52	77.34	87.18	3.74	4.38	9.06	11.54	12.32
肇庆	Zhaoqing	132.71	113.31	133.49	112.16	96.12	19.33	16.39	20.67	16.89	13.68
清远	Qingyuan	201.79	217.04	297.83	295.75	312.16	29.31	31.43	46.11	44.48	44.44
潮州	Chaozhou	34.85	29.41	48.40	54.31	52.25	5.07	4.26	7.48	8.17	7.44
揭阳	Jieyang	16.15	13.23	24.99	37.20	98.40	2.35	1.91	3.87	5.43	13.82
云浮	Yunfu	46.82	50.82	50.67	50.37	40.27	6.78	7.38	7.83	7.51	5.71
按经济区域分	By Region										
珠三角	Pearl River Delta	27111.43	26338.82	30794.14	28333.57	27108.30	3932.20	3806.84	4766.24	4253.73	3851.97
粤东	Eastern Region	267.70	262.58	314.53	291.01	351.53	38.89	37.86	48.67	43.69	49.83
粤西	Western Region	265.85	332.61	472.05	577.87	656.14	38.58	48.27	73.10	87.09	93.16
粤北	Northern Region	427.34	446.90	560.58	520.50	526.96	62.05	64.70	86.78	78.14	74.96

6-13 各市外商投资企业出口总额

Total Value of Exports of Enterprises with Foreign Investment by City

市别	City	亿元人民币 RMB100 million					亿美元 USD100 million				
		2019	2020	2021	2022	2023	2019	2020	2021	2022	2023
全　省	**Provincial Total**	**18091.14**	**16894.23**	**18854.71**	**18350.46**	**17115.94**	**2624.36**	**2440.74**	**2918.51**	**2756.09**	**2432.97**
广　州	Guangzhou	1942.16	1622.36	1910.52	1874.07	1778.58	282.03	234.37	295.63	282.10	253.18
深　圳	Shenzhen	6296.18	6253.07	6677.36	6819.80	6639.52	912.28	904.33	1033.84	1020.15	942.73
珠　海	Zhuhai	748.34	702.53	747.33	825.77	820.45	108.53	101.57	115.69	123.76	116.78
汕　头	Shantou	70.04	54.17	55.23	53.47	54.30	10.17	7.82	8.55	8.03	7.72
佛　山	Foshan	1279.29	1228.98	1442.58	1327.92	1229.76	185.81	177.35	223.20	200.43	175.08
韶　关	Shaoguan	46.05	39.11	49.05	44.36	40.39	6.67	5.64	7.59	6.68	5.72
河　源	Heyuan	136.48	125.73	142.30	140.30	117.69	19.81	18.14	22.02	21.14	16.71
梅　州	Meizhou	28.09	24.43	26.60	25.27	22.73	4.08	3.53	4.12	3.82	3.23
惠　州	Huizhou	1491.07	1305.07	1562.47	1383.42	1301.24	216.68	188.57	241.86	208.25	185.03
汕　尾	Shanwei	79.21	65.52	88.07	73.46	67.57	11.49	9.47	13.64	11.01	9.60
东　莞	Dongguan	3991.99	3727.47	4080.36	3662.84	3123.81	578.96	537.95	631.56	551.29	444.07
中　山	Zhongshan	977.86	882.02	1009.53	1075.14	954.23	142.02	127.25	156.25	162.17	135.78
江　门	Jiangmen	579.06	533.62	667.32	651.00	601.65	84.07	77.08	103.28	98.03	85.55
阳　江	Yangjiang	10.69	12.25	20.83	17.36	14.17	1.55	1.77	3.22	2.62	2.02
湛　江	Zhanjiang	44.32	26.24	27.25	27.12	29.33	6.43	3.78	4.22	4.06	4.18
茂　名	Maoming	10.46	7.95	7.89	8.89	6.88	1.52	1.15	1.22	1.34	0.98
肇　庆	Zhaoqing	121.36	86.91	105.83	111.48	109.06	17.63	12.56	16.38	16.78	15.50
清　远	Qingyuan	143.82	128.56	148.52	161.15	136.01	20.88	18.57	22.99	24.24	19.35
潮　州	Chaozhou	15.85	10.40	10.22	9.18	8.03	2.30	1.50	1.58	1.38	1.14
揭　阳	Jieyang	40.42	25.75	25.70	21.01	25.46	5.88	3.71	3.98	3.16	3.61
云　浮	Yunfu	38.41	32.08	49.74	37.45	35.10	5.57	4.65	7.70	5.66	4.98
按经济区域分	By Region										
珠三角	Pearl River Delta	17427.30	16342.04	18203.30	17731.44	16558.30	2528.00	2361.02	2817.68	2662.96	2353.71
粤　东	Eastern Region	205.52	155.84	179.23	157.13	155.35	29.84	22.50	27.75	23.58	22.08
粤　西	Western Region	65.47	46.44	55.96	53.37	50.38	9.50	6.70	8.66	8.02	7.17
粤　北	Northern Region	392.85	349.92	416.21	408.52	351.91	57.01	50.52	64.42	61.53	50.01

6-14 各市外商投资企业进口总额

Total Value of Imports of Enterprises with Foreign Investment by City

市 别	City	亿元人民币 RMB100 million					亿美元 USD100 million				
		2019	2020	2021	2022	2023	2019	2020	2021	2022	2023
全 省	**Provincial Total**	**11877.37**	**10986.57**	**12726.58**	**11991.48**	**10847.31**	**1723.27**	**1589.37**	**1970.19**	**1800.48**	**1542.27**
广 州	Guangzhou	2277.74	1864.22	1950.82	1803.58	1538.28	330.88	269.10	301.78	271.61	218.72
深 圳	Shenzhen	4497.17	4267.82	5081.87	4618.06	4513.22	651.56	618.05	786.81	691.17	641.20
珠 海	Zhuhai	696.52	633.76	753.09	661.40	641.25	101.02	91.60	116.58	99.53	91.05
汕 头	Shantou	39.72	32.60	32.08	42.91	37.06	5.78	4.70	4.96	6.49	5.28
佛 山	Foshan	527.16	481.82	569.39	479.88	416.38	76.52	69.71	88.13	72.43	59.24
韶 关	Shaoguan	17.15	14.69	20.81	18.11	14.59	2.49	2.12	3.22	2.72	2.07
河 源	Heyuan	38.48	34.93	45.55	36.68	26.01	5.57	5.06	7.06	5.52	3.69
梅 州	Meizhou	8.55	8.63	9.84	8.77	10.36	1.24	1.24	1.52	1.32	1.47
惠 州	Huizhou	687.88	550.20	623.30	603.08	532.52	100.08	79.67	96.50	90.74	75.76
汕 尾	Shanwei	75.03	64.42	60.76	47.91	46.12	10.89	9.29	9.41	7.20	6.54
东 莞	Dongguan	2228.27	2305.81	2719.63	2796.13	2257.50	323.43	333.56	421.15	420.14	321.24
中 山	Zhongshan	357.48	303.27	351.13	342.66	247.39	51.91	43.79	54.35	51.60	35.23
江 门	Jiangmen	171.52	181.31	188.18	197.54	196.08	24.92	26.23	29.13	29.66	27.90
阳 江	Yangjiang	24.73	25.61	30.63	32.54	27.08	3.60	3.68	4.74	4.85	3.87
湛 江	Zhanjiang	47.57	64.98	118.98	127.67	184.68	6.88	9.53	18.44	19.21	26.40
茂 名	Maoming	4.62	9.74	19.70	24.71	17.83	0.67	1.41	3.04	3.67	2.54
肇 庆	Zhaoqing	57.78	48.41	44.86	43.42	45.10	8.43	6.99	6.94	6.53	6.42
清 远	Qingyuan	71.12	70.84	84.52	79.11	68.77	10.31	10.23	13.09	11.96	9.82
潮 州	Chaozhou	19.65	6.93	10.48	16.12	19.68	2.86	1.00	1.62	2.42	2.81
揭 阳	Jieyang	5.44	3.31	3.36	5.60	3.39	0.79	0.48	0.52	0.84	0.48
云 浮	Yunfu	23.79	13.29	7.59	5.61	4.02	3.45	1.92	1.17	0.85	0.57
按经济区域分	By Region										
珠 三 角	Pearl River Delta	11501.51	10636.61	12282.28	11545.75	10387.72	1668.74	1538.70	1901.38	1733.42	1476.74
粤 东	Eastern Region	139.85	107.26	106.69	112.54	106.26	20.33	15.47	16.51	16.96	15.11
粤 西	Western Region	76.92	100.32	169.31	184.92	229.59	11.15	14.63	26.23	27.73	32.81
粤 北	Northern Region	159.08	142.38	168.30	148.28	123.74	23.06	20.57	26.07	22.36	17.61

6−15 外商投资企业进出口主要指标（2023年）

Main Indicators on Imports and Exports of Enterprises with Foreign Investment(2023)

项目	Item	亿元人民币 RMB 100 million			亿美元 USD 100 million		
		进出口总额 Total	出口 Exports	进口 Imports	进出口总额 Total	出口 Exports	进口 Imports
全　省	**Provincial Total**	**27963.24**	**17115.94**	**10847.31**	**3975.24**	**2432.97**	**1542.27**
按贸易方式分	By Customs Regime						
一般贸易	Ordinary Trade	9285.96	5959.72	3326.23	1320.64	847.68	472.96
来料加工	Processing and Assembling with Customer's Materials	1137.91	670.58	467.33	161.85	95.34	66.50
进料加工	Processing and Assembling with Import Materials	13315.80	9055.53	4260.27	1891.54	1286.70	604.84
加工设备	Processing Equipments	5.10		5.10	0.73		0.73
外资设备	Foreign-funded Equipments	10.06		10.06	1.45		1.45
保税仓库	Bonded Warehouse	4136.89	1393.58	2743.32	588.94	198.08	390.85
其他	Others	20.54	10.69	9.85	2.92	1.52	1.40
按经济类型分	By Type of Ownership						
合作经营企业	Joint Ventures	166.66	139.90	26.76	23.70	19.89	3.81
合资经营企业	Cooperative Enterprises	7467.76	4415.98	3051.78	1064.34	629.51	434.84
外资(独资)企业	Enterprises with Sole Foreign Investment	20328.83	12560.06	7768.76	2887.20	1783.58	1103.62
按产品类型分	By Type of Product						
#机电产品	Machanical and Electrical Products	20727.27	13427.30	7299.96	2946.12	1908.64	1037.48
高新技术产品	High and New-tech Products	12267.55	6636.46	5631.09	1742.78	942.36	800.43
#计算机与通信技术	Computer and Communication Technology	4906.54	4281.22	625.31	696.25	607.62	88.64
电子技术	Electronic Technology	5866.35	1565.95	4300.40	834.10	222.51	611.59
按主要国家(地区)分	By Main Country (Region)						
亚洲	**Asia**	**18034.28**	**9664.10**	**8370.18**	**2562.96**	**1373.07**	**1189.89**
#中国香港	Hong Kong, China	5394.66	5314.55	80.11	765.57	754.21	11.36
中国澳门	Macao, China	45.06	42.97	2.09	6.41	6.11	0.30
中国台湾	Taiwan, China	2590.32	343.91	2246.41	368.60	48.90	319.71
日本	Japan	2251.10	984.95	1266.14	319.84	140.10	179.74
韩国	Republic of Korea	1503.40	362.59	1140.81	213.83	51.61	162.22
东盟	Association of Southeast Asian Nations	3576.99	1717.92	1859.07	508.41	244.30	264.11
中东十七国	The Seventeen Countries of the Middle East	822.91	528.54	294.37	117.35	75.39	41.96
非洲	**Africa**	**510.59**	**274.06**	**236.53**	**72.71**	**39.07**	**33.65**
欧洲	**Europe**	**4080.36**	**3019.36**	**1061.01**	**580.28**	**429.47**	**150.80**
#欧盟	European Union	3253.35	2381.04	872.31	462.71	338.76	123.95
#英国	United Kingdom	423.84	376.59	47.25	60.22	53.50	6.71
德国	Germany	879.87	547.20	332.67	125.10	77.88	47.22
法国	France	362.47	205.75	156.72	51.50	29.25	22.25
意大利	Italy	261.84	168.00	93.83	37.28	23.93	13.35
荷兰	Netherlands	667.68	605.74	61.94	94.95	86.12	8.83
芬兰	Finland	21.33	9.38	11.95	3.03	1.34	1.70
瑞士	Switzerland	121.15	35.45	85.70	17.23	5.05	12.19
俄罗斯	Russia	231.18	188.36	42.82	32.88	26.77	6.11
南美洲	**Sorth America**	**1407.46**	**976.76**	**430.70**	**200.22**	**138.90**	**61.33**
北美洲	**North America**	**3364.68**	**2856.80**	**507.89**	**478.68**	**406.31**	**72.37**
#加拿大	Canada	278.36	232.15	46.21	39.69	33.08	6.61
美国	United States of America	3086.30	2624.62	461.68	438.98	373.23	65.75
大洋洲及其他	**Oceania and Others**	**565.87**	**324.86**	**241.01**	**80.39**	**46.16**	**34.23**
#澳大利亚	Australia	458.02	284.74	173.28	65.05	40.45	24.60
新西兰	New Zealand	77.80	31.58	46.22	11.08	4.49	6.58

6-16 外商投资企业出口主要商品数量和金额（2023年）

Volume and Value of Main Export Commodities of Enterprises with Foreign Investment (2023)

商品名称	Item	数量 Volume	金额 Value 万元人民币 RMB10 000	万美元 USD 10 000
肉类(包含杂碎) (吨)	Meat Products (Including Minced Meat) (ton)	15970	47979	6818
水产品 (吨)	Aquatic Products (ton)	46780	251948	35846
蔬菜及食用菌 (吨)	Vegetables and Edible Fungi (ton)	82188	88991	12658
干鲜瓜果及坚果 (吨)	Dried and Fresh Fruits and Nuts (ton)	11631	29162	4151
茶叶 (吨)	Tea Leaves (ton)	928	4216	599
粮食 (吨)	Grain (ton)	77744	34536	4909
罐头 (吨)	Canned Products (ton)	7908	11184	1591
酒类及饮料	Liquor and Drinks		665324	94450
烟草及其制品 (吨)	Tobacco and Tobacco Products (ton)	18	1371	195
制盐 (吨)	Salt (ton)	1841	1634	232
水泥及水泥熟料 (吨)	Cement and Cement Clinker (ton)	1403885	58135	8263
钨品 (吨)	Tungsten Products (ton)	1	131	18
成品油 (吨)	Refined Oil (ton)	836520	524076	74311
氧化铝 (吨)	Alumina (ton)	50	168	24
稀土及其制品 (吨)	Rare Earths and their Products (ton)	492	36164	5133
基本有机化学品	Basic Organic Chemical Products		386919	55122
医药材及药品 (吨)	Medicinal Materials and Drugs (ton)	58264	327039	46566
肥料 (吨)	Fertilizer (ton)	100555	22961	3243
合成有机染料 (吨)	Synthetic Organic Dyes (ton)	594	4490	641
美容化妆品及洗护用品 (吨)	Cosmetics and Skincare Products (ton)	196202	538015	76466
塑料制品 (吨)	Plastic Products	1315521	3808461	541609
橡胶轮胎 (吨)	Rubber Tires (ton)	103770	180059	25660
皮革、毛皮及其制品	Leather, Furs, and their Products		343965	48884
箱包及类似容器 (吨)	Luggage Bags and Similar Containers (ton)	102015	1183716	168231
木及其制品 (吨)	Wood and Wood Products (ton)	132613	277128	39334
植物材料编结品 (吨)	Woven Plant Material Products (ton)	1300	6235	888
纸浆、纸及其制品 (吨)	Paper Pulp, Paper, and their Products (ton)	702032	1073575	152630
纺织原料 (吨)	Textile Raw Materials (ton)	2995	7357	1038
纺织纱线、织物及其制品	Textile Yarn, Fabric, and their Products		2681889	381663
服装及衣着附件	Clothing and Clothing Accessories		2597665	369172
鞋靴 (吨)	Footwear (ton)	81317	1375133	195767
帽类 (千个)	Hats (1000 units)	152400	207584	29539
伞 (吨)	Umbrellas (ton)	4267	23589	3352
花岗岩石材及其制品 (吨)	Granite Materials and Products (ton)	10443	7184	1019
陶瓷产品 (吨)	Pottery Products (ton)	456975	262552	37260
玻璃及其制品	Glass and Glassware		1074425	152533
珍珠、宝石及半宝石	Pearls, Precious Stones and Semi-precious Stones		443620	63623
贵金属或包贵金属的首饰(千克)	Precious Metals or Jeweler with Precious Metals (kg)	127994	3437458	488237

6-16 续表 continued

商品名称	Item	数量 Volume	金额 Value 万元人民币 RMB10 000	金额 Value 万美元 USD 10 000
钢材 (吨)	Steel (ton)	535403	504679	71831
未锻轧铜及铜材 (吨)	Unwrought Copper and Copper Materials (ton)	47436	306441	43638
未锻轧铝及铝材 (吨)	Unwrought Aluminum and Aluminum Materials (ton)	254223	557396	79277
家具及其零件	Furniture and their Parts		2196089	311862
玩具	Toys		2906020	411840
体育用品及设备	Sports Equipment and Devices		979530	139607
笔及其零件	Pens and Pen Parts		52015	7410
机械基础件	Basic Mechanical Parts		679838	96620
手用或机用工具 (吨)	Hand or Machine Tools (ton)	53180	385805	54836
农业机械 (千台)	Agricultural Machinery (1000 sets)	26444	111708	15972
食品加工机械 (千台)	Food Processing Machinery (1000 sets)	299	62756	8912
包装机械	Packaging Machinery		114191	16188
印刷、装订机械及其零件	Printing, Binding Machinery and their Parts		3337731	475603
通用机械设备	General Mechanical Equipment		3666877	523623
纺织机械及其零件	Textile Machinery and their Parts		90394	12814
缝制机械及其零件	Sewing Machinery and their Parts		12464	1774
机床 (千台)	Machine Tools (1000 sets)	466	142935	20285
自动数据处理设备及其零部件	Automatic Data Processing Equipment and their Parts		15729902	2238438
电工器材	Electrical Equipment		14608345	2079239
手机 (千台)	Mobile Phones (1000 sets)	47620	12213162	1724155
家用电器	Household Appliances		13515132	1922340
音视频设备及其零件	Audiovisual Equipment and their Parts		3051995	433387
电子元件	Electrical Components		18148571	2578974
集装箱 (千个)	Containers (1000 units)	211	634087	90257
摩托车 (千辆)	Motorcycles (1000 units)	1776	749234	106434
自行车 (千辆)	Bicycles (1000 units)	351	49921	7102
摩托车及自行车的零配件	Motorcycle and Bicycle Parts		644507	91887
汽车 (包含底盘)	Automobiles (Including Chassis)		2440708	345452
汽车零配件	Automobile Parts		2317199	328883
婴孩车及其零件 (吨)	Baby Carriages and their Parts (ton)	29818	185834	26354
船舶	Ships		139372	19860
眼镜及其零件	Eyeglasses and their Parts		602055	85634
液晶平板显示模组 (千个)	Liquid Crystal Display Modules (1000 units)	372546	4242515	603140
计量检测分析自控仪器及器具	Automated Measurement, Detection, Analysis Devices and Appliances		2041733	290687
医疗仪器及器械	Medical Devices and Equipment		1503953	213978
钟表及其零件	Clocks and their Parts		1189525	168898
灯具、照明装置及其零件	Lamps, Lighting Devices, and their Parts		1358463	192867
游戏机及其零附件	Gaming Consoles and their Parts		787310	112129

6-17 外商投资企业进口主要商品数量和金额（2023年）

Volume and Value of Main Import Commodities by Enterprises with Foreign Investment (2023)

商品名称	Item	数量 Volume	金额 Value 万元人民币 RMB10 000	万美元 USD 10 000
肉类(包含杂碎) (吨)	Meat Products (Including Minced Products) (ton)	41232	214798	30716
#牛肉及牛杂碎 (吨)	Beef and Minced Beef Products (ton)	26948	184519	26442
猪肉及猪杂碎 (吨)	Pork and Minced Pork Products (ton)	4374	10391	1477
水产品 (吨)	Aquatic Products (ton)	53920	159027	22744
#冻鱼 (吨)	Frozen Fish (ton)	16865	22854	3259
乳品 (吨)	Dairy Products (ton)	151250	998780	142341
#奶粉 (吨)	Milk Powder (ton)	69060	893112	127269
干鲜瓜果及坚果 (吨)	Dried and Fresh Fruit and Nuts (ton)	121307	369279	52583
粮食 (吨)	Grain (ton)	1833213	735783	104440
#小麦 (吨)	Wheat (ton)	167907	44707	6463
大麦 (吨)	Barley (ton)	8211	1520	211
大豆 (吨)	Soybeans (ton)	1552209	643319	91180
食用植物油 (吨)	Edible Vegetable Oils (ton)	546144	368496	52232
#棕榈油 (吨)	Palm Oil (ton)	451536	287775	40745
食糖 (吨)	Sugar (ton)	26059	12545	1767
酒类及饮料	Liquor and Drinks		247404	35094
#啤酒 (千升)	Beer (1000 liters)	3526	2820	403
制盐 (吨)	Salt (ton)	1864	710	100
金属矿及矿砂 (吨)	Metal Ores and Other Ores (ton)	22803452	1904558	269421
铁矿砂及其精矿 (吨)	Iron Ore and Iron Ore Concentrate (ton)	19124343	1567271	221521
煤及褐煤 (吨)	Coal and Lignite (ton)	14384950	943027	133614
原油 (吨)	Crude Oil (ton)	4219225	1770345	253718
成品油 (吨)	Refined Oil (ton)	195855	151947	21740
基本有机化学品	Basic Organic Chemicals		1432219	204441
#二甲苯 (吨)	Xylene (ton)	872781	636876	90885
医药材及药品 (吨)	Medicinal Materials and Drugs (ton)	24933	1206012	171389
肥料 (吨)	Fertilizer (ton)	801177	271776	39091
#氯化钾 (吨)	Potassium Chloride (ton)	784231	266566	38336
美容化妆品及洗护用品 (吨)	Cosmetics and Skincare Products (ton)	11281	141845	20307
初级形状的塑料 (吨)	Plastics in their Initial Form (ton)	2214113	3143362	447520
塑料制品 (吨)	Plastic Products	135208	1477037	209743
天然及合成橡胶(包括胶乳)(吨)	Natural and Synthetic Rubber (Including Latex) (ton)	82181	146824	20903
皮革、毛皮及其制品 (吨)	Leather, Furs, and their Products	47411	213151	30350
#牛皮革及马皮革 (吨)	Cow Leather and Horse Leather (ton)	43987	179263	25526
木及其制品 (吨)	Wood and Wood Products (ton)	210067	71639	10177
#锯材 (吨)	Saws (ton)	67748	33532	4774
纸浆、纸及其制品 (吨)	Paper Pulp, Paper, and their Products (ton)	4892873	1763362	251394
#纸浆 (吨)	Paper Pulp (ton)	3730296	1269533	181173

6－17 续表 continued

商品名称	Item	数量 Volume	金额 Value 万元人民币 RMB10 000	金额 Value 万美元 USD 10 000
纺织原料 (吨)	Textile Raw Materials (ton)	17750	27446	3919
#棉花 (吨)	Cotton (ton)	8399	12490	1791
纺织纱线、织物及其制品	Yarn, Fabric, and their Products	352224	1106082	157400
#纺织纱线 (吨)	Textile Yarn (ton)	146196	453561	64569
服装及衣着附件	Clothing and Clothing Accessories	70215	198199	28167
玻璃及其制品	Glass and Glassware	165333	1056493	150325
#玻璃纤维及其制品 (吨)	Glass Fibre and Glass Fibre Products (ton)	26576	100697	14317
珍珠、宝石及半宝石	Pearls, Precious Stones, and Semi-precious Stones	124013	1279590	182609
#钻石	Diamonds		1203633	171840
钢材 (吨)	Steel (ton)	1187517	971393	138170
未锻轧铜及铜材 (吨)	Unwrought Copper and Copper Materials (ton)	225984	1667675	236635
未锻轧铝及铝材 (吨)	Unwrought Aluminium and Aluminium Materials (ton)	66184	196648	27902
机械基础件	Basic Mechanical Parts	627888	573617	81590
农业机械 (千台)	Agricultural Machinery (1000 sets)	413	6844	983
食品加工机械 (千台)	Food Processing Machinery (1000 sets)	14	58107	8163
包装机械 (千台)	Packaging Machinery (1000 sets)	1	31160	4468
印刷、装订机械及其零件	Printing, Binding Machinery and their Parts	13141	615313	87583
#打印机、复印机及一体机(千台)	Printers, Copiers, and All-in-one Machines (1000 sets)	229	64568	9220
通用机械设备	General Mechanical Equipment	96270	717593	101639
#阀门及类似装置 (千套)	Valves and Similar Devices (1000 sets)	49050	218711	31166
机床 (千台)	Machine Tools (1000 sets)	3	178829	25367
自动数据处理设备及其零部件	Automatic Data Processing Equipment and their Parts	26431	2294411	326953
存储部件 (千台)	Storage Components (1000 sets)	4880	273573	38943
#自动数据处理设备的零件、附件 (吨)	Accessories and Parts of Automatic Data Processing Equipment (ton)	8240	1313367	187324
半导体制造设备 (千台)	Semiconductor Manufacturing Equipment (1000 units)	2	525394	74638
#制造平板显示器用的机器及装置 (千台)	Flat Panel Display Manufacturing Equipment and Devices (1000 sets)	1	91575	13061
电工器材	Electrical Equipment		3684284	523848
#电气控制装置	Electrical Control Devices		1733719	246443
音视频设备及其零件	Audiovisual Equipment and their Parts		1934270	272352
#电子元件	Electrical Components		44449079	6321366
二极管及类似半导体器件 (千个)	Diodes and Similar Semiconductor Devices (1000 units)	67347953	3375162	479974
#集成电路 (千个)	Integrated Circuits (1000 units)	63294112	37224290	5294577
汽车(包含底盘) (辆)	Automobiles (Including Chassis) (unit)	9	3192	443
汽车零配件	Automobile Parts		1254838	178137
船舶	Ships		13472	1928
液晶平板显示模组 (千个)	Liquid Crystal Display Modules (1000 units)	184153	1836215	261123
计量检测分析自控仪器及器具	Automatic Measuring, Detection, Analysis Devices and Equipment		1279558	181953
医疗仪器及器械	Medical Devices and Equipment		173707	24714
钟表及其零件	Clocks and their Parts		333893	47375
手表 (千只)	Wristwatches (1000 units)	3343	59408	8454

6-18 私营企业进出口主要指标（2023年）

Main Indicators on Imports and Exports of Private Enterprises (2023)

项目	Item	亿元人民币 RMB100 million			亿美元 USD 100 million		
		进出口总额 Total	出口 Exports	进口 Imports	进出口总额 Total	出口 Exports	进口 Imports
全　省	**Provincial Total**	**49194.42**	**33489.26**	**15705.15**	**6990.58**	**4760.14**	**2230.44**
按贸易方式分	By Customs Regime						
一般贸易	Ordinary Trade	34951.03	25830.88	9120.15	4966.85	3670.48	1296.37
来料加工	Processing and Assembling with Customer's Materials	577.01	308.03	268.98	82.00	43.77	38.22
进料加工	Processing and Assembling with Import Materials	3927.60	2455.60	1472.00	558.71	349.46	209.25
加工设备	Processing Equipments	0.31		0.31	0.04		0.04
保税仓库	Bonded Warehouse	8760.06	3979.48	4780.58	1242.68	565.11	677.57
其他	Others	955.36	904.62	50.74	137.01	129.82	7.20
按产品类型分	By Type of Product						
#机电产品	Machanical and Electrical Products	29459.78	19277.62	10182.16	4185.44	2740.77	1444.67
#自动数据处理设备及其零部件	Automatic Data Processing Machine and Components	2830.08	1791.05	1039.03	401.21	254.30	146.92
高新技术产品	High and New-tech Products	17246.51	8669.16	8577.35	2448.24	1231.21	1217.03
#计算机与通信技术	Computer and Communication Technology	6644.11	5290.96	1353.15	943.05	751.48	191.57
电子技术	Electronic Technology	8511.93	2251.82	6260.10	1208.71	319.85	888.86
按主要国家(地区)分	By Main Country (Region)						
亚洲	**Asia**	**27906.96**	**16028.59**	**11878.37**	**3964.99**	**2278.72**	**1686.28**
#中国香港	Hong Kong, China	4590.79	4455.21	135.57	652.13	632.86	19.27
中国澳门	Macao, China	57.01	56.43	0.58	8.10	8.01	0.08
中国台湾	Taiwan, China	3620.37	578.23	3042.14	513.54	81.99	431.55
日本	Japan	1734.82	826.62	908.20	246.49	117.54	128.95
韩国	Republic of Korea	1877.48	706.18	1171.31	266.65	100.37	166.27
东盟	Association of Southeast Asian Nations	8961.03	5347.15	3613.88	1274.64	761.12	513.52
中东十七国	The Seventeen Countries of the Middle East	2429.05	2098.78	330.27	345.18	298.51	46.67
非洲	**Africa**	**1846.36**	**1530.30**	**316.06**	**263.31**	**218.33**	**44.98**
欧洲	**Europe**	**8054.89**	**6482.70**	**1572.19**	**1144.38**	**921.39**	**222.99**
#欧盟	European Union	5594.15	4495.36	1098.79	795.21	639.21	156.00
#英国	United Kingdom	1046.35	959.99	86.36	148.67	136.41	12.26
德国	Germany	1182.61	842.02	340.59	167.95	119.63	48.32
法国	France	644.85	481.38	163.47	91.63	68.40	23.22
意大利	Italy	569.66	470.62	99.04	81.09	67.01	14.07
荷兰	Netherlands	950.28	824.80	125.48	134.97	117.30	17.67
俄罗斯	Russia	967.28	857.86	109.42	137.24	121.70	15.54
南美洲	**Sorth America**	**2753.64**	**2058.99**	**694.65**	**391.29**	**292.30**	**98.98**
北美洲	**North America**	**7168.02**	**6393.51**	**774.51**	**1018.44**	**908.01**	**110.43**
#加拿大	Canada	619.95	497.31	122.63	88.16	70.60	17.56
美国	United States of America	6542.46	5894.31	648.15	929.49	837.15	92.34
大洋洲及其他	**Oceania and others**	**1464.54**	**995.17**	**469.37**	**208.18**	**141.40**	**66.78**
#澳大利亚	Australia	1259.38	882.74	376.64	178.98	125.42	53.56
新西兰	New Zealand	148.13	89.23	58.90	21.09	12.67	8.42

6-19 外商投资情况

Utilization of Foreign Capital

年份 Year	新设企业数 (个) Number of Newly Established Foreign-invested Enterprises (unit)	合同外资金额 (万美元) Amount of Contracted Foreign Capital (USD 10000)	实际外资金额 (万美元) Amount of Foreign Capital Actually Utilized (USD 10000)
1979	70	14616	3074
1980	188	120046	12320
1981	236	156206	17326
1982	151	147698	17123
1983	412	61552	24523
1984	1105	116958	54163
1985	1640	200073	51529
1986	774	85902	64392
1987	1186	124647	59396
1988	2741	224196	91906
1989	2438	243813	115644
1990	3042	268958	145984
1991	4554	490530	182286
1992	9769	1885764	355150
1993	16768	3314887	749805
1994	10558	2382441	939708
1995	8177	2483244	1018028
1996	4608	1554584	1162362
1997	3744	769202	1171083
1998	4349	916180	1202005
1999	3013	617451	1220300
2000	4245	868393	1223720
2001	5317	1343463	1297240
2002	6613	1617119	1311071
2003	7306	2178926	1557779
2004	8322	1936046	1001158
2005	8384	2374365	1236391
2006	8452	2456820	1451065
2007	9506	3393817	1712603
2008	6999	2863991	1916703
2009	4346	1755834	1953460
2010	5641	2460075	2026098
2011	7035	3469238	2179836
2012	6043	3499424	2354911
2013	5520	3631343	2495210
2014	6016	4305905	2687144
2015	7029	5611000	2687546
2016	8078	8667477	2334921
2017	15599	7308672	2290668
2018	35774	5900.98②	1450.88②
2019	14350	5523.84	1522.00
2020	12864	5032.99	1620.29
2021	16155	4894.14	1840.02
2022	13365	4051.57	1819.02
2023	21685	4516.85	1591.64

注：1.2002年起，实际使用外资中企业投资总额内的境外借款只包括外方股东贷款。2004年起，实际使用外资金额统计口径调整，与历史数据不可比。

2.2018年起，实际使用外资金额使用商务部反馈人民币数据，单位为亿元。

Notes:a)Starting from 2002, overseas loans within the total investment amount of enterprises in actual use of foreign capital only include loans from foreign shareholders. Since 2004, the statistical caliber of actual use of foreign capital has been adjusted and cannot be compared with historical data.

b)Since 2018, the actual amount of foreign investment used has been reported in RMB by the Ministry of Commerce, with a unit of billions of yuan.

6-20 分行业外商直接投资（2023年）
Foreign Direct Investment by Sector (2023)

指 标	Item	新设企业数（个）Number of Newly Established Foreign-invested Enterprises (unit)	合同外资金额（万元）Amount of Contracted Foreign Capital (RMB 10000)	实际外资金额（万元）Amount of Foreign Capital Actually Utilized (RMB 10000)
全 省	**Provincial Total**	**21685**	**45168468**	**15916400**
农、林、牧、渔业	Farming,Forestry,Anima Husbandry and Fishery	72	194734	3624
采矿业	Mining	2	7415	150734
制造业	Manufacture	1078	11318193	4921501
电力、热力、燃气及水生产和供应业	Production and Supply of Electric Power, Gas and Water	60	1110138	132435
建筑业	Construction	339	791633	67344
批发和零售业	Wholesale and Retail Trades	8702	14062689	620783
交通运输、仓储和邮政业	Transport, Storage and Postal Services	414	469757	462734
住宿和餐饮业	Hotels and Catering Services	649	120997	101987
信息传输、软件和信息技术服务业	Information Transmission, Computer Services and Software	1786	1406854	1246677
金融业	Finance	135	1055840	755578
房地产业	Real Estate	381	379571	1471657
租赁和商务服务业	Leasing and Business Services	4191	7758139	2841839
科学研究和技术服务业	Scientific Research, Technical Services	2422	6122046	2874674
水利、环境和公共设施管理业	Management of Water Conservancy,Environment and Public Facilities	33	-84760	75566
居民服务、修理和其他服务业	Services to Households,Repair and Other Services	464	6045	13789
教育	Education	54	23794	4434
卫生和社会工作	Health and Social Service	58	110489	39827
文化、体育和娱乐业	Culture, Sports and Entertainment	845	314894	131217
公共管理、社会保障和社会组织	Public Administration,Social Security and Social Organizations			

6-21 分国家(地区)实际使用外资金额

Actual Value of Foreign Capital Used in Countries and Regions

单位：万美元　　(USD 10000)

指　　标	Item	2000	2010	2015	2021	2022	2023
合　计	**Total**	**1223720**	**2026098**	**2687546**	**18400192**	**18190177**	**15916400**
亚洲	**Asia**	**927071**	**1486723**	**2268764**	**16972216**	**16705805**	**14163834**
#中国香港	Hong Kong, China	744826	1291738	2047856	14314569	15308147	11421527
中国台湾	Taiwan, China	49746	24543	10525	43919	34491	42638
中国澳门	Macao, China	26137	30189	73718	1200837	490977	331096
日本	Japan	30852	51044	45514	226567	202781	143598
新加坡	Singapore	49115	46482	47343	769122	644005	692276
韩国	Republic of Korea	13671	20658	34770	405758	13028	134198
文莱	Brunei		8825	3133	3287	110	
马来西亚	Malaysia	4993	5133	4541	748	666	2521
泰国	Thailand	2895	998	822	2433	914	3653
印度尼西亚	Indonesia	3352	877	36	29	1129	350
阿联酋	United Arab Emirates	100	5370	10	39	174	1390551
菲律宾	Philippines	191	91	5		441	100
印度	India	964	69	148	2406	494	385
非洲	**Africa**	**4272**	**16972**	**12060**	**29763**	**24720**	**25392**
#毛里求斯	Mauritius	4576	14738	7327	17554	10965	14085
塞舌尔	Seychelles		1772	4635	12072	13755	11307
欧洲	**Europe**	**38643**	**78713**	**83864**	**629418**	**642562**	**1022831**
#荷兰	Netherlands	7886	9646	7246	36216	78847	9985
英国	United Kingdom	8258	1859	13139	70093	57821	274977
法国	France	4551	52008	21078	11318	172	143614
德国	Germany	10057	3657	33898	292691	401620	541674
瑞士	Switzerland	3349	2839	1191	51117	75254	25614
意大利	Italy		1736	1344	2194	624	5670
西班牙	Spain	44	2089	444	4536	606	13155
芬兰	Finland	2302	18		31062	52	225
卢森堡	Luxembourg	90	660	860	116900	376	3442
爱尔兰	Ireland		2010	3762	3637		160
瑞典	Sweden	360	500	647	4799	1356	393
奥地利	Austria	101	1000		3600	25262	152
比利时	Belgium	499	60	129			49
丹麦	Denmark		201	11	455	32	10
南美洲	**Sorth America**	**161983**	**303059**	**142932**	**576009**	**633176**	**510798**
#维尔京群岛	Virgin Islands	149200	270979	123429	498419	571883	253840
开曼群岛	Cayman Islands	6694	24644	16671	74566	60009	253881
巴哈马	Bahamas	3543	1649	1019			
巴巴多斯	Barbados		3254	701	346		
巴拿马	Panama	1544	1953	288			
北美洲	**North America**	**74453**	**40816**	**35221**	**113355**	**66101**	**88768**
#美国	United States of America	66972	25388	19049	103948	47486	63563
百慕大	Bermuda	2320	13341	15808	800	13172	3674
加拿大	Canada	5161	2087	364	8607	5443	21531
大洋洲	**Oceania**	**14510**	**53171**	**57284**	**79429**	**117813**	**104777**
#萨摩亚	Samoa	8942	49714	54362	72567	116810	52383
澳大利亚	Australia	4697	2869	2538	800	631	51003
马绍尔群岛	Marshall Islands	680	183	384			
新西兰	New Zealand	86	181			372	1391
其它	**Others**	**2788**	**46644**	**87276**	**2**		
#投资性公司投资	Investment Companies		35196	87119			
创业投资公司投资	Resuccess Investments Limited			157			

注：2018年起，实际使用外资金额使用商务部反馈人民币数据，单位为万元。

Notes: Since 2018, the actual amount of foreign investment used has been reported in RMB by the Ministry of Commerce, with a unit of ten thousand of yuan.

6-22 各市外商直接投资

Foreign Direct Investment by City

市别	City	2022			2023		
		新设企业数(个) Number of Newly Established Foreign-invested Enterprises (unit)	合同外资金额(万元) Amount of Contracted Foreign Capital (RMB 10000)	实际外资金额(万元) Amount of Foreign Capital Actually Utilized (RMB 10000)	新设企业数(个) Number of Newly Established Foreign-invested Enterprises (unit)	合同外资金额(万元) Amount of Contracted Foreign Capital (RMB 10000)	实际外资金额(万元) Amount of Foreign Capital Actually Utilized (RMB 10000)
广州	Guangzhou	3442	12921431	5741290	6629	18175946	4832227
深圳	Shenzhen	4289	13903531	7143307	8002	9436456	6262117
珠海	Zhuhai	1942	3949588	877322	2219	2883244	805996
汕头	Shantou	58	156191	19247	59	74581	54664
佛山	Foshan	727	1485306	731415	968	4681924	626438
韶关	Shaoguan	43	235947	51832	29	161662	23821
河源	Heyuan	36	352467	113835	46	27873	23394
梅州	Meizhou	23	5214	11507	28	44260	12918
惠州	Huizhou	364	1548920	1039938	528	869204	889244
汕尾	Shanwei	53	128589	28390	64	81294	32671
东莞	Dongguan	1104	1057170	788673	1369	5699059	722121
中山	Zhongshan	581	576393	416276	847	942834	352146
江门	Jiangmen	395	1247381	352032	555	424732	305647
阳江	Yangjiang	27	69637	60702	36	15114	17544
湛江	Zhanjiang	37	136741	408219	40	23926	462378
茂名	Maoming	29	1020606	18886	18	7882	10455
肇庆	Zhaoqing	90	732121	110570	117	395340	148803
清远	Qingyuan	63	775631	111487	66	131510	115523
潮州	Chaozhou	5	68873	70183	10	17866	8685
揭阳	Jieyang	12	2953	43405	14	781225	39831
云浮	Yunfu	45	141039	51661	41	292536	19632
按经济区域分	By Region						
珠三角	Pearl River Delta	12934	37421841	17200823	21234	43508739	14944739
粤东	Eastern Region	128	356606	161225	175	999226	148769
粤西	Western Region	93	1226984	487807	94	46922	490377
粤北	Northern Region	210	1510298	340322	182	613581	182370

6–23 分行业外商投资企业工商注册登记情况（2023年末）
Registration Status of Enterprises with Foreign Investment by Sector (Year-end of 2023)

行　业	Sector	企业数（户）Number of Registered Enterprises (unit)	投资总额（亿美元）Total Investment (USD 100 million)	注册资本（亿美元）Registered Capital (USD 100 million)	#外方 Capital Invested by Foreign Partners
全　省	**Provincial Total**	**199057**	**23059.11**	**16253.07**	**10946.51**
农、林、牧、渔业	Farming,Forestry,Anima Husbandry and Fishery	1780	588.53	206.42	195.73
采矿业	Mining	69	24.30	21.14	18.40
制造业	Manufacture	35161	3783.27	2328.35	1599.03
电力、热力、燃气及水生产和供应业	Production and Supply of Electric Power, Gas and Water	754	735.58	313.90	122.32
建筑业	Construction	3103	297.63	227.27	92.03
批发和零售业	Wholesale and Retail Trades	66762	6972.90	5548.27	5193.73
交通运输、仓储和邮政业	Transport, Storage and Postal Services	4565	362.90	243.49	129.96
住宿和餐饮业	Hotels and Catering Services	9590	68.33	51.60	34.57
信息传输、软件和信息技术服务业	Information Transmission, Computer Services and Software	14284	982.55	688.66	363.16
金融业	Finance	3579	961.61	1019.53	495.58
房地产业	Real Estate	5992	1773.36	1305.93	583.07
租赁和商务服务业	Leasing and Business Services	28443	4887.12	3224.02	1462.78
科学研究和技术服务业	Scientific Research, Technical Services	17099	1305.85	844.98	494.45
水利、环境和公共设施管理业	Management of Water Conservancy,Environment and Public Facilities	348	65.56	40.38	32.02
居民服务、修理和其他服务业	Services to Households,Repair and Other Services	3098	86.66	72.38	49.87
教育	Education	338	5.43	4.79	3.09
卫生和社会工作	Health and Social Service	202	35.49	23.27	13.45
文化、体育和娱乐业	Culture, Sports and Entertainment	3632	118.88	86.24	61.16
其他	Others	258	3.18	2.46	2.12

6-24 各市外商投资企业工商注册登记情况（2023年末）

Registration Status of Enterprises with Foreign Investment by City(Year-end of 2023)

市别	City	企业数(户) Number of Registered Enterprises(unit)	投资总额 (亿美元) Total Investment (USD 100 million)	注册资本 (亿美元) Registered Capital (USD 100 million)	#外方 Capital Invested by Foreign Partners
全省	**Provincial Total**	**199057**	**23059.11**	**16253.07**	**10946.51**
广州	Guangzhou	43664	4633.95	3288.73	717.05
深圳	Shenzhen	73535	5974.33	4179.51	2235.11
珠海	Zhuhai	18509	7260.59	5899.44	5630.85
汕头	Shantou	1395	99.56	73.31	55.77
佛山	Foshan	9219	1016.21	548.53	444.04
韶关	Shaoguan	1033	53.28	36.45	28.44
河源	Heyuan	1951	98.41	62.97	55.25
梅州	Meizhou	3270	49.79	35.49	31.16
惠州	Huizhou	8407	1033.94	382.51	311.48
汕尾	Shanwei	896	40.53	32.70	28.95
东莞	Dongguan	16036	875.78	634.90	578.64
中山	Zhongshan	6310	248.48	198.33	163.72
江门	Jiangmen	5148	533.91	263.37	191.60
阳江	Yangjiang	698	224.95	67.13	33.21
湛江	Zhanjiang	1027	207.03	100.16	76.13
茂名	Maoming	1530	61.73	49.41	40.36
肇庆	Zhaoqing	2764	218.14	174.64	164.95
清远	Qingyuan	1641	144.67	88.86	71.68
潮州	Chaozhou	577	26.01	18.59	15.63
揭阳	Jieyang	722	53.66	28.07	24.83
云浮	Yunfu	650	135.46	26.70	21.39
局本部	Unclassified by Region	75	68.71	63.27	26.27

6-25 一类口岸开放使用情况（2023年末）
Opening and Operating Status of Category-1 Ports (Year-end of 2023)

市别 City		个数 Number	口岸类型 Name of Ports				
			水运 Water Transport		陆运 Land Transport		空运 Air Transport
合计	**Total**	**52**	31		16		5
广州	Guangzhou	6	广州港口岸	Guangzhou Port	广州火车东站铁路口岸	Guangzhou East Railway Station for Passenger Service	白云国际机场 Baiyun International Airport
			广州南沙港口岸	Nansha Port			
			广州莲花山港口岸	Lianhuashan Port			
			增城新塘港客运口岸	Xintang Port			
深圳	Shenzhen	16	蛇口工业区码头	Shekou Port	罗湖	Luohu	深圳宝安国际机场 Shenzhen International Airport
			赤湾码头	Chiwan Port	文锦渡	Wenjindu	
			大铲湾港区	Dachan Bay Port	沙头角	Shatoujiao	
			妈湾码头	Mawan Port	皇岗	Huanggang	
			盐田码头	Yantian Port	深圳湾	Shenzhen Bay	
			大亚湾核电站专用码头	Dayawan Port	福田	Futian	
					广深港高铁西九龙站	Guangzhou-Shenzhen-Hong Kong Express Rail Link West Kowloon Terminus	
					莲塘	Liantang	
					深圳(笋岗)铁路口岸	Shenzhen(Sungang) Railway Station	
珠海	Zhuhai	6	珠海港口岸	Zhuhai Port	拱北	Gongbei	
					横琴	Hengqin	
					珠澳跨境工业区专用口岸	The Industrial Zone Dedicated port cross-border between The Pearl River Delta and Macao	
					港珠澳大桥珠海公路口岸	Zhuhai Port of Hong Kong Zhuhai Macao Bridge	
					珠海青茂口岸	Qingmao Port	
汕头	Shantou	2	汕头港口岸	Shantou Port			
			潮阳港口岸	Chaoyang Port			
梅州	Meizhou	1					梅县机场 Meixian Airport
惠州	Huizhou	1	惠州港口岸	Huizhou Port			
汕尾	Shanwei	1	汕尾港口岸	Shanwei Port			
东莞	Dongguan	2	虎门港口岸	Humen Port	东莞常平铁路客运	Dongguan Changping Railway Stations for Passenger Service	
中山	Zhongshan	1	中山港口岸	Zhongshan Port			
江门	Jiangmen	5	江门客运港口岸	Jiangmen Port			
			开平三埠港客运口岸	Sanfu Port			
			台山广海港口岸	Guanghai Port			
			鹤山港客运口岸	Heshan Port			
			新会港口岸	Xinhui Port			
佛山	Foshan	3	顺德容奇港口岸	Shunde Port			
			南海港口岸	Nanhai Port			
			高明港客运口岸	Gaoming Port			
阳江	Yangjiang	1	阳江港口岸	Yangjiang Port			
湛江	Zhanjiang	2	湛江港口岸	Zhanjiang Port			湛江机场 Zhanjiang Airport
茂名	Maoming	1	茂名港口岸	Maoming Port			
肇庆	Zhaoqing	1	肇庆港客运口岸	Zhaoqing Port			
潮州	Chaozhou	1	潮州港口岸	Chaozhou Port			
揭阳	Jieyang	2	揭阳港口岸	Jieyang Port			揭阳潮汕国际机场 Jieyang International Airport

6-26 对外经济技术合作情况

Economic and Technical Cooperation with Foreign Countries and Regions

年 份 Year	对外承包工程 Contracted Projects				对外劳务合作 Labor Services		
	签订合同数 (个) Number of Contracts Signed (unit)	合同金额 (万美元) Contracted Value (USD 10000)	营业金额 (万美元) Value of Turnover (USD 10000)	年末在外人数 (人) Number of Persons Abroad at the Year-end (person)	劳务人员合同工资总额 (万美元) Total Wages of Contract Workers (USD 10000)	劳务人员实际收入总额 (万美元) Actual Total Income of Contract Workers (USD 10000)	年末在外人数 (人) Number of Persons Abroad at the Year-end (person)
1985	28	1897	2491	305	424	433	1197
1990	23	5953	7586	688	6055	3189	8045
1995	29	19183	10924	850	20593	17775	33263
1996	37	14823	9474	1680	11784	19365	23319
1997	67	22435	10940	354	17356	14743	22857
1998	28	13331	17526	566	12925	14464	20816
1999	63	52961	21857	603	9327	13230	19128
2000	86	36555	34515	634	12941	10777	19564
2001	250	53924	26192	641	13271	11752	30695
2002	165	64827	58986	643	19114	17059	18922
2003	193	97055	86898	730	23132	21926	21738
2004	810	168338	161287	856	27392	28315	17043
2005	2061	326752	247189	606	32762	30878	20469
2006	1625	458442	344170	752	41898	37030	27024
2007	757	597733	546069	946	80824	62927	27880
2008	331	844352	686045	886	68209	58420	33691
2009	556	814859	758799	2105	45718	59469	33124
2010	605	986740	820815	4554	76575	58428	33901
2011	528	1343526	1134158	4017	46578	46445	38621
2012	517	1905053	1605342	3863	46643	38600	44301
2013	617	2366492	2286507	3243	53917	44689	54272
2014	1139	1524873	1241121	3405	138820	66218	72788
2015	1937	2072350	1987790	3633	139705	117787	81600
2016	1503	2198726	1816382	4350	65540	89185	80468
2017	1151	2218294	1809649	6293	72805	86660	79440
2018	1136	1914713	1756733	10507	67494	85623	82329
2019	1030	2556123	1670589	9025	73640	92860	84216
2020	878	1873148	1566539	10542	55850	79177	60035
2021	787	1835162	1562286	2303	63696	87394	10601
2022	859	1979411	1620215	8617	44027	88198	58453
2023	961	1771343	1445662	3490	63216	98046	65794

注：1.2009年以后，“对外承包工程”包含“对外设计咨询”。
　　2.2011年对外劳务合作统计口径调整。

Note: a) After 2009, foreign design consultation is included in foreign contracted projects.
　　b) The statistics coverage of foreign labor service has been adjusted in 2011.

6–27 分国别(地区)对外直接投资

Foreign Direct Investment by Country (Region)

国家(地区)	Country of Region	企业(机构)个数 (个) Number of Companies(Institutions) (unit)			对外直接投资额 (万美元) Amount of Overseas Direct Investment (USD 10000)		
		2021	2022	2023	2021	2022	2023
合计	**Total**	**1075**	**1230**	**1690**	**1696707**	**2207193**	**2383177**
亚洲	**Asia**	**887**	**970**	**1388**	**1128470**	**1557865**	**1619402**
#中国香港	Hong Kong, China	712	743	896	1067363	1511149	1515825
中国澳门	Macao, China	29	29	27	6752	6912	9499
印度尼西亚	Indonesia	5	14	34	2799	947	7516
泰国	Thailand	7	11	73	3653	1467	14066
新加坡	Singapore	32	48	111	29299	17719	53416
韩国	Republic of Korea	14	9	22	1453	1733	690
日本	Japan	15	33	32	1778	1207	2210
中国台湾	Taiwan, China	5	1	2	184	18	45
马来西亚	Malaysia	11	6	19	4143	2532	1705
印度	India	7	7	1	42	1809	5
越南	Vietnam	26	41	135	6162	5337	8813
柬埔寨	Cambodia	3	3	4	3144	4978	4035
以色列	Israel	3	1	1	473	945	548
老挝	Laos	1	2	2	306	55	599
非洲	**Africa**	**20**	**18**	**19**	**1343**	**210**	**1255**
#加纳	Ghana	2	0		222		
肯尼亚	Kenya	2	1		30	6	6
塞舌尔	Seychelles	3	0		5	87	
欧洲	**Europe**	**59**	**87**	**105**	**38388**	**20941**	**29028**
#法国	France	2	1	9	108	479	42
爱尔兰	Ireland			1	1308		1073
荷兰	Netherlands		9	12		2274	4831
俄罗斯	Russia	4		14	1		84
德国	Germany	15	35	29	8056	3702	5786
英国	United Kingdom	12	9	10	179	121	3766
卢森堡	Luxembourg				1270	242	
意大利	Italy	5	4	6	2084	1961	1326
瑞士	Switzerland	2	4	3	1	142	208
瑞典	Sweden	2	3	2	2838	6411	7851
挪威	Norway			1	47		
波兰	Poland	4	1	1	1464	3804	1646
匈牙利	Hungary	1	3	8	1934	1236	1176
拉丁美洲	**Latin America**	**43**	**45**	**45**	**104955**	**103392**	**144537**
#英属维尔京群岛	Virgin Islands	2	4	5	64397	35384	82921
开曼群岛	Cayman Islands	29	30	14	38285	65666	59561
巴西	Brazil	2	5	5	906	10	
秘鲁	Peru	2	1		190		696
墨西哥	Mexico	6	5	17	160	542	552
智利	Chile	1		1	50		356
北美洲	**North America**	**64**	**104**	**121**	**14287**	**27331**	**22219**
#美国	United States of America	58	94	116	12796	26352	21349
加拿大	Canada	5	10	4	1490	979	870
大洋洲	**Oceania**	**2**	**6**	**12**	**5105**	**7374**	**6465**
#新西兰	New Zealand		1		185	12	143
澳大利亚	Australia	1	5	11	1539	5161	6117
巴布亚新几内亚	Papua New Guinea				3380	2200	200
利润再投资分摊	**Reinvested profit sharing**				**404160**	**490080**	**560270**

6-28 分行业对外直接投资(2023年)

Foreign Direct Investment by Sector (2023)

分组指标	Indexes by Group	企业(机构)个数(个) Number of Companies (Institutions) (unit)	对外直接投资额(万美元) Amount of Overseas Direct Investment (USD 10 000)
全　省	**Provincial Total**	**1690**	**2383177**
农、林、牧、渔业	Agricultural, Forestry, Husbandry, and Fishing Industries	8	1296
采矿业	Mining Industry	2	27451
制造业	Manufacturing Industry	350	166553
电力、热力、燃气及水的生产和供应业	Electricity, Heat, Gas, and Water Production and Supply Industries	5	20136
建筑业	Construction Industry	13	10406
批发和零售业	Wholesale and Retail Industries	755	894509
交通运输、仓储和邮政业	Transportation, Storage, and Postal Industries	54	16548
住宿和餐饮业	Accommodation and Catering Industries	3	2983
信息传输、软件和信息技术服务业	Information Transmission, Software, and Information Technology Industries	132	134857
金融业	Financial Industry	4	10199
房地产业	Real Estate Industry		463
租赁和商务服务业	Leasing and Business Services Industries	95	494402
科学研究和技术服务业	Scientific Research and Technical Services Industries	81	15141
水利、环境和公共设施管理业	Water Conservation, Environment, and Public Facility Management Industries	4	6.2512
居民服务、修理和其他服务业	Resident Services, Repairs, and Other Service Industries	5	27061
教育	Education	3	1
卫生和社会工作	Health and Social Work	5	794
文化、体育和娱乐业	Culture, Sports and Entertainment Industries	5	102
公共管理、社会保障和社会组织	Public Management, Social Security, Social Organization		
其他	Others	166	
利润再投资分摊	Profit Reinvestment and Sharing		560270

主要统计指标解释

货物进出口总额 指实际进出我国国境的货物总金额。包括对外贸易实际进出口货物，来料加工装配进出口货物，国家间、联合国及国际组织无偿援助物资和赠送品，华侨、港澳台同胞和外籍华人捐赠品，租赁期满归承租人所有的租赁货物，进料加工进出口货物，边境地方贸易及边境地区小额贸易进出口货物，中外合资企业、中外合作经营企业、外商独资经营企业进出口货物和公用物品，到、离岸价格在规定限额以上的进出口货样和广告品(无商业价值、无使用价值和免费提供出口的除外)，从保税仓库提取在中国境内销售的进口货物，以及其他进出口货物。该指标可以观察一个国家在对外贸易方面的总规模。我国规定出口货物按离岸价格统计，进口货物按到岸价格统计。

商品目的地进口额和商品货源地出口额 目的地进口额指进口货物的消费、使用或最终抵运地的实际进口额；货源地出口额指出口货物的产地或原始发货地的实际出口额。

利用外资 指我国政府、部门、企业和其他经济组织通过对外借款、吸收客商直接投资以及向境外发行债券、股票等方式筹借的境外资金。

外资的形式可以是现汇、实物、工业产权或专有技术等有形资本和无形资本。

我国自有外汇和中国银行自有外汇资金发放的外汇贷款购置国外设备和材料，华侨、港澳同胞的捐赠，联合国或其他国际组织的无偿赠送资金、无偿援建的项目均不属于外资范围 。

利用外资的方式有：对外借款，外国（或港澳地区）企业和经济组织或个人在我国境内开办独资企业、与我国境内的企业或组织共同开办合资企业、合作经营(企业)项目或合作开发资源，以及补偿贸易、国际租赁等。

补偿贸易 是以商品或劳务偿还贷款的一种贸易方式。即由客商提供设备、原材料、生产技术，以这些设备、原材料、生产技术生产的产品或是用双方协商的其他产品价值去支付 （偿还）进口设备、原材料价款。

对外借款 指我国政府、部门、企业和中国银行等单位向国际金融组织 、外国政府、企业等借用的长期、短期资本，到期需还本付息。借款按不同渠道划分为：①外国政府贷款； ②国际金融组织贷款；③外国银行贷款；④出口信贷；⑤发行债券。

外商直接投资 指外国企业和经济组织或个人（包括华侨、港澳同胞以及我在境外注册的企业）按我国有关政策、法规，在我国境内开办外商独资企业，与我国境内的企业或经济组织共同举办中外合资企业、合作经营企业或合作开发资源的投资，以及外商从企业得到收益的再投资。2002 年起“外商直接投资”统计口径调整，“企业投资总额内的境外借款”只包括“企业投资总额内直接投资者对企业的贷款,即外方股东贷款”。不包括“直接投资者提供担保的第三方对企业的贷款即外方股东担保贷款”和“其他方式的企业境外借款即其他境外借款。”

国际租赁 指出租者用自有资金，或向银行借款购买资本设备租给承租者在约定的期限内使用，承租者依约按期付给出租者一定租金，在租赁期内设备的使用属于承租者，设备的所有权属于出租者，租期满后，出租者对设备具有支配权：收回、作价出卖或赠送企业。

对外直接投资 指我国企业、团体等(简称境内投资主体) 在国外及港澳台地区以现金、实物、无形资产等方式投资，并以控制国(境)外企业的经营管理权为核心的经济活动。对外直接投资的内涵主要体现在一经济体通过投资于另一经济体而实现其持久利益的目标。

Explanatory Notes on Main Statistical Indicators

Total Import and Export of Goods refer to the real value of commodities imported and exported across the border of China. They include the actual imports and exports through foreign trade, imported and exported goods under the processing and assembling trades and materials, supplies and gifts as aid given gratis between governments and by the United Nations and other international organizations, and contributions donated by overseas Chinese, compatriots in Hong Kong and Macao and Chinese with foreign citizenship, leasing commodities owned by tenant at the expiration of leasing period, the imported and exported commodities processed with imported materials, commodities trading in border areas, the imported and exported commodities and articles for public use of the Sino-foreign joint ventures, cooperative enterprises and ventures with sole foreign investment. Also included is import or export of samples and advertising goods for which CIF or FOB value are beyond the permitted ceiling (excluding goods of no trading or use value and free commodities for export), imported goods sold in China from bonded warehouses and other imported or exported goods. The indicator of the total imports and exports at customs can be used to observe the total size of external trade in a country. In accordance with the stipulation of the Chinese government, imports are calculated at CIF, while exports are calculated at FOB.

Import or Export Value by Location of China's Foreign Trade Managing Units refers to actual value of imports and exports carried out by corporations which have been registered by the local Customs house and are vested with right to run import export business.

Utilization of Foreign Capital refers to funds financed from abroad by means of loans, foreign direct investment, and issuing bonds and shares undertaken by the Chinese governments at all levels, various departments, enterprises and other economic units.

The types of foreign capital include tangible capital and intangible capital, such as remittance, goods, industrial property rights and know-how.

Those excluded are the purchases of foreign equipment and materials with loans from state-owned foreign exchange and foreign exchange owned by the Bank of China, donations by overseas Chinese, compatriots in Hong Kong and Macao, and funds and projects as aid given gratis by the United Nations and other international organizations.

Utilization of foreign capital takes the forms of loans from abroad, sole investment in enterprises in the boundary of China by foreign (or Hong Kong and Macao) enterprises, economic organizations or individuals, investment in Sino-foreign joint ventures, cooperative projects (enterprises), cooperative exploitation of natural resources with enterprises or organizations in China, compensation trade and international lease, etc.

Compensation Trade refers to a kind of trade returning loans with commodities or services, i.e. imported equipment, raw materials and production technology provided by foreign entrepreneurs are repaid (returned) by means of the products produced with such equipment, raw materials and production technology or by means of the value of other products negotiated by both sides.

Foreign Loans refer to long-term capital and short-term capital borrowed from international financial organizations, foreign governments and enterprises by the Chinese governments at all levels, by various departments, enterprises and the Bank of China, etc, and repaid with interest at maturity. Foreign loans can be divided according to channels into: ①loans from foreign governments; ②loans from international financial organizations; ③loans from foreign banks; ④export credit; ⑤bonds and shares issued abroad.

Foreign Direct Investment refers to investment inside China by foreign enterprises and economic organizations or individuals (including overseas Chinese, compatriots from Hong Kong and Macao, and Chinese enterprises registered abroad), following the relevant policies and laws of China, for the establishment of foreign sole investment enterprises, Sino-foreign joint ventures and cooperative enterprises or for cooperative exploitation of resources with enterprises or economic organizations in China, and re-investment of foreign entrepreneurs with the profits gained from such enterprises and corporations. Starting from 2002, the foreign direct investment statistic has been adjusted such that the overseas borrowings in total investment of enterprises only include loans to the enterprises by direct investors or, in other terms, loans by foreign shareholders, but exclude loans from the third party guaranteed by the direct investors or, in other terms, loans guaranteed by the foreign shareholders, and overseas borrowings by enterprises in other manners or, in other terms, other overseas borrowings.

International Lease refers to the lease of which tenants rent the equipment purchased by lessors with their own money or loans from banks during a fixed period and repay a sum of leasing expenses to lessors according to contracts. During the leasing period, tenants have the right to use the equipment while lessors maintain possession of the equipment. At the expiration of the leasing period, lessors have the right to dispose the equipment: take it back, sell it at a fixed price, or donate it to an enterprise.

Overseas Direct Investment refers to investment made by domestic enterprises and organizations (referred to as domestic investors) in foreign countries and Hong Kong SAR, Macao SAR and Taiwan province in forms of cash, physical investment and intangible assets, and the economic activities centring on operation and management of those enterprises are under the control of domestic investors. The content of overseas direct investment mainly reflects one economic entity by investing in another economic entity to achieve its goal of lasting interest.

七、能源、资源和环境

ENERGY, RESOURCES AND ENVIRONMENT

七　能源、资源和环境

简要说明

一、本篇资料反映广东自然资源状况、能源生产、能源消费、能耗水平和生态环境事业等情况。能源情况主要包括：能源生产、消费及品种构成，分行业能源消费总量，综合能源平衡，各市能源单耗，能源生产和消费弹性系数，能源加工转换效率，生活用能源消费等资料。自然资源包括土地 、气候、森林、水利、矿产资源情况。环保部分主要包括水环境、大气环境、生态环境、城市环境、农村环境、自然灾害等。

二、本篇资料由广东省统计局综合统计处、能源统计处根据有关资料和调查结果整理提供。

三、能源资料取自全省《地区能源平衡表》《工业企业能源购进、消费及库存表》等。地区能源平衡表编制范围为辖区内生产和消费能源的单位；规模以上工业企业的能源消费根据国家统计局制定的报表制度由统计系统搜集资料逐级汇总上报；加工转换消费来源于《工业企业能源购进、消费及库存附表》；其他数据来源于有关厅(局)、公司或企业。矿产、土地资源、海洋资料由省自然资源厅提供；气象资料由省气象局提供；森林资源资料由省林业局提供；水利资料由省水利厅提供；环保事业情况由省生态环境厅提供；城市建设情况由省住房和城乡建设厅提供。

四、关于数据口径与计算的说明：

1．2015 年以后的数据已按第四次全国经济普查结果进行调整。

2．能源生产与消费弹性系数分别按能源生产、消费增长速度与地区生产总值增长速度计算。

3．在地区能源平衡表中，进口量和出口量采用海关统计数据，电力折算标准煤系数按平均发电煤耗计算。

4．能源加工转换效率表中的电力折算标准煤系数采用当量值计算，每千瓦小时折 0.1229 千克标准煤。

五、2023 年能源相关数据未经国家统计局核定，暂缺。

7 Energy ,Resources and Environment

Brief Introduction

Ⅰ. The data in this chapter reflect the natural resource, energy production, consumption, and efficiency and environmental protection of Guangdong Province. The data on energy mainly including the energy production and consumption and their composition, the energy consumption by sector, the overall balance of energy, energy consumption per unit by city, the elasticity ratios of energy production and consumption, the efficiency of energy conversion and the consumption of energy for non-production use, etc. The data on natural resource cover land, climate, forest, water conservancy and mineral resources. The data on environmental protection mainly include water environment, atmospheric environment, ecological environment, urban environment, rural environment, natural disasters, etc.

Ⅱ. The data in this chapter are prepared and provided by the Division of Comprehensive Statistics of Statistics Bureau of Guangdong Province and the Division of Energy Statistics of Statistics Bureau of Guangdong Province.

Ⅲ. The data in this chapter come from the Energy Balance Sheet of the whole province and the Sheets of Energy Purchase, Consumption and Storage of Key Energy Consumption Industrial Enterprises. The coverage of the regional energy balance includes the units that produce and consume energy. Among them, the data on the energy consumption of industrial enterprises above designated size are collected by the statistical agencies in accordance with the statistical reporting scheme stipulated by the National Bureau of Statistics and tabulated and reported to the higher authorities level by level; the data on the energy processing, transformation and consumption are derived from the Sheets of Energy Purchase, Consumption and Storage of Key Energy Consumption Industrial

Enterprises; other data are provided by related government departments, companies and enterprises. The data on mineral and land resources an ocean are provided by Department of Natural Resources of Guangdong Province. The data on meteorological phenomena are provided by the Meteorological Bureau of Guangdong Province. The data on forest are provided by the Forestry Administration of Guangdong Province. The data on water conservancy are provided by the Water Resources Department of Guangdong Province. The data on environmental protection are provided by Department of Ecology and Environment of Guangdong Province. The data on urban construction are provided by Department of Housing and Urban Rural Development of Guangdong Province.

Ⅳ. Data coverage and calculation:

(1) Since 2015,data have been adjusted in accordance with the figures from the third china economics census.

(2) The elasticity ratio of energy production is calculated as the quotient of the growth rate of energy production divided by the growth rate of GDP; and the elasticity ratio of energy consumption is calculated as the quotient of the growth rate of energy consumption divided by the growth rate of GDP.

(3) In the energy balance sheet, the data on the imports and exports are data from the customs statistics.The ratio for converting electric power into the standard coal equivalent is calculated according to the average consumption of coal for generating electricity.

(4) In the table on the efficiency of energy conversion, the ratio for converting electric power into the standard coal equivalent is calculated on the basis of heat value equivalent.One kilowatt is equal to 0.1229 kg SCE.

Ⅴ.The energy related data for 2023 has not been approved by the National Bureau of Statistics and is currently unavailable.

7-1 能源主要指标

Main Indicators of Energy

项　　目	item	2020	2021	2022
一、能源生产	**Production of Energy**			
(一)一次能源生产量	Primary Energy Output			
原油 (万吨)	Crude Oil (10000 tons)	1613.15	1744.68	1884.62
天然气 (亿立方米)	Natural Gas (100 million cu.m)	131.59	132.48	124.39
一次电 (亿千瓦时)	Primary Electricity (100 million kwh)	1622.79	1667.66	1896.53
(二)二次能源生产量	Secondary Energy Output			
原油加工量 (万吨)	Crude Oil Processing Capacity (10000 tons)	6211.95	6740.95	6560.33
汽油 (万吨)	Gasoline (10000 tons)	1206.19	1417.41	1371.76
煤油 (万吨)	Kerosene (10000 tons)	668.74	633.73	532.74
柴油 (万吨)	Diesel Oil (10000 tons)	1592.53	1649.54	1964.18
燃料油 (万吨)	Fuel Oil (10000 tons)	576.73	644.22	568.29
液化石油气 (万吨)	Liquefied Petroleum Gas (10000 tons)	464.49	503.72	468.50
发电量 (亿千瓦时)	Power Generation (100 million kwh)	3603.12	4638.57	4469.17
二、能源消费 (万吨标准煤)	**Consumption of Energy (10000 tons of SCE)**			
能源消费总量	Total Energy Consumption	34502.92	36821.42	36519.05
第一产业	Primary Industry	670.30	711.81	746.20
第二产业	Secondary Industry	20510.49	21881.43	21920.27
第三产业	Tertiary Industry	7634.13	8343.72	7867.70
居民消费量	Household Consumption	5688.01	5884.46	5984.88
三、节能减排 (%)	**Energy Conservation (%)**			
单位GDP能耗上升或下降(±)	Energy Consumption per Unit of GDP rises or decreases (±)	-1.16	-1.20	-2.60
规模以上工业单位工业增加值能耗上升或下降(±)	Energy Consumption per Unit of Industrial Value-added rises or decreases (±)	1.21	1.70	-3.00
单位GDP电耗上升或下降(±)	Electricity Consumption per Unit of GDP rises or decreases (±)	1.16	5.20	-1.90

7-2 能源生产总量及构成

Total Production of Energy and its Composition

项　目	Item	2000	2005	2010	2015	2020	2021	2022
能源生产总量 (万吨标准煤)	**Total Energy Production (10000 tons of SCE)**	**3711.69**	**4758.79**	**4858.07**	**6862.51**	**8563.01**	**8892.72**	**9647.31**
构　成 (%)	Composition (%)	100.0	100.0	100.0	100.0	100.0	100.0	100.0
原　煤	Coal	8.0	7.2					
原　油	Crude Oil	53.6	44.1	37.8	32.8	26.9	28.0	27.9
天然气	Natural Gas	11.3	12.5	21.5	18.7	17.7	18.1	15.6
一次电力及其他能源	Primary Electricity and Other Energy	27.1	36.2	40.7	48.5	55.4	53.9	56.5

7-3 能源消费总量及构成
Total Consumption of Energy and Its Composition

年份 Year	一次能源消费量(万吨标准煤) Primary Energy Consumption (10000 tons of SCE)	构成(%) Composition(%)				终端能源消费量(万吨标准煤) Final Energy Consumption (10000 tons of SCE)	构成(%) Composition(%)			
		原煤 Coal	原油 Crude Oil	天然气 Natural Gas	一次电力及其他能源 Primary Electricity and Other Energy		原煤 Coal	油品 Oil Products	电力 Elect-ricity	其他 Others
1990	3690.25	56.5	35.3		8.2	3936.44	33.6	22.4	33.0	11.0
1995	6147.61	56.4	28.5	0.2	14.9	7062.28	27.0	20.9	39.7	12.4
2000	7983.46	52.2	35.0	0.2	12.6	9080.20	17.1	22.6	45.4	14.9
2001	8169.60	52.5	34.0		13.5	9775.15	15.9	22.6	46.1	15.4
2002	9036.40	51.9	31.0		17.1	10861.68	14.5	21.6	49.2	14.7
2003	10462.09	53.5	28.6	0.2	17.7	12414.48	17.8	22.6	44.5	15.1
2004	12013.14	51.4	28.4	0.2	20.0	14487.74	11.7	20.7	52.6	15.0
2005	13086.58	52.8	26.1	0.3	20.8	17255.84	10.9	23.6	50.7	14.8
2006	15281.00	50.4	26.2	1.3	22.1	19254.03	12.5	23.7	48.7	15.1
2007	17344.10	52.0	24.2	3.5	20.3	21427.33	12.0	22.2	49.3	16.5
2008	17679.13	50.8	24.6	4.1	20.5	22671.76	13.8	21.2	48.5	16.5
2009	19235.86	46.5	27.5	5.4	20.6	23943.39	12.2	20.9	46.3	20.6
2010	21942.15	45.2	29.0	5.7	20.1	24594.92	9.7	18.8	50.4	21.1
2011	23318.44	50.2	27.0	6.4	16.4	26223.64	10.3	16.8	51.5	21.4
2012	23786.60	46.4	27.1	6.4	20.1	26763.90	9.7	16.7	52.2	21.4
2013	24930.93	46.4	27.1	6.5	20.0	27666.36	10.4	16.8	51.0	21.8
2014	25636.29	43.7	26.6	6.8	22.9	28669.57	10.2	16.6	53.5	19.7
2015	26999.64	40.2	25.9	7.1	26.8	29359.74	10.0	16.8	52.2	21.0
2016	28179.17	38.2	25.6	7.8	28.4	30700.98	9.8	18.1	52.6	19.5
2017	29253.74	38.7	25.4	8.2	27.7	31645.79	8.1	17.7	54.5	19.7
2018	30154.66	37.2	28.1	8.3	26.4	32760.73	7.2	17.2	54.6	21.0
2019	31122.99	34.2	25.9	8.7	31.2	33359.42	6.4	16.9	57.1	19.6
2020	32818.22	31.3	27.2	10.3	31.2	33774.90	6.3	15.6	58.0	20.1
2021	36221.32	35.0	26.8	11.4	26.8	35955.63	5.2	13.6	61.0	20.2
2022	36230.97	33.5	26.2	11.3	29.0	35700.97	4.8	11.3	61.3	22.6

7-4 综合能源平衡表

Overall Energy Balance Sheet

单位：万吨标准煤 (10000 tons of SCE)

项　目	Item	2000	2010	2015	2020	2021	2022
可供本地区消费的能源量	**Total Energy Available for Consumption by Locality**	**9447.70**	**25445.22**	**30117.44**	**34502.92**	**36821.42**	**36519.05**
年初库存量	Stock at the Year-beginning	675.20	1347.93	1635.41	2810.98	2389.88	2243.64
一次能源生产量	Primary Energy Output	3711.69	4858.07	7126.26	8563.01	8892.72	9647.31
外省调入量	Allocation from Other Provinces	5628.27	15570.94	20486.80	18114.15	19247.95	22186.34
进口量	Imports	2757.39	8112.34	6732.49	18952.08	20027.99	18737.66
境内轮船和飞机在境外加油量	Petroleum Consumed by Chinese Airplanes and Ships Abroad		183.44	220.81	117.84	175.81	305.26
本省调出量(-)	Allocation over Other Provinces(-)	-1599.39	-1294.98	-2392.60	-9703.98	-9369.68	-12205.82
出口量(-)	Exports(-)	-980.31	-1700.12	-1377.99	-1819.78	-2145.51	-1628.38
境外轮船和飞机在境内加油量(-)	Petroleum Consumed by Foreign Airplanes and Ships in China(-)	-62.51	-275.16	-336.16	-110.38	-158.04	-304.70
年末库存量(-)	Stock at the Year-end(-)	-779.26	-1357.25	-1977.58	-2421.02	-2239.69	-2462.26
加工转换投入(-)产出(+)量	**Input Output in Processing and Transformation**	**-35.74**	**-92.50**	**-0.11**	**-42.04**	**-72.39**	**-0.41**
火力发电	Thermal Power						
供热	Heating		-90.80	-128.38	-223.60	-216.53	-250.51
洗选煤	Coal Washing						
炼焦	Coking	-3.85	-2.25	-8.76	-54.66	-43.07	-25.41
炼油及煤制油	Petroleum Refining	-26.89	205.83	-185.30	-408.96	-463.28	-500.75
制气	Gas Production	-5.00	-1.08	-31.76	-35.07	-57.87	-78.43
回收能	Recovery of Energy	96.59	123.70	365.40	680.70	709.15	855.33
损失量	**Losses**	**331.76**	**757.80**	**757.59**	**685.97**	**793.40**	**817.67**
#运输和输配损失	Losses in Transmission	318.75	732.46	741.70	654.40	696.47	740.62
终端消费量	**End-use**	**9080.20**	**24594.92**	**29359.74**	**33774.90**	**35955.63**	**35700.97**
第一产业	Primary Industry	353.56	400.60	501.98	670.30	711.81	746.20
农、林、牧、渔业	Farming, Forestry, Animal Husbandry and Fishery	353.56	400.60	501.98	670.30	711.81	746.20
第二产业	Secondary Industry	5790.91	16452.13	18179.56	19791.89	21025.50	21123.25
工业	Industry	5693.02	15813.16	17445.74	19056.24	20304.99	20545.42
#用作原料材料	As Raw Materials and Fuel	86.44	990.06	586.76	1328.70	1193.32	1430.02
建筑业	Construction	97.90	638.97	733.82	735.65	720.51	577.83
第三产业	Tertiary Industry	1648.93	4749.44	6256.26	7624.71	8333.86	7846.63
交通运输仓储及邮电通信业	Transport, Storage, Postal and Telecommunication Services	957.92	2332.91	3137.15	3395.70	3307.71	2743.23
批发和零售贸易业、餐饮业	Wholesale and Retail Trade and Catering Services	403.21	1202.83	1479.01	1765.40	2096.29	2136.42
其他	Others	287.81	1213.70	1640.10	2463.61	2929.85	2966.98
生活消费	Residential Consumption	1286.80	2992.75	4421.95	5688.01	5884.46	5984.88
城镇	Urban Areas	818.33	1896.70	2796.08	3527.24	3650.28	3703.40
乡村	Rural Areas	468.45	1096.05	1625.86	2160.77	2234.18	2281.48
平衡差额	**Balance**						
消费量合计	**Total Energy Consumption**	**9447.70**	**25445.22**	**30117.44**	**34502.92**	**36821.42**	**36519.05**

7-5 分行业能源消费总量和原煤、电力消费量（2022年）

Consumption of Total Energy, Coal and Electricity by Sector (2022)

行业	Sector	能源消费总量（万吨标准煤）Total Energy Consumption (10000 tons of SCE)	原煤消费量（万吨）Coal Consumption (10000 tons)	电力消费量（亿千瓦小时）Electricity Consumption (100 million kwh)
消费总量	**Total**	**36519.05**	**18628.88**	**7870.34**
农、林、牧、渔业	**Farming,Forestry,Animal Husbandry and Fishery**	**746.20**	**39.74**	**164.62**
工业合计	**Industry**	**21350.59**	**18570.43**	**4565.47**
采矿业	**Mining and Quarrying**	**224.70**	**5.58**	**24.02**
煤炭开采和洗选业	Mining and Washing of Coal			
石油和天然气开采业	Extraction of Petroleum and Natural Gas	137.14		0.99
黑色金属矿采选业	Mining and Dressing of Ferrous Metal Ores	12.99		3.04
有色金属矿采选业	Mining and Dressing of Nonferrous Metal Ores	18.52	1.46	5.69
非金属矿采选业	Mining and Dressing of Nonmetal Ores	52.78	4.12	14.16
开采专业及辅助性活动	Auxiliary Minning Operations Mining	3.08		0.14
其他采矿业	Mining and Dressing of Other Ores	0.18		
制造业	**Manufacturing**	**18325.62**	**3646.17**	**3627.39**
农副食品加工业	Processing of Farm and Sideline Food	275.89	12.49	62.81
食品制造业	Manufacture of Food	185.75	19.89	42.01
酒、饮料和精制茶制造业	Manufacture of Wine, Beverage and Tea	99.69	6.68	23.72
烟草制品业	Tobacco Products	8.36		2.21
纺织业	Textile Industry	536.53	169.60	106.31
纺织服装、服饰业	Manufacture of Textile Garments, Footwear and	116.79	11.53	32.03
皮革、毛皮、羽毛(绒)及其制品业	Leather, Fur, Feather, Down and Related Products	99.47	1.15	29.91
木材加工及木、竹、藤、棕、草制品业	Timber Processing, Bamboo, Cane, Palm Fiber & Straw Products	81.19	0.80	23.74
家具制造业	Manufacture of Furniture	100.84	0.66	31.33
造纸及纸制品业	Papermaking and Paper Products	936.71	652.85	194.31
印刷业和记录媒介的复制	Printing and Record Medium Reproduction	122.79	0.37	36.73
文教、工美、体育和娱乐用品制造业	Manufacture of Cultural, Educational and Sports Articles	151.60	0.22	48.20
石油加工、炼焦及核燃料加工业	Petroleum Refining, Coking, and Nuclear Fuel Processing	2305.68	448.70	122.41
化学原料及化学制品制造业	Manufacture of Raw Chemical Materials and Chemical Products	1925.81	95.61	232.07
医药制造业	Manufacture of Medicines	133.66	4.13	34.51
化学纤维制造业	Manufacture of Chemical Fibers	55.83	2.08	14.24
橡胶和塑料制品业	Rubber Products	871.15	20.89	266.36
非金属矿物制品业	Nonmetal Mineral Products	2778.88	1507.78	364.59
黑色金属冶炼及压延加工业	Smelting and Pressing of Ferrous Metals	2256.15	575.18	314.00
有色金属冶炼及压延加工业	Smelting and Pressing of Nonferrous Metals	590.18	80.18	136.60
金属制品业	Metal Products	791.96	13.63	232.62
通用设备制造业	Manufacture of General-purpose Machinery	209.96	5.54	66.57
专用设备制造业	Manufacture of Special-purpose Machinery	245.28	2.69	80.49
汽车制造业	Manufacture of Automobile	330.28		104.57
铁路、船舶、航空航天和其他运输设备制造业	Manufacture of Railway ,Ship,Aeronautics and Other Transport Equipment	63.08	0.04	16.56
电气机械及器材制造业	Manufacture of Electrical Machinery and Equipment	787.29	0.51	255.50
通信设备、计算机及其他电子设备制造业	Manufacture of Communication Equipment, Computers and Other Electronic Equipment	2068.37	3.98	698.61
仪器仪表制造业	Manufacture of Instruments and Meters	58.59		18.89
其他制造业	Handicraft and Other Manufactures	37.94	1.20	10.90
废弃资源综合利用业	Recycling and Disposal of Waste	94.87	7.79	23.04
金属制品、机械和设备修理业	Manufacture of Metal Products,Machinery and Equipment Maintenance	5.07		1.55
电力、燃气及水的生产和供应业	**Production and Supply of Electric Power,Gas and Water**	**2800.27**	**14918.68**	**914.06**
电力、热力的生产和供应业	Production and Supply of Electric Power and Heat Power	2504.09	14905.37	816.73
燃气生产和供应业	Production and Supply of Gas	27.33	0.58	6.42
水的生产和供应业	Production and Supply of Water	268.86	12.73	90.91
建筑业	**Construction**	**577.83**	**2.85**	**104.26**
交通运输、仓储及邮政业	**Transport, Storage,Postal and Telecommunication Services**	**2756.15**		**178.41**
批发和零售贸易餐饮业	**Wholesale and Retail Trade and Catering Services**	**2136.42**	**3.24**	**520.30**
其他行业	**Others**	**2966.98**	**2.12**	**984.33**
生活消费	**Non-production Consumption**	**5984.88**	**10.50**	**1352.95**

7-6 各市电力消费量

Electricity Consumption by City

单位：亿千瓦小时 (100 million kwh)

市 别	City	2000	2005	2010	2015	2018	2019	2020	2021	2022
全 省	**Provincial Total**	**1334.58**	**2673.56**	**4060.13**	**5310.69**	**6323.35**	**6695.85**	**6926.12**	**7866.63**	**7870.34**
广 州	Guangzhou	238.78	425.67	625.90	779.32	936.90	1005.58	996.72	1119.73	1118.76
深 圳	Shenzhen	190.35	440.21	663.55	806.68	907.19	972.98	983.34	1103.40	1073.82
珠 海	Zhuhai	30.82	61.58	102.26	145.37	175.99	189.91	193.20	218.22	224.64
汕 头	Shantou	43.91	87.60	136.81	178.01	209.36	211.99	218.46	249.30	251.14
佛 山	Foshan	168.84	316.29	463.08	587.84	690.85	702.65	710.30	780.79	758.91
韶 关	Shaoguan	35.81	58.72	84.06	111.31	133.64	144.23	154.09	167.61	189.35
河 源	Heyuan	9.27	23.90	51.52	78.06	89.84	97.40	99.38	115.75	117.57
梅 州	Meizhou	22.70	40.40	60.88	77.98	99.11	104.67	112.07	123.41	118.98
惠 州	Huizhou	43.53	105.22	192.46	290.62	408.38	425.88	447.84	510.36	516.62
汕 尾	Shanwei	9.35	16.87	29.73	47.05	56.83	60.56	65.95	73.91	75.48
东 莞	Dongguan	179.78	419.83	562.00	666.84	806.64	850.70	873.90	1001.18	967.71
中 山	Zhongshan	54.54	123.63	186.65	245.51	293.01	310.04	316.58	357.17	344.71
江 门	Jiangmen	64.65	113.63	165.21	237.13	281.78	294.71	309.07	350.84	342.41
阳 江	Yangjiang	12.09	22.46	40.43	98.21	119.84	134.26	145.20	148.99	155.71
湛 江	Zhanjiang	24.15	49.09	78.68	116.04	196.43	212.65	237.97	280.77	294.72
茂 名	Maoming	29.98	40.11	65.80	98.40	115.18	123.63	133.38	152.87	153.93
肇 庆	Zhaoqing	24.00	48.58	105.08	152.30	171.81	180.44	182.28	210.64	211.98
清 远	Qingyuan	22.60	59.47	125.53	179.27	198.72	216.03	240.18	276.33	262.98
潮 州	Chaozhou	13.95	33.17	59.16	75.59	91.10	95.59	101.11	115.34	114.67
揭 阳	Jieyang	22.51	51.13	98.68	152.71	155.88	157.06	166.94	188.19	195.43
云 浮	Yunfu	12.14	21.55	34.89	57.81	68.58	74.45	78.56	85.17	95.26
按经济区域分	By Region									
珠 三 角	Pearl River Delta	995.29	2054.64	3066.18	3911.61	4672.54	4932.88	5013.23	5652.34	5559.56
粤 东	Eastern Region	89.72	188.77	324.38	453.34	513.18	525.21	552.46	626.74	636.72
粤 西	Western Region	66.22	111.66	184.91	312.65	431.45	470.54	516.55	582.63	604.36
粤 北	Northern Region	102.52	204.04	356.88	504.43	589.89	636.79	684.29	768.27	784.14

注：由于各市电力消费量不包含不分区域线损，全省数不等于分市数合计。

Note: Because the electricity consumption by region doesn't include line losses , the sum of electricity consumption by cities is different from the provincial total.

7-7 各市单位GDP能耗增长速度

Growth Rate of Energy Consumption Per Unit GDP by City

单位：% (%)

市别	City	2010	2013	2014	2015	2016	2017	2018	2019	2020	2021	2022
全省	**Provincial Total**	**-2.9**	**-4.6**	**-3.6**	**-5.7**	**-3.6**	**-3.7**	**-3.4**	**-3.5**	**-1.2**	**-1.2**	**-2.6**
广州	Guangzhou	-4.6	-5.1	-3.5	-4.5	-5.0	-4.8	-3.2	-3.9	-4.2	-1.8	-3.1
深圳	Shenzhen	-2.9	-5.1	-4.4	-3.3	-4.2	-4.2	-4.2	-3.5	-5.5	1.0	-5.8
珠海	Zhuhai	-3.7	-5.0	-4.1	-2.8	-3.9	-4.2	-1.3	-3.1	-0.4	-2.1	-0.2
汕头	Shantou	-3.2	-4.0	-3.8	-6.8	-3.0	-5.0	-4.1	-2.8	-2.2	-0.3	2.8
佛山	Foshan	-4.4	-4.5	-4.4	-5.6	-6.6	-5.1	-5.2	-4.9	-5.3	-1.7	-3.7
韶关	Shaoguan	-1.6	-4.3	-5.0	-8.0	-3.8	3.2	1.8	-1.0	-1.5	-5.4	-1.1
河源	Heyuan	-1.1	-3.7	-2.2	-4.1	-4.1	-4.2	0.1	-0.5	-8.3	5.6	-1.8
梅州	Meizhou	-3.2	-4.5	-3.7	-5.9	-3.8	-4.8	12.8	0.0	2.2	-2.2	-3.3
惠州	Huizhou	-5.8	-4.4	-3.7	-7.1	-1.5	6.3	10.2	1.7	2.3	-5.3	-5.0
汕尾	Shanwei	-2.0	-5.7	-1.1	2.0	-3.0	-0.9	-4.6	1.4	-0.7	-3.2	-0.7
东莞	Dongguan	-2.0	-5.4	-5.9	-7.9	-4.7	-4.9	-5.6	-4.5	-2.9	-4.0	-1.9
中山	Zhongshan	-1.5	-4.0	-3.8	-3.9	-3.9	-3.7	-3.8	-1.3	-6.2	-0.3	-4.0
江门	Jiangmen	-2.3	-4.5	-3.0	-6.6	-4.5	-4.6	-4.9	-2.5	-2.5	-2.3	-3.3
阳江	Yangjiang	-1.0	-4.0	-3.4	-4.1	7.2	5.5	5.6	4.0	-1.1	-12.7	2.8
湛江	Zhanjiang	-0.3	-4.0	-4.0	-2.6	38.3	8.8	-3.8	-1.7	11.4	13.6	9.8
茂名	Maoming	-4.3	-4.2	-2.4	-7.4	-2.8	-4.4	-0.8	-3.8	-7.1	-5.0	-7.9
肇庆	Zhaoqing	-2.4	-4.0	-3.5	-4.5	-5.4	-2.0	-6.9	-3.5	-2.6	-8.0	-2.5
清远	Qingyuan	-2.0	-2.8	-3.0	-7.7	-4.0	-3.9	3.6	-3.1	-3.1	-8.0	-9.7
潮州	Chaozhou	-3.3	-4.8	-3.5	-6.7	-4.1	-3.8	-4.3	-3.5	-2.1	-2.2	-3.5
揭阳	Jieyang	-2.2	-4.5	-2.0	-6.4	-4.4	2.8	-6.9	-3.5	-4.8	0.8	10.5
云浮	Yunfu	-1.5	-3.9	-3.1	-2.9	-4.8	-4.2	-5.2	-4.1	-3.6	-6.2	2.8

注：本表为当年节能考核确认数。
Note: Data in this table is the confirmed figure of energy saving assessment in the current year.

7-8 各市单位GDP电耗增长速度

Growth Rate of Electricity Consumption per Unit of GDP by City

单位：% (%)

市别	City	2010	2013	2014	2015	2016	2017	2018	2019	2020	2021	2022
全省	**Provincial Total**	**0.0**	**-3.6**	**0.6**	**-6.1**	**-1.7**	**-1.2**	**-0.6**	**-0.2**	**1.2**	**5.2**	**-1.9**
广州	Guangzhou	-2.5	-8.2	-0.8	-6.1	-2.4	-1.3	-2.3	0.5	-3.5	3.9	-1.1
深圳	Shenzhen	1.0	-8.3	-0.6	-5.0	-4.2	-4.8	-3.6	-0.4	-1.9	5.2	-5.9
珠海	Zhuhai	-1.2	-6.2	0.0	-1.6	-3.1	-2.5	0.2	1.0	-1.2	5.6	0.7
汕头	Shantou	-0.6	-5.4	-0.8	-5.8	-1.3	-3.6	-2.2	-4.6	1.0	7.5	-0.3
佛山	Foshan	-2.8	-5.1	-1.4	-4.0	-2.5	0.1	-3.5	-4.9	-0.5	1.5	-4.8
韶关	Shaoguan	2.4	0.8	0.0	-12.0	-5.5	1.0	7.2	2.0	3.7	0.1	1.6
河源	Heyuan	3.5	0.3	3.0	-3.0	-1.7	-1.5	7.2	2.8	0.7	7.9	0.3
梅州	Meizhou	-4.7	-5.3	1.1	-6.2	0.6	-0.5	8.1	2.1	5.4	3.8	-4.2
惠州	Huizhou	-1.6	-3.8	1.1	-3.6	2.8	5.8	4.6	0.1	3.6	3.5	-2.7
汕尾	Shanwei	-5.8	-4.5	6.6	-0.6	0.1	0.5	-1.1	-0.1	3.5	0.8	0.7
东莞	Dongguan	2.8	-6.2	-1.5	-6.5	-2.6	0.2	-1.3	-1.8	1.6	5.9	-4.0
中山	Zhongshan	1.4	-4.4	1.4	-4.7	-2.0	1.1	-1.0	4.6	0.6	4.3	-4.0
江门	Jiangmen	1.6	-3.7	2.0	-4.0	-2.4	-0.6	-2.2	0.1	2.5	4.7	-5.5
阳江	Yangjiang	5.7	4.5	6.4	-0.2	0.1	0.9	2.5	3.5	3.5	-5.3	3.6
湛江	Zhanjiang	-0.1	-6.2	1.4	-2.3	22.4	10.8	2.1	4.1	9.8	8.6	3.8
茂名	Maoming	-4.7	-6.3	4.8	-3.9	-1.4	-4.3	2.1	2.8	6.3	6.5	0.2
肇庆	Zhaoqing	1.7	-2.5	-0.4	-9.9	-0.4	0.7	-4.5	-1.2	-1.9	4.6	-0.5
清远	Qingyuan	-2.3	1.7	2.8	-4.9	0.0	-12.6	7.8	2.2	2.1	6.6	-5.8
潮州	Chaozhou	0.9	-7.1	1.1	-6.4	-1.3	0.3	0.9	-0.1	4.5	4.4	-2.8
揭阳	Jieyang	-3.6	-1.8	3.7	-11.0	-0.9	-12.0	-0.5	-2.2	6.1	6.2	5.2
云浮	Yunfu	0.2	1.7	1.6	-2.9	-1.1	0.2	2.9	2.3	1.4	0.3	9.5

7-9 各市单位工业增加值能耗增长速度

Growth Rate of Energy Consumption per Unit of Industrial Value-added by City

单位：% (%)

市 别	City	2010	2013	2014	2015	2016	2017	2018	2019	2020	2021	2022
全 省	**Provincial Total**	**-6.9**	**-5.0**	**-9.2**	**-10.5**	**-3.7**	**0.0**	**-2.4**	**-5.2**	**1.2**	**1.7**	**-3.0**
广 州	Guangzhou	-12.6	-10.9	-11.9	-13.0	-6.6	-4.9	-6.5	-7.5	-1.7	-3.7	-3.7
深 圳	Shenzhen	-3.7	-9.5	-8.5	-11.1	-5.0	-0.8	-11.2	-3.9	-4.8	5.5	-5.2
珠 海	Zhuhai	-10.5	-9.2	-8.5	-1.9	-7.1	-6.8	-8.8	-9.6	-1.2	6.6	-7.5
汕 头	Shantou	18.7	5.4	-11.2	-16.0	-16.8	4.9	3.3	-11.2	-0.8	2.7	0.5
佛 山	Foshan	-10.5	-11.4	-12.5	-13.8	-8.3	-6.4	-8.8	-8.9	-8.3	-3.9	-11.1
韶 关	Shaoguan	-2.1	-10.6	-12.8	-8.7	-0.5	12.5	4.5	-2.2	2.8	2.2	-5.4
河 源	Heyuan	-1.1	-15.9	-19.3	-13.3	-9.7	1.4	-2.8	-14.2	-12.6	35.9	27.0
梅 州	Meizhou	-15.3	-3.2	-14.9	-15.5	1.5	-23.4	26.2	4.1	4.6	6.9	-6.7
惠 州	Huizhou	-16.9	-18.2	-14.1	-12.3	-4.6	10.3	11.6	6.1	5.3	-9.4	-7.6
汕 尾	Shanwei	-14.2	-30.7	-14.9	26.2	-2.2	14.8	-4.7	21.2	2.0	-0.3	3.9
东 莞	Dongguan	-10.9	-8.4	-9.7	-10.9	-3.9	-7.9	-9.2	-11.9	-3.2	-1.6	2.2
中 山	Zhongshan	-3.8	-12.3	-3.8	4.9	-1.6	-1.6	-6.0	-2.3	-2.0	-10.8	-10.3
江 门	Jiangmen	-12.9	-0.5	-17.5	-14.9	-10.9	-4.8	0.0	-10.3	0.7	5.5	1.4
阳 江	Yangjiang	59.0	-16.7	-1.2	-10.3	4.6	5.5	8.0	-11.1	-4.5	-12.5	1.9
湛 江	Zhanjiang	-4.3	-7.4	-17.8	-11.4	43.4	13.1	-3.7	-1.3	17.9	16.4	13.4
茂 名	Maoming	-9.9	-11.5	-5.0	-11.6	-6.5	-3.1	2.8	-2.2	5.3	5.9	-0.4
肇 庆	Zhaoqing	-7.7	-9.3	-9.8	-12.9	-8.4	-0.5	-8.2	-7.2	0.3	-16.6	-6.5
清 远	Qingyuan	-16.3	-0.7	-9.5	-9.2	-7.4	-0.7	-1.6	-5.5	-3.9	-10.2	-9.8
潮 州	Chaozhou	17.9	-16.1	-21.1	-13.2	-11.5	11.5	-3.8	-3.9	-8.4	6.2	-6.8
揭 阳	Jieyang	-15.5	24.3	-18.6	-15.5	-17.5	15.1	-5.7	-6.5	4.4	9.8	35.0
云 浮	Yunfu	-9.7	-21.3	-14.2	-10.3	-7.6	-2.4	-8.8	-11.5	-3.4	-8.6	-2.1

7-10 平均每天各种能源消费量

Average Daily Energy Consumption by Variety

能源品种	Energy Variety	2000	2005	2010	2015	2020	2021	2022
合 计(吨标准煤)	**Total (ton of SCE)**	**248773**	**472363**	**721776**	**804376**	**925340**	**985086**	**978109**
煤 炭 (吨)	Coal (Ton)	59590	78227	143273	135415	100542	75952	70515
焦 炭 (吨)	Coke (Ton)	3973	8058	13314	14875	27718	25546	29460
原 油 (吨)	Crude Oil (Ton)	250	178	480	635	772	808	1555
燃料油 (吨)	Fuel Oil (Ton)	9248	18288	13141	8253	7812	10123	8603
汽 油 (吨)	Gasoline (Ton)	8226	19330	29693	33601	41242	34725	28164
煤 油 (吨)	Kerosene (Ton)	2444	4212	5532	7510	7655	9984	9140
柴 油 (吨)	Diesel Oil (Ton)	18726	34920	45370	43303	42118	37197	29895
液化石油气 (吨)	Liquefied Petroleum Gas(Ton)	8720	16676	16023	18510	16956	16671	21535
电 力(万千瓦时)	Electricity (10000 kwh)	33978	69671	105290	139035	183624	208886	208683

7−11 平均每人年生活用能源

Annual per Capita Energy Consumption of Households

能源品种	Energy Variety	2000	2005	2010	2015	2020	2021	2022
合 计(千克标准煤)	**Total (kg of SCE)**	**148.90**	**227.85**	**290.97**	**381.75**	**452.99**	**465.03**	**472.35**
煤 炭 (千克)	Coal (kg)	9.63	10.54	6.14	5.75	5.17	3.54	1.17
汽 油 (千克)	Gasoline (kg)	4.42	14.57	36.95	46.50	62.03	49.45	40.41
煤 油 (千克)	Kerosene (kg)	0.24	0.33	0.35	0.35	0.26	0.23	0.17
柴 油 (千克)	Diesel Oil (kg)	0.57	0.98	1.39	1.65	1.67	1.55	1.90
液化石油气 (千克)	Liquefied Petroleum Gas(kg)	31.47	43.66	27.42	40.19	33.54	33.78	39.16
电 力 (千瓦时)	Electricity (kwh)	239.09	359.06	536.60	730.31	939.33	1040.97	1067.80

7−12 分品种生活能源年消费总量

Annual Total Energy Consumption of Households by Variety

能源品种	Energy Variety	2000	2005	2010	2015	2020	2021	2022
合 计(万吨标准煤)	**Total (10000 tons of SCE)**	**1286.80**	**2100.39**	**2992.75**	**4421.95**	**5688.01**	**5884.46**	**5984.88**
煤 炭 (万吨)	Coal (10000 tons)	83.22	96.46	63.19	66.57	64.91	44.77	14.77
汽 油 (万吨)	Gasoline (10000 tons)	38.20	133.36	380.05	538.63	778.93	625.71	512.07
煤 油 (万吨)	Kerosene (10000 tons)	2.10	2.98	3.60	4.11	3.30	2.87	2.16
柴 油 (万吨)	Diesel Oil (10000 tons)	4.90	8.93	14.30	19.10	20.97	19.58	24.13
液化石油气 (万吨)	Liquefied Petroleum Gas(10000 tons)	271.96	399.55	282.01	465.57	421.12	427.45	496.19
电 力(亿千瓦小时)	Electricity (100 million kwh)	206.62	328.62	551.92	845.96	1179.47	1317.24	1352.95

7-13　能源加工转换效率

Efficiency of Energy Conversion

单位：%　　　　　　　　　　　　　　　　　　　　　　　　　　　　(%)

年 份 Year	火力发电 Thermal Power Generation	供 热 Heating	炼 焦 Coking	炼 油 Petroleum Refining	制 气 Gas Production
1990	31.13	79.21	93.48	99.44	
1995	31.85	80.07	90.93	99.89	86.17
2000	37.20	87.19	94.35	99.02	79.18
2001	37.21	85.09	95.23	99.12	77.90
2002	36.36	76.40	94.27	98.40	80.08
2003	40.69	71.43	82.36	98.57	78.67
2004	35.53	86.10	91.53	99.29	79.70
2005	36.22	95.99	96.66	99.53	79.18
2006	37.74	88.49	96.95	99.80	95.40
2007	38.80	70.66	99.02	99.79	97.22
2008	38.00	77.34	98.43	99.10	95.65
2009	38.69	82.15	98.31	99.58	93.47
2010	38.90	82.80	99.08	98.12	87.81
2011	38.22	79.19	98.69	98.54	89.87
2012	38.49	78.26	97.57	98.17	89.77
2013	39.66	79.57	96.01	98.48	91.00
2014	39.72	75.73	96.15	97.42	71.51
2015	40.62	84.02	97.15	97.69	57.39
2016	40.78	83.32	97.91	99.03	60.99
2017	40.79	84.41	96.56	95.78	62.77
2018	41.70	81.59	92.63	99.47	57.40
2019	41.58	79.64	93.56	97.10	62.80
2020	42.04	82.00	93.10	96.43	64.00
2021	42.75	85.02	94.79	97.07	65.00
2022	42.80	83.48	97.46	96.65	58.81

7-14 能源生产弹性系数

Elasticity Ratio of Energy Production

年份 Year	能源生产比上年增长(%) Growth Rate of Energy Production over Preceding Year(%)	电力生产比上年增长(%) Growth Rate of Electricity Production over Preceding Year(%)	本省生产总值比上年增长(%) Growth Rate of Gross Domestic Product(GDP) over Preceding Year(%)	能源生产弹性系数 Elasticity Ratio of Energy Production	电力生产弹性系数 Elasticity Ratio of Electricity Production
1986	1.0	8.0	12.7	0.08	0.63
1990	0.3	15.3	11.6	0.02	1.32
1995	14.7	6.6	15.6	0.94	0.42
1996	43.3	10.7	11.3	3.83	0.95
1997	8.5	8.0	11.2	0.76	0.71
1998	-4.1	5.6	10.8		0.52
1999	-10.3	9.8	10.1		0.97
2000	5.8	18.7	11.5	0.50	1.63
2001	-8.2	5.9	10.5		0.56
2002	6.5	12.4	12.4	0.52	1.00
2003	12.7	17.7	14.8	0.86	1.20
2004	18.6	11.9	14.8	1.26	0.80
2005	-6.7	7.4	13.8		0.54
2006	-8.1	8.5	14.6		0.58
2007	-5.7	8.9	14.7		0.61
2008	12.5	-0.4	10.1	1.24	
2009	-0.6	-0.6	9.7		
2010	10.6	20.1	12.4	0.85	1.62
2011	-0.2	15.6	10.0		1.56
2012	5.0	-1.8	8.2	0.61	
2013	5.4	6.7	8.5	0.64	0.79
2014	4.3	0.5	7.8	0.55	0.06
2015	22.7	0.5	8.0	2.84	0.06
2016	4.0	5.7	7.5	0.53	0.76
2017	-1.4	6.4	7.5		0.85
2018	0.6	3.5	6.8	0.09	0.51
2019	18.3	7.1	6.2	2.96	1.14
2020	2.2	7.1	2.3	0.96	1.51
2021	3.9	20.7	8.1	0.48	2.58
2022	8.5	0.9	1.9	4.47	0.50

7–15 能源消费弹性系数

Elasticity Ratio of Energy Consumption

年份 Year	能源消费比上年增长（%） Growth Rate of Energy Consumption over Preceding Year(%)	电力消费比上年增长(%) Growth Rate of Electricity Consumption over Preceding Year(%)	本省生产总值比上年增长(%) Growth Rate of Gross Domestic Product(GDP) over Preceding Year(%)	能源消费弹性系数 Elasticity Ratio of Energy Consumption	电力消费弹性系数 Elasticity Ratio of Electricity Consumption
1986	8.4	4.7	12.7	0.66	0.37
1990	4.1	14.3	11.6	0.35	1.24
1995	9.2	7.6	15.6	0.59	0.49
1996	5.5	8.9	11.3	0.48	0.79
1997	2.7	7.1	11.2	0.24	0.64
1998	5.3	7.5	10.8	0.49	0.70
1999	4.3	10.0	10.1	0.42	0.99
2000	8.2	22.9	11.5	0.71	1.99
2001	7.7	9.3	10.5	0.74	0.88
2002	11.6	15.7	12.4	0.93	1.27
2003	15.4	20.3	14.8	1.04	1.37
2004	16.1	17.5	14.8	1.09	1.18
2005	16.8	12.0	13.8	1.22	0.87
2006	11.2	12.4	14.6	0.77	0.85
2007	10.9	13.0	14.7	0.74	0.88
2008	5.3	3.3	10.1	0.52	0.32
2009	6.9	2.9	9.7	0.71	0.30
2010	8.9	12.5	12.4	0.72	1.00
2011	5.8	8.3	10.0	0.58	0.83
2012	2.3	5.0	8.2	0.28	0.61
2013	3.6	4.5	8.5	0.42	0.53
2014	3.9	8.4	7.8	0.50	1.08
2015	1.9	1.4	8.0	0.24	0.18
2016	3.6	5.6	7.5	0.48	0.75
2017	3.5	6.2	7.5	0.47	0.83
2018	3.2	6.1	6.8	0.47	0.90
2019	2.4	5.9	6.2	0.39	0.95
2020	1.1	3.4	2.3	0.46	1.50
2021	6.7	13.6	8.1	0.84	1.70
2022	-0.8	0.0	1.9	0.00	0.02

7-16 自然资源

Natural Resources

项目		Item		2022	2023
一、土地资源和海洋		**Land Resources and Sea**			
土地面积	(万平方公里)	Total Land Area	(10000 sq.km)	17.98	17.98
耕地	(万公顷)	Cultivated Land	(10000 hectares)	189.97	190.63
林地	(万公顷)	Afforested Land	(10000 hectares)	1074.23	1072.88
园地	(万公顷)	Plantation	(10000 hectares)	131.66	129.40
牧草地	(万公顷)	Grass Land	(10000 hectares)	0.04	0.04
海域总面积	(万平方公里)	Total Area of Sea	(10000 sq.km)	41.93	41.93
海洋滩涂面积	(万公顷)	Sea Beach Area	(10000 hectares)	18.02	18.02
海岛面积	(平方公里)	Area of Islands	(sq.km)	1513.17	1513.17
大陆海岸线长度	(公里)	Length of Continental Coastline	(km)	4084.48	4084.48
岛屿岸线长度	(公里)	Length of Island Coastline	(km)	2378.71	2378.71
岛屿个数	(个)	Number of Islands	(unit)	1963	1963
二、气候		**Climate**			
年平均降雨量	(毫米)	Annual Average Precipitation	(mm)	2057.6	1819.2
年平均气温	(摄氏度)	Annual Average Temperature	(℃)	22.2	22.7
年日照时数	(小时)	Annual Sunshine Hours	(hour)	1856.3	1780.8
三、森林		**Forest**			
森林蓄积量	(亿立方米)	Total Standing Stock Volume	(100 million cu.m)		
森林覆盖率	(%)	Forest Coverage Rate	(%)		
四、水力水产		**Hydropower and Aquatic Products**			
水能资源理论蕴藏量	(万千瓦)	Theoretical Hydropower Resources	(10000 kw)	1137.2	1137.2
#技术可开发量		Developable Resources		864.6	864.6
五、矿产		**Mineral Resources**			
煤保有资源储量	(万吨)	Ensured Reserve of Coal	(10000 tons)	48383.59	48793.31
铁矿石保有资源储量	(万吨)	Ensured Reserve of Iron Ore	(10000 tons)	58972.31	37278.91
硫铁矿保有资源储量	(万吨)	Ensured Reserve of Pyrite Ore	(10000 tons)	31119.84	31136.18

注：1.表中土地面积、耕地、林地、园地、牧草地数据为2022年数据。
2.海域总面积包括内水领海专属经济区面积。
3.大陆海岸线长度来源于2022年省政府批复岸线；海岛面积、岛岸线长度、岛屿个数来源于2013年广东省海岛地名普查；海域总面积包括内水领海专属经济区面积。
4.森林覆盖率、森林蓄积量数据由林草湿调查监测工作产生，并由国家林业局统一发布各省林草湿调查监测成果，2022年、2023年相关数据尚未发布。
5.煤保有资源储量变动原因是2023年度新增压覆及国情调查成果数据调整入库，铁矿石保有资源储量变动主要原因是(兴宁霞岚钒钛磁铁矿)国情调查成果数据调整入库。

Notes: a) The data of Total Land Area, Cultivated Land, Afforested Land, Plantation, Grass Land in the table is based on the data of 2022.
b) Total Area of Sea includes the area of exclusive economic zone of internal waters and territorial waters.
c) The length of continental coastline approved by the Guangdong Provincial Government in 2022; the area of islands, the length of the island coastline, and the number of islands are from the geographical name survey of Guangdong Province in 2013; the total area of sea includes the area of the exclusive economic zone of internal waters and territorial waters.
d)The data on forest area and forest volume are generated by the forest and grass moisture survey and monitoring work,and the results of forest and grass moisture survey and monitoring in each province are uniformly released by the National Forestry Administration.The relevant data for 2022 and 2023 have not been released yet.
e)The reason for the change in coal reserves is that the 2023 annual addition of the overlay and the adjustment and storage of national survey results. The main reason for the change in iron ore reserves is the adjustment and storage of the national survey results of (Xingning Xialan Vanadium-Titanium Magnetite).

7-17 各地区年平均气温

Average Temperature by Region

单位：摄氏度 (℃)

年份 Year	粤北 Northern Regions	粤东北 North Eastern Regions	粤西北 North Western Regions	粤东 Eastern Regions	粤中 Central Regions	粤西 Western Regions
1980	20.7	21.5	22.5	21.2	22.2	23.4
1985	20.2	20.9	22.0	21.1	21.6	22.6
1990	21.1	21.5	22.8	21.8	22.6	23.4
1995	20.0	20.0	22.2	21.6	22.3	23.0
1996	19.9	21.4	22.4	21.9	21.6	23.3
1997	20.4	21.3	22.7	22.1	22.0	23.7
1998	21.2	22.5	23.3	23.0	22.8	24.5
1999	20.8	21.9	22.7	22.6	22.5	24.0
2000	20.4	21.9	22.6	22.5	22.5	23.8
2001	20.5	22.0	22.5	22.7	22.6	23.8
2002	21.0	22.3	22.8	23.0	23.0	24.1
2003	20.9	21.9	22.9	22.6	23.0	24.4
2004	20.8	21.6	22.6	22.6	22.8	23.2
2005	20.5	21.6	22.5	22.3	22.8	23.0
2006	20.8	22.1	23.1	22.8	23.2	23.4
2007	21.2	22.0	23.0	22.9	23.2	23.2
2008	20.5	21.5	22.1	22.3	22.5	22.4
2009	20.6	22.3	22.9	22.6	23.0	23.3
2010	20.0	21.8	22.4	22.3	22.5	23.3
2011	19.6	21.7	22.3	22.1	21.4	22.4
2012	19.6	22.0	22.4	22.3	21.7	23.2
2013	20.0	21.2	22.7	22.6	21.5	23.0
2014	20.4	21.7	22.8	22.8	21.7	23.3
2015	20.8	22.0	23.4	23.5	22.3	24.3
2016	20.7	21.7	22.5	23.3	22.0	23.6
2017	20.8	22.0	22.6	23.5	22.1	23.7
2018	21.2	21.7	20.7	22.7	22.4	22.9
2019	21.4	22.0	20.9	23.1	22.9	23.7
2020	21.2	22.5	23.1	23.9	22.7	24.3
2021	21.4	23.0	23.3	24.2	22.9	24.2
2022	20.8	21.9	22.6	23.4	22.1	23.3
2023	21.1	22.3	23.2	23.8	22.7	24.0

7–18　各地区年降雨量

Annual Precipitation by Region

单位：毫米　　(mm)

年份 Year	粤北 Northern Regions	粤东北 North Eastern Regions	粤西北 North Western Regions	粤东 Eastern Regions	粤中 Central Regions	粤西 Western Regions
1980	1459.4	1461.7	1586.1	1369.1	1492.2	2274.0
1985	1360.2	1607.8	1726.9	1481.3	1706.0	2411.3
1990	1436.6	1709.0	1284.8	2236.9	1239.5	1510.2
1995	1506.9	1171.0	1766.4	1512.2	1752.4	2082.9
1996	1633.1	1361.5	1693.1	1409.0	1683.4	1222.6
1997	2045.3	1847.5	1815.3	2040.9	1997.3	2344.3
1998	1862.3	1458.2	1737.5	1593.6	1736.1	1266.4
1999	1314.3	1033.8	1318.7	1517.4	1620.4	1392.6
2000	1565.8	1850.9	1318.2	1486.7	1798.9	1762.7
2001	1689.8	1560.3	1889.2	1947.9	2678.9	2314.5
2002	1814.9	1110.3	1480.9	1409.7	1866.7	2263.3
2003	1388.2	1415.2	1251.8	1406.6	1338.7	1372.4
2004	1156.3	1251.8	1034.7	1379.7	1636.5	1068.5
2005	1772.2	1647.3	1905.2	1631.3	1986.2	1387.3
2006	1782.8	2040.2	1727.0	2507.7	2175.7	1149.8
2007	1502.3	1399.2	1252.4	1482.2	1370.3	1620.8
2008	1553.1	1300.2	2221.0	2123.6	2284.0	1865.2
2009	1275.5	1246.7	1440.4	927.9	1472.6	1849.9
2010	2104.4	1416.1	1419.6	1350.3	2353.6	1952.3
2011	1443.0	1233.1	1277.2	1027.0	1632.3	1408.5
2012	2056.3	1460.5	1919.2	1247.1	1813.9	2068.6
2013	1654.0	1930.2	1736.2	1887.2	2095.4	2084.2
2014	1517.0	1164.9	1788.2	1416.5	2234.0	1468.9
2015	2128.7	1696.3	1848.1	1446.6	2471.9	1328.9
2016	2428.9	2410.3	2132.5	2174.7	2939.7	1820.0
2017	1397.2	1396.3	1275.8	1419.0	2067.4	1760.7
2018	1547.0	1364.9	1691.3	1672.6	1795.1	1902.7
2019	1963.4	1872.2	1988.1	1721.9	1918.4	1716.0
2020	1719.5	1122.7	1057.4	1207.5	1916.2	1568.9
2021	1168.9	823.4	1064.3	923.5	1544.1	1123.8
2022	2423.9	1841.3	1666.1	2024.4	1959.7	1928.4
2023	2065.1	1819.3	1451.8	1687.5	1900.6	2361.9

7-19 各地区年日照时数

Annual Sunshine Hours by Region

单位：小时 (hour)

年份 Year	粤 北 Northern Regions	粤东北 North Eastern Regions	粤西北 North Western Regions	粤 东 Eastern Regions	粤 中 Central Regions	粤 西 Western Regions
1980	1754.1	1811.1	1945.8	1989.2	1921.8	2036.5
1985	1701.6	1926.7	1613.3	1900.6	1406.0	1868.4
1990	1613.9	1893.1	1542.8	1921.3	1648.7	1877.4
1995	1420.6	1868.7	1704.6	2038.3	1559.6	1828.3
1996	1626.5	1965.7	1796.9	2094.8	1564.7	2042.3
1997	1349.1	1490.2	1454.9	1985.8	1209.8	1895.1
1998	1578.3	1689.6	1546.1	1917.5	1469.4	1994.0
1999	1564.0	1819.7	1699.0	2237.0	1599.5	2050.7
2000	1497.2	1672.6	1714.1	2126.3	1609.2	1855.3
2001	1613.0	1884.0	1559.2	2199.8	1651.0	1794.6
2002	1506.4	1813.2	1521.7	2266.6	1566.5	1783.8
2003	1821.1	2030.1	1762.6	2341.5	1741.6	2144.5
2004	1818.5	2117.1	1640.2	2433.5	1767.4	2024.7
2005	1491.2	1736.4	1345.6	1849.5	1288.5	1784.4
2006	1487.7	1779.4	1454.8	1843.5	1328.7	1664.3
2007	1736.3	1750.6	1722.4	1961.2	1616.0	1778.7
2008	1545.0	1853.1	1638.8	1852.1	1482.2	1864.4
2009	1852.9	1962.9	1531.8	2059.8	1671.8	1981.8
2010	1631.0	1676.9	1356.5	1855.5	1484.0	1878.4
2011	1783.8	1901.1	1709.7	2077.9	1878.4	1822.3
2012	1501.0	1660.3	1361.1	1650.4	1471.2	1544.0
2013	1731.5	1827.8	1624.2	1865.8	1582.9	1811.2
2014	1886.2	1997.5	1744.5	1957.8	1613.6	1991.5
2015	1540.8	1740.4	1583.0	2010.7	1594.3	2008.1
2016	1629.2	1553.6	1466.2	1701.0	1451.8	1963.9
2017	1738.9	1831.4	1605.4	1994.6	1671.5	1891.9
2018	1609.7	1700.5	1541.2	2066.9	1556.8	1687.7
2019	1653.8	1757.2	1566.6	1971.3	1660.3	1771.2
2020	1581.8	1830.7	1724.0	2426.4	1661.4	1803.9
2021	1898.0	2142.3	1948.9	2567.0	1946.8	2080.8
2022	1684.6	1851.6	1779.5	2431.4	1774.6	1801.8
2023	1884.0	1675.7	1677.8	2527.5	1683.4	1742.0

7–20 各市土地面积和人口密度

Land Area and Population Density by City

市别	City	土地面积(平方公里) Land Area (sq.km)	人口密度（人/平方公里） Population Density (persons/sq.km)								
			2000	2005	2010	2015	2019	2020	2021	2022	2023
全省	**Provincial Total**	**179800.00**	**486**	**511**	**581**	**650**	**695**	**702**	**705**	**704**	**707**
广州	Guangzhou	7238.46	1337	1277	1744	2200	2530	2589	2599	2588	2601
深圳	Shenzhen	1987.01	3596	4239	5311	7081	8611	8877	8899	8889	8953
珠海	Zhuhai	1725.07	758	839	944	1095	1352	1420	1430	1436	1446
汕头	Shantou	2204.70	2263	2395	2400	2481	2492	2497	2509	2514	2521
佛山	Foshan	3797.79	1400	1507	1871	2276	2483	2506	2531	2515	2532
韶关	Shaoguan	18412.66	149	159	154	154	155	155	155	155	155
河源	Heyuan	15653.63	143	176	189	186	182	181	181	182	181
梅州	Meizhou	15864.51	240	259	267	257	247	244	244	243	243
惠州	Huizhou	11350.36	288	332	405	485	526	534	534	533	535
汕尾	Shanwei	4865.56	465	531	600	569	553	549	552	551	553
东莞	Dongguan	2460.38	2615	2662	3328	4063	4249	4261	4283	4242	4262
中山	Zhongshan	1780.99	1313	1352	1735	2226	2463	2488	2508	2488	2503
江门	Jiangmen	9535.19	414	430	467	482	498	504	507	506	506
阳江	Yangjiang	7966.79	278	297	304	317	325	327	329	329	329
湛江	Zhanjiang	13263.80	487	536	530	527	526	526	530	530	534
茂名	Maoming	11451.80	457	510	510	519	535	540	543	545	546
肇庆	Zhaoqing	14891.43	227	247	265	269	275	276	277	277	277
清远	Qingyuan	19035.48	164	188	193	203	208	209	209	209	209
潮州	Chaozhou	3159.89	780	810	862	826	817	812	815	815	815
揭阳	Jieyang	5266.10	999	1068	1117	1099	1070	1059	1067	1070	1074
云浮	Yunfu	7785.16	277	301	304	304	306	306	307	308	308

注：1．2000、2010、2020年所使用人口数据为第五次、第六次、第七次全国人口普查结果，2005年使用人口数据为广东省2005年全国1%人口抽样调查结果。2015–2019年人口数据根据第七次全国人口普查结果修正后使用。

2．表中土地面积数为2022年数据，2023年计算人口密度所使用的土地面积为2022年数据。

Note: a) The population data used in 2000、2010 and 2020 are the results of the 5th、6th and 7th Population Censuses, the population data used in 2005 is the result of 1% national population sample survey in Guangdong Province in 2005. The population data of 2015-2019 are used according to revised results of the 7th National Census.

b) The number of land area in table is based on the data of 2022, all land areas used in population density in 2023 are the data of 2022.

7—21 水资源及供水用水基本情况

Water Resources, Water Supply and Water use

项　　目	Item	2010	2015	2021	2022	2023
年平均降水量　(毫米)	Precipitation per Year (mm)	1927	1876	1421	2114	1893
水资源总量　(亿立方米)	Total Amount of Water Resource (100 million cu.m)	1998.8	1933.4	1221.1	2223.6	1956.0
#地表水资源量	Surface Water Resources	1989.5	1923.4	1211.3	2213.3	1946.3
地下水资源量	Groundwater Resources	478.3	461.4	301.3	546.2	483.0
人均水资源量　(立方米/人)	Per Capita Amount of Water Resource (cu.m/person)	1915	1782	966	1755	1542
供水总量　(亿立方米)	Water Supply (100 million cu.m)	469.0	443.1	407.0	401.7	400.4
地表水	Surface Water	446.4	426.0	394.0	383.5	382.0
地下水	Groundwater	21.3	15.3	8.6	6.5	5.3
其他	Others	1.3	1.7	4.4	11.7	13.1
用水总量　(亿立方米)	Total Water Consumption (100 million cu.m)	469.0	443.1	407.0	401.7	400.4
#农业用水	Agriculture	231.3	227.0	204.2	198.7	197.5
工业用水	Industry	138.8	112.5	78.2	73.4	73.6
生活用水	Living	90.4	98.3	117.9	116.7	115.9
生态环境补水	Ecology	8.5	5.3	6.7	12.9	13.4
人均用水量　(立方米/人)	Per Capita Water Consumption (cu.m/person)	450	411	322	317	316
万元GDP用水量　(立方米/万元)	Water Consumption per 10000 Yuan of GDP (cu.m/10000 yuan)	103	61	33	31	30
万元工业增加值用水量　(立方米/万元)	Water Consumption per 10000 Yuan of Value-added of Industry (cu.m/10000 yuan)	65	37	17	15	15

7-22 环境保护基本情况

Basic Conditions of Environmental Protection

项　目	item	2010	2015	2021	2022	2023
水环境	**Water Environment**					
优良水体比例 (%)	Proportion of Excellent Water (%)					
地表水国考断面	National Examination Section of Surface water		77.5	90.5	92.6	92.6
地表水省考断面	Provincial Section of Surface Water		76.2	87.5	92.2	91.8
劣V类水体比例 (%)	Proportion of Inferior Class V water (%)					
地表水国考断面	National Examination Section of Surface water		8.5	1.4	0.0	0.0
地表水省考断面	Provincial Section of Surface Water		9.8	1.2	0.0	0.0
大气环境	**Atmospheric Environment**					
二氧化硫浓度 (微克/立方米)	Sulfur Dioxide Concentration (microgram / cubic meter)		12	8	8	7
二氧化氮浓度 (微克/立方米)	Nitrogen Dioxide Concentration (microgram / cubic meter)		24	22	19	19
颗粒物PM10浓度 (微克/立方米)	Respirable Suspended Particulates Concentration (microgram / cubic meter)		47	40	34	37
颗粒物PM2.5浓度(微克/立方米)	Fine Suspended Particulates Concentration (microgram / cubic meter)		31	22	20	21
一氧化碳浓度 (毫克/立方米)	Carbon Monoxide Concentration (milligram / cubic meter)		1.3	0.9	0.9	0.8
臭氧浓度 (微克/立方米)	Ozone Concentration (microgram / cubic meter)		126	144	157	143
空气质量达二级标准城市数 (个)	Number of Cities Meeting Grade II Air Quality Standard (unit)	21	16	18	14	17
生态环境	**Ecological Environment**					
人均耕地面积 (亩)	Per Capita Area of Cultivated Land (mu)	0.37	0.36	0.23	0.22	0.23
新增水土流失治理面积 (千公顷)	Area of Soil Erosion under Control (1000 hectares)	44.56	72.61	80.83	86.85	80.88
森林面积 (万公顷)	Forest Area (10000 hectares)	1036.28	1086.11	1054.70		
森林覆盖率 (%)	Forest Coverage Rate (%)	57.00	58.88	58.74		
人均森林面积 (公顷)	Per Capita Forest Area (hectare)	0.1	0.1	0.1		
活立木蓄积量 (万立方米)	Volume of Standing Forest Stock (10000 cu.m)	43936	56636	62824		
森林蓄积量 (万立方米)	Stock Volume of Forest (10000 cu.m)	43190	56128	62370		
当年造林面积 (万公顷)	Afforested Area in Current Year (10000 hectares)	30.77	107.34	17.56	17.72	11.99
自然保护区数 (个)	Number of Natural Reserves (unit)	357	377	377	377	377
自然保护区面积 (万公顷)	Area of Natural Reserves (10000 hectares)	164.44	168.89	169.50	169.50	169.50

注：森林面积、森林覆盖率、人均森林面积、活立木蓄积量、森林蓄积量数据由林草湿调查监测工作产生，并由国家林业局统一发布各省林草湿调查监测成果，2022年、2023年相关数据尚未发布。

Notes: The data on forest area, forest coverage, per capita forest area, standing timber volume, and forest volume are generated by the forest and grass moisture survey and monitoring work, and the results of forest and grass moisture survey and monitoring in each province are uniformly released by the National Forestry Administration. The relevant data for 2022 and 2023 have not been released yet.

7-22 续表 continued

项　目	item	2010	2015	2021	2022	2023
城市环境	**Urban Environment**					
城市供水普及率 (%)	Popularization Rate of Tap Water in Urban Areas (%)	98.4	98.5	100.0	100.0	100.0
城市污水排放量 (万吨)	Volume of Municipal Sewage Discharge (10000 tons)	506546	671363	961591	999541	975162
城市污水处理量 (万吨)	Volume of Municipal Sewage Disposal (10000 tons)	436041	628706	944597	983837	976550
城市污水处理厂集中处理率(%)	Rate of Municipal Sewage Disposal (%)	73.1	93.3	97.6	98.0	100.0
城市生活垃圾无害化处理率(%)	Rate of Harmless Disposal of Urban Domestic Waste (%)	72.1	91.6	100.0	100.0	100.0
城市燃气普及率 (%)	Popularization Rate of Gas in Urban Areas (%)	95.8	97.6	98.2	98.6	98.9
城市人均公园绿地面积(平方米)	Per Capita Urban Public Green Area (sq.m)	13.29	17.40	17.49	17.68	17.95
建成区绿化覆盖率 (%)	Green Coverage Rate in Built-up Areas (%)	41.3	41.4	42.3	43.9	40.9
城市公共交通车辆运营数 (标台)	Number of Public Transportation Vehicles (Unit)	45850	62947	76570	74032	70779
农村环境	**Rural Environment**					
农村自来水普及率 (%)	Popularization Rate of Tap Water in Rural Areas (%)	59.5	83.4	99.1	99.3	99.3
无害化卫生厕所普及率 (%)	Popularization Rate of Harmless Sanitary Toilets (%)	77.7	87.2	99.4	95.9	97.0
农村沼气池产气总量 (万立方米)	Total Output of Biogas from Rural Biogas Pools (10000 cu.m)	18724	36617	33661	44900	56646
自然灾害	**Natural Disasters**					
地质灾害次数 (次)	Number of Geological Disasters (unit)	600	191	3	352	23
地质灾害直接经济损失 (万元)	Direct Economic Loss due to Geological Disasters (10000 yuan)	22732	3666	21	16261	1568
海洋灾害发生次数 (次)	Number of Marine Disasters (time)	14	9	35	38	3
海洋灾害直接经济损失 (亿元)	Direct Economic Loss due to Marine Disasters (100 million yuan)		28.77	0.28	7.65	1.83
森林火灾次数 (次)	Number of Forest Fires (time)	59	273	98	45	11

注：1.森林面积、森林覆盖率、人均森林面积、活立木蓄积量、森林蓄积量等数据由林草湿调查监测工作产生，并由国家林业局统一发布调查监测成果，2022年、2023年相关数据尚未发布。

2.2022年农村卫生厕所普及率的统计参照《农村三格式户厕建设技术规范》(GBT 38836—2020)开展。

3.2023年，海洋灾害发生次数为各灾种造成损失的过程次数。

Note: a)Data on forest area, forest coverage rate, per capita forest area, volume of standing forest stock and stock volume of forest in 2022 are temporarily lacking.

b)The statistics of the penetration rate of rural sanitary toilets in 2022 is carried out according to the Technical Code for the Construction of Rural Three-format Household Toilets(GBT 38836-2020).

c)In 2023, the number of occurrences of marine disasters refers to the number of processes in which various disasters cause losses.

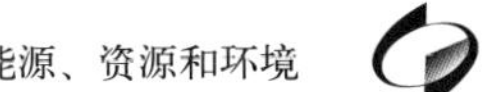

7-23 各市水环境质量情况（2023年）

Statistics on Water Environment Quality by City(2023)

单位：%　　(%)

市别	City	国控地表水断面 State Controlled Surface Water Sections		省考地表水断面 Provincial Surface Water Section	
		优良率 Excellent Rate	劣V类比例 Proportion of Inferior to Class V	优良率 Excellent Rate	劣V类比例 Proportion of Inferior to Class V
全省	**Provincial Total**	**92.6**	**0.0**	**91.8**	**0.0**
广州	Guangzhou	92.3	0.0	85.0	0.0
深圳	Shenzhen	100.0	0.0	100.0	0.0
珠海	Zhuhai	100.0	0.0	100.0	0.0
汕头	Shantou	80.0	0.0	85.7	0.0
佛山	Foshan	85.7	0.0	92.9	0.0
韶关	Shaoguan	100.0	0.0	100.0	0.0
河源	Heyuan	100.0	0.0	100.0	0.0
梅州	Meizhou	100.0	0.0	100.0	0.0
惠州	Huizhou	100.0	0.0	94.7	0.0
汕尾	Shanwei	100.0	0.0	100.0	0.0
东莞	Dongguan	71.4	0.0	77.8	0.0
中山	Zhongshan	100.0	0.0	83.3	0.0
江门	Jiangmen	100.0	0.0	100.0	0.0
阳江	Yangjiang	100.0	0.0	100.0	0.0
湛江	Zhanjiang	100.0	0.0	83.3	0.0
茂名	Maoming	81.8	0.0	80.0	0.0
肇庆	Zhaoqing	100.0	0.0	93.3	0.0
清远	Qingyuan	100.0	0.0	90.9	0.0
潮州	Chaozhou	75.0	0.0	85.7	0.0
揭阳	Jieyang	40.0	0.0	63.6	0.0
云浮	Yunfu	100.0	0.0	100.0	0.0

7−24 各市大气环境质量情况（2023年）

Statistics on Atmospheric Environmental Quality by City(2023)

市 别	City	SO_2年平均浓度（μg/m^3）Annual Average Concentration of Sulfur Dioxide (μg/m^3)	NO_2年平均浓度（μg/m^3）Annual Average Concentration of Nitrogen Dioxide (μg/m^3)	颗粒物PM10年平均浓度（μg/m^3）Annual Average Concentration of Respirable Suspended Particulates (μg/m^3)	颗粒物PM2.5年平均浓度（μg/m^3）Annual Average Concentration of Fine Suspended Particulates (μg/m^3)	O_3-8h第90百分位数浓度（μg/m^3）O_3-8h 90th Percentile Concentration (μg/m^3)	CO第95百分位数浓度（mg/m^3）95th Percentile Concentration of CO (mg/m^3)	空气质量达到及好于二级的天数(天) Days with Air Quality Reaching or Better than Grade II (day)	AQI达标率(%) AQI Compliance Rate (%)
全 省	**Provincial Total**	**7**	**19**	**37**	**21**	**143**	**0.8**	**7263**	**94.8**
广 州	Guangzhou	6	29	41	23	159	0.9	330	90.4
深 圳	Shenzhen	5	21	35	18	131	0.8	357	97.8
珠 海	Zhuhai	6	19	33	18	152	0.7	335	91.8
汕 头	Shantou	8	15	35	20	141	0.9	358	98.1
佛 山	Foshan	6	29	39	23	166	0.9	320	87.7
韶 关	Shaoguan	12	14	38	24	126	0.9	358	98.1
河 源	Heyuan	5	15	38	20	120	0.8	362	99.2
梅 州	Meizhou	7	18	31	19	120	0.8	364	99.7
惠 州	Huizhou	6	16	36	19	130	0.8	359	98.4
汕 尾	Shanwei	8	9	30	17	134	0.7	360	98.6
东 莞	Dongguan	8	25	38	21	168	0.8	324	88.8
中 山	Zhongshan	5	21	35	20	163	0.8	324	88.8
江 门	Jiangmen	6	25	41	22	172	0.9	313	85.8
阳 江	Yangjiang	6	17	36	21	135	0.8	353	96.7
湛 江	Zhanjiang	8	12	33	20	130	0.8	355	97.3
茂 名	Maoming	10	12	36	21	130	0.8	358	98.1
肇 庆	Zhaoqing	9	24	38	23	157	0.7	332	91.0
清 远	Qingyuan	7	18	39	23	147	0.8	341	93.4
潮 州	Chaozhou	7	14	37	24	144	0.8	352	96.4
揭 阳	Jieyang	8	18	47	26	146	0.9	353	96.7
云 浮	Yunfu	11	20	39	21	138	0.8	355	97.3

7-25 各市城市建设基本情况

Basic Statistics on Urban Sanitation by City

市别	City	城市污水处理率（%） Rate of Sewage Treatment				城市生活垃圾无害化处理率（%） Rate of Consumption Waste Treatment			
		2010	2015	2022	2023	2010	2015	2022	2023
全省	**Province Total**	**73.1**	**93.7**	**98.4**	**98.5**	**72.1**	**91.6**	**100.0**	**100.0**
广州	Guangzhou	88.1	93.2	99.4	99.4	92.0	95.2	100.0	100.0
深圳	Shenzhen	88.9	96.6	96.1	96.1	94.6	100.0	100.0	100.0
珠海	Zhuhai	84.7	95.7	99.2	99.2	92.3	100.0	100.0	100.0
汕头	Shantou	57.9	90.2	99.1	99.1	64.4	92.6	100.0	100.0
佛山	Foshan	79.7	94.4	104.1	104.1	95.6	100.0	100.0	100.0
韶关	Shaoguan	53.6	86.2	100.0	100.0	100.0	100.0	100.0	100.0
河源	Heyuan	43.0	92.9	96.9	96.9	96.5	100.0	100.0	100.0
梅州	Meizhou	33.7	88.6	100.0	100.0	100.0	100.0	100.0	100.0
惠州	Huizhou	71.5	97.6	90.7	90.7	100.0	100.0	100.0	100.0
汕尾	Shanwei	18.6	89.1	98.7	98.7		100.0	100.0	100.0
东莞	Dongguan	91.1	96.5	98.0	98.0	100.0	100.0	100.0	100.0
中山	Zhongshan	85.1	96.0	99.1	99.1	100.0	100.0	100.0	100.0
江门	Jiangmen	63.5	91.6	98.1	98.1	100.0	100.0	100.0	100.0
阳江	Yangjiang	54.6	85.5	100.0	100.0	100.0	100.0	100.0	100.0
湛江	Zhanjiang	39.6	88.5	99.6	99.6	97.4	100.0	100.0	100.0
茂名	Maoming	34.4	88.4	123.2	123.2		100.0	100.0	100.0
肇庆	Zhaoqing	70.5	85.1	99.0	99.0	83.8	100.0	100.0	100.0
清远	Qingyuan	70.4	87.6	97.9	97.9	100.0	100.0	100.0	100.0
潮州	Chaozhou	33.5	79.7	120.2	120.2	100.0	79.3	100.0	100.0
揭阳	Jieyang	20.8	89.8	96.9	96.9	90.0	95.0	100.0	100.0
云浮	Yunfu	63.7	93.1	99.1	99.1	100.0	100.0	100.0	100.0

7−25 续表 continued

市别	City	城市公共交通车辆标准运营数（标台） Number of Public Transportation Vehicles (unit)				城市人均公园绿地面积（平方米） Per Capital Area of Parks and Green Land in City (sq.m)			
		2010	2015	2022	2023	2010	2015	2022	2023
全省	**Province Total**	**45850**	**62947**	**74032**	**70779**	**13.29**	**17.40**	**17.68**	**17.95**
广州	Guangzhou	10232	16179	18138	17112	11.87	21.82	23.66	23.66
深圳	Shenzhen	14677	17943	18564	17905	16.40	16.91	12.58	12.58
珠海	Zhuhai	1557	2349	3205	3175	13.70	19.50	22.25	22.25
汕头	Shantou	1111	1253	2225	2301	12.20	15.01	15.25	15.34
佛山	Foshan	3715	6783	6984	6195	10.20	14.69	19.58	19.58
韶关	Shaoguan	460	635	749	731	11.80	12.50	16.75	16.79
河源	Heyuan	294	330	520	520	12.10	12.55	13.88	15.45
梅州	Meizhou	238	925	1758	1341	11.80	16.70	16.95	19.24
惠州	Huizhou	1124	2446	3045	3118	11.10	17.75	16.14	16.95
汕尾	Shanwei	199	344	1102	1102	10.70	13.48	11.66	15.60
东莞	Dongguan	6129	5346	6650	6623	15.30	19.36	19.56	19.56
中山	Zhongshan	2151	2436	2902	2873	11.90	18.39	15.05	15.05
江门	Jiangmen	924	1524	1872	1665	11.00	17.75	20.39	20.79
阳江	Yangjiang	143	242	399	398	10.60	11.17	20.99	25.79
湛江	Zhanjiang	735	1167	1095	1121	12.70	13.94	17.19	20.04
茂名	Maoming	392	511	1032	913	10.00	13.74	17.71	18.28
肇庆	Zhaoqing	443	814	1187	1146	22.70	20.73	19.24	23.64
清远	Qingyuan	633	778	1064	1027	11.30	13.03	14.81	14.87
潮州	Chaozhou	140	192	380	370	10.30	10.57	13.92	14.17
揭阳	Jieyang	377	387	718	718	12.90	8.65	15.15	15.11
云浮	Yunfu	176	362	444	427	12.10	12.70	19.55	17.98

注：标台营运数为不含轨道交通数。
Note: Data of track transport is not included in the number of vehicles.

主要统计指标解释

能源生产总量 指一定时期内全国（地区）一次能源生产量的总和，是观察全国（地区）能源生产水平、规模、构成和发展速度的总量指标。一次能源生产量包括原煤、原油、天然气、水电、核能及其他动力能（如风能、地热能等）发电量。不包括低热值燃料生产量、生物质能、太阳能等的利用和由一次能源加工转换而成的二次能源产量。

能源消费总量 指一定时期内全国（地区）生产和生活消费的各种能源的总和，是观察能源消费水平、构成和增长速度的总量指标，能源消费总量包括原煤和原油及其制品、天然气、电力。不包括低热值燃料、生物质能和太阳能等的利用 。能源消费总量分为三部分，即终端能源消费量、能源加工转换损失量和损失量。

(1)终端能源消费量 指一定时期内全国（地区）生产和生活消费的各种能源在扣除了用于加工转换二次能源消费量和损失量以后的数量。

(2)能源加工转换损失量 指一定时期内全国（地区）投入加工转换的各种能源数量之和与产出各种能源产品之和的差额。它是观察能源在加工转换过程中损失量变化的指标。

(3)能源损失量 指一定时期内能源在输送、分配、储存过程中发生的损失和由客观原因造成的各种损失量。不包括各种气体能源放空、放散量。

能源生产弹性系数 是研究能源生产增长速度与国民经济增长速度之间关系的指标。计算公式：

$$\text{能源生产弹性系数}=\frac{\text{能源生产总量增长速度}}{\text{国民经济增长速度}}$$

国民经济增长速度，可根据不同的目的或需要，用国民生产总值，国内生产总值等指标来计算，本资料是采用国内生产总值指标计算的。

电力生产弹性系数 是研究电力生产增长速度与国民经济增长速度之间关系的指标。一般来说，电力的发展应当快于国民经济的发展，也就是说电力应超前发展。计算公式：

$$\text{电力生产弹性系数}=\frac{\text{电力生产量增长速度}}{\text{国民经济增长速度}}$$

能源消费弹性系数 是反映能源消费增长速度与国民经济增长速度之间比例关系的指标。计算公式：

$$\text{能源消费弹性系数}=\frac{\text{能源消费量增长速度}}{\text{国民经济增长速度}}$$

电力消费弹性系数 是反映电力消费增长速度与国民经济增长速度之间比例关系的指标。计算公式：

$$\text{电力消费弹性系数}=\frac{\text{电力消费量增长速度}}{\text{国民经济增长速度}}$$

能源加工转换效率 指一定时期内能源经过加工、转换后，产出的各种能源产品的数量与同期内投入加工转换的各种能源数量的比率。它是观察能源加工转换装置和生产工艺先进与落后、管理水平高低等的重要指标。计算公式：

$$\text{能源加工转换效率}=\frac{\text{能源加工、转换产出量}}{\text{能源加工、转换投入量}}\times 100\%$$

土地资源 土地指陆地的表层部分，它主要由岩石、岩石的风化物和土壤构成。土地资源按利用类型可以分为农用地、建筑用地和未利用地。农用地包括耕地、园地、林地、牧草地和水面。建筑用地包括居民点及工矿用地、交通用地和水利设施用地。未利用地指农用地和建筑用地以外的土地，包括滩涂、荒漠、戈壁、冰川和石山等。

耕地面积 指经过开垦用以种植农作物并经常进行耕耘的土地面积。包括种有作物的土地面积、休闲地、新开荒地和抛荒未满三年的土地面积。

林业用地面积 指生长乔木、竹类、灌木、沿海红树林等林木的土地面积，包括有林地、灌木林、疏林地、未成林造林地、迹地、苗圃等。

草地面积 指牧区和农区用于放牧牲畜或割草，植被盖度在5% 以上的草原、草坡、草山等面积。包括天然的和人工种植或改良的草地面积。

森林资源 指森林、林木、林地以及依托森林、林木、林地生存的野生动物、植物和微生物。林木指树木和竹子。森林指以乔木为主体的植物群落，是集生的乔木及与共同作用的植物、动物、微生物和土壤、气候等的总体。

活立木总蓄积量 指一定范围内土地上全部树木蓄积的总量，包括森林蓄积、疏林蓄积、散生木蓄积和四旁树蓄积。

森林覆盖率 指一个国家或地区森林面积占土地总面积的百分比。森林覆盖率是反映森林资源的丰富程度和生态平衡状况的重要指标。在计算森林覆盖率时，森林面积包括郁闭度0.2 以上的乔木林地面积和竹林地面积，国家特别规定的灌木林地面积、农田林网以及四旁(村旁、路旁、水旁、宅旁)林木的覆盖面积。计算公式为:

$$\text{森林覆盖率(\%)}=\frac{\text{森林面积}}{\text{土地总面积}}\times 100\%$$

森林面积 指由乔木树种构成，郁闭度0.2 以上(含0.2)的林地或冠幅宽度10 米以上的林带的面积，即有林地面积。森林面积包括天然起源和人工起源的针叶林面积、阔叶林面积、针阔混交林面积和竹林面积，不包括灌木林地面积和疏林地面积。

森林蓄积量 指一定森林面积上存在着的林木树干部分的总材积。它是反映一个国家或地区森林资源总规模和水平的基本指标之一，也是反映森林资源的丰富程度、衡量森林生态环境优劣的重要依据。

水资源 水在自然界中以固体、液体和气态三种聚集状态存在，分布于海洋、陆地(包括土壤)以及大气之中，通过水循环形成水资源。水资源包括经人类控制并直接可供灌溉、发电、给水、航运、养殖等用途的地表水和地下水，以及江河、湖泊、井、泉、潮汐、港湾和养殖水域等。水资源是发展国民经济不可缺少的重要自然资源。

矿产资源 矿产资源指由地质作用形成的，具有利用价值的，呈固态、液态、气态的自然资源，是社会发展的重要物质基础。

矿产基础储量 基础储量是查明矿产资源的一部分。它能满足现行采矿和生产所需的指标要求，是控制的、探明的并通过可行性或预可行性研究认为属于经济的、边界经济的部分，用未扣除设计、采矿损失的数量表表示。

矿产保有资源储量 指查明的矿产资源储量（资源储量=基础储量+资源量）扣除已开采部分损失量和加减应勘查，重算或其它原因增减量而得出的年底实有资源储量。

Explanatory Notes on Main Statistical Indicators

Total Energy Production refers to the total production of primary energy by all energy producing enterprises in the country (region) in a given period of time. It is a comprehensive indicator of the capacity, scale, composition and development speed of energy production of the country (region). The production of primary energy includes that of coal, crude oil, natural gas, hydropower and electricity generated by nuclear energy and other means such as wind power and geothermal power. However, it excludes the production of fuel of low calorific value, bioenergy, solar energy and secondary energy converted from primary energy.

Total Domestic Energy Consumption refers to the total consumption of energy of various kinds by production sectors and households in the country (region) in a given period of time. It is a comprehensive indicator of the scale, composition and development speed of energy consumption. The total energy consumption includes that of coal, crude oil and their products, natural gas and electricity, but excludes the consumption of fuel of low calorific value, bioenergy and solar energy. Total domestic energy consumption can be divided into three parts:

(1) Final Energy Consumption: This refers to the total energy consumption by production sectors and households in the country (region) in a given period of time, excluding primary energy consumption and loss in the process of conversion into secondary energy.

(2)Loss During the Process of Energy Conversion: This refers to the total input of various kinds of energy for conversion minus the total output of various kinds of energy in the country (region) in a given period of time. It is an indicator of the loss that occurs during the process of energy conversion.

(3)Loss: This refers to the total loss of energy during the course of energy transmission, distribution and storage and the loss caused by any objective reason in a given period of time, excluding the loss of various kinds of gas due to gas discharges and stocktaking.

Elasticity Ratio of Energy Production is an indicator of the relationship between the growth rate of energy production and the growth rate of the national economy. The formula is:

$$\text{Elasticity Ratio of Energy Production} = \frac{\text{Growth Rate of Energy Production}}{\text{Growth Rate of National Economy}}$$

The average annual growth rate of the national economy can be shown by the gross national product, gross domestic product and other indicators, depending on the purposes or needs. The gross domestic product is used in the calculation of the ratio in this chapter.

Elasticity Ratio of Electricity Production is an indicator of the relationship between the growth rate of electricity production and the growth rate of the national economy. Generally speaking, the growth rate of electricity production should be higher than that of the national economy; in other words, electricity production should develop in advance of the national economy. Its formula is:

$$\text{Elasticity Ratio of Electricity Production} = \frac{\text{Growth Rate of Electricity Production}}{\text{Growth Rate of National Economy}}$$

Elasticity Ratio of Energy Consumption is an indicator of the relationship between the growth rate of energy consumption and the growth rate of the national economy. The formula is:

$$\text{Elasticity Ratio of Energy Consumption} = \frac{\text{Growth Rate of Energy Consumption}}{\text{Growth Rate of National Economy}}$$

Elasticity Ratio of Electricity Consumption is an indicator of the relationship between the growth rate of electricity consumption and the growth rate of the national economy. The formula is:

$$\text{Elasticity Ratio of Electricity Consumption} = \frac{\text{Growth Rate of Electricity Consumption}}{\text{Growth Rate of National Economy}}$$

Efficiency of Energy Processing and Conversion refers to the ratio of the total output of energy products of various kinds after processing and conversion to the total input of energy of various kinds for processing and conversion in the same reference period. It is an important indicator of the current conditions of energy processing and conversion equipment, production technique and management. The formula is:

$$\text{Efficiency of Energy Processing \& Conversion} = \frac{\text{Output of Energy after Processing \& Conversion}}{\text{Input of Energy for Processing \& Conversion}} \times 100\%$$

Land Resource Land refers to the surface of the earth, consisting of mainly rocks and its weathering and earth. Land resource can be classified, by its utilization, as land for agriculture, land for construction and unused land. Land for agriculture includes cultivated land, plantation, forestland, grassland and waters. Land for construction includes land for residential purpose, for manufacturing and mining, for transportation and for water conservancy projects. Unused land refers to land other than land for agriculture and construction, including beaches, deserts, Gobi, glaciers and rock mountains.

Area of Cultivated Land refers to area of land reclaimed for the regular cultivation of various farm crops, including crop-cover land, fallow, newly reclaimed land and land laid idle for less than 3 years.

Area of Afforested Land refers to land for trees, bamboos, bushes and mangrove including forest-cover land, bush-covered land, sparse forest land, land planned for forestation, slash and nurseries of young trees.

Area of Grassland refers to areas of grassland, grass-slopes and grass-covered hills with a vegetation-covering rate of over 5% that are used for animal husbandry or harvesting of grass. It includes natural, cultivated and improved grassland areas.

Forest Resource refers to forests, trees, forestland and wild animals, plants and microorganism that live on forests and trees. Trees include trees and bamboos. Forest refers to the population of clusters of trees and other plants, animals and microorganism as well as the earth and climate that have interactions with the trees.

Total Standing Stock Volume refers to the total stock volume of trees growing in land, including trees in forests, tress in sparse forests, scattered trees and trees planted by the side of villages, farm houses and along roads and rivers.

Forest Coverage Rate refers to the ratio of area of afforested land to total land area. It is a very important indicator that reflects the status of abundance of forest resource and ecosystem balance. Forest area includes the area of trees and bamboo growing with a canopy density above 0.2, the area of shrubby trees according to regulations of the government, the area of forest land inside farm land and the area of trees planted by the side of villages, farm houses and along roads and rivers. The formula for calculating forest coverage rate is as follows:

$$\text{Forest Coverage Rate (\%)} = \frac{\text{Area of Afforested Land}}{\text{Area of Total Land}} \times 100\%$$

Forest Area refers to wooded area, i.e. the area of forest where trees and bamboo grow with a canopy density above 0.2 (inclusive) or a crown width above 10 meters, including natural and planted coniferous forest, broad-leaved forest, mixed forest, and bamboo groves, but excluding shrubbery and open forest.

Stock Volume of Forest refers to total stock volume of wood growing in forest area, which shows the total size and level of forest resources of a country or a region. It is also an important indicator of the richness of forest resource and the status of forest ecological environment.

Water Resource Water exists in the nature in solid, liquid and gaseous states, is distributed in the ocean, land (including earth) and air, and constitutes water resource through circulation. Water resource includes surface water and underground water that is controlled by human beings for irrigation, power-generation, water supply, navigation and cultivation. It also includes rivers, lakes, wells, springs, tides, gulfs and water area for cultivation. Water resource as an indispensable natural resource for the development of national economy.

Mineral Resources refer to useful natural resources enriched due to geological processes, in the form of solid, liquid or gas. Minerals are important material basis for social development.

Basic Reserves of Mineral Resources Basic reserves are part of total identified mineral resources that meet present mining and production standards, which is the part of reserve controlled, proven, and found to be of economic or marginal value through feasibility assessment or pre-feasibility study. Basic reserves are indicated as a figure including designing and mining loss.

Ensured Reserves of Mineral Resources refer to the actual reserves of mineral resources at the year-end, calculated as the proven reserves of mineral resources (Reserves of Mineral Resources = Basic Reserves + Resource) minus losses in previous extraction processes, plus or minus increases or losses due to exploration, recalculation or other reasons.

八、财政、银行和保险

GOVERNMENT FINANCE, BANKING AND INSURANCE

八 财政、银行和保险

简要说明

一、本篇资料反映广东地方公共财政预算收支、银行、保险等方面的基本情况。

二、本篇资料由广东省统计局综合统计处负责整理、编辑。

三、资料来源：

财政资料根据广东省财政厅提供的历年《广东省财政总决算报表》有关项目加工整理。

银行资料由中国人民银行广州分行提供。

保险业务资料由国家金融监督管理总局广东监管局提供

8 Government Finance，Banking and Insurance

Brief Introduction

Ⅰ. The data in this chapter show the basic situation of local government general budgetary revenue and expenditure, banking and insurance of Guangdong Province.

Ⅱ. The data in this chapter are prepared by the Division of Comprehensive Statistics of Statistics Bureau of Guangdong Province.

Ⅲ. Data sources:

The data on local government finance are prepared in accordance with the related tables of the Total Final Accounts of Government Finance of Guangdong provided by Guangdong Provincial Department of Finance.

The data on banking are provided by Guangzhou Branch of the People's Bank of China.

The data on insurance are provided by Guangdong Financial Supervisory Authority.

8-1 地方一般公共预算收支和增长速度
Local Government General Public Budget Revenue and Expenditure and Their Growth Rates

单位：亿元 (100 million yuan)

年份 Year	地方一般公共预算收入 Local Government General Public Budget Revenue	#税收收入 Taxes	地方一般公共预算支出 Local Government General Public Budget Expenditure	收支差额 Balance	增长速度（%）Growth Rate (%) 地方一般公共预算收入 Local General Government Public Budget Revenue	地方一般公共预算支出 Local General Government Public Budget Expenditure	地方一般公共预算收入占地区生产总值的比重(%) Percentage of Budgetary Revenue to GDP (%)
1978	41.82	25.78	28.70	13.12	17.9	42.6	22.5
1979	36.25	25.98	29.88	6.37	-13.3	4.1	17.3
1980	37.79	27.72	27.04	10.75	4.2	-9.5	15.1
1981	41.01	30.84	29.60	11.41	8.5	9.5	14.1
1982	42.23	34.72	33.34	8.89	3.0	12.6	12.4
1983	44.29	38.52	37.45	6.84	4.9	12.3	12.0
1984	49.28	43.59	47.18	2.10	11.3	26.0	10.7
1985	69.27	65.25	66.74	2.53	40.6	41.5	12.0
1986	82.41	73.29	89.55	-7.14	19.0	34.2	12.3
1987	95.88	88.65	96.59	-0.71	16.3	7.9	11.3
1988	107.57	119.17	115.20	-7.63	12.2	19.3	9.3
1989	136.87	145.02	141.16	-4.29	27.2	22.5	9.9
1990	131.02	135.62	150.69	-19.67	-4.3	6.8	8.4
1991	177.35	158.31	182.48	-5.13	35.4	21.1	9.4
1992	222.64	195.98	219.61	3.03	25.5	20.3	9.1
1993	346.56	310.78	331.27	15.29	55.7	50.8	10.0
1994	298.70	275.06	416.83	-118.13	-13.8	25.8	6.5
1995	382.34	353.64	525.63	-143.29	28.0	26.1	6.4
1996	479.45	438.25	601.23	-121.78	25.4	14.4	7.0
1997	543.95	494.76	682.66	-138.71	13.5	13.5	7.0
1998	640.75	545.62	825.61	-184.86	17.8	20.9	7.5
1999	766.19	645.28	1034.44	-268.25	19.6	25.3	8.3
2000	910.56	798.61	1069.86	-159.30	18.8	3.4	8.4
2001	1160.51	1014.72	1321.33	-160.82	27.5	23.5	9.6
2002	1201.61	1032.33	1521.08	-319.47	3.5	15.1	8.8
2003	1315.52	1109.50	1695.63	-380.11	9.5	11.5	8.2
2004	1418.51	1191.55	1852.95	-434.44	7.8	9.3	7.6
2005	1807.20	1526.97	2289.07	-481.87	27.4	23.5	8.2
2006	2179.46	1850.44	2553.34	-373.88	20.6	11.5	8.4
2007	2785.80	2415.47	3159.57	-373.77	27.8	23.7	8.8
2008	3310.32	2864.79	3778.57	-468.25	18.8	19.6	9.0
2009	3649.81	3130.61	4334.37	-684.56	10.3	14.7	9.2
2010	4517.04	3803.47	5421.54	-904.50	23.8	25.1	9.8
2011	5514.84	4548.66	6712.40	-1197.56	22.1	23.8	10.4
2012	6229.18	5073.88	7387.86	-1158.68	13.0	10.1	10.9
2013	7081.47	5767.94	8411.00	-1329.53	13.7	13.8	11.3
2014	8065.08	6510.47	9152.64	-1087.56	13.9	8.8	11.8
2015	9366.78	7377.07	12827.80	-3461.01	11.9	40.1	12.5
2016	10390.35	8098.63	13446.09	-3055.74	10.3	4.8	12.6
2017	11320.35	8871.89	15037.48	-3717.13	10.9	11.8	12.4
2018	12105.26	9737.51	15729.26	-3624.00	7.9	4.6	12.1
2019	12654.53	10063.95	17297.85	-4643.32	4.5	10.0	11.8
2020	12923.85	9881.95	17430.79	-4506.94	2.1	0.8	11.7
2021	14105.04	10785.23	18247.01	-4141.97	9.1	4.7	11.3
2022	13260.88	9286.11	18533.08	-5272.20	-6.0	1.6	10.2
2023	13850.78	10244.77	18527.03	-4676.25	4.4	0.0	10.2

注：2015年起，地方公共财政预算收入和地方公共财政预算支出统一更名为地方一般公共预算收入和地方一般公共预算支出，财政收入按可比口径计算。

Note: From 2015, the name of local government budgetary revenue and local government budgetary expenditure have been changed to local public budgetary revenue and local public budgetary expenditure.Growth rates of revenue are caculated by comparable caliber.

8-2 地方一般公共预算收支基本情况

Basic Items of General Public Budget Revenue and Expenditure

单位：亿元 (100 million yuan)

指　　标	Item	2010	2015	2019	2020	2021	2022	2023
一、地方一般公共预算收入	**General Public Budget Revenue**	**4517.04**	**9366.78**	**12654.53**	**12923.85**	**14105.04**	**13260.88**	**13850.78**
税收收入	Tax Revenue	3803.47	7377.07	10063.95	9881.95	10785.23	9286.11	10244.77
#增值税	Value-added Tax	657.82	1339.16	3977.07	3693.94	4091.37	3114.09	4291.82
企业所得税	Corporate Income Tax	678.75	1303.11	2001.21	1946.60	2111.31	1880.53	1784.12
个人所得税	Individual Income Tax	287.26	510.14	656.19	760.88	916.19	985.30	946.13
城市维护建设税	City Maintenance and Construction Tax	135.97	457.05	598.98	581.28	630.05	558.98	598.22
房产税	House Property Tax	122.44	241.00	356.76	315.94	374.14	430.69	470.67
印花税	Stamp Tax	69.93	141.41	152.10	166.46	196.79	201.21	223.82
土地增值税	Land Appreciation Tax	189.79	576.75	1402.89	1375.09	1392.05	1243.62	1033.79
耕地占用税	Farm Land Occupation Tax	56.03	95.38	58.34	58.71	50.96	59.92	67.01
契税	Deed Tax	235.51	427.24	640.89	783.82	809.80	597.03	621.88
非税收入	Non-tax Revenue	713.57	1989.71	2590.58	3041.90	3319.80	3974.77	3606.00
专项收入	Special Program Receipts	97.35	598.77	892.51	974.77	1199.34	1217.41	1086.09
行政事业性收费收入	Charge of Administrative and Units	293.43	408.19	292.06	226.87	292.42	284.35	297.21
罚没收入	Penalty Receipts	95.62	155.77	231.11	238.46	263.19	418.65	338.45
国有资本经营收入	Operation Income from State-owned Assets	90.00	62.70	90.03	93.26	101.15	204.73	132.44
国有资源(资产)有偿使用收入	Income from Use of State-owned Resources Assets	81.88	355.19	731.60	1190.99	1110.55	1472.94	1277.18
其他收入	Other Non-tax Revenue	55.29	409.09	353.28	317.54	353.14	376.69	474.64
二、地方一般公共预算支出	**General Public Budget Expenditure**	**5421.54**	**12827.80**	**17297.85**	**17430.79**	**18247.01**	**18533.08**	**18527.03**
#一般公共服务	Expenditure for General Public Services	685.39	1018.91	1855.32	1889.53	1828.89	1773.74	1718.76
教育	Expenditure for Education	921.48	2040.65	3210.51	3510.56	3796.69	3871.14	4004.45
科学技术	Expenditure for Science and Technology	214.44	569.55	1168.79	955.73	982.76	983.78	980.46
文化旅游体育与传媒	Expenditure for Culture, Tourism, Sports and Media	166.16	194.58	350.33	417.22	395.59	350.19	360.52
社会保障和就业	Expenditure for Social Safety Net and Employment Effort	469.58	1064.91	1703.48	1807.20	2131.89	2153.96	2265.67
卫生健康	Expenditure for Health Care	304.04	918.36	1579.60	1772.99	1857.10	2081.25	2021.59
节能环保	Expenditure for Energy Conservation and Environment Protection	239.16	322.33	747.44	517.76	493.55	464.89	444.65
城乡社区	Expenditure for Urban and Rural Community Affairs	407.64	1174.16	2413.84	1574.89	1556.64	1429.03	1367.66
农林水	Expenditure for Agriculture, Forestry and Water Conservancy	325.02	811.90	957.68	1125.81	1109.47	1067.57	1076.77
交通运输	Expenditure for Transportation	318.17	1982.63	525.23	652.43	728.22	759.61	614.73
其他支出	Other Expenditure	331.54	428.10	39.55	30.47	43.99	46.77	34.14

8-3 各市地方一般公共预算收支

Local Government General Budgetary Revenue and Expenditure by City

单位：亿元 (100 million yuan)

市别	City	地方一般公共预算收入 Local Government General Budgetary Revenue								
		2000	2005	2010	2015	2019	2020	2021	2022	2023
全　省	**Provincial Total**	**910.56**	**1807.20**	**4517.04**	**9366.78**	**12654.53**	**12923.85**	**14105.04**	**13260.88**	**13850.78**
广　州	Guangzhou	200.55	371.26	872.65	1349.47	1699.04	1722.79	1884.26	1855.10	1945.06
深　圳	Shenzhen	221.92	412.38	1106.82	2726.85	3773.38	3857.46	4257.70	4012.44	4112.92
珠　海	Zhuhai	24.23	48.97	124.53	269.96	344.49	379.13	448.19	437.41	482.51
汕　头	Shantou	18.94	29.44	72.65	131.26	138.25	143.47	146.35	127.98	133.07
佛　山	Foshan	59.53	130.85	306.05	557.55	731.62	753.56	808.26	796.76	800.77
韶　关	Shaoguan	8.63	19.93	47.81	85.23	101.05	105.12	109.08	89.40	101.15
河　源	Heyuan	2.55	8.52	25.09	67.48	77.48	79.81	84.30	69.32	72.91
梅　州	Meizhou	7.18	15.18	38.95	103.59	91.59	88.19	95.01	82.22	92.72
惠　州	Huizhou	12.94	34.72	131.23	340.02	400.86	412.25	455.39	441.73	473.30
汕　尾	Shanwei	4.16	7.09	26.23	28.83	42.45	46.01	52.77	61.30	66.52
东　莞	Dongguan	30.22	103.97	277.84	517.97	673.27	694.75	769.57	766.13	805.09
中　山	Zhongshan	17.46	54.26	139.38	287.51	283.42	287.57	316.47	316.04	332.98
江　门	Jiangmen	21.24	41.63	104.29	199.01	256.83	264.00	279.87	263.03	277.17
阳　江	Yangjiang	3.89	8.70	26.77	67.93	64.30	65.70	77.67	76.35	78.71
湛　江	Zhanjiang	12.44	24.01	66.23	121.86	131.27	137.78	160.40	136.94	155.63
茂　名	Maoming	9.08	21.26	51.95	113.92	139.89	142.66	148.42	140.69	145.48
肇　庆	Zhaoqing	10.97	20.44	76.80	143.36	114.21	124.51	146.46	160.84	176.56
清　远	Qingyuan	4.53	13.25	72.79	108.38	118.54	123.62	137.42	141.01	152.00
潮　州	Chaozhou	4.60	8.64	23.25	47.20	48.01	48.63	51.77	49.22	59.67
揭　阳	Jieyang	9.24	11.19	38.65	77.40	73.02	73.97	79.31	71.39	101.11
云　浮	Yunfu	3.65	9.33	23.54	58.70	60.48	65.89	75.24	99.83	92.94
按经济区域分	By Region									
珠三角	Pearl River Delta	599.06	1218.48	3139.58	6391.70	8277.11	8496.03	9366.17	9049.47	9406.36
粤　东	Eastern Region	36.94	56.38	160.78	284.69	301.73	312.09	330.21	309.90	360.36
粤　西	Western Region	25.41	53.96	144.95	303.71	335.46	346.15	386.49	353.99	379.82
粤　北	Northern Region	26.54	66.21	208.18	423.38	449.14	462.62	501.05	481.78	511.71

8–3 续表 continued

单位：亿元 (100 million yuan)

市别	City	地方一般公共预算支出 Local Government General Budgetary Expenditure								
		2000	2005	2010	2015	2019	2020	2021	2022	2023
全　省	**Provincial Total**	**1069.86**	**2289.07**	**5421.54**	**12827.80**	**17297.85**	**17430.79**	**18247.01**	**18533.08**	**18527.03**
广　州	Guangzhou	240.72	438.41	977.32	1727.72	2865.33	2952.65	3021.18	3022.45	2971.65
深　圳	Shenzhen	225.04	599.16	1266.07	3521.67	4552.73	4178.42	4570.22	4997.38	5012.43
珠　海	Zhuhai	31.14	57.77	166.41	388.77	615.74	677.62	786.66	754.13	671.86
汕　头	Shantou	27.90	50.14	121.71	280.98	386.54	427.26	412.92	379.75	372.46
佛　山	Foshan	72.48	150.85	363.35	799.93	941.32	1003.04	1072.01	1022.33	982.86
韶　关	Shaoguan	19.94	44.55	100.24	287.07	377.59	370.14	370.19	356.47	368.43
河　源	Heyuan	16.78	37.00	94.55	268.38	370.22	361.76	347.08	335.92	333.61
梅　州	Meizhou	23.84	46.25	117.98	376.37	443.84	474.35	443.07	449.51	425.16
惠　州	Huizhou	20.14	52.41	185.44	486.07	614.86	637.37	663.31	693.03	726.73
汕　尾	Shanwei	9.99	20.05	56.51	212.95	278.92	266.51	279.62	296.72	266.44
东　莞	Dongguan	33.61	117.04	289.83	581.24	863.01	840.33	882.53	861.60	905.85
中　山	Zhongshan	19.24	56.71	145.85	355.37	411.74	375.63	472.48	463.10	465.87
江　门	Jiangmen	28.18	54.24	132.98	292.90	421.24	442.38	460.25	450.67	455.24
阳　江	Yangjiang	11.00	23.17	64.92	170.91	242.34	249.84	242.62	271.39	263.75
湛　江	Zhanjiang	27.82	57.95	153.65	412.36	503.10	538.59	547.39	535.56	545.37
茂　名	Maoming	20.67	45.28	122.49	346.78	458.12	479.75	489.54	510.14	513.78
肇　庆	Zhaoqing	20.09	40.64	127.66	267.71	351.65	430.58	396.80	397.56	416.91
清　远	Qingyuan	16.35	38.15	132.81	292.59	395.28	411.84	406.78	423.79	428.74
潮　州	Chaozhou	11.31	21.36	55.99	147.67	197.16	217.17	209.97	214.93	201.80
揭　阳	Jieyang	19.50	30.99	94.68	276.88	349.69	374.48	365.75	374.84	386.86
云　浮	Yunfu	11.18	23.87	69.28	157.42	242.99	263.10	255.68	273.54	257.35
按经济区域分	By Region									
珠三角	Pearl River Delta	690.64	1567.23	3654.91	8421.36	11637.61	11538.02	12325.44	12662.25	12609.39
粤　东	Eastern Region	68.70	122.50	328.89	918.47	1212.31	1285.41	1268.25	1266.24	1227.55
粤　西	Western Region	59.49	126.40	341.06	930.04	1203.57	1268.18	1279.55	1317.09	1322.91
粤　北	Northern Region	88.09	189.83	514.86	1381.84	1829.92	1881.20	1822.80	1839.23	1813.29

8-4 各市人均地方一般公共预算收入

Per Capita Local Government General Public Budget Revenue by City

单位：元 (yuan)

市 别	City	2000	2005	2010	2015	2019	2020	2021	2022	2023
全 省	**Provincial Total**	**1087.68**	**1974.59**	**4390.34**	**8683.80**	**11067.94**	**10292.55**	**11146.70**	**10466.03**	**10922.12**
广 州	Guangzhou	2061.72	3875.93	7100.70	10153.45	11248.07	9299.20	10035.75	9882.06	10356.76
深 圳	Shenzhen	3327.64	5064.37	10892.78	24613.26	28515.59	22209.02	24112.41	22705.45	23202.82
珠 海	Zhuhai	2024.57	3492.54	8025.47	16621.83	17599.19	15858.65	18232.99	17694.79	19411.77
汕 头	Shantou	409.83	596.51	1368.64	2370.24	2446.25	2609.28	2652.74	2311.78	2397.73
佛 山	Foshan	1146.57	2265.69	4349.20	7544.00	9108.59	7953.07	8449.55	8314.83	8355.40
韶 关	Shaoguan	314.70	686.57	1683.27	2918.61	3352.84	3684.42	3816.95	3124.79	3536.95
河 源	Heyuan	111.86	311.21	860.81	2199.23	2499.49	2808.12	2970.08	2439.81	2567.20
梅 州	Meizhou	188.06	370.01	924.97	2391.27	2090.60	2264.01	2452.61	2125.89	2406.02
惠 州	Huizhou	408.85	946.27	2931.87	7171.79	8256.63	6853.94	7512.70	7291.51	7807.84
汕 尾	Shanwei	170.37	255.84	893.66	956.42	1413.00	1717.59	1970.40	2283.23	2475.66
东 莞	Dongguan	503.97	1585.20	3454.53	6241.63	7988.12	6636.08	7322.12	7305.60	7695.99
中 山	Zhongshan	762.08	2231.98	4578.83	8981.32	8472.91	6522.11	7113.32	7103.52	7491.81
江 门	Jiangmen	540.87	1014.97	2365.62	4407.32	5566.01	5524.66	5807.00	5447.34	5747.71
阳 江	Yangjiang	179.12	375.62	1116.06	2711.43	2508.51	2528.64	2972.00	2912.67	3000.40
湛 江	Zhanjiang	207.35	361.18	950.34	1686.16	1786.90	1973.61	2289.50	1947.05	2205.34
茂 名	Maoming	173.63	366.48	887.70	1878.43	2198.76	2319.25	2393.93	2258.69	2329.46
肇 庆	Zhaoqing	325.95	558.68	1979.41	3541.77	2739.21	3033.31	3552.04	3895.28	4275.12
清 远	Qingyuan	143.50	372.24	1972.39	2832.14	3055.15	3118.16	3454.22	3539.13	3813.03
潮 州	Chaozhou	192.52	343.30	877.50	1760.93	1806.18	1888.80	2014.12	1911.50	2316.37
揭 阳	Jieyang	178.24	200.52	660.97	1280.02	1197.53	1319.44	1416.77	1269.08	1791.52
云 浮	Yunfu	169.61	400.53	1002.33	2393.45	2384.84	2764.31	3149.97	4168.42	3878.18
按经济区域分	By Region									
珠 三 角	Pearl River Delta	1442.48	2688.72	5717.85	10984.52	12985.86	10957.32	11943.50	11535.31	11983.24
粤 东	Eastern Region	252.38	356.63	960.44	1647.57	1732.96	1907.79	2017.93	1887.15	2189.81
粤 西	Western Region	189.61	365.50	952.37	1922.57	2061.61	2200.44	2443.18	2228.63	2384.99
粤 北	Northern Region	187.58	423.54	1300.73	2550.51	2655.95	2902.57	3143.97	3020.76	3211.03

注：本表按年中常住人口数计算。
Note: The data in this table are calculated by permanent population of the year.

8-5 各市财政收支（2023年）

单位：亿元

项　　目	Item	全　省 Provincial Total	广　州 Guangzhou
一、地方一般公共预算收入	**General Public Budget Revenue of Local Governments**	**13850.78**	**1945.06**
税收收入	Tax Revenue	10244.77	1370.80
#增值税	Value-added Tax	4291.82	451.41
企业所得税	Corporate Income Tax	1784.12	190.88
个人所得税	Individual Income Tax	946.13	99.00
城市维护建设税	City Maintenance and Construction Tax	598.22	139.44
房产税	House Property Tax	470.67	133.57
土地增值税	Land Appreciation Tax	1033.79	101.70
耕地占用税	Farm Land Occupation Tax	67.01	13.19
契税	Deed Tax	621.88	146.64
非税收入	Non-tax Revenue	3606.00	574.26
专项收入	Special Program Receipts	1086.09	205.76
行政性收费收入	Charge of Administrative and Units	297.21	42.61
罚没收入	Penalty Receipts	338.45	57.83
国有资本经营收入	Operation Income from State-owned Assets	132.44	35.08
国有资源(资产)有偿使用收入	Income from Use of State-owned Resources Assets	1277.18	85.56
其他收入	Other Non-tax Revenue	474.64	147.42
二、地方一般公共预算支出	**General Public Budget Expenditure of Local Governments**	**18527.03**	**2971.65**
#一般公共服务	Expenditure for General Public Services	1718.76	283.51
教育	Expenditure for Education	4004.45	643.39
科学技术	Expenditure for Science and Technology	980.46	194.96
文化旅游体育与传媒	Expenditure for Culture, Tourism, Sports and Media	360.52	51.90
社会保障和就业	Expenditure for Social Safety Net and Employment Effort	2265.67	347.10
卫生健康	Expenditure for Health Care	2021.59	364.70
节能环保	Expenditure for Energy Conservation and Environment Protection	444.65	52.72
城乡社区	Expenditure for Urban and Rural Community Affairs	1367.66	246.11
农林水	Expenditure for Agriculture, Forestry and Water Conservancy	1076.77	94.04
交通运输	Expenditure for Transportation	614.73	46.21

Basic Conditions of Local Government General Public Budget Revenue and Expenditure by City(2023)

(100 million yuan)

深圳 Shenzhen	珠海 Zhuhai	汕头 Shantou	佛山 Foshan	韶关 Shaoguan	河源 Heyuan	梅州 Meizhou	惠州 Huizhou	汕尾 Shanwei
4112.92	**482.51**	**133.07**	**800.77**	**101.15**	**72.91**	**92.72**	**473.30**	**66.52**
3467.68	300.29	83.75	464.57	52.03	38.18	51.26	282.57	31.74
1330.36	87.80	29.95	163.05	16.93	13.14	15.43	103.39	9.47
715.49	54.30	7.74	49.70	3.11	3.25	3.75	24.87	2.42
505.75	25.51	3.27	21.24	1.58	0.98	1.41	8.52	0.72
188.71	26.53	8.38	44.75	7.58	3.25	7.97	27.99	2.23
113.07	18.39	7.99	50.36	4.82	3.33	3.14	22.11	2.49
352.49	31.44	6.53	33.69	2.39	2.09	4.37	29.63	3.22
2.66	1.96	1.99	2.63	1.73	2.50	2.76	5.85	2.70
163.88	38.25	9.48	56.87	5.46	4.61	6.32	38.00	5.04
645.24	182.22	49.32	336.20	49.12	34.73	41.46	190.73	34.78
259.31	116.80	7.12	45.01	5.91	3.02	7.05	54.66	1.95
59.28	6.23	6.25	17.19	3.53	3.03	3.27	10.42	3.18
41.13	11.22	8.04	20.22	12.17	9.91	4.67	21.72	4.75
16.44	1.78	0.43	29.27	0.47	0.01	…	8.20	0.84
134.19	39.98	23.76	171.20	19.20	16.25	22.34	68.42	17.48
134.90	6.21	3.71	53.30	7.84	2.51	4.14	27.31	6.58
5012.43	**671.86**	**372.46**	**982.86**	**368.43**	**333.61**	**425.16**	**726.73**	**266.44**
400.62	67.35	39.64	116.99	42.34	35.14	44.53	74.98	24.69
1001.45	113.82	101.39	212.42	64.03	74.44	92.07	151.40	59.77
454.94	57.65	3.62	57.36	2.61	1.98	2.20	21.21	3.04
127.45	11.70	4.96	17.87	5.74	2.99	6.41	14.03	3.14
303.92	97.86	68.29	110.55	72.71	60.05	95.88	88.95	47.53
619.45	40.33	50.00	109.06	41.06	35.75	51.87	73.24	34.54
181.48	7.46	3.87	15.10	12.00	3.63	3.68	17.11	1.51
585.36	71.42	20.47	83.04	9.75	15.65	13.98	89.79	18.00
99.62	20.30	25.20	36.94	57.75	42.58	52.40	53.08	32.24
170.27	27.41	7.84	40.47	11.09	14.90	12.88	22.29	8.54

8-5 续表

单位：亿元

项 目	Item	东 莞 Dongguan	中 山 Zhongshan
一、地方一般公共预算收入	**General Public Budget Revenue of Local Governments**	**805.09**	**332.98**
税收收入	Tax Revenue	605.40	209.70
#增值税	Value-added Tax	269.43	83.53
企业所得税	Corporate Income Tax	60.46	20.58
个人所得税	Individual Income Tax	30.27	8.05
城市维护建设税	City Maintenance and Construction Tax	55.36	19.07
房产税	House Property Tax	35.64	21.79
土地增值税	Land Appriciation Tax	61.12	16.91
耕地占用税	Farm Land Occupation Tax	1.96	1.44
契税	Deed Tax	50.72	24.15
非税收入	Non-tax Revenue	199.69	123.29
专项收入	Special Program Receipts	67.07	17.65
行政性收费收入	Charge of Administrative and Units	23.26	10.50
罚没收入	Penalty Receipts	15.87	11.55
国有资本经营收入	Operation Income from State-owned Assets	17.43	
国有资源(资产)有偿使用收入	Income from Use of State-owned Resources Assets	66.66	65.20
其他收入	Other Non-tax Revenue	9.40	18.38
二、地方一般公共预算支出	**General Public Budget Expenditure of Local Governments**	**905.85**	**465.87**
#一般公共服务	Expenditure for General Public Services	95.78	42.19
教育	Expenditure for Education	233.64	96.21
科学技术	Expenditure for Science and Technology	34.61	29.51
文化旅游体育与传媒	Expenditure for Culture, Tourism, Sports and Media	20.35	7.88
社会保障和就业	Expenditure for Social Safety Net and Employment Effort	60.03	51.22
卫生健康	Expenditure for Health Care	85.44	38.08
节能环保	Expenditure for Energy Conservation and Environment Protection	43.08	10.02
城乡社区	Expenditure for Urban and Rural Community Affairs	47.08	59.48
农林水	Expenditure for Agriculture, Forestry and Water Conservancy	38.07	24.21
交通运输	Expenditure for Transportation	33.34	16.01

continued

(100 million yuan)

江门 Jiangmen	阳江 Yangjiang	湛江 Zhanjiang	茂名 Maoming	肇庆 Zhaoqing	清远 Qingyuan	潮州 Chaozhou	揭阳 Jieyang	云浮 Yunfu
277.17	**78.71**	**155.63**	**145.48**	**176.56**	**152.00**	**59.67**	**101.11**	**92.94**
154.33	51.85	90.39	68.82	77.90	80.36	31.62	43.88	31.73
57.89	18.05	32.84	20.19	27.65	26.87	11.56	11.56	8.88
15.50	7.08	5.04	5.56	6.72	6.94	2.76	3.70	2.63
4.92	1.29	2.77	1.81	2.72	2.40	1.16	1.11	1.38
13.86	4.62	12.58	10.37	6.91	6.95	3.16	5.89	2.37
15.87	3.43	6.82	3.16	7.84	6.86	3.07	4.01	2.90
9.47	2.93	8.06	8.25	3.81	8.50	1.65	3.29	1.47
2.93	2.61	3.01	4.06	2.55	1.24	1.65	2.87	4.73
17.21	6.00	10.02	7.47	10.00	11.23	2.55	4.77	3.22
122.85	26.86	65.24	76.66	98.66	71.64	28.05	57.23	61.21
20.24	3.61	11.33	12.70	5.70	6.41	2.84	6.73	2.19
7.27	3.49	5.25	7.42	4.58	3.35	1.29	3.05	1.09
15.18	5.61	13.46	7.82	6.62	9.46	5.77	7.45	4.42
13.58	…	2.84	1.06	2.39	0.03	0.04	1.84	0.19
63.17	12.50	23.83	43.37	77.07	39.92	16.69	36.73	48.55
3.40	1.65	8.53	4.29	2.30	12.47	1.41	1.43	4.77
455.24	**263.75**	**545.37**	**513.78**	**416.91**	**428.74**	**201.80**	**386.86**	**257.35**
46.03	26.41	54.69	44.33	45.25	41.65	21.90	31.55	32.46
90.11	52.86	127.44	140.91	87.90	100.58	47.15	90.67	54.82
12.72	1.64	1.64	1.89	6.36	2.53	1.09	1.72	2.38
6.90	5.04	5.04	7.50	5.61	5.33	2.48	3.61	2.32
88.22	48.05	118.07	92.55	73.04	69.50	35.68	74.99	46.56
49.71	30.92	71.91	66.41	47.99	48.38	26.28	55.89	30.50
5.24	1.83	5.46	17.06	18.85	5.98	1.35	13.38	2.26
11.86	6.43	21.36	9.89	16.09	12.99	8.07	8.91	9.99
39.18	36.34	42.52	50.28	46.71	61.27	22.47	30.59	31.26
23.02	8.26	18.47	11.60	9.46	11.69	8.80	17.14	7.69

8-6 历年金融机构存贷款

Deposits and Loans in All Financial Institutions

单位：亿元　　　　(100million yuan)

年 份 Year	金融机构本外币存款余额 Deposits in Renminbi and Foreign Currencies in All Financial Institutions	#住户存款 Savings Deposit by Household	金融机构本外币贷款余额 Loans and Loans in Renminbi and Foreign Currencies in Financial Institutions	金融机构人民币存款余额 Deposits in Renminbi Currencies in Financial Institutions	#人民币住户存款 Savings Deposit by Household in Renminbi	金融机构人民币贷款余额 Loans in Renminbi Currencies in Financial Institutions
2000	19083.64	10031.68	13227.62	16919.98	8667.29	11787.14
2001	21714.85	11386.03	14472.08	19449.34	9930.12	13192.74
2002	25409.90	13372.85	16840.39	22975.88	11819.09	15314.56
2003	29640.83	15590.68	20126.24	27240.23	14061.77	18287.58
2004	33252.01	17631.07	21955.28	30869.62	16193.41	19671.52
2005	38119.91	20267.76	23261.21	35958.71	19051.35	20965.55
2006	43262.20	22677.19	25935.19	41146.58	21584.60	23617.49
2007	48955.03	23013.34	30617.27	47016.48	22242.70	27497.88
2008	56119.28	28181.18	33755.62	54309.57	27481.56	30964.62
2009	69691.46	32136.32	44510.22	67742.59	31411.40	39683.65
2010	82019.40	36965.75	51799.30	79957.97	36318.66	47191.56
2011	91590.15	41061.56	58615.27	89168.60	40405.07	53411.83
2012	105099.55	46265.58	67077.08	99934.60	45533.78	59967.26
2013	119685.15	50638.64	75664.16	114855.02	49891.35	68491.93
2014	127881.47	53215.87	84921.79	121964.85	52410.55	77889.50
2015	160388.22	55008.70	95661.12	153551.79	54238.30	89289.27
2016	179829.19	59768.75	110928.41	171024.47	58618.89	103649.79
2017	194535.75	62942.27	126031.95	184779.60	61890.08	118978.62
2018	208051.16	70293.46	145169.39	199576.08	69231.95	139100.04
2019	232458.64	78959.14	167994.58	222962.37	77943.89	162378.43
2020	267638.26	88976.65	195680.62	257851.63	87969.94	189802.41
2021	293169.22	97598.57	222234.29	282489.30	96634.05	215784.19
2022	322357.66	113554.76	245722.94	312286.48	112555.17	239605.98
2023	350887.61	126625.54	271561.63	341361.26	125616.81	265275.42

注：2015年前，住户存款主要为居民储蓄存款。
Note：Before 2015, the savings by households are mainly savings by residents.

8–7 金融机构本外币存贷款余额

Deposits and Loans in Renminbi and Foreign Currencies in All Financial Institutions

单位：亿元　　　　(100million yuan)

指　　标	Item	2020	2021	2022	2023
一、各项存款	**Total Deposits**	**267638.26**	**293169.22**	**322357.66**	**350887.61**
境内存款	Domestic Deposits	257410.78	282596.96	311848.67	340894.49
住户存款	Deposits of Households	88976.65	97598.57	113554.76	126625.54
活期存款	Demand Deposits	46576.09	49607.97	54921.52	55453.50
定期及其他存款	Time & Other Deposits	42400.57	47990.60	58633.24	71172.05
非金融企业存款	Deposits of Non-financial Enterprises	102596.79	110133.55	120746.78	128674.82
活期存款	Demand Deposits	28669.72	29772.63	29956.91	27641.98
定期及其他存款	Time & Other Deposits	73927.07	80360.92	90789.87	101032.84
广义政府存款	Deposits of Government	38421.43	41917.79	44130.53	46450.73
财政性存款	Fiscal Deposits	4304.07	5140.81	4389.18	3490.66
机关团体存款	Deposits of Government Departments &	34117.36	36776.99	39741.35	42960.07
非银行业金融机构存款	Deposits of Non-banking Financial Institutions	27415.91	32947.06	33416.60	39143.39
境外存款	Overseas Deposits	10227.49	10572.25	10509.00	9993.12
二、各项贷款	**Total Loans**	**195680.62**	**222234.29**	**245722.94**	**271561.63**
境内贷款	Domestic Loans	192014.72	218200.07	241522.58	267066.34
住户贷款	Loans to Households	82517.46	93239.77	98214.21	105920.93
#短期贷款	Short-term Loans	13205.25	14771.61	14459.37	16109.32
中长期贷款	Mid & Long-term Loans	69312.21	78468.16	83754.84	89811.61
非金融企业及机关团体贷款	Loans to Non-financial Enterprises and	109221.81	124834.12	143029.86	160828.99
#短期贷款	Short-term Loans	31123.74	32697.21	34246.93	37574.46
中长期贷款	Mid & Long-term Loans	68304.93	79496.95	92867.50	106455.87
非银行业金融机构贷款	Loans to Non-banking Financial Institutions	275.45	126.18	278.51	316.42
境外贷款	Overseas Loans	3665.90	4034.22	4200.36	4495.29

注：2015年起银行资金来源项目使用新的分类。
Note: Since 2015, new categorization is applied to items of bank fund sources.

8-8 金融机构人民币存贷款余额

Deposits and Loans in Renminbi in All Financial Institutions

单位：亿元 (100 million yuan)

指　　标	Item	2020	2021	2022	2023
一、各项存款	**Total Deposits**	**257851.63**	**282489.30**	**312286.48**	**341361.26**
境内存款	Domestic Deposits	251502.64	275598.99	304470.53	333739.02
住户存款	Deposits of Households	87969.94	96634.05	112555.17	125616.81
活期存款	Demand Deposits	45943.18	48985.03	54318.44	54927.88
定期及其他存款	Time & Other Deposits	42026.76	47649.03	58236.72	70688.93
非金融企业存款	Deposits of Non-financial Enterprises	97912.35	104492.67	114585.73	122921.66
活期存款	Demand Deposits	26713.28	27374.28	27633.52	25589.57
定期及其他存款	Time & Other Deposits	71199.07	77118.39	86952.21	97332.10
广义政府存款	Deposits of Government	38409.77	41908.58	44120.07	46439.82
财政性存款	Fiscal Deposits	4304.07	5140.81	4389.18	3490.66
机关团体存款	Deposits of Government Departments & Organizations	34105.70	36767.77	39730.88	42949.16
非银行业金融机构存款	Deposits of Non-banking Financial Institutions	27210.58	32563.69	33209.56	38760.73
境外存款	Overseas Deposits	6349.00	6890.31	7815.95	7622.24
二、各项贷款	**Total Loans**	**189802.41**	**215784.19**	**239605.98**	**265275.42**
境内贷款	Domestic Loans	188651.84	214464.29	237918.53	262974.64
住户贷款	Loans to Households	82512.79	93234.78	98207.90	105912.79
#短期贷款	Short-term Loans	13201.52	14767.38	14453.98	16101.70
中长期贷款	Mid & Long-term Loans	69311.27	78467.40	83753.91	89811.09
非金融企业及机关团体贷款	Loans to Non-financial Enterprises and Government Departments & Organizations	105863.59	121103.34	139434.22	156747.21
#短期贷款	Short-term Loans	28699.38	29969.33	31554.60	34389.65
中长期贷款	Mid & Long-term Loans	67510.75	78625.19	92093.74	105713.18
非银行业金融机构贷款	Loans to Non-banking Financial Institutions	275.45	126.18	276.42	314.65
境外贷款	Overseas Loans	1150.58	1319.90	1687.45	2300.78

注：2015年起银行资金来源项目使用新的分类。
Note: Since 2015, new categorization is applied to items of bank fund sources.

8-9 各市中资金融机构基本情况

Basic Conditions of Chinese-funded Financial Institutions by City

市别	City	2005				2010			
		机构数(个) Number of Financial Institutions	年末从业人员(人) Number of Employed Persons at the Year-end	人民币存款(亿元) Total Deposits (100 million yuan)	人民币贷款(亿元) Total Loans (100 million yuan)	机构数(个) Number of Financial Institutions	年末从业人员(人) Number of Employed Persons at the Year-end	人民币存款(亿元) Total Deposits (100 million yuan)	人民币贷款(亿元) Total Loans (100 million yuan)
全省合计	**Provincial Total**	**15433**	**222738**	**35783.57**	**20745.27**	**14983**	**258254**	**78285.89**	**46099.26**
广州	Guangzhou	2053	45800	11065.22	6873.34	2395	58412	22775.49	14597.74
深圳	Shenzhen	1119	28354	8478.18	6168.03	1286	41483	20210.75	13708.16
珠海	Zhuhai	417	6798	925.47	424.33	406	7664	2542.56	1203.85
汕头	Shantou	655	9196	955.34	391.08	632	9476	1849.14	627.91
佛山	Foshan	1913	21732	3770.74	2056.29	1775	25815	8293.02	4729.61
韶关	Shaoguan	406	5153	461.78	166.55	401	5317	903.67	346.28
河源	Heyuan	349	3759	204.20	107.99	325	3828	496.83	335.32
梅州	Meizhou	635	7373	429.79	206.37	529	6371	835.07	330.25
惠州	Huizhou	664	8012	781.79	367.23	650	9065	2038.58	1096.21
汕尾	Shanwei	246	2937	140.77	57.21	217	2965	326.96	130.20
东莞	Dongguan	1262	14985	2933.40	1500.52	1221	19395	5915.54	3302.49
中山	Zhongshan	586	7837	1131.19	479.02	568	9017	2596.88	1324.65
江门	Jiangmen	906	11627	1163.76	534.17	819	11194	2214.97	973.75
阳江	Yangjiang	289	3986	245.37	99.66	268	3806	564.19	283.93
湛江	Zhanjiang	931	10663	705.32	285.97	780	10321	1556.00	714.40
茂名	Maoming	717	7915	521.02	225.46	612	7670	1025.39	361.30
肇庆	Zhaoqing	551	7120	478.15	229.43	494	6874	1057.35	642.04
清远	Qingyuan	471	5510	386.23	175.08	447	5620	986.45	510.26
潮州	Chaozhou	304	4087	324.04	132.34	275	4187	649.81	205.91
揭阳	Jieyang	613	6120	468.15	169.19	586	6178	963.79	400.68
云浮	Yunfu	346	3774	213.66	96.02	297	3596	483.45	274.32
按经济区域分	By Region								
珠三角	Pearl River Delta	9471	152265	30727.90	18632.36	9614	188919	67645.13	41578.51
粤东	Eastern Region	1818	22340	1888.30	749.81	1710	22806	3789.69	1364.70
粤西	Western Region	1937	22564	1471.71	611.09	1660	21797	3145.59	1359.62
粤北	Northern Region	2207	25569	1695.66	752.01	1999	24732	3705.47	1796.43

8-9 续表 continued

市别	City	2022 机构数(个) Number of Financial Institutions	2022 年末从业人员(人) Number of Employed Persons at the Year-end	2022 人民币存款(亿元) Total Deposits (100 million yuan)	2022 人民币贷款(亿元) Total Loans (100 million yuan)	2023 机构数(个) Number of Financial Institutions	2023 年末从业人员(人) Number of Employed Persons at the Year-end	2023 人民币存款(亿元) Total Deposits (100 million yuan)	2023 人民币贷款(亿元) Total Loans (100 million yuan)
全省合计	**Provincial Total**	**16296**	**348922**	**308385.92**	**236227.69**	**16207**	**351300**	**337625.92**	**262102.14**
广州	Guangzhou	2678	93659	77119.84	66682.86	2683	92475	83412.49	74602.88
深圳	Shenzhen	1896	66555	116577.32	78704.75	1898	69849	126997.38	87616.27
珠海	Zhuhai	496	11408	11408.41	10030.38	497	11482	11820.96	10839.91
汕头	Shantou	634	10892	4948.44	2765.58	630	10761	5295.70	3029.78
佛山	Foshan	1704	31305	23200.95	17968.20	1688	31430	26877.67	19683.38
韶关	Shaoguan	407	5407	2413.05	1640.09	399	5394	2696.72	1792.15
河源	Heyuan	348	4652	1630.84	1743.69	344	4655	1731.22	1827.34
梅州	Meizhou	569	6870	2799.87	1967.44	565	6919	3077.54	2217.77
惠州	Huizhou	746	12440	7774.16	9055.26	745	12577	8897.63	10082.36
汕尾	Shanwei	207	2956	1059.78	982.59	208	2940	1141.15	1134.85
东莞	Dongguan	1393	25802	22339.83	15655.23	1390	25865	25061.19	17283.52
中山	Zhongshan	612	11557	7712.98	6784.89	611	11563	8585.77	7484.02
江门	Jiangmen	862	12551	6412.91	5458.29	849	12636	7114.02	6003.89
阳江	Yangjiang	275	4195	1964.66	1720.02	270	4162	2150.42	1901.00
湛江	Zhanjiang	736	10743	4358.81	3649.89	734	10846	4698.16	3987.47
茂名	Maoming	588	7991	3678.62	2409.42	576	7917	3905.30	2613.60
肇庆	Zhaoqing	511	8063	3382.11	2926.97	503	8026	3658.95	3216.11
清远	Qingyuan	458	6702	3032.78	2715.37	456	6785	3340.02	2983.35
潮州	Chaozhou	274	4386	1883.90	734.61	258	4250	2050.34	843.50
揭阳	Jieyang	597	7004	3042.14	1410.73	597	6964	3278.12	1550.15
云浮	Yunfu	305	3784	1644.54	1221.45	306	3804	1835.19	1408.85
按经济区域分	By Region								
珠三角	Pearl River Delta	10898	273340	275928.50	213266.828	10864	275903	302426.05	236812.33
粤东	Eastern Region	1712	25238	10934.26	5893.52	1693	24915	11765.31	6558.27
粤西	Western Region	1599	22929	10002.08	7779.32	1580	22925	10753.88	8502.07
粤北	Northern Region	2087	27415	11521.07	9288.03	2070	27557	12680.69	10229.47

注：1. 本表存贷款统计口径为中资金融机构人民币存贷款。
2. 机构数和年末从业人员统计范围为银行业及相关金融机构(不含人民银行、外资银行及资产管理公司)。

Notes: a) Deposits and loans in this table refer to the deposits and loans in Renminbi in domestic-funded financial institutions.
b) The number of financial institutions and the number of employed persons at the year-end refer to those in banking and related financial institutions (excluding the People's Bank of China, foreign-funded banks and assets management companies).

8-10 各市金融机构本外币存贷款

Deposits and Loans in Renminbi and Foreign Currencies in All Financial Institutions by City

单位：亿元 (100 million yuan)

市 别	City	各项存款 Total Deposits								
		2000	2005	2010	2015	2019	2020	2021	2022	2023
全省合计	**Provincial Total**	**19083.64**	**38119.91**	**82019.40**	**160388.22**	**232458.64**	**267638.26**	**293169.22**	**322357.66**	**350887.61**
广 州	Guangzhou	6200.47	11734.10	23953.96	42843.67	59131.20	67798.81	74988.86	80495.07	86638.33
深 圳	Shenzhen	3942.00	9486.76	21937.89	57778.90	83942.45	101897.31	112545.17	123400.52	133350.52
珠 海	Zhuhai	521.71	1014.08	2748.70	5383.73	9047.24	9604.51	10496.05	11794.30	12182.88
汕 头	Shantou	600.21	995.64	1873.03	2857.20	3861.01	4130.81	4516.63	5045.42	5382.54
佛 山	Foshan	2119.08	3906.93	8462.33	11867.67	16948.10	19161.40	20606.98	23787.77	27524.35
韶 关	Shaoguan	263.73	468.35	907.75	1532.91	1944.17	2089.98	2231.08	2423.78	2705.05
河 源	Heyuan	91.12	205.94	500.02	988.90	1448.09	1544.34	1567.98	1647.28	1749.55
梅 州	Meizhou	219.47	438.71	839.63	1565.28	2251.36	2438.24	2579.03	2807.60	3085.59
惠 州	Huizhou	394.44	823.96	2090.14	3836.10	6558.61	7235.61	7809.67	8396.63	9648.97
汕 尾	Shanwei	78.19	144.45	332.70	631.03	1002.60	1073.29	1057.07	1062.96	1145.02
东 莞	Dongguan	1327.79	3036.77	6077.87	9968.80	16426.44	18232.83	20315.59	23514.02	26125.61
中 山	Zhongshan	619.44	1186.76	2665.35	4378.36	6345.05	6921.69	7332.85	8267.18	9044.94
江 门	Jiangmen	805.18	1279.67	2285.75	3766.81	4946.81	5475.45	5864.34	6570.65	7261.47
阳 江	Yangjiang	142.73	248.75	575.32	1014.74	1486.24	1639.46	1744.28	1973.00	2157.23
湛 江	Zhanjiang	408.90	716.97	1565.19	2684.61	3651.54	3938.27	4191.05	4377.76	4714.90
茂 名	Maoming	332.55	524.90	1028.67	1974.75	3012.91	3246.33	3432.91	3686.02	3911.92
肇 庆	Zhaoqing	281.64	493.23	1072.54	1785.01	2642.47	2893.08	3052.70	3429.96	3693.68
清 远	Qingyuan	213.85	393.96	995.36	1699.82	2564.42	2710.50	2827.48	3085.55	3382.19
潮 州	Chaozhou	162.70	328.97	653.27	1076.19	1489.43	1621.68	1735.33	1895.52	2059.58
揭 阳	Jieyang	240.07	473.60	967.03	1837.87	2429.00	2599.43	2770.96	3048.35	3284.10
云 浮	Yunfu	118.37	217.40	486.93	915.88	1329.49	1385.24	1503.20	1648.32	1839.18
按经济区域分	By Region									
珠 三 角	Pearl River Delta	16211.75	32962.25	71294.51	141609.04	205988.39	239220.69	263012.21	289656.10	315470.76
粤 东	Eastern Region	1081.18	1942.66	3826.04	6402.29	8782.04	9425.22	10080.00	11052.26	11871.24
粤 西	Western Region	884.18	1490.63	3169.17	5674.10	8150.69	8824.06	9368.24	10036.79	10784.05
粤 北	Northern Region	906.54	1724.37	3729.68	6702.78	9537.52	10168.30	10708.77	11612.52	12761.56

8-10 续表 continued

单位：亿元 (100 million yuan)

市 别	City	各项贷款 Total Loans								
		2000	2005	2010	2015	2019	2020	2021	2022	2023
全省合计	**Provincial Total**	**13227.62**	**23261.21**	**51799.30**	**95661.12**	**167994.58**	**195680.62**	**222234.29**	**245722.94**	**271561.63**
广 州	Guangzhou	4241.87	7622.20	16284.31	27296.16	47103.31	54387.64	61399.61	68918.60	76674.23
深 圳	Shenzhen	3032.13	7596.72	16808.12	32449.04	59461.39	68020.54	77240.78	83422.99	92140.89
珠 海	Zhuhai	349.20	486.72	1472.54	2969.70	6358.61	7626.26	8909.80	10312.70	11090.38
汕 头	Shantou	476.66	421.36	661.52	1199.00	2168.92	2220.33	2516.74	2812.05	3070.64
佛 山	Foshan	1581.90	2122.74	4868.99	7950.53	12175.18	14507.62	16474.11	18234.52	19981.36
韶 关	Shaoguan	149.23	169.68	376.06	731.84	1110.56	1316.85	1504.19	1651.32	1800.76
河 源	Heyuan	62.19	108.13	338.69	801.08	1346.12	1572.17	1671.36	1756.15	1832.81
梅 州	Meizhou	147.02	206.44	331.10	736.41	1352.38	1588.81	1758.09	1969.06	2217.87
惠 州	Huizhou	221.42	409.44	1225.71	2701.60	5848.89	7183.93	8478.86	9479.08	10783.89
汕 尾	Shanwei	68.74	57.21	131.12	306.14	521.64	680.92	819.04	984.03	1135.13
东 莞	Dongguan	642.33	1540.48	3441.99	5980.90	10132.14	12777.12	14931.21	16780.23	18401.74
中 山	Zhongshan	382.09	498.05	1373.62	2894.32	4912.91	5711.18	6486.49	7055.21	7812.37
江 门	Jiangmen	574.26	565.45	1032.46	2218.01	3667.71	4390.98	4970.31	5497.83	6041.75
阳 江	Yangjiang	89.71	100.66	292.24	757.74	1173.23	1353.97	1522.11	1722.80	1904.95
湛 江	Zhanjiang	294.70	310.03	721.00	1568.76	2508.25	2932.33	3153.76	3660.83	3993.04
茂 名	Maoming	211.96	230.93	362.40	858.33	1582.35	1871.39	2126.26	2412.27	2617.51
肇 庆	Zhaoqing	217.44	232.13	652.01	1281.52	2156.79	2485.60	2639.61	2939.68	3229.54
清 远	Qingyuan	150.82	179.13	520.62	1061.23	1886.24	2218.01	2487.61	2739.91	3025.45
潮 州	Chaozhou	118.57	137.20	219.41	369.04	467.17	549.47	657.41	738.59	844.63
揭 阳	Jieyang	131.25	169.40	407.06	931.72	1182.07	1236.62	1358.28	1412.24	1551.52
云 浮	Yunfu	84.12	97.10	278.34	598.05	878.74	1048.88	1128.67	1222.87	1411.16
按经济区域分	By Region									
珠 三 角	Pearl River Delta	11242.64	21073.93	47159.74	85741.78	151816.93	177090.87	201530.79	222640.84	246156.16
粤 东	Eastern Region	795.23	785.17	1419.10	2805.90	4339.79	4687.33	5351.47	5946.91	6601.92
粤 西	Western Region	596.37	641.62	1375.65	3184.82	5263.82	6157.70	6802.13	7795.89	8515.50
粤 北	Northern Region	593.39	760.49	1844.81	3928.63	6574.04	7744.72	8549.91	9339.30	10288.05

8-11 各市金融机构住户存款

Savings Deposit by Household in All Financial Institutions by City

单位：亿元 (100 million yuan)

市别	City	中外资金融机构本外币住户存款 Savings Deposit by Household in Renminbi and Foreign Currencies in All Financial Institutions								
		2000	2005	2010	2015	2019	2020	2021	2022	2023
全省合计	**Provincial Total**	**10031.68**	**20267.76**	**36965.75**	**55008.70**	**78959.14**	**88976.65**	**97598.57**	**113554.76**	**126625.54**
广州	Guangzhou	2683.38	5475.77	9302.33	13602.38	18383.44	21177.97	23151.08	26878.13	30117.66
深圳	Shenzhen	1391.78	3525.70	6918.19	9680.24	16327.05	19031.88	20834.08	24928.72	27668.14
珠海	Zhuhai	262.41	513.72	982.54	1322.97	1985.20	2243.02	2498.01	2949.27	3312.26
汕头	Shantou	401.88	765.26	1305.62	1918.05	2614.33	2825.22	3066.23	3504.56	3884.01
佛山	Foshan	1359.52	2465.51	4460.82	6232.20	8383.03	9259.24	10124.60	11843.25	13465.18
韶关	Shaoguan	172.46	320.00	562.11	925.18	1315.94	1459.06	1607.29	1820.97	2028.74
河源	Heyuan	71.32	146.36	314.33	591.09	864.07	950.91	1045.01	1163.96	1260.48
梅州	Meizhou	166.95	326.86	582.20	1061.20	1517.82	1679.03	1864.83	2088.83	2323.80
惠州	Huizhou	276.61	548.27	1044.17	1729.01	2614.95	2910.72	3244.63	3753.98	4195.86
汕尾	Shanwei	58.89	111.83	231.32	388.93	534.84	582.34	628.54	711.20	782.43
东莞	Dongguan	753.78	1796.69	3425.89	4630.69	6365.70	6998.52	7655.09	9071.89	10153.62
中山	Zhongshan	409.23	764.69	1462.96	2108.53	2896.31	3246.66	3560.37	4155.30	4676.12
江门	Jiangmen	607.54	951.96	1516.72	2270.52	3059.53	3394.16	3757.84	4266.61	4743.08
阳江	Yangjiang	107.92	192.35	386.82	665.27	976.68	1102.18	1217.15	1382.16	1528.03
湛江	Zhanjiang	310.23	514.85	945.28	1684.28	2339.16	2525.38	2771.94	3104.97	3397.13
茂名	Maoming	251.70	413.71	752.61	1413.64	1996.80	2192.91	2426.31	2725.01	2960.54
肇庆	Zhaoqing	197.68	347.39	657.31	1160.94	1645.21	1787.68	1992.83	2248.07	2474.72
清远	Qingyuan	152.70	279.69	593.11	1013.87	1517.73	1676.20	1848.61	2081.13	2271.94
潮州	Chaozhou	111.07	246.32	461.35	748.54	1016.19	1116.17	1222.22	1402.82	1573.32
揭阳	Jieyang	190.83	392.24	716.17	1251.86	1734.69	1870.86	2048.80	2320.41	2547.23
云浮	Yunfu	93.82	168.58	343.92	609.30	870.46	946.56	1033.09	1153.53	1261.23
按经济区域分	By Region									
珠三角	Pearl River Delta	7941.93	16389.71	29770.92	42737.49	61660.42	70049.84	76818.54	90095.22	100806.65
粤东	Eastern Region	762.66	1515.65	2714.46	4307.37	5900.06	6394.59	6965.80	7938.99	8787.00
粤西	Western Region	669.84	1120.91	2084.70	3763.19	5312.63	5820.47	6415.40	7212.14	7885.71
粤北	Northern Region	657.25	1241.49	2395.67	4200.64	6086.03	6711.76	7398.83	8308.40	9146.19

8-11 续表 continued

单位：亿元 (100 million yuan)

市 别	City	中资金融机构人民币住户存款 Savings Deposit by Household in Renminbi in Chinese-funded Financial Institutions								
		2000	2005	2010	2015	2019	2020	2021	2022	2023
全省合计	**Provincial Total**	**8667.29**	**19051.35**	**36219.15**	**54114.45**	**77790.28**	**87826.30**	**96486.15**	**112381.27**	**125382.78**
广 州	Guangzhou	2239.64	5024.69	9013.15	13236.26	17903.24	20703.72	22696.13	26401.54	29611.69
深 圳	Shenzhen	1082.43	3229.38	6717.05	9429.42	15971.13	18674.43	20484.90	24544.92	27250.61
珠 海	Zhuhai	216.08	480.87	957.58	1296.96	1950.23	2209.72	2465.54	2914.90	3273.34
汕 头	Shantou	351.40	733.50	1291.11	1897.90	2592.37	2802.94	3045.15	3482.50	3862.66
佛 山	Foshan	1216.98	2358.78	4406.34	6170.92	8306.48	9185.36	10053.82	11770.37	13389.41
韶 关	Shaoguan	165.47	313.97	559.16	921.64	1311.80	1455.19	1603.75	1817.44	2025.40
河 源	Heyuan	69.96	145.12	313.64	590.09	863.11	949.95	1044.09	1163.02	1259.50
梅 州	Meizhou	155.14	318.77	578.33	1057.84	1514.10	1675.55	1861.56	2085.53	2320.44
惠 州	Huizhou	249.31	522.21	1031.63	1717.05	2599.07	2895.98	3230.42	3739.44	4181.16
汕 尾	Shanwei	54.18	108.39	229.73	385.72	532.67	580.30	625.57	709.41	781.21
东 莞	Dongguan	672.07	1728.28	3384.45	4587.86	6308.80	6944.74	7603.58	9019.34	10099.20
中 山	Zhongshan	354.65	725.06	1442.18	2082.30	2866.87	3217.59	3532.27	4126.79	4646.47
江 门	Jiangmen	483.75	851.93	1461.98	2228.65	3011.77	3348.82	3713.01	4221.58	4700.07
阳 江	Yangjiang	104.99	189.91	385.69	663.22	974.68	1100.25	1215.29	1380.36	1526.22
湛 江	Zhanjiang	298.14	505.70	940.08	1675.56	2329.34	2516.73	2763.52	3096.37	3388.80
茂 名	Maoming	247.45	410.02	750.67	1410.49	1993.71	2189.85	2423.38	2722.04	2957.56
肇 庆	Zhaoqing	184.21	335.91	650.23	1151.53	1636.17	1779.19	1984.74	2239.84	2466.41
清 远	Qingyuan	146.27	273.86	590.26	1010.55	1513.83	1672.42	1844.92	2077.44	2268.27
潮 州	Chaozhou	104.19	242.65	459.60	744.83	1011.24	1111.19	1217.59	1399.16	1570.15
揭 阳	Jieyang	180.82	387.29	714.16	1247.84	1730.83	1867.38	2045.39	2317.29	2544.28
云 浮	Yunfu	90.13	165.09	342.13	607.82	868.86	944.99	1031.56	1151.99	1259.90
按经济区域分	By Region									
珠 三 角	Pearl River Delta	6699.12	15257.09	29064.60	41900.94	60553.76	68959.55	75764.41	88978.71	99618.37
粤 东	Eastern Region	690.59	1471.82	2694.60	4276.29	5867.10	6361.81	6933.69	7908.35	8758.30
粤 西	Western Region	650.58	1105.62	2076.44	3749.27	5297.73	5806.83	6402.19	7198.77	7872.59
粤 北	Northern Region	626.97	1216.81	2383.51	4187.95	6071.69	6698.11	7385.86	8295.43	9133.52

8-12 财产保险公司主要指标

Main Indicators of Property Insurance Companies

单位：万元 (10000 yuan)

项　目	Item	2020 保费收入 Premium Income	2020 赔款支出 Indemnity Expenditure	2021 保费收入 Premium Income	2021 赔款支出 Indemnity Expenditure
合　计	**Total**	**15540749.10**	**9300861.80**	**16162145.15**	**9269796.23**
企业财产保险	Enterprise Property Insurance	795692.90	337640.99	871085.52	367995.38
家庭财产保险	Household Property Insurance	123852.11	51618.44	139119.85	59634.32
#投资型家财险	Of Which: Investment-Linked Household Property Insurance	209.94	100.90	332.23	48.50
机动车辆保险	Motor Vehicle Insurance	9289970.36	5268930.42	9067603.25	5665520.84
工程保险	Project Insurance	222866.03	123111.41	246614.23	121676.47
责任保险	Liability Insurance	1350390.88	481196.97	1578364.74	645465.10
信用保险	Credit Insurance	393167.30	273109.91	409657.71	116910.98
保证保险	Guarantee Insurance	692276.82	1439051.39	471839.57	493981.50
#机动车辆消费贷款保证保险	Of Which: Motor Vehicle Consumption Loan Guarantee Insurance	468.51	9104.92	373.31	-1327.18
个人贷款抵押房屋保证保险	Personal Loan Home Mortgage Guarantee Insurance	233.49	29.40	27.16	9.63
船舶保险	Ship Insurance	66021.87	33693.26	62585.61	44302.37
货物运输保险	Freight Transport Insurance	144588.33	66686.97	205967.37	90788.05
特殊风险保险	Peculiar Risk Insurance	231570.91	104803.11	189015.06	66699.20
农业保险	Agriculture Insurance	267447.12	141322.47	483778.60	247499.63
健康险	Health Insurance	1085692.57	684118.60	1342157.14	918064.21
意外伤害保险	Accident Injury Insurance	722298.68	197367.52	860881.05	251506.67
其他险	Other Property Insurance	154913.21	98210.35	233475.44	179751.52

8-12 续表 continued

单位：万元 (10000 yuan)

项　目	Item	2022 保费收入 Premium Income	2022 赔款支出 Indemnity Expenditure	2023 保费收入 Premium Income	2023 赔款支出 Indemnity Expenditure
合　计	**Total**	**17807307.13**	**10049442.80**	**19052153.79**	**11775506.91**
企业财产保险	Enterprise Property Insurance	932947.97	407063.66	1015805.22	424976.41
家庭财产保险	Household Property Insurance	228049.37	47285.92	341135.57	118267.20
#投资型家财险	Of Which: Investment-Linked Household Property Insurance	246.64	3.28	409.95	67.44
机动车辆保险	Motor Vehicle Insurance	9664915.76	5844835.69	10274687.36	6615359.83
工程保险	Project Insurance	268807.52	92822.72	277281.88	114533.50
责任保险	Liability Insurance	1827164.53	732709.51	2021413.94	969873.31
信用保险	Credit Insurance	503318.20	138071.10	440066.43	181036.94
保证保险	Guarantee Insurance	491917.88	635329.83	146827.26	566912.09
#机动车辆消费贷款保证保险	Of Which: Motor Vehicle Consumption Loan Guarantee Insurance	403.83	-606.73		62.28
个人贷款抵押房屋保证保险	Personal Loan Home Mortgage Guarantee Insurance	142.29	-815.49	118.43	1.76
船舶保险	Ship Insurance	81930.19	28432.77	77692.65	33157.49
货物运输保险	Freight Transport Insurance	269613.24	126173.86	304040.93	136880.34
特殊风险保险	Peculiar Risk Insurance	210781.90	56664.73	184209.99	81517.57
农业保险	Agriculture Insurance	819655.59	497839.18	1013320.07	760086.35
健康险	Health Insurance	1410894.10	926997.96	1603617.32	979496.57
意外伤害保险	Accident Injury Insurance	741969.44	290242.01	654997.46	319874.54
其他险	Other Property Insurance	355341.41	224973.89	697057.71	473534.77

注：因部分机构正在风险处置，表中2021年保险统计数据均不包括该部分机构数据。
Note: As some institutions are under risk disposal, the insurance statistics of 2021 in the table do not include the data of these institutions.

8-13 人身保险公司主要指标
Main Indicators of Life Insurance Companies

单位：亿元 (100 million yuan)

项 目	Item	2020	2021	2022	2023
保费收入	**Premium Income**	**4098.78**	**3963.50**	**4113.43**	**4650.82**
按险种分	Premium by Line of Business:				
寿险	Life Insurance	3062.64	2921.43	3022.68	3521.76
个人业务	Personal Business	3052.12	2912.23	3014.20	3512.40
新单保费	New Business Premium	1189.49	1129.28	1106.56	1367.37
续期保费	Renewal Premium	1862.63	1782.95	1907.63	2145.03
团体业务	Group Business	10.53	9.21	8.48	9.36
新单保费	New Business Premium	8.43	6.57	5.84	6.57
续期保费	Renewal Premium	2.10	2.64	2.64	2.80
意外伤害险	Accident Injury Insurance	103.39	97.38	85.95	75.94
一年期以内业务	Within One-year	15.74	13.47	10.79	10.18
一年期业务	One Year	45.27	44.25	39.24	34.13
一年以上业务	Over One-year Period Business	42.37	39.65	35.93	31.63
健康险	Health Insurance	932.75	944.69	1004.79	1053.12
一年期以内及一年期业务	Within One Year and One-year Period Business	171.37	165.95	206.96	212.79
个人业务	Personal Business	81.81	74.62	90.41	101.30
团体业务	Group Business	89.56	91.33	116.56	111.49
一年期以上业务	Over One-year Period Business	761.38	778.74	797.83	840.34
个人业务	Personal Business	728.70	759.35	779.24	819.10
团体业务	Group Business	32.69	19.39	18.59	21.24
按新型产品分：	Premium by New Product:				
寿险保费收入合计	Total Life Insurance Premium Income	3062.64	2921.43	3022.68	3521.76
普通寿险	Ordinary Insurance	1725.99	1816.49	2104.84	2645.73
新单保费	New Business Premium	582.89	635.45	726.46	972.07
续期保费	Renewal Premium	1143.09	1181.04	1378.38	1673.66
分红寿险	Dividend Insurance	1324.96	1093.88	906.28	863.70
新单保费	New Business Premium	613.49	498.78	383.45	398.58
续期保费	Renewal Premium	711.47	595.10	522.83	465.12
投资连结保险	Investment Link Insurance	1.37	1.37	1.39	1.42
万能寿险	Universal Life Insurance	10.32	9.70	10.17	10.91
赔付支出	**Total Payment Expenditure**	**659.43**	**954.09**	**740.14**	**1018.80**
赔款支出	Total Indemnity Expenditure	112.56	131.51	140.57	162.84
意外伤害险	Accident Injury Insurance	14.80	15.79	17.48	18.18
一年期以内业务	Within One-year Period Business	3.96	3.97	4.42	3.55
一年期业务	One-year Period Business	10.84	11.81	13.06	14.64
一年期以内及一年期健康险	Within One Year and One-year Period Health Insurance Business	97.76	115.72	123.09	144.66
个人业务	Personal Business	27.24	32.66	38.78	41.22
团体业务	Group Business	70.52	83.06	84.31	103.44
死伤医疗给付合计	Total Payment for Death, Injury and Medical Treatment	129.56	175.01	191.09	216.37
寿险	Life Insurance	30.26	34.25	36.28	47.87
个人业务	Personal Business	26.98	31.05	32.92	43.83
团体业务	Group Business	3.28	3.20	3.36	4.04
一年期以上健康险	Over One-year Period Health Insurance	99.30	140.77	154.82	168.50
个人业务	Personal Business	97.76	137.91	150.90	163.85
团体业务	Group Business	1.53	2.86	3.92	4.65
满期给付合计	Total Mature Payment	306.68	538.22	285.96	426.68
寿险	Life Insurance	248.17	260.92	250.63	422.19
个人业务	Personal Business	245.48	257.52	246.10	417.40
团体业务	Group Business	2.69	3.40	4.53	4.79
一年期以上健康险	Over One-year Period Health Insurance	58.51	277.31	35.33	4.49
个人业务	Personal Business	58.51	277.31	35.32	4.49
团体业务	Group Business			…	…
年金给付合计	Total Annuity Payment	110.59	109.32	122.52	212.91
个人业务	Personal Business	107.09	104.72	118.96	208.55
团体业务	Group Business	3.49	4.60	3.57	4.36
退保金	**Withdrawal Amount Insured**	**372.69**	**388.14**	**604.60**	**592.39**
寿险	Life Insurance	351.68	360.06	575.10	556.24
个人业务	Personal Business	351.03	357.26	574.77	555.87
团体业务	Group Business	0.65	2.80	0.33	0.37
一年期以上健康险	Over One-year Period Health Insurance	21.01	28.09	29.50	36.15

注：因部分机构正在风险处置，表中2021年保险统计数据均不包括该部分机构数据。
Note: As some institutions are under risk disposal, the insurance statistics of 2021 in the table do not include the data of these institutions.

8-14 保险业务主要指标

Main Indicators of Insurance Business

指　　标	Indicators	2016	2017	2018	2019	2020	2021	2022	2023
保费收入　（亿元）	**Premium of Insurance (100 million yuan)**	**3820.51**	**4304.60**	**4663.89**	**5496.70**	**5652.86**	**5578.96**	**5894.16**	**6556.04**
财产险	Property Insurance	945.52	1105.34	1271.17	1433.18	1373.28	1395.91	1565.44	1679.35
人寿险	Life Insurance	2038.11	2533.14	2571.73	3011.38	3062.64	2920.67	3022.68	3521.76
健康险	Health Insurance	723.85	527.79	648.14	857.14	1041.32	1078.91	1145.88	1213.49
人身意外伤害险	Personal Accident Insurance	113.02	138.34	172.85	194.99	175.62	183.46	160.15	141.44
各项赔款和给付（亿元）	**Payment (100 million yuan)**	**1035.42**	**1142.38**	**1403.46**	**1425.25**	**1589.47**	**1881.04**	**1745.09**	**2196.34**
财产险	Property Insurance	469.07	549.07	744.73	765.58	841.94	810.02	883.22	1047.61
人寿险	Life Insurance	449.50	450.70	477.64	405.98	389.01	404.48	409.43	682.97
健康险	Health Insurance	97.16	118.98	152.29	222.30	323.98	625.60	405.94	415.59
人身意外伤害险	Personal Accident Insurance	19.70	23.63	28.80	31.38	34.54	40.94	46.50	50.17
保险公司数　（家）	**Number of Insurance Companies (unit)**	**103**	**109**	**111**	**113**	**114**	**118**	**118**	**118**
#财产保险公司	Property Insurance Companies	47	51	52	53	54	55	55	55
人身保险公司	Life Insurance Companies	56	58	59	60	60	63	63	63
#中资保险公司	Domestic Funded Insurance Companies	68	74	76	78	79	82	82	82
外资保险公司	Foreign-funded Insurance Companies	35	35	35	35	35	36	36	36
保险公司总资产（亿元）	**Total Assets of Insurance Companies(100 million yuan)**	**10811.14**	**12101.88**	**13037.68**	**14884.76**	**16916.68**	**18619.97**	**20662.10**	**22485.57**
#财产险公司	Property Insurance Companies	1017.09	1058.64	1110.77	1196.67	1345.15	1404.12	1596.39	1680.28
寿险公司	Life Insurance Companies	9472.37	10583.70	11529.09	13179.93	14892.66	16411.30	18105.24	19833.45
保险公司分支机构（家）	**Number of Institutions of Insurance Companies (Unit)**	**5815**	**6005**	**6098**	**6167**	**6306**	**6256**	**5959**	**5713**
从业人员数　（万人）	**Employed Persons (person)**	**69.64**	**76.56**	**81.40**	**82.16**	**79.15**	**54.37**	**44.72**	**39.46**

注：“保险公司分支机构(家)”统计指标从2014年起进行了调整，包括省级分公司、地市级分公司和中心支公司、支公司、营业部、营销服务部及电销专属机构。

Note: The number of institutions of insurance companies were adjusted from 2014, including the provincial branch, municipal branch,central branch, sales department, marketing department and telemarketing exclusive agency.

8-15 分市原保险保费收入和赔付支出情况（2023年）
Premium of Primary Insurance and Payment by City (2023)

单位：亿元 (100 million yuan)

地 区	Region	原保险保费收入 Premium of Primary Insurance			赔付支出 Payment		
		小计 Sub-total	财产险业务 Property Insurance	人身险业务 Life Insurance	小计 Sub-total	财产险业务 Property Insurance	人身险业务 Life Insurance
全 省	**Provincial Total**	**6556.04**	**1679.35**	**4876.68**	**2196.35**	**1047.61**	**1148.73**
广 州	Guangzhou	1741.85	381.70	1360.15	558.91	251.89	307.03
深 圳	Shenzhen	1719.56	442.69	1276.87	561.57	264.54	297.03
珠 海	Zhuhai	191.06	42.94	148.12	59.30	27.73	31.58
汕 头	Shantou	139.18	33.93	105.26	47.00	18.51	28.49
佛 山	Foshan	665.55	157.85	507.70	193.43	96.27	97.17
韶 关	Shaoguan	66.55	20.07	46.48	26.50	13.01	13.49
河 源	Heyuan	40.84	17.39	23.45	19.46	10.64	8.82
梅 州	Meizhou	67.32	23.09	44.23	27.82	14.16	13.66
惠 州	Huizhou	194.99	61.24	133.75	72.07	37.36	34.71
汕 尾	Shanwei	29.68	11.38	18.30	16.31	7.32	8.99
东 莞	Dongguan	608.58	167.05	441.53	188.12	106.72	81.40
中 山	Zhongshan	258.35	66.78	191.57	75.36	39.44	35.92
江 门	Jiangmen	194.51	45.98	148.52	69.58	27.56	42.02
阳 江	Yangjiang	59.35	16.99	42.36	30.33	11.01	19.32
湛 江	Zhanjiang	120.89	40.04	80.84	59.66	27.08	32.59
茂 名	Maoming	111.61	36.75	74.86	54.20	25.67	28.53
肇 庆	Zhaoqing	92.45	29.03	63.42	36.67	16.63	20.04
清 远	Qingyuan	79.06	28.49	50.57	33.50	17.76	15.74
潮 州	Chaozhou	57.05	16.04	41.00	18.83	9.21	9.62
揭 阳	Jieyang	78.40	24.43	53.97	31.05	15.24	15.81
云 浮	Yunfu	39.21	15.48	23.73	16.69	9.88	6.81

注：赔付支出不包括直保公司的分保赔付支出。
Note: The payment does not include the reinsurance payment of the direct insurance company.

主要统计指标解释

一般公共预算收入 指国家财政参与社会产品分配所取得的收入，是实现国家职能的财力保证。主要包括：

（1）各项税收：包括国内增值税、国内消费税、进口货物增值税和消费税、出口货物退增值税和消费税、营业税、企业所得税、个人所得税、资源税、城市维护建设税、房产税、印花税、城镇土地使用税、土地增值税、车船税、船舶吨税、车辆购置税、关税、耕地占用税、契税、烟叶税等。财政收入按现行分税制财政体制划分为中央本级收入和地方本级收入。

（2）非税收入：包括专项收入、行政事业性收费、罚没收入和其他收入。

一般公共预算支出 指国家财政将筹集起来的资金进行分配使用，以满足经济建设和各项事业的需要。主要包括：一般公共服务、外交、国防、公共安全、教育、科学技术、文化体育与传媒、社会保障和就业、医疗卫生与计划生育、节能环保、城乡社区、农林水、交通运输、资源勘探信息等、商业服务业等、金融、援助其他地区、国土海洋气象等、住房保障、粮油物资储备、政府债务付息等方面的支出。财政支出根据政府在经济和社会活动中的不同职权，划分为中央财政支出和地方财政支出。

信贷资金 指金融机构以信用方式集聚和分配的货币资金。金融机构信贷资金的来源有各项存款、金融债券、对国家金融机构负债、流通中现金、其他项目等；信贷自己的运用有各项贷款、有价证券及投资、黄金占款、外汇买卖、财政借款及在国家金融机构中的资产等。

存款 指企业、机关、团体或居民根据资金必须收回的原则，把货币资金存入银行或其他信用机构保管并取得一定利息的一种信用活动形式。根据存款对象或性质的不同可划分为住户存款、非金融企业存款、政府存款、非银行业金融存款等科目。它是银行信贷资金的主要来源。

贷款 指银行或其他信贷机构根据资金必须归还的原则，按一定利率，为企业、个人等提供资金的一种信用活动形式。我国银行贷款分为短期贷款、中长期贷款、融资租赁、票据融资、各项垫款、境外贷款等。

住户存款 个人客户在其他存款性公司开立账户并存入资金或货币，由其他存款性公司出具存款凭证，个人客户凭存款凭证可以支取本金或利息的存款。

保险金额 指保险人承担赔偿或者给付保险金责任的最高限额。

保费 指投保人为取得保险人在约定范围内所承担赔偿责任而支付给保险人的费用。

赔款 指保险人根据保险合同的规定，向被保险人支付的赔偿保险责任损失的金额。

给付 包括死伤医疗给付和满期给付。死伤医疗给付是指保险人根据人寿保险及长期健康保险合同的规定，因被保险人在保险期内发生保险责任范围内的保险事故支付给被保险人（或受益人）的金额。满期给付是指被保险人生存期满，保险人按人寿保险合同规定支付给被保险人的满期保险金额。

Explanatory Notes on Main Statistical Indicators

General Public Budgetary Revenue refers to income for the government finance through participating in the distribution of social products. It is the financial guarantee to ensure government functioning. The contents of government revenue include the following main items:

(1) Various tax revenues, including domestic value added tax (VAT), domestic consumption tax, VAT and consumption tax from imports, VAT and consumption tax rebate for exports, business tax, corporate income tax, individual income tax, resource tax, city maintenance and construct tax, house property tax, stamp tax, urban land

use tax, land appreciation tax, tax on vehicles and boat operation, ship tonnage tax, vehicle purchase tax, tariffs, farm land occupation tax, deed tax, and tobacco leaf tax, etc.

(2) Non-tax revenue, including special program receipts, charge of administrative and institutional units, penalty receipts and others non-tax receipts.

General Public Budgetary Expenditure refers to the distribution and use of the funds which the government finance has raised, so as to meet the needs of economic construction and various undertakings. It includes the following main items: expenditure for general public services, expenditure for foreign affairs, expenditure for national defence expenditure for public security, expenditure for education, expenditure for science and technology, expenditure for culture, sport and media, expenditure for social safety net and employment effort, expenditure for medical and health care and family planning, expenditure for energy conservation and environment protection, expenditure for urban and rural community affairs, expenditure for agriculture, forestry and water conservancy, expenditure for transportation, expenditure for resource exploration and information, expenditure for affairs of commerce and services, expenditure for finance, aid to other regions, expenditure for land, ocean and weather, expenditure for housing security, expenditure for grain & oil reserves, interest payment for public debts. General public budget expenditure is divided into general public budget expenditure of central government and general public budget expenditure of local government according to the different functions of the governments played in economic and social activities.

Credit Funds refer to the monetary funds accumulated and distributed in the means of credit by the financial institutions. The sources of credit funds include various deposits, financial bonds, liabilities to international financial institutions, currency in circulation, other items. The uses of credit funds include loans, securities and investment, position for bullion purchase, foreign exchange trading, advances to treasury, and assets with international financial institutions.

Deposit is a form of credit by which enterprises, institutions, organizations or households can put money into banks and other credit institutions for safekeeping and interest earning under the principle of free withdrawal. According to different depositors, deposits are divided into household deposits, non financial enterprise deposits, government deposits, non banking financial institutions deposits. Deposits are major sources of the credit funds of banks.

Loan is a form of credit by which banks and other credit institutions provide funds at certain interest rate to enterprises and individuals in the light of the principle of unconditional repayment. Loans from Chinese banks include short-term loan, medium-term and long-term loans, financial lease, bill financing, various money advanced, foreign loans.

Savings Deposits refer to the capital which is deposited in the account opened in the reserve corporation by the individual with a deposit certificate as the proof, the principal and interest of which can be withdrew with the deposit certificate.

Amount Insured refers to the maximum that the insurant will get for the claim of the case insured.

Premium is the fee paid by the insurant to the insurer to obtain the obligation of compensation from the insurance within the agreed terms. is the compensation paid by the insurer to the insurant in accordance with the insurance contract.

Settled Claim is the compensation paid by the insurer to the insurant in accordance with the insurance contract.

Payment includes payment for death, injury or medical treatment and payment at maturity. Payment for death, injury or medical treatment refers to the money paid to the insurant (or the beneficiary) in accordance with the life or health insurance contract when the insurant encounters accidents within the insured period covered in the contract. Payment at maturity refers to the payment to the insurant in accordance with the life insurance contract at the end of the insured period.

九、价格

PRICE

九 价格

简要说明

一、本篇资料反映生产、流通、消费与投资等环节的价格变动情况。主要包括居民消费价格指数、工业生产者出厂价格指数、工业生产者购进价格指数、农产品生产者价格指数。

二、本篇资料由国家统计局广东调查总队消费价格调查处和生产投资价格调查处整理提供。

三、居民消费价格指数采用分层随机抽样调查方法编制，即在全省选择不同经济区域的市、县以及有代表性的商品和服务项目作为样本，对市场价格进行经常性调查，以样本推断总体。

四、工业生产者出厂价格指数和工业生产者购进价格指数均采用重点调查与典型调查相结合的方法统计。

五、农产品生产者价格指数采用抽样调查和重点调查相结合的调查方法进行统计。

9 Price

Brief Introduction

I. The data in this chapter reflect price changes in production, circulation,consumption and investment, including mainly consumer price indices,price indices of means of agricultural production, producer price indices for manufactured goods, producer price indices for purchased goods, producers' price indices for farm products.

II. The data are prepared and provided by the Division of Consumers Price Survey and the Division of Production Price Survey under Guangdong Survey Office of the National Bureau of Statistics.

III. The data for the calculation of consumer price indices in the province are collected through stratified random sampling. Cities and counties distributed in different economic regions of the province are selected as sample areas, and representative commodities and services are selected as sample commodities and services. Regular surveys are conducted to collect data on market prices. The data on the population are estimated on the basis of the sample.

IV. The data for the calculation of producer price indices for manufactured goods and producer price indices for purchased goods are all collected through key-point survey combined with typical survey.

V. The data for the calculation of producers' price indices of farm products are collected through sampling survey combined with key-point survey.

9-1 各种价格指数
Price Indices

上年=100 (preceding year=100)

年份 Year	居民消费价格指数 Consumer Price Indices	城市居民消费价格指数 Urban	农村居民消费价格指数 Rural	工业生产者出厂价格指数 Producer Price Index for Industrial Products	工业生产者购进价格指数 Purchasing Price Index for Industrial Products
1978		100.3			
1979		104.6			
1980		109.5			
1981		106.3			
1982		102.6			
1983		102.8			
1984	101.3	101.9	100.4		
1985	114.8	117.1	111.2		
1986	104.9	104.7	105.3		
1987	111.2	112.8	109.7		
1988	129.4	129.5	129.3		
1989	122.1	121.9	122.4		
1990	97.5	97.4	97.6		
1991	101.2	102.3	99.9		
1992	107.3	108.4	105.9		
1993	121.6	122.0	120.6		
1994	121.7	121.0	122.5		
1995	114.0	113.1	115.3		
1996	107.0	107.2	106.5		
1997	101.9	102.1	101.5	100.1	97.3
1998	98.2	98.3	98.1	94.8	91.4
1999	98.2	98.4	97.7	97.7	97.8
2000	101.4	102.2	100.0	103.4	110.9
2001	99.3	99.2	99.6	98.5	99.1
2002	98.6	98.6	98.6	96.5	96.3
2003	100.6	100.7	100.4	99.3	104.1
2004	103.0	102.6	103.7	101.7	110.6
2005	102.3	102.0	102.7	101.5	105.0
2006	101.8	101.8	101.6	101.4	103.6
2007	103.7	103.7	103.5	101.3	103.3
2008	105.6	105.5	105.8	103.1	107.9
2009	97.7	97.6	97.8	95.8	93.8
2010	103.1	103.1	103.2	103.2	107.3
2011	105.3	105.3	105.6	103.7	107.3
2012	102.8	102.8	102.9	99.5	99.5
2013	102.5	102.4	102.7	98.8	98.2
2014	102.3	102.3	102.1	98.9	98.8
2015	101.5	101.6	101.3	96.8	95.3
2016	102.3	102.4	102.0	99.4	98.0
2017	101.5	101.7	100.8	103.3	105.3
2018	102.2	102.2	101.9	101.8	102.5
2019	103.4	103.1	104.6	100.2	99.2
2020	102.6	102.6	103.0	99.0	97.4
2021	100.8	101.0	100.1	103.4	108.0
2022	102.2	102.2	102.3	103.0	104.1
2023	100.4	100.6	99.6	98.5	97.6

9-2 各种价格定基指数

Fixed-base Price Indices

年份 Year	居民消费价格指数(1983年为100) Consumer Price Indices (1983=100)	城市居民消费价格指数(1983年为100) Urban (1983=100)	农村居民消费价格指数(1983年为100) Rural (1983=100)	工业生产者出厂价格指数(1996年为100) Producer Price Index for Industrial Products (1996=100)	工业生产者购进价格指数(1996年为100) Purchasing Price Index for Industrial Products (1996=100)
1978					
1979					
1980					
1981					
1982					
1983	100.0	100.0	100.0		
1984	101.3	101.9	100.4		
1985	116.3	119.3	111.6		
1986	122.0	124.9	117.6		
1987	135.7	140.9	129.0		
1988	175.5	182.5	166.8		
1989	214.3	222.5	204.1		
1990	209.0	216.7	199.2		
1991	211.5	221.7	199.0		
1992	226.9	240.3	210.7		
1993	275.9	293.1	254.2		
1994	335.8	354.7	311.3		
1995	382.8	401.2	359.0		
1996	409.6	430.1	382.3	100.0	100.0
1997	417.4	439.1	388.1	100.1	97.3
1998	409.9	431.6	380.7	94.9	88.9
1999	402.5	424.7	371.9	92.7	86.9
2000	408.1	434.1	371.9	95.9	96.4
2001	405.3	430.6	370.4	94.5	95.5
2002	399.6	424.6	365.3	91.2	92.0
2003	402.0	427.5	366.7	90.6	95.8
2004	414.1	438.6	380.3	92.1	106.0
2005	423.6	447.4	390.5	93.5	111.3
2006	431.2	455.5	396.8	94.8	115.3
2007	447.2	472.3	410.7	96.0	119.1
2008	472.2	498.3	434.5	99.0	128.4
2009	461.3	486.3	424.9	94.9	120.4
2010	475.6	501.4	438.5	97.9	129.2
2011	500.8	528.0	463.1	101.4	138.6
2012	514.8	542.8	476.5	100.9	137.9
2013	527.7	555.8	489.4	99.7	135.4
2014	539.8	568.6	499.7	98.6	134.0
2015	547.9	577.7	506.2	95.4	127.7
2016	560.5	591.6	516.3	94.8	125.1
2017	568.9	601.7	520.4	97.9	131.8
2018	581.4	614.9	530.3	99.7	135.1
2019	601.2	634.0	554.7	99.9	134.0
2020	616.9	650.4	571.4	98.9	130.5
2021	621.8	656.9	572.0	102.3	140.9
2022	635.5	671.4	585.2	105.3	146.7
2023	638.0	675.4	582.9	103.8	143.3

9-3 居民消费价格分类指数（2023年）

Consumer Price Indices by Category (2023)

上年=100 (preceding year=100)

项 目	Item	全省 Provincial Indices	城市 Urban Indices	农村 Rural Indices
居民消费价格总指数	**Consumer Price Index**	**100.4**	**100.6**	**99.6**
非食品烟酒价格指数	**Non food,tobacco and alcohol price index**	**100.0**	**100.2**	**99.2**
服务价格指数	**Service Price Index**	**100.7**	**100.9**	**99.9**
消费品价格指数	**Consumer Goods Price Index**	**100.2**	**100.4**	**99.4**
扣除鲜菜鲜果价格指数	**Price Index Deducting Fresh Vegetables and Fruits**	**100.3**	**100.5**	**99.5**
食品烟酒	**Foods,tobacco and alcohol**	**101.4**	**101.6**	**100.3**
食品	Foods	100.7	100.9	100.1
粮食	Grain	100.3	100.0	101.2
#大米	Rice	99.5	98.8	101.6
粮食制品	Grain Products	101.9	102.2	100.2
薯类	Tubers	105.3	105.1	106.5
豆类	beans	99.8	99.8	100.0
食用油	edible oil	100.9	101.4	99.4
菜及食用菌	Vegetables and Edible Fungi	99.8	99.7	100.4
#鲜菜	Fresh Vegetables	99.6	99.5	100.4
畜肉类	Neat of animal	94.7	95.1	93.7
#猪肉	Pork	91.5	92.0	90.1
禽肉类	Meat of poultries	102.7	102.6	103.0
水产品	Aquatic Products	101.4	101.5	101.2
蛋类	Eggs	103.0	103.0	102.8
奶类	Milk	103.0	103.4	101.0
干鲜瓜果类	Dried and Fresh Melons and Fruits	105.0	105.5	102.9
#鲜果	Fresh Fruits	105.7	106.2	103.3
糖果糕点类	Candy and pastry	101.5	101.6	100.9
调味品	Condiment	101.2	101.3	100.8
其他食品类	Other Foods	100.8	100.9	100.3
茶及饮料	Tea and Beverages	100.7	100.5	101.8
烟酒	Tobacco and Alcohol	100.8	100.9	100.6
卷烟	Cigarettes	101.1	101.3	100.7
酒类	Alcohol	99.7	99.7	99.9
在外餐饮	Outside catering	102.8	103.0	100.6
衣着	**Clothing**	**101.8**	**102.1**	**100.0**
服装	Garments	101.9	102.2	100.4
衣着材料及配件	Clothing Materials and Accessories	100.1	99.9	101.2
衣着服务费	Clothing Services Fee	101.2	101.4	98.8
鞋类	Footwear	101.0	101.5	98.5
鞋类服务	Footwear Services	101.1	101.3	99.9
居住	**Residence**	**99.5**	**99.8**	**98.1**
租赁房房租	Rental housing	99.4	99.6	97.4
住房保养维修及管理	Housing maintenance and management	101.2	101.3	100.8
水电燃料	Hydropower fuel	99.6	99.8	98.5
自有住房	Own housing	99.2	99.5	97.2

9−3 续表 continued

上年=100 (preceding year=100)

项 目	Item	全 省 Provincial Indices	城 市 Urban Indices	农 村 Rural Indices
生活用品及服务	**Daily Necessities and Services**	**99.9**	**99.8**	**100.3**
家具及室内装饰品	Furniture and Interior Decorations	100.3	100.4	100.0
家具	Furniture	100.3	100.4	100.0
室内装饰品	Interior Decorations	101.0	101.0	100.6
家用器具	Home Appliances	98.3	98.2	98.9
家用纺织品	Home Textiles	97.9	97.7	99.3
家庭日用杂品	Household Groceries	100.2	100.1	100.6
个人护理用品	Personal-care Supply	100.1	99.9	101.2
家庭服务	Domestic Service	101.5	101.4	102.4
交通通信	**Transportation and Communication**	**97.7**	**97.9**	**96.8**
交通	Transportation	97.3	97.4	96.2
交通工具	The Traffic Tools	95.7	95.5	96.5
交通工具用燃料	The Vehicles Fuel	94.8	94.8	94.5
交通工具使用和维修	Vehicle usage and Maintenance	100.0	100.1	99.3
交通费	Transportation	103.9	104.1	102.1
通信	Communication	99.3	99.4	98.5
通信工具	Communication Tools	97.7	98.0	95.7
通信服务	Communication Service	99.8	99.9	99.1
邮递服务	Postal Service	99.9	99.9	99.9
教育文化娱乐	**Education Culture and Entertainment**	**102.7**	**102.7**	**102.8**
教育	Education	101.9	101.6	103.1
教育用品	Education Supplies	103.8	104.1	102.4
教育服务	Education Services	101.8	101.5	103.1
文化娱乐	Cultural Entertainment	104.2	104.5	102.1
文娱耐用消费品	Recreational Consumer Goods	97.7	97.8	97.0
其他文娱用品	Other Entertainment Items	100.6	100.8	99.6
文化娱乐服务	Cultural Entertainment Service	101.5	101.7	99.9
旅游	Tourism	111.9	111.8	113.4
医疗保健	**Health care**	**100.4**	**100.5**	**100.4**
药品及医疗器具	Medicines and Medical Instruments	101.8	101.8	102.0
中药	Traditional Chinese Medicine	109.4	110.4	106.1
西药	Western Medicines	101.9	101.6	102.7
滋补保健品	Nourishing Health Products	99.7	99.9	98.4
医疗卫生器具	Medical Appliance	96.7	96.8	96.2
保健器具	Health Care Appliances	100.2	100.3	100.1
医疗服务	Medical Services	100.0	100.0	100.0
其他用品及服务	**Other Goods and Services**	**102.3**	**102.6**	**100.7**
其他用品	Other Products	103.0	103.3	101.4
其他服务	Other Service Class	101.8	102.0	99.9

9-4 各市居民消费价格分类指数（2023年）

Consumer Price Indices by Category and by City (2023)

上年=100 (preceding year=100)

市别	City	总指数 General Indices	服务价格 Service Price	食品烟酒 Foods Tobacco and Alcohol	食品 Foods	#粮食 Grain	食用油 Edible Oil	鲜菜 Vegetables	畜肉类 Meat of Livestock	禽肉类 Meat of Poultry	水产品 Aquatic Products	蛋类 Eggs
广 州	Guangzhou	101.0	101.2	102.0	100.9	98.1	102.6	97.8	95.5	102.3	101.6	102.1
深 圳	Shenzhen	100.8	100.6	101.9	101.3	103.3	101.1	100.0	95.0	102.5	101.8	103.2
珠 海	Zhuhai	100.5	102.0	100.9	100.4	97.5	99.4	96.0	91.5	104.4	104.4	100.9
汕 头	Shantou	101.0	100.8	101.7	101.9	100.3	101.3	101.5	96.1	103.2	100.7	100.8
佛 山	Foshan	100.1	100.5	101.5	101.2	100.2	101.6	100.4	96.1	103.8	101.5	106.1
韶 关	Shaoguan	99.7	100.4	100.1	99.8	100.6	97.5	104.5	90.2	103.7	100.9	102.3
河 源	Heyuan	99.8	100.1	100.9	101.3	96.1	103.2	98.5	93.8	106.1	104.6	101.0
梅 州	Meizhou	100.0	100.2	100.6	100.4	96.5	102.8	102.0	92.1	107.9	103.0	103.1
惠 州	Huizhou	100.2	101.4	100.9	100.4	100.9	102.3	102.2	91.5	100.3	102.5	104.7
汕 尾	Shanwei	100.2	100.8	100.7	100.1	96.8	97.3	100.5	98.2	101.6	97.8	100.6
东 莞	Dongguan	99.9	100.9	100.0	99.0	100.8	101.0	95.2	98.1	100.2	96.5	105.7
中 山	Zhongshan	100.4	101.2	101.3	101.2	100.8	105.3	99.5	94.2	102.7	103.2	101.6
江 门	Jiangmen	100.2	101.0	100.1	98.8	100.0	93.6	101.8	92.0	100.1	100.0	96.8
阳 江	Yangjiang	99.2	100.4	99.7	99.9	99.1	99.6	99.9	94.4	104.1	97.5	103.3
湛 江	Zhanjiang	100.1	100.2	101.1	100.2	99.3	101.4	100.3	97.0	100.7	98.7	102.7
茂 名	Maoming	100.3	101.5	100.8	100.6	100.4	101.2	100.5	93.0	102.9	102.6	102.6
肇 庆	Zhaoqing	100.5	100.3	101.5	100.6	99.8	100.7	101.5	93.3	102.8	99.1	101.6
清 远	Qingyuan	99.9	100.6	100.6	100.1	97.2	97.5	94.8	94.5	102.6	102.4	104.1
潮 州	Chaozhou	100.1	101.0	100.5	100.7	99.9	101.9	100.8	95.2	100.7	103.5	100.8
揭 阳	Jieyang	99.8	99.9	100.7	100.0	100.9	99.9	100.8	94.7	101.6	102.1	100.0
云 浮	Yunfu	99.8	100.8	100.6	100.7	97.4	99.8	103.0	94.7	102.2	101.5	99.5

9-4 续表 continued

上年=100 (preceding year=100)

市别	City	干鲜瓜果类 Fruits and Nuts	茶及饮料 Tea and Beverages	烟酒 Tobacco and Alcohol	在外餐饮 Dining Out	衣着 Clothing	居住 Housing	生活用品及服务 Articles for Daily Use and Services	交通通信 Transport and Communi-cations	教育文化娱乐 Education Culture and Recreation	医疗保健 Health Care	其他用品及服务 Other Articles and Services
广 州	Guangzhou	104.6	99.5	101.5	104.1	102.2	99.6	99.6	98.5	104.2	100.5	103.4
深 圳	Shenzhen	106.6	101.5	100.1	103.0	103.9	100.1	100.1	97.3	102.9	100.3	102.0
珠 海	Zhuhai	102.6	101.8	101.3	101.7	99.5	101.0	99.5	96.6	104.0	100.7	102.2
汕 头	Shantou	106.2	101.1	101.9	101.3	102.7	99.5	99.0	98.8	102.1	101.6	103.1
佛 山	Foshan	107.9	101.0	100.2	102.4	101.1	99.7	99.7	98.1	99.5	99.9	102.5
韶 关	Shaoguan	102.4	99.3	101.1	100.7	101.2	99.0	99.7	97.6	101.2	100.6	101.8
河 源	Heyuan	105.7	98.8	102.4	99.4	97.6	98.0	98.1	98.1	100.1	103.0	101.9
梅 州	Meizhou	99.6	101.0	100.7	100.9	102.4	98.6	99.3	97.7	101.7	101.0	102.1
惠 州	Huizhou	107.9	92.3	100.5	103.2	98.8	99.9	99.3	97.6	103.3	100.2	102.8
汕 尾	Shanwei	104.5	102.8	100.2	102.3	99.8	99.2	98.9	97.7	101.6	101.8	102.1
东 莞	Dongguan	100.0	103.2	102.6	101.2	99.3	99.8	101.0	97.7	101.4	101.1	101.7
中 山	Zhongshan	105.5	102.3	99.9	101.6	100.2	99.7	101.0	97.1	103.1	100.8	102.0
江 门	Jiangmen	100.6	100.8	103.4	101.9	99.8	99.5	102.2	98.2	103.0	102.0	101.0
阳 江	Yangjiang	104.1	101.1	99.9	99.0	96.4	99.1	99.0	97.8	100.5	100.2	100.4
湛 江	Zhanjiang	102.7	101.5	100.7	103.2	98.1	99.2	99.7	97.6	101.5	100.8	101.8
茂 名	Maoming	101.4	101.6	102.8	101.0	99.6	99.3	100.7	97.0	104.7	100.0	101.2
肇 庆	Zhaoqing	113.0	101.4	98.2	103.7	105.6	97.4	100.2	98.0	104.8	100.4	103.1
清 远	Qingyuan	107.0	98.0	102.2	101.3	99.4	100.0	99.7	97.5	100.8	100.2	101.8
潮 州	Chaozhou	104.4	102.6	99.0	100.2	99.4	99.6	99.1	97.8	102.6	99.8	100.9
揭 阳	Jieyang	100.1	98.8	102.8	102.0	98.0	97.9	100.0	98.5	101.7	100.3	100.4
云 浮	Yunfu	107.2	100.5	99.5	100.7	96.2	99.3	98.7	97.6	101.9	100.1	102.3

9-5 各市服务项目价格分类指数（2023年）

Service Price Indices by Category and by City (2023)

上年=100 (preceding year=100)

市 别	City	服务价格 Service Price	#租赁房房租 Rent of Rental Housing	家庭服务 Household Services	交通费 Traffic Fee	通信服务 Communication Services	邮递服务 Postal Service	教育服务 Education Service	文化娱乐服务 Cultural and Recreational Services	旅游 Tourism	医疗服务 Medical Service	其他服务 Other Service
广 州	Guangzhou	101.2	99.3	100.3	108.4	99.6	100.1	102.7	103.5	113.4	99.7	103.5
深 圳	Shenzhen	100.6	99.8	100.2	100.1	100.0	100.0	101.2	100.7	117.0	100.0	101.6
珠 海	Zhuhai	102.0	101.1	102.5	102.8	100.0	100.0	102.3	101.6	122.8	100.0	101.0
汕 头	Shantou	100.8	97.9	100.3	105.6	100.0	100.0	100.8	100.6	110.6	100.0	103.2
佛 山	Foshan	100.5	99.6	105.3	107.7	100.1	100.0	99.7	99.4	99.7	100.0	101.0
韶 关	Shaoguan	100.4	99.9	100.0	106.1	98.7	99.2	100.3	101.8	105.5	100.0	99.8
河 源	Heyuan	100.1	96.8	100.9	107.7	100.0	99.5	101.5	98.7	90.5	103.0	101.1
梅 州	Meizhou	100.2	98.7	100.3	105.1	100.0	100.0	100.2	100.4	115.2	99.8	100.4
惠 州	Huizhou	101.4	99.7	102.0	101.8	100.2	99.9	101.8	103.0	122.5	100.8	103.4
汕 尾	Shanwei	100.8	100.5	99.3	102.3	99.5	96.0	102.4	100.4	105.6	102.0	100.3
东 莞	Dongguan	100.9	99.5	107.0	100.5	100.4	99.0	101.2	101.5	105.8	100.0	100.1
中 山	Zhongshan	101.2	99.1	104.0	106.1	99.1	99.7	102.2	100.5	115.5	100.0	100.3
江 门	Jiangmen	101.0	99.3	108.8	106.2	99.8	100.0	103.4	99.9	102.3	101.5	98.9
阳 江	Yangjiang	100.4	100.0	99.2	107.1	100.0	100.0	100.2	101.1	102.8	100.0	100.1
湛 江	Zhanjiang	100.2	99.8	100.2	104.0	100.0	100.0	100.4	99.6	110.0	100.0	100.1
茂 名	Maoming	101.5	99.7	100.1	104.5	100.0	97.5	105.1	102.2	113.0	100.0	99.3
肇 庆	Zhaoqing	100.3	97.7	102.9	105.7	100.0	99.8	107.2	97.5	103.5	99.9	101.6
清 远	Qingyuan	100.6	100.8	99.9	105.6	100.0	100.0	100.4	99.7	106.0	100.3	99.6
潮 州	Chaozhou	101.0	99.7	100.6	105.9	100.0	98.1	100.8	102.0	122.8	100.0	102.6
揭 阳	Jieyang	99.9	97.2	102.3	104.1	100.0	100.9	101.5	99.0	110.6	100.1	101.1
云 浮	Yunfu	100.8	97.4	102.5	108.2	98.9	100.0	101.2	101.7	116.6	100.0	100.8

9-6 工业生产者出厂价格指数
Producer Price Indices for Industrial Products

上年=100 (preceding year=100)

项 目	Item	2018	2019	2020	2021	2022	2023
工业生产者出厂价格指数	**Producer Price Index for Industrial Products**	**101.8**	**100.2**	**99.0**	**103.4**	**103.0**	**98.5**
按轻重工业分	**Grouped by Light and Heavy Industries**						
轻工业	Light Industry	100.7	100.7	99.7	101.7	102.3	100.5
以农产品为原料	Using Farm Products as Raw Materials	101.2	101.4	100.3	101.8	103.2	99.5
以非农产品为原料	Using Non-farm Products as Raw Materials	100.3	100.2	99.3	101.7	101.8	101.0
重工业	Heavy Industry	102.4	99.9	98.6	104.2	103.3	97.6
采 掘	Mining and Quarrying	108.8	100.2	92.9	118.5	121.5	97.2
原 料	Raw Materials	104.6	98.1	94.5	110.9	112.0	98.4
加 工	Processing	101.6	100.4	99.9	102.6	101.1	97.5
按生产生活资料分	**Grouped by Production and Living Materials**						
生产资料	Means of Production	102.6	100.0	98.6	105.0	104.2	98.0
采 掘	Mining and Quarrying	108.8	100.2	92.9	118.5	121.5	97.2
原 料	Raw Materials	104.6	98.0	94.2	110.9	112.0	98.3
加 工	Processing	101.8	100.5	99.9	103.5	102.2	97.9
生活资料	Living Materials	100.5	100.5	99.7	100.4	100.6	99.6
食 品	Food	101.0	102.3	102.7	101.5	102.4	99.3
衣 着	Clothing	99.8	102.2	99.0	98.4	102.6	101.4
一般日用品	Articles for Daily Use	100.4	101.3	100.8	100.6	102.0	102.6
耐用消费品	Durable Consumer Goods	100.5	99.0	98.4	100.3	99.1	98.0
按工业部门分	**Grouped by Industrial Sectors**						
冶金工业	Metallurgical Industry	106.6	100.6	100.2	115.7	104.9	96.7
电力工业	Power Industry	96.0	98.8	97.5	98.8	105.2	104.2
石油工业	Petroleum Industry	115.0	95.9	83.8	124.5	131.0	93.7
化学工业	Chemical Industry	103.0	99.1	98.1	106.2	102.3	96.4
机械工业	Machine Manufacturing Industry	100.0	100.2	99.4	100.6	101.0	98.4
建筑材料工业	Building Materials Industry	106.4	100.2	100.1	104.0	96.8	95.5
森林工业	Timber Industry	100.8	101.2	99.9	100.4	102.5	100.1
食品工业	Food Industry	101.1	102.0	102.9	103.5	103.8	99.5
纺织工业	Textile Industry	101.7	101.7	99.1	99.9	104.7	100.6
缝纫工业	Tailoring Industry	100.4	102.3	98.9	98.8	103.2	100.9
皮革工业	Leather Industry	98.7	102.3	99.2	96.2	101.3	103.1
造纸工业	Paper Making Industry	105.7	96.0	96.5	106.0	101.2	95.2
文教艺术用品工业	Industry for Cultural, Educational & Art Articles	100.0	102.7	101.0	100.6	101.9	102.0
其它工业	Others	98.0	103.0	104.4	101.1	101.6	104.2

9-7 工业生产者购进价格指数

Purchasing Price Indices for Industrial Producers

上年=100 (preceding year=100)

项 目	Item	2018	2019	2020
工业生产者购进价格指数	**Producer Price Index for Purchased Goods**	**102.5**	**99.2**	**97.4**
按材料类别分	**Grouped by Type of Material**			
燃料、动力类	Fuels and Power	103.7	99.7	91.4
黑色金属材料类	Ferrous Materials	104.8	101.1	98.8
#钢材	Steel	105.0	98.2	98.1
其它	Others	104.4	106.0	100.1
有色金属材料和电线类	Nonferrous Materials and Wires	104.2	96.9	99.9
化工原料类	Chemical Materials	103.4	97.3	94.6
木材及纸浆类	Timber and Paper Pulp	106.2	96.2	96.2
建筑材料及非金属矿类	Building Materials and Nonmetal Minerals	115.2	103.4	102.4
其它工业原材料及半成品类	Other Raw Materials and Semi-finished Products	100.3	99.2	99.3
农副产品类	Agricultural Products	99.0	100.6	103.6
纺织原料类	Textile Raw Materials	103.0	100.2	96.4

9-7 续表 continued

上年=100 (preceding year=100)

项 目	Item	2021	2022	2023
工业生产者购进价格指数	**Producer Price Index for Purchased Goods**	**108.0**	**104.1**	**97.6**
按材料类别分	**Grouped by Type of Material**			
燃料、动力类	Fuels and Power	118.4	117.9	96.8
黑色金属材料类	Ferrous Materials	119.5	98.8	92.6
#钢材	Steel	119.5	99.2	92.2
其它	Others	120.6	93.1	98.1
有色金属材料和电线类	Nonferrous Materials and Wires	126.4	102.5	98.6
化工原料类	Chemical Materials	109.8	104.5	93.9
木材及纸浆类	Timber and Paper Pulp	104.7	108.6	97.7
建筑材料及非金属矿类	Building Materials and Nonmetal Minerals	102.1	99.6	96.8
其它工业原材料及半成品类	Other Raw Materials and Semi-finished Products	102.8	102.3	99.4
农副产品类	Agricultural Products	99.5	104.1	95.1
纺织原料类	Textile Raw Materials	100.0	101.9	100.3

9-8 分行业工业生产者出厂价格指数

Producer Price Indices for Industrial Products by Sector

上年=100 (preceding year=100)

项　目	Item	2020	2021	2022	2023
工业生产者出厂价格指数	**Producer Price Index for Manufactured Goods**	**99.0**	**103.4**	**103.0**	**98.5**
按工业行业分	**Grouped by Industrial Sector**				
#石油和天然气开采业	Extraction of Petroleum and Natural Gas	82.6	123.5	131.1	97.1
黑色金属矿采选业	Mining and Processing of Ferrous Metal Ores	115.9	155.9	82.9	98.8
有色金属矿采选业	Mining and Processing of Non-ferrous Metal Ores	106.3	110.5	104.0	90.0
非金属矿采选业	Mining and Processing of Nonmetal Ores	102.5	99.2	98.8	99.0
农副食品加工业	Processing of Foods from Agricultural Products	104.7	107.3	106.5	98.4
食品制造业	Processing of Foodstuff	99.9	100.1	102.8	99.8
酒、饮料和精制茶制造业	Manufacture of Liquor, Beverages and Refined Tea	102.4	99.4	100.5	100.4
烟草制品业	Manufacture of Tobacco	103.1	102.1	100.3	100.0
纺织业	Textile Industry	99.2	99.5	106.2	100.0
纺织服装、服饰业	Manufacture of Textile, Wearing Apparel and Accessories	98.8	98.6	101.9	101.2
皮革、毛皮、羽毛及其制品和制鞋业	Manufacture of Leather,Fur, Feather and Related Products and Footware	99.3	98.4	101.6	102.7
木材加工及木、竹、藤、棕、草制品业	Processing of Timber, Manufacture of Wood, Bamboo, Rattan, Palm and Straw Products	99.4	103.6	102.6	99.1
家具制造业	Manufacture of Furniture	98.7	98.7	100.6	100.6
造纸和纸制品业	Manufacture of Paper and Paper Products	96.5	106.0	101.2	95.2
印刷和记录媒介复制业	Printing, Reproduction of Recording Media	99.8	99.5	101.3	101.7
文教、工美、体育和娱乐用品制造业	Manufacture of Articles for Culture, Education, Arts and Crafts, Sport and Entertainment Activities	104.9	102.8	102.5	106.7
石油加工、炼焦和核燃料加工业	Processing of Petroleum, Coking, Processing of Nuclear Fuel	82.2	130.0	135.6	92.7
化学原料和化学制品制造业	Manufacture of Raw Chemical Materials and Chemical Products	97.1	112.1	103.3	95.1
医药制造业	Manufacture of Medicines	101.4	97.6	99.4	99.5
化学纤维制造业	Manufacture of Chemical Fibers	89.4	114.3	99.7	88.1
橡胶和塑料制品业	Manufacture of Rubber and Plastic Products	98.1	102.3	101.9	97.0
非金属矿物制品业	Manufacture of Non-metallic Mineral Products	99.9	103.9	97.3	95.8
黑色金属冶炼和压延加工业	Smelting and Pressing of Ferrous Metals	98.3	123.3	109.4	95.6
有色金属冶炼和压延加工业	Smelting and Pressing of Nonferrous Metals	101.2	123.5	105.6	96.3
金属制品业	Manufacture of Metal Products	100.1	107.6	101.9	95.9
通用设备制造业	Manufacture of General-purpose Machinery	101.2	101.3	101.2	100.8
专用设备制造业	Manufacture of Special-purpose Machinery	100.3	100.3	100.6	99.7
汽车制造业	Manufacture of Automobiles	101.4	99.5	100.6	98.2
铁路、船舶、航空航天和其他运输设备制造业	Manufacture of Railway, Ship, Aerospace and Other Electronic Equipment	100.3	101.0	101.8	98.4
电气机械和器材制造业	Manufacture of Electrical Machinery and Equipment	97.7	101.4	105.3	101.0
计算机、通信和其他电子设备制造业	Manufacture of Communication Equipment, Computers and Other Electronic Equipment	99.6	100.2	99.5	97.4
仪器仪表制造业	Manufacture of Measuring Instruments and Machinery	98.0	98.7	101.1	102.0
其他制造业	Other Manufacturing	98.8	99.4	102.8	99.6
废弃资源综合利用业	Utilization of Waste Resources	98.9	113.9	103.5	98.8
金属制品、机械和设备修理业	Repair Service of Metal Products,Machinery and Equipment	120.3	99.0	103.2	101.7
电力、热力生产和供应业	Production and Supply of Electric Power and Heat Power	97.6	98.8	105.2	104.2
燃气生产和供应业	Production and Supply of Gas	93.7	110.3	118.5	94.3
水的生产和供应业	Production and Supply of Water	100.0	100.8	100.7	100.2

9-9 农产品生产者价格指数

Producer Price Indices for Farm Products

上年=100 (preceding year=100)

项 目	Item	2018	2019	2020	2021	2022	2023
农产品生产者价格指数	**Producer Price Indices for Farm Products**	**101.3**	**107.3**	**104.7**	**98.8**	**100.1**	**98.0**
农业产品	**Farm Products**	**100.1**	**103.5**	**99.8**	**100.8**	**102.8**	**97.4**
谷物	Cereal	101.0	98.3	100.5	104.1	101.8	100.4
#稻谷	Rice	101.0	98.3	100.5	104.1	101.6	100.5
薯类	Potato	106.3	103.1	99.4	95.5	98.8	107.3
油料	Oil-Bearing Crops	102.2	103.8	106.2	100.9	101.0	104.4
豆类	Beans	102.2	99.4	102.3	106.6	102.2	97.6
糖料	Sugar Crops	91.4	93.6	105.0	101.0	104.0	102.6
未加工烟草	Raw Tobacco	97.5	102.8	101.8	104.9	102.1	109.7
蔬菜及食用菌	Vegetables & Edible Fungi	101.1	102.3	100.4	103.3	101.6	98.2
#叶菜类蔬菜	Leaf Vegetable	103.1	103.2	99.0	102.8	103.6	97.4
白菜类蔬菜	Chinese Cabbage Vegetable	100.6	102.3	101.0	102.6	101.3	97.8
芥菜类蔬菜	Mustard Vegetable	99.2	100.7	101.3	106.5	100.8	93.2
甘蓝类蔬菜	Brassica Vegetable	100.7	98.6	102.8	103.6	97.4	101.7
根茎类蔬菜	Root Vegetable	104.9	92.8	98.5	102.7	101.0	96.1
瓜菜类蔬菜	Cucurbita Vegetable	98.6	104.8	101.5	100.4	101.9	98.1
豆类蔬菜	Bean Vegetable	99.2	105.6	97.7	108.8	102.1	99.6
茄果类蔬菜	Solanaceous Vegetable	103.0	113.1	94.3	102.7	102.6	95.1
莴苣及菊苣类蔬菜	Lettuce Vegetable	102.9	101.3	108.7	100.0	102.5	96.4
葱蒜类蔬菜	Bulb Vegetable	102.1	97.1	101.7	106.9	100.1	90.3
花卉	Flowers	101.6	94.5	102.3	96.0	99.5	96.6
盆景及园艺产品	Potted Landscape and Gardening Products	99.2	94.1	93.2	98.8	100.8	96.4
水果及坚果	Fruit and Nuts	95.0	124.0	96.7	93.7	105.2	94.5
茶及饮料原料	Tea and Beverage Raw Meterials	104.6	102.2	99.8	101.6	102.6	100.5
林业产品	**Forestry Products**	**99.4**	**98.0**	**99.5**	**109.3**	**99.8**	**98.7**
育种和育苗	Seed Breeding and Seedling	100.1	98.2	103.9	102.0	99.9	98.5
木材采伐产品	Wood Logging	101.2	99.9	98.4	108.0	97.8	97.2
竹材采伐产品	Bamboo Logging	100.5	100.1	96.1	102.5	100.5	99.9
林产品	Forestry Products	93.2	91.2	99.4	127.1	100.1	98.9
饲养动物及其产品	**Farm Animal and Products**	**101.6**	**121.0**	**119.5**	**88.2**	**92.0**	**93.6**
活牲畜	Live Animals	89.7	140.5	157.9	69.1	83.5	86.4
#猪	Pig	89.7	140.5	157.9	69.1	83.5	86.4
活家禽	Live Birds	107.5	109.3	89.0	103.1	102.0	103.0
#鸡	Chicken	103.9	108.8	92.0	103.2	102.1	101.5
鸭	Duck	111.9	107.5	89.3	107.0	101.5	94.4
畜禽产品	Animal and Bird Products	120.3	95.7	88.7	104.3	103.5	98.9
#鸡蛋	Chicken Eggs	112.9	99.7	94.7	100.4	103.1	97.4
鸭蛋	Duck Eggs	138.4	85.9	74.0	113.9	110.7	104.1
渔业产品	**Fishery Products**	**103.6**	**102.1**	**99.2**	**105.0**	**101.6**	**100.1**
海水养殖产品	Marine Farm Products	103.2	103.5	97.3	102.4	101.3	101.8
#海水养殖鱼	Marine Farm Fish	104.6	105.1	99.3	101.3	98.1	101.9
海水养殖虾	Marine Farm Shrimp	100.3	99.1	99.6	101.5	103.5	103.2
海水捕捞产品	Marine Catching Products	105.6	105.2	101.2	106.0	101.6	99.0
#海水捕捞鲜鱼	Marine Catching Fish	106.3	105.7	100.5	101.4	100.9	98.7
海水捕捞虾	Marine Catching Shrimp	103.4	105.0	105.8	105.8	119.4	101.0
淡水养殖产品	Freshwater Farm Products	101.9	100.4	98.5	104.3	101.9	99.3
#养殖淡水鱼	Freshwater Fram Fish	102.0	99.4	101.5	105.2	101.3	98.0
淡水养殖虾	Freshwater Fram Shrimp	101.3	104.0	87.1	100.6	103.6	101.7
淡水捕捞产品	Freshwater Catching Products	109.9	100.2	106.2	110.1		
#捕捞淡水鱼	Freshwater Catching Fish	112.4	100.0	107.0	102.3		
淡水捕捞鲜虾	Freshwater Catching Shrimp	106.7	100.1	102.5	110.1		

主要统计指标解释

居民消费价格指数 是度量生活消费品及服务项目价格水平随着时间而变动的相对数，反映居民家庭购买的消费品及服务项目价格水平的变动情况。该指数是宏观经济分析、决策、调控和价格总水平监测以及国民经济核算的重要指标，其按年度计算的变动率通常被用来作为反映通货膨胀(或紧缩)程度的指标。

城市居民消费价格指数 是反映城市居民家庭所购买的生活消费品和服务项目价格变动趋势和变动程度的相对数。编制该指数，可以观察和分析消费品的零售价格和服务项目价格变动对城市居民生活消费支出的影响，作为研究城市居民生活和制定工资政策的依据。

农村居民消费价格指数 是反映农村居民家庭所购买的生活消费品和服务项目价格变动趋势和变动程度的相对数。编制该指数，可以观察农村消费品的零售价格和服务项目价格变动对农村居民生活消费支出的影响，反映农村居民生活水平的实际变化情况，为分析和研究农村居民生活问题提供依据。

工业生产者出厂价格指数 是反映工业企业产品第一次出售时的出厂价格变化趋势和变动幅度的相对数（2010 年前称工业品出厂价格指数），是综合了工业企业出售给本企业以外所有单位和个人的各种产品价格指数计算取得。是反映某一时期工业生产领域价格变动情况的重要经济指标，也是制定有关经济政策和国民经济核算的重要依据。

工业生产者购进价格指数 是反映工业企业作为中间投入产品购进价格的变化趋势和变动幅度的相对数（2010 年前称原材料、燃料、动力购进价格指数）。反映工业企业作为生产投入而从物资交易市场和能源、原材料生产企业购买原材料，燃料和动力产品时，所支付的价格水平变动趋势和程度的重要指标，是扣除工业企业物质消耗成本中的价格变动影响的重要依据。

农产品生产者价格指数 是反映农产品生产者第一手(直接)出售其产品时实际获得的单位产品价格。开展农产品生产者价格调查是为了全面收集农产品生产者价格资料，客观反映农产品生产者价格水平和结构变动情况，满足农业与国民经济核算需要，为各级政府制定农业保护与农产品流通政策提供决策依据，向社会各界提供优质的农产品价格信息服务。

Explanatory Notes on Main Statistical Indicators

Consumer Price Indices measure the relative change with time in prices of consumer goods and services, reflecting the rates of change in consumer goods and services purchased by households. It is an important indicator for macroeconomic analysis, decision-making, regularization and control, supervision of general price level and national economic accounting. The annualized rates of change are generally considered as an indicator of inflation or deflation.

Consumer Price Indices of Urban Households reflect the trend and degree of changes in prices of consumer goods and services purchased by urban households and can be used to observe and analyze the impact of price changes in consumer goods and services on urban household living expenditures, thus providing the basis for policy making concerning the living cost and the wages of urban staff and workers.

Consumer Price Indices of Rural Households reflect the trend and degree of changes in prices of consumer goods and services purchased by rural households and can be used to observe and analyze the impact of change in prices of consumer goods and services on living expenditure and actual changes in the living standards of rural residents, thus providing the basis for analysis and research on the conditions of life in rural areas.

Producer Price Indices for Manufactured Goods reflect the trend and degree of changes in general ex-factory prices of all manufactured goods on first sale (it was referred to as Ex-factory Price Indices for Industrial Goods). It is calculated on the basis of sales of manufactured goods by an industrial enterprise to all units outside the enterprise, as well as sales of consumer goods to residents.It is an import index reflecting the price changes on the course of industrial production, and provides important data for economic policy making and national economic accounting

Producer Price Indices for Purchased Goods reflect the trend and degree of changes in prices paid by industrial enterprises when they purchase production input (it was referred to as Purchasing Price Indices of Raw Materials, Fuels and Power). They reflect changes in the level and degree of prices paid by industrial enterprises when they purchase production input such as raw materials, fuels and power from the market or from other energy or raw materials producing enterprises. These indices provide an important basis for measuring the material consumption of industrial enterprises after removing the influence of price changes.

Producer Price Indices of Agricultural Products refer to the actual prices per unit of agricultural products at which the producers of the agricultural products directly sell them. The purpose of conducting the survey of producer prices of agricultural products is to comprehensively collect the data on the producer prices of agricultural products, objectively reflect the situations of the level and structural changes of the producer prices of agricultural products, meet the needs of conducting the agricultural accounts and national accounts, provide the government at different levels with the base data for making the policies of protecting agriculture and circulation of agricultural products and provide the various social circles with the high quality information on the prices of agricultural products.

十、人民生活

PEOPLE'S LIVING CONDITIONS

十 人民生活

简要说明

一、本篇资料反映广东居民生活状况，主要内容包括广东全体居民及分城乡居民家庭人口、收入与消费支出结构、住房面积和主要耐用消费品拥有量等。

二、本篇资料由国家统计局广东调查总队居民收支调查处整理提供。

三、居民调查资料采用二相抽样和多阶段抽样相结合的调查方法统计。

四、2013 年国家统计局实行城乡住户一体化调查改革，将过去城镇与农村分别开展的调查体系，按照统一指标、统一方法、统一标准、统一调查、统一程序的原则，整合为城乡一体化住户调查新体系。由于新旧调查体系在调查范围和对象、城乡划分标准、样本抽选方法、计算和汇总方式、指标名称和口径等都发生了变化，新旧口径指标数据衔接困难。

五、旧调查体系的农村居民纯收入指标在新的调查体系中统一为城乡可比的可支配收入，旧调查体系中的城乡经营性收入、财产性收入与转移性收入在新的调查体系中统一为经营净收入、财产净收入与转移净收入。

六、2013 年起为新口径数据，2013 年以前的为旧调查体系的数据。

七、按照国家统计局统一部署，2022 年开展了住户调查大样本轮换，2023 年是全面启用新调查样本的第一年。由于住户调查以居民收入为核心指标开展调查， 2023 年部分指标波动较大。

10 People's Living Conditions

Brief Introduction

Ⅰ. The data in this chapter show the basic conditions of the people’s livelihood in the urban and rural areas of Guangdong Province. The main contents include urban and rural households population, per capita income and consumption expenditure structure, housing area and possession of the major consumer goods.

Ⅱ.The data in this chapter are prepared and provided by Division of Income and Expenditure Survey and under Guangdong Survey Office of the National Bureau of Statistics.

Ⅲ.The survey data of urban and rural residents are collected through two-phase sampling scheme combined with multi-stage sampling scheme.

Ⅳ.The National Bureau of Statistics of China started an integrated reform of household survey in 2013, including both rural and urban households. According to the principle of unified index, unified standard, unified survey, unified software, unified release, the separate urban and rural household surveys are changed to the integrated household income and expenditure survey. Because there are great difference of survey scope and object, survey methodology, sample selection, data collection methodology between the integrated and the separate household survey, the data produced by the integrated system of household survey are not comparable to those produced by the separate urban and rural household surveys prior to 2013.

V.The net income of rural households of the old household survey are integrated to the disposal income of rural households in the new household survey since 2013. Income from properties, transfers and business of the old household survey are unified to net income from properties, transfers and business in the new household survey.

Ⅵ.Data before 2013 are produced by the old survey system , data since 2013 are new scope.

VII. In accordance with the unified deployment of the National Bureau of Statistics of China, the large sample rotation of household survey was carried out in 2022, and 2023 is the first year of full implementation of the new survey sample. Since the household survey is conducted with residents' income as the core indicator, it has led to significant fluctuations in some indicators in 2023.

10-1 全省居民家庭基本情况
Basic Conditions of Households Province Wide

指 标	Item	2018	2019	2020	2021	2022	2023
调查户数 （户）	**Survey of households (households)**	**7900**	**7900**	**7900**	**7900**	**7900**	**7900**
平均每户常住人口 （人）	Average Number of per Permanent Household (person)	3.26	3.28	3.29	3.46	3.47	3.12
平均每户就业人口 （人）	Average Number of Employed Persons per Household (person)	1.75	1.74	1.70	1.80	1.78	1.55
人均可支配收入（元）	**Per Capita Disposable Income (yuan)**	**35809.9**	**39014.3**	**41028.6**	**44993.3**	**47064.6**	**49327.4**
1.工资性收入	Income of Wages and Salaries	24749.0	26554.3	27824.4	30777.3	32200.8	33662.9
2.经营净收入	Net Business Income	4734.5	5154.7	5037.4	5729.1	5977.5	6328.4
3.财产净收入	Net Income from Properties	4131.4	4776.9	5339.1	5831.3	6107.7	6411.9
4.转移净收入	Net Income from Transfers	2194.9	2528.4	2827.7	2655.6	2778.6	2924.2
可支配收入构成 (%)	**Composition of Disposable Income (%)**	**100.0**	**100.0**	**100.0**	**100.0**	**100.0**	**100.0**
1.工资性收入	Income of Wages and Salaries	69.1	68.1	67.8	68.4	68.4	68.3
2.经营净收入	Net Business Income	13.2	13.2	12.3	12.7	12.7	12.8
3.财产净收入	Net Income from Properties	11.5	12.2	13.0	13.0	13.0	13.0
4.转移净收入	Net Income from Transfers	6.1	6.5	6.9	5.9	5.9	5.9
人均消费支出 （元）	**Per Capita Consumption Expenditure (yuan)**	**26054.0**	**28994.7**	**28491.9**	**31589.3**	**32168.7**	**34331.5**
1.食品烟酒	Food,Tobacco and Liquor	8480.8	9369.2	9629.3	10484.6	11025.8	11137.1
2.衣着	Clothing	1135.3	1192.2	1044.5	1278.0	1178.3	1290.4
3.居住	Living	6643.3	7329.1	7733.0	8189.6	8406.2	8849.0
4.生活用品及服务	Daily Necessities and Services	1440.8	1560.2	1560.6	1614.1	1636.0	1692.9
5.交通通信	Transportation and Telecommunication	3423.9	3833.6	3808.7	4164.6	4174.3	4864.5
6.教育文化娱乐	Education,Culture and Entertainment	2750.9	3244.4	2442.9	3241.6	3196.3	3538.1
7.医疗保健	Health Service	1520.8	1770.4	1677.9	1900.9	1783.0	2119.7
8.其他用品和服务	Other Necessities and Services	658.2	695.5	595.1	715.9	768.8	839.8
消费支出构成 (%)	**Composition of Consumption Expenditure (%)**	**100.0**	**100.0**	**100.0**	**100.0**	**100.0**	**100.0**
1.食品烟酒	Food,Tobacco and Liquor	32.6	32.3	33.8	33.2	34.3	32.4
2.衣着	Clothing	4.4	4.1	3.7	4.0	3.7	3.8
3.居住	Living	25.5	25.3	27.1	25.9	26.1	25.8
4.生活用品及服务	Daily Necessities and Services	5.5	5.4	5.4	5.1	5.1	4.9
5.交通通信	Transportation and Telecommunication	13.1	13.2	13.4	13.2	13.0	14.2
6.教育文化娱乐	Education,Culture and Entertainment	10.6	11.2	8.6	10.3	9.9	10.3
7.医疗保健	Health Service	5.8	6.1	5.9	6.0	5.5	6.2
8.其他用品和服务	Other Necessities and Services	2.5	2.4	2.1	2.3	2.4	2.4

10-2 按收入五等份分组的全省居民人均可支配收入

Per Capita Disposable Income of Households Province Wide by Income Quintile

单位：元 (yuan)

年份 Year	低收入户 (20%) Low Income Households (20%)	中等偏下户 (20%) Lower Middle Income Households (20%)	中等收入户 (20%) Middle Income Households (20%)	中等偏上户 (20%) Upper Middle Income Households (20%)	高收入户 (20%) High Income Households (20%)
2016	9544.7	19574.7	30598.5	41989.6	68599.3
2017	10534.3	20963.3	32339.4	45235.8	75774.6
2018	11241.7	21673.8	33984.3	49984.2	82444.3
2019	11824.3	23226.2	36697.8	54261.2	89717.5
2020	12665.7	23627.3	37656.8	55938.4	93242.9
2021	14229.0	26527.9	40839.1	60156.0	98481.3
2022	14617.0	27922.3	42696.4	63101.8	104311.9
2023	15407.5	29227.6	44328.3	65506.3	108280.8

10-3 全省居民人均主要食品消费量

Per Capita Consumption of Major Foods Province Wide

单位:千克 (Kg)

指 标	Item	2018	2019	2020	2021	2022	2023
粮食	Grain	108.67	115.90	128.21	111.59	106.47	111.51
谷物	Cereal	101.08	106.67	118.36	103.75	98.98	102.63
薯类	Tuber	1.54	1.65	1.62	1.29	1.26	1.44
豆类	Beans and the Products	6.05	7.59	8.22	6.54	6.22	7.44
油脂类	Oil and Fats	9.16	9.03	9.94	10.35	10.05	9.30
#植物油	Vegetable Oil	8.58	8.47	9.50	9.78	9.57	8.84
蔬菜及菜制品	Vegetable and Mushroom	100.57	109.45	113.01	97.86	101.15	104.40
#鲜菜	Fresh Vegetables	97.19	105.74	109.33	95.02	98.53	101.37
肉类	Products of Meat	40.99	38.73	33.61	37.58	42.76	49.65
#猪肉	Pork	34.02	30.71	25.96	29.61	34.20	39.73
禽类	Poultry	21.08	25.92	31.12	24.56	24.34	24.25
#鸡	Chick	13.74	16.62	19.54	15.71	15.68	15.27
水产品	Aquatic Products	22.03	28.61	30.01	27.55	24.43	27.01
#鱼类	Fresh	16.35	21.05	22.28	20.19	16.68	18.65
蛋类及蛋制品	Eggs and Egg Products	7.39	8.37	9.87	8.40	8.77	9.75
#鲜蛋	Fresh Eggs	7.06	8.01	9.50	8.09	8.50	9.43
奶及奶制品	Milk and Dairy Products	8.63	8.83	9.59	12.85	9.28	9.41
#鲜奶	Fresh Milk	4.65	5.36	6.40	9.18	6.71	6.70
鲜瓜果	Fresh Melons and Fruits	35.66	43.04	43.55	41.35	40.82	46.51
食糖	Sugar	1.56	1.55	1.58	1.15	1.04	0.93

10-4 全省居民平均每百户年末主要耐用消费品拥有量

Main Durable Consumer Goods Owned per 100 Households Province wide

指　标	Item	2018	2019	2020	2021	2022	2023
家用汽车　(辆)	Car (set)	36.94	41.27	42.68	47.63	53.04	52.12
摩托车　(辆)	Motorcycle (set)	67.25	66.44	65.54	63.55	61.95	41.30
助力车　(台)	Electric Bicycle (set)	34.60	39.65	41.77	54.64	57.70	59.38
洗衣机　(台)	Washing Machine (set)	89.73	92.65	93.16	98.08	98.27	91.26
电冰箱(柜)　(台)	Refrigerator (set)	94.41	97.64	98.23	103.16	103.57	96.04
微波炉　(台)	Microwave Oven (set)	39.16	41.12	41.82	42.84	43.02	32.66
彩色电视机　(台)	Color Television (set)	109.07	110.19	110.48	108.36	108.84	85.14
空调　(台)	Air Conditioner (set)	176.07	187.85	190.13	224.33	229.07	206.17
热水器　(台)	Water Heater (unit)	99.43	101.52	104.22	104.65	105.59	99.67
排油烟机　(台)	Fume hood (set)	65.54	68.33	69.39	72.29	73.14	65.74
移动电话　(部)	Mobile Phone (set)	268.23	270.56	268.44	280.13	281.85	246.26
计算机　(台)	Computer (set)	69.34	72.59	74.33	67.81	68.07	63.22
照相机　(台)	Camera (set)	15.88	16.26	16.21	11.41	11.76	9.56

10-5 各市全体居民人均可支配收入

Per Capita Disposable Income of Households by City

单位：元 (yuan)

市别	City	2018	2019	2020	2021	2022	2023
全省	**Provincial Total**	**35809.9**	**39014.3**	**41028.6**	**44993.3**	**47064.6**	**49327.4**
广州	Guangzhou	55276.1	60073.8	63289.2	68908.3	71357.9	74836.7
深圳	Shenzhen	57543.6	62522.4	64877.7	70847.3	72718.2	76910.3
珠海	Zhuhai	48107.1	52495.1	55936.1	61390.0	62976.1	64974.8
汕头	Shantou	24428.0	26612.8	28220.5	30969.7	32653.8	33652.9
佛山	Foshan	49629.5	54042.7	56244.8	61700.2	64150.2	67462.7
韶关	Shaoguan	23676.0	25805.5	27546.2	30211.5	31411.1	32966.0
河源	Heyuan	19397.1	21052.3	22291.1	24626.5	25825.1	27563.5
梅州	Meizhou	21217.0	22903.9	23872.6	26209.8	27431.1	28777.5
惠州	Huizhou	33929.9	37159.6	39745.4	43350.5	44890.4	46636.5
汕尾	Shanwei	21001.1	22782.9	24427.0	27422.8	29020.1	30757.1
东莞	Dongguan	49331.0	53657.2	56533.1	62126.5	63832.9	65701.3
中山	Zhongshan	46865.0	50477.6	52753.6	57900.8	59764.0	62378.8
江门	Jiangmen	29546.9	32323.3	33666.5	37068.4	38756.2	40783.9
阳江	Yangjiang	23281.8	25131.1	26591.4	29167.9	30514.4	31766.5
湛江	Zhanjiang	21426.9	23320.4	24986.3	27646.3	28861.4	29733.4
茂名	Maoming	21349.9	23179.0	24600.4	26728.6	27787.9	29124.3
肇庆	Zhaoqing	24070.9	26121.5	27496.2	30394.1	31469.8	32562.0
清远	Qingyuan	22369.4	24362.0	26055.0	28741.3	29911.6	31464.8
潮州	Chaozhou	20895.1	22542.4	23302.5	25083.7	26420.0	27979.4
揭阳	Jieyang	20042.3	21341.1	21821.5	23780.5	24788.2	25797.1
云浮	Yunfu	19239.1	20938.1	22306.2	24610.9	25951.9	27187.7
按经济区域分	By Region						
珠三角	Pearl River Delta	47911.0	52213.7	54809.6	60729.7	62700.0	65654.7
粤东	Eastern Region	21754.2	23483.6	24575.6	27006.0	28388.3	29597.8
粤西	Western Region	21691.0	23550.9	25087.4	27538.1	28713.6	29829.7
粤北	Northern Region	21288.0	23120.3	24504.7	27038.0	28256.0	29745.8

注：按照国家统计局的统一部署，广东省分市县城乡一体化住户调查工作从2013年底正式启动，从2014年开始正式对外发布分市全体居民人均可支配收入数据。

Note: Under the unified deployment by NBS, Guangdong province started an integrated household survey by city and county since 2013,including both urban and rural households. Since 2014 the data of per capita disposal income and expenditures of all households in the province by city is released officially after the transitional period.

10−6 各市全体居民人均可支配收入来源（2023年）
Per Capita Disposable Income of Households by Sources and City (2023)

单位：元 (yuan)

地　区	City	可支配收入 Disposable Income	工资性收入 Income of Wages and Salaries	经营净收入 Net Business Income	财产净收入 Net Income from Property	转移净收入 Net Income from Transfer
全　省	**Provincial Total**	**49327.4**	**33662.9**	**6328.4**	**6411.9**	**2924.2**
广　州	Guangzhou	74836.7	49472.3	4572.0	14570.1	6222.2
深　圳	Shenzhen	76910.0	65008.6	7276.6	6883.9	-2259.1
珠　海	Zhuhai	64974.8	47337.7	5062.0	8624.2	3950.9
汕　头	Shantou	33652.9	23360.8	4199.6	1972.3	4120.2
佛　山	Foshan	67462.7	41305.6	8423.0	12950.2	4783.8
韶　关	Shaoguan	32966.0	20407.3	6161.9	1658.9	4737.8
河　源	Heyuan	27563.5	17084.2	4858.8	934.0	4686.5
梅　州	Meizhou	28777.6	16194.4	4971.8	1277.8	6333.6
惠　州	Huizhou	46636.5	31059.9	8661.7	4650.0	2265.0
汕　尾	Shanwei	30757.1	17707.7	6593.9	1398.5	5057.0
东　莞	Dongguan	65701.3	46456.3	6996.2	12516.6	-267.9
中　山	Zhongshan	62378.8	42534.0	7464.7	7291.8	5088.3
江　门	Jiangmen	40783.9	29012.8	3955.0	3449.8	4366.3
阳　江	Yangjiang	31766.5	18432.3	7528.6	1747.0	4058.7
湛　江	Zhanjiang	29733.4	16111.5	5783.3	1743.4	6095.1
茂　名	Maoming	29124.3	16891.6	4843.1	1428.7	5960.8
肇　庆	Zhaoqing	32562.0	20415.5	5577.4	1817.6	4751.5
清　远	Qingyuan	31464.8	19572.9	6172.4	1442.3	4277.3
潮　州	Chaozhou	27979.4	16601.3	4994.7	1608.5	4774.8
揭　阳	Jieyang	25797.1	14726.6	5449.9	1249.6	4370.9
云　浮	Yunfu	27187.7	18152.0	4281.3	1293.4	3461.0

10–7 各市全体居民人均消费支出
Per Capita Consumption Expenditure of Households by City

单位：元 (yuan)

市别	City	2018	2019	2020	2021	2022	2023
全省	**Provincial Total**	**26054.0**	**28994.7**	**28491.9**	**31589.3**	**32168.7**	**34331.5**
广州	Guangzhou	39467.1	42308.7	41400.3	44253.1	44036.6	46570.8
深圳	Shenzhen	40535.0	43112.7	40581.1	46285.7	44792.9	49013.0
珠海	Zhuhai	35081.4	38211.8	36359.7	42333.7	41333.3	41943.2
汕头	Shantou	19186.8	20944.5	21256.8	22493.0	22824.0	23075.3
佛山	Foshan	34052.6	37160.3	36936.0	40545.2	41129.2	43329.8
韶关	Shaoguan	17207.8	18727.2	18800.2	21335.8	21486.7	22455.2
河源	Heyuan	14593.5	15604.9	16003.5	18030.4	18426.3	19450.7
梅州	Meizhou	15912.5	16822.5	17071.0	18931.3	19624.1	20694.1
惠州	Huizhou	24461.9	26610.7	26232.4	29175.7	29408.0	29744.5
汕尾	Shanwei	16414.2	17834.1	18773.8	20497.6	21635.4	23094.5
东莞	Dongguan	33208.9	35729.7	34259.8	39078.9	39432.5	40294.6
中山	Zhongshan	31057.9	33959.0	32735.5	37852.7	38648.1	39164.9
江门	Jiangmen	19751.6	21647.4	21898.7	24192.8	24538.9	26063.2
阳江	Yangjiang	17850.1	18918.8	19181.0	21018.8	21371.9	21987.8
湛江	Zhanjiang	15302.6	16312.4	16559.7	18858.3	19141.6	19769.5
茂名	Maoming	15440.7	16517.1	17014.9	18276.5	18740.1	19543.8
肇庆	Zhaoqing	15505.6	17021.7	16777.3	19094.7	19592.8	20449.8
清远	Qingyuan	16709.5	17981.4	18247.9	20404.0	20710.6	21648.9
潮州	Chaozhou	15616.1	16840.8	17472.2	18887.9	19568.3	20727.9
揭阳	Jieyang	14574.3	15140.1	15565.8	17824.2	18662.0	18925.5
云浮	Yunfu	13672.1	14882.9	14833.8	16428.5	16840.2	17638.4

注：按照国家统计局的统一部署，广东省分市县城乡一体化住户调查工作从2013年底正式启动，从2014年开始正式对外发布分市全体居民人均消费支出数据。

Note: Under the unified deployment by NBS, Guangdong province started an integrated household survey by city and county since 2013, including both urban and rural households. Since 2014 the data of per capita disposal income and expenditures of all households in the province by city is released officially after the transitional period.

10-8 城镇居民家庭基本情况

Basic Situation of Urban Households

指 标	Item	2018	2019	2020	2021	2022	2023
调查户数 （户）	**Survey of households (household)**	**5550**	**5550**	**5550**	**5550**	**5550**	**5550**
平均每户常住人口（人）	Average number of residents per Permanent Household (person)	3.18	3.21	3.23	3.35	3.37	2.98
平均每户就业人口（人）	Average Number of Employed Persons per Permanent Household (person)	1.73	1.73	1.69	1.77	1.75	1.49
人均可支配收入 （元）	**Per Capita Disposable Income (yuan)**	**44341.0**	**48117.6**	**50257.0**	**54853.6**	**56905.3**	**59306.6**
1.工资性收入	Income of Wages and Salaries	32180.1	34151.9	35429.3	38605.8	40017.6	41580.5
2.经营净收入	Net Business Income	4872.6	5473.8	5237.3	5855.2	6069.1	6422.4
3.财产净收入	Income from Properties	5816.6	6686.2	7425.9	8020.1	8304.6	8664.6
4.转移净收入	Income from Transfers	1471.7	1805.7	2164.4	2372.5	2514.0	2639.1
人均消费支出 （元）	**Per Capita Consumption Expenditure (yuan)**	**30924.3**	**34424.1**	**33511.3**	**36621.1**	**36936.2**	**39333.3**
1.食品烟酒	Food,Tobacco and Liquor	9780.2	10757.5	10794.7	11622.0	12129.8	12290.4
2.衣着	Clothing	1415.3	1480.8	1282.1	1519.9	1381.4	1559.1
3.居住	Living	8147.8	8961.6	9457.9	9696.4	9925.7	10328.6
4.生活用品及服务	Daily Necessities and Services	1726.2	1894.8	1895.3	1874.8	1905.8	2011.1
5.交通通信	Transportation and Telecommunication	4107.3	4597.1	4626.3	5008.5	4888.5	5660.9
6.教育文化娱乐	Education,Culture and Entertainment	3335.7	3984.5	2958.7	3872.8	3747.8	4114.7
7.医疗保健	Health Service	1591.3	1883.0	1748.6	2143.7	2019.2	2350.3
8.其他用品和服务	Other Necessities and Services	820.5	864.9	747.7	882.9	937.8	1018.4
消费支出构成 （%）	**Composition of Consumption Expenditure**	**100.0**	**100.0**	**100.0**	**100.0**	**100.0**	**100.0**
1.食品烟酒	Food,Tobacco and Liquor	31.6	31.2	32.2	31.7	32.8	31.2
2.衣着	Clothing	4.6	4.3	3.8	4.1	3.7	4.0
3.居住	Living	26.3	26.0	28.2	26.5	26.9	26.2
4.生活用品及服务	Daily Necessities and Services	5.6	5.5	5.7	5.1	5.2	5.1
5.交通通信	Transportation and Telecommunication	13.3	13.4	13.8	13.7	13.2	14.4
6.教育文化娱乐	Education,Culture and Entertainment	10.8	11.6	8.8	10.6	10.2	10.5
7.医疗保健	Health Service	5.1	5.5	5.2	5.9	5.5	6.0
8.其他用品和服务	Other Necessities and Services	2.7	2.5	2.3	2.4	2.5	2.6

10-9 历年城镇居民人均可支配收入及生活消费支出(1978-2012年)

Per Capita Disposable Income and Consumption Expenditure of Urban Households (1978-2012)

年份 Year	人均可支配收入(元) Per Capita Disposable Income (yuan)	指数 Index 名义增长(上年为100) Nominal Growth (preceding year=100)	实际增长(上年为100) Real Growth (preceding year=100)	实际增长(1978年为100) Real Growth (1978=100)	人均消费支出(元) Per Capita Consumption Expenditure (yuan)	指数 Index 名义增长(上年为100) Nominal Growth (preceding year=100)	实际增长(上年为100) Real Growth (preceding year=100)	恩格尔系数(%) Engle Coefficient (%)
1978	412.1	101.0	96.6	100.0	400.0	106.3	101.5	66.6
1979	416.3	101.0	96.6	96.6	425.0	106.3	101.5	67.0
1980	472.6	113.5	103.7	100.1	485.8	114.3	104.5	65.5
1981	560.7	118.6	111.6	111.7	517.4	106.5	100.2	65.8
1982	631.5	112.6	109.8	122.7	592.1	114.4	111.5	64.2
1983	714.2	113.1	110.0	135.0	660.1	111.5	108.5	64.5
1984	818.4	114.6	112.4	151.8	744.4	112.8	110.7	63.6
1985	954.1	116.6	99.6	151.1	889.6	119.5	102.1	58.3
1986	1102.1	115.5	110.3	166.7	998.9	112.3	107.2	58.6
1987	1320.9	119.9	106.3	177.1	1215.8	121.7	107.9	56.7
1988	1583.1	119.9	92.6	163.9	1507.0	123.9	95.7	56.7
1989	2086.2	131.8	108.1	177.2	1921.1	127.5	104.6	56.5
1990	2303.2	110.4	113.3	200.8	1983.9	103.3	106.0	57.2
1991	2752.2	119.5	116.8	234.6	2388.8	120.4	117.7	53.1
1992	3476.7	126.3	116.5	273.4	2830.6	118.5	110.4	51.5
1993	4632.4	133.2	109.2	298.6	3777.4	133.4	110.3	48.9
1994	6367.1	137.4	113.6	339.2	5181.3	137.2	113.4	46.4
1995	7438.7	116.8	103.3	350.4	6253.7	120.7	106.7	48.0
1996	8157.8	109.7	102.3	358.4	6736.1	107.7	100.5	47.3
1997	8561.7	105.0	102.8	368.4	6853.5	101.7	99.7	46.0
1998	8839.7	103.2	105.0	387.0	7054.1	102.9	104.7	44.1
1999	9125.9	103.2	104.9	406.0	7517.8	106.6	108.3	40.6
2000	9761.6	107.0	104.7	424.9	8016.9	106.6	104.3	38.6
2001	10415.2	106.7	107.6	457.0	8099.6	101.0	101.8	38.1
2002	11137.2	109.1	110.6	495.7	8988.5	111.0	112.6	38.5
2003	12380.4	111.2	110.4	547.2	9636.2	107.2	106.5	37.2
2004	13627.7	110.1	107.3	587.0	10694.8	111.0	108.2	37.0
2005	14769.9	108.4	106.3	623.8	11809.9	110.4	108.2	36.1
2006	16015.6	108.4	106.5	664.3	12432.2	105.3	103.4	36.2
2007	17699.3	110.5	106.6	707.9	14336.9	115.3	111.2	35.3
2008	19732.9	111.5	105.7	748.3	15528.0	108.3	102.7	37.8
2009	21574.7	109.3	112.0	838.1	16857.5	108.6	111.3	36.9
2010	23897.8	110.8	107.5	901.0	18489.5	109.7	106.4	36.5
2011	26897.5	112.6	106.9	963.2	20251.8	109.5	104.0	36.9
2012	30226.7	112.4	109.3	1052.8	22396.4	110.6	107.6	36.9

10-10 全省城镇居民人均主要食品消费量
Per Capita Consumption of Major Foods of Urban Households

单位:千克 (Kg)

指标	Item	2018	2019	2020	2021	2022	2023
粮食	Grain	93.89	100.79	108.86	94.50	90.41	98.91
谷物	Cereal	86.28	91.70	99.56	86.98	83.30	90.22
薯类	Tuber	1.54	1.71	1.75	1.40	1.36	1.49
豆类	Beans and the Products	6.07	7.38	7.55	6.13	5.75	7.20
油脂类	Oil and Fats	8.16	8.42	9.14	9.30	9.26	8.45
#植物油	Vegetable Oil	7.77	7.97	8.81	8.91	8.91	8.06
蔬菜及菜制品	Vegetable and Mushroom	98.52	110.64	113.70	94.22	96.60	99.00
#鲜菜	Fresh Vegetables	94.86	106.65	109.81	91.22	93.82	95.81
肉类	Products of Meat	40.71	39.44	34.35	36.56	40.86	46.67
#猪肉	Pork	33.07	30.56	25.81	27.97	31.75	36.28
禽类	Poultry	19.80	23.86	28.06	21.93	22.31	21.99
#鸡	Chick	13.06	15.69	18.06	14.19	14.55	13.95
水产品	Aquatic Products	23.06	29.49	30.07	28.74	24.33	25.95
#鱼类	Fresh	16.76	21.19	21.71	20.84	16.15	17.26
蛋类及制品	Eggs and Egg Products	7.58	8.66	10.19	8.52	8.83	9.74
#鲜蛋	Fresh Eggs	7.19	8.24	9.76	8.17	8.52	9.37
奶及奶制品	Milk and Dairy Products	10.76	10.80	11.75	14.97	10.91	11.20
#鲜奶	Fresh Milk	5.79	6.55	7.84	10.61	7.90	7.98
鲜瓜果	Fresh Melons and Fruits	41.07	49.30	49.18	44.89	43.51	51.96
食糖	Sugar	1.41	1.40	1.45	1.07	0.94	0.86

10-11 全省城镇居民平均每百户年末主要耐用消费品拥有量
Main Durable Consumer Goods Owned per 100 Urban Households at the Year-end

项目	Item	2018	2019	2020	2021	2022	2023
家用汽车 (辆)	Car (set)	42.92	47.63	48.88	53.77	59.15	58.05
摩托车 (辆)	Motorcycle (set)	46.42	45.55	44.90	45.13	43.93	36.85
助力车 (台)	Electric Bicycle (set)	34.08	39.31	41.50	53.95	56.74	55.83
洗衣机 (台)	Washing Machine (set)	91.84	93.75	94.33	98.65	98.68	96.58
电冰箱 (台)	Refrigerator (set)	95.04	97.91	98.55	103.27	103.68	100.12
微波炉 (台)	Microwave Oven (set)	44.28	46.14	46.91	46.15	46.14	33.22
彩色电视机 (台)	Color Television (set)	105.94	107.57	108.23	106.94	107.40	90.02
空调 (台)	Air Conditioner (set)	202.39	212.11	213.87	244.28	248.54	232.17
热水器 (台)	Water Heater (unit)	101.71	102.99	105.27	105.84	106.49	103.40
排油烟机 (台)	Fume Hood (set)	72.47	75.09	75.91	77.53	78.26	75.04
移动电话 (部)	Mobile Telephone (set)	258.88	263.99	264.56	274.77	276.37	251.96
计算机 (台)	Computer (set)	83.66	86.82	88.63	80.19	80.19	76.04
照相机 (台)	Camera (set)	20.50	21.21	21.42	14.82	15.05	11.21

10-12 各市城镇居民人均可支配收入

Per Capita Disposable Income of Urban Households by City

单位：元 (yuan)

市　别	City	2018	2019	2020	2021	2022	2023
全　省	**Provincial Total**	**44341.0**	**48117.6**	**50257.0**	**54853.6**	**56905.3**	**59306.6**
广　州	Guangzhou	59982.1	65052.1	68304.1	74416.2	76849.4	80500.9
深　圳	Shenzhen	57543.6	62522.4	64877.7	70847.3	72718.2	76910.0
珠　海	Zhuhai	50713.0	55219.3	58474.7	64233.7	65743.2	67772.6
汕　头	Shantou	29077.3	31415.8	32921.9	35600.7	37036.9	38069.9
佛　山	Foshan	50736.9	55232.8	57444.9	62942.3	65416.8	68643.4
韶　关	Shaoguan	30287.3	32633.9	34418.2	37623.5	38742.0	40304.6
河　源	Heyuan	25491.8	27128.5	28018.2	30445.7	31517.6	33195.1
梅　州	Meizhou	27385.3	29235.3	29942.2	32751.5	33923.6	35128.8
惠　州	Huizhou	39573.6	42999.4	45474.5	49243.0	50811.1	52621.0
汕　尾	Shanwei	26012.3	28051.3	29860.3	33081.8	34766.3	36594.7
东　莞	Dongguan	50721.3	55155.9	58051.9	63739.8	65405.9	67286.0
中　山	Zhongshan	48803.6	52502.4	54737.3	60322.7	62195.7	64856.4
江　门	Jiangmen	35465.8	38595.2	39922.9	43621.8	45399.8	47727.3
阳　江	Yangjiang	29360.1	31255.7	32310.8	35069.1	36319.1	37521.8
湛　江	Zhanjiang	29046.3	31240.7	32925.6	35988.8	37098.6	37497.7
茂　名	Maoming	27163.4	29404.9	30733.0	33423.9	34303.5	35348.5
肇　庆	Zhaoqing	30679.6	33259.8	34752.0	37791.4	38711.1	39678.8
清　远	Qingyuan	29377.0	31597.1	33159.2	36171.6	37244.0	38734.6
潮　州	Chaozhou	24170.2	25827.7	26440.2	28403.1	29758.2	31377.5
揭　阳	Jieyang	25425.2	26745.5	27066.4	29397.1	30273.1	31305.2
云　浮	Yunfu	24946.5	26806.5	28329.8	30951.9	32380.5	33628.1
按经济区域分	By Region						
珠三角	Pearl River Delta	52129.1	56638.7	59225.1	65118.6	67092.6	70194.8
粤　东	Eastern Region	26694.2	28569.8	29622.2	32240.7	33521.5	34767.1
粤　西	Western Region	28404.7	30552.5	31971.0	34861.6	35906.0	36697.5
粤　北	Northern Region	27826.9	29828.0	31095.7	34008.9	35151.8	36592.4

注：按照国家统计局的统一部署，广东省分市县城乡一体化住户调查工作从2013年底正式启动，从2014年开始正式对外发布分市城镇居民人均可支配收入数据。

Note: Under the unified deployment by NBS, Guangdong province started an integrated household survey by city and county since 2013,including both urban and rural households . Since 2014 the data of per capita disposal income of all households in the province by city is released officially after the transitional period.

10-13 各市城镇居民人均可支配收入来源（2023年）

Per Capita Disposable Income of Urban Households by Sources and City (2023)

单位：元 (yuan)

地 区	City	可支配收入 Disposable Income	工资性收入 Income of Wages and Salaries	经营净收入 Net Business Income	财产净收入 Net Income from Property	转移净收入 Net Income from Transfer
全 省	**Provincial Total**	**59306.6**	**41580.5**	**6422.4**	**8664.6**	**2639.1**
广 州	Guangzhou	80500.9	52784.4	4591.8	16237.0	6887.7
深 圳	Shenzhen	76910.0	65008.6	7276.6	6883.9	-2259.1
珠 海	Zhuhai	67772.6	49625.1	4962.6	9095.1	4089.8
汕 头	Shantou	38069.9	25564.6	5195.3	2841.7	4468.3
佛 山	Foshan	68643.4	42023.4	8479.6	13230.9	4909.4
韶 关	Shaoguan	40304.6	27203.9	4980.1	2182.2	5938.4
河 源	Heyuan	33195.1	22064.0	4728.0	1625.0	4778.1
梅 州	Meizhou	35128.8	20789.9	5067.2	2372.2	6899.5
惠 州	Huizhou	52621.0	35783.4	8957.5	5754.7	2125.5
汕 尾	Shanwei	36594.7	20877.5	7589.0	2247.5	5880.7
东 莞	Dongguan	67286.0	47150.0	7241.5	13141.0	-246.5
中 山	Zhongshan	64856.4	44167.2	7717.9	7588.2	5383.1
江 门	Jiangmen	47727.3	33646.6	4194.6	4552.0	5334.0
阳 江	Yangjiang	37521.8	23237.3	6503.0	3048.8	4732.8
湛 江	Zhanjiang	37497.7	22255.3	5156.3	3405.8	6680.4
茂 名	Maoming	35348.5	23198.9	5863.4	2318.8	3967.3
肇 庆	Zhaoqing	39678.8	26624.5	4801.1	2920.4	5332.8
清 远	Qingyuan	38734.6	25519.5	5904.7	2307.8	5002.7
潮 州	Chaozhou	31377.5	18995.9	4064.3	2432.7	5884.5
揭 阳	Jieyang	31305.2	17497.0	6723.8	2323.7	4760.7
云 浮	Yunfu	33628.1	23104.0	3783.0	2830.0	3911.0

10-14 各市城镇居民人均消费支出
Per Capita Consumption Expenditure of Urban Households by City

单位：元 (yuan)

市　别	City	2018	2019	2020	2021	2022	2023
全　省	**Provincial Total**	**30924.3**	**34424.1**	**33511.3**	**36621.1**	**36936.2**	**39333.3**
广　州	Guangzhou	42181.0	45049.3	44283.4	47161.9	46825.2	49480.3
深　圳	Shenzhen	40535.0	43112.7	40581.1	46285.7	44792.9	49013.0
珠　海	Zhuhai	36818.8	40030.5	37777.6	43956.5	42856.5	43525.6
汕　头	Shantou	21998.3	23853.7	24049.9	25268.0	25094.0	25119.3
佛　山	Foshan	34803.5	37970.2	37664.0	41327.2	41897.2	44120.2
韶　关	Shaoguan	20808.0	22472.7	22162.1	25079.0	25168.5	26098.9
河　源	Heyuan	17343.1	18227.6	18320.0	20165.0	20214.2	21063.0
梅　州	Meizhou	18659.0	19447.4	19479.0	21415.2	22063.9	23123.0
惠　州	Huizhou	27772.5	30008.8	29369.0	32431.0	32578.6	32810.0
汕　尾	Shanwei	19800.8	21421.5	22492.5	24292.0	25379.2	26786.0
东　莞	Dongguan	33675.1	36198.4	34706.3	39802.6	40131.4	40983.0
中　山	Zhongshan	32180.4	35173.2	33773.6	39143.7	39887.3	40365.9
江　门	Jiangmen	23237.4	25679.4	25477.6	27912.1	28182.6	29843.1
阳　江	Yangjiang	21782.2	22838.0	22895.4	23892.6	23908.9	24306.0
湛　江	Zhanjiang	20214.0	21058.9	21006.8	23270.4	23422.2	23736.6
茂　名	Maoming	18022.0	19256.0	19440.4	20638.6	20789.8	21452.5
肇　庆	Zhaoqing	19984.4	21685.4	20990.2	23028.1	23385.0	24147.4
清　远	Qingyuan	20270.2	21620.2	21774.1	23987.5	24146.0	25063.5
潮　州	Chaozhou	17386.4	18569.1	19109.3	20533.8	21147.1	22276.8
揭　阳	Jieyang	16907.5	17183.7	17416.5	19781.6	20393.5	20469.6
云　浮	Yunfu	16398.4	17638.7	17536.5	19057.1	19149.6	20043.1

注：按照国家统计局的统一部署，广东省分市县城乡一体化住户调查工作从2013年底正式启动，从2014年开始正式对外发布分市城镇居民人均消费支出数据。

Note: Under the unified deployment by NBS, Guangdong province started an integrated household survey by city and county since 2013, including both urban and rural households. Since 2014 the data of per capita expenditures of all households in the province by city is released officially after the transitional period.

10-15 农村居民家庭基本情况
Basic Conditions of Rural Households

指标	Item	2018	2019	2020	2021	2022	2023
调查户数 （户）	**Survey of households (household)**	**2350**	**2350**	**2350**	**2350**	**2350**	**2350**
平均每户常住人口 （人）	Average number of residents per Permanent Household (person)	3.45	3.47	3.45	3.74	3.72	3.57
平均每户就业人口 （人）	Average Number of Employed Persons per Permanent Household (person)	1.81	1.76	1.72	1.88	1.86	1.73
人均可支配收入 （元）	**Per Capita Disposable Income (yuan)**	**17167.7**	**18818.4**	**20143.4**	**22306.0**	**23597.8**	**25141.8**
1.工资性收入	Income of Wages and Salaries	8510.7	9698.7	10613.5	12765.0	13560.2	14473.8
2.经营净收入	Net Business Income	4432.7	4446.9	4584.9	5438.8	5759.3	6100.6
3.财产净收入	Income from Properties	448.9	541.0	616.1	795.3	868.8	952.2
4.转移净收入	Income from Transfers	3775.5	4131.7	4328.9	3306.8	3409.5	3615.2
人均消费支出 （元）	**Per Capita Consumption Expenditure (yuan)**	**15411.3**	**16949.4**	**17132.3**	**20011.8**	**20800.0**	**22209.1**
1.食品烟酒	Food,Tobacco and Liquor	5641.2	6289.3	6991.8	7867.4	8393.1	8342.1
2.衣着	Clothing	523.6	552.0	506.9	721.4	694.0	639.1
3.居住	Living	3355.8	3707.4	3829.2	4722.4	4782.7	5263.1
4.生活用品及服务	Daily Necessities and Services	817.0	817.9	803.2	1014.2	992.5	921.6
5.交通通信	Transportation and Telecommunication	1930.4	2139.8	1958.1	2222.9	2471.2	2934.4
6.教育文化娱乐	Education,Culture and Entertainment	1473.0	1602.7	1275.5	1789.4	1881.0	2140.8
7.医疗保健	Health Service	1366.7	1520.7	1517.9	1342.2	1219.6	1560.9
8.其他用品和服务	Other Necessities and Services	303.6	319.8	249.8	331.8	365.9	407.0
消费支出构成 （%）	**Composition of Consumption Expenditure**	**100.0**	**100.0**	**100.0**	**100.0**	**100.0**	**100.0**
1.食品烟酒	Food,Tobacco and Liquor	36.6	37.1	40.8	39.3	40.3	37.6
2.衣着	Clothing	3.4	3.3	3.0	3.6	3.3	2.9
3.居住	Living	21.8	21.9	22.3	23.6	23.0	23.7
4.生活用品及服务	Daily Necessities and Services	5.3	4.8	4.7	5.1	4.8	4.2
5.交通通信	Transportation and Telecommunication	12.5	12.6	11.4	11.1	11.9	13.2
6.教育文化娱乐	Education,Culture and Entertainment	9.6	9.5	7.4	8.9	9.0	9.6
7.医疗保健	Health Service	8.9	9.0	8.9	6.7	5.9	7.0
8.其他用品和服务	Other Necessities and Services	2.0	1.9	1.5	1.7	1.8	1.8

注：2013年起为新口径数据。
Note: Since 2013, the relative data of rural households have been calculated according to the new standard.

10–16 历年农村居民人均纯收入及生活消费支出（1978–2012年）

Per Capita Income and Consumption Expenditure of Rural Households (1978-2012)

年份 Year	人均纯收入（元） Per Capita Net Income (yuan)	指数 Index			人均消费支出（元） Per Capita Living Expenditure (yuan)	指数 Index		恩格尔系数（%） Engle Coefficient (%)
		名义增长（上年为100） Nominal Growth (Preceding year=100)	实际增长（上年为100） Real Growth (Preceding year=100)	实际增长（1978年为100） Real Growth (1978=100)		名义增长（上年为100） Nominal Growth (Preceding year=100)	实际增长（上年为100） Real Growth (Preceding year=100)	
1978	193.3	107.9		100.0	184.9	97.4		61.7
1979	222.7	115.2	113.6	113.6	205.2	111.0	110.1	59.9
1980	274.4	123.2	119.4	135.6	222.2	108.3	103.9	60.4
1981	325.4	118.6	111.4	151.1	266.1	119.7	112.1	59.3
1982	381.8	117.3	112.7	170.3	312.4	117.4	116.2	58.4
1983	395.9	103.7	107.0	182.2	328.8	105.2	106.3	60.3
1984	425.3	107.4	107.2	195.3	346.2	105.3	105.0	59.3
1985	495.3	116.5	109.8	214.5	388.0	112.1	105.7	60.4
1986	546.4	110.3	107.6	230.8	454.1	117.0	111.1	58.8
1987	662.2	121.2	111.1	256.4	545.3	120.1	109.5	57.3
1988	808.7	122.1	102.7	263.3	684.7	125.6	103.2	55.2
1989	955.0	118.1	102.0	268.6	870.6	127.2	107.3	53.7
1990	1043.0	109.2	101.6	272.9	932.6	107.1	99.7	57.7
1991	1143.1	109.6	109.4	298.5	942.4	101.1	101.2	57.4
1992	1307.7	114.4	110.4	329.6	1060.3	112.5	108.8	54.0
1993	1674.8	128.1	106.1	349.7	1391.0	131.2	106.8	52.8
1994	2181.5	130.3	103.8	363.0	1882.0	135.3	103.6	55.6
1995	2699.2	123.7	106.5	386.6	2255.0	119.8	105.3	54.5
1996	3183.5	117.9	107.6	415.9	2584.2	114.6	106.9	51.6
1997	3467.7	108.9	104.2	433.4	2617.7	101.3	100.3	52.3
1998	3527.1	101.7	103.4	448.2	2683.2	102.5	103.8	51.1
1999	3628.9	102.9	106.2	475.9	2645.9	98.6	101.7	50.7
2000	3654.5	100.7	100.9	480.2	2646.0	100.0	100.0	49.8
2001	3769.8	103.2	103.5	497.0	2703.4	102.2	102.5	49.9
2002	3911.9	103.8	105.1	522.4	2825.0	104.5	106.0	47.6
2003	4054.6	103.6	103.4	540.1	2927.4	103.6	103.4	47.9
2004	4365.9	107.7	104.0	561.8	3240.8	110.7	106.7	48.8
2005	4690.5	107.4	104.5	587.0	3707.7	114.4	111.4	48.3
2006	5079.8	108.3	106.4	624.6	3886.0	104.8	103.2	48.6
2007	5624.0	110.7	106.5	665.5	4202.3	108.1	104.5	49.7
2008	6399.8	113.8	107.6	715.8	4873.0	115.9	109.6	49.0
2009	6906.9	107.9	110.7	792.4	5019.8	103.0	105.3	48.3
2010	7890.3	114.2	110.3	874.0	5515.6	109.9	106.5	47.7
2011	9371.7	118.8	111.9	978.0	6725.6	121.9	115.5	49.1
2012	10542.8	112.5	109.3	1069.0	7458.6	110.9	107.8	49.1

注：本表数据来源于2013年之前分别开展的城镇住户调查和农村住户调查。

Note: The data shown in the table are compiled on the basis of the urban and rural household surveys before year 2013.

10-17 全省农村居民人均主要食品消费量

Per Capita Consumption of Major Foods of Rural Households

单位:千克 (Kg)

指 标	Item	2018	2019	2020	2021	2022	2023
粮食	Grain	140.98	149.44	171.99	150.91	144.76	142.05
谷物	Cereal	133.41	139.86	160.93	142.35	136.38	132.71
薯类	Tuber	1.56	1.52	1.32	1.05	1.05	1.32
豆类	Beans and the Products	6.02	8.05	9.74	7.50	7.33	8.02
油脂类	Oil and Fats	11.34	10.40	11.76	12.75	11.94	11.35
#植物油	Vegetable Oil	10.37	9.56	11.06	11.78	11.15	10.71
蔬菜及菜制品	Vegetable and Mushroom	105.04	106.80	111.45	106.24	112.01	117.46
#鲜菜	Fresh Vegetables	102.29	103.70	108.25	103.75	109.76	114.86
肉类	Products of Meat	41.62	37.14	31.92	39.93	47.28	56.85
#猪肉	Pork	36.12	31.06	26.32	33.39	40.06	48.08
禽类	Poultry	23.87	30.49	38.04	30.62	29.17	29.75
#鸡	Chick	15.25	18.68	22.88	19.23	18.37	18.45
水产品	Aquatic Products	19.79	26.64	29.86	24.81	24.67	29.58
#鱼类	Fresh	15.47	20.73	23.56	18.70	17.94	22.03
蛋类及蛋制品	Eggs ang Egg Products	6.96	7.73	9.14	8.13	8.62	9.76
#鲜蛋	Fresh Eggs	6.78	7.50	8.92	7.92	8.45	9.56
奶及奶制品	Milk and Dairy Products	3.99	4.48	4.72	7.97	5.39	5.07
#鲜奶	Fresh Milk	2.16	2.72	3.14	5.88	3.87	3.59
鲜瓜果	Fresh Melons and Fruits	23.83	29.16	30.81	33.18	34.41	33.30
食糖	Sugar	1.90	1.88	1.87	1.33	1.26	1.11

10-18 全省农村居民平均每百户年末主要耐用品拥有量

Main Durable Consumer Goods Owned per 100 Rural Households at the Year-end

项 目	Item	2018	2019	2020	2021	2022	2023
家用汽车 (辆)	Car (set)	22.73	26.01	27.69	31.84	36.93	44.23
摩托车 (辆)	Motorcycle (set)	116.73	116.58	115.45	110.87	109.43	93.17
助力车 (台)	Electric Bicycle (set)	35.84	40.49	42.42	56.40	60.22	70.87
洗衣机 (台)	Washing Machine (set)	84.71	89.98	90.32	96.62	97.18	98.58
电冰箱(柜) (台)	Refrigerator (set)	92.94	97.00	97.48	102.86	103.27	104.11
微波炉 (台)	Microwave Oven (set)	27.01	29.09	29.52	34.33	34.81	30.85
彩色电视机 (台)	Color Television (set)	116.51	116.47	115.93	112.01	112.65	109.63
空调 (台)	Air Conditioner (set)	113.53	129.63	132.71	173.09	177.77	185.26
热水器 (台)	Water Heater (unit)	94.02	97.99	101.70	101.59	103.20	103.76
排油烟机 (台)	Fume hood (set)	49.07	52.12	53.62	58.82	59.68	61.53
移动电话 (部)	Mobile Phone (set)	290.44	286.34	277.85	293.90	296.27	289.26
计算机 (台)	Computer (set)	35.29	38.45	39.75	36.02	36.14	32.15
照相机 (台)	Camera (set)	4.88	4.38	3.60	2.65	3.11	4.21

10−19 各市农村居民人均可支配收入

Per Capita Disposal Income of Rural Households by City

单位：元 (yuan)

市别	City	2018	2019	2020	2021	2022	2023
全省	**Provincial Total**	**17167.7**	**18818.4**	**20143.4**	**22306.0**	**23597.8**	**25141.8**
广州	Guangzhou	26020.1	28867.9	31266.3	34533.3	36292.3	38606.7
深圳	Shenzhen						
珠海	Zhuhai	26198.4	29069.3	31118.6	34394.0	35828.6	38025.2
汕头	Shantou	16246.1	17735.3	18962.5	20819.2	22056.8	22969.9
佛山	Foshan	28764.7	31503.4	33440.2	37067.0	38971.3	41423.4
韶关	Shaoguan	15433.7	16940.1	18288.7	20252.9	21234.3	22603.3
河源	Heyuan	14620.3	16030.3	17313.4	19146.3	20189.6	21875.0
梅州	Meizhou	15173.3	16447.2	17430.1	19241.2	20289.6	21706.9
惠州	Huizhou	21039.1	23027.4	24925.1	27580.0	28963.7	30530.0
汕尾	Shanwei	14851.5	16304.7	17732.3	19884.5	21226.8	22741.3
东莞	Dongguan	32276.9	35904.5	38827.2	43187.8	45135.8	46864.7
中山	Zhongshan	32263.3	35121.6	37632.8	41749.9	43490.2	45770.2
江门	Jiangmen	18153.6	19873.3	21129.4	23376.4	24742.2	26130.0
阳江	Yangjiang	16799.1	18331.9	19981.8	22195.6	23431.1	24657.1
湛江	Zhanjiang	15888.9	17343.0	18758.2	20692.7	21713.2	22762.0
茂名	Maoming	16950.8	18482.2	19621.2	21561.2	22444.0	23856.2
肇庆	Zhaoqing	17695.7	19217.0	20627.5	22688.7	23653.4	24808.8
清远	Qingyuan	15162.9	16523.8	17881.3	19841.2	20803.4	22099.3
潮州	Chaozhou	14944.5	16359.6	17265.7	19133.6	20274.8	21721.5
揭阳	Jieyang	14421.7	15675.4	16311.9	18015.8	18959.3	19846.7
云浮	Yunfu	15240.3	16646.2	17776.9	19675.1	20786.9	21908.7
按经济区域分	By Region						
珠三角	Pearl River Delta	22805.6	25025.8	26856.5	30464.7	31956.7	33682.3
粤东	Eastern Region	15013.2	16386.8	17357.1	19211.4	20335.4	21422.9
粤西	Western Region	16434.7	17932.4	19267.8	21261.0	22254.3	23478.8
粤北	Northern Region	15111.5	16490.8	17698.0	19599.6	20627.7	22007.6

注：1.按照国家统计局的统一部署广东省分市县城乡一体化住户调查工作从2013年底正式启动，从2014年开始正式对外发布分市农村居民人均可支配收入数据，不再发布分市农村居民人均纯收入数据，这两项收入指标数据在调查范围、调查方法和统计口径上均有一定变化，不完全可比。

2.深圳因完全城市化，无相关数据。

Note: a)Under the unified deployment by NBS, Guangdong province started an integrated household survey by city and county since the end of the 2013, including both urban and rural households. Since 2014 the data of per capita disposal income and expenditures of all households in the province by city is released officially after the transitional period. The coverage, methodology and definitions used in the integrated rural survey are different from the survey prior to 2013, therefore the disposable income of rural household of 2014 are different from the net income of rural household prior to 2013.

b)There is no data of Shenzhen city due to its totally urbanization.

10-20 各市农村居民人均可支配收入来源（2023年）

Per Capita Disposable Income of Rural Households by Sources and City(2023)

单位：元 (yuan)

地区	City	可支配收入 Disposable Income	工资性收入 Income of Wages and Salaries	经营净收入 Net Business Income	财产净收入 Net Income from Property	转移净收入 Net Income from Transfer
全省	**Provincial Total**	**25141.8**	**14473.8**	**6100.6**	**952.2**	**3615.2**
广州	Guangzhou	38606.7	28286.7	4445.8	3908.3	1965.9
深圳	Shenzhen					
珠海	Zhuhai	38025.2	25304.8	6019.6	4088.0	2612.8
汕头	Shantou	22969.9	16852.1	2713.4	626.3	2778.1
佛山	Foshan	41423.4	27006.9	6458.6	5676.6	2281.3
韶关	Shaoguan	22603.3	10810.0	7830.8	920.0	3042.5
河源	Heyuan	21875.0	12054.0	4991.0	236.0	4594.0
梅州	Meizhou	21706.9	11078.3	4865.5	60.6	5702.5
惠州	Huizhou	30530.0	18343.2	7865.6	1676.9	2644.3
汕尾	Shanwei	22741.3	13355.0	5227.4	232.7	3926.1
东莞	Dongguan	46864.7	38210.7	4081.0	5094.7	-521.7
中山	Zhongshan	45770.2	31586.0	5767.0	5304.8	3112.4
江门	Jiangmen	26130.0	19233.2	3449.1	1123.7	2324.0
阳江	Yangjiang	24657.1	12496.7	8795.6	138.8	3226.0
湛江	Zhanjiang	22762.0	10595.2	6346.3	250.9	5569.5
茂名	Maoming	23856.2	11553.3	3979.5	675.4	7648.1
肇庆	Zhaoqing	24808.8	13651.3	6423.0	616.3	4118.3
清远	Qingyuan	22099.3	11912.0	6517.3	327.2	3342.8
潮州	Chaozhou	21721.5	12191.5	6708.2	90.7	2731.0
揭阳	Jieyang	19846.7	11733.8	4073.7	89.3	3949.9
云浮	Yunfu	21908.7	14093.0	4689.7	33.9	3092.1

10-21 全省各市农村居民人均消费支出

Per Capita Consumption Expenditure of Rural Households by City

单位：元 (yuan)

市 别	City	2018	2019	2020	2021	2022	2023
全 省	**Provincial Total**	**15411.3**	**16949.4**	**17132.3**	**20011.8**	**20800.0**	**22209.1**
广 州	Guangzhou	20633.9	22521.9	22990.1	26099.2	26229.7	27960.9
深 圳	Shenzhen						
珠 海	Zhuhai	20474.7	22573.0	22498.4	26928.2	26389.0	26701.3
汕 头	Shantou	14054.2	15373.1	15743.2	16914.0	17267.0	18186.3
佛 山	Foshan	19905.6	21822.5	22258.9	25035.2	25861.4	27585.1
韶 关	Shaoguan	12719.5	13864.3	14271.2	16306.6	16375.7	17309.9
河 源	Heyuan	12438.4	13437.2	13990.0	16020.0	16656.2	17822.0
梅 州	Meizhou	13221.5	14145.7	14515.1	16285.3	16940.3	17990.6
惠 州	Huizhou	16900.2	18387.4	18118.6	20462.9	20879.3	21494.0
汕 尾	Shanwei	12258.2	13422.8	14191.6	15443.0	16557.8	18025.7
东 莞	Dongguan	25354.5	27720.6	26890.2	30583.7	31124.8	32111.3
中 山	Zhongshan	22603.3	24750.6	24824.9	29243.7	30355.0	31113.9
江 门	Jiangmen	13041.6	13643.5	14727.1	16422.2	16853.1	18085.8
阳 江	Yangjiang	13656.4	14603.2	14888.4	17623.3	18276.2	19124.0
湛 江	Zhanjiang	11732.8	12730.1	13071.1	15180.8	15426.9	16207.5
茂 名	Maoming	13487.4	14450.9	15045.5	16453.4	17059.1	17928.3
肇 庆	Zhaoqing	11358.5	12510.3	12789.0	14997.4	15499.4	16421.6
清 远	Qingyuan	13047.7	14039.3	14190.8	16111.6	16443.2	17250.0
潮 州	Chaozhou	12399.6	13588.0	14322.4	15937.7	16662.8	17875.4
揭 阳	Jieyang	12138.1	12997.6	13621.7	15815.3	16821.9	17257.4
云 浮	Yunfu	11761.9	12867.5	12801.6	14382.1	14984.8	15667.4

注：按照国家统计局的统一部署，广东省分市县城乡一体化住户调查工作从2013年底正式启动，从2014年开始正式对外发布分市农村居民人均消费支出数据。

Note: Under the unified deployment by NBS, Guangdong province started an integrated household survey by city and county since the end of the 2013 including both urban and rural households. Since 2014 the data of per capita disposal income and expenditures of all households in the province by city is released officially after the transitional period.

10-22 全省、城镇、农村居民人均可支配收入及生活消费支出(2013-2023年)

Per Capita Disposable Income and Consumption Expenditure of Households (2013-2023)

年份 Year	人均可支配收入(元) Per Capita Disposable Income (yuan)	指数 Index 名义增长(上年为100) Nominal Growth (Preceding year=100)	指数 Index 实际增长(上年为100) Real Growth (Preceding year=100)	人均消费支出(元) Per Capita Consumption Expenditure (yuan)	指数 Index 名义增长(上年为100) Nominal Growth (Preceding year=100)	指数 Index 实际增长(上年为100) Real Growth (Preceding year=100)	恩格尔系数(%) Engle Coefficient (%)
全省居民 Provincial Household							
2013	23420.7	110.1	107.4	17421.0	108.9	106.2	35.0
2014	25685.0	109.7	107.2	19205.5	110.2	107.7	34.3
2015	27858.9	108.5	106.9	20975.7	109.2	107.6	34.5
2016	30295.8	108.7	106.3	23448.4	111.8	109.3	34.2
2017	33003.3	108.9	107.3	24819.6	105.8	104.2	33.5
2018	35809.9	108.5	106.2	26054.0	105.0	102.7	32.6
2019	39014.3	108.9	105.3	28994.7	111.3	107.6	32.3
2020	41028.6	105.2	102.5	28491.9	98.3	95.8	33.8
2021	44993.3	109.7	108.8	31589.3	110.9	110.0	33.2
2022	47064.6	104.6	102.4	32168.7	101.8	99.6	34.3
2023	49327.4	104.8	104.4	34331.5	106.7	106.3	32.4
城镇居民 Urban Household							
2013	29537.3	109.5	106.9	21621.5	107.8	105.3	33.6
2014	32148.1	108.8	106.4	23611.7	109.2	106.7	33.2
2015	34757.2	108.1	106.4	25673.1	108.7	107.0	33.2
2016	37684.3	108.4	105.9	28613.3	111.5	108.8	32.9
2017	40975.1	108.7	106.9	30197.9	105.5	103.7	32.2
2018	44341.0	108.2	105.9	30924.3	102.4	100.2	31.6
2019	48117.6	108.5	105.2	34424.1	111.3	108.0	31.2
2020	50257.0	104.4	101.8	33511.3	97.3	94.9	32.2
2021	54853.6	109.1	108.1	36621.1	109.3	108.2	31.7
2022	56905.3	103.7	101.5	36936.2	100.9	98.7	32.8
2023	59306.6	104.2	103.6	39333.3	106.5	105.9	31.2
农村居民 Rural Household							
2013	11067.8	110.7	107.8	8937.8	111.9	109.0	42.1
2014	12245.6	110.6	108.3	10043.2	112.4	110.1	39.5
2015	13360.4	109.1	107.7	11103.0	110.6	109.2	40.6
2016	14512.2	108.6	106.5	12414.8	111.8	109.6	40.4
2017	15779.7	108.7	107.8	13199.6	106.3	105.5	40.2
2018	17167.7	108.8	106.8	15411.3	116.8	114.6	36.6
2019	18818.4	109.6	104.8	16949.4	110.0	105.2	37.1
2020	20143.4	107.0	103.9	17132.3	101.1	98.1	40.8
2021	22306.0	110.7	110.6	20011.8	116.8	116.7	39.3
2022	23597.8	105.8	103.4	20800.0	103.9	101.6	40.3
2023	25141.8	106.5	107.0	22209.1	106.8	107.3	37.6

注：本表数据来源于自2013年起开展的城乡一体化住户收支和生活状况调查。

Notes: The data shown in the table are compiled on the basis of the integrated household income and expenditure survey carried out since 2013, including both urban and rural households.

主要统计指标解释

一、城乡一体化住户收支与生活状况调查指标解释

从2012年四季度起，国家统计局对分别进行的城乡住户调查实施了一体化改革，规范了城乡划分范围，统一了城乡居民收入指标名称、分类和统计标准，建立了城乡统一的一体化住户调查，并据此采集全国居民有关数据。

（一）居民可支配收入

居民可支配收入指居民可用于最终消费支出和储蓄的总和，即居民可用于自由支配的收入。既包括现金收入，也包括实物收入。按照收入的来源，可支配收入包含四项，分别为：工资性收入、经营净收入、财产净收入和转移净收入。

工资性收入 指就业人员通过各种途径得到的全部劳动报酬和各种福利，包括受雇于单位或个人、从事各种自由职业、兼职和零星劳动得到的全部劳动报酬和福利。

经营净收入 指住户或住户成员从事生产经营活动所获得的净收入，是全部经营收入中扣除经营费用、生产性固定资产折旧和生产税之后得到的净收入。计算公式为：

经营净收入=经营收入-经营费用-生产性固定资产折旧-生产税

财产净收入 指住户或住户成员将其所拥有的金融资产、住房等非金融资产和自然资源交由其他机构单位、住户或个人支配而获得的回报并扣除相关的费用之后得到的净收入。财产净收入包括利息净收入、红利收入、储蓄性保险净收益、转让承包土地经营权租金净收入、出租房屋净收入、出租其他资产净收入和自有住房折算净租金等。财产净收入不包括转让资产所有权的溢价所得。

转移净收入 计算公式为：转移净收入=转移性收入-转移性支出

转移性收入 指国家、单位、社会团体对住户的各种经常性转移支付和住户之间的经常性收入转移。包括养老金或退休金、社会救济和补助、政策性生产补贴、政策性生活补贴、救灾款、经常性捐赠和赔偿、报销医疗费、住户之间的赡养收入，本住户非常住成员寄回带回的收入等。转移性收入不包括住户之间的实物馈赠。

转移性支出 指调查户对国家、单位、住户或个人的经常性或义务性转移支付。包括缴纳的税款、各项社会保障支出、赡养支出、经常性捐赠和赔偿支出以及其他经常转移支出等。

（二）居民消费支出

居民消费支出是指居民用于满足家庭日常生活消费需要的全部支出，既包括现金消费支出，也包括实物消费支出。消费支出可划分为食品烟酒、衣着、居住、生活用品及服务、交通通信、教育文化娱乐、医疗保健以及其他用品及服务八大类。

食品烟酒 指用于各种食品和烟草、酒类的支出。

衣着 指与居民穿着有关的支出，包括服装、服装材料、鞋类、其他衣类及配件、衣着相关加工服务的支出。

居住 指与居住有关的支出，包括房租、水、电、燃料、物业管理等方面的支出，也包括自有住房折算租金。

生活用品及服务 指家庭及个人的各类生活品及家庭服务。包括家具及室内装饰品、家用器具、家用纺织品、家庭日用杂品、个人用品和家庭服务。

交通通信 指用于交通和通信工具及相关的各种服务费、维修费和车辆保险等支出。

教育文化娱乐 指用于教育和文化娱乐方面的支出。

医疗保健 指用于医疗和保健的药品、用品和服务的总费用。包括医疗器具及药品，以及医疗服务。

其他用品及服务 指无法直接归入上述各类支出的其他用品与服务支出。

二、2012 年及以前的分城镇和农村住户调查指标解释

2012 年及以前年份，中国的住户调查一直分城乡分别开展。由于分别调查，农村与城镇居民收入、支出等指标的统计口径有所不同，数据也不完全可比，城镇调查城镇居民可支配收入，农村调查农村居民纯收入。城镇居民收入与支出数据，指现金收入或现金支出，不包括实物收支；其中，计算城镇居民人均可支配收入和消费支出时，不包括自有住房折算租金，也不包括购建房支出。农村居民收入与支出数据，分为总收支和现金收支，即农村居民的总收支部分包括了自产自用的实物收支；其中，计算农村居民人均纯收入和消费支出时，也不包括自有住房折算租金，但农村居民居住消费支出中，包括了购建房支出。为了保持历史数据的可比，本年鉴中 2012 年及以前年份的数据和指标解释仍保持了原城镇住户调查和农村住户调查方案的原貌。

（一）城镇住户调查

城镇家庭人口 指居住在一起，经济上合在一起共同生活的家庭成员。凡计算为家庭人口的成员其全部收支都包括在本家庭中。

城镇居民家庭可支配收入 指家庭成员得到可用于最终消费支出和其他非义务性支出以及储蓄的总和，即居民家庭可以用来自由支配的收入。它是家庭总收入扣除交纳的个人所得税、个人交纳的社会保障支出以及记账补贴后的收入。计算公式为：

城镇居民家庭可支配收入=家庭总收入-交纳个人所得税-个人交纳的社会保障支出-记账补贴

（二）农村住户调查

农村住户 指农村常住户。农村常住户指长期(一年以上)居住在乡镇(不包括城关镇)行政管理区域内的住户，以及长期居住在城关镇所辖行政村范围内的农村住户。户口不在本地而在本地居住一年及以上的住户也包括在本地农村常住户范围内；有本地户口，但举家外出谋生一年以上的住户，无论是否保留承包耕地都不包括在本地农村住户范围内。

农村居民家庭纯收入 指农村住户当年从各个来源得到的总收入相应地扣除所发生的费用后的收入总和。计算公式为：

农村居民家庭纯收入=总收入-家庭经营费用支出-税费支出-生产性固定资产折旧-赠送农村内部亲友

纯收入主要用于再生产投入和当年生活消费支出，也可用于储蓄和各种非义务性支出。“农民人均纯收入”是按人口平均的纯收入水平，反映的是一个地区农村居民的平均收入水平。

Explanatory Notes on Main Statistical Indicators

Ⅰ. Integrated Urban and Rural Households Survey on Income and Expenditures and Living Conditions

Since the fourth quarter of 2012, the NBS has launched its reform on the household survey programme, to form an integrated survey, instead of the two separate urban and rural household surveys. The reform regulates the division of urban and rural areas, integrates the concepts, classifications and standards, conducts the integrated household survey, and collects household data in the whole country thereafter.

1. Disposable Income of Households

Disposable Income of Households refers to the income of households for purpose of final expenditure and savings. It includes income both in cash and in kind. By sources of income, disposable income includes four categories: income from wages and salaries, net business income, net income from properties and net income from transfer.

Income from Wages and Salaries refers to remuneration of labour and salaries from all kinds of sources, including those employed by other units or individuals, freelance work, part-time jobs, and sporadic labour.

Net Business Income refers to net income earned by households and their members engaged in production and business activities. It refers to the net income of operating revenue minus operating costs, depreciation of productive fixed assets, and production tax. The formula is:

Net Business Income=Operating Revenue-Operating Costs-Depreciation of Productive Fixed Assets-Production Tax

Net Income from Properties refers to the net income received as returns by households or members of financial assets, non-financial assets such as housing, to other institutions, households or individuals, and minus relevant costs. Net income from properties includes net income of interest, bonus income, net income of saving insurance, net income of rents of transferring management right of contract land, income of renting housing, income of renting other assets, net converted rents of self-owned housing. Net income from properties do not include premium of transferring ownership of assets.

Net Income from Transfer The formula is:

Net Income from Transfer=Income from Transfers-Expenditure from Transfer

Income from Transfer refers to the regular transfer from country, institutions, social communities to households and between households. It includes old-age and retirement pension, disaster relief funds, regular donation and compensation, applying for medical fees, supporting income between households, income from non-usual-residing members of households, etc. Income from transfer do not include presents in kinds between households.

Expenditure from Transfer refers to regular or deontic transfer from households to country, institutions, households or individuals. It includes taxes paid, expenditure of all kinds of social security, supporting expenditure, regular donation and compensation and other regular transfer expenditure, etc.

2. Consumption Expenditure of Households

Consumption Expenditure of Households refers to all expenditure of households for living expenditure to satisfy family daily living. It includes expenditure in cash and in kind. It includes eight categories: food, tobacco and liquor, clothing, residence, household facilities, articles and services, transport and communications, education, cultural and recreational activities, health care and medical services, and miscellaneous goods and services.

Food, Tobacco and Liquor refers to expenditure for food, tobacco and liquor of all kinds.

Clothing refers to expenditure related to clothing, including clothes, clothing materials, footwear, other clothing and accessories, processing services related to clothing.

Residence refers to expenditure related to residence, including housing rents, water, electricity, fuel, property management, and including converted self-owned housing rents.

Household Facilities, Articles and Services refers to expenditure for family and individual articles for living purpose and family services. It includes furniture and interior decoration, home appliances, home textiles, household miscellaneous daily articles, personal articles, and family services.

Transport and Communications refers to expenditure for transport and communication and related services, maintenance and repairs, and vehicle insurance.

Education, Cultural and Recreational Activities refers to expenditure on education, cultural and recreational activities.

Health Care and Medical Services refers to expenditure on drugs, supplies and services of medical and health care. It includes medical appliances and drugs, and medical services.

Miscellaneous Goods and Services refers to expenditure of all kinds of expenditure of other articles and services that can not divided into the category above.

II. Explanatory on Indicators before 2012

Prior to 2012, household surveys in China were conducted separately in urban and rural areas. Statistical coverage of indicators of household income and expenditure of urban and rural households were different, data were not comparable completely. Disposable income was surveyed in urban households, and net income was surveyed in rural households. Income and expenditure of urban households refer to that in cash, not including physical payments. Among which, when calculating per capita disposable income and consumption, self-owned housing conversion rental is not included, and expenditure of purchasing housing is not included either. Income and expenditure of rural households are divided into that of total and in cash, that is, total income and expenditure include self occupied physical payments. Among which, when computing per capita net income and expenditure of rural households, self-owned housing conversion rental is not included, but purchasing of housing is included in consumption expenditure of rural households.

For comparable reason, data prior to 2012 in this yearbook were still original urban households and rural households survey.

1. Urban Household Survey

Population of Urban Households refer to members of households living and sharing economically together in the urban areas. All the income and expenditure of all the members of such households are included in the income and expenditure of the household.

Disposable Income of Urban Households refers to the actual income at the disposal of members of the households which can be used for final consumption, other non-compulsory expenditure and savings. This equals to total income minus income tax, personal contribution to social security and subsidy for keeping diaries in being a sample household. The following formula is used:

Disposable Income of Urban Households= total household income - income tax - personal contribution to social security - subsidy for keeping diaries for a sampled household

2. Rural Household Survey

Rural Households refer to usual resident households in rural areas. Usual resident households in rural areas are households residing on a long term basis(for more than one year) in the areas under the administration of township governments (not including county towns), and in the areas under the administration of villages in county towns. Households residing in the current addresses for over one year with their household registration in other places are still considered as resident households of the locality. For households with their household registration in one place but all members of the households having moved away to make a living in another place for over one year, they will not be included in the rural households of the area where they are registered, irrespective of whether they still keep their contracted land.

Net Income of Rural Households refers to the total income of rural households from all sources minus all corresponding expenses. The formula for calculation is as follows:

Net income of rural households = total income - household operation expenses - taxes and fees-depreciation of fixed assets for production - gifts to rural relatives.

Net income is mainly used as input for reinvestment in production and as consumption expenditure of the year, and also used for savings and non-compulsory expenses of various forms. "Per capita net income of farmers" is the level of net income averaged by population, reflecting the average income level of rural population in a given area.

十一、农业

AGRICULTURE

十一　农业

简要说明

一、本篇资料反映广东省农业生产和农村经济的基本情况。内容主要包括农业产值、主要产品产量、农业自然灾害等方面的统计资料。

二、本篇资料主要由广东省统计局农村社会经济统计处，国家统计局广东调查总队农业调查处、农村调查处整理提供。

三、本篇资料根据国家统计局农业统计报表制度填报，统计范围包括各市县区各种经济类型的全部农林牧渔业生产活动。

四、根据《全国农业普查条例》，本篇资料的 1996 年部分数据以第一次全国农业普查结果为基础做了调整，2006 年部分数据以第二次全国农业普查结果为基础做了调整，2007-2017 年部分数据以第三次全国农业普查结果为基础做了调整。

11 Agriculture

Brief Introduction

Ⅰ.The data in this chapter show the basic conditions of agricultural production and rural economy in Guangdong Province, including mainly rural labor force, output value of agriculture, output of major products, as well as statistics on natural disasters in agriculture enterprises.

Ⅱ.The data in this chapter are mainly prepared and provided by the rural social and Economic Statistics Department of the Guangdong Provincial Bureau of statistics, the agricultural investigation department and the rural investigation department of the Guangdong Survey Corps of the National Bureau of Statistics.

Ⅲ.This data is filled according to the agricultural statistical reporting system of the National Bureau of Statistics, and the statistical scope includes all agricultural, forestry, animal husbandry and fishery production activities of various economic types in cities, counties and districts.

Ⅳ. Some data of 1996 in this chapter are adjusted in accordance with the regulations of the first national agricultural census，some data of 2006 in this chapter are adjusted in accordance with the regulations of the second national agricultural census， some data from 2007-2017 in this chapter are adjusted in accordance with the regulations of the third national agricultural census.

11-1 农业主要指标

Main Indicators of Agriculture

指 标	Item	2000	2010	2015	2021	2022	2023
化肥施用量(折纯)(万吨)	Consumption of Chemical Fertilizers (100 percent equivalent,10000 tons)	176.20	233.42	238.17	212.87	208.74	206.79
#氮肥	Nitrogenous Fertilizer	95.89	94.93	90.78	80.06	78.26	77.25
磷肥	Phosphate Fertilizer	18.36	24.75	29.03	25.98	25.19	24.80
钾肥	Potash Fertilizer	35.84	46.74	47.00	40.80	40.21	39.95
农药使用量 (万吨)	Consumption of Pesticides (10000 tons)	8.47	9.10	9.23	7.74	7.60	7.44
农林牧渔业总产值(亿元)	Gross Output Value of Agriculture (100 million yuan)	1701.18	3697.18	5303.63	8305.84	8892.29	9202.09
农林牧渔业增加值(亿元)	Value-added of Agriculture (100 million yuan)	1005.14	2254.49	3275.05	5151.27	5541.58	5753.60
农作物总播种面积(万亩)	Total Sown Area (10000 mu)	7735.35	6394.16	6291.83	6747.53	6830.20	6880.91
粮食作物	Grain Corps	4649.83	3579.49	3289.94	3319.55	3345.43	3344.26
经济作物	Economics Corps	2940.05	2814.67	3001.88	3427.98	3484.77	3536.65
人工造林面积 (万亩)	Afforested Area in Barren Mountains(10000 mu)	25.76	142.72	177.69	29.61	15.48	22.37
主要产品产量 (万吨)	Output of Major Products (10000 tons)						
粮食	Grain	1822.33	1249.15	1211.66	1279.87	1291.54	1285.19
糖蔗	Sugarcane	1137.59	1064.09	1093.58	1118.20	1107.76	1087.43
花生	Peanuts	77.68	81.59	94.48	115.87	115.93	119.54
烟叶	Tobacco	6.21	5.00	4.52	3.88	3.71	3.74
蔬菜	Vegetables	2214.80	2550.50	2994.65	3855.73	3999.11	4099.33
园林水果	Fruits	643.52	1049.21	1298.52	1826.73	1895.18	1991.87
水产品	Aquatic Products	593.19	729.03	803.71	884.52	894.03	924.02
猪肉	Pork	206.85	285.14	296.31	263.23	279.81	298.00

注：1.2004年起粮食播种面积含大豆，下表同。
2.经济作物包括甘蔗、油料作物、麻类、烟叶、中草药材、蔬菜、瓜果类、其他农作物，下表同。
3.2023年农林牧渔业增加值为快报数。

Notes: a) Since 2004, the sown area of grain has included that of soybeans. The same applies to the following tables.
b) Economics crops include sugarcane, oil crops, hemp, tobacco leaves, chinese herbal medicine vegetables, melons and fruits, and other crops, the same below.
c) In 2023, the Value-added of Agriculture is the result of express report.

11-2 各市农村基层组织情况（2023年）
Basic Conditions of Rural Grassroots Units by City (2023)

市别	City	乡镇个数（个）Number of Townships (unit)	村民委员会个数（个）Number of Villagers' Committees (unit)
全省	**Provincial Total**	**1123**	**19436**
广州	Guangzhou	34	1145
深圳	Shenzhen		
珠海	Zhuhai	15	122
汕头	Shantou	30	558
佛山	Foshan	21	329
韶关	Shaoguan	95	1207
河源	Heyuan	95	1251
梅州	Meizhou	104	2048
惠州	Huizhou	49	1043
汕尾	Shanwei	40	728
东莞	Dongguan	28	350
中山	Zhongshan	15	150
江门	Jiangmen	61	1056
阳江	Yangjiang	38	710
湛江	Zhanjiang	84	1638
茂名	Maoming	86	1628
肇庆	Zhaoqing	88	1255
清远	Qingyuan	80	1031
潮州	Chaozhou	41	894
揭阳	Jieyang	64	1446
云浮	Yunfu	55	847
按经济区域分	By Region		
珠三角	Pearl River Delta	311	5450
粤东	Eastern Region	175	3626
粤西	Western Region	208	3976
粤北	Northern Region	429	6384

11-3 农业生产条件

Agricultural Production Basic Conditions

指 标	Item	2020	2021	2022	2023
农业机械化情况	**Mechanization of Agriculture**				
农业机械总动力 (万千瓦)	Total Agricultural Machinery Power (10 000 kw)	2495.43	2524.48	2556.34	2586.04
机耕面积 (千公顷)	Total Area Cultivated Using Machinery (10 000 hectares)	3825.98	3877.57	3980.79	4091.52
机播面积 (千公顷)	Total Area Sown Using Machinery (1 000 hectares)	504.99	616.27	721.93	900.98
农用物资使用情况	**Use of Agricultural Materials**				
化肥施用量(折纯量) (万吨)	Consumption of Chemical Fertilizers(pure) (10 000 tons)	219.80	212.87	208.74	206.79
农用塑料薄膜使用量 (万吨)	Plastic Agricultural Film Used (10 000 tons)	4.26	4.30	4.53	4.35
农用柴油使用量 (万吨)	Diesel Used in Agriculture (10 000 tons)	85.81	85.42	85.99	86.23
农药使用量 (万吨)	Consumption of Pesticides (10 000 tons)	8.32	7.74	7.60	7.44
农田水利情况	**Agricultural Water Conservation**				
耕地灌溉面积 (千公顷)	Irrigated Area of Cultivated Land (10 000 hectares)	1776.46	1776.46	1529.21	1560.24
高效节水灌溉建设任务 (千公顷)	Construction task of efficient and water-saving irrigation (10 000 hectares)	5.34	7.39	3.61	4.11
除涝面积 (千公顷)	Areas with Flood Prevention Measures (10 000 hectares)	543.82	552.74	535.06	536.93
新增水土流失治理面积 (千公顷)	Areas Newly Treated for Water and Soil Erosion (10 000 hectares)	95.63	80.83	86.85	80.88
堤防长度 (公里)	Total Length of Dikes (10 000 km)	31929.09	31910.76	30304.25	17625.72
堤防保护耕地面积 (千公顷)	Dike protection Area of Cultivated Land(10 000 hectares)	1135.29	1136.61	1101.76	1104.92

注：2023年起，堤防长度指标仅统计全省1至5级堤防的长度，与历史数据不可比。

Notes: Starting from 2023, the embankment length index only measures the length of level 1 to level 5 embankments in the province, which is incomparable to historical data.

11-4 农业自然灾害情况

Statistics on Agriculture Covered and Affected by Natural Disasters

项 目	Item	2000	2010	2021	2022	2023
农作物受灾面积 (万亩)	Area of Farm Crops Covered by Natural Disasters(10000 mu)	948.43	916.21	119.56	383.16	326.20
#绝收面积	Area without Output	84.14	106.45	22.61	67.79	26.88
受灾人口 (万人)	Number of Persons Covered by Natural Disasters (10000 persons)	1801.00	1197.00	96.05	442.17	448.66
紧急转移安置人口(万人)	Number of Persons Receiving Evacuation and Re-settlement (10000 persons)	27.73	71.61	0.89	25.47	29.20
因灾死亡人口 (人)	Death Toll in Natural Disasters (person)	102	177	2	19	5
因灾伤病人口 (人)	Number of Wounded Persons in Natural Disasters (person)	14454	1121	2	4	
倒塌房屋 (间)	Number of Broken Buildings (room)	27743	73666	267	6551	1497
损坏房屋 (间)	Number of Damaged Buildings (room)	74052	137066	1778	3090	5730
因灾死亡大牲畜(头、只)	Number of Large Livestock Killed in Natural Disasters (head)	62417	74002	2388	3412	21448
直接经济损失 (亿元)	Volume of Direct Economic Loss (100 million yuan)	38.20	180.01	25.59	191.77	170.19

11-5 农林牧渔业总产值

Gross Output Value of Agriculture, Forestry, Animal Husbandry and Fishery

单位：亿元 (100 million yuan)

年份 Year	农林牧渔业总产值 Total	农业产值 Farming	林业产值 Forestry	牧业产值 Animal Husbandry	渔业产值 Fishery	农林牧渔专业及辅助性活动产值 Professional and Support Activities for Agriculture, Forestry, Animal Husbandry, Fishery
1978	85.94	59.56	4.98	15.98	5.42	
1979	91.53	67.19	7.67	13.58	3.09	
1980	126.25	97.15	6.83	17.75	4.52	
1981	133.85	99.33	7.81	21.62	5.09	
1982	135.52	98.33	8.33	21.73	7.13	
1983	169.96	120.06	10.72	28.57	10.61	
1984	200.07	141.22	12.13	33.81	12.91	
1985	245.21	149.09	21.09	54.68	20.35	
1986	279.15	168.68	24.38	60.74	25.35	
1987	348.61	214.47	16.74	78.26	39.14	
1988	473.78	277.38	27.66	114.28	54.46	
1989	548.60	323.15	28.00	134.60	62.85	
1990	600.71	359.39	28.46	143.68	69.18	
1991	654.82	388.90	29.64	156.08	80.20	
1992	737.11	428.99	32.86	175.36	99.90	
1993	899.03	486.46	35.51	223.16	153.90	
1994	1151.38	628.17	41.07	279.98	202.16	
1995	1445.48	777.72	46.12	349.11	272.53	
1996	1577.89	825.60	49.64	398.12	304.53	
1997	1656.46	851.35	52.10	425.67	327.34	
1998	1705.44	861.97	54.65	441.61	347.21	
1999	1745.02	859.66	58.77	457.51	369.08	
2000	1701.18	807.94	59.64	450.18	383.42	
2001	1722.35	817.95	56.78	457.56	390.06	
2002	1781.06	841.77	57.09	465.91	416.29	
2003	1908.66	851.72	55.72	482.83	432.74	85.65
2004	2154.79	959.97	61.72	571.09	466.45	95.56
2005	2447.57	1109.18	66.25	638.61	523.79	109.74
2006	2536.27	1235.40	67.60	623.34	519.03	90.90
2007	2810.45	1268.70	116.96	781.97	540.58	102.24
2008	3276.02	1398.82	125.23	983.84	650.23	117.89
2009	3301.86	1442.40	139.95	939.67	657.65	122.18
2010	3697.18	1668.66	180.20	978.33	737.01	132.97
2011	4301.86	1910.21	213.71	1193.73	835.41	148.80
2012	4550.29	2060.91	228.75	1189.80	908.12	162.71
2013	4802.01	2229.64	256.99	1168.73	968.42	178.23
2014	5053.72	2357.16	289.66	1145.87	1068.00	193.03
2015	5303.63	2490.20	308.72	1195.97	1102.12	206.62
2016	5817.55	2763.79	330.04	1318.89	1179.15	225.68
2017	5969.87	2889.97	356.14	1202.30	1276.11	245.34
2018	6318.12	3089.57	390.62	1184.72	1383.81	269.39
2019	7175.89	3530.21	408.48	1404.13	1524.78	308.30
2020	7901.92	3769.26	414.29	1778.18	1581.54	358.64
2021	8305.84	3951.14	495.44	1707.82	1747.34	404.10
2022	8892.29	4308.23	549.15	1680.24	1898.24	456.43
2023	9202.09	4430.96	562.69	1696.79	2005.31	506.35

11-6 农林牧渔业总产值指数（1978年＝100）
Indices of Gross Output Value of Agriculture, Forestry, Animal Husbandry and Fishery (1978=100)

1978年＝100 (year of 1978=100)

年份 Year	农林牧渔业总产值 Total	农业产值 Farming	林业产值 Forestry	牧业产值 Animal Husbandry	渔业产值 Fishery	农林牧渔专业及辅助性活动产值 Professional and Support Activities for Agriculture, Forestry, Animal Husbandry, Fishery
1978	100.0	100.0	100.0	100.0	100.0	
1979	99.2	99.4	85.1	104.6	93.7	
1980	110.2	111.8	108.3	104.4	102.8	
1981	112.8	110.3	119.6	122.9	111.9	
1982	131.2	127.4	133.4	148.6	135.0	
1983	134.6	127.2	140.4	159.8	164.3	
1984	147.1	138.9	147.6	175.5	185.5	
1985	157.8	145.5	154.8	202.2	216.2	
1986	167.5	151.0	173.4	219.6	257.0	
1987	183.6	165.8	166.9	237.7	313.2	
1988	197.7	173.4	223.2	259.2	350.3	
1989	213.2	186.9	232.3	279.4	389.9	
1990	228.9	201.5	215.7	306.2	429.3	
1991	243.0	211.9	213.8	332.6	470.1	
1992	257.7	220.3	218.9	357.8	536.5	
1993	267.6	213.7	222.6	398.9	644.5	
1994	279.5	219.5	227.5	415.1	716.3	
1995	302.7	237.1	239.6	443.5	800.1	
1996	320.9	245.0	246.5	485.9	882.9	
1997	342.7	263.7	249.2	509.5	953.5	
1998	359.3	272.7	258.1	535.8	1033.7	
1999	379.1	286.8	271.8	563.9	1101.9	
2000	389.3	288.6	281.3	579.6	1184.5	
2001	400.1	295.6	294.0	592.7	1230.1	
2002	426.1	323.4	285.8	601.4	1310.6	
2003	438.2	331.6	277.8	614.8	1367.5	100.0
2004	457.9	350.5	287.2	625.9	1433.1	107.8
2005	479.9	362.3	295.5	660.4	1514.2	120.5
2006	499.1	375.2	280.8	680.7	1605.1	132.3
2007	515.5	385.5	289.1	701.2	1670.8	143.1
2008	536.1	392.4	289.9	750.8	1749.5	155.0
2009	562.9	414.3	310.6	779.3	1839.0	163.2
2010	586.9	434.2	324.5	803.9	1921.4	171.4
2011	609.9	458.6	351.1	795.6	2023.4	180.8
2012	632.7	476.3	373.0	811.3	2123.6	191.1
2013	647.0	490.9	393.7	796.8	2211.8	203.2
2014	666.4	512.8	413.2	788.5	2292.0	213.5
2015	687.0	534.0	437.6	785.6	2369.7	224.7
2016	707.1	554.6	467.1	777.7	2451.0	238.3
2017	730.8	580.3	490.1	771.7	2542.1	255.3
2018	761.2	609.8	521.8	780.5	2634.9	274.3
2019	787.7	645.5	548.4	739.9	2734.3	303.6
2020	819.3	681.8	555.1	716.3	2891.0	344.8
2021	877.7	713.7	559.4	824.6	3023.8	385.5
2022	919.5	743.7	603.3	856.7	3162.4	427.1
2023	966.8	770.0	653.0	916.8	3317.9	472.5

注：本表按可比价格计算。
Note: The indices are calculated at comparable prices.

11-7 农林牧渔业总产值指数（上年=100）

Indices of Gross Output Value of Agriculture, Forestry, Animal Husbandry and Fishery (preceding year=100)

上年=100 (preceding year=100)

年份 Year	农林牧渔业总产值 Total	农业产值 Farming	林业产值 Forestry	牧业产值 Animal Husbandry	渔业产值 Fishery	农林牧渔专业及辅助性活动产值 Professional and Support Activities for Agriculture, Forestry, Animal Husbandry, Fishery
1979	99.2	99.4	85.1	104.6	93.7	
1980	111.1	112.5	127.3	99.8	109.7	
1981	102.4	98.7	110.4	117.6	108.9	
1982	116.3	115.5	111.5	120.9	120.6	
1983	102.6	99.9	105.2	107.6	121.7	
1984	109.3	109.2	105.1	109.8	112.9	
1985	107.3	104.8	104.9	115.2	116.5	
1986	106.1	103.8	112.0	108.6	118.9	
1987	109.6	109.8	96.3	108.2	121.9	
1988	107.7	104.6	133.7	109.0	111.8	
1989	107.8	107.8	104.1	107.8	111.3	
1990	107.4	107.8	92.9	109.6	110.1	
1991	106.2	105.1	99.1	108.6	109.5	
1992	106.0	103.9	102.4	107.6	114.1	
1993	103.8	97.0	101.7	111.5	120.1	
1994	104.4	102.7	102.2	104.1	111.1	
1995	108.3	108.0	105.3	106.8	111.7	
1996	106.0	103.3	102.9	109.6	110.3	
1997	106.8	107.6	101.1	104.8	108.0	
1998	104.8	103.4	103.6	105.2	108.4	
1999	105.5	105.2	105.3	105.2	106.6	
2000	102.7	100.6	103.5	102.8	107.5	
2001	102.8	102.4	104.5	102.2	103.8	
2002	106.5	109.4	97.2	101.5	106.5	
2003	102.8	102.5	97.2	102.2	104.3	
2004	104.5	105.7	103.4	101.8	104.8	107.8
2005	104.8	103.4	102.9	105.5	105.7	111.8
2006	104.0	103.6	95.0	103.1	106.0	109.8
2007	103.3	102.7	103.0	103.0	104.1	108.2
2008	104.0	101.8	100.3	107.1	104.7	108.3
2009	105.0	105.6	107.1	103.8	105.1	105.3
2010	104.3	104.8	104.5	103.2	104.5	105.0
2011	103.9	105.6	108.2	99.0	105.3	105.5
2012	103.7	103.9	106.3	102.0	105.0	105.7
2013	102.3	103.1	105.5	98.2	104.2	106.3
2014	103.0	104.5	105.0	99.0	103.6	105.1
2015	103.1	104.1	105.9	99.6	103.4	105.2
2016	102.9	103.9	106.8	99.0	103.4	106.1
2017	103.3	104.6	104.9	99.2	103.7	107.1
2018	104.2	105.1	106.5	101.1	103.7	107.4
2019	103.5	105.8	105.1	94.8	103.8	110.7
2020	104.0	105.6	101.2	96.8	105.7	113.6
2021	107.1	104.7	100.8	115.1	104.6	111.8
2022	104.8	104.2	107.8	103.9	104.6	110.8
2023	105.1	103.5	108.2	107.0	104.9	110.6

注：本表按可比价格计算。
Note: The indices are calculated at comparable prices.

11-8 各市农林牧渔业总产值（2023年）

Gross Output Value of Farming, Forestry, Animal Husbandry and Fishery by City (2023)

单位：亿元 (100 million yuan)

市 别	City	农林牧渔业总产值 Total	农业产值 Farming	林业产值 Forestry	牧业产值 Animal Husbandry	渔业产值 Fishery	农林牧渔专业及辅助性活动产值 Professional and Support Activities for Agriculture, Forestry, Animal Husbandry, Fishery
全 省	**Provincial Total**	**9202.09**	**4430.96**	**562.69**	**1696.79**	**2005.31**	**506.35**
广 州	Guangzhou	582.79	311.84	8.12	37.51	129.91	95.40
深 圳	Shenzhen	49.96	15.78	0.78	2.17	28.78	2.45
珠 海	Zhuhai	129.78	13.24	0.25	4.09	100.57	11.63
汕 头	Shantou	267.14	129.09	0.48	35.72	83.18	18.67
佛 山	Foshan	449.21	152.12	1.38	61.82	195.56	38.34
韶 关	Shaoguan	393.21	225.10	36.65	112.23	14.07	5.15
河 源	Heyuan	268.46	151.77	47.96	56.10	7.88	4.75
梅 州	Meizhou	422.10	284.79	21.56	90.26	13.40	12.09
惠 州	Huizhou	458.28	300.14	20.60	66.60	63.27	7.66
汕 尾	Shanwei	321.52	120.69	7.64	34.96	140.14	18.10
东 莞	Dongguan	56.02	41.02	0.34	1.28	11.58	1.79
中 山	Zhongshan	154.78	52.04	0.09	2.81	96.39	3.46
江 门	Jiangmen	632.63	188.23	13.95	134.80	267.78	27.87
阳 江	Yangjiang	425.91	114.77	11.57	81.12	201.30	17.15
湛 江	Zhanjiang	1134.81	606.91	20.49	163.57	290.15	53.68
茂 名	Maoming	1153.06	608.37	97.48	261.36	142.35	43.50
肇 庆	Zhaoqing	780.54	356.28	118.29	164.58	98.95	42.44
清 远	Qingyuan	570.74	281.51	55.86	168.52	23.66	41.20
潮 州	Chaozhou	222.34	134.41	2.21	23.58	48.95	13.18
揭 阳	Jieyang	364.25	214.35	39.57	51.10	32.40	26.83
云 浮	Yunfu	364.56	128.51	57.42	142.60	15.04	20.99
按经济区域分	By Region						
珠 三 角	Pearl River Delta	3293.99	1430.68	163.80	475.67	992.79	231.05
粤 东	Eastern Region	1175.25	598.54	49.90	145.36	304.66	76.79
粤 西	Western Region	2713.79	1330.06	129.53	506.05	633.81	114.34
粤 北	Northern Region	2019.07	1071.68	219.46	569.71	74.05	84.18

注：本表按当年价格计算。
Note: Data in this table are calculated at current prices.

11-9 各市农林牧渔业总产值指数(2023年)

Indices of Gross Output Value of Agriculture,Forestry, Animal Husbandry and Fishery by City (2023)

上年=100 (preceding year=100)

市别	City	农林牧渔业总产值 Total	农业产值 Farming	林业产值 Forestry	牧业产值 Animal Husbandry	渔业产值 Fishery	农林牧渔专业及辅助性活动产值 Professional and Support Activities for Agriculture, Forestry, Animal Husbandry, Fishery
全 省	**Provincial Total**	**105.1**	**103.5**	**108.2**	**107.0**	**104.9**	**110.6**
广 州	Guangzhou	104.2	103.1	178.7	103.3	100.7	110.3
深 圳	Shenzhen	112.5	108.2	136.5	51.8	122.2	108.9
珠 海	Zhuhai	107.6	87.5	75.7	113.5	110.7	107.1
汕 头	Shantou	104.0	103.0	124.9	108.2	103.0	107.9
佛 山	Foshan	105.5	105.0	97.0	102.9	105.3	114.3
韶 关	Shaoguan	106.6	104.5	108.0	110.3	103.8	111.8
河 源	Heyuan	106.6	103.7	110.6	110.0	112.6	111.5
梅 州	Meizhou	105.9	104.5	114.5	108.6	101.1	109.5
惠 州	Huizhou	106.5	104.8	130.7	108.5	105.1	114.2
汕 尾	Shanwei	104.9	103.1	100.8	106.3	105.7	110.5
东 莞	Dongguan	103.5	103.3	129.5	103.8	103.3	106.4
中 山	Zhongshan	105.4	104.1	105.0	87.6	106.7	106.6
江 门	Jiangmen	107.1	105.5	108.8	112.2	104.8	116.0
阳 江	Yangjiang	103.3	99.0	97.9	111.4	102.3	110.7
湛 江	Zhanjiang	103.2	101.1	100.0	107.5	104.5	109.6
茂 名	Maoming	104.5	104.3	108.6	103.1	103.4	112.5
肇 庆	Zhaoqing	104.8	103.4	106.1	106.5	103.7	109.5
清 远	Qingyuan	106.2	104.1	107.5	108.4	107.0	108.5
潮 州	Chaozhou	105.3	105.2	109.4	104.5	104.2	110.4
揭 阳	Jieyang	105.0	103.7	106.7	106.5	104.8	110.5
云 浮	Yunfu	106.0	104.7	107.2	106.7	100.4	109.6
按经济区域分	By Region						
珠 三 角	Pearl River Delta	105.7	104.0	111.1	107.2	105.5	111.3
粤 东	Eastern Region	104.8	103.7	106.1	106.5	104.6	109.9
粤 西	Western Region	103.8	102.3	106.1	105.8	103.5	110.8
粤 北	Northern Region	106.2	104.3	108.8	108.5	104.5	109.3

注：本表按可比价格计算。
Note: The indices are calculated at comparable prices.

11-10 农作物播种面积
Total Sown Area of Farm Crops

单位：万亩 (10000 mu)

年份 Year	农作物总播种面积 Total Sown Area	一、粮食作物 Grain Crops	#稻谷 Rice	#薯类 Tubers	#大豆 Soybean
1978	9962.46	7603.47	5790.39	873.02	163.71
1979	9492.62	7300.54	5691.88	845.65	185.91
1980	8954.84	6908.02	5596.10	800.67	198.18
1981	8567.83	6548.40	5450.29	767.07	199.33
1982	8539.77	6475.65	5373.51	778.51	218.52
1983	8364.03	6485.66	5406.97	780.98	197.43
1984	8313.00	6269.47	5272.01	765.51	193.21
1985	8036.82	5750.76	4815.81	730.83	175.22
1986	8037.18	5731.76	4804.77	745.48	177.59
1987	8064.78	5679.94	4750.06	743.22	174.25
1988	8063.89	5598.29	4678.26	726.61	172.60
1989	8322.71	5777.18	4768.32	743.93	173.64
1990	8507.35	5822.06	4763.67	751.70	172.44
1991	8489.09	5643.92	4596.92	746.74	163.30
1992	8231.36	5303.82	4313.79	710.56	157.48
1993	7718.41	4840.76	3944.83	681.66	160.54
1994	7807.99	4959.10	4005.47	747.93	157.12
1995	7957.19	5052.24	4052.13	775.96	155.84
1996	8156.22	5120.09	4066.33	778.70	155.04
1997	8267.25	5144.06	4055.92	772.52	149.14
1998	8310.73	5147.65	4029.10	768.09	146.06
1999	7894.24	4912.04	3836.30	697.22	144.52
2000	7735.35	4649.83	3619.05	640.15	145.46
2001	7868.21	4634.79	3638.28	661.15	132.19
2002	7207.37	4021.44	3151.22	582.81	102.14
2003	7294.58	4012.81	3144.56	578.14	114.54
2004	7211.96	4184.55	3208.50	581.55	120.60
2005	7223.06	4179.75	3206.40	579.75	125.70
2006	6573.85	3700.00	2912.90	468.40	96.90
2007	6444.51	3662.24	2895.53	448.58	85.95
2008	6410.77	3638.75	2896.11	425.09	81.17
2009	6416.17	3638.09	2900.39	404.84	73.18
2010	6394.16	3579.49	2877.21	392.65	72.66
2011	6367.10	3524.67	2847.03	372.05	63.76
2012	6372.63	3497.08	2847.31	355.91	61.87
2013	6363.36	3399.78	2774.98	339.63	58.22
2014	6337.79	3346.61	2740.15	333.84	54.53
2015	6291.83	3289.94	2707.15	319.78	51.71
2016	6271.95	3266.67	2709.05	304.07	48.47
2017	6341.26	3254.59	2708.13	300.04	46.74
2018	6419.04	3226.56	2681.09	299.72	47.68
2019	6536.07	3240.96	2690.51	303.74	48.86
2020	6677.71	3307.03	2751.65	304.33	48.92
2021	6747.53	3319.55	2741.13	317.08	48.95
2022	6830.20	3345.43	2753.84	324.51	52.05
2023	6880.91	3344.26	2741.42	330.52	53.79

11-10 续表 continued

单位：万亩 (10000 mu)

年份 Year	二、经济作物 Economic Crops	#糖蔗 Sugarcane	#花生 Peanuts	#烟叶 Tobacco	#蔬菜 Vegetables
1978	2195.28	258.96	486.62	69.19	
1979	2006.17	227.15	519.73	59.44	
1980	1848.64	218.57	553.24	38.62	
1981	1820.10	272.52	595.41	45.06	
1982	1845.60	331.53	588.01	48.73	
1983	1680.94	312.86	489.74	43.25	
1984	1850.32	341.02	523.56	39.06	
1985	2110.84	442.83	545.78	55.25	
1986	2127.83	405.07	560.80	41.87	
1987	2210.59	344.72	533.13	41.42	
1988	2293.00	354.90	497.82	61.39	
1989	2371.89	338.02	486.05	72.25	
1990	2512.85	419.73	485.96	68.55	776.00
1991	2681.87	453.90	472.15	81.93	867.95
1992	2770.06	461.14	471.88	79.08	946.88
1993	2717.11	353.65	499.78	73.92	1057.02
1994	2691.77	325.62	505.35	53.15	1147.53
1995	2749.11	320.18	499.60	44.33	1244.96
1996	2881.09	329.28	497.42	45.10	1348.64
1997	2974.06	334.02	499.70	55.45	1416.62
1998	3017.02	325.59	510.83	50.30	1484.82
1999	2837.68	261.47	468.50	42.72	1441.85
2000	2940.05	239.60	496.61	46.64	1515.15
2001	3101.23	215.25	511.57	53.48	1685.69
2002	3083.79	222.66	472.49	46.27	1692.00
2003	3167.23	198.29	488.66	44.86	1792.29
2004	3027.41	193.45	462.20	47.42	1720.01
2005	3043.31	188.08	464.11	47.47	1744.08
2006	2873.85	195.13	462.28	30.23	1627.80
2007	2782.27	206.37	446.50	28.62	1570.07
2008	2772.02	203.87	455.75	33.57	1612.13
2009	2778.08	203.79	459.64	34.44	1621.20
2010	2814.67	205.08	461.08	32.54	1651.25
2011	2842.42	211.58	461.80	32.31	1662.82
2012	2875.55	219.42	466.41	31.22	1669.40
2013	2963.58	231.18	469.80	29.99	1736.59
2014	2991.19	225.68	470.91	28.23	1772.00
2015	3001.88	215.36	474.87	27.42	1782.70
2016	3005.28	214.36	471.77	26.71	1784.79
2017	3086.67	219.36	478.65	26.11	1840.83
2018	3192.48	223.17	498.73	26.21	1908.37
2019	3295.11	220.60	510.77	25.10	1980.78
2020	3370.68	205.18	521.36	24.73	2045.32
2021	3427.98	192.60	524.52	23.77	2088.37
2022	3484.77	189.14	520.19	22.98	2142.56
2023	3536.65	183.93	530.25	22.65	2180.59

11-11 主要农产品产量

Output of Major Farm Products

单位：万吨 (10000 tons)

年份 Year	粮食作物 Grain Crops	#稻谷 Rice	#薯类 Tubers	#大豆 Soybean	糖蔗 Sugarcane	花生 Peanuts	烟叶 Tobacco	蔬菜 Vegetables	茶叶 Tea	园林水果 Fruits
1978	1509.51	1328.56	121.04	7.99	835.42	35.17	4.73		0.92	29.40
1979	1605.36	1435.22	125.15	9.56	742.90	40.70	4.00		0.89	26.20
1980	1681.91	1523.92	123.68	11.47	834.73	50.00	2.72		1.00	29.10
1981	1521.00	1372.22	122.53	12.01	1235.50	57.39	3.68		1.13	39.20
1982	1795.72	1627.37	138.98	14.44	1496.10	61.90	4.67		1.31	46.30
1983	1817.48	1673.12	138.98	10.80	1159.83	48.08	3.41		1.45	53.00
1984	1819.33	1666.08	130.21	11.90	1454.15	53.40	3.50		1.61	73.90
1985	1604.37	1454.29	131.88	11.32	1831.40	57.07	4.89		1.75	116.28
1986	1567.00	1421.55	128.01	12.27	1622.13	60.40	3.50		2.03	185.50
1987	1701.81	1536.46	146.48	12.43	1338.60	53.50	4.05		2.28	264.10
1988	1636.70	1472.95	143.42	12.32	1538.68	51.80	5.80		2.39	277.98
1989	1817.21	1630.29	153.47	13.25	1681.34	55.38	7.15	916.88	2.35	275.83
1990	1896.29	1687.00	167.05	13.87	2093.46	57.95	7.08	976.83	2.59	328.58
1991	1873.50	1651.65	176.59	12.60	2286.38	56.11	8.46	1106.19	2.67	394.19
1992	1810.40	1602.27	170.28	13.94	2271.06	60.30	8.62	1203.54	2.87	453.62
1993	1629.11	1425.81	169.20	15.28	1603.11	66.02	7.70	1367.22	3.07	402.44
1994	1662.66	1434.04	194.68	15.44	1397.22	63.71	5.30	1509.93	3.32	401.55
1995	1803.33	1553.90	209.40	16.50	1472.21	69.98	5.04	1703.86	3.96	414.51
1996	1891.43	1626.29	210.28	17.32	1392.00	73.05	5.29	1865.10	3.62	381.17
1997	1966.75	1669.33	228.35	17.61	1629.27	74.10	7.33	1995.99	3.66	414.48
1998	1884.13	1688.53	238.28	17.32	1616.94	69.38	6.61	2011.13	3.89	453.12
1999	1935.82	1630.13	214.38	17.91	1218.30	73.31	5.80	2109.68	4.06	622.68
2000	1822.33	1528.53	199.05	18.73	1137.59	77.68	6.21	2214.80	4.21	643.52
2001	1721.55	1441.35	198.15	17.36	1073.38	79.73	6.79	2377.60	4.15	590.74
2002	1484.16	1243.46	171.02	12.67	1136.45	75.19	6.08	2442.53	4.24	698.91
2003	1488.00	1250.38	166.77	14.92	952.87	80.73	6.00	2584.20	4.14	718.59
2004	1390.00	1123.13	180.28	18.10	940.77	76.47	6.27	2557.65	4.04	787.85
2005	1394.97	1116.99	185.48	18.87	946.02	75.86	6.30	2596.02	4.45	831.69
2006	1242.42	1015.90	150.48	14.92	1025.66	76.54	4.23	2380.56	4.74	893.47
2007	1267.03	1041.38	148.04	12.64	1078.06	75.45	4.07	2316.01	4.91	934.12
2008	1210.02	994.97	136.91	12.10	1043.21	77.93	4.71	2355.51	4.88	948.32
2009	1261.99	1044.00	133.43	11.08	1062.73	79.58	4.98	2446.67	5.20	1004.99
2010	1249.15	1041.80	129.01	11.20	1064.09	81.59	5.00	2550.50	5.38	1049.21
2011	1275.73	1072.65	122.86	9.60	1111.28	83.72	5.00	2633.02	6.04	1100.20
2012	1295.69	1097.00	120.06	10.15	1164.49	86.66	5.06	2722.03	6.39	1147.12
2013	1202.48	1012.80	112.48	9.88	1218.46	89.17	4.83	2808.09	7.09	1206.39
2014	1229.97	1053.29	106.12	9.45	1159.89	91.77	4.61	2898.53	7.51	1248.18
2015	1211.66	1040.82	102.34	9.03	1093.58	94.48	4.52	2994.65	8.07	1298.52
2016	1204.22	1039.53	96.53	8.63	1096.56	95.48	4.40	3036.45	8.92	1331.99
2017	1208.56	1046.34	95.43	8.48	1144.14	98.42	4.26	3177.49	9.29	1421.23
2018	1193.49	1032.07	94.67	8.71	1207.97	104.40	4.33	3330.24	9.99	1547.81
2019	1240.80	1075.05	97.41	9.04	1241.64	108.69	4.17	3527.96	11.08	1644.38
2020	1267.56	1099.58	97.29	9.10	1176.25	112.05	4.12	3706.85	12.82	1756.16
2021	1279.87	1104.41	102.72	8.64	1118.20	115.87	3.88	3855.73	13.95	1826.73
2022	1291.54	1108.63	107.01	9.27	1107.76	115.93	3.71	3999.11	16.08	1895.18
2023	1285.19	1096.89	109.88	9.64	1087.43	119.54	3.74	4099.33	17.89	1991.87

11-12 主要畜产品和水产品产量

Output of Major Farm Products

单位：万吨 Units: (10000 tons)

年份 Year	肉类 Meat	#猪肉 Pork	牛奶 Cow Milk	水产品 Aquatic Products	海水产品 Seawater Aquatic Products	淡水产品 Freshwater Aquatic Products
1978	48.45	48.09	1.66	65.50	46.47	19.03
1979	58.96	58.30	1.90	57.44	36.71	20.73
1980	63.20	62.62	2.18	63.34	41.54	21.80
1981	69.61	69.10	2.56	64.17	39.63	24.54
1982	76.85	76.20	2.88	76.32	47.12	29.20
1983	85.24	84.50	3.16	85.61	51.58	34.03
1984	90.00	89.00	3.89	95.63	54.33	41.30
1985	128.12	97.59	4.09	109.44	58.74	50.70
1986	154.16	106.60	4.39	136.54	78.18	58.36
1987	154.15	114.12	4.55	155.36	90.17	65.19
1988	172.45	124.64	4.99	174.66	102.02	72.64
1989	181.66	132.40	5.08	189.75	113.47	76.28
1990	202.45	145.35	5.51	207.66	124.53	83.13
1991	225.08	158.01	6.03	225.31	135.11	90.20
1992	245.69	166.22	5.72	251.06	147.42	103.64
1993	271.46	173.89	5.71	280.75	158.46	122.29
1994	278.50	176.89	5.71	314.10	174.80	139.30
1995	305.06	188.75	5.49	354.34	197.21	157.13
1996	252.03	162.03	5.81	395.08	218.39	176.69
1997	275.62	176.59	6.03	520.96	330.66	190.30
1998	305.45	197.53	6.97	554.28	346.20	208.07
1999	315.86	204.40	7.77	575.95	355.37	220.58
2000	324.48	206.85	9.19	593.19	360.45	232.73
2001	333.25	213.65	10.18	609.67	367.07	242.60
2002	343.63	220.17	10.82	628.06	374.36	253.70
2003	358.50	232.77	10.55	648.55	379.21	269.34
2004	365.32	242.14	10.94	664.56	381.79	282.78
2005	384.31	256.28	11.64	695.23	397.95	297.28
2006	382.08	251.46	12.00	658.84	373.59	285.25
2007	388.60	237.41	12.17	664.34	373.12	291.22
2008	418.32	258.39	13.62	680.41	376.81	303.60
2009	436.92	268.98	14.75	702.60	387.15	315.45
2010	454.86	285.14	14.95	729.03	401.50	327.53
2011	451.65	282.93	14.95	762.53	418.23	344.31
2012	464.13	291.09	14.33	739.35	408.92	330.43
2013	459.22	295.09	14.46	764.29	418.58	345.71
2014	456.69	302.86	14.20	783.22	426.44	356.78
2015	454.71	296.31	13.61	803.71	434.71	369.00
2016	448.70	288.24	13.61	818.29	441.54	376.75
2017	444.08	277.96	13.88	833.54	451.81	381.73
2018	449.90	281.52	13.89	842.44	449.17	393.28
2019	412.12	221.93	13.92	866.40	455.49	410.91
2020	400.99	192.42	15.10	875.81	450.53	425.28
2021	457.42	263.23	17.23	884.52	455.04	429.47
2022	481.01	279.81	19.81	894.03	458.29	435.74
2023	507.46	298.00	20.25	924.02	478.15	445.87

注：2012—2017年水产品数据以第三次全国农业普查数据为基础做了调整。下表同。

Note: From 2012 to 2017, data of aquatic products are adjusted in accordance with the Third National Agricultural Census. The same applies to the following tables.

11-13 主要农作物播种面积、亩产及总产量

Sown Area, Yield per Mu and Total Output of Major Farm Crops

单位：万亩、公斤、万吨 (10000 mu, kg, 10000 tons)

作物名称	Farm Crop	2010			2022			2023		
		播种面积 Sown Area	亩产 Yield per Mu	总产量 Total Output	播种面积 Sown Area	亩产 Yield per Mu	总产量 Total Output	播种面积 Sown Area	亩产 Yield per Mu	总产量 Total Output
农作物播种面积	**Total Sown Area**	**6394.16**			**6830.20**			**6880.91**		
粮食作物	**Grain Crops**	**3579.49**	**349**	**1249.15**	**3345.43**	**386**	**1291.54**	**3344.26**	**384**	**1285.19**
稻谷	Rice	2877.21	362	1041.80	2753.84	403	1108.63	2741.42	400	1096.89
早稻	Early Rice	1386.98	362	502.04	1296.34	401	520.09	1298.93	408	529.70
晚稻	Late Rice	1490.23	362	539.76	1457.50	404	588.54	1442.49	393	567.19
小麦	Wheat	1.30	191	0.25	0.63	235	0.15	0.99	214	0.21
玉米	Corn	209.12	296	61.94	197.86	320	63.41	201.04	326	65.47
薯类(折粮)	Tubers	392.65	329	129.01	324.51	330	107.01	330.52	332	109.88
大豆	Soybean	72.66	154	11.20	52.05	178	9.27	53.79	179	9.64
经济作物	**Economic Crops**	**2814.67**			**3484.77**			**3536.65**		
甘蔗	Sugarcane and Fruit Cane	233.16	5253	1224.73	220.79	5852	1292.05	213.80	5945	1271.08
#糖蔗	Sugarcane	205.08	5189	1064.09	189.14	5857	1107.76	183.93	5912	1087.43
油料作物	Oil-bearing Crops	477.28	175	83.34	532.82	220	117.43	543.15	223	121.01
#花生	Peanuts	461.08	177	81.59	520.19	223	115.93	530.25	225	119.54
麻类	Fiber Crops	0.29	164	0.05	0.06	245	0.01	0.07	218	0.02
烟叶	Tobacco	32.54	154	5.00	22.98	162	3.71	22.65	165	3.74
中草药材	Chinese Herbal Medicine	16.92			102.74			111.67		
蔬菜	Vegetables	1651.25	1544	2550.50	2142.56	1867	3999.11	2180.59	1880	4099.33
瓜果类	Melons and Fruits	57.67	1724	99.43	64.91	2052	133.20	65.77	2067	135.92
其他农作物	Other Crops	345.56			397.91			398.94		
#木薯	Cassava	114.94	1223	140.61	91.47	1450	132.67	90.27	1457	131.55

11−14 各市主要农作物播种面积、亩产及总产量（2023年）

Sown Area, Yield per Mu and Total Output of Major Farm Crops by City (2023)

单位：亩、公斤、吨 (mu, kg, ton)

市别	City	粮食作物 Grain Crops 播种面积 Sown Area	亩产 Yield per Mu	总产量 Total Output	#稻谷 Rice 播种面积 Sown Area	亩产 Yield per Mu	总产量 Total Output
全省	**Provincial Total**	**33442616**	**384**	**12851860**	**27414205**	**400**	**10968910**
广州	Guangzhou	451261	337	151919	360091	345	124247
深圳	Shenzhen	23816	297	7073	14726	282	4150
珠海	Zhuhai	80512	369	29737	66670	397	26463
汕头	Shantou	1035528	447	462581	690567	467	322731
佛山	Foshan	145118	350	50777	104095	372	38768
韶关	Shaoguan	1819576	415	755180	1534904	437	670429
河源	Heyuan	2005800	406	814587	1836469	420	771714
梅州	Meizhou	2766426	412	1138411	2428360	433	1050726
惠州	Huizhou	1713388	360	616639	1275493	368	469927
汕尾	Shanwei	1247332	349	435275	1033786	360	372013
东莞	Dongguan	33870	330	11179	24106	368	8883
中山	Zhongshan	45216	351	15883	37709	365	13773
江门	Jiangmen	2810803	352	988631	2523802	361	910496
阳江	Yangjiang	1818294	349	635348	1604316	362	580923
湛江	Zhanjiang	4251104	357	1518963	3357751	366	1228811
茂名	Maoming	3768965	406	1532053	3151002	424	1335360
肇庆	Zhaoqing	2999605	408	1225315	2521029	428	1078089
清远	Qingyuan	2271496	324	736764	1832838	346	634603
潮州	Chaozhou	641838	431	276581	481617	462	222668
揭阳	Jieyang	1970084	410	807046	1217258	426	518645
云浮	Yunfu	1542584	416	641921	1317616	444	585491
按经济区域分	By Region						
珠三角	Pearl River Delta	8303589	409	3097152	6927721	429	2674796
粤东	Eastern Region	4894782	411	1981482	3423228	427	1436057
粤西	Western Region	9838363	407	3686364	8113069	425	3145094
粤北	Northern Region	10405882	417	4086862	8950187	445	3712963

11-14 续表 1 continued

单位：亩、公斤、吨 (mu, kg, ton)

市 别	City	#大豆 Soybean 播种面积 Sown Area	亩产 Yield per Mu	总产量 Total Output	经济作物 Economic Crops 播种面积 Sown Area	#糖蔗 Sugarcane 播种面积 Sown Area	亩产 Yield per Mu	总产量 Total Output
全 省	**Provincial Total**	**537911**	**179**	**96437**	**35366486**	**1839309**	**5912**	**10874280**
广 州	Guangzhou	6751	173	1169	2726866			
深 圳	Shenzhen	477	155	74	151861	116	2888	335
珠 海	Zhuhai	2868	181	520	130361			
汕 头	Shantou	6558	186	1220	748408			
佛 山	Foshan	1557	156	243	826761			
韶 关	Shaoguan	48337	183	8830	2102066	6115	5536	33852
河 源	Heyuan	40719	190	7744	1140106	5067	5008	25376
梅 州	Meizhou	61727	174	10738	2023683	350	2049	717
惠 州	Huizhou	21851	166	3627	2258946	6929	7536	52218
汕 尾	Shanwei	20620	180	3705	1149472	1050	4841	5083
东 莞	Dongguan	1682	148	249	330374			
中 山	Zhongshan	851	172	146	375795	87	3736	325
江 门	Jiangmen	33524	184	6182	1942498	10732	6432	69028
阳 江	Yangjiang	50136	172	8614	1382801	2424	4686	11359
湛 江	Zhanjiang	29667	166	4925	5789073	1674781	5948	9962365
茂 名	Maoming	45041	168	7552	3331649	99963	5176	517388
肇 庆	Zhaoqing	36178	177	6415	2777013	2043	5089	10397
清 远	Qingyuan	52743	189	9943	3595335	29652	6267	185837
潮 州	Chaozhou	12230	207	2528	322006			
揭 阳	Jieyang	42247	187	7896	1133457			
云 浮	Yunfu	22148	186	4117	1127953			
按经济区域分	By Region							
珠 三 角	Pearl River Delta	105739	178	18625	11520476	19907	6646	132303
粤 东	Eastern Region	81654	188	15349	3353343	1050	4841	5083
粤 西	Western Region	124844	169	21091	10503524	1777168	5903	10491112
粤 北	Northern Region	225674	187	41372	9989143	41184	5968	245782

11-14 续表 2 continued

单位：亩、公斤、吨 (mu, kg, ton)

市别	City	#花生 Peanuts 播种面积 Sown Area	亩产 Yield per Mu	总产量 Total Output	#烟叶 Tobacco 播种面积 Sown Area	亩产 Yield per Mu	总产量 Total Output
全　省	**Provincial Total**	**5302538**	**225**	**1195425**	**226466**	**165**	**37367**
广　州	Guangzhou	49986	198	9899			
深　圳	Shenzhen	3277	166	543			
珠　海	Zhuhai	2870	255	733			
汕　头	Shantou	18594	171	3184			
佛　山	Foshan	10582	209	2217	13	615	8
韶　关	Shaoguan	553752	251	139180	134624	162	21816
河　源	Heyuan	369324	217	80189			
梅　州	Meizhou	200302	198	39722	58653	164	9643
惠　州	Huizhou	264341	205	54172			
汕　尾	Shanwei	196605	177	34701			
东　莞	Dongguan	574	218	125			
中　山	Zhongshan	245	302	74			
江　门	Jiangmen	194593	193	37507	6	183	1
阳　江	Yangjiang	315268	160	50436	85	200	17
湛　江	Zhanjiang	982469	261	256384	535	161	86
茂　名	Maoming	694385	235	162980	6710	215	1442
肇　庆	Zhaoqing	432744	220	95129	16288	169	2758
清　远	Qingyuan	580647	225	130671	9487	166	1576
潮　州	Chaozhou	29833	181	5405			
揭　阳	Jieyang	132159	279	36838	65	292	19
云　浮	Yunfu	269988	205	55336			
按经济区域分	By Region						
珠 三 角	Pearl River Delta	959212	209	200398	16307	170	2767
粤　东	Eastern Region	377191	212	80129	65	292	19
粤　西	Western Region	1992122	236	469800	7330	211	1545
粤　北	Northern Region	1974013	225	445098	202764	163	33035

11-14 续表 3 continued

单位：亩、公斤、吨 (mu, kg, ton)

市 别	City	#木薯 Cassava			#蔬菜 Vegetables		
		播种面积 Sown Area	亩产 Yield per Mu	总产量 Total Output	播种面积 Sown Area	亩产 Yield per Mu	总产量 Total Output
全 省	**Provincial Total**	**902674**	**1457**	**1315495**	**21805907**	**1880**	**40993332**
广 州	Guangzhou	1532	1223	1873	2238246	1850	4141279
深 圳	Shenzhen	344	1355	466	139244	1238	172427
珠 海	Zhuhai	32	831	27	106587	1290	137531
汕 头	Shantou	310	3435	1065	705765	2578	1819586
佛 山	Foshan	197	1832	361	508001	1706	866829
韶 关	Shaoguan	8732	1681	14678	959012	1613	1547185
河 源	Heyuan	35327	944	33344	626678	1357	850679
梅 州	Meizhou	97649	1173	114557	1155659	2318	2678941
惠 州	Huizhou	993	1920	1907	1898476	1891	3590734
汕 尾	Shanwei	24393	2344	57176	861342	1811	1559569
东 莞	Dongguan				301316	1400	421699
中 山	Zhongshan	61	1246	76	225047	1675	377031
江 门	Jiangmen	31775	1578	50138	1153208	1753	2021126
阳 江	Yangjiang	48587	1077	52320	870748	1163	1012303
湛 江	Zhanjiang	141159	1954	275802	2499258	1876	4689035
茂 名	Maoming	78052	1380	107683	1960415	2022	3964935
肇 庆	Zhaoqing	231336	1355	313555	1512613	2208	3339907
清 远	Qingyuan	59533	1338	79634	2506294	1670	4185061
潮 州	Chaozhou	2414	1206	2912	248276	2323	576745
揭 阳	Jieyang	8296	1653	13717	904497	2610	2360929
云 浮	Yunfu	131952	1472	194205	425226	1599	679802
按经济区域分	By Region						
珠 三 角	Pearl River Delta	266270	1384	368402	8082737	1864	15068564
粤 东	Eastern Region	35413	2114	74870	2719880	2322	6316828
粤 西	Western Region	267798	1627	435805	5330421	1813	9666273
粤 北	Northern Region	333193	1310	436418	5672869	1752	9941668

11-15 造林面积及主要林产品产量

Area of Afforestation and Output of Major Forest Products

项　目	Item	2000	2010	2015	2021	2022	2023
人工造林面积　（万亩）	Artificial Afforestation Area (10000 mu)	25.76	142.72	177.69	29.61	15.48	22.37
年末实有育苗面积（万亩）	Actual Area of Seedlings Raising at the Year-end (10000 mu)	3.12	4.54	12.17	3.63	2.70	10.21
主要林产品产量	Output of Major Forest Products						
油茶籽　（吨）	Tea-oil Seeds (ton)	26268	82417	149374	177622	179745	199441
竹笋干　（吨）	Dried Bamboo Shoots (ton)	14132	30291	39805	66153	99634	104300
板栗　（吨）	Chinese Chestnuts (ton)	5440	10616	21229	55592	55092	69584
松香类产品　（万吨）	Rosin Products (10000 tons)	9.61	12.91	15.62	18.64	14.61	16.42
木材竹材产量	Output of Wood and Bamboo						
木材　（万立方米）	Wood (10000 cubic meters)	275	655	791	1264	1254	1376
大径竹　（万根）	Large Diameter Bamboo (10000 sticks)	6809	13252	12754	30907	41665	43882

11-16 水产养殖面积和水产品产量

Area of Cultivation and Output of Aquatic Products

指　标	Item	2000	2010	2015	2021	2022	2023
水产品产量（万吨）	**Output of Aquatic Products(10000 tons)**	**593.19**	**729.03**	**803.71**	**884.52**	**894.03**	**924.02**
海水产品	Seawater Aquatic Products	360.45	401.50	434.71	455.04	458.29	478.15
捕捞	Catches	191.48	152.43	154.00	118.80	118.61	120.87
养殖	Artificially Cultured	168.97	249.07	280.71	336.24	339.68	357.28
淡水产品	Freshwater Aquatic Products	232.73	327.53	369.00	429.47	435.74	445.87
捕捞	Catches	13.52	12.86	12.26	8.91	7.68	7.44
养殖	Artificially Cultured	219.21	314.67	356.74	420.57	428.06	438.42
养殖面积　（万亩）	**Area of Cultivation (10000 mu)**	**846.76**	**845.12**	**734.88**	**713.43**	**710.49**	**716.02**
海水养殖	Seawater	292.33	298.89	247.76	248.58	249.90	258.20
淡水养殖	Freshwater	554.43	546.24	487.12	464.85	460.59	457.82

11−17 牲畜头数及肉类产量

Number of Livestock and Output of Meat

项目	Item	2000	2010	2015	2021	2022	2023
牛年末存栏头数（万头）	**Number of Cattle and Buffaloes (at the year-end) (10000 heads)**	**420.64**	**175.49**	**132.92**	**112.99**	**108.55**	**98.50**
肉牛	Beef Cattle	416.92	169.91	127.13	106.79	102.35	92.37
奶牛	Milch Cows	3.72	5.57	5.79	6.20	6.20	6.13
牛奶产量（万吨）	**Output of Milk (10000 tons)**	**9.19**	**14.95**	**13.61**	**17.23**	**19.81**	**20.25**
山羊年末存栏只数（万只）	**Number of Goats on Hand at the Year-end (10000 heads)**	**29.33**	**50.52**	**83.55**	**88.64**	**85.12**	**83.82**
生猪年末存栏头数（万头）	**Number of Hogs at the Year-end (10000 heads)**	**2034.79**	**2332.51**	**2308.54**	**2075.48**	**2195.86**	**2049.20**
#能繁殖母猪	Number of Female Hogs with Fertility	143.75	262.65	242.52	191.18	204.38	195.79
肉猪出栏头数（万头）	**Number of Slaughtered Fattened Hogs (10000 heads)**	**2954.98**	**3863.23**	**3959.62**	**3336.63**	**3496.79**	**3794.01**
家禽年末存栏（亿只）	**Poultry at year-end (100 million heads)**	**3.89**	**4.09**	**3.74**	**3.94**	**3.88**	**4.02**
出售和自宰的家禽（亿只）	**Poultry sold or slaughtered (100 million heads)**	**9.29**	**11.75**	**10.48**	**12.80**	**13.37**	**13.74**
禽蛋产量（万吨）	**Poultry Eggs (10 000 tons)**	**33.08**	**35.54**	**36.40**	**43.66**	**47.20**	**49.91**
肉类产量（万吨）	**Output of Meat (10000 tons)**	**324.48**	**454.86**	**454.71**	**457.42**	**481.01**	**507.46**
#猪肉	Pork	206.85	285.14	296.31	263.23	279.81	298.00
牛肉	Beef	5.17	4.97	4.14	4.37	4.53	4.43
羊肉	Mutton	0.43	1.24	1.83	1.96	2.00	1.94
禽肉	Meat of Poultry	111.50	158.04	145.01	182.19	189.48	194.54
兔肉	Rabbit Meat	0.53	0.65	0.90	0.68	0.57	0.55

11-18 各市人工造林面积、水产品产量、牲畜头数及猪肉产量（2023年）
Area of Afforestation, Output of Aquatic Products, Number of Livestock and Output of Pork by City (2023)

市 别	City	人工造林面积（万亩）Artificial Afforestation Area (10000 mu)	水产品产量（万吨）Output of Aquatic Products (10000 tons)	#淡水养殖 Freshwater	牛年末存栏头数（万头）Number of Cattles and Buffalos at the Year-end (10000 heads)	生猪年末存栏头数（万头）Number of Hogs at the Year-end (10000 heads)	肉猪出栏头数（万头）Number of Slaughtered Fattened Hogs (10000 heads)	猪肉产量（万吨）Output of Pork (10000 tons)
全 省	**Provincial Total**	**22.37**	**924.02**	**438.42**	**98.50**	**2049.20**	**3794.01**	**298.00**
广 州	Guangzhou	0.22	48.37	34.51	1.22	55.88	69.84	5.32
深 圳	Shenzhen	0.02	8.71	0.69	0.14	0.61	5.41	0.44
珠 海	Zhuhai	0.02	35.86	18.66	…	7.43	12.16	0.88
汕 头	Shantou	0.18	47.69	9.39	0.29	29.35	61.18	4.80
佛 山	Foshan	0.02	80.27	79.71	0.37	50.53	100.73	7.98
韶 关	Shaoguan	3.33	8.48	8.25	3.46	185.84	313.27	24.52
河 源	Heyuan	3.56	5.19	4.93	6.04	97.37	152.40	11.82
梅 州	Meizhou	0.71	11.00	10.08	9.00	119.03	219.56	17.33
惠 州	Huizhou	0.61	22.01	14.73	3.64	74.48	152.57	11.86
汕 尾	Shanwei	2.51	61.76	5.18	6.28	48.72	99.21	7.83
东 莞	Dongguan		5.20	4.44	0.01	1.27	1.85	0.15
中 山	Zhongshan		39.49	39.33	0.02	0.86	1.59	0.12
江 门	Jiangmen	0.19	91.95	54.84	1.79	125.80	241.20	18.82
阳 江	Yangjiang	0.20	120.68	10.23	6.65	161.48	291.46	23.15
湛 江	Zhanjiang	0.82	128.49	17.91	17.35	284.74	449.96	34.81
茂 名	Maoming	0.67	94.49	35.79	13.04	280.28	614.87	49.21
肇 庆	Zhaoqing	3.47	52.93	52.62	15.23	156.43	328.49	25.77
清 远	Qingyuan	3.13	14.44	14.27	7.55	175.40	323.38	25.24
潮 州	Chaozhou	0.22	21.62	4.81	0.53	23.54	43.52	3.52
揭 阳	Jieyang	0.97	15.30	8.09	3.24	68.96	127.93	10.08
云 浮	Yunfu	1.52	10.09	9.98	2.64	101.20	183.42	14.36
按经济区域分	By Region							
珠三角	Pearl River Delta	4.55	384.80	299.53	22.43	473.30	913.84	71.33
粤 东	Eastern Region	3.88	146.37	27.47	10.34	170.57	331.84	26.23
粤 西	Western Region	1.69	343.66	63.93	37.04	726.50	1356.29	107.17
粤 北	Northern Region	12.25	49.20	47.51	28.69	678.83	1192.03	93.27

注：分市人工造林数据未包括当地国家级自然保护区和省属林场完成量。
Note: The artificial afforestation data by city do not include the completed amount of local national nature reserves and provincial forest farms.

11-19 茶叶、桑、园林水果面积及产量

Planted Area and Output of Tea, Mulberry and Fruits

指 标	Item	2000	2010	2015	2021	2022	2023
茶叶年末实有面积 (万亩)	Planted Area of Tea at the Year-end (10000 mu)	64.80	62.76	78.07	133.90	149.19	168.98
茶叶总产量 (万吨)	Output of Tea (10000 tons)	4.21	5.38	8.07	13.95	16.08	17.89
桑地年末实有面积 (万亩)	Planted Area of Mulberries at the Year-end (10000 mu)	26.89	47.73	51.25	31.00	31.18	30.09
桑叶产量 (万吨)	Output of mulberry leaves (10000 tons)	51.25	94.35	113.54	87.77	90.05	88.17
园林水果年末实有面积(万亩)	Planted Area of Fruits at the Year-end (10000 mu)	1502.35	1510.61	1452.71	1576.14	1603.68	1642.32
园林水果总产量 (万吨)	Gross Output of Fruits (10000 tons)	643.52	1049.21	1298.52	1826.73	1895.18	1991.87
#柑橘橙年末实有面积 (万亩)	Planted Area of Citruses at the Year-end (10000 mu)	123.34	326.83	296.62	287.95	287.33	289.82
柑橘橙总产量 (万吨)	Output of Citruses (10000 tons)	81.06	259.34	317.53	399.72	420.18	433.97
香(大)蕉年末实有面积 (万亩)	Planted Area of Bananas at the Year-end (10000 mu)	151.51	171.85	162.22	167.13	165.95	159.50
香(大)蕉总产量 (万吨)	Output of Bananas (10000 tons)	235.30	334.13	357.83	483.30	488.55	478.34
菠萝年末实有面积 (万亩)	Planted Area of Pineapples at the Year-end (10000 mu)	44.58	38.81	44.58	58.87	58.73	61.42
菠萝总产量 (万吨)	Output of Pineapples (10000 tons)	47.53	63.21	83.76	125.98	129.47	131.96
荔枝年末实有面积 (万亩)	Planted Area of Lychees at the Year-end (10000 mu)	474.83	390.99	371.82	393.98	406.84	419.89
荔枝总产量 (万吨)	Output of Lychees (10000 tons)	64.75	96.53	116.18	151.62	146.74	163.41
龙眼年末实有面积 (万亩)	Planted Area of Longans at the Year-end (10000 mu)	236.31	182.45	170.54	172.39	172.64	172.57
龙眼总产量 (万吨)	Output of Longans (10000 tons)	34.68	58.22	76.04	104.23	96.05	106.23

11-20 各市园林水果面积及产量（2023年）
Planted Area and Output of Fruits by City (2023)

单位：万亩、万吨 (10000 mu，10000 tons)

市别	City	园林水果 Fruits 年末面积 Year-end Area	园林水果 Fruits 总产量 Total Output	#柑橘橙 Citrus 年末面积 Year-end Area	#柑橘橙 Citrus 总产量 Total Output	#香(大)蕉 Banana 年末面积 Year-end Area	#香(大)蕉 Banana 总产量 Total Output
全　省	**Provincial Total**	**1642.32**	**1991.87**	**289.82**	**433.97**	**159.50**	**478.34**
广　州	Guangzhou	107.26	84.46	6.20	8.87	6.88	27.20
深　圳	Shenzhen	5.45	4.10	0.41	0.62	0.18	0.28
珠　海	Zhuhai	7.34	8.49	0.07	0.07	0.80	2.65
汕　头	Shantou	22.05	34.09	1.16	2.41	3.12	6.73
佛　山	Foshan	2.27	4.47	0.18	0.32	0.75	2.43
韶　关	Shaoguan	72.60	75.28	33.96	39.31	0.67	0.65
河　源	Heyuan	58.32	49.13	14.22	14.26	1.39	1.22
梅　州	Meizhou	133.42	171.61	12.20	16.91	5.73	8.47
惠　州	Huizhou	110.74	111.65	27.74	31.63	14.68	39.47
汕　尾	Shanwei	57.41	39.15	1.58	4.50	3.55	4.53
东　莞	Dongguan	20.19	7.19	0.03	0.02	2.11	3.60
中　山	Zhongshan	5.39	12.29	0.14	0.29	1.54	5.28
江　门	Jiangmen	42.56	46.27	17.56	21.21	4.83	9.39
阳　江	Yangjiang	76.19	45.24	7.01	9.74	7.82	12.25
湛　江	Zhanjiang	177.03	340.93	8.75	12.13	37.87	120.84
茂　名	Maoming	370.43	476.65	15.00	18.43	41.54	186.92
肇　庆	Zhaoqing	122.82	224.53	83.99	174.19	10.65	19.19
清　远	Qingyuan	71.87	90.80	32.87	43.54	2.96	5.74
潮　州	Chaozhou	24.53	28.91	1.66	2.54	0.89	3.13
揭　阳	Jieyang	88.48	80.46	6.76	10.13	6.20	11.70
云　浮	Yunfu	65.97	56.17	18.33	22.85	5.34	6.67
按经济区域分	By Region						
珠 三 角	Pearl River Delta	424.02	503.44	136.32	237.23	42.43	109.48
粤　东	Eastern Region	192.47	182.63	11.15	19.57	13.76	26.09
粤　西	Western Region	623.65	862.81	30.77	40.30	87.23	320.00
粤　北	Northern Region	402.18	442.99	111.58	136.86	16.09	22.76

11-20 续表 continued

单位：万亩、万吨 (10000 mu，10000 tons)

市 别	City	#菠萝 Pineapple		#荔枝 Lychee		#龙眼 Longan	
		年末面积 Year-end Area	总产量 Total Output	年末面积 Year-end Area	总产量 Total Output	年末面积 Year-end Area	总产量 Total Output
全 省	**Provincial Total**	**61.42**	**131.96**	**419.89**	**163.41**	**172.57**	**106.23**
广 州	Guangzhou	0.04	0.15	56.69	11.81	12.04	4.48
深 圳	Shenzhen	0.15	0.13	3.31	1.25	0.48	0.27
珠 海	Zhuhai	0.02	0.11	3.98	0.64	0.75	0.15
汕 头	Shantou	…	…	4.93	1.27	0.69	0.68
佛 山	Foshan	0.01	0.02	0.19	0.12	0.42	0.29
韶 关	Shaoguan	…	…	0.01	0.01	0.19	0.12
河 源	Heyuan	0.04		5.24	0.95	1.66	0.74
梅 州	Meizhou	0.23	0.13	4.49	2.05	5.21	3.63
惠 州	Huizhou	0.38	0.52	38.24	12.28	13.32	7.04
汕 尾	Shanwei	2.25	1.40	24.81	12.40	3.70	2.83
东 莞	Dongguan			15.60	2.44	1.72	0.52
中 山	Zhongshan	0.42	0.66	1.09	0.52	0.69	0.50
江 门	Jiangmen	0.08	0.13	8.02	2.77	5.38	1.81
阳 江	Yangjiang	0.05	0.04	32.12	8.61	14.74	5.64
湛 江	Zhanjiang	50.42	117.45	39.19	25.16	5.76	4.24
茂 名	Maoming	0.09	0.13	142.69	62.09	81.78	56.27
肇 庆	Zhaoqing	0.77	0.65	2.78	3.07	3.36	2.70
清 远	Qingyuan	0.01	0.01	2.40	1.32	1.48	1.05
潮 州	Chaozhou	0.83	0.91	3.50	2.58	5.42	5.99
揭 阳	Jieyang	5.47	9.27	18.12	8.32	7.88	3.95
云 浮	Yunfu	0.15	0.26	12.52	3.76	5.89	3.31
按经济区域分	By Region						
珠 三 角	Pearl River Delta	1.87	2.36	129.88	34.90	38.16	17.77
粤 东	Eastern Region	8.55	11.58	51.35	24.57	17.70	13.46
粤 西	Western Region	50.56	117.62	214.00	95.86	102.28	66.14
粤 北	Northern Region	0.44	0.40	24.65	8.08	14.44	8.86

11-21 主要农产品产量与最高年份比较（2023年）
Output of Major Farm Products in Comparison with Peak Year (2023)

指 标	Item	2023	新中国成立以来最高年份 Peak Year since 1949		
			年份 Year	产量 Output	2023年为新中国成立以来最高年份% Percentage of 2023 to Peak Year%
粮食总产量 （万吨）	**Total Output of Grain (10000 tons)**	**1285.19**	**1997**	**1966.75**	**65.3**
#稻谷	Output of Rice	1096.89	1998	1688.53	65.0
#早稻	Early Rice	529.70	1983	862.25	61.4
晚稻	Late Rice	567.19	1998	866.51	65.5
薯类	Tubers	109.88	1998	238.28	46.1
经济作物 （万吨）	**Economic Crops (10000 tons)**				
甘蔗	Sugarcane and Fruit Canes	1271.08	1992	2376.62	53.5
#糖蔗	Sugarcane	1087.43	1992	2271.06	47.9
油料作物	Oil-bearing Crops	121.01	2022	117.43	103.1
#花生	Peanuts	119.54	2022	115.93	103.1
烟叶	Tobacco	3.74	1992	8.62	43.3
蔬菜 （万吨）	Vegetables (10000 tons)	4099.33	2022	3999.11	102.5
园林水果 （万吨）	**Fruits (10000 tons)**	**1991.87**	**2022**	**1895.18**	**105.1**
水产品 （万吨）	**Aquatic Products (10000 tons)**	**924.02**	**2022**	**894.03**	**103.4**
生猪年末存栏量 （万头）	**Number of Hogs at the Year-end (10000 heads)**	**2049.20**	**2009**	**2455.11**	**83.5**
生猪出栏头数 （万头）	**Number of Slaughtered Fattened Hogs (10000 heads)**	**3794.01**	**2014**	**4062.02**	**93.4**
猪肉产量 （万吨）	**Output of Pork (10000 tons)**	**298.00**	**2014**	**302.86**	**98.4**
家禽年末存栏 （亿只）	**Poultry at year-end (100 million heads)**	**4.02**	**2010**	**4.09**	**98.4**
出售和自宰的家禽（亿只）	**Poultry sold or slaughtered(100 million heads)**	**13.74**	**2020**	**13.74**	**100.0**
禽肉产量 （万吨）	**Output of Poultry Meat (10 000 tons)**	**194.54**	**2020**	**195.27**	**99.6**

11−22 农林牧渔业分项产值
Agricultural Production Basic Conditions

单位：亿元 (100 million yuan)

指 标	Item	2020	2021	2022	2023
农林牧渔业总产值	**Gross Output Value of Agriculture**	**7901.92**	**8305.84**	**8892.29**	**9202.09**
农业产值	**Farming**	**3769.26**	**3951.14**	**4308.23**	**4430.96**
谷物及其他作物	Cereal and other Crops	768.96	783.80	812.49	828.30
#谷物	Cereal	375.02	390.66	401.97	402.34
薯类	Tubers	98.20	98.32	106.71	115.90
豆类	Beans	9.13	9.33	9.93	10.06
糖料	Sugar Crops	84.14	82.02	82.72	83.18
油料	Oil Bearing Crops	105.44	110.10	111.67	119.36
蔬菜园艺作物	Horticulture Vegetables	1682.44	1834.07	1972.57	1998.19
#蔬菜(含菜用瓜、食用菌)	Vegetables	1464.81	1574.19	1680.55	1691.82
水果、坚果、饮料和香料作物	Fruits, Nuts, Drink, and Spice Crops	1194.48	1208.42	1372.15	1443.94
#水果(含果用瓜)、坚果	Fruits (Including Fruit Melons), Nuts	1084.18	1057.52	1187.11	1236.46
中草药材	Chinese Medicinal Herbs	123.38	124.85	151.03	160.53
林业产值	**Forestry**	**414.29**	**495.44**	**549.15**	**562.69**
林木的培育和种植	Planting and Nurturing of Trees	35.14	32.49	35.75	45.13
竹木采运	Lumbering and Transport of Bamboo	134.76	165.29	174.51	180.40
林产品	Forestry Production	244.38	297.67	338.89	337.15
牧业产值	**Animal Husbandry**	**1778.18**	**1707.82**	**1680.24**	**1696.79**
牲畜饲养	Breeding and Raising of Domestic Animals	54.97	56.49	63.03	62.62
猪的饲养	Raising of Swine	1000.35	940.13	874.34	804.53
家禽饲养	Raising of Poultry	632.64	633.00	670.02	759.48
其他畜牧业	Raising of Other Animals	90.22	78.19	72.85	70.16
渔业产值	**Fishery**	**1581.54**	**1747.34**	**1898.24**	**2005.31**
海水产品	Seawater Aquatic Production	793.73	909.96	997.50	1068.40
淡水产品	Freshwater Aquatic Production	787.81	837.38	900.73	936.91
农林牧渔专业及辅助性活动产值	**Professional and Auxiliary Activities of Agriculture, Forestry,Animal Husbandry, and Fishery Industries**	**358.64**	**404.10**	**456.43**	**506.35**

主要统计指标解释

农林牧渔业总产值　是以货币表现的农林牧渔业的全部产品总量和对农林牧渔业生产活动进行的各种支持性服务活动的价值。它反映一定时期内农林牧渔业生产总规模和总成果，是观察农林牧渔业生产水平和发展速度，研究农林牧渔业内部比例关系、农林牧渔业与工业、农林牧渔业与国家建设、人民生活比例关系的重要指标，同时也是计算农林牧渔业劳动生产率和农林牧渔业增加值的基础资料。

农林牧渔业总产值的计算，一般采用“产品法”，即凡有产品产量的，都按单位产品价格乘产量的办法求得每种产品产量的产值，然后相加求得各业的产值，最后各业相加求出农林牧渔业总产值。

农作物播种面积　指农业生产经营者在日历年度内收获的农作物在全部土地（耕地或非耕地）上的播种或移植面积。凡是本年内收获的作物，无论是本年还是上年播种，都算为当年播种面积，但不包括本年播种，下年收获的作物面积。

农作物产量　指农业生产经营者日历年度内生产的农作物数量。

Explanatory Notes on Main Statistical Indicators

Gross Output Value of Agriculture Forestry, Animal Husbandry and Fishery　refers to the total volume of products of farming, forestry, animal husbandry, and fishery and the value of various services supporting the production of farming, forestry, animal husbandry and fishery in monetary terms, which reflects the total scale and total results of farming, forestry, animal husbandry and fishery production during a given period of time. It is an important indicator to observe the production level and development speed of farming, forestry, animal husbandry and fishery, to study the internal structure of farming, forestry, animal husbandry and fishery, and to review the proportionate relationship of farming, forestry, animal husbandry and fishery to industry, to national construction and to people's life. It is also the foundation for calculating the labor productivity and value-added of farming, forestry, animal husbandry and fishery.

Generally, the gross output value of farming, forestry, animal husbandry and fishery is calculated with the production approach. Where applicable, the gross output value of each single product is obtained by multiplying the output of each product by its price. These values are then summed up to obtain the output value of each sector. The sum of output values of all sectors is the gross output value of farming, forestry, animal husbandry and fishery.

Sown Area of Crops　refers to area of all land (cultivated or non-cultivated area) sown or transplanted with crops that are harvested within the calendar year by agricultural producers. All crops harvested within the year are counted as sown area, regardless of being sown in this year or the previous year. Crops sown this year but will be harvested in the coming year are excluded.

Crops Output　refers to total output of crops produced by agricultural producers within a calendar year.

十二、工业

INDUSTRY

十二 工业

简要说明

一、本篇主要包括如下资料：1. 全省及各地市全部工业和规模以上工业生产主要指标总量及速度。2. 规模以上工业主要产品产量。3. 全省及各地市规模以上工业主要经济效益指标。4. 规模以上工业企业按主要经济类型和企业规模分组的主要财务指标。5. 规模以上工业中高技术制造业、先进制造业主要经济指标。

二、本篇资料由广东省统计局工业交通统计处整理提供。

三、本篇工业资料是根据国家统计局工业统计报表制度填报。2011 年定报及以前数据经各市、县统计局布置、收集、汇总整理，2011 年起通过网上直报系统收集、汇总整理。其中 1995 年度资料通过第三次全国工业普查取得，2004 年数据根据第一次全国经济普查取得，2008 年数据根据第二次全国经济普查取得。2013 年数据根据第三次全国经济普查取得，2018 年数据根据 2018 年广东省第四次全国经济普查取得。

四、规模以上工业法人单位的统计范围。1998 年至 2006 年为全部国有和年主营业务收入 500 万元及以上的非国有工业企业；2007 至 2010 年为年主营业务收入 500 万元及以上的工业企业（即规模以上工业企业）；从 2011 年开始，为年主营业务收入 2000 万元及以上的工业企业（即规模以上工业企业）；2021 年起，为年主营业务收入 2000 万元及以上的工业企业和个体经营户（即规模以上工业法人单位）。

五、从 2017 年年报起，工业行业分类按 2017 年《国民经济行业分类标准》划分；企业规模划分按 2017 年《统计上大中小微型企业划分办法》标准执行，增加了微型企业分组。

12 Industry

Brief Introduction

Ⅰ. This chapter covers the following data: (1) Principal aggregate indicators and growth rates of industrial production of total industry and industry above designated size of the province and cities; (2) Output of major products of industry above designated size; (3) Main indicators on economic benefits of industry above designated size of the province and cities; (4) Main financial indicators on industry above designated size grouped by sector and scale; (5) Main economic indicators on advanced manufacturing industries and hi-tech manufacturing industries above designated size;

Ⅱ. The data in this chapter are prepared and provided by the Division of Industry and Transport Statistics of Statistics Bureau of Guangdong Province.

III. The data in this chapter are compiled mainly in accordance with the industrial statistical reporting scheme stipulated by the National Bureau of Statistics. The annual data of 2011 and before 2011 are collected, tabulated and prepared by the municipal and county statistical bureaus. Since 2011, the annual data are collected, tabulated and prepared by the network reporting system. Of which the annual data of 1995 were collected in the Third National Industrial Census and the data of 2004 were collected in the First National Economic Census of Guangdong, the data of 2008 were collected in the Second National Economic Census of Guangdong, the data of 2013 were collected in the Third National Economic Census of Guangdong, the data of 2018 were collected in the Fourth Economic Census of Guangdong.

IV. Industrial legal entities above designated size refers to all State-owned industrial enterprises and non-State-owned industrial enterprises with revenue from principal business over 5 million yuan from 1998 to 2006. For 2007 to 2010, the scopes of industrial statistics were all industrial enterprises with revenue from principal business over 5 million yuan, (or the industrial enterprises above designated size). Since 2011, the scope is adjusted to all industrial enterprises with revenue from principal business above 20 million yuan (i.e. industrial enterprises above designated size). From 2021, the scope is industrial enterprise and self-employed household with an annual main business income of 20 million yuan or more(i.e. industrial legal entities above designated size).

V. Industrial sectors since 2017 in this chapter has been categorized in accordance with the 2017 Industrial Classification of the National Economy and the size of industrial enterprises have been categorized in accordance with the 2017 Interim Regulations on Statistical Categorization of Large, Medium , Small and Micro Industrial Enterprises. Micro industrial enterprises are added.

12-1 工业主要指标

Main Indicators of Industry

指 标	Item	2000	2010	2015	2021	2022	2023
全部工业	**All Industrial Enterprises**						
企业单位数 (个)	Number of Enterprises (unit)	380231	481022	582813	674522	732757	
	(100 million yuan)						
规模以上工业	**Industrial Enterprises above Designated Size**						
企业单位数 (个)	Number of Enterprises (unit)	19695	53418	42134	66329	70725	71996
亏损企业数 (个)	Number of Loss-making Enterprises (unit)	4805	6385	5850	10759	14953	16762
工业总产值 (亿元)	Gross Industrial Output Value (100 million yuan)	12480.93	85824.64	124649.16	171979.82	180933.44	185154.19
工业销售产值 (亿元)	Sales Output Value of Industry (100 million yuan)	12156.19	83646.51	121049.68	164660.77	173713.57	178191.72
出口交货值 (亿元)	Export Delivery Value (100 million yuan)	4634.44	25919.08	32035.16	37553.99	38598.36	36716.99
营业收入 (亿元)	Business Revenue (100 million yuan)	12480.93	85824.64	124649.16	173649.71	183027.35	185496.87
资产总计 (亿元)	Total Assets (100 million yuan)	14370.57	62626.90	95411.22	175746.01	196419.19	211484.21
流动资产合计 (亿元)	Average Balance of Circulating Funds (100 million yuan)	6891.49	34339.97	54715.38	105030.92	117937.22	126344.46
固定资产合计 (亿元)	Average Balance of Net Value of Fixed Assets (100 million yuan)	5884.78	22407.53	26943.69	32626.99	36649.71	38315.11
负债总计 (亿元)	Total Liabilities (100 million yuan)	8272.36	35073.74	54747.90	100629.77	114686.14	124245.14
所有者权益合计(亿元)	Total Creditors' Equity (100 million yuan)	6098.21	27461.84	40239.01	75120.93	81498.85	87246.87
利润总额 (亿元)	Total Profits (100 million yuan)	564.75	6239.64	7723.16	11278.35	10329.25	11595.24
亏损企业亏损额(亿元)	Loss Value of Loss-making Enterprises (100 million yuan)	156.03	227.26	510.18	1219.85	1801.76	1582.05
利税总额 (亿元)	Total Pre-tax Profits (100 million yuan)	1042.77	9418.42	12375.00	16325.16	15857.14	17448.34
应交增值税 (亿元)	Value-added Tax Payable (100 million yuan)	360.83	2280.56	3284.50	3259.11	3598.56	3749.15
所得税费用 (亿元)	Fee of Income Tax Payable (100 million yuan)	62.79	820.89	1179.43	1511.50	1303.74	1427.36
本年应付工资总额 (亿元)	Total Salary Payable in Current Year (100 million yuan)	676.06	5747.72	9888.11	15585.50	16983.35	17862.46
就业人员平均人数 (万人)	Average Employed Persons (10000 persons)	572.89	1568.00	1439.33	1343.58	1332.56	1297.06

注：1.2011年起，规模以上工业统计口径从年主营业务收入500万元及以上调整为2000万元及以上工业企业，2021年调整为主业务收入2000万元及以上工业企业和工业个体经营户，为反映可比口径速度，本表规模以上工业主要指标使用快报增速，全部工业数据含个体数据。

2.2011年起，本年应付工资总额指标数据为本年应付职工薪酬；所得税费用数据2014年以前为应交所得税。

3.本表中营业收入数据2017年及以前为主营业务收入数据，2018年后为营业收入数据。

Notes: a) Since 2011, the annual principal business revenue of industrial enterprises above designated size is changed from industrial enterprises of 5 million yuan or above to 20 million yuan or above. It is adjusted to industrial enterprises and industrial self-employed households with main business income of 20 million yuan and above in 2021. Growth rates in this table are calculated at current price with flash statistics report in order to compare the rate. Data on all industrial enterprises include self-employed individuals.

b) Total salary payable in current year from 2011 are total employee pay payable and income tax payable are tax expenses.Data of fee of income tax payable before 2014 are income tax payable.

c) The indicator was Revenue from Principal Business in 2017 and before,and are Business Revenue since 2018.

12-2 规模以上工业企业单位数和产值
Number of Industrial Enterprises above Designated Size and Their Gross Output Values

项 目	Item	2000	2010	2021	2022	2023
工业企业单位数 （个）	**Total Number of Industrial Enterprises (unit)**	**19695**	**53418**	**66329**	**70725**	**71996**
按登记注册统计类别分	By Registered Statistical Categories					
总计中：#国有控股工业企业	Of the Total:State-holding Industrial Enterprises	3320	1279	1439	1573	1646
内资企业	Domestic Invested Enterprises	11282	34477	54455	58989	60699
港澳台投资企业	Enterprises with Investment from Hong Kong, Macao and Taiwan	6731	13151	7994	7942	7723
外商投资企业	Foreign Invested Enterprises	1682	5790	3880	3794	3494
其他统计类别	Other Statistical Categories					80
按轻重工业分	Grouped by Light and Heavy Industries					
轻工业	Light Industry	12255	29678	29844	31685	32045
重工业	Heavy Industry	7440	23740	36485	39040	39951
按企业规模分	Grouped by Size of Enterprises					
大型企业	Large Enterprises	823	524	1564	1438	1389
中型企业	Medium Enterprises	1228	6968	6812	6449	6414
小微型企业	Small and Micro Enterprises	17644	45926	57953	62838	64193
工业总产值 （亿元）	**Gross Industrial Output Value (100 million yuan)**	**12480.93**	**85824.64**	**171979.82**	**180933.44**	**185154.19**
按登记注册统计类别分	By Registered Statistical Categories					
总计中：#国有控股工业企业	Of the Total:State-holding Industrial Enterprises	3126.12	13166.37	28733.57	32513.46	35543.39
内资企业	Domestic Invested Enterprises	5206.58	40305.41	114549.08	121529.11	130038.00
港澳台投资企业	Enterprises with Investment from Hong Kong, Macao and Taiwan	4747.30	21813.34	29834.65	31506.28	26963.13
外商投资企业	Foreign Invested Enterprises	2527.06	23705.89	27596.08	27898.05	28128.28
其他统计类别	Other Statistical Categories					24.79
按轻重工业分	Grouped by Light and Heavy Industries					
轻工业	Light Industry	6607.84	32867.30	53378.95	54766.14	55123.30
重工业	Heavy Industry	5873.09	52957.34	118600.86	126167.29	130030.89
按企业规模分	Grouped by Size of Enterprises					
大型企业	Large Enterprises	4523.92	28306.79	77076.51	82354.91	84290.38
中型企业	Medium Enterprises	1427.65	28566.98	38215.85	40038.23	40405.19
小微型企业	Small and Micro Enterprises	6529.37	28950.88	56687.45	58540.30	60458.62

注：1.2011年起，规模以上工业统计口径从年主营业务收入500万元及以上调整为2000万元及以上工业企业,2021年调整为主业务收入2000万元及以上工业企业和工业个体经营户。

2.企业规模划分：2003年以前为一个标准，2003-2010年为一个标准，2011年起采用新的标准，并增加微型企业.

3.本表登记注册统计类别按《关于市场主体统计分类的划分规定》(国统字〔2023〕14号)执行。

Note: a) Since 2011,the annual principal business revenue of industrial enterprises above designated size is changed from industrial enterprises of 5 million yuan or above to 20 million yuan or above. It is adjusted to industrial enterprises and industrial self-employed households with main business income of 20 million yuan and above in 2021.

b) Size of Industrial enterprise categorization: The standard prior to 2003 is not the same as the period from 2003 to 2010. Since 2011, New standard is adopted and micro-enterprises is added.

c) The registered statistical categories of this table is implemented in accordance with the Regulations onStatistics the Classification of Market Entity(Guotongzi [2023] No. 14).

12-3 全部工业总产值和指数
Gross Industrial Output Value of All Industrial Enterprises and Theirs Indices

年份 Year	绝对数（亿元） Absolute Figures (100 million yuan)			指数（1978年＝100） Indices(1978=100)	
	全部工业总产值 Gross Industrial Output Value	#国有控股工业企业 State-holding Industry Enterprises	#国有工业 State-owned Industry	全部工业总产值 Gross Industrial Output Value	#国有工业 State-owned Industry
1978	206.56		131.83	100.0	100.0
1979	221.46		142.64	107.5	106.1
1980	248.68		146.95	117.4	109.2
1981	282.95		165.53	134.5	120.3
1982	313.76		178.78	145.7	129.5
1983	356.91		204.68	163.4	144.1
1984	433.40		240.19	196.4	164.0
1985	534.72		298.42	249.6	194.0
1986	632.89		334.59	288.3	209.7
1987	878.29		427.10	384.6	255.4
1988	1318.90		594.98	519.3	316.7
1989	1647.24		714.93	603.9	335.8
1990	1902.25		765.43	707.1	366.9
1991	2524.12		973.59	909.6	442.1
1992	3479.39		1202.46	1243.0	532.5
1993	5237.37		1445.38	1731.0	552.4
1994	7273.95		1562.24	2305.9	536.8
1995	9720.54		1709.89	2880.8	539.8
1995(新规定) (New Stipulations)	8849.90		1465.82		
1996	10530.93		1544.58	3404.9	549.8
1997	12372.69		1574.39	4040.7	590.0
1998	13799.16		1453.79	4708.5	526.3
1999	15303.33	3025.68	1427.42	5385.9	487.2
2000	16904.47	3126.12	1536.50	6376.7	472.1
2001	18909.91	3309.51	1186.24	7428.9	374.8
2002	21788.71	3369.50	1217.66	8847.8	392.4
2003	27375.56	4017.54	979.19	11281.8	379.3
2004	34443.48	6039.24	1862.55	13958.7	709.5
2005	41661.74	6375.54	2068.75	16634.5	776.4
2006	51131.94	7253.17	2923.76	20137.8	1082.3
2007	62759.92	8603.94	2791.73	24399.0	1267.4
2008	74414.31	11144.50	2877.31	27636.7	1267.0
2009	75886.62	10790.11	3654.86	29405.4	1280.4
2010	93462.97	13166.37	4595.82	35110.0	1554.0
2011	103493.35	13927.70	5102.02	39358.3	1765.3
2012	105049.54	15529.16	5938.25	43490.9	1899.5
2013	119139.72	17525.16	1242.18	48796.8	2076.2
2014	130081.02	18225.94	635.82	52944.5	2153.0
2015	135308.14	17032.30	605.34	54956.4	2200.4
2016	144926.09	17172.18	665.85	58418.7	2347.8
2017	148173.99	19525.92	802.95	65078.4	2014.4
2018	148876.81	20855.98	153.00	70610.1	2433.4
2019	157662.91	21270.03	240.20	73858.2	2762.0
2020	155210.54	21191.00	633.27	73569.1	3134.1
2021	182919.33	28733.57	801.98	81220.3	3773.5
2022	193108.50	32513.46	941.32	82194.9	4079.1
2023	198238.45	35543.39	193.08	85400.5	4446.2

注：1.工业总产值按当年价计算。2023年起，国有工业统计口径依据《关于市场主体统计分类的划分规定》(国统字[2023]14号)调整，总量数据与历史数据不可比，指数按同口径可比价计算。
2.2000年起全部工业总产值中规模以下部分为抽样调查数。

Notes: a) The total industrial output value is calculated at the current price. Since 2023, the statistical caliber of state-owned industries has been adjusted in accordance with the Regulations onStatistics the Classification of Market Entity(Guotongzi [2023] No. 14).
b) Since 2000, data of the industrial enterprises below designated size in the gross industrial output value have been obtained from sample surveys.

12-4 规模以上工业总产值和指数

Gross Output Value of Industrial Enterprises above Designated Size and Their Indices

单位:亿元 (100 million yuan)

年份 Year	工业总产值 Gross Industrial Output Value	轻工业 Light Industry	重工业 Heavy Industry	#大中型工业 Large and Medium-sized Industry	指数(1978年=100) Indices (1978=100)	轻工业 Light Industry	重工业 Heavy Industry	#大中型工业 Large and Medium-sized Industry
1978	180.73	102.32	78.41	49.34	100.0	100.0	100.0	100.0
1979	194.64	110.28	84.36	54.91	105.8	105.3	106.4	109.5
1980	212.69	128.17	84.52	56.33	115.8	127.7	100.7	103.1
1981	241.93	152.97	88.96	66.89	128.7	151.3	102.1	133.0
1982	263.02	164.17	98.85	75.37	139.9	164.2	111.2	148.5
1983	293.70	180.60	113.10	92.78	157.1	184.5	124.7	181.5
1984	359.87	223.29	136.58	110.63	188.1	226.1	142.8	209.9
1985	471.83	289.68	182.15	166.11	236.0	279.6	179.8	302.0
1986	550.49	344.70	205.79	210.27	269.5	327.7	194.7	379.7
1987	747.47	472.45	275.02	299.19	350.1	426.5	252.2	522.3
1988	1118.00	718.03	399.97	459.74	472.5	582.1	332.2	720.2
1989	1399.45	893.20	506.25	622.42	543.2	594.3	389.2	863.6
1990	1605.80	1057.02	548.78	734.35	637.6	795.5	435.8	1042.2
1991	2144.93	1371.46	773.47	1057.02	820.0	1009.7	622.1	1476.1
1992	2884.93	1796.12	1088.23	1408.48	1096.0	1331.0	854.4	1980.5
1993	4252.70	2515.77	1736.93	1891.29	1470.7	1751.6	1188.8	2412.8
1994	5565.48	3224.69	2340.79	2563.27	1819.1	2135.9	1507.6	2863.3
1995(原规定) (Original Stipulations)	7189.24	4148.78	3040.46	3227.59	2274.1	2581.8	1993.2	3519.7
1995(新规定) (New Stipulations)	6502.97	3776.94	2726.03	2824.61				
1996	7490.49	4344.25	3146.24	3470.81	2625.4	2989.5	2290.2	4253.6
1997	8442.32	4914.09	3528.23	3950.86	3045.3	3470.5	2652.8	5176.4
1998	9738.56	5765.51	3973.05	4169.16	3508.2	3866.1	3228.5	5927.0
1999	10538.17	6011.06	4527.11	4711.94	4016.9	4299.1	3861.3	7070.9
2000	12480.93	6607.84	5873.09	5951.56	4757.4	4737.6	5027.4	8590.8

12-4 续表 continued

单位:亿元 (100 million yuan)

年份 Year	工业总产值 Gross Industrial Output Value	轻工业 Light Industry	重工业 Heavy Industry	#大中型工业 Large and Medium-sized Industry	指数(1978年=100) Indices (1978=100)	轻工业 Light Industry	重工业 Heavy Industry	#大中型工业 Large and Medium-sized Industry
2001	14035.35	7165.90	6869.44	7534.70	5637.5	5400.9	6234.0	12181.8
2002	16378.60	8161.63	8216.97	8755.02	6787.6	6313.7	7742.6	14472.0
2003	21513.46	9959.51	11553.95	14353.53	9051.9	7845.4	11063.4	19955.4
2004	29554.92	12146.01	17408.91	19799.88	12228.7	9549.6	15380.9	27054.8
2005	35942.74	14506.76	21435.97	24403.13	14652.0	11434.3	17914.1	32852.0
2006	44674.75	17148.09	27526.65	30828.93	17963.7	13549.8	21927.5	40937.6
2007	55252.86	21221.12	34031.74	37718.60	21931.9	16667.6	26370.0	49436.3
2008	65424.61	25035.86	40388.76	43866.65	25188.6	19373.2	29468.8	55765.6
2009	68275.77	26685.86	41589.91	44755.10	27430.4	20806.8	32415.7	57494.3
2010	85824.64	32867.30	52957.34	56873.77	33437.7	25200.5	39064.6	70824.4
2011	94871.68	36005.33	58866.35	67492.96	38954.9	29333.4	45549.3	79606.6
2012	95602.09	35817.39	59784.70	70178.27	43162.0	32032.1	49147.7	86134.3
2013	109673.07	41669.48	68003.59	76417.82	48686.7	36420.5	55192.9	95695.2
2014	119713.04	45756.65	73956.39	85194.40	53019.8	39953.3	59829.1	103446.5
2015	124649.16	47604.61	77044.55	88503.28	54981.5	41471.5	62042.8	106239.6
2016	133768.04	50237.52	83530.51	94758.85	58555.4	43379.2	66758.0	112826.4
2017	135722.42	47827.76	87894.65	95951.23	65582.0	47587.0	75703.6	126252.8
2018	140398.93	44520.43	95878.50	99544.89	71156.5	50394.6	83046.9	133954.2
2019	146121.72	46185.68	99936.04	101521.68	74429.7	51956.9	87531.4	144335.9
2020	148469.69	45387.73	103081.95	101762.61	75546.1	52216.6	89194.5	147800.0
2021	171979.82	53378.95	118600.86	115292.36	83176.3	58743.7	97222.0	160658.6
2022	180933.44	54766.14	126167.29	122393.14	83924.8	57745.1	99263.7	165317.7
2023	185154.19	55123.30	130030.89	124695.57	87281.8	58091.5	104723.2	172922.3

注：1.工业总产值按当年价格计算，指数按同口径可比价计算。

2.1997年以前为乡及乡以上工业，2011年起规模以上工业统计口径从年主营业务收入500万元及以上调整为2000万元及以上，2021年调整为主业务收入2000万元及以上工业企业和工业个体经营户。

Notes: a) Gross industrial output values are calculated at current prices, whereas their indices are calculated at comparable prices of the same caliber.

b) Data prior to 1997 refer to the industrial enterprises at or above the township level.Since 2011,the annual principal business revenue of 20 industrial enterprises above designated size is changed from industrial enterprises of 5 million yuan or above to million yuan or above. It is adjusted to industrial enterprises and industrial self-employed households with main business income of 20 million yuan and above in 2021.

12-5 规模以上工业产品产量

Output of Industrial Products of Enterprises above Designated Size

产品名称		Item		2000	2010	2021	2022	2023
化学纤维	(万吨)	Chemical Fiber	(10000 tons)	45.00	44.54	84.71	75.51	71.85
#合成纤维	(万吨)	Synthetic Fiber	(10000 tons)	45.00	42.45	55.27	51.93	53.16
纱	(万吨)	Yarn	(10000 tons)	16.99	45.16	25.27	25.42	22.53
布	(亿米)	Cloth	(100 million m)	16.99	28.27	25.75	20.17	16.30
#棉布	(亿米)	Pure Cotton Cloth	(100 million m)	7.49	19.54	11.37	8.85	6.65
蚕丝	(万吨)	Silk	(10000 tons)	0.05	0.17	0.04	0.03	0.01
呢绒	(万米)	Woolen Piece Goods	(10000 m)	676.00	13.00	694.50	631.50	813.20
服装	(亿件)	Clothing	(100 million pieces)	21.99	70.26	39.16	35.20	33.24
皮革鞋靴	(亿双)	Leather Shoes and Boots	(100 million pairs)	9.05	12.18	3.36	3.64	3.95
机制纸及纸板	(万吨)	Machine-made Paper and Paperboard	(10000 tons)	260.30	1434.68	2410.29	2374.14	2509.21
家用电冰箱	(万台)	Household Refrigerators	(10000 sets)	320.70	1457.76	2091.56	1773.35	2195.00
家用冷柜	(万台)	Freezers	(10000 sets)		180.14	554.31	464.34	562.03
家用洗衣机	(万台)	Household Washing Machines	(10000 sets)	244.18	467.83	757.57	686.72	785.56
家用吸尘器	(万台)	Vacuum Cleaners	(10000 sets)	251.80	2626.67	2551.32	2321.83	2800.81
家用电风扇	(万台)	Electric Fans	(10000 sets)	6759.02	14813.38	21170.92	16057.12	16899.49
房间空气调节器	(万台)	House Air Conditioners	(10000 sets)	697.91	5477.85	6736.25	6637.70	7438.47
家用吸排油烟机	(万台)	Smoke Absorbers	(10000 sets)	43.39	1324.67	2427.27	2328.77	1748.33
电饭锅	(万个)	Electric Rice Cookers	(10000 sets)		15207.47	10357.51	9445.49	10231.17
微波炉	(万台)	Microwave Ovens	(10000 sets)	906.51	5341.00	9140.69	9108.53	9430.41
程控交换机	(万线)	Program Controlled Switchboards	(10000 lines)	3554.88	1602.61	591.11	829.71	445.42
电话单机	(万部)	Telephone Sets	(10000 sets)	7700.05	14766.80	4758.81	3730.57	2759.33
移动通信手持机(手机)	(万台)	Mobile Telephone	(10000 units)	1001.30	48626.59	66965.36	62690.03	65066.15
#智能手机	(万台)	Smart Telephone	(10000 units)			52476.53	50603.90	49380.09
微型计算机设备	(万台)	Micro-computers Equipment	(10000 units)	169.74	3581.11	5935.41	6948.85	7458.10
服务器	(万台)	Servers	(10000 units)		2.98	148.36	85.22	236.78
集成电路	(亿块)	Semiconductor Integrated Circuit	(100 million pieces)	11.76	161.01	539.39	516.87	697.80
彩色电视机	(万部)	Color TV Sets	(10000 sets)	1531.53	4494.78	9810.91	10792.02	11211.09
#智能电视	(万台)	Smart TV	(10000 sets)			7418.27	7957.95	8736.13
数字激光音、视盘机	(万台)	Laser Digital Audio,Video Disc Machine	(10000sets)	637.69	7589.01	572.78	351.82	308.95
组合音响	(万部)	Hi-fi Stereo Component System	(10000 sets)	2344.58	9713.01	17252.45	15545.19	13584.15
照相机	(万架)	Cameras	(10000 sets)	3545.88	3798.93	529.65	444.43	792.51
#数码照相机	(万台)	Digital Cameras	(10000 sets)		3687.89	466.00	360.02	430.33
表	(万只)	Watches	(10000 units)	19123.23	11892.26	8032.13	8238.43	8296.91
日用玻璃制品	(万吨)	Daily Use Glassware	(10000 tons)	51.46	150.93	112.86	103.57	113.57
合成洗涤剂	(万吨)	Synthetic Detergents	(10000 tons)	26.31	224.61	324.62	325.08	390.88
精制食用植物油	(万吨)	Refined Edible Vegetable oil	(10000 tons)	7.87	244.21	756.40	711.04	782.81
成品糖	(万吨)	Refined Sugar	(10000 tons)	91.30	91.66	131.42	119.16	103.40
食用盐	(万吨)	Edible Salt	(10000 tons)			0.18	0.47	4.68
卷烟	(万箱)	Cigarettes	(10000 units)	177.30	260.69	258.30	259.30	260.46
罐头	(万吨)	Canned Food	(10000 tons)	7.11	30.18	22.87	17.12	15.62
饮料酒	(万千升)	Alcoholic Beverages (mixed weight)	(10000 kiloliter)	178.66	415.80	428.86	414.88	468.93
#白酒	(万千升)	Spirits	(10000 kiloliter)	17.88	10.27	10.74	10.48	5.37
啤酒	(万千升)	Beer	(10000 kiloliter)	158.89	401.40	408.25	394.11	454.46
乳制品	(万吨)	Dairy Products	(10000 tons)	1.29	58.12	82.74	77.86	78.05
中成药	(万吨)	Traditional Chinese Patent Medicine	(10000 tons)	6.05	19.01	24.41	22.37	23.39
化学药品原药	(万吨)	Chemical Active Pharmaceutical Ingredient	(10000 tons)	1.94	4.78	11.73	9.61	3.66

12−5 续表 continued

产品名称	Item	2000	2010	2021	2022	2023
农用氮、磷、钾化学肥料(折纯)(万吨)	Chemical Fertilizer (10000 tons)	34.65	62.15	6.44	5.52	12.80
#磷肥(折五氧化二磷100%) (万吨)	Phosphate Fertilizer (10000 tons)	18.67	50.66	2.45	3.77	6.02
化学农药原药(折有效成分100%)(万吨)	Chemical Pesticide (10000 tons)	0.84	0.86	2.28	3.10	3.84
乙烯 (万吨)	Ethylene (10000 tons)	54.85	203.96	417.75	391.15	501.57
合成橡胶 (万吨)	Synthetic Rubber (10000 tons)	5.45	38.36	72.78	70.33	92.94
橡胶轮胎外胎 (万条)	Tires (10000 pieces)	359.13	6907.25	3277.46	3404.11	3905.52
交流电动机 (万千瓦)	Alternating Current Motors (10000 kw)	236.21	753.39	5185.75	8191.64	5458.03
汽车 (万辆)	Motor Vehicles (10000 units)	3.94	156.29	338.46	415.37	518.30
#载货汽车 (万辆)	Trucks (10000 units)	0.53	0.34	0.82	0.63	1.05
客车 (万辆)	Buses (10000 units)	0.18	0.20	0.45	0.75	0.20
轿车 (万辆)	Cars (10000 units)	3.22	132.67	183.34	235.02	269.74
#新能源汽车 (万辆)	New Energy Vehicle (10000 units)			53.54	129.73	253.00
城市轨道车辆 (辆)	Urban Rail Vehicle (unit)			246	172	116
民用钢质船舶 (万载重吨)	Civil Steel ship (10000 deadweight ton)		177.18	71.73	82.56	510.57
摩托车整车 (万辆)	Motorcycles (10000 units)	146.31	917.60	732.23	628.72	630.27
两轮脚踏自行车 (万辆)	Bicycles (10000 units)	1038.00	788.75	884.83	901.50	721.57
生铁 (万吨)	Pig Iron (10000 tons)	201.57	806.68	2053.64	2420.90	2437.57
粗钢 (万吨)	Crude Steel (10000 tons)	286.99	1239.34	3178.33	3571.77	4448.54
钢材 (万吨)	Rolled Steel Products (10000 tons)	406.28	2918.89	5111.18	5627.44	6192.39
十种有色金属 (万吨)	Ten Kinds of Nonferrous Metals(10000 tons)		45.31	49.99	53.29	73.96
铝材 (万吨)	Aluminum (10000 tons)		496.85	510.11	553.07	555.73
汽车用发动机 (万千瓦)	Automotive engines (10000 kw)		8727.56	24047.87	26369.58	25483.89
工业机器人 (万套)	Industrial Robots (10000 sets)			12.44	16.57	20.13
光纤 (万千米)	Optical fiber (10000 km)			672.97	1261.15	1402.94
光缆 (万芯千米)	Optical Cable (10000 km)		835.99	2975.71	3356.84	3806.89
太阳能电池(光伏电池) (万千瓦)	Solar cells (photovoltaic cells) (10000 kw)			216.46	320.56	344.06
水泥 (万吨)	Cement (10000 tons)	5872.00	11536.67	17005.20	15131.17	14251.58
平板玻璃 (万重量箱)	Plate Glass (10000 wt.cases)	632.59	7821.07	11083.79	10336.04	8931.64
硫酸(折100%) (万吨)	Sulphuric Acid (10000 tons)	138.75	236.74	251.57	237.38	260.86
纯碱(碳酸钠) (万吨)	Soda Ash (10000 tons)	24.28	40.01	57.28	55.66	64.56
烧碱(折100%) (万吨)	Caustic Soda (10000 tons)	16.43	27.62	34.56	33.98	34.73

注：1.纱包括纯棉纱、棉混纺纱、化学纤维纱，不包括棉线、代用纤维纱和手工纺纱。
2.布包括纯棉布、棉混纺布、化学纤维布，不包括代用纤维布、手工织布。
3.农用化肥按有效成分100%计算。
4.2023年起，表统计口径调整为钟表与计时仪器，与历史数据不可比。

Notes: a) Yarn includes pure and blended cotton yarn, chemical fiber yarn, but excludes cotton thread, substitute fiber yarn and handmade yarn.
b) Cloth includes pure and blended cotton cloth,chemical fiber cloth and canvas,but excludes substitute fiber cloth,hand-woven cloth and cord fabric.
c) Output of chemical fertilizers is calculated on the basis of 100 percent effective content equivalent.
d) Starting from 2023, the statistical caliber of the table was adjusted to include clocks and timing instruments, which is no longer comparable to historical data.

12-6 各市规模以上工业企业单位数和工业总产值

Number and Gross Output Value of Industrial Enterprises above Designated Size by City

市别	City	工业企业单位数（个） Number of Industrial Enterprises (unit)								
		2000	2005	2010	2015	2019	2020	2021	2022	2023
广　州	Guangzhou	4531	5240	6969	4644	5802	6208	6757	6878	6873
深　圳	Shenzhen	1834	5214	8249	6539	10337	11255	13027	13790	14188
珠　海	Zhuhai	771	992	1347	1023	1388	1492	1655	1792	1778
汕　头	Shantou	794	1490	2580	1771	1972	1928	2061	2181	2225
佛　山	Foshan	2180	5148	7684	5787	7902	8020	9370	9851	9884
韶　关	Shaoguan	406	392	559	628	475	504	603	641	660
河　源	Heyuan	148	226	440	575	567	581	623	627	642
梅　州	Meizhou	371	392	521	440	474	505	536	547	557
惠　州	Huizhou	689	1243	1853	1893	2764	3055	3873	4365	4466
汕　尾	Shanwei	94	179	452	238	244	258	289	316	325
东　莞	Dongguan	1663	4504	5899	5688	10658	11525	12778	13844	14180
中　山	Zhongshan	1074	3291	5063	3045	3635	3868	4626	4959	5025
江　门	Jiangmen	1599	2365	3246	2036	2458	2535	2903	3264	3536
阳　江	Yangjiang	250	498	596	571	334	386	461	512	504
湛　江	Zhanjiang	458	578	850	828	870	780	788	815	824
茂　名	Maoming	447	590	792	957	810	751	652	674	693
肇　庆	Zhaoqing	981	684	1131	1110	1269	1321	1446	1562	1634
清　远	Qingyuan	304	426	813	611	772	834	949	1034	1059
潮　州	Chaozhou	326	727	1245	890	936	939	1035	1075	1035
揭　阳	Jieyang	455	714	2525	2030	1393	1376	1464	1572	1470
云　浮	Yunfu	320	264	604	830	355	383	433	426	438
按经济区域分	By Region									
珠三角	Pearl River Delta	15322	28681	41441	31765	46213	49279	56435	60305	61564
粤　东	Eastern Region	1669	3110	6802	4929	4545	4501	4849	5144	5055
粤　西	Western Region	1155	1666	2238	2356	2014	1917	1901	2001	2021
粤　北	Northern Region	1549	1700	2937	3084	2643	2807	3144	3275	3356

注：2011年起，规模以上工业统计口径从年主营业务收入500万元及以上调整为2000万元及以上工业企业，2021年为主业务收入2000万元及以上工业企业和工业个体经营户。

Note: Since 2011, the annual principal business revenue of industrial enterprises above designated size is changed from industrial enterprises of 5 million yuan or above to 20 million yuan or above. It is adjusted to industrial enterprises and industrial self-employed households with main business income of 20 million yuan and above in 2021.

12-6 续表 continued

市 别	City	工业总产值（亿元） Gross Industrial Output Value（100 million yuan）								
		2000	2005	2010	2015	2019	2020	2021	2022	2023
广 州	Guangzhou	2568.57	6032.05	13831.25	18424.73	19407.64	20310.16	23121	23928.58	24380.91
深 圳	Shenzhen	2566.93	9867.55	18526.82	25542.44	37326.16	38460.79	42453.96	46259.43	49192.69
珠 海	Zhuhai	630.17	1569.56	2976.18	3966.02	4646.99	4565.80	5272.44	5916.09	6142.00
汕 头	Shantou	344.34	761.37	1897.57	2968.80	3060.82	2985.44	3378.2	3404.18	3018.87
佛 山	Foshan	1560.55	4780.88	14527.47	19544.95	23222.05	23037.41	26312.48	27965.42	28147.67
韶 关	Shaoguan	151.01	393.36	773.37	1221.78	1210.17	1256.83	1645.23	1617.80	1675.29
河 源	Heyuan	35.81	182.10	832.73	1443.02	1352.91	1244.61	1459.68	1459.82	1529.63
梅 州	Meizhou	81.81	206.98	455.97	704.76	713.19	725.80	865.46	858.68	950.00
惠 州	Huizhou	657.83	1428.66	3905.17	7044.73	7431.43	7714.43	9949.28	11099.46	11186.85
汕 尾	Shanwei	30.08	113.45	432.42	1166.08	1236.29	1180.04	1462.56	1251.04	1086.39
东 莞	Dongguan	914.64	3940.11	7739.09	12744.42	21561.78	21862.96	24513.14	24772.97	24609.55
中 山	Zhongshan	532.95	2221.45	5023.63	6345.28	5162.50	5375.84	6619.31	6772.54	7119.98
江 门	Jiangmen	871.15	1453.25	3828.91	3998.76	4246.64	4382.58	5451.19	5631.70	5876.22
阳 江	Yangjiang	66.17	213.82	693.46	1990.04	1237.44	1526.51	2124.62	2320.70	2375.24
湛 江	Zhanjiang	269.10	644.27	1404.95	2272.40	2231.12	2102.93	2951.8	3371.13	3206.97
茂 名	Maoming	373.22	702.04	1360.15	2328.05	1988.87	1771.25	2231.07	2477.57	2484.53
肇 庆	Zhaoqing	392.04	321.20	1744.19	4034.37	3123.28	3272.42	4272.96	4385.41	4487.73
清 远	Qingyuan	77.51	364.34	2887.04	1680.13	2003.40	2173.68	2864.73	2833.26	3013.69
潮 州	Chaozhou	73.88	293.72	723.12	1325.80	1543.11	1196.57	1458.8	1387.93	1279.06
揭 阳	Jieyang	136.46	298.82	1794.82	4803.12	2873.24	2745.02	2900.65	2502.81	2626.76
云 浮	Yunfu	146.71	153.77	466.34	1099.49	542.68	578.59	671.27	716.92	764.14
按经济区域分	By Region									
珠三角	Pearl River Delta	10694.83	31614.71	72102.70	101645.70	126128.47	128982.41	147965.76	156731.60	161143.61
粤 东	Eastern Region	584.76	1467.36	4847.93	10263.80	8713.46	8107.07	9200.2	8545.96	8011.09
粤 西	Western Region	708.49	1560.13	3458.56	6590.49	5457.43	5400.69	7307.49	8169.40	8066.74
粤 北	Northern Region	492.85	1300.55	5415.45	6149.17	5822.36	5979.52	7506.36	7486.48	7932.75

注：本表产值按当年价格计算。

Note: Data of gross industrial output value in this table are calculated at current prices.

12-7 各市规模以上工业企业单位数（2023年）

单位：个

项 目	Item	全省 Provincial Total	广州 Guangzhou
总 计	**Total**	**71996**	**6873**
按登记注册统计类别分	By Registered Statistical Categories		
总计中：#国有控股工业企业	Of the Total:State-holding Industrial Enterprises	1646	349
#内资企业	Domestic Invested Enterprises	60699	5700
港澳台投资企业	Enterprises with Investment from Hong Kong,Macao and Taiwan	7723	600
外商投资企业	Foreign Invested Enterprises	3494	571
按轻重工业分	Grouped by Light and Heavy Industries		
轻工业	Light Industry	32045	3290
重工业	Heavy Industry	39951	3583
按企业规模分	Grouped by Size of Enterprises		
大型企业	Large Enterprises	1389	157
中型企业	Medium Enterprises	6414	588
小微型企业	Small and Micro Enterprises	64193	6128
按行业分	Grouped by Sector		
煤炭开采和洗选业	Mining and Washing of Coal		
石油和天然气开采业	Extraction of Petroleum and Natural Gas	3	
黑色金属矿采选业	Mining and Dressing of Ferrous Metal Ores	9	
有色金属矿采选业	Mining and Dressing of Nonferrous Metal Ores	29	
非金属矿采选业	Mining and Dressing of Nonmetal Ores	216	5
开采专业及辅助性活动	Mining Specialized and Auxiliary Operations	7	
其他采矿业	Mining and Dressing of Other Ores		
农副食品加工业	Processing of Farm and Sideline Food	1338	147
食品制造业	Manufacture of Food	1007	193
酒、饮料和精制茶制造业	Manufacture of Wine, Beverage and Refined Tea	230	38
烟草制品业	Tobacco Products	98	1
纺织业	Textile Industry	1756	132
纺织服装、服饰业	Manufacture of Textile Garments, Footwear and Headgear	2484	413
皮革、毛皮、羽毛及其制品和制鞋业	Leather, Fur, Feather, Down and Related Products	1755	335
木材加工和木、竹、藤、棕、草制品业	Timber Processing, Bamboo, Cane, Palm Fiber & Straw Products	537	44
家具制造业	Manufacture of Furniture	1838	142
造纸和纸制品业	Papermaking and Paper Products	1566	150
印刷和记录媒介复制业	Printing and Record Medium Reproduction	1179	117
文教、工美、体育和娱乐用品制造业	Manufacture of Cultural, Educational,Sports and Entertainment Articles	2094	142
石油、煤炭及其他燃料加工业	Petroleum, Coal and other Fuel Processing	123	16
化学原料和化学制品制造业	Manufacture of Raw Chemical Materials and Chemical Products	3496	710
医药制造业	Manufacture of Medicines	642	155
化学纤维制造业	Manufacture of Chemical Fibers	95	9
橡胶和塑料制品业	Rubber and Plastic Products	6461	451
非金属矿物制品业	Nonmetal Mineral Products	3904	286
黑色金属冶炼和压延加工业	Smelting and Pressing of Ferrous Metals	592	36
有色金属冶炼和压延加工业	Smelting and Pressing of Nonferrous Metals	1273	69
金属制品业	Metal Products	7166	377
通用设备制造业	Manufacture of General-purpose Machinery	4218	470
专用设备制造业	Manufacture of Special-purpose Machinery	4230	445
汽车制造业	Manufacture of Automobile	1202	354
铁路、船舶、航空航天和其他运输设备制造业	Manufacture of Railway ,Ship,Aeronautics and Other Transport equipment	543	88
电气机械和器材制造业	Manufacture of Electrical Machinery and Equipment	8463	524
计算机、通信和其他电子设备制造业	Manufacture of Communication Equipment, Computers and Other Electronic Equipment	9966	670
仪器仪表制造业	Manufacture of Instruments and Meters	1234	120
其他制造业	Other Manufactures	526	34
废弃资源综合利用业	Comprehensive Utilization of Waste	283	20
金属制品、机械和设备修理业	Manufacture of Metal Products,Machinery and Equipment Maintenance	99	28
电力、热力生产和供应业	Production and Supply of Electric Power and Heat Power	604	64
燃气生产和供应业	Production and Supply of Gas	324	47
水的生产和供应业	Production and Supply of Water	406	41

注：本表登记注册统计类别按《关于市场主体统计分类的划分规定》(国统字〔2023〕14号)执行。

Number of Industrial Enterprises above Designated Size by City (2023)

(unit)

深 圳 Shenzhen	珠 海 Zhuhai	汕 头 Shantou	佛 山 Foshan	韶 关 Shaoguan	河 源 Heyuan	梅 州 Meizhou	惠 州 Huizhou	汕 尾 Shanwei
14188	**1778**	**2225**	**9884**	**660**	**642**	**557**	**4466**	**325**
234	72	48	134	84	25	36	85	35
12079	1312	2067	8959	590	511	519	3571	277
1498	291	109	599	55	115	26	661	42
610	175	45	308	15	16	12	204	6
4197	600	1794	4565	150	222	172	1988	168
9991	1178	431	5319	510	420	385	2478	157
305	67	14	149	13	20	7	128	11
1247	249	104	841	65	91	53	445	20
12636	1462	2107	8894	582	531	497	3893	294
1	1							
	1			1	5			
				7	2	3		
		1	2	5	9	13	28	7
3	1							
57	33	49	142	17	20	25	56	24
50	36	76	114	9	12	14	27	12
16	10	5	28	4	5	11	14	2
88		2		2		1	2	
65	15	288	478	8	10	10	65	13
161	31	522	254	3	17	6	61	23
75	1	10	143	3	6	4	209	5
20	6	1	78	17	17	4	57	5
106	9	8	617		8	6	257	1
228	27	71	193	11	8	5	86	5
223	36	80	115	2	8	5	54	3
414	16	273	90	18	32	19	187	23
7	7	1	19			1	8	
279	140	89	471	125	13	14	230	6
115	34	22	69	7	9	12	19	
1	5	3	17		2	1	5	
976	131	292	767	31	51	18	540	24
215	72	53	556	85	106	122	274	44
33	5	3	228	7	14	6	14	
133	16	5	407	19	9	3	52	1
855	110	38	1571	71	31	15	410	30
995	118	48	763	27	30	11	161	5
1336	116	62	605	20	40	19	147	6
119	33	10	258	5	3	18	69	
110	26	2	67	1	1		46	2
2002	232	74	1269	32	44	29	476	14
4579	374	45	328	36	77	109	733	28
573	68	3	65	3	9	3	55	
186	2	11	24	3	9	1	35	1
23	14	22	37	17	2	8	17	3
19	5	3	2	3			5	2
38	23	21	32	46	20	23	29	16
38	13	6	21	7	10	9	10	4
49	11	26	54	8	3	9	28	16

Ntote: The registered statistical categories of this table is implemented in accordance with the Regulations onStatistics the Classification of Market Entity(Guotongzi [2023] No. 14).

12-7 续表

单位：个

项　目	Item	东 莞 Dongguan	中 山 Zhongshan
总　计	**Total**	**14180**	**5025**
按登记注册统计类别分	By Registered Statistical Categories		
总计中：#国有控股工业企业	Of the Total:State-holding Industrial Enterprises	65	45
#内资企业	Domestic Invested Enterprises	11100	4225
港澳台投资企业	Enterprises with Investment from Hong Kong,Macao and Taiwan	2145	520
外商投资企业	Foreign Invested Enterprises	928	277
按轻重工业分	Grouped by Light and Heavy Industries		
轻工业	Light Industry	6017	3189
重工业	Heavy Industry	8163	1836
按企业规模分	Grouped by Size of Enterprises		
大型企业	Large Enterprises	271	87
中型企业	Medium Enterprises	1373	438
小微型企业	Small and Micro Enterprises	12536	4500
按行业分	Grouped by Sector		
煤炭开采和洗选业	Mining and Washing of Coal		
石油和天然气开采业	Extraction of Petroleum and Natural Gas		
黑色金属矿采选业	Mining and Dressing of Ferrous Metal Ores		
有色金属矿采选业	Mining and Dressing of Nonferrous Metal Ores		
非金属矿采选业	Mining and Dressing of Nonmetal Ores	1	
开采专业及辅助性活动	Mining Specialized and Auxiliary Operations		
其他采矿业	Mining and Dressing of Other Ores		
农副食品加工业	Processing of Farm and Sideline Food	103	37
食品制造业	Manufacture of Food	108	47
酒、饮料和精制茶制造业	Manufacture of Wine, Beverage and Refined Tea	17	12
烟草制品业	Tobacco Products		1
纺织业	Textile Industry	229	126
纺织服装、服饰业	Manufacture of Textile Garments, Footwear and Headgear	438	270
皮革、毛皮、羽毛及其制品和制鞋业	Leather, Fur, Feather, Down and Related Products	480	77
木材加工和木、竹、藤、棕、草制品业	Timber Processing, Bamboo, Cane, Palm Fiber & Straw Products	69	28
家具制造业	Manufacture of Furniture	374	150
造纸和纸制品业	Papermaking and Paper Products	419	120
印刷和记录媒介复制业	Printing and Record Medium Reproduction	275	87
文教、工美、体育和娱乐用品制造业	Manufacture of Cultural, Educational,Sports and Entertainment Articles	585	138
石油、煤炭及其他燃料加工业	Petroleum, Coal and other Fuel Processing	18	7
化学原料和化学制品制造业	Manufacture of Raw Chemical Materials and Chemical Products	521	183
医药制造业	Manufacture of Medicines	27	37
化学纤维制造业	Manufacture of Chemical Fibers	26	6
橡胶和塑料制品业	Rubber and Plastic Products	1887	478
非金属矿物制品业	Nonmetal Mineral Products	321	160
黑色金属冶炼和压延加工业	Smelting and Pressing of Ferrous Metals	68	19
有色金属冶炼和压延加工业	Smelting and Pressing of Nonferrous Metals	221	53
金属制品业	Metal Products	1532	547
通用设备制造业	Manufacture of General-purpose Machinery	969	282
专用设备制造业	Manufacture of Special-purpose Machinery	1009	184
汽车制造业	Manufacture of Automobile	145	60
铁路、船舶、航空航天和其他运输设备制造业	Manufacture of Railway ,Ship,Aeronautics and Other Transport equipment	47	11
电气机械和器材制造业	Manufacture of Electrical Machinery and Equipment	1540	1396
计算机、通信和其他电子设备制造业	Manufacture of Communication Equipment, Computers and Other Electronic Equipment	2247	332
仪器仪表制造业	Manufacture of Instruments and Meters	243	68
其他制造业	Other Manufactures	136	51
废弃资源综合利用业	Comprehensive Utilization of Waste	7	2
金属制品、机械和设备修理业	Manufacture of Metal Products,Machinery and Equipment Maintenance	15	3
电力、热力生产和供应业	Production and Supply of Electric Power and Heat Power	32	15
燃气生产和供应业	Production and Supply of Gas	44	11
水的生产和供应业	Production and Supply of Water	27	27

12-7 continued

(unit)

江 门 Jiangmen	阳 江 Yangjiang	湛 江 Zhanjiang	茂 名 Maoming	肇 庆 Zhaoqing	清 远 Qingyuan	潮 州 Chaozhou	揭 阳 Jieyang	云 浮 Yunfu
3536	**504**	**824**	**693**	**1634**	**1059**	**1035**	**1470**	**438**
45	41	108	63	48	48	21	36	24
2830	456	758	655	1444	881	994	1398	373
543	34	38	28	133	136	35	59	56
156	14	28	10	56	40	5	9	9
1887	279	438	332	589	375	718	948	127
1649	225	386	361	1045	684	317	522	311
58	7	9	4	30	30	4	6	12
286	57	62	35	173	137	42	65	43
3192	440	753	654	1431	892	989	1399	383
		1						
				1	1			
		9	4	2	1			1
27	6	22	35	21	19	4	3	8
2		1						
108	51	150	152	37	38	43	36	13
68	12	18	19	34	11	69	70	8
13	3	8	2	14	10	10	7	1
		1						
111	1	11	9	38	37	6	95	9
70	10	3	11	16	6	32	131	6
55	5	43	27	28	36	44	167	2
47	5	44	24	29	14	4	16	8
95		13	1	28	17	2	3	1
103	10	22	5	44	8	31	16	4
51		11	3	9	9	68	22	1
44	1	3	10	31	28	13	22	5
5		3	25	1	1		4	
200	13	31	74	163	144	25	20	45
20	2	13	29	9	10	7	29	17
7				1	3		7	2
305	37	24	34	101	110	65	128	11
213	41	125	120	200	178	410	163	160
29	20	4	3	11	16	12	63	1
72	3	4	2	116	50	13	14	11
713	160	24	23	284	54	90	205	26
149	25	7	5	80	38	9	16	10
85	3	16	7	61	21	3	31	14
43	1	7		35	33		1	8
119	2		1	3	14		3	
446	32	111	5	62	26	14	120	15
221	2	2	15	86	37	7	20	18
10			1	7	2	1	2	1
18		2	1	5	4	1	2	
14	7	14	6	22	23	3	13	9
7		6		1				
32	34	47	23	28	40	11	20	10
12	7	10	7	14	12	31	5	6
22	11	14	10	12	8	7	16	7

12-8 各市规模以上工业总产值（2023年）

单位：亿元

项 目	Item	全 省 Provincial Total	广 州 Guangzhou
总 计	**Total**	**185154.19**	**24380.91**
按登记注册统计类别分	By Registered Statistical Categories		
总计中：#国有控股工业企业	Of the Total:State-holding Industrial Enterprises	35543.39	11455.37
#内资企业	Domestic Invested Enterprises	130038.00	14298.13
港澳台投资企业	Enterprises with Investment from Hong Kong,Macao and Taiwan	26963.13	2140.03
外商投资企业	Foreign Invested Enterprises	28128.28	7941.88
按轻重工业分	Grouped by Light and Heavy Industries		
轻工业	Light Industry	55123.30	5772.05
重工业	Heavy Industry	130030.89	18608.86
按企业规模分	Grouped by Size of Enterprises		
大型企业	Large Enterprises	84290.38	12480.64
中型企业	Medium Enterprises	40405.19	4071.76
小微型企业	Small and Micro Enterprises	60458.62	7828.51
按行业分	Grouped by Sector		
煤炭开采和洗选业	Mining and Washing of Coal		
石油和天然气开采业	Extraction of Petroleum and Natural Gas	1061.26	
黑色金属矿采选业	Mining and Dressing of Ferrous Metal Ores	45.70	
有色金属矿采选业	Mining and Dressing of Nonferrous Metal Ores	92.65	
非金属矿采选业	Mining and Dressing of Nonmetal Ores	256.38	12.77
开采专业及辅助性活动	Mining Specialized and Auxiliary Operations	57.05	
其他采矿业	Mining and Dressing of Other Ores		
农副食品加工业	Processing of Farm and Sideline Food	4328.56	458.39
食品制造业	Manufacture of Food	2180.43	604.45
酒、饮料和精制茶制造业	Manufacture of Wine, Beverage and Refined Tea	1246.30	385.13
烟草制品业	Tobacco Products	824.76	260.48
纺织业	Textile Industry	2257.43	130.99
纺织服装、服饰业	Manufacture of Textile Garments, Footwear and Headgear	2409.95	266.73
皮革、毛皮、羽毛及其制品和制鞋业	Leather, Fur, Feather, Down and Related Products	1439.01	161.88
木材加工和木、竹、藤、棕、草制品业	Timber Processing, Bamboo, Cane, Palm Fiber & Straw Products	398.52	27.46
家具制造业	Manufacture of Furniture	2150.43	356.60
造纸和纸制品业	Papermaking and Paper Products	2637.44	162.03
印刷和记录媒介复制业	Printing and Record Medium Reproduction	1310.68	125.24
文教、工美、体育和娱乐用品制造业	Manufacture of Cultural, Educational,Sports and Entertainment Articles	4020.44	134.15
石油、煤炭及其他燃料加工业	Petroleum, Coal and other Fuel Processing	5493.51	663.25
化学原料和化学制品制造业	Manufacture of Raw Chemical Materials and Chemical Products	7384.32	1329.56
医药制造业	Manufacture of Medicines	2017.40	572.63
化学纤维制造业	Manufacture of Chemical Fibers	191.27	8.03
橡胶和塑料制品业	Rubber and Plastic Products	6118.03	570.83
非金属矿物制品业	Nonmetal Mineral Products	6351.17	545.11
黑色金属冶炼和压延加工业	Smelting and Pressing of Ferrous Metals	4591.48	270.66
有色金属冶炼和压延加工业	Smelting and Pressing of Nonferrous Metals	3973.63	785.26
金属制品业	Metal Products	8794.14	433.49
通用设备制造业	Manufacture of General-purpose Machinery	6157.39	907.16
专用设备制造业	Manufacture of Special-purpose Machinery	5936.59	481.76
汽车制造业	Manufacture of Automobile	12846.58	6394.93
铁路、船舶、航空航天和其他运输设备制造业	Manufacture of Railway ,Ship,Aeronautics and Other Transport equipment	1595.38	628.03
电气机械和器材制造业	Manufacture of Electrical Machinery and Equipment	22192.47	1330.60
计算机、通信和其他电子设备制造业	Manufacture of Communication Equipment, Computers and Other Electronic Equipment	47168.02	2627.89
仪器仪表制造业	Manufacture of Instruments and Meters	1503.82	142.91
其他制造业	Other Manufactures	636.39	23.46
废弃资源综合利用业	Comprehensive Utilization of Waste	783.85	49.25
金属制品、机械和设备修理业	Manufacture of Metal Products,Machinery and Equipment Maintenance	302.55	115.83
电力、热力生产和供应业	Production and Supply of Electric Power and Heat Power	10511.89	2064.48
燃气生产和供应业	Production and Supply of Gas	3075.62	1217.03
水的生产和供应业	Production and Supply of Water	811.69	132.45

注：1.本表产值按当年价格计算。
2.本表登记注册统计类别按《关于市场主体统计分类的划分规定》(国统字〔2023〕14号)执行。

Gross Output Value of Industry above Designated Size by City (2023)

(100 million yuan)

深 圳 Shenzhen	珠 海 Zhuhai	汕 头 Shantou	佛 山 Foshan	韶 关 Shaoguan	河 源 Heyuan	梅 州 Meizhou	惠 州 Huizhou	汕 尾 Shanwei
49192.69	**6142.00**	**3018.87**	**28147.67**	**1675.29**	**1529.63**	**950.00**	**11186.85**	**1086.39**
6127.11	864.15	451.47	2183.45	812.90	183.71	271.54	2624.90	186.60
33078.99	4145.21	2712.19	22116.60	1450.61	1114.86	882.41	6990.46	665.30
7394.89	847.27	219.44	3520.25	112.44	291.35	36.44	2396.76	272.20
8718.49	1149.53	86.13	2507.04	112.24	123.43	31.15	1791.32	148.89
8876.85	2059.85	1946.70	14278.27	269.79	310.12	258.60	2451.96	364.25
40315.83	4082.15	1072.18	13869.40	1405.50	1219.50	691.40	8734.89	722.14
27389.34	2703.86	384.60	10082.79	673.19	638.37	177.41	6419.07	471.27
8114.35	1391.89	774.38	9556.20	468.21	371.35	383.07	1700.85	255.85
13688.99	2046.26	1859.89	8508.68	533.89	519.91	389.51	3066.94	359.27
650.71	156.91							
	12.62			0.21	32.17			
				39.90	3.64	8.34		
		1.31	1.10	2.66	6.29	6.30	40.54	15.34
42.46	2.57							
236.46	126.61	119.89	613.03	31.95	27.15	46.83	108.92	35.42
83.98	88.06	84.99	412.48	9.98	19.36	14.73	18.67	15.17
183.08	21.81	5.64	250.38	3.61	41.75	22.96	72.23	1.91
336.20		2.68		80.98		93.97	6.20	
109.49	13.87	301.99	954.62	12.60	6.72	4.49	32.89	33.69
262.42	22.27	523.28	450.77	1.64	16.75	9.01	53.13	43.07
83.99	0.21	8.53	236.28	1.29	21.75	5.24	129.65	2.07
15.68	5.38	0.25	90.52	22.68	8.49	1.07	38.39	6.66
83.31	21.66	4.52	783.68		7.66	1.69	183.36	0.22
125.88	70.50	91.88	334.18	14.15	8.62	5.74	67.85	7.57
264.49	19.13	76.91	226.96	3.15	8.19	2.62	46.10	5.14
2316.73	18.79	264.14	234.04	26.78	69.57	6.59	122.09	31.45
42.51	105.11	0.29	161.95			0.20	1159.30	
356.68	505.53	196.59	1273.00	157.54	14.61	8.54	1174.34	10.16
426.06	204.58	59.76	227.06	12.16	13.77	11.13	42.40	
0.94	74.04	5.18	25.48		0.62	0.40	2.12	
790.11	140.42	294.29	1311.35	25.97	35.98	13.92	445.68	34.34
615.33	128.36	98.00	1664.88	71.01	98.00	98.98	325.38	49.26
39.41	112.02	4.29	781.40	436.14	170.93	20.37	37.77	
307.52	86.82	4.26	1029.17	139.57	7.76	19.32	55.03	2.78
1052.10	161.27	29.87	2943.60	89.87	36.55	7.90	284.58	18.07
1316.72	247.88	25.58	1480.27	41.25	24.08	8.93	146.44	89.13
2484.09	176.03	71.27	989.95	16.88	39.84	9.80	284.24	4.58
3473.28	72.83	42.58	1611.22	2.40	7.65	27.87	173.42	
211.14	52.70	0.23	90.72	0.30	1.30		71.25	17.66
3976.06	1700.67	108.85	7378.44	67.22	69.93	41.52	1298.84	161.39
25878.36	1018.36	123.45	754.19	76.18	529.92	231.83	4021.16	285.65
670.16	100.06	1.13	146.24	9.16	10.27	1.58	42.89	
314.55	0.63	25.36	26.63	1.27	6.77	0.27	18.84	0.23
143.25	13.51	26.04	264.97	33.96	4.00	5.41	26.97	1.40
22.71	126.26	3.29	2.83	0.84			1.92	0.79
1486.14	327.93	369.71	781.15	229.84	170.88	201.87	596.18	204.03
634.91	185.09	7.09	353.22	7.68	7.20	4.88	27.76	2.61
155.76	21.49	35.76	261.92	4.46	1.47	5.68	30.34	6.61

Note: a)Data in this table are calculated at current prices.

b)The registered statistical categories of this table is implemented in accordance with the Regulations onStatistics the Classification of Market Entity(Guotongzi [2023] No. 14).

12-8 续表

单位：亿元

项 目	Item	东 莞 Dongguan	中 山 Zhongshan
总 计	**Total**	**24609.55**	**7119.98**
按登记注册统计类别分	By Registered Statistical Categories		
总计中：#国有控股工业企业	Of the Total:State-holding Industrial Enterprises	1478.66	552.64
#内资企业	Domestic Invested Enterprises	17397.05	4600.75
港澳台投资企业	Enterprises with Investment from Hong Kong,Macao and Taiwan	4700.70	1062.50
外商投资企业	Foreign Invested Enterprises	2507.71	1455.92
按轻重工业分	Grouped by Light and Heavy Industries		
轻工业	Light Industry	7286.19	3435.01
重工业	Heavy Industry	17323.36	3684.97
按企业规模分	Grouped by Size of Enterprises		
大型企业	Large Enterprises	10528.40	2711.25
中型企业	Medium Enterprises	5266.94	1564.49
小微型企业	Small and Micro Enterprises	8814.21	2844.23
按行业分	Grouped by Sector		
煤炭开采和洗选业	Mining and Washing of Coal		
石油和天然气开采业	Extraction of Petroleum and Natural Gas		
黑色金属矿采选业	Mining and Dressing of Ferrous Metal Ores		
有色金属矿采选业	Mining and Dressing of Nonferrous Metal Ores		
非金属矿采选业	Mining and Dressing of Nonmetal Ores	0.41	
开采专业及辅助性活动	Mining Specialized and Auxiliary Operations		
其他采矿业	Mining and Dressing of Other Ores		
农副食品加工业	Processing of Farm and Sideline Food	869.90	63.96
食品制造业	Manufacture of Food	243.18	72.35
酒、饮料和精制茶制造业	Manufacture of Wine, Beverage and Refined Tea	89.93	44.96
烟草制品业	Tobacco Products		13.76
纺织业	Textile Industry	204.32	96.24
纺织服装、服饰业	Manufacture of Textile Garments, Footwear and Headgear	388.52	169.55
皮革、毛皮、羽毛及其制品和制鞋业	Leather, Fur, Feather, Down and Related Products	336.16	50.01
木材加工和木、竹、藤、棕、草制品业	Timber Processing, Bamboo, Cane, Palm Fiber & Straw Products	41.28	18.40
家具制造业	Manufacture of Furniture	354.64	163.63
造纸和纸制品业	Papermaking and Paper Products	933.27	108.27
印刷和记录媒介复制业	Printing and Record Medium Reproduction	309.40	57.41
文教、工美、体育和娱乐用品制造业	Manufacture of Cultural, Educational,Sports and Entertainment Articles	498.26	143.03
石油、煤炭及其他燃料加工业	Petroleum, Coal and other Fuel Processing	15.88	6.54
化学原料和化学制品制造业	Manufacture of Raw Chemical Materials and Chemical Products	656.00	297.88
医药制造业	Manufacture of Medicines	63.35	89.81
化学纤维制造业	Manufacture of Chemical Fibers	21.73	1.31
橡胶和塑料制品业	Rubber and Plastic Products	1326.95	392.03
非金属矿物制品业	Nonmetal Mineral Products	524.79	224.61
黑色金属冶炼和压延加工业	Smelting and Pressing of Ferrous Metals	70.19	127.43
有色金属冶炼和压延加工业	Smelting and Pressing of Nonferrous Metals	270.25	61.77
金属制品业	Metal Products	1402.36	410.72
通用设备制造业	Manufacture of General-purpose Machinery	1056.18	410.47
专用设备制造业	Manufacture of Special-purpose Machinery	969.61	135.48
汽车制造业	Manufacture of Automobile	385.02	159.99
铁路、船舶、航空航天和其他运输设备制造业	Manufacture of Railway ,Ship,Aeronautics and Other Transport equipment	83.29	19.96
电气机械和器材制造业	Manufacture of Electrical Machinery and Equipment	2252.51	2257.15
计算机、通信和其他电子设备制造业	Manufacture of Communication Equipment, Computers and Other Electronic Equipment	9515.71	904.36
仪器仪表制造业	Manufacture of Instruments and Meters	274.59	87.78
其他制造业	Other Manufactures	140.47	52.03
废弃资源综合利用业	Comprehensive Utilization of Waste	3.71	3.75
金属制品、机械和设备修理业	Manufacture of Metal Products,Machinery and Equipment Maintenance	21.52	1.31
电力、热力生产和供应业	Production and Supply of Electric Power and Heat Power	1036.71	398.88
燃气生产和供应业	Production and Supply of Gas	192.77	51.09
水的生产和供应业	Production and Supply of Water	56.70	24.05

12-8 continued

(100 million yuan)

江 门 Jiangmen	阳 江 Yangjiang	湛 江 Zhanjiang	茂 名 Maoming	肇 庆 Zhaoqing	清 远 Qingyuan	潮 州 Chaozhou	揭 阳 Jieyang	云 浮 Yunfu
5876.22	**2375.24**	**3206.97**	**2484.53**	**4487.73**	**3013.69**	**1279.06**	**2626.76**	**764.14**
691.48	1383.83	2004.92	1642.90	547.19	454.38	218.69	1253.46	154.05
3770.30	2039.57	1859.45	2409.39	3863.34	2294.23	1172.59	2544.43	632.15
1519.05	247.73	994.29	27.98	433.68	542.37	40.09	62.90	100.76
584.87	87.95	353.23	47.16	190.49	176.32	66.19	17.11	31.22
2359.32	363.32	818.31	352.18	1510.76	783.76	609.46	833.61	182.93
3516.91	2011.93	2388.67	2132.35	2976.97	2229.93	669.60	1793.15	581.21
1652.59	880.87	2100.34	1473.87	1045.50	747.57	168.67	1254.99	305.79
1617.10	1016.45	360.62	421.98	1286.86	1128.79	201.71	271.93	180.39
2606.53	477.92	746.01	588.67	2155.36	1137.33	908.68	1099.84	277.96
		253.63						
				0.54	0.17			
		8.77	12.00	16.90	1.14			1.95
52.09	5.46	31.40	12.15	24.67	25.04	1.39	2.38	15.07
5.14		6.87						
301.23	163.40	447.61	253.50	126.71	129.70	74.90	58.73	34.27
204.42	57.01	17.54	10.06	74.51	7.86	67.23	70.73	3.66
25.70	1.80	12.30	0.65	35.71	28.17	11.15	6.99	0.43
		30.50						
117.76	1.04	5.45	2.98	101.24	44.87	2.73	76.23	3.22
47.58	6.58	5.15	17.48	19.75	1.37	10.55	88.56	5.79
36.72	3.87	18.73	5.67	51.21	97.78	30.42	156.75	0.80
31.83	3.33	15.17	8.50	32.59	13.28	1.08	8.72	7.75
77.52		13.63	0.13	43.03	52.21	0.66	2.13	0.16
324.92	14.75	154.31	3.50	100.72	25.86	35.01	16.68	31.76
53.98		9.17	0.84	26.06	8.81	48.96	17.71	0.41
24.45	0.59	0.81	5.35	40.44	47.31	6.49	20.07	9.28
3.81		917.11	1465.68	0.30	0.25		951.32	
412.09	10.52	73.02	314.60	262.36	250.23	26.28	9.93	44.83
31.26	3.23	32.77	21.64	37.61	61.41	8.62	69.40	28.73
26.23				1.67	1.31		20.79	1.40
236.11	14.27	13.61	21.42	173.95	140.52	38.97	86.59	10.71
318.05	67.37	100.08	55.62	473.68	339.06	299.39	125.86	128.38
82.66	1188.63	610.76	8.24	17.20	287.97	21.26	211.11	93.06
164.09	34.79	2.03	0.58	348.78	476.29	102.18	13.16	62.22
706.18	138.67	9.95	7.40	744.96	72.46	74.38	124.51	45.25
151.71	35.52	4.04	2.98	120.09	59.44	13.15	7.54	8.82
97.74	1.45	5.60	13.61	100.01	13.91	0.57	31.01	9.16
108.36	0.45	10.62		267.64	75.62		0.35	32.36
333.06	1.72		0.34	1.97	78.69		3.03	
645.40	111.19	53.42	2.65	511.57	77.65	22.38	103.44	21.56
588.73	0.93	2.75	6.17	264.36	231.67	59.32	9.39	37.62
4.30			0.16	7.06	1.36	3.04	0.63	0.50
14.76		0.16	0.16	3.45	5.69	0.37	1.28	
31.50	4.29	26.47	2.65	79.28	35.49	2.76	21.95	3.23
2.00		2.94		0.31				
538.54	482.24	290.04	214.47	268.18	270.15	189.42	277.98	113.08
56.41	16.69	9.70	8.00	99.59	46.20	122.07	20.00	5.65
19.86	5.46	10.85	5.32	9.63	4.72	4.33	11.79	3.02

12-9 规模以上工业企业主要经济指标

年份 Year	全部就业人员平均人数(万人) Annual Average Number of Employed Persons (10000 persons)	总产值(亿元) Gross Output Value of Industry (100 million yuan)	固定资产原价(亿元) Original Value of Fixed Assets (100 million yuan)	营业收入(亿元) Business Revenue (100 million yuan)	利润总额(亿元) Total Profits (100 million yuan)
1978	170.51	168.91	111.42		16.78
1979	171.76	181.96	129.09	170.09	15.21
1980	182.39	198.83	136.59	189.97	19.41
1981	189.08	226.26	152.58	215.09	21.18
1982	194.33	245.54	172.00	231.20	22.44
1983	197.50	275.25	226.58	226.91	26.17
1984	241.42	336.45	221.46	313.33	30.44
1985	298.66	438.91	269.13	412.77	39.09
1986	323.16	522.35	335.19	498.80	37.74
1987	353.95	711.04	433.95	692.47	51.35
1988	382.19	1056.47	540.37	1016.20	68.67
1989	387.90	1321.33	700.66	1222.20	60.42
1990	390.28	1379.98	843.88	1287.91	37.04
1991	433.18	2018.62	1339.04	1875.02	71.83
1992	450.99	2696.47	1485.36	2537.84	115.34
1993	478.39	4085.35	2099.09	3920.98	211.80
1994	537.57	5325.35	3309.63	4826.68	210.36
1995	537.83	6325.19	4298.15	6195.84	171.87
1996	529.13	7308.51	5066.23	6808.08	178.75
1997	522.94	8201.71	5904.95	7767.79	270.90
1998	548.59	9738.56	6968.36	9243.42	224.89
1999	537.77	10538.17	7399.10	10208.99	356.79
2000	572.89	12480.93	8005.77	12380.65	564.75
2001	578.94	14035.35	8655.82	13891.46	595.60
2002	644.39	16378.60	9550.47	16247.73	769.09
2003	741.17	21513.46	10768.77	21566.93	1075.41
2004	996.44	29554.92	12713.34	28998.45	1449.96
2005	1085.65	35942.74	14453.16	34781.58	1693.99
2006	1203.58	44674.75	17824.33	43550.87	2217.73
2007	1307.40	55252.86	19763.42	53927.94	3061.60
2008	1493.38	65424.61	24529.17	63371.65	3272.60
2009	1436.02	68275.77	26293.23	66117.81	4204.40
2010	1568.00	85824.64	33489.49	84114.85	6239.64
2011	1463.86	94871.68	33244.26	92996.88	5874.03
2012	1452.16	95602.09	35983.70	93821.74	5464.90
2013	1455.81	109673.07	39339.68	106361.21	6496.42
2014	1455.78	119713.04	43635.95	115451.13	7014.99
2015	1439.33	124649.16	48104.10	119157.86	7723.16
2016	1417.84	133768.04	52729.34	129151.31	8383.04
2017	1403.19	135722.42	52619.74	133924.37	8864.36
2018	1341.31	140398.93	53725.45	142597.86	8748.68
2019	1315.80	146121.72	58026.73	146726.43	9140.48
2020	1277.06	148469.69	62452.78	149930.12	9572.09
2021	1343.58	171979.82	68125.54	173649.71	11278.35
2022	1332.56	180933.44	74967.63	183027.35	10329.25
2023	1297.06	185154.19	79455.88	185496.87	11595.24

注：1.利税总额包括增值税。
2.全员劳动生产率按工业总产值计算。
3.1997年以前为独立核算工业企业，1998年起统计口径改为年主营业务收入500万元及以上的规模以上工业，2011年调整为年主营业务收入2000万元及以上工业企业,2021年调整为主业务收入2000万元及以上工业企业和工业个体经营户。
4.本表中营业收入数据2017年及以前为主营业务收入数据，2018年后为营业收入数据。

Main Indicators of Industrial Enterprises above Designated Size

利税总额 (亿元) Total Pre-tax Profits (100 million yuan)	百元固定资产实现利税 (元) Pre-tax Profits per 100 yuan of Original Value of Fixed Assets	总资产贡献率 (%) Ratio of Total Assets to Industrial Output (%)	产值利税率 (%) Ratio of Pre-tax Profits to Gross Output Value (%)	百元营业收入实现利税 (元) Pre-tax Profits per 100 yuan of Business Revenue (yuan)	全员劳动生产率 (元/人) Overall Labor Produc-tivity (yuan/person)
32.91	29.54		19.48		9906
34.48	26.71		18.45	20.27	10594
38.51	28.19		19.37	20.27	10901
42.12	27.60		18.61	19.58	11966
44.62	25.94		18.17	19.30	12635
48.59	21.45		17.65	21.42	13937
56.83	25.66		16.89	18.14	13936
75.99	29.23		17.31	18.41	14696
80.90	24.14		15.49	16.22	16164
102.24	23.56		14.38	14.76	20089
140.65	26.03		13.31	13.84	27643
138.71	19.80		10.50	11.35	34064
121.50	14.40		8.80	9.43	35359
188.08	14.05		9.32	10.03	46600
248.78	22.32		9.23	9.80	59790
397.40	18.93		9.73	10.14	85398
478.41	14.46		8.89	9.91	99063
445.53	10.37		7.04	7.19	117606
489.26	9.66		6.69	7.19	138123
617.90	10.46	7.54	7.53	7.95	156838
622.82	8.94	7.37	6.40	6.74	177520
778.94	10.53	7.62	7.39	7.63	195961
1042.77	13.03	8.86	8.35	8.42	217859
1139.98	13.17	8.70	8.12	8.21	242432
1380.24	14.45	9.17	8.43	8.50	254172
1850.90	17.19	10.42	8.60	8.56	290264
2329.79	18.33	10.52	7.90	8.03	296605
2877.81	19.91	11.29	8.01	8.27	331071
3907.10	21.92	12.24	8.75	8.97	371182
5105.93	25.83	13.59	9.24	9.46	422616
6136.69	25.02	14.32	9.38	9.68	438098
6793.59	25.84	14.18	9.95	10.27	475451
9418.42	28.12	15.63	10.97	11.20	547351
9608.33	28.9	14.98	10.13	10.33	648093
9383.63	26.08	13.94	9.82	10.00	658344
11008.36	27.98	14.53	10.04	10.35	753347
11663.66	26.73	13.97	9.74	10.10	822329
12375.00	25.73	13.58	9.93	10.39	866022
13150.85	24.94	12.98	9.83	10.18	943464
13769.27	26.17	12.45	10.15	10.28	967242
13706.38	25.51	11.56	9.31	9.61	1046730
13766.51	23.72	10.49	9.42	9.38	1110516
14119.76	22.61	9.82	9.51	9.42	1162590
16325.16	23.96	9.71	9.49	9.40	1280012
15857.14	21.15	8.47	8.76	8.66	1357788
17448.34	21.96	8.57	9.42	9.41	1427491

Note:a) Total pre-tax profits include value-added tax.

b) The overall labor productivity is calculated by gross output value of industry.

c) From 1998 to 2010, data are statistics of industrial enterprises above designated size with annual principal business revenue of over 5 million yuan, while data prior to 1997 are statistics of industrial enterprises with independent accounting systems. Since 2011, data are statistics of legal person industrial enterprises with annual principal business revenue of over 20 million yuan. It is adjusted to industrial enterprises and industrial self-employed households with main business income of 20 million yuan and above in 2021.

d) The indicator was Revenue from Principal Business in 2017 and before,and are Business Revenue since 2018.

12-10 规模以上国有控股工业企业主要经济指标

年份 Year	全部就业人员平均人数（万人） Annual Average Number of Employed Persons (10000 persons)	总产值（亿元） Gross Output Value of Industry (100 million yuan)	固定资产原价（亿元） Original Value of Fixed Assets (100 million yuan)	营业收入（亿元） Business Revenue (100 million yuan)	利润总额（亿元） Total Profits (100 million yuan)
1978	120.35	122.28	96.06		
1979	121.97	132.30	103.51	126.87	
1980	126.09	136.30	107.27	127.97	
1981	132.60	153.54	118.82	147.85	
1982	139.90	165.82	131.82	158.43	
1983	142.18	188.09	147.53	178.04	
1984	143.08	222.35	162.13	205.73	
1985	144.14	277.87	203.80	265.05	
1986	150.14	312.74	235.47	305.42	
1987	156.48	400.55	294.46	402.63	
1988	162.43	555.41	328.58	545.00	
1989	162.85	670.95	404.50	631.61	
1990	163.80	713.88	488.36	689.83	
1991	173.85	906.72	612.24	853.62	
1992	171.60	1118.86	751.42	1073.94	
1993	153.26	1371.58	856.85	1372.66	
1994	152.25	1498.80	1076.47	1400.87	
1995	142.83	1396.35	1315.16	1499.25	
1996	137.50	1476.12	1599.77	1555.28	
1997	124.71	1505.06	1794.89	1657.79	
1998	102.67	1453.79	1790.91	1616.64	
1999	128.16	3025.68	3520.17	3153.04	
2000	104.39	3126.12	3513.50	3583.55	226.08
2001	91.77	3236.65	3982.54	3757.95	241.30
2002	83.25	3264.46	3942.57	3800.38	224.39
2003	75.20	3949.03	4603.66	4717.48	623.49
2004	72.53	6039.24	4913.92	6031.47	423.55
2005	69.42	6375.54	5153.83	6261.70	387.31
2006	60.80	7253.17	6557.86	6887.69	672.39
2007	60.86	8603.94	6702.65	8258.85	926.24
2008	77.84	11144.50	8327.10	11045.88	782.48
2009	75.33	10790.11	9249.22	10637.39	861.47
2010	78.89	13166.37	10456.03	13418.41	1235.97
2011	82.98	13927.70	10891.43	13871.28	723.19
2012	82.87	15529.16	12395.46	15602.52	700.33
2013	81.67	17525.16	13124.26	17095.26	1105.5
2014	79.95	18225.94	14561.95	17804.39	1081.26
2015	83.23	17032.30	15949.18	16453.02	1196.46
2016	82.67	17172.18	17041.31	16266.66	1437.99
2017	78.17	19525.92	17858.14	19783.07	1597.99
2018	74.93	20855.98	19117.62	22071.06	1559.97
2019	71.17	21270.03	20440.64	21286.03	1343.26
2020	68.68	21191.00	21222.22	21279.76	1250.19
2021	74.91	28733.57	24230.32	28816.61	1676.42
2022	76.62	32513.46	27246.31	32626.42	1436.88
2023	76.39	35543.39	29965.90	35370.72	1626.89

注：1.1998年以前为国有工业，1999年起为国有及国有控股工业，2007年起改为国有控股工业。
　　2.全员劳动生产率按工业总产值计算。

Main Indicators of State-owned and State-holding Industrial Enterprises above Designated Size

利税总额 (亿元) Total Pre-tax Profits (100 million yuan)	百元固定资产实现利税 (元) Pre-tax Profits per 100 yuan of Original Value of Fixed Assets (yuan)	总资产贡献率 (%) Ratio of Total Assets to Industrial Output Value (%)	产值利税率 (%) Ratio of Pre-tax Profits to Gross Output Value (%)	百元主营业务收入实现利税 (元) Pre-tax Profits per 100 yuan of Principal Business Revenue (yuan)	全员劳动生产率 (元/人) Overall Labor Produc-tivity (yuan/person)
26.09	27.16		21.34		10160
26.89	25.96		20.31	21.18	10847
28.33	25.90		20.57	22.19	10810
31.18	26.24		20.31	21.09	11579
33.29	25.26		20.08	21.01	11853
38.18	25.88		20.30	21.45	13229
44.02	27.15		19.80	21.39	15540
56.34	27.64		20.28	21.26	19278
59.70	25.36		19.09	19.55	20830
72.44	24.60		18.09	17.99	25598
91.05	27.71		16.39	16.71	34194
94.11	23.26		14.93	14.90	41200
84.35	17.27		11.82	12.23	43582
116.26	18.99		12.82	13.62	52155
131.24	17.47		11.73	12.22	65202
169.40	19.77		12.35	12.34	89494
176.81	16.42		11.80	12.62	98443
160.57	12.21		11.50	10.71	97763
139.01	8.69		9.42	8.94	107354
160.92	8.97		10.69	9.71	120685
163.10	9.11		11.22	10.09	141598
376.11	10.68	8.63	12.34	11.93	236086
433.35	12.33	9.09	13.86	12.09	299465
486.46	12.21	9.53	15.03	12.94	352692
483.25	12.26	9.34	14.80	12.72	392127
623.49	13.54	10.88	15.79	13.22	525137
779.41	15.86	12.39	12.91	12.92	832654
800.26	15.53	13.03	12.55	12.78	918401
1213.73	18.50	14.89	16.73	17.62	1192956
1603.72	23.92	17.68	18.63	19.41	1413727
1676.74	20.14	15.49	15.05	15.18	1431719
1747.60	18.89	14.73	16.20	16.43	1432379
2398.44	22.94	17.21	18.22	17.87	1668953
1963.69	18.03	13.54	14.10	14.16	1678441
2172.26	17.52	14.03	13.99	13.92	1873918
2800.64	21.34	16.57	15.98	16.38	2145850
2810.73	19.30	15.61	15.42	15.79	2279667
2660.82	16.68	13.53	15.62	16.17	2046414
2889.08	16.95	13.36	16.82	17.76	2077196
3144.43	17.61	13.04	16.10	15.89	2497879
3150.36	16.48	12.93	14.93	14.27	2783395
2636.84	12.90	10.21	12.40	12.39	2988623
2512.04	11.84	9.16	11.85	11.80	3085469
3387.13	13.98	9.40	11.79	11.75	3835746
3311.11	12.15	8.16	10.18	10.15	4243469
3873.04	12.92	8.69	10.90	10.95	4652885

Note: a)Data prior to 1998 are statistics of state-owned industrial enterprises,data since 1999 are statistics of state-owned and state-holding industrial enterprises, and data since 2007 are statistics of state-holding industrial enterprises.
b) The overall labor productivity is calculated by gross output value of industry.

12-11 规模以上工业企业主要经济指标（2023年）

单位：亿元

项目	Item	企业单位数（个）Number of Enterprises (unit)	工业总产值（当年价）Gross Industrial Output Value (at current prices)
全　省	**Provincial Total**	**71996**	**185154.19**
按登记注册统计类别分	By Registered Statistical Categories		
总计中：#国有控股工业企业	Of the Total:State-holding Industrial Enterprises	1646	35543.39
#内资企业	Domestic Invested Enterprises	60699	130038.00
港澳台投资企业	Enterprises with Investment from Hong Kong,Macao and Taiwan	7723	26963.13
外商投资企业	Foreign Invested Enterprises	3494	28128.28
按轻重工业分	Grouped by Light and Heavy Industries		
轻工业	Light Industry	32045	55123.30
重工业	Heavy Industry	39951	130030.89
按企业规模分	Grouped by Size of Enterprises		
大型企业	Large Enterprises	1389	84290.38
中型企业	Medium Enterprises	6414	40405.19
小微型企业	Small and Micro Enterprises	64193	60458.62
按行业分	Grouped by Sector		
煤炭开采和洗选业	Mining and Washing of Coal		
石油和天然气开采业	Extraction of Petroleum and Natural Gas	3	1061.26
黑色金属矿采选业	Mining and Dressing of Ferrous Metal Ores	9	45.70
有色金属矿采选业	Mining and Dressing of Nonferrous Metal Ores	29	92.65
非金属矿采选业	Mining and Dressing of Nonmetal Ores	216	256.38
开采专业及辅助性活动	Mining Specialized and Auxiliary Operations	7	57.05
其他采矿业	Mining and Dressing of Other Ores		
农副食品加工业	Processing of Farm and Sideline Food	1338	4328.56
食品制造业	Manufacture of Food	1007	2180.43
酒、饮料和精制茶制造业	Manufacture of Wine, Beverage and Refined Tea	230	1246.30
烟草制品业	Tobacco Products	98	824.76
纺织业	Textile Industry	1756	2257.43
纺织服装、服饰业	Manufacture of Textile Garments, Footwear and Headgear	2484	2409.95
皮革、毛皮、羽毛及其制品和制鞋业	Leather, Fur, Feather, Down and Related Products	1755	1439.01
木材加工和木、竹、藤、棕、草制品业	Timber Processing, Bamboo, Cane, Palm Fiber & Straw Products	537	398.52
家具制造业	Manufacture of Furniture	1838	2150.43
造纸和纸制品业	Papermaking and Paper Products	1566	2637.44
印刷和记录媒介复制业	Printing and Record Medium Reproduction	1179	1310.68
文教、工美、体育和娱乐用品制造业	Manufacture of Cultural, Educational,Sports and Entertainment Articles	2094	4020.44
石油、煤炭及其他燃料加工业	Petroleum, Coal and other Fuel Processing	123	5493.51
化学原料和化学制品制造业	Manufacture of Raw Chemical Materials and Chemical Products	3496	7384.32
医药制造业	Manufacture of Medicines	642	2017.40
化学纤维制造业	Manufacture of Chemical Fibers	95	191.27
橡胶和塑料制品业	Rubber and Plastic Products	6461	6118.03
非金属矿物制品业	Nonmetal Mineral Products	3904	6351.17
黑色金属冶炼和压延加工业	Smelting and Pressing of Ferrous Metals	592	4591.48
有色金属冶炼和压延加工业	Smelting and Pressing of Nonferrous Metals	1273	3973.63
金属制品业	Metal Products	7166	8794.14
通用设备制造业	Manufacture of General-purpose Machinery	4218	6157.39
专用设备制造业	Manufacture of Special-purpose Machinery	4230	5936.59
汽车制造业	Manufacture of Automobile	1202	12846.58
铁路、船舶、航空航天和其他运输设备制造业	Manufacture of Railway ,Ship,Aeronautics and Other Transport equipment	543	1595.38
电气机械和器材制造业	Manufacture of Electrical Machinery and Equipment	8463	22192.47
计算机、通信和其他电子设备制造业	Manufacture of Communication Equipment, Computers and Other Electronic Equipment	9966	47168.02
仪器仪表制造业	Manufacture of Instruments and Meters	1234	1503.82
其他制造业	Other Manufactures	526	636.39
废弃资源综合利用业	Comprehensive Utilization of Waste	283	783.85
金属制品、机械和设备修理业	Manufacture of Metal Products,Machinery and Equipment Maintenance	99	302.55
电力、热力生产和供应业	Production and Supply of Electric Power and Heat Power	604	10511.89
燃气生产和供应业	Production and Supply of Gas	324	3075.62
水的生产和供应业	Production and Supply of Water	406	811.69

注：本表登记注册统计类别按《关于市场主体统计分类的划分规定》(国统字〔2023〕14号)执行。

Main Economic Indicators of Industrial Enterprises above Designated Size (2023)

(100 million yuan)

年末资产总计 Total Assets at the Year-end	流动资产合计 Total Working Capital	营业收入 Business Revenue	营业成本 Cost of Business	税金及附加 Tax and Extra Charges on Main Business	利润总额 Total Profits	利税总额 Total Pre-tax Profits	本年应交增值税 Value-added Tax Payable in Current Year	全部就业人员年平均人数(万人) Annual Average Number of Employed Persons (10000 persons)
211484.21	**126344.46**	**185496.87**	**154245.29**	**2103.95**	**11595.24**	**17448.34**	**3749.15**	**1297.06**
47170.62	16915.03	35370.72	30519.91	1340.56	1626.89	3873.04	905.59	76.39
151612.60	89390.37	129446.52	107324.60	1396.67	8082.79	12225.30	2745.84	860.67
29984.58	18355.80	26674.59	21859.58	337.48	2012.34	2886.68	536.85	281.88
29875.03	18588.50	29352.74	25040.16	369.74	1499.63	2335.34	465.97	154.51
54496.64	35206.35	54533.39	43778.50	599.93	3551.15	5467.93	1316.85	545.19
156987.57	91138.11	130963.49	110466.79	1504.02	8044.09	11980.41	2432.30	751.88
108504.74	61953.14	85009.40	68997.33	1485.77	7147.60	10493.59	1860.22	418.44
43036.08	25580.03	40393.27	33529.55	389.00	2449.33	3636.97	798.65	345.78
59943.39	38811.29	60094.21	51718.41	229.18	1998.31	3317.77	1090.28	532.85
1669.15	417.73	973.90	344.17	82.08	537.97	702.56	82.51	0.55
50.81	29.46	45.25	35.22	0.39	6.32	8.18	1.47	0.10
113.62	35.23	95.16	66.37	3.23	16.16	25.39	6.00	0.58
468.07	153.69	240.73	164.73	7.15	23.22	39.41	9.04	1.32
105.91	62.90	56.24	43.45	0.11	9.37	10.43	0.95	0.17
2860.96	1896.42	4770.20	4459.40	8.71	107.50	148.77	32.56	15.05
2226.69	1309.48	2398.02	1645.36	14.69	232.25	336.30	89.36	19.46
1246.28	734.95	1311.38	960.17	24.08	124.21	189.47	41.18	7.43
673.33	525.11	822.98	321.13	341.22	78.25	477.54	58.07	4.07
1729.41	1055.69	2136.08	1825.57	9.82	113.79	172.25	48.64	22.21
1702.38	1243.40	2209.83	1785.02	12.29	97.41	167.37	57.67	41.59
792.57	595.78	1396.18	1200.75	6.10	49.53	80.53	24.90	30.59
426.32	266.66	381.46	331.83	1.88	13.40	24.50	9.22	4.62
2306.16	1517.27	2090.64	1706.62	10.50	121.09	176.65	45.06	29.61
2637.17	1471.71	2453.72	2183.95	10.37	29.59	96.45	56.49	19.00
1621.06	978.50	1265.19	1046.66	6.01	81.56	113.87	26.29	18.65
2649.68	2107.05	4056.29	3631.67	11.55	105.20	152.37	35.62	47.22
2720.72	920.92	5599.09	4697.80	697.14	98.21	1103.38	308.03	2.45
7839.61	4367.45	7597.59	6260.59	39.96	384.88	614.89	190.05	34.71
4466.24	2397.20	1937.89	1052.00	15.42	249.90	344.51	79.18	16.70
213.23	102.65	187.93	158.92	0.89	14.16	18.81	3.76	1.34
6144.30	3789.89	5987.08	5002.85	25.21	314.83	455.44	115.39	77.72
7350.30	4508.06	6052.55	5161.07	31.13	266.22	451.99	154.64	49.24
2474.98	1157.78	4621.68	4370.92	14.84	90.44	158.17	52.89	7.87
2287.21	1673.81	4277.11	4033.29	7.14	60.07	100.73	33.53	14.55
6556.37	4501.24	8610.65	7434.52	35.39	379.24	586.02	171.39	92.17
6906.15	5023.19	6076.04	4893.80	24.50	402.45	542.41	115.47	59.94
8251.90	5950.75	5615.13	4170.93	28.47	609.56	772.76	134.74	65.35
10917.78	7678.42	13315.83	11617.85	293.92	529.21	1052.15	229.02	49.11
2102.75	1518.44	1626.75	1431.74	6.68	66.22	89.84	16.93	11.07
24749.46	16807.53	21702.98	17611.94	89.80	1584.71	2207.51	533.00	174.15
62221.23	42400.91	47689.96	38846.36	174.93	3628.09	4399.55	596.53	317.53
2181.41	1605.49	1541.49	1146.41	7.48	111.59	158.05	38.97	20.27
682.46	525.02	611.63	482.63	2.75	40.98	54.31	10.58	9.47
600.80	359.17	790.49	730.80	2.33	19.63	32.16	10.21	2.29
361.61	250.30	313.43	263.91	1.50	22.39	31.39	7.50	2.77
23697.26	4807.42	10617.81	9540.96	45.15	726.43	1058.72	287.15	17.11
1777.57	650.20	3166.36	2953.73	3.43	145.80	166.88	17.65	2.47
3701.32	947.61	854.17	630.21	5.72	103.38	126.59	17.49	6.57

Note: The registered statistical categories of this table is implemented in accordance with the Regulations onStatistics the Classification of Market Entity(Guotongzi [2023] No. 14).

12-12 规模以上国有控股工业企业主要经济指标（2023年）

单位：亿元

项目	Item	企业单位数（个）Number of Enterprises (unit)	工业总产值（当年价）Gross Industrial Output Value (at current prices)
全省	**Provincial Total**	**1646**	**35543.39**
按轻重工业分	Grouped by Light and Heavy Industries		
轻工业	Light Industry	341	2500.04
重工业	Heavy Industry	1305	33043.35
按企业规模分	Grouped by Size of Enterprises		
大型企业	Large Enterprises	143	24821.75
中型企业	Medium Enterprises	269	4488.68
小微型企业	Small and Micro Enterprises	1234	6232.95
按行业分	Grouped by Sector		
煤炭开采和洗选业	Mining and Washing of Coal		
石油和天然气开采业	Extraction of Petroleum and Natural Gas		
黑色金属矿采选业	Mining and Dressing of Ferrous Metal Ores	1	1.30
有色金属矿采选业	Mining and Dressing of Nonferrous Metal Ores	8	58.89
非金属矿采选业	Mining and Dressing of Nonmetal Ores	21	44.16
开采专业及辅助性活动	Mining Specialized and Auxiliary Operations	4	46.61
其他采矿业	Mining and Dressing of Other Ores		
农副食品加工业	Processing of Farm and Sideline Food	124	453.13
食品制造业	Manufacture of Food	28	128.96
酒、饮料和精制茶制造业	Manufacture of Wine, Beverage and Refined Tea	22	194.58
烟草制品业	Tobacco Products	6	550.01
纺织业	Textile Industry	2	58.31
纺织服装、服饰业	Manufacture of Textile Garments, Footwear and Headgear	3	2.73
皮革、毛皮、羽毛及其制品和制鞋业	Leather, Fur, Feather, Down and Related Products		
木材加工和木、竹、藤、棕、草制品业	Timber Processing, Bamboo, Cane, Palm Fiber & Straw Products	7	5.96
家具制造业	Manufacture of Furniture	1	0.66
造纸和纸制品业	Papermaking and Paper Products	10	123.26
印刷和记录媒介复制业	Printing and Record Medium Reproduction	22	42.07
文教、工美、体育和娱乐用品制造业	Manufacture of Cultural, Educational,Sports and Entertainment Articles	9	180.36
石油、煤炭及其他燃料加工业	Petroleum, Coal and other Fuel Processing	9	5015.67
化学原料和化学制品制造业	Manufacture of Raw Chemical Materials and Chemical Products	55	877.08
医药制造业	Manufacture of Medicines	43	369.71
化学纤维制造业	Manufacture of Chemical Fibers	1	29.38
橡胶和塑料制品业	Rubber and Plastic Products	34	116.99
非金属矿物制品业	Nonmetal Mineral Products	82	194.90
黑色金属冶炼和压延加工业	Smelting and Pressing of Ferrous Metals	17	2191.21
有色金属冶炼和压延加工业	Smelting and Pressing of Nonferrous Metals	29	1130.27
金属制品业	Metal Products	60	342.30
通用设备制造业	Manufacture of General-purpose Machinery	34	170.72
专用设备制造业	Manufacture of Special-purpose Machinery	33	155.09
汽车制造业	Manufacture of Automobile	43	5073.83
铁路、船舶、航空航天和其他运输设备制造业	Manufacture of Railway ,Ship,Aeronautics and Other Transport equipment	30	555.47
电气机械和器材制造业	Manufacture of Electrical Machinery and Equipment	70	430.85
计算机、通信和其他电子设备制造业	Manufacture of Communication Equipment, Computers and Other Electronic Equipment	134	4680.99
仪器仪表制造业	Manufacture of Instruments and Meters	9	35.02
其他制造业	Other Manufactures	3	5.40
废弃资源综合利用业	Comprehensive Utilization of Waste	20	67.63
金属制品、机械和设备修理业	Manufacture of Metal Products,Machinery and Equipment Maintenance	19	90.64
电力、热力生产和供应业	Production and Supply of Electric Power and Heat Power	354	9374.66
燃气生产和供应业	Production and Supply of Gas	83	2185.92
水的生产和供应业	Production and Supply of Water	216	558.67

Main Economic Indicators of State-holding Industrial Enterprises above Designated Size (2023)

(100 million yuan)

年末资产总计 Total Assets at the Year-end	流动资产合计 Total Working Capital	营业收入 Business Revenue	营业成本 Cost of Business	税金及附加 Tax and Other Charges on Principal Business	利润总额 Total Profits	利税总额 Total Pre-tax Profits	本年应交增值税 Value-added Tax Payable in Current Year	全部就业人员年平均人数(万人) Annual Average Number of Employed Persons (10000 persons)
47170.62	**16915.03**	**35370.72**	**30519.91**	**1340.56**	**1626.89**	**3873.04**	**905.59**	**76.39**
3144.93	1715.49	2528.28	1724.96	349.86	209.70	660.48	100.91	11.12
44025.69	15199.55	32842.44	28794.95	990.70	1417.19	3212.56	804.68	65.27
30981.43	11020.97	24121.46	20801.29	1111.03	989.17	2780.67	680.47	50.28
7078.28	2884.12	4541.92	3648.92	205.61	317.12	646.03	123.30	14.97
9110.91	3009.94	6707.35	6069.70	23.93	320.60	446.35	101.82	11.15
0.79	0.15	1.11	0.67		0.22	0.30	0.08	0.01
87.16	19.85	60.62	36.68	2.91	14.80	21.90	4.19	0.44
196.78	37.96	43.19	33.68	1.29	2.44	6.21	2.48	0.26
95.76	55.52	46.61	36.20	0.09	7.65	8.21	0.48	0.12
164.64	95.99	466.31	441.13	1.28	11.08	14.48	2.13	1.02
223.07	77.69	131.75	103.38	0.85	18.00	23.28	4.42	1.52
293.70	210.04	182.51	132.03	5.51	28.07	39.72	6.13	0.64
479.94	357.13	553.77	132.59	336.03	39.79	431.99	56.16	0.54
17.90	5.29	57.77	47.19	0.19	8.08	10.41	2.13	0.16
3.68	2.54	2.41	2.14	0.02	-0.30	-0.18	0.11	0.08
47.95	16.73	8.46	7.23	0.13	0.83	1.15	0.20	0.47
1.44	0.70	0.65	0.56		0.04	0.06	0.02	0.04
302.44	137.98	138.81	135.33	0.46	-1.82	-0.60	0.75	0.46
175.73	82.50	44.14	34.56	0.34	2.01	3.65	1.30	0.57
46.94	35.56	181.76	176.97	0.22	0.88	1.73	0.64	0.38
2315.24	670.20	5038.08	4186.63	679.64	88.68	1071.95	303.63	1.67
735.46	207.99	890.24	863.80	5.06	-11.20	30.26	36.39	1.10
1062.39	481.98	362.76	167.85	3.47	81.21	106.51	21.83	2.59
18.76	7.85	29.95	20.53	0.22	7.39	8.91	1.31	0.04
205.26	95.64	121.79	97.49	0.83	8.75	11.44	1.86	1.57
362.65	180.46	201.41	173.55	1.52	6.72	13.07	4.83	0.93
1266.36	385.33	2219.45	2138.49	4.84	22.49	53.82	26.49	1.99
412.85	316.60	1351.43	1331.74	1.40	2.50	6.32	2.41	0.71
464.81	302.21	383.58	343.61	1.75	10.72	16.15	3.68	1.79
396.07	242.35	188.78	160.52	0.82	5.26	8.84	2.76	1.25
355.46	235.97	143.11	114.40	0.82	14.74	18.82	3.26	0.79
3056.36	1934.53	4984.63	4353.70	217.18	212.35	528.75	99.22	7.31
1042.79	752.71	605.54	571.56	1.40	3.21	6.56	1.95	1.57
444.55	321.77	453.26	398.48	1.58	17.38	25.08	6.12	2.58
6860.83	4293.35	4004.01	3002.43	22.52	257.71	310.35	30.11	20.81
51.87	39.46	34.94	25.15	0.20	1.51	2.86	1.14	0.26
6.57	5.11	5.33	4.32	0.02	0.27	0.40	0.12	0.05
85.54	32.99	75.98	69.02	0.36	1.62	3.00	1.01	0.23
149.84	92.95	90.10	79.42	0.62	3.95	7.27	2.70	0.92
21590.00	4060.32	9416.02	8529.29	40.00	604.30	893.98	249.67	15.18
1204.01	383.63	2253.22	2106.10	2.48	108.04	121.72	11.19	1.27
2945.00	736.03	597.26	461.48	4.52	47.50	64.69	12.67	5.09

12-13 规模以上“三资”工业企业主要经济指标（2023年）

单位：亿元

项　　目	Item	企业单位数（个）Number of Enterprises (unit)	工业总产值（当年价）Gross Industrial Output Value (at current prices)
全　省	**Provincial Total**	**11217**	**55091.40**
按登记注册统计类别分	By Registered Statistical Categories		
港澳台投资企业	Enterprises with Investment from Hong Kong,Macao and Taiwan	7723	26963.13
外商投资企业	Foreign Invested Enterprises	3494	28128.28
按轻重工业分	Grouped by Light and Heavy Industries		
轻工业	Light Industry	5403	15381.94
重工业	Heavy Industry	5814	39709.46
按企业规模分	Grouped by Size of Enterprises		
大型企业	Large Enterprises	645	33217.50
中型企业	Medium Enterprises	2264	11742.62
小微型企业	Small and Micro Enterprises	8308	10131.29
按行业分	Grouped by Sector		
煤炭开采和洗选业	Mining and Washing of Coal		
石油和天然气开采业	Extraction of Petroleum and Natural Gas	2	904.35
黑色金属矿采选业	Mining and Dressing of Ferrous Metal Ores	1	0.54
有色金属矿采选业	Mining and Dressing of Nonferrous Metal Ores	2	2.08
非金属矿采选业	Mining and Dressing of Nonmetal Ores	8	5.89
开采专业及辅助性活动	Mining Specialized and Auxiliary Operations	2	8.29
其他采矿业	Mining and Dressing of Other Ores		
农副食品加工业	Processing of Farm and Sideline Food	123	999.30
食品制造业	Manufacture of Food	190	1008.36
酒、饮料和精制茶制造业	Manufacture of Wine, Beverage and Refined Tea	57	734.93
烟草制品业	Tobacco Products	1	4.30
纺织业	Textile Industry	302	590.94
纺织服装、服饰业	Manufacture of Textile Garments, Footwear and Headgear	441	716.79
皮革、毛皮、羽毛及其制品和制鞋业	Leather, Fur, Feather, Down and Related Products	306	532.70
木材加工和木、竹、藤、棕、草制品业	Timber Processing, Bamboo, Cane, Palm Fiber & Straw Products	49	50.08
家具制造业	Manufacture of Furniture	239	518.48
造纸和纸制品业	Papermaking and Paper Products	250	952.23
印刷和记录媒介复制业	Printing and Record Medium Reproduction	186	310.51
文教、工美、体育和娱乐用品制造业	Manufacture of Cultural, Educational,Sports and Entertainment Articles	624	1645.78
石油、煤炭及其他燃料加工业	Petroleum, Coal and other Fuel Processing	20	1043.94
化学原料和化学制品制造业	Manufacture of Raw Chemical Materials and Chemical Products	547	2798.12
医药制造业	Manufacture of Medicines	114	643.68
化学纤维制造业	Manufacture of Chemical Fibers	20	88.18
橡胶和塑料制品业	Rubber and Plastic Products	1154	1627.40
非金属矿物制品业	Nonmetal Mineral Products	326	895.84
黑色金属冶炼和压延加工业	Smelting and Pressing of Ferrous Metals	60	672.51
有色金属冶炼和压延加工业	Smelting and Pressing of Nonferrous Metals	131	594.49
金属制品业	Metal Products	915	1782.79
通用设备制造业	Manufacture of General-purpose Machinery	560	1793.97
专用设备制造业	Manufacture of Special-purpose Machinery	605	1568.00
汽车制造业	Manufacture of Automobile	400	9522.16
铁路、船舶、航空航天和其他运输设备制造业	Manufacture of Railway ,Ship,Aeronautics and Other Transport equipment	101	360.17
电气机械和器材制造业	Manufacture of Electrical Machinery and Equipment	1194	4636.36
计算机、通信和其他电子设备制造业	Manufacture of Communication Equipment, Computers and Other Electronic Equipment	1719	15480.86
仪器仪表制造业	Manufacture of Instruments and Meters	234	441.82
其他制造业	Other Manufactures	110	216.59
废弃资源综合利用业	Comprehensive Utilization of Waste	16	143.69
金属制品、机械和设备修理业	Manufacture of Metal Products,Machinery and Equipment Maintenance	16	180.94
电力、热力生产和供应业	Production and Supply of Electric Power and Heat Power	90	861.06
燃气生产和供应业	Production and Supply of Gas	67	666.46
水的生产和供应业	Production and Supply of Water	35	86.85

注：本表登记注册统计类别按《关于市场主体统计分类的划分规定》(国统字〔2023〕14号)执行。

Main Economic Indicators of Foreign-funded Industrial Enterprises above Designated Size (2023)

(100 million yuan)

年末资产总计 Total Assets at the Year-end	流动资产合计 Total Working Capital	营业收入 Business Revenue	营业成本 Cost of Business	税金及附加 Tax and Other Charges on Principal Business	利润总额 Total Profits	利税总额 Total Pre-tax Profits	本年应交增值税 Value-added Tax Payable in Current Year	全部就业人员年平均人数(万人) Annual Average Number of Employed Persons (10000 persons)
59859.61	**36944.30**	**56027.33**	**46899.73**	**707.23**	**3511.98**	**5222.02**	**1002.82**	**436.39**
29984.58	18355.80	26674.59	21859.58	337.48	2012.34	2886.68	536.85	281.88
29875.03	18588.50	29352.74	25040.16	369.74	1499.63	2335.34	465.97	154.51
16909.46	10903.51	15726.23	12434.02	90.78	1047.80	1446.82	308.24	190.28
42950.16	26040.79	40301.10	34465.71	616.45	2464.18	3775.20	694.58	246.11
34835.26	21368.72	33648.00	28157.70	587.08	2356.79	3553.48	609.61	205.34
13907.31	8229.35	12014.97	9908.41	67.65	755.42	1039.31	216.24	131.56
11117.04	7346.23	10364.35	8833.62	52.50	399.77	629.24	176.97	99.49
1262.13	134.50	885.98	310.47	73.69	486.18	639.26	79.39	0.53
3.65	0.99	0.47	0.40	0.01	0.04	0.08	0.03	
4.58	1.13	2.11	1.80	0.08	-0.21	0.01	0.14	0.03
9.61	5.55	5.84	4.14	0.18	0.36	0.76	0.21	0.05
22.17	16.64	8.29	5.45	0.01	2.24	2.71	0.45	0.06
649.93	456.83	1107.88	1055.41	1.90	11.65	17.28	3.72	2.29
954.30	626.16	1233.67	731.24	8.77	124.77	187.48	53.94	7.98
618.22	371.02	805.39	580.91	12.15	63.58	100.81	25.07	4.52
3.71	3.33	4.25	3.86	0.02	0.03	0.05		0.14
623.96	414.96	559.61	475.17	3.27	26.51	40.42	10.64	7.83
562.74	427.28	688.30	566.74	4.09	28.90	49.60	16.62	15.90
352.41	252.65	525.72	435.98	2.91	24.70	36.51	8.91	14.09
50.63	35.52	47.84	40.35	0.50	1.86	3.56	1.20	0.65
602.23	424.51	510.22	417.29	3.07	41.60	52.43	7.76	7.53
1116.91	637.09	902.66	800.92	4.52	11.38	38.60	22.69	5.98
521.50	327.90	314.57	252.16	1.93	17.75	25.87	6.19	7.01
1303.00	1075.33	1667.49	1464.76	5.94	48.69	65.13	10.49	25.14
669.33	244.01	1051.39	849.06	171.06	7.06	270.05	91.94	0.47
3325.20	1754.11	3002.98	2427.34	15.33	149.60	259.56	94.63	9.75
1107.16	664.74	616.93	319.99	5.00	78.76	109.41	25.65	5.28
94.04	42.04	87.63	70.73	0.47	10.94	13.29	1.88	0.55
2107.07	1267.31	1630.53	1334.58	8.66	97.95	129.99	23.38	26.93
1468.25	871.82	870.62	720.48	5.82	69.44	96.91	21.65	7.42
458.64	259.89	739.72	716.96	1.90	2.84	11.76	7.02	1.24
472.54	353.47	606.72	552.52	1.40	18.26	26.44	6.78	3.52
1566.60	1078.64	1797.97	1528.39	8.52	93.52	134.19	32.15	24.00
1794.61	1389.99	1813.61	1482.62	7.94	140.88	176.06	27.24	17.35
2185.14	1423.53	1524.34	1121.32	9.28	236.38	272.70	27.05	17.78
7140.90	5412.43	9996.81	8639.02	263.55	481.90	929.16	183.70	30.44
465.82	315.52	388.38	329.37	2.50	26.69	30.51	1.32	3.93
5865.77	3778.94	4632.99	3944.57	20.14	256.72	323.89	47.04	51.97
17515.19	11088.75	15317.18	13595.32	49.85	636.89	784.62	97.88	122.01
447.53	345.83	456.17	359.16	2.28	38.48	48.41	7.66	7.12
333.40	287.70	212.42	160.64	0.86	16.10	18.53	1.57	2.74
75.77	37.12	152.59	138.84	0.62	7.29	9.71	1.80	0.31
163.52	119.66	182.08	150.66	0.82	17.11	21.26	3.32	1.14
2815.63	601.67	878.60	645.66	6.49	143.47	192.48	42.52	1.33
806.27	317.05	708.12	622.63	1.41	58.08	67.48	7.99	0.99
319.56	78.69	89.26	42.80	0.30	33.57	35.07	1.19	0.43

Note: The registered statistical categories of this table is implemented in accordance with the Regulations onStatistics the Classification of Market Entity(Guotongzi [2023] No. 14).

12-14 规模以上私营工业企业主要经济指标（2023年）

单位：亿元

项　　目	Item	企业单位数（个） Number of Enterprises (unit)	工业总产值（当年价） Gross Industrial Output Value (at current prices)
全　省	**Provincial Total**	**50821**	**70889.56**
按轻重工业分	Grouped by Light & Heavy Industries		
轻工业	Light Industry	23275	28612.50
重工业	Heavy Industry	27546	42277.06
按企业规模分	Grouped by Size of Enterprises		
大型企业	Large Enterprises	338	19358.40
中型企业	Medium Enterprises	2674	16368.53
小微型企业	Small and Micro Enterprises	47809	35162.63
按行业分	Grouped by Sector		
煤炭开采和洗选业	Mining and Washing of Coal		
石油和天然气开采业	Extraction of Petroleum and Natural Gas		
黑色金属矿采选业	Mining and Dressing of Ferrous Metal Ores	4	15.89
有色金属矿采选业	Mining and Dressing of Nonferrous Metal Ores	17	21.32
非金属矿采选业	Mining and Dressing of Nonmetal Ores	141	115.06
开采专业及辅助性活动	Mining Specialized and Auxiliary Operations	2	5.14
其他采矿业	Mining and Dressing of Other Ores		
农副食品加工业	Processing of Farm and Sideline Food	753	1314.26
食品制造业	Manufacture of Food	640	812.17
酒、饮料和精制茶制造业	Manufacture of Wine, Beverage and Refined Tea	103	158.53
烟草制品业	Tobacco Products	80	189.26
纺织业	Textile Industry	1345	1400.39
纺织服装、服饰业	Manufacture of Textile Garments, Footwear and Headgear	1931	1558.93
皮革、毛皮、羽毛及其制品和制鞋业	Leather, Fur, Feather, Down and Related Products	1368	840.75
木材加工和木、竹、藤、棕、草制品业	Timber Processing, Bamboo, Cane, Palm Fiber & Straw Products	427	280.77
家具制造业	Manufacture of Furniture	1429	1341.82
造纸和纸制品业	Papermaking and Paper Products	1191	1177.59
印刷和记录媒介复制业	Printing and Record Medium Reproduction	889	752.09
文教、工美、体育和娱乐用品制造业	Manufacture of Cultural, Educational,Sports and Entertainment Articles	1334	1914.16
石油、煤炭及其他燃料加工业	Petroleum, Coal and other Fuel Processing	74	156.33
化学原料和化学制品制造业	Manufacture of Raw Chemical Materials and Chemical Products	2370	2832.46
医药制造业	Manufacture of Medicines	324	583.94
化学纤维制造业	Manufacture of Chemical Fibers	66	80.39
橡胶和塑料制品业	Rubber and Plastic Products	4741	3730.70
非金属矿物制品业	Nonmetal Mineral Products	2958	3799.12
黑色金属冶炼和压延加工业	Smelting and Pressing of Ferrous Metals	467	1293.09
有色金属冶炼和压延加工业	Smelting and Pressing of Nonferrous Metals	996	1680.55
金属制品业	Metal Products	5558	5432.25
通用设备制造业	Manufacture of General-purpose Machinery	3119	3262.77
专用设备制造业	Manufacture of Special-purpose Machinery	3016	2854.49
汽车制造业	Manufacture of Automobile	551	866.69
铁路、船舶、航空航天和其他运输设备制造业	Manufacture of Railway ,Ship,Aeronautics and Other Transport equipment	343	365.53
电气机械和器材制造业	Manufacture of Electrical Machinery and Equipment	6236	12533.02
计算机、通信和其他电子设备制造业	Manufacture of Communication Equipment, Computers and Other Electronic Equipment	6715	17665.20
仪器仪表制造业	Manufacture of Instruments and Meters	803	717.98
其他制造业	Other Manufactures	356	319.69
废弃资源综合利用业	Comprehensive Utilization of Waste	190	343.06
金属制品、机械和设备修理业	Manufacture of Metal Products,Machinery and Equipment Maintenance	54	30.43
电力、热力生产和供应业	Production and Supply of Electric Power and Heat Power	72	166.14
燃气生产和供应业	Production and Supply of Gas	92	231.47
水的生产和供应业	Production and Supply of Water	66	46.10

Main Economic Indicators of Private Industrial Enterprises above Designated Size (2023)

(100 million yuan)

年末资产总计 Total Assets at the Year-end	流动资产合计 Total working Capital	营业收入 Business Revenue	营业成本 Cost of Business	税金及附加 Tax and Other Charges on Principal Business	利润总额 Total Profits	利税总额 Total Pre-tax Profits	本年应交增值税 Value-added Tax Payable in Current Year	全部就业人员年平均人数(万人) Annual Average Number of Employed Persons (10000 persons)
68973.16	**47432.62**	**68727.73**	**55918.48**	**287.96**	**4273.56**	**6085.84**	**1524.32**	**590.68**
22196.18	15097.44	27120.20	22337.87	117.69	1574.32	2389.24	697.24	272.43
46776.99	32335.18	41607.53	33580.60	170.27	2699.25	3696.60	827.08	318.25
25914.85	16825.99	18592.18	13392.09	99.03	2266.70	2911.55	545.82	98.49
14335.72	9090.40	16146.39	13475.72	78.25	998.54	1401.85	325.07	133.43
28722.60	21516.24	33989.15	29050.67	110.69	1008.32	1772.44	653.43	358.76
18.69	12.20	14.28	8.44	0.21	4.23	5.22	0.77	0.07
12.93	7.12	21.33	18.40	0.16	0.95	1.70	0.58	0.07
124.51	59.72	107.17	78.53	2.59	6.90	13.06	3.57	0.69
1.64	1.50	4.34	4.09	0.01	0.09	0.22	0.12	
899.06	605.50	1425.91	1317.04	2.74	32.17	47.41	12.50	6.90
801.90	465.41	809.30	635.06	4.08	73.78	102.66	24.80	8.00
173.44	85.66	158.69	128.53	2.76	8.67	15.79	4.36	1.36
123.37	110.60	189.92	139.09	4.56	18.28	24.29	1.45	2.64
918.74	534.74	1321.63	1143.99	5.56	71.07	107.90	31.27	12.36
975.56	724.35	1392.17	1132.76	7.40	61.94	105.71	36.36	23.16
395.46	307.25	804.68	709.04	2.86	22.59	39.72	14.27	14.83
227.04	153.21	267.88	233.31	1.01	9.81	17.26	6.44	2.88
1262.38	886.46	1297.76	1070.01	5.52	64.69	98.28	28.06	17.60
830.09	515.74	1074.00	947.20	3.88	24.09	51.91	23.95	10.00
594.64	363.16	706.21	593.65	3.17	32.73	51.49	15.59	8.78
1090.91	853.02	1924.07	1746.36	4.43	37.31	61.76	20.02	18.52
119.26	61.86	171.28	158.21	0.74	4.85	7.77	2.18	0.33
2674.97	1669.12	2770.86	2231.63	16.05	168.82	249.04	64.17	18.27
1251.83	728.46	550.72	339.33	3.73	84.61	105.22	16.88	5.34
83.07	44.75	71.77	61.45	0.30	3.64	5.91	1.97	0.66
2933.05	1894.48	3608.18	3053.47	13.35	179.62	270.99	78.02	40.24
3703.14	2408.86	3566.28	3067.83	16.57	113.87	221.38	90.94	30.07
602.39	404.62	1231.24	1120.31	8.03	50.55	76.24	17.66	3.97
785.97	583.58	1633.99	1523.65	2.76	21.81	41.89	17.32	7.78
3401.36	2352.53	5219.70	4512.12	21.22	215.14	349.43	113.08	55.19
3532.41	2572.70	3163.39	2520.28	12.10	200.16	280.12	67.85	32.66
3508.79	2629.56	2682.41	2025.79	12.26	218.35	304.89	74.28	32.71
1070.84	747.95	886.19	740.53	4.12	33.24	55.06	17.69	8.21
377.83	278.78	356.41	297.50	1.75	15.59	25.12	7.78	3.62
10743.95	7626.50	11601.39	9296.03	47.13	816.29	1225.63	362.21	89.39
23495.16	16340.62	17812.08	13531.06	69.52	1568.37	1963.47	325.58	116.34
1054.77	795.61	719.63	515.70	3.36	55.46	80.22	21.40	9.29
243.69	168.00	315.15	258.78	1.46	15.93	24.52	7.13	5.52
267.39	171.48	335.27	306.20	0.96	9.03	15.50	5.51	1.28
51.37	33.32	33.17	26.22	0.17	1.64	3.24	1.44	0.76
335.91	116.05	173.40	144.72	0.98	17.10	23.43	5.35	0.46
82.04	51.27	258.07	249.22	0.23	4.24	5.54	1.07	0.23
203.62	66.88	47.82	32.98	0.26	5.94	6.89	0.69	0.50

12－15　规模以上大中型工业企业主要经济指标（2023年）

单位：亿元

项　　目	Item	企业单位数（个）Number of Enterprises (unit)	工业总产值（当年价）Gross Industrial Output Value (at current prices)
全　省	**Provincial Total**	**7803**	**124695.57**
按轻重工业分	Grouped by Light & Heavy Industry		
轻工业	Light Industry	3481	33286.23
重工业	Heavy Industry	4322	91409.35
按企业规模分	Grouped by Size of Enterprises		
大型企业	Large	1389	84290.38
中型企业	Medium	6414	40405.19
按行业分	Grouped by Sector		
煤炭开采和洗选业	Mining and Washing of Coal		
石油和天然气开采业	Extraction of Petroleum and Natural Gas	2	904.35
黑色金属矿采选业	Mining and Dressing of Ferrous Metal Ores	1	8.82
有色金属矿采选业	Mining and Dressing of Nonferrous Metal Ores	4	50.88
非金属矿采选业	Mining and Dressing of Nonmetal Ores	5	53.03
开采专业及辅助性活动	Mining Specialized and Auxiliary Operations	2	39.47
其他采矿业	Mining and Dressing of Other Ores		
农副食品加工业	Processing of Farm and Sideline Food	109	1456.51
食品制造业	Manufacture of Food	138	1427.77
酒、饮料和精制茶制造业	Manufacture of Wine, Beverage and Refined Tea	50	975.35
烟草制品业	Tobacco Products	39	748.76
纺织业	Textile Industry	133	1125.24
纺织服装、服饰业	Manufacture of Textile Garments, Footwear and Headgear	260	1265.94
皮革、毛皮、羽毛及其制品和制鞋业	Leather, Fur, Feather, Down and Related Products	176	643.84
木材加工和木、竹、藤、棕、草制品业	Timber Processing, Bamboo, Cane, Palm Fiber & Straw Products	16	91.49
家具制造业	Manufacture of Furniture	201	1247.61
造纸和纸制品业	Papermaking and Paper Products	108	1393.47
印刷和记录媒介复制业	Printing and Record Medium Reproduction	118	714.77
文教、工美、体育和娱乐用品制造业	Manufacture of Cultural, Educational,Sports and Entertainment Articles	342	2097.76
石油、煤炭及其他燃料加工业	Petroleum, Coal and other Fuel Processing	11	5192.82
化学原料和化学制品制造业	Manufacture of Raw Chemical Materials and Chemical Products	210	3440.97
医药制造业	Manufacture of Medicines	144	1522.40
化学纤维制造业	Manufacture of Chemical Fibers	13	114.31
橡胶和塑料制品业	Rubber and Plastic Products	484	2407.51
非金属矿物制品业	Nonmetal Mineral Products	306	2963.90
黑色金属冶炼和压延加工业	Smelting and Pressing of Ferrous Metals	47	3466.37
有色金属冶炼和压延加工业	Smelting and Pressing of Nonferrous Metals	77	1388.72
金属制品业	Metal Products	548	3914.47
通用设备制造业	Manufacture of General-purpose Machinery	372	3701.33
专用设备制造业	Manufacture of Special-purpose Machinery	408	3491.17
汽车制造业	Manufacture of Automobile	323	11698.21
铁路、船舶、航空航天和其他运输设备制造业	Manufacture of Railway ,Ship,Aeronautics and Other Transport equipment	76	1155.20
电气机械和器材制造业	Manufacture of Electrical Machinery and Equipment	1040	16519.51
计算机、通信和其他电子设备制造业	Manufacture of Communication Equipment, Computers and Other Electronic Equipment	1661	38400.54
仪器仪表制造业	Manufacture of Instruments and Meters	157	713.42
其他制造业	Other Manufactures	67	349.39
废弃资源综合利用业	Comprehensive Utilization of Waste	12	265.22
金属制品、机械和设备修理业	Manufacture of Metal Products,Machinery and Equipment Maintenance	20	258.65
电力、热力生产和供应业	Production and Supply of Electric Power and Heat Power	69	8602.50
燃气生产和供应业	Production and Supply of Gas	8	358.24
水的生产和供应业	Production and Supply of Water	46	525.67

Main Economic Indicators of Large and Medium-sized Industrial Enterprises above Designated Size (2023)

(100 million yuan)

年末资产总计 Total Assets at the Year-end	流动资产合计 Total Working Capital	营业收入 Business Revenue	营业成本 Cost of Business	税金及附加 Tax and Other Charges	利润总额 Total Profits	利税总额 Total Pre-tax Profits	本年应交增值税 Value-added Tax Payable in Current Year	全部就业人员年平均人数(万人) Annual Average Number of Employed Persons (10000 persons)
151540.82	**87533.17**	**125402.67**	**102526.88**	**1874.77**	**9596.93**	**14130.57**	**2658.87**	**764.21**
37056.56	23101.08	33139.59	25410.08	518.01	2973.02	4427.77	936.75	293.61
114484.26	64432.09	92263.08	77116.80	1356.76	6623.92	9702.79	1722.12	470.60
108504.74	61953.14	85009.40	68997.33	1485.77	7147.60	10493.59	1860.22	418.44
43036.08	25580.03	40393.27	33529.55	389.00	2449.33	3636.97	798.65	345.78
1262.13	134.50	885.98	310.47	73.69	486.18	639.26	79.39	0.53
5.87	4.01	4.90	3.71	0.01	0.50	0.62	0.10	0.04
74.71	12.17	51.91	32.26	1.71	12.63	17.95	3.61	0.41
89.25	37.51	51.65	27.64	1.77	10.46	14.32	2.09	0.34
83.07	46.27	39.47	29.86	0.04	7.14	7.61	0.43	0.12
1140.09	678.49	1609.51	1482.37	3.68	56.96	73.53	12.88	5.63
1501.93	880.83	1650.11	1040.71	10.95	199.55	279.37	68.88	11.31
839.78	529.97	1021.32	729.21	17.68	101.67	152.32	32.97	5.47
594.14	460.29	746.40	269.60	337.02	68.70	462.09	56.37	3.31
768.85	463.88	1101.32	923.79	5.03	83.36	115.35	26.96	9.46
965.16	659.37	1165.31	892.39	8.31	69.34	112.34	34.69	20.78
381.41	265.92	634.26	533.83	3.70	31.07	46.33	11.56	15.50
98.83	55.09	89.39	74.76	0.54	6.02	9.15	2.58	1.07
1540.17	1000.70	1237.58	989.22	6.70	106.29	140.61	27.62	15.44
1728.38	857.92	1282.63	1152.21	6.60	8.53	48.47	33.34	7.56
922.57	537.07	671.21	544.95	3.43	69.40	86.40	13.57	9.40
1709.00	1349.18	2109.77	1831.33	7.91	83.08	109.78	18.79	28.26
2515.30	782.31	5210.47	4343.90	687.89	86.91	1079.11	304.31	1.88
4050.05	1922.16	3625.75	2952.98	21.17	202.55	332.83	109.11	12.22
3550.95	1851.71	1472.73	774.50	12.05	220.98	294.83	61.80	11.81
140.61	59.69	119.26	99.08	0.58	12.21	15.04	2.24	0.66
3012.78	1634.29	2423.68	2000.41	12.78	191.85	248.65	44.02	31.72
3607.51	1821.28	2831.76	2413.61	15.49	184.04	264.58	65.05	22.01
1969.58	775.23	3493.37	3308.46	12.80	66.54	120.22	40.88	4.86
1042.47	711.17	1491.72	1359.95	3.45	38.52	56.86	14.90	7.33
3183.51	1991.62	3884.85	3283.78	19.90	263.39	364.84	81.54	40.06
4220.52	2982.92	3667.43	2967.81	15.71	293.95	366.10	56.44	30.44
4977.71	3519.06	3249.94	2360.66	18.19	489.55	581.10	73.37	33.09
9583.51	6790.03	12161.91	10623.47	289.27	491.78	986.79	205.74	39.84
1642.20	1179.09	1213.40	1077.88	4.97	53.59	68.47	9.91	6.70
19411.12	12769.83	16144.28	12895.04	72.22	1435.79	1944.82	436.81	108.87
52618.41	35196.50	38792.61	31140.87	153.10	3448.41	4074.95	473.45	241.57
1218.37	856.27	752.50	577.62	3.73	52.08	71.78	15.97	10.38
481.92	366.84	338.35	259.10	1.71	29.84	36.77	5.21	5.16
218.94	120.72	269.75	247.02	0.97	9.58	14.42	3.87	0.73
294.64	205.34	261.27	221.99	1.27	19.55	26.53	5.71	2.09
17358.30	3431.65	8718.78	8025.99	34.04	510.36	751.23	206.83	13.60
528.51	121.86	391.70	333.19	1.00	28.91	33.76	3.85	0.81
2208.59	470.41	534.43	391.26	3.73	65.66	81.40	12.00	3.78

12-16 规模以上高技术制造业主要经济指标（2023年）

单位：亿元

项　　目	Item	企业单位数（个）Number of Enterprises (unit)	工业总产值（当年价）Gross Industrial Output Value (at current prices)
高技术制造业合计	**Total**	**13710**	**56429.20**
信息化学品制造	**Manufacture of Information Chemical Products**	**8**	**5.89**
医药制造业	**Manufacture of Medicines**	**642**	**2017.40**
#化学药品制造	Manufacture of Chemical Medicines	153	672.96
中成药生产	Manufacture of Traditional Chinese Patent Medicines	100	479.91
生物药品制品制造	Manufacture of Biological and Biochemical Products	105	407.85
航空航天器及设备制造	**Manufacture of Aircraft and Spacecraft**	**32**	**223.63**
飞机制造	Manufacture of Aircraft	5	16.88
航天器制造	Manufacture of Spacecraft	2	3.13
航空、航天相关设备制造	Manufacture of Aircraft and Spacecraft related products	6	6.95
其他航空航天器制造	Manufacture of Air Vehicle	11	24.18
航空航天器修理	Repair of Aircraft and Spacecraft	8	172.49
电子及通信设备制造业	**Manufacture of Electronic and Communication Equipment**	**9818**	**46728.26**
电子工业专用设备制造	Equipment for Electronic Industry	699	1324.29
光纤、光缆及锂离子电池制造	Optical Fiber,Cable Manufacturing	613	2932.72
通信设备、雷达及配套设备制造	Manufacture of Communication Equipment	867	21201.80
#通信系统设备制造	Manufacture of Communication Transmission Equipment	362	3668.10
通信终端设备制造	Manufacture of Communication Exchange Equipment	492	17515.51
雷达及配套设备制造	Manufacture of Radar Equipment	13	18.20
广播电视设备制造	Manufacture of Broadcasting and Television Equipment	235	586.06
非专业视听设备制造	Manufacture of Audio-visual Equipment	674	2458.67
电子器件制造	Manufacture of Electronic Parts	2118	6852.79
电子元件及电子专用材料制造	Manufacture of Electronic component and Electronic Specialized Materials	3332	8482.27
智能消费设备制造	Manufacturing of Intelligent Consumption Equipment	449	1427.60
其他电子设备制造	Manufacture of Electronic Devices	831	1462.05
电子计算机及办公设备制造业	**Manufacture of Computers and Office Equipment**	**1534**	**4920.76**
计算机整机制造	Manufacture of Complete Computers	224	1600.00
计算机零部件制造	Manufacture of Computer part Equipment	468	1006.88
计算机外围设备制造	Manufacture of Computer Peripheral Equipment	484	1360.98
工业控制计算机及系统制造	Manufacture of Industrial Control Computer and System	49	35.67
信息安全设备制造	Manufacture of Information Security Equipment	30	33.41
其他计算机制造	Other computer equipment	161	554.48
办公设备制造	Manufacture of Office Equipment	118	329.35
医疗设备及仪器仪表制造业	**Manufacture of Medical Equipment, Instruments and Meters**	**1676**	**2533.27**
#医疗仪器设备及器械制造	Manufacture of Medical Equipment and Appliances	657	1260.94
通用仪器仪表制造	Manufacture of General Measuring Instruments and Machinery	632	749.52
专用仪器仪表制造	Manufacture of Special Measuring Instruments and Machinery	210	217.23

Main Indicators on High-tech Manufacturing Enterprises above Designated Size (2023)

(100 million yuan)

年末资产总计 Total Assets at the Year-end	流动资产合计 Total Working Capital	营业收入 Business Revenue	营业成本 Cost of Business	税金及附加 Tax and Other Charges	利润总额 Total Profits	利税总额 Total Pre-tax Profits	本年应交增值税 Value-added Tax Payable in Current Year	全部就业人员年平均人数(万人) Annual Average Number of Employed Persons (10000 persons)
76690.01	**51864.53**	**56644.11**	**45361.60**	**220.23**	**4461.26**	**5486.95**	**805.47**	**397.33**
8.29	**5.23**	**4.77**	**4.04**	**0.02**	**0.22**	**0.29**	**0.06**	**0.07**
4466.24	**2397.20**	**1937.89**	**1052.00**	**15.42**	**249.90**	**344.51**	**79.18**	**16.70**
1475.18	728.40	627.10	333.92	5.09	106.02	140.40	29.29	4.61
980.67	511.84	470.10	264.28	4.62	63.71	93.81	25.48	4.32
1111.86	585.60	405.41	152.44	2.64	15.69	32.68	14.34	2.94
316.33	**212.93**	**232.81**	**188.66**	**1.01**	**23.94**	**28.65**	**3.70**	**1.44**
75.15	45.04	27.03	23.03	0.06	2.36	2.52	0.10	0.23
4.55	3.56	1.60	1.37	0.00	-0.12	-0.15	-0.03	0.01
31.45	17.73	9.44	6.55	0.07	1.30	1.60	0.23	0.10
37.14	23.90	18.65	13.36	0.10	2.08	2.52	0.35	0.17
168.03	122.72	176.10	144.35	0.78	18.32	22.15	3.05	0.94
63322.24	**43054.15**	**46889.70**	**37969.19**	**176.08**	**3674.23**	**4458.57**	**608.27**	**315.70**
2008.59	1675.38	1189.28	917.33	5.16	96.19	127.77	26.41	13.26
3665.30	2471.90	2886.42	2518.41	8.30	92.01	133.50	33.18	17.89
29564.62	21859.66	21819.17	16437.89	87.45	2675.11	3071.37	308.81	85.15
3714.59	2837.85	2982.98	2230.06	19.14	175.43	220.70	26.13	21.43
25800.33	18979.32	18816.64	14193.79	68.21	2498.71	2849.09	282.17	63.46
49.70	42.49	19.55	14.03	0.09	0.97	1.58	0.51	0.25
519.83	394.05	594.23	470.54	2.30	37.13	46.75	7.32	4.97
2545.58	1877.79	2503.50	2243.71	6.79	61.76	87.87	19.32	18.58
11488.60	5842.29	6390.28	5571.75	23.92	168.41	262.51	70.18	52.46
10726.72	6665.26	8626.41	7459.41	32.50	395.80	536.45	108.16	96.48
1346.86	1078.53	1458.62	1190.51	4.70	63.10	80.92	13.11	9.55
1456.14	1189.28	1421.79	1159.64	4.96	84.71	111.44	21.77	17.37
4836.81	**3652.02**	**5096.35**	**4507.73**	**13.45**	**182.10**	**244.26**	**48.72**	**35.33**
1419.38	1112.69	1663.34	1550.13	2.40	32.98	41.06	5.68	4.29
738.38	612.55	997.16	879.85	2.70	34.29	43.79	6.81	11.28
1475.93	1060.94	1470.67	1292.16	4.33	57.80	81.85	19.72	10.73
55.29	47.24	36.45	25.94	0.14	3.77	5.07	1.17	0.37
55.43	44.90	32.89	25.00	0.10	0.28	0.79	0.40	0.27
625.85	477.78	570.53	460.51	2.34	32.68	47.43	12.41	4.70
466.55	295.93	325.32	274.16	1.44	20.30	24.27	2.54	3.70
3740.10	**2542.99**	**2482.59**	**1639.98**	**14.26**	**330.88**	**410.68**	**65.55**	**28.08**
1827.90	1120.96	1165.81	668.77	7.99	230.12	269.08	30.97	13.47
1141.25	834.60	767.89	556.01	3.79	57.91	85.13	23.43	8.17
412.43	319.52	236.87	162.95	1.12	18.07	25.46	6.27	3.03

12–17 规模以上先进制造业主要经济指标（2023年）

单位：亿元

项目	Item	企业单位数（个）Number of Enterprises (unit)	工业总产值（当年价）Gross Industrial Output Value (at current prices)	年末资产总计 Total Assets at the Year-end
合计	**Total**	**42704**	**102399.75**	**118023.95**
高端电子信息制造业	**Manufacture of Advanced Electronic Equipment and Communication Equipment**	**7147**	**39685.93**	**55404.96**
集成电路及关键元器件	Integrated Circuits and Key Components	6097	16766.67	23920.62
信息通信设备	Communication Equipment	854	21183.60	29514.92
新型显示	New-Type Displays	196	1735.66	1969.42
先进装备制造业	**Manufacture of Advanced Equipment**	**11610**	**32707.89**	**35179.11**
智能制造装备	Intelligent Manufacturing Equipment	3517	5544.39	7950.28
船舶与海洋工程装备	Equipment for Ships and Marine Engineering	90	612.69	1141.16
节能环保装备	Equipment for Energy Conservation and Environmental Protection	1406	2764.37	3179.06
轨道交通设备	Equipment for Rail Transportation	34	82.82	181.72
航空装备	Equipment for Aviation	58	472.04	452.29
新能源装备	Equipment for New Energy	1975	3874.02	4664.58
汽车制造	Automobiles	1202	12846.58	10917.78
卫星及应用	Satellites and Applications	615	3973.59	4122.05
重要基础件	Critical Basic Components	2713	2537.39	2570.19
石油化工产业	**Petrochemical Manufacturing**	**3402**	**12270.46**	**9938.27**
先进轻纺制造业	**Manufacture of Advanced Light Textiles**	**12416**	**11696.22**	**10975.77**
绿色食品饮料	Green Foods and Drinks	2663	2385.27	1956.69
高附加值纺织服装	High Added-value Textile Clothing	6099	1979.15	1418.00
环保多功能家具	Environmental Friendly and Multi-purpose Furniture	1838	645.13	691.85
智能节能型家电	Intelligent Energy Saving Household Appliances	1816	6686.67	6909.23
新材料制造业	**Manufacture of New Materials**	**8577**	**9636.71**	**8486.94**
高端精品钢材	High-end Fine Steel	567	3284.24	1874.58
高性能复合材料及特种功能材料	High Performance Composite Materials and Special Purpose Materials	8003	6333.87	6587.38
战略前沿材料	Strategic Materials	7	18.60	24.99
生物医药及高性能医疗器械	**Manufacture of Biological Medicines and Advanced Medical Equipment**	**1395**	**2750.09**	**5146.22**
生物制药	Biological Medicine	642	1613.92	3572.99
高性能医疗器械	Advanced Medical Equipment	753	1136.18	1573.23

Main Indicators on Advanced Manufacturing Enterprises above Designated Size (2023)

(100 million yuan)

流动资产合计 Total Working Capital	营业收入 Business Revenue	营业成本 Cost of Business	税金及附加 Tax and Other Charges on Principal Business	利润总额 Total Profits	利税总额 Total Pre-tax Profits	本年应交增值税 Value-added Tax Payable in Current Year	全部就业人员年平均人数(万人) Annual Average Number of Employed Persons (10000 persons)
77123.49	**102711.70**	**83959.23**	**1351.69**	**7002.99**	**10459.21**	**2104.53**	**829.95**
36904.91	**39967.72**	**32182.79**	**152.89**	**3377.84**	**4053.86**	**523.12**	**254.54**
13645.22	16346.57	14130.56	61.06	660.40	921.78	200.31	161.33
21817.17	21799.62	16423.85	87.35	2674.14	3069.79	308.30	84.90
1442.52	1821.54	1628.37	4.47	43.31	62.29	14.51	8.31
24970.93	**31911.34**	**26278.38**	**381.03**	**1907.64**	**2855.39**	**566.72**	**230.01**
5677.97	5292.22	3868.10	26.82	585.81	737.91	125.28	56.14
788.47	649.07	604.92	1.77	10.07	15.07	3.24	2.22
2165.61	2599.21	2196.07	9.94	142.85	194.49	41.70	24.98
137.02	86.56	71.82	0.54	3.80	6.20	1.87	0.62
371.27	483.86	404.48	1.87	22.40	25.44	1.17	2.09
3243.97	3695.30	2991.78	14.38	262.73	347.09	69.99	34.55
7678.42	13315.83	11617.85	293.92	529.21	1052.15	229.02	49.11
3156.88	3300.88	2470.98	20.61	191.37	244.13	32.16	25.92
1751.33	2488.42	2052.38	11.20	159.40	232.90	62.30	34.37
4912.03	**12550.48**	**10512.07**	**734.22**	**416.46**	**1629.27**	**478.59**	**34.14**
7538.91	**11666.30**	**9220.91**	**58.94**	**1002.03**	**1426.48**	**365.51**	**225.90**
1221.75	2599.48	2162.90	14.47	142.33	207.16	50.37	42.83
980.90	1868.15	1556.27	9.28	93.86	146.28	43.14	95.56
455.18	627.19	511.99	3.15	36.33	52.99	13.52	29.61
4881.08	6571.48	4989.76	32.04	729.51	1020.04	258.49	57.91
4936.60	**9489.19**	**8339.18**	**36.65**	**382.55**	**577.75**	**158.56**	**103.38**
853.78	3316.23	3135.52	11.29	66.48	117.92	40.15	7.31
4062.26	6156.08	5188.78	25.30	315.37	458.76	118.09	95.98
20.56	16.88	14.88	0.06	0.70	1.07	0.31	0.09
2880.86	**2609.11**	**1486.99**	**19.44**	**388.66**	**496.83**	**88.73**	**34.30**
1917.76	1550.31	841.60	12.34	199.92	275.61	63.35	16.70
963.10	1058.80	645.39	7.10	188.74	221.22	25.38	17.59

12-18 规模以上工业企业主要经济效益指标（2023年）

项　　目	Item
全　省	**Provincial Total**
按登记注册统计类别分	By Registered Statistical Categories
总计中：#国有控股工业企业	Of the Total:State-holding Industrial Enterprises
#内资企业	Domestic Invested Enterprises
港澳台投资企业	Enterprises with Investment from Hong Kong,Macao and Taiwan
外商投资企业	Foreign Invested Enterprises
按轻重工业分	Grouped by Light and Heavy Industries
轻工业	Light Industry
重工业	Heavy Industry
按企业规模分	Grouped by Size of Enterprises
大型企业	Large Enterprises
中型企业	Medium Enterprises
小微型企业	Small and Micro Enterprises
按行业分	Grouped by Sector
煤炭开采和洗选业	Mining and Washing of Coal
石油和天然气开采业	Extraction of Petroleum and Natural Gas
黑色金属矿采选业	Mining and Dressing of Ferrous Metal Ores
有色金属矿采选业	Mining and Dressing of Nonferrous Metal Ores
非金属矿采选业	Mining and Dressing of Nonmetal Ores
开采专业及辅助性活动	Mining Specialized and Auxiliary Operations
其他采矿业	Mining and Dressing of Other Ores
农副食品加工业	Processing of Farm and Sideline Food
食品制造业	Manufacture of Food
酒、饮料和精制茶制造业	Manufacture of Wine, Beverage and Refined Tea
烟草制品业	Tobacco Products
纺织业	Textile Industry
纺织服装、服饰业	Manufacture of Textile Garments, Footwear and Headgear
皮革、毛皮、羽毛及其制品和制鞋业	Leather, Fur, Feather, Down and Related Products
木材加工和木、竹、藤、棕、草制品业	Timber Processing, Bamboo, Cane, Palm Fiber & Straw Products
家具制造业	Manufacture of Furniture
造纸和纸制品业	Papermaking and Paper Products
印刷和记录媒介复制业	Printing and Record Medium Reproduction
文教、工美、体育和娱乐用品制造业	Manufacture of Cultural, Educational,Sports and Entertainment Articles
石油、煤炭及其他燃料加工业	Petroleum, Coal and other Fuel Processing
化学原料和化学制品制造业	Manufacture of Raw Chemical Materials and Chemical Products
医药制造业	Manufacture of Medicines
化学纤维制造业	Manufacture of Chemical Fibers
橡胶和塑料制品业	Rubber and Plastic Products
非金属矿物制品业	Nonmetal Mineral Products
黑色金属冶炼和压延加工业	Smelting and Pressing of Ferrous Metals
有色金属冶炼和压延加工业	Smelting and Pressing of Nonferrous Metals
金属制品业	Metal Products
通用设备制造业	Manufacture of General-purpose Machinery
专用设备制造业	Manufacture of Special-purpose Machinery
汽车制造业	Manufacture of Automobile
铁路、船舶、航空航天和其他运输设备制造业	Manufacture of Railway ,Ship,Aeronautics and Other Transport equipment
电气机械和器材制造业	Manufacture of Electrical Machinery and Equipment
计算机、通信和其他电子设备制造业	Manufacture of Communication Equipment, Computers and Other Electronic Equipment
仪器仪表制造业	Manufacture of Instruments and Meters
其他制造业	Other Manufactures
废弃资源综合利用业	Comprehensive Utilization of Waste
金属制品、机械和设备修理业	Manufacture of Metal Products,Machinery and Equipment Maintenance
电力、热力生产和供应业	Production and Supply of Electric Power and Heat Power
燃气生产和供应业	Production and Supply of Gas
水的生产和供应业	Production and Supply of Water

注：1.本表登记注册统计类别按《关于市场主体统计分类的划分规定》(国统字〔2023〕14号)执行。
2.全员劳动生产率按工业总产值计算。

Main Indicators on Economic Benefit of Industrial Enterprises above Designated Size (2023)

总资产贡献率 (%) Ratio of Total Assets to Industrial Output Value (%)	资产负债率 (%) Assets-Liability Ratio (%)	成本费用利润率 (%) Ratio of Profits to Industrial Costs (%)	全员劳动生产率 (元/人) Overall Labor Productivity (yuan/person)	产品销售率 (%) Proportion of Products Sold (%)
8.57	**58.75**	**6.63**	**1427491**	**96.24**
8.69	57.88	4.97	4652885	97.74
8.41	60.47	6.59	1510893	95.94
9.86	50.68	8.19	956546	95.88
8.07	58.13	5.43	1820483	97.99
10.23	54.92	6.99	1011084	95.03
7.99	60.08	6.49	1729410	96.73
9.82	59.52	9.06	2014396	96.36
8.93	53.12	6.50	1168523	95.49
6.05	61.40	3.44	1134627	96.52
42.00	78.66	145.29	19295636	97.74
17.13	57.16	16.43	4570000	100.44
22.94	61.99	21.29	1597414	98.28
8.98	64.31	11.09	1942273	96.00
9.96	28.63	19.74	3355882	99.99
5.69	65.69	2.30	2876120	98.26
15.33	46.38	10.70	1120468	97.01
15.34	48.09	10.56	1677389	97.16
70.29	28.66	19.45	2026437	97.46
10.32	56.39	5.64	1016403	94.67
10.07	50.29	4.63	579454	91.62
10.42	61.19	3.69	470418	97.53
6.42	59.84	3.63	862597	96.61
8.04	62.00	6.09	726251	97.04
4.27	56.40	1.22	1388126	94.75
7.32	45.50	6.74	702777	96.12
6.17	66.01	2.66	851427	95.05
41.44	57.82	2.04	22422490	98.64
8.34	54.36	5.34	2127433	97.89
7.94	42.35	14.46	1208024	90.93
9.04	45.53	8.12	1427388	94.93
7.89	50.68	5.53	787189	96.51
6.62	62.52	4.62	1289840	96.36
6.87	59.96	2.00	5834155	96.73
5.02	73.06	1.43	2731017	97.67
9.37	59.63	4.62	954122	96.61
8.08	56.67	7.05	1027259	95.06
9.51	52.01	11.84	908430	93.83
9.57	65.34	4.23	2615879	98.72
4.09	63.54	4.24	1441174	96.28
8.95	59.69	7.85	1274331	92.91
7.26	59.74	7.91	1485467	96.09
7.56	48.74	7.72	741894	96.76
8.12	44.97	7.20	672006	93.87
6.29	66.90	2.55	3422926	98.36
9.04	59.00	7.66	1092238	100.50
5.34	61.14	7.24	6143711	99.36
9.73	53.90	4.79	12451903	99.91
4.52	58.74	13.44	1235449	97.75

Ntote: a)The registered statistical categories of this table is implemented in accordance with the Regulations onStatistics the Classification of Market Entity(Guotongzi [2023] No. 14).

b)The overall labor productivity is calculated by gross output value of industry.

12-19 规模以上制造业工业企业主要经济指标

Main Economic Indicators of Manufacturing Enterprises above Designated Size

项目	Item	2000	2010	2015	2021	2022	2023
企业单位数 (个)	Number of Enterprises (unit)	18571	52102	42134	64919	69188	70398
工业总产值 (亿元)	Gross Industrial Output Value (100 million yuan)	11352.62	79504.12	124649.16	159796.90	166828.59	169241.95
营业收入 (亿元)	Business Revenue (100 million yuan)	10865.66	77730.85	120886.73	161397.04	168816.49	169447.26
资产总计 (亿元)	Total Assets (100 million yuan)	11653.11	52734.31	95411.22	148971.08	167339.96	179900.50
流动资产合计 (亿元)	Total Liquid Assets (100 million yuan)		32414.52	54715.38	99693.71	111726.52	119240.23
固定资产净额 (亿元)	Total Fixed Assets (100 million yuan)		16420.14	26943.69	21734.04	24030.33	24925.48
负债总计 (亿元)	Total Liabilities (100 million yuan)	6950.47	29407.47	54747.90	84636.43	96623.44	104881.26
所有者权益合计 (亿元)	Total Creditors' Equity (100 million yuan)	4576.24	23243.24	40239.01	64335.99	70483.21	75027.04
利润总额 (亿元)	Total Profits (100 million yuan)	348.92	5313.74	7723.16	10371.61	9106.84	10026.58
亏损企业亏损额 (亿元)	Loss Value of Loss-making Enterprises (100 million yuan)	131.89	195.53	510.18	1035.17	1553.64	1501.50
利税总额 (亿元)	Total Pre-tax Profits (100 million yuan)	729.92	8150.46	12375.00	15076.96	14146.68	15310.17
应交增值税 (亿元)	Value-added Tax Payable(100 million yuan)	277.66	2003.07	3284.50	3011.58	3227.47	3326.89
从业人员平均人数 (万人)	Average Employed Persons (10000 persons)	546.03	1533.72	1439.33	1314.70	1303.60	1268.19

注：1.工业总产值按当年价格计算。2011年统计口径从年业务收入500万元及以上调整为2000万元及以上工业企业，2021年为主业务收入2000万元，2021年为主业务收入2000万元及以上工业企业和工业个体经营户。

2.本表中营业收入指标数据2017年及以前为主营业务收入数据，2018年后为营业收入数据。

Note: a) Gross industrial output values are calculated at current prices.Since 2011,the annual principal business revenue of industrial enterprises above designated size is changed from industrial enterprises of 5 million yuan or above to 20 million yuan or above. It is adjusted to industrial enterp and industrial self-employed households with main business income of 20 million yuan and above in 2021.

b) The indicator was Revenue from Principal Business in 2017 and before,and are Business Revenue since 2018.

12-20 各市规模以上工业企业主要经济指标（2023年）

Main Economic Indicators of Industrial Enterprises above Designated Size by City (2023)

单位：亿元 (100 million yuan)

市 别	City	营业收入 Business Revenue	营业成本 Cost of Principal Business	资产合计 Total Assets	负债合计 Total Liabilities	利润总额 Total Profits	利税总额 Total Pre-tax Profits	全部就业人员年平均人数(万人) Annual Average Number of Employed Persons (10000 persons)
广 州	Guangzhou	25393.92	21057.40	33154.50	18565.54	1391.66	2448.42	124.77
深 圳	Shenzhen	49451.26	39255.23	66564.96	38462.98	3794.23	4864.82	296.09
珠 海	Zhuhai	6683.51	5290.17	10648.60	6334.61	633.27	815.09	43.32
汕 头	Shantou	2705.08	2296.15	3226.90	1618.38	145.61	213.19	26.01
佛 山	Foshan	27393.71	23093.51	20657.76	11660.79	1904.10	2742.02	154.80
韶 关	Shaoguan	1769.39	1543.20	2202.68	1456.87	47.25	143.75	11.65
河 源	Heyuan	1449.87	1273.55	1363.76	897.50	73.74	110.00	16.25
梅 州	Meizhou	957.03	780.25	1467.87	807.21	33.11	125.76	8.71
惠 州	Huizhou	10968.00	9664.34	10590.32	6422.72	337.34	744.03	102.66
汕 尾	Shanwei	1007.36	907.50	1278.45	847.59	38.08	51.66	5.76
东 莞	Dongguan	24981.77	20992.58	25375.36	15935.33	1777.07	2295.41	262.63
中 山	Zhongshan	6803.91	5721.35	7099.26	4246.43	326.23	486.48	82.43
江 门	Jiangmen	5601.27	4769.71	6736.66	4103.83	223.04	389.50	53.46
阳 江	Yangjiang	2336.36	2030.45	2948.77	1853.04	152.90	203.99	8.48
湛 江	Zhanjiang	3364.09	2842.77	4187.54	2688.90	150.78	525.35	10.36
茂 名	Maoming	2618.83	2304.18	1552.64	884.62	69.94	373.33	6.90
肇 庆	Zhaoqing	4251.92	3672.80	3923.24	2313.11	207.08	318.09	27.50
清 远	Qingyuan	3275.38	2864.58	3906.32	2564.83	133.22	199.93	22.76
潮 州	Chaozhou	1205.03	1055.27	1164.48	531.23	64.69	97.25	11.53
揭 阳	Jieyang	2468.41	2112.83	2497.39	1490.80	72.63	259.90	13.47
云 浮	Yunfu	810.80	717.48	936.74	558.84	19.26	40.36	7.53
按经济区域分	By Region							
珠 三 角	Pearl River Delta	161529.27	133517.09	184750.65	108045.34	10594.03	15103.87	1147.66
粤 东	Eastern Region	7385.87	6371.75	8167.23	4487.99	321.01	622.00	56.76
粤 西	Western Region	8319.27	7177.40	8688.96	5426.55	373.62	1102.67	25.75
粤 北	Northern Region	8262.46	7179.06	9877.38	6285.26	306.58	619.79	66.90

12-21 各市规模以上私营工业企业主要经济指标（2023年）
Main Economic Indicators of Private Industrial Enterprises above Designated Size by City (2023)

单位：亿元 (100 million yuan)

市别	City	营业收入 Business Revenue	营业成本 Cost of Business	资产合计 Total Assets	负债合计 Total Liabilities	利润总额 Total Profits	利税总额 Total Pre-tax Profits	全部就业人员年平均人数(万人) Annual Average Number of Employed Persons (10000 persons)
广州	Guangzhou	4722.72	3794.63	5217.17	2896.27	269.21	378.54	45.46
深圳	Shenzhen	23060.10	17639.39	29603.09	18203.51	1852.07	2359.31	150.58
珠海	Zhuhai	1395.01	1150.10	2194.42	1237.97	65.74	96.72	14.24
汕头	Shantou	1690.29	1420.67	1405.50	676.00	85.38	128.16	18.44
佛山	Foshan	16635.55	13775.48	11621.09	6843.17	1256.55	1831.57	95.57
韶关	Shaoguan	374.87	329.89	398.47	282.88	7.30	16.42	3.52
河源	Heyuan	489.09	412.75	404.10	281.01	33.41	49.34	5.02
梅州	Meizhou	328.23	288.46	523.42	332.87	2.51	12.01	4.76
惠州	Huizhou	2360.17	2030.96	2071.40	1420.73	77.51	127.67	31.89
汕尾	Shanwei	267.79	243.15	215.28	140.25	9.60	14.17	1.78
东莞	Dongguan	7204.08	6070.57	6584.11	4267.09	239.80	421.77	101.24
中山	Zhongshan	2376.17	2006.47	2112.73	1403.69	61.96	125.02	39.33
江门	Jiangmen	1875.70	1610.70	1768.21	1129.31	53.37	106.37	23.00
阳江	Yangjiang	229.85	198.99	205.64	121.64	9.04	14.44	4.04
湛江	Zhanjiang	440.19	393.43	477.33	365.18	3.99	14.18	4.89
茂名	Maoming	364.84	325.31	343.41	210.17	9.55	18.31	3.68
肇庆	Zhaoqing	2027.38	1705.44	1255.52	746.00	126.86	187.54	13.52
清远	Qingyuan	827.15	723.09	767.09	573.80	21.78	40.53	6.61
潮州	Chaozhou	746.55	651.44	632.20	263.19	40.97	60.17	9.04
揭阳	Jieyang	1079.77	939.84	935.89	484.91	43.85	74.80	10.99
云浮	Yunfu	232.21	207.72	237.11	146.07	3.11	8.81	3.08
按经济区域分	By Region							
珠三角	Pearl River Delta	61656.89	49783.73	62427.74	38147.74	4003.08	5634.5	514.82
粤东	Eastern Region	3784.4	3255.1	3188.86	1564.35	179.79	277.31	40.25
粤西	Western Region	1034.89	917.73	1026.37	697	22.58	46.92	12.61
粤北	Northern Region	2251.55	1961.91	2330.19	1616.62	68.11	127.11	23.00

12-22 各市规模以上工业企业主要经济效益指标（2023年）

Main Indicators on Economic Benefit of Industrial Enterprises above Designated Size by City (2023)

市别	City	总资产贡献率 (%) Ratio of Total Assets to Industrial Output Value (%)	资产负债率 (%) Assets-Liability Ratio (%)	成本费用利润率 (%) Ratio of Profits to Industrial Costs (%)	全员劳动生产率 (元/人) Overall Labor Productivity (yuan/person)	产品销售率 (%) Proportion of Products Sold (%)
全　省	**Provincial Total**	**8.57**	**58.75**	**6.63**	**1427491**	**96.24**
广　州	Guangzhou	7.61	56.00	5.86	1954068	98.11
深　圳	Shenzhen	7.58	57.78	8.09	1661410	96.43
珠　海	Zhuhai	7.55	59.49	10.45	1417821	92.53
汕　头	Shantou	7.13	50.15	5.69	1160657	90.77
佛　山	Foshan	13.67	56.45	7.47	1818325	96.75
韶　关	Shaoguan	7.31	66.14	2.82	1438017	96.61
河　源	Heyuan	8.76	65.81	5.37	941311	95.72
梅　州	Meizhou	9.31	54.99	3.83	1090700	99.95
惠　州	Huizhou	7.40	60.65	3.22	1089699	95.07
汕　尾	Shanwei	4.86	66.30	3.95	1886094	97.36
东　莞	Dongguan	9.14	62.80	7.43	937043	95.93
中　山	Zhongshan	7.19	59.82	5.03	863761	92.43
江　门	Jiangmen	6.55	60.92	4.15	1099181	95.17
阳　江	Yangjiang	7.98	62.84	7.01	2800991	96.71
湛　江	Zhanjiang	13.31	64.21	5.00	3095531	101.15
茂　名	Maoming	24.80	56.97	2.92	3600768	98.80
肇　庆	Zhaoqing	8.71	58.96	5.12	1631902	95.56
清　远	Qingyuan	5.73	65.66	4.28	1324117	97.83
潮　州	Chaozhou	8.71	45.62	5.71	1109332	95.23
揭　阳	Jieyang	11.23	59.69	3.23	1950082	93.84
云　浮	Yunfu	4.80	59.66	2.43	1014794	99.11

注：全员劳动生产率按工业总产值计算。
Note: The overall labor productivity is calculated by gross output value of industry.

12-22 续表 continued

市　别	City	总资产贡献率比去年增减(百分点) Percentage Gain in Ratio of Total Assets to Industrial Output Value over Preceding Year	资产负债率比去年增减(百分点) Percentage Gain in Assets-Liability Ratio over Preceding Year	成本费用利润率比去年增减(百分点) Percentage Gain in Ratio of Profits to Industrial Costs over Preceding Year	全员劳动生产率比去年增长(%) Growth in Overall Labor Productivity over Preceding Year (%)	产品销售率比去年增减(百分点) Percentage Gain in Proportion of Products Sold over Preceding Year
全　省	**Provincial Total**	**0.10**	**0.36**	**0.65**	**5.1**	**-0.16**
广　州	Guangzhou	-0.95	0.61	-0.64	4.2	-0.92
深　圳	Shenzhen	0.11	0.59	0.54	9.0	0.02
珠　海	Zhuhai	0.17	-1.76	0.65	6.8	-2.08
汕　头	Shantou	-2.43	0.21	-1.13	-5.8	-1.73
佛　山	Foshan	-1.16	-0.62	-0.33	1.6	0.63
韶　关	Shaoguan	0.99	0.31	1.55	5.4	-1.78
河　源	Heyuan	0.48	3.07	1.53	7.7	0.42
梅　州	Meizhou	0.47	1.60	0.49	12.3	1.66
惠　州	Huizhou	0.20	-1.24	0.28	0.2	0.75
汕　尾	Shanwei	1.58	-1.08	2.74	22.1	2.98
东　莞	Dongguan	2.52	1.19	3.67	3.5	0.03
中　山	Zhongshan	-0.63	1.39	0.26	7.5	-3.25
江　门	Jiangmen	-0.25	0.77	0.46	2.6	0.02
阳　江	Yangjiang	0.48	-3.68	0.25	5.9	-1.87
湛　江	Zhanjiang	0.25	-1.88	-1.00	-2.6	0.55
茂　名	Maoming	9.51	1.49	2.73	3.9	-0.21
肇　庆	Zhaoqing	0.53	-0.56	0.83	4.2	-0.82
清　远	Qingyuan	-1.81	4.36	-0.94	11.1	0.34
潮　州	Chaozhou	-2.35	1.61	-1.07	-0.8	-0.06
揭　阳	Jieyang	4.01	2.67	-0.49	28.0	2.70
云　浮	Yunfu	0.69	3.20	1.12	9.7	-0.75

12−23 各市规模以上国有控股工业企业主要经济效益指标（2023年）

Main Indicators on Economic Benefit of State-holding Industrial Enterprises above Designated Size by City (2023)

市 别	City	总资产贡献率 (%) Ratio of Total Assets to Industrial Output Value (%)	资产负债率 (%) Assets-Liability Ratio (%)	成本费用利润率 (%) Ratio of Profits to Industrial Costs (%)	全员劳动生产率 (元/人) Overall Labor Productivity (yuan/person)	产品销售率 (%) Proportion of Products Sold (%)
全 省	**Provincial Total**	**8.69**	**57.88**	**4.97**	**4652885**	**97.74**
广 州	Guangzhou	7.34	58.52	5.05	5169391	98.29
深 圳	Shenzhen	7.10	55.34	9.30	3568497	92.41
珠 海	Zhuhai	5.34	52.40	4.30	3097312	98.78
汕 头	Shantou	6.07	53.97	6.63	3179366	95.52
佛 山	Foshan	6.35	53.52	3.32	4158952	99.57
韶 关	Shaoguan	10.68	65.04	3.25	3277823	95.17
河 源	Heyuan	7.20	67.71	5.11	4272326	98.35
梅 州	Meizhou	21.02	52.69	7.80	3394250	108.62
惠 州	Huizhou	15.28	56.92	2.00	6481235	100.98
汕 尾	Shanwei	4.81	65.20	6.68	4665000	97.87
东 莞	Dongguan	4.81	60.61	2.54	2703218	98.24
中 山	Zhongshan	6.50	57.86	4.22	2971183	99.49
江 门	Jiangmen	4.00	66.53	2.81	4869577	98.15
阳 江	Yangjiang	7.46	63.50	8.01	9677133	95.82
湛 江	Zhanjiang	17.81	54.65	2.83	8284793	102.49
茂 名	Maoming	41.46	50.79	3.48	11409028	99.66
肇 庆	Zhaoqing	5.69	46.93	5.50	2358578	98.86
清 远	Qingyuan	4.52	65.28	3.31	4286604	100.12
潮 州	Chaozhou	8.48	59.08	7.12	5206905	99.87
揭 阳	Jieyang	13.79	64.64	2.09	13056875	96.62
云 浮	Yunfu	5.90	51.71	3.18	2370000	99.32

注：全员劳动生产率按工业总产值计算。
Note: The overall labor productivity is calculated by gross output value of industry.

12-24 各市规模以上按登记注册统计类别分工业企业资产（2023年）

Total Assets of Industrial Enterprises above Designated Size by Registered Statistical Categories and by City (2023)

单位：亿元 (100 million yuan)

市 别	City	资产合计 Total Assets	总计中：#国有控股工业企业 Of the Total: State-holding Industry Enterprises	#内资企业 Domestic Invested Enterprises	港澳台投资企业 Enterprises with Investment from Hong Kong, Macao and Taiwan	外商投资企业 Foreign Invested Enterprises
广 州	Guangzhou	33154.50	17357.07	23696.51	2681.33	6776.35
深 圳	Shenzhen	66564.96	9038.96	45803.42	9656.12	11105.25
珠 海	Zhuhai	10648.60	1165.39	8651.26	991.33	1006.00
汕 头	Shantou	3226.90	759.93	2715.09	408.34	103.02
佛 山	Foshan	20657.76	2163.01	16046.87	2829.05	1779.84
韶 关	Shaoguan	2202.68	1043.19	1944.32	168.39	89.98
河 源	Heyuan	1363.76	261.62	1046.63	258.60	58.54
梅 州	Meizhou	1467.87	442.59	1353.10	77.72	37.05
惠 州	Huizhou	10590.32	2168.96	6406.04	2307.00	1872.68
汕 尾	Shanwei	1278.45	465.40	816.15	276.42	185.88
东 莞	Dongguan	25375.36	1703.75	19025.03	4380.88	1967.28
中 山	Zhongshan	7099.26	630.56	4189.71	1288.58	1620.79
江 门	Jiangmen	6736.66	1671.29	3608.72	1657.89	1469.10
阳 江	Yangjiang	2948.77	2060.15	2087.95	806.06	54.76
湛 江	Zhanjiang	4187.54	2138.84	2718.62	674.68	794.24
茂 名	Maoming	1552.64	803.71	1386.68	46.67	119.30
肇 庆	Zhaoqing	3923.24	847.42	3280.38	376.61	266.07
清 远	Qingyuan	3906.32	603.24	2670.90	736.47	498.60
潮 州	Chaozhou	1164.48	274.16	1067.09	71.85	25.43
揭 阳	Jieyang	2497.39	1382.02	2395.53	83.82	17.53
云 浮	Yunfu	936.74	189.36	702.61	206.80	27.34
按经济区域分	By Region					
珠 三 角	Pearl River Delta	184750.65	36746.40	130707.94	26168.79	27863.37
粤 东	Eastern Region	8167.23	2881.52	6993.86	840.42	331.86
粤 西	Western Region	8688.96	5002.70	6193.25	1527.41	968.30
粤 北	Northern Region	9877.38	2539.99	7717.56	1447.97	711.50

注：本表登记注册统计类别按《关于市场主体统计分类的划分规定》(国统字〔2023〕14号)执行。

Ntote: The registered statistical categories of this table is implemented in accordance with the Regulations onStatistics the Classification of Market Entity(Guotongzi [2023] No. 14).

12-25 各市规模以上大中型工业企业产值资产（2023年）

Gross Output Value and Total Assets of Large and Medium-sized Industrial Enterprises above Designated Size by City (2023)

单位：亿元 (100 million yuan)

市 别	City	企业个数（个）Number of Enterprises (unit)	#大型 Large sized	工业总产值（当年价）Gross Industrial Output Value (at current prices)	#大型 Large sized	资产总计 Total Assets	#大型 Large sized
全 省	**Provincial Total**	**7803**	**1389**	**124695.57**	**84290.38**	**151540.82**	**108504.74**
广 州	Guangzhou	745	157	16552.40	12480.64	25706.92	20531.24
深 圳	Shenzhen	1552	305	35503.69	27389.34	52115.29	40376.81
珠 海	Zhuhai	316	67	4095.75	2703.86	7775.73	5378.94
汕 头	Shantou	118	14	1158.98	384.60	1048.76	382.73
佛 山	Foshan	990	149	19638.99	10082.79	14455.33	8892.88
韶 关	Shaoguan	78	13	1141.40	673.19	1213.51	562.01
河 源	Heyuan	111	20	1009.71	638.37	738.72	442.05
梅 州	Meizhou	60	7	560.48	177.41	799.88	312.08
惠 州	Huizhou	573	128	8119.92	6419.07	7401.10	5581.50
汕 尾	Shanwei	31	11	727.12	471.27	746.91	505.34
东 莞	Dongguan	1644	271	15795.35	10528.40	18144.49	13111.33
中 山	Zhongshan	525	87	4275.75	2711.25	4507.79	3045.55
江 门	Jiangmen	344	58	3269.69	1652.59	4139.64	1657.33
阳 江	Yangjiang	64	7	1897.32	880.87	1687.69	1092.24
湛 江	Zhanjiang	71	9	2460.96	2100.34	2940.35	2117.88
茂 名	Maoming	39	4	1895.85	1473.87	999.22	589.97
肇 庆	Zhaoqing	203	30	2332.36	1045.50	2123.00	1302.30
清 远	Qingyuan	167	30	1876.36	747.57	2396.60	699.47
潮 州	Chaozhou	46	4	370.38	168.67	513.84	281.19
揭 阳	Jieyang	71	6	1526.92	1254.99	1540.33	1284.01
云 浮	Yunfu	55	12	486.18	305.79	545.73	357.88
按经济区域分	By Region						
珠 三 角	Pearl River Delta	6892	1252	109583.90	75013.45	136369.29	99877.88
粤 东	Eastern Region	266	35	3783.40	2279.53	3849.83	2453.28
粤 西	Western Region	174	20	6254.14	4455.08	5627.25	3800.09
粤 北	Northern Region	471	82	5074.14	2542.32	5694.44	2373.50

12-26 规模以上工业主要产品生产能力

Main Industrial Products above Designated Size

名称	Item	2020	2021	2022	2023
天然原油 (万吨)	Crude Oil (10 000 tons)	1696.60	1857.88	1927.48	2087.93
卷烟 (亿支)	Cigarettes (100 million pieces)	1616.40	1611.76	1640.93	1595.36
棉纺锭 (万锭)	Cotton Hasp (10 000 ingots)	50.32	44.42	47.21	46.36
气流纺锭 (万头)	Rotor Hasp (10 000 ingots)	1.94	2.78	2.97	3.37
棉布织机 (万台)	Printing and Dyeing Cotton Cloth (10 000 sets)	1.86	2.88	2.04	1.78
原油加工能力 (万吨)	Crude Oil Processing Capacity (10 000 tons)	7160.54	7138.12	9205.59	9190.09
焦炭 (万吨)	Coke (10 000 tons)	626.00	786.00	786.00	796.00
烧碱(折100%) (万吨)	Caustic Soda (10 000 tons)	37.40	37.40	33.40	33.10
农用氮、磷、钾化肥 (万吨)	Chemical Fertilizers (10 000 tons)	60.50	30.71	34.27	65.37
初级形态塑料 (万吨)	Primary Plastic (10 000 tons)	906.68	932.91	971.43	1278.22
化学纤维 (万吨)	Chemical Fibre (10 000 tons)	77.54	84.60	122.76	125.08
硅酸盐水泥熟料 (万吨)	Clinker (10 000 tons)	11302.28	11257.50	11376.29	11150.59
水泥 (万吨)	Cement (10 000 tons)	22161.03	22612.75	23480.72	22444.90
平板玻璃 (万重量箱)	Plate Glass (10 000 weight cases)	10746.76	14493.47	11629.01	11537.42
生铁 (万吨)	Pig Iron (10 000 tons)	2000.00	1950.80	2352.00	2352.00
粗钢 (万吨)	Crude Steel (10 000 tons)	4644.66	4909.36	4668.36	5784.85
钢材 (万吨)	Rolled Steel (10 000 tons)	6270.86	6750.80	6796.90	8106.66
金属切削机床 (万台)	Metal- cutting Machine Tools (10 000 tons)	5.82	6.83	10.48	24.32
汽车 (万辆)	Motor Vehicles (10 000 sets)	363.00	379.60	455.96	572.38
#乘用车 (万辆)	Passenger Vehicle (10 000 sets)	358.70	367.00	443.15	560.15
新能源乘用车 (万辆)	New energy Passenger Vehicle (10 000 sets)	36.30	41.00	107.00	240.00
商用车 (万辆)	Commercial vehicle (10 000 sets)	3.80	12.10	12.81	12.23
新能源商用车 (万辆)	New energy Commercial Vehicle (10 000 sets)	2.22	2.52	2.96	2.70
民用钢质船舶 (万载重吨)	Civil Steel Ship (10 000 tons)	188.38	193.96	179.86	212.52
太阳能电池 (万千瓦)	Solar Cells (10 000kw)	388.06	827.07	625.40	1035.89
家用电冰箱 (万台)	Household Refrigerators (10 000 sets)	2518.88	2490.10	2547.74	2668.47
房间空气调节器 (万台)	Air Conditioners (10 000 sets)	11084.01	10319.57	10710.08	10710.69
微型计算机设备 (万台)	Micro Computer Equipment (10 000 sets)	8006.55	8298.74	10112.46	9425.18
移动通信手持机(手机)(万台)	Mobile Telephones (10 000 sets)	66804.00	67565.07	61498.03	67199.16
彩色电视机 (万台)	Color TV Set (10 000 sets)	13687.49	13113.82	13771.02	14599.78
发电设备容量总计 (万千瓦)	Installed Capacity of Power Generation(10 000 Kw)	12866.83	13970.00	14798.19	16061.87
#火电设备容量 (万千瓦)	Thermal Power (10 000 Kw)	9580.73	10183.91	10665.34	11405.80
水电设备容量 (万千瓦)	Hydropower (10 000 Kw)	959.24	941.49	961.15	990.39
核电设备容量 (万千瓦)	Nuclear Power (10 000 Kw)	1613.81	1613.81	1613.81	1613.81
风电设备容量 (万千瓦)	Wind Power (10 000 Kw)	424.56	883.20	1224.25	1284.67

注：农用氮、磷、钾化肥指农用氮、磷、钾化学肥料总计(折纯)。

Note: Output of chemical fertilizers is calculated on the basis of 100 percent effective content equivalent.

主要统计指标解释

工业 指从事自然资源的开采，对采掘品和农产品进行加工和再加工的物质生产部门。具体包括：(1)对自然资源的开采，如采矿、晒盐、森林采伐等（但不包括禽兽捕猎和水产捕捞）；(2)对农副产品的加工、再加工，如粮油加工、食品加工、轧花、缫丝、纺织、制革等；(3)对采掘品的加工、再加工，如炼铁、炼钢、化工生产、石油加工、机器制造、木材加工等，以及电力、自来水、煤气的生产和供应等；(4)对工业品的修理、翻新，如机器设备的修理、交通运输工具（包括小卧车）的修理等。

1984 年以前农村的村及村以下办工业归属农业，1984 年以后划归工业。

工业统计调查单位 工业统计调查单位分为两类：独立核算法人工业企业和工业生产活动单位。

(1)独立核算法人工业企业　是指从事工业生产经营活动的单位。独立核算法人工业企业应同时具备以下条件：①依法成立，有自己的名称、组织机构和场所，能够承担民事责任；②独立拥有和使用资产，承担负债，有权与其他单位签订合同；③独立核算盈亏，并能够编制资产负债表。

(2)工业生产活动单位　是指在一个场所从事一种或主要从事一种工业生产活动的经济单位。它包括独立核算工业企业按主营业务活动(即工业生产活动)划分的主营业务活动单位和非工业企业所属的工业生产活动单位（即原非独立核算工业生产单位）。工业生产活动单位，一般应同时具备以下三个条件：①具有一个场所，从事一种或主要从事一种工业活动；②单独组织工业生产、经营或业务活动；③单独核算收入和支出。

轻工业 指主要提供生活消费品和制作手工工具的工业。按其所使用的原料不同，可分为两大类：(1)以农产品为原料的轻工业，是指直接或间接以农产品为基本原料的轻工业。主要包括食品制造、饮料制造、烟草加工、纺织、缝纫、皮革和毛皮制作、造纸以及印刷等工业；(2)以非农产品为原料的轻工业，是指以工业品为原料的轻工业。主要包括文教体育用品、化学药品制造、合成纤维制造、日用化学制品、日用玻璃制品、日用金属制品、手工工具制造、医疗器械制造、文化和办公用机械制造等工业。

重工业 是指为国民经济各部门提供物质技术基础的主要生产资料的工业。按其生产性质和产品用途，可分为下列三类：(1)采掘（伐）工业，是指对自然资源的开采，包括石油开采、煤炭开采、金属矿开采、非金属矿开采和木材采伐等工业；(2)原材料工业，指向国民经济各部门提供基本材料、动力和燃料的工业。包括金属冶炼及加工、炼焦及焦炭化学、化工原料、水泥、人造板以及电力、石油和煤炭加工等工业；(3)加工工业，是指对工业原材料进行再加工制造的工业。包括装备国民经济各部门的机械设备制造工业、金属结构、水泥制品等工业，以及为农业提供的生产资料如化肥、农药等工业。

根据上述划分原则，修理业中以重工业产品为修理作业对象的划为重工业，反之划为轻工业。

工业总产值 是以货币表现的工业企业在一定时期内生产的已出售或可供出售工业产品总量，它反映一定时间内工业生产的总规模和总水平。它包括：在本企业内不再进行加工，经检验、包装入库（规定不需包装的产品除外）的成品价值，对外加工费收入，自制半成品、在产品期末期初差额价值。工业总产值采用“工厂法”计算，即以工业企业作为一个整体，按企业工业生产活动的最终成果来计算，企业内部不允许重复计算，不能把企业内部各个车间（分厂）生产的成果相加。但在企业之间、行业之间、地区之间存在着重复计算。

轻重工业总产值的划分也是按“工厂法”计算的，即一个工业企业在正常情况下生产的主要产品的性质属于轻工业，则该企业的全部总产值作为轻工业总产值；一个工业企业生产的主要产品的性质属于重工业，则该企业的全部总产值作为重工业总产值。

工业销售产值（当年价格） 是以货币形式表现的，工业企业在本年内销售的本企业生产的工业产品或提供工业性劳务价值的总价值量。工业销售产值包括的内容为：

（1）销售成品价值：指企业在报告期内实际销售（包括本期生产和非本期生产）的全部成品、半成品的总价值，即按报告期产品的实际销售数量乘以不含增值税（销项税额）的产品实际销售平均单价计算。销售成品价值中包括企业生产的自制设备及提供给本企业在建工程、其他非工业部门和生活福利部门等单位使用的成品价值，但不包括用订货者来料加工，并且只收取加工费的成品（半成品）价值。

（2）对外加工费收入：指企业在报告期内完成的对外承接的工业品加工（包括用定货者来料加工的产品）的加工费收入；对外工业品修理作业可收取的加工费收入和对内非工业部门提供的加工修理、设备安装等收入。对外加工费收入按不含增值税（销项税额）的价格计算。

对于以对外加工生产为主，对外加工费收入所占比重较大的企业，如果对外加工费收入出现跨年度支付的情况，为保证总产值生产口径计算的准确性，则应将对外加工费收入按实际情况调整，记录本年应实际收取的对外加工费收入。

出口交货值 指工业企业交给外贸部门或自营（委托）出口（包括销往香港、澳门、台湾），用外汇价格结算的产品价值，以及外商来样、来料加工、来件装配和补偿贸易等生产的产品价值。在计算出口交货值时，要把外汇价格按交易时的汇率折成人民币计算。

流动资产合计 资产满足以下条件之一应归为流动资产：（1）预计在一个正常营业周期中变现、出售或耗用，主要包括存货、应收账款等；（2）主要为交易目的而持有；（3）预计在资产负债表日起一年内（含一年）变现；（4）自资产负债日起一年内，交换其他资产或清偿负债的能力不受限制的现金或现金等价物。包括货币资金、应收票据、应收账款、存货等项目。来源于“资产负债表”中“流动资产合计”项目的期末余额数。

应收账款 指企业因销售商品、提供劳务等经营活动所形成的债权，包括应向客户收取的货款、增值税款和为客户代垫的运杂费等。来源于会计“资产负债表”中“应收账款”项目的期末余额数。

存货 指企业在日常活动中持有以备出售的产成品或商品、处在生产过程中的在产品、在生产过程或提供劳务过程中耗用的材料或物料等，通常包括原材料、在产品、半成品、产成品、商品以及周转材料等。来源于会计“资产负债表”中“存货”项目的期末余额数。

产成品 指企业已经完成全部生产过程并验收入库，可以按照合同规定的条件送交订货单位，或者可以作为商品对外销售的产品。来源于会计“产成品”科目的借方余额。

固定资产合计 指企业为生产商品、提供劳务、出租或经营管理而持有的，使用寿命超过一个会计年度的有形资产。包括使用期限超过一年的房屋、建筑物、机器、机械、运输工具以及其他与生产、经营有关的设备、器具、工具等。固定资产合计是时点指标，表示固定资产经过扣减折旧、减值准备等后的期末余额。执行《企业会计准则》或《小企业会计准则》的企业，来源于会计“资产负债表”中“固定资产”项目的期末余额数。

资产总计 指企业过去的交易或者事项形成的、由企业拥有或者控制的、预期会给企业带来经济利益的资源。资产一般按流动性（资产的变现或耗用时间长短）分为流动资产和非流动资产。其中流动资产可分为货币资金、交易性金融资产、应收票据、应收账款、预付款项、其他应收款、存货等；非流动资产可分为长期股权投资、固定资产、无形资产及其他非流动资产等。来源于会计“资产负债表”中“资产总计”项目的期末余额数。

负债合计 指企业过去的交易或者事项形成的，预期会导致经济利益流出企业的现时义务。负债一般按偿还期长短分为流动负债和非流动负债。来源于会计“资产负债表”中“负债合计”项目的期末余额数。

流动负债合计 负债满足下列条件之一的应归为流动负债：（1）预计在一个正常营业周期中清偿；（2）主要为交易目的而持有；（3）自资产负债表日起一年内到期应予清偿；（4）企业无权自主地将清偿推迟至资产负债表日后一年以上。包括短期借款、应付票据、应付账款、应付职工薪酬、应交税费等项目。来源于会计“资产负债表”中“流动负债合计”项目的期末余额数。

营业收入 指企业经营主要业务和其他业务所确认的收入总额。营业收入合计包括“主营业务收入”和“其他业务收入”。来源于会计“利润表”中“营业收入”项目的本期金额数。

营业成本 指企业从事销售商品、提供劳务和让渡资产使用权等生产经营活动发生的实际成本。“营业成本”应当与“营业收入”进行配比。包括“主营业务成本”和“其他业务成本”。根据会计“利润表”中“营业成本”项目的本年累计数填报。

利润总额 指企业在一定会计期间的经营成果，是生产经营过程中各种收入扣除各种耗费后的盈余，反映企业在报告期内实现的盈亏总额。来源于会计“利润表”中“利润总额”项目的本期金额数。

本年应交增值税 指企业按税法规定，从事货物销售或提供加工、修理修配劳务等增加货物价值的活动本期应交纳的税金。计算公式为：

本年应交增值税=销项税额－（进项税额－进项税额转出）－出口抵减内销产品应纳税额－减免税款+出口退税

本年进项税额：指工业企业在报告期内购入货物或接受应税劳务而支付的、准予从销项税额中抵扣的增值税额。

本年销项税额：指工业企业在报告期内销售货物或提供应税劳务应收取的增值税额。

利税总额 指企业利润总额、产品销售税金及附加和应交增值税之和。

总资产贡献率 是指企业一定时期内全部资产获利能力，是企业经营业绩和管理水平的集中体现，是评价和考核企业盈利能力的核心指标。计算公式为：

$$总资产贡献率（\%）=\frac{利润总额+税金总额+利息支出}{平均资产总额}\times 100\%$$

税金总额为产品销售税金及附加与应交增值税之和，平均资产总额为期初、期末资产总计的算术平均值 。

资产负债率 是指反映企业经营风险的大小，反映企业利用债权人提供的资金从事经营活动的能力。计算公式为：

$$资产负债率（\%）=\frac{负债总计}{资产总计}\times 100\%$$

资产及负债均为报告期末数。

成本费用利润率 是指工业企业投入生产成本及费用的经济效益，同时也反映企业降低成本所取得的经济效益。计算公式为：

$$成本费用利润率（\%）=\frac{利润总额}{成本费用总额}\times 100\%$$

成本费用总额为主营业务成本和营业费用、管理费用、财务费用三项期间费用。

全员劳动生产率 是指反映企业的生产效率和劳动投入的经济效益。一般用平均每人一年创造的工业总产值表示。计算公式为：

$$全员劳动生产率（元/人）=\frac{工业总产值}{全部职工平均人数}\times 100\%$$

全部职工平均人数为企业在报告期内全部从业人员的平均人数，计算公式为：

$$全部从业人员年平均人数=\frac{1至12月各月全部从业人员平均人数之和}{12}$$

或：

$$全部从业人员年平均人数=\frac{1至12月各月月初、月末全部从业人员之和}{24}$$

工业产品销售率 是指反映工业产品已实现销售的程度，是分析工业产销衔接情况、研究工业产品满足社会需求的指标。计算公式为：

$$产品销售率（\%）=\frac{现价工业销售产值}{现价工业总产值}\times 100\%$$

Explanatory Notes on Main Statistical Indicators

Industry refers to the material production sector which is engaged in extraction of natural resources and processing and reprocessing of minerals and agricultural products. It includes: (1) Extraction of natural resources, such as mining, salt production, and logging (but excluding hunting and fishing); (2) Processing and reprocessing of farm and sideline produces, such as rice husking, flour milling, wine making, oil pressing, cotton ginning, silk reeling, spinning and weaving, and leather making; (3) Manufacture of industrial products, such as steel making,iron smelting, chemicals manufacturing, petroleum processing, machine building, timber processing; and production and supply of electricity, water and gas; (4) Repair and renovation of industrial products, such as the repair of machinery and means of transport (including cars).

Prior to 1984, industrial enterprises run by villages and cooperative organizations under village were classified into agriculture. Since 1984, these enterprises have been grouped into industry.

Units of Industrial Statistics Survey These are classified into two categories: corporate industrial enterprises with independent accounting system and industrial establishments.

(1) Corporate industrial enterprises with independent accounting system refer to enterprises engaging in industrial production activities which simultaneously meet the following requirements: ①They are established legally, having their own names, organizations, location, able to take civil liability; ②They possess and use their assets independently, assume liabilities, and are entitled to sign contracts with other units; ③They are financially independent and compile their own balance sheets.

(2) Industrial establishments refer to economic units located in one single place and engaged entirely or primarily in one kind of industrial production activity, including units engaged in main business activities (industrial production activities) under industrial enterprises with independent accounting system and units engaged in industrial production activities under non-industrial enterprises (formerly industrial establishments with dependent accounting system). Industrial establishments generally meet the following requirements simultaneously: ① They have each one location and are engaged entirely or primarily in one kind of industrial activity each; ② They operate and manage their industrial production activities separately; ③ They have accounts of income and expenditure separately.

Light Industry refers to the industry that produces consumer goods and hand tools. It consists of two categories, depending on the materials used:

(1) Industries using farm products as raw materials. These are branches of light industry which directly or indirectly use farm products as basic raw materials, including the manufacture of food and beverages, tobacco processing, textile, clothing, fur and leather manufacturing, paper making, printing, etc.

(2) Industries using non-farm products as raw materials. These are branches of light industry which use manufactured goods as raw materials, including the manufacture of cultural, educational and sports articles, chemicals, synthetic fiber, chemical products for daily use, glass products for daily use, metal products for daily use, hand tools, medical apparatus and instruments, and the manufacture of cultural and clerical machinery.

Heavy Industry refers to the industry which produces capital goods and provides various sectors of the national economy with necessary material and technical basis. It consists of the following three branches according to the purpose of production or the use of products:

(1) Mining, quarrying and logging industry refers to the industry that extracts natural resources, including extraction of petroleum, coal, metal and non-metal ores, and logging.

(2) Raw materials industry refers to the industry that provides various sectors of the national economy with raw materials, fuels and power. It includes smelting and processing of metals, coking and coke chemistry, chemical materials and building materials such as cement, plywood, and power, petroleum refining and coal dressing.

(3) Manufacturing industry refers to the industry that processes raw materials. It includes machine-building industry which equips sectors of the national economy, industries of metal structure and cement products, industries producing means of agricultural production, such as chemical fertilizers and pesticides.

According to the above principle of classification, repairing trades engaged primarily in repairing products of heavy industry are classified into heavy industry, while those engaged in repairing products of light industry are classified into light industry.

Gross Industrial Output Value refers to the total volume of industrial products sold or available for sale in monetary terms during a given period, which reflects the total achievements and overall scale of industrial production during a given period. It includes the value of the finished products in the enterprises, which are not to be further processed and have been inspected, packed and put in storage (where applicable), the income from external processing and the value gain of semi-finished products at the end of the reference period over the beginning. The gross industrial output value is calculated by the factory approach, i.e. the whole industrial enterprise is regarded as the basic accounting unit in calculating the gross industrial output value. No double calculations are to be made within the same enterprise and the output value of different workshops (branch factories) should not be added. However, this approach does not exclude the possibility of double calculations between enterprises, sectors and regions.

Output value of light and heavy industries is also classified by the factory approach. Under normal conditions, if the major products of an industrial enterprise belong to light industry products, the gross output value of that enterprise is classified wholly into light industry; the same principle applies to heavy industry.

Sales Value of Industry (Current Price) refers to refers to the total value of industrial products sold or industrial services provided in monetary terms within the current year. It includes:

(1) Sales Value of Finished Products. Sale value of finished products refers to the total value of finished and semi-finished products sold within the reporting period (including those produced within and outside the period). It equals the actual sales volume of products sold within the reporting period timing the actual average sales price (excluding value added or sales tax). It includes the equipment made by the enterprise itself, as well as the finished products provided to the projects under construction, non-industrial departments and welfare department, and excludes the value of finished or semi-finished products of external processing with supplied materials that produces only processing charges.

(2) Income from External Processing: refers to income from contracted external processing of industrial products (including processing of industrial products using materials from the clients), and the income from industrial repairing work provided to other units. Income from external processing is calculated using information from the item “products sales income” in the enterprise accounting at the prices excluding value-added tax.

For an enterprise whose main business is external processing and the charges of external processing constitute a large proportion of its income, in case of cross-year payment, the income of external processing charges shall be adjusted and the actual income of external processing charges of the current year shall be recorded to ensure the accuracy of the coverage of gross industrial output.

Export Delivery Value refers to the value of the products that an industrial enterprises have delivered to export units or have exported on its own or per procuration (including those sold to Hong Kong, Macaw and Taiwan), and the value of the products from processing and compensation trades(processing with given materials or samples, assembling supplied components). In calculating the export delivery value, the foreign exchanges shall be converted into yuan at current exchange rates.

Total Current Assets refer to the assets that meet one of the following requirements: (1) expected to be cashed, sold or used in a normal operation cycle, mainly including inventory and accounts receivable; (2) be owned for trading purpose mainly; (3) expected to be cashed in one year (including one year) from the day of the Balance Sheet; (4) unlimited cash or cash equivalents that can be exchanged with other assets or being capable of settling debts during one year since the day of the Balance Sheet. Included are monetary capital, notes receivable, accounts receivable and inventories. Data on this indicator can be obtained from the year-end figures of Total Current Assets in the Balance Sheet of accounting records.

Accounts Receivable refers to creditor's rights formed by business activities such as selling goods, providing labor, which include payment for goods that should be charged to the customer, value-added tax and advance freight for the clients. It comes from the ending balance of Accounts Receivable in Balance Sheet of accounting records.

Inventories refers to finished goods or commodities held in preparation for sale in enterprises' daily activities, goods in the production process, material or the physical materials consumed in the production process or in the process of providing labor, usually include raw materials, goods in the production process, semi-finished products, finished products, goods and materials in flow. It comes from the ending balance of Inventory in Balance Sheet of accounting records.

Finished Goods refers to the products that the enterprises have completed all of the production process and accepted and put in storage, and can be sent to the ordering units in accordance with the contract stipulations, or can be on sale. It comes from the debit balance of Finished Products of accounting.

Fixed Assets refers to houses, buildings machines, vehicles and other equipment, appliances and tools related to production and operation that have been used for more than one year. It also includes articles that are not major equipment of production or operation, but the value of which exceeds 2000 yuan and the service period of which exceeds 2 years. Data can be obtained from the year-end figures of Fixed Assets in the Balance Sheet of accounting records.

Total Assets refer to all resources that are owned or controlled by enterprises through previous trades or transactions with expectation of making economic profits. Classified by the degree of liquidity, total assets include current assets and non-current assets. Current assets can be classified into monetary capital, trading financial assets, notes receivable, accounts receivable, advanced payments, other receivables and inventories. Non-current assets can be divided into long-term equity investment, fixed assets, intangible assets and other non-current assets. Data on this indicator can be obtained from the year-end figures of total assets in the Balance Sheet of accounting records.

Total Liabilities refer to payable liabilities of enterprises that accumulated from previous trades or transactions with expectation of economic profits leaking out. In terms of payment, it can be divided into liquid liabilities and long-term liabilities. Data on this indicator can be obtained from the year-end figures of total liabilities in the Balance Sheet of accounting records. It comes from the debit balance of Total Liabilities in the Balance Sheet of accounting records.

Total Liquid Liabilities refer to total debt payable by enterprises within an operating cycle of one year or over one year, including short-term loans, payables and advance payments, wages payable, taxes payable and profits payable, etc. Data can be obtained from the year-end figures of Total Liquid Liabilities in the Balance Sheet of accounting records.

Business Revenue refers to the revenue from the sales of products (or commodities) and from rendering of industrial services by industrial enterprises. It is classified into two categories: principal business revenue (or basic business revenue) and other business revenue (or additional business revenue). It comes from current amount of Business Revenue in income statement.

Business Cost refers to the total cost incurred by an enterprise in its principal business and other business operations.It includes "Cost of principal business" and "Cost of other business".It come from this year's cumulative report of "operating cost" items from the "income statement".

Total Profits refers to the operation results in a certain accounting period, and it is the balance of various incomes minus various spending in the course of operation, reflecting the total profits and losses of enterprises in reference period. Data are obtained from the amount of total profits in the profit statement of the accounting record of enterprise.

Value-added Tax Payable refers to the amount of the value-added tax which should be paid by the enterprises according to tax laws during the reference period of selling goods or providing such services as processing, repairing or assembling that add value to goods. The formula used is:

$$\text{Value-added Tax Payable} = \text{Output Tax} - (\text{Input Tax} - \text{Input Tax Returns}) - \text{Export Deduct Domestic Sales Goods Tax} - \text{Tax Deduction} + \text{Export Tax Refund}$$

Amount of Input Tax at Current Year refers to the VAT an industrial enterprise pays for purchasing goods or receiving taxable services within the reference period, which is allowed to be deducted from the amount of output tax.

Amount of Output Tax at Current Year refers to the VAT an industrial enterprise pays for selling goods or providing taxable services within the reference period.

Total Pre-Tax Profits refers to the sum of total profits, sales tax as well as additional and payable value-added taxes.

Ratio of Total Assets to Industrial Output Value refers to the profit-making capability of all assets of the enterprise. As a core indicator for the evaluation and assessment of the profit-making potential of the enterprise, it is a focused reflection of the performance and management efficiency of the enterprise. This ratio is calculated as follows:

$$\text{Ratio of Total Assets to Industrial Output Value (\%)} = \left(\frac{\text{Total Profits} + \text{Total Taxes} + \text{Interest Expenditure}}{\text{Average Assets}}\right) \times 100\% \times \left(\frac{12}{\text{cumulative number of months}}\right)$$

where Total Taxes are the sum of tax and extra charges on the sales of products and value-added tax payable; and Average Assets are the arithmetic mean of beginning assets and ending assets.

Ratio of Capital Maintenance and Appreciation is an important indicator of the changes of net assets of an enterprise and a focused reflection of the development capability of enterprises. It is the ratio of total creditors' equity at the end of the reference period to that of the same period of the previous year, calculated as follows:

$$\text{Ratio of Capital Maintenance and Appreciation (\%)} = \left(\frac{\text{Total Creditors' Equity at the End of the Reference Period}}{\text{Total Creditors' Equity of the Same Period of the Previous Year}}\right) \times 100\%$$

where Creditors' equity is equal to the total assets of the enterprise minus its total liabilities.

Assets-Liability Ratio reflects both the operation risk and the capability of the enterprise in making use of the capital from the creditors. It is calculated as follows:

$$\text{Assets-Liability Ratio(\%)} = \left(\frac{\text{Total Debts}}{\text{Total Assets}}\right) \times 100\%$$

where both assets and debts are figures at the end of the reference period.

Ratio of Profits to Industrial Costs refers to the ratio of profits realized in a given period to the total production costs of industrial enterprises in the same period, which also reflects the economic benefit attained by the enterprises from reduced costs. This ratio is calculated as follows:

$$\text{Ratio of Profits to Industrial Costs (\%)} = \left(\frac{\text{Total Profits}}{\text{Total Costs}}\right) \times 100\%$$

where Total costs are the sum of cost of products sold, marketing cost, management cost and financial cost.

Value-added Labor Productivity reflects the production efficiency of the enterprise and economic benefit of its labor input. It is usually expressed as the industrial gross output value created by an average member of an industrial enterprise in a year. The formula used is:

$$\begin{array}{c}\text{Value-added Labor Productivity} \\ \text{(yuan/person)}\end{array} = \left(\frac{\text{Gross output Value of Industry}}{\text{Average Number of Staff and Workers}}\right) \times \left(\frac{12}{\text{Cumulative Number of Months}}\right)$$

Average Number of Staff and Workers refers to the average number of all employed persons by an industrial enterprise within the reference period. The formula used is:

$$\text{Average Number of Staff and Workers} = \frac{\text{Sum of Average Monthly Numbers from January to December}}{12}$$

Or

$$\begin{array}{c}\text{Average Number of} \\ \text{Staff and Workers}\end{array} = \frac{\text{Sum of Average Numbers at the Beginning and End of Each Month from January to December}}{24}$$

Proportion of Products Sold refers to the sales of industrial products to the gross industrial output value, and is used to analyze the linkage between production and sales and the extent to which the needs of the society are met by the supply of industrial products. It is calculated as follows:

$$\text{Proportion of Products Sold (\%)} = \left(\frac{\text{Value of Industrial Sales at Current Prices}}{\text{Gross Industrial Output Value at Current Prices}}\right) \times 100\%$$

十三、建筑业

CONSTRUCTION

十三 建筑业

简要说明

一、本篇资料反映广东省建筑业发展的基本情况。主要内容包括全省和各市建筑业企业生产经营的情况，主要指标有企业个数、就业人员数、建筑业总产值、房屋建筑面积、房屋建筑施工新开工面积、利润总额、利税总额和建筑业劳动生产率等。

二、本篇资料由广东省统计局固定资产投资统计处整理提供。

三、本篇资料是根据国家统计局制定的《建筑业统计报表制度》整理汇总的。统计范围包括：广东境内具有法人资格的独立核算建筑业企业和辖区内建筑业法人所属的产业活动单位。

四、从 2004 年开始到 2018 年止，统计范围为具有建筑业资质的独立核算建筑业企业（包括具有总承包和专业承包资质和劳务分包资质的独立核算建筑业企业）。从 2019 年开始，统计范围为具有总承包和专业承包资质的独立核算建筑业企业。

13 Construction

Brief Introduction

Ⅰ. The data in this chapter show the development of the construction industry in Guangdong Province. They cover mainly the statistics of production and management of the enterprises of construction of the whole province and its cities, including the number of enterprises, the number of employed persons, gross output value of construction, floor space of buildings, value-added of construction, total profits and total pre-tax profits, construction enterprise labor productivity, etc.

Ⅱ. The data in this chapter are prepared and provided by the Division of Investment and Construction Statistics of Statistics Bureau of Guangdong Province.

Ⅲ. The data in this chapter are collected in accordance with the Reporting Scheme of Construction Statistics stipulated by the National Bureau of Statistics. The coverage of construction statistics includes construction enterprises with legal person qualifications and independent accounting system and industrial establishments affiliated with corporate construction enterprises under the jurisdiction of Guangdong Province.

Ⅳ. From 2004 to 2018, the scope of the construction statistics include all construction enterprises with construction qualifications and independent accounting system (including independent accounting construction enterprises with general contracting and professional contracting qualification and labor subcontracting qualification). Starting from 2019, the statistical scope is independent accounting construction enterprises with general contracting and professional contracting qualifications.

13-1 建筑业企业生产情况

Production Conditions of Construction Enterprises

项 目	Item	2022 合计 Total of 2022	2022 #内资企业 Domestic Invested Enterprises	2023 合计 Total of 2023	2023 #内资企业 Domestic Invested Enterprises
企业个数 (个)	**Number of Construction Enterprises (unit)**	**10960**	**10876**	**12352**	**12249**
建筑业合同情况	**Contracts of Construction**				
签订的合同额 (亿元)	Value of Contracts Signed (100 million yuan)	68170.24	66815.86	75934.32	74291.63
上年结转合同额 (亿元)	Value of Contracts Carried-over from the Previous Year (100 million yuan)	35748.13	34908.44	43888.54	42742.13
本年新签合同额 (亿元)	Value of Newly-signed Contracts in Current Year (100 million yuan)	32422.11	31907.42	32045.78	31549.50
承包工程完成情况	**Contracted Projects Completed**				
直接从建设单位承揽工程完成产值 (亿元)	Completed Output Value of Contracted Projects Directly from Construction Units (100 million yuan)	22478.24	22005.33	25468.71	25011.16
其中：自行完成施工产值 (亿元)	Output Value of Self-completed Projects (100 million yuan)	20253.66	19930.51	22244.51	21906.77
分包出去工程的产值 (亿元)	Output Value of Outsourcing Projects (100 million yuan)	2224.59	2074.82	3224.21	3104.39
从建设单位以外承揽工程完成产值 (亿元)	Completed Output Value of Contracted Projects outside Construction Units (100 million yuan)	2702.85	2664.95	3154.70	3139.94
建筑业总产值 (亿元)	**Gross Output Value of Construction (100 million yuan)**	**22956.50**	**22595.46**	**25399.21**	**25046.71**
#装配式建筑工程产值 (亿元)	Output value of prefabricated construction (100 million yuan)	476.15	475.65	631.58	626.73
#装饰装修产值 (亿元)	Output Value of Decoration Projects (100 million yuan)	1549.76	1525.77	1767.89	1753.15
#在外省完成的产值 (亿元)	Output Value Completed in Other Provinces (100 million yuan)	5262.14	5032.58	5724.80	5506.05
建筑工程产值 (亿元)	Output Value of Construction Projects (100 million yuan)	20398.87	20072.97	22593.12	22274.54
安装工程产值 (亿元)	Output Value of Installation Projects (100 million yuan)	1965.54	1932.27	2186.00	2158.58
其他产值 (亿元)	Other Output Values (100 million yuan)	592.10	590.23	620.08	613.58
竣工产值 (亿元)	**Output Value Completed (100 million yuan)**	**7261.45**	**7024.84**	**8478.53**	**8276.39**
房屋建筑施工面积 (万平方米)	**Floor Space of Buildings under Construction (10000 sq.m)**	**107372.69**	**100300.30**	**117914.56**	**113792.43**
#新开工面积 (万平方米)	Floor Space of Newly-started Buildings (10000 sq.m)	30605.05	29210.63	30613.46	29464.67
劳动人员情况	**Labor Force**				
从事建筑业活动的就业人员平均人数 (万人)	Average Number of Employed Persons in the Main Business Activities (10000 persons)	398.31	395.49	439.15	436.17

13-2 建筑业企业主要指标

Main Indicators on Construction Enterprises

年份 Year	建筑业企业单位数(个) Number of Construction Enterprises (unit)	建筑业企业总产值(亿元) Gross Output Value of Construction Enterprises (100 million yuan)	建筑业企业增加值(亿元) Value-added of Construction Enterprises (100 million yuan)	建筑业企业利税总额(亿元) Total Pre-tax Profits of Construction Enterprises (100 million yuan)
1978	178	5.47	10.49	0.20
1979	188	6.32	9.29	0.23
1980	204	8.88	12.66	0.32
1981	224	13.44	16.74	0.49
1982	246	19.66	22.24	0.72
1983	269	24.51	26.45	0.90
1984	357	36.83	33.22	1.31
1985	462	50.45	44.01	1.54
1986	448	57.14	47.42	1.28
1987	492	65.96	56.58	1.56
1988	596	86.74	73.82	2.74
1989	646	125.65	90.07	3.62
1990	686	113.40	92.45	3.12
1991	705	137.30	107.12	4.33
1992	910	216.56	201.04	9.65
1993	1766	459.95	318.05	23.03
1994	1587	535.75	387.80	31.29
1995	1618	635.83	451.40	39.47
1996	2031	632.16	464.66	35.74
1997	2399	732.97	468.97	38.26
1998	2961	800.00	502.87	43.11
1999	3283	954.44	526.56	53.06
2000	4593	944.61	537.06	58.24
2001	3699	1179.03	565.75	84.51
2002	4019	1418.41	596.03	88.95
2003	4488	1702.87	710.77	127.48
2004	4166	1901.86	780.81	143.75
2005	4182	2200.58	847.44	164.38
2006	4172	2594.04	934.97	191.62
2007	4326	3005.32	1073.17	256.59
2008	4470	3375.03	1208.40	205.07
2009	4508	3826.83	1350.61	329.00
2010	4551	4742.09	1574.96	393.87
2011	4589	5804.21	1755.04	470.75
2012	4637	6564.37	1876.07	517.82
2013	4977	7927.13	2260.48	653.70
2014	4982	8440.29	2496.15	675.99
2015	4926	8984.86	2684.40	724.74
2016	5054	9805.00	2909.50	736.98
2017	5606	11571.33	3289.32	851.86
2018	6509	14199.49	3849.75	1083.08
2019	7171	16633.41	4333.96	1041.77
2020	8334	18429.84	4651.50	1024.55
2021	9674	21346.12	5170.10	938.58
2022	10960	22956.50	5247.57	996.42
2023	12352	25399.21	5892.49	1015.91

13-3 按登记注册统计类别分建筑业企业主要经济指标（2023年）

Main Economic Indicators of Construction Enterprises by Registration Statistical Categories (2023)

项目	Item	合计 Total	内资企业 Domestic Invested Enterprises
企业个数 （个）	Number of Construction Enterprises (unit)	12352	12249
签订的合同额 （亿元）	Value of Contracts Signed (100 million yuan)	75934.32	74291.63
#本年新签合同额 （亿元）	Value of Newly-signed Contracts in Current Year (100 million yuan)	32045.78	31549.50
建筑业总产值 （亿元）	Gross Output Value of Construction (100 million yuan)	25399.21	25046.71
#建筑工程	Construction Projects	22593.12	22274.54
安装工程	Installation Projects	2186.00	2158.58
竣工产值 （亿元）	Output Value Completed (100 million yuan)	8478.53	8276.39
房屋建筑施工面积（万平方米）	Floor Space of Buildings under Construction (10000 sq.m)	117914.56	113792.43
#本年新开工面积	Floor Space of Newly-started Buildings this year (10000 sq.m)	30613.46	29464.67
房屋建筑竣工面积（万平方米）	Floor Space of Buildings Completed (10000 sq.m)	27303.13	26445.17
从事建筑业活动的平均人数 （万人）	Average Number of Employed Persons in the Main Business Activities (10000 persons)	439.15	436.17

注：本表登记注册统计类别按《关于市场主体统计分类的划分规定》(国统字〔2023〕14号)执行。

Ntote: The registered statistical categories of this table is implemented in accordance with the Regulations onStatistics the Classification of Market Entity(Guotongzi [2023] No. 14).

13-3 续表 continued

项目	Item	港澳台商投资企业 Investment Enterprises from Hong Kong,Macao and Taiwan	外商投资企业 Foreign Funded Enterprises
企业个数 （个）	Number of Construction Enterprises (unit)	87	16
签订的合同额 （亿元）	Value of Contracts Signed (100 million yuan)	968.76	673.94
#本年新签合同额 （亿元）	Value of Newly-signed Contracts in Current Year (100 million yuan)	374.19	122.09
建筑业总产值 （亿元）	Gross Output Value of Construction (100 million yuan)	210.50	141.99
#建筑工程	Construction Projects	179.50	139.08
安装工程	Installation Projects	24.91	2.51
竣工产值 （亿元）	Output Value Completed (100 million yuan)	104.44	97.70
房屋建筑施工面积(万平方米)	Floor Space of Buildings under Construction (10000 sq.m)	2746.75	1375.38
#本年新开工面积	Floor Space of Newly-started Buildings this year (10000 sq.m)	822.61	326.18
房屋建筑竣工面积(万平方米)	Floor Space of Buildings Completed (10000 sq.m)	326.01	531.96
从事建筑业活动的平均人数 （万人）	Average Number of Employed Persons in the Main Business Activities (10000 persons)	1.95	1.04

13-4 按登记注册统计类别分建筑业企业财务状况（2023年）
Financial Situation of Construction Enterprises by Registration Statistical Categories (2023)

单位：亿元 (100 million yuan)

项目	Item	合计 Total	内资企业 Domestic Invested Enterprises	港澳台商投资企业 Investment Enterprises from Hong Kong,Macao and Taiwan	外商投资企业 Foreign Funded Enterprises
年初存货	Inventory at the beginning of the year	2499.14	2285.82	27.28	186.04
流动资产合计	Total Current Assets	29846.79	27965.61	1033.36	847.81
#存货	Inventory	2563.07	2331.11	33.80	198.16
固定资产原价合计	Total Original Value of Fixed Assets	1516.25	1491.80	20.68	3.77
累计折旧	Accumulated Depreciation	755.25	741.50	11.74	2.01
#本年折旧	Depreciation for the Current Year	115.13	113.81	0.97	0.35
在建工程	Construction In Progress	232.14	218.62	13.25	0.26
资产总计	Total Assets	36359.99	34288.70	1211.09	860.20
流动负债合计	Total Current Liabilities	24783.73	23359.64	729.70	694.39
非流动负债合计	Total Non-current Liabilities	1865.96	1728.63	136.85	0.48
负债合计	Total liabilities	28134.72	26554.55	880.47	699.70
所有者权益合计	Total Owner's Equity	8219.49	7728.37	330.62	160.50
主营业务收入	Main Business Income	24362.61	23851.84	347.40	163.36
主营业务成本	Main Business Cost	22454.35	21992.64	307.42	154.29
主营业务税金及附加	Main Business Taxes and Surcharges	61.72	60.92	0.52	0.28
其他业务利润	Other Business Profits	15.04	14.42	0.62	
销售费用	Selling Expenses	52.58	51.79	0.53	0.25
管理费用	Administration Expenses	761.01	748.22	9.61	3.18
财务费用	Financial Expenses	147.54	136.73	9.83	0.98
营业利润	Operating Profit	519.14	507.24	12.23	-0.33
利润总额	Total Profit	493.72	482.06	11.76	-0.10
所得税费用	Income Tax Expenses	95.21	92.95	2.05	0.21
应付职工薪酬	Payroll Payable	3212.69	3183.23	17.42	12.03
应交增值税	Value-Added Tax Payable	449.61	443.04	4.64	1.92

注：本表登记注册统计类别按《关于市场主体统计分类的划分规定》(国统字〔2023〕14号)执行。

Ntote: The registered statistical categories of this table is implemented in accordance with the Regulations onStatistics the Classification of Market Entity(Guotongzi [2023] No. 14).

13-5 按行业分建筑业企业主要经济指标和财务状况（2023年）

Main Economic Indicators and Financial Situation of Construction Enterprises by Sector (2023)

单位：亿元　　(100 million yuan)

项　　目	Item	合计 Total	房屋建筑业 housing industry	土木工程建筑业 Civil engineering and construction industry
企业个数　(个)	Number of Construction Enterprises　(unit)	12352	4919	2936
签订的合同额　(亿元)	Value of Contracts Signed　(100 million yuan)	75934.32	35324.68	32369.10
#本年新签合同额	Value of Newly-signed Contracts in Current Year　(100 million yuan)	32045.78	15475.84	12068.99
建筑业总产值	Gross Output Value of Construction　(100 million yuan)	25399.21	12952.47	8442.03
#建筑工程	Construction Projects	22593.12	11996.34	7780.87
安装工程	Installation Projects	2186.00	708.89	465.71
竣工产值	Output Value Completed　(100 million yuan)	8478.53	5592.82	1831.86
房屋建筑施工面积(万平方米)	Floor Space of Buildings under Construction　(10000 sq.m)	117914.56	99292.00	13085.19
#本年新开工面积	Floor Space of Newly-started Buildings this year (10000 sq.m)	30613.46	24155.80	2875.67
房屋建筑竣工面积(万平方米)	Floor Space of Buildings Completed　(10000 sq.m)	27303.13	22279.45	3971.42
从事建筑业活动的平均人数　(万人)	Average Number of Employed Persons in the Main Business Activities　(10000 persons)	439.15	226.11	130.82
年初存货	Inventory at the beginning of the year	2499.14	1480.69	572.82
流动资产合计	Total Current Assets	29846.79	15136.84	9498.79
#存货	Inventory	2563.07	1542.35	600.36
固定资产原价合计	Total Original Value of Fixed Assets	1516.25	509.33	706.99
累计折旧	Accumulated Depreciation	755.25	242.33	372.30
#本年折旧	Depreciation for the Current Year	115.13	38.43	53.18
在建工程	Construction In Progress	232.14	90.63	103.61
资产总计	Total Assets	36359.99	17370.70	13062.36
流动负债合计	Total Current Liabilities	24783.73	12236.60	8702.98
非流动负债合计	Total Non-current Liabilities	1865.96	707.49	987.58
负债合计	Total liabilities	28134.72	13786.72	9972.25
所有者权益合计	Total Owner's Equity	8219.49	3581.36	3089.07
主营业务收入	Main Business Income	24362.61	11831.69	8481.29
主营业务成本	Main Business Cost	22454.35	11004.07	7791.96
主营业务税金及附加	Main Business Taxes and Surcharges	61.72	35.20	16.71
其他业务利润	Other Business Profits	15.04	5.56	4.86
销售费用	Selling Expenses	52.58	13.35	10.38
管理费用	Administration Expenses	761.01	305.11	213.15
财务费用	Financial Expenses	147.54	71.60	38.51
营业利润	Operating Profit	519.14	209.56	233.77
利润总额	Total Profit	493.72	205.55	227.74
所得税费用	Income Tax Expenses	95.21	42.62	33.92
应付职工薪酬	Payroll Payable	3212.69	1676.29	1007.38
应交增值税	Value-Added Tax Payable	449.61	224.76	131.57

13-5 续表 continued

单位：亿元 (100 million yuan)

项目	Item	建筑安装业 Construction and installation industry	建筑装饰、装修和其他建筑业 Building decoration, decoration, and other construction industries
企业个数 (个)	Number of Construction Enterprises (unit)	1677	2820
签订的合同额 (亿元)	Value of Contracts Signed (100 million yuan)	2610.87	5629.67
#本年新签合同额	Value of Newly-signed Contracts in Current Year (100 million yuan)	1581.63	2919.33
建筑业总产值	Gross Output Value of Construction (100 million yuan)	1302.65	2702.05
#建筑工程	Construction Projects	516.50	2299.41
安装工程	Installation Projects	729.58	281.83
竣工产值	Output Value Completed (100 million yuan)	398.49	655.35
房屋建筑施工面积(万平方米)	Floor Space of Buildings under Construction (10000 sq.m)	2771.07	2766.30
#本年新开工面积	Floor Space of Newly-started Buildings this year (10000 sq.m)	2157.73	1424.26
房屋建筑竣工面积(万平方米)	Floor Space of Buildings Completed (10000 sq.m)	304.98	747.28
从事建筑业活动的平均人数 (万人)	Average Number of Employed Persons in the Main Business Activities (10000 persons)	23.81	58.42
年初存货	Inventory at the beginning of the year	150.92	294.72
流动资产合计	Total Current Assets	1653.59	3557.57
#存货	Inventory	152.28	268.08
固定资产原价合计	Total Original Value of Fixed Assets	125.15	174.77
累计折旧	Accumulated Depreciation	66.46	74.16
#本年折旧	Depreciation for the Current Year	10.23	13.29
在建工程	Construction In Progress	7.56	30.33
资产总计	Total Assets	1897.17	4029.76
流动负债合计	Total Current Liabilities	1169.96	2674.20
非流动负债合计	Total Non-current Liabilities	46.90	123.99
负债合计	Total liabilities	1309.69	3066.05
所有者权益合计	Total Owner's Equity	587.15	961.91
主营业务收入	Main Business Income	1442.07	2607.56
主营业务成本	Main Business Cost	1283.54	2374.78
主营业务税金及附加	Main Business Taxes and Surcharges	3.19	6.62
其他业务利润	Other Business Profits	2.58	2.04
销售费用	Selling Expenses	10.60	18.24
管理费用	Administration Expenses	101.74	141.00
财务费用	Financial Expenses	7.31	30.12
营业利润	Operating Profit	27.93	47.88
利润总额	Total Profit	28.55	31.87
所得税费用	Income Tax Expenses	6.63	12.04
应付职工薪酬	Payroll Payable	189.67	339.35
应交增值税	Value-Added Tax Payable	33.78	59.49

13-6 各市建筑业企业个数

Number of Construction Enterprises by City

单位：个 (unit)

市别	City	2000	2005	2010	2015	2019	2020	2021	2022	2023
全省	**Provincial Total**	**4593**	**4182**	**4551**	**4926**	**7171**	**8334**	**9674**	**10960**	**12352**
广州	Guangzhou	757	764	779	877	1330	1639	2011	2203	2431
深圳	Shenzhen	447	604	808	776	1262	1389	1501	1788	2066
珠海	Zhuhai	143	165	144	393	407	510	517	584	603
汕头	Shantou	271	199	212	175	174	175	187	198	214
佛山	Foshan	248	502	497	427	612	719	802	858	887
韶关	Shaoguan	110	66	76	94	187	257	335	352	356
河源	Heyuan	117	82	85	104	135	160	168	186	225
梅州	Meizhou	154	111	146	151	181	191	194	201	279
惠州	Huizhou	241	124	111	103	259	328	663	902	994
汕尾	Shanwei	100	43	38	36	41	58	87	128	125
东莞	Dongguan	183	361	444	540	949	1017	1096	1181	1289
中山	Zhongshan	385	273	314	319	395	460	509	601	705
江门	Jiangmen	342	156	165	164	235	269	286	328	372
阳江	Yangjiang	122	91	95	113	108	142	172	194	208
湛江	Zhanjiang	238	125	106	127	195	211	241	264	276
茂名	Maoming	146	100	97	129	206	219	252	286	486
肇庆	Zhaoqing	136	122	119	90	117	142	169	176	211
清远	Qingyuan	136	74	80	88	123	153	174	204	222
潮州	Chaozhou	139	90	83	66	61	61	63	67	81
揭阳	Jieyang	121	84	107	111	142	166	175	178	216
云浮	Yunfu	57	46	45	43	52	68	72	81	106
按经济区域分	By Region									
珠三角	Pearl River Delta	2882	3071	3381	3689	5566	6473	7554	8621	9558
粤东	Eastern Region	631	416	440	388	418	460	512	571	636
粤西	Western Region	506	316	298	369	509	572	665	744	970
粤北	Northern Region	574	379	432	480	678	829	943	1024	1188

13-7 各市建筑业企业总产值
Gross Output Value of Construction Enterprises by City

单位：亿元 (100 million yuan)

市别	City	2000	2005	2010	2015	2019	2020	2021	2022	2023
全　省	**Provincial Total**	**944.61**	**2200.58**	**4742.09**	**8984.86**	**16633.41**	**18429.84**	**21346.12**	**22956.50**	**25399.21**
广　州	Guangzhou	256.13	633.99	1296.19	2546.94	5304.90	5961.63	7069.68	7522.52	8777.79
深　圳	Shenzhen	153.02	545.62	1460.99	2275.20	4361.44	4772.22	5412.91	6243.27	7113.35
珠　海	Zhuhai	33.11	52.48	100.81	477.45	986.91	1106.13	1235.98	1359.03	1456.46
汕　头	Shantou	80.67	127.78	219.12	405.52	713.30	787.63	827.85	752.91	618.37
佛　山	Foshan	73.08	154.68	315.42	497.09	616.92	713.07	880.15	986.79	1082.63
韶　关	Shaoguan	24.14	29.25	102.76	214.35	213.35	239.64	271.26	235.34	228.43
河　源	Heyuan	5.74	17.01	20.68	69.31	138.34	138.69	160.89	170.49	147.51
梅　州	Meizhou	15.14	54.81	125.91	241.12	392.94	402.36	400.61	341.53	375.67
惠　州	Huizhou	20.35	46.94	69.83	141.29	237.03	273.55	425.69	524.32	685.81
汕　尾	Shanwei	5.49	6.95	15.44	14.41	43.77	55.64	62.15	54.29	53.30
东　莞	Dongguan	40.45	84.35	122.06	224.59	562.68	664.48	842.63	960.57	1072.80
中　山	Zhongshan	26.20	73.41	133.70	153.67	256.81	313.35	404.56	495.18	568.55
江　门	Jiangmen	47.18	56.06	119.18	225.24	316.38	334.60	367.51	428.76	502.57
阳　江	Yangjiang	18.80	32.97	66.18	120.05	133.89	117.91	124.08	110.94	111.67
湛　江	Zhanjiang	45.61	75.96	168.08	461.75	838.24	881.02	967.14	929.02	797.78
茂　名	Maoming	39.05	92.14	134.67	481.04	938.44	1024.10	1227.18	1216.25	1172.59
肇　庆	Zhaoqing	15.40	39.99	99.40	125.49	169.03	183.33	210.89	202.01	185.44
清　远	Qingyuan	11.49	20.19	52.78	101.72	142.50	198.03	207.30	183.53	196.31
潮　州	Chaozhou	12.71	18.99	25.98	43.84	50.70	51.29	54.36	57.89	64.73
揭　阳	Jieyang	12.24	21.78	75.06	133.02	152.24	139.38	103.36	88.96	91.18
云　浮	Yunfu	8.61	15.20	17.85	31.75	63.60	71.79	89.95	92.88	96.26
按经济区域分	By Region									
珠三角	Pearl River Delta	664.92	1687.53	3717.58	6666.97	12812.10	14322.35	16850.00	18722.46	21445.41
粤　东	Eastern Region	111.11	175.50	335.60	596.79	960.01	1033.94	1047.71	954.05	827.58
粤　西	Western Region	103.46	201.08	368.93	1062.85	1910.58	2023.03	2318.39	2256.22	2082.03
粤　北	Northern Region	65.12	136.47	319.98	658.26	950.72	1050.52	1130.01	1023.77	1044.18

13-8 各市建筑业企业营业收入(2023年)

Operating Revenue of Construction Enterprises by City(2023)

单位：亿元 (100 million yuan)

市别	City	营业收入 Operating Revenue	#主营业务收入 Main Business Income	营业成本 Operating Costs	#主营业务成本 Main Business Costs	其他营业收入 Other Operating Income	#其他业务利润 Other Business Profits
全省	**Provincial Total**	**25217.85**	**24362.61**	**23318.18**	**22454.35**	**855.25**	**15.04**
广州	Guangzhou	8992.51	8845.78	8407.13	8212.01	146.73	7.30
深圳	Shenzhen	7413.04	7177.59	6839.07	6600.82	235.45	4.50
珠海	Zhuhai	1504.26	1474.18	1358.26	1332.82	30.08	0.76
汕头	Shantou	514.95	454.82	476.15	417.58	60.13	0.11
佛山	Foshan	1079.41	1040.40	980.70	948.24	39.01	2.02
韶关	Shaoguan	209.67	196.01	192.03	179.30	13.66	0.07
河源	Heyuan	128.40	112.24	112.36	97.70	16.16	0.02
梅州	Meizhou	356.69	333.85	318.37	300.09	22.84	0.34
惠州	Huizhou	639.75	582.09	586.70	535.00	57.65	0.32
汕尾	Shanwei	41.59	35.69	37.12	32.01	5.90	
东莞	Dongguan	1009.77	952.17	913.00	860.15	57.60	0.20
中山	Zhongshan	579.33	554.09	526.00	505.67	25.24	0.28
江门	Jiangmen	331.42	317.83	299.86	287.45	13.59	0.14
阳江	Yangjiang	106.37	99.47	97.58	90.43	6.90	0.00
湛江	Zhanjiang	691.11	675.50	658.87	645.35	15.62	0.07
茂名	Maoming	1052.40	1009.42	1004.15	962.52	42.98	0.07
肇庆	Zhaoqing	131.41	123.81	122.47	113.69	7.60	0.00
清远	Qingyuan	203.97	188.84	180.73	167.18	15.12	0.06
潮州	Chaozhou	61.69	58.85	57.02	53.64	2.85	0.00
揭阳	Jieyang	82.10	46.19	75.51	41.16	35.91	0.06
云浮	Yunfu	88.02	83.79	75.11	71.55	4.23	-1.29
按经济区域分	By Region						
珠三角	Pearl River Delta	21680.89	21067.93	20033.18	19395.86	612.96	15.52
粤东	Eastern Region	700.33	595.55	645.80	544.39	104.78	0.17
粤西	Western Region	1849.89	1784.39	1760.60	1698.29	65.50	0.14
粤北	Northern Region	986.74	914.74	878.61	815.81	72.01	-0.80

13-9 各市建筑业企业利税总额

Total Pre-tax Profits of Construction Enterprises by City

单位：亿元 (100 million yuan)

市别	City	2000	2005	2010	2015	2019	2020	2021	2022	2023
全省	**Provincial Total**	**58.24**	**164.38**	**393.87**	**724.74**	**1041.77**	**1024.55**	**938.58**	**996.42**	**1015.91**
广州	Guangzhou	15.17	45.42	118.16	171.85	224.60	264.28	247.84	223.58	281.51
深圳	Shenzhen	13.79	39.76	105.09	212.92	259.51	211.86	144.15	270.58	241.57
珠海	Zhuhai	1.43	4.16	7.44	34.12	60.08	64.95	72.06	87.76	95.91
汕头	Shantou	4.14	9.86	17.64	32.64	91.92	80.07	56.42	33.04	42.94
佛山	Foshan	4.70	14.31	30.47	38.40	42.93	34.07	44.83	46.34	39.57
韶关	Shaoguan	2.00	1.57	6.66	14.55	10.06	12.58	10.38	12.15	11.28
河源	Heyuan	0.53	1.23	2.08	10.72	16.94	12.70	12.02	13.00	11.70
梅州	Meizhou	0.81	6.47	13.70	26.53	39.87	39.26	31.95	27.83	24.27
惠州	Huizhou	1.02	3.63	4.96	5.44	12.69	16.16	17.92	21.70	32.33
汕尾	Shanwei	0.58	0.58	1.43	1.29	4.28	3.42	4.08	3.40	3.33
东莞	Dongguan	2.25	6.36	9.80	17.09	36.91	36.86	42.77	36.60	43.64
中山	Zhongshan	1.53	6.09	13.71	11.87	20.90	20.82	21.99	20.75	19.19
江门	Jiangmen	2.37	3.79	9.61	20.34	22.75	21.11	20.11	20.84	20.35
阳江	Yangjiang	1.15	3.24	6.26	9.09	14.60	10.98	9.44	6.79	5.42
湛江	Zhanjiang	1.69	3.80	10.69	23.94	42.30	49.68	52.60	43.49	39.20
茂名	Maoming	1.82	5.97	10.01	52.94	88.22	81.99	82.86	75.33	61.95
肇庆	Zhaoqing	0.77	2.55	6.32	7.79	7.96	9.48	10.25	8.95	6.43
清远	Qingyuan	0.40	1.20	6.24	5.78	11.91	28.83	35.21	20.73	17.36
潮州	Chaozhou	0.66	1.17	2.12	3.18	5.01	4.32	3.67	3.65	3.49
揭阳	Jieyang	0.73	2.09	9.48	21.01	20.31	13.17	9.35	8.48	5.54
云浮	Yunfu	0.70	1.13	1.98	3.26	8.01	7.96	8.71	11.41	8.92
按经济区域分	By Region									
珠三角	Pearl River Delta	43.03	126.06	305.57	519.81	688.33	679.59	621.90	737.11	780.50
粤东	Eastern Region	6.11	13.70	30.68	58.12	121.52	100.98	73.53	48.58	55.30
粤西	Western Region	4.66	13.01	26.96	85.97	145.13	142.66	144.89	125.61	106.57
粤北	Northern Region	4.44	11.61	30.66	60.84	86.79	101.33	98.26	85.12	73.54

13–10 各市建筑业企业利润总额

Total Profits of Construction Enterprises by City

单位：亿元 (100 million yuan)

市 别	City	2000	2005	2010	2015	2019	2020	2021	2022	2023
全 省	**Provincial Total**	**22.73**	**70.53**	**205.47**	**396.36**	**570.14**	**541.11**	**445.33**	**504.07**	**493.72**
广 州	Guangzhou	5.20	18.64	65.51	96.23	122.71	150.99	139.73	121.54	157.46
深 圳	Shenzhen	7.57	15.65	50.44	115.51	154.70	116.91	40.88	154.51	102.34
珠 海	Zhuhai	0.37	1.98	3.47	19.05	44.06	48.90	53.58	60.91	69.89
汕 头	Shantou	1.36	3.74	8.23	15.63	61.77	45.36	29.21	13.83	21.67
佛 山	Foshan	2.00	6.54	19.27	24.99	23.06	15.36	19.22	20.66	14.18
韶 关	Shaoguan	0.23	0.43	2.95	5.44	4.23	4.97	3.97	4.19	4.29
河 源	Heyuan	0.29	0.48	0.95	7.71	9.39	7.28	6.89	7.26	6.70
梅 州	Meizhou	0.21	4.56	8.44	17.08	26.08	27.66	20.12	17.97	14.23
惠 州	Huizhou	0.35	1.02	1.68	2.37	4.88	7.31	7.86	8.63	15.25
汕 尾	Shanwei	0.22	0.18	0.56	0.55	1.38	1.13	1.72	1.53	1.33
东 莞	Dongguan	1.14	3.81	5.78	9.67	20.81	17.34	18.46	10.99	16.83
中 山	Zhongshan	0.78	3.63	7.46	6.25	14.61	14.09	14.51	11.04	7.56
江 门	Jiangmen	0.34	1.55	4.88	11.33	11.10	10.47	9.73	9.73	9.73
阳 江	Yangjiang	0.61	1.38	3.59	4.71	5.58	4.47	4.81	3.15	2.19
湛 江	Zhanjiang	0.28	1.19	3.76	8.68	13.16	11.34	13.08	11.14	9.48
茂 名	Maoming	0.77	2.49	4.43	27.67	29.41	22.01	18.72	17.36	18.65
肇 庆	Zhaoqing	0.09	0.65	2.51	3.26	2.65	3.47	3.58	2.48	1.34
清 远	Qingyuan	0.01	0.46	3.44	3.24	3.75	19.50	27.21	13.98	10.70
潮 州	Chaozhou	0.28	0.49	1.12	1.77	1.61	2.25	1.71	1.78	1.69
揭 阳	Jieyang	0.26	1.22	5.90	13.46	11.29	5.51	4.42	3.42	2.08
云 浮	Yunfu	0.37	0.43	1.10	1.77	3.89	4.79	5.92	7.96	6.13
按经济区域分	By Region									
珠 三 角	Pearl River Delta	17.84	53.48	161.00	288.67	398.59	384.84	307.55	400.48	394.57
粤 东	Eastern Region	2.12	5.62	15.81	31.41	76.06	54.25	37.06	20.56	26.77
粤 西	Western Region	1.66	5.06	11.78	41.05	48.16	37.82	36.61	31.65	30.32
粤 北	Northern Region	1.11	6.36	16.87	35.23	47.34	64.20	64.11	51.37	42.06

13−11 各市建筑业企业房屋建筑施工面积

Floor Space of Buildings under Construction by Construction Enterprises by City

单位：万平方米 (10000 sq.m)

市别	City	2000	2005	2010	2015	2019	2020	2021	2022	2023
全省	**Provincial Total**	**16333.82**	**26886.00**	**33140.39**	**50461.59**	**84392.33**	**91890.63**	**105978.61**	**107372.69**	**117914.56**
广州	Guangzhou	3161.25	5311.14	7135.48	15163.70	32046.22	35123.20	39243.58	38614.01	36651.55
深圳	Shenzhen	1999.65	4800.07	5980.34	7682.65	15901.54	16948.79	20769.52	22419.28	37915.31
珠海	Zhuhai	733.57	625.51	877.39	1969.64	1826.83	2374.35	3972.99	2947.55	2909.09
汕头	Shantou	1477.16	2176.29	2381.63	4218.81	5976.68	5992.08	5896.33	5152.85	4182.02
佛山	Foshan	1763.57	2782.45	3335.62	2731.91	3240.81	5141.61	8638.64	9626.77	5398.52
韶关	Shaoguan	362.44	424.57	781.78	1063.36	1201.06	955.25	1149.05	1039.68	853.79
河源	Heyuan	79.80	294.41	218.83	453.06	647.47	567.99	639.97	529.74	768.39
梅州	Meizhou	273.56	776.23	1315.80	1632.23	2242.01	2017.01	1749.27	1461.86	1473.51
惠州	Huizhou	366.05	772.13	942.90	1162.39	1522.36	2529.10	3538.18	3177.93	4202.74
汕尾	Shanwei	127.42	114.77	175.11	118.61	284.54	250.63	217.73	211.80	169.84
东莞	Dongguan	1217.56	1234.98	733.44	1045.99	1517.73	2269.60	2845.68	3954.25	4898.09
中山	Zhongshan	400.99	945.60	601.02	470.87	654.55	919.87	1505.28	3138.46	2670.38
江门	Jiangmen	1329.02	1585.95	1640.13	2457.27	2401.03	2554.04	2173.77	2353.38	2779.52
阳江	Yangjiang	270.81	525.95	825.31	920.64	732.08	760.53	673.78	542.04	498.77
湛江	Zhanjiang	857.19	1399.47	1943.66	3361.23	5243.37	4840.73	4330.77	3951.85	4011.09
茂名	Maoming	734.43	1395.55	1770.78	3264.79	6021.54	5768.60	5792.18	5526.36	5926.80
肇庆	Zhaoqing	386.93	531.11	728.47	640.44	586.08	514.49	498.22	508.22	470.12
清远	Qingyuan	249.02	466.45	632.87	562.07	728.31	754.23	915.57	942.90	826.21
潮州	Chaozhou	217.15	206.67	373.12	597.67	507.10	586.08	565.22	532.41	548.61
揭阳	Jieyang	193.91	277.75	559.41	638.29	599.14	539.17	370.64	304.68	252.23
云浮	Yunfu	132.34	238.96	187.29	305.99	511.88	483.28	492.23	436.68	507.97
按经济区域分	By Region									
珠三角	Pearl River Delta	11358.59	18588.94	21974.80	33324.85	59697.16	68375.04	83185.86	86739.85	97895.33
粤东	Eastern Region	2015.64	2775.47	3489.27	5573.38	7367.46	7367.96	7049.92	6201.74	5152.70
粤西	Western Region	1862.43	3320.97	4539.75	7546.67	11996.99	11369.86	10796.73	10020.25	10436.67
粤北	Northern Region	1097.16	2200.62	3136.57	4016.70	5330.73	4777.76	4946.10	4410.86	4429.87

13-12 各市建筑业企业房屋建筑施工新开工面积

Floor Space of Buildings Started This Year by Construction Enterprises by City

单位：万平方米 (10000 sq.m)

市别	City	2000	2005	2010	2015	2019	2020	2021	2022	2023
全　省	**Provincial Total**	**6423.16**	**11879.41**	**14529.68**	**15802.23**	**26469.33**	**29175.62**	**30525.21**	**30605.05**	**30613.46**
广　州	Guangzhou	1153.97	2313.48	2995.47	3473.80	7929.47	9866.93	8959.73	9825.71	7818.49
深　圳	Shenzhen	791.59	1933.19	2443.02	1833.43	5229.78	5669.14	5361.42	8057.59	11066.66
珠　海	Zhuhai	236.23	298.50	476.92	687.28	535.43	804.74	1363.85	923.15	599.03
汕　头	Shantou	576.48	942.72	1129.55	1421.14	2051.94	1631.85	1606.44	826.09	670.45
佛　山	Foshan	943.98	1230.74	931.63	682.05	971.21	1709.02	3721.59	2179.74	1491.73
韶　关	Shaoguan	160.10	196.57	360.77	551.67	350.82	270.43	294.38	249.37	202.67
河　源	Heyuan	40.48	151.18	126.65	283.87	380.26	284.69	309.44	224.06	304.10
梅　州	Meizhou	124.38	323.52	655.48	541.14	996.67	652.37	572.65	288.56	291.11
惠　州	Huizhou	185.75	380.49	444.14	325.94	437.96	1248.76	1021.09	982.89	1266.73
汕　尾	Shanwei	84.60	50.11	122.07	55.53	65.10	86.18	84.32	94.52	67.45
东　莞	Dongguan		589.95	345.07	328.25	708.78	1120.94	1222.85	1396.47	1612.29
中　山	Zhongshan	200.38	503.83	287.82	212.48	248.78	410.65	592.32	1138.25	979.62
江　门	Jiangmen	668.83	631.55	833.99	928.62	690.12	528.54	664.31	905.35	910.96
阳　江	Yangjiang	354.20	249.55	369.70	326.31	225.77	150.17	123.05	158.77	102.49
湛　江	Zhanjiang	290.52	639.64	922.67	1299.72	2326.96	1726.68	1680.67	935.41	1033.61
茂　名	Maoming	138.54	600.67	848.76	1614.28	2212.01	1970.72	2080.79	1792.89	1598.33
肇　庆	Zhaoqing	115.93	248.72	298.32	337.26	260.08	178.64	159.06	171.20	181.15
清　远	Qingyuan	97.89	235.35	318.47	269.03	229.65	281.33	330.25	199.11	161.19
潮　州	Chaozhou	99.95	96.79	134.94	98.21	56.54	148.70	85.38	51.76	79.20
揭　阳	Jieyang	108.93	147.23	388.76	408.95	405.94	337.88	184.71	99.95	89.81
云　浮	Yunfu	50.43	115.64	95.48	123.25	156.06	97.25	106.91	104.21	86.40
按经济区域分	By Region									
珠三角	Pearl River Delta	4296.66	8130.45	9056.38	8809.12	17011.62	21537.36	23066.21	25580.37	25926.65
粤　东	Eastern Region	869.96	1236.84	1775.32	1983.84	2579.51	2204.62	1960.85	1072.32	906.91
粤　西	Western Region	783.26	1489.86	2141.14	3240.31	4764.74	3847.57	3884.52	2887.06	2734.44
粤　北	Northern Region	473.28	1022.26	1556.84	1768.97	2113.47	1586.07	1613.63	1065.30	1045.47

13-13 各市建筑业企业劳动生产率

Labor Productivity of Construction Enterprises by City

单位：元/人 (yuan/person)

市别	City	2000	2005	2010	2015	2019	2020	2021	2022	2023
全省	**Provincial Total**	**70137**	**132056**	**239595**	**382570**	**475704**	**493524**	**541866**	**576342**	**578372**
广州	Guangzhou	91086	204454	315033	552068	574751	573454	623186	681875	687401
深圳	Shenzhen	107549	183515	300502	345823	474309	484905	527352	575034	595171
珠海	Zhuhai	85936	162503	228342	385938	448816	415380	534504	486602	516860
汕头	Shantou	56057	99266	159623	296273	454946	498467	522338	544946	413347
佛山	Foshan	86795	115051	285616	586097	641674	714819	757575	766971	699333
韶关	Shaoguan	57743	83704	189045	313316	320481	315172	349030	360597	381252
河源	Heyuan	33395	82741	121383	280999	354389	334064	335343	331741	286836
梅州	Meizhou	44258	78866	141903	327465	405335	405034	480570	433026	413246
惠州	Huizhou	60374	119974	217933	406527	490286	559940	595367	543417	543356
汕尾	Shanwei	46496	51367	116927	211873	235210	329961	355300	351846	380791
东莞	Dongguan	64176	108136	218052	263489	410150	457503	484333	488335	569055
中山	Zhongshan	73597	119772	249502	333178	510957	534601	620575	576016	522711
江门	Jiangmen	49612	64418	147038	336038	425974	425780	469581	525951	420745
阳江	Yangjiang	59689	78360	123368	241168	293671	269880	315154	305884	330322
湛江	Zhanjiang	57160	98452	173336	315036	355164	405312	419062	523488	472651
茂名	Maoming	46992	90457	170522	396918	517968	572739	605481	640703	600928
肇庆	Zhaoqing	46380	107435	257334	385010	431525	522676	527241	543245	452453
清远	Qingyuan	42073	90596	158598	266337	310542	439627	384343	371505	403893
潮州	Chaozhou	57817	91838	146120	237822	197879	241983	251802	282466	316743
揭阳	Jieyang	40672	57368	131884	242247	275180	260243	257864	231980	249715
云浮	Yunfu	49773	74640	101721	204748	299633	268503	313760	338307	324130
按经济区域分	By Region									
珠三角	Pearl River Delta	82426	156714	283028	418380	510891	519647	573671	604975	614011
粤东	Eastern Region	53458	87357	149042	274993	374504	414196	440862	449102	375238
粤西	Western Region	55234	90945	160692	334707	412842	459920	490318	559067	523487
粤北	Northern Region	47252	81395	151686	298647	352562	363911	387438	375857	372188

主要统计指标解释

建筑业总产值 是以货币表现的建筑业企业在一定时期内生产的建筑业产品和服务的总和。建筑业总产值包括三部分内容：

⑴建筑工程产值：指列入建筑工程预算内的各种工程价值。

⑵安装工程产值：指设备安装工程价值以及将预制品部件安装成建筑工程产品的价值，但不包括被安装设备、被安装部品部件本身的价值。

⑶其他产值：建筑业总产值中除建筑工程、安装工程以外的产值。包括房屋构筑物修理产值、非标准设备制造产值、总包企业向分包企业收取的管理费以及不能明确划分的施工活动所完成的产值。

①房屋构筑物修理产值：指房屋和构筑物的修理所完成的价值，但不包括被修理房屋构筑物的本身价值和生产设备的修理价值。

②非标准设备制造产值：指加工制造没有定型的非标准生产设备的加工费和原材料价值以及附属加工厂为本企业承建工程制作的非标准设备的价值。

竣工产值 一般是以单位工程为对象，当该工程按照设计所规定的工程内容全部完成，达到了设计规定的交工条件，经有关部门检查验收鉴定合格的单位工程价值，即为竣工产值。

房屋施工面积 指在报告期内施工的全部房屋建筑面积，它包括本期新开工的房屋面积、上期跨入本期继续施工的房屋面积、上期停缓建在本期恢复施工的房屋面积、本期竣工的房屋面积以及本期施工后又停缓建的房屋面积。

房屋新开工面积 指报告期内本年新开工建设的房屋建筑面积，以单位工程为核算对象。不包括在上年开工跨入本年继续施工的房屋建筑面积和上年停缓建而在本年恢复施工的房屋建筑面积。房屋的开工应以房屋正式开始破土刨槽（地基处理或打永久桩）的日期为准。房屋新开工面积指整栋房屋的全部建筑面积，不能分割计算。

从事建筑业活动的就业人员平均人数 指建筑业企业(或单位)报告期实际拥有的、与建筑施工活动有关的人员的平均人数，包括参加本企业(或单位)建筑施工活动的非本企业(或单位)人员，但不包括企业内部社会服务性机构的人员以及由本企业支付工资但所从事的工作与本企业生产基本无关的人员。

年末就业人员中工程技术人员 指负担工程技术和工程技术管理工作，并具有工程技术工作能力的人员。

利润总额 指企业在生产经营过程中各种收入扣除各种耗费后的盈余，反映企业在报告期内实现的亏盈总额，包括营业利润、补贴收入、投资净收益和营业外收支净额。

工程结算税金及附加 指因从事建筑业生产活动，取得工程价款结算收入而按规定应该交纳的营业税、城市维护建设税等以及随同营业税金一并计算交纳的教育费附加等。

应交增值税 指按照税法规定，以销售货物、服务、无形资产、不动产或提供加工、修理修配劳务的增值额和货物进口金额为计税依据而课征的一种流转税。指按照税法规定，针对销售货物或提供加工、修理修配劳务以及进口货物实现的增值额，企业在报告期内应交纳的税金。填报本指标时，应按权责发生制核算企业本期应负担的增值税，按销项税额与进项税额之间的差额填写。如果一般纳税人企业进项税大于销项税，致使应交税金出现负数时，该项一律填零，不填负数。

应交增值税=销项税额-(进项税额-进项税额转出)-出口抵减内销产品应纳税额-减免税款+出口退税

利税总额=工程结算税金及附加+应交增值税+利润总额

建筑业全员劳动生产率=建筑业总产值÷计算建筑业劳动生产率的平均人数

Explanatory Notes on Main Statistical Indicators

Gross Output Value of Construction refers to the sum in monetary terms of construction products and services completed by construction enterprises during a given period of time. It includes:

(1) Output value of construction projects, which is the value of various projects covered by the project budgets.

(2) Output value of equipment installation projects refers to the value of the installation of equipment and the value of installing prefabricated parts into construction engineering products. It does not include the value of the equipment and the part itself.

(3) Other output values, which are output values other than output value of construction projects and output value of installation projects, including output value of house and building repair, output value of non-standard equipment manufacture, management expenses received by overall contractor enterprises from subcontractor enterprises and output value completed in unclassified construction activities.

①Output value of house and building repair is the value created through the repairs of houses and buildings, excluding the value of houses or buildings being repaired and the value of the repair of production equipment.

②Output value of non-standard equipment manufacture is the value of non-standard production equipment with unique specifications (including raw materials and manufacturing costs), and equipment manufactured by subsidiary workshops for construction projects contracted by construction enterprises.

Output Value Completed refers to the value of unit project completed, which has come up to the designed standards for putting into use and has been checked and accepted as qualified project by related departments.

Floor Space of Buildings under Construction refers to the floor space of buildings under construction during the reference period, including newly started buildings, buildings started earlier and continued into the reference period, buildings suspended in preceding periods but resumed during the reference period, buildings completed during the reference period, and buildings started and then suspended during the reference period.

Floor Space of Buildings Started This Year refers to the total floor space area of the buildings started in the year by real estate development companies. It excludes the buildings started in previous years and continued in the year, and the buildings suspended in previous years but restarted in the year. The start of a construction is defined by the date of ground breaking or pile driving. The floor space of the building includes that of the entire building.

Average Number of Persons for Labor Productivity Calculation of the Construction Industry refers to the average number of persons actually employed in the construction enterprises (units) and engaged in related activities of construction in the reference period, including non-staff personnel engaged in the construction activities of the enterprises (units), but excluding personnel employed in social service institutions of the enterprises and those receiving remunerations therefrom but engaged in activities basically irrelevant to the production of the enterprises.

Number of Engineering Technical Personnel Employed at the Year-end refers to personnel capable of and engaged in engineering technical work and related management.

Total Profits refer to the surplus of various incomes in the production and operation of the enterprises after deducting all expenses. This reflects the total profits or losses realized by the enterprises in the reference period, including profits from operation, income from subsidies, net investment earnings and net income from activities other than operations.

Taxes and Extra Charges on Project Settlement Accounts refer to business tax, city maintenance and construction tax and extra charges for education calculated and paid with business tax, which should be borne by the enterprises obtaining project settlement incomes from the production activities of construction.

Value added tax payable According to the tax law refers to, in order to sell goods, services, intangible assets, real estate or providing processing, repairs and replacement services appreciation and the amount of goods imported for a turnover tax assessed on profits realized from tax basis.In accordance with the provisions of the tax law, the enterprise shall pay the tax in the report period according to the value added value of goods sold or provided for processing, repair and repair services and import goods.When filling in this index, the value added tax shall be calculated according to the accrual basis of accrual basis, and the difference between the output tax and the input tax shall be filled in.If the average taxpayer enterprise enters into a tax more than the sales tax, resulting in the negative tax payable, the item will be filled to zero, and no negative value will be filled.

Value added tax payable = sales tax - (input tax - input tax) - export offset shall be tax payable - tax deduction Export tax rebate

Total Pre-tax Profits = Taxes and Extra Charges on Project Settlement Accounts +Value added tax payable + Total Profits

Overall Labor Productivity of Construction = Gross Output Value of Construction ÷ Average Number of Persons for Labor Productivity Calculation

十四、规模以上服务业

SERVICE ENTERPRISES ABOVE DESIGNATED SIZE

十四 规模以上服务业

简要说明

一、本篇资料主要反映规模以上服务业的基本情况、财务状况、从业人员及劳动报酬情况等。

二、本篇资料由广东省统计局服务业统计处整理、编辑。

三、据国家统计报表制度，2012 年规模以上服务业年报首次纳入“一套表”联网直报系统。规模以上服务业统计范围：辖区内年营业收入 2000 万元及以上服务业法人单位。包括：交通运输、仓储和邮政业，信息传输、软件和信息技术服务业，水利、环境和公共设施管理业，卫生。辖区内年营业收入 1000 万元及以上服务业法人单位。包括：租赁和商务服务业，科学研究和技术服务业，教育，以及物业管理、房地产中介服务、房地产租赁经营和其他房地产业。辖区内年营业收入 500 万元及以上服务业法人单位。包括：居民服务、修理和其他服务业，文化、体育和娱乐业，社会工作。调查方法为符合上述条件企业的全面调查。

14 Service Enterprises Above Designated Size

Brief Introduction

Ⅰ. This data in this chapter reflect the basic information, financial condition, employed persons, labor remuneration and ecommerce transactions of some service enterprises above designated size.

Ⅱ. Data of some service enterprises above designated size are prepared and edited by the Division of Service Statistics of Statistics Bureau of Guangdong Province.

Ⅲ. According to the National Statistical Reporting System, some service enterprises above designated size have been integrated into the "network reporting" system since 2012. Statistics coverage of some service enterprises above designated size: All the service legal entity with annual business revenue of 20 million yuan or above within the jurisdiction, including transport, storage and postal services, information transmission, software and information technology services, management of water conservancy, environment and public facilities, hygiene. All the service legal entity with annual business revenue of 10 million yuan or above within the jurisdiction, including leasing and business services, scientific research and technical services, education, estate management, real estate agent services, real estate intermediary services, own real estate business activities and other real estate,etc.All the service legal entity with annual business revenue of 5 million yuan or above within the jurisdiction, including households service, repair and other services, culture, sports and entertainment services, social work. Survey method is a comprehensive survey.

14-1 规模以上服务业企业财务指标
Main Financial Indicators of Service Enterprises above Designated Size

单位：亿元 (100 million yuan)

项　　目	Item	2020	2021	2022	2023	2023年比2022年增长(%) Growth Rate in 2023 Over 2022(%)
年初存货	**Inventory at Year-beginning**	**2747.27**	**3169.54**	**4200.69**		
期末资产负债	**Closing Balance**					
固定资产原价	Original Value of Fixed Assets	37402.65	39758.55	43348.30	43949.02	4.2
本年折旧	Depreciation Drawn in Current Year	1752.55	1872.23	1915.25		
资产总计	Total Assets	163089.18	182956.23	197977.09	204472.89	4.1
负债合计	Total Liabilities	90997.01	103752.20	114026.95	115352.59	3.4
所有者权益合计	Total Creditors'Equity	72092.17	79204.03	83949.85	89120.28	5.0
损益及分配	**Profits and Loss**					
营业收入	Business Revenue	35728.23	44419.85	46722.88	50205.08	8.1
营业成本	Business Costs	25677.66	32352.12	34881.30	36699.48	5.7
税金及附加	Tax and Extra Charges	226.93	269.94	273.73	326.21	18.6
销售费用	Sales Expenses	1973.81	2439.96	2486.28	2661.29	7.5
管理费用	Management Expenses	3817.65	4641.61	4710.37	4621.86	-2.1
财务费用	Financial Expenses	1029.83	1026.18	1105.68	1116.61	1.7
其中：利息收入	Interest Revenue	607.03	730.38	746.82		
利息支出	Interest Expense	1408.93	1539.25	1613.21		
投资收益(损失以“–”号记)	Investment Income(loss with “-”mark)	3009.38	2982.87	2995.11	3123.15	7.5
营业利润	Business Profits	5068.14	5339.28	4720.94	6293.51	35.6
利润总额	Total Profits	5180.83	5316.25	4802.85	6192.70	30.9
所得税费用	Income Taxes Payable	588.00	632.66	648.85	753.26	16.4
人工成本及增值税	**Labor Cost and Value-added Tax**					
应付职工薪酬(本年贷方累计发生额)	Total Wages Payable(Credit Accumulated Amount in this year)	7522.62	8898.92	9802.91	9794.79	2.0
应交增值税(本期累计发生额)	Value-added Tax Payable	766.86	960.12	1170.85	1139.45	8.8

注：增速按可比口径计算。
Note: The growth rates are calculated on comparable coverage.

14-2 规模以上服务业企业分行业主要指标（2023年）

单位：亿元

项目	Item	企业单位数(个) Number of Enterprises (unit)	营业收入 Business Revenue 总量 Total	2023年比2022年增长(%) Growth Rate in 2023 Over 2022(%)
全 省	**Provincial Total**	**35303**	**50205.08**	**8.1**
按经济类型分	Grouped by Ownership			
内资企业	Domestic-funded Enterprises	32568	41618.30	7.3
#国有企业	State-owned Enterprises	803	1915.02	14.2
集体企业	Collective-owned Enterprises	640	265.74	6.8
有限责任公司	Limited Liability Corporations	8850	17282.15	15.4
私营企业	Private Enterprises	20640	17337.53	-2.4
港澳台商投资企业	Enterprises with Investment from Hong Kong, Macao and Taiwan	1843	6461.38	12.8
外商投资企业	Enterprises with Foreign Investment	892	2125.41	10.7
按行业分	Grouped by Sector			
交通运输、仓储和邮政业	Transport, Storage and Postal Services	5774	12447.84	6.3
铁路运输业	Railway Transport Service	21	1322.64	43.4
#铁路旅客运输	Railway Passenger Transport	9	1275.02	44.7
铁路货物运输	Railway Freight Transport	11	44.20	22.2
道路运输业	Road Transport Services	1891	2491.91	7.8
#城市公共交通运输	Urban Public Transport	156	478.21	25.9
公路旅客运输	Highway Passenger Transport	114	57.34	3.7
道路货物运输	Road Freight Transport	1467	1185.71	-1.2
水上运输业	Waterway Transport Service	283	939.49	4.6
#水上旅客运输	Waterway Passenger Transport	21	19.21	197.8
水上货物运输	Waterway Freight Transport	156	611.45	5.2
航空运输业	Air Transport Service	38	1874.57	66.2
#航空客货运输	Air Passenger and Freight Transport	15	1714.93	69.4
管道运输业	Pipeline Transport Service	5	38.50	0.6
多式联运和运输代理业	Multimodal Transport and Transport Agency Industry	2540	3785.99	-16.0
#运输代理业	Transportation Agency	2492	3479.22	-17.4
装卸搬运和仓储业	Handling and Storage	671	700.14	6.9
邮政业	Postal Service	325	1294.60	4.1
#快递服务	Express Service	282	1023.41	1.5
信息传输、软件和信息技术服务业	Information Transmission, Software and Information Technology Services	5515	18398.54	11.4
电信、广播电视和卫星传输服务	Telecommunications, Broadcasting Television and Satellite Transmission Services	314	2475.54	4.7
#电信	Telecommunications	290	2375.60	4.4
互联网和相关服务	Internet and Related Services	908	6016.99	9.7
#互联网信息服务	Internet Information Services	397	4028.91	12.7
软件和信息技术服务业	Software and Information Technology Services	4293	9906.01	14.4
#软件开发	Software Development	2515	5663.98	8.9
信息系统集成和物联网技术服务	Information System Integration and Internet of Things Technology Services	641	1001.69	10.2
信息技术咨询服务	Information Technology Consulting Services	444	1962.94	50.6
房地产业(不含房地产开发经营)	Realty Industry	5783	3939.40	6.7
#物业管理业	Property Management Industry	2379	2134.96	7.6
房地产中介服务业	Real Estate Agent Services	567	387.59	3.2

Main Indicators of Service Enterprises above Designated Size by Sector(2023)

(100 million yuan)

营业成本 Business Costs		税金及附加 Tax and Extra Charges		销售费用 Selling Expenses		管理费用 Management Expenses	
总量 Total	2023年比2022年增长(%) Growth Rate in 2023 Over 2022(%)	总量 Total	2023年比2022年增长(%) Growth Rate in 2023 Over 2022(%)	总量 Total	2023年比2022年增长(%) Growth Rate in 2023 Over 2022(%)	总量 Total	2023年比2022年增长(%) Growth Rate in 2023 Over 2022(%)
36699.48	**5.7**	**326.21**	**18.6**	**2661.29**	**7.5**	**4621.86**	**-2.1**
32075.56	6.0	264.65	18.7	1873.20	-4.7	3755.53	-2.3
1587.43	16.9	15.35	24.5	38.29	14.2	168.58	-1.8
77.70	5.1	6.56	9.6	2.60	-14.7	55.28	10.3
13497.65	13.9	136.76	28.0	641.54	0.4	1256.74	-1.8
13238.03	-3.2	76.65	7.6	974.50	-10.4	1780.16	-3.1
3279.25	1.3	44.58	21.7	681.22	65.1	607.42	-4.0
1344.67	9.0	16.97	10.0	106.87	10.0	258.91	4.8
11199.57	0.6	44.87	37.6	191.23	4.9	639.00	0.3
1192.59	15.7	1.80	195.8	0.39	-58.6	24.30	16.9
1143.00	15.9	1.63	255.1	0.35	-62.2	22.04	18.7
46.42	17.5	0.17	15.2	0.03	109.9	2.08	1.7
2260.89	2.6	22.42	46.9	31.92	-14.3	164.04	-2.5
688.53	3.1	15.46	78.7	4.30	-24.0	46.26	-6.1
58.69	-6.4	0.58	43.1	0.46	-25.6	11.60	-8.6
1061.34	-1.0	2.28	-6.8	25.65	-12.2	75.46	-2.0
759.81	7.1	3.42	10.8	4.36	-5.1	64.33	11.7
18.88	37.8	0.06	48.7	0.69	68.5	1.87	5.7
541.38	8.6	1.09	-2.3	2.50	-6.0	34.89	20.8
1755.23	28.5	5.83	77.8	66.06	40.3	48.33	1.5
1619.19	31.2	3.68	96.4	64.11	41.7	39.79	1.2
19.78	7.9	0.13	-5.8	0.05	-6.3	1.67	20.3
3470.78	-16.6	2.90	13.1	57.37	-8.4	191.81	-2.1
3179.78	-18.1	2.50	9.4	54.17	-8.1	179.41	-2.2
558.53	10.0	6.36	10.5	18.02	4.2	60.60	-2.9
1181.96	3.7	2.00	4.1	13.07	5.2	83.91	1.0
942.40	1.5	0.71	5.8	11.74	3.7	59.96	-0.4
11395.33	9.9	77.84	18.2	1670.85	11.7	1398.20	-4.5
1692.49	5.0	8.73	18.7	180.40	-2.1	117.62	2.2
1618.26	4.7	8.56	18.9	173.85	-2.6	103.92	2.5
3556.30	2.7	36.52	32.7	524.77	-11.8	409.50	-5.2
2398.46	1.5	31.91	34.1	166.67	-3.4	200.98	-12.9
6146.54	16.2	32.60	5.2	965.68	34.7	871.08	-4.9
2913.08	4.2	21.53	11.2	756.00	44.5	521.44	-7.1
758.32	12.4	3.25	9.8	41.43	9.3	83.11	3.0
1658.98	63.3	3.51	-6.6	59.76	8.4	83.44	-8.6
2762.69	7.9	80.35	6.7	111.84	-5.3	577.14	-3.2
1677.61	8.9	16.57	-6.0	37.83	-7.7	236.33	-2.3
300.38	4.4	1.53	5.5	33.18	-10.7	42.92	-26.4

14-2 续表 1

单位：亿元

项　　目	Item	财务费用 Financial Expenses	
		总量 Total	2023年比2022年增长(%) Growth Rate in 2023 Over 2022(%)
全　省	**Provincial Total**	**1116.61**	**1.7**
按经济类型分	Grouped by Ownership		
内资企业	Domestic-funded Enterprises	1044.90	3.7
#国有企业	State-owned Enterprises	61.69	7.5
集体企业	Collective-owned Enterprises	2.66	-0.9
有限责任公司	Limited Liability Corporations	663.44	9.9
私营企业	Private Enterprises	169.95	3.6
港澳台商投资企业	Enterprises with Investment from Hong Kong,Macao and Taiwan	33.09	-39.4
外商投资企业	Enterprises with Foreign Investment	38.62	7.6
按行业分	Grouped by Sector		
交通运输、仓储和邮政业	Transport, Storage and Postal Services	478.01	0.9
铁路运输业	Railway Transport Service	36.37	0.6
#铁路旅客运输	Railway Passenger Transport	29.90	2.6
铁路货物运输	Railway Freight Transport	6.47	-7.5
道路运输业	Road Transport Services	280.84	3.5
#城市公共交通运输	Urban Public Transport	106.99	12.1
公路旅客运输	Highway Passenger Transport	2.45	-15.5
道路货物运输	Road Freight Transport	6.03	-3.6
水上运输业	Waterway Transport Service	29.96	198.9
#水上旅客运输	Waterway Passenger Transport	1.17	-12.7
水上货物运输	Waterway Freight Transport	23.95	832.6
航空运输业	Air Transport Service	85.67	-25.8
#航空客货运输	Air passenger and freight Transport	79.10	-27.4
管道运输业	Pipeline Transport Service	3.86	2.5
多式联运和运输代理业	Multimodal Transport and Transport Agency Industry	7.43	222.0
#运输代理业	Transportation Agency	6.01	721.5
装卸搬运和仓储业	Handling and Storage	27.73	-1.8
邮政业	Postal Service	6.15	-4.0
#快递服务	Express Service	4.39	2.9
信息传输、软件和信息技术服务业	Information Transmission, Software and Information Technology Services	-66.48	7.4
电信、广播电视和卫星传输服务	Telecommunications, Broadcasting Television and Satellite Transmission Services	-7.78	22.0
#电信	Telecommunications	-9.22	17.9
互联网和相关服务	Internet and Related Services	-27.67	32.6
#互联网信息服务	Internet Information Services	-33.75	29.8
软件和信息技术服务业	Software and Information Technology Services	-31.02	-49.2
#软件开发	Software Development	-29.16	-25.6
信息系统集成和物联网技术服务	Information System Integration and Internet of Things Technology Services	0.31	-51.3
信息技术咨询服务	Information Technology Consulting services	-1.28	-292.1
房地产业(不含房地产开发经营)	Realty Industry	248.27	-19.0
#物业管理业	Property Management Industry	38.88	-8.4
房地产中介服务业	Real Estate Agent Services	-3.78	-986.9

14-2 1 continued

(100 million yuan)

利润总额 Total Profits		所得税费用 Income Taxes Payable		应付职工薪酬 Total Wages Payable		应交增值税 Value-added Taxes Payable		期末用工人数 (万人) Total number of employed persons at the year-end (10000 persons)
总量 Total	2023年比2022年增长(%) Growth Rate in 2023 Over 2022(%)	总量 Total	2023年比2022年增长(%) Growth Rate in 2023 Over 2022(%)	总量 Total	2023年比2022年增长(%) Growth Rate in 2023 Over 2022(%)	总量 Total	2023年比2022年增长(%) Growth Rate in 2023 Over 2022(%)	
6192.70	**30.9**	**753.26**	**16.4**	**9794.79**	**2.0**	**1139.45**	**8.8**	**626.75**
4135.46	31.6	482.64	8.5	7990.02	1.5	918.62	9.7	562.12
353.38	32.3	33.61	24.0	477.85	3.5	51.34	22.1	27.89
130.06	11.7	3.96	38.1	46.35	5.1	6.62	8.4	5.89
1869.55	49.9	259.82	17.0	3201.13	2.3	407.18	12.2	198.97
686.47	-12.9	118.04	-4.2	3122.96	-0.6	353.70	6.0	271.24
1671.96	39.1	206.60	38.4	1222.93	4.0	174.91	7.2	43.14
385.27	-0.2	64.02	20.1	581.85	5.1	45.92	-1.9	21.48
473.23	395.7	125.91	13.3	1772.65	0.6	177.23	12.1	103.40
58.00	147.2	10.63	3674.0	257.55	9.3	74.35	210.8	13.77
67.45	158.1	10.11	13584.5	247.63	9.3	70.52	337.9	13.22
-9.52	-39.9	0.51	147.0	9.65	8.7	3.83	-50.6	0.54
121.87	131.6	46.48	6.8	520.69	-8.3	50.44	-39.3	38.37
-71.71	29.4	0.65	-79.5	291.09	-13.0	7.68	-58.4	18.05
3.81	182.8	0.72	-35.2	28.96	-5.8	1.90	70.0	3.21
15.94	8.3	4.79	-10.8	113.33	-4.1	16.96	-9.9	11.14
109.64	-0.2	21.80	33.9	128.32	0.7	7.55	-23.5	4.54
-2.25	75.5	-0.63	-330.3	6.23	12.1	0.15	-29.3	0.29
18.73	-22.1	4.40	496.5	63.72	-3.1	3.86	20.6	1.70
-21.08	94.5	8.18	-6.0	343.28	9.5	12.17	105.5	11.42
-37.08	89.7	4.49	-70.4	298.68	9.4	8.03	193.2	9.70
13.15	-22.7	3.23	-26.8	3.55	15.4	0.23	40.2	0.10
67.27	-39.0	14.20	-26.3	270.06	-1.3	14.34		18.72
67.68	-38.1	13.66	-27.2	207.15	2.3	12.01	-6.5	13.96
64.14	97.4	14.21	8.4	98.09	-1.6	12.85	-4.7	7.69
60.24	120.8	7.19	30.1	151.11	6.5	5.31	-28.0	8.79
56.51	94.0	7.51	14.5	79.32	0.9	4.38	-28.3	5.63
2705.71	27.7	345.25	18.0	3028.72	2.2	439.54	9.1	106.60
495.44	-2.3	108.21	1.5	304.75	3.8	60.47	-9.8	11.26
492.17	-2.0	108.50	1.7	277.41	4.1	59.45	-10.9	9.83
1227.31	57.3	156.27	53.1	626.17	1.2	150.44	31.1	18.09
1111.82	54.1	144.74	58.0	386.21	1.3	116.92	36.2	6.52
982.95	18.2	80.76	-3.8	2097.81	2.3	228.63	3.5	77.25
761.33	17.7	55.04	-1.9	1366.66	2.2	154.90	2.6	45.22
61.82	-1.0	6.57	-12.2	184.11	7.5	21.54	7.1	8.42
76.14	32.9	6.52	-19.3	217.48	0.7	20.96	11.8	9.51
439.26	41.4	89.81	40.7	945.44	-0.2	144.45	6.3	97.13
117.70	-15.8	35.41	3.4	711.20	4.0	68.47	3.5	83.48
89.87	110.8	7.68	3219.8	85.63	-25.8	13.31	10.7	4.48

14−2 续表 2

单位：亿元

项　　目	Item	企业单位数(个) Number of Enterprises (unit)	营业收入 Business Revenue 总量 Total	2023年比2022年增长(%) Growth Rate in 2023 Over 2022(%)
租赁和商务服务业	Leasing and Business Services	9282	8623.71	8.2
租赁业	Leasing	642	289.62	-2.4
#机械设备经营租赁	Machinery Equipment Operating Leasing	627	277.11	-1.7
商务服务业	Business Services	8640	8334.08	8.6
#组织管理服务	Organizational Management Services	1550	1431.67	9.1
咨询与调查	Consultation and Investigation	1189	756.92	-3.5
广告业	Advertising	1140	1668.41	7.6
其他商务服务	Other Business Services	732	693.83	53.1
科学研究和技术服务业	Scientific Research and Technical Services	4044	3822.82	1.1
研究和试验发展	Research and Experimental Development	403	450.01	24.5
#工程和技术研究和试验发展	Engineering and Technology Research and Experimental Development	244	327.74	25.0
专业技术服务业	Professional Technical Services	3065	2933.18	-2.6
科技推广和应用服务业	Services of Science and Technology Exchanges and Promotion	576	439.63	7.7
水利环境和公共设施管理业	Management of Water Conservancy, Environment and Public Facilities	585	641.51	1.3
水利管理业	Management of Water Conservancy	21	28.40	13.5
生态保护和环境治理业	Ecological Protection and Environmental Treatment	169	123.90	-7.7
#环境治理业	Environmental Treatment	167	120.95	-8.9
公共设施管理业	Management of Public Facilities	384	350.52	-0.1
土地管理业	Management of Land	11	138.69	12.6
居民服务、修理和其他服务业	Households' service, Repair and Other Services	1411	491.27	7.9
居民服务业	Services to Households	350	139.76	18.4
机动车、电子产品和日用产品修理业	Motor Vehicle, Electronic Products and Consumer Products repair	422	126.79	3.8
#汽车、摩托车等修理与维护	Automobile, Motorcycle and Others Repair and Maintenance	287	56.03	1.8
其他服务业	Other Services	639	224.72	4.6
教育	Education	841	431.20	8.9
#中等教育	Secondary Education	175	136.10	10.5
高等教育	Higher Education	14	25.01	24.1
卫生和社会工作	Health and Social Work	767	708.77	-9.2
卫生	Health	651	684.97	-9.3
#医院	Hospital	392	478.34	10.1
基层医疗卫生服务	Primary Health Care Services	117	64.69	14.2
社会工作	Social Work	116	23.81	-6.6
文化、体育和娱乐业	Culture, Sports and Entertainment	1301	700.02	38.6
新闻和出版业	News and Publication	99	107.66	6.6
#出版业	Publication	91	101.28	6.3
广播、电视、电影和影视录音制作业	Production of Radio, Television, Film and Video Recording	411	211.82	43.9
文化艺术业	Culture and Arts	156	48.50	87.6
体育	Sports	212	92.69	5.1
娱乐业	Entertainment	423	239.35	67.4

14-2 2 continued

(100 million yuan)

营业成本 Business Costs		税金及附加 Tax and Extra Charges		销售费用 Selling Expenses		管理费用 Management Expenses	
总量 Total	2023年比2022年增长(%) Growth Rate in 2023 Over 2022(%)	总量 Total	2023年比2022年增长(%) Growth Rate in 2023 Over 2022(%)	总量 Total	2023年比2022年增长(%) Growth Rate in 2023 Over 2022(%)	总量 Total	2023年比2022年增长(%) Growth Rate in 2023 Over 2022(%)
6523.23	9.4	64.77	10.6	314.61	-1.5	1049.22	-3.1
221.21	-0.6	1.21	6.8	19.06	-5.0	34.97	-2.6
212.72	0.4	1.06	-5.4	16.90	-2.8	34.01	-2.2
6302.02	9.8	63.56	10.7	295.55	-1.3	1014.25	-3.1
677.58	8.1	29.38	15.9	27.52	4.4	373.59	1.8
421.82	-1.9	3.25	2.4	80.67	-3.2	187.21	-5.3
1528.30	8.3	5.46	0.8	53.81	8.7	62.76	-5.2
575.59	63.8	1.78	20.2	31.53	15.8	52.83	-0.2
2775.13	0.9	15.62	1.7	153.83	1.8	483.13	0.9
296.04	32.9	1.92	5.0	23.25	11.7	50.70	8.2
233.11	32.6	1.46	3.7	7.69	16.4	31.18	9.3
2160.14	-4.5	11.92	0.1	101.34	-1.5	364.52	-0.7
318.95	20.8	1.78	10.3	29.25	6.4	67.91	5.1
455.94	-0.1	30.36	75.7	12.77	-5.8	56.66	-4.8
18.96	11.4	0.23	55.4	0.10	-29.2	4.17	-8.9
91.71	-5.3	0.64	8.8	2.77	-10.4	14.18	-6.9
90.15	-5.6	0.61	8.0	2.58	-13.7	13.92	-6.8
274.65	-0.6	1.46	21.4	5.43	-12.9	34.68	-2.8
70.62	6.6	28.03	82.7	4.48	9.4	3.63	-9.7
355.98	6.9	1.97	-0.7	43.60	7.0	73.40	0.3
83.09	13.4	0.42	0.5	27.11	23.6	24.09	1.0
98.82	4.8	0.41	5.2	10.10	-14.6	14.82	2.5
41.57	3.0	0.16	-2.5	4.63	-20.3	9.38	7.7
174.08	5.1	1.14	-3.0	6.39	-8.7	34.49	-1.1
270.52	9.7	0.81	22.0	30.35	0.1	107.86	0.7
98.57	11.7	0.08	35.3	0.92	23.6	35.40	4.3
16.84	19.8	0.05	-8.8	0.14	8.0	5.21	23.0
489.32	-10.1	1.03	18.3	76.63	-1.5	111.68	3.3
471.11	-10.2	1.01	18.1	75.86	-1.4	105.97	4.2
343.50	7.3	0.85	26.5	43.13	12.4	78.54	7.4
40.81	11.2	0.02	25.9	11.90	13.5	10.62	9.2
18.21	-8.1	0.02	31.6	0.77	-6.4	5.71	-10.3
471.76	27.5	8.58	30.4	55.57	21.2	125.58	7.4
77.42	5.7	1.21	-2.4	6.62	31.3	24.41	14.2
72.38	5.0	0.93	-4.1	6.42	28.0	21.22	15.8
169.82	44.2	1.76	15.1	11.41	7.7	20.58	-0.5
37.75	91.8	0.28	87.3	5.05	112.1	8.27	-3.8
46.58	4.6	3.17	7.8	12.23	-5.2	27.93	-5.6
140.20	22.3	2.16	199.8	20.26	35.7	44.40	21.1

14-2 续表 3

单位：亿元

项　　目	item	财务费用 Financial Expenses	
		总量 Total	2023年比2022年增长(%) Growth Rate in 2023 Over 2022(%)
租赁和商务服务业	Leasing and Business Services	377.08	21.2
租赁业	Leasing	10.52	-9.6
#机械设备经营租赁	Machinery Equipment Operating Leasing	10.44	-9.7
商务服务业	Business Services	366.56	22.4
#组织管理服务	Organizational Management Services	282.79	27.4
咨询与调查	Consultation and Investigation	18.24	38.9
广告业	Advertising	-0.58	64.2
其他商务服务业	Other Business Services	5.87	339.0
科学研究和技术服务业	Scientific Research and Technical Services	18.43	-33.9
研究和试验发展	Research and Experimental Development	-0.16	-278.4
#工程和技术研究和试验发展	Engineering and Technology Research and Experimental Development	-1.56	-12.1
专业技术服务业	Professional Technical Services	6.43	-36.8
科技推广和应用服务业	Services of Science and Technology Exchanges and Promotion	12.16	-31.0
水利环境和公共设施管理业	Management of Water Conservancy, Environment and Public Facilities	31.84	39.2
水利管理业	Management of Water Conservancy	5.43	50.1
生态保护和环境治理业	Ecological Protection and Environmental Treatment	3.28	-9.9
#环境治理业	Environmental Treatment	3.21	-9.4
公共设施管理业	Management of Public Facilities	13.56	12.6
土地管理业	Management of Land	9.57	168.1
居民服务、修理和其他服务业	Households' service, Repair and Other Services	4.26	29.8
居民服务业	Services to Households	1.99	32.0
机动车、电子产品和日用产品修理业	Motor Vehicle, Electronic Products and Consumer Products repair	0.75	35.9
#汽车、摩托车等修理与维护	Automobile, Motorcycle and Others Repair and Maintenance	0.35	10.3
其他服务业	Other Services	1.52	24.2
教育	Education	6.79	-17.3
#中等教育	Secondary Education	2.86	-4.3
高等教育	Higher Education	1.06	-6.5
卫生和社会工作	Health and Social Work	10.14	-2.3
卫生	Health	9.62	-2.9
#医院	Hospital	7.36	-6.4
基层医疗卫生服务	Primary Health Care Services	0.51	15.3
社会工作	Social Work	0.52	10.0
文化、体育和娱乐业	Culture, Sports and Entertainment	8.27	30.30
新闻和出版业	News and Publication	-1.40	8.80
#出版业	Publication	-1.32	-19.90
广播、电视、电影和影视录音制作业	Production of Radio, Television, Film and Video Recording	4.36	-11.40
文化艺术业	Culture and Arts	0.42	211.30
体育	Sports	3.85	-10.10
娱乐业	Entertainment	1.05	172.70

14-2 3 continued

(100 million yuan)

利润总额 Total Profits		所得税费用 Income Taxes Payable		应付职工薪酬 Total Wages Payable		应交增值税 Value-added Tax Payable		期末用工人数（万人） Total number of employed persons at the year-end (10000 persons)
总量 Total	2023年比2022年增长(%) Growth Rate in 2023 Over 2022(%)	总量 Total	2023年比2022年增长(%) Growth Rate in 2023 Over 2022(%)	总量 Total	2023年比2022年增长(%) Growth Rate in 2023 Over 2022(%)	总量 Total	2023年比2022年增长(%) Growth Rate in 2023 Over 2022(%)	
2074.51	3.8	113.33	6.8	2077.95	4.9	205.23	8.3	182.38
4.07	-61.6	3.79	-20.3	37.30	-5.2	9.36	4.6	2.97
3.85	-65.6	3.65	-23.2	35.54	-3.6	8.91	3.3	2.88
2070.44	4.1	109.54	8.1	2040.65	5.1	195.88	8.5	179.41
1596.84	1.4	42.30	6.0	339.79	4.0	53.86	6.8	18.12
69.95	-31.3	10.23	13.8	266.43	-6.8	23.65	3.5	14.19
23.16	-4.1	5.29	-28.4	109.34	-18.9	11.17	25.9	4.27
48.21	41.2	1.75	-82.1	71.48	7.0	10.33	13.1	5.78
301.65	-0.8	34.83	-16.7	1069.70	0.2	111.79	5.6	50.44
41.98	-19.7	7.09	-8.8	99.54	6.6	8.87	-1.1	3.47
44.38	-6.1	5.67	-4.6	63.75	8.5	5.93	-10.6	2.05
237.97	-0.6	22.67	-21.4	852.16	-0.9	84.63	-3.3	42.32
21.70	75.2	5.06	-1.9	118.00	3.2	18.29	95.2	4.65
101.15	38.0	17.66	41.0	140.82	0.5	22.00	4.2	18.05
7.30	552.4	0.26	-32.7	6.66	1.3	1.07	2.5	0.33
27.07	81.1	5.92	229.0	20.12	-4.8	2.79	-7.4	1.27
9.38	-33.1	1.50	-11.6	19.26	-5.5	2.67	-8.9	1.20
35.92	37.1	5.82	13.5	111.33	1.5	10.79	-6.5	16.36
30.87	-0.5	5.67	8.6	2.70	1.0	7.35	33.2	0.09
10.03	165.7	3.71	38.1	192.89	4.5	15.39	7.9	30.65
1.61	141.0	1.81	101.5	46.35	5.0	2.42	-1.8	4.97
1.62	317.7	0.51	-33.8	23.29	-1.0	4.16	10.7	2.18
-0.04	76.4	0.24	-32.3	10.03	-9.9	1.77	9.4	1.07
6.80	-7.1	1.39	36.0	123.24	5.3	8.82	9.5	23.50
15.41	2779.4	4.34	33.0	185.69	6.6	5.59	15.6	12.95
-0.62	65.6	0.66	95.5	65.90	12.9	0.12	-35.6	4.50
1.90	111.5	0.34	207.5	8.30	10.5	0.25	135.1	0.55
9.68	-57.9	6.27	-33.3	227.10	-3.3	2.49	61.8	15.45
10.58	-55.7	6.21	-33.7	214.29	-2.9	2.36	70.2	13.50
3.77	141.0	4.33	26.3	161.99	7.9	1.21	254.5	10.36
0.80	201.1	0.36	68.8	17.10	15.7	0.39	114.8	1.16
-0.91	4.5	0.06	94.4	12.80	-8.8	0.13	-13.8	1.95
62.07	7.5	12.17	207.7	153.84	6.5	15.73	16.0	9.70
19.20	10.8	2.16	21.3	36.75	2.7	3.12	26.4	1.27
19.06	12.8	2.09	17.7	32.51	2.8	2.91	28.6	1.12
6.58	205.5	1.55	54.4	27.22	0.4	2.98	-10.4	1.72
0.63	148.9	0.27	17.3	10.70	15.2	0.94	14.0	0.77
2.09	160.5	1.49	34.0	32.29	-0.6	3.10	-22.8	2.59
33.57	-34.6	6.71	4175.3	46.88	17.8	5.59	91.7	3.35

14−3 规模以上服务业企业分行业营业收入

Business Revenue of Service Enterprises above Designated Size by Sector

单位：亿元 (100 million yuan)

项　目	Item	营业收入 Business Revenue 2018	2019	2020
全　省	**Provincial Total**	**28553.34**	**33516.56**	**35728.23**
按行业分	Grouped by Sector			
交通运输、仓储和邮政业	Traffic, Transport, Storage and Post	8264.88	8708.66	8704.79
信息传输、软件和信息技术服务业	Information Transfer, Software and Information Technology Services	8522.24	10665.72	12482.65
房地产业(不含房地产开发经营)	Realty Industry	2002.50	2598.26	3016.96
租赁和商务服务业	Tenancy and Business Services	5351.76	6195.57	6096.01
科学研究和技术服务业	Scientific Research and Technical Service	2579.68	3084.71	3293.50
水利、环境和公共设施管理业	Management of Water Conservancy, Environment and Public Facilities	380.08	460.72	516.40
居民服务、修理和其他服务业	Resident Services, Repair and other Services	292.23	369.21	372.62
教育	Education	333.38	398.25	405.97
卫生和社会工作	Health and Social Work	324.20	406.93	428.23
文化、体育和娱乐业	Culture, Sports and Entertainment	502.38	628.51	411.09

14−3 续表 continued

单位：亿元 (100 million yuan)

项　目	Item	营业收入 Business Revenue 2021	2022	2023
全　省	**Provincial Total**	**44419.85**	**46722.88**	**50205.08**
按行业分	Grouped by Sector			
交通运输、仓储和邮政业	Traffic, Transport, Storage and Post	11391.18	11679.85	12447.84
信息传输、软件和信息技术服务业	Information Transfer, Software and Information Technology Services	15107.78	16580.39	18398.54
房地产业(不含房地产开发经营)	Realty Industry	3577.55	3702.70	3939.40
租赁和商务服务业	Tenancy and Business Services	7819.10	8137.07	8623.71
科学研究和技术服务业	Scientific Research and Technical Service	3840.64	3755.05	3822.82
水利、环境和公共设施管理业	Management of Water Conservancy, Environment and Public Facilities	643.37	666.93	641.51
居民服务、修理和其他服务业	Resident Services, Repair and other Services	445.97	472.21	491.27
教育	Education	471.35	437.71	431.20
卫生和社会工作	Health and Social Work	565.79	780.36	708.77
文化、体育和娱乐业	Culture, Sports and Entertainment	557.12	510.61	700.02

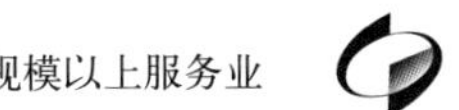

14-4 规模以上服务业企业分行业营业利润

Business Profits of Service Enterprises above Designated Size by Sector

单位：亿元 (100 million yuan)

项　　目	Item	营业利润 Business Profits 2018	2019	2020
全　省	**Provincial Total**	**4450.17**	**5035.18**	**5068.14**
按行业分	Grouped by Sector			
交通运输、仓储和邮政业	Traffic, Transport, Storage and Post	490.76	591.81	209.63
信息传输、软件和信息技术服务业	Information Transfer, Software and Information Technology Services	1628.82	1985.38	2109.54
房地产业(不含房地产开发经营)	Realty Industry	423.91	337.80	527.37
租赁和商务服务业	Tenancy and Business Services	1543.85	1760.50	1882.80
科学研究和技术服务业	Scientific Research and Technical Service	294.48	251.66	321.02
水利、环境和公共设施管理业	Management of Water Conservancy, Environment and Public Facilities	44.28	39.92	51.95
居民服务、修理和其他服务业	Resident Services, Repair and other Services	13.76	14.30	11.17
教育	Education	5.42	0.04	-10.18
卫生和社会工作	Health and Social Work	10.26	8.83	8.32
文化、体育和娱乐业	Culture, Sports and Entertainment	-5.37	44.94	-43.49

14-4 续表 continued

单位：亿元 (100 million yuan)

项　　目	Item	营业利润 Business Profits 2021	2022	2023
全　省	**Provincial Total**	**5339.28**	**4720.94**	**6293.51**
按行业分	Grouped by Sector			
交通运输、仓储和邮政业	Traffic, Transport, Storage and Post	282.52	-154.85	448.55
信息传输、软件和信息技术服务业	Information Transfer, Software and Information Technology Services	2025.74	2150.01	2866.10
房地产业(不含房地产开发经营)	Realty Industry	475.32	260.71	407.35
租赁和商务服务业	Tenancy and Business Services	2146.27	2015.59	2089.79
科学研究和技术服务业	Scientific Research and Technical Service	313.00	288.62	297.41
水利、环境和公共设施管理业	Management of Water Conservancy, Environment and Public Facilities	58.48	72.56	84.11
居民服务、修理和其他服务业	Resident Services, Repair and other Services	9.51	2.85	9.78
教育	Education	-3.24	6.07	14.29
卫生和社会工作	Health and Social Work	20.67	29.00	16.06
文化、体育和娱乐业	Culture, Sports and Entertainment	11.02	50.38	60.07

14-5 规模以上服务业企业分行业应付职工薪酬

Total Wages Payable of Service Enterprises above Designated Size by Sector

单位：亿元 (100 million yuan)

项　　目	Item	应付职工薪酬 Total Wages Payable		
		2018	2019	2020
全　省	**Provincial Total**	**5919.15**	**6883.07**	**7522.62**
按行业分	Grouped by Sector			
交通运输、仓储和邮政业	Traffic, Transport, Storage and Post	1585.44	1507.99	1455.49
信息传输、软件和信息技术服务业	Information Transfer, Software and Information Technology Services	1439.38	1844.25	2151.83
房地产业(不含房地产开发经营)	Realty Industry	645.54	737.74	836.82
租赁和商务服务业	Tenancy and Business Services	1066.75	1344.03	1505.35
科学研究和技术服务业	Scientific Research and Technical Service	636.47	762.46	853.26
水利、环境和公共设施管理业	Management of Water Conservancy, Environment and Public Facilities	68.45	86.14	104.55
居民服务、修理和其他服务业	Resident Services, Repair and other Services	108.59	135.47	152.26
教育	Education	148.68	175.39	188.88
卫生和社会工作	Health and Social Work	95.77	122.33	134.60
文化、体育和娱乐业	Culture, Sports and Entertainment	124.09	167.27	139.58

14-5 续表 continued

单位：亿元 (100 million yuan)

项　　目	Item	应付职工薪酬 Total Wages Payable		
		2021	2022	2023
全　省	**Provincial Total**	**8898.92**	**9802.91**	**9794.79**
按行业分	Grouped by Sector			
交通运输、仓储和邮政业	Traffic, Transport, Storage and Post	1622.86	1776.47	1772.65
信息传输、软件和信息技术服务业	Information Transfer, Software and Information Technology Services	2677.49	3031.30	3028.72
房地产业(不含房地产开发经营)	Realty Industry	932.83	982.71	945.44
租赁和商务服务业	Tenancy and Business Services	1792.73	2023.07	2077.95
科学研究和技术服务业	Scientific Research and Technical Service	1021.38	1087.94	1069.70
水利、环境和公共设施管理业	Management of Water Conservancy, Environment and Public Facilities	131.72	144.36	140.82
居民服务、修理和其他服务业	Resident Services, Repair and other Services	172.37	186.86	192.89
教育	Education	212.76	193.83	185.69
卫生和社会工作	Health and Social Work	179.31	233.13	227.10
文化、体育和娱乐业	Culture, Sports and Entertainment	155.47	143.24	153.84

14-6 规模以上服务业企业分行业就业人员平均人数

Average number of Employed Persons of Service Enterprises above Designated Size by Sector

单位：万人 (10000 persons)

项　　目	Item	就业人员平均人数 Average Number of Employed Persons		
		2018	2019	2020
全　省	**Provincial Total**	**496.20**	**539.58**	**590.85**
按行业分	Grouped by Sector			
交通运输、仓储和邮政业	Traffic, Transport, Storage and Post	115.67	109.32	109.12
信息传输、软件和信息技术服务业	Information Transfer, Software and Information Technology Services	77.34	87.44	95.74
房地产业(不含房地产开发经营)	Realty Industry	83.39	88.93	96.13
租赁和商务服务业	Tenancy and Business Services	112.96	133.59	160.23
科学研究和技术服务业	Scientific Research and Technical Service	41.91	45.92	48.72
水利、环境和公共设施管理业	Management of Water Conservancy, Environment and Public Facilities	10.93	12.57	15.89
居民服务、修理和其他服务业	Resident Services, Repair and other Services	21.64	25.09	27.30
教育	Education	13.94	15.38	16.38
卫生和社会工作	Health and Social Work	9.03	10.43	11.66
文化、体育和娱乐业	Culture, Sports and Entertainment	9.39	10.92	9.69

注：本表中，2020年及以前为就业人员平均人数，2021年起改为期末用工人数，与历史数据不具可比性。
Notes: In this chart, the average number of employed persons in 2020 and before is changed to the number of employees at the year-end since 2021, which is not comparable with historical data.

14-6 续表 continued

单位：万人 (10000 persons)

项　　目	Item	期末用工人数 The number of Employed Persons at the Year-end		
		2021	2022	2023
全　省	**Provincial Total**	**620.58**	**639.52**	**626.75**
按行业分	Grouped by Sector			
交通运输、仓储和邮政业	Traffic, Transport, Storage and Post	105.67	107.55	103.40
信息传输、软件和信息技术服务业	Information Transfer, Software and Information Technology Services	109.49	108.35	106.60
房地产业(不含房地产开发经营)	Realty Industry	98.98	100.04	97.13
租赁和商务服务业	Tenancy and Business Services	164.52	179.81	182.38
科学研究和技术服务业	Scientific Research and Technical Service	54.82	53.46	50.44
水利、环境和公共设施管理业	Management of Water Conservancy, Environment and Public Facilities	17.94	19.09	18.05
居民服务、修理和其他服务业	Resident Services, Repair and other Services	28.88	29.67	30.65
教育	Education	15.71	14.64	12.95
卫生和社会工作	Health and Social Work	14.14	17.16	15.45
文化、体育和娱乐业	Culture, Sports and Entertainment	10.43	9.75	9.70

14-7 各市规模以上服务业企业主要指标（2023年）

单位：亿元

市别	City	企业单位数（个）Number of Enterprises (unit)	营业收入 Business Revenue 总量 Total	营业收入 Business Revenue 2023年比2022年增长(%) Growth Rate in 2023 Over 2022(%)	营业成本 Business Costs 总量 Total	营业成本 Business Costs 2023年比2022年增长(%) Growth Rate in 2023 Over 2022(%)
广州	Guangzhou	13009	18994.25	10.2	14700.19	7.7
深圳	Shenzhen	11200	22701.79	6.7	15927.05	3.3
珠海	Zhuhai	1307	1535.42	14.8	1015.15	14.6
汕头	Shantou	564	348.94	1.5	266.87	-0.5
佛山	Foshan	2244	1436.56	3.5	1062.44	4.4
韶关	Shaoguan	185	108.70	2.0	86.16	0.6
河源	Heyuan	110	80.45	1.7	49.85	-0.2
梅州	Meizhou	85	89.37	9.8	77.85	17.7
惠州	Huizhou	1212	650.56	5.9	521.16	14.8
汕尾	Shanwei	186	116.94	12.0	98.69	10.4
东莞	Dongguan	2481	2243.36	9.3	1481.16	8.0
中山	Zhongshan	903	503.66	1.8	382.19	2.1
江门	Jiangmen	407	263.75	11.6	189.57	9.7
阳江	Yangjiang	118	82.20	-2.9	62.28	-5.0
湛江	Zhanjiang	372	300.63	2.6	215.04	-2.9
茂名	Maoming	253	162.20	7.5	121.94	5.4
肇庆	Zhaoqing	137	139.16	14.2	105.51	14.3
清远	Qingyuan	269	218.77	2.9	160.35	4.1
潮州	Chaozhou	56	59.54	3.6	47.78	2.7
揭阳	Jieyang	136	121.00	-0.2	94.75	-0.4
云浮	Yunfu	69	47.83	4.7	33.52	1.1
按经济区域分	By Region					
珠三角	Pearl River Delta	32900	48468.51	8.3	35384.41	5.8
粤东	Eastern Region	942	646.42	3.1	508.08	1.8
粤西	Western Region	743	545.03	3.1	399.25	-0.9
粤北	Northern Region	718	545.12	3.8	407.73	4.8

Main Indicators of Service Enterprises above Designated Size by City (2023)

(100 million yuan)

税金及附加 Tax and Extra Charges		销售费用 Selling Expenses		管理费用 Management Expenses	
总量 Total	2023年比2022年增长(%) Growth Rate in 2023 Over 2022(%)	总量 Total	2023年比2022年增长(%) Growth Rate in 2023 Over 2022(%)	总量 Total	2023年比2022年增长(%) Growth Rate in 2023 Over 2022(%)
109.42	16.6	845.62	0.6	1704.25	1.5
126.73	17.4	1486.03	14.8	2024.60	-4.8
38.38	59.4	59.67	7.6	180.93	-5.9
1.89	-2.2	19.99	-4.6	32.20	-1.0
14.41	10.5	65.56	3.5	166.67	-2.6
0.49	11.2	3.41	-17.7	11.91	0.6
0.32	-9.3	2.86	0.7	22.38	-0.6
0.34	1.1	3.23	6.1	8.25	0.3
6.45	9.1	18.40	-3.4	70.00	2.4
0.57	35.7	3.79	19.1	14.05	14.2
14.01	0.1	78.64	-14.6	200.90	-5.4
4.64	-5.4	22.10	-8.9	57.23	1.9
2.46	6.9	8.63	-6.1	27.13	0.9
0.35	-0.7	3.66	-7.8	7.86	-6.0
1.92	11.8	10.62	6.1	31.24	1.5
0.61	16.0	7.84	9.0	13.41	-2.4
0.94	13.1	4.71	-4.8	12.27	3.2
1.37	15.1	6.20	5.1	19.60	-1.5
0.21	-1.9	2.74	-10.1	3.42	1.9
0.41	-7.0	5.56	15.5	8.26	-12.7
0.28	4.0	2.04	-10.7	5.29	5.3
317.44	18.9	2589.36	7.7	4443.99	-2.2
3.08	2.4	32.08	0.2	57.93	0.5
2.88	10.9	22.12	4.5	52.52	-0.7
2.81	8.1	17.73	-2.6	67.43	-0.1

14-7 续表

单位：亿元

市别	City	财务费用 Financial Expenses 总量 Total	财务费用 Financial Expenses 2023年比2022年增长(%) Growth Rate in 2023 Over 2022(%)	利润总额 Total Profits 总量 Total	利润总额 Total Profits 2023年比2022年增长(%) Growth Rate in 2023 Over 2022(%)
广州	Guangzhou	471.34	0.8	1729.68	30.7
深圳	Shenzhen	345.06	-0.6	3329.09	42.2
珠海	Zhuhai	53.59	16.5	234.63	19.5
汕头	Shantou	8.09	-20.9	7.49	37.6
佛山	Foshan	51.66	8.3	141.73	19.4
韶关	Shaoguan	4.15	-6.5	3.06	297.1
河源	Heyuan	1.26	-10.7	3.52	-11.6
梅州	Meizhou	9.20	33.1	-10.34	-185.4
惠州	Huizhou	45.51	-1.1	100.15	-39.6
汕尾	Shanwei	3.35	57.1	-1.11	-2055.7
东莞	Dongguan	59.02	-0.9	446.20	9.3
中山	Zhongshan	11.62	3.9	66.12	22.7
江门	Jiangmen	13.82	12.5	28.03	45.5
阳江	Yangjiang	0.89	-3.7	7.27	8.5
湛江	Zhanjiang	11.34	27.2	36.63	25.9
茂名	Maoming	2.17	-19.7	17.05	36.4
肇庆	Zhaoqing	2.80	-1.0	14.47	31.6
清远	Qingyuan	19.53	7.4	17.45	-2.4
潮州	Chaozhou	0.54	9.2	4.13	10.0
揭阳	Jieyang	0.72	2.6	11.05	-3.8
云浮	Yunfu	0.97	19.3	6.39	44.2
按经济区域分	By Region				
珠三角	Pearl River Delta	1054.41	1.3	6090.10	31.3
粤东	Eastern Region	12.69	-6.4	21.56	4.5
粤西	Western Region	14.40	14.8	60.95	26.2
粤北	Northern Region	35.11	10.5	20.08	-14.4

14-7 continued

(100 million yuan)

<table>
<tr><th colspan="2">所得税费用
Income Taxes Payable</th><th colspan="2">应付职工薪酬
Total Wages Payable</th><th colspan="2">应交增值税
Value-added Tax Payable</th><th rowspan="2">期末用工人数
(万人)
Total number of employed persons at the year-end
(10000 persons)</th></tr>
<tr><th>总量
Total</th><th>2023年比2022年增长(%)
Growth Rate in 2023 Over 2022(%)</th><th>总量
Total</th><th>2023年比2022年增长(%)
Growth Rate in 2023 Over 2022(%)</th><th>总量
Total</th><th>2023年比2022年增长(%)
Growth Rate in 2023 Over 2022(%)</th></tr>
<tr><td>247.38</td><td>9.7</td><td>3870.53</td><td>4.0</td><td>429.40</td><td>9.0</td><td>243.33</td></tr>
<tr><td>338.91</td><td>26.2</td><td>4184.42</td><td>-0.1</td><td>521.67</td><td>13.5</td><td>233.92</td></tr>
<tr><td>34.96</td><td>15.1</td><td>379.84</td><td>4.2</td><td>44.58</td><td>12.4</td><td>23.84</td></tr>
<tr><td>5.36</td><td>1.2</td><td>70.54</td><td>0.2</td><td>5.46</td><td>-5.4</td><td>6.20</td></tr>
<tr><td>23.72</td><td>-0.6</td><td>309.73</td><td>-2.4</td><td>35.44</td><td>2.7</td><td>28.78</td></tr>
<tr><td>1.34</td><td>54.0</td><td>23.63</td><td>1.9</td><td>2.81</td><td>-66.9</td><td>2.39</td></tr>
<tr><td>1.37</td><td>9.0</td><td>14.12</td><td>-2.9</td><td>1.51</td><td>24.4</td><td>1.45</td></tr>
<tr><td>1.80</td><td>6.5</td><td>17.70</td><td>6.0</td><td>2.20</td><td>11.6</td><td>1.46</td></tr>
<tr><td>15.27</td><td>25.8</td><td>124.54</td><td>1.6</td><td>15.46</td><td>3.4</td><td>12.49</td></tr>
<tr><td>1.20</td><td>24.1</td><td>29.43</td><td>5.4</td><td>2.88</td><td>85.0</td><td>2.50</td></tr>
<tr><td>42.37</td><td>-1.2</td><td>386.58</td><td>5.8</td><td>40.31</td><td>-9.4</td><td>34.08</td></tr>
<tr><td>7.88</td><td>2.4</td><td>112.09</td><td>-1.0</td><td>9.79</td><td>2.7</td><td>11.07</td></tr>
<tr><td>6.07</td><td>20.7</td><td>53.27</td><td>5.1</td><td>4.91</td><td>-4.6</td><td>4.82</td></tr>
<tr><td>1.41</td><td>10.8</td><td>19.85</td><td>-12.8</td><td>2.39</td><td>5.7</td><td>1.91</td></tr>
<tr><td>8.50</td><td>38.9</td><td>67.72</td><td>6.1</td><td>6.44</td><td>-32.5</td><td>5.19</td></tr>
<tr><td>3.13</td><td>20.3</td><td>34.54</td><td>14.1</td><td>2.52</td><td>-26.5</td><td>3.74</td></tr>
<tr><td>3.18</td><td>15.5</td><td>23.69</td><td>4.2</td><td>3.11</td><td>7.2</td><td>2.06</td></tr>
<tr><td>4.39</td><td>-5.8</td><td>35.41</td><td>10.1</td><td>5.83</td><td>2.0</td><td>3.87</td></tr>
<tr><td>1.05</td><td>26.5</td><td>8.67</td><td>7.9</td><td>0.57</td><td>1.1</td><td>1.00</td></tr>
<tr><td>2.81</td><td>27.6</td><td>17.75</td><td>-8.7</td><td>0.82</td><td>-19.1</td><td>1.75</td></tr>
<tr><td>1.17</td><td>19.4</td><td>10.75</td><td>0.8</td><td>1.36</td><td>7.4</td><td>0.90</td></tr>
<tr><td></td><td></td><td></td><td></td><td></td><td></td><td></td></tr>
<tr><td>719.74</td><td>16.3</td><td>9444.68</td><td>2.0</td><td>1104.67</td><td>9.9</td><td>594.38</td></tr>
<tr><td>10.41</td><td>12.1</td><td>126.38</td><td>0.5</td><td>9.74</td><td>9.2</td><td>11.45</td></tr>
<tr><td>13.03</td><td>30.5</td><td>122.11</td><td>4.5</td><td>11.36</td><td>-25.5</td><td>10.84</td></tr>
<tr><td>10.08</td><td>6.5</td><td>101.63</td><td>4.5</td><td>13.69</td><td>-26.6</td><td>10.08</td></tr>
</table>

主要统计指标解释

期末用工人数 指报告期最后一日 24 时企业实际拥有的、参与本企业生产经营活动的人员数，无论是否从本企业领取劳动报酬均视为用工人数。该指标为时点指标，不包括最后一日当天及以前已经不再参与本企业生产经营活动的人员。包括企业的正式人员、劳务派遣人员和其他临时人员。

Explanatory Notes on Main Statistical Indicators

The number of Employed Persons at the Year-end refers to the number of personnel actually owned by the enterprise and participating in the production and business activities of the enterprise at 24 on the last day of the reporting period, whether or not they receive labor remuneration from the enterprise shall be regarded as the number of employees. This indicator is a time point indicator, excluding the personnel who have ceased to participate in the production and business activities of the enterprise on the last day and before. It includes the enterprise's regular personnel, labor dispatch personnel and other temporary personnel.

十五、运输和邮电

TRANSPORTATION, POSTAL AND TELECOMMUNICATION SERVICES

十五 运输和邮电

简要说明

一、本篇资料反映广东运输和邮电通信业发展的基本状况。

交通运输业资料主要包括：运输线路里程、运输设备拥有量、货物运输量和旅客运输量、港口设备和吞吐量、航站吞吐量等。

邮电通信业资料主要包括：邮电通信主要工具及设备情况，主要邮电业务完成情况，邮电通信发展水平等。

二、资料调查范围和统计单位

1. 铁路资料：包括国家铁路、地方铁路和合资铁路运营情况，不含军用铁路及由厂矿企事业单位自建的铁路专用线和专用铁道。

2. 公路、水路、港口资料：(1)公路和水路线路里程为年末通车和通航里程数。公路里程、桥梁、渡口统计从2006年起包括农村公路。(2)民用汽车拥有量，根据公安交通管理局所属车管部门登记注册的车辆资料整理；(3)民用运输船舶拥有量，不含渔船、水上施工作业船，根据水上航运管理部门登记注册的船舶资料整理；(4)公路、水路客货运输量资料，包括在广东公路水路运输管理部门注册登记或审批备案的、从事营业性公路、水路客、货运输的营业性运输工具(包括个体联户)所完成的运输量。此部分数据2005年之前由统计局收集整理，2005年起改由省交通运输厅通过抽样调查方法负责收集整理。2009年，交通运输部统一部署更换调查方法收集整理。2014-2015年，按交通运输部要求，公路水路客货运输量采用经济调查结果进行推算。2016年，公路水路客货运输量采用2015年专项调查结果进行推算。2020年客货运输量中，公路货物运输量根据2019年道路货物运输量专项调查结果推算，海洋水路客货运输量统计方式改为企业一套表联网直报，管道运输纳统增加6家企业，增速按可比口径计算。2021年，道路货物运输量统计方法调整为“规上企业全面调查+规下业户波动推算”。每次更换调查方法，均会导致公路水路客货运输量数据与以往不可比，使用时敬请注意。(5)港口设备及吞吐量，根据各地港务管理部门注册的港口企业和从事港口生产活动单位的资料整理。2019年起，港口统计数据采集方式改为企业一套表联网直报，统计范围是辖区内各港口。

3. 管道运输资料：包括输原油、输成品油、输天然气、输其他气体的管线长度、输送能力及完成的运输量。数据主要来源于中国石油天然气集团公司和中国石油化工集团公司所属的本地各管道运输单位。

4. 民航运输资料：统计对象为在广东境内注册、从事民用航空运输飞行和通用飞行的航空运输企业和民用航空机场，不包括在境内运输飞行的国内其他航空公司及外国航空公司。统计范围为各航空公司从事国内运输、港澳台运输、国际运输的定期航班航线条数及里程、运输量及期末飞机在册架数、民用航空机场航班起降架次和客货吞吐量等。

5. 邮电通信资料：包括全省电信和邮政运营企业为社会公众提供的各类电信和邮政服务，不含专用网业务资料。资料主要来源于省通信管理局、邮政管理局以及邮政、电信、移动、联通等运营单位。

三、本篇资料由广东省统计局服务业统计处整理、编辑。资料主要来源于省内民航、铁路、公路、水运、港口、公安、邮政、通信等行业主管部门以及各有关单位。

15 Transportation,Postal and Telecommunication Services

Brief Introduction

Ⅰ. The data in this chapter cover mainly the basic conditions of the development of transport, postal and telecommunication services in Guangdong Province.

The data on transport cover mainly the route length of five means of transportation, the possession of transport equipment, the freight and passenger traffic the possession of port equipment and the volume of freight handled in ports, the passenger and freight throughput of airports, etc.

The data on postal and telecommunication services cover mainly major means and equipment of post and telecommunications, achievements of main businesses of postal and telecommunication services, and the level of development of postal and telecommunication services, etc.

Ⅱ. Coverage and Statistical Units

1. Data on railway transportation: including the operation and management of the national, local and joint-venture railways, but excluding the railways for military purpose, lines built by factories, mines, enterprises and institutions for exclusive use, and special railways.

2. Data on highways, waterways and ports: (1) The length of highways and waterways refer to the length open to traffic or navigation at the end of the year. The Statistical of length of highways,bridges,ferries from 2006 include rural highway. (2) The data on the possession of civil motor vehicles are compiled according to registration data of vehicles at the divisions of vehicle management under the traffic management departments of public security authorities. (3) The data on the possession of civil vessels exclusive of fishing boats and engineering ships over water are compiled according to registration data of vessels at the authorities of navigation and port management. (4) The data on the volume of transportation by highways and waterways, including all enterprises, institutions, and individuals (or individual partnerships) registered in Guangdong for passenger and freight transportation by highways and waterways, were collected and prepared by the Bureau of Statistics before 2005. Since 2005, the data were collected and prepared by the Department of Transport of Guangdong through sample survey. Since 2009, the data are collected and prepared in accordance with the new survey method stipulated by the Ministry of Transport. Since 2015, the data are prepared according to the third economic census of Guangdong Province.In the passenger and cargo traffic in 2020, cargo traffic by highway have been calculated according special survey of road cargo traffic in 2019,statistics of passenger and cargo traffic by waterway have been obtained by corporations reporting directly online,pipeline transportation enterprises increased by 6,the growth rate is calculated by comparable coverage.In 2021, the statistical method of road freight transport volume have adjusted to "comprehensive survey of Enterprises above Designated Size + fluctuating calculation of enterprises below Designated Size". Since the new survey method has new criteria for survey target and urban-rural division, the data are not comparable with those of the previous years. (5) The data on possession of port equipment and production capacity and handling capacity of ports are compiled according to registration data of port enterprises and production units at local port authorities. Starting in 2019, data related to ports have been compiled from direct online reporting by port enterprises, with the statistical scope being ports within each jurisdiction.

3. Data on pipeline transport: the data on pipeline transport cover the length, transport capacity and the volume transported of pipelines of petroleum (crude oil), petroleum products, natural gas and other gases. The data are mainly provided by enterprises engaged in the pipeline transport subordinate to the China National Petroleum Corporation and China Petrochemical Corporation.

4. Data on civil aviation transport: data on civil aviation transport include air transport enterprises and civil airports registered for civil aviation transport and general aviation, excluding other domestic aviation companies and foreign aviation companies engaged in air transport within Chinese territory. The statistics cover regular flights of domestic transport, transport between the mainland of China and Hong Kong, Macao and Taiwan, and international transport managed by various aviation companies, concerning the number of lines, length, transport volume, number of registered aircrafts at the end of the reference period, sorties at civil airports, and volumes of passenger and freight handled at civil airports.

5. Data on post and telecommunications: data in this category include telecommunications and postal services rendered to the public by telecommunications and postal enterprises of the whole province, but exclude services provided through dedicated networks. Statistics are mainly provided by Guangdong Communications Administration and corresponding enterprises, including China Post, China Telecom, China Mobile, China Unicom ,and China Netcom.

Ⅲ. The data in this chapter are prepared and compiled by the Division of Service Industry Statistics of Statistics Bureau of Guangdong Province. Raw data are mainly provided by authorities and related enterprises and institutions within the province of civil aviation, railways, highways, waterways, ports, public securities, and post and telecommunications.

15-1 运输邮电主要指标

Main Indicators on Transport, Postal and Telecommunication Services

指标	Item	2000	2010	2022	2023	2023年比2022年增长% Growth Rate in 2023 over 2022 (%)
铁路营业里程 (公里)	Length of Railways in Operation (km)	1942	2297	5158	5452	5.7
公路通车里程 (公里)	Length of Highways (km)	102606	190144	223081	223391	0.1
内河通航里程 (公里)	Length of Navigable Inland Waterways (km)	13696	13596	12266	12266	0.0
民航航线里程 (万公里)	Length of Civil Aviation Routes (10000 km)	50.03	180.74	273.44	330.60	20.9
管道输油(气)里程 (公里)	Length of Petroleum and Gas Pipelines (km)	1535.57	6033.62	11769.84	12075.71	2.6
港口码头泊位 (个)	Number of Berths in Coastal Ports (unit)	3191	3082	2252	2327	3.3
#万吨级泊位	Berths at 10000 Ton Class	126	245	368	401	9.0
码头泊位长度 (米)	Length of Quay Line (m)	180238	252762	244557	249656	2.1
公路桥梁 (座)	Number of Highway Bridges (unit)	19668	42330	62112	67834	9.2
#永久式	Permanent	19656	42233	62049	67805	9.3
民用汽车 (万辆)	Number of Civil Motor Vehicles (10000 units)	172.91	783.50	2898.36	3069.11	5.9
机动船舶数 (艘)	Number of Motor Vessels (unit)	21733	8793	6359	6097	-4.1
吨位数 (万净载重吨)	Tonnage (10000 dead weight ton)	526.88	1140.71	2305.98	1924.25	-16.6
民用运输飞机 (架)	Number of Civil Aircrafts (unit)	106	441	909	921	1.3
移动电话交换机容量 (万户)	Capacity of Mobile Telephone Exchanges (10000 subscribers)	1825.40	14766.90	24521.58	24521.58	0.0
固定电话用户 (万户)	Subscribers of Local Fixed Telephones	1414.94	3169.14	1944.08	1783.72	-8.2
固定互联网宽带接入用户 (万户)	Subscribers of Fixed Internet Broadband (10000 subscribers)	216.41	1523.22	4628.72	4824.35	4.2
移动互联网用户 (万户)	Subscribers of Mobile Internet (10000 subscribers)			15097.28	15723.88	4.2
移动电话用户 (万户)	Subscribers of Mobile Telephones (10000 subscribers)	1357.26	9710.09	16650.76	17048.20	2.4
客运量 (万人)	Passenger Traffic (10000 persons)	164791	467049	47632	82680	73.6
旅客周转量 (亿人公里)	Passenger-kilometers (100 million passenger-km)	1218.59	3342.23	1621.36	3530.74	117.8
货运量 (万吨)	Freight Traffic (10000 tons)	119216	205034	364199	382401	5.0
货物周转量 (亿吨公里)	Freight Ton-kilometers (100 million ton-km)	3064.51	5933.88	28438.62	29668.13	4.3
港口货物吞吐量 (万吨)	Volume of Freight Handled in Ports (10000 tons)	31649	122258	204802	221462	8.1
港口旅客吞吐量 (万人)	Volume of Passengers Handled in Ports (10000 persons)	1670.32	2483.21	1464.19	3021.56	106.4
航站旅客吞吐量 (万人)	Volume of Passengers Handled at Airports (10000 persons)	2142.84	7188.64	5824.95	14141.54	142.8
邮电业务总量 (亿元)	Business Volume of Postal and Telecommunication Services (100 million yuan)	757.22	4832.94	5063.13	5669.45	12.0
邮政 (亿元)	Postal Service (100 million yuan)	50.40	118.57	3112.87	3645.36	17.1
电信 (亿元)	Telecommunication Service (100 million yuan)	706.82	4714.37	1950.26	2024.09	3.8

注：1.邮电业务总量1988年及以前按1980年不变价格计算，1989—2000年按1990年不变价格计算，2001—2010年按2000年不变价格计算，2011—2016年按2010年不变价格计算，2017年起，电信业务总量按2015年不变价格计算，邮政业务总量仍按2010年不变价格计算。2021年起，按2020年不变价计算。2022年起，电信业务总量按上年不变价计算。增速按可比价格计算。

2.2017年起，铁路客运量和货运量改为按发送量计算，客运量货运量数据与往年不可比。增长速度按可比口径计算。

3.从2019年起，港口统计数据采集方式改为企业一套表联网直报，统计范围是辖区内各港口，增长速度按可比口径计算。

Notes:a) The business volume of postal and telecommunication services in and before 1998 was calculated at 1980 constant prices, that from 1998 to 2000 was calculated at 1990 constant prices, that from 2001 to 2010 was calculated at 2000 constant prices and that from 2011 to 2016 was calculated at 2010 constant prices. Since 2017, the total amount of telecommunications was calculated at 2015 constant prices, while the total amount of postal business was calculated at 2010 constant prices. From 2021, that was calculated at 2020 constant prices. In 2022, the total amount of telecommunications was calculated at last year's constant prices.The growth rate was calculated at comparable prices.

b) Since 2017, passenger and cargo traffic by rail have been calculated according traffic sent, as such, data of cargo and passenger traffic by rail is incomparable with previous years. Growth rate is calculated with a comparable prices.

c) Since 2019, dockyard statistics have been obtained by corporations reporting directly online, the statistical scope of the data is organized by dockyards within each jurisdiction, growth rates are calculated with comparable data.

15-2 全社会旅客运输量
Total Passenger Traffic

年份 Year	客运量(万人) Passenger Traffic (10000 persons)					旅客周转量（亿人公里） Passenger-kilometers (100 million passenger-km)				
	合计 Total	铁路 Railways	公路 Highways	水路 Waterways	民航 Civil Aviation	合计 Total	铁路 Railways	公路 Highways	水路 Waterways	民航 Civil Aviation
1985	49848	3357	41826	4427	238	270.23	50.41	178.27	20.46	21.09
1986	126890	3742	113561	9295	292	450.35	56.70	346.81	19.82	27.02
1987	158715	4129	144684	9557	345	796.86	66.98	678.04	21.20	30.64
1988	218915	4828	204278	9420	389	402.34	82.53	261.18	22.43	36.20
1989	66727	4882	58110	3377	358	447.62	84.38	309.25	20.50	33.49
1990	78046	4467	70681	2428	470	453.21	82.56	307.40	19.68	43.57
1991	83460	5004	75570	2317	569	526.66	102.11	348.85	20.89	54.81
1992	93678	6243	83128	3503	804	624.55	131.99	385.76	25.75	81.05
1993	95468	6835	84708	3078	847	696.92	161.04	422.88	25.60	87.40
1994	125036	6920	111447	5636	1033	929.48	164.11	619.52	33.21	112.64
1995	130998	6283	118406	5146	1163	936.29	163.11	613.07	31.13	128.98
1996	128831	5593	117815	4232	1191	938.65	153.86	626.60	20.65	137.54
1997	123649	6201	113259	3032	1157	957.20	177.61	616.48	17.21	145.90
1998	132462	6743	121795	2729	1195	994.84	194.16	630.65	13.87	156.16
1999	148636	7553	137324	2605	1154	1082.14	212.13	700.74	13.62	155.65
2000	164791	12165	148945	2363	1318	1218.59	241.51	780.74	11.65	184.69
2001	178676	12783	161967	2382	1544	1342.12	252.37	858.86	11.40	219.49
2002	188657	13310	171191	2347	1809	1490.34	273.19	945.16	11.31	260.68
2003	191202	12935	174288	2208	1771	1505.83	267.14	983.67	11.41	243.61
2004	202414	15142	183012	1827	2433	1738.21	308.38	1076.06	10.17	343.60
2005	212104	16106	189881	2062	4055	2122.14	327.74	1190.73	9.54	594.13
2006	197314	15109	175567	2073	4565	2245.37	347.60	1212.76	12.14	672.87
2007	211215	16762	186835	2071	5548	2626.71	387.61	1410.72	10.98	817.40
2008	238375	13739	216902	1902	5832	2844.79	420.12	1566.73	9.80	848.14
2009	428705	13394	406704	1873	6734	2853.30	407.72	1470.06	7.06	968.46
2010	467049	14956	442224	2241	7628	3342.23	456.46	1736.34	8.36	1141.07
2011	522095	17902	493618	2594	7981	3851.84	505.16	2082.68	9.63	1254.37
2012	586299	18528	556510	2725	8535	4372.06	514.88	2470.11	10.01	1377.06
2013	636816	20459	604934	2426	8997	4852.41	565.91	2776.08	10.23	1500.19
2014	193363	23744	157234	2613	9771	3967.28	670.78	1629.79	10.67	1656.05
2015	207345	26536	168028	2728	10054	4335.79	747.05	1769.61	10.50	1808.63
2016	144262	28954	102094	2648	10566	3842.58	793.44	1079.80	10.34	1959.00
2017	148549	28476	105919	2733	11420	4140.29	872.08	1129.53	10.85	2127.82
2018	154682	33745	105249	2775	12913	4501.97	953.75	1120.71	11.13	2416.38
2019	155770	38213	101012	2614	13931	4764.98	1023.05	1092.97	9.71	2639.26
2020	87777	22609	54946	1345	8878	2617.23	630.33	556.31	4.27	1426.32
2021	62126	23977	27567	1580	9002	2352.19	670.39	265.96	4.51	1411.33
2022	47632	17526	23730	884	5492	1621.36	526.81	193.83	2.31	898.40
2023	82680	36351	30583	2774	12972	3530.74	1014.11	253.09	8.56	2254.98

15-3 旅客运输量指数

Indices of Passenger Traffic

上年=100 (preceding year=100)

年份 Year	客运量 Passenger Traffic					旅客周转量 Passenger-kilometers				
	合计 Total	铁路 Railways	公路 Highways	水路 Waterways	民航 Civil Aviation	合计 Total	铁路 Railways	公路 Highways	水路 Waterways	民航 Civil Aviation
1978	107.9	105.6	109.0	104.8	144.8	110.4	112.8	109.8	102.3	151.9
1979	114.9	115.5	116.0	109.2	144.2	123.5	129.1	119.8	117.1	165.2
1980	117.3	101.0	125.2	97.7	118.6	121.2	120.4	128.0	109.3	97.4
1981	107.4	100.0	110.0	99.1	125.1	110.9	109.0	112.2	106.0	121.0
1982	119.7	95.7	126.6	99.9	122.4	111.8	102.6	117.1	102.4	125.4
1983	107.2	107.2	108.6	96.4	89.6	111.9	117.8	114.0	99.7	94.6
1984	119.7	109.2	124.4	87.3	142.9	125.6	115.3	130.4	98.3	183.2
1985	109.2	112.6	109.1	103.6	131.6	118.1	121.3	116.1	101.0	148.7
1986	90.0	102.8	88.2	91.7	125.2	95.0	106.7	86.0	91.4	130.8
1987	125.1	110.3	127.4	102.8	118.2	176.9	118.1	195.5	107.0	113.4
1988	137.9	116.9	141.2	98.6	112.8	50.5	123.2	38.5	105.8	118.1
1989	30.5	101.1	28.4	35.8	92.0	111.3	102.2	118.4	91.4	92.5
1990	117.0	91.5	121.6	71.9	131.3	101.2	97.8	99.4	96.0	130.1
1991	106.9	112.0	106.9	95.4	121.1	116.2	123.7	113.5	106.1	125.8
1992	112.2	124.8	110.0	151.2	141.3	118.6	129.3	110.6	123.3	147.9
1993	101.9	109.5	101.9	87.9	105.3	111.6	122.0	109.6	99.4	107.8
1994	131.0	101.2	131.6	183.1	122.0	133.4	101.9	146.5	129.7	128.9
1995	104.8	90.8	106.2	91.3	112.6	100.7	99.4	99.0	93.7	114.5
1996	98.3	89.0	99.5	82.2	102.4	100.3	94.3	102.2	66.3	106.6
1997	96.0	110.9	96.1	71.6	97.1	102.0	115.4	98.4	83.3	106.1
1998	107.1	108.7	107.5	90.0	103.3	103.9	109.3	102.3	80.6	107.0
1999	112.2	112.0	112.8	95.5	96.6	108.8	109.3	111.1	98.2	99.7
2000	108.4	111.9	108.5	90.7	114.2	112.6	113.8	111.4	85.5	118.7
2001	108.4	105.1	108.7	100.8	117.1	110.1	104.5	110.0	97.9	118.8
2002	105.6	104.1	105.7	98.5	117.2	111.0	108.2	110.0	99.2	118.8
2003	101.3	97.2	101.8	94.1	97.9	101.0	97.8	104.1	100.9	93.5
2004	105.9	117.1	105.0	82.7	137.4	115.4	115.4	109.4	89.1	141.0
2005	104.8	106.4	103.8	112.9	166.7	122.1	106.3	110.7	93.8	172.9
2006	122.3	93.8	126.2	101.7	112.6	109.9	106.1	109.1	124.0	113.3
2007	107.0	110.9	106.4	99.9	121.5	117.0	111.5	116.3	90.4	121.5
2008	115.4	114.0	116.1	91.8	105.1	108.3	108.4	111.1	89.3	103.8
2009	88.5	97.5	87.8	117.6	115.4	111.8	97.0	115.2	93.6	114.2
2010	108.9	111.7	108.7	119.6	113.3	117.1	112.0	118.1	118.4	117.8
2011	111.8	119.7	111.6	115.8	104.6	115.2	110.7	119.9	115.2	109.9
2012	112.3	103.5	112.7	105.1	106.9	113.5	101.9	118.6	103.9	109.8
2013	108.6	110.4	108.7	89.0	105.4	111.0	109.9	112.4	102.2	108.9
2014	110.4	116.1	109.6	116.3	108.6	112.1	118.5	111.4	116.2	110.4
2015	107.2	111.8	106.9	104.4	102.9	109.3	111.4	108.6	98.4	109.2
2016	105.0	109.1	104.1	97.1	105.1	106.7	106.2	104.3	98.5	108.3
2017	105.6	112.1	103.7	103.2	108.1	107.6	109.4	104.6	104.9	108.6
2018	103.9	118.5	99.4	101.5	110.2	107.5	109.4	99.2	102.6	111.1
2019	100.7	113.2	96.0	94.2	107.9	105.8	107.3	97.5	87.2	109.2
2020	56.3	59.2	54.4	49.1	63.7	54.9	61.6	50.9	42.6	54.0
2021	70.8	106.1	50.2	117.5	101.4	89.9	106.4	47.8	105.5	98.9
2022	76.7	73.1	86.1	56.0	61.0	68.9	78.6	72.9	51.3	63.7
2023	173.6	207.4	128.9	313.8	236.2	217.8	192.5	130.6	369.9	251.0

15-4 各市客运量

Passenger Traffic by City

单位：万人 (10000 persons)

市别	City	2005	2010	2015	2019	2020	2021	2022	2023
全省	**Provincial Total**	**161357**	**467049**	**207345**	**155770**	**87777**	**62126**	**47632**	**82680**
广州	Guangzhou	22583	47872	85170	25658	18063	6731	6772	8270
深圳	Shenzhen	9500	151404	7040	6907	5266	4636	4523	5687
珠海	Zhuhai	4874	19078	4017	3121	1406	1003	695	3779
汕头	Shantou	1991	2539	1642	1676	1133	305	263	351
佛山	Foshan	11472	25166	5387	4359	1448	2000	1780	2349
韶关	Shaoguan	2280	10200	5515	5638	2934	1173	892	963
河源	Heyuan	1969	3294	3257	2980	783	992	855	954
梅州	Meizhou	3550	4399	2859	2598	863	340	272	352
惠州	Huizhou	5049	12763	6799	4686	926	889	563	820
汕尾	Shanwei	3800	7250	1237	1221	514	537	580	972
东莞	Dongguan	30951	77446	5071	3276	831	899	704	901
中山	Zhongshan	9200	13258	1822	1488	523	624	441	651
江门	Jiangmen	8249	18096	10272	8935	5127	1360	936	1132
阳江	Yangjiang	1585	4111	1586	1594	532	266	165	264
湛江	Zhanjiang	6413	12745	9026	9439	3729	2674	1851	2290
茂名	Maoming	5079	6830	6367	6753	5783	1419	960	835
肇庆	Zhaoqing	4436	6388	3119	2722	1245	813	555	575
清远	Qingyuan	1959	9874	3088	3251	2390	1182	829	1015
潮州	Chaozhou	733	2056	2255	1953	797	156	146	252
揭阳	Jieyang	3014	4789	2041	2398	1381	658	507	561
云浮	Yunfu	2509	4907	3188	2972	619	489	326	384
不分地区	Unclassified	20161	22584	36589	52144	31487	32979	23018	49323
按经济区域分	By Region								
珠三角	Pearl River Delta	126475	394055	165285	113296	66321	51934	39987	73488
粤东	Eastern Region	9538	16634	7175	7248	3825	1656	1495	2135
粤西	Western Region	13077	23686	16979	17787	10044	4359	2976	3389
粤北	Northern Region	12267	32674	17907	17440	7588	4177	3175	3669

注：分市数据仅含公路和水路运输，铁路和民航运输在“不分地区”反映。下表同。

Note: Data by city only include the figures of highway and waterway transportation, whereas data of railway and civil aviation transportation are reflected in the category “Unclassified by Region”. The same applies to the following table.

15-5 各市旅客周转量

Passenger-kilometers by City

单位：亿人公里 (100 million passenger-km)

市别	City	2005	2010	2015	2019	2020	2021	2022	2023
全　省	**Provincial Total**	**2043.23**	**3342.23**	**4335.79**	**4764.98**	**2617.23**	**2352.19**	**1621.36**	**3530.74**
广　州	Guangzhou	193.24	461.34	861.08	263.18	180.69	66.86	56.97	60.42
深　圳	Shenzhen	71.42	242.13	144.31	134.93	60.08	31.85	22.98	30.08
珠　海	Zhuhai	41.69	68.90	69.18	47.94	22.60	8.60	5.35	24.43
汕　头	Shantou	21.08	51.67	22.45	23.42	17.02	6.80	5.06	6.18
佛　山	Foshan	50.94	82.76	59.31	57.88	16.53	18.76	15.08	20.98
韶　关	Shaoguan	14.17	40.41	28.55	29.17	15.38	5.91	3.86	4.95
河　源	Heyuan	36.97	38.18	38.44	37.55	11.10	10.93	9.06	10.10
梅　州	Meizhou	41.73	51.79	39.52	35.70	12.17	5.53	3.98	5.69
惠　州	Huizhou	35.97	49.46	57.43	40.80	10.01	8.95	4.54	6.11
汕　尾	Shanwei	26.90	52.98	14.05	15.66	6.79	6.03	6.19	9.84
东　莞	Dongguan	158.53	129.07	81.55	42.29	11.46	9.49	6.44	10.35
中　山	Zhongshan	48.84	88.99	21.77	23.36	8.75	5.55	3.62	6.18
江　门	Jiangmen	60.30	58.99	64.71	58.54	33.12	9.88	6.37	8.28
阳　江	Yangjiang	26.29	21.80	11.01	10.96	4.13	3.37	2.12	3.50
湛　江	Zhanjiang	62.10	82.45	95.49	105.51	37.75	20.76	11.29	13.39
茂　名	Maoming	64.83	61.47	59.23	63.27	56.27	21.20	13.29	12.80
肇　庆	Zhaoqing	25.40	33.22	14.71	12.73	6.36	7.41	4.60	5.50
清　远	Qingyuan	35.45	38.68	24.08	26.23	20.26	10.95	6.54	9.46
潮　州	Chaozhou	19.37	23.93	27.53	24.93	11.13	3.21	2.61	5.85
揭　阳	Jieyang	67.53	37.28	22.22	25.84	12.33	4.03	3.47	4.07
云　浮	Yunfu	18.62	29.21	23.49	22.77	6.63	4.39	2.71	3.50
不分地区	Unclassified	921.87	1597.53	2555.68	3662.31	2056.65	2081.72	1425.21	3269.09
按经济区域分	By Region								
珠三角	Pearl River Delta	1608.20	2812.37	3929.73	4343.96	2406.25	2249.09	1551.16	3441.41
粤　东	Eastern Region	134.87	165.86	86.25	89.85	47.28	20.06	17.33	25.94
粤　西	Western Region	153.23	165.72	165.73	179.74	98.15	45.33	26.71	29.69
粤　北	Northern Region	146.93	198.27	154.08	151.43	65.55	37.71	26.15	33.71

15-6 全社会货物运输量

Total Freight Traffic

年份 Year	货运量(万吨) Freight Traffic (10000 tons)						货物周转量(亿吨公里) Freight Ton-kilometers (100 million ton-km)					
	合计 Total	铁路 Railways	公路 Highways	水路 Waterways	民航 Civil Aviation	管道 Pipelines	合计 Total	铁路 Railways	公路 Highways	水路 Waterways	民航 Civil Aviation	管道 Pipelines
1985	58726	3000	42813	12045	4	864	1767.86	102.29	156.45	1503.47	0.38	5.27
1986	65078	4269	49030	10831	4	944	1845.33	130.02	127.28	1581.60	0.45	5.98
1987	74571	4493	57393	11664	5	1016	1982.59	142.56	179.41	1653.81	0.54	6.27
1988	79811	4504	57717	16583	6	1001	2209.11	151.55	216.22	1834.41	0.67	6.26
1989	85054	4888	63254	15820	6	1086	2419.57	168.39	301.16	1942.79	0.71	6.52
1990	85809	4803	63709	16198	8	1091	2598.88	179.54	346.27	2065.69	0.90	6.48
1991	94136	5347	69784	17718	10	1277	3181.83	206.18	386.49	2580.79	1.06	7.31
1992	113119	6089	84181	21346	12	1491	3560.59	239.34	583.36	2727.97	1.41	8.51
1993	125273	6595	87567	29660	14	1437	3797.09	261.91	428.17	3097.19	1.70	8.12
1994	119901	6971	81361	30165	20	1384	4326.09	280.31	443.54	3592.35	2.39	7.50
1995	111063	7634	68884	32952	21	1572	4642.91	290.78	352.45	3990.19	2.75	6.74
1996	95598	8138	60131	25699	24	1606	3761.09	294.12	327.81	3129.27	3.27	6.62
1997	99763	8430	62728	26873	25	1707	3837.78	294.45	341.08	3185.26	3.99	13.00
1998	101933	8288	65682	25669	28	2266	3453.92	290.65	371.08	2750.19	4.90	37.10
1999	106334	8150	70626	24857	31	2670	2980.69	282.68	426.70	2223.75	5.45	42.11
2000	119216	15172	75365	25696	31	2952	3064.51	295.97	472.49	2247.86	6.45	41.74
2001	131621	15435	86555	26434	35	3162	3221.47	296.79	522.89	2350.73	7.54	43.52
2002	137032	14790	92736	26263	42	3201	3229.39	277.87	576.35	2323.27	9.94	41.96
2003	143964	15375	97806	27412	42	3329	3666.83	285.02	614.01	2719.83	11.76	36.21
2004	156094	19495	102843	29783	49	3924	4148.54	341.26	657.49	3091.39	13.22	45.18
2005	158470	18647	105581	30179	73	3989	4359.97	319.68	781.41	3195.85	17.45	45.58
2006	145911	16170	97461	27503	79	4698	4162.77	333.12	742.67	2964.89	18.70	103.39
2007	165426	16480	112611	30893	87	5355	4430.93	337.31	906.84	3043.53	20.14	123.11
2008	176279	11545	126068	32318	85	6263	4520.12	344.96	1064.55	2878.85	18.38	213.38
2009	179722	11254	125433	36623	90	6322	4942.83	309.55	1518.43	2937.94	18.83	158.08
2010	205034	12170	142389	43092	116	7267	5933.88	329.49	1753.40	3642.22	32.98	175.79
2011	234978	12034	166567	48856	118	7403	7113.29	322.25	2150.04	4427.64	37.00	176.36
2012	266359	12002	189034	57737	128	7458	9780.56	306.04	2434.95	6820.29	42.40	176.89
2013	305833	12042	217630	68378	131	7652	12495.93	301.55	2875.68	9104.57	44.20	169.94
2014	353732	11143	257135	77220	144	8090	15020.92	274.81	3113.84	11407.80	51.05	173.42
2015	376434	10072	279983	78093	149	8137	15130.59	253.90	3454.99	11190.91	56.47	174.33
2016	377645	10135	272826	85633	160	8891	22032.27	254.41	3381.92	18160.35	61.85	173.74
2017	400601	7254	288904	94871	166	9407	28192.23	261.97	3636.89	24011.92	68.73	212.71
2018	424996	7617	304743	102352	226	10058	28644.77	267.99	3890.32	24177.41	80.53	228.53
2019	446018	8185	319279	108371	238	9944	29230.88	297.35	4113.62	24508.26	82.98	228.67
2020	356221	7845	231171	103759	238	13209	27575.18	278.44	2524.20	24404.83	85.93	281.78
2021	398420	9919	267489	107206	240	13564	28388.06	356.53	2980.46	24688.52	92.35	270.20
2022	364199	9374	242474	97628	221	14503	28438.62	362.74	2710.33	25005.04	89.09	271.42
2023	382401	9633	252809	105880	246	13831	29668.13	370.84	2850.49	26083.05	86.88	276.87

15-7 货物运输量指数

Indices of Freight Traffic

上年=100 (preceding year=100)

年份 Year	货运量 Freight Traffic						货物周转量 Freight Ton-kilometers					
	合计 Total	铁路 Railways	公路 Highways	水路 Waterways	民航 Civil Aviation	管道 Pipelines	合计 Total	铁路 Railways	公路 Highways	水路 Waterways	民航 Civil Aviation	管道 Pipelines
1978	96.3	109.2	74.9	104.5	126.6		110.9	110.9	93.0	111.1	140.0	
1979	92.1	103.5	88.9	87.2	100.0	197.2	138.4	103.5	96.6	141.9	142.9	192.9
1980	101.4	93.8	85.3	111.3	151.0	151.4	98.2	99.1	90.7	98.1	100.0	596.3
1981	92.2	84.8	87.0	93.1	102.6	165.3	84.3	92.7	93.8	83.5	100.0	280.7
1982	104.6	107.8	98.1	105.7	125.8	105.7	104.9	105.4	105.3	104.9	130.0	103.8
1983	100.4	104.9	92.4	100.5	118.5	108.7	110.1	108.8	87.6	110.3	123.1	109.8
1984	100.0	108.6	92.6	98.4	133.8	105.3	98.8	112.2	84.7	97.9	162.5	101.9
1985	177.1	105.5	225.5	115.1	133.3	101.2	109.2	111.8	206.5	104.0	146.2	100.4
1986	110.8	142.3	114.5	89.9	100.0	109.3	104.4	127.1	81.4	105.2	118.4	113.5
1987	114.6	105.2	117.1	107.7	125.0	107.6	107.4	109.6	141.0	104.6	120.0	104.8
1988	107.0	100.2	100.6	142.2	120.0	98.5	111.4	106.3	120.5	110.9	124.1	99.8
1989	106.6	108.5	109.6	95.4	100.0	108.5	109.5	111.1	139.3	105.9	106.0	104.2
1990	100.9	98.3	100.7	102.4	133.3	100.5	107.4	106.6	115.0	106.3	126.8	99.4
1991	109.7	111.3	109.5	109.4	125.0	117.0	122.4	114.8	111.6	124.9	117.8	112.8
1992	120.2	113.9	120.6	120.5	120.0	116.8	111.9	116.1	150.9	105.7	133.0	116.4
1993	110.7	108.3	104.0	138.9	116.7	96.4	106.6	109.4	73.4	113.5	120.6	95.4
1994	95.7	105.7	92.9	101.7	142.9	96.3	113.9	107.0	103.6	116.0	140.6	92.4
1995	92.6	109.5	84.7	109.2	105.0	113.6	107.3	103.7	79.5	111.1	115.1	89.9
1996	86.1	106.6	87.3	78.0	114.3	102.2	81.0	101.1	93.0	78.4	118.9	98.2
1997	104.4	103.6	104.3	104.6	104.2	106.3	102.0	100.1	104.0	101.8	122.0	196.4
1998	102.2	98.3	104.7	95.5	112.0	132.7	90.0	98.7	108.8	86.3	122.8	285.4
1999	104.3	98.3	107.5	96.8	110.7	117.8	86.3	97.3	115.0	80.9	111.2	113.5
2000	106.0	106.0	106.7	103.4	100.0	110.6	102.8	104.7	110.7	101.1	118.3	99.1
2001	110.4	101.7	114.8	102.9	112.9	107.1	105.1	100.3	110.7	104.6	116.9	104.3
2002	104.1	95.8	107.1	99.4	120.0	101.2	100.2	93.6	110.2	98.8	131.8	96.4
2003	105.1	104.0	105.5	104.4	100.0	104.0	113.5	102.6	106.5	117.1	118.3	86.3
2004	108.4	126.8	105.1	108.6	116.7	117.9	113.1	119.7	107.1	113.7	112.4	124.8
2005	101.5	95.7	102.7	101.3	149.0	101.7	105.1	93.7	118.8	103.4	132.0	100.9
2006	108.9	86.7	114.8	104.1	108.1	117.8	106.3	104.2	114.9	102.7	107.2	226.8
2007	113.4	101.9	115.5	112.3	110.5	114.0	106.4	101.3	122.1	102.7	107.7	119.1
2008	109.9	102.3	111.9	104.6	97.1	112.3	100.7	102.3	117.4	94.6	91.3	117.3
2009	117.3	97.5	123.7	107.9	106.8	101.0	107.7	89.7	123.9	102.9	102.4	106.3
2010	114.1	108.1	113.5	117.7	128.1	114.9	120.1	106.4	115.5	124.0	175.1	111.2
2011	114.6	98.9	117.0	113.4	102.4	101.9	119.9	97.8	122.6	121.6	112.2	100.3
2012	111.5	99.7	113.5	109.1	107.9	100.7	116.0	95.0	113.3	119.5	114.6	100.3
2013	114.8	100.3	115.1	118.4	102.7	102.6	127.8	98.5	118.1	133.5	104.2	96.1
2014	107.8	92.5	107.4	112.2	110.0	105.7	123.0	91.1	116.7	126.3	115.5	102.0
2015	106.4	90.4	108.9	101.1	102.9	100.6	100.7	92.4	111.0	98.1	110.6	100.5
2016	108.0	100.6	106.6	113.4	107.6	109.3	150.2	100.2	108.8	164.0	109.5	99.7
2017	106.9	101.3	105.9	110.8	103.7	105.8	128.0	104.3	107.5	132.2	111.1	122.4
2018	106.1	105.0	105.5	107.9	106.5	106.9	101.6	99.7	107.0	100.7	107.3	107.4
2019	104.9	107.5	104.8	105.9	105.6	98.9	102.0	111.0	105.7	101.4	103.0	100.1
2020	95.0	95.8	96.4	91.7	99.8	97.9	99.8	93.6	98.4	99.9	103.6	109.1
2021	111.8	126.4	115.7	103.3	100.9	102.7	102.9	128.0	118.1	101.2	107.5	95.9
2022	91.4	94.5	90.6	91.1	92.0	106.9	100.2	101.7	90.9	101.3	96.5	100.5
2023	105.0	102.8	104.3	108.5	111.3	95.4	104.3	102.2	105.2	104.3	97.5	102.0

15-8 各市货运量
Freight Traffic by City

单位：万吨 (10000 tons)

市 别	City	2005	2010	2015	2019	2020	2021	2022	2023
全 省	**Provincial Total**	**133992**	**205034**	**376434**	**446018**	**356221**	**398420**	**364199**	**382401**
广 州	Guangzhou	28026	51335	94303	132922	89191	93968	85820	87833
深 圳	Shenzhen	7837	25706	32331	33982	41150	43657	40617	42751
珠 海	Zhuhai	2225	7038	11626	12883	7575	7947	7089	9482
汕 头	Shantou	1703	3087	6469	7533	7704	8651	7297	7589
佛 山	Foshan	17354	19153	29428	33311	23779	27128	26179	28090
韶 关	Shaoguan	3251	6364	19024	22570	10298	9358	8628	8788
河 源	Heyuan	986	2244	6509	6879	4372	6548	5769	6142
梅 州	Meizhou	3751	4092	7820	9070	9310	11211	10235	10337
惠 州	Huizhou	4786	11104	23435	27853	21387	24483	21844	23931
汕 尾	Shanwei	1106	1232	2536	3071	2260	3662	3221	3759
东 莞	Dongguan	5127	9312	15923	17653	17139	17449	15115	15045
中 山	Zhongshan	5985	7820	17963	11529	10666	10661	9668	9587
江 门	Jiangmen	5626	7458	15407	16901	17921	18568	17805	17988
阳 江	Yangjiang	417	1752	11385	10538	5499	7415	6623	6989
湛 江	Zhanjiang	5016	6808	16528	22177	18652	20726	17705	19494
茂 名	Maoming	4388	4365	9895	12486	10303	13236	12290	12795
肇 庆	Zhaoqing	3689	2869	7303	8509	8096	9705	8759	10012
清 远	Qingyuan	3200	7155	15267	19443	17594	25774	21697	23131
潮 州	Chaozhou	1310	2339	4928	6385	2795	2775	2541	2635
揭 阳	Jieyang	2213	1945	3898	4813	2422	2870	2876	2914
云 浮	Yunfu	3286	2303	6099	7141	6817	8903	8326	9399
不分地区	Unclassified	22710	19553	18358	18368	21291	23724	24097	23710
按经济区域分	By Region								
珠 三 角	Pearl River Delta	103365	161348	266078	313912	258195	277290	256992	268429
粤 东	Eastern Region	6332	8603	17831	21802	15181	17958	15934	16898
粤 西	Western Region	9821	12925	37808	45201	34454	41377	36618	39278
粤 北	Northern Region	14474	22158	54719	65103	48391	61795	54655	57797

注：分市数据仅含公路和水路运输，铁路、民航和管道运输在“不分地区”反映。下表同。

Note: Data by city only include the figures of highway and waterway transportation, whereas data of railway, civil aviation and pipeline transportation are reflected in the category “Unclassified by Region”. The same applies to the following table.

15-9 各市货物周转量

Freight Ton-kilometers by City

单位：亿吨公里 (100 million ton-km)

市别	City	2005	2010	2015	2019	2020	2021	2022	2023
全　省	**Provincial Total**	**3917.43**	**5933.88**	**15130.59**	**29230.88**	**27575.18**	**28388.06**	**28438.62**	**29668.13**
广　州	Guangzhou	2431.16	2032.86	8225.53	21737.17	21525.32	21760.26	22053.63	22770.23
深　圳	Shenzhen	317.28	1627.56	2241.11	2174.03	1987.07	2169.88	2212.30	2420.42
珠　海	Zhuhai	84.89	168.12	167.01	237.64	442.37	459.28	335.21	462.93
汕　头	Shantou	38.41	101.79	170.80	175.31	78.41	83.43	78.30	75.27
佛　山	Foshan	182.11	152.08	266.40	336.53	238.96	295.92	306.27	346.13
韶　关	Shaoguan	26.97	118.91	359.42	430.09	187.06	161.56	149.26	147.27
河　源	Heyuan	8.48	34.02	87.46	97.83	36.39	56.01	52.71	55.81
梅　州	Meizhou	45.95	73.69	177.60	195.06	89.27	119.92	111.81	119.73
惠　州	Huizhou	40.29	152.97	476.75	505.40	375.63	409.37	410.35	418.70
汕　尾	Shanwei	8.60	13.44	29.30	36.06	20.58	31.23	27.24	38.33
东　莞	Dongguan	32.94	109.03	508.71	535.47	528.77	507.04	459.27	481.76
中　山	Zhongshan	43.03	64.81	167.46	98.83	74.55	82.26	76.01	85.67
江　门	Jiangmen	70.96	112.55	182.29	178.22	158.20	157.17	147.55	155.38
阳　江	Yangjiang	2.98	39.93	195.05	100.76	37.08	47.88	43.28	48.91
湛　江	Zhanjiang	57.47	177.54	469.13	595.97	398.17	461.70	445.82	448.17
茂　名	Maoming	23.78	92.42	211.71	283.52	227.90	279.39	256.84	254.63
肇　庆	Zhaoqing	24.87	38.56	76.11	84.95	67.78	80.94	81.10	98.32
清　远	Qingyuan	29.37	118.19	262.28	321.25	183.13	264.47	217.76	244.86
潮　州	Chaozhou	25.27	103.37	234.40	326.98	168.69	111.81	111.01	116.06
揭　阳	Jieyang	22.64	26.93	77.53	89.13	23.96	28.11	44.02	45.20
云　浮	Yunfu	17.26	36.83	59.85	81.69	79.77	101.38	95.63	99.76
不分地区	Unclassified	382.72	538.26	484.69	608.99	646.15	719.08	723.25	734.60
按经济区域分	By Region								
珠三角	Pearl River Delta	3610.25	4996.80	12796.07	26497.23	26044.79	26641.18	26804.96	27974.14
粤　东	Eastern Region	94.92	245.54	512.03	627.47	291.64	254.58	260.57	274.86
粤　西	Western Region	84.22	309.90	875.89	980.25	663.14	788.97	745.94	751.70
粤　北	Northern Region	128.04	381.64	946.61	1125.93	575.62	703.33	627.16	667.43

15-10 运输工具和线路拥有量

Number of Means of Transport and Length of Transport Routes

项　目	Item	2000	2010	2015	2021	2022	2023
铁　路	**Railways**						
铁路机车 (台)	Number of Locomotives (unit)	538	448	350	319	297	280
铁路营业里程 (公里)	Length of Railways in Operation (km)	1942	2297	3859	5101	5158	5452
中央铁路	National Railways	694	629	629	633	633	658
地方铁路	Local Railways	1248	1668	3230	4468	4525	4794
公　路	**Highways**						
公路通车里程 (公里)	Length of Highways (km)	102606	190144	216023	222987	223081	223391
民用汽车 (万辆)	Civil Motor Vehicles (10000 units)	172.91	783.50	1472.33	2702.55	2898.36	3069.11
#载客汽车 (万辆)	Passenger Vehicles (10000 units)	85.34	629.30	1290.57	2410.37	2602.63	2774.30
(万客位)	Passenger Vehicle Seats (10000 seats)	796.92	4148.85	7572.21	13376.17	14301.67	15163.63
#轿车 (万辆)	Sedan Cars (10000 units)	25.39	380.46	820.12	1464.24	1576.00	1775.91
载货汽车 (万辆)	Freight Vehicles (10000 units)	84.38	147.53	174.90	281.77	285.08	284.11
(万吨位)	Tonnage of Freight Vehicles (10000 tonnages)	351.75	268.23	354.81	781.61	778.12	769.08
水　运	**Waterways**						
内河通航里程 (公里)	Length of Navigable Inland Waterways (km)	13696	13596	12150	12266	12266	12266
机动船 (艘)	Number of Motor Vessels (unit)	21733	8793	8716	6646	6359	6097
(万净载重吨)	Tonnage of Motor Vessels (1000 dead weight tonnage)	526.88	1140.71	2703.55	2369.96	2305.98	1924.25
(客位)	Number of Motor Vessel Seats (seat)	149004	65960	80219	80824	78925	79023
(总功率万千瓦)	Total Power (10000 kws)	307.42	420.54	688.33	619.56	609.66	531.91
民　航	**Civil Aviation**						
民用航空航线条数 (条)	Number of Civil Aviation Routes (line)	329	815	963	1629	1591	1827
民用航空航线里程(万公里)	Length of Civil Aviation Routes(10000 kms)	50.03	180.74	237.29	339.56	273.44	330.60
民用运输飞机 (架)	Number of Civil Aircrafts (unit)	106	441	625	901	909	921
管　道	**Pipelines**						
条　数 (条)	Number of Pipelines (line)	45	105	116	154	156	149
输油(气)里程 (公里)	Length of Petroleum and Gas Pipelines (km)	1535.57	6033.62	6500.90	9664.23	11769.84	12075.71

15-11 各市民用汽车拥有量（2023年）
Possession of Civil Vehicles by City (2023)

单位：辆 (unit)

市别	City	民用汽车总计 Total	载客汽车 Passenger Vehicles	#轿车 Sedan Cars	按车型分 By Vehicle Type 大型 Large	中型 Medium	小型 Small	微型 Minibuses
全　省	**Provincial Total**	**30691133**	**27742955**	**17759123**	**139794**	**35638**	**27517682**	**49841**
广　州	Guangzhou	3722701	3237764	1780034	30547	5776	3194603	6838
深　圳	Shenzhen	4102723	3541150	1983759	28647	4068	3502595	5840
珠　海	Zhuhai	947253	879503	574225	7509	995	870982	17
汕　头	Shantou	1096205	988396	657948	4142	1152	980591	2511
佛　山	Foshan	3637743	3376455	2195788	10688	2196	3356426	7145
韶　关	Shaoguan	564807	518340	343223	1970	1289	514011	1070
河　源	Heyuan	584394	530658	374933	1811	991	526869	987
梅　州	Meizhou	749091	664511	468485	2419	1147	659588	1357
惠　州	Huizhou	1828873	1704994	1134534	6330	1263	1694963	2438
汕　尾	Shanwei	395589	370931	252970	2206	561	367522	642
东　莞	Dongguan	4149792	3897381	2453717	15096	2534	3876330	3421
中　山	Zhongshan	1575204	1433559	954574	4712	735	1424661	3451
江　门	Jiangmen	1179026	1067117	747246	3526	957	1060024	2610
阳　江	Yangjiang	595183	537175	399012	1222	341	534647	965
湛　江	Zhanjiang	984328	888820	628122	3253	1269	883109	1189
茂　名	Maoming	1050995	952150	698016	2423	2545	945046	2136
肇　庆	Zhaoqing	763289	683613	458724	2546	1098	678955	1014
清　远	Qingyuan	920257	826041	544277	3355	1522	819399	1765
潮　州	Chaozhou	503987	445170	301027	990	346	441863	1971
揭　阳	Jieyang	825613	742421	492592	2984	1014	737116	1307
云　浮	Yunfu	479427	428264	308449	1212	942	424944	1166
不分地区	Unclassified	34653	28542	7468	2206	2897	23438	1
按经济区域分	By Region							
珠三角	Pearl River Delta	21941257	19850078	12290069	111807	22519	19682977	32775
粤　东	Eastern Region	2821394	2546918	1704537	10322	3073	2527092	6431
粤　西	Western Region	2630506	2378145	1725150	6898	4155	2362802	4290
粤　北	Northern Region	3297976	2967814	2039367	10767	5891	2944811	6345

15-11 续表 continued

单位：辆 (unit)

市 别	City	载货汽车 Freight Vehicles	按车型分 By Vehicle Type 重型 Heavy	中型 Medium	轻型 Light	微型 Mini Trucks	其他汽车 Others
全 省	**Provincial Total**	**2841094**	**540739**	**81433**	**2213086**	**5836**	**107084**
广 州	Guangzhou	464974	95579	16086	352468	841	19963
深 圳	Shenzhen	542436	124167	9334	408163	772	19137
珠 海	Zhuhai	64264	12690	1271	50302	1	3486
汕 头	Shantou	105597	9510	1456	92681	1950	2212
佛 山	Foshan	252339	44222	9828	198205	84	8949
韶 关	Shaoguan	44352	8837	738	34744	33	2115
河 源	Heyuan	50360	10753	1370	38155	82	3376
梅 州	Meizhou	82000	15215	1296	65302	187	2580
惠 州	Huizhou	117529	26024	3153	88284	68	6350
汕 尾	Shanwei	23186	4449	857	17844	36	1472
东 莞	Dongguan	243734	47185	11844	184593	112	8677
中 山	Zhongshan	138436	16971	4475	116940	50	3209
江 门	Jiangmen	108631	19539	3358	85665	69	3278
阳 江	Yangjiang	55680	12469	1761	41361	89	2328
湛 江	Zhanjiang	91918	14507	3274	74095	42	3590
茂 名	Maoming	95165	17733	2527	74842	63	3680
肇 庆	Zhaoqing	77659	15106	2902	59636	15	2017
清 远	Qingyuan	90730	23720	2335	64624	51	3486
潮 州	Chaozhou	56754	3136	769	52500	349	2063
揭 阳	Jieyang	81058	6997	1552	72344	165	2134
云 浮	Yunfu	49621	11909	1099	35836	777	1542
不分地区	Unclassified	4671	21	148	4502		1440
按经济区域分	By Region						
珠 三 角	Pearl River Delta	2014673	401504	62399	1548758	2012	76506
粤 东	Eastern Region	266595	24092	4634	235369	2500	7881
粤 西	Western Region	242763	44709	7562	190298	194	9598
粤 北	Northern Region	317063	70434	6838	238661	1130	13099

15-12 各市私人汽车拥有量（2023年）

Possession of Private Vehicles by City (2023)

单位：辆 (unit)

市别	City	汽车总计 Total	载客汽车 Passenger Vehicles	#轿车 Sedan Cars	载货汽车 Freight Vehicles	其它汽车 Others
全省	**Provincial Total**	**27073797**	**25610915**	**16652552**	**1430167**	**32715**
广州	Guangzhou	2991583	2811391	1546305	175014	5178
深圳	Shenzhen	3266571	3169139	1800625	94825	2607
珠海	Zhuhai	843613	805468	536834	37350	795
汕头	Shantou	1032659	954730	642930	77153	776
佛山	Foshan	3284283	3142601	2071146	139449	2233
韶关	Shaoguan	522205	492353	331228	29047	805
河源	Heyuan	535734	498397	356943	35304	2033
梅州	Meizhou	686196	625485	446888	59517	1194
惠州	Huizhou	1638988	1578874	1064430	58461	1653
汕尾	Shanwei	367673	350632	242035	16384	657
东莞	Dongguan	3688579	3562918	2274796	123491	2170
中山	Zhongshan	1434248	1351990	913333	81413	845
江门	Jiangmen	1076454	1010287	720851	65213	954
阳江	Yangjiang	567083	522707	392574	43311	1065
湛江	Zhanjiang	935488	860229	615825	73154	2105
茂名	Maoming	989683	915930	677831	71475	2278
肇庆	Zhaoqing	696441	650132	443658	45525	784
清远	Qingyuan	817244	758526	507471	57261	1457
潮州	Chaozhou	481078	432271	295121	47660	1147
揭阳	Jieyang	780833	712866	476830	66670	1297
云浮	Yunfu	437161	403989	294898	32490	682
按经济区域分	By Region					
珠三角	Pearl River Delta	18920760	18082800	11371978	820741	17219
粤东	Eastern Region	2662243	2450499	1656916	207867	3877
粤西	Western Region	2492254	2298866	1686230	187940	5448
粤北	Northern Region	2998540	2778750	1937428	213619	6171

15–13 各市公路基本情况（2023年）

Basic Conditions of Highways by City (2023)

单位：公里 (km)

市别	City	通车里程 Length of Highways	按等级分 By Class		按路面分 By Pavement			桥梁 Bridges	
			等级路 Expressways and Class I to IV Highways	等外路 Highways below Class IV	有铺装路面 Paved Highways	简易铺装路面 Simply-paved Highways	未铺装路面 Unpaved Highways	座 Number (unit)	米 Span (meter)
全省	**Provincial Total**	**223391**	**223383**	**8**	**223001**	**315**	**75**	**67834**	**8491498**
广州	Guangzhou	8422	8422		8421	0		4787	1149192
深圳	Shenzhen	721	721		721			1135	290078
珠海	Zhuhai	1527	1527		1527			752	322607
汕头	Shantou	4099	4096	2	4096		2	1626	306306
佛山	Foshan	4806	4806		4806			3655	866074
韶关	Shaoguan	17388	17388		17388			3435	365198
河源	Heyuan	17666	17666		17625	5	36	4951	395762
梅州	Meizhou	21045	21045		20928	113	3	5431	436231
惠州	Huizhou	13976	13976		13973	2	1	4732	469161
汕尾	Shanwei	6031	6031		6009	19	4	1681	112568
东莞	Dongguan	3541	3541		3541			2115	519233
中山	Zhongshan	2853	2853		2853			1791	457850
江门	Jiangmen	10020	10014	6	10019	0		4284	464184
阳江	Yangjiang	10891	10891		10835	54	2	3266	202990
湛江	Zhanjiang	22957	22957		22882	66	8	3396	261877
茂名	Maoming	19521	19521		19517	4		5199	325059
肇庆	Zhaoqing	14378	14378		14329	49	0	4052	428866
清远	Qingyuan	20866	20866		20855	1	10	4738	431034
潮州	Chaozhou	5654	5654		5651	0	3	1475	185484
揭阳	Jieyang	8014	8014		8007	0	6	2884	242568
云浮	Yunfu	9017	9017		9017	1		2449	259177
按经济区域分	By Region								
珠三角	Pearl River Delta	60243	60238	6	60191	51	1	27303	4967245
粤东	Eastern Region	23798	23795	2	23764	19	15	7666	846926
粤西	Western Region	53368	53368		53233	124	10	11861	789926
粤北	Northern Region	85982	85982		85813	120	48	21004	1887401

15-14 公路通车里程和桥梁数

Length of Highways and Number of Bridges

项目	Item	2000	2010	2015	2020	2021	2022	2023
通车里程 （公里）	**Length of Highways (km)**	**102606**	**190144**	**216023**	**221873**	**222987**	**223081**	**223391**
按等级分	By Class							
等级路	Expressways and Class Ito IV Highways	93695	170144	201456	221651	222779	223013	223383
高速公路	Expressways	1186	4839	7021	10488	11042	11211	11481
一 级	First Class	5391	10126	10936	12021	12421	13337	13710
二 级	Second Class	13397	19082	19213	19636	19374	19122	18066
三 级	Third Class	9156	16089	18662	22403	23945	25299	27711
四 级	Fourth Class	64565	120008	145624	157103	155997	154045	152415
等外公路	Highways below Class IV	8911	19999	14567	222	208	67	8
按路面分	By Pavement							
有铺装路面	Paved Highways		123784	147976	221024	222320	222463	223001
简易铺装路面	Simply-paved Highways		5721	9418	685	575	543	315
未铺装路面	Unpaved Highways		60638	58629	164	92	75	75
桥 梁 （座）	**Number of Bridges (unit)**	**19668**	**42330**	**45589**	**50036**	**51302**	**62112**	**67834**
（米）	Span of Bridges (m)	819770	2340261	3205460	4693655	4924474	6779767	8491498
#永久式 （座）	Number of Permanent Bridges (unit)	19656	42233	45501	49939	51243	62049	67805
（米）	Span of Permanent Bridges (m)	819502	2337490	3202958	4691065	4923071	6778053	8490823
半永久式 （座）	Number of Semi-permanent Bridges (unit)	12	52	48	67	31	33	19
（米）	Span of Semi-permanent Bridges (m)	268	1391	1266	1575	751	714	410
渡 口 （个）	**Number of Ferries (unit)**	**33**	**71**	**79**	**67**	**64**	**56**	**60**

15-15 输油(气)管道长度和运输量

Length and Traffic of Petroleum and Gas Pipelines

项目	Item	2000	2010	2015	2020	2021	2022	2023
总 计	**Total**							
条 数 (条)	Number of Pipelines (line)	45	105	116	156	154	156	149
输送里程 (公里)	Length of Pipelines (km)	1535.57	6033.62	6500.90	10136.90	9664.23	11769.84	12075.71
输油(气)量 (万吨)	Pipeline Traffic (10000 tons)	2952	7267	8137	13209	13564	14503	13831
输油(气)周转量(万吨公里)	Ton-kilometers (10000 ton-km)	417432	1757891	1743309	2817764	2701993	2714244	2768667
原油管道	**Crude Oil Pipelines**							
条 数 (条)	Number of Pipelines (line)	7	17	25	44	45	45	45
输送里程 (公里)	Length of Pipelines (km)	352.67	634.18	595.38	741.80	745.80	841.61	841.61
输油量 (万吨)	Pipeline Traffic (10000 tons)	1912	3364	4474	6347	5970	6322	5477
输油周转量 (万吨公里)	Ton-kilometers (10000 ton-km)	189623	352764	382146	450767	422756	428914	387682
成品油管道	**Refined Oil Pipelines**							
条 数 (条)	Number of Pipelines (line)	27	62	53	44	48	45	45
输送里程 (公里)	Length of Pipelines (km)	211.00	3925.88	4283.67	6300.69	7357.59	6628.99	6628.99
输油量 (万吨)	Pipeline Traffic (10000 tons)	663	3015	3431	3439	4306	3526	3825
输油周转量 (万吨公里)	Ton-kilometers (10000 ton-km)	13250	1153210	1247144	1810463	1769311	1590619	1727489
其他管道	**Other Pipelines**							
条 数 (条)	Number of Pipelines (line)	11	26	38	68	61	66	59
输送里程 (公里)	Length of Pipelines (km)	971.90	1473.56	1621.85	3094.41	1560.84	4299.24	4605.11
输气量 (万吨)	Pipeline Traffic (10000 tons)	377	887	233	3423	3288	4655	4530
输气周转量 (万吨公里)	Ton-kilometers(10000 ton-km)	214559	251917	114020	556533	509926	694710	653495

15−16 民航航站吞吐量

Throughput of Civil Aviation Airports

年 份 Year	合 计 Total			进 港 In-port			出 港 Out-port		
	架次 (万次) Sorties (10000 sorties)	旅客 (万人) Passenger Traffic (10000 persons)	货物 (万吨) Freight Traffic (10000 tons)	架次 (万次) Sorties (10000 sorties)	旅客 (万人) Passenger Traffic (10000 persons)	货物 (万吨) Freight Traffic (10000 tons)	架次 (万次) Sorties (10000 sorties)	旅客 (万人) Passenger Traffic (10000 persons)	货物 (万吨) Freight Traffic (10000 tons)
1980	1.60	161	2.90	0.80	81	1.40	0.80	80	1.50
1985	4.00	318	6.20	2.00	160	3.00	2.00	158	3.20
1990	6.20	687	13.50	3.10	343	5.90	3.10	344	7.60
1995	17.70	1963	39.50	8.80	963	14.10	8.90	1000	25.40
1996	18.20	2025	45.60	9.10	993	15.90	9.10	1032	29.70
1997	19.00	1981	49.00	9.50	974	16.70	9.50	1007	32.30
1998	20.80	2010	55.80	10.40	986	20.80	10.40	1024	35.00
1999	22.20	1929	63.70	11.10	942	25.60	11.10	987	38.10
2000	23.60	2143	73.00	11.80	1044	30.90	11.80	1099	42.10
2001	25.10	2344	81.00	12.50	1136	33.90	12.60	1208	47.10
2002	28.00	2731	95.70	14.00	1340	40.40	14.00	1391	55.30
2003	28.10	2751	82.40	14.10	1351	34.90	14.00	1400	47.50
2004	34.70	3661	115.80	17.30	1801	50.80	17.40	1860	65.00
2005	38.40	4100	133.00	19.20	2023	58.60	19.20	2077	74.40
2006	42.36	4599	151.13	21.18	2262	64.40	21.18	2337	86.70
2007	46.61	5407	133.20	23.30	2614	53.00	23.31	2793	80.20
2008	49.33	5738	130.47	24.60	2756	52.70	24.60	2982	77.78
2009	54.20	6462	158.50	27.10	3150	65.30	27.10	3312	93.20
2010	58.56	7189	198.40	29.30	3533	83.00	29.30	3655	115.50
2011	61.18	7768	203.96	30.59	3837	84.56	30.59	3931	119.40
2012	65.60	8283	213.59	32.79	4090	86.81	32.81	4193	126.78
2013	70.83	9124	226.75	35.41	4502	91.96	35.42	4622	134.79
2014	76.90	9924	246.27	38.45	4877	99.93	38.45	5047	146.34
2015	79.90	10494	260.26	39.95	5170	108.06	39.96	5324	152.20
2016	85.65	11440	284.36	42.82	5642	118.26	42.83	5798	166.10
2017	94.30	12940	301.27	47.15	6408	125.95	47.15	6532	175.32
2018	100.29	14184	319.22	50.14	7019	133.28	50.15	7165	185.94
2019	105.69	15303	329.75	52.84	7560	133.22	52.85	7743	196.54
2020	84.16	9942	323.89	42.06	4990	126.96	42.10	4952	196.94
2021	85.01	9594	369.93	42.47	4764	138.70	42.53	4830	231.23
2022	60.41	5825	345.60	30.21	2873	126.43	30.21	2952	219.17
2023	105.28	14142	371.29	52.63	7007	126.07	52.64	7134	245.22

15-17 港口泊位及吞吐量

Berth and Throughput of Coastal Ports

项　目	Item	2000	2010	2015	2021	2022	2023
码头泊位合计　（个）	**Number of Berths (unit)**	**3191**	**3082**	**3093**	**2295**	**2252**	**2327**
沿海港口	**Coastal Ports**	**1373**	**1884**	**2005**	**1488**	**1476**	**1548**
#广州港	Guangzhou Port	141	633	584	497	493	541
湛江港	Zhanjiang Port	41	184	174	162	162	166
汕头港	Shantou Port	28	91	92	37	35	36
深圳港	Shenzhen Port	121	172	156	164	172	172
内河港口	**Ports of Inland Rivers**	**1818**	**1198**	**1088**	**807**	**776**	**779**
万吨级码头泊位合计（个）	**Berths at 10000 Ton Class (unit)**	**126**	**245**	**291**	**349**	**368**	**401**
沿海港口	**Coastal Ports**	**126**	**245**	**291**	**349**	**368**	**401**
#广州港	Guangzhou Port	32	62	74	80	83	86
湛江港	Zhanjiang Port	24	31	33	44	44	64
汕头港	Shantou Port	6	18	19	14	14	15
深圳港	Shenzhen Port	34	69	67	74	76	77
内河港口	**Ports of Inland Rivers**						
码头泊位长度　（米）	**Length of Quay Line (m)**	**180238**	**252762**	**266828**	**241392**	**244557**	**249656**
沿海港口	**Coastal Ports**	**105193**	**176753**	**200025**	**186842**	**191119**	**198204**
#广州港	Guangzhou Port	13496	51673	51722	40283	40265	42398
湛江港	Zhanjiang Port	6635	17458	18419	23577	23577	24182
汕头港	Shantou Port	3152	9715	9898	6029	5900	6178
深圳港	Shenzhen Port	17150	31377	30627	33736	34925	35269
内河港口	**Ports of Inland Rivers**	**75045**	**76009**	**66803**	**54550**	**53438**	**51451**
货物吞吐量合计　（万吨）	**Total Volume of Freight Handled (10000 tons)**	**31649**	**122258**	**171109**	**209600**	**204802**	**221462**
沿海港口	**Coastal Ports**	**25495**	**105300**	**142059**	**181604**	**175517**	**188392**
#广州港	Guangzhou Port	11128	42526	50053	62367	62906	64283
湛江港	Zhanjiang Port	2038	13638	22036	25555	25376	28273
汕头港	Shantou Port	1284	3509	5181	4138	4019	3879
深圳港	Shenzhen Port	4224	22097	21706	27838	27243	28664
内河港口	**Ports of Inland Rivers**	**6154**	**16958**	**29050**	**27996**	**29284**	**33070**
集装箱吞吐量合计(万TEU)	**Total Volume of Containers Handled (10000 TEUS)**	**862.68**	**4360.14**	**5512.12**	**7078.20**	**7064.83**	**7209.26**
沿海港口	**Coastal Ports**	**655.15**	**3867.77**	**4914.73**	**6428.94**	**6490.04**	**6567.51**
#广州港	Guangzhou Port	142.98	1270.00	1739.66	2417.96	2460.17	2510.57
湛江港	Zhanjiang Port	7.48	32.01	60.12	140.47	153.54	158.13
汕头港	Shantou Port	11.44	93.50	117.86	179.99	176.50	175.82
深圳港	Shenzhen Port	395.84	2250.96	2420.45	2876.76	3003.62	2988.00
内河港口	**Ports of Inland Rivers**	**207.53**	**492.37**	**597.38**	**649.25**	**574.80**	**641.75**
旅客吞吐量合计　（万人）	**Total Volume of Passengers Handled(10000 persons)**	**1670.32**	**2483.21**	**3432.96**	**1849.17**	**1464.19**	**3021.56**
沿海港口	**Coastal Ports**	**1330.81**	**2109.39**	**2867.17**	**1849.17**	**1464.19**	**3010.58**
#广州港	Guangzhou Port	15.00	79.01	61.32	3.81	1.66	22.24
湛江港	Zhanjiang Port	29.60	1051.41	1299.79	1252.53	1185.45	1928.30
汕头港	Shantou Port	5.50					
深圳港	Shenzhen Port	203.36	333.88	586.52	259.92	113.31	488.09
内河港口	**Ports of Inland Rivers**	**339.51**	**373.82**	**565.79**			**10.97**

注：从2019年起，港口统计数据采集方式改为企业一套表联网直报，统计范围是辖区内各港口。
Note: From 2019, the port statistical data collection method are changed to online reporting, and the statistical scope is all ports within the jurisdiction.

15-18 各市港口货物吞吐量
Freight Throughput of Ports by City

单位：万吨 (10000 tons)

市别	City	2000	2005	2010	2015	2019	2020	2021	2022	2023
全省	**Provincial Total**	**31649**	**70926**	**122258**	**171109**	**191819**	**202226**	**209600**	**204802**	**221462**
广州	Guangzhou	12455	27283	42526	52096	62687	63643	65130	65592	67498
深圳	Shenzhen	5697	15351	22098	21706	25785	26506	27838	27243	28664
珠海	Zhuhai	1770	3557	6056	11209	13838	13367	12826	10237	11886
汕头	Shantou	1284	1736	3509	5181	3155	3351	4138	4019	3879
佛山	Foshan	2033	3951	5410	6147	9636	9285	9341	8559	10203
韶关	Shaoguan	131	118	40	62	98	299	291	419	889
河源	Heyuan	45	49							
梅州	Meizhou	145	306	132	114					
惠州	Huizhou	825	1515	4673	7013	8956	9636	9644	9005	9158
汕尾	Shanwei	25	107	489	858	1310	1274	1666	1751	1851
东莞	Dongguan	746	2280	5657	13149	19808	19857	18896	17021	19551
中山	Zhongshan	635	2072	4798	7319	1547	1312	1434	1539	1842
江门	Jiangmen	879	2438	4965	7525	6832	10698	10510	9628	10348
阳江	Yangjiang	68	222	799	2139	3235	3350	3403	3838	3687
湛江	Zhanjiang	2688	6620	13638	22036	21570	23391	25555	25376	28273
茂名	Maoming	1104	1360	2284	2685	2508	2683	2887	3162	3175
肇庆	Zhaoqing	189	520	1597	2945	4057	4789	4657	4982	5050
清远	Qingyuan	193	461	639	2927	1462	1864	2570	2478	2512
潮州	Chaozhou	60	80	635	1144	824	1366	1737	1708	1633
揭阳	Jieyang	266	248	1290	2851	1898	2370	2768	2990	5957
云浮	Yunfu	411	654	1023	2002	2613	3186	4307	5257	5406
按经济区域分	By Region									
珠三角	Pearl River Delta	25229	58966	97779	129108	153147	159092	160276	153805	164200
粤东	Eastern Region	1635	2171	5924	10035	7187	8361	10310	10468	13320
粤西	Western Region	3860	8202	16721	26860	27312	29424	31845	32376	35135
粤北	Northern Region	925	1588	1834	5106	4173	5349	7169	8153	8807

15−19 各市城市公共交通情况（2023年）

Basic Statistics on Public Transportation in Cities by City (2023)

市别	City	公共汽电车 Public Bus and Trolly Bus				出租汽车 Taxi	
		运营车辆(辆) Number of Vehicles under Operation (unit)	运营线路条数(条) Number of operating lines	运营线路长度(公里) Length under Operation (Km)	客运量(万人) Passenger Traffic (10000 persons)	运营车辆(辆) Number of Vehicles in Operation (unit)	客运量(万人) Passengers Transported (10000 persons)
全　省	**Provincial Total**	**63120**	**5689**	**122074**	**336521**	**51174**	**74767**
广　州	Guangzhou	14076	1372	24505	108543	18827	32113
深　圳	Shenzhen	15354	942	19591	82118	20625	28188
珠　海	Zhuhai	2498	216	4480	29352	3387	5468
汕　头	Shantou	2087	156	4910	10082	803	808
佛　山	Foshan	6088	635	13738	26899	1562	1172
韶　关	Shaoguan	694	118	2164	3345	192	210
河　源	Heyuan	510	60	1181	1329	154	366
梅　州	Meizhou	1384	214	5517	6522	133	144
惠　州	Huizhou	2867	222	6856	13495	986	889
汕　尾	Shanwei	1105	108	2903	3132	259	274
东　莞	Dongguan	6330	373	7323	14848	1021	2156
中　山	Zhongshan	2618	226	4299	10340	487	318
江　门	Jiangmen	1604	227	4965	7364	175	340
阳　江	Yangjiang	405	74	1385	864	79	85
湛　江	Zhanjiang	1056	112	2483	3031	406	913
茂　名	Maoming	927	109	2943	1955	1031	359
肇　庆	Zhaoqing	1021	145	3981	5604	139	159
清　远	Qingyuan	978	188	3971	3732	430	565
潮　州	Chaozhou	381	51	1311	1107	277	114
揭　阳	Jieyang	716	61	1859	1989	102	72
云　浮	Yunfu	421	80	1709	870	99	55
按经济区域分	By Region						
珠三角	Pearl River Delta	52456	4358	89738	298563	47209	70803
粤　东	Eastern Region	4289	376	10983	16310	1441	1268
粤　西	Western Region	2388	295	6811	5850	1516	1357
粤　北	Northern Region	3987	660	14542	15798	1008	1338

15−19 续表 continued

市 别	City	轨道交通 Subway, Light Rail and Streetcar 运营车数(辆) Number of Vehicles under Operation (unit)	运营线路条数(条) Number of operating lines	运营线路长度(公里) Length under Operation (km)	客运量(万人) Passengers Transported (10000 persons)	客运轮渡 Passenger Ferryboat 运营船舶(艘) Number of Vehicles under Operation (unit)	客运量(万人) Passengers Transported (10000 persons)
全 省	**Provincial Total**	**8809**	**41**	**1382**	**596798**	**52**	**1550**
广 州	Guangzhou	3762	18	675	313791	44	1251
深 圳	Shenzhen	4492	17	567	271030		
珠 海	Zhuhai	30	1	9			
汕 头	Shantou					4	288
佛 山	Foshan	405	4	94	7443		
韶 关	Shaoguan						
河 源	Heyuan						
梅 州	Meizhou						
惠 州	Huizhou						
汕 尾	Shanwei						
东 莞	Dongguan	120	1	38	4534		
中 山	Zhongshan						
江 门	Jiangmen						
阳 江	Yangjiang						
湛 江	Zhanjiang					4	11
茂 名	Maoming						
肇 庆	Zhaoqing						
清 远	Qingyuan						
潮 州	Chaozhou						
揭 阳	Jieyang						
云 浮	Yunfu						
按经济区域分	By Region						
珠 三 角	Pearl River Delta	8809	41	1383	596797	44	1251
粤 东	Eastern Region					4	288
粤 西	Western Region					4	11
粤 北	Northern Region						

15-20 邮电业务总量和指数

Business Volume of Postal and Telecommunication Services and Their Indices

年份 Year	邮电业务总量(亿元) Business Volume of Postal and Telecommunication Services (100million yuan)			指数(上年=100) Indices (preceding year=100)		
	合计 Total	邮政 Postal Services	电信 Telecommunication Services	合计 Total	邮政 Postal Services	电信 Telecommunication Services
1978	0.90			103.4		
1979	0.96			106.7		
1980	1.05			109.4		
1981	1.15			109.5		
1982	1.17			101.7		
1983	1.31			112.0		
1984	1.56			119.1		
1985	2.05			131.4		
1986	2.54			123.9		
1987	3.49			137.4		
1988	5.11			146.4		
1989	10.33	0.75	9.58	135.9	90.4	141.5
1990	26.30	3.91	22.39	254.6	521.3	233.7
1991	38.89	4.60	34.29	147.9	117.6	153.1
1992	57.06	5.59	51.47	146.7	121.5	150.1
1993	94.25	7.10	87.15	165.2	127.0	169.3
1994	142.78	8.32	134.46	151.5	117.2	154.3
1995	204.93	9.63	202.60	143.5	115.7	150.7
1996	265.56	10.92	254.64	129.6	113.4	125.7
1997	330.38	11.44	318.94	124.4	104.8	125.3
1998	418.18	15.20	402.98	126.6	132.9	126.3
1999	542.65	19.72	522.93	129.8	129.8	129.8
2000	757.22	50.40	706.82	139.5	255.5	135.2
2001	782.67	42.13	740.54	129.9	105.1	131.7
2002	917.87	48.36	869.51	117.3	114.8	117.4
2003	1202.52	54.33	1148.19	131.0	112.3	132.1
2004	1781.78	55.12	1726.66	148.2	101.5	150.4
2005	2121.94	59.82	2062.12	119.1	108.5	119.4
2006	2540.54	69.48	2471.06	119.7	116.1	119.8
2007	3070.55	77.30	2993.25	120.9	111.3	121.1
2008	3564.85	87.97	3476.88	116.1	113.8	116.2
2009	3938.15	101.16	3837.00	110.5	115.0	110.4
2010	4832.94	118.57	4714.37	122.9	125.2	122.7
2011	1918.01	291.36	1626.65	116.4	129.9	114.3
2012	2174.67	395.18	1779.49	113.4	135.6	109.4
2013	2507.99	592.00	1915.99	115.3	149.8	107.7
2014	3394.39	859.81	2534.58	120.4	145.2	113.7
2015	4397.09	1228.75	3168.34	129.5	142.9	125.0
2016	6892.41	1886.25	5006.16	156.7	153.5	158.0
2017	6107.19	2526.29	3580.90	158.0	133.9	181.0
2018	11010.28	3215.75	7794.53	180.3	127.3	217.7
2019	16451.23	4403.44	12047.79	149.4	136.9	154.6
2020	20833.11	5807.81	15025.30	126.6	131.9	124.7
2021	4954.59	3021.10	1933.49	126.5	125.9	127.5
2022	5063.13	3112.87	1950.26	108.5	103.0	118.6
2023	5669.45	3645.36	2024.09	112.0	117.1	103.8

注：1.邮电业务总量1988年及以前按1980年不变价格计算，1989—2000年按1990年不变价格计算，2001—2010年按2000年不变价格计算，2011—2016年按2010年不变价格计算，2017年起，电信业务总量按2015年不变价格计算，邮政业务总量仍按2010年不变价格计算。2021年起，按2020年不变价计算。2022年起，电信按照上年不变价就计算。指数按可比价格计算。

2.统计范围是辖区内全社会所有从事电信运营企业和国家邮政企业，以及获得快递业务经营许可的快递服务企业。

Notes:a) The business volume of postal and telecommunication services in and before 1998 was calculated at 1980 constant prices, that from 1998 to 2000 was calculated at 1990 constant prices, that from 2001 to 2010 was calculated at 2000 constant prices and that from 2011 to 2016 was calculated at 2010 constant prices. Since 2017,the total amount of telecommunications was calculated at 2015 constant prices, while the total amount of postal business was calculated at 2010 constant prices. From 2022,that was calculated at last year's constant prices. The index was calculated at comparable prices.

b) The statistical coverages of business volume of postal and Telecommunication services are all telecom enter prises, the national postal enterprises and express mail enterprises with express license.

15–21 各市邮电业务总量

Business Volume of Postal and Telecommunication Services by City

单位：亿元 (100 million yuan)

市别	City	2000	2010	2015	2019	2020	2021	2022	2023
全省	**Provincial Total**	**757.22**	**4832.94**	**4397.09**	**16451.23**	**20833.11**	**4954.59**	**5063.13**	**5669.45**
广州	Guangzhou	168.26	1051.65	1092.94	3814.51	4707.38	1298.94	1266.65	1419.44
深圳	Shenzhen	154.20	1031.26	1069.43	3998.91	4917.38	1273.12	1281.50	1460.09
珠海	Zhuhai	22.31	137.61	91.22	315.81	403.91	71.55	66.57	72.44
汕头	Shantou	36.61	173.81	134.46	537.54	735.30	210.94	232.51	270.26
佛山	Foshan	66.29	428.72	282.87	1050.49	1336.25	288.80	311.75	331.72
韶关	Shaoguan	11.11	69.58	45.17	170.58	219.63	35.74	36.80	38.93
河源	Heyuan	6.26	46.33	41.85	170.72	217.26	35.02	35.63	36.35
梅州	Meizhou	12.87	52.48	68.43	207.09	255.72	46.91	48.44	50.49
惠州	Huizhou	27.19	201.02	146.50	606.36	786.86	137.20	143.04	156.88
汕尾	Shanwei	11.10	48.01	38.05	140.18	184.88	33.69	35.79	41.23
东莞	Dongguan	74.05	674.09	475.59	1947.19	2562.96	521.90	532.09	606.34
中山	Zhongshan	30.10	194.98	156.64	628.18	784.05	141.22	157.53	180.95
江门	Jiangmen	32.02	135.08	102.06	382.65	462.90	80.23	83.59	89.83
阳江	Yangjiang	8.60	50.67	45.30	165.89	216.27	43.43	48.62	57.27
湛江	Zhanjiang	19.38	116.85	122.72	465.47	580.50	85.91	89.30	93.55
茂名	Maoming	13.21	87.27	86.71	356.74	441.01	68.30	72.07	77.01
肇庆	Zhaoqing	13.22	95.05	69.81	270.97	342.96	60.55	63.23	70.38
清远	Qingyuan	9.96	56.06	61.24	235.91	301.45	47.94	50.75	53.63
潮州	Chaozhou	12.78	54.52	46.13	197.87	272.79	70.47	78.98	88.54
揭阳	Jieyang	20.81	94.01	96.30	575.54	830.84	305.00	325.62	357.75
云浮	Yunfu	6.89	33.91	37.69	130.19	164.37	25.90	27.17	28.44
不分地区	Unclassified			85.99	82.42	108.45	71.83	75.50	87.95
按经济区域分	By Region								
珠三角	Pearl River Delta	587.64	3949.45	3573.05	13097.48	16413.10	3945.34	3981.44	4476.01
粤东	Eastern Region	81.31	370.35	314.94	1451.14	2023.82	620.10	672.90	757.78
粤西	Western Region	41.19	254.79	254.72	988.11	1237.77	197.63	209.99	227.83
粤北	Northern Region	47.09	258.35	254.38	914.50	1158.43	191.52	198.80	207.84

15—22 各市邮电业务情况（2023年）

Conditions of Postal and Telecommunication Services by City (2023)

市别	City	业务总量（亿元）Business Volume of Postal and Telecommunication Services (100million yuan)	#电信 Business Volume of Telecommunications	函件（万件）Number of Letters (10000 pcs)	报刊累计数（万份）Newspaper and Magazine Issue (10000 copies)	快递（万件）Pieces of Express Mail Services (10000 pcs)	移动电话用户（万户）Subscribers of Mobile Telephones (10000 subscribers)	互联网宽带接入用户(万户) Subscribers of Fixed Internet Broadband (10000 subscribers)	移动互联网用户（万户）Subscribers of Mobile Internet (10000 subscribers)
全　省	**Provincial Total**	**5669.45**	**2024.09**	**11365.07**	**72241.07**	**3456728.98**	**17048.20**	**4824.35**	**15723.88**
广　州	Guangzhou	1419.44	414.81	3664.73	19297.33	1145019.13	3323.30	817.88	3061.40
深　圳	Shenzhen	1460.09	405.75	1913.85	9291.86	636835.63	2969.63	682.65	2732.86
珠　海	Zhuhai	72.44	50.00	1413.93	1650.85	19386.84	396.87	126.55	367.57
汕　头	Shantou	270.26	56.33	106.56	3506.73	297773.44	651.59	185.09	614.46
佛　山	Foshan	331.72	141.39	1024.54	3953.27	182708.30	1290.86	368.98	1196.32
韶　关	Shaoguan	38.93	28.12	98.63	1806.45	4200.61	301.22	102.64	275.13
河　源	Heyuan	36.35	27.04	17.19	3754.25	5232.63	272.98	92.91	255.46
梅　州	Meizhou	50.49	34.09	127.49	1576.88	9807.80	410.35	135.40	365.66
惠　州	Huizhou	156.88	91.48	169.09	3808.02	69155.97	747.47	279.87	711.09
汕　尾	Shanwei	41.23	23.00	18.57	658.68	19030.85	250.07	79.14	234.76
东　莞	Dongguan	606.34	205.52	1613.11	2863.24	343032.62	1677.75	453.86	1549.54
中　山	Zhongshan	180.95	80.33	120.68	2242.74	110307.35	702.70	227.31	658.29
江　门	Jiangmen	89.83	57.98	413.87	3863.06	24044.94	564.29	195.78	514.29
阳　江	Yangjiang	57.27	24.69	106.90	1111.17	36725.33	266.46	95.34	244.98
湛　江	Zhanjiang	93.55	69.38	90.11	2591.21	14937.43	727.75	214.48	662.87
茂　名	Maoming	77.01	53.36	152.66	1972.78	12241.53	604.78	162.26	544.75
肇　庆	Zhaoqing	70.38	41.52	122.20	1679.66	23239.29	428.08	136.81	386.41
清　远	Qingyuan	53.63	39.78	106.23	3059.85	7722.88	401.64	129.91	377.39
潮　州	Chaozhou	88.54	25.06	23.04	1674.59	85842.21	281.94	93.35	258.77
揭　阳	Jieyang	357.75	45.35	27.32	1037.97	407226.91	547.94	166.52	505.02
云　浮	Yunfu	28.44	21.14	34.37	840.48	2257.27	230.53	77.62	206.87
不分地区	Unclassified	87.95	87.95						
按经济区域分	By Region								
珠三角	Pearl River Delta	4476.01	1576.73	10456.00	48650.03	2553730.07	12100.94	3289.69	11177.76
粤　东	Eastern Region	757.78	149.75	175.49	6877.97	809873.42	1731.55	524.10	1613.01
粤　西	Western Region	227.83	147.43	349.67	5675.16	63904.30	1598.99	472.08	1452.60
粤　北	Northern Region	207.84	150.18	383.91	11037.91	29221.19	1616.72	538.48	1480.51

15-23 邮政通信业基本情况

Basic Conditions of Postal and Telecommunication Services

项目	Item	2000	2010	2015	2021	2022	2023
邮政业务量	**Business Volume of Postal Services**						
函件 (万件)	Number of Letters (10000 pcs)	106603	76204	64547	13008	11037	11365
包裹 (万件)	Package (10000 pcs)		332	182	225	271	318
快递 (亿件)	Pieces of Express Mail Services (10000 pcs)	0.13	5.91	50.13	294.57	301.36	345.67
报刊累计数 (万份)	Newspaper and Magazine Circulation (10000 copies)	107755	87895	91159	69919	71214	72241
全省平均每人每年发函件数 (件)	Annual Number of Per Capita Letter Mailed (pcs)	13.80	8.31	5.95	1.00	0.90	0.90
全省平均每百人每年订报刊数 (份)	Annual Average Number of Newspapers and Magazines Subscribed per 100 Persons(copies)	15.10	8.21	8.40	4.20	4.90	5.69
电信业务量	**Business Volume of Telecommunication Services**						
长途光缆线路长度 (公里)	Length of Long-distance Optical Cable Routes (km)		46289	52662	57870	62060	66124
移动电话交换机容量(万户)	Capacity of Mobile Telephone Exchanges (10000 subscribers)	1825.40	14766.90	22025.80	23803.81	24521.58	24521.58
固定电话用户 (万户)	Number of Subscribers of Local Telephones (10000 subscribers)	1414.94	3169.14	2807.11	2072.20	1944.08	1783.72
移动电话用户 (万户)	Number of Mobile Telephones Subscribers (10000 subscribers)	1357.26	9710.09	15009.75	16267.80	16650.76	17048.20
固定互联网宽带接入用户 (万户)	Broadband Subscribers of Internet (10000 subscribers)	216.41	1523.22	2285.19	4277.71	4628.72	4824.35
移动互联网用户 (万户)	Number of Mobile Broadband Internet Subscribers (10000 subscribers)		6918.7	10950.25	15070.27	15097.28	15723.88
固定电话普及率 (户/百人)	Popularization Rate of Local Telephones (subscribers/100 persons)	18.40	30.38	25.87	16.34	15.36	14.09
移动电话普及率 (户/百人)	Popularization Rate of Mobile Telephones (subscribers/100 persons)	17.61	93.09	138.35	128.25	131.56	134.69

注：2020年前广东省邮路总长度(单程)指标由省邮政集团公司报送，不含单独机要，不含速递邮路长度，2021年该指标由省邮政管理局汇总后报送，包含邮政邮路(含单独机要邮路)、速递邮路。

Note: Before 2020，the total length (one-way) of postal routes in Guangdong Province submitted by the provincial postal group company，excluding Individual confidential information and the length of express postal routes，In 2021,the index submitted by the provincial postal administration after being summarized, including postal routes (including separate confidential postal routes) and express postal routes。

主要统计指标解释

铁路营业里程 又称营业长度(包括正式营业和临时营业里程)，指办理客货运输业务的铁路正线总长度。凡是全线或部分建成双线及以上的线路，以第一线的实际长度计算；复线、站线、段管线、岔线和特殊用途线以及不计算运费的联络线都不计算营业里程。该指标可以反映铁路运输业基础设施的发展水平，也是计算客货周转量、运输密度和机车车辆运用效率等指标的基础资料。

公路通车里程 指在一定时期内实际达到《公路工程技术标准 JTJ01-88》规定的等级公路，并经公路主管部门正式验收交付使用的公路里程数。包括大中城市的郊区公路以及通过小城镇街道部分的公路里程和桥梁、渡口的长度，不包括大中城市的街道、厂矿、林区生产用道和农业生产用道的里程。两条或多条公路共同经由同一路段，只计算一次，不得重复计算里程长度。该指标可以反映公路建设的发展规模，也是计算运输网密度等指标的基础资料。

内河航道里程 也称内河通航里程，指在一定时期内，能通航运输船舶及排筏的天然河流、湖泊水库、运河及通航渠道的长度。包括全年季节性通航累计三个月以上的航道，不包括仅供零散流放竹、木排的河道。该指标可以反映内河水运网的规模、水平和发展情况。

民用航空航线里程 指民航运输定期班机飞行的航线长度的总和。航线长度按机场之间的距离计算，通常有两种计算方法：一是将每条航线长度相加称为重复计算航线里程；一是将两线或两条以上航线经过同一区段里程，只计算一次航线长度称为不重复计算航线里程。一般常用的是后者，该指标可以确切反映民航运输网的规模，是表明民航事业为国民经济服务和方便人民生活程度的主要指标。

输油(气)管道里程 指油品(或天然气)的实际输送距离，一般按输油(气)管道的单线长度计算。若包括复线和备用线长度则称为输油(气)管道延展长度，是指管道铺设的实际长度。我们通常使用的是不包括复线的“输油(气)管道里程”，该指标可以反映管道运输的发展规模和水平。

货(客)运量 指在一定时期内，各种运输工具实际运送的货物(旅客)数量。该指标是反映运输业为国民经济和人民生活服务的数量指标，也是制定和检查运输生产计划、研究运输发展规模和速度的重要指标。货运按吨计算，客运按人计算。货物不论运输距离长短、货物类别，均按实际重量统计。旅客不论行程远近或票价多少，均按一人一次客运量统计；半价票、小孩票也按一人统计。

货物(旅客)周转量 指在一定时期内，由各种运输工具运送的货物(旅客)数量与其相应运输距离的乘积之总和。该指标可以反映运输业生产的总成果，也是编制和检查运输生产计划，计算运输效率、劳动生产率以及核算运输单位成本的主要基础资料。计算货物(旅客)周转量通常按发出站与到达站之间的最短距离，也就是计费距离计算。计算公式为：

货物（旅客）周转量=Σ（货物（旅客）运输量×运输距离）

港口货物吞吐量 指经水运进出港区范围，并经过装卸的货物数量，包括邮件及办理托运手续的行李、包裹以及补给运输船舶的燃料、物料和淡水。货物吞吐量按货物流向分为进口、出口吞吐量，按货物交流性质分为外贸货物吞吐量和国内贸易货物吞吐量。货物吞吐量的货类构成及其流向，是衡量港口生产能力大小的重要指标。

港口集装箱吞吐量 指用集装箱装载货物、按箱数表示的港口货物吞吐量。计量单位为国际标准箱（TEU）。将各种不同规格尺寸的集装箱自然箱数，按换算比例折合成 TUE（TWENTY FT EQUAL TO UNIT 的缩写）统计，即折合成 20 英尺标准箱统计，换算比例为：40 英尺箱为 1:2，35 英尺箱为 1:1.75，20 英尺箱为 1:1，10 英尺箱为 1:0.5。

民用汽车 指报告期末，在公安交通管理部门按照《机动车注册登记工作规范》，已注册登记领有民用车辆牌照的全部汽车数量。汽车统计的主要分类：根据汽车结构分为载客汽车、载货汽车及其他汽车；根据汽车所有者不同分为个人(私人)汽车、单位汽车；根据汽车的使用性质分为营运汽车、非营运汽车；根据汽车大小规格不同载客汽车分为大型、中型、小型和微型，载货汽车分为重型、中型、轻型和微型。

机动船 又称自航船，指装有各种发动机推进装置，以机械动力行驶的船舶。

驳船 指本身无动力装置，或只设简易动力装置，依靠拖船或推船带动的平底船。

船舶净载重量 指报告期末所拥有船舶的总载重量减去燃（物）料、淡水、粮食及供应品、人员及其行李等的重量及船舶常数后，能够装载货物的实际重量。

沿海港口 指位于海沿岸，具有一定设施和条件，供船舶停靠、旅客上下、货物装卸、生活物料供应等作业的港口。

内河港口 指位于江、河、湖沿岸，具有一定设施和条件，供船舶停靠、旅客上下、货物装卸、生活物料供应等作业的港口。

民用航空航线条数 民用航空航线指出于商业的目的，运输飞机从地球表面一点(起飞)飞到另一点(终点)的航行线路。应同时具备三个条件：一是有运输飞机定期飞行，二是有足以保证运输飞机飞行和起降所需要的机场及地面设施，三是经过批准并在一个航季中正常执行。计算条数时，来回程计为一条。分为国内航线、国际航线和地区航线。

民航运输飞机 从事公共航空运输的民用飞机。分为大中型飞机和小型飞机，大中型飞机指 100 座及以上的运输飞机，小型飞机指 100 座以下的运输飞机。

城市公共交通 指城市中供公众乘用的、经济方便的各种交通方式的总称。包括公共汽车、电车、轨道交通（地铁、轻轨、有轨电车、磁悬浮、索道、缆车等）、出租汽车、公共轮渡等客运交通设施。

运营线路网长度 指公共交通线路所通过的运营线路净长度。计算公式：运营线路网长度=运营线路总长度－Σ重复的线路长度

运营线路总长度 指全部运营线路长度之和。计算公式：运营线路长度=Σ各条运营线路长度=Σ〔1/2（上行起点至终点里程+下行起点至终点里程+上下行终点掉头里程）。单向行驶的环行线路长度等于起点至终点里程与终点下客站至起点里程之和的一半，不包括折返、试车、联络线等非运营线路。

运营车辆数 指城市中用于公共交通运营业务的全部车辆数。地铁和轻轨在统计时一自然节为一辆。出租汽车指已经领取出租汽车专用牌照的运营车辆，包括技术完好的、在修的、长期行驶的以及拟报废尚未经上级机关批准的车辆。

轮渡运营船舶数 指用于城市客渡运营业务的全部船舶数。不含旅游客轮（长途旅游、市内供游人游览江、河、湖泊的船只）。

城市公共交通客运总量 指报告期内城市公共交通各种运输方式运送乘客的总人次。

邮电业务总量 指以价值量形式表现的邮电通信企业为社会提供各类邮电通信服务的总数量。邮电业务量按专业分类包括函件、包件、汇票、报刊发行、邮政快件、特快专递、邮政储蓄、集邮、公众电报、用户电报、传真、长途电话、出租电路、无线寻呼、移动电话、分组交换数据通信、出租代维等。计算方法为各类产品乘以相应的平均单价(不变价)之和，再加上出租电路和设备、代用户维护电话交换机和线路等的服务收入。该指标综合反映了一定时期邮电业务发展的总成果，是研究邮电业务量构成和发展趋势的重要指标。计算公式为：

邮电业务总量=Σ（各类邮电业务量×不变单价）+出租代维及其他业务收入
=邮政业务总量+通信业务总量

移动电话用户 指通过移动电话交换机进入移动电话网、占用移动电话号码的各类电话用户。包括签约用户和智能网预付费用户。一个移动电话号码统计为一户。

本地电话用户 指接入本地电信运营商固定电话网上的电话用户。包括：住宅用户、单位用户、公用电话用户等。

国际互联网用户 包括互联网窄带拨号用户和互联网宽带接入用户。互联网窄带拨号用户又分为互联网注册拨号用户、互联网主叫电话记费用户、互联网上网卡用户等几种。互联网注册拨号用户指由基础电信运营商用户提供的，使用固定帐号上网的一种方式，由用户到运营商的营业厅或业务代理商处申请办理，获得拨号上网帐号及密码，用户根据该帐号及密码拨叫上网特服号，通过认证获得动态 IP 地址接入宽带互联网。互联网主叫电话记费用户指用户不需要到运营商的营业厅或业务代理商处申请办理，只需要拨打某一运营商已经开通的主叫特服号码即可上网，上网费用随主叫电话收取。互联网上网卡用户指使用上网卡上的帐号和密码认证，通过 PSTN、N-ISDN 等方式接入宽带互联网的用户。互联网宽带接入用户指采用分组交换网、DDN 网、帧中继/ATM 网以及模拟专线、数字专线等方式，不经过基础电信运营商的宽带 IP 城域网，直接接入宽带互联网节点的用户，不含 XDSL、专线和 LAN 专线用户。

移动电话交换机容量 指移动电话交换机根据一定话务模型和交换机处理能力计算出来的最大同时服务用户的数量。

Explanatory Notes on Main Statistical Indicators

Length of Railways in Operation refers to the total length of the trunk line under passenger and freight transportation (including both regular operations and temporary operations). In the case of wholly or partially double or multiple track railways, calculation is based on the actual length of the first track, regardless of other tracks, station sidings, tracks under the charge of stations, branch lines, special-purpose lines and non-payable connecting lines. The length of railways in operation is an important indicator of the development of infrastructure for railway transport, as well as the foundation for the calculation of passenger-kilometers and freight ton-kilometers, traffic density and utilization efficiency of locomotives and carriages.

Length of Highways refers to the length of highways built in conformity with the grades specified by the Technical Standards JTJ01-88 for Highway Engineering, formally checked and accepted by highway authorities and put into use. The length of highways includes that of suburban highways at large and medium sized cities and highways passing through streets at small cities and towns, as well as the span of bridges and ferries. However, it does not include the length of streets in large and medium sized cities and highways built for production purposes at factories, mines, forest areas and agricultural areas. If two or more highways share the same segment, the length of the shared segment is only calculated for once and no duplication is allowed. The length of highways is an important indicator of the scale of development of highway construction, as well as the foundation for the calculation of transport network density and other indicators.

Length of Navigable Inland Waterways refers to the length of natural rivers, lakes, reservoirs, canals, and ditches open to navigation during a given period, which enables the transport by ships and rafts. This includes channels open to seasonal navigation for an accumulative period of over 3 months in a year, but excludes river courses used exclusively for wood or bamboo rafts on an irregular basis. This indicator reflects the scale, level and development situation of the inland waterway network.

Length of Civil Aviation Routes refers to the length of all routes for regular civil aviation flights. Calculation of route lengths is based on the distance between airports, usually in either of the following ways: duplicated calculation of route lengths, which directly sums up the length of every single air route, or singular calculation of route lengths, which calculates the same segments of aviation routes shared by two or more routes only once. In general practice, the latter is used, as it can precisely reflect the size of the civil aviation network and indicate the extent to which civil aviation serves the national economy and the needs of the people.

Length of Petroleum and Gas Pipelines refers to the actual transport distance of oil or gas products, generally calculated as the length of single pipelines. Inclusion of double pipelines and alternate pipeline in the calculation is termed the extension length of petroleum and gas pipelines, which indicates the actual length of the pipelines built. In general practice, the “Length of Petroleum and Gas Pipelines” exclusive of double pipelines is used, which reflects the scale and degree of development in pipeline transport.

Freight (Passenger) Traffic refers to the volume of freight (passengers) transported with various means. This indicator provides a quantitative measure of how the transport industry serves the national economy and the needs of the people, as well as an important reference for drafting and checking production plans in the transport industry and for studying the scale and speed of development in the transport industry. Freight transport is calculated in tons and passenger traffic is calculated in the number of persons. Freight transport is calculated in the actual weight of goods regardless of traveling distances and types of freight, while passenger traffic is calculated as the number of individuals traveling once, regardless of traveling distances, ticket prices, whether the passengers are traveling with half-price tickets or child tickets.

Freight Ton-kilometers (Passenger-kilometers) refer to the sum of the products of the volume of transported cargo (passengers) multiplied by the transport distance. These are important indicators of the total achievements of the transport industry, as well as the major foundation for drafting and checking production plans in the transport industry and for calculating the efficiency, labor productivity and the cost of transport enterprises. Normally, the shortest distance between the departure station and the destination station (i.e. the payable distance) is the basis to calculate the freight ton-kilometers and passenger-kilometers on. These indicators are calculated as follows:

Freight Ton-kilometers (Passenger-kilometers) = Σ (Freight (Passenger) Traffic $\times$ Transport Distance)

Volume of Freight Handled in Ports refers to the volume of cargo passing in and out of the harbor area that undergoes the loading and unloading processes, including mails, checked baggage and bales, as well as fuel, material and fresh water supplies to ships. The volume of freight handled may be classified by direction of flow as import volume and export volume, or by nature of cargo as volume of freight for domestic trade and volume of freight for foreign trade. The classification of volume of freight handled and its direction of flow are important indicators of the production capacity of ports.

Volume of Container Handled in Ports refers to the volume of freight handled in Ports that are loaded and unloaded in containers.The unit of measurement is TEU. The number of natural containers of various sizes of containers is converted into TEU (TWENTY FT EQUAL TO UNIT) according to the conversion ratio, that is to say, the conversion ratio is 1:2 for 40 foot container, 1:1.75 for 35 foot container, 1:1 for 20 foot container, and 1:0.5 for 10 foot container.

Possession of Civil Motor Vehicles refers to the total number of vehicles that are registered at transport management offices under the public security authorities and provided with civil vehicle licenses and tags according to the Work Standard for Motor Vehicles Registration at the end of the reference period. Major categories of vehicle are: passenger vehicles, freight vehicles and other vehicles in terms of structure; private vehicles and organization-owned vehicles in terms of ownership; commercial vehicles and non-commercial vehicles in terms of use; large, medium, small and mini passenger vehicles, and heavy, medium, light and mini trucks in terms of size.

Motor Vessels refer to vessels installed with power units and propelled by mechanical power. It is also known as self-propelled vessels.

Barges refer to flat-bottomed vessels driven by drawers or propellers. It has no power units or has only simple power units.

Dead Weight Tonnage of Vessels refers to the actual tonnage all the vessels within the reference period are capable of carrying. It equals the tonnage of all the vessels minus that of fuel, material and fresh water, foods, supplies, persons and luggage on vessels.

Coastal Seaports refer to seaports located alongside the coasts that have the right facilities and conditions for vessel mooning, passenger boarding and alighting, cargo loading and unloading, and supply of daily life materials.

Inland Ports refer to ports located along rivers and lakes that have the right facilities and conditions for vessel mooning, passenger boarding and alighting, cargo loading and unloading, and supply of daily life materials.

Number of Civil Aviation Routes refers to the number of all routes of commercial civil aviation flights from one point of the earth to another. Civil aviation routes shall meet three conditions. Firstly, there shall be regular flights. Secondly, there shall be adequate airport and ground facilities to ensure the flight, takeoff and landing. Thirdly, the flights are approved and carried out normally during the flight season. Singular calculation is used in calculating the number of routes. Civil aviation routes are divided into domestic routes, international routes and regional routes.

Civil Aviation Aircraft refer to aircraft used in public civil aero transport. They are divided into large and medium sized aircraft and small sized aircraft. The former refer to those with 100 seats and above, and the latter refer to those with less than 100 seats.

Urban Public Transportation refers to all the economical transport taken by the public in cities. It includes bus, trolley bus, rail transport (subway, light rail, streetcar, magnetically levitated trains, cableway, telpher, etc.), taxi, ferry boast, etc.

Length of Public Transportation Network refers to the net length covered by the public transportation routes. The following formula is used:

Length of Public Transportation Network=Length of Public Transportation under Operation - Σ Length of Repeated Routes

Length of Public Transportation under Operation refers to the sum of all public transportation routes under operation. The following formula is used:

Length of Public Transportation under Operation= - Σ (1/2 (length from starting station to terminal of forward trip+length from terminal to beginning station of backward trip+length of take-turning of both trips)

Number of Vehicles under Operation refers to the total number of vehicles under operation in public transportation in cities. For subway and light rail, each compartment is calculated as one unit. Taxi refers to all those with special operation license, including those in good condition, under maintenance, in long-term operation and with pending approval for writing-off.

Number of Ferry Boats refer to the total number of boats for ferry operation., excluding the long-distance or intra-city cruiser.

Total Passenger Traffic in Cities refers to the total number of persons transported by public transportation in cities.

Business Volume of Postal and Telecommunication Services refers to the total amount of postal and telecommunication services, expressed in value terms, provided by postal and telecommunication enterprises for the society. Postal and telecommunication services can be classified as letters, parcels, remittance, delivery of newspapers and magazines, fast mail service, express mail service, savings deposits, stamps for collection, public and individual telegraph service, facsimiles, long-distance telephone service, leasing of telephone lines, urban paging service, mobile telephone service, data communication through packet networks, network elements lease and maintenance, etc. To calculate the volume, the business volume of each product is multiplied by its average unit price (at constant prices), summed, and added to income from other services such as leasing of telephone lines and equipment, maintenance of telephone switchboards and lines on behalf of customers. This indicator reflects the overall achievements of postal and telecommunication services during a given period, and is an important reference for studying the composition of business volume and the development trend of postal and telecommunication services. This volume is calculated as follows:

Business Volume of Postal and Telecommunication Services = Σ (Business Volume of Each Product × Constant Unit Price) + Income from Leasing, Maintenance, and Other Services = Business Volume of Postal Services + Business Volume of Telecommunication Services

Mobile Telephone Subscribers refer to persons who own mobile telephone numbers and are connected with the mobile telephone communication network through mobile telephone switchboards, including contracted subscribers and pre-paid subscribers for intelligent network. One mobile telephone number is calculated as one subscriber.

Local Telephone Subscribers refer to subscribers that are connected to the local telecommunication service provider through fix line network, including household subscribers, institutional subscribers and public telephones.

Number of Internet Subscribers include both narrow-band dial-up users and broad-band access users of the internet. Narrow-band dial-up users are further classified into registered dial-up users, pay-per-calling users, and pre-pay card users. Registered dial-up service enables internet access through fixed accounts provided by basic telecommunication operators. Users of this service apply to the operators or their agents for accounts and passwords, with which they dial special numbers for internet connection and acquire dynamic IP addresses through authentification to gain access to the broad-band internet. Pre-pay calling service implies that instead of applying to the operators or their agents, users only need to dial a certain operator's special numbers to gain access to the internet and pay internet fees together with their calling fees. Pre-pay card users refer to those connected to the broad-band internet through PSTN and N-ISDN networks with accounts and passwords provided by the pre-pay cards. Broad-band access users (exclusive of XDSL and LAN users) refer to users directly connected to broad-band internet nodes through packet networks, DDN networks, frame relay/ATM networks, and special analog or digital lines, bypassing the broad-band IP MAN provided by basic telecommunication operators.

Capacity of Mobile Telephone Exchanges refers to the maximum number of subscribers that can be served simultaneously, calculated according to a certain calling model and the handling capacity of the mobile telephone exchanges.

十六、批发和零售业

WHOLESALE AND RETAIL TRADES

十六　批发零售业

简要说明

一、本篇资料反映包括批发零售业商品流通情况、社会消费品零售总额等。

二、本篇资料主要根据国家统计局《批发和零售业统计报表制度》进行搜集和加工整理。资料中限额以上批发和零售业采用全面调查的方法自下而上逐级综合汇总而得。

三、各表的调查范围：

限额以上批发和零售业统计限额标准：批发业年销售额2000万元及以上；零售业年销售额500万元及以上。

商品购、销、存总额表为各种经济类型的限额以上批发零售业法人。

社会消费品零售总额表为各种经济类型的法人及产业活动单位、个体户对城乡居民和社会集团的零售。

四、本篇资料由广东省统计局贸易外经统计处整理提供。

16 Wholesale and Retail Trades

Brief Introduction

I. The date in this chapter show the development of Guangdong's domestic market， including mainly the circulation of commodities in the wholesale and retail trades and the total retail sales of consumer goods， etc.

II. The data are collected and processed in accordance with the Statistical Reporting Scheme on Wholesale and Retail Trades stipulated by the National Bureau of Statistics. Data on basic conditions for all corporate enterprises of wholesale, retail above the designated size are collected through comprehensive reporting systems and data are reported level by level in a bottom-up manner.

III. The statistical coverage in this chapter comes as follows:

Criteria for wholesale and retail sale trades above designated size is defined as follows： wholesale trade with annual sales of 20 million yuan or above, retail sale trade with annual sales of 5 million yuan or above.

The table of total purchase, sales, and inventory of goods refers to the legal entities of wholesale and retail businesses above the quota for various economic types.

The table of total retail sales of consumer goods includes the retail sales of corporate units, establishments and individuals of various types of ownership to urban and rural residents and institutions.

Ⅳ. The data in this chapter are prepared and provided by the Division of Trade and External Economic Relations Statistics of Statistics Bureau of Guangdong Province.

16-1 批发零售业主要指标
Main Indicators on Domestic Trade

指　　标	Item	2000	2010	2015	2021	2022	2023
社会消费品零售总额（亿元）	**Total Retail Sales of Consumer Goods (100 million yuan)**	**4320.73**	**16991.39**	**30326.76**	**44187.71**	**44882.92**	**47494.86**
按消费形态分	By pattern						
商品零售	Retail Sales			26574.66	39427.05	40327.24	41731.42
餐饮收入	Catering Income			3752.09	4760.66	4555.68	5763.44
按城乡分	By Urban and Rural Area						
城镇	Urban Areas	3292.69	14766.77	27089.25	38923.93	39286.68	41385.83
乡村	Rural Areas	1028.04	2224.62	3237.50	5263.78	5596.24	6109.03
限额以上批发零售业企业商品销售总额（亿元）	**Total Sales of Commodities of Wholesale and Retail Trades Enterprises above Designated Size (100 million yuan)**		**32108.52**	**64201.29**	**140582.60**	**137793.66**	**165558.32**
按行业分	By Sector						
限额以上批发业销售额	Sales in Wholesale Trade above Designated Size		25799.00	52907.49	124338.77	121677.39	146030.64
限额以上零售业销售额	Sales in Retail Trade above Designated Size		6309.52	11293.80	16243.83	16116.27	19527.68
限额以上连锁总店数（个）	**Number of General Chain Stores above Designated Size (unit)**		**206**	**386**	**416**	**415**	**574**
限额以上连锁门店数（个）	**Number of Branch Chain Stores above Designated Size (unit)**		**23096**	**25903**	**35112**	**36927**	**46734**
限额以上连锁店销售总额（亿元）	**Total Sales of Chain Stores above Designated Size (100 million yuan)**		**3502.08**	**5241.15**	**3827.81**	**4015.93**	**4696.04**
#零售额	Retail Value		2980.36	4420.51	3002.13	2967.19	3062.60
亿元以上商品交易市场成交额（亿元）	**Transaction Value of Commodity Markets above 100 Million Yuan (100 million yuan)**		**4828.13**	**5576.63**	**5534.20**	**5174.43**	**5379.18**

16-2 按城乡分社会消费品零售总额

Total Retail Sales of Consumer Goods by Urban and Rural Area

单位：亿元 (100 million yuan)

年份 Year	社会消费品零售总额 Total Retail Sales of Consumer Goods	按城乡分 By Urban and Rural Area	
		城镇 Urban Areas	乡村 Rural Areas
1978	79.86	38.42	41.44
1979	92.69	43.25	49.44
1980	117.67	66.72	50.95
1981	142.38	71.19	71.19
1982	164.23	82.77	81.46
1983	183.62	97.32	86.30
1984	226.13	131.61	94.52
1985	289.23	178.45	110.78
1986	327.02	172.67	154.35
1987	405.19	214.34	190.85
1988	568.07	306.19	261.88
1989	636.15	345.43	290.72
1990	667.36	457.34	210.02
1991	786.64	531.57	255.07
1992	1109.55	809.96	299.59
1993	1515.73	1137.96	377.78
1994	1984.58	1511.22	473.36
1995	2465.76	1865.49	600.27
1996	2754.06	2093.87	660.19
1997	3112.79	2363.79	749.00
1998	3530.86	2689.95	840.91
1999	3885.99	2962.03	923.96
2000	4320.73	3292.69	1028.04
2001	4783.01	3641.78	1141.23
2002	5301.86	4048.11	1253.76
2003	5918.30	4544.02	1374.28
2004	6741.88	5201.17	1540.71
2005	7777.23	5997.87	1779.36
2006	9019.22	6950.06	2069.16
2007	10509.88	8107.94	2401.94
2008	12699.80	9809.61	2890.20
2009	14531.85	11328.71	3203.14
2010	16991.39	14766.77	2224.62
2011	19693.70	17201.99	2491.71
2012	21954.29	19479.27	2475.02
2013	24589.96	21917.34	2672.62
2014	27436.68	24486.93	2949.75
2015	30326.76	27089.25	3237.50
2016	33303.21	29759.18	3544.02
2017	36598.59	32708.58	3890.01
2018	39767.12	35543.82	4223.30
2019	42951.75	38314.75	4637.00
2020	40207.85	35904.43	4303.42
2021	44187.71	38923.93	5263.78
2022	44882.92	39286.68	5596.24
2023	47494.86	41385.83	6109.03

16-3 各市社会消费品零售总额（2023年）
Total Retail Sales of Consumer Goods by City (2023)

单位：亿元 (100 million yuan)

市别	City	社会消费品零售总额 Total Retail Sales of Consumer Goods	按消费形态分 By Sector		按城乡分 By Urban and Rural Area	
			商品零售 Retail Sales	餐饮收入 Catering Income	城镇 Urban Area	乡村 Rural Area
广州	Guangzhou	11012.62	10105.53	907.09	10627.01	385.61
深圳	Shenzhen	10486.19	9375.77	1110.42	10465.22	20.97
珠海	Zhuhai	1078.97	960.15	118.82	1048.76	30.21
汕头	Shantou	1546.28	1385.16	161.12	1117.15	429.13
佛山	Foshan	3734.48	3449.74	284.74	3615.17	119.31
韶关	Shaoguan	506.75	464.02	42.73	433.48	73.27
河源	Heyuan	388.14	356.32	31.81	296.32	91.81
梅州	Meizhou	694.81	630.79	64.01	483.84	210.96
惠州	Huizhou	2144.90	1873.57	271.33	1820.16	324.74
汕尾	Shanwei	491.45	422.89	68.56	357.63	133.82
东莞	Dongguan	4408.12	4026.50	381.62	3967.62	440.50
中山	Zhongshan	1643.91	1513.84	130.07	1495.22	148.69
江门	Jiangmen	1347.90	1213.11	134.79	1043.27	304.63
阳江	Yangjiang	502.91	444.54	58.37	386.24	116.67
湛江	Zhanjiang	1950.54	1712.70	237.84	1573.28	377.26
茂名	Maoming	1599.99	1380.44	219.55	1127.24	472.75
肇庆	Zhaoqing	1180.60	1114.74	65.86	947.80	232.80
清远	Qingyuan	601.41	561.00	40.40	493.90	107.50
潮州	Chaozhou	508.97	468.86	40.11	417.18	91.78
揭阳	Jieyang	1098.85	1052.49	46.35	785.82	313.03
云浮	Yunfu	397.50	361.41	36.09	292.31	105.19
按经济区域分	By Region					
珠三角	Pearl River Delta	37037.68	33632.95	3404.74	35030.23	2007.46
粤东	Eastern Region	3645.54	3329.40	316.14	2677.78	967.76
粤西	Western Region	4053.44	3537.68	515.76	3086.76	966.68
粤北	Northern Region	2588.59	2373.54	215.04	1999.85	588.73

16-4 各市社会消费品零售总额

Total Retail Sales of Consumer Goods by City

单位：亿元 (100 million yuan)

市 别	City	2000	2005	2010	2015	2019	2020	2021	2022	2023
广 州	Guangzhou	1079.59	1765.01	3809.04	6994.42	9551.57	9218.66	10122.56	10298.15	11012.62
深 圳	Shenzhen	854.79	1757.85	3646.89	6419.78	9144.46	8664.83	9498.12	9708.28	10486.19
珠 海	Zhuhai	121.33	210.43	421.33	741.78	996.30	921.26	1048.24	1044.67	1078.97
汕 头	Shantou	208.62	304.14	639.03	1101.82	1562.73	1417.06	1503.84	1485.03	1546.28
佛 山	Foshan	340.06	609.45	1470.02	2585.63	3685.27	3289.09	3556.66	3593.57	3734.48
韶 关	Shaoguan	75.98	111.72	219.10	359.20	477.55	445.25	488.16	493.97	506.75
河 源	Heyuan	38.91	74.41	153.54	271.31	386.83	360.74	387.62	378.01	388.14
梅 州	Meizhou	67.16	126.76	284.21	490.54	689.33	634.88	654.37	656.82	694.81
惠 州	Huizhou	143.35	291.29	652.02	1258.11	1924.55	1746.08	1978.92	2040.52	2144.90
汕 尾	Shanwei	60.56	98.42	219.60	339.09	442.26	435.65	477.30	475.53	491.45
东 莞	Dongguan	271.05	608.38	1456.27	2622.65	4003.89	3740.14	4239.24	4254.87	4408.12
中 山	Zhongshan	156.97	311.11	700.88	1206.61	1617.09	1407.22	1530.11	1593.42	1643.91
江 门	Jiangmen	191.38	301.36	542.35	854.97	1206.96	1162.62	1278.10	1309.05	1347.90
阳 江	Yangjiang	69.80	115.53	229.27	376.57	502.25	451.18	482.71	495.63	502.91
湛 江	Zhanjiang	174.57	289.73	657.45	1198.96	1717.27	1638.76	1784.46	1826.63	1950.54
茂 名	Maoming	134.85	241.37	554.67	1010.03	1440.68	1356.48	1497.32	1509.89	1599.99
肇 庆	Zhaoqing	86.31	162.25	362.34	727.62	1107.52	1062.16	1160.82	1117.07	1180.60
清 远	Qingyuan	67.35	105.37	265.04	420.67	573.94	520.09	579.62	581.16	601.41
潮 州	Chaozhou	58.70	93.58	201.06	345.92	490.84	444.88	480.70	487.08	508.97
揭 阳	Jieyang	80.38	131.34	365.23	751.47	1069.76	955.16	1055.76	1066.13	1098.85
云 浮	Yunfu	39.05	67.75	142.08	249.62	360.69	337.24	375.50	384.19	397.50
按经济区域分	By Region									
珠 三 角	Pearl River Delta	3244.82	6017.12	13061.13	23411.58	33237.60	31212.06	34412.76	34959.60	37037.68
粤 东	Eastern Region	408.25	627.48	1424.92	2538.30	3565.60	3252.74	3517.59	3513.77	3645.54
粤 西	Western Region	379.22	646.63	1441.38	2585.55	3660.20	3446.43	3764.49	3832.16	4053.44
粤 北	Northern Region	288.44	486.01	1063.96	1791.33	2488.35	2298.21	2485.28	2494.15	2588.59

16−5 限额以上批发和零售业商品销售总额

Total Sales of Commodities of Wholesale and Retail Trades above Designated Size

单位：亿元 (100 million yuan)

项　目	Item	2010	2015	2021	2022	2023
限额以上单位	**Establishments above Designated Size**	**30316.84**	**66166.10**	**133208.82**	**143519.85**	**159730.99**
食品、饮料、烟酒类	Food, Beverages, Tobacco and Liquor	2635.17	7097.34	11307.32	12541.48	14566.45
粮油类	Grain and Edible Oil	366.51	1134.22	1712.15	2031.89	2353.63
肉禽蛋类	Meat, Poultry and Eggs	230.13	703.26	1373.81	1787.91	2252.30
饮料类	Beverages	192.76	1046.10	1079.32	1087.45	1247.34
烟酒类	Tobacco and Liquor	1175.56	1939.10	2847.79	2997.90	3146.88
其它食品类	Other Food	670.21	2274.66	3340.34	4636.34	5566.30
服装鞋帽、针纺织品类	Garments,Footwear,Headgear,Knitwear and Textiles	1869.06	5244.01	3600.19	3496.41	3807.21
服装类	Garments	1133.19	3451.73	2183.39	1918.92	2024.68
鞋帽类	Footwear and Headgear	206.49	689.94	648.41	600.08	643.22
针、纺织品类	Knitwear and Textiles	529.38	1102.34	772.07	977.42	1139.31
化妆品类	Cosmetics	138.83	401.67	796.74	790.04	972.05
金银珠宝类	Gold, Silver and Jewelry	221.13	1280.64	1381.26	1401.30	1659.36
日用品类	Daily-use Articles	762.55	2347.19	2970.17	3142.29	3229.27
#洗涤用品类	Detergents	232.11				
儿童玩具类	Toys for Children	32.61	96.89			
五金、电料类	Hardware and Electrical Appliances	266.24	761.81	1250.84	1384.23	1427.38
体育、娱乐用品类	Sports and Recreational Articles	153.92	168.46	451.05	409.42	463.27
书报杂志类	Newspapers and Magazines	77.67	161.28	191.57	205.74	216.13
电子出版物及音像制品类	E-journals and Video Products	23.12	29.96	17.32	10.20	11.45
家用电器和音像器材类	Household Appliances and Video Appliances	1221.85	2459.14	3783.35	3673.59	3932.03
中西药品类	Traditional Chinese and Western Medicines	1248.10	2957.35	4958.16	5274.60	5428.64
#西药	Western Medicines	848.37	1939.97	3430.88	3762.64	3859.69
中草药及中成药	Traditional Chinese Medicines	256.71	659.07	787.90	881.52	931.20
文化办公用品类	Articles for Cultural and Office Use	637.27	3586.88	3192.55	3135.73	3466.50
家具类	Furniture	189.07	542.19	765.24	726.42	777.50
通讯器材类	Communication Appliances	719.27	3176.14	5599.90	5511.20	5934.89
煤炭及制品类	Coal and Related Products	1144.17	1293.35	2807.68	3015.13	3078.07
木材及制品类	Timber and Related Products	60.20	163.68	743.07	818.39	753.66
石油及制品类	Petroleum and Related Products	7779.83	7792.01	12347.91	14253.75	14396.81
化工材料及制品类	Chemical Materials and Products	1566.66	3952.91	8902.66	9663.72	10605.76
金属材料类	Metal Materials	4380.16	8268.17	37741.11	38508.14	46819.12
建筑及装潢材料类	Construction and Decoration Materials	432.07	1171.45	3811.46	3270.53	3384.11
机电产品及设备类	Mechanical and Electrical Products and Equipment	1235.24	2888.60	7584.80	8196.37	8231.73
汽车类	Motor Vehicles	2773.14	6494.43	12781.05	16680.58	18959.67
种子饲料类	Seeds and Feedstuff	53.57	208.81	659.18	842.18	997.06
棉麻类	Cotton and Hemp	20.81	93.09	278.08	262.26	293.54
其它类	Others	707.74	3625.54	5286.17	6306.15	6319.35

注：本表数据为2023年快报数。
Note: The data in this table come from express reports.

16-6 限额以上批发零售业商品批发额

Total Wholesale Value of Commodities of Wholesale and Retail Trades

单位：亿元 (100 million yuan)

项　目	Item	2010	2015	2021	2022	2023
限额以上单位	**Establishments above Designated Size**	**24600.85**	**53553.50**	**117680.13**	**126808.10**	**142296.01**
食品、饮料、烟酒类	Food, Beverages, Tobacco and Liquor	2067.13	5863.76	9444.53	10469.26	12305.42
粮油类	Grain and Edible Oil	279.88	928.33	1538.31	1836.05	2126.57
肉禽蛋类	Meat, Poultry and Eggs	168.66	536.39	1199.33	1562.08	2000.50
饮料类	Beverages	134.29	907.60	820.44	806.60	959.79
烟酒类	Tobacco and Liquor	1065.75	1737.72	2507.17	2639.84	2807.94
其它食品类	Other Food	418.55	1753.72	2534.95	3624.68	4410.61
服装鞋帽、针纺织品类	Garments,Footwear,Headgear,Knitwear and Textiles	1385.88	3993.25	2612.60	2641.46	2828.94
服装类	Garments	786.06	2606.88	1462.88	1301.90	1304.26
鞋帽类	Footwear and Headgear	117.36	415.44	465.54	439.41	469.29
针、纺织品类	Knitwear and Textiles	482.46	970.93	687.87	900.15	1055.38
化妆品类	Cosmetics	56.22	228.49	432.74	420.13	496.95
金银珠宝类	Gold, Silver and Jewelry	151.49	1045.36	1025.64	1039.81	1256.46
日用品类	Daily-use Articles	569.53	1760.89	2134.73	2274.36	2316.91
#洗涤用品类	Detergents	166.98				
儿童玩具类	Toys for Children	19.52	61.29			
五金、电料类	Hardware and Electrical Appliances	241.86	635.55	1216.88	1349.27	1400.49
体育、娱乐用品类	Sports and Recreational Articles	131.35	97.62	279.94	257.63	294.99
书报杂志类	Newspapers and Magazines	50.89	109.76	117.79	126.87	127.93
电子出版物及音像制品类	E-journals and Video Products	16.38	14.56	15.94	8.50	9.97
家用电器和音像器材类	Household Appliances and Video Appliances	790.44	1742.73	2851.61	2703.46	2915.74
中西药品类	Traditional Chinese and Western Medicines	957.64	2349.21	4231.42	4432.71	4567.88
#西药	Western Medicines	651.83	1524.78	2922.80	3158.77	3224.01
中草药及中成药	Traditional Chinese Medicines	216.34	571.22	694.51	772.54	824.10
文化办公用品类	Articles for Cultural and Office Use	570.14	3229.34	2651.04	2592.18	2925.45
家具类	Furniture	156.89	392.91	606.45	567.23	605.65
通讯器材类	Communication Appliances	639.96	2731.33	4698.99	4487.87	4807.29
煤炭及制品类	Coal and Related Products	1137.75	1264.48	2807.67	3015.13	3077.93
木材及制品类	Timber and Related Products	60.20	163.68	743.07	818.39	753.66
石油及制品类	Petroleum and Related Products	6488.12	5822.76	10266.37	11867.42	12047.13
化工材料及制品类	Chemical Materials and Products	1566.66	3952.91	8902.66	9663.72	10605.76
金属材料类	Metal Materials	4380.16	8268.17	37741.11	38508.14	46819.12
建筑及装潢材料类	Construction and Decoration Materials	392.48	1021.24	3744.73	3200.17	3326.72
机电产品及设备类	Mechanical and Electrical Products and Equipment	1200.20	2741.70	7536.06	8134.55	8163.19
汽车类	Motor Vehicles	920.60	2720.82	7551.10	10986.64	13240.10
种子饲料类	Seeds and Feedstuff	53.57	208.81	659.18	842.18	997.06
棉麻类	Cotton and Hemp	20.81	92.93	278.08	262.26	293.54
其它类	Others	594.50	3101.24	5129.81	6138.75	6111.75

注：本表数据为2023年快报数。
Note: The data in this table come from express reports.

16-7 限额以上批发零售业商品零售额

Total Retail Value of Commodities of Wholesale and Retail Trades

单位：亿元 (100 million yuan)

项　目	Item	2010	2015	2021	2022	2023
限额以上单位	**Establishments above Designated Size**	**5715.99**	**12612.60**	**15528.69**	**16711.75**	**17434.98**
食品、饮料、烟酒类	Food, Beverages, Tobacco and Liquor	568.04	1233.58	1862.79	2072.22	2261.02
粮油类	Grain and Edible Oil	86.63	205.89	173.84	195.83	227.05
肉禽蛋类	Meat, Poultry and Eggs	61.47	166.87	174.48	225.82	251.80
饮料类	Beverages	58.47	138.50	258.88	280.85	287.55
烟酒类	Tobacco and Liquor	109.81	201.38	340.63	358.06	338.94
其它食品类	Other Food	251.66	520.94	805.39	1011.65	1155.69
服装鞋帽、针纺织品类	Garments,Footwear,Headgear,Knitwear and Textiles	483.18	1250.76	987.59	854.95	978.27
服装类	Garments	347.13	844.85	720.51	617.02	720.42
鞋帽类	Footwear and Headgear	89.13	274.50	182.87	160.67	173.92
针、纺织品类	Knitwear and Textiles	46.92	131.41	84.20	77.27	83.93
化妆品类	Cosmetics	82.61	173.18	364.00	369.91	475.10
金银珠宝类	Gold, Silver and Jewelry	69.64	235.28	355.62	361.49	402.89
日用品类	Daily-use Articles	193.02	586.30	835.44	867.94	912.37
#洗涤用品类	Detergents	65.13				
儿童玩具类	Toys for Children	13.09	35.60			
五金、电料类	Hardware and Electrical Appliances	24.38	126.26	33.96	34.96	26.89
体育、娱乐用品类	Sports and Recreational Articles	22.57	70.84	171.11	151.79	168.27
书报杂志类	Newspapers and Magazines	26.78	51.52	73.77	78.87	88.20
电子出版物及音像制品类	E-journals and Video Products	6.74	15.40	1.39	1.69	1.48
家用电器和音像器材类	Household Appliances and Video Appliances	431.41	716.41	931.74	970.14	1016.29
中西药品类	Traditional Chinese and Western Medicines	290.46	608.14	726.74	841.89	860.76
#西药	Western Medicines	196.54	415.19	508.08	603.87	635.68
中草药及中成药	Traditional Chinese Medicines	40.37	87.85	93.39	108.98	107.10
文化办公用品类	Articles for Cultural and Office Use	67.13	357.54	541.51	543.54	541.05
家具类	Furniture	32.18	149.28	158.79	159.19	171.84
通讯器材类	Communication Appliances	79.31	444.81	900.91	1023.34	1127.61
煤炭及制品类	Coal and Related Products	6.42	28.87	0.01		0.15
木材及制品类	Timber and Related Products					
石油及制品类	Petroleum and Related Products	1291.71	1969.25	2081.54	2386.33	2349.68
化工材料及制品类	Chemical Materials and Products					
金属材料类	Metal Materials					
建筑及装潢材料类	Construction and Decoration Materials	39.59	150.21	66.73	70.36	57.40
机电产品及设备类	Mechanical and Electrical Products and Equipment	35.04	146.90	48.74	61.82	68.53
汽车类	Motor Vehicles	1852.54	3773.61	5229.94	5693.93	5719.58
种子饲料类	Seeds and Feedstuff					
棉麻类	Cotton and Hemp		0.16			
其它类	Others	113.24	524.30	156.36	167.40	207.60

注：本表数据为2023年快报数。
Note: The data in this table come from express reports.

16-8 限额以上批发企业商品购、销、存总额（2023年）

Total Purchases, Sales and Inventory of Enterprises above Designated Size in Wholesale Trade (2023)

单位：亿元 (100 million yuan)

项目	Item	企业单位数（个）Number of Enterprises (unit)	购进总额 Total Purchases	#进口 Imports	商品销售总额 Total Sales of Commodities
批发业合计	**Total Wholesale Trade**	**45291**	**141856.24**	**7014.27**	**146030.64**
按登记注册统计类别分组	By Registration Statistical Categories				
内资企业	Domestic-funded	42977	129595.84	5641.47	133833.14
有限责任公司	Limited Liability Corporations	42131	123116.45	5322.91	127231.09
股份有限公司	Share-holding Corporations Ltd.	468	5644.45	311.18	5678.63
非公司企业法人	Non Corporate Legal Entity	141	572.90	2.66	640.39
个人独资企业	Sole Proprietorship Enterprises	149	115.40	2.83	128.92
合伙企业	Partnership Enterprises	85	146.02	1.89	153.45
其他内资企业	Other Domestic Invested Enterprises	NA	0.61		0.65
港澳台投资企业	Enterprises with Investment from Hong Kong, Macao and Taiwan	1555	6171.60	804.31	6898.95
外商投资企业	Foreign Invested Enterprises	744	6083.08	568.49	5292.61
其他统计类别	Other Statistical Categories	15	5.72		5.94
按国民经济行业分组	By Economic Sector				
农、林、牧、渔产品批发	Wholesale of Farm and Livestock Products	1062	3158.57	236.91	2972.31
食品、饮料及烟草制品批发业	Wholesale of Food, Beverages and Tobacco Products	4970	10934.11	947.76	12018.46
#米、面制品及食用油批发业	Wholesale of Rice, Flour Products and Edible Oil	610	1153.23	44.81	1185.56
烟草制品批发业	Wholesale of Tobacco Products	46	1466.46	5.63	2014.18
纺织、服装及日用品批发业	Wholesale of Textiles, Garments and Daily-use Products	5412	7509.17	164.44	8325.74
#服装批发业	Wholesale of Garments	683	1510.03	17.25	1624.17
家用视听设备批发	Wholesale of Household Audio-visual Equipments	296	381.16	9.93	407.13
日用家电批发	Wholesale of Household Appliances	964	2002.75	18.03	2131.60
文化、体育用品及器材批发业	Wholesale of Cultural and Sports Articles and Appliances	1592	2448.72	67.85	2715.31
医药及医疗器材批发业	Wholesale of Medicines and Medical Appliances and Chemical Products	2502	5182.20	362.70	5712.41
矿产品、建材及化工产品批发	Wholesale of Mineral Products, Building Materials	17986	77658.41	2087.18	77823.91
#煤炭及制品批发业	Wholesale of Coal and Related Products	338	2807.30	367.00	2889.27
石油及制品批发业	Wholesale of Petroleum and Related Products	1333	13981.18	549.28	12735.94
金属及金属矿批发业	Wholesale of Metal and Related Products	6971	45602.50	734.52	46015.11
建材批发业	Wholesale of Building Materials	3246	4720.21	59.34	5017.31
化肥批发业	Wholesale of Chemical Fertilizers	124	265.82	2.48	291.00
机械设备、五金交电及电子产品批发业	Wholesale of Machinery, Hardware, Electric and Electronic Products	10288	30815.94	2056.37	32172.12
#汽车及零配件批发	Wholesale of Motor Vehicles and Parts	955	13995.50	68.64	14434.42
计算机、软件及辅助设备批发业	Wholesale of Computers, Software and Assistant Equipments	1128	2043.38	135.30	2104.86
贸易经纪与代理	Trade Broker and Agency	309	2096.13	1007.06	2132.40
其他批发业	Other Wholesale Trades	1170	2053.00	84.00	2157.98

注：1.本表登记注册统计类别按《关于市场主体统计分类的划分规定》(国统字〔2023〕14号)执行。
2.NA表示企业个数小于或等于3。

Ntote: a) The registered statistical categories of this table is implemented in accordance with the Regulations onStatistics the Classification of Market Entity(Guotongzi [2023] No. 14).
b) NA refers to less than or equal to three.

16-8 续表 continued

单位：亿元 (100 million yuan)

项　　目	Item	批发额 Wholesale Trade	#出口 Exports	零售额 Retail Trade	年末库存总额 Inventory at the Year-end
批发业合计	**Total Wholesale Trade**	**144212.11**	**5727.57**	**1818.53**	**5939.75**
按登记注册统计类别分组	By Registration Statistical Categories				
内资企业	Domestic Invested Enterprises	132473.46	5101.62	1359.68	5226.26
有限责任公司	Limited Liability Corporations	126042.82	4930.73	1188.27	4900.27
股份有限公司	Share-holding Corporations Ltd.	5517.92	161.90	160.71	273.33
非公司企业法人	Non Corporate Legal Entity	634.71	2.97	5.68	34.65
个人独资企业	Sole Proprietorship Enterprises	125.08	2.51	3.84	9.59
合伙企业	Partnership Enterprises	152.28	3.50	1.18	8.30
其他内资企业	Other Domestic Invested Enterprises	0.65			0.12
港澳台投资企业	Enterprises with Investment from Hong Kong, Macao and Taiwan	6714.44	255.60	184.51	476.93
外商投资企业	Foreign Invested Enterprises	5018.31	370.34	274.30	236.24
其他统计类别	Other Statistical Categories	5.89		0.04	0.32
按国民经济行业分组	By Economic Sector				
农、林、牧、渔产品批发	Wholesale of Farm and Livestock Products	2956.69	43.21	15.62	219.10
食品、饮料及烟草制品批发业	Wholesale of Food, Beverages and Tobacco Products	11799.48	169.30	218.98	963.58
#米、面制品及食用油批发业	Wholesale of Rice, Flour Products and Edible Oil	1162.78	4.76	22.78	164.76
烟草制品批发业	Wholesale of Tobacco Products	2012.87	9.44	1.31	202.41
纺织、服装及日用品批发业	Wholesale of Textiles, Garments and Daily-use Products	7996.07	1561.62	329.66	601.59
#服装批发业	Wholesale of Garments	1575.52	265.37	48.64	113.15
家用视听设备批发	Wholesale of Household Audio-visual Equipments	398.55	129.12	8.58	22.59
日用家电批发	Wholesale of Household Appliances	1999.06	300.94	132.54	146.66
文化、体育用品及器材批发业	Wholesale of Cultural and Sports Articles and Appliances	2545.76	158.87	169.54	393.02
医药及医疗器材批发业	Wholesale of Medicines and Medical Appliances and Chemical Products	5621.37	65.73	91.04	510.82
矿产品、建材及化工产品批发	Wholesale of Mineral Products, Building Materials	77224.21	766.83	599.70	1866.13
#煤炭及制品批发业	Wholesale of Coal and Related Products	2884.85	1.13	4.42	77.59
石油及制品批发业	Wholesale of Petroleum and Related Products	12339.38	171.35	396.56	345.09
金属及金属矿批发业	Wholesale of Metal and Related Products	45923.39	126.65	91.72	779.04
建材批发业	Wholesale of Building Materials	4968.15	199.76	49.16	271.15
化肥批发业	Wholesale of Chemical Fertilizers	290.79	2.61	0.22	22.93
机械设备、五金交电及电子产品批发业	Wholesale of Machinery, Hardware, Electric and Electronic Products	31817.83	2561.65	354.29	1233.44
#汽车及零配件批发	Wholesale of Motor Vehicles and Parts	14361.99	184.11	72.43	160.43
计算机、软件及辅助设备批发业	Wholesale of Computers, Software and Assistant Equipments	2067.38	240.39	37.47	186.45
贸易经纪与代理	Trade Broker and Agency	2130.02	211.58	2.38	64.82
其他批发业	Other Wholesale Trades	2120.66	188.79	37.32	87.26

16-9 限额以上零售企业商品购、销、存总额（2023年）

Total Purchases, Sales and Inventory of Enterprises above Designated Size in Retail Trade (2023)

单位：亿元 (100 million yuan)

项目	Item	企业单位数(个) Number of Enterprises (unit)	购进总额 Total Purchases	#进口 Imports	商品销售总额 Total Sales of Commodities
零售业合计	**Total Retail Trade**	**12106**	**16528.92**	**412.52**	**19527.68**
按登记注册统计类别分组	By Registration Statistical Categories				
内资企业	Domestic Invested Enterprises	11578	13563.44	267.62	15884.02
有限责任公司	Limited Liability Corporations	10676	12358.23	265.90	13722.65
股份有限公司	Share-holding Corporations Ltd.	122	952.32	1.73	1596.41
非公司企业法人	Non Corporate Legal Entity	165	82.77		367.22
个人独资企业	Sole Proprietorship Enterprises	546	140.86		164.91
合伙企业	Partnership Enterprises	67	27.77		31.14
其他内资企业	Other Domestic Invested Enterprises	NA	1.49		1.69
港澳台投资企业	Enterprises with Investment from Hong Kong, Macao and Taiwan	353	1785.84	112.62	2048.02
外商投资企业	Foreign Invested Enterprises	171	1179.47	32.28	1595.09
其他统计类别	Other Statistical Categories	4	0.18		0.55
按国民经济行业分组	By Economic Sector				
综合零售业	Comprehensive Retail Trade	800	1436.22	28.96	1664.47
#百货零售	Retail of General Merchandise	350	685.28	0.01	822.82
超级市场零售	Retail in Supermarkets	354	581.38	28.95	645.34
食品、饮料及烟草制品专门零售业	Retail of Food, Beverages and Tobacco Products	929	511.47	10.58	661.21
纺织、服装及日用品专门零售业	Retail of Textiles, Garments and Daily-use Products	760	582.04	8.88	871.21
#服装零售	Retail of Garments	330	259.80	3.58	407.64
文化、体育用品及器材专门零售业	Retail of Cultural and Sports Articles and Appliances	506	220.14	0.34	286.69
#体育用品及器材零售	Retail of Sports Articles and Appliances	30	10.53		15.18
图书、报刊零售	Retail of Books	186	66.52		75.54
医药及医疗器材专门零售业	Retail of Medicines and Medical Appliances	517	456.59	0.80	612.01
#西药零售	Retail of Western Medicines	409	421.11	0.55	557.52
中药零售	Retail of Traditional Chinese Medicines	57	18.85		27.73
汽车、摩托车、燃料及零配件零售业	Retail of Motor Vehicles, Motorcycles and Parts	5254	8016.89	288.37	9300.91
#汽车新车零售	Retail of Motor Vehicles	3380	6233.45	286.67	6185.80
机动车燃油零售	Retail of Motor Vehicle Fuels	1499	1614.41	0.95	2924.57
家用电器及电子产品专门零售业	Retail of Household Appliances and Electronic Products	1186	711.01	26.15	785.41
#家用视听设备零售	Retail of Household Audio-visual Equipments	46	38.67	3.59	39.91
日用家电零售	Retail of Household Appliances	517	219.10	0.00	251.75
计算机、软件及辅助设备零售业	Retail of Computers, Software and Assistant Equipments	261	89.37	0.33	92.00
通讯设备零售	Retail of Communication Equipments	257	320.84	21.94	349.33
五金、家具及室内装修材料专门零售业	Retail of Hardware, Furniture and Interior Decoration Materials	378	117.07	1.47	161.20
货摊、无店铺及其他零售业	Stall,Non-shop and Other Retails	1776	4477.50	47.00	5184.57

注：1.本表登记注册统计类别按《关于市场主体统计分类的划分规定》(国统字〔2023〕14号)执行。
2.NA表示企业个数小于或等于3。

Ntote: a) The registered statistical categories of this table is implemented in accordance with the Regulations onStatistics the Classification of Market Entity(Guotongzi [2023] No. 14).
b) NA refers to less than or equal to three.

16-9 续表 continued

单位：亿元 (100 million yuan)

项目	Item	批发额 Wholesale Trade	#出口 Exports	零售额 Retail Trade	年末库存总额 Inventory at the Year-end
零售业合计	**Total Retail Trade**	**3043.15**	**25.14**	**16484.53**	**1357.77**
按登记注册统计类别分组	By Registration Statistical Categories				
内资企业	Domestic Invested Enterprises	2503.65	21.23	13380.37	1127.68
有限责任公司	Limited Liability Corporations	1800.23	21.09	11922.42	1064.91
股份有限公司	Share-holding Corporations Ltd.	542.30	0.15	1054.11	50.03
非公司企业法人	Non Corporate Legal Entity	130.87		236.35	5.56
个人独资企业	Sole Proprietorship Enterprises	24.77		140.14	5.81
合伙企业	Partnership Enterprises	5.32		25.82	1.36
其他内资企业	Other Domestic Invested Enterprises	0.17		1.52	0.01
港澳台投资企业	Enterprises with Investment from Hong Kong, Macao and Taiwan	232.72	3.63	1815.30	124.54
外商投资企业	Foreign Invested Enterprises	306.49	0.28	1288.61	105.21
其他统计类别	Other Statistical Categories	0.29		0.26	0.34
按国民经济行业分组	By Economic Sector				
综合零售业	Comprehensive Retail Trade	222.38	0.07	1442.09	118.23
#百货零售	Retail of General Merchandise	15.92	0.07	806.90	54.39
超级市场零售	Retail in Supermarkets	174.25		471.09	52.56
食品、饮料及烟草制品专门零售业	Retail of Food, Beverages and Tobacco Products	151.44	0.01	509.77	59.83
纺织、服装及日用品专门零售业	Retail of Textiles, Garments and Daily-use Products	171.79	1.76	699.43	145.02
#服装零售	Retail of Garments	80.05	0.79	327.58	74.07
文化、体育用品及器材专门零售业	Retail of Cultural and Sports Articles and Appliances	42.75	2.51	243.94	49.98
#体育用品及器材零售	Retail of Sports Articles and Appliances	2.24	0.53	12.94	3.11
图书零售	Retail of Books	5.47		70.06	13.89
医药及医疗器材专门零售业	Retail of Medicines and Medical Appliances	90.27		521.75	68.13
#西药零售	Retail of Western Medicines	80.64		476.88	61.33
中药零售	Retail of Traditional Chinese Medicines	3.04		24.69	4.08
汽车、摩托车、燃料及零配件零售业	Retail of Motor Vehicles, Motorcycles and Parts	1575.48	3.35	7725.43	626.26
#汽车新车零售	Retail of Motor Vehicles	608.12	2.15	5577.69	561.82
机动车燃油零售	Retail of Motor Vehicle Fuels	943.56	0.01	1981.02	43.02
家用电器及电子产品专门零售业	Retail of Household Appliances and Electronic Products	192.64	8.45	592.77	106.60
#家用视听设备零售	Retail of Household Audio-visual Equipments	8.27	1.01	31.64	10.05
日用家电零售	Retail of Household Appliances	42.53	0.08	209.22	33.91
计算机、软件及辅助设备零售业	Retail of Computers, Software and Assistant Equipments	15.81	6.54	76.18	7.90
通讯设备零售	Retail of Communication Equipments	108.77	0.24	240.57	45.79
五金、家具及室内装修材料专门零售业	Retail of Hardware, Furniture and Interior Decoration Materials	37.23	3.02	123.97	16.02
货摊、无店铺及其他零售业	Stall,Non-shop and Other Retails	559.17	6.00	4625.40	167.71

16-10 各市限额以上批发零售企业商品购、销、存总额（2023年）

Total Purchases, Sales and Inventory of Enterprises above Designated Size in Wholesale and Retail Trades by City (2023)

单位：亿元 (100 million yuan)

市别	City	商品购进总额 Total Purchases	#进口 Imports	商品销售总额 Total Sales	批发额 Wholesale Trade	#出口 Exports	零售额 Retail Trade	年末库存总额 Inventory at the Year-end
合 计	**Total**	**158385.16**	**7426.79**	**165558.32**	**147255.26**	**5752.71**	**18303.06**	**7297.52**
批发业	**Wholesale Trade**	**141856.24**	**7014.27**	**146030.64**	**144212.11**	**5727.57**	**1818.53**	**5939.75**
广 州	Guangzhou	58802.76	1979.06	59099.06	58359.68	1093.61	739.39	2249.70
深 圳	Shenzhen	41991.90	3697.17	43609.57	43203.67	2374.52	405.90	1880.30
珠 海	Zhuhai	4841.56	168.45	5114.86	5068.84	328.89	46.03	178.06
汕 头	Shantou	1730.29	117.15	1839.39	1821.38	49.86	18.00	104.53
佛 山	Foshan	17253.16	270.06	17930.89	17662.42	568.13	268.47	628.61
韶 关	Shaoguan	524.19	2.15	642.27	605.20	1.12	37.07	26.18
河 源	Heyuan	66.44	0.46	85.21	84.81	5.28	0.40	3.90
梅 州	Meizhou	249.54	1.00	287.82	281.45	0.01	6.37	10.89
惠 州	Huizhou	2036.82	178.91	2199.53	2091.12	51.33	108.41	68.22
汕 尾	Shanwei	106.84	0.27	128.26	126.50		1.76	6.06
东 莞	Dongguan	5877.06	224.51	6195.58	6133.09	534.09	62.49	331.41
中 山	Zhongshan	1751.35	67.86	1836.97	1810.67	370.13	26.30	100.94
江 门	Jiangmen	1131.57	59.58	1191.77	1153.12	258.99	38.64	87.48
阳 江	Yangjiang	207.43	0.88	237.03	236.26	46.78	0.77	11.16
湛 江	Zhanjiang	987.57	55.28	1051.00	1028.37	16.45	22.63	67.62
茂 名	Maoming	1904.48	12.44	1980.96	1971.93	0.02	9.03	60.15
肇 庆	Zhaoqing	908.92	32.13	959.85	951.15	16.29	8.70	26.90
清 远	Qingyuan	559.59	109.56	602.89	600.57	6.85	2.32	31.97
潮 州	Chaozhou	118.46	5.16	138.77	137.54	4.00	1.23	5.66
揭 阳	Jieyang	650.93	31.13	723.71	710.52	1.21	13.19	54.03
云 浮	Yunfu	155.39	1.06	175.24	173.81		1.43	5.99
零售业	**Retail Trade**	**16528.92**	**412.52**	**19527.68**	**3043.15**	**25.15**	**16484.53**	**1357.77**
广 州	Guangzhou	5150.86	123.13	6126.94	846.30	7.57	5280.64	381.04
深 圳	Shenzhen	5175.62	139.22	5795.57	1057.30	4.34	4738.27	460.27
珠 海	Zhuhai	392.84	4.92	499.71	64.48	7.73	435.23	39.60
汕 头	Shantou	257.78	0.38	291.51	42.41	0.28	249.10	24.11
佛 山	Foshan	976.79	40.25	1087.44	138.86	1.65	948.59	90.54
韶 关	Shaoguan	92.01	0.15	97.21	12.40		84.81	10.87
河 源	Heyuan	123.63	1.88	134.11	41.40		92.72	8.58
梅 州	Meizhou	88.71	2.83	145.06	32.44		112.61	9.91
惠 州	Huizhou	631.50	10.14	722.06	99.56	0.86	622.50	48.68
汕 尾	Shanwei	55.41	0.16	79.69	14.32		65.37	5.25
东 莞	Dongguan	1434.38	62.72	1644.07	151.49	0.07	1492.58	103.21
中 山	Zhongshan	525.14	7.34	665.35	119.93	0.01	545.42	41.27
江 门	Jiangmen	346.84	3.47	460.57	77.08	0.27	383.48	30.81
阳 江	Yangjiang	82.50	0.65	142.80	41.09		101.71	9.13
湛 江	Zhanjiang	171.93	3.53	277.92	50.66		227.26	19.52
茂 名	Maoming	160.63	4.59	272.40	65.15		207.25	19.36
肇 庆	Zhaoqing	332.48	1.35	428.03	55.37		372.66	15.46
清 远	Qingyuan	118.38	2.15	196.93	62.24		134.69	13.45
潮 州	Chaozhou	87.60	1.42	94.46	20.44	0.01	74.02	7.23
揭 阳	Jieyang	227.37	2.00	259.58	28.96	2.35	230.62	13.09
云 浮	Yunfu	96.52	0.24	106.28	21.27		85.01	6.39

 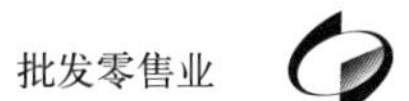

16-11 限额以上连锁批发零售业经营情况（2023年）

Business of Chain Stores above Designated Size in Wholesale and Retail Trade (2023)

项目	Item	连锁总店数（个）Number of General Chain Stores (unit)	销售总额（亿元）Total Sales Revenue (100 million yuan)	#零售额（亿元）Retail Sales (100 million yuan)	营业面积（万平方米）Operational Area (10 000 sq.m)
批发零售业合计	**Wholesale and Retail Trade**	**574**	**4696.04**	**3062.60**	**1487.48**
按登记注册统计类别分组	By Registration Statistical Categories				
内资企业	Domestic Invested Enterprises	505	3067.59	1979.94	883.98
有限责任公司	Limited Liability Corporations	466	1693.62	1127.64	632.33
股份有限公司	Share-holding Corporations Ltd.	33	1027.36	644.34	171.60
非公司企业法人	Non Corporate Legal Entity	4	339.77	201.12	76.00
个人独资企业	Sole Proprietorship Enterprises	NA	0.26	0.26	0.10
合伙企业	Partnership Enterprises				
其他内资企业	Other Domestic Invested Enterprises	NA	6.59	6.59	3.95
港澳台投资企业	Enterprises with Investment from Hong Kong, Macao and Taiwan	46	905.19	580.89	307.38
外商投资企业	Foreign Invested Enterprises	23	723.26	501.77	296.11
其他统计类别	Other Statistical Categories				
按零售业态分	By Type of Operation				
便利店	Convenience Store	25	75.83	64.03	72.90
超市	Supermarket	68	624.91	470.94	376.47
百货店	Department Store	18	329.33	294.07	331.19
专业店	Specialty Store	340	2505.57	1739.45	493.88
品牌专卖店	Brand Exclusive Store	97	632.94	240.16	122.34
其他	Other Store	26	527.47	253.96	90.70

注：1.本表登记注册统计类别按《关于市场主体统计分类的划分规定》（国统字〔2023〕14号）执行。
2.NA表示企业个数小于或等于3。

Ntote: a) The registered statistical categories of this table is implemented in accordance with the Regulations onStatistics the Classification of Market Entity(Guotongzi [2023] No. 14).
b) NA refers to less than or equal to three.

16−11 续表 continued

项 目	Item	从业人数（人）Number of Employed Persons (person)	连锁门店数（个）Number of Branch Chain Stores (unit)	直营店（个）Under Direct Management (unit)	加盟店（个）Through License Arrangement (unit)
批发零售业合计	**Retail Trade**	**244132**	**46734**	**35357**	**11377**
按注册登记类型分	By Status of Registration				
内资企业	Domestic Invested Enterprises	173358	39570	29351	10219
有限责任公司	Limited Liability Corporations	146232	34234	24818	9416
股份有限公司	Share-holding Corporations Ltd.	22754	4617	3815	802
非公司企业法人	Non Corporate Legal Entity	3015	327	326	NA
个人独资企业	Sole Proprietorship Enterprises	44	13	13	
合伙企业	Partnership Enterprises				
其他内资企业	Other Domestic Invested Enterprises	1313	379	379	
港澳台投资企业	Enterprises with Investment from Hong Kong, Macao and Taiwan	40789	5452	4576	876
外商投资企业	Foreign Invested Enterprises	29985	1712	1430	282
其他统计类别	Other Statistical Categories				
按零售业态分	By Type of Operation				
便利店	Convenience Store	10953	4431	2686	1745
超市	Supermarket	43384	1430	1426	4
百货店	Department Store	19421	1083	963	120
专业店	Specialty Store	103281	22992	18244	4748
品牌专卖店	Brand Exclusive Store	33740	10391	5911	4480
其他	Other Store	33353	6407	6127	280

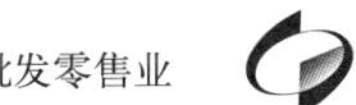

16-12 亿元以上商品交易市场成交额

Turnover of Commodity Exchange Markets with Transaction Value over 100 Million Yuan

单位：亿元 (100 million yuan)

项目	Item	2005	2010	2015
合计	**Total**	**1948.95**	**4828.13**	**5576.63**
食品、饮料、烟酒类	Food, Beverages, Tobacco and Liquor	853.12	1591.87	1933.27
#粮油类	Grain and Edible Oil	136.45	192.61	172.99
服装鞋帽、针、纺织品类	Garments,Footwear,Headgear,Knitwear and Textiles	457.60	1028.01	1294.61
化妆品类	Cosmetics	8.18	15.69	18.67
金银珠宝类	Gold, Silver and Jewelry	1.14	47.17	21.98
日用品类	Daily-use Articles	42.93	209.48	197.15
五金、电料类	Hardware and Electrical Appliances	19.07	121.51	191.98
体育、娱乐用品类	Sports and Recreational Articles	5.09	7.44	10.09
书报杂志类	Newspapers and Magazines	2.37	4.75	2.64
电子出版物及音像制品类	E-journals and Video Products	2.22	5.84	11.52
家用电器和音像器材类	Household Appliances and Video Appliances	15.20	33.88	19.31
中西药品类	Traditional Chinese and Western Medicines	13.24	12.49	16.39
#中草药及中成药类	Chinese Herbal Medicines and Chinese Patent Medicines	12.52	11.76	13.49
文化办公用品类	Articles for Cultural and Office Use	62.63	66.35	57.66
家具类	Furniture	3.03	9.05	8.28
通讯器材类	Communication Appliances	2.24	52.00	38.80
煤炭及制品类	Coal and Related Products			0.17
木材及制品类	Timber and Related Products	34.84	45.27	70.78
化工材料及制品类	Chemical Materials and Products	5.11	388.17	431.15
金属材料类	Metal Materials	82.11	485.52	418.28
建筑及装潢材料类	Construction and Decoration Materials	43.93	73.64	110.99
机电产品及设备类	Mechanical and Electrical Products and Equipments	17.68	28.11	47.40
汽车类	Motor Vehicles	175.68	531.59	555.89
种子饲料类	Seeds and Feedstuff		0.07	0.08
其他类	Others	101.54	70.23	119.54

16-12 续表 continued

单位：亿元 (100 million yuan)

项　　目	Item	2021	2022	2023
合　计	**Total**	**5534.20**	**5174.19**	**5379.18**
食品、饮料、烟酒类	Food, Beverages, Tobacco and Liquor	2230.54	2327.72	2401.74
#粮油类	Grain and Edible Oil	157.87	159.89	150.34
服装鞋帽、针、纺织品类	Garments,Footwear,Headgear,Knitwear and Textiles	1439.38	1215.22	1290.64
化妆品类	Cosmetics	13.90	11.48	10.97
金银珠宝类	Gold, Silver and Jewelry	35.25	29.23	23.46
日用品类	Daily-use Articles	163.63	160.34	188.12
五金、电料类	Hardware and Electrical Appliances	143.90	125.50	100.63
体育、娱乐用品类	Sports and Recreational Articles	6.43	3.69	4.03
书报杂志类	Newspapers and Magazines	1.32	1.81	2.77
电子出版物及音像制品类	E-journals and Video Products	0.42	0.49	0.37
家用电器和音像器材类	Household Appliances and Video Appliances	9.01	6.81	6.22
中西药品类	Traditional Chinese and Western Medicines	21.08	20.66	21.87
#中草药及中成药类	Chinese Herbal Medicines and Chinese Patent Medicines	20.42	19.94	21.05
文化办公用品类	Articles for Cultural and Office Use	13.38	13.98	13.80
家具类	Furniture	13.60	26.90	40.72
通讯器材类	Communication Appliances	9.66	9.60	9.52
煤炭及制品类	Coal and Related Products			
木材及制品类	Timber and Related Products	31.10	29.33	28.13
化工材料及制品类	Chemical Materials and Products	409.25	348.36	326.58
金属材料类	Metal Materials	159.23	82.00	73.62
建筑及装潢材料类	Construction and Decoration Materials	144.95	139.37	171.87
机电产品及设备类	Mechanical and Electrical Products and Equipments	48.28	50.99	54.03
汽车类	Motor Vehicles	489.38	416.33	493.84
种子饲料类	Seeds and Feedstuff	0.15	0.27	0.29
其他类	Others	150.36	154.13	115.95

16−13 限额以上批发零售企业财务状况（2023年）

Financial Indicators of Enterprises above Designated Size in Wholesale and Retail Trades Services (2023)

单位：亿元 (100 million yuan)

项　目	Item	批发零售业合计 Wholesale and Retail Trades	批发业 Wholesale Trade	零售业 Retail Trade
企业数　（个）	Number of Enterprises　(unit)	57397	45291	12106
年初存货	Inventory at the Year-beginning	7205.63	5876.81	1328.83
流动资产合计	Circulating Assets	59025.46	51849.96	7175.50
#存货	Inventory	7357.61	5997.53	1360.09
固定资产原价	Original Value of Fixed Assets	3475.26	2364.47	1110.79
累计折旧	Accumulated Depreciation	1606.55	1068.80	537.75
#本年折旧	Depreciation Drawn in Current Year	238.34	158.33	80.01
资产合计	Total Assets	73287.60	63549.88	9737.71
负债合计	Total Liabilities	56035.97	48822.18	7213.79
所有者权益合计	Total Creditors' Equity	17251.70	14727.69	2524.01
实收资本	Paid-up Capital	13605.88	9749.45	3856.43
#个人资本	Personal Capital	2404.55	1500.46	904.09
营业收入	Business Revenue	149785.23	131909.48	17875.75
#主营业务收入	Main Business Revenue	148625.17	131102.36	17522.81
营业成本	Business Costs	141771.84	126270.81	15501.03
营业税金及附加	Tax and Extra Charges on Business	390.95	337.41	53.54
其它业务利润	Profits from Other Businesses	297.23	126.83	170.39
销售费用	Marketing Expenses	4234.48	2534.67	1699.81
管理费用	Management Expenses	2202.42	1668.64	533.78
财务费用	Financial Expenses	254.28	184.42	69.86
#利息支出	Interests	352.07	300.28	51.80
营业利润	Business Profits	1403.60	1347.28	56.32
营业外收入	Non-operating Revenue	106.23	74.10	32.13
利润总额	Total Profits	1434.13	1365.85	68.28
应交所得税	Income Taxes Payable	278.94	237.66	41.29
本年应付职工薪酬	Total Wages Payable in Current Year	2575.77	1821.67	754.10
本年应交增值税	Value-added Tax Payable in Current Year	950.40	734.53	215.87

16-14 限额以上批发企业财务状况（2023年）

单位:亿元

项目	Item	企业数（个）Number of Enterprises	年初库存 Beginning Inventory	流动资产合计 Circulating Assets
批发业合计	**Total Wholesale Trade**	**45291**	**5876.81**	**51849.96**
按登记注册统计类别分组	By Registration Statistical Categories			
内资企业	Domestic Invested Enterprises	42977	5087.91	45564.17
有限责任公司	Limited Liability Corporations	42131	4672.21	41908.42
股份有限公司	Share-holding Corporations Ltd.	468	362.78	3329.53
非公司企业法人	Non Corporate Legal Entity	141	29.11	224.09
个人独资企业	Sole Proprietorship Enterprises	149	14.79	47.27
合伙企业	Partnership Enterprises	85	8.91	53.02
其他内资企业	Other Domestic Invested Enterprises	NA	0.10	1.84
港澳台投资企业	Enterprises with Investment from Hong Kong, Macao and Taiwan	1555	492.01	3684.75
外商投资企业	Foreign Invested Enterprises	744	296.69	2599.61
其他统计类别	Other Statistical Categories	15	0.20	1.43
按国民经济行业分	By Economic Sector			
农林牧产品批发业	Wholesale of Farm and Livestock Products	1062	207.44	796.75
食品、饮料及烟草制品批发业	Wholesale of Food, Beverages and Tobacco Products	4970	796.33	4675.45
#米、面制品及食用油批发业	Wholesale of Rice, Flour Products and Edible Oil	610	183.71	501.55
烟草制品批发业	Wholesale of Tobacco Products	46	46.01	403.57
纺织、服装及日用品批发业	Wholesale of Textiles, Garments and Daily-use Products	5412	619.67	4163.67
#服装批发业	Wholesale of Garments	683	108.79	734.39
家用视听设备批发	Wholesale of Household Audio-visual Equipments	296	22.03	261.10
日用家电批发	Wholesale of Household Appliances	964	152.27	1043.60
文化、体育用品及器材批发业	Wholesale of Cultural and Sports Articles and Appliances	1592	348.05	1164.59
医药及医疗器材批发业	Wholesale of Medicines and Medical Appliances	2502	495.15	3159.91
矿产品、建材及化工产品批发	Wholesale of Mineral Products, Building Materials and Chemical Products	17986	2006.29	21373.42
#煤炭及制品批发业	Wholesale of Coal and Related Products	338	81.06	847.74
石油及制品批发业	Wholesale of Petroleum and Related Products	1333	458.64	2357.93
金属及金属矿批发业	Wholesale of Metal and Related Products	6971	776.99	10627.63
建材批发业	Wholesale of Building Materials	3246	261.64	4480.16
化肥批发业	Wholesale of Chemical Fertilizers	124	22.29	103.89
机械设备、五金交电及电子产品批发业	Wholesale of Machinery, Hardware, Electric and Electronic Products	10288	1253.46	14553.82
汽车零配件批发业	Wholesale of Motor Vehicles and Parts	955	171.87	6174.44
计算机、软件及辅助设备批发业	Wholesale of Computers, Software and Assistant Equipments	1128	159.65	942.65
贸易经纪与代理	Trade Broker and Agency	309	59.63	1025.68
其他批发业	Other Wholesale Trades	1170	90.77	936.67

注:1.本表登记注册统计类别按《关于市场主体统计分类的划分规定》(国统字〔2023〕14号)执行。
2.NA表示企业个数小于或等于3。

Financial Indicators of Enterprises above Designated Size in Wholesale Trade (2023)

(100 million yuan)

固定资产原价 Original Value of Fixed Assets	累计折旧		资产合计 Total Assets	负债合计 Total Liabilities	所有者权益合计 Total Creditors' Equity	实收资本 Paid-up Capital	营业收入 Business Revenue	主营业务收入 Main Business Revenue
	Accumulated Depreciation	本年折旧 Depreciation Drawn in Current Year						
2364.47	**1068.80**	**158.33**	**63549.88**	**48822.18**	**14727.69**	**9749.45**	**131909.48**	**131102.36**
1854.22	819.63	128.98	54943.59	43389.38	11554.20	8366.36	119599.49	119004.14
1475.28	640.16	107.72	48452.76	39933.42	8519.34	7623.19	113457.45	112951.20
346.59	163.65	19.39	6081.59	3269.87	2811.73	711.49	5313.20	5226.03
25.76	13.62	1.37	291.11	91.50	199.61	21.92	568.49	567.39
4.17	1.29	0.29	57.58	45.54	12.03	5.08	121.05	120.73
2.17	0.85	0.19	58.45	48.14	10.31	4.37	138.71	138.20
0.26	0.07	0.02	2.10	0.92	1.18	0.30	0.59	0.59
168.63	72.85	10.65	5055.19	3098.15	1957.04	859.04	6286.24	6205.03
341.22	176.13	18.68	3549.34	2333.62	1215.72	523.85	6017.94	5887.40
0.39	0.19	0.02	1.76	1.03	0.73	0.21	5.80	5.79
81.93	26.06	4.29	1221.37	777.23	444.14	364.84	2799.90	2793.78
373.63	158.35	24.28	5663.73	3904.50	1759.44	969.63	11160.25	11005.21
101.21	31.29	3.93	663.89	458.83	205.06	378.09	1120.24	1110.39
64.18	34.74	3.92	476.01	99.57	376.44	6.08	1797.06	1795.38
187.85	78.94	13.41	5010.25	3790.63	1219.62	698.58	7673.67	7573.43
32.73	13.76	1.75	845.63	594.85	250.78	83.99	1480.58	1462.10
7.49	3.39	0.62	434.03	331.17	102.86	74.96	380.21	377.17
36.05	13.38	3.08	1137.74	963.87	173.87	74.34	1959.11	1945.90
53.94	27.21	4.37	1310.74	995.87	314.88	175.87	2463.76	2443.94
163.85	74.98	12.95	3751.00	2653.66	1097.35	483.20	5121.57	5062.38
1081.68	505.65	64.80	27014.63	21144.49	5870.14	4437.77	70328.81	70068.19
56.61	11.57	2.59	1600.76	1075.43	525.33	192.94	2539.12	2536.17
485.40	266.38	28.43	3464.68	2391.12	1073.54	628.30	12908.49	12787.39
267.42	111.09	14.88	12753.98	10769.14	1984.85	2320.73	40513.60	40427.80
135.44	44.17	9.13	5460.79	4283.49	1177.30	734.29	4516.89	4491.47
2.79	1.53	0.17	198.47	96.11	102.37	21.04	266.20	265.72
361.67	170.49	30.01	16776.26	13653.53	3122.51	2192.34	28629.16	28437.01
46.94	20.37	3.99	6535.12	6240.18	294.94	353.02	12650.33	12576.97
25.74	12.76	3.13	1061.66	860.98	200.68	351.97	1936.40	1928.83
25.95	10.14	1.24	1298.93	1014.16	284.77	103.37	1807.94	1800.01
33.96	16.97	2.99	1502.97	888.13	614.84	323.85	1924.42	1918.41

Ntote: a) The registered statistical categories of this table is implemented in accordance with the Regulations onStatistics the Classification of Market Entity(Guotongzi [2023] No. 14).

b) NA refers to less than or equal to three.

16-14 续表

单位:亿元

项　　目	Item	营业成本 Business Costs	营业税金及附加 Tax and Extra Charges on Business	其他业务利润 Profits from Other Businesses
批发业合计	**Total Wholesale Trade**	**126270.81**	**337.41**	**126.83**
按登记注册类型分	By Status of Registration			
内资企业	Domestic Invested Enterprises	115096.69	313.93	33.77
有限责任公司	Limited Liability Corporations	109390.13	284.72	26.62
股份有限公司	Share-holding Corporations Ltd.	4955.87	9.08	6.68
非公司企业法人	Non Corporate Legal Entity	502.64	19.90	0.41
个人独资企业	Sole Proprietorship Enterprises	115.84	0.10	0.04
合伙企业	Partnership Enterprises	131.65	0.13	0.01
其他内资企业	Other Domestic Invested Enterprises	0.56	...	
港澳台投资企业	Enterprises with Investment from Hong Kong, Macao and Taiwan	5645.83	14.78	31.72
外商投资企业	Foreign Invested Enterprises	5522.93	8.71	61.34
其他统计类别	Other Statistical Categories	5.35	...	
按国民经济行业分	By Economic Sector			
农林牧产品批发业	Wholesale of Farm and Livestock Products	2723.51	1.58	1.45
食品、饮料及烟草制品批发业	Wholesale of Food, Beverages and Tobacco Products	9943.51	223.26	58.85
#米、面制品及食用油批发业	Wholesale of Rice, Flour Products and Edible Oil	1074.82	1.01	1.20
烟草制品批发业	Wholesale of Tobacco Products	1317.66	212.28	0.14
纺织、服装及日用品批发业	Wholesale of Textiles, Garments and Daily-use Products	6800.65	13.49	35.58
#服装批发业	Wholesale of Garments	1342.73	2.81	12.50
家用视听设备批发	Wholesale of Household Audio-visual Equipments	341.57	0.71	0.17
日用家电批发	Wholesale of Household Appliances	1798.56	3.11	2.10
文化、体育用品及器材批发业	Wholesale of Cultural and Sports Articles and Appliances	2257.22	7.19	2.21
医药及医疗器材批发业	Wholesale of Medicines and Medical Appliances	4515.34	10.62	16.00
矿产品、建材及化工产品批发	Wholesale of Mineral Products, Building Materials and Chemical Products	69019.17	51.80	41.88
#煤炭及制品批发业	Wholesale of Coal and Related Products	2489.41	2.98	0.36
石油及制品批发业	Wholesale of Petroleum and Related Products	12590.08	9.71	22.24
金属及金属矿批发业	Wholesale of Metal and Related Products	40237.47	24.92	8.23
建材批发业	Wholesale of Building Materials	4253.90	5.85	4.39
化肥批发业	Wholesale of Chemical Fertilizers	253.24	0.25	0.55
机械设备、五金交电及电子产品批发业	Wholesale of Machinery, Hardware, Electric and Electronic Products	27436.24	26.45	34.37
汽车零配件批发业	Wholesale of Motor Vehicles and Parts	12424.78	9.27	14.58
计算机、软件及辅助设备批发业	Wholesale of Computers, Software and Assistant Equipments	1836.34	1.97	1.37
贸易经纪与代理	Trade Broker and Agency	1753.64	0.89	1.94
其他批发业	Other Wholesale Trades	1821.53	2.11	-65.43

16-14 continued

(100 million yuan)

销售费用 Marketing Expenses	管理费用 Manag-ement Expenses	财务费用 Financial Expenses	营业利润 Business Profits	营业外收入 Non-operating revenue	利润总额 Total Profits	应交所得税 Income Taxes Payable	本年应付职工薪酬 Staff Salary Payable in Current Year	本年应交增值税 Value-added Tax Payable in Current Year
2534.67	**1668.64**	**184.42**	**1347.28**	**74.10**	**1365.85**	**237.66**	**1821.67**	**734.53**
1994.49	1367.02	168.85	887.39	60.55	902.35	181.17	1422.08	615.86
1803.51	1278.10	141.82	682.96	53.48	695.18	158.09	1257.12	553.88
180.52	72.62	29.77	163.80	5.25	165.01	14.37	148.15	52.12
6.50	11.34	-3.31	37.87	0.47	38.18	8.50	13.01	7.83
1.87	2.21	0.25	0.68	0.04	0.69	0.08	1.61	1.09
2.04	2.70	0.33	2.14	1.32	3.42	0.14	2.16	0.94
0.05	0.04		-0.06	0.00	-0.13	0.00	0.03	0.00
316.47	174.93	1.31	261.28	7.35	262.77	31.83	237.76	73.46
223.47	126.57	14.25	198.53	6.20	200.64	24.65	161.70	45.20
0.24	0.12	0.01	0.08	...	0.09	...	0.13	...
23.26	29.73	8.78	23.91	1.77	23.98	4.92	24.94	5.03
425.03	331.50	7.45	328.00	10.53	333.07	77.24	336.66	135.30
28.28	18.53	6.44	4.51	2.09	5.06	1.43	20.62	5.11
27.50	86.05	-10.01	166.69	0.19	167.22	48.61	94.85	67.46
470.87	263.69	6.18	182.60	9.89	183.78	27.10	306.31	93.45
70.03	52.21	-1.39	74.19	3.73	76.33	5.27	77.82	17.39
18.46	13.22	3.22	10.74	0.50	10.89	0.81	17.75	3.14
97.81	32.40	0.49	21.76	1.48	22.41	4.34	48.42	18.72
104.03	64.13	5.38	30.25	1.95	31.08	4.08	74.82	21.22
305.00	161.21	12.01	151.29	3.42	149.94	25.96	176.63	74.75
610.20	372.33	111.26	325.49	27.39	330.17	63.50	403.77	226.22
16.06	19.32	13.62	14.29	3.68	15.39	2.75	12.99	12.84
183.37	43.08	22.06	82.46	4.75	81.49	21.78	100.45	64.88
96.71	99.71	40.37	56.17	12.56	61.72	11.13	95.67	62.12
137.48	79.86	20.08	83.85	2.96	83.92	10.84	76.82	36.45
4.68	4.68	0.50	7.86	0.11	7.93	0.59	4.11	0.62
532.39	393.12	16.72	262.96	17.29	270.46	29.52	450.57	156.42
202.42	31.95	-12.09	-0.23	1.75	-0.18	-4.90	52.83	26.86
35.06	38.17	2.99	16.97	1.17	16.55	2.93	45.75	17.26
17.92	16.28	9.25	13.88	0.73	14.51	2.02	14.19	7.18
45.97	36.66	7.40	28.88	1.12	28.88	3.31	33.79	14.98

16-15 限额以上零售企业财务状况（2023年）

单位：亿元

项　目	Item	企业数(个) Number of Enterprises (unit)	年初库存 Beginning Inventory	流动资产合计 Circulating Assets
零售业合计	**Total Retail Trade**	**12106**	**1328.83**	**7175.50**
按登记注册统计类别分组	By Registration Statistical Categories			
内资企业	Domestic Invested Enterprises	11578	1104.19	5697.78
有限责任公司	Limited Liability Corporations	10676	1024.28	5024.35
股份有限公司	Share-holding Corporations Ltd.	122	63.77	549.39
非公司企业法人	Non Corporate Legal Entity	165	7.64	85.34
个人独资企业	Sole Proprietorship Enterprises	546	7.38	30.94
合伙企业	Partnership Enterprises	67	1.10	7.05
其他内资企业	Other Domestic Invested Enterprises	NA	0.02	0.72
港澳台投资企业	Enterprises with Investment from Hong Kong, Macao and Taiwan	353	131.48	689.65
外商投资企业	Foreign Invested Enterprises	171	92.91	787.44
其他统计类别	Other Statistical Categories	4	0.25	0.64
按国民经济行业分	By Economic Sector			
综合零售业	Comprehensive Retail	800	121.80	1078.72
#百货零售业	Retail of General Merchandise	350	53.49	583.45
超级市场零售业	Retail in Supermarkets	354	58.23	409.50
食品、饮料及烟草制品专门零售业	Retail of Food, Beverages and Tobacco Products	929	64.88	390.05
纺织、服装及日用品专门零售业	Retail of Textiles, Garments and Daily-use Products	760	143.85	552.88
#服装零售业	Retail of Garments	330	74.43	317.45
文化、体育用品及器材专门零售业	Retail of Cultural and Sports Articles and Appliances	506	48.54	211.79
#体育用品及器材零售	Retail of Sports Articles and Appliances	30	3.04	8.13
图书零售业	Retail of Books	186	13.72	65.64
医药及医疗器材专门零售业	Retail of Medicines and Medical Appliances	517	70.43	273.37
#西药零售	Retail of Western Medicines	409	62.80	248.28
中药零售	Retail of Traditional Chinese Medicines	57	4.73	12.03
汽车、摩托车、燃料及零配件专门零售业	Retail of Motor Vehicles, Motorcycles and Parts	5254	584.36	2775.27
#汽车新车零售	Retail of Motor Vehicles	3380	505.27	1981.71
机动车燃油零售	Retail of Fuel Oil of Motor Vehicles	1499	55.95	646.44
家用电器及电子产品专门零售业	Retail of Household Appliances and Electronic Products	1186	106.73	434.67
#家用视听设备零售	Retail of Household Audio-visual Equipments	46	9.03	17.51
日用家电零售	Retail of Household Appliances	517	35.08	179.48
计算机、软件及辅助设备零售业	Retail of Computers, Software and Assistant Equipments	261	8.45	46.90
通讯设备零售业	Retail of Communication Equipments	257	43.79	163.73
五金、家具及室内装修材料专门零售业	Retail of Hardware, Furniture and Interior Decoration Materials	378	15.98	76.96
货摊、无店铺及其他零售业	Stall,Non-shop and Other Retails	1776	172.25	1381.79

注：1.本表登记注册统计类别按《关于市场主体统计分类的划分规定》(国统字〔2023〕14号)执行。
2.NA表示企业个数小于或等于3。

Financial Indicators of Enterprises above Designated Size in Retail Trade (2023)

(100 million yuan)

固定资产原价 Original Value of Fixed Assets	累计折旧 Accumulated Depreciation	本年折旧 Depreciation Drawn in Current Year	资产合计 Total Assets	负债合计 Total Liabilities	所有者权益合计 Total Creditors' Equity	实收资本 Paid-up Capital	营业收入 Business Revenue	主营业务收入 Main Business Revenue
1110.79	**537.75**	**80.01**	**9737.71**	**7213.79**	**2524.01**	**3856.43**	**17875.75**	**17522.81**
828.03	387.63	58.73	7519.17	5550.39	1968.87	3391.54	14547.60	14287.12
680.78	312.78	50.41	6438.50	5198.32	1240.27	3319.66	12650.73	12425.07
113.01	58.60	6.38	909.60	379.10	530.50	64.11	1393.30	1365.30
25.27	12.22	1.22	124.09	-58.60	182.69	2.44	324.17	318.02
7.50	3.18	0.60	38.27	25.78	12.49	4.17	150.49	149.84
1.31	0.73	0.09	7.95	5.78	2.17	1.10	27.40	27.38
0.15	0.11	0.01	0.76	0.01	0.75	0.05	1.50	1.50
113.82	67.89	9.89	1029.04	782.45	246.59	193.95	1887.67	1840.42
168.87	82.21	11.38	1188.75	880.38	308.38	270.93	1439.93	1394.73
0.08	0.02	0.01	0.75	0.58	0.17	…	0.54	0.54
241.36	142.67	13.97	1677.54	1313.77	363.77	327.49	1488.37	1423.60
113.13	65.55	4.50	973.55	675.98	297.57	142.53	676.26	647.25
115.61	69.93	7.50	596.32	526.14	70.17	152.84	629.93	603.23
51.56	24.47	3.36	529.51	295.43	234.09	79.38	580.51	574.74
41.28	25.32	4.30	681.96	576.88	105.09	610.98	791.55	774.81
21.66	12.40	1.42	403.48	345.18	58.31	546.72	383.47	374.21
37.49	18.57	1.74	305.91	158.97	146.94	56.40	270.68	265.96
2.89	2.12	0.14	10.99	9.81	1.18	1.86	13.67	13.57
30.66	14.17	1.19	134.37	72.25	62.12	33.52	78.34	75.61
38.71	11.45	2.15	345.99	287.00	58.99	29.23	564.80	555.75
36.02	10.53	1.94	315.89	260.68	55.21	25.30	515.44	507.52
1.89	0.62	0.16	16.31	15.08	1.23	2.58	24.73	24.15
552.17	257.07	45.86	4011.64	2748.37	1263.27	2331.99	8571.88	8371.36
287.09	131.73	29.06	2447.01	2102.59	344.42	1141.93	5785.00	5633.40
228.62	113.11	12.93	1369.04	533.28	835.76	1087.26	2601.23	2556.85
17.96	10.01	1.36	475.14	428.72	46.48	67.60	710.08	702.72
0.87	0.34	0.05	20.48	13.54	6.94	19.77	34.86	34.25
10.53	5.77	0.60	199.30	179.55	19.75	23.02	220.46	217.87
2.21	1.27	0.25	50.76	39.44	11.32	10.18	85.73	84.71
2.93	1.82	0.32	176.27	173.00	3.32	11.37	318.31	315.43
26.64	9.57	1.35	110.23	93.90	16.33	41.73	149.50	146.97
103.62	38.63	5.91	1599.79	1310.76	289.06	311.64	4748.36	4706.91

Ntote: a) The registered statistical categories of this table is implemented in accordance with the Regulations onStatistics the Classification of Market Entity(Guotongzi [2023] No. 14).

b) NA refers to less than or equal to three.

16－15　续表

单位:亿元

项　　目	Item	营业成本 Business Costs	营业税金及附加 Tax and Extra Charges on Business	其它业务利润 Profits from Other Businesses
零售业合计	**Total Retail Trade**	**15501.03**	**53.54**	**170.39**
按登记注册统计类别分组	By Registration Statistical Categories			
内资企业	Domestic Invested Enterprises	12786.15	40.34	131.89
有限责任公司	Limited Liability Corporations	11103.39	33.93	128.79
股份有限公司	Share-holding Corporations Ltd.	1240.99	3.88	2.80
非公司企业法人	Non Corporate Legal Entity	291.33	0.59	0.01
个人独资企业	Sole Proprietorship Enterprises	125.65	1.88	0.27
合伙企业	Partnership Enterprises	23.47	0.06	0.02
其他内资企业	Other Domestic Invested Enterprises	1.33	0.00	0.00
港澳台投资企业	Enterprises with Investment from Hong Kong, Macao and Taiwan	1581.87	8.07	20.95
外商投资企业	Foreign Invested Enterprises	1132.61	5.12	17.55
其他统计类别	Other Statistical Categories	0.40	…	
按国民经济行业分	By Economic Sector			
综合零售业	Comprehensive Retail	1183.74	5.15	84.01
#百货零售业	Retail of General Merchandise	517.51	3.58	24.16
超级市场零售业	Retail in Supermarkets	526.19	1.21	56.47
食品、饮料及烟草制品专门零售业	Retail of Food, Beverages and Tobacco Products	433.01	1.99	1.60
纺织、服装及日用品专门零售业	Retail of Textiles, Garments and Daily-use Products	509.75	2.98	6.28
#服装零售业	Retail of Garments	234.06	1.45	3.54
文化、体育用品及器材专门零售业	Retail of Cultural and Sports Articles and Appliances	197.82	4.75	2.68
#体育用品及器材零售	Retail of Sports Articles and Appliances	9.44	0.06	0.00
图书零售业	Retail of Books	57.96	0.39	1.84
医药及医疗器材专门零售业	Retail of Medicines and Medical Appliances	417.45	1.24	2.29
#西药零售	Retail of Western Medicines	382.45	1.12	2.25
中药零售	Retail of Traditional Chinese Medicines	17.16	0.05	0.03
汽车、摩托车、燃料及零配件专门零售业	Retail of Motor Vehicles, Motorcycles and Parts	7965.29	24.63	57.27
#汽车新车零售	Retail of Motor Vehicles	5441.97	17.76	52.60
机动车燃油零售	Retail of Fuel Oil of Motor Vehicles	2351.32	6.63	4.13
家用电器及电子产品专门零售业	Retail of Household Appliances and Electronic Products	633.84	0.82	1.60
#家用视听设备零售	Retail of Household Audio-visual Equipments	31.06	0.03	0.19
日用家电零售	Retail of Household Appliances	190.84	0.34	0.73
计算机、软件及辅助设备零售业	Retail of Computers, Software and Assistant Equipments	76.30	0.11	0.11
通讯设备零售业	Retail of Communication Equipments	293.35	0.26	0.56
五金、家具及室内装修材料专门零售业	Retail of Hardware, Furniture and Interior Decoration Materials	107.66	0.82	0.39
货摊、无店铺及其他零售业	Stall,Non-shop and Other Retails	4052.48	11.15	14.25

注:本表登记注册统计类别按《关于市场主体统计分类的划分规定》(国统字〔2023〕14号)执行。

16-15 continued

(100 million yuan)

销售费用 Marketing Expenses	管理费用 Manag-ement Expenses	财务费用 Financial Expenses	营业利润 Business Profits	营业外收入 Non-operating revenue	利润总额 Total Profits	应交所得税 Income Taxes Payable	本年应付职工薪酬 Staff Salary Payable in Current Year	本年应交增值税 Value-added Tax Payable in Current Year
1699.81	**533.78**	**69.86**	**56.32**	**32.13**	**68.28**	**41.29**	**754.10**	**215.87**
1236.31	408.53	52.97	55.85	25.28	64.64	32.57	588.21	168.71
1110.10	372.46	46.08	6.31	24.11	16.17	29.29	513.18	140.41
101.78	23.08	5.18	28.94	0.98	28.40	1.31	51.36	21.86
14.66	5.03	0.90	12.40	0.09	12.15	0.91	17.28	3.16
8.01	6.90	0.73	7.06	0.09	6.76	0.93	5.14	2.78
1.68	1.00	0.07	1.12	0.02	1.13	0.13	1.19	0.48
0.08	0.06	0.00	0.02	0.00	0.02	0.00	0.06	0.02
219.36	69.72	4.16	7.69	3.83	9.83	4.25	105.39	24.25
244.13	55.51	12.72	-7.33	3.01	-6.30	4.47	60.46	22.90
0.02	0.01	...	0.11		0.11		0.04	...
226.65	61.09	14.98	2.21	4.46	2.99	5.23	103.76	18.10
108.26	29.14	7.00	13.36	2.04	13.49	5.03	45.83	9.81
88.87	22.23	7.39	-15.24	2.12	-14.43	-0.38	46.66	5.86
95.07	34.19	1.35	22.75	2.79	23.90	4.15	42.79	13.50
211.49	54.99	4.79	10.65	4.97	14.43	3.62	87.50	20.47
109.39	29.91	3.36	3.28	2.12	5.42	1.55	44.86	9.79
39.93	26.34	0.79	8.35	0.55	8.32	1.42	29.29	5.43
2.40	1.47	0.17	0.00	0.02	0.00	0.06	1.51	0.53
8.23	10.36	0.00	2.99	0.32	3.25	0.26	10.55	0.73
113.56	23.08	2.09	11.81	1.21	12.32	3.00	62.16	10.12
103.80	19.45	1.86	11.29	1.16	11.80	2.82	56.68	8.84
4.69	2.03	0.16	0.46	0.04	0.48	0.10	3.75	0.48
387.10	187.36	38.60	-19.77	11.56	-16.49	11.63	277.03	80.56
251.34	136.04	24.57	-81.69	9.43	-77.18	2.48	194.45	40.85
127.73	41.40	12.54	67.13	1.49	65.54	9.01	74.00	37.77
48.66	25.22	3.62	-2.51	1.13	-2.12	0.25	30.98	6.79
3.36	0.92	0.13	-0.20	0.04	-0.16	0.01	1.37	0.24
19.51	9.22	1.62	-0.80	0.52	-0.50	-0.17	9.41	2.54
4.12	4.94	0.50	-0.74	0.22	-0.85	0.09	4.73	1.10
17.08	7.65	1.25	-1.27	0.29	-1.10	0.26	11.89	1.76
30.33	11.11	1.00	-1.95	0.21	-1.92	0.47	12.86	3.52
547.01	110.40	2.63	24.78	5.23	26.84	11.52	107.74	57.38

Ntote: The registered statistical categories of this table is implemented in accordance with the Regulations onStatistics the Classification of Market Entity(Guotongzi [2023] No. 14).

16-16 各市限额以上批发零售企业财务状况（2023年）

单位:亿元

市 别	City	企业数(个) Number of Enterprises (unit)	年初库存 Beginning Inventory	流动资产合计 Circulating Assets	固定资产原价 Original Value of Fixed Assets
批发零售业合计	**Total Wholesale and Retail Trades**	**57397**	**7205.63**	**59025.46**	**3475.26**
批发业	**Wholesale Trade**	**45291**	**5876.81**	**51849.96**	**2364.47**
广 州	Guangzhou	14281	2142.00	14444.65	866.48
深 圳	Shenzhen	12602	1844.60	22420.03	671.50
珠 海	Zhuhai	1302	197.68	2126.50	75.19
汕 头	Shantou	985	130.38	487.82	45.70
佛 山	Foshan	5779	600.43	5410.50	163.37
韶 关	Shaoguan	248	23.73	169.14	18.49
河 源	Heyuan	54	4.31	56.37	3.26
梅 州	Meizhou	165	15.30	107.18	14.77
惠 州	Huizhou	1052	74.29	649.06	66.24
汕 尾	Shanwei	85	5.84	46.12	4.41
东 莞	Dongguan	3927	348.05	2393.56	174.38
中 山	Zhongshan	1094	96.83	711.49	45.55
江 门	Jiangmen	909	75.57	566.78	43.76
阳 江	Yangjiang	197	12.93	68.42	16.24
湛 江	Zhanjiang	652	62.81	447.80	41.40
茂 名	Maoming	825	71.62	568.77	22.30
肇 庆	Zhaoqing	290	57.53	464.27	39.25
清 远	Qingyuan	308	36.73	301.45	12.50
潮 州	Chaozhou	78	6.70	33.80	6.68
揭 阳	Jieyang	385	57.23	320.33	13.46
云 浮	Yunfu	73	12.25	55.93	19.51
零售业	**Retail Trade**	**12106**	**1328.83**	**7175.50**	**1110.79**
广 州	Guangzhou	2576	357.31	2048.05	304.00
深 圳	Shenzhen	2439	454.59	2682.03	267.19
珠 海	Zhuhai	388	36.65	338.31	31.43
汕 头	Shantou	386	25.40	79.25	22.49
佛 山	Foshan	944	91.23	344.41	74.33
韶 关	Shaoguan	266	9.95	43.32	8.95
河 源	Heyuan	162	10.09	142.54	12.99
梅 州	Meizhou	201	10.91	35.29	15.94
惠 州	Huizhou	850	47.55	211.81	51.47
汕 尾	Shanwei	134	5.99	21.29	7.01
东 莞	Dongguan	892	99.23	422.73	107.56
中 山	Zhongshan	420	39.33	193.33	37.30
江 门	Jiangmen	526	32.75	169.44	37.73
阳 江	Yangjiang	172	9.62	25.94	11.98
湛 江	Zhanjiang	309	23.07	134.76	24.37
茂 名	Maoming	346	19.01	68.78	23.12
肇 庆	Zhaoqing	238	14.43	86.81	21.82
清 远	Qingyuan	222	12.68	40.35	19.47
潮 州	Chaozhou	146	7.73	18.69	8.20
揭 阳	Jieyang	320	14.22	46.00	13.26
云 浮	Yunfu	169	7.07	22.38	10.17

Financial Indicators of Enterprises above Designated Size in Wholesale and Retail Trades by City (2023)

(100 million yuan)

累计折旧 Accumulated Depreciation	#本年折旧 Depreciation Drawn in Current Year	资产合计 Total Assets	负债合计 Total Liabilities	所有者权益合计 Total Creditors' Equity	实收资本 Paid-up Capital	营业收入 Business Revenue	主营业务收入 Main Business Revenue
1606.55	**238.34**	**73287.60**	**56035.97**	**17251.70**	**13605.88**	**149785.23**	**148625.17**
1068.80	**158.33**	**63549.88**	**48822.18**	**14727.69**	**9749.45**	**131909.48**	**131102.36**
409.09	58.19	17796.23	13664.86	4131.58	2121.20	54053.81	53792.10
316.13	45.40	27399.33	21465.56	5933.56	4599.93	38879.03	38615.78
27.91	4.66	2474.48	1849.41	625.07	269.58	4566.88	4514.40
21.20	2.53	583.34	372.64	210.70	88.66	1645.10	1641.86
66.56	11.16	5977.14	5031.21	945.93	960.69	15996.98	15917.56
7.97	1.61	211.08	172.12	38.96	34.46	562.12	555.23
1.55	0.27	74.94	29.11	45.82	5.15	76.76	76.50
6.81	0.95	129.21	95.57	33.64	9.47	259.87	258.65
23.85	4.24	824.78	615.40	209.38	164.91	1996.24	1990.32
1.75	0.76	51.57	39.44	12.13	3.17	113.83	113.47
77.81	11.65	3256.86	2300.88	955.98	615.85	5662.79	5614.12
22.48	3.75	941.96	652.50	289.46	98.69	1690.93	1665.03
17.61	2.78	904.98	451.17	453.79	329.27	1091.83	1086.67
8.33	1.18	85.36	57.61	27.75	12.38	231.29	230.58
16.68	2.41	636.83	424.73	212.11	196.69	950.48	912.91
9.02	1.66	634.06	417.52	216.54	139.85	1789.65	1782.15
9.50	1.74	698.87	531.29	167.58	21.65	859.59	856.11
4.92	0.78	370.00	277.93	92.07	32.93	540.17	538.72
3.16	0.51	44.74	27.52	17.22	4.69	126.70	126.46
6.15	0.96	344.79	294.18	50.61	23.35	648.59	647.21
10.33	1.14	109.35	51.54	57.81	16.88	166.85	166.53
537.75	**80.01**	**9737.71**	**7213.79**	**2524.01**	**3856.43**	**17875.75**	**17522.81**
139.03	22.08	2838.13	2231.47	606.66	602.78	5593.90	5491.30
139.96	20.42	3440.38	2640.66	799.77	633.23	5350.12	5263.82
15.78	2.69	394.77	268.07	126.70	43.83	458.67	450.93
9.89	1.59	105.81	67.77	38.05	16.21	264.03	259.17
39.74	5.24	456.14	369.89	86.25	1721.07	1011.26	985.22
5.05	0.72	55.45	43.93	11.53	14.34	91.40	89.55
6.01	0.80	161.27	133.19	28.11	37.31	123.10	119.91
7.82	0.97	249.55	239.90	9.65	8.22	132.47	130.20
23.48	3.86	306.75	204.31	102.44	51.93	656.40	640.88
3.32	0.45	27.99	18.38	9.62	2.30	71.98	71.06
45.74	7.37	567.88	369.56	198.31	183.32	1508.99	1465.85
18.41	2.80	262.71	145.94	116.76	35.80	568.97	557.45
19.54	2.36	223.69	151.51	72.19	50.64	420.29	409.52
6.63	0.98	50.16	29.17	21.00	4.88	131.20	128.06
10.93	1.74	185.34	85.68	99.66	269.98	251.17	245.57
10.18	1.84	102.86	36.52	66.34	62.00	251.16	244.44
11.91	1.12	109.77	57.35	52.42	91.54	390.87	379.86
9.61	0.92	70.15	27.61	42.54	9.05	177.77	172.84
4.72	0.54	27.75	23.72	4.04	4.11	86.93	85.79
4.88	0.81	62.64	45.28	17.36	8.09	238.99	237.09
5.12	0.70	38.53	23.91	14.62	5.79	96.07	94.31

16-16 续表

单位:亿元

市 别	City	营业成本 Business Costs	营业税金及附加 Tax and Extra Charges on Business	其他业务利润 Profits from Other Businesses	销售费用 Marketing Expenses
批发零售业合计	**Total Wholesale and Retail Trades**	**141771.84**	**390.95**	**297.23**	**4234.48**
批发业	**Wholesale Trade**	**126270.81**	**337.41**	**126.83**	**2534.67**
广 州	Guangzhou	52041.44	78.66	85.67	1074.72
深 圳	Shenzhen	37044.42	68.10	81.80	699.51
珠 海	Zhuhai	4356.08	10.93	2.54	99.30
汕 头	Shantou	1545.39	14.36	0.89	34.32
佛 山	Foshan	15549.74	27.21	7.84	248.52
韶 关	Shaoguan	523.30	6.52	0.32	12.14
河 源	Heyuan	60.54	5.81	0.01	1.98
梅 州	Meizhou	230.12	8.08	0.08	8.37
惠 州	Huizhou	1889.87	11.56	0.81	41.95
汕 尾	Shanwei	96.84	5.90		2.74
东 莞	Dongguan	5324.90	21.90	-59.44	145.79
中 山	Zhongshan	1569.70	8.45	3.42	57.72
江 门	Jiangmen	1014.54	9.75	0.70	30.34
阳 江	Yangjiang	209.76	4.29	0.05	5.89
湛 江	Zhanjiang	900.29	8.90	0.58	16.72
茂 名	Maoming	1739.49	7.43	0.52	13.67
肇 庆	Zhaoqing	820.32	7.52	0.06	10.32
清 远	Qingyuan	505.79	7.12	0.16	8.36
潮 州	Chaozhou	108.79	5.64	0.17	3.19
揭 阳	Jieyang	587.11	14.97	0.33	16.72
云 浮	Yunfu	152.34	4.33	0.33	2.40
零售业	**Retail Trade**	**15501.03**	**53.54**	**170.39**	**1699.81**
广 州	Guangzhou	4788.16	16.12	37.69	635.25
深 圳	Shenzhen	4597.66	19.19	32.76	531.39
珠 海	Zhuhai	390.29	1.22	11.93	39.00
汕 头	Shantou	236.05	1.19	1.32	18.49
佛 山	Foshan	887.50	3.56	9.50	84.68
韶 关	Shaoguan	79.19	0.12	0.59	8.27
河 源	Heyuan	110.56	0.21	0.46	6.90
梅 州	Meizhou	120.07	0.23	0.35	8.37
惠 州	Huizhou	578.26	1.37	4.64	50.37
汕 尾	Shanwei	64.65	0.11	0.17	3.92
东 莞	Dongguan	1358.50	2.85	24.42	105.17
中 山	Zhongshan	477.69	1.59	4.36	62.87
江 门	Jiangmen	371.48	0.85	35.19	36.96
阳 江	Yangjiang	118.19	0.20	0.54	7.97
湛 江	Zhanjiang	221.47	0.43	1.73	18.41
茂 名	Maoming	226.82	0.46	0.58	13.85
肇 庆	Zhaoqing	344.41	0.76	1.55	31.51
清 远	Qingyuan	159.14	0.31	1.49	11.49
潮 州	Chaozhou	80.02	0.14	0.26	5.05
揭 阳	Jieyang	204.51	2.49	0.63	13.65
云 浮	Yunfu	86.43	0.14	0.23	6.27

16-16 continued

(100 million yuan)

管理费用 Management Expenses	财务费用 Financial Expenses	营业利润 Business Profits	营业外收入 Non-operating revenue	利润总额 Total Profits	应交所得税 Income Taxes Payable	本年应付职工薪酬 Staff Salary Payable in Current Year	本年应交增值税 Value-added Tax Payable in Current Year
2202.42	**254.28**	**1403.60**	**106.23**	**1434.13**	**278.94**	**2575.77**	**950.40**
1668.64	**184.42**	**1347.28**	**74.10**	**1365.85**	**237.66**	**1821.67**	**734.53**
575.71	56.14	413.07	26.93	421.41	82.55	661.76	259.92
605.87	73.97	537.89	22.82	546.30	75.73	651.14	218.83
49.62	5.14	65.41	6.20	68.20	13.96	56.98	32.76
23.03	2.92	26.65	0.60	26.44	5.56	18.55	10.49
119.84	12.73	55.99	8.49	57.63	14.01	129.86	59.17
12.57	1.40	5.93	0.18	5.87	1.89	15.62	5.38
4.53	0.12	3.66	0.03	3.63	1.31	4.42	2.03
9.71	0.76	3.31	0.17	3.36	1.61	11.32	3.62
26.40	2.53	22.20	1.12	22.77	4.22	30.37	20.59
4.26	0.16	3.92	0.02	3.90	1.29	4.84	2.42
107.91	12.36	78.53	2.74	77.18	12.75	97.91	48.65
30.15	2.18	25.21	1.28	25.72	3.53	40.31	18.30
20.52	3.74	35.71	0.83	36.22	3.72	20.66	9.75
7.15	0.48	3.76	0.11	3.44	1.15	8.28	2.27
17.90	3.01	4.87	0.62	4.23	2.49	15.43	11.19
11.06	2.33	17.50	0.45	16.00	1.81	12.29	6.66
9.93	1.39	6.01	0.78	6.52	2.16	11.58	7.24
10.67	1.59	13.45	0.46	13.27	1.81	10.59	4.61
4.29	0.07	5.23	0.05	5.22	1.36	3.19	2.11
11.70	1.19	16.68	0.18	16.45	3.96	9.03	7.00
5.82	0.23	2.31	0.03	2.09	0.79	7.54	1.55
533.78	**69.86**	**56.32**	**32.13**	**68.28**	**41.29**	**754.10**	**215.87**
166.96	20.13	-25.30	11.28	-19.93	10.70	226.40	76.67
174.77	20.17	24.13	8.62	26.69	12.58	241.81	60.18
16.52	1.47	12.30	0.76	12.65	3.35	22.92	5.53
7.94	0.83	0.36	0.23	0.39	0.44	9.56	2.81
35.25	4.77	2.58	2.49	4.29	2.48	43.13	13.62
3.72	0.54	-0.49	0.19	-0.44	0.09	6.00	1.03
2.92	0.83	1.74	0.27	1.16	0.16	5.22	1.44
3.46	0.58	-0.18	0.25	-0.10	0.09	5.99	1.54
17.88	3.68	4.76	0.59	4.84	0.91	28.32	7.09
2.32	0.28	0.53	0.06	0.52	0.14	3.22	1.18
31.77	6.27	5.54	2.68	5.79	3.22	47.54	14.99
16.37	2.35	10.13	1.02	10.45	2.69	22.35	9.46
11.56	1.72	-2.21	1.76	-0.71	1.06	20.16	4.59
2.56	0.45	1.84	0.22	1.93	0.31	5.33	1.40
6.51	1.22	3.29	0.45	3.46	0.45	23.91	2.63
5.79	0.93	3.57	0.38	3.50	0.65	10.71	2.71
10.95	0.65	3.02	0.36	3.21	0.87	9.08	3.66
5.59	0.67	0.74	0.20	0.77	0.29	8.41	1.56
1.42	0.28	0.03	0.10	0.08	0.06	3.41	0.75
6.98	1.53	9.72	0.12	9.62	0.58	6.05	2.05
2.53	0.49	0.21	0.11	0.13	0.16	4.59	0.98

主要统计指标解释

社会消费品零售总额　指各种经济类型的批发零售业、住宿餐饮业和其他行业的企业（单位）或个体户，售予城乡居民用于生活消费和社会集团用于公共消费的商品金额的总和。

批发零售业商品购进总额　指从本企业以外的单位和个人购进（包括从国外直接进口）作为转卖或加工后转卖的商品金额。本指标由“从生产者购进额” “从批发零售业购进额” “进口额”和“其他购进”组成。 这个指标反映批发零售企业从国内、国外市场上购进商品的总量。

批发零售业商品销售总额　指售予本企业以外的单位和个人的商品金额（包括对国（境）外直接出口及售给本单位消费用的商品）。本指标由“对生产经营单位批发额” “对批发零售业批发额” “出口额”和“对居民和社会集团商品零售额”项目组成。这个指标反映批发零售业在国内市场上销售商品以及出口商品的总量。

批发　指除零售以外的一切商品销售活动。包括对生产经营单位批发、对批发零售业批发和出口。

对生产经营单位批发　指售给国民经济和社会各部门作为生产或经营使用的商品。

零售　指出售城乡居民用于生活消费商品和社会集团直接用于公用消费商品的活动。

批发零售业年末库存总额　指批发零售企业已取得所有权的全部商品。这个指标反映批发零售贸易企业的商品库存情况，对市场商品供应的保证程度。

批发零售业住宿餐饮业法人单位　指各种经济类型独立核算法人批发零售企业、住宿餐饮企业的单位个数。法人单位应同时具备以下条件：1. 依法成立，有自己的名称、组织机构和场所，能够独立承担民事责任；2. 独立拥有和使用资产，承担负债，有权与其他单位签订合同；3. 独立核算盈亏，并能够编制资产负债表。

批发业　是指从工农业生产者或从商品流通企业单位和个体户购进商品，转卖给工业、农业、建筑业、运输邮电业、住宿餐饮业、服务业等生产经营单位作为生产经营用，以及将商品转卖给其他批发企业或零售企业的商品流通企业(单位)和个体户。

零售业　是指从工农业生产者、批发业或居民购进商品，转卖给城乡居民作为生活消费和售给社会集团作为公共消费的商品流通企业(单位)和个体户。

Explanatory Notes on Main Statistical Indicators

Total Retail Sales of Consumer Goods　refer to the sum of retail sales of consumer goods sold by enterprises (establishments) or individuals in wholesale，retail trade，accommodations, catering services and other industries of various types of ownership to urban and rural households for living consumption and to social institutions for public consumption.

Total Purchases of Commodities by Wholesale and Retail Trades　refer to the purchases of commodities from other establishments or individuals (including direct import from abroad) for the purpose of reselling，either with or without further processing of the commodities purchased. This indicator includes the purchases from producers，the purchases from wholesale and retail trades，imports and other purchases. It is used to show the total value of purchases of commodities by wholesale and retail establishments from domestic and overseas markets.

Total Sales of Commodities by Wholesale and Retail Trades　refer to the value of commodities sold to other establishments and individuals (including direct export and commodities sold to the sellers themselves for consumption). This indicator includes the value of wholesale to production and operation units， the value of wholesale to wholesale and retail trades， exports and retail sales to urban and rural households and social institutions. It is an indicator of the total value of sales of commodities at domestic markets and export.

Wholesale refers to all selling activities of commodities except retail trade， including wholesale to production and operation units， wholesale to wholesale and retail trades and export.

Wholesale to Production and Operation Units refers to commodities sold to departments of national economy and social departments for their production and operation.

Retail Sale refers to the selling of commodities to urban and rural households for living consumption and to social institutions for direct public consumption.

Total Inventory of Wholesale and Retail Trades at the Year-end refers to the total commodities possessed by wholesale and retail enterprises， which reflects the commodity stock level of various wholesale and retail enterprises and the potential for market supply.

Corporate Units in Wholesale and Retail Trades, Accommodations and Catering Services refer to the number of corporate enterprises of various types of ownership in the wholesale and retail trades, accommodations and catering services with independent accounting systems. An enterprise can be called a corporate enterprise only when it simultaneously meets the following requirements: (1)It is established according to law, with its own name， organization and location for business operation, as well as the capability to independently assume civil responsibility; (2)It owns and uses its assets independently, assumes liabilities and is entitled to sign contracts with other units; (3)It has an independent accounting system and is able to compile balance sheets.

Wholesale Trade refers to the commodity circulation enterprises (establishments) and individuals which purchase commodities from producers in industry and agriculture or from commodity circulation enterprises and individuals for the purpose of reselling them to establishments in industry， agriculture， construction， transportation， postal and telecommunications services， accommodations and catering services and other services for their production and operation as well as reselling them to other wholesale or retail enterprises.

Retail Trade refers to the commodity circulation enterprises (establishments) and individuals which purchase commodities from producers in industry and agriculture， wholesale trade or residents for the purpose of reselling them to urban and rural households for living consumption and to social institutions for public consumption.

十七、住宿餐饮业和旅游

HOTELS, CATERING SERVICES AND TOURISM

十七　住宿餐饮业和旅游

简要说明

一、本篇资料主要反映住宿和餐饮业的基本情况、经营情况和旅游产业的发展情况。主要内容包括：限额以上住宿和餐饮业基本情况、经营情况、财务情况；连锁餐饮业经营情况；经广东口岸入境游客人数（港澳台和外国人）、城市接待国内外旅游人数、旅行社组织接待人数以及旅游收入等基本情况。

二、本篇资料来源

本篇资料中住宿和餐饮业主要根据国家统计局《住宿和餐饮业统计报表制度》进行搜集和加工整理；旅游资料主要由广东省文化和旅游厅提供。

三、本篇资料的统计范围

限额以上住宿和餐饮业的企业、个体户；餐饮连锁集团；旅行社、星级饭店和旅游者。住宿业年营业额 200 万元及以上；餐饮业年营业额 200 万元及以上。

四、本篇的调查方法

限额以上住宿和餐饮业资料采用全面调查的方法自下而上逐级综合汇总而得，限额以下企业及个体户资料采用抽样调查方法推算而得。旅游部门基本情况、住宿设施接待人数、旅行社接待人数由各基层企业上报汇总，城市接待旅游人数、国内外旅游收入根据抽样调查资料测算。

五、本篇资料由广东省统计局贸易外经统计处整理、编辑。

17 Hotels,Catering Services and Tourism

Brief Introduction

Ⅰ. Data in this chapter reflect the development of hotel and catering services and tourism in China. They mainly include: the basic conditions, operating and financial status of hotel and catering services above the designated size; the operating status of chain catering services; number of international tourists entering China through ports in Guangdong (including foreigners, Chinese compatriots from Hong Kong, Macao and Taiwan), number of domestic and international tourists received by cities, number of tourists received by travel agencies, and earnings from tourism, etc.

Ⅱ. Data sources :

The data are collected and processed in accordance with the Statistical Reporting Scheme on Accommodations and Catering Services stipulated by the National Bureau of Statistics. The data in this chapter are provided by the Department of Culture and Tourism of Guangdong Province.

Ⅲ. The statistical coverage in this chapter comes as follows:

Data in this chapter cover the enterprises of hotel and catering services above the designated size, self-employed households of hotel and catering services; chain catering services, travel agencies, star-rated hotels and tourists; hotels with annual turnover of 2 million yuan or above, and catering services with annual turnover of 2 million yuan or above.

Ⅳ. The statistical coverage in this chapter comes as follows:

Data on basic conditions for all corporate enterprises of accommodations and catering services above the designated size are collected through comprehensive reporting systems and data are reported level by level in a bottom-up manner. Data on small-size enterprises and individual enterprises below the designated size are collected through sample surveys. Basic statistics on tourist agencies, the number of tourists received by lodging facilities, and the number of tourists received by travel agencies are summaries of reports from various enterprises, whereas the number of tourists received by cities and earnings from domestic and international tourism are estimates from sample surveys.

V. The data in this chapter are prepared and edited by the Division of Trade and External Economic Relations Statistics of Statistics Bureau of Guangdong Province.

17-1 住宿、餐饮业、旅游主要指标
Main Indicators on Hotels, Catering Services and Tourism

指　标	Item	2000	2010	2015	2020	2021	2022	2023
限额以上住宿餐饮业营业额（亿元）	**Business Revenue from Hotels and Catering Services above Designated Size (100 million yuan)**		**901.95**	**1600.72**	**1424.61**	**1756.22**	**1765.90**	**2330.64**
#客房收入	Revenue from Accommodations		189.48	326.56	254.85	315.85	325.74	427.33
餐费收入	Revenue from Restaurants		645.66	1153.00	1031.14	1255.00	1260.98	1685.79
商品销售收入	Revenue from Sales of Commodities		15.17	30.78	54.20	77.26	78.83	97.42
旅行社数（个）	**Number of Travel Agencies (unit)**	**504**	**1292**	**2150**	**3425**	**3605**	**3764**	**4473**
旅行社从业人员（人）	**Engaged Persons of Travel Agencies (person)**		**37841**	**62779**	**52805**	**48418**	**39081**	**36614**
星级宾馆(酒店)数(个)	**Number of Star-rated Hotels (unit)**	**750**	**1209**	**972**	**613**	**549**	**501**	**478**
接待过夜旅游者人数（万人次）	**Number of Tourists Staying Overnight Received (10000 person-times)**	**7662.95**	**21283.05**	**36225.18**	**23059.46**	**25701.06**	**20307.15**	**33824.15**
入境过夜游客	Inbound Tourists	1198.94	3141.09	3445.36	468.85	320.44	190.16	1634.82
外国人	Foreigners	212.85	732.25	781.83	80.46	64.48	44.46	286.16
港澳同胞	Chinese Compatriots from Hong Kong and Macao	813.84	2091.07	2382.48	341.30	229.08	127.05	1292.33
台湾同胞	Chinese Compatriots from Taiwan	172.25	316.74	281.05	47.09	26.87	18.653	56.33
国内旅游者	Domestic Tourists	6464.01	18141.96	32779.82	22590.61	25380.63	20116.99	32189.34
旅游收入（亿元）	**Earnings from Tourism (100 million yuan)**	**1149.95**	**3809.44**	**9080.76**	**4690.59**	**5433.73**	**4213.51**	**9525.58**
国际旅游收入	Foreign Exchange Earnings	340.08	844.85	1104.16	162.28	144.51	116.84	776.50
国内旅游收入	Domestic Tourism Earnings	809.87	2964.59	7976.60	4528.31	5289.21	4096.67	8749.08

注：2020年起，接待过夜旅游者人数统计口径调整，由联网住宿企业根据公安系统网身份证登记信息统计过夜人数。接待过夜旅游者人数、旅游收入均与2019年以前年份不可比。

Note: From the year of 2020, the statistic caliber on the number of tourists staying overnight has been changed, networked hotels record the number according to ID card registration information in public security system, therefore the number of tourists staying overnight and earnings from tourism are incomparable with those in the year of 2019.

17-2 限额以上住宿业经营情况（2023年）
Business of Hotels above Designated Size (2023)

单位：亿元 (100 million yuan)

项 目	Item	企业(单位)数(个) Number of Enterprises (unit)	营业额合计 Business Revenue	#客房收入 Revenue from Hotels	#餐费收入 Revenue from Restaurants	#商品销售收入 Revenue from Sales of Commodities
住宿业合计	**Hotels**	**4105**	**674.41**	**412.66**	**164.62**	**14.17**
按登记注册统计类别分	By Registered Statistical Categories					
内资企业	Domestic Invested Enterprises	3914	584.29	367.54	135.48	11.79
有限责任公司	Limited Liability Corporations	3634	548.66	348.34	126.44	10.25
股份有限公司	Share-holding Corporations Ltd.	25	14.04	6.18	4.01	0.94
非公司企业法人	Non Corporate Legal Entity	51	7.47	3.69	1.96	0.12
个人独资企业	Sole Proprietorship Enterprises	169	11.61	7.59	2.64	0.48
合伙企业	Partnership Enterprises	35	2.52	1.74	0.43	0.01
其他内资企业	Other Domestic Invested Enterprises					
港澳台投资企业	Enterprises with Investment from Hong Kong, Macao and Taiwan	153	61.11	29.88	21.38	2.03
外商投资企业	Foreign Invested Enterprises	38	29.00	15.24	7.76	0.36
其他统计类别	Other Statistical Categories					
按国民经济行业分	By Sector					
旅游饭店	Tourist Hotel	1766	461.96	247.14	140.11	10.46
一般旅馆	General Hotels	2138	193.87	152.02	21.95	2.77
民宿服务	Home Lodging Services	64	2.68	1.98	0.49	0.08
其他住宿业	Others	137	15.90	11.51	2.08	0.86

注：1.其他住宿业包含露营地服务(以下相关表同)。
2.本表登记注册统计类别按《关于市场主体统计分类的划分规定》(国统字〔2023〕14号)执行。

Ntote: a)Other accommodation services include campground services (the same as the following related tables).
b)The registered statistical categories of this table is implemented in accordance with the Regulations onStatistics the Classification of Market Entity(Guotongzi [2023] No. 14).

17-3 限额以上餐饮业经营情况（2023年）

Business of Catering Services Enterprises above Designated Size (2023)

单位：亿元　　(100 million yuan)

项　目	Item	企业(单位)数(个) Number of Enterprises (unit)	营业额 Business Revenue	#客房收入 Revenue from Hotels	#餐费收入 Revenue from Restaurants	#商品销售收入 Revenue from Sales of Commodities
餐饮业合计	**Catering Services**	**8142**	**1656.23**	**14.67**	**1521.17**	**83.25**
按登记注册统计类别分	By Registered Statistical Categories					
内资企业	Domestic Invested Enterprises	7760	1243.62	13.93	1132.27	70.48
有限责任公司	Limited Liability Corporations	7040	1181.42	12.95	1074.97	68.45
股份有限公司	Share-holding Corporations Ltd.	25	8.91		7.06	1.10
非公司企业法人	Non Corporate Legal Entity	58	8.07	0.14	6.81	0.40
个人独资企业	Sole Proprietorship Enterprises	549	35.30	0.79	33.69	0.51
合伙企业	Partnership Enterprises	86	9.71	0.06	9.53	0.03
其他内资企业	Other Domestic Invested Enterprises	NA	0.21		0.21	
港澳台投资企业	Enterprises with Investment from Hong Kong, Macao and Taiwan	305	253.21	0.50	236.34	9.79
外商投资企业	Foreign Invested Enterprises	77	159.40	0.23	152.56	2.98
其他统计类别	Other Statistical Categories					
按国民经济行业分	By Sector					
正餐服务	Restaurant	6707	954.61	14.52	900.68	22.44
快餐服务	Fast Food	276	298.14		286.29	4.01
饮料及冷饮服务	Beverages and Cold Drinks	224	152.95	0.01	138.45	8.89
餐饮配送及外卖送餐服务	Catering Distribution and Delivery Service	547	166.53	0.08	126.99	34.51
其他餐饮业	Others	388	84.00	0.06	68.76	13.40

注：1.本表登记注册统计类别按《关于市场主体统计分类的划分规定》(国统字〔2023〕14号)执行。
2.NA表示企业个数小于或等于3。

Ntote: a) The registered statistical categories of this table is implemented in accordance with the Regulations onStatistics the Classification of Market Entity(Guotongzi [2023] No. 14).
b) NA refers to less than or equal to three.

17-4 各市限额以上住宿餐饮业经营情况（2023年）

Business of Enterprises above Designated Size of Hotels and Catering Services by City (2023)

单位：亿元 (100 million yuan)

市别	Item	企业(单位)数(个) Number of Enterprises (unit)	营业额 Business Revenue	#客房收入 Revenue from Hotels	#餐费收入 Revenue from Restaurants	#商品销售收入 Revenue from Sales of Commodities
合　计	**Total**	**12247**	**2330.64**	**427.33**	**1685.79**	**97.42**
住宿业	**Accommodation**	**4105**	**674.41**	**412.66**	**164.62**	**14.17**
广　州	Guangzhou	969	206.57	120.92	47.10	5.29
深　圳	Shenzhen	825	173.79	117.36	35.21	0.95
珠　海	Zhuhai	209	36.60	22.96	8.48	0.67
汕　头	Shantou	180	19.77	14.22	4.39	0.21
佛　山	Foshan	311	42.86	24.10	12.91	1.80
韶　关	Shaoguan	129	10.99	6.66	2.68	0.27
河　源	Heyuan	66	6.60	4.04	1.93	0.29
梅　州	Meizhou	69	5.84	3.31	1.83	0.15
惠　州	Huizhou	293	35.71	23.35	8.55	0.61
汕　尾	Shanwei	73	4.81	3.52	1.05	...
东　莞	Dongguan	275	49.58	23.94	17.60	1.58
中　山	Zhongshan	137	15.51	8.63	4.71	0.35
江　门	Jiangmen	113	14.09	7.09	4.64	0.80
阳　江	Yangjiang	23	2.88	2.27	0.47	0.03
湛　江	Zhanjiang	78	9.41	5.79	2.71	0.30
茂　名	Maoming	65	6.02	3.68	1.57	0.11
肇　庆	Zhaoqing	71	5.18	3.18	1.65	0.11
清　远	Qingyuan	80	13.50	7.98	3.88	0.12
潮　州	Chaozhou	50	3.87	3.05	0.58	0.01
揭　阳	Jieyang	60	5.90	3.75	1.46	0.27
云　浮	Yunfu	29	4.91	2.85	1.25	0.25
餐饮业	**Catering Service**	**8142**	**1656.23**	**14.67**	**1521.17**	**83.25**
广　州	Guangzhou	2194	598.83	3.84	546.46	35.56
深　圳	Shenzhen	1975	562.71	2.37	528.47	16.87
珠　海	Zhuhai	297	44.07	0.05	40.43	2.88
汕　头	Shantou	216	23.34		22.31	0.99
佛　山	Foshan	909	97.68	0.55	87.21	8.90
韶　关	Shaoguan	145	7.77	0.23	7.05	0.30
河　源	Heyuan	51	3.78	0.24	3.39	0.07
梅　州	Meizhou	56	3.47	0.17	3.28	0.01
惠　州	Huizhou	379	39.80	1.98	35.59	1.11
汕　尾	Shanwei	99	6.90	0.23	6.50	0.13
东　莞	Dongguan	760	135.96	0.67	122.27	10.85
中　山	Zhongshan	380	52.72	0.09	48.72	2.73
江　门	Jiangmen	214	30.22	0.21	28.14	1.15
阳　江	Yangjiang	46	6.79	0.52	5.50	0.40
湛　江	Zhanjiang	131	15.49	1.31	13.34	0.34
茂　名	Maoming	80	5.60	0.43	4.87	0.25
肇　庆	Zhaoqing	68	6.41	0.33	5.67	0.26
清　远	Qingyuan	40	5.67	0.62	4.65	0.18
潮　州	Chaozhou	30	2.66	...	2.64	0.02
揭　阳	Jieyang	52	4.55	0.67	3.08	0.24
云　浮	Yunfu	20	1.79	0.14	1.60	0.02

17-5 限额以上连锁住宿餐饮业经营情况（2023年）

Business of Chain Stores above Designated Size in Hotels and Catering Services (2023)

项　目	Item	连锁总店数（个）Number of General Chain Stores (unit)	营业额（亿元）Total Business Revenue (100 million yuan)	#零售额（亿元）Retail Sales (100 million yuan)	营业面积（平方米）Operational Area (sq.m)
住宿餐饮业合计	**Catering Service**	**208**	**517.91**	**501.28**	**258.24**
按登记注册统计类别分	By Registered Statistical Categories				
内资企业	Domestic Invested Enterprises	146	209.59	200.39	90.29
有限责任公司	Limited Liability Corporations	142	199.04	189.91	81.58
股份有限公司	Share-holding Corporations Ltd.	NA	9.14	9.14	7.37
非公司企业法人	Non Corporate Legal Entity				
个人独资企业	Sole Proprietorship Enterprises	NA	0.93	0.86	1.20
合伙企业	Partnership Enterprises	NA	0.49	0.49	0.14
其他内资企业	Other Domestic Invested Enterprises				
港澳台投资企业	Enterprises with Investment from Hong Kong, Macao and Taiwan	42	170.49	165.24	95.55
外商投资企业	Foreign Invested Enterprises	20	137.83	135.64	72.40
其他统计类别	Other Statistical Categories				
按国民经济行业分	By Sector				
正餐服务	Restaurant	115	149.98	144.68	73.61
快餐服务	Fast Food	52	247.97	240.97	133.02
饮料及冷饮服务	Beverages and Cold Drinks	26	115.41	111.16	50.10
餐饮配送及外卖送餐服务	Catering Distribution and Delivery Service	NA	0.42	0.42	0.78
其他餐饮业	Others	12	4.13	4.05	0.73

注：1.本表登记注册统计类别按《关于市场主体统计分类的划分规定》(国统字〔2023〕14号)执行。
2.NA表示企业个数小于或等于3。

Ntote: a) The registered statistical categories of this table is implemented in accordance with the Regulations onStatistics the Classification of Market Entity(Guotongzi [2023] No. 14).
b) NA refers to less than or equal to three.

17−5 续表 continued

项 目	Item	就业人数（人）Number of Employed Persons (person)	连锁门店数（个）Number of Branch Chain Stores (unit)	直营店（个）Under Direct Management (unit)	加盟店（个）Through License Arrangement (unit)
住宿餐饮业合计	**Catering Service**	**192585**	**10757**	**10471**	**286**
按登记注册统计类别分	By Registered Statistical Categories				
内资企业	Domestic Invested Enterprises	58130	4595	4380	215
有限责任公司	Limited Liability Corporations	55495	4541	4348	193
股份有限公司	Share-holding Corporations Ltd.	2080	27	5	22
非公司企业法人	Non Corporate Legal Entity				
个人独资企业	Sole Proprietorship Enterprises	447	NA	NA	
合伙企业	Partnership Enterprises	108	25	25	
其他内资企业	Other Domestic Invested Enterprises				
港澳台投资企业	Enterprises with Investment from Hong Kong, Macao and Taiwan	79462	3384	3317	67
外商投资企业	Foreign Invested Enterprises	54993	2778	2774	4
其他统计类别	Other Statistical Categories				
按国民经济行业分	By Sector				
正餐服务	Restaurant	40325	1699	1652	47
快餐服务	Fast Food	119230	4903	4741	162
饮料及冷饮服务	Beverages and Cold Drinks	31737	3935	3881	54
餐饮配送及外卖送餐服务	Catering Distribution and Delivery Service	445	47	46	NA
其他餐饮业	Others	848	173	151	22

17-6 限额以上住宿餐饮企业财务状况（2023年）

Financial Indicators of Enterprises above Designated Size in Hotels and Catering Services (2023)

单位：亿元 (100 million yuan)

项　目	Item	住宿和餐饮业合计 Total Hotels and Catering Services	住宿业 Hotels Services	餐饮业 Catering Services
企业数（个）	Number of Enterprises (unit)	12247	4105	8142
年初存货	Inventory at the Year-beginning	104.77	70.37	34.40
流动资产合计	Circulating Assets	1858.97	1116.57	742.40
#存货	Inventory	108.41	68.35	40.06
固定资产原价	Original Value of Fixed Assets	1396.44	1093.20	303.23
累计折旧	Accumulated Depreciation	749.92	591.90	158.03
#本年折旧	Depreciation Drawn in Current Year	63.43	42.35	21.08
资产合计	Total Assets	3502.79	2232.69	1270.11
负债合计	Total Liabilities	3067.66	2061.03	1006.63
所有者权益合计	Total Creditors' Equity	437.56	172.24	265.32
实收资本	Paid-up Capital	1856.40	1516.86	339.55
#个人资本	Personal Capital	225.31	169.09	56.21
营业收入	Business Revenue	2217.59	644.10	1573.49
#主营业务收入	Main Business Revenue	2179.71	625.23	1554.48
营业成本	Business Costs	1162.42	298.09	864.33
营业税金及附加	Tax and Extra Charges on Business	10.04	7.35	2.68
其他业务利润	Profits from Other Businesses	18.11	10.43	7.68
销售费用	Marketing Expenses	613.44	152.08	461.36
管理费用	Management Expenses	425.42	200.83	224.58
财务费用	Financial Expenses	38.83	27.48	11.35
#利息支出	Interests	26.09	19.10	6.99
营业利润	Business Profits	-20.66	-35.84	15.17
营业外收入	Non-operating Revenue	19.49	7.11	12.38
利润总额	Total Profits	-11.26	-31.52	20.26
所得税费用	Income Taxes Expenses	12.83	4.91	7.92
本年应付职工薪酬	Total Wages Payable in Current Year	565.97	185.50	380.47

17-7 限额以上住宿企业财务状况（2023年）

单位：亿元

项　目	Item	企业数（个）Number of Enterprises (unit)	年初库存 Beginning Inventory	流动资产合计 Circulating Assets	固定资产原价 Original Value of Fixed Assets
住宿业合计	Total Hotels	4105	70.37	1116.57	1093.20
按登记注册统计类别分	By Registered Statistical Categories				
内资企业	Domestic Invested Enterprises	3914	62.74	900.35	807.54
有限责任公司	Limited Liability Corporations	3634	61.89	857.18	734.74
股份有限公司	Share-holding Corporations Ltd.	25	0.21	20.85	27.09
非公司企业法人	Non Corporate Legal Entity	51	0.30	10.81	28.89
个人独资企业	Sole Proprietorship Enterprises	169	0.28	9.11	11.91
合伙企业	Partnership Enterprises	35	0.06	2.39	4.92
其他内资企业	Other Domestic Invested Enterprises				
港澳台投资企业	Enterprises with Investment from Hong Kong, Macao and Taiwan	153	7.10	113.01	223.51
外商投资企业	Foreign Invested Enterprises	38	0.53	103.21	62.15
其他统计类别	Other Statistical Categories				
按国民经济行业分	By Economic Sector				
旅游饭店	Tourist Hotel	1766	57.57	831.67	918.90
一般旅馆	General Hotels	2138	12.44	257.92	156.70
民宿服务	Home Lodging Services	64	0.06	3.20	1.20
其他住宿业	Others	137	0.30	23.78	16.40
按控股情况分	By Holdings				
国有控股	State Holdings	225	2.98	135.29	214.44
集体控股	Collective Holdings	48	0.10	18.97	11.10
私人控股	Private Holdings	3642	37.46	701.39	562.50
港澳台商控股	Hongkong,Macaw and Taiwan Holdings	144	29.28	151.28	242.52
外商控股	Foreign Holdings	46	0.56	109.62	62.65
其他	Others				
按星级分	By Star Rating				
五星	Five Star	164	12.92	280.86	336.91
四星	Four Star	373	20.41	160.55	137.14
三星	Three Star	500	5.79	62.84	76.93
二星	Two Star	62	0.03	2.30	2.75
一星	One Star	28	0.02	1.60	3.13
其他	Others	2978	31.20	608.42	536.34

注：本表登记注册统计类别按《关于市场主体统计分类的划分规定》(国统字〔2023〕14号)执行。

Financial Indicators of Hotels above Designated Size (2023)

(100 million yuan)

累计折旧 Accumulated Depreciation	本年折旧 Depreciation Drawn in Current Year	资产合计 Total Assets	负债合计 Total Liabilities	所有者权益合计 Total Creditors' Equity	实收资本 Paid-up Capital	营业收入 Business Revenue	主营业务收入 Main Business Revenue
591.90	42.35	2232.69	2061.03	172.24	1516.86	644.10	625.23
428.63	34.62	1812.94	1679.97	133.55	1353.96	558.23	541.72
384.85	30.33	1711.27	1607.07	104.77	1324.93	524.82	508.98
17.24	0.87	52.82	15.66	37.16	18.37	13.27	13.24
16.64	2.28	27.17	40.50	-13.33	6.97	6.87	6.45
6.50	0.82	17.57	11.47	6.10	3.23	10.84	10.65
3.40	0.33	4.11	5.25	-1.14	0.45	2.43	2.39
132.62	5.68	261.53	253.97	7.55	119.61	59.19	57.08
30.65	2.05	158.22	127.09	31.13	43.29	26.68	26.42
511.81	31.36	1751.77	1595.89	155.89	1035.44	439.99	426.08
72.83	9.16	431.44	418.10	13.92	471.75	186.00	181.14
0.30	0.12	5.46	5.22	0.25	1.09	2.71	2.69
6.95	1.71	44.00	41.82	2.18	8.57	15.40	15.32
128.55	8.21	422.92	228.94	193.97	145.31	116.25	113.86
7.13	0.57	28.90	32.43	-3.54	2.89	9.43	8.89
289.99	25.16	1288.47	1352.42	-63.37	1160.70	428.19	415.97
135.78	6.28	324.53	307.50	17.03	165.12	59.57	56.49
30.44	2.14	167.87	139.73	28.15	42.84	30.65	30.02
193.33	9.43	571.03	504.33	66.69	628.99	134.39	129.78
83.63	5.79	328.69	295.06	33.63	127.82	84.03	82.03
45.22	3.84	123.74	122.22	1.60	71.29	43.23	42.18
1.28	0.15	4.86	2.94	1.92	2.20	3.33	3.18
1.17	0.07	6.73	4.12	2.61	0.52	1.75	1.73
267.26	23.07	1197.64	1132.36	65.78	686.03	377.36	366.31

Ntote: The registered statistical categories of this table is implemented in accordance with the Regulations onStatistics the Classification of Market Entity(Guotongzi [2023] No. 14).

17-7 续表

单位：亿元

项目	Item	营业成本 Business Costs	营业税金及附加 Tax and Extra Charges on Business	其他业务利润 Profits from Other Businesses	销售费用 Marketing Expenses
住宿业合计	Total Hotels	298.09	7.35	10.43	152.08
按登记注册统计类别分	By Registered Statistical Categories				
内资企业	Domestic Invested Enterprises	263.71	5.79	7.71	131.40
有限责任公司	Limited Liability Corporations	245.70	5.19	7.58	123.77
股份有限公司	Share-holding Corporations Ltd.	8.58	0.30	...	1.32
非公司企业法人	Non Corporate Legal Entity	2.91	0.08	0.05	3.43
个人独资企业	Sole Proprietorship Enterprises	5.54	0.17	0.08	2.25
合伙企业	Partnership Enterprises	0.98	0.04	0.01	0.64
其他内资企业	Other Domestic Invested Enterprises				
港澳台投资企业	Enterprises with Investment from Hong Kong, Macao and Taiwan	23.98	1.11	2.64	15.33
外商投资企业	Foreign Invested Enterprises	10.39	0.45	0.07	5.35
其他统计类别	Other Statistical Categories				
按国民经济行业分	By Economic Sector				
旅游饭店	Tourist Hotel	196.18	6.20	9.04	111.45
一般旅馆	General Hotels	91.25	1.03	1.28	37.43
民宿服务	Home Lodging Services	1.58	...	0.01	0.42
其他住宿业	Others	9.08	0.12	0.10	2.79
按控股情况分	By Holdings				
国有控股	State Holdings	61.05	2.08	1.56	23.71
集体控股	Collective Holdings	3.92	0.10	...	1.83
私人控股	Private Holdings	196.94	3.39	4.84	103.80
港澳台商控股	Hongkong,Macaw and Taiwan Holdings	22.98	1.33	3.63	16.71
外商控股	Foreign Holdings	13.19	0.45	0.39	6.03
其他	Others				
按星级分	By Star Rating				
五星	Five Star	54.52	2.27	2.49	29.48
四星	Four Star	37.87	1.21	1.34	22.58
三星	Three Star	22.38	0.36	1.03	9.40
二星	Two Star	1.98	0.03	....	0.61
一星	One Star	0.88	0.03		0.20
其他	Others	180.46	3.46	5.57	89.82

17-7 continued

(100 million yuan)

管理费用 Management Expenses	财务费用 Financial Expenses	营业利润 Business Profits	营业外收入 Non-operating revenue	利润总额 Total Profits	所得税费用 Income Taxes Expenses	本年应付职工薪酬 Staff Salary Payable in Current Year
200.83	27.48	-35.84	7.11	-31.52	4.91	185.50
171.45	23.04	-31.62	6.29	-27.81	3.83	160.03
160.15	22.54	-18.11	4.98	-15.12	3.41	146.33
3.41	-0.19	-0.13	0.02	-0.11	0.20	5.15
4.77	0.51	-13.70	1.24	-12.92	0.05	5.04
2.33	0.14	0.40	0.03	0.41	0.17	2.84
0.79	0.05	-0.08	0.02	-0.07	0.01	0.68
20.17	2.58	-3.72	0.54	-3.36	0.85	18.02
9.21	1.86	-0.49	0.28	-0.35	0.23	7.45
134.34	22.36	-25.15	5.31	-21.94	3.83	132.52
61.69	4.40	-10.30	1.28	-9.64	1.09	47.93
0.84	0.06	-0.18	0.02	-0.18	...	0.89
3.96	0.66	-0.21	0.50	0.24	-0.01	4.17
33.11	2.08	-9.84	2.13	-8.61	2.17	43.78
2.96	0.91	-0.42	0.05	-0.35	0.05	2.57
134.55	17.72	-18.56	3.77	-16.39	1.62	113.29
20.62	4.96	-6.69	0.55	-6.31	0.72	17.47
9.59	1.80	-0.32	0.60	0.14	0.35	8.40
42.50	7.86	-0.02	1.15	0.32	1.90	38.12
23.55	3.96	-4.25	0.61	-4.00	0.61	25.84
16.31	1.14	-14.41	0.62	-14.09	0.57	15.69
0.65	0.02	0.07	0.01	0.07	0.02	0.76
0.61	...	0.10	0.01	0.11	...	0.52
117.21	14.50	-17.32	4.71	-13.94	1.82	104.57

17–8 限额以上餐饮企业财务状况（2023年）

单位：亿元

项　目	Item	企业数（个）Number of Enterprises (unit)	年初库存 Beginning Inventory	流动资产合计 Circulating Assets	固定资产原价 Original Value of Fixed Assets
餐饮业合计	**Total Catering Services**	**8142**	**34.40**	**742.40**	**303.23**
按登记注册统计类别分	**By Registered Statistical Categories**				
内资企业	Domestic Invested Enterprises	7760	28.80	619.16	197.05
有限责任公司	Limited Liability Corporations	7040	27.14	564.57	184.01
股份有限公司	Share-holding Corporations Ltd.	25	0.22	36.77	3.11
非公司企业法人	Non Corporate Legal Entity	58	0.17	3.04	0.73
个人独资企业	Sole Proprietorship Enterprises	549	0.70	11.77	6.83
合伙企业	Partnership Enterprises	86	0.56	2.98	2.34
其他内资企业	Other Domestic Invested Enterprises	NA	...	0.03	0.03
港澳台投资企业	Enterprises with Investment from Hong Kong, Macao and Taiwan	305	3.35	97.77	76.67
外商投资企业	Foreign Invested Enterprises	77	2.25	25.47	29.51
其他统计类别	Other Statistical Categories				
按国民经济行业分	By Economic Sector				
正餐服务	Dinner Service	6707	23.80	488.98	199.02
快餐服务	Fast Food Service	276	3.50	78.40	73.38
饮料及冷饮服务	Beverage and Cold Drink Service	224	2.22	69.84	15.70
餐饮配送及外卖送餐服务	Food and Beverage Distribution and Takeout Service	547	3.35	74.32	10.11
其他餐饮业	Other Services	388	1.53	30.87	5.02
按控股情况分	By Holdings				
国有控股	State Holdings	85	0.89	114.43	36.37
集体控股	Collective Holdings	29	0.06	12.32	0.84
私人控股	Private Holdings	7654	28.31	502.39	159.80
港澳台商控股	Hongkong,Macaw and Taiwan Holdings	286	3.24	88.53	77.11
外商控股	Foreign Holdings	86	1.90	24.73	29.11
其他	Others	NA			

注：1.本表登记注册统计类别按《关于市场主体统计分类的划分规定》(国统字〔2023〕14号)执行。
2.NA表示企业个数小于或等于3。

Financial Indicators of Catering Services Enterprises above Designated Size (2023)

(100 million yuan)

累计折旧 Accumulated Depreciation	本年折旧 Depreciation Drawn in Current Year	资产合计 Total Assets	负债合计 Total Liabilities	所有者权益合计 Total Creditors' Equity	实收资本 Paid-up Capital	营业收入 Business Revenue	主营业务收入 Main Business Revenue
158.03	**21.08**	**1270.11**	**1006.63**	**265.32**	**339.55**	**1573.49**	**1554.48**
97.76	15.01	940.33	785.51	156.66	265.48	1184.22	1168.72
91.70	14.01	859.56	741.57	119.83	254.43	1125.47	1111.45
1.33	0.20	53.34	21.90	31.44	6.55	8.48	7.84
0.54	0.03	4.73	3.71	1.02	0.96	7.58	7.23
3.07	0.50	17.90	14.32	3.58	2.35	33.45	33.07
1.10	0.27	4.76	3.95	0.81	1.16	9.05	8.92
0.02	...	0.04	0.06	-0.02	0.03	0.20	0.20
45.93	3.96	234.42	146.13	88.29	44.75	238.93	237.98
14.34	2.12	95.36	74.99	20.37	29.31	150.34	147.79
103.01	13.49	817.82	692.73	125.25	266.12	910.86	899.80
38.56	3.63	221.60	153.03	68.57	28.08	281.86	279.46
8.74	1.91	105.83	66.51	40.99	16.63	145.09	141.65
4.92	1.40	87.86	68.61	19.26	20.33	155.52	154.45
2.80	0.65	37.00	25.74	11.25	8.39	80.16	79.12
14.67	1.64	221.01	108.61	112.41	44.79	54.63	53.62
0.49	0.09	14.18	11.90	2.28	0.89	4.98	4.66
83.16	13.27	717.95	667.70	52.10	221.88	1130.70	1116.18
46.04	3.95	224.17	144.27	79.90	42.15	232.13	231.19
13.67	2.13	92.79	74.15	18.64	29.84	151.05	148.83

Ntote: a) The registered statistical categories of this table is implemented in accordance with the Regulations onStatistics the Classification of Market Entity(Guotongzi [2023] No. 14).
b) NA refers to less than or equal to three.

17-8 续表

单位：亿元

项　目	Item	营业成本 Business Costs	营业税金及附加 Tax and Extra Charges on Business	其他业务利润 Profits from Other Businesses	销售费用 Marketing Expenses
餐饮业合计	**Total Catering Services**	**864.33**	**2.68**	**7.68**	**461.36**
按登记注册统计类别分	By Registered Statistical Categories				
内资企业	Domestic Invested Enterprises	694.52	2.36	7.21	290.45
有限责任公司	Limited Liability Corporations	658.64	2.05	7.14	278.40
股份有限公司	Share-holding Corporations Ltd.	5.80	0.05		0.90
非公司企业法人	Non Corporate Legal Entity	4.52	0.05	0.05	1.90
个人独资企业	Sole Proprietorship Enterprises	20.65	0.18	0.02	6.48
合伙企业	Partnership Enterprises	4.82	0.03	0.01	2.69
其他内资企业	Other Domestic Invested Enterprises	0.09	…		0.08
港澳台投资企业	Enterprises with Investment from Hong Kong, Macao and Taiwan	86.87	0.23	0.39	121.58
外商投资企业	Foreign Invested Enterprises	82.95	0.10	0.09	49.32
其他统计类别	Other Statistical Categories				
按国民经济行业分	By Economic Sector				
正餐服务	Dinner Service	487.21	2.07	2.57	267.58
快餐服务	Fast Food Service	136.27	0.24	2.13	107.75
饮料及冷饮服务	Beverage and Cold Drink Service	63.95	0.07	2.66	60.06
餐饮配送及外卖送餐服务	Food and Beverage Distribution and Takeout Service	121.28	0.20	0.17	14.18
其他餐饮业	Other Services	55.63	0.11	0.15	11.79
按控股情况分	By Holdings				
国有控股	State Holdings	41.94	0.37	0.33	6.58
集体控股	Collective Holdings	3.07	0.11	…	1.06
私人控股	Private Holdings	653.10	1.90	6.91	285.34
港澳台商控股	Hongkong,Macaw and Taiwan Holdings	82.26	0.21	0.39	120.28
外商控股	Foreign Holdings	83.97	0.09	0.05	48.11
其他	Others				

17-8 continued

(100 million yuan)

管理费用 Management Expenses	财务费用 Financial Expenses	营业利润 Business Profits	营业外收入 Non-operating revenue	利润总额 Total Profits	所得税费用 Income Taxes Expenses	本年应付职工薪酬 Staff Salary Payable in Current Year
224.58	**11.35**	**15.17**	**12.38**	**20.26**	**7.92**	**380.47**
191.03	7.75	2.53	10.25	6.71	3.94	277.51
180.20	7.80	-3.74	9.91	0.19	3.61	261.32
2.03	-0.35	6.60	0.03	6.63	0.14	2.95
1.94	0.03	-0.85	0.10	-0.75	0.06	2.12
5.39	0.20	0.50	0.16	0.60	0.12	8.64
1.44	0.06	0.02	0.05	0.06	0.01	2.43
0.03	0.01	-0.01	…	-0.01		0.05
18.32	1.93	11.64	1.51	12.53	3.34	62.80
15.23	1.67	1.01	0.61	1.02	0.64	40.15
153.13	7.01	-1.89	9.49	1.79	3.05	229.15
27.53	3.60	7.26	0.78	7.56	2.24	73.93
13.84	-0.05	7.38	1.18	8.09	2.09	31.29
18.89	0.56	0.24	0.57	0.58	0.30	29.62
11.18	0.23	2.18	0.36	2.23	0.23	16.47
7.61	-0.11	1.24	0.78	1.88	-0.70	17.17
1.44	…	-0.68	4.16	0.15	0.24	1.51
182.44	7.89	1.30	5.33	4.04	4.37	260.97
17.57	1.94	11.60	1.47	12.45	3.30	60.95
15.52	1.64	1.71	0.63	1.73	0.71	39.87

17-9 各市限额以上住宿和餐饮企业财务状况（2023年）

单位：亿元

市 别	City	企业数（个）Number of Enterprises (unit)	年初库存 Beginning Inventory	流动资产合计 Circulating Assets	固定资产原价 Original Value of Fixed Assets
住宿餐饮业合计	**Total Hotels and Catering Services**	**12247**	**104.77**	**1858.97**	**1396.44**
住宿业	**Hotels**	**4105**	**70.37**	**1116.57**	**1093.20**
广 州	Guangzhou	969	32.75	326.45	280.89
深 圳	Shenzhen	825	2.34	395.84	263.52
珠 海	Zhuhai	209	1.04	49.09	73.43
汕 头	Shantou	180	0.45	14.27	30.83
佛 山	Foshan	311	1.61	69.00	73.04
韶 关	Shaoguan	129	0.87	8.93	15.87
河 源	Heyuan	66	1.09	10.28	10.41
梅 州	Meizhou	69	0.42	13.00	12.85
惠 州	Huizhou	293	11.05	59.45	55.15
汕 尾	Shanwei	73	0.12	4.18	9.40
东 莞	Dongguan	275	10.27	61.82	110.75
中 山	Zhongshan	137	0.22	9.43	34.07
江 门	Jiangmen	113	0.41	17.15	28.73
阳 江	Yangjiang	23	0.03	2.83	5.67
湛 江	Zhanjiang	78	0.36	22.15	24.88
茂 名	Maoming	65	0.26	7.04	6.57
肇 庆	Zhaoqing	71	0.15	9.55	7.99
清 远	Qingyuan	80	0.40	19.28	28.65
潮 州	Chaozhou	50	3.36	5.25	6.50
揭 阳	Jieyang	60	0.13	4.41	6.35
云 浮	Yunfu	29	3.03	7.13	7.68
餐饮业	**Catering Services**	**8142**	**34.40**	**742.40**	**303.23**
广 州	Guangzhou	2194	10.42	223.78	100.06
深 圳	Shenzhen	1975	11.18	316.51	81.38
珠 海	Zhuhai	297	1.17	17.88	4.80
汕 头	Shantou	216	0.38	4.86	2.04
佛 山	Foshan	909	2.75	35.39	17.65
韶 关	Shaoguan	145	0.34	3.17	3.16
河 源	Heyuan	51	0.07	1.89	1.34
梅 州	Meizhou	56	0.14	2.30	1.14
惠 州	Huizhou	379	1.07	17.46	16.10
汕 尾	Shanwei	99	0.16	2.55	0.78
东 莞	Dongguan	760	3.19	54.73	25.80
中 山	Zhongshan	380	1.10	16.52	11.05
江 门	Jiangmen	214	0.93	10.78	7.21
阳 江	Yangjiang	46	0.19	4.23	2.95
湛 江	Zhanjiang	131	0.51	7.69	12.99
茂 名	Maoming	80	0.15	4.65	5.20
肇 庆	Zhaoqing	68	0.27	7.47	2.20
清 远	Qingyuan	40	0.19	6.83	2.65
潮 州	Chaozhou	30	0.07	0.49	0.44
揭 阳	Jieyang	52	0.06	2.49	2.43
云 浮	Yunfu	20	0.07	0.73	1.85

Financial Indicators of Enterprises above Designated Size of Hotels and Catering Services by City (2023)

(100 million yuan)

累计折旧 Accumulated Depreciation	#本年折旧 Depreciation Drawn in Current Year	资产合计 Total Assets	负债合计 Total Liabilities	所有者权益合计 Total Creditors' Equity	实收资本 Paid-up Capital	营业收入 Business Revenue	主营业务收入 Main Business Revenue
749.92	**63.43**	**3502.79**	**3067.66**	**437.56**	**1856.40**	**2217.59**	**2179.71**
591.90	**42.35**	**2232.69**	**2061.03**	**172.24**	**1516.86**	**644.10**	**625.23**
156.05	9.92	658.18	523.07	135.40	195.15	197.27	190.35
142.79	11.40	664.29	628.07	36.43	807.19	169.55	164.66
40.29	1.84	130.82	113.82	17.01	76.83	35.35	34.37
14.98	0.90	38.09	40.07	-1.98	14.27	18.62	18.19
44.59	2.82	125.21	124.12	1.09	87.59	40.95	39.95
7.06	0.75	24.75	22.64	2.11	6.75	10.51	10.21
5.52	0.43	22.93	19.12	3.82	5.25	6.34	6.28
6.78	0.51	23.07	24.72	-1.65	2.08	5.40	5.31
26.34	2.03	100.80	111.33	-10.53	14.31	31.32	30.79
4.00	0.55	12.07	7.86	4.22	1.64	4.64	4.54
65.90	4.15	134.14	176.85	-42.63	39.59	47.24	46.06
17.00	1.31	33.72	31.22	2.50	24.81	14.25	13.92
17.28	1.47	40.10	39.18	0.92	39.88	13.46	12.85
2.52	0.31	7.13	6.96	0.17	2.48	2.73	2.66
9.45	0.96	54.70	47.30	7.41	56.10	8.84	8.49
2.43	0.43	18.85	23.38	-4.53	1.26	5.83	5.81
4.15	0.27	17.99	18.03	-0.04	4.07	5.13	5.01
14.52	1.31	65.89	70.69	-4.80	121.31	12.84	12.25
3.35	0.37	25.65	10.86	14.80	3.48	3.73	3.71
4.05	0.28	12.84	9.67	3.17	5.27	5.26	5.13
2.84	0.33	21.45	12.09	9.35	7.57	4.83	4.67
158.03	**21.08**	**1270.11**	**1006.63**	**265.32**	**339.55**	**1573.49**	**1554.48**
56.12	6.99	435.47	329.66	105.81	71.98	567.13	563.26
43.83	5.96	490.60	384.27	108.17	112.96	538.12	529.13
2.97	0.45	23.83	23.96	-0.13	19.45	42.57	41.88
0.83	0.19	7.20	4.82	2.38	1.20	21.69	21.57
7.82	1.08	55.55	51.86	3.69	9.82	90.14	88.76
1.55	0.21	7.51	5.93	1.58	1.57	7.51	7.48
0.53	0.07	3.64	2.62	1.02	0.72	3.66	3.64
0.61	0.15	3.16	3.22	-0.06	0.69	3.40	3.40
8.81	1.09	30.61	28.12	2.49	54.85	38.18	37.45
0.36	0.09	3.44	2.99	0.45	0.34	6.37	6.36
10.58	1.63	96.82	59.71	37.12	31.72	129.17	127.13
4.48	0.83	28.06	24.73	3.33	3.89	50.13	50.07
3.25	0.59	19.39	16.90	2.49	4.15	28.85	28.72
1.45	0.17	9.35	8.49	0.86	0.62	6.46	6.26
8.11	0.62	15.60	17.80	-2.19	7.92	14.43	13.99
1.59	0.36	10.29	9.04	1.25	4.12	5.47	5.45
1.15	0.13	10.12	11.28	-1.15	11.12	6.15	5.95
1.47	0.14	12.51	15.76	-3.26	1.09	5.46	5.40
0.14	0.03	0.86	0.46	0.39	0.20	2.54	2.54
1.46	0.08	4.17	2.36	1.80	1.01	4.33	4.30
0.89	0.21	1.93	2.64	-0.71	0.14	1.73	1.72

17−9 续表

单位：亿元

市别	City	营业成本 Business Costs	营业税金及附加 Tax and Extra Charges on Business	其他业务利润 Profits from Other Businesses	销售费用 Marketing Expenses
住宿餐饮业合计	**Total Hotels and Catering Services**	**1162.42**	**10.04**	**18.11**	**613.44**
住宿业	**Hotels**	**298.09**	**7.35**	**10.43**	**152.08**
广　州	Guangzhou	86.39	2.70	4.66	44.45
深　圳	Shenzhen	82.69	1.45	1.30	35.73
珠　海	Zhuhai	16.89	0.41	0.29	9.15
汕　头	Shantou	7.96	0.22	…	4.67
佛　山	Foshan	19.58	0.49	1.01	10.20
韶　关	Shaoguan	4.79	0.10	0.04	2.62
河　源	Heyuan	2.61	0.05	0.01	2.35
梅　州	Meizhou	2.91	0.05	0.04	0.93
惠　州	Huizhou	13.84	0.33	0.01	8.33
汕　尾	Shanwei	2.52	0.06	…	0.85
东　莞	Dongguan	19.13	0.54	0.73	13.59
中　山	Zhongshan	7.02	0.07	0.02	3.66
江　门	Jiangmen	6.12	0.19	0.15	3.27
阳　江	Yangjiang	1.17	0.05	0.02	0.76
湛　江	Zhanjiang	2.99	0.16	0.11	3.09
茂　名	Maoming	3.40	0.06	…	1.10
肇　庆	Zhaoqing	2.90	0.05	0.09	1.53
清　远	Qingyuan	6.16	0.17	1.75	3.61
潮　州	Chaozhou	2.10	0.09	0.09	0.83
揭　阳	Jieyang	3.77	0.06	0.03	0.40
云　浮	Yunfu	3.14	0.04	0.08	0.96
餐饮业	**Catering Services**	**864.33**	**2.68**	**7.68**	**461.36**
广　州	Guangzhou	292.69	0.74	2.82	176.81
深　圳	Shenzhen	272.82	0.80	3.88	190.92
珠　海	Zhuhai	25.56	0.04	…	9.97
汕　头	Shantou	15.73	0.07	0.01	3.44
佛　山	Foshan	56.66	0.24	0.05	18.83
韶　关	Shaoguan	4.99	0.02	0.05	1.11
河　源	Heyuan	2.52	0.01	…	0.48
梅　州	Meizhou	2.59	0.02		0.33
惠　州	Huizhou	23.26	0.11	0.13	7.43
汕　尾	Shanwei	4.27	0.03		1.12
东　莞	Dongguan	88.13	0.19	0.32	19.86
中　山	Zhongshan	31.20	0.08	0.03	12.77
江　门	Jiangmen	16.97	0.06	0.13	7.66
阳　江	Yangjiang	3.63	0.03	0.01	1.36
湛　江	Zhanjiang	7.44	0.10	0.03	4.02
茂　名	Maoming	3.16	0.03		1.10
肇　庆	Zhaoqing	3.78	0.01	0.19	1.26
清　远	Qingyuan	2.83	0.01	0.03	1.67
潮　州	Chaozhou	2.04	0.01	…	0.18
揭　阳	Jieyang	2.92	0.07		0.73
云　浮	Yunfu	1.14	0.01	…	0.32

17-9 continued

(100 million yuan)

管理费用 Management Expenses	财务费用 Financial Expenses	营业利润 Business Profits	营业外收入 Non-operating revenue	利润总额 Total Profits	所得税费用 Income Taxes Expenses	本年应付职工薪酬 Staff Salary Payable in Current Year
425.42	**38.83**	**-20.66**	**19.49**	**-11.26**	**12.83**	**565.97**
200.83	**27.48**	**-35.84**	**7.11**	**-31.52**	**4.91**	**185.50**
59.72	7.74	-0.06	2.29	1.13	2.53	57.60
55.74	8.89	-14.25	1.98	-12.73	1.26	45.62
11.59	0.96	-3.48	0.18	-3.40	0.10	11.69
4.53	0.77	0.33	0.15	0.42	0.05	4.25
13.48	1.03	-3.63	0.98	-2.96	0.24	12.05
3.73	0.37	-1.04	0.22	-0.84	0.02	3.25
1.73	0.30	-0.75	0.16	-0.63	0.01	1.98
2.05	0.80	-1.32	0.04	-1.30	...	1.81
9.84	1.09	-1.55	0.31	-1.40	0.21	9.07
1.56	0.03	-0.37	0.04	-0.33	...	1.59
14.71	2.69	-3.32	0.17	-3.26	0.32	13.42
4.37	0.25	-1.05	0.14	-0.95	0.02	4.48
4.12	0.77	-0.73	0.09	-0.69	0.06	3.88
0.94	0.10	-0.28	...	-0.30	...	0.73
3.18	0.28	-0.79	0.03	-0.77	0.01	2.93
1.50	0.13	-0.35	0.06	-0.32	0.02	1.87
1.36	0.36	-1.18	0.05	-1.16	...	1.64
3.89	0.59	-1.42	0.18	-1.44	-0.01	4.12
0.83	0.05	-0.17	0.02	-0.16	0.02	0.87
0.98	0.03	...	0.02	0.02	0.02	1.19
0.99	0.26	-0.44	...	-0.44	...	1.48
224.58	**11.35**	**15.17**	**12.38**	**20.26**	**7.92**	**380.47**
82.16	3.79	19.79	2.86	21.39	4.61	131.58
72.37	3.50	-5.55	7.47	-3.13	1.43	139.23
7.17	0.42	-0.50	0.22	-0.37	0.20	10.77
1.75	0.08	0.57	0.04	0.59	0.09	3.18
13.54	0.66	0.16	0.42	0.46	0.31	19.48
1.32	0.07	...	0.06	0.02	0.01	1.84
0.58	0.04	0.03	0.01	0.04	0.02	0.89
0.38	0.03	0.05	0.01	0.06	...	0.76
6.94	0.43	0.15	0.09	0.17	0.17	10.06
0.91	0.05	-0.02	0.02	-0.02	0.01	1.40
19.37	0.66	0.98	0.52	1.16	0.72	27.92
5.88	0.19	0.05	0.36	0.31	0.19	12.95
4.06	0.32	-0.09	0.08	-0.03	0.14	7.61
1.37	0.10	-0.03	0.02	-0.02	0.01	2.04
3.00	0.33	-0.47	0.04	-0.45	-0.04	4.09
0.88	0.13	0.39	0.04	0.39	0.02	1.83
1.05	0.15	-0.29	0.07	-0.17	0.01	1.56
1.08	0.25	-0.33	0.02	-0.41	-0.01	1.62
0.20	0.01	0.11	...	0.11	0.01	0.50
0.35	0.11	0.15	0.01	0.16	0.01	0.70
0.24	0.03	0.01	0.01	-0.01	...	0.45

17-10 各市限额以上住宿餐饮业营业额

Business of Enterprises above Designated Size of Hotels and Catering Services by City

单位：亿元 (100 million yuan)

市别	Item	2022 住宿业 Hotels Service	2022 餐饮业 Catering Service	2023 住宿业 Hotels Service	2023 餐饮业 Catering Service
广州	Guangzhou	142.57	379.57	206.57	598.83
深圳	Shenzhen	127.94	407.08	173.79	562.71
珠海	Zhuhai	23.63	39.85	36.60	44.07
汕头	Shantou	13.19	19.97	19.77	23.34
佛山	Foshan	30.78	81.51	42.86	97.68
韶关	Shaoguan	8.36	7.22	10.99	7.77
河源	Heyuan	5.28	6.35	6.60	3.78
梅州	Meizhou	3.51	3.02	5.84	3.47
惠州	Huizhou	23.32	35.42	35.71	39.80
汕尾	Shanwei	3.79	7.67	4.81	6.90
东莞	Dongguan	40.59	119.46	49.58	135.96
中山	Zhongshan	11.83	43.31	15.51	52.72
江门	Jiangmen	12.04	28.93	14.09	30.22
阳江	Yangjiang	2.50	7.67	2.88	6.79
湛江	Zhanjiang	7.35	15.18	9.41	15.49
茂名	Maoming	4.17	8.46	6.02	5.60
肇庆	Zhaoqing	4.55	8.03	5.18	6.41
清远	Qingyuan	9.52	6.33	13.50	5.67
潮州	Chaozhou	1.99	1.88	3.87	2.66
揭阳	Jieyang	4.83	6.43	5.90	4.55
云浮	Yunfu	3.87	2.49	4.91	1.79
按经济区域分	By Region				
珠三角	Pearl River Delta	417.25	1143.17	579.90	1568.40
粤东	Eastern Region	23.81	35.95	34.36	37.46
粤西	Western Region	14.03	31.32	18.31	27.88
粤北	North Region	30.54	25.40	41.84	22.49

17-11 旅游部门基本情况

Basic Statistics on Tourism-related Agencies

指 标	Item	2000	2010	2015	2021	2022	2023
宾馆(酒店) (家)	Number of Hotels (unit)	2655	9179	16440	17692	18314	21320
按星级分：白金五星	By Star Rating:Platinum Five Star		1	1	1	1	1
五星	Five Star	19	93	116	94	90	85
四星	Four Star	61	194	178	136	127	130
三星	Three Star	283	661	566	292	263	242
二星	Two Star	339	246	107	25	20	20
一星	One Star	48	14	4	1		
未评星级	Unrated	1905	7970	15468	17143	17813	20842
宾馆(酒店)接待能力	Reception Capability of Hotels						
客房 (间)	Number of Guest Rooms (unit)	202277	565582	982628	1173307	1447484	1530504
床位 (张)	Number of Beds (unit)	401718	938389	1535288	1742855	2125534	2181108
旅行社 (家)	Number of Travel Agencies (unit)	504	1292	2150	3605	3764	4473

注：星级宾馆(酒店)指2023年底止已得到国家文化和旅游部或广东省文化和旅游厅批准的，不包已报未批部分。

Note: Star-rated hotels refer to those approved by the National Culture And Tourism Ministry or Guangdong Provincial Culture and Tourism Department by the end of 2023, excluding hotels under examination.

17-12 城市接待外国游客人数

Number of Foreign Visitors Received by Cities

单位：人次 (person-time)

国 别	Country	2000	2005	2010	2015	2021	2022	2023
总计	**Total**	**2128501**	**4639133**	**7322478**	**7818342**	**584893**	**444588**	**2861670**
日本	Japan	413833	962727	1077329	892362	124329	127194	115565
韩国	Republic of Korea	71841	239213	418115	474549	35948	24402	305834
菲律宾	Philippines	20793	30847	47184	59613	3005	3332	48650
新加坡	Singapore	93762	179559	284832	285197	20670	12833	156477
泰国	Thailand	48341	150502	134313	147501	7182	5699	74293
印度尼西亚	Indonesia	63159	128428	158879	118720	2706	2649	88201
马来西亚	Malaysia	110384	220598	421556	351926	12942	11008	164579
美国	United States	196362	361224	645783	710768	59688	44013	256743
加拿大	Canada	35968	67844	133138	133020	14451	11845	60495
英国	United Kingdom	59123	105238	138353	146989	13530	8130	71543
法国	France	43578	99158	119850	148791	10191	7836	47907
德国	Germany	44707	87158	118332	142266	18498	14063	51041
意大利	Italy	19792	56071	86454	78488	6973	7383	32930
俄罗斯	Russia	10407	26692	58568	84489	11856	9323	83995
澳大利亚	Australia	34595	73346	149780	138169	9844	10611	60167
新西兰	New Zealand	5835	15702	24119	30740	3313	3195	15299
其他	Others	856021	1834826	3305893	3874754	229767	141072	1227951

17-13 各市旅游宾馆(酒店)住宿设施（2023年）

Lodging Facilities of Tourist Hotels by City (2023)

市别	City	宾馆(酒店)(个) Number of Hotels (unit)	#白金五星级 Platinum Five Star	五星级 Five Star	四星级 Four Star	三星级 Three Star	二星级 Two Star	一星级 One Star	客房(间) Number of Rooms (unit)	床位(张) Number of Beds (unit)
全　省	**Provincial Total**	**21320**	**1**	**85**	**130**	**242**	**20**		**1530504**	**2181108**
广　州	Guangzhou	4439	1	24	31	57	11		302155	425524
深　圳	Shenzhen	3570		20	14	17	3		337763	433783
珠　海	Zhuhai	581		4	7	19			59922	86132
汕　头	Shantou	290		2	5	11			29876	41163
佛　山	Foshan	1027		8	12	10			86747	121371
韶　关	Shaoguan	641			2	28			35019	55051
河　源	Heyuan	704		1	2	11	2		36303	59898
梅　州	Meizhou	682		2	8	17			31195	47736
惠　州	Huizhou	1468		4	5	7			99817	140657
汕　尾	Shanwei	801		1	2	8			32567	48375
东　莞	Dongguan	1593		7	7				134900	179100
中　山	Zhongshan	557		2	1	8	1		43665	58894
江　门	Jiangmen	795		2	1	5			40903	62828
阳　江	Yangjiang	716		2	2	6			41372	77867
湛　江	Zhanjiang	689		2	6	7	1		47242	71285
茂　名	Maoming	601		1	2	3			37927	70166
肇　庆	Zhaoqing	546		1	7	17	1		39719	59531
清　远	Qingyuan	765		1	4	3			39686	65960
潮　州	Chaozhou	252			5	4	1		11709	16690
揭　阳	Jieyang	297		1	4	1			22350	30117
云　浮	Yunfu	306			3	3			19667	28980
按经济区域分	By Region									
珠 三 角	Pearl River Delta	14576	1	72	85	140	16		1145591	1567820
粤　东	Eastern Region	1640		4	16	24	1		96502	136345
粤　西	Western Region	2006		5	10	16	1		126541	219318
粤　北	Northern Region	3098		4	19	62	2		161870	257625

17-14　各市接待过夜旅游者人数

Number of Overnight Tourists by City

单位：万人次　　(10000 person-times)

市　别	City	2022 合计 Total	2022 入境游客 Overseas Tourist Arrivals	2022 国内游客 Domestic Tourists	2023 合计 Total	2023 入境游客 Overseas Tourist Arrivals	2023 国内游客 Domestic Tourists
全　省	**Provincial Total**	**20307.15**	**190.16**	**20116.99**	**33824.15**	**1634.82**	**32189.34**
广　州	Guangzhou	4956.94	71.08	4885.86	8261.85	274.13	7987.72
深　圳	Shenzhen	4896.03	55.13	4840.90	7735.81	714.21	7021.60
珠　海	Zhuhai	608.08	18.35	589.73	1746.928	146.124	1600.80
汕　头	Shantou	383.62	1.56	382.06	733.48	29.39	704.09
佛　山	Foshan	1250.65	5.55	1245.11	2001.11	91.43	1909.68
韶　关	Shaoguan	362.81	0.60	362.21	572.68	7.63	565.05
河　源	Heyuan	267.45	0.33	267.13	443.63	7.76	435.87
梅　州	Meizhou	231.69	0.42	231.27	464.67	7.09	457.58
惠　州	Huizhou	1079.94	4.84	1075.10	1939.37	61.25	1878.12
汕　尾	Shanwei	331.40	2.20	329.20	349.88	18.92	330.96
东　莞	Dongguan	1588.44	7.43	1581.01	2513.35	80.42	2432.93
中　山	Zhongshan	512.94	7.87	505.07	892.44	62.59	829.85
江　门	Jiangmen	638.91	3.65	635.26	945.42	62.13	883.29
阳　江	Yangjiang	404.63	1.34	403.30	692.62	5.63	686.99
湛　江	Zhanjiang	657.80	0.74	657.06	1131.84	5.71	1126.13
茂　名	Maoming	464.23	0.44	463.78	775.26	3.38	771.88
肇　庆	Zhaoqing	455.46	1.98	453.48	707.33	16.08	691.25
清　远	Qingyuan	480.17	1.57	478.60	767.44	19.49	747.95
潮　州	Chaozhou	167.75	0.44	167.31	336.97	8.04	328.93
揭　阳	Jieyang	267.47	0.36	267.11	379.925	5.763	374.16
云　浮	Yunfu	300.72	4.29	296.44	432.15	7.65	424.50
按经济区域分	By Region						
珠 三 角	Pearl River Delta	15987.39	175.87	15811.52	26743.61	1508.36	25235.24
粤　东	Eastern Region	1150.25	4.57	1145.68	1800.26	62.11	1738.14
粤　西	Western Region	1526.66	2.52	1524.15	2599.72	14.72	2585.00
粤　北	Northern Region	1642.85	7.20	1635.64	2680.57	49.62	2630.95

17-15 各市旅游业收入

Tourism Earnings by City

单位：亿元　　(100 million yuan)

市　别	City	收入合计 Total Earnings 2022	收入合计 Total Earnings 2023	国际旅游收入 Foreign Exchange Earnings 2022	国际旅游收入 Foreign Exchange Earnings 2023	国内旅游收入 Domestic Tourism Earnings 2022	国内旅游收入 Domestic Tourism Earnings 2023
全　省	**Provincial Total**	**4213.51**	**9525.58**	**116.84**	**776.50**	**4096.67**	**8749.08**
广　州	Guangzhou	1196.10	2922.86	40.43	194.19	1155.67	2728.67
深　圳	Shenzhen	1161.50	2381.25	32.28	266.93	1129.22	2114.32
珠　海	Zhuhai	114.06	529.19	5.77	70.54	108.29	458.65
汕　头	Shantou	71.33	155.51	0.95	12.33	70.38	143.18
佛　山	Foshan	284.25	530.35	2.27	44.32	281.98	486.03
韶　关	Shaoguan	50.48	118.47	0.36	3.38	50.11	115.09
河　源	Heyuan	41.60	108.98	0.89	3.37	40.71	105.61
梅　州	Meizhou	40.64	117.51	0.25	3.37	40.39	114.14
惠　州	Huizhou	168.18	419.68	4.06	21.62	164.12	398.06
汕　尾	Shanwei	49.43	88.48	5.78	8.15	43.65	80.33
东　莞	Dongguan	307.41	548.39	6.46	41.96	300.94	506.43
中　山	Zhongshan	95.16	184.17	6.07	22.79	89.09	161.38
江　门	Jiangmen	94.88	250.21	1.38	50.78	93.51	199.43
阳　江	Yangjiang	68.93	146.92	0.37	2.64	68.56	144.28
湛　江	Zhanjiang	113.04	250.07	0.38	2.73	112.66	247.34
茂　名	Maoming	82.14	172.85	0.24	1.56	81.91	171.29
肇　庆	Zhaoqing	74.95	165.79	0.90	7.14	74.05	158.65
清　远	Qingyuan	91.49	166.55	6.26	8.69	85.22	157.86
潮　州	Chaozhou	17.89	69.73	0.18	3.86	17.71	65.87
揭　阳	Jieyang	40.33	92.03	0.03	2.72	40.30	89.31
云　浮	Yunfu	49.72	106.56	1.52	3.40	48.20	103.16
按经济区域分	By Region						
珠 三 角	Pearl River Delta	3496.49	7931.91	99.62	720.29	3396.87	7211.62
粤　东	Eastern Region	178.98	405.76	6.94	27.07	172.04	378.69
粤　西	Western Region	264.11	569.84	0.99	6.93	263.13	562.91
粤　北	Northern Region	273.93	618.07	9.29	22.21	264.63	595.86

17−16 各市国际旅游外汇收入

Foreign Exchange Earnings from International Tourism by City

单位：万美元 (USD 10000)

市 别	City	2000	2005	2010	2015	2019	2020	2021	2022	2023
全 省	**Provincial Total**	**411221**	**639739**	**1243154**	**1788466**	**2052131**	**235267**	**224002**	**173705**	**1101928**
广 州	Guangzhou	150580	229400	468858	569601	653027	80595	62311	60107	275578
深 圳	Shenzhen	141669	200869	318058	496837	500331	94272	101563	47990	378807
珠 海	Zhuhai	39395	70148	122339	96263	164980	15750	17934	8586	100101
汕 头	Shantou	11705	5950	5016	8927	21001	1430	1023	1418	17500
佛 山	Foshan	15973	34485	72896	137548	108054	5122	4084	3375	62894
韶 关	Shaoguan	351	2782	10309	2848	3108	949	788	539	4797
河 源	Heyuan	798	850	1389	1420	4098	172	93	1322	4789
梅 州	Meizhou	1487	1975	2962	10321	19542	1779	525	372	4785
惠 州	Huizhou	5333	16549	50168	88494	106940	3177	2651	6041	30676
汕 尾	Shanwei	387	455	1175	2538	3996	1522	4765	8595	11571
东 莞	Dongguan	7618	28189	67592	157743	159108	11696	13317	9610	59540
中 山	Zhongshan	14692	21027	27591	29843	30528	2518	1636	9026	32339
江 门	Jiangmen	8295	10521	47657	96887	176782	6802	3269	2049	72069
阳 江	Yangjiang	230	852	1876	3729	4841	491	692	549	3749
湛 江	Zhanjiang	1004	1483	2716	7305	12521	810	773	562	3877
茂 名	Maoming	169	676	1198	1739	3338	317	322	350	2220
肇 庆	Zhaoqing	6264	4718	12440	32231	21960	1693	620	1332	10137
清 远	Qingyuan	834	2051	11062	15608	11592	1199	1815	9313	12333
潮 州	Chaozhou	3071	5264	13207	22296	37193	973	794	265	5481
揭 阳	Jieyang	701	587	2150	1820	3361	318	316	43	3857
云 浮	Yunfu	665	907	2499	4468	5830	3682	4713	2263	4830
按经济区域分	By Region									
珠 三 角	Pearl River Delta	389819	615907	1187597	1705447	1921710	221625	207384	148114	1022140
粤 东	Eastern Region	15864	12256	21547	35581	65551	4243	6898	10321	38409
粤 西	Western Region	1403	3012	5790	12773	20700	1618	1787	1461	9845
粤 北	Northern Region	4135	8564	28220	34665	44170	7781	7934	13809	31534

注：本表数为广东省文化和旅游厅抽样调查测算数。
Note: Data in this table are obtained from the sample surveys of Guangdong Provincial Culture and Tourism Department.

主要统计指标解释

住宿业 是指为顾客提供临时住宿服务的企业(单位)和个体户。

餐饮业 是指从事食品的烹饪、调制并直接售给居民和社会集团的企业(单位)和个体户。

入境旅游人数 指来我国参观、访问、旅行、探亲、访友、休养 、考察、参加会议和从事经济、科技、文化、教育、体育、宗教等活动的外国人、华侨、港澳台同胞的人数。不包括外国在我国的常驻机构，如使领馆、通讯社、企业办事处的工作人员；来我国常驻的外国专家、留学生以及在岸逗留不过夜人员。

国际旅游外汇收入 指入境旅游的外国人、华侨、港澳台同胞在中国大陆旅游过程中发生的一切旅游支出，对于国家来说就是国际旅游外汇收入。

Explanatory Notes on Main Statistical Indicators

Hotel Services refers to the enterprises (establishments) and individuals engaged in providing temporary accommodation to customers.

Catering Services refer to the enterprises (establishments) and individuals engaged in food cooking , seasoning and selling food directly to households and social institutions.

Number of Overseas Visitor Arrivals refers to the number of foreigners, overseas Chinese, Chinese compatriots from Hong Kong, Macao and Taiwan coming to China for sight-seeing, visits, tours, family reunions, gatherings of friends, recuperation, inspection, conferences and other activities in the nature of business, science and technology, culture, education, sports, and religion. The statistics excludes representatives and employees of resident institutions of foreign countries in China such as embassies, consulates, news agencies and offices of foreign companies and organizations, as well as long-term foreign experts or students residing in China, and persons in transition without staying overnight in China.

Foreign Exchange Earnings from International Tourism refer to the total expenditures of foreigners, overseas Chinese, Chinese compatriots from Hong Kong, Macao and Taiwan during their stay in the mainland of China, or earnings of foreign exchange from international tourism in terms of national economy.

十八、房地产业

REAL ESTATE

十八　房地产业

简要说明

一、本篇资料反映广东省房地产开发企业经营活动情况，主要包括房地产开发企业土地开发和购置情况、投资规模及完成情况、房屋建筑情况及商品房销售情况等。

二、本篇资料由广东省统计局固定资产投资统计处整理提供。

三、本篇统计资料是根据《房地产开发统计报表制度》搜集和加工整理而得，全部数据采用全面调查的统计方法。

18 Real Estate

Brief Introduction

I. The information within this section reflects the operation and activities of real estate development enterprises within the Guangdong Province. The information focuses on the land development and purchasing activities of real estate development enterprises, the scope of investments and their completion, the construction of buildings, and the sale of commodity buildings

II. The information within this section was edited and provided by the Statistics Office on Investment in Fixed Assets from the Guangdong Statistics Bureau

III. The statistical information within this section was collected and further edited in accordance to the "Real Estate Development Statistics Reporting System," all data has been compiled by full investigation.

18-1 房地产开发主要指标
Main Indicators on Real Estate Development

项目	Item	2000	2010	2015	2021	2022	2023
本年完成投资额 (亿元)	**Investment Completed in Current Year (100 million yuan)**	**858.61**	**3659.69**	**8538.47**	**17465.85**	**15096.93**	**13693.33**
#住宅	Residential Buildings	593.74	2539.03	5890.51	12438.31	10834.24	9942.27
本年实际到位资金(亿元)	**Total Actual Funds in Place This Year (100 million yuan)**	**1064.51**	**7426.13**	**14164.30**	**28156.22**	**18866.75**	**18186.79**
#国内贷款	Domestic Loans	228.53	1256.11	2577.81	4377.99	2806.34	2857.43
利用外资	Foreign Investment	39.16	90.85	26.65	15.19	13.07	17.89
自筹资金	Self-raising Funds	287.71	1582.94	3933.40	9183.75	7125.12	5993.29
定金及预收款	Deposit and Advances Received	423.32	1537.64	4656.66	9589.35	5799.01	6020.35
个人按揭贷款	Personal Mortgage Loan		974.17	2322.61	4231.62	2677.94	2775.16
其他到位资金	Others	85.79	1984.42	647.17	758.32	445.26	522.68
房屋建筑面积(万平方米)	**Floor Space of Buildings (10000 sq.m)**						
施工面积	Floor Space under Construction	9922.12	29301.36	57941.86	94247.53	88662.69	82899.11
#住宅	Residential Buildings	7400.38	22253.76	40388.82	63828.96	59483.86	55301.26
竣工面积	Floor Space Completed	3161.39	5659.10	6044.43	8043.47	8161.12	8283.72
#住宅	Residential Buildings	2598.52	4589.22	4435.40	5587.55	5641.97	5566.03
竣工房屋价值 (亿元)	**Value of Buildings Completed (100 million yuan)**	**511.46**	**1587.46**	**2256.69**	**4291.48**	**4779.71**	**4813.82**
#住宅	Residential Buildings	415.94	1276.09	1639.45	3094.66	3356.40	3321.73
新建商品房销售面积 (万平方米)	**Floor Space of Newly-built Commercial Buildings Sold (10000 sq.m)**	**2259.95**	**7321.76**	**11681.01**	**14011.26**	**10591.11**	**9582.01**
#住宅	Residential Buildings	2009.34	6552.81	10497.62	11826.26	8568.72	7665.55
新建商品房销售额 (亿元)	**Total Sales of Newly-built Commercial Buildings (100 million yuan)**	**729.50**	**5480.77**	**11442.80**	**22320.27**	**15870.47**	**15103.05**
#住宅	Residential Buildings	597.36	4589.82	9967.32	19457.63	13428.51	12976.46

注：2000年其他到位资金包括个人按揭贷款。
Note: Others funds in place in 2000 include personal mortgage loan.

18–2 按用途分房地产开发企业房屋建筑及销售情况

Situation of Real Estate Development, Corporate Building Construction and Sales by Purpose

指　标	Item	2005	2010	2015	2021	2022	2023
房屋施工面积　（万平方米）	**Floor Space under Construction (10000 sq.m)**	**15110.04**	**29301.36**	**57941.86**	**94247.53**	**88662.69**	**82899.11**
#住宅	Residential Buildings	11399.99	22253.76	40388.82	63828.96	59483.86	55301.26
办公楼	Office Buildings	691.43	946.33	2607.81	6103.22	5751.13	5439.13
商业营业用房	Commercial Retail Buildings	1756.51	2621.92	6208.54	7828.19	7185.81	6715.27
房屋新开工面积（万平方米）	**Newly Started Constructing Floor Space (10000 sq.m)**	**4989.82**	**9904.38**	**12676.74**	**16097.26**	**8535.40**	**6883.83**
#住宅	Residential Buildings	4010.39	7826.80	8681.76	11392.51	5688.99	4726.95
办公楼	Office Buildings	99.04	160.47	566.83	584.57	465.10	382.69
商业营业用房	Commercial Retail Buildings	494.79	688.69	1573.31	1009.17	601.35	515.54
房屋竣工面积　（万平方米）	**Floor Space Completed (10000 sq.m)**	**4385.16**	**5659.10**	**6044.43**	**8043.47**	**8161.12**	**8283.72**
#住宅	Residential Buildings	3476.73	4589.22	4435.40	5587.55	5641.97	5566.03
办公楼	Office Buildings	118.20	120.07	237.18	419.80	378.22	493.78
商业营业用房	Commercial Retail Buildings	427.16	474.79	504.54	627.82	668.40	648.18
竣工房屋价值　（亿元）	**Value of Buildings Completed (100 million yuan)**	**829.35**	**1587.46**	**2256.69**	**4291.48**	**4779.71**	**4813.82**
#住宅	Residential Buildings	632.53	1276.08	1639.45	3094.66	3356.40	3321.73
办公楼	Office Buildings	29.84	42.50	114.29	320.52	371.95	441.58
商业营业用房	Commercial Retail Buildings	98.59	154.56	234.71	371.91	484.53	419.48
新建商品房销售面积（万平方米）	**Floor Space of Newly-built Commercial Buildings Sold (10000 sq.m)**	**5038.91**	**7321.76**	**11681.01**	**14011.26**	**10591.11**	**9582.01**
#住宅	Residential Buildings	4546.32	6552.81	10497.62	11826.26	8568.72	7665.55
办公楼	Office Buildings	107.76	163.03	311.12	457.52	454.02	332.41
商业营业用房	Commercial Retail Buildings	277.08	371.91	479.21	725.69	656.75	581.05
新建商品房销售额（亿元）	**Total Sales of Newly-built Commercial Buildings (100 million yuan)**	**2238.66**	**5480.77**	**11442.80**	**22320.27**	**15870.47**	**15103.05**
#住宅	Residential Buildings	1886.39	4589.82	9967.32	19457.63	13428.51	12976.46
办公楼	Office Buildings	89.61	248.43	583.87	1076.79	1077.22	725.28
商业营业用房	Commercial Retail Buildings	224.58	483.00	624.73	1143.97	848.19	865.00

18-3 按登记注册统计类别分组房地产开发情况（2023年）
Real Estate Development By Registration Statistical Categories (2023)

单位：亿元 (100 million yuan)

指 标	Item	完成投资额 Investment Completed	#住宅 Residential Buildings	房屋施工面积（万平方米）Floor Space of Buildings under Construction (10000 sq.m)
全 省	**Provincial Total**	**13693.33**	**9942.27**	**82899.11**
按登记注册统计类别分组	By Registration Status Categories			
内 资	Domestic-funded	13006.50	9509.42	76616.76
港、澳、台商投资	Funds from Hong Kong,Macao and Taiwan	558.33	356.10	4998.01
外商投资	Foreign Funded	128.49	76.75	1284.34

注：本表登记注册统计类别按《关于市场主体统计分类的划分规定》(国统字〔2023〕14号)执行。
Ntote: The registered statistical categories of this table is implemented in accordance with the Regulations onStatistics the Classification of Market Entity(Guotongzi [2023] No. 14).

18-3 续表 continued

单位：亿元 (100 million yuan)

指 标	Item	房屋竣工面积（万平方米）Floor Space of Buildings Completed (10000 sq.m)	#住宅 Residential Buildings	竣工房屋价值 Value of Buildings Completed	#住宅 Residential Buildings
全 省	**Provincial Total**	**8283.72**	**5566.03**	**4813.82**	**3321.73**
按登记注册统计类别分组	By Registration Status Categories				
内 资	Domestic-funded	7839.84	5370.11	4568.96	3225.11
港、澳、台商投资	Funds from Hong Kong,Macao and Taiwan	344.08	126.71	210.36	68.68
外商投资	Foreign Funded	99.79	69.21	34.50	27.94

18-4 各市房地产开发企业投资总规模及完成情况（2023年）
The Total Investment Scale and Completion Status of Real Estate Development Enterprises By City (2023)

单位：亿元 (100 million yuan)

市别	City	计划总投资 Planned Total Investment	自开始建设至本年底累计完成投资 Accumulated Investment Completed From the Beginning of Construction to the End of this Year	本年完成投资 Completed Investment this Year	建筑安装工程 Construction and Installation	设备工器具购置 Purchase of Equipment and Instruments	其他费用 Others	土地购置费 Land Acquisition Fee
全　省	**Provincial Total**	**137490.32**	**102751.49**	**13693.33**	**7121.28**	**118.97**	**6453.08**	**5293.26**
广　州	Guangzhou	36215.52	26561.71	3311.45	1145.74	10.18	2155.53	1780.64
深　圳	Shenzhen	27305.04	20786.05	3824.48	1628.66	6.20	2189.62	1810.48
珠　海	Zhuhai	7921.52	5931.93	510.24	338.98	4.97	166.29	105.86
汕　头	Shantou	2397.93	2096.13	318.10	252.43	4.19	61.48	49.46
佛　山	Foshan	13023.16	10670.80	1277.02	751.63	17.63	507.75	429.02
韶　关	Shaoguan	1731.74	1356.11	108.80	90.26	1.83	16.71	11.97
河　源	Heyuan	1454.40	873.79	132.43	121.68	1.58	9.16	3.22
梅　州	Meizhou	1966.75	1389.42	94.43	76.33	1.81	16.29	10.90
惠　州	Huizhou	9449.10	6984.39	1025.46	721.13	26.86	277.48	227.94
汕　尾	Shanwei	1339.03	822.06	110.71	88.33	6.36	16.02	8.02
东　莞	Dongguan	7735.00	5922.99	903.61	319.18	2.73	581.71	543.37
中　山	Zhongshan	4236.42	3073.46	295.52	176.15	1.68	117.69	93.06
江　门	Jiangmen	4422.22	3477.84	398.71	319.95	4.92	73.85	59.36
阳　江	Yangjiang	1303.20	864.70	77.05	65.78	0.98	10.30	4.82
湛　江	Zhanjiang	3570.69	2292.98	327.36	254.17	3.18	70.02	39.05
茂　名	Maoming	3216.91	1945.45	262.31	183.92	5.58	72.81	45.08
肇　庆	Zhaoqing	3218.52	2427.48	207.38	178.47	8.00	20.91	15.30
清　远	Qingyuan	3723.49	2895.33	250.77	180.92	2.25	67.60	42.78
潮　州	Chaozhou	695.58	589.13	50.12	45.04	0.79	4.29	1.68
揭　阳	Jieyang	1366.97	1040.80	130.41	111.00	5.88	13.53	8.56
云　浮	Yunfu	1197.13	748.93	76.98	71.55	1.36	4.07	2.69
按经济区域分	By Region							
珠三角	Pearl River Delta	113526.50	85836.65	11753.86	5579.88	83.17	6090.82	5065.03
粤　东	Eastern Region	5799.51	4548.12	609.34	496.80	17.22	95.31	67.73
粤　西	Western Region	8090.81	5103.13	666.72	503.86	9.74	153.13	88.95
粤　北	Northern Region	10073.50	7263.59	663.40	540.74	8.84	113.82	71.56

18-5 各市房地产开发投资情况（2023年）

Investment in Real Estate Development by City (2023)

单位：亿元 (100 million yuan)

市别	City	完成投资额 Investment Completed	按用途分 By use #住宅 Residential Buildings	#办公楼 Office Buildings	#商业营业用房 Buildings for Business Use
全省	**Provincial Total**	**13693.33**	**9942.27**	**864.80**	**1041.90**
广州	Guangzhou	3311.45	2411.91	227.18	193.83
深圳	Shenzhen	3824.48	2444.31	420.87	398.44
珠海	Zhuhai	510.24	321.79	61.59	54.21
汕头	Shantou	318.10	252.41	3.42	13.93
佛山	Foshan	1277.02	992.69	41.59	100.32
韶关	Shaoguan	108.80	87.68	2.43	11.69
河源	Heyuan	132.43	106.53	2.50	7.75
梅州	Meizhou	94.43	75.80	0.31	9.11
惠州	Huizhou	1025.46	848.62	14.12	50.18
汕尾	Shanwei	110.71	92.10	0.55	7.13
东莞	Dongguan	903.61	674.23	64.70	39.94
中山	Zhongshan	295.52	229.17	6.01	17.88
江门	Jiangmen	398.71	312.89	6.37	35.62
阳江	Yangjiang	77.05	68.43	0.14	4.26
湛江	Zhanjiang	327.36	258.99	1.87	16.98
茂名	Maoming	262.31	205.49	3.98	24.33
肇庆	Zhaoqing	207.38	173.22	3.17	14.48
清远	Qingyuan	250.77	188.34	0.73	22.21
潮州	Chaozhou	50.12	36.37	1.64	4.64
揭阳	Jieyang	130.41	98.77	1.52	8.24
云浮	Yunfu	76.98	62.52	0.09	6.73
按经济区域分	By Region				
珠三角	Pearl River Delta	11753.86	8408.84	845.61	904.90
粤东	Eastern Region	609.34	479.65	7.14	33.94
粤西	Western Region	666.72	532.91	5.99	45.56
粤北	Northern Region	663.40	520.87	6.06	57.49

18-6 各市房地产开发房屋建筑面积及价值（2023年）
Floor Space and Value of Buildings in Real Estate Development by City (2023)

市别	City	房屋建筑面积(万平方米) Floor Space of Buildings(10000 sq.m) 施工面积 Floor Space of Buildings under Construction	竣工面积 Floor Space of Buildings Completed	#住宅 Residential Buildings	竣工房屋价值(亿元) Value of Buildings Completed (100 million yuan)	#住宅 Residential Buildings
全　省	**Provincial Total**	**82899.11**	**8283.72**	**5566.03**	**4813.82**	**3321.73**
广　州	Guangzhou	12676.79	1013.04	510.07	689.23	399.89
深　圳	Shenzhen	11183.21	978.32	535.10	1172.30	673.62
珠　海	Zhuhai	3202.38	385.84	266.80	291.01	212.21
汕　头	Shantou	3310.24	650.01	424.06	334.72	225.25
佛　山	Foshan	7116.48	559.49	339.16	363.54	270.43
韶　关	Shaoguan	1899.11	203.24	158.10	69.26	54.63
河　源	Heyuan	1808.53	216.44	138.33	91.53	63.17
梅　州	Meizhou	2034.24	274.54	222.17	93.51	77.46
惠　州	Huizhou	7735.25	652.61	509.97	324.86	269.13
汕　尾	Shanwei	1232.80	103.90	76.58	39.15	35.80
东　莞	Dongguan	3935.53	306.78	211.31	272.75	223.81
中　山	Zhongshan	3534.37	259.49	161.71	101.92	66.65
江　门	Jiangmen	3764.84	463.92	325.68	170.76	127.22
阳　江	Yangjiang	1411.75	136.13	113.42	38.10	32.79
湛　江	Zhanjiang	3826.92	253.45	186.58	119.38	96.47
茂　名	Maoming	3497.86	448.50	321.13	159.58	113.99
肇　庆	Zhaoqing	3198.69	460.08	353.16	154.66	118.25
清　远	Qingyuan	3983.86	370.67	266.78	135.53	101.47
潮　州	Chaozhou	736.22	185.22	160.93	37.77	30.33
揭　阳	Jieyang	1273.46	149.15	110.41	83.09	70.57
云　浮	Yunfu	1536.60	212.89	174.59	71.18	58.58
按经济区域分	By Region					
珠三角	Pearl River Delta	56347.54	5079.57	3212.95	3541.02	2361.21
粤　东	Eastern Region	6552.71	1088.28	771.98	494.73	361.95
粤　西	Western Region	8736.52	838.08	621.13	317.06	243.25
粤　北	Northern Region	11262.33	1277.79	959.98	461.01	355.32

18-7 按用途分新建商品房销售情况（2023年）

Newly-built Commercial Buildings Sold by Use (2023)

指　标	Item	全省 Provincial Total	按登记注册统计类别分组 By Registration Status Categories 内资 Domestic-funded Economy	港、澳、台商投资 Funds from Hong Kong, Macao and Taiwan	外商投资 Foreign Funded
新建商品房销售面积（万平方米）	**Floor Space of Newly-built Commercial Buildings Sold (10000 sq.m)**	**9582.01**	**9041.50**	**423.24**	**117.26**
#住宅	Residential Buildings	7665.55	7276.28	318.00	71.27
办公楼	Office Buildings	332.41	299.55	25.65	7.22
商业营业用房	Commercial Retail Buildings	581.05	538.08	35.10	7.87
新建商品房销售额（亿元）	**Total Sales of Newly-built Commercial Buildings (100 million yuan)**	**15103.05**	**14135.86**	**823.77**	**143.42**
#住宅	Residential Buildings	12976.46	12269.88	613.28	93.30
办公楼	Office Buildings	725.28	662.58	53.49	9.21
商业营业用房	Commercial Retail Buildings	865.00	730.33	125.73	8.95

注：本表登记注册统计类别按《关于市场主体统计分类的划分规定》(国统字〔2023〕14号)执行。

Ntote: The registered statistical categories of this table is implemented in accordance with the Regulations onStatistics the Classification of Market Entity (Guotongzi [2023] No. 14).

18-8 各市新建商品房屋销售情况（2023年）
Sales of Newly-built Commercial Buildings by City (2023)

市别	City	新建商品房销售面积（万平方米）Floor Space of Newly-built Commercial Buildings Sold (10000 sq.m)	#住宅 Residential Buildings	新建商品房销售额（亿元）Total Sales of Newly-built Commercial Buildings (100 million yuan)	#住宅 Residential Buildings
全　省	**Provincial Total**	**9582.01**	**7665.55**	**15103.05**	**12976.46**
广　州	Guangzhou	1404.49	1067.71	4078.66	3462.91
深　圳	Shenzhen	784.14	602.53	3493.64	2942.24
珠　海	Zhuhai	271.02	216.82	638.85	542.35
汕　头	Shantou	363.01	319.57	344.43	294.64
佛　山	Foshan	1014.78	746.00	1499.83	1300.30
韶　关	Shaoguan	204.92	181.17	118.57	102.59
河　源	Heyuan	223.07	181.93	118.80	105.22
梅　州	Meizhou	241.59	222.83	137.46	125.86
惠　州	Huizhou	1138.57	908.53	1143.14	1002.55
汕　尾	Shanwei	230.93	218.10	165.64	150.18
东　莞	Dongguan	361.61	298.56	915.22	839.81
中　山	Zhongshan	464.83	345.63	536.60	457.36
江　门	Jiangmen	583.01	457.81	426.64	371.34
阳　江	Yangjiang	205.37	186.52	113.31	103.67
湛　江	Zhanjiang	383.50	326.97	349.28	301.11
茂　名	Maoming	345.12	312.99	225.02	202.12
肇　庆	Zhaoqing	410.58	313.73	231.49	185.30
清　远	Qingyuan	445.65	328.15	273.78	222.75
潮　州	Chaozhou	116.79	87.71	66.35	59.69
揭　阳	Jieyang	193.76	183.94	134.03	124.43
云　浮	Yunfu	195.28	158.35	92.30	80.06
按经济区域分	By Region				
珠三角	Pearl River Delta	6433.02	4957.31	12964.07	11104.15
粤　东	Eastern Region	904.50	809.31	710.46	628.94
粤　西	Western Region	933.98	826.49	687.60	606.90
粤　北	Northern Region	1310.51	1072.44	740.92	636.48

主要统计指标解释

土地购置费 指房地产开发企业通过各种方式取得土地使用权而支付的费用。土地购置费按实际发生额填报，分期付款的应分期计入。项目分期开发的，只计入与本期项目有关的土地购置费。前期支付的土地购置费，项目纳入统计后计入。

房地产开发投资 指房地产开发企业本年完成的全部用于房屋建设工程、土地开发工程的投资额以及公益性建筑和土地购置费等的投资。

本年实际到位资金 指房地产开发企业本年实际到位的，可用于房地产开发的各种货币资金。包括国内贷款、利用外资、自筹资金、定金及预收款、个人按揭贷款和其他资金。

房屋施工面积 指房地产开发企业本年施工的全部房屋建筑面积。包括本年新开工的房屋建筑面积、上年跨入本年继续施工的房屋建筑面积、上年停缓建在本年恢复施工的房屋建筑面积、本年竣工的房屋建筑面积以及本年施工后又停缓建的房屋建筑面积。多层建筑应填各层建筑面积之和。

房屋新开工面积 指房地产开发企业本年新开工建设的房屋建筑面积，以单位工程为核算对象。不包括在上年开工跨入本年继续施工的房屋建筑面积和上年停缓建而在本年恢复施工的房屋建筑面积。房屋的开工应以房屋正式开始破土刨槽（地基处理或打永久桩）的日期为准。房屋新开工面积指整栋房屋的全部建筑面积，不能分割计算。

房屋竣工面积 指房地产开发企业本年按照设计要求已全部完工，达到住人和使用条件，经验收鉴定合格或达到竣工验收标准，可正式移交使用的各栋房屋建筑面积的总和。

新建商品房销售面积 指房地产开发企业本年出售商品房屋的合同总面积(即双方签署的正式买卖合同中所确定的建筑面积)。

新建商品房销售额 指房地产开发企业本年出售商品房屋的合同总价款(即双方签署的正式买卖合同中所确定的合同总价)。该指标与商品房销售面积同口径。

Explanatory Notes on Main Statistical Indicators

Land Purchase Fee refers to fees paid by real estate development enterprises for obtaining land use rights in various ways. The land purchase fee shall be filled in according to the actual amount, which paid by installments shall be counted by stages. If the project is developed by stages, only included the land purchase fees related to the current project. The land purchase fees paid in the previous period are included after the statistics.

Real Estate Development Investment refers to total investments completed by real estate development enterprises in this year for housing construction projects, land development projects, public welfare buildings and land acquisition costs.

Funds Actually Paid in this year refers to various monetary funds that actually in place by real estate development enterprises this year and available for real estate development. Including domestic loans, utilization of foreign capital, self raised funds, deposits and advances, personal mortgage loans and other funds.

Building Area under Construction refers to total area of houses constructed by real estate development enterprises in this year. Including the building area of newly started houses in this year, houses continued to be constructed from previous year to this year, houses suspended from construction in the previous year and resumed in this year, houses completed in this year and houses suspended from construction after construction in this year. For multi-storey buildings, the area of each floor shall be filled into total area.

New Construction Area refers to building area of the newly constructed houses of the real estate development enterprises in this year, which is accounted for by the unit project. It does not include the building area of houses that started in previous year and continued construction in current year and stopped construction in previous year and resumed construction in current year. The commencement of the house shall be subject to the date when the house officially starts the earth breaking and trenching (foundation treatment or permanent pile driving). The newly started area of the house refers to the total construction area of the whole house which cannot be calculated separately.

Building Area Completed refers to total area of each building that the real estate development enterprise has completed in accordance with the design requirements this year, has reached the occupancy and use conditions, passed the acceptance appraisal or reached the completion acceptance standard, and can be officially handed over for use.

Floor Space of Newly-built Commercial Buildings Sold refers to total contracted area of commercial buildings sold by real estate development enterprises in this year (i.e. the building area determined in the formal sales contract signed by both parties).

Total Sales of Newly-built Commercial Buildings refers to total contract price of the commercial building sold by the real estate development enterprise this year (i.e. the total contract price determined in the formal sales contract signed by both parties). This indicator use the same caliber as area of commercial building sold.

十九、教育和科技

EDUCATION AND TECHNOLOGY

十九　教育和科技

简要说明

一、本篇资料主要反映广东教育、科学技术活动基本情况。

二、本篇资料主要包括：

1. 高、中、初等教育，幼儿教育和各种类型的各级成人教育，指标主要包括各级各类的学校数、在校生数、招生数、毕业生数、教职工数和专任教师数等。

2. 科技成果奖励和技术市场情况，专利申请受理量和批准量，研究与开发机构基本情况，高校研究与发展人员及经费，科协系统科技活动情况等数据。

三、本篇资料由广东省统计局社会和科技统计处负责整理、编辑。

四、统计资料来源：

教育统计资料根据广东省教育厅、广东省人力资源和社会保障厅提供的统计年报加工整理。科技统计资料根据广东省科技厅、广东省人力资源和社会保障厅、广东省教育厅、广东省科协等部门提供的统计年报加工整理。

19 Education and Technology

Brief Introduction

I. The data in this chapter show the basic conditions on the development Guangdong's education, science and technology.

II. The data in this chapter mainly include:

(1) The data on tertiary, secondary, primary, and kindergarten education and various types of adult education at all levels, including the number of schools, the number of students enrolled, the number of new enrollments, the number of graduates, the number of staff and workers, and the number of full-time teachers of various levels and categories.

(2) The data on scientific and technological achievements and prizes, conditions of technological markets, numbers of patent applications accepted and granted, basic conditions of R&D institutions, R&D personnel and funds in universities and colleges, and scientific and technological activities of associations of science and technology, etc.

III. The data are prepared and edited by the Division of Social, Scientific and Technological Statistics of Statistics Bureau of Guangdong Province.

IV. Data sources:

Data on education are processed and prepared in accordance with the annual statistical reports provided by Guangdong Provincial Department of Education and Guangdong Provincial Department of Human Resources and Social Security. Data on science and technology are processed and prepared in accordance with the annual statistical reports provided by Guangdong Provincial Department of Sciencc and Technology, Guangdong Provincial Department of Human Resources and Social Security，Guangdong Provincial Department of Education, Guangdong Provincial Department of Personnel and Guangdong Provincial Association of Science and Technology.

19-1 教育、科技主要指标

Main Indicators on Education, Science and Technology

指　　标	Item	2000	2010	2015	2021	2022	2023
在校学生数　（万人）	Number of Total Enrollment　(10000 persons)						
普通本专科	Regular Institutions of Higher Education	29.95	142.66	185.64	253.98	267.09	260.14
成人本专科	Institutions of Higher Education for Adults	20.14	46.40	66.45	97.51	110.27	116.79
中等学校	Secondary Schools	541.72	939.23	736.79	783.17	824.62	861.91
#普通中学	Regular Secondary Schools	460.69	709.05	560.72	629.98	665.38	699.53
高等教育毛入学率(%)	Gross Enrollment Rate of High Education　(%)	11.35	28.00	33.00	57.65	60.07	63.10
高中毛入学率　(%)	Gross Enrollment Rate of Senior Secondary Schools　(%)	38.70	86.20	95.70	97.71	97.58	97.17
学龄儿童入学率　(%)	Percentage of School-age Children Enrolled　(%)	99.70	99.95	99.98	100.00	99.93	100.00
每万人口普通本专科在校学生数　(人)	Number of Students Enrolled in Regular Institutions of Higher Education per 10000 Population　(person)	41.19	140.83	173.10	201.55	210.35	205.27
研究与实验发展(R&D)人员　(万人)	Number of R&D Personnel　(10000 persons)		44.66	68.02	124.85	133.98	158.27
R&D人员全时当量　(万人年)	Full-time Equivalent of (R&D Personnel　(10 000 man-year)	7.11	36.47	50.17	88.52	97.25	120.24
研究与实验发展(R&D)经费内部支出(亿元)	R&D Expenditure Internal Expenditure　(100 million yuan)	107.12	808.75	1798.17	4002.18	4411.90	4802.62
#基础研究	Basic Research		16.72	54.21	274.27	239.62	266.74
应用研究	Applied Research		37.32	165.00	356.72	415.74	359.57
试验发展	Experimental Development		754.70	1478.96	3371.19	3756.54	4176.30
#政府资金	Government Funds	101.38	65.76	145.85	474.26	495.50	519.20
企业资金	Enterprises Funds	86.44	708.93	1606.21	3462.49	3845.82	4187.32
R&D经费支出占地区生产总值比例　(%)	Percentage of Research and Development Expenditure in Provincial GDP　(%)	0.99	1.74	2.43	3.21	3.42	3.54
省级及以上科技奖励成果　(项)	Number of Achievements in Science and Technology Awarded by Provincial-level and Higher Agencies(item)	289	296	269	176	190	245
专利授权量　(件)	Number of Patent Granted　(piece)	15799	119346	241176	872209	837276	703695
#发明专利	Inventions	261	13691	33477	102850	115080	143141
技术合同成交额(亿元)	Transaction Value of Technological Contracts　(100 million yuan)	48.21	242.50	663.53	4292.73	4525.42	4438.13

注：1.R&D经费支出占地区生产总值比例指标历史数据，已根据修订后的地区生产总值数据进行调整。

2.中等学校含中等职业学校、技工学校、普通高中、初中。

Note: a) Historical statistics on ratio of expenditure on R&D to GDP have been adjusted according to amended GDP statistics.

b) Secondary Schools include Secondary Technical Vocational Schools, Skilled Workers Schools, Ordinary High Schools and Junior High School.

19−2 各级各类学校在校学生数

Number of Total Enrollment by Level and Type of School

单位：万人 (10000 persons)

年份 Year	普通高等学校 General Colleges and Universities	中等学校 Secondary Schools			小学 Primary Schools
		中等职业教育学校 Vocational Secondary Schools	技工学校 Technical Schools	普通中学 Regular Secondary Schools	
1978	3.07	3.64		313.32	743.02
1979	3.79	4.51	0.71	268.73	743.81
1980	4.10	6.28	1.61	252.11	748.86
1981	4.47	6.12	1.39	218.71	734.78
1982	4.09	6.51	0.99	200.19	723.03
1983	4.56	9.96	0.92	199.59	705.34
1984	5.47	12.99	1.01	220.69	692.73
1985	6.99	18.01	1.45	236.45	671.25
1986	7.83	28.22	1.45	249.93	670.62
1987	8.63	34.26	2.63	252.60	677.37
1988	9.72	37.63	3.40	244.23	688.72
1989	10.04	42.09	3.93	235.73	715.15
1990	9.59	45.27	5.22	234.03	747.29
1991	9.27	44.74	5.63	238.28	788.93
1992	9.74	46.29	6.58	255.02	808.98
1993	11.70	50.24	7.68	277.19	832.14
1994	13.75	55.89	9.57	307.38	862.21
1995	15.18	66.67	11.10	339.46	883.19
1996	16.40	67.30	12.28	373.19	897.64
1997	17.47	72.70	13.29	400.85	911.34
1998	18.50	70.50	14.50	423.61	918.02
1999	22.08	69.50	23.00	443.91	920.96
2000	29.95	65.57	15.46	460.69	929.93
2001	38.19	62.00	16.67	489.70	952.98
2002	46.78	61.20	17.82	513.40	979.61
2003	58.78	63.08	23.90	545.91	1025.37
2004	72.69	65.54	28.11	580.86	1049.62
2005	87.47	71.02	32.81	611.69	1067.03
2006	100.86	80.84	38.16	639.29	1056.99
2007	111.97	90.76	45.81	655.38	1017.62
2008	121.64	100.08	53.54	679.65	956.47
2009	133.41	120.46	64.11	696.11	887.65
2010	142.66	154.78	75.56	709.05	848.55
2011	152.73	152.05	85.13	699.47	822.06
2012	161.68	149.57	88.52	668.40	808.24
2013	170.99	140.89	87.62	625.24	807.94
2014	179.42	128.22	62.26	590.77	831.91
2015	185.64	117.21	58.86	560.72	868.88
2016	189.29	106.57	53.26	545.22	905.22
2017	192.58	99.39	55.37	545.37	941.96
2018	196.32	86.73	54.27	556.18	988.37
2019	205.40	85.97	57.77	572.77	1033.43
2020	240.02	86.68	60.89	595.82	1057.11
2021	253.98	90.30	62.88	629.98	1079.01
2022	267.09	94.22	65.01	665.38	1084.05
2023	260.14	96.51	65.87	699.53	1110.52

注：1.普通高等学校包括大学，学院，独立学院，职业本科学校，高等专科院校，高等职业学校，其他普通高教机构，在校学生人数指普通本、专科人数，下同。

2.中等职业教育学校包括调整后中等职业学校，中等技术学校，中等师范学校，成人中等专业学校，职业高中学校，残疾人中等职业学校，技工学校，附设中职班，其他中职机构，下同；1986年前缺成人中专数据。

Notes: a) General colleges and universities include universities, colleges, independent colleges, vocational colleges, vocational colleges, higher vocational schools and other general institutions of higher education. The number of students in school refers to the number of students in regular universities with full undergraduate courses and colleges with specialized courses.The same applies to the following tables.

b) Secondary vocational education schools include adjusted secondary vocational schools, secondary technical schools, secondary normal schools, adult secondary specialized schools, vocational high schools, secondary vocational schools for the disabled, technical schools, secondary affiliated vocational classes, and other secondary vocational institutions, the same below; There are no adult secondary school data before 1986.

19–3 各级各类学校情况

Statistics on Various Levels and Types of Schools

项　目	Item	2000	2005	2010	2015	2021	2022	2023
普通高等学校	**Institutions of Higher Education**							
学校数　(所)	Number of Schools (unit)	52	111	131	143	160	161	162
毕业生数　(万人)	Number of Graduates (10000 persons)	5.00	15.71	33.42	47.69	57.44	63.38	86.08
本科	Universities with Full Undergraduate Courses	2.40	6.11	15.29	22.41	28.22	32.10	33.57
专科	Colleges with Specialized Courses	2.60	9.60	18.13	25.28	29.22	31.27	52.51
招生数　(万人)	Number of New Enrollments (10000 persons)	12.08	30.70	44.02	56.15	75.19	79.56	83.20
本科	Universities with Full Undergraduate Courses	5.01	13.65	21.70	27.54	35.46	39.00	40.37
专科	Colleges with Specialized Courses	7.07	17.04	22.31	28.61	39.73	40.55	42.83
在校学生数(万人)	Number of Enrolled Students (10000 persons)	29.95	87.47	142.66	185.64	253.98	267.09	260.14
本科	Universities with Full Undergraduate Courses	15.03	42.86	77.86	104.08	128.57	134.65	140.62
专科	Colleges with Specialized Courses	14.92	44.61	64.80	81.56	125.41	132.44	119.51
教职工数　(万人)	Number of Teachers and Staff (10000 persons)	4.68	9.08	11.40	14.54	19.03	19.81	20.57
#专任教师	Full-time Teachers	2.04	5.43	7.86	9.89	12.88	13.59	14.35
中等职业教育	**Vocational Secondary Schools**							
学校数　(所)	Number of Schools (unit)	658	641	566	481	382	372	372
毕业生数　(万人)	Number of Graduates (10000 persons)	21.54	18.91	33.17	41.73	26.05	27.19	27.73
招生数　(万人)	Number of New Enrollment (10000 persons)	21.10	27.93	74.13	39.54	33.60	34.91	33.65
在校学生数(万人)	Number of Total Enrollment (10000 persons)	65.57	71.02	154.78	117.21	90.30	94.22	96.51
教职工数　(万人)	Number of Teachers and Staff (10000 persons)	5.70	4.91	5.86	5.78	5.72	5.76	5.91
#专任教师	Full-time Teachers	3.70	3.37	4.35	4.50	4.49	4.59	4.72
技工学校	**Technical Schools**							
学校数　(所)	Number of Schools (unit)	186	191	246	163	148	148	148
毕业生数　(万人)	Number of Graduates (10000 persons)	4.28	9.60	12.80	14.46	15.45	17.33	17.66
招生数　(万人)	Number of New Enrollments (10000 persons)	5.84	12.90	28.20	19.94	21.94	22.28	22.85
在校学生数(万人)	Number of Total Enrollment (10000 persons)	15.46	32.81	75.56	58.86	62.88	65.01	65.87
教职工数　(万人)	Number of Teachers and Staff (10000 persons)	1.07	1.46	2.78	2.94	3.27	3.41	3.48
#专任教师	Full-time Teachers	0.68	1.03	1.98	2.10	2.49	2.63	2.73
普通中学	**Regular Secondary Schools**							
学校数　(所)	Number of Schools (unit)	3964	4282	4334	4434	4908	5024	5110
毕业生数　(万人)	Number of Graduates (10000 persons)	131.82	174.33	210.23	201.96	185.57	196.30	204.77
招生数　(万人)	Number of New Enrollments (10000 persons)	171.16	219.64	241.96	182.89	225.14	236.55	243.61
在校学生数(万人)	Number of Total Enrollment (10000 persons)	460.69	611.69	709.05	560.72	629.98	665.38	699.53
教职工数　(万人)	Number of Teachers and Staff (10000 persons)	27.57	36.03	44.53	47.54	70.93	73.72	76.91
#专任教师	Full-time Teachers	22.86	30.73	39.15	42.67	47.25	49.26	51.32

注：1.普通高等学校含大学，学院，独立学院，职业本科学校，高等专科院校，高等职业学校，其他普通高教机构。(下同)

2.根据教育部指标解释，对高等教育教职工取数口径从2012年开始调整为全口径教职工数，2011年及以前年份取校本部教职工数。(下同)

3.自2020年起，九年一贯制学校、十二年一贯制学校的教职工数计入普通中学教职工数；专任教师数则按教育层次进行归类。(下同)

Notes: a) General colleges and universities include universities, colleges, independent colleges, vocational colleges, higher vocational schools and other general institutions of higher education. The same applies to the following tables.

b)According to the explanation of Ministry of Education indicators, the teachers and staff of higher education began to adjust to the whole caliber from 2012, fetched the number of main campus teachers and staff in 2011 and before. (The same below)

c) Since 2020,the number of teachers and staff in regular secondary schools include the number in nine-year and twelve-year education schools; The number of full-time teachers are grouped by education level. (The same below)

19-3 续表 continued

项 目	Item	2000	2005	2010	2015	2021	2022	2023
小学	**Primary Schools**							
学校数 (万所)	Number of Schools (10000 units)	2.42	2.12	1.68	1.01	1.06	1.06	1.07
毕业生数 (万人)	Number of Graduates (10000 persons)	148.48	167.43	174.19	121.49	159.08	166.09	169.30
招生数 (万人)	Number of New Enrollments (10000 persons)	155.73	164.16	135.92	165.80	183.80	175.91	199.91
在校学生数 (万人)	Number of Students Enrolled (10000 persons)	929.93	1067.03	848.55	868.88	1079.01	1084.05	1110.52
教职工数 (万人)	Number of Teachers and Staff (10000 persons)	42.08	46.37	48.78	51.44	51.15	51.70	52.76
#专任教师	Full-time Teachers	36.41	40.38	43.07	46.86	59.22	60.20	61.34
学龄儿童	**School-age Children**							
学龄儿童总数 (万人)	Total number (10000 persons)	905.39	1026.90	801.82	836.09	1027.88	1041.14	1071.48
已入学学龄儿童数 (万人)	Primary School Enrollment number (10000 persons)	902.65	1023.60	801.45	835.93	1027.88	1040.28	1071.48
学龄儿童入学率 (%)	Enrollment Rate (%)	99.70	99.68	99.95	99.98	100.00	99.92	100.00
小学毕业生	**Primary School Graduates**							
小学毕业生人数 (万人)	Number of Graduates (10000 persons)	148.48	167.43	174.19	121.49	159.08	166.09	169.30
已升学人数 (万人)	Number of Students Entering into Junior Secondary Schools (10000 persons)	142.77	162.66	166.37	116.45	154.62	161.63	165.19
幼儿园	**Kindergartens**							
幼儿园数 (所)	Number of Kindergartens (unit)	12027	10359	11161	16368	21101	21566	21662
在园幼儿数 (万人)	Number of Children in Kindergartens (10000 persons)	214.18	213.92	227.23	402.28	500.39	498.05	458.62
教职工数 (万人)	Number of Teachers and Staff (10000 persons)	12.91	15.90	23.68	43.62	65.28	66.78	65.15
#专任教师	Full-time Teachers	8.36	9.18	13.63	24.07	34.51	35.10	33.70
特殊教育学校	**Special Schools**							
特殊教育学校数 (所)	Number of Schools (unit)	61	67	75	116	150	152	154
招生数 (人)	Number of New Enrollments (persons)	2000	3363	3666	7303	13198	13087	13657
在校学生数 (人)	Number of Total Enrollment (persons)	27507	25752	26064	36048	71170	74455	76278

注：1.特殊教育学校是指盲人学校，聋人学校，弱智学校，其他特教学校，附设特教班

2.学龄儿童总数取6—11岁校内外学龄人口数，已入学学龄儿童数取6—11岁在校学龄人口数。

3.自2020年起，小学教职工数仅统计小学及小学教学点的教职工数；专任教师数则按教育层次进行归类。

Notes: a)Special schools refer to separate institutions providing regular or vocational primary and secondary education for blinded, dumb or mentally-retarded children, or other children and adolescents in need of special care in education.

b)The total number of School-age Children is the School-age population inside and outside the school aged 6-11,the Primary School Enrollment number is the School-age population aged 6-11.

c) Since 2020, the number of teachers and staff in primary school only counted the number in primary school and primary school place; The number of full-time teachers are grouped by education level.

19-4 研究生教育情况
Statistics on Postgraduate Education

项目	Item	2000	2005	2010	2015	2021	2022	2023
培养单位数（个）	**Number of Institutions of Postgraduate Education (unit)**	**26**	**29**	**31**	**28**	**30**	**32**	**32**
高等学校	Institutions of Higher Education	18	21	23	25	27	29	29
科研单位	Research Institutions	8	8	8	3	3	3	3
招生数（人）	**Number of New Enrollments (person)**	**5672**	**17054**	**25798**	**30650**	**64501**	**68644**	**72058**
博士	Doctor	1053	2802	3307	3540	7023	7687	8445
高等学校	Institutions of Higher Education	1001	2599	3117	3532	7015	7676	8434
科研单位	Research Institutions	52	203	190	8	8	11	11
硕士	Master	4619	14252	22491	27110	57478	60957	63613
高等学校	Institutions of Higher Education	4510	13953	22135	27018	57340	60767	63410
科研单位	Research Institutions	109	299	356	92	138	190	203
在校学生数（人）	**Number of Enrolled Students (person)**	**13023**	**43942**	**72455**	**89404**	**174309**	**195410**	**209528**
博士	Doctor	2558	9049	12341	14474	25020	27906	30877
高等学校	Institutions of Higher Education	2445	8406	11706	14443	24996	27877	30842
科研单位	Research Institutions	113	643	635	31	24	29	35
硕士	Master	10405	34893	60114	74930	149289	167504	178651
高等学校	Institutions of Higher Education	10161	34066	59159	74682	148888	167042	178111
科研单位	Research Institutions	244	827	955	248	401	462	540
毕业生数（人）	**Number of Graduates (person)**	**2182**	**9489**	**17862**	**26174**	**38911**	**45084**	**54905**
博士	Doctor	417	1342	2436	2947	3735	4506	5180
高等学校	Institutions of Higher Education	387	1241	2288	2937	3724	4500	5175
科研单位	Research Institutions	30	101	148	10	11	6	5
硕士	Master	1765	8147	15426	23227	35176	40578	49725
高等学校	Institutions of Higher Education	1692	7941	15158	23151	35071	40454	49601
科研单位	Research Institutions	73	206	268	76	105	124	124

注：2014年起中国科学院大学下辖广州化学研究所、南海海洋研究所、华南植物研究所、广州能源研究所和广州地球化学研究所的教育事业报表统一归口中国科学院大学管理，并调整2013年起数据，从2013年起研究生数据均不含以上培养研究生单位数据。

Notes: Since 2014,Guangzhou Institute of Chemistry,South China Sea Institute of Oceanography,South China Institute of Botany,Guangzhou Institute of Energy and the Guangzhou Institute of Geochemistry's education statistics are under the centralized to the University of Chinese Academy of Sciences and since 2013 data has been adjusted and the number of students has excluded the number of students in these institutions.

19-5 各级各类继续教育在校学生数
Number of Total Enrollment by Level and Type of Continuing Education

单位：人 (person)

项目	Item	2000	2005	2010	2015	2021	2022	2023
成人高等教育	**Higher Education for Adults**	**201410**	**295618**	**463987**	**664495**	**975147**	**1102687**	**1167907**
成人高等学校	Institutions of Higher Education for Adults	84057	30081	22025	17556	25174	25944	26059
开放大学	The Open University	34242	10740	10980	10256	12956	12378	10494
职工高等学校	Schools of Higher Education for Staff and Workers	17147	6865	6344	5411	12218	13566	15565
管理干部学院	Colleges for Management Cadres	20142	2686	4398				
教育学院	Teachers' Colleges	12526	9790	303	1889			
普通、职业高等学校	Regular HEIs	117353	265537	441962	646939	949973	1076743	1141848
函授	Correspondence	51028	100260	173761	281334	538311	681925	739019
业余	Spare time Schools	43063	141532	265713	365605	411662	394818	402829
脱产	Full-time Courses for Adults	23262	23745	2488				
网络教育本专科	**Online Education**		**43663**	**66875**	**93857**	**398939**	**457604**	**512912**
本科	Universities with Full Undergraduate Courses		34627	34263	42732	87502	107329	144740
专科	Colleges with Specialized Courses		9036	32612	51125	311437	350275	368172
成人中等教育	**Secondary Education for Adults**	**44006**		**29105**	**7341**	**4943**	**5249**	**5280**
成人中专学校	Specialized Secondary Schools for Adults			27327	7341	4943	5249	5280
成人中学	Secondary Schools for Adults	44006		5358				

注：2021年起，广东开放大学学生统计从成人教育学生调整为网络教育学生。

Notes: From 2021, the scope of student statistics in Guangdong Open University have been adjusted from adult education students to online education students.

19-6 高等学校情况（2023年）

Statistics on Institutions of Higher Education (2023)

项目	Item	学校数(所) Number of Schools (unit)	毕业生数(人) Number of Graduates (person)	招生数(人) Number of New Enrollments (person)	在校学生数(人) Number of Total Enrollment (person)	教职工数(人) Number of Teachers and Staff (person)	#专任教师 Full-time Teachers
总计	**Total**	**162**	**860826**	**831973**	**2601372**	**205665**	**143477**
#女性	Female		429199	420367	1311298	106386	73897
按隶属关系分	**Grouped by Relation of Leadership**						
中央属	Under Central Government	4	23985	26858	104451	21701	10903
地方属	Under Local Government	158	836841	805115	2496921	183964	132574
按学校类别分	**Grouped by Type of Institution**						
综合大学	University	73	384294	363697	1079338	94468	60847
理工院校	Science and Engineering College	36	239714	217359	688816	45750	34666
农业院校	Agriculture College	4	31396	27354	111831	8134	6231
医药院校	Medicine College	12	37967	39702	146018	14715	10973
师范院校	Teacher Education College	10	50887	50097	176707	14849	9979
语文院校	Language and Literature College	2	7074	8929	30357	3162	2072
财经院校	Economics and Finance College	14	93063	102849	302936	18078	14431
政法院校	Politics and Law College	2	3643	3336	12367	980	536
体育院校	Physical Culture College	3	4919	4456	14289	1651	1035
艺术院校	Art College	6	7869	14194	38713	3878	2707
其他	Others						
总计中：普通高等职业(专科)学校	General higher vocational (technical) schools	93	472770	410697	1141557	66615	54341

19-7 中等学校情况（2023年）

Statistics on Secondary Schools (2023)

项目	Item	学校数(所) Number of Schools (unit)	毕业生数(人) Number of Graduates (person)	招生数(人) Number of New Enrollments (person)	在校学生数(人) Number of Total Enrollment (person)	教职工数(人) Number of Teachers and Staff (person)	#专任教师 Full-time Teachers
中等职业教育	**Vocational Secondary Education**	**372**	**277277**	**336508**	**965071**	**59122**	**47182**
调整后中等职业学校	Vocational Secondary Schools after Adjustment	232	163745	201585	582141	36617	28762
普通中专	General Secondary Schools	52	37421	46901	125211	6616	4639
成人中等专业学校	Specialized Secondary Schools for Adults	1	1500	1764	5280	244	210
职业高中学校	Vocational Senior Secondary Schools	87	61571	74618	212451	14799	12076
其他机构	Other Institutions	20	6868	5101	21097	846	661
附设中职班	Affiliated Vocational Class	46	6172	6539	18891		834
技工学校	**Technical Schools**	**148**	**176647**	**228488**	**658749**	**34800**	**27305**
普通中学	**Regular Secondary Schools**	**5110**	**2047688**	**2436121**	**6995324**	**769125**	**513198**
#高中	Senior Schools	1165	664568	784251	2228677	319755	172114

注：1．2011年起增加附设中职班。其他机构和附设中职班不计学校数。普通中专包括中等技术学校和中等师范学校。
2．自2020年起，九年一贯制学校教职工数计入普通初中教职工数、十二年一贯制学校及完全中学学校的教职工数计入普通高中教职工数；专任教师数则按教育层次进行归类。

Note: a) Since 2011, the item of Affiliated Vocational Class is added. The number of schools of other institutions and affiliated secondary vocational classes is not included in the total number schools of vocational secondary education. The general secondary schools include the secondary technical schools and secondary normal schools.

b)Since 2020, the number of teachers and staff in ordinary junior middle school include the number in nine-year education schools, the number of teachers and staff in ordinary high school include the number in twelve-year education school and complete secondary schools; the number of full-time teachers are grouped by education level.

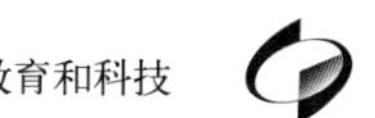

19—8 各市普通中学情况（2023年）

Statistics on Regular Secondary Schools by City (2023)

市别	City	学校数（所）Number of Schools (unit)	毕业生数（人）Number of Graduates (person)	高中 Senior Secondary Schools	初中 Junior Secondary Schools	招生数（人）Number of New Enrollments (person)
广州	Guangzhou	566	186663	53426	133237	232734
深圳	Shenzhen	554	183442	55118	128324	245090
珠海	Zhuhai	100	37982	11766	26216	47584
汕头	Shantou	316	125970	45989	79981	141565
佛山	Foshan	243	128411	43785	84626	156297
韶关	Shaoguan	153	53940	17502	36438	63955
河源	Heyuan	201	75974	24799	51175	81844
梅州	Meizhou	242	88306	29267	59039	94615
惠州	Huizhou	315	117821	37689	80132	139024
汕尾	Shanwei	169	57622	18708	38914	65979
东莞	Dongguan	268	115053	35224	79829	151493
中山	Zhongshan	117	61203	18674	42529	75922
江门	Jiangmen	203	76883	27891	48992	87130
阳江	Yangjiang	124	53089	16966	36123	65721
湛江	Zhanjiang	302	140765	43034	97731	170332
茂名	Maoming	279	150833	53383	97450	171600
肇庆	Zhaoqing	210	86600	27470	59130	96302
清远	Qingyuan	195	77988	23568	54420	99444
潮州	Chaozhou	143	47403	17133	30270	49800
揭阳	Jieyang	303	128869	47701	81168	137788
云浮	Yunfu	107	52871	15475	37396	61902
按经济区域分	By Region					
珠三角	Pearl River Delta	2576	994058	311043	683015	1231576
粤东	Eastern Region	931	359864	129531	230333	395132
粤西	Western Region	705	344687	113383	231304	407653
粤北	Northern Region	898	349079	110611	238468	401760

19－8 续表 continued

市 别	City	在校学生数（人）Number of Total Enrollment (person)	高中 Senior Secondary Schools	初中 Junior Secondary Schools	教职工数（人）Number of Teachers and Staff (person)	#专任教师 Full-time Teachers
广 州	Guangzhou	643034	183621	459413	81598	50932
深 圳	Shenzhen	669228	222909	446319	111616	54446
珠 海	Zhuhai	130500	42721	87779	13533	9903
汕 头	Shantou	416622	151912	264710	42912	30350
佛 山	Foshan	437883	142477	295406	51243	32854
韶 关	Shaoguan	185471	56025	129446	16318	13202
河 源	Heyuan	248189	85478	162711	25171	18769
梅 州	Meizhou	281309	92763	188546	26152	21523
惠 州	Huizhou	406202	124887	281315	44284	28980
汕 尾	Shanwei	197218	61579	135639	19550	13954
东 莞	Dongguan	425776	130066	295710	59787	30241
中 山	Zhongshan	211336	62055	149281	23746	14841
江 门	Jiangmen	251248	87727	163521	24188	18306
阳 江	Yangjiang	188526	59382	129144	18835	12531
湛 江	Zhanjiang	493270	144109	349161	41974	32201
茂 名	Maoming	505341	161108	344233	45478	37730
肇 庆	Zhaoqing	286542	84281	202261	28459	19709
清 远	Qingyuan	277512	82577	194935	26020	18934
潮 州	Chaozhou	150483	54227	96256	15028	11708
揭 阳	Jieyang	410266	146115	264151	38430	29610
云 浮	Yunfu	179368	52658	126710	14803	12474
按经济区域分	By Region					
珠三角	Pearl River Delta	3461749	1080744	2381005	438454	260212
粤 东	Eastern Region	1174589	413833	760756	115920	85622
粤 西	Western Region	1187137	364599	822538	106287	82462
粤 北	Northern Region	1171849	369501	802348	108464	84902

注：自2020年起，九年一贯制学校、十二年一贯制学校的教职工数计入普通中学教职工数；专任教师数则按教育层次进行归类。

Note: Since 2020, the number of teachers and staff in regular secondary schools include the number in nine-year and twelve-year education schools; the number of full-time teachers are grouped by education level.

19—9 各市中等职业教育基本情况（2023年）

Basic Statistics on Vocational Secondary Education by City (2023)

市　别	City	学校数（所）Number of Schools (unit)	毕业生数（人）Number of Graduates (person)	招生数（人）Number of New Enrollments (person)	在校学生数（人）Number of Total Enrollment (person)	教职工数（人）Number of Teachers and Staff (person)	#专任教师 Full-time Teachers
广　州	Guangzhou	75	53150	43364	148862	8509	6529
深　圳	Shenzhen	16	12338	15080	44099	4373	3009
珠　海	Zhuhai	8	6816	7060	20348	1300	1032
汕　头	Shantou	16	8780	14175	36257	2435	1958
佛　山	Foshan	28	20833	24135	69817	5514	4141
韶　关	Shaoguan	13	11186	11775	33995	2136	1888
河　源	Heyuan	15	8497	13787	36441	2097	1563
梅　州	Meizhou	14	7895	9591	25912	1241	1001
惠　州	Huizhou	26	15411	21900	59975	3329	2624
汕　尾	Shanwei	10	5159	7649	20479	1184	1033
东　莞	Dongguan	21	17105	22631	65554	4558	3521
中　山	Zhongshan	7	8090	10378	29582	1887	1568
江　门	Jiangmen	16	9906	12586	34476	2026	1778
阳　江	Yangjiang	6	5283	6567	19079	971	815
湛　江	Zhanjiang	33	20617	29555	78129	3728	3055
茂　名	Maoming	12	19590	24867	71538	4150	3544
肇　庆	Zhaoqing	14	18654	23779	66379	3437	2909
清　远	Qingyuan	14	10376	13789	38614	2395	2073
潮　州	Chaozhou	7	3160	4714	13074	784	573
揭　阳	Jieyang	12	8077	10572	30310	1927	1620
云　浮	Yunfu	9	6354	8554	22151	1141	948
按经济区域分	By Region						
珠三角	Pearl River Delta	211	162303	180913	539092	34933	27111
粤　东	Eastern Region	45	25176	37110	100120	6330	5184
粤　西	Western Region	51	45490	60989	168746	8849	7414
粤　北	Northern Region	65	44308	57496	157113	9010	7473

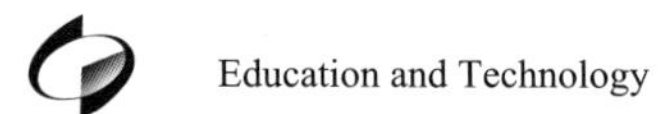

19-10 各市小学情况（2023年）
Statistics on Primary Schools by City (2023)

市别	City	学校数（所）Number of Schools (unit)	毕业生数（人）Number of Graduates (person)	招生数（人）Number of New Enrollments (person)	在校学生数（人）Number of Total Enrollment (person)	教职工数（人）Number of Teachers and Staff (person)	专任教师 Full-time Teachers
广州	Guangzhou	1008	176673	272459	1294475	63203	71311
深圳	Shenzhen	359	167112	236985	1226562	36649	69873
珠海	Zhuhai	150	30912	44550	219365	11084	11717
汕头	Shantou	721	89688	94481	581000	24166	30051
佛山	Foshan	430	106567	150410	731857	38293	39726
韶关	Shaoguan	215	44900	46651	266712	14422	15289
河源	Heyuan	347	50762	44943	288362	17577	20465
梅州	Meizhou	437	60765	59919	364293	20081	21557
惠州	Huizhou	605	99356	110684	639349	26927	33997
汕尾	Shanwei	444	45621	45231	289301	16148	17275
东莞	Dongguan	344	125950	152140	836752	36384	45064
中山	Zhongshan	214	55383	73562	378230	15842	18861
江门	Jiangmen	340	57592	71176	371238	16716	18699
阳江	Yangjiang	171	43783	42140	253738	11260	14670
湛江	Zhanjiang	914	119833	130671	788303	39059	42306
茂名	Maoming	1511	116034	112998	706660	42898	41282
肇庆	Zhaoqing	235	68383	66584	403114	18918	21523
清远	Qingyuan	354	68704	72611	426735	21523	23127
潮州	Chaozhou	495	32147	36012	212276	10608	11573
揭阳	Jieyang	1212	89090	94768	571380	29792	30173
云浮	Yunfu	184	43783	40117	255541	16019	14872
按经济区域分	By Region						
珠三角	Pearl River Delta	3685	887928	1178550	6100942	264016	330771
粤东	Eastern Region	2872	256546	270492	1653957	80714	89072
粤西	Western Region	2596	279650	285809	1748701	93217	98258
粤北	Northern Region	1537	268914	264241	1601643	89622	95310

注：自2020年起，小学教职工数仅统计小学及小学教学点的教职工数；专任教师数则按教育层次进行归类。

Note: Since 2020, the number of teachers and staff in primary school only counted the number in primary school and primary school place; The number of full-time teachers are grouped by education level.

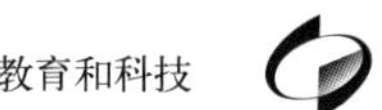

19—11 各市学龄儿童入学情况

Statistics on School-age Children Enrolled in Schools by City

市别	City	2022			2023		
		学龄儿童人数(人) Number of School-age Children (person)	已入学人数(人) Number of School-age Children Enrolled in Schools (person)	入学率(%) Enrollment Rate (%)	学龄儿童人数(人) Number of School-age Children (person)	已入学人数(人) Number of School-age Children Enrolled in Schools (person)	入学率(%) Enrollment Rate (%)
广州	Guangzhou	1183978	1183978	100.0	1272905	1272905	100.0
深圳	Shenzhen	1143995	1143995	100.0	1203935	1203935	100.0
珠海	Zhuhai	197743	197743	100.0	213969	213969	100.0
汕头	Shantou	557060	557060	100.0	558227	558227	100.0
佛山	Foshan	671336	671336	100.0	717983	717983	100.0
韶关	Shaoguan	257132	257132	100.0	259200	259200	100.0
河源	Heyuan	282371	282371	100.0	276541	276541	100.0
梅州	Meizhou	320967	317064	98.8	329572	329572	100.0
惠州	Huizhou	623819	623819	100.0	630838	630838	100.0
汕尾	Shanwei	286828	282214	98.4	280690	280690	100.0
东莞	Dongguan	818057	818058	100.0	823079	823079	100.0
中山	Zhongshan	355435	355435	100.0	373932	373932	100.0
江门	Jiangmen	348233	348233	100.0	360550	360550	100.0
阳江	Yangjiang	242902	242902	100.0	240935	240935	100.0
湛江	Zhanjiang	746423	746423	100.0	755921	755921	100.0
茂名	Maoming	682536	682533	100.0	706624	706624	100.0
肇庆	Zhaoqing	343323	343323	100.0	358563	358563	100.0
清远	Qingyuan	402645	402645	100.0	406099	406099	100.0
潮州	Chaozhou	197274	197274	100.0	200493	200493	100.0
揭阳	Jieyang	535307	535278	100.0	536551	536551	100.0
云浮	Yunfu	214024	214024	100.0	208219	208219	100.0
按经济区域分	By Region						
珠三角	Pearl River Delta	5685919	5685920	100.0	5955754	5955754	100.0
粤东	Eastern Region	1576469	1571826	99.7	1575961	1575961	100.0
粤西	Western Region	1671861	1671858	100.0	1703480	1703480	100.0
粤北	Northern Region	1477139	1473236	99.7	1479631	1479631	100.0

注：学龄人口数取校内外学龄人口6—11岁人口数；已入学人数取在校学龄人口6—11岁人口数。

Note: The School-age population is the School-age population inside and outside school aged 6-11; the Primary School Enrollment number is the School-age population aged 6-11.

19-12 研究与试验发展(R&D)基本情况

Basic Statistics on Research and Development (R&D)

指　　标	Item	2010	2015	2020	2022	2023
研究与试验发展(R&D)活动人员 (人)	**Number of R&D Personnel (person)**	**446579**	**680237**	**1175441**	**1339797**	**1582687**
按活动主体分组	By Activity Subject					
政府属科研机构	Basic Statistics on Research and Development Institutions under Government Departments	9488	15739	30356	35461	39032
高等学校	Higher Education	33865	57346	85733	104249	133090
企业	Enterprises	359476	534293	1036259	1172752	1379000
其他	Others	43750	72859	23093	27335	31565
研究与试验发展(R&D)经费内部支出 (亿元)	**Internal Expenditure on R&D (100 million yuan)**	**808.75**	**1798.17**	**3479.88**	**4411.90**	**4802.62**
按活动主体分组	By Activity Subject					
政府属科研机构	Basic Statistics on Research and Development Institutions under Government Departments	21.35	63.98	180.04	206.99	202.58
高等学校	Higher Education	28.58	62.97	202.94	238.46	259.17
企业	Enterprises	703.68	1520.55	2998.60	3841.61	4184.47
其他	Others	55.14	150.67	98.31	124.84	156.39
按活动类型分组	By Activity Type					
基础研究	Basic Research	16.72	54.21	204.10	239.62	266.74
应用研究	Applied Research	37.32	165.00	319.89	415.74	359.57
试验发展	Experimental Development	754.70	1478.96	2955.90	3756.54	4176.3

19−13 公有经济企业、事业单位专业技术人员年末人数

Number of Professional and Technical Personnel in State-owned Enterprises and Institutions at the Year-end

单位：人 (person)

年份 Year	专业技术人员 Professional and Technical Personnel	#工程技术人员 Engineering	#农业技术人员 Agriculture	#科学技术人员 Scientific Research	#卫生技术人员 Health Care	#教学人员 Teaching
1978	211149	48836	16017	7852	53068	80287
1979	211117	48641	16975	7277	53155	79748
1980	291939	56144	18176	7356	61445	86192
1981	303892	60071	19017	6763	63536	97109
1982	328455	70699	19431	7822	69056	102178
1983	547038	85327	21636	5744	74183	109210
1984	579740	89348	22505	5573	79806	120016
1985	642542	102506	23030	6431	86174	133013
1986	656380	108210	23854	6368	89545	313009
1987	664085	118601	23553	6231	93553	333245
1988	674085	119167	19478	4904	85092	313419
1989	810130	137803	20644	5986	90751	364965
1990	838403	145535	21194	5731	92912	379894
1991	814651	140906	13050	4810	93141	398276
1992	883821	149916	13749	4566	104334	412681
1993	957725	163440	14246	4388	117959	434036
1994	1017804	174960	14670	4118	128079	460702
1995	1077848	180530	15219	4425	134586	511418
1996	1167583	186156	15449	4610	147155	573934
1997	1223897	191954	15779	4443	156889	613121
1998	1262343	190486	15703	4413	165721	649873
1999	1291078	184304	15660	4585	171461	677110
2000	1297804	180223	15083	4705	175521	696005
2001	1285708	168354	14151	4467	181703	710967
2002	1274140	160458	13386	4425	184192	721719
2003	1264983	135621	12575	4918	202548	734721
2004	1374679	149214	17321	5253	238886	774022
2005	1399042	146411	17407	5434	248547	791255
2006	1375416	137802	16999	5163	246679	805397
2007	1391934	140828	17311	5711	246480	824462
2008	1419852	144941	16701	5745	260940	837059
2009	1462861	153563	15805	5984	268796	856665
2010	1458044	149724	14084	4551	259131	885446
2011	1448011	151700	13475	5260	253992	879621
2012	1459018	151998	12256	5021	264976	861104
2013	1455605	139807	12538	3813	269147	888962
2014	1493095	155964	12772	5850	283499	888862
2015	1449255	139817	16076	6139	288384	928348
2016	1486082	151883	16681	7340	308402	893189
2017	1551010	169994	13161	10992	306208	897089
2018	1643815	178876	12111	12286	298778	883820
2019	1560074	195106	12001	7752	301505	901015
2020	1604988	214557	12214	8900	308073	913578
2021	1619331	215319	10926	6071	313637	924604
2022	1686386	246043	12223	4623	318987	942882
2023	1735136	255687	12670	6112	324584	965629

注：本表未包中央单位专业技术人员数。
Note: Data in this table do not include professional and technical personnel from the central units stationed in Guangdong.

19－14 高层次人才情况

Statistics on High-level Talents

单位：人 (person)

项　目	Item	2000	2005	2010	2015	2021	2022	2023
享受国家津贴新增人数	Number of Persons Granted State Allowances	164		137				133
高级职称批准人数	Number of Persons with Senior Professional Titles	6111	19336	19031	16581	36756	47679	64592
博士后招收人数	Number of Persons in Working Stations for Post-doctoral Research	163	380	560	1297	4427	4519	5768
博士生情况	Status of Doctorate Students							
招生数	Number of New Enrollments	1053	2802	3307	3540	7023	7687	8445
在校生	Number of Enrolled Students	2558	9049	12341	14474	25020	27906	30877
毕业生	Number of Graduates	417	1342	2436	2947	3735	4506	5180

注：享受国家津贴的人数从2003年起逢双年评比一次。
Note: The number of persons granted state allowances has been appraised every double-digital year since 2003.

19－15 各类技术合同签订情况

Statistics on Technical Contracts Signed by Type

项　目	Item	2000	2005	2010	2015	2021	2022	2023
技术合同项目数（项）	**Number of Technical Contracts (item)**	**5464**	**14432**	**17558**	**17344**	**49261**	**47892**	**49604**
技术开发合同	Technical Development Contracts	921	5983	11629	13786	19366	19054	21244
技术咨询合同	Technical Consultation Contracts	572	1279	1649	430	5699	3606	2872
技术转让合同	Technical Transfer Contracts	297	639	868	1242	2083	2446	1676
技术许可合同	Technology License Contract							881
技术服务合同	Technical Service Contracts	3674	6531	3412	1886	22113	22786	22931
技术合同金额（万元）	**Value of Technical Contracts (10000 yuan)**	**482104**	**1124740**	**2425045**	**6635253**	**42927258**	**45254248**	**44381271**
技术开发合同	Technical Development Contracts	142107	571458	1961788	2359626	14024662	15936000	17104340
技术咨询合同	Technical Consultation Contracts	12530	31696	48539	17050	417379	457788	233859
技术转让合同	Technical Transfer Contracts	110279	288881	344264	2923722	7683299	5576242	3346451
技术许可合同	Technology License Contract							1538794
技术服务合同	Technical Service Contracts	217188	232705	70454	1334855	20801917	23284218	22157827

19–16 科技成果项数

Number of Achievements for Scientific and Technological Research

单位：项 (item)

项　目	Item	2000	2005	2010	2015	2021	2022	2023
国家级科技奖励成果	**National Prizes for Scientific and Technological Research Achievements**	**24**	**15**	**36**	**32**			**53**
国际合作奖	National Cooperation Prize							
国家发明奖	National Invention Prize		1	2	5			9
国家自然科学奖	National Prize for Natural Sciences		1	1	5			6
国家科技进步奖	National Prize for Progress in Science and Technology	24	13	33	22			38
省级重大科技成果	**Major Provincial Scientific and Technological Achievements**				**2133**	**2546**	**2601**	**1736**
基础理论成果	Achievements in Fundamental Theory				126	602	605	385
应用技术成果	Achievements in Applied Technology				1990	1779	1787	1209
软科学成果	Achievements in Soft Sciences				17	165	209	142
省级科技奖励成果	**Provincial Prizes for Scientific and Technological Achievements**	**265**	**288**	**260**	**237**	**176**	**190**	**192**
省科技进步奖	Provincial Prize for Progress in Science and Technology	265	288	260	237	142	132	132
农业方面	Agriculture	46	51	31	31	11	10	10
工业方面	Industry	113	117	145	148	96	86	88
医药卫生方面	Medicine and Health Care	72	68	65	42	31	30	32
其他	Others	34	52	19	16	4	6	2

注：省级重大科技成果为全社会口径。
Note: Data of major provincial scientific and technological achievements are the whole society caliber.

19–17 县级政府部门属研究与开发机构基本情况

Basic Statistics on Research and Development Institutions under Government Departments at County Level

项　目	Item	2000	2005	2010	2015	2021	2022	2023
机构数 (个)	Number of Institutions (unit)	183	166	143	124	90	82	78
职工总数 (人)	Number of Staff and Workers(person)	4379	3433	2798	2054	1517	1326	1181
科技活动人员(人)	Scientists and Engineers (person)			1390	1119	1120	984	960
经费收入 (万元)	Funds (10000 yuan)	13409	12229	16592	27162	37671	31421	32505
#来自政府的经费	Government Funds	5426	5187	9605	17467	27776	25670	29601

19-18 县级以上政府部门属研究与开发机构基本情况
Basic Statistics on Research and Development Institutions under Government Departments at and above County Level

项目	Item	2000	2005	2010	2015	2021	2022	2023
总计	**Total**							
机构数 (个)	Number of Institutions (unit)	296	192	181	184	196	192	187
职工总数 (人)	Number of Staff and Workers (person)	24926	14216	16922	22582	33417	33387	34078
科技活动人员 (人)	Scientists and Engineers			12819	17929	30496	29912	31177
经费收入 (万元)	Funds (10000 yuan)	358844	384866	665228	1450489	2934065	2474107	2457409
#政府拨款	Government Appropriations	98386	153946	332815	781376	2172171	1769817	1653489
经费支出 (万元)	Expenditures (10000 yuan)	330098	363973	674994	1363744	2712108	2542894	2432439
科技经费支出(万元)	Expenditures on Purchase of Assets(10000 yuan)			408216	962263	2475991	2334988	2230825
自然科学及技术领域	**Natural Sciences and Technology**							
机构数 (个)	Number of Institutions (unit)	263	163	156	158	176	171	166
职工总数 (人)	Number of Staff and Workers (person)	23623	13026	15601	21011	31816	31750	32453
科技活动人员 (人)	Scientists and Engineers			11738	16675	29020	28381	29661
经费收入 (万元)	Funds (10000 yuan)	345582	360334	626119	1375436	2834725	2370984	2357864
#政府拨款	Government Appropriations	89595	137906	306735	728278	2091386	1682902	1575432
经费支出 (万元)	Expenditures (10000 yuan)	317219	341823	634843	1297806	2610756	2437020	2324111
科技经费支出(万元)	Expenditures on Purchase of Assets(10000 yuan)			378555	919010	2394432	2254960	2150537
社会及人文科学领域	**Social Sciences and Humanities**							
机构数 (个)	Number of Institutions (unit)	16	13	10	10	11	12	12
职工总数 (人)	Number of Staff and Workers (person)	780	655	645	675	1045	1084	1090
科技活动人员 (人)	Scientists and Engineers			567	616	928	980	985
经费收入 (万元)	Funds (10000 yuan)	6906	10914	18906	32129	72870	78231	76157
#政府拨款	Government Appropriations	5908	9370	14003	26643	64383	70197	62699
经费支出 (万元)	Expenditures (10000 yuan)	6897	10207	17585	30830	74386	79306	83221
科技经费支出(万元)	Expenditures on Purchase of Assets(10000 yuan)			14334	23636	57684	56714	58267
科技情报和文献机构	**Scientific-Technological Information and Literature Institutions**							
机构数 (个)	Number of Institutions (unit)	17	16	15	16	9	9	9
职工总数 (人)	Number of Staff and Workers (person)	523	535	676	896	556	553	535
科技活动人员 (人)	Scientists and Engineers			514	638	548	551	531
经费收入 (万元)	Funds (10000 yuan)	6356	13619	20203	42923	26470	24893	23389
#政府拨款	Government Appropriations	2883	6670	12078	26455	16402	16718	15358
经费支出 (万元)	Expenditures (10000 yuan)	5982	11944	22566	35108	26966	26568	25108
科技经费支出(万元)	Expenditures on Purchase of Assets(10000 yuan)			15327	19618	23875	23313	22022

19－19　各市县级及以上政府部门属研究与开发机构基本情况

Basic Statistics on Research and Development Institutions under Government Departments at and above County Level by City

市 别	City	2022						
		机构数(个) Number of Institutions (unit)	就业人员(人) Number of Employed Persons (person)	#科技活动人员(人) R&D Personnel (person)	经费收入(万元) Funds (10000 yuan)	#政府拨款 Government Appropriations	经费支出(万元) Expenditures (10000 yuan)	科技经费支出(万元) R&D Expenditure (10000 yuan)
全 省	**Provincial Total**	**274**	**34713**	**30896**	**2505528**	**1795487**	**2575425**	**2360266**
广 州	Guangzhou	89	20487	18405	1494958	920068	1529699	1377904
深 圳	Shenzhen	14	6068	5383	408821	306802	394753	367012
珠 海	Zhuhai	3	323	291	22485	21211	49717	45145
汕 头	Shantou	12	548	494	66720	65657	71059	69038
佛 山	Foshan	7	1164	1117	104290	102143	149345	145498
韶 关	Shaoguan	15	327	281	8974	7135	9187	7156
河 源	Heyuan	10	130	101	1775	1691	1775	1524
梅 州	Meizhou	22	348	311	8970	8230	9113	7423
惠 州	Huizhou	15	666	639	74958	83054	58061	56434
汕 尾	Shanwei	5	81	67	3392	3384	2076	1887
东 莞	Dongguan	11	2222	1866	105992	79424	141858	132979
中 山	Zhongshan	2	143	117	5385	4698	5236	4341
江 门	Jiangmen	9	245	174	8723	7057	9089	6963
阳 江	Yangjiang	4	163	145	12982	12485	10892	10557
湛 江	Zhanjiang	14	955	772	153484	146492	105465	101986
茂 名	Maoming	10	232	188	7594	6951	7804	6234
肇 庆	Zhaoqing	11	166	143	4887	4754	5862	5118
清 远	Qingyuan	6	68	58	1538	1377	1511	1020
潮 州	Chaozhou	6	163	147	4924	4837	4661	4044
揭 阳	Jieyang	6	154	144	2496	2458	2631	2395
云 浮	Yunfu	3	60	53	2183	5581	5635	5612

19－19 续表 continued

市别	City	2023 机构数(个) Number of Institutions (unit)	就业人员(人) Number of Employed Persons (person)	#科技活动人员(人) R&D Personnel (person)	经费收入(万元) Funds (10000 yuan)	#政府拨款 Government Appropr-iations	经费支出(万元) Expenditures (10000 yuan)	科技经费支出(万元) R&D Expenditure (10000 yuan)
全省合计	**Provincial Total**	**265**	**35259**	**32137**	**2489914**	**1683089**	**2469596**	**2260104**
广州	Guangzhou	86	21010	19371	1515536	922836	1492538	1358195
深圳	Shenzhen	16	6413	5826	455944	322969	463759	425935
珠海	Zhuhai	3	346	317	53729	52160	57231	54676
汕头	Shantou	11	520	485	24819	24025	27039	24932
佛山	Foshan	7	1152	1050	92961	73268	101048	97095
韶关	Shaoguan	13	278	237	9294	6752	9370	7155
河源	Heyuan	9	110	83	1517	1419	1473	1196
梅州	Meizhou	21	326	294	9747	8767	10539	9001
惠州	Huizhou	14	344	317	15535	14332	31697	30579
汕尾	Shanwei	6	107	87	7723	7674	5225	4797
东莞	Dongguan	10	2350	2066	142539	100194	125244	111165
中山	Zhongshan	2	119	104	5630	3996	6729	5863
江门	Jiangmen	9	242	184	8482	6599	8901	7317
阳江	Yangjiang	4	197	182	8125	3768	10435	10087
湛江	Zhanjiang	14	981	821	117245	111032	90843	86986
茂名	Maoming	10	224	215	7364	10433	11568	10894
肇庆	Zhaoqing	11	167	150	5802	5662	6253	5519
清远	Qingyuan	6	84	77	1546	1353	1534	1191
潮州	Chaozhou	5	107	94	2668	2378	4230	3887
揭阳	Jieyang	5	137	137	2530	2496	2636	2411
云浮	Yunfu	3	45	40	1179	975	1305	1222

19-20 三种专利申请量与授权量

Three Types of Patent Application and Granted

单位：件 (item)

年份 Year	申请量 Number of Patent Applications	发明 Inventions	实用新型 Utility Models	外观设计 Designs	授权量 Number of Patent Applic-ations Granted	发明 Inventions	实用新型 Utility Models	外观设计 Designs
1990	1948	231	1001	716	889	40	571	278
1995	7729	463	2367	4899	4611	57	1446	3108
2000	21123	1760	6033	13330	15799	261	4797	10741
2001	27596	2549	8144	16903	18259	301	5246	12712
2002	34339	3806	9972	20561	22760	351	6396	16013
2003	43186	6181	12985	24020	29235	953	7921	20361
2004	52201	8093	14682	29426	31446	1941	9307	20198
2005	72220	12887	18951	40382	36894	1876	11017	24001
2006	90886	21351	23886	45649	43516	2441	15644	25431
2007	102449	26692	25389	50368	56451	3714	21636	31101
2008	103883	28099	28883	46901	62031	7604	25072	29355
2009	125673	32247	39027	54399	83621	11355	27438	44828
2010	152907	40866	47706	64335	119346	13691	43901	61754
2011	196275	52012	67336	76927	128415	18242	51402	58771
2012	229514	60448	78731	90335	153598	22153	65946	65499
2013	264265	68990	93592	101683	170430	20084	77503	72843
2014	278351	75148	96136	107067	179953	22276	83202	74475
2015	355939	103941	135717	116281	241176	33477	105254	102445
2016	505667	155581	203609	146477	259032	38626	118157	102249
2017	627819	182639	283560	161620	332648	45740	169017	117891
2018	793819	216469	367938	209412	478082	53259	268508	156315
2019	807700	203311	369143	235246	527389	59742	282740	184907
2020	967204	215926	470055	281223	709725	70695	380882	258148
2021	980634	242551	456220	281863	872209	102850	484320	285039
2022	993480	236957	465463	291060	837276	115080	457716	264480
2023	963732	240223	427462	296047	703695	143141	324931	235623

注：2017年起，专利申请量统计口径调整为国家知识产权局受理的按规定缴足申请费、符合进入初步审查阶段条件的专利申请数量，2017年前，该口径数据称为专利申请受理量。

Note: Starting from 2017, the statistic for the number of patent applications accepted only includes patents that have passed initial review conditions and paid application fees as stipulated by the State Intellectual Property Office. Data before 2017 of this coverage were named as number of patent applications accepted. Since 2020, the State Intellectual Property Office will no longer feed back the data of patent applications in each province.

19−21 分市全社会研究与试验发展人员与经费

Personnel and Intramural Expenditure on R&D by City

市 别	City	2022			
		R&D活动人员 (人) Number of R&D Personnel (person)	#企业 Enterprises	R&D经费内部支出 (亿元) Internal Expenditure on R&D(100 million yuan)	#企业 Enterprises
全 省	**Provincial Total**	**1339797**	**1172752**	**4411.90**	**3841.61**
广 州	Guangzhou	278740	175695	988.36	625.02
深 圳	Shenzhen	466248	444557	1880.49	1786.01
珠 海	Zhuhai	45746	41935	118.07	111.66
汕 头	Shantou	16140	12946	36.28	26.46
佛 山	Foshan	101655	94930	359.53	330.49
韶 关	Shaoguan	7162	5411	13.94	12.35
河 源	Heyuan	5206	4919	8.26	7.81
梅 州	Meizhou	3417	2346	8.08	4.68
惠 州	Huizhou	85352	82935	185.71	176.38
汕 尾	Shanwei	2508	2231	9.85	9.76
东 莞	Dongguan	186715	180823	458.72	439.92
中 山	Zhongshan	43245	40777	100.66	94.92
江 门	Jiangmen	35792	33578	91.40	81.40
阳 江	Yangjiang	3552	3023	8.07	7.53
湛 江	Zhanjiang	10436	4498	31.97	24.76
茂 名	Maoming	8510	6338	14.92	10.60
肇 庆	Zhaoqing	15826	13512	37.37	35.15
清 远	Qingyuan	9396	9117	22.06	21.08
潮 州	Chaozhou	3669	3202	8.01	6.21
揭 阳	Jieyang	6161	5998	22.99	22.88
云 浮	Yunfu	4321	3981	7.16	6.54

19−21 续表 continued

市 别	City	2023			
		R&D活动人员（人）Number of R&D Personnel (person)	#企业 Enterprises	R&D经费内部支出（亿元）Internal Expenditure on R&D(100 million yuan)	#企业 Enterprises
全 省	**Provincial Total**	**1582687**	**1379000**	**4802.62**	**4184.47**
广 州	Guangzhou	349873	223563	1042.99	686.57
深 圳	Shenzhen	551528	521495	2236.61	2086.61
珠 海	Zhuhai	66388	62765	171.79	165.02
汕 头	Shantou	17424	13406	38.06	25.47
佛 山	Foshan	119125	112340	280.48	250.91
韶 关	Shaoguan	9397	7558	16.06	13.76
河 源	Heyuan	5236	4916	6.08	5.70
梅 州	Meizhou	4210	3148	7.99	5.10
惠 州	Huizhou	86228	84058	174.19	168.72
汕 尾	Shanwei	2732	2467	8.49	8.08
东 莞	Dongguan	191264	184554	447.80	431.92
中 山	Zhongshan	57908	55113	127.17	116.45
江 门	Jiangmen	40086	37589	79.79	72.30
阳 江	Yangjiang	5300	4695	13.53	12.56
湛 江	Zhanjiang	14435	5836	41.26	33.63
茂 名	Maoming	11221	8781	15.12	11.36
肇 庆	Zhaoqing	22583	20236	46.92	45.14
清 远	Qingyuan	12297	12039	20.92	20.05
潮 州	Chaozhou	4574	4110	8.66	6.83
揭 阳	Jieyang	5706	5490	11.17	11.09
云 浮	Yunfu	5172	4841	7.55	7.21

19-22 规模以上工业企业的科技活动基本情况

Basic Statistics on Science and Technology Activities of Industrial Enterprises above Designated size

指标		Item		2020	2021	2022
企业基本情况		**Statistics on Industrial Enterprises**				
有R&D活动企业数	(个)	Number of Enterprises with R&D Activities	(unit)	23081	26688	22742
有R&D活动企业所占比重	(%)	Percentage of Enterprises with R&D Activities	(%)	39.5	40.3	33.1
R&D活动情况		**Statistics on R&D Activities**				
R&D人员全时当量	(万人年)	Full-time Equivalent of R&D Personnel	(10 000 man-years)	70.00	70.91	77.26
R&D经费支出	(亿元)	Expenditure on R&D	(100 million yuan)	2499.95	2902.18	3217.75
R&D经费支出与主营业务收入之比	(%)	Percentage of Expenditure on R&D to Sales Revenue	(%)	1.67	1.67	1.79
R&D项目数	(项)	R&D Projects	(item)	132120	146858	116888
R&D项目经费支出	(亿元)	Expenditure on R&D Projects	(100 million yuan)	2566.01	3091.68	3554.68
企业办R&D机构情况		**Statistics on R&D Institutions**				
机构数	(个)	Number of R&D Institutions	(units)	28262	32938	32434
机构人员数	(万人)	R&D Personnel	(10 000 persons)	108.99	122.41	110.99
机构经费支出	(亿元)	Expenditure on R&D	(100 million yuan)	4274.02	5046.84	4068.20
新产品开发及生产情况		Statistics on New Products Development and Production				
新产品开发项目数	(个)	Number of New Products	(unit)	166140	201009	221782
新产品开发经费支出	(亿元)	Expenditure on New Products Development	100 million yuan)	4127.13	4636.98	5159.47
新产品销售收入	(亿元)	Sales Revenue of New Products	(100 million yuan)	44313.05	49684.90	48075.11
#新产品出口		Export		13132.99	14296.30	13011.14
专利情况		**Statistics on Patents**				
专利申请数	(件)	Number of Patent Applications	(piece)	305665	340935	354470
#发明专利		Inventions		127497	139727	149075
有效发明专利数	(件)	Number of Inventions in Force	(piece)	435509	511717	572589
技术获取和技术改造情况		**Statistics on Technology Acquisition and Technology Reconstruction**				
引进国外技术经费支出	(亿元)	Expenditure for Acquisition of Foreign Technology	(100 million yuan)	211.15	167.28	100.95
引进技术消化吸收经费支出	(亿元)	Expenditure for Assimilation of Technology	(100 million yuan)	2.99	2.70	2.25
购买国内技术经费支出	(亿元)	Expenditure for Purchase of Domestic Technology	(100 million yuan)	233.89	152.77	153.85
技术改造经费支出	(亿元)	Expenditure for Technical Renovation	(100 million yuan)	668.89	612.70	541.34

19-23 规模以上工业企业研究与发展经费内部支出

Internal Expenditures of Industrial Enterprises Above Designated Size

单位：亿元 (100 million yuan)

指　　标	Item	2020	2021	2022
总　计	**Totals**	**2499.95**	**2902.18**	**3217.75**
按登记注册类型分	**By Status of Registration**			
内资企业	Domestic Funded	1892.69	2179.69	2404.00
国有企业	State-owned Enterprises	7.25	12.39	5.20
集体企业	Collective-owned Enterprises	0.46	0.17	0.14
股份合作企业	Cooperative Enterprises	0.67	0.27	0.14
联营企业	Joint Ownership Enterprises	0.18	0.30	0.29
有限责任公司	Limited Liability Enterprises	780.31	897.35	1066.90
#国有独资	State Sole Funded Corporations	28.23	27.38	30.41
股份有限公司	Share-holding Corporations Limited	315.07	319.91	367.87
私营企业	Private Enterprises	788.74	949.17	963.02
其他企业	Other Enterprises	0.01	0.13	0.44
港、澳、台商投资企业	Enterprises with Funds from Hong Kong,Macao, and Taiwan	332.32	360.15	427.96
外商投资企业	Foreign Funded Enterprises	274.95	362.34	385.80
按企业规模分	**By Size of Enterprises**			
大型企业	Large Enterprises	1429.55	1684.46	1940.26
中型企业	Medium-sized Enterprises	487.25	549.18	599.92
小微型企业	Small Enterprises	583.15	668.55	677.57
按行业分	**By Industry**			
采矿业	**Mining**	**6.91**	**7.34**	**12.51**
煤炭开采和洗选业	Mining and Washing of Coal			
石油和天然气开采业	Extraction Petroleum and Natural Gas	5.29	4.87	8.67
黑色金属矿采选业	Mining and Processing of Ferrous Metal Ores	…	0.02	0.03
有色金属矿采选业	Mining and Processing of Non-ferrous Metal Ores	0.57	1.28	1.50
非金属矿采选业	Mining and Processing of Non-metal Ores	0.60	0.85	1.56
开采辅助活动	Support Activities for Mining	0.45	0.33	0.74
其他采矿业	Mining of Other Ores			
制造业	**Manufacturing**	**2461.82**	**2862.10**	**3163.55**
农副食品加工业	Processing of Food from Agricultural Products	23.70	22.69	24.54
食品制造业	Manufacture of Foods	20.40	21.44	20.90
酒、饮料和精制茶制造业	Manufacture of Liquor, Beverages and Refined Tea	4.47	4.75	6.70
烟草制品业	Manufacture of Tobacco	4.16	2.10	2.97
纺织业	Manufacture of Textile	10.86	12.54	10.75
纺织服装、服饰业	Manufacture of Textile, Wearing Apparel, and Accessories	13.59	15.14	17.39

19－23　续表　continued

单位：亿元　(100 million yuan)

指　　标	Item	2020	2021	2022
皮革、毛皮、羽毛及其制品和制鞋业	Manufacture of Leather, Fur, Feather and Related Products and Footwear	11.69	12.68	14.30
木材加工和木、竹、藤、棕、草制品业	Processing of Timber, Manufacture of Wood,Bamboo, Rattan, Palm and Straw Products	3.72	6.53	3.83
家具制造业	Manufacture of Furniture	26.34	30.03	29.33
造纸和纸制品业	Manufacture of Paper and Paper Products	14.37	17.83	17.36
印刷和记录媒介复制业	Printing and Reproduction of Recording Media	18.48	13.56	19.19
文教、工美、体育和娱乐用品制造业	Manufacture of Articles for Culture, Education, Arts and Crafts, Sport and Entertainment Activities	12.89	14.62	13.30
石油加工、炼焦和核燃料加工业	Processing of Petroleum, Coking and Processing of Nuclear Fuel	4.72	5.54	4.56
化学原料和化学制品制造业	Manufacture of Raw Chemical Materials and Chemical Products	47.14	61.39	59.32
医药制造业	Manufacture of Medicines	58.73	80.35	96.06
化学纤维制造业	Manufacture of Chemical Fibers	2.10	3.10	1.71
橡胶和塑料制品业	Manufacture of Rubber and Plastics Products	83.57	97.23	97.72
非金属矿物制品业	Manufacture of Non-metallic Mineral Products	35.71	44.95	38.97
黑色金属冶炼和压延加工业	Smelting and Pressing of Ferrous Metals	9.36	11.09	19.41
有色金属冶炼和压延加工业	Smelting and Pressing of Non-ferrous Metals	11.68	18.81	16.62
金属制品业	Manufacture of Metal Products	78.04	98.64	101.54
通用设备制造业	Manufacture of General Purpose Machinery	105.36	121.34	124.23
专用设备制造业	Manufacture of Special Purpose Machinery	122.58	133.32	160.85
汽车制造业	Manufacture of Automobiles	129.57	169.51	226.79
铁路、船舶、航空航天和其他运输设备制造业	Manufacture of Railway, Ship, Aerospace and Other Transport Equipment	22.79	26.19	20.38
电气机械和器材制造业	Manufacture of Electrical Machinery and Apparatus	342.93	364.99	405.64
计算机、通信和其他电子设备制造业	Manufacture of Computers, Communication and Other Electronic Equipment	1182.61	1392.61	1539.58
仪器仪表制造业	Manufacture of Measuring Instruments and Machinery	45.71	43.32	51.63
其他制造业	Other Manufacture	7.26	8.17	8.09
废弃资源综合利用业	Utilization of Waste Resources	3.34	4.32	5.88
金属制品、机械和设备修理业	Repair Service of Metal Products, Machinery and Equipment	3.96	3.34	4.01
电力、热力、燃气及水生产和供应业	**Production and Supply of Electric Power, Heat Power, and Water**	**31.22**	**32.74**	**41.70**
电力、热力生产和供应业	Production and Supply of Electric Power and Heat Power	19.88	22.23	27.04
燃气生产和供应业	Production and Supply of Gas	7.22	7.19	10.91
水的生产和供应业	Production and Supply of Water	4.11	3.32	3.75

19-24 分市规模以上工业企业R&D活动人员和经费

R&D Personnel and Expenditure of Industrial Enterprises by City

市别	City	R&D活动人员(人) Number of R&D Personnel (person)			R&D经费内部支出(亿元) Internal Expenditure on R&D(100 million yuan)		
		2020	2021	2022	2020	2021	2022
全省	**Provincial Total**	**911222**	**957403**	**1026944**	**2499.95**	**2902.18**	**3217.75**
广州	Guangzhou	105364	96735	116321	315.11	377.92	401.00
深圳	Shenzhen	345344	351055	380604	1157.31	1259.73	1491.38
珠海	Zhuhai	34522	29707	36860	93.94	84.41	94.42
汕头	Shantou	11822	10549	11052	18.45	20.93	20.53
佛山	Foshan	98761	93184	91194	238.86	298.07	305.48
韶关	Shaoguan	5870	5587	5305	13.13	14.05	11.90
河源	Heyuan	2180	5182	4836	4.26	8.68	7.61
梅州	Meizhou	1574	2530	2257	2.77	5.61	3.88
惠州	Huizhou	57344	70360	81864	115.26	157.30	170.23
汕尾	Shanwei	1731	1603	2227	6.08	8.25	9.57
东莞	Dongguan	135841	175876	173176	308.42	405.61	411.00
中山	Zhongshan	32129	33794	39942	68.03	75.16	91.33
江门	Jiangmen	37269	37617	33327	70.13	82.33	73.21
阳江	Yangjiang	2045	2372	2938	5.23	4.46	7.29
湛江	Zhanjiang	2454	2763	4144	9.85	10.65	23.90
茂名	Maoming	6452	5868	5727	10.11	10.10	8.63
肇庆	Zhaoqing	10340	11159	13478	21.19	26.69	34.73
清远	Qingyuan	7831	8739	8875	14.01	19.71	19.11
潮州	Chaozhou	3692	3326	3194	4.57	5.84	4.68
揭阳	Jieyang	6606	5903	5818	20.82	20.22	22.74
云浮	Yunfu	2051	3494	3805	2.43	6.45	5.13
按经济区域分	By Region						
珠三角	Pearl River Delta	856914	899487	966766	2388.24	2767.22	3072.79
粤东	Eastern Region	23851	21381	22291	49.92	55.24	57.52
粤西	Western Region	10951	11003	12809	25.18	25.22	39.81
粤北	Northern Region	19506	25532	25078	36.60	54.50	47.63

19-25 分市规模以上工业企业新产品开发与销售情况(2022年)

New Products Development and Sale by Industrial Enterprises by City(2022)

单位：亿元 (100 million yuan)

市别	City	新产品开发项目数(项) New Products (unit)	新产品开发经费支出 Expenditure on New Products Development	新产品销售收入 Sale Revenue of New Products	#出口 Exports
全省	**Provincial Total**	**221782**	**5159.47**	**48075.11**	**13011.14**
广州	Guangzhou	26824	567.02	6653.26	836.67
深圳	Shenzhen	64256	2399.24	15400.83	5750.80
珠海	Zhuhai	7382	171.90	1969.56	615.11
汕头	Shantou	3297	35.60	452.83	87.73
佛山	Foshan	28253	490.67	5448.51	1099.56
韶关	Shaoguan	1602	28.26	226.70	34.24
河源	Heyuan	1360	13.91	169.89	43.00
梅州	Meizhou	702	10.23	155.75	16.49
惠州	Huizhou	13467	245.50	3319.96	1210.46
汕尾	Shanwei	288	14.15	174.01	58.19
东莞	Dongguan	36897	663.02	8856.10	2010.01
中山	Zhongshan	13009	156.42	1592.67	534.38
江门	Jiangmen	10331	120.25	1397.64	419.68
阳江	Yangjiang	662	41.47	137.21	16.61
湛江	Zhanjiang	1303	34.06	245.62	11.67
茂名	Maoming	1022	15.45	116.77	10.24
肇庆	Zhaoqing	4517	57.05	659.60	59.65
清远	Qingyuan	2627	45.57	698.52	123.52
潮州	Chaozhou	1232	10.70	117.14	35.53
揭阳	Jieyang	1877	28.18	196.18	17.90
云浮	Yunfu	874	10.81	86.35	19.70
按经济区域分	By Region				
珠三角	Pearl River Delta	204936	4871.07	45298.13	12536.32
粤东	Eastern Region	6694	88.62	940.16	199.34
粤西	Western Region	2987	90.99	499.60	38.52
粤北	Northern Region	7165	108.79	1337.22	236.96

19–26 科协机构及活动情况

Statistics on Associations for Science and Technology and Their Activities

项　目	Item	2000	2005	2010	2015	2022	2023
科协机构　（个）	**Number of Associations for Science and Technology (unit)**	**357**	**196**	**1026**	**142**	**141**	**141**
省科协	Provincial Associations	1	1	1	1	1	1
市科协	City Associations	21	21	21	21	21	21
县(市、区)科协	County (County-level City, District)Associations	123	120	121	120	119	119
厂矿科协	Factory and Mine Associations	212	54	883			
各级学会　（个）	**Number of Learned Societies (unit)**	**880**	**953**	**931**	**2417**	**1783**	**1804**
省级学会	Provincial Learned Societies	146	**151**	151	151	206	222
市级学会	City Learned Societies	734	802	780	838	1042	1069
县级学会	County Learned Societies				1428	535	513
农村专业技术协会　（个）	**Rural Specialized Technological Societies (unit)**	**2900**	**1948**	**1440**	**1360**	**332**	**222**
科协活动开展情况	**Activities of Associations for Science and Technology**						
举办各类学术交流会（次）	Number of Academic Meetings Held (time)	4769	1232	677	1466	2000	2224
举办科技科普展览（次）	Number of Scientific and Technological Popularization Exhibitions Lectures (time)	2258	2319	3582	1561	1078	1332
青少年科技竞赛（次）	Number of Scientific and Technological Competitions for Adolescents (time)	1286	760	407	327	276	326
参加科协各类活动人次（万人次）	**Number of Participants in Activities Organized by Associations for Science and Technology (person-time)**	**836.76**	**871.69**	**1116.45**	**864.15**	**13617.56**	**12080.00**
参加各类学术交流会	Number of Participants in Academic Meetings	50.52	17.00	29.50	33.57	965.90	665.57
参加各类科技培训	Number of Participants in Training Programs	65.47	46.95	25.20	32.59	26.19	13.19
参加各类科普活动	Number of Participants in Scientific and Technological Popularization Activities	720.77	807.74	1061.75	797.99	12625.47	11401.23
主办科技期刊　（种）	**Publications of Academic Journals and Scientific and Technological Popularization Readings (kind)**	**582**	**216**	**611**	**110**	**42**	**44**
科技期刊总印数（万册、万份）	Number of Academic Journals and Scientific and Technological Popularization Readings Issued (10000 copies)	562	522	513	303	48	46

注：1.2013年，科协机构数不包括厂矿科协。
　　2.2013年起，主办科技期刊只统计在新闻出版机构注册登记，有正式刊号或内部准印证并由本单位直接主办、负责编辑的期刊。
　　3.各类科技培训统计口径变更为实用技术培训。

Note: a) In 2013, factory and mice associations are not included in number of associations for science and technology.
b)From 2013,publications of academic journals and scientific and technological popularization readings refer only to those with official numbers registered by press and publication or those with internal permit directly edited by the unit.
c)The scope of participants in training programs has been changed to operative technology training.

主要统计指标解释

普通高等学校 指按照国家规定的设置标准和审批程序批准举办，通过国家统一招生考试，收高中毕业生为主要培养对象，实施高等教育的全日制大学、独立设置的学院和高等专科学校，高等职业学校和其他机构。

成人高等学校 指按照国家有关规定审批、招收通过全国成人高教统一招生考试的具有高中毕业或同等学力的在职从业人员利用脱产、半脱产、业余或函授等多种形式对其实施高等学历教育，培养高等教育专科或本科毕业水平的专门人才，修业年限、课程设置和总学时的数按高等学历教育要求付诸实施的学校。包括广播电视大学、职工高等学校、农民高等学校、管理干部学院、教育学院、独立设置的函授学院等。

小学学龄儿童入学率 指调查范围内已入小学学习的学龄儿童占校内外学龄儿童总数（包括弱智儿童在内，但不包括盲聋哑儿童）的比重。

研究与试验发展(R&D) 指在科学技术领域，为增加知识总量，以及运用这些知识去创造新的应用进行的系统的创造性的活动，包括基础研究、应用研究、试验发展三类活动。国际上通常采用R&D活动的规模和强度指标反映一国的科技实力和核心竞争力。

基础研究 指为了获得关于现象和可观察事实的基本原理的新知识(揭示客观事物的本质、运动规律，获得新发现、新学说)而进行的实验性或理论性研究，它不以任何专门或特定的应用或使用为目的。其成果以科学论文和科学著作为主要形式。用来反映知识的原始创新能力。

应用研究 指为获得新知识而进行的创造性研究，主要针对某一特定的目的或目标。应用研究是为了确定基础研究成果可能的用途，或是为达到预定的目标探索应采取的新方法(原理性)或新途径。其成果形式以科学论文、专著、原理性模型或发明专利为主。用来反映对基础研究成果应用途径的探索。

试验发展 指利用从基础研究、应用研究和实际经验所获得的现有知识，为产生新的产品、材料和装置，建立新的工艺、系统和服务，以及对已产生和建立的上述各项作实质性的改进而进行的系统性工作。其成果形式主要是专利、专有技术、具有新产品基本特征的产品原型或具有新装置基本特征的原始样机等。在社会科学领域，试验发展是指把通过基础研究、应用研究获得的知识转变成可以实施的计划(包括为进行检验和评估实施示范项目)的过程。人文科学领域没有对应的试验发展活动。主要反映将科研成果转化为技术和产品的能力，是科技推动经济社会发展的物化成果。

R&D人员 指参与研究与试验发展项目研究、管理和辅助工作的人员，包括项目(课题)组人员，企业科技行政管理人员和直接为项目(课题)活动提供服务的辅助人员。反映投入从事拥有自主知识产权的研究开发活动的人力规模。

R&D人员全时当量 指全时人员数加非全时人员按工作量折算为全时人员数的总和。例如：有两个全时人员和三个非全时人员(工作时间分别为20%、30%和70%)，则全时当量为2+0.2+0.3+0.7=3.2人年。为国际上比较科技人力投入而制定的可比指标。

R&D经费支出合计 指调查单位用于内部开展R&D活动（基础研究、应用研究和试验发展）的实际支出。包括用于R&D项目（课题）活动的直接支出，以及间接用于R&D活动的管理费、服务费、与R&D有关的基本建设支出以及外协加工费等。不包括生产性活动支出、归还贷款支出以及与外单位合作或委托外单位进行R&D活动而转拨给对方的经费支出。

R&D经费支出中政府资金 指R&D经费内部支出中来自各级政府部门的各类资金，包括财政科学技术拨款、科学基金、教育等部门事业费以及政府部门预算外资金的实际支出。

R&D经费支出中企业资金 指R&D经费内部支出中来自本企业的自有资金和接受其他企业委托而获得的经费，以及科研院所、高校等事业单位从企业获得的资金的实际支出。

新产品销售收入 指报告期企业销售新产品实现的销售收入。新产品是指采用新技术原理、新设计构思研制、生产的全新产品，或在结构、材质、工艺等某一方面比原有产品有明显改进，从而显著提高了产品性能或扩大了使用功能的产品。既包括经政府有关部门认定并在有效期内的新产品，也包括企业自行研制开发，未经政府有关部门认定，从投产之日起一年之内的新产品。

专利 是专利权的简称，是对发明人的发明创造经审查合格后，由专利局依据专利法授予发明人和设计人对该项发明创造享有的专有权。包括发明、实用新型和外观设计。反映拥有自主知识产权的科技和设计成果情况。

发明（专利） 指对产品、方法或者其改进所提出的新的技术方案。是国际通行的反映拥有自主知识产权技术的核心指标。

实用新型（专利） 指对产品的形状、构造或者其结合所提出的适于实用的新的技术方案。反映具有一定技术含量的技术成果情况。

外观设计（专利） 指对产品的形状、图案、色彩或者其结合所作出的富有美感并适于工业上应用的新设计。反映拥有自主知识产权的外观设计成果情况。

Explanatory Notes on Main Statistical Indicators

Regular Institutions of Higher Education refer to educational establishments set up according to government standards and evaluation and approval procedures, mainly enrolling graduates from senior secondary schools through uniform national matriculation examinations and providing higher education. Such institutions include full-time universities, independent colleges, technical colleges, professional colleges, and other institutions.

Institutions of Higher Learning for Adults refer to educational establishments approved according to relevant government rules, enrolling staff and workers with senior secondary or equivalent education through uniform national matriculation examinations, and providing them with regular higher education in various forms such as full-time, part-time, spare-time and correspondence courses in accordance with requirements of regular higher education in years of education, curricula, and total learning hours, so that they meet the standards for graduation of universities or junior colleges. Institutions of higher learning for adults include radio and TV universities, colleges for staff and workers, colleges for farmers, colleges for management cadres, teachers' colleges, and independent correspondence colleges.

Enrollment Rate of Primary School-age Children refers to the proportion of school-age children enrolled at primary schools in the total number of school-age children both in and outside schools (including retarded children, but excluding blind, deaf and dumb children).

Research and Development (R&D) refers to systematic and creative activities in the field of science and technology aiming at increasing the knowledge and using the knowledge for new application. R&D includes 3 categories of activities: basic research, applied research and experiments and development. The scale and intensity of R&D are widely used internationally to reflect the strength of S&T and the core competitiveness of a country in the world.

Basic Research refers to empirical or theoretical research aiming at obtaining new knowledge on the fundamental principles regarding phenomena or observable facts to reveal the intrinsic nature and underlying laws and to acquire new discoveries or new theories. Basic research takes no specific or designated application as the aim of the research. Results of basic research are mainly released or disseminated in the form of scientific papers or monographs. This indicator reflects the innovation capacity for original knowledge.

Applied Research refers to creative research aiming at obtaining new knowledge on a specific objective or target. Purpose of the applied research is to identify the possible uses of results from basic research, or to explore new (fundamental) methods or new approaches. Results of applied research are expressed in the form of scientific papers, monographs, fundamental models or invention patents. This indicator reflects the exploration of ways to apply the results of basic research.

Experiments and Development refer to systematic activities aiming at using the knowledge from basic and applied researches or from practical experience to develop new products, materials and equipment, to establish new production process, systems and services, or to make substantial improvement on the existing products, process or services. Results of experiment and development activities are embodied in patents, exclusive technology, and monotype of new products or equipment. In social sciences, experiment and development activities refer to the process of converting the knowledge from basic or applied researches into feasible programmes (including conduct of demonstration projects for assessment and evaluation). There are no experiment and development activities in the science of humanities. This indicator reflects the capability of transferring the results of S&T into technique and products, and measures the realization of S&T in spearheading the economic and social development.

R & D Personnel refer to persons engaged in research, management and supporting activities of R & D, including persons in the project teams, persons engaged in the management of S&T activities of enterprises and supporting staff providing direct service to the research projects. This indicator reflects the size of personnel engaged in R&D activities with independent intellectual property.

Full-time Equivalent of R&D Personnel refers to the sum of the full-time persons and the full-time equivalent of part-time persons converted by workload. For instance, if there are 2 full-time persons and 3 part-time workers (20%, 30% and 70% of working hours respectively on R&D activities), the full-time equivalent are 2+0.2+0.3+0.7=3.2 person-years. This is an internationally comparable indicator of S&T manpower input.

Total Expenditure of Funds on R&D refers to the real expenditure of surveyed units on their own R&D activities (basic research, applied research, experiments and development) including direct expenditure on R&D activities, indirect expenditure of management and services on R&D activities, expenditure on capital construction and material processing by others. Excluding the expenditure on production activities, return of loan, and fees transferred to cooperated or entrusted agencies on R&D activities.

Expenditure of Government Funds on R&D refers to the expenditure of funds on R&D activities from government agencies at different levels, including appropriate funds on science and technology from financial departments, scientific funds, operating expenses from education departments and the real expenditure of extra budgetary funds from government agencies.

Expenditure of Funds of Enterprises on R&D refers to the expenditure of funds on R&D activities from self-raised funds of enterprises and funds from other enterprises through entrustment, and the expenditure of funds of institutions, such as institution of scientific research and universities, from enterprises.

Sales Income of New Products refers to the sales income of new products of the enterprises at the reference period. New products refer to products developed and produced with new technologies and designs or improved in structure, material, process or other aspects so that their performance are improved or their functions expanded. New products include those affirmed by government authorities in their validity period and also those developed by enterprises without the affirmation of government authorities within one year after they are put into production.

Patent is an abbreviation for the patent right and refers to the exclusive right of ownership by the inventors or designers for the creation or inventions, given from the patent offices after due process of assessment and approval in accordance with the Patent Law. Patents are granted for inventions, utility models and designs. This indicator reflects the achievements of S&T and design with independent intellectual property.

Patented Inventions refer to new technical proposals to the products or methods or their modifications. This is universal core indicator reflecting the technologies with independent intellectual property.

Patented Utility Models refer to the practical and new technical proposals on the shape and structure of the product or the combination of both. This indicator reflects the condition of technological results with certain technical content.

Designs refer to the aesthetics and industrially applicable new designs for the shape, pattern and colour of the product, or their combinations. This indicator reflects the appearance design achievements with independent intellectual property.

二十、文化与体育

CULTURE AND SPORTS

二十　文化与体育

简要说明

一、本篇资料主要反映文化事业和体育的基本情况。

二、本篇资料主要包括：

1. 文化艺术、文物、图书馆、新闻出版、广播、电影、电视等文化事业的机构、人员及业务活动开展情况等。

2. 体育系统职工人数、群众体育活动开展情况及运动竞技成绩等。

三、本篇资料由广东省统计局社会和科技统计处负责整理、编辑。

四、统计资料来源：

文化、体育统计资料根据广东省文化和旅游厅、广东省广播电视局、广东省体育局及广东省档案局等有关部门提供的统计年报加工整理。

20 Culture and Sports

Brief Introduction

I. The data in this chapter show the basic conditions on the development Guangdong's cultural undertakings. as well as sports.

II. The data in this chapter mainly include:

(1) The data on institutions, personnel and business activities of culture and arts, cultural relics, libraries, news and publication, radio, film and television, etc.

(2) The number of staff and workers in sports departments， mass sports and athletics sports， etc.

III. The data are prepared and edited by the Division of Social, Scientific and Technological Statistics of Statistics Bureau of Guangdong Province.

IV. Data sources:

The data on culture and sport are processed and prepared in accordance with the annual statistical reports provided by the Department of Culture and Tourism of Guangdong Province, Radio and Television Administration of Guangdong Province, Guangdong Provincial Bureau of Sports, Guangdong Provincial Bureau of Archives and the related departments.

20-1 文化、体育主要指标

Main Indicators on Culture and Education

指　　标	Item	2000	2010	2015	2022	2023
电影放映单位 (个)	Number of Film Projection Units (unit)	1626	1392	1793	3032	3293
文化和旅游部门所属艺术表演团体 (个)	Art Performance Groups Affiliated with the Cultural and Tourism Sector (unit)	138	133	72	76	74
文化馆 (个)	Number of Cultural Centers (unit)	118	129	146	144	144
公共图书馆 (个)	Number of Public Libraries (unit)	125	133	140	150	150
公共图书馆藏量 (万册、件)	Holdings of Public Libraries (10000 volumes)	2330	4615	7008	14253	15129
博物馆（含美术馆） (个)	Number of Museums (including arts museum) (unit)	131	169	193	393	277
博物馆藏品数(含美术馆) (万件)	Holdings of Museums (including arts museum) (10000 pieces)	49.09	84.46	101.83	277.42	267.71
全省每万人拥有公共文化设施面积 (平方米)	Area of Public Cultural Facilities per 10000 People (Sq m)		416.00	1189.24	1477.57	1496.06
档案馆 (个)	Number of Archives (unit)	161	205	217	190	191
利用档案 (万卷次)	Archives Utilized (10000 volume-times)	36.32	301.00	495.00	847.48	718.80
图书出版量 (万册)	Number of Books Published (10000 copies)	26978	23134	31287	50591	55342
杂志出版量 (万册)	Number of Magazines Published (10000 copies)	26299	21201	14458	9113	7992
报纸出版量 (亿份)	Number of Newspapers Published (100 million copies)	34.63	45.59	32.77	13.19	12.74
广播电台 (座)	Number of Radio Stations (unit)	106	22	22	2	2
电视台 (座)	Number of TV Stations (unit)	67	24	24	3	3
广播电视台 (座)	Number of Radio and Television Stations	83	79		95	95
广播综合人口覆盖率 (%)	Overall Population Coverage Rate of Radio (%)	96.0	98.0	99.9	99.98	99.98
电视综合人口覆盖率 (%)	Overall Population Coverage Rate of Television (%)	96.4	98.0	99.9	99.98	99.98
举办全民健身活动次数 (次)	Number of National Body-building Activities Held (time)		9477	5000	2258	4500
全省人均拥有体育场地面积 (平方米)	Per Capita Area of Sports Venues (Sqm)	1.91	2.01		2.68	2.80

注：1.2012年，艺术表演团体统计口径调整为事业单位和省直企业中的文化部门艺术表演团体。2013年起，统计口径调整为公有制艺术表演团体(事业)和公有制艺术表演团体(企业)。2023年起为文化和旅游部门所属艺术表演团体(事业)和文化和旅游部门所属艺术表演团体(企业)。以下相关表同。

2.2019年起博物馆的统计范围增加了民办博物馆。2023年起博物馆统计口径调整为国有博物馆。以下相关表同。

3.2019年起，广播电台、电视台数据只包含独立的广播电台和电视台，广播电台和电视台合并机构纳入广播电视台统计。

Note: a) In 2012, the statistical criteria for art performance groups were adjusted to include cultural department art performance groups in public institutions and provincial enterprises. Since 2013, the statistical criteria have been adjusted to include public owned art performance groups (institutions) and public owned art performance groups (enterprises). Starting from 2023, it will become an art performance group (business) under the Ministry of Culture and Tourism and an art performance group (enterprise) under the Ministry of Culture and Tourism. The following related tables are the same.

b)Since 2019,the statistical scope of museums has increased to include private museums. Starting from 2023,the statistical caliber of museums will be adjusted to state-owned museums. The following related tables are the same.

c)Since 2019,the number of radio stations and the number of television stations only include independent radio and television stations, and the combined institutions of radio and television stations are included in the radio and television stations.

e)According to the change in the statistical caliber of the National Cultural Relics and Tourism Statistics Direct Reporting System, since 2023, the coverage of art performance troupes has been adjusted，only for art performance troupes(undertakings) under the Ministry of Culture and Tourism and art performance troupes(enterprises) under the Ministry of Culture and Tourism.

f)According to the change in the statistical caliber of the National Cultural Relics and Tourism Statistics Direct Reporting System, since 2023, the statistical caliber of museums have adjusted to state-owned museums.

20-2 文化艺术、文物事业机构数

Number of Institutions of Culture, Arts and Cultural Relics

单位：个 (unit)

年份 Year	电影放映单位 Film Projection Units	文化和旅游部门所属艺术表演团体 Art Performance Groups Affiliated with the Cultural and Tourism Sector	文化馆 Cultural Centers	公共图书馆 Public Libraries	博物馆 Museums	档案馆 Archives
1978	6346	172	124	76	30	
1980	7375	195	113	97	26	
1985	6037	171	123	117	106	
1990	4024	130	113	103	106	138
1991	4041	122	110	104	107	147
1992	3917	125	113	108	108	150
1993	3974	126	115	110	108	148
1994	3750	132	116	111	111	156
1995	3668	134	115	114	113	155
1996	3670	136	115	115	114	157
1997	3463	138	117	119	117	157
1998	3621	139	117	120	122	157
1999	2938	140	117	121	128	162
2000	1626	138	118	125	131	161
2001	1794	139	118	129	140	175
2002	904	141	120	131	140	185
2003	840	144	117	129	144	185
2004	684	140	119	128	143	185
2005	720	139	117	129	146	185
2006	1542	138	120	129	147	186
2007	1844	128	122	130	153	186
2008	1450	130	121	132	152	188
2009	1265	127	128	133	160	197
2010	1392	133	129	133	169	205
2011	1357	100	134	134	161	209
2012	1419	61	137	137	168	209
2013	1506	75	147	137	191	214
2014	1673	72	147	138	192	218
2015	1793	72	146	140	193	217
2016	1974	72	146	142	192	192
2017	2323	74	146	143	197	192
2018	2490	74	145	143	199	188
2019	2666	72	145	146	259	189
2020	2845	71	144	148	324	186
2021	2839	76	144	150	385	189
2022	3032	76	144	150	393	190
2023	3293	74	144	150	277	191

注：2009年起，博物馆包含美术馆；2023年起，博物馆统计口径为国有博物馆。
Note:Since 2009, museums have included art galleries; Starting from 2023, the statistical caliber of museums was state-owned museums.

20-3 文化和旅游部门所属艺术表演团体演出基本情况（2023年）

Basic Performance Information of Art Performance Groups Affiliated with the Cultural and Tourism Sector (2023)

项　目	Item	剧团数(个) Number of Troupes (unit)	国内演出场次(万场) Number of Domestic Performances (10000 shows)	#到农村演出 Shows in Rural Areas	国内演出观众人次(万人次) Number of Domestic Spectators (10000 person-times)
合　计	**Total**	**74**	**1.05**	**0.51**	**845.18**
文化和旅游部门所属艺术表演团体(事业)	Art Performance Groups Affiliated with the Cultural and Tourism Sector (Institution)	28	0.36	0.14	371.60
文化和旅游部门所属艺术表演团体(企业)	Art Performance Groups Affiliated with the Cultural and Tourism Sector (Enterprises)	46	0.69	0.37	473.58
按剧种分	**By Type of Art Performance Troupe**				
话剧、儿童剧、滑稽剧类	Modern Drama, Children Drama, Farce Drama	3	0.01		9.19
歌舞、音乐类	Dance, Music	21	0.27	0.05	178.41
京剧、昆曲类	Beijing Opera, Kunqu Opera				
地方戏曲类	Local Opera	40	0.63	0.40	566.03
杂技、魔术、马戏类	Magic, Acrobatics, Circus	3	0.04	0.01	18.20
曲艺类	Chinese Folk Art	5	0.06	0.01	23.07
乌兰牧骑	Nei Monggol Cultural Troupe Mounted on Horseback				
综合性艺术表演团体	Comprehensive Art Troupes	2	0.06	0.03	50.28

20-4 文化、文物机构及人员数（2023年）

Number of Institutions and Personnel in Culture and Cultural Relics (2023)

项　目	Item	合计 Total		文化部门 Cultural Departments		其他部门 Others	
		机构数(个) Number of Institutions (unit)	人数(人) Number of Personnel (person)	机构数(个) Number of Institutions (unit)	人数(人) Number of Personnel (person)	机构数(个) Number of Institutions (unit)	人数(人) Number of Personnel (person)
总　计	**Total**	**2548**	**44136**	**2506**	**43552**	**42**	**584**
文化合计	**Culture**	**2293**	**37719**	**2275**	**37560**	**18**	**159**
艺术事业	Arts	118	5937	118	5937		
图书馆事业	Libraries	150	5413	150	5413		
群众文化事业	Mass Culture	1762	15678	1762	15678		
艺术教育业	Art Education	2	328	2	328		
文艺科研	Scientific Research on Arts	7	100	7	100		
艺术展览创作机构	Art Exhibition Creative Agency	61	800	43	641	18	159
文化行政主管部门	Administrative Department	153	8592	153	8592		
其他文化机构	Other Agencies	40	871	40	871		
文物合计	**Cultural Relics**	**255**	**6417**	**231**	**5992**	**24**	**425**
文物科研机构	Institutions for Cultural Relics	4	199	4	199		
文物保护管理机构	Agencies of Cultural Relics Preservation	25	327	25	327		
博物馆	Museums	223	5812	199	5387	24	425
其他文物机构	Other Agencies	3	79	3	79		

20-5 公共图书馆、群众文化事业机构及人员数（2023年）

Number of Institutions and Personnel in Public Libraries and Mass Culture (2023)

项目	Item	合计 Total		文化部门 Cultural Departments		其他部门 Others	
		机构数（个） Number of Institutions (unit)	人数（人） Number of Personnel (person)	机构数（个） Number of Institutions (unit)	人数（人） Number of Personnel (person)	机构数（个） Number of Institutions (unit)	人数（人） Number of Personnel (person)
图书馆事业	**Libraries**	**150**	**5413**	**150**	**5413**		
#少儿图书馆	Children's Libraries	5	240	5	240		
群众文化事业	**Mass Culture**	**1762**	**15678**	**1762**	**15678**		
群众艺术馆、文化馆	Mass Art Centers	144	2646	144	2646		
文化站	Cultural Stations	1618	13032	1618	13032		

20-6 各市文化、文物事业机构数（2023年）

Number of Institutions in Culture and Cultural Relics by City (2023)

单位：个 (unit)

市别	City	文化和旅游部门所属艺术表演团体 Art Performance Groups Affiliated with the Cultural and Tourism Sector	文化馆 Cultural Centers	公共图书馆 Public Libraries	博物馆（含美术馆） Museums (including art museums)	档案馆 Archives
全省	**Provincial Total**	**74**	**144**	**150**	**277**	**191**
广州	Guangzhou	7	12	13	45	16
深圳	Shenzhen	3	10	12	51	11
珠海	Zhuhai	2	4	4	5	5
汕头	Shantou	6	8	8	11	10
佛山	Foshan	1	6	6	13	8
韶关	Shaoguan	2	11	11	12	12
河源	Heyuan	5	7	7	8	8
梅州	Meizhou	6	9	10	19	14
惠州	Huizhou		6	6	9	8
汕尾	Shanwei	4	5	5	7	5
东莞	Dongguan		1	1	10	2
中山	Zhongshan		1	1	4	2
江门	Jiangmen	1	8	8	13	13
阳江	Yangjiang	1	5	5	7	6
湛江	Zhanjiang	8	10	11	13	14
茂名	Maoming	6	6	6	6	7
肇庆	Zhaoqing	2	9	9	14	10
清远	Qingyuan	4	9	10	9	10
潮州	Chaozhou	1	4	4	6	5
揭阳	Jieyang	5	6	6	7	6
云浮	Yunfu	1	6	6	6	6
省直属单位	Units Directly under Provincial Government	9	1	1	2	13
按经济区域分	By Region					
珠三角	Pearl River Delta	16	57	60	164	75
粤东	Eastern Region	16	23	23	31	26
粤西	Western Region	15	21	22	26	27
粤北	Northern Region	18	42	44	54	50

注：各区域不包省直单位部分。
Note: By Region does not include agencies directly under provincial jurisdiction.

20–7 各市文化、文物事业机构的人员数（2023年）

Number of Personnel in Culture and Cultural Relics by City (2023)

单位：人 (person)

市 别	City	文化和旅游部门所属艺术表演团体 Art Performance Groups Affiliated with the Cultural and Tourism Sector	文化馆 Cultural Centers	公共图书馆 Public Libraries	博物馆（含美术馆） Museums (including art museums)	档案馆 Archives
全 省	**Provincial Total**	**4513**	**2646**	**5413**	**6495**	**2722**
广 州	Guangzhou	815	235	927	1357	443
深 圳	Shenzhen	374	360	1582	1093	154
珠 海	Zhuhai	269	75	125	168	64
汕 头	Shantou	214	107	120	232	136
佛 山	Foshan	51	147	344	555	165
韶 关	Shaoguan	78	179	107	232	126
河 源	Heyuan	157	119	183	128	78
梅 州	Meizhou	152	158	163	282	134
惠 州	Huizhou		171	140	198	116
汕 尾	Shanwei	213	69	80	101	57
东 莞	Dongguan		84	174	382	24
中 山	Zhongshan		29	53	114	112
江 门	Jiangmen	56	107	166	220	164
阳 江	Yangjiang	39	73	76	202	90
湛 江	Zhanjiang	353	114	137	206	133
茂 名	Maoming	170	66	137	70	90
肇 庆	Zhaoqing	72	128	171	260	123
清 远	Qingyuan	86	129	122	107	93
潮 州	Chaozhou	53	56	72	131	41
揭 阳	Jieyang	152	110	128	111	73
云 浮	Yunfu	44	83	100	79	69
省直属单位	Units Dircctly under Provincial Government	1165	47	306	267	237
按经济区域分	By Region					
珠 三 角	Pearl River Delta	1637	1336	3682	4347	1365
粤 东	Eastern Region	632	342	400	575	307
粤 西	Western Region	562	253	350	478	313
粤 北	Northern Region	517	668	675	828	500

注：各区域不包省直单位部分。
Note: By Region does not include agencies directly under provincial jurisdiction.

20-8 图书、杂志、报纸出版数量

Number of Books, Magazines and Newspapers Published

项 目	Item	2000	2005	2010	2015	2021	2022	2023
图书出版	**Books Published**							
种数 (种)	Number of Publications (kind)	4374	5908	6354	10089	11565	10557	12081
总印数 (万册)	Total Printed Copies(10000 copies)	26978	22600	23134	31287	50566	50591	55341
总印张数(千印张)	Total Printed Sheets (1000 sheets)	1482942	1514191	1597301	2434970	3982308	3967554	4707826
杂志出版	**Magazines Published**							
种数 (种)	Number of Publications (kind)	337	366	380	382	380	380	380
总印数 (万册)	Total Printed Copies(10000 copies)	26299	20371	21201	14458	9539	9113	7992
总印张数(千印张)	Total Printed Sheets (1000 sheets)	919514	116814	1251752	844427	475097	452947	400033
报纸出版	**Newspapers Published**							
种数 (种)	Number of Publications (kind)	101	102	100	100	92	92	90
总印数 (万份)	Total Printed Copies(10000 copies)	346268	398152	455912	327660	144834	131893	127418
总印张数(千印张)	Total Printed Sheets (1000 sheets)	17669099	28996964	43788152	20081573	4601690	3726676	3433496

注：1.本表图书种数、总印数和总印张不包含非“中国标准书号”部分。
　　2.2000年开始报纸出版统计不包校报、院报。
Note:a)Total Printed Copies and Total Printed Sheets does not include publications without “China International Standard Book Number”.
　　b)Since 2000, the number of newspaper published does not include that of college or institute newspaper.

20-9 图书出版情况（2023年）

Statistics on Books Published (2023)

门 类	Category	图书出版种数(种) Number of Publications (kind)	#新出 New Public-ations	总印数(万册) Total Printed Copies (10000 copies)	总印张数(千印张) Total Printed Sheets (1000 sheets)
合 计	**Total**	**12081**	**5089**	**55342**	**4707826**
马克思主义、列宁主义、毛泽东思想	Marxism, Leninism and Mao Zedong Thought	32	9	12	2250
哲学	Philosophy	153	73	167	16598
社会科学总论	General Social Sciences	78	47	34	4382
政治、法律	Politics and Law	283	186	931	64775
军事	Military Affairs	25	12	239	18325
经济	Economy	574	393	561	88574
文化、科学、教育、体育	Culture, Science, Education and Sports	6748	1820	48169	3942267
语言、文字	Language, Philology	220	93	208	29410
文学	Literature	1646	953	3408	372281
艺术	Arts	492	350	476	53483
历史、地理	History and Geography	608	393	556	46262
自然科学总论	General Natural Sciences	12	7	6	1624
数理科学、化学	Mathematics, Physics and Chemistry	47	22	20	1913
天文学、地理科学	Astronomy and Geology	51	39	26	3652
生物科学	Biological Science	69	50	50	5570
医药、卫生	Medicine and Health Care	422	283	149	20305
农业科学	Agricultural Science	55	40	18	1779
工业技术	Industrial Technology	377	183	158	22997
交通运输	Transportation	34	18	7	741
航空、航天	Aeronautics and Aerospace	12	10	25	2074
环境科学	Environmental Science	41	25	19	1783
综合性图书	General Books	102	83	101	6782

注：本表图书种数、总印数和总印张不包含非“中国标准书号”部分。
Notes: Total Printed Copies and Total Printed Sheets does not include publications without “China International Standard Book Number”.

20−10 杂志出版情况（2023年）

Statistics on Magazines Published (2023)

项　目	Item	种数（种）Number of Publications (kind)	平均期印数（万册）Average Printed Copies per Issue (10000 copies)	总印数（万册）Total Printed Copies (10000 copies)	总印张数（千印张）Total Printed Sheets (1000 sheets)
合　计	**Total**	**380**	**345**	**7992**	**400033**
综　合	General	26	5	110	6109
哲学、社会科学	Philosophy, Social Sciences	97	169	3832	186678
自然科学、技术	Natural Sciences, Technology	180	114	2840	144616
文化、教育	Culture, Education	46	46	1106	52821
文学、艺术	Literature, Arts	31	10	104	9809

20−11 报纸出版情况（2023年）

Statistics on Newspapers Published (2023)

项　目	Item	种数(种) Number of Publications (kind)	平均期印数(万册) Average Printed Copies per Issue (10000 copies)	总印数(万册) Total Printed Copies (10000 copies)	总印张数(千印张) Total Printed Sheets (1000 sheets)
合　计	**Total**	**90**	**468**	**127418**	**3433496**
按类型分	**By Type**				
综合类	General Newspapers	44	381	116055	3122288
专业类	Specialized Newspapers	28	35	6004	219876
生活服务类	Life Service Newspapers	10	5	233	16168
读者对象类	Reader Oriented Newspapers	7	45	4809	68843
文摘类	Digest Newspapers	1	3	316	6322
按范围分	**By Region**				
省　级	Provincial-level Newspapers	28	206	52609	1700285
市　级	City-level Newspapers	62	263	74809	1733211

注：根据《全国报纸出版统计调查制度(2019)》，将报纸分为“综合类”“专业类”“生活服务类”“读者对象类”“文摘类”(以上为非高校校报）和“高校校报”六类。本表不包含高校校报。其中以前年度将“综合类”“生活服务类”“读者对象类”对应以前年度的“综合报”，将“文摘类”“专业类”对应以前年度的“专业报”。

Note: According to the 《National Newspaper Publishing Statistical Survey System (2019)》, newspapers are divided into six categories: "General", "Specialized", "Life Service", " Reader Oriented", "Digest"(the above are not college newspapers) and "college newspapers". This table does not include college newspapers. In the previous year, "General", "Life Service" and " Reader Oriented" correspond to "General Newspaper" , and "Digest" and "Specialized Newspaper" correspond to "Specialized Newspapers".

20-12 广播、电视事业发展情况

Statistics on Radio and Television Stations

项　目	Item	2000	2010	2015	2019	2020	2021	2022	2023
广播电台（座）	Number of Radio Stations (set)	106	22	22	2	2	2	2	2
中波广播发射台和转播台（座）	Number of Medium Wave Radio Transmission Stations and Relaying Stations (set)	10	21	27	26	22	22	28	24
电视台（座）	Number of Television Stations (set)	67	24	24	3	3	3	3	3
100瓦及以上电视发射台和转播台（座）	Number of Television Transmission and Relaying Stations at 1000 W and above (set)	49	83	83	103	95	95	98	105
广播电视台（座）	Number of Radio and Television Stations (set)	83	79	79	95	95	95	95	95
有线广播电视用户（万户）	Number of Subscribers to Cable Radio and Television (10000 subscribers)		1702	2089	1767	1706	1710	1536	1734
数字电视用户（万户）	Number of Subscribers to Digital Television (10000 subscribers)		950	1622	1705	1639	1642	1477	1656

注：1000瓦及以上电视发射台和转播台，从2006年起改为100瓦以上(含100瓦)电视发射台和转播台。

Note: Television transmission and relaying stations at 1000 W and above since 2006 have been replaced by television transmission and relaying stations at 100W and above.

20-13 广播电台宣传基本情况（2023年）

Basic Statistics on Radio Stations (2023)

项　目	Item	广播电视台（座） Number of Radio and TV Stations (set)	广播电台（座） Number of Radio Stations (set)	节目套数（套） Number of Programs (set)	平均每日播音时间（小时） Average Daily Broadcasting Hours (hour)	#自办节目时间 Self-produced Programs	#新闻节目 News Programs	#专题节目 Special Subject Programs	#文艺节目 Programs of Entertainment
合　计	**Total**	**95**	**2**	**140**	**2288**	**1720**	**451**	**389**	**283**
省　级	Provincial Level	1		9	216	205	25	67	28
市　级	City Level	19	2	59	1078	964	167	189	118
县　级	County Level	75		72	994	551	259	133	137

20−14 电视台宣传基本情况（2023年）

Basic Statistics on Television Stations (2023)

项 目	Item	广播电视台（座） Number of Radio and TV Stations (set)	电视台（座） Television Stations (set)	节目套数（套） Number of Programs (set)	平均每日播出音时间(小时) Average Daily Broadcasting Hours (hour)	#自办节目时间 Self-produced Programs	#新闻节目 News Programs	#专题节目 Special Subject Programs	#文艺节目 Entertainment Programs
合 计	**Total**	**95**	**3**	**146**	**2277**	**659**	**353**	**335**	**56**
省 级	Provincial Level	1		13	283	121	37	40	4
市 级	City Level	19	3	61	1069	329	163	169	30
县 级	County Level	75		72	925	209	153	127	23

20−15 各市广播、电视事业机构数（2023年）

Number of Institutions of Radio and Television by City (2023)

单位：座 (set)

市 别	City	广播电台 Number of Radio Stations	中波广播发射台和转播台 Number of Medium Wave Radio Transmission Stations and Relaying Stations	电视台 Number of Television Stations	100瓦及以上电视发射台和转播台 Number of Television Transmission and Relaying Stations at 100 W and above	广播电视台 Number of Radio and Television Stations
广 州	Guangzhou				7	5
深 圳	Shenzhen	1	2	2	1	
珠 海	Zhuhai				1	2
汕 头	Shantou				3	4
佛 山	Foshan	1		1	7	
韶 关	Shaoguan				12	9
河 源	Heyuan				7	6
梅 州	Meizhou		3		4	8
惠 州	Huizhou				6	5
汕 尾	Shanwei				4	4
东 莞	Dongguan				1	1
中 山	Zhongshan				1	1
江 门	Jiangmen				3	6
阳 江	Yangjiang				2	4
湛 江	Zhanjiang		1		11	6
茂 名	Maoming				3	5
肇 庆	Zhaoqing				7	7
清 远	Qingyuan				8	8
潮 州	Chaozhou				2	3
揭 阳	Jieyang				5	5
云 浮	Yunfu				4	5
省直属单位	Units Directly under Provincial Government		18		6	1

20-16 体育事业情况

Statistics on Sports

指　　标	Item	2010	2015	2021	2022	2023
体育系统年末职工人数（人）	**Number of Staff and Workers in Sports Departments at the Year-end (person)**	**9405**	**10620**	**11987**	**10917**	**10173**
正式运动员	Official Athletes	1036	1649	2085	2208	2324
体育教练员	Sports Coaches	1094	1485	1942	1949	2032
专职文化教师	Full-time Teachers for Literacy Classes	918	907	898	807	813
科技人员	Scientific and Technological Personnel	113	114	91	105	115
医务人员	Medical Personnel	97	60	110	112	142
管理人员	Administrative Personnel	3328	4401	5076	4023	3134
其他人员	Others	2819	2004	1785	1713	1613
体育比赛成绩	**Achievements in Sports Tournament**					
破世界纪录（项）	Number of World Records Chalked Up (item)	1	1	3		1
获世界冠军（人次）	Number of World Championships Won (person-time)	27	27	10	14	30
破亚洲纪录（项）	Number of Asian Records Chalked Up (item)	2	4	6		5
破全国纪录（项次）	Number of National Records Chalked Up (item-time)	5	5	8	1	1
获得全国冠军（项次）	Number of National Championships Won (item-time)	132	124	124	70	161
体育活动开展情况	**Sports Meets and Activities**					
举办全民健身活动次数（次）	Number of National Body-building Activities Held (time)	9477	5000	2000	2258	4500

主要统计指标解释

文化事业机构 指从事专业文化工作和为专业文化工作服务的独立建制的单独核算的单位。不包括这些单位另外举办独立核算的其他机构和各部门的业余文化组织。

文化和旅游部门所属艺术表演团体 是指由文化和旅游部门主办或实行行业管理（经文化和旅游行政部门审批并领取营业性演出许可证），专门从事表演艺术等活动的各类专业艺术表演团体，含民间职业剧团（不包括群众业余文艺表演团队）。

电影放映单位 指具有放映机器设备、固定或不固定的放映场所与专职或兼职的放映技术人员，经有关部门登记批准，经常为一定的观众对象放映电影的机构。包括经批准对外开放进行营业，并与电影发行放映管理机构分帐的专用放映单位和军委系统租片单位。

艺术表演观众人数（人次） 指售票、包场等有演出收入的场次和政府采纳的公益性演出场次及参加汇演等无演出收入的公开演出场次，不包括彩排审查和内部观摩演出的观看人次数。

Explanatory Notes on Main Statistical Indicators

Cultural Institutions refer to units which have their own organizational system and independent accounting system and specialize in or serve cultural development. They exclude other establishments with independent accounting system run by these cultural institutions and amateur cultural groups established by various departments.

Art Performance Groups refers to various professional artistic performance groups organized or managed by the cultural and tourism departments (approved by the cultural and tourism administrative departments and obtaining commercial performance licenses), specializing in performing arts and other activities, including folk professional theater troupes (excluding amateur cultural performance teams).

Film Projection Units refer to units with film projection equipment, full or part-time projectionists, permanent or non-permanent cinemas, approved by and registered with related administrative departments to show films regularly for certain groups of audience, including film projection units which have been approved to give commercial shows and share profits with administrative agencies of film circulation and projection, as well as film renting units of the military system.

Number of Spectators at Art Performance (person-time) refers to the number of attendants at commercial shows, completely booked shows or free shows given in minority national areas, excluding the number of spectators at rehearsals for examination and internal shows for study.

二十一、卫生、社会福利、社会保障和其他

PUBLIC HEALTH, SOCIAL WELFARE, SOCIAL INSURANCE AND OTHERS

二十一　卫生、社会福利、社会保障和其他

简要说明

一、本篇资料主要反映广东卫生、社会福利、社会保险、安全生产及其他事业的发展情况。

二、本篇资料由广东省统计局社会和科技统计处负责整理、编辑。

三、卫生部分主要包括卫生事业机构、床位及人员数等，资料由广东省卫生健康委员会提供。

四、社会福利部分主要包括各种社会福利事业情况、城乡基层社会保障情况、婚姻登记状况等，资料由广东省民政厅提供。

五、社会保险部分主要包括城乡基本养老保险、失业保险、城乡基本医疗保险等基金征缴收入和参保人数，资料由广东省人力资源和社会保障厅提供。

六、亿元生产总值安全生产事故死亡率数据由广东省应急管理厅提供。

七、其他部分主要包括司法工作开展情况和交通、火灾事故发生情况等，资料由广东省司法厅 、广东省公安厅提供。

21 Public Health,Social Welfare,Social Insurance and Others

Brief Introduction

I. The data in this chapter mainly show the development of Guangdong's public health，social welfare，social security, safe production and other undertakings.

II. The data are prepared by the Division of Social，Scientific and Technological Statistics of Statistics Bureau of Guangdong Province.

III. The data on public health mainly include the number of health institutions，hospital beds and personnel，etc. The data are provided by Health Department of Guangdong Province.

IV. The data on social welfare mainly include the social welfare services，grassroots social security in urban and rural areas and marriage registration status，etc. The data are provided by Guangdong Provincial Department of Civil Affairs.

Ⅴ.The data on social security mainly include the statistics on basic pension insurance for urban and rural residents, the unemployment insurance, the amount collected and percentage of collection and the number of persons participating in urban and rural basic medical care insurance.The data is provided by Guangdong Provincial Department of Human Resources and Social Security.

Ⅵ. The rate of death from work safety accidents per 100 million yuan of GDP is provided by the Department of Emergency Management of Guangdong Province.

Ⅶ. Other data mainly include judicial conditions and basic statistics on traffic and fire accidents，etc. The data are provided by Guangdong Provincial Department of Justice and Guangdong Provincial Department of Public Security.

21-1 卫生、社会福利和其他主要指标

Main Indicators of Sports, Public Health, Social Welfare, Environmental Protection and Others

指　标	Item	2000	2010	2021	2022	2023
医疗卫生机构数 (个)	Number of Health Care Institutions (unit)	8984	44880	57955	59531	62862
#医院、卫生院	Hospitals	2426	2444	2935	2981	3044
医疗卫生机构床位数 (万张)	Number of Beds in Health Care Institutions (10000 units)	16.81	30.01	58.90	60.83	62.86
#医院、卫生院床位	Hospital Beds	15.72	27.71	54.66	56.41	58.34
卫生技术人员数 (万人)	Number of Medical Technical Personnel (10000 persons)	26.50	45.55	87.58	91.84	97.91
#执业(助理)医师	Licensed Physicians & Physician Assistants	11.12	17.51	32.09	33.52	35.95
平均每千人口有卫生机构床位数 (张)	Number of Beds in health Institutions per 1000 Population (bed)	1.94	2.87	4.64	4.81	4.95
平均每千人口有卫生技术人员数 (人)	Number of Medical Technical Personnel per 1000 Population (person)	3.07	4.36	6.90	7.26	7.71
#执业(助理)医师	Licensed Physicians & Physician Assistants	1.29	1.68	2.53	2.65	2.83
社会救助总人数 (万人)	Total Number under Social Relief (10000 persons)	154.70	288.00	173.95	162.77	156.14
全省常住人口社保卡持卡率(%)	Percentage of Permanent Provincial Residents with Social Security Card (%)		17.34	94.20	94.39	97.20
登记结婚件数 (对)	Registered Marriages (couple)	562118	857146	591124	573050	632192
离婚总数 (对)	Registered Divorces (couple)	47521	127048	167209	184511	226080
执业律师人数 (人)	Number of Full-time Lawyers (person)	7292	20230	61946	70680	79357
公证人员数 (人)	Number of Notarial Personnel (person)	1380	1694	2928	3052	3106
人民调解委员会调解人员数 (人)	Number of Mediators of People's Mediation Committees (person)	135192	194224	182304	184727	191693
亿元生产总值生产安全事故死亡率	Rate of Death from Work Safety Accidents per 100 Million Yuan of Gross Regional Product	1.080	0.153	0.019	0.016	0.016
交通事故发生数 (起)	Number of Traffic Accidents (unit)	66072	30480	48206	38782	44104
交通事故损失折款 (万元)	Losses from Traffic Accidents Converted into Cash (10000 yuan)	27526	8051	10534	8649	11220
火灾事故发生数 (起)	Number of Fire Accidents (unit)	8622	6065	64134	55629	57785
火灾事故损失折款 (万元)	Losses from Fire Accidents Converted into Cash (10000 yuan)	10065	17500	79931	70995	71742

注：2010年起医疗卫生机构、人员数总数含村卫生室数，千人口数据分母为常住人口。

Note: Since 2010,Data of village clinics was included in the total number of health care institutions and their personnel. The population of per 1000 persons used in this table are resident population.

21-2 医疗卫生机构、床位及人员数

Number of Health Care Institutions, Beds and Personnel

年份 Year	机构（个） Health Institutions (unit)	#医院及卫生院 Hospitals	床位（张） Beds (bed)	#医院及卫生院床位 Hospital Beds	卫生工作人员（人） Medical Personnel (person)	#卫生技术人员 Medical Technical Personnel
1978	6949	1968	90645	84120	159583	126606
1979	7304	1974	91955	85144	171703	136568
1980	7649	1988	92506	84999	181480	144537
1981	8045	2002	94794	87010	191370	151971
1982	8331	2014	97441	88688	202162	160710
1983	8443	2037	100042	90851	208506	166543
1984	8525	2042	103231	93770	213193	170495
1985	8479	1853	107702	98231	220593	175337
1986	8713	1860	110022	99632	225526	180045
1987	8705	1880	114773	104932	230444	184126
1988	8820	1906	119328	109280	234807	187307
1989	8948	1886	122055	111816	240581	192147
1990	8989	1885	124015	114056	244039	194771
1991	9032	1906	129774	119079	249717	199051
1992	8989	1943	135527	124835	257043	205110
1993	8572	1968	139812	129317	267432	211874
1994	8720	2231	144865	134334	277398	220153
1995	8848	2267	148825	137756	288715	229894
1996	8921	2319	151553	141221	196108	237623
1997	8942	2348	155313	144496	305562	245862
1998	8805	2373	158351	147604	313737	252213
1999	8699	2415	162398	151367	320432	258591
2000	8984	2426	168143	157164	327065	264990
2001	8638	2444	172735	162197	330418	268347
2002	15500	2415	180791	165498	323294	262633
2003	15409	2410	188543	172981	336175	273620
2004	15744	2391	200056	183107	348203	283351
2005	16318	2428	209741	192551	364520	297334
2006	16953	2433	221886	204071	408972	332829
2007	16490	2435	234179	216951	452080	360674
2008	15821	2428	250497	231583	479462	383876
2009	16238	2442	271972	250364	513997	413444
2010	44880	2444	300083	277126	593503	455524
2011	45935	2411	325038	298070	627347	486356
2012	46556	2437	355274	324744	664825	520243
2013	47855	2447	378367	346478	710288	555498
2014	48087	2482	405707	372637	734345	584356
2015	48367	2539	435666	400745	771034	620004
2016	49124	2581	465228	428423	821880	667525
2017	49926	2666	492113	453022	866925	709894
2018	51527	2745	516973	477526	921703	757840
2019	53928	2817	545190	503893	964914	795132
2020	55900	2875	564701	523883	1009408	832061
2021	57955	2935	588953	546566	1062390	875803
2022	59531	2981	608258	564076	1111769	918430
2023	62862	3044	628574	583401	1173017	979076

注：从2002年开始，机构数中包含个体诊所机构数；从2010年开始机构、人员总计中含村卫生室数。

Note: Since 2002, the number of institutions has included the number of individual clinics;since 2010,number of village clinics was included in health care institutions.

21-3 医疗卫生机构、床位和人员数（2023年）
Number of Health Care Institutions, Beds and Personnel (2023)

机构类别	Type of Institution	机构（个） Number of Institutions (unit)	床位数（张） Beds (bed)	在岗职工（人） Employed Staff and Workers (person)	#卫生技术人员 Medical Technical Personnel	#执业(助理)医师 Licensed Physicians & Physician Assistants
医疗卫生机构数	**Health Care Institutions**	**62862**	**628574**	**1173017**	**979076**	**359481**
医　院	Hospitals	1874	515591	688029	573647	188082
卫生院	Health Centers	1170	67810	108354	94096	33902
康复医疗机构	Rehabilitation Medical Institution	14	458	918	524	179
社区卫生服务中心	Community Health Service Centers	736	9814	57964	50359	20884
社区卫生服务站	Community Health Service Stations	2058	22	14878	13976	6894
门诊部、诊所、卫生所等	Outpatient Departments and Clinics	30784	174	166732	150172	71890
#诊所	Outpatient Departments	21317		74116	68592	35122
卫生所(医务室)	Clinics (Medical Stations)	2736		10963	10158	5103
急救中心(站)	Emergency Centers (Stations)	67		1237	713	167
采供血机构	Blood Taking and Supply Agencies	50		3094	2354	264
妇幼保健机构	Maternity and Child Care Centers	133	28560	60391	51222	16782
专科疾病防治院(所、站)	Specialized Prevention and Treatment Stations	123	6145	9347	7182	2705
疾病预防控制机构	Disease Prevention and Control Centers (Antiepidemic Stations)	147		11880	9064	4532
卫生监督所	Sanitation Supervision Stations	149		4515	3017	
卫生监督检验(监测、检测)所(站)	Sanitation Supervision Quarantine Stations					
医学科学研究机构	Research Institutions of Medical Science	10		146	37	19
医学在职培训机构	On-the-job Medical Training Institutions	4		633	129	17
健康教育所(站、中心)	Health Education Stations (Centers)	44		637	261	117
村卫生室	Rural Medical Stations	25127		32852	15113	11903
其他卫生机构	Other Health Agencies	372		11410	7210	1144

注：1.总数中含村卫生室数。
　　2.康复医疗机构包括疗养院和康复医疗中心。

Note: a) Number of village clinics was included in health care institutions.
　　b) Rehabilitation medical institutions include sanatoriums and rehabilitation medical centers.

21-4 各市医疗卫生机构、床位和人员数（2023年）

Number of Health Care Institutions, Beds and Personnel by City (2023)

市 别	City	机构（个）Number of Institutions (unit)	#医院 Hospitals	床位数（张）Beds (bed)	#医院床位 Hospital Beds	在岗职工（人）Employed Staff and Workers (person)	#卫生技术人员 Medical Technical Personnel	#执业(助理)医师 Licensed Physicians & Physician Assistants
全 省	**Provincial Total**	**62862**	**1874**	**628574**	**515591**	**1173017**	**979076**	**359481**
广 州	Guangzhou	6677	331	117071	106785	247839	204254	71850
深 圳	Shenzhen	6113	159	56296	52408	152926	125989	50626
珠 海	Zhuhai	1161	46	13446	12190	29437	24689	9490
汕 头	Shantou	2275	68	23693	21075	39956	34147	13239
佛 山	Foshan	3083	143	42248	39419	83238	71693	26308
韶 关	Shaoguan	2158	54	22553	17179	31673	26187	8580
河 源	Heyuan	2255	69	20855	13476	29600	24962	8280
梅 州	Meizhou	2951	67	24753	17719	37399	31315	11316
惠 州	Huizhou	4114	84	25753	19948	55215	47378	18129
汕 尾	Shanwei	1647	44	12199	8759	20636	16509	5802
东 莞	Dongguan	4199	126	35997	34725	82805	70184	27409
中 山	Zhongshan	1517	69	16683	16594	36054	31855	12230
江 门	Jiangmen	1842	60	27355	20366	46523	40137	14499
阳 江	Yangjiang	1861	60	16016	12839	23445	18835	6577
湛 江	Zhanjiang	3957	136	46557	35995	65412	54127	17793
茂 名	Maoming	4026	83	40383	24646	47250	39306	14679
肇 庆	Zhaoqing	3267	69	21527	16054	38290	31071	10470
清 远	Qingyuan	2762	66	19445	13073	33542	28120	9872
潮 州	Chaozhou	2205	34	7986	5906	16031	12310	4926
揭 阳	Jieyang	3327	75	25353	18592	35286	28916	11416
云 浮	Yunfu	1465	31	12405	7843	20460	17092	5990
按经济区域分	By Region							
珠三角	Pearl River Delta	31973	1087	356376	318489	772327	647250	241011
粤 东	Eastern Region	9454	221	69231	54332	111909	91882	35383
粤 西	Western Region	9844	279	102956	73480	136107	112268	39049
粤 北	Northern Region	11591	287	100011	69290	152674	127676	44038

注：机构、人员数含村卫生室数。
Note: Number of village clinics was included in health care institutions.

21-5 各类医疗卫生机构、床位和人员数

Number of Health Institutions, Beds and Personnel by Type

指　　标	Item	2000	2005	2010	2015	2021	2022	2023
医疗卫生机构数（个）	**Number of Institutions (unit)**	**8984**	**40175**	**44880**	**48367**	**57955**	**59531**	**62862**
#医院	Hospitals	746	965	1088	1323	1762	1812	1874
卫生院	Health Centers	1680	1463	1356	1216	1173	1169	1170
门诊部、诊所、卫生所	Clinics, Health Stations and Community Health	5710	12224	11056	14068	25782	27434	30784
专科疾病防治院	Specialized Disease Prevention &Treatment Institution	158	157	147	131	128	124	123
疾病预防控制机构	Sanitation and Anti-epidemic Institutions	171	134	134	137	142	145	147
妇幼保健机构	Maternity and Child Care Centers	31	125	126	130	130	132	133
医学科学研究机构	Research Institutions of Medical Science	20	20	18	17	10	10	10
村卫生室	Rural Medical Stations	28913	23763	28339	27178	25448	25304	25127
床位数（张）	**Number of Beds (unit)**	**168143**	**209573**	**300083**	**435666**	**588953**	**608258**	**628574**
在岗职工（人）	**Employed Staff and Workers (person)**	**327065**	**364401**	**593503**	**771034**	**1062390**	**1111769**	**1173017**
卫生技术人员	Medical Technical Personnel	264990	271230	455524	620004	875803	918430	979076
#执业(助理)医师	Licensed Physicians & Physician Assistants	111172	120875	175100	229389	320923	335181	359481
注册护士	Nurses	83198	98681	168043	254430	402047	420790	450646
其他技术人员	Other Technical Personnel	8910	42559	54491	50033	54729	55549	55146
管理人员	Administrative Personnel	24320	21617	29541	30638	38236	40223	41544
工勤人员	Logistics Personnel	28845	28995	53947	70359	93622	97567	97251

注：从2002年开始，机构数中包含个体诊所机构数；门诊部(所)含门诊部、诊所、卫生所、医务室、护理站等；妇幼保健院归入妇幼保健机构统计；医生指执业(助理)医师。2008年起，门诊部(所)含护理站，不含社区卫生服务站(纳入其他卫生机构)。2010年起机构、人员数含村卫生室数。2021年起，管理人员为仅从事管理人员数。

Note: Since 2002, the number of institutions has included the number of individual clinics, covered in the category of outpatient departments (clinics); maternity and child care centers have been included in the number of maternity and child care institutions; doctors have referred to certified (assistant) doctors; and since 2008, clinics include nurse stations, but exclude community health stations, which is listed as Other Healthcare Institutions. Since 2010,Number of village clinics was included in health care institutions. Since 2021,the number of managers only includes the persons who are engaged in management.

21−6 各市社会保险基金征缴收入(2023年)

Amount Collected of Security Insurance (2023)

单位：万元 (10000 yuan)

市别	City	城镇职工基本养老保险基金征缴收入 Amount Collected of Urban Employee Basic Pension Insurance	城乡居民基本养老保险基金征缴收入 Amount Collected of Basic Pension Insurance for Urban and Rural Residents	城镇职工基本医疗保险基金征缴收入 Amount Collected of Urban Employee Basic Medical Insurance	城乡居民基本医疗保险基金征缴收入 Amount Collected of Basic Medical Care Insurance for Urban and Rural Residents	失业保险基金征缴收入 Amount Collected of Unemployment Insurance	工伤保险基金征缴收入 Amount Collected of Work Injury Insurance
全省	**Provincial Total**	**63248164**	**730884**	**17447369**	**2852520**	**1565604**	**868061**
广州	Guangzhou	13213772	185338	4827148	235768	470172	175194
深圳	Shenzhen	16569471	1123	5729557	412430	357691	224849
珠海	Zhuhai	2047648	18617	495307	32734	55612	24475
汕头	Shantou	1024602	33687	302857	146579	25966	9210
佛山	Foshan	4959756	52103	1191114	149404	122398	69384
韶关	Shaoguan	745545	21551	191941	78284	15794	10550
河源	Heyuan	606640	19429	145555	86557	11369	7190
梅州	Meizhou	856240	21738	196943	139833	15801	7820
惠州	Huizhou	2550277	40978	588778	92140	53549	35318
汕尾	Shanwei	339601	24655	78713	91987	6269	4415
东莞	Dongguan	6664626	18967	1342239	102297	218143	134744
中山	Zhongshan	2428416	9019	484369	91682	63995	38104
江门	Jiangmen	1631404	26041	424599	93568	32822	21419
阳江	Yangjiang	509586	28168	120952	81965	10078	7624
湛江	Zhanjiang	1055085	45464	282805	222879	22652	10606
茂名	Maoming	848957	39560	234866	216059	19188	9225
肇庆	Zhaoqing	939246	32990	240873	118636	19438	12701
清远	Qingyuan	940413	44279	253604	120042	19970	13016
潮州	Chaozhou	462549	14144	108567	77100	9377	4293
揭阳	Jieyang	634439	32669	97293	183788	8155	5118
云浮	Yunfu	419298	20362	109286	78787	7165	5085
省直	Directly under Provincial Government	3800592					37720
按经济区域分	By Region						
珠三角	Pearl River Delta	51004617	385176	15323985	1328659	1393821	736189
粤东	Eastern Region	2461191	105155	587430	499455	49766	23037
粤西	Western Region	2413628	113193	638623	520903	51918	27454
粤北	Northern Region	3568136	127360	897331	503503	70098	43661

注：1.各区域数据不包含省直单位部分；本表生育保险收入不再单独填列，合并在职工医保收入中体现。
2.珠海、佛山、东莞、中山建立城乡一体化基本医疗保险制度，本表中4市居民基本医疗基金合并在职工基本医疗基金统计。

Note: a)The data of each region does not include the agencies directly under provincial jurisdiction. The Maternity Insurance income in this table are no longer filled in individually, consolidated in the Medical Care Insurance income of employees.

b)Zhuhai, Foshan, Dongguan and Zhongshan have established the urban-rural integrated basic medical insurance system.In this table, the urban employee medical care insurance in the four cities include the basic medical care insurance for urban and rural residents.

21-7 各市社会保险参保人数（2023年）

Number of Persons Participating in Social Insurance by City (2023)

单位：万人 (10000 persons)

市别	City	城镇职工基本养老保险参保人数 Urban Employee Basic Pension Insurance Contributors	城乡居民基本养老保险参保人数 Basic Pension Insurance for Urban and Rural Residents Contributors	城镇职工基本医疗保险 Urban Employees Basic Medical Care Insurance Contributors	城乡居民基本医疗保险参保人数 Basic Medical Care Insurance for Urban and Rural Residents Contributors	失业保险参保人数 Unemployment Insurance Contributors	工伤保险参保人数 Work Injury Insurance Contributors	生育保险参保人数 Maternity Insurance Contributors
全　省	**Provincial Total**	**5368.88**	**2760.03**	**4848.20**	**6192.69**	**3794.76**	**4270.30**	**3902.78**
广　州	Guangzhou	901.52	134.19	925.78	488.43	718.69	763.47	702.86
深　圳	Shenzhen	1439.76	1.34	1440.32	297.95	1269.40	1325.84	1286.50
珠　海	Zhuhai	157.86	11.24	163.82	76.47	123.09	130.68	126.42
汕　头	Shantou	108.24	238.77	90.44	394.53	56.52	83.26	62.70
佛　山	Foshan	461.70	70.69	419.88	239.50	329.54	374.06	335.51
韶　关	Shaoguan	78.82	103.87	70.71	215.93	37.38	47.94	42.48
河　源	Heyuan	57.29	131.67	46.27	239.37	29.61	40.79	43.39
梅　州	Meizhou	109.45	164.84	53.42	356.89	39.63	49.02	39.63
惠　州	Huizhou	224.79	115.62	220.93	241.55	166.50	189.12	193.12
汕　尾	Shanwei	35.31	103.00	25.38	239.42	13.48	20.35	18.97
东　莞	Dongguan	630.03	4.62	572.62	97.80	455.07	497.54	446.94
中　山	Zhongshan	247.42	1.15	199.78	124.22	169.50	194.15	173.50
江　门	Jiangmen	173.30	148.95	170.12	234.42	105.96	122.71	115.35
阳　江	Yangjiang	45.60	126.51	35.38	222.89	21.11	36.00	26.75
湛　江	Zhanjiang	112.48	288.60	88.49	598.43	51.08	59.34	57.49
茂　名	Maoming	86.75	275.62	61.53	567.40	37.26	45.87	41.05
肇　庆	Zhaoqing	94.84	166.36	87.54	314.02	56.58	72.55	62.65
清　远	Qingyuan	93.03	185.66	82.28	310.33	51.10	63.18	58.75
潮　州	Chaozhou	55.34	114.32	33.23	207.78	24.07	28.36	23.37
揭　阳	Jieyang	66.08	252.91	29.28	512.41	19.67	32.45	21.18
云　浮	Yunfu	38.90	120.10	31.00	212.94	19.51	24.94	24.17
省　直	Directly under Provincial Government	150.35					68.69	
按经济区域分	By Region							
珠三角	Pearl River Delta	4331.22	654.16	4200.79	2114.37	3394.35	3670.12	3442.84
粤　东	Eastern Region	264.97	709.00	178.34	1354.14	113.74	164.42	126.22
粤　西	Western Region	244.84	690.73	185.40	1388.72	109.45	141.20	125.29
粤　北	Northern Region	377.49	706.13	283.68	1335.46	177.23	225.87	208.43

注：1.各区域不包省直单位部分。
　　2.2012年8月起，新型社会农村养老保险和城镇居民社会养老保险制度全覆盖工作全面启动，合并为城乡居民社会养老保险。

Note: a) “By Region” does not include agencies directly under provincial jurisdiction.
　　b) Since August 2012,system of new old-age insurance and urban basic pension insurance have started completely, and called basic pension insurance for urban and rural residents as total.

21-8 优抚、社会救济和福利事业情况

Statistics on Preferential Treatment and Resettlement, Social Relief and Welfare

项 目	Item	2010	2015	2020	2021	2022	2023
优抚事业	**Preferential Treatment and Resettlement**						
优抚事业单位数 (个)	Number of Institutions for Preferential Treatment and Resettlement (unit)			39	42	42	42
优抚事业单位服务对象人数 (人次)	Number of Persons Adopted by Preferential Treatment and Resettlement Institutions (person-time)			35347	42090	49679	50629
优抚事业费用 (万元)	Expenses on Preferential Treatment and Resettlement (10000 yuan)			542804	585915	631784	696188
社会救助	**Social Relief**						
社会救助总人数 (万人)	Total Number under Social Relief (10000 persons)	288.00	227.25	180.35	173.95	162.77	156.14
城乡居民最低生活保障人数 (万人)	Number of Urban and Rural Residents Receiving Minimum Income Relief (10000 persons)	224.70	183.30	142.97	142.33	130.62	124.53
城镇	Urban Areas	40.70	29.69	15.21	15.00	14.78	14.60
农村	Rural Areas	184.00	153.60	127.76	127.33	115.84	109.93
城乡居民最低生活保障家庭户数 (万户)	Number of Urban and Rural Households Receiving Minimum Income Relief (10000 households)	91.80	86.39	59.52	58.63	54.29	52.04
城镇	Urban Areas	17.30	15.19	8.17	7.93	7.75	7.66
农村	Rural Areas	74.50	71.20	51.35	50.70	46.54	44.38
城乡居民最低生活保障金支出 (万元)	Expenditures on Minimum Income Relief for Urban and Rural Residents (10000 yuan)	244490	553022	827367	794511	831586	819203
城镇	Urban Areas	79665	159530	151952	145289	150282	152096
农村	Rural Areas	164825	393493	675415	649222	681305	667107
社会福利支出 (亿元)	Expenses on Social Welfare (100 million yuan)		40.89	117.74	131.47	143.42	147.91
社会救助支出 (亿元)	Expenses on Social Relief (100 million yuan)		94.79	124.34	118.65	125.51	124.26

21－8 续表 continued

项　目	Item	2010	2015	2020	2021	2022	2023
社会工作机构情况	**Social Welfare**						
提供住宿的社会工作机构（个）	Number of Social Welfare Institutions with Accommodations (unit)	2514	1588	2039	2109	2058	2076
编制登记	Registered with State Office for Scopes	256	1282	1440	1455	1363	1325
工商登记	Registered with Industry and Commerce Administration	27	48	215	272	304	356
民政登记	Registered with Civil Affairs Administration	1791	220	359	354	355	345
一个机构多块牌子	Multiple Brands within One Organization	440	38	24	28	36	50
提供住宿的社会服务机构年末在院人数（人）	Number of People Taken in by Social Welfare Institutions with Accommodations at the year-end (person)	92224	92043	102212	101126	98395	103496
编制登记	Registered with State Office for Scopes	26402	61360	50335	47844	44786	43364
工商登记	Registered with Industry and Commerce Administration	3188	8481	19506	21160	23295	28820
民政登记	Registered with Civil Affairs Administration	51516	20525	32065	31555	29866	30209
一个机构多块牌子	Multiple Brands within One Organization	11118	1677	306	567	448	1103
社区服务	**Community Service**						
社区综合服务机构和设施总数（个）	Number of Community Nursing Service Facilities and Institution (unit)	15960	57108	30978	31894	31950	32063
社区服务指导中心	Community Service Guidance Centers		29	18	17	18	19
社区服务中心	Community Service Centers	1366	2893	1863	2073	2108	2129
社区服务站	Community Service Stations	1632	13284	26605	27146	27116	27223
社区专项服务机构和设施数	Number of Community Special Service Facilities and Institution	12962	40281	2492	2658	2708	2692
社区养老服务机构和设施数（个）	Number of Community Nursing Service Facilities and Institution (unit)			22364	21450	21808	21414
未登记和挂靠的特困人员救助供养机构	Unregistered and Affiliated Rescue and Feeding Institutions for the Poor People			16	11	11	8
全托服务社区养老服务机构和设施	Total Care Community Nursing Service Facilities and Institution			1442	1579	1587	1589
日间照料社区养老服务机构和设施	Daily Care Community Nursing.Service Facilities and Institution			14917	13698	13672	12851
社区养老机构和设施	Community Nursing Facilities and Insitution		621				
互助型养老设施	Community Mutual Aid Nursing Facilities			3931	3936	3928	3663
其他社区养老服务设施	Other Community Service Facilities			2058	2226	2610	3303

注：1.2013年起，社会福利收养性事业单位数和社会福利收养性事业单位收养人数指标分别修改为提供住宿的社会服务机构数和提供住宿的社会服务机构年末在院人数。

2.2015年以前，一个机构多块牌子的机构为未登记注册机构。

3.2019年以前社区服务机构和设施总数包括(1)社区服务指导中心；(2)社区服务中心；(3)社区服务站；(4)未登记注册的特困人员供养机构；(5)社区养老照料机构和设施；(6)社区互助型养老设施；(7)其他社区服务机构和设施，数据填至2019年。从2020年起，根据《民政事业统计调查制度》，将社区综合服务机构和设施与社区养老服务机构和设施分开单独统计，2020年按新的口径进行填报。

Note: a) Since 2013, the indicator of number of social welfare institutions and number of people taken in by social welfare institutions are amended as the indicator of social welfare institutions with accommodations and number of people taken in by social welfare institutions with accommodations at year-end respectively.

b)Before 2015, the organizations with multiple brands are unregistered organizations.

c)The total number of community service facilities and institutions before 2019 includes(1)Community Service Guidance Centers;(2)Community Service Centers; (3)Community Service Stations; (4)Unregistered Feeding Institutions for the Poor People; (5)Community Nursing Facilities and Institution; (6)Community Mutual Aid Nursing Facilities;(7)Other Community Service Facilities, data to 2019. Since 2020，according to the Statistical Survey System of Civil Affairs, counted the Community Comprehensive Service Facilities and the Community Nursing Service Facilities and Institution separately and fill in new caliber in 2000.

21-9 婚姻登记情况

Statistics on Marriage Registration

项　　目	Item	2010	2015	2021	2022	2023
登记结婚件数　（对）	**Marriage Registration Number　(couple)**	**857146**	**840411**	**591124**	**573050**	**632192**
内地居民登记结婚件数	Mainland Residents Marriage Registration Number	850448	832694	586212	567609	622253
涉外及华侨、港澳台居民登记结婚件数	Marriage Registration Number with Foreigners, Overseas Chinese and Citizens of HongKong, Macao and Taiwan	6698	7717	4912	5441	9939
登记结婚人数　（人）	**Nmber of Persons Registered　(person)**	**1714292**	**1680822**	**1182248**	**1146100**	**1264384**
按居住地分类	By Place of Residence					
内地居民登记结婚人数	Number of mainland residents registered	1700896	1665442	1172424	1135218	1244506
涉外及华侨、港澳台居民登记结婚中	Number of Registered Marriages Involving Foreigners and Overseas Chinese, Hong Kong, Macao and Taiwan residents					
内地居民	Mainland Residents	6676	7676	4901	5435	9933
#女性	Female	5241	5324	2570	2838	5212
香港居民	Hongkong Residents	1552	2436	1575	1972	4728
澳门居民	Macao Residents	765	827	616	594	695
台湾居民	Taiwan Residents	770	840	356	465	761
华侨	Overseas Chinese	1069	1526	106	202	379
外国人	Foreigners	2564	2129	2270	2214	3382
按婚前状况分类	By pre marital status					
初婚人数	Number of First Marriages	1583025	1501835	987392	968785	1071125
再婚人数	Number of Remarriages	131267	178987	194856	177315	193259
#女性	Female	57536	85208	103362	95841	107295
恢复结婚件数　（对）	Resumption of Marriages　(couple)	12764	27356	23364	23330	25716
按年龄分类	By age					
#20～24	20～24	549611	490868	184422	146421	138038
25～29	25～29	703191	718631	521992	520238	573473
30～34	30～34	237064	230655	258661	276867	322140
35～39	35～39	105735	90905	94449	96641	110261
40以上	above 40	118691	149763	122724	105933	120472
离婚总数　（对）	**Total Number of Divorce　(couple)**	**127048**	**193360**	**167209**	**184511**	**226080**
民政离婚登记　（对）	Registered Divorce　(couple)	100759	167544	144933	158096	190684
内地居民登记离婚　（对）	Number of Mainland Residents Registered Divorces　(couple)	99536	166142	144402	157504	189276
涉外及华侨、港澳台居民登记离婚　（对）	Divorce from Foreigners,Overseas Chinese and Citizens of Hong Kong, Macao and Taiwan　(couple)	1223	1402	531	592	1408
#外国人　（人）	Foreigners　(person)	397	290	138	194	300
法院调解离婚　（对）	Divorces through Law Court Mediation　(couple)	17644	15268	11821	15465	22560
法院判决离婚　（对）	Divorces through Law Court Judgment　(couple)	8645	10548	10455	10950	12836

21-10 律师、公证、基层司法基本情况

Basic Statistics on Lawyers, Notarization, Grassroots Judicial Work

项目	Item	2005	2010	2015	2021	2022	2023
律师工作	**Lawyers**						
律师事务所 （个）	Number of Law Offices (unit)	1110	1668	2290	3857	4136	4473
执业律师 （人）	Number of Full-time Lawyers (person)	15779	20230	28221	61946	70680	79357
担任常年法律顾问 （家）	Number of Units as Permanent Legal Advisors(unit)	20533	36484	59664	100925	105979	98792
民事案件诉讼代理 （件）	Agent of Civil Cases (case)	61800	150817	225385	866545	903404	1068447
非诉讼代理 （件）	Agent of Non-litigious Legal Affairs (case)	157212	126726	174951	390888	374785	292615
刑事诉讼辩护及代理(件)	Defender of Criminal Cases (case)	18675	38116	30739		103753	149432
公证工作	**Notarization**						
公证处 （个）	Number of Notary Offices (unit)	114	139	146	154	154	153
工作人员（公证员、公证员助理） （人）	Number of Notarial Personnel (person)	1374	1694	2190	2928	3052	3106
出证总数 （件）	Number of Notarized Documents (case)	1055486	1358974	1525912	1305061	1120370	1431751
国内公证	Domestic Notary	636337	912609	1044876	1066235	906707	1068621
涉外及涉台港澳公证	Foreign-related and Hong Kong, Macao and	419149	490745	481036	238826	213663	363130
基层司法行政工作	**Grassroots Judicial Work**						
基层司法所 （个）	Number of Law Service Offices (unit)	1647	1617	1616	1628	1629	1630
工作人员 （人）	Number of Personnel Working in Law Service Offices (person)	4938	4976	6036	8896	8961	9062
人民调解委员会 （个）	Number of People's Mediation Committees (unit)	28923	33789	32549	31689	31827	32646
调解人员 （人）	Number of Mediators (person)	163459	194224	181205	182304	184727	191693
调解纠纷总数 （件）	Number of Disputes Mediated (case)	169991	384531	326174	489348	417242	460121

注：自2021年起，司法部统计报表中将值班律师法律帮助案件以及法律援助受援人数不列入受理案件总数以及法律援助受援人数统计。

Note: Since 2021, the Ministry of Justice has excluded the legal assistance cases of duty lawyers and the number of legal aid recipients from the total number of cases accepted and the number of legal aid recipients in the statistical statements.

21－11　交通事故发生情况（2023年）

Statistics on Traffic Accidents (2023)

项　　目	Item	合计 Total	按道路横断面位置分 By Cross-section Location of Roads				按事故发生道路类型分 By Type of Roads Where Accidents Occurs			
			机动车道 Roads for Motored Vehicles	非机动车道 Roads for Non-motored Vehicles	混合道 Mixed Roads	其他道 Others	高速公路 Express Highways	等级公路 Classified Highways	城市道路 Urban Roads	其他路 Others
发生　（起）	Number of Traffic Accidents (case)	44104	31325	1736	9572	1471	1039	14736	25626	2703
死亡　（人）	Number of Deaths (person)	7681	5877	211	1287	306	433	3236	3548	464
受伤　（人）	Number of Injuries (person)	43478	30275	1894	9987	1322	1149	15445	24118	2766
损失折款（万元）	Losses Converted into Cash (10000 yuan)	11220	9013	292	1326	589	2668	3311	4868	373
平均每起事故损失（元）	Average Loss per Traffic Accident (yuan)	2544	2877	1682	1386	4002	25676	2247	1900	1379

注：1.等级公路分为一至四级公路和等外公路；
2.城市道路包括城市快速路和一般城市道路；
3.其他路包括单位小区自建路、公共停车场、公共广场、乡道、村道、田间地头、农垦区等区域。

Notes: a) Classified highways refer to highways of Class I to IV and Unclassified Highway.
b) Urban roads include express roads and normal roads in urban areas.
c) Other roads include roads within residential neighborhoods, public parking lots, squares, country roads, village roads, farm roads and reclaimed areas.

21－12　火灾事故发生情况（2023年）

Statistics on Fire Accidents (2023)

项　　目	Item	合计 Total	特大 Extraordinarily Serious Accidents	重大 Serious Accidents	较大 Relatively Serious Accidents	一般 Ordinary Accidents
发生　（起）	Number of Traffic Accidents (case)	57785			5	57780
死亡　（人）	Number of Deaths (person)	118			21	97
受伤　（人）	Number of Injuries (person)	294				294
损失折款（万元）	Losses Converted into Cash(10000 yuan)	71742			134	71608
平均每起事故损失(元)	Average Loss per Traffic Accident(yuan)	12415			27	12393

21-13 各市亿元生产总值生产安全事故死亡率

Rate of Death from Work Safety Accidents per 100 Million Yuan of Gross Domestic Product by City

单位：% (%)

市别	City	2010	2014	2015	2016	2017	2018	2019	2020	2021	2022	2023
全省	**Provincial Rate**	**0.153**	**0.092**	**0.085**	**0.050**	**0.041**	**0.034**	**0.029**	**0.023**	**0.019**	**0.016**	**0.016**
广州	Guangzhou	0.104	0.056	0.051	0.026	0.021	0.016	0.015	0.013	0.012	0.010	0.009
深圳	Shenzhen	0.071	0.033	0.032	0.020	0.014	0.012	0.011	0.010	0.008	0.007	0.005
珠海	Zhuhai	0.111	0.067	0.060	0.036	0.029	0.022	0.017	0.017	0.019	0.013	0.012
汕头	Shantou	0.181	0.110	0.107	0.035	0.044	0.035	0.027	0.027	0.014	0.012	0.012
佛山	Foshan	0.129	0.061	0.058	0.032	0.029	0.034	0.028	0.023	0.018	0.009	0.009
韶关	Shaoguan	0.356	0.196	0.170	0.116	0.113	0.104	0.091	0.062	0.057	0.045	0.050
河源	Heyuan	0.260	0.167	0.135	0.087	0.099	0.085	0.104	0.102	0.066	0.074	0.072
梅州	Meizhou	0.286	0.182	0.175	0.063	0.047	0.041	0.031	0.023	0.018	0.039	0.049
惠州	Huizhou	0.200	0.104	0.098	0.066	0.061	0.049	0.041	0.038	0.027	0.022	0.018
汕尾	Shanwei	0.302	0.198	0.188	0.139	0.167	0.102	0.089	0.062	0.048	0.034	0.036
东莞	Dongguan	0.135	0.089	0.084	0.052	0.043	0.039	0.028	0.021	0.016	0.012	0.009
中山	Zhongshan	0.185	0.114	0.108	0.065	0.047	0.049	0.057	0.056	0.045	0.028	0.022
江门	Jiangmen	0.261	0.174	0.162	0.080	0.061	0.036	0.029	0.024	0.016	0.037	0.027
阳江	Yangjiang	0.278	0.139	0.137	0.122	0.085	0.077	0.093	0.069	0.059	0.066	0.055
湛江	Zhanjiang	0.167	0.095	0.091	0.070	0.055	0.051	0.051	0.029	0.033	0.022	0.027
茂名	Maoming	0.190	0.109	0.104	0.043	0.032	0.028	0.025	0.020	0.013	0.014	0.033
肇庆	Zhaoqing	0.241	0.133	0.127	0.094	0.064	0.059	0.057	0.040	0.032	0.034	0.044
清远	Qingyuan	0.199	0.154	0.158	0.195	0.187	0.144	0.119	0.077	0.045	0.075	0.067
潮州	Chaozhou	0.172	0.155	0.156	0.070	0.052	0.049	0.051	0.036	0.035	0.025	0.036
揭阳	Jieyang	0.207	0.110	0.103	0.037	0.043	0.044	0.051	0.029	0.030	0.032	0.036
云浮	Yunfu	0.383	0.199	0.169	0.164	0.139	0.151	0.124	0.085	0.063	0.040	0.036

注：1.2005—2015年全省生产安全事故包括工矿商贸、道路交通、火灾、铁路路外、水上交通及渔业船舶死亡人数；各市生产安全事故包括工矿商贸、道路交通、火灾事故死亡人数。

2.2016年原国家安全监管总局开展生产安全事故统计改革，调整了生产安全事故统计范围。

Note:a) Work safety accidents from 2005 to 2015 of the Province include the number of deaths related to industry, mining,traffic,fire,railway,water traffic and fishing boats accidents, and work safety accidents of each city include the number of deaths related to mining, traffic and fire accidents.

b)Due to the statistics reform of production safety accident conducted by State Administration of Work Safety in 2016, the statistical coverage of production safety accident has been adjusted.

主要统计指标解释

卫生技术人员 指卫生事业机构支付工资的全部固定职工和合同制职工，现任职务为卫生技术工作的专业人员。包括中医师、西医师、中西医结合高级医师、护师、中药师、西药师、检验师、其他技师、中医士、西医士、护士、助产士、中药剂士、西药剂士、检验士、其他技士、其他中医、护理员、中药剂员、西药剂员、检验员，其他初级卫生技术人员。

医生 指经卫生部门审查合格，具有执业资格的医疗专业人员。

提供住宿的社会服务活动机构 根据《2014 年社会服务业统计制度》，提供住宿的社会服务活动机构包括：为老年人与残疾人提供收留抚养服务的机构、为智障与精神病人提供收留抚养服务的机构、为儿童提供收留抚养和救助服务机构以及其他提供住宿的服务机构。

律师 指受聘参加法律顾问处工作，提任法律顾问、刑（民）事代理人、刑事辩护人，办理非诉讼事件、解答法律询问，代写法律事务文书等主要从事律师事务的司法人员。

公证人员 指在国家公证机关依法办理公证事务的司法人员。包括公证员、助理公证员和在公证处工作的其他人员。

调解人员 在人民调解委员会担负调解民间一般民事纠纷和轻微违法行为所引起的纠纷的工作人员。包括调解委员会的委员和调解小组的调解员。

亿元生产总值生产安全事故死亡率 指一定时期内，每生产亿元生产总值，因各类生产安全事故造成的死亡人数。

Explanatory Notes on Main Statistical Indicators

Medical Technical Personnel refer to all permanent and contract medical staff and workers employed by medical institutions，including doctors of Chinese and Western medicine，senior doctors who integrate traditional Chinese therapeutics with Western therapeutics in practice，senior nurses，pharmacists of Chinese and Western medicine，laboratory specialists，other specialists，paramedics of Chinese and Western medicine，nurses，midwives，druggists in Chinese and Western medicine，laboratory technicians，other technicians，other practitioners of Chinese medicine，nursing attendants，pharmacological workers of Chinese and Western medicine，laboratory workers，and other primary medical personnel.

Doctors refer to qualified medical professionals approved to practice by public health departments.

Social Welfare Institutions with Accommodations In accordance with Statistical System of Social Service in 2014，Social Welfare Institutions with Accommodations includes: Institutions taking care of old people and handicapped people, institutions taking care of retarded people and mental patients, institutions adopting and salving children and other social welfare institutions with accommodations. That is, from 1995 to 2012 the caliber is Number of Social Welfare Institutions (unit); since 2013, due to the change of system in Ministry of Civil Affairs，the caliber changes to Social Welfare Institutions with Accommodations .

Lawyers refer to legal workers who are employed by legal counseling firms to act as legal advisers，agents in criminal or civil lawsuits，or defenders in criminal lawsuits，or to handle non litigious legal affairs，to advise on matters of law or to write legal papers for others.

Notary Personnel refer to judicial workers of the state notary offices handling notarization work according to law. They include notaries，assistant notaries，and other people working for notary offices.

Mediators refer to workers on people’s mediation committees responsible for mediating in civil disputes and cases of slight infraction of the law. They include members of the mediation committees and mediators of mediation groups.

Rate of Death from Work Safety Accidents per 100 Million Yuan of Gross Domestic Product refers to the number of deaths due to various work safety accidents in the production process of every 100 million yuan of gross domestic product within a certain period.

二十二、区域经济主要指标

MAJOR ECONOMIC REGIONS

二十二　区域主要经济指标

简要说明

一、本篇主要反映广东境内主要区域社会经济发展的基本情况，内容主要包括：珠三角、广州和深圳、粤东、粤西、粤北、山区县以及少数民族县等经济区域的主要统计指标数据。

二、本篇资料分别由广东省统计局各有关专业处整理提供，综合统计处负责编辑。

三、本篇资料根据国家统计局制定的各有关专业统计报表制度填报汇总而成。

四、本篇各项指标数据为各经济区域汇总数，由于部分年份各市生产总值等指标汇总数不等于全省数，因此仅适合反映该地区发展变化情况。

22 Major Economic Regions

Brief Introduction

Ⅰ. The data in this chapter mainly reflect the basic conditions of social and economic development of main economic regions in Guangdong, including the main indicators on the cities of the Pearl River Delta, Guangzhou and Shenzhen, the Eastern and Western and Northern Region, counties in mountainous areas and minority counties.

II. The data in this chapter are prepared and provided by the related specialized divisions and compiled by the Division of Comprehensive Statistics of Statistics Bureau of Guangdong Province.

Ⅲ. The data in this chapter are tabulated and reported in accordance with the various statistical reporting schemes stipulated by the National Bureau of Statistics.

Ⅳ. The indicators in this chapter are overall figures of various economic regions that only reflect the status of development of the corresponding regions, as the provincial total is not equal to the sum of indicators of various cities, such as gross domestic product.

22-1 区域主要经济指标
Main Indicators on Regional Economies

指 标	Item	2022 珠三角 Pearl River Delta	粤东 Eastern Region	粤西 Western Region	粤北 Northern Region
土地面积 (平方公里)	Land Area (sq.km.)	54767	15496	32682	76751
年末常住人口 (万人)	Permanent Population at the Year-end (10000 persons)	7829.43	1643.42	1589.58	1594.37
#城镇人口 (万人)	Urban Population (10000 persons)	6848.95	1006.82	763.71	845.92
地区生产总值 (亿元)	Gross Domestic Product (100 million yuan)	104983.11	7959.90	9155.27	7415.27
第一产业	Primary Industry	1838.39	670.35	1645.14	1196.21
第二产业	Secondary Industry	43244.01	3390.60	3384.76	2601.35
第三产业	Tertiary Industry	59900.71	3898.95	4125.37	3617.71
人均地区生产总值 (元)	Per Capita GDP (yuan)	133821	48473	57640	46494
地区生产总值指数 (上年=100)	Index of Gross Domestic Product (preceding year=100)	102.2	100.8	100.9	101.1
第一产业	Primary Industry	104.8	105.6	104.5	105.1
第二产业	Secondary Industry	102.1	98.2	96.6	99.2
第三产业	Tertiary Industry	102.2	102.3	102.5	101.1
人均地区生产总值指数 (上年=100)	Index of Per Capita Gross Domestic Product (preceding year=100)	102.2	100.5	100.5	101.1
固定资产投资同比上年增长(%)	Growth Rate of Investment in Fixed Assets (%)	0.4	-13.4	-10.6	-14.4
#房地产开发投资 (亿元)	Investment in Real Estate Development (100 million yuan)	12927.69	750.85	684.18	734.21
社会消费品零售总额 (亿元)	Total Amount of Retail Sales of Consumer Goods (100 million yuan)	34959.60	3513.77	3832.16	2494.15
出口总额 (亿元)	Total Exports (100 million yuan)	50836.84	1065.66	445.15	722.61
进口总额 (亿元)	Total Imports (100 million yuan)	28333.57	291.01	577.87	520.50
实际外商直接投资 (亿元)	Foreign Direct Investment Actually Utilized (100 million yuan)	1720.08	16.12	48.78	34.03
地方一般公共预算收入 (亿元)	Local Public Budgetary Revenue (100 million yuan)	9049.47	309.90	353.99	481.78
地方一般公共预算支出 (亿元)	Local Public Budgetary Expenditure (100 million yuan)	12662.25	1266.24	1317.09	1839.23
金融机构本外币存款 (亿元)	Deposits in Renminbi and Foreign Currencies in All Financial Institutions (100 million yuan)	289656.10	11052.26	10036.79	11612.52
#本外币住户存款	Savings Deposits by Resident	90095.22	7938.99	7212.14	8308.40
金融机构本外币贷款 (亿元)	Loans in Renminbi and Foreign Currencies in All Financial Institutions (100 million yuan)	222640.84	5946.91	7795.89	9339.30
全体居民人均可支配收入 (元)	Per Capita Disposable Income of Households (yuan)	62700.0	28388.3	28713.6	28256.0
城镇居民人均可支配收入 (元)	Per Capita Disposable Income of Urban Households (yuan)	67092.6	33521.5	35906.0	35151.8
农村居民人均可支配收入 (元)	Per Capita Disposable Income of Rural Households (yuan)	31956.7	20335.4	22254.3	20627.7

22-1 续表 continued

指　标	Item	2023 珠三角 Pearl River Delta	2023 粤　东 Eastern Region	2023 粤　西 Western Region	2023 粤　北 Northern Region
土地面积 (平方公里)	Land Area (sq.km.)	54767	15496	32682	76751
年末常住人口 (万人)	Permanent Population at the Year-end (10000 persons)	7869.76	1647.86	1595.54	1592.84
#城镇人口 (万人)	Urban Population (10000 persons)	6912.10	1018.23	785.74	866.80
地区生产总值 (亿元)	Gross Domestic Product (100 million yuan)	110214.70	8390.78	9362.60	7705.08
第一产业	Primary Industry	1913.38	696.29	1688.04	1242.99
第二产业	Secondary Industry	44701.01	3634.93	3402.62	2698.70
第三产业	Tertiary Industry	63600.32	4059.55	4271.93	3763.40
人均地区生产总值 (元)	Per Capita GDP (yuan)	140408	50988	58790	48350
地区生产总值指数（上年=100）	Index of Gross Domestic Product (preceding year=100)	104.8	105.0	103.4	104.6
第一产业	Primary Industry	104.9	104.0	104.1	105.9
第二产业	Secondary Industry	104.8	106.7	102.2	105.2
第三产业	Tertiary Industry	104.8	103.9	103.9	103.8
人均地区生产总值指数 （上年=100）	Index of Per Capita Gross Domestic Product (preceding year=100)	104.8	104.8	103.1	104.7
固定资产投资同比上年增长(%)	Growth Rate of Investment in Fixed Assets (%)	2.4	-3.2	8.6	4.4
#房地产开发投资 (亿元)	Investment in Real Estate Development (100 million yuan)	11753.86	609.34	666.72	663.40
社会消费品零售总额 (亿元)	Total Amount of Retail Sales of Consumer Goods (100 million yuan)	37037.68	3645.54	4053.44	2588.59
出口总额 (亿元)	Total Exports (100 million yuan)	52334.49	977.71	397.29	664.83
进口总额 (亿元)	Total Imports (100 million yuan)	27108.30	351.53	656.14	526.96
实际外商直接投资 (亿元)	Foreign Direct Investment Actually Utilized (100 million yuan)	1494.47	14.88	49.04	18.24
地方一般公共预算收入 (亿元)	Local Public Budgetary Revenue (100 million yuan)	9406.36	360.36	379.82	511.71
地方一般公共预算支出 (亿元)	Local Public Budgetary Expenditure (100 million yuan)	12609.39	1227.55	1322.91	1813.29
金融机构本外币存款 (亿元)	Deposits in Renminbi and Foreign Currencies in All Financial Institutions (100 million yuan)	315470.76	11871.24	10784.05	12761.56
#本外币住户存款	Savings Deposits by Resident	100806.65	8787.00	7885.71	9146.19
金融机构本外币贷款 (亿元)	Loans in Renminbi and Foreign Currencies in All Financial Institutions (100 million yuan)	246156.16	6601.92	8515.50	10288.05
全体居民人均可支配收入 (元)	Per Capita Disposable Income of Households (yuan)	65654.7	29597.8	29829.7	29745.8
城镇居民人均可支配收入 (元)	Per Capita Disposable Income of Urban Households (yuan)	70194.8	34767.1	36697.5	36592.4
农村居民人均可支配收入 (元)	Per Capita Disposable Income of Rural Households (yuan)	33682.3	21422.9	23478.8	22007.6

注：本表地区生产总值、工业增加值绝对数按当年价格计算，指数按可比价格计算，下表同。

Notes: The figures in value terms on GDP and value-added of industry are calculated at current prices, whereas the index are calculated at comparable prices.The same applies to the following tables.

22-2 区域主要经济指标占全省比重

Percentage of Main Regional Economic Indicators to the Provincial Total

单位：% (%)

指　　标	Item	2022 珠三角占全省比重 Percentage of Pearl River Delta to the Whole Province	粤东占全省比重 Percentage of Eastern Region to the Whole Province	粤西占全省比重 Percentage of Western Region to the Whole Province	粤北占全省比重 Percentage of Northern Region to the Whole Province
土地面积	Land Area	30.5	8.6	18.2	42.7
年末常住人口	Permanent Population at the Year-end	61.9	13.0	12.5	12.6
#城镇人口	Urban Population	72.4	10.6	8.1	8.9
地区生产总值	Gross Domestic Product	81.1	6.1	7.1	5.7
第一产业	Primary Industry	34.4	12.5	30.7	22.4
第二产业	Secondary Industry	82.2	6.4	6.4	4.9
第三产业	Tertiary Industry	83.7	5.4	5.8	5.1
固定资产投资总额	Investment in Fixed Assets	78.6	8.3	6.0	7.1
#房地产开发投资	Investment in Real Estate Development	85.6	5.0	4.5	4.9
社会消费品零售总额	Total Retail Sales of Consumer Goods	78.0	7.8	8.6	5.6
出口总额	Total Exports	95.8	2.0	0.8	1.4
进口总额	Total Imports	95.3	1.0	1.9	1.8
实际外商直接投资	Foreign Direct Investment Actually Utilized	94.6	0.9	2.7	1.9
地方一般公共预算收入	Local Public Budgetary Revenue	88.8	3.0	3.5	4.7
地方一般公共预算支出	Local Public Budgetary Expenditure	74.1	7.4	7.7	10.8
金融机构本外币存款	Deposits in Renminbi and Foreign Currencies in All Financial Institutions	89.9	3.4	3.1	3.6
#本外币住户存款	Savings Deposits by Resident	79.3	7.0	6.4	7.3
金融机构本外币贷款	Loans in Renminbi and Foreign Currencies in All Financial Institutions	90.6	2.4	3.2	3.8

22-2 续表 continued

单位：% (%)

指 标	Item	2023 珠三角占全省比重 Percentage of Pearl River Delta to the Whole Province	2023 粤东占全省比重 Percentage of Eastern Region to the Whole Province	2023 粤西占全省比重 Percentage of Western Region to the Whole Province	2023 粤北占全省比重 Percentage of Northern Region to the Whole Province
土地面积	Land Area	30.5	8.6	18.2	42.7
年末常住人口	Permanent Population at the Year-end	61.9	13.0	12.6	12.5
#城镇人口	Urban Population	72.1	10.6	8.2	9.1
地区生产总值	Gross Domestic Product	81.2	6.2	6.9	5.7
第一产业	Primary Industry	34.5	12.6	30.5	22.4
第二产业	Secondary Industry	82.1	6.7	6.3	5.0
第三产业	Tertiary Industry	84.0	5.4	5.6	5.0
固定资产投资总额	Investment in Fixed Assets	78.6	7.8	6.3	7.2
#房地产开发投资	Investment in Real Estate Development	85.8	4.4	4.9	4.8
社会消费品零售总额	Total Retail Sales of Consumer Goods	78.3	7.7	8.6	5.5
出口总额	Total Exports	96.2	1.8	0.7	1.2
进口总额	Total Imports	94.6	1.2	2.3	1.8
实际外商直接投资	Foreign Direct Investment Actually Utilized	94.8	0.9	3.1	1.2
地方一般公共预算收入	Local Public Budgetary Revenue	88.3	3.4	3.6	4.8
地方一般公共预算支出	Local Public Budgetary Expenditure	74.3	7.2	7.8	10.7
金融机构本外币存款	Deposits in Renminbi and Foreign Currencies in All Financial Institutions	89.9	3.4	3.1	3.6
#本外币住户存款	Savings Deposits by Resident	79.6	6.9	6.2	7.2
金融机构本外币贷款	Loans in Renminbi and Foreign Currencies in All Financial Institutions	90.6	2.4	3.1	3.8

注：各指标在计算分区域占全省比重时，分母为21个市相加的合计数。

Notes: While calculating the percentage of each indicator of Pearl River Delta, East Wing, West Wing and Mountainous Areas to the whole province, the denominator is the sum of 21 cities.

22-3 珠三角主要经济指标

Main Economic Indicators of the Pearl River Delta Economic Zone

年份 Year	年末常住人口 (万人) Permanent Population at the Year-end (10000 persons)	#城镇人口 Urban Population	年末户籍总人口 (万人) Total Population with Residence Registration at the Year-end (10000 persons)	城镇单位就业人员 (万人) Employed Persons in Urban Areas (10000 persons)
1990	2369.93	1696.63	2371.57	
1995	3292.03		2372.76	
2000	4289.78	2981.23	2563.60	495.46
2005	4547.14	3516.06	2763.32	636.10
2006	4735.47	3771.33	2821.27	675.38
2007	4930.68	3919.89	2872.47	718.88
2008	5138.48	4119.52	2920.82	724.38
2009	5361.72	4375.17	2967.02	767.05
2010	5622.95	4650.64	3024.57	823.67
2011	5937.94	4935.29	3073.87	927.40
2012	6216.60	5183.35	3105.01	969.59
2013	6446.86	5390.61	3156.02	1552.80
2014	6664.86	5590.56	3207.94	1555.45
2015	6868.51	5797.80	3265.69	1532.73
2016	7101.24	6018.53	3350.52	1547.13
2017	7338.07	6240.51	3475.10	1560.00
2018	7545.46	6463.52	3628.04	1603.20
2019	7683.95	6616.26	3767.72	1699.00
2020	7823.54	6825.60	3892.19	1719.68
2021	7860.60	6875.67	4015.66	1746.73
2022	7829.43	6848.95	4118.15	1717.30
2023	7869.76	6912.10	4224.39	1664.83

注：2011—2019年年末常住人口根据2020年第七次全国人口普查初步汇总数进行平滑调整，城镇人口也作了相应的调整。

Note: The year-end populations from 2011 to 2019 have been adjusted in accordance with the preliminary sum figure obtained from the 7th National Population Census and the same applied to urban population.

22-3 续表 1 continued

年份 Year	地区生产总值 (亿元) Gross Domestic Product (100 million yuan)	第一产业 Primary Industry	第二产业 Secondary Industry	第三产业 Tertiary Industry	人均地区生产总值 (元) Per Capita Gross Domestic Product(yuan)
1990	1006.89	153.77	441.65	411.46	4612
1995	4077.74	346.94	1984.48	1746.32	13019
2000	8471.28	460.17	4044.38	3966.73	20369
2005	18426.64	559.23	9377.60	8489.80	40661
2006	21866.00	567.69	11266.58	10031.73	47112
2007	25971.88	631.40	13165.60	12174.88	53738
2008	30212.28	698.72	15107.89	14405.68	60010
2009	32478.00	694.61	15709.73	16073.65	61862
2010	38028.65	772.96	18655.55	18600.14	69281
2011	43890.08	876.91	21430.14	21583.03	76014
2012	47939.37	928.85	22670.54	24339.99	78967
2013	53472.83	984.03	24809.05	27679.75	84537
2014	57844.44	1030.07	26763.44	30050.94	88318
2015	62541.37	1073.87	28097.17	33370.33	92510
2016	68196.86	1153.92	29741.79	37301.15	97721
2017	74953.26	1181.53	32004.91	41766.82	103863
2018	80440.72	1265.53	34038.02	45137.18	108094
2019	87213.05	1430.38	35748.98	50033.69	114532
2020	89850.38	1576.19	35942.30	52331.89	115880
2021	100914.59	1705.36	41360.66	57848.57	128684
2022	104983.11	1838.39	43244.01	59900.71	133821
2023	110214.70	1913.38	44701.01	63600.32	140408

22-3 续表 2 continued

年份 Year	地区生产总值指数(上年=100) Index of Gross Domestic Product (preceding year=100)	第一产业 Primary Industry	第二产业 Secondary Industry	第三产业 Tertiary Industry	人均地区生产总值指数(上年=100) Index of Per Capita Gross Domestic Product(preceding year=100)
1990	117.3	107.4	119.9	118.6	116.1
1995	120.5	108.2	122.5	120.1	112.1
2000	113.9	104.4	114.6	114.1	106.5
2005	115.7	103.6	118.3	113.7	114.6
2006	116.8	98.5	118.7	115.8	113.9
2007	116.3	100.6	116.0	117.5	112.0
2008	112.8	101.7	111.9	114.5	107.9
2009	110.9	104.0	109.6	112.5	106.3
2010	113.1	104.1	115.5	110.9	108.2
2011	111.1	103.9	112.1	110.3	105.6
2012	109.5	103.3	108.8	110.4	104.1
2013	110.7	102.6	111.2	110.6	106.3
2014	108.6	102.9	108.7	108.7	104.9
2015	108.6	102.8	107.5	109.8	105.2
2016	108.0	102.2	107.2	108.9	104.6
2017	107.8	103.1	107.2	108.5	104.3
2018	106.8	104.8	107.2	106.4	103.6
2019	106.4	104.1	104.7	107.9	104.0
2020	102.4	105.3	101.7	102.9	100.5
2021	108.0	109.4	109.5	107.0	106.8
2022	102.2	104.8	102.1	102.2	102.2
2023	104.8	104.9	104.8	104.8	104.8

22-3 续表 3 continued

年份 Year	公路通车里程(公里) Total Length of Highways in Operation (km)	货运量(万吨) Freight Traffic (10000 tons)	邮电业务总量(亿元) Total Business Volume of Postal and Telecommunication Services (100 million yuan)	本地电话年末用户(万户) Number of Subscribers of Local Telephones at the Year-end (10000 subscribers)	移动电话年末用户 (万户) Number of Subscribers of Mobile Telephones at the Year-end (10000 subscribers)	房地产开发投资(亿元) Investment in Real Estate Development (100 million yuan)	社会消费品零售总额(亿元) Total Retail Sales of Consumer Goods (100 million yuan)
1990							424.35
1995	20323		152.60				1793.50
2000	29029		587.64				3244.82
2005	32312	103365	1738.94	2355.10	5317.71		6017.12
2006	52139	113275	2068.19	2559.62	5497.75		6983.89
2007	53106	122408	2348.22	2651.33	6075.36		8136.58
2008	53418	120916	2754.77	2529.77	6463.22		9820.96
2009	54261	142733	2983.47	2400.25	6867.61	2583.17	11177.86
2010	55848	161348	3949.45	2269.84	7457.64	3118.66	13061.13
2011	56380	182281	1544.39	2284.31	8285.85	4022.87	15125.61
2012	58590	203570	1730.31	2295.29	9573.16	4483.67	16934.22
2013	59555	243500	2019.89	2288.94	11228.38	5362.75	19023.38
2014	61548	254491	2751.65	2195.47	11318.90	6293.55	21253.37
2015	63054	266078	3573.05	2086.68	11437.39	7075.57	23411.58
2016	63631	271565	5487.87	1954.24	10933.74	8601.16	25748.56
2017	64119	287210	4997.13	1801.51	10828.40	9827.78	28335.47
2018	62670	303566	8872.90	1659.62	12248.45	11490.33	30796.88
2019	61498	313912	13097.48	1706.89	11855.06	12849.54	33237.60
2020	62196	258195	16413.10	1579.55	10971.73	14106.37	31212.07
2021	62335	277290	3945.34	1540.60	11466.09	14202.86	34412.76
2022	62387	256992	3981.44	1447.76	11719.68	12927.69	34959.60
2023	60243	268429	4476.01	1318.07	12100.94	11753.86	37037.68

22-3 续表 4 continued

年份 Year	出口总额(亿美元) Total Exports (USD 100 million)	出口总额(亿元) Total Exports (100 million yuan)	进口总额(亿美元) Total Imports (USD 100 million)	进口总额(亿元) Total Imports (100 million yuan)	实际外商直接投资额(亿美元) Foreign Direct Investment Actually Utilized (USD 100 million)	实际外商直接投资额(亿元) Foreign Direct Investment Actually Utilized (RMB 100 million)	地方一般公共预算收入(亿元) Local Public General Budgetary Revenue (100 million yuan)
1990	222.21		196.77		12.36		97.98
1995	513.31		429.29		79.47		275.26
2000	849.41		744.75		103.87		599.06
2005	2277.37		1841.56		113.34		1218.48
2006	2891.30		2185.61		130.86		1460.77
2007	3547.70		2564.64		151.88		1882.01
2008	3886.85		2699.72		169.21		2248.16
2009	3417.76		2431.96		175.08		2522.29
2010	4318.02		3197.18		183.47		3139.58
2011	5066.23		3680.77		195.29		3674.70
2012	5477.01		3960.17		215.53		4129.09
2013	6070.93	37698.26	4403.39	27354.02	230.62		4669.16
2014	6137.68	37699.81	4153.86	25514.90	248.61		5375.37
2015	6084.61	37799.60	3664.45	22773.16	256.24		6391.70
2016	5651.27	37313.11	3450.83	22808.94	225.90		6923.98
2017	5902.36	39982.03	3709.88	25107.91	218.11		7455.96
2018	6147.40	40607.96	4238.33	27964.07		1350.73	7915.51
2019	5969.27	41172.79	3932.20	27111.43		1459.98	8277.81
2020	5972.54	41343.22	3806.84	26338.82		1551.42	8496.03
2021	7429.60	48011.36	4766.24	30794.14		1747.69	9366.17
2022	7624.97	50836.84	4253.73	28333.57		1720.08	9049.47
2023	7439.27	52334.49	3851.97	27108.30		1494.47	9406.36

22-3 续表 5 continued

年份 Year	地方一般公共预算支出(亿元) Local Public Genera Budgetary Expenditure (100 million yuan)	金融机构本外币存款(亿元) Deposits in Renminbi and Foreign Currencies in All Financial Institutions (100 million yuan)	#本外币住户存款(亿元) Savings Deposits by Urban and Rural Residents (100 million yuan)	金融机构本外币贷款(亿元) Loans in Renminbi and Foreign Currencies in All Financial Institutions (100 million yuan)	全体居民人均可支配收入(元) Per Capita Disposable Income of Households (yuan)	城镇居民人均可支配收入(元) Per Capita Annual Disposable Income of Urban Households (yuan)	农村居民人均可支配收入(元) Per Capita Disposable Income of Rural Households (yuan)
1990	80.03						
1995	322.81						
2000	690.64	16211.75	7941.93	11227.42			
2005	1567.23	32962.25	16389.71	21073.93			
2006	1714.73	37367.68	18306.14	23613.32			
2007	2145.82	42555.31	18485.09	27982.87			
2008	2550.77	48512.14	22711.25	31044.80			
2009	2882.33	60618.78	25914.62	40608.44			
2010	3654.91	71294.51	29770.92	47159.74			
2011	4444.97	79575.13	33015.57	53133.57			
2012	4798.40	91585.24	37059.20	60568.45			
2013	5240.59	104255.28	40218.90	67988.65			
2014	5973.23	110800.56	41899.85	76017.12	33642.1	37063.7	15754.0
2015	8421.36	141609.04	42737.49	85741.78	36662.0	40284.5	17296.4
2016	9285.10	158966.41	46321.96	100149.59	40109.1	43967.4	19063.7
2017	10329.95	171937.41	48505.37	113683.01	43840.1	47926.9	20813.5
2018	10608.94	183537.91	54607.65	131084.22	47911.0	52129.1	22805.6
2019	11637.61	205988.39	61660.42	151816.93	52213.7	56638.7	25025.8
2020	11538.02	239220.69	70049.84	177090.87	54809.6	59225.1	26856.5
2021	12325.44	263012.21	76818.54	201530.79	60729.7	65118.6	30464.7
2022	12662.25	289656.10	90095.22	222640.84	62700.0	67092.6	31956.7
2023	12609.39	315470.76	100806.65	246156.16	65654.7	70194.8	33682.3

22-4 珠三角工业企业主要指标（2023年）

单位：亿元

项　目	Item	企业单位数（个）Number of Enterprises (unit)
总　计	**Total**	**61564**
按登记注册类别分	Grouped by Registered Statistical Categories	
总计中：#国有控股工业企业	Of the Total:State-holding Industrial Enterprises	1077
#内资企业	Domestic Invested Enterprises	51220
港澳台投资企业	Enterprises with Investment from Hong Kong,Macao and Taiwan	6990
外商投资企业	Foreign Invested Enterprises	3285
按轻重工业分	Grouped by Light and Heavy Industry	
轻工业	Light Industry	26322
重工业	Heavy Industry	35242
按企业规模分	Grouped by Size of Enterprise	
大型企业	Large	1252
中型企业	Medium	5640
小微型企业	Small and Micro	54672
按行业分	Grouped by Sector	
煤炭开采和洗选业	Mining and Washing of Coal	
石油和天然气开采业	Extraction of Petroleum and Natural Gas	2
黑色金属矿采选业	Mining and Dressing of Ferrous Metal Ores	2
有色金属矿采选业	Mining and Dressing of Nonferrous Metal Ores	2
非金属矿采选业	Mining and Dressing of Nonmetal Ores	84
开采专业及辅助性活动	Mining Specialized and Auxiliary Operations	6
其他采矿业	Mining and Dressing of Other Ores	
农副食品加工业	Processing of Farm and Sideline Food	720
食品制造业	Manufacture of Food	677
酒、饮料和精制茶制造业	Manufacture of Beverage	162
烟草制品业	Tobacco Products	92
纺织业	Textile Industry	1259
纺织服装、服饰业	Manufacture of Textile Garments, Footwear and Headgear	1714
皮革、毛皮、羽毛及其制品和制鞋业	Leather, Fur, Feather, Down and Related Products	1403
木材加工和木、竹、藤、棕、草制品业	Timber Processing, Bamboo, Cane, Palm Fiber & Straw Products	378
家具制造业	Manufacture of Furniture	1778
造纸和纸制品业	Papermaking and Paper Products	1370
印刷和记录媒介复制业	Printing and Record Medium Reproduction	967
文教、工美、体育和娱乐用品制造业	Manufacture of Cultural, Educational and Sports Articles	1647
石油、煤炭及其他燃料加工业	Petroleum, Coal and other Fuel Processing	88
化学原料和化学制品制造业	Manufacture of Raw Chemical Materials and Chemical Products	2897
医药制造业	Manufacture of Medicines	485
化学纤维制造业	Manufacture of Chemical Fibers	77
橡胶和塑料制品业	Plastic Products	5636
非金属矿物制品业	Nonmetal Mineral Products	2297
黑色金属冶炼和压延加工业	Smelting and Pressing of Ferrous Metals	443
有色金属冶炼和压延加工业	Smelting and Pressing of Nonferrous Metals	1139
金属制品业	Metal Products	6399
通用设备制造业	Manufacture of General-purpose Machinery	3987
专用设备制造业	Manufacture of Special-purpose Machinery	3988
汽车制造业	Manufacture of Automobile	1116
铁路、船舶、航空航天和其他运输设备制造业	Manufacture of Railway ,Ship,Aeronautics and Other Transport Equipment	517
电气机械和器材制造业	Manufacture of Electrical Machinery and Equipment	7947
计算机、通信和其他电子设备制造业	Manufacture of Communication Equipment, Computers and Other Electronic Equipment	9570
仪器仪表制造业	Manufacture of Instruments and Meters	1209
其他制造业	Other Manufactures	491
废弃资源综合利用业	Comprehensive Utilization of Waste	156
金属制品、机械和设备修理业	Manufacture of Metal Products,Machinery and Equipment Maintenance	85
电力、热力生产和供应业	Production and Supply of Electric Power and Heat Power	293
燃气生产和供应业	Production and Supply of Gas	210
水的生产和供应业	Production and Supply of Water	271

注：1.本表统计范围为年主营业务收入2000万元及以上的工业法人企业。
　　2.本表登记注册统计类别按《关于市场主体统计分类的划分规定》(国统字〔2023〕14号)执行。

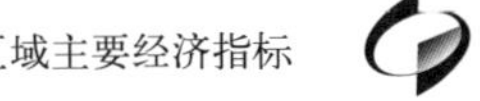

Main Indicators of Industrial Enterprises of the Pearl River Delta (2023)

(100 million yuan)

#亏损企业 Loss-making Enterprises	工业总产值 (当年价) Gross Industrial Output Value (at current prices)	年末资产总计 Total Assets at the Year-end	#产成品 Finished Products	流动资产合计 Total Current Asserts	年末负债合计 Total Liabilities at the Year-end
14696	**161143.61**	**184750.65**	**7395.04**	**114893.55**	**108045.34**
204	26524.95	36746.40	738.55	14540.04	21069.09
11813	110260.84	130707.94	4823.78	80467.40	78769.66
1979	24015.14	26168.79	1490.17	16684.02	13376.17
894	26847.24	27863.37	1080.47	17733.50	15891.58
6563	48030.27	47849.54	2658.16	31282.96	26188.70
8133	113113.34	136901.10	4736.88	83610.59	81856.64
139	75013.45	99877.88	3349.10	59018.74	59610.49
1108	34570.44	36491.41	1692.10	22329.05	18979.27
13449	51559.71	48381.35	2353.83	33545.76	29455.57
	807.63	1197.38	2.43	370.47	841.16
	13.15	12.12	0.78	4.96	2.67
	16.90	6.50	0.04	3.69	3.87
22	131.58	272.89	4.70	82.05	178.08
	50.17	101.30	0.17	59.17	25.71
170	2905.21	1772.23	80.29	1145.07	1080.59
180	1802.10	1832.55	81.81	1091.71	860.88
24	1108.93	1068.79	42.17	647.18	506.82
17	616.64	472.49	16.20	384.86	154.49
361	1761.41	1319.74	82.76	818.81	671.73
520	1680.72	1362.83	148.36	1004.76	707.74
284	1086.10	598.34	43.63	465.08	385.59
97	301.53	312.19	18.02	194.92	177.68
479	2067.42	2096.97	88.76	1458.46	1254.51
367	2227.62	2068.03	92.93	1204.83	1156.25
293	1128.77	1358.74	43.78	851.56	653.33
465	3532.00	2238.54	578.51	1878.40	1557.70
24	2158.64	921.98	40.91	443.90	581.03
511	6267.46	5983.24	235.43	3460.07	3128.10
145	1694.77	3763.48	158.83	1979.48	1544.65
26	161.56	173.41	11.63	84.64	74.83
1192	5387.42	5497.22	232.66	3444.65	2772.72
595	4820.19	5485.76	227.73	3387.40	3507.02
116	1538.74	843.97	59.67	543.74	560.17
247	3108.69	1731.66	95.23	1310.34	1261.24
1463	8139.26	5998.37	332.02	4186.60	3571.32
871	5836.92	6593.11	401.60	4826.59	3733.30
998	5718.92	7850.17	436.24	5665.50	4042.94
273	12646.68	10708.08	334.96	7545.69	7026.62
124	1492.12	2050.59	43.52	1475.13	1303.12
1806	21351.25	23871.50	1052.98	16183.74	14190.53
2446	45573.13	60171.86	2167.22	41136.49	36006.55
273	1476.00	2155.98	144.24	1587.78	1055.03
104	594.82	657.57	26.03	509.98	294.68
56	616.19	423.59	34.44	271.29	288.73
13	294.69	352.50	12.77	244.10	208.36
42	7498.19	16900.59	4.57	3561.11	10062.16
36	2817.86	1521.03	15.07	578.01	828.50
56	712.22	3003.34	1.96	801.34	1784.94

Notes: a) The statistical coverage of industry refers to the legal person industrial enterprises with annual main business revenue over 20 million yuan.
b) The registered statistical categories of this table is implemented in accordance with the Regulations onStatistics the Classification of Market Entity(Guotongzi [2023] No. 14).

22-4 续表

单位：亿元

项 目	Item	营业收入 Business Revenue
总 计	**Total**	**161529.27**
按登记注册类型分	Grouped by Registered Statistical Categories	
总计中：#国有控股工业企业	Of the Total:State-holding Industrial Enterprises	26221.85
#内资企业	Domestic Invested Enterprises	109723.62
港澳台投资企业	Enterprises with Investment from Hong Kong,Macao and Taiwan	23883.24
外商投资企业	Foreign Invested Enterprises	27902.45
按轻重工业分	Grouped by Light and Heavy Industry	
轻工业	Light Industry	47712.45
重工业	Heavy Industry	113816.82
按企业规模分	Grouped by Size of Enterprise	
大型企业	Large	75769.37
中型企业	Medium	34432.90
小微型企业	Small and Micro	51327.00
按行业分	Grouped by Sector	
煤炭开采和洗选业	Mining and Washing of Coal	
石油和天然气开采业	Extraction of Petroleum and Natural Gas	725.17
黑色金属矿采选业	Mining and Dressing of Ferrous Metal Ores	15.56
有色金属矿采选业	Mining and Dressing of Nonferrous Metal Ores	16.43
非金属矿采选业	Mining and Dressing of Nonmetal Ores	117.00
开采专业及辅助性活动	Mining Specialized and Auxiliary Operations	49.37
其他采矿业	Mining and Dressing of Other Ores	
农副食品加工业	Processing of Farm and Sideline Food	3224.34
食品制造业	Manufacture of Food	2032.86
酒、饮料和精制茶制造业	Manufacture of Beverage	1167.85
烟草制品业	Tobacco Products	613.98
纺织业	Textile Industry	1690.14
纺织服装、服饰业	Manufacture of Textile Garments, Footwear and Headgear	1573.01
皮革、毛皮、羽毛及其制品和制鞋业	Leather, Fur, Feather, Down and Related Products	1057.93
木材加工和木、竹、藤、棕、草制品业	Timber Processing, Bamboo, Cane, Palm Fiber & Straw Products	282.99
家具制造业	Manufacture of Furniture	2010.46
造纸和纸制品业	Papermaking and Paper Products	2063.72
印刷和记录媒介复制业	Printing and Record Medium Reproduction	1094.40
文教、工美、体育和娱乐用品制造业	Manufacture of Cultural, Educational and Sports Articles	3640.98
石油、煤炭及其他燃料加工业	Petroleum, Coal and other Fuel Processing	2164.77
化学原料和化学制品制造业	Manufacture of Raw Chemical Materials and Chemical Products	6295.69
医药制造业	Manufacture of Medicines	1645.42
化学纤维制造业	Manufacture of Chemical Fibers	166.01
橡胶和塑料制品业	Plastic Products	5308.01
非金属矿物制品业	Nonmetal Mineral Products	4590.31
黑色金属冶炼和压延加工业	Smelting and Pressing of Ferrous Metals	1587.23
有色金属冶炼和压延加工业	Smelting and Pressing of Nonferrous Metals	3384.69
金属制品业	Metal Products	7969.06
通用设备制造业	Manufacture of General-purpose Machinery	5783.84
专用设备制造业	Manufacture of Special-purpose Machinery	5404.16
汽车制造业	Manufacture of Automobile	13120.25
铁路、船舶、航空航天和其他运输设备制造业	Manufacture of Railway ,Ship,Aeronautics and Other Transport equipment	1528.66
电气机械和器材制造业	Manufacture of Electrical Machinery and Equipment	20885.51
计算机、通信和其他电子设备制造业	Manufacture of Communication Equipment, Computers and Other Electronic Equipment	46158.17
仪器仪表制造业	Manufacture of Instruments and Meters	1514.21
其他制造业	Other Manufactures	573.22
废弃资源综合利用业	Comprehensive Utilization of Waste	621.36
金属制品、机械和设备修理业	Manufacture of Metal Products,Machinery and Equipment Maintenance	305.32
电力、热力生产和供应业	Production and Supply of Electric Power and Heat Power	7488.35
燃气生产和供应业	Production and Supply of Gas	2905.24
水的生产和供应业	Production and Supply of Water	753.59

22-4 continued

(100 million yuan)

税金及附加 Tax and Extra Charges	利润总额 Total Profits	#亏损总额 Total Losses	利税总额 Total Pretax Profits	本年应交增值税 Value-added Tax Payable in Current Year	全部从业人员年平均人数（万人） Annual Average Number of Employed Persons (10000 persons)
1410.02	**10594.03**	**1403.92**	**15103.87**	**3099.82**	**1147.66**
748.05	1275.76	219.94	2560.52	536.71	62.50
903.55	7376.93	907.81	10547.27	2266.78	745.63
163.37	1851.38	178.42	2420.52	405.76	254.96
343.06	1365.34	317.64	2135.26	426.86	147.07
441.78	3282.07	417.64	4902.95	1179.10	464.34
968.24	7311.96	986.28	10200.93	1920.73	683.32
991.35	6766.98	333.51	9274.26	1515.93	385.75
231.82	2175.70	401.29	3076.83	669.31	304.39
186.85	1651.35	669.12	2752.78	914.58	457.51
58.93	434.52		554.65	61.20	0.34
0.06	1.48		1.87	0.33	0.01
0.03	0.05		0.10	0.02	0.06
3.97	16.59	1.85	25.20	4.64	0.42
0.07	8.64		9.48	0.76	0.14
5.93	96.22	13.91	124.35	22.20	7.80
12.60	206.88	14.40	298.23	78.75	15.26
22.00	105.86	0.90	163.84	35.97	6.58
216.49	61.50	2.37	314.93	36.95	3.82
7.86	98.12	14.46	147.76	41.78	17.27
7.86	69.62	21.99	122.47	44.98	31.13
4.80	38.63	6.74	61.98	18.55	23.15
1.44	10.71	2.02	18.95	6.81	3.44
9.71	120.53	16.68	172.91	42.68	28.13
8.65	29.20	24.78	86.50	48.64	16.39
4.72	74.89	11.20	101.43	21.82	16.47
8.66	90.57	19.11	126.52	27.28	36.21
247.69	51.39	5.16	387.18	88.10	1.22
33.68	358.81	71.48	553.61	161.12	29.00
12.90	220.43	73.30	302.55	69.23	13.77
0.76	13.32	2.60	17.04	2.96	1.12
22.06	277.99	46.58	403.21	103.16	69.76
21.82	209.12	44.29	344.16	113.22	33.30
4.43	35.36	14.36	60.41	20.62	3.83
5.52	49.04	16.12	82.58	28.01	12.18
32.54	359.67	44.20	552.04	159.84	82.87
23.36	384.58	58.26	519.68	111.74	57.08
27.24	599.22	81.65	755.46	129.00	61.95
292.78	515.40	139.22	1032.13	223.95	46.54
6.49	59.46	12.93	81.71	15.76	10.59
85.70	1553.96	146.49	2162.42	522.75	165.34
168.60	3577.82	405.49	4324.60	578.18	301.69
7.34	109.04	23.46	154.87	38.49	19.79
2.38	39.32	4.06	51.86	10.16	8.92
1.52	11.60	5.57	19.85	6.74	1.43
1.47	22.28	0.95	30.96	7.22	2.54
30.13	462.11	42.41	680.05	187.82	11.31
3.04	124.00	3.08	140.11	13.07	1.85
4.81	96.10	11.84	116.22	15.30	4.96

22−5 广州、深圳主要经济指标（2023年）

Main Economic Indicators of Guangzhou and Shenzhen (2023)

指标	Item	合计 Total	广州 Guangzhou	深圳 Shenzhen
土地面积 (平方公里)	Land Area (sq.km)	9225.47	7238.46	1987.01
年末常住人口 (万人)	Permanent Population at the Year-end (10000 persons)	3661.71	1882.70	1779.01
#城镇人口	Urban Population	3408.86	1633.34	1775.52
年末户籍总人口 (万人)	Total Population with Residence Registration at the Year-end (10000 persons)	1744.00	1056.61	687.39
城镇单位就业人员 (万人)	Employed Persons in Urban Areas (10000 persons)	900.92	411.19	489.73
地区生产总值 (亿元)	Gross Domestic Product (100 million yuan)	64962.13	30355.73	34606.40
第一产业	Primary Industry	342.49	317.78	24.71
第二产业	Secondary Industry	20791.03	7775.71	13015.32
第三产业	Tertiary Industry	43828.61	22262.23	21566.38
人均地区生产总值 (元)	Per Capita Gross Domestic Product (yuan)	177947	161634	195230
地区生产总值指数 (上年=100)	Index of Gross Domestic Product (preceding year=100)	105.3	104.6	106.0
第一产业	Primary Industry	103.4	103.5	102.6
第二产业	Secondary Industry	105.0	102.6	106.5
第三产业	Tertiary Industry	105.5	105.3	105.6
人均地区生产总值指数 (上年=100)	Index of Per Capita Gross Domestic Product (preceding year=100)	105.1	104.5	105.6
公路通车里程 (公里)	Total Length of Highways in Operation (km)	9143	8422	721
民用汽车拥有量 (万辆)	Number of Civil Vehicles Owned (100 million unit)	782.54	372.27	410.27
#私人汽车拥有量	Number of Private Vehicles Owned	625.82	299.16	326.66
邮电业务总量 (亿元)	Total Business Volume of Postal and Telecommunication (100 million yuan)	2879.52	1419.44	1460.09
本地电话年末用户 (万户)	Number of Subscribers of Local Telephones at the Year-end (10000 subscribers)	630.52	277.71	352.81
移动电话年末用户 (万户)	Number of Subscribers of Mobile Telephones at the Year-end (10000 subscribers)	6292.94	3323.30	2969.63
房地产开发投资 (亿元)	Investment in Real Estate Development (100 million yuan)	7135.92	3311.45	3824.48
社会消费品零售总额 (亿元)	Total Retail Sales of Consumer Good (100 million yuan)	21498.81	11012.62	10486.19
出口总额 (亿元)	Total Exports (100 million yuan)	31046.10	6501.57	24544.53
进口总额 (亿元)	Total Imports (100 million yuan)	18564.60	4411.53	14153.08
实际外商直接投资额 (亿元)	Foreign Direct Investment Actually Utilized (100 million yuan)	1109.43	483.22	626.21
地方一般公共预算收入 (亿元)	Local Public Budgetary Revenue (100 million yuan)	6057.98	1945.06	4112.92
地方一般公共预算支出 (亿元)	Local Public Budgetary Expenditure (100 million yuan)	7984.08	2971.65	5012.43
金融机构本外币存款 (亿元)	Deposits in Renminbi and Foreign Currencies in All Financial Institutions (100 million yuan)	219988.85	86638.33	133350.52
#本外币住户存款	Savings Deposits by Residents	57785.80	30117.66	27668.14
金融机构本外币贷款 (亿元)	Loans in Renminbi and Foreign Currencies in All Financial Institutions (100 million yuan)	168815.13	76674.23	92140.89
全体居民人均可支配收入 (元)	Per Capita Disposable Income of Households (yuan)		74836.7	76910.3
城镇居民人均可支配收入 (元)	Per Capita Disposable Income of Urban Households (yuan)		80500.9	76910.3
农村居民人均可支配 收入 (元)	Per Capita Disposable Income of Rural Households (yuan)		38606.7	

 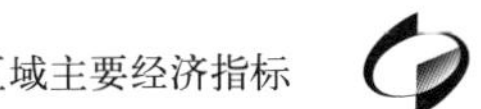

22-6 粤东西北主要经济指标

Main Economic Indicators of the East and West and Northern Region

年份 Year	年末常住人口 (万人) Permanent Population at the Year-end (10000 persons)	#城镇人口 Urban Population	年末户籍总人口 (万人) Total Population with Residence Registration at the Year-end (10000 persons)	城镇单位就业人员 (万人) Employed Persons in Urban Areas (10000 persons)
2000	4235.41	1787.22	4934.94	274.48
2001	4357.08		4970.09	262.55
2002	4427.40		5024.37	254.28
2003	4499.14		5062.96	255.45
2004	4594.16		5090.66	257.74
2005	4646.85	2098.62	5136.32	266.15
2006	4706.60	2191.04	5227.44	277.04
2007	4728.84	2202.07	5283.58	280.72
2008	4755.00	2216.23	5346.26	281.78
2009	4768.46	2256.19	5398.98	287.98
2010	4817.99	2259.21	5496.98	294.85
2011	4818.06	2268.59	5563.33	310.82
2012	4824.41	2275.05	5530.87	334.39
2013	4823.14	2283.13	5603.44	403.50
2014	4824.14	2293.19	5678.95	407.20
2015	4809.50	2319.58	5742.67	404.70
2016	4806.76	2334.93	5814.38	410.44
2017	4802.92	2348.03	5841.81	403.10
2018	4802.54	2403.58	5874.08	390.93
2019	4805.05	2457.00	5895.69	365.59
2020	4800.46	2538.38	5916.46	365.58
2021	4823.40	2590.85	5931.29	364.17
2022	4827.37	2616.45	5931.57	349.35
2023	4836.24	2670.77	5921.82	325.17

22-6 续表 1 continued

年份 Year	地区生产总值 (亿元) Gross Domestic Product (100 million yuan)	第一产业 Primary Industry	第二产业 Secondary Industry	第三产业 Tertiary Industry	人均地区生产总值 (元) Per Capita Gross Domestic Product(yuan)
2000	2775.18	726.47	1054.10	994.61	6576
2001	2967.84	745.05	1141.98	1080.80	6908
2002	3181.57	778.07	1224.68	1178.82	7244
2003	3550.67	818.69	1426.03	1305.94	7955
2004	4083.32	897.96	1681.55	1503.81	8981
2005	4640.29	901.99	1989.52	1748.77	10043
2006	5464.89	957.22	2523.24	1984.43	11685
2007	6465.64	1062.06	3058.40	2345.19	13705
2008	7630.76	1208.84	3618.56	2803.36	16092
2009	8129.39	1256.17	3640.60	3232.62	17072
2010	9529.29	1433.71	4282.62	3812.96	19867
2011	11183.63	1667.60	4969.43	4546.59	23181
2012	12348.50	1808.63	5394.13	5145.74	25579
2013	13729.70	1916.89	6061.82	5750.99	28425
2014	14929.56	2018.70	6632.09	6278.78	30911
2015	15722.21	2145.60	6686.52	6890.10	32598
2016	16998.21	2345.85	6939.89	7712.48	35308
2017	18311.86	2428.58	7074.33	8808.96	38087
2018	19504.50	2570.99	7361.29	9572.22	40611
2019	20773.87	2920.23	7619.23	10234.41	43245
2020	21301.25	3156.55	7925.75	10218.95	44352
2021	23804.94	3279.34	9195.13	11330.47	49471
2022	24530.44	3511.70	9376.71	11642.03	50836
2023	25458.46	3627.32	9736.25	12094.88	52689

22-6 续表 2 continued

年份 Year	地区生产总值指数(上年=100) Index of Gross Domestic Product (preceding year=100)	第一产业 Primary Industry	第二产业 Secondary Industry	第三产业 Tertiary Industry	人均地区生产总值指数(上年=100) Index of Per Capita Gross Domestic Product (preceding year=100)
2000	108.2	105.3	108.1	110.4	107.5
2001	106.4	104.8	105.5	108.5	105.0
2002	108.5	105.4	109.3	109.9	106.5
2003	110.8	104.4	114.8	111.1	109.5
2004	112.3	104.5	115.8	113.5	110.4
2005	113.7	103.6	117.8	115.3	112.3
2006	115.3	104.7	121.3	114.0	114.6
2007	115.5	103.6	119.5	116.2	115.1
2008	111.5	103.1	111.6	115.0	111.0
2009	111.3	105.5	109.8	115.1	110.8
2010	114.1	105.0	116.3	114.7	113.3
2011	112.1	104.5	114.0	112.9	111.5
2012	110.3	104.8	112.9	109.1	110.2
2013	112.0	103.5	114.9	111.4	111.9
2014	109.3	103.6	111.7	108.0	109.3
2015	107.9	103.6	107.4	109.9	108.1
2016	107.4	103.0	105.9	110.3	107.6
2017	106.7	103.8	104.5	109.5	106.8
2018	105.2	104.5	104.7	105.9	105.3
2019	105.1	103.5	103.7	106.8	105.1
2020	102.2	103.3	103.1	101.2	102.2
2021	107.9	107.0	107.7	108.5	107.7
2022	100.9	104.9	98.0	102.0	100.7
2023	104.3	104.7	104.8	103.9	104.2

22-6 续表 3 continued

年份 Year	公路通车里程(公里) Total Length of Highways in Operation (km)	货运量(万吨) Freight Traffic (10000 tons)	邮电业务总量(亿元) Total Business Volume of Postal and Telecommunication Services (100 million yuan)	本地电话年末用户(万户) Number of Subscribers of Local Telephones at the Year-end (10000 subscribers)	移动电话年末用户 (万户) Number of Subscribers of Mobile Telephones at the Year-end (10000 subscribers)	房地产开发投资(亿元) Investment in Real Estate Development (100 million yuan)	社会消费品零售总额(亿元) Total Retail Sales of Consumer Goods (100 million yuan)
2000	69133		169.58	549.37		73.33	1075.91
2001	70449	48307	168.33	641.30	543.26	80.39	1153.03
2002	73076	50111	189.63	730.86	706.06	95.52	1245.99
2003	74106	52616	236.67	848.28	888.71	99.40	1348.52
2004	74690	54202	333.87	1210.00	1317.44	112.74	1526.88
2005	77369	30627	383.01	1083.96	1448.30	142.70	1760.11
2006	124739	32636	472.35	1073.86	1620.17	179.68	2035.34
2007	128900	38046	722.32	1091.75	1766.69	281.61	2373.30
2008	129736	42258	810.08	1043.60	1932.03	370.54	2878.84
2009	130699	36989	954.68	966.38	2071.24	378.15	3353.98
2010	134296	43686	883.49	899.35	2252.45	541.04	3930.26
2011	134345	52697	373.62	862.85	2507.03	787.04	4568.09
2012	136354	62789	444.36	840.51	2894.83	869.12	5020.07
2013	143359	75952	488.10	810.96	3477.68	1126.85	5566.58
2014	150546	99242	642.75	753.98	3624.47	1344.90	6183.31
2015	152969	110358	824.04	720.43	3572.36	1462.90	6915.18
2016	154454	106080	1404.54	655.48	3415.21	1706.63	7554.65
2017	155461	113392	1110.06	604.59	3970.45	2247.92	8263.13
2018	155029	121430	2137.38	551.81	4574.81	2921.86	8970.24
2019	158793	132107	3353.75	596.40	4677.99	3002.62	9714.15
2020	159677	98026	4420.01	552.32	4565.20	3206.37	8997.37
2021	160652	121130	1009.25	531.60	4801.71	3262.99	9767.36
2022	160694	107207	1081.68	496.33	4931.08	2169.23	9840.08
2023	163148	113972	1193.45	465.65	4947.26	1939.46	10287.58

22-6　续表 4　continued

年份 Year	出口总额(亿美元) Total Exports (USD 100 million)	出口总额(亿元) Total Exports (RMB 100 million)	进口总额(亿美元) Total Imports (USD 100 million)	进口总额(亿元) Total Imports (RMB 100 million)	实际外商直接投资额(亿美元) Foreign Direct Investment Actually Utilized (USD 100 million)	实际外商直接投资额(亿元) Foreign Direct Investment Actually Utilized (RMB 100 million)	地方一般公共预算收入(亿元) Local Public General Budgetary Revenue (100 million yuan)
2000	69.08		37.19		13.70		88.89
2001	44.39		33.12		14.14		101.53
2002	56.43		32.16		15.68		108.83
2003	75.08		42.24		19.14		121.96
2004	87.72		56.63		9.96		133.47
2005	104.22		57.72		10.30		176.54
2006	128.17		68.39		14.25		219.70
2007	151.51		87.60		19.38		278.37
2008	169.80		95.44		22.24		338.91
2009	171.79		91.17		20.27		400.35
2010	213.89		122.04		19.14		513.91
2011	253.04		137.41		22.70		619.29
2012	263.49		142.31		19.96		718.42
2013	292.71	1815.70	151.20	938.21	18.90		842.56
2014	323.19	1985.26	151.11	928.13	20.10		949.18
2015	347.11	2158.67	128.79	799.23	12.51		1011.79
2016	334.75	2209.97	116.13	768.50	7.59		990.73
2017	326.32	2210.49	128.22	868.34	10.95		1059.05
2018	317.61	2098.56	141.30	931.50		97.41	1058.94
2019	325.28	2242.59	139.52	960.89		60.59	1086.33
2020	310.04	2146.99	150.83	1042.09		68.87	1120.85
2021	361.53	2336.96	208.55	1347.16		88.59	1217.74
2022	336.33	2233.42	208.92	1389.38		98.94	1145.66
2023	290.01	2039.82	217.94	1534.63		82.15	1251.90

22-6　续表 5　continued

年份 Year	地方一般公共预算支出(亿元) Local Public Genera Budgetary Expenditure (100 million yuan)	金融机构本外币存款(亿元) Deposits in Renminbi and Foreign Currencies in All Financial Institutions (100 million yuan)	#本外币住户存款(亿元) Savings Deposits by Urban and Rural Residents (100 million yuan)	金融机构本外币贷款(亿元) Loans in Renminbi and Foreign Currencies in All Financial Institutions (100 million yuan)	全体居民人均可支配收入(元) Per Capita Disposable Income of Households (yuan)	城镇居民人均可支配 收入(元) Per Capita Disposable Income of Urban Households (yuan)	农村居民人均可支配收入(元) Per Capita Disposable Income of Rural Households (yuan)
2000	216.28	2871.90	2089.75	1984.98			
2001	239.76	3149.51	2321.72	2011.43			
2002	300.61	3511.40	2638.20	2134.33			
2003	348.73	4066.83	3037.48	2353.51			
2004	386.45	4547.77	3438.04	2312.68			
2005	438.76	5157.66	3878.05	2187.28			
2006	538.75	5894.51	4371.05	2321.86			
2007	673.46	6399.72	4528.21	2634.39			
2008	801.64	7607.15	5469.95	2791.07			
2009	965.51	9072.69	6221.71	3901.78			
2010	1184.81	10724.89	7194.83	4639.56			
2011	1464.85	12015.02	8045.99	5481.70			
2012	1726.82	13514.31	9206.38	6508.63			
2013	1983.95	15429.88	10419.74	7675.51			
2014	2323.42	17080.90	11316.03	8904.68	15397.9	20239.9	10935.7
2015	3230.36	18779.17	12271.21	9919.34	16843.9	22018.2	12019.1
2016	3263.41	20862.78	13446.79	10778.82	18364.5	23871.9	13147.1
2017	3473.17	22598.34	14436.89	12348.94	19948.4	25767.5	14297.8
2018	3882.98	24513.25	15685.83	14085.18	21578.1	27522.0	15570.2
2019	4245.80	26470.25	17298.73	16177.66	23383.7	29523.1	16992.8
2020	4434.79	28417.57	18926.81	18589.75	24716.7	30759.0	18176.9
2021	4370.61	30157.00	20780.03	20703.50	27191.4	33564.5	20112.8
2022	4422.56	32701.56	23459.54	23082.10	28451.6	34739.8	21153.3
2023	4363.76	35416.85	25818.90	25405.47	29723.1	35920.7	22388.8

22-7 粤东主要经济指标

Main Economic Indicators of the Eastern Region

指　　标		Item		2022	2023	2023年比2022年增长% Growth Rate in 2023 over 2022
土地面积	(平方公里)	Land Area	(sq.km)	15496	15496	0.0
年末常住人口	(万人)	Permanent Population at the Year-end	(10000 persons)	1643.42	1647.86	0.3
#城镇人口		Urban Population		1006.82	1018.23	1.1
年末户籍总人口	(万人)	Total Population with Residence Registration at the Year-end	(10000 persons)	1930.83	1928.82	-0.1
城镇单位就业人员	(万人)	Employed Persons in Urban Areas	(10000 persons)	108.80	94.74	-12.9
地区生产总值	(亿元)	Gross Domestic Product	(100 million yuan)	7959.90	8390.78	5.0
第一产业		Primary Industry		670.35	696.29	4.0
第二产业		Secondary Industry		3390.60	3634.93	6.7
第三产业		Tertiary Industry		3898.95	4059.55	3.9
人均地区生产总值	(元)	Per Capita Gross Domestic Product	(yuan)	48473	50988	4.8
地区生产总值指数	(上年=100)	Index of Gross Domestic Product	(preceding year=100)	100.8	105.0	
第一产业		Primary Industry		105.6	104.0	
第二产业		Secondary Industry		98.2	106.7	
第三产业		Tertiary Industry		102.3	103.9	
人均地区生产总值指数	(上年=100)	Index of Per Capita Gross Domestic Product	(preceding year=100)	100.5	104.8	
公路通车里程	(公里)	Total Length of Highways in Operation	(km)	23121	23798	2.9
邮电业务总量	(亿元)	Total Business Volume of Postal and Telecommunication	(100 million yuan)	672.90	757.78	12.6
本地电话年末用户	(万户)	Number of Subscribers of Local Telephones at the Year-end	(10000 subscribers)	197.36	187.19	-5.2
移动电话年末用户	(万户)	Number of Subscribers of Mobile Telephones at the Year-end	(10000 subscribers)	1722.21	1731.55	0.5
房地产开发投资	(亿元)	Investment in Real Estate Development	(100 million yuan)	750.85	609.34	-18.8
社会消费品零售总额	(亿元)	Total Retail Sales of Consumer Goods	(100 million yuan)	3513.77	3645.54	3.8
出口总额	(亿元)	Total Exports	(100 million yuan)	1065.66	977.71	-8.3
进口总额	(亿元)	Total Imports	(100 million yuan)	291.01	351.53	20.8
实际外商直接投资额	(亿元)	Foreign Direct Investment Actually Utilized	(100 million yuan)	16.12	14.88	-7.7
地方一般公共预算收入	(亿元)	Local Public Budgetary Revenue	(100 million yuan)	309.90	360.36	16.3
地方一般公共预算支出	(亿元)	Local Public Budgetary Expenditure	(100 million yuan)	1266.24	1227.55	-3.1
金融机构本外币存款	(亿元)	Deposits in Renminbi and Foreign Currencies in All Financial Institutions	(100 million yuan)	11052.26	11871.24	7.4
#住户存款		Savings Deposits by Residents		7938.99	8787.00	10.7
金融机构本外币贷款	(亿元)	Loans in Renminbi and Foreign Currencies in All Financial Institutions	(100 million yuan)	5946.91	6601.92	11.0
全体居民人均可支配收入	(元)	Per Capita Disposable Income of Households	(yuan)	28388.3	29597.8	4.3
城镇居民人均可支配收入	(元)	Per Capita Disposable Income of Urban Households	(yuan)	33521.5	34767.1	3.7
农村居民人均可支配收入	(元)	Per Capita Disposable Income of Rural Households	(yuan)	20335.4	21422.9	5.3

22-8 粤西主要经济指标

Main Economic Indicators of the Western Region

指　　标		Item		2022	2023	2023年比2022年增长% Growth Rate in 2023 over 2022
土地面积	(平方公里)	Land Area	(sq.km)	32682	32682	0.0
年末常住人口	(万人)	Permanent Population at the Year-end	(10000 persons)	1589.58	1595.54	0.4
#城镇人口		Urban Population		763.71	785.74	2.9
年末户籍总人口	(万人)	Total Population with Residence Registration at the Year-end	(10000 persons)	1998.48	1998.82	0.0
城镇单位就业人员	(万人)	Employed Persons in Urban Areas	(10000 persons)	107.70	102.19	-5.1
地区生产总值	(亿元)	Gross Domestic Product	(100 million yuan)	9155.27	9362.60	3.4
第一产业		Primary Industry		1645.14	1688.04	4.1
第二产业		Secondary Industry		3384.76	3402.62	2.2
第三产业		Tertiary Industry		4125.37	4271.93	3.9
人均地区生产总值	(元)	Per Capita Gross Domestic Product	(yuan)	57640	58790	3.1
地区生产总值指数	(上年=100)	Index of Gross Domestic Product	(preceding year=100)	100.9	103.4	
第一产业		Primary Industry		104.5	104.1	
第二产业		Secondary Industry		96.6	102.2	
第三产业		Tertiary Industry		102.5	103.9	
人均地区生产总值指数	(上年=100)	Index of Per Capita Gross Domestic Product	(preceding year=100)	100.5	103.1	
公路通车里程	(公里)	Total Length of Highways in Operation	(km)	52550	53368	1.6
邮电业务总量	(亿元)	Total Business Volume of Postal and Telecommunication	(100 million yuan)	209.99	227.83	8.5
本地电话年末用户	(万户)	Number of Subscribers of Local Telephones at the Year-end	(10000 subscribers)	138.37	128.49	-7.1
移动电话年末用户	(万户)	Number of Subscribers of Mobile Telephones at the Year-end	(10000 subscribers)	1605.20	1598.99	-0.4
房地产开发投资	(亿元)	Investment in Real Estate Development	(100 million yuan)	684.18	666.72	-2.6
社会消费品零售总额	(亿元)	Total Retail Sales of Consumer Goods	(100 million yuan)	3832.16	4053.44	5.8
出口总额	(亿元)	Total Exports	(100 million yuan)	445.15	397.29	-10.8
进口总额	(亿元)	Total Imports	(100 million yuan)	577.87	656.14	13.5
实际外商直接投资额	(亿元)	Foreign Direct Investment Actually Utilized	(100 million yuan)	48.78	49.04	0.5
地方一般公共预算收入	(亿元)	Local Public Budgetary Revenue	(100 million yuan)	353.99	379.82	7.3
地方一般公共预算支出	(亿元)	Local Public Budgetary Expenditure	(100 million yuan)	1317.09	1322.91	0.4
金融机构本外币存款	(亿元)	Deposits in Renminbi and Foreign Currencies in All Financial Institutions	(100 million yuan)	10036.79	10784.05	7.4
#本外币住户存款		Savings Deposits by Residents		7212.14	7885.71	9.3
金融机构本外币贷款	(亿元)	Loans in Renminbi and Foreign Currencies in All Financial Institutions	(100 million yuan)	7795.89	8515.50	9.2
全体居民人均可支配收入	(元)	Per Capita Disposable Income of Households	(yuan)	28713.6	29829.7	3.9
城镇居民人均可支配收入	(元)	Per Capita Disposable Income of Urban Households	(yuan)	35906.0	36697.5	2.2
农村居民人均可支配收入	(元)	Per Capita Disposable Income of Rural Households	(yuan)	22254.3	23478.8	5.5

22-9 粤北主要经济指标

Main Economic Indicators of the Northern Region

指标	Item	2022	2023	2023年比2022年增长% Growth Rate in 2023 over 2022
土地面积 (平方公里)	Land Area (sq.km)	76751	76751	0.0
年末常住人口 (万人)	Permanent Population at the Year-end (10000 persons)	1594.37	1592.84	-0.1
#城镇人口	Urban Population	845.92	866.80	2.5
年末户籍总人口 (万人)	Total Population with Residence Registration at the Year-end (10000 persons)	2002.26	1994.17	-0.4
城镇单位就业人员 (万人)	Employed Persons in Urban Areas (10000 persons)	132.85	128.23	-3.5
地区生产总值 (亿元)	Gross Domestic Product (100 million yuan)	7415.27	7705.08	4.6
第一产业	Primary Industry	1196.21	1242.99	5.9
第二产业	Secondary Industry	2601.35	2698.70	5.2
第三产业	Tertiary Industry	3617.71	3763.40	3.8
人均地区生产总值 (元)	Per Capita Gross Domestic Product (yuan)	46494	48350	4.7
地区生产总值指数 (上年=100)	Index of Gross Domestic Product (preceding year=100)	101.1	104.6	
第一产业	Primary Industry	105.1	105.9	
第二产业	Secondary Industry	99.2	105.2	
第三产业	Tertiary Industry	101.1	103.8	
人均地区生产总值指数 (上年=100)	Index of Per Capita Gross Domestic Product (preceding year=100)	101.1	104.7	
公路通车里程 (公里)	Total Length of Highways in Operation (km)	85023	85982	1.1
邮电业务总量 (亿元)	Total Business Volume of Postal and Telecommunication (100 million yuan)	198.80	207.84	4.5
本地电话年末用户 (万户)	Number of Subscribers of Local Telephones at the Year-end (10000 subscribers)	160.60	149.97	-6.6
移动电话年末用户 (万户)	Number of Subscribers of Mobile Telephones at the Year-end (10000 subscribers)	1603.67	1616.72	0.8
房地产开发投资 (亿元)	Investment in Real Estate Development (100 million yuan)	734.21	663.40	-9.6
社会消费品零售总额 (亿元)	Total Retail Sales of Consumer Goods (100 million yuan)	2494.15	2588.59	3.8
出口总额 (亿元)	Total Exports (100 million yuan)	722.61	664.83	-8.0
进口总额 (亿元)	Total Imports (100 million yuan)	520.50	526.96	1.2
实际外商直接投资额 (亿元)	Foreign Direct Investment Actually Utilized (100 million yuan)	34.03	18.24	-46.4
地方一般公共预算收入 (亿元)	Local Public Budgetary Revenue (100 million yuan)	481.78	511.71	6.2
地方一般公共预算支出 (亿元)	Local Public Budgetary Expenditure (100 million yuan)	1839.23	1813.29	-1.4
金融机构本外币存款 (亿元)	Deposits in Renminbi and Foreign Currencies in All Financial Institutions (100 million yuan)	11612.52	12761.56	9.9
#本外币住户存款	Savings Deposits by Residents	8308.40	9146.19	10.1
金融机构本外币贷款 (亿元)	Loans in Renminbi and Foreign Currencies in All Financial Institution (100 million yuan)	9339.30	10288.05	10.2
全体居民人均可支配收入 (元)	Per Capita Disposable Income of Households (yuan)	28256.0	29745.8	5.3
城镇居民人均可支配收入 (元)	Per Capita Disposable Income of Urban Households (yuan)	35151.8	36592.4	4.1
农村居民人均可支配收入 (元)	Per Capita Disposable Income of Rural Households (yuan)	20627.7	22007.6	6.7

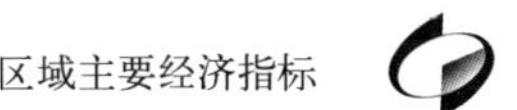

22–10 山区县(市、区)主要经济指标
Main Economic Indicators of Counties (County-level Cities and Districts) in Mountainous Areas

指标	Item	2022	2023	2023年比2022年增长% Growth Rate in 2023 over 2022
年末户籍总人口 (万人)	Total Population with Residence Registration at the Year-end (10000 persons)	3489.60	3474.25	-0.4
地区生产总值 (亿元)	Gross Domestic Product (100 million yuan)	12183.88	12654.61	4.5
第一产业	Primary Industry	2386.43	2468.21	5.4
第二产业	Secondary Industry	4166.61	4283.10	4.5
第三产业	Tertiary Industry	5630.84	5903.30	4.0
人均地区生产总值 (元)	Per Capita Gross Domestic Product (yuan)	45679	47454	4.5
地区生产总值指数 (上年=100)	Index of Gross Domestic Product (preceding year=100)	101.5	104.5	
第一产业	Primary Industry	105.1	105.4	
第二产业	Secondary Industry	98.2	104.5	
第三产业	Tertiary Industry	102.2	104.0	
人均地区生产总值指数(上年=100)	Index of Per Capita Gross Domestic Product(preceding year=100)	101.3	104.5	
房地产开发投资 (亿元)	Investment in Real Estate Development (100 million yuan)	932.50	786.03	-15.7
社会消费品零售总额 (亿元)	Total Retail Sales of Consumer Goods (100 million yuan)	4302.32	4543.86	5.6
地方一般公共预算收入 (亿元)	Local Public Budgetary Revenue (100 million yuan)	570.18	586.00	2.8
地方一般公共预算支出 (亿元)	Local Public Budgetary Expenditure (100 million yuan)	2490.97	2434.28	-2.3

注：50个山区县(市、区)包括:从化区、南澳县、曲江区、乐昌市、南雄市、仁化县、始兴县、翁源县、新丰县、乳源县、东源县、和平县、龙川县、紫金县、连平县、梅江区、梅县区、兴宁市、平远县、蕉岭县、大埔县、丰顺县、五华县、惠东县、龙门县、海丰县、陆河县、阳春市、信宜市、高州市、高要区、广宁县、德庆县、封开县、怀集县、清新区、英德市、连州市、佛冈县、阳山县、连山县、连南县、潮安区、饶平县、普宁市、揭西县、云安区、罗定市、新兴县、郁南县。

Notes: Counties(county-level cities and districts)in mountainous areas total 50, including Conghua District, Nan'ao County,Qujiang District,Lechang City,Nanxiong City, Renhua County, Shixing County, Wengyuan County, Xinfeng County, Ruyuan County,Dongyuan County, Heping County, Longchuan County, Zijin County, Lianping County, Meijiang District, Meixian County,Xingning City, Pingyuan County,Jiaoling County,Dabu County,Fengshun County,Wuhua County,Huidong County,Longmen County,Haifeng County,Luhe County,Yangchun City,Xinyi City,Gaozhou City, Gaoyao City, Guangning County, Deqing County, Fengkai County, Huaiji County, Qingxin County, Yingde City, Lianzhou City, Fogang County, Yangshan County, Lianshan County, Liannan County, Chao'an District, Raoping County, Puning City, Jiexi County, Yun'an District, Luoding City, Xinxing County and Yunan County.

22-11 少数民族县主要经济指标（2023年）
Main Economic Indicators of Minority Counties (2023)

指标	Item	合计 Total	乳源县 Ruyuan County	连山县 Lianshan County	连南县 Liannan County
土地面积（平方公里）	Land Area (sq.km)	2459	2299	1218	1241
年末户籍总人口（万人）	Total Population with Residence Registration at the Year-end (10000 persons)	53.52	23.31	12.52	17.70
少数民族人口（万人）	Population of Minority Nationalities (10000 persons)	21.46	2.89	8.25	10.32
地区生产总值（亿元）	Gross Domestic Product (100 million yuan)	240.56	115.55	50.94	74.06
第一产业	Primary Industry	36.31	11.68	11.53	13.09
第二产业	Secondary Industry	87.94	57.09	12.28	18.57
第三产业	Tertiary Industry	116.31	46.78	27.12	42.40
人均地区生产总值（元）	Per Capita Gross Domestic Product (yuan)	57290	61205	53314	54640
地区生产总值指数（上年=100）	Index of Gross Domestic Product (preceding year=100)	101.3	100.2	104.6	101.2
第一产业	Primary Industry	106.4	111.4	103.8	104.1
第二产业	Secondary Industry	96.7	94.0	113.3	96.1
第三产业	Tertiary Industry	103.2	104.8	101.1	102.5
人均地区生产总值指数（上年=100）	Index of Per Capita Gross Domestic Product (preceding year=100)	101.1	99.9	104.5	101.1
公路通车里程（公里）	Total Length of Highways in Operation (km)	3925	1748	1026	1151
本地电话年末用户（户）	Number of Subscribers of Local Telephones at the Year-end (subscriber)	40592	24271	6010	10311
移动电话年末用户（户）	Number of Subscribers of Mobile Telephones at the Year-end (subscriber)	405897	179239	101347	125311
房地产开发投资（亿元）	Investment in Real Estate Development (100 million yuan)	3.88	2.29	0.56	1.03
社会消费品零售总额（亿元）	Total Retail Sales of Consumer Goods (100 million yuan)	41.22	23.70	5.68	11.85
地方一般公共预算收入（亿元）	Local Public Budgetary Revenue (100 million yuan)	10.89	5.52	2.48	2.90
地方一般公共预算支出（亿元）	Local Public Budgetary Expenditure (100 million yuan)	70.96	28.34	18.84	23.78
农村居民人均可支配收入（元）	Per Capita Annual Disposable Income of Rural Residents (yuan)		21710	18980	19114
普通中学（所）	Number of Regular Secondary Schools (unit)	27	8	10	9
在校学生数（人）	Number of Students Enrolled in Regular Secondary Schools (person)	28007	11536	6645	9826
小学（所）	Number of Primary Schools (unit)	50	12	8	30
在校学生数（人）	Number of Students Enrolled in Primary Schools (person)	42976	18197	9858	14921

二十三、县（市、区）主要经济指标

COUNTIES AND DISTRICTS UNDER CITY ADMINISTRATION

二十三　县（市、区）主要经济指标

简要说明

一、本篇资料反映广东县（市、区）经济发展基本情况，主要包括：各县（市、区）的地区生产总值、农林牧渔业总产值、主要农产品产量、规模以上工业生产、房地产开发、社会消费品零售总额、财政收支、居民可支配收入等内容。

二、本篇资料由广东省统计局及国家统计局广东调查总队各有关专业处整理提供，综合统计处负责编辑。

三、本篇资料依据国家统计局制定的各有关专业年度报表制度填报汇总而成。

四、本篇所列县（市、区）是由民政部门批准设立的行政区，部分指标数据不含功能区，存在汇总数不等于全市数情况。

23 Counties and Districts Under City Administration

Brief Introduction

I. The data in this chapter show the basic conditions of the economic development of counties and districts under city administration in Guangdong Province, mainly including gross domestic product, gross output value of industry and agriculture, output of major agriculture products, real estate development investment, total retail sales of consumer goods, number and wages of fully employed staff and workers, local government budgetary revenue and expenditure, etc.

II. The data in this chapter are prepared and provided by the related specialized divisions and compiled by the Division of Comprehensive Statistics of Statistics Bureau of Guangdong Province.

III. The data in this chapter are reported and compiled in accordance with related specialized annual report schemes formulated by the National Bureau of Statistics.

IV. The counties (cities, districts) listed in this article are administrative regions approved by the civil affairs department. Some indicator data does not include functional areas, and there is a situation where the total number does not equal the number of cities in the city.

23-1 各县(市、区)地区生产总值
Gross Domestic Product by County (County-level City and District)

县(市、区)	County (County-level City and District)	地区生产总值(亿元) Gross Domestic Product (100 million yuan) 2022	2023	指数(上年=100) Index (preceding year=100) 2022	2023
广州市	Guangzhou				
越秀区	Yuexiu District	3651.44	3810.24	100.1	104.5
海珠区	Haizhu District	2511.74	2720.16	101.4	108.6
荔湾区	Liwan District	1216.87	1277.93	101.1	104.8
天河区	Tianhe District	6221.95	6551.26	102.4	105.1
白云区	Baiyun District	2494.34	2812.01	97.1	108.1
黄埔区	Huangpu District	4267.55	4315.17	100.8	101.2
花都区	Huadu District	1771.44	1801.51	98.9	102.1
番禺区	Panyu District	2711.72	2866.95	101.4	104.6
南沙区	Nansha District	2252.49	2323.54	104.2	104.3
从化区	Conghua District	408.78	424.48	98.0	104.7
增城区	Zengcheng District	1324.74	1452.46	103.9	108.5
深圳市	Shenzhen				
福田区	Futian District	5503.65	5704.55	102.8	102.8
罗湖区	Luohu District	2600.26	2808.19	102.7	107.2
盐田区	Yantian District	809.64	850.02	104.0	105.3
南山区	Nanshan District	8153.86	8566.02	103.3	105.1
宝安区	Baoan District	4686.10	5202.01	102.7	108.5
龙岗区	Longgang District	5149.01	5483.77	102.8	106.2
龙华区	Longhua District	2951.92	3010.72	102.9	102.0
坪山区	Pingshan District	1128.16	1329.89	114.0	118.0
光明区	Guangming District	1403.24	1526.64	105.6	109.0
珠海市	Zhuhai				
香洲区	Xiangzhou District	2697.82	2819.14	101.6	104.2
金湾区	Jinwan District	867.23	887.08	103.4	102.0
斗门区	Doumen District	505.13	527.00	104.2	104.5
汕头市	Shantou				
金平区	Jinping District	611.50	637.56	101.6	104.3
龙湖区	Longhu District	620.05	645.34	100.9	104.8
澄海区	Chenghai District	520.94	557.31	104.0	106.0
濠江区	Haojiang District	185.41	187.50	98.4	102.0
潮阳区	Chaoyang District	535.09	555.70	99.1	104.2
潮南区	Chaonan District	524.50	536.41	102.4	102.5
南澳县	Nanao County	37.17	38.50	101.7	104.0
佛山市	Foshan				
禅城区	Chancheng District	2274.43	2387.50	103.1	105.6
南海区	Nanhai District	3761.40	3930.50	102.7	104.3
顺德区	Shunde District	4144.18	4317.01	100.7	104.5
高明区	Gaoming District	1044.44	1100.50	103.6	106.0
三水区	Sanshui District	1470.55	1540.63	102.2	105.6
韶关市	Shaoguan				
浈江区	Zhengjiang District	229.13	237.91	99.8	104.5
武江区	Wujiang District	310.35	320.07	101.0	104.1
曲江区	Qujiang District	193.78	210.18	89.5	109.7
乐昌市	Lechang City	138.26	146.03	100.7	105.7
南雄市	Nanxiong City	134.37	135.90	101.3	102.5
仁化县	Renhua County	123.77	126.86	109.2	103.5
始兴县	Shixing County	100.76	103.09	101.2	103.5
翁源县	Wengyuan County	132.76	140.11	101.5	105.5
新丰县	Xinfeng County	82.05	85.14	99.1	103.8
乳源县	Ruyuan County	118.23	115.55	106.5	100.2

注：海丰县不包含深汕合作区地区生产总值数据。
Notes: GDP of Shenzhen-Shanwei Cooperation Zone not included Haifeng county.

23-1 续表 1 continued

县(市、区)	County (County-level City and District)	地区生产总值(亿元) Gross Domestic Product (100 million yuan) 2022	2023	指数(上年=100) Index(preceding year=100) 2022	2023
河源市	Heyuan				
源城区	Yuancheng District	535.44	546.04	101.5	102.5
东源县	Dongyuan County	173.35	181.68	102.9	105.4
和平县	Heping County	129.76	135.22	100.2	105.0
龙川县	Longchuan County	172.44	181.62	100.3	106.0
紫金县	Zijin County	190.53	197.45	100.4	104.0
连平县	Lianping County	100.86	106.20	101.1	104.6
梅州市	Meizhou				
梅江区	Meijiang District	289.08	304.98	100.4	106.0
梅县区	Meixian District	239.26	258.48	100.3	107.6
兴宁市	Xingning City	202.23	213.07	101.3	106.2
平远县	Pingyuan County	87.37	93.72	100.8	106.6
蕉岭县	Jiaoling County	106.28	114.37	99.8	107.6
大埔县	Dabu County	101.45	106.85	100.6	105.4
丰顺县	Fengshun County	120.06	132.41	100.4	109.5
五华县	Wuhua County	180.05	184.55	101.8	104.5
惠州市	Huizhou				
惠城区	Huicheng District	1949.28	2078.91	104.4	107.0
惠阳区	Huiyang District	1705.84	1755.97	105.0	105.0
惠东县	Huidong County	733.85	762.13	102.3	104.6
博罗县	Boluo County	810.79	838.89	103.8	104.8
龙门县	Longmen County	200.52	203.78	105.1	102.6
汕尾市	Shanwei				
市城区	Urban District	363.87	394.79	100.4	106.0
陆丰市	Lufeng City	417.69	445.25	96.7	103.9
海丰县	Haifeng County	417.10	445.05	101.3	103.9
陆河县	Luhe County	132.00	145.75	128.7	108.7
江门市	Jiangmen				
蓬江区	Pengjiang District	878.92	918.24	104.4	104.2
江海区	Jianghai District	300.11	306.28	102.5	103.8
新会区	Xinhui District	943.63	1011.25	103.5	107.2
台山市	Taishan City	514.50	547.40	103.1	106.3
开平市	Kaiping City	457.57	500.36	103.0	105.5
鹤山市	Heshan City	460.51	502.87	103.3	106.2
恩平市	Enping City	219.18	235.85	103.1	106.3
阳江市	Yangjiang				
江城区	Jiangcheng District	576.26	593.30	101.2	104.5
阳东区	Yangdong District	351.94	349.87	100.2	101.1
阳春市	Yangchun City	358.05	363.03	99.0	103.6
阳西县	Yangxi County	255.40	275.59	103.8	106.1

23-1 续表 2 continued

县(市、区)	County (County-level City and District)	地区生产总值(亿元) Gross Domestic Product (100 million yuan)		指数(上年=100) Index(preceding year=100)	
		2022	2023	2022	2023
湛江市	Zhanjiang				
赤坎区	Chikan District	364.00	380.39	102.0	103.0
霞山区	Xiashan District	447.03	457.99	101.1	102.6
麻章区	Mazhang District	602.84	618.20	87.7	101.4
坡头区	Potou District	414.33	398.48	107.5	102.4
雷州市	Leizhou City	369.53	386.42	102.4	103.6
廉江市	Lianjiang County	541.68	555.76	102.4	105.0
吴川市	Wuchuan City	306.59	314.89	101.2	102.7
遂溪县	Suixi County	421.64	426.43	102.3	100.8
徐闻县	Xuwen County	243.19	255.02	109.5	103.5
茂名市	Maoming				
茂南区	Maonan District	1156.15	1152.55	96.9	103.1
电白区	Dianbai District	810.80	840.26	103.0	104.1
信宜市	Xinyi City	550.08	566.29	102.1	104.2
高州市	Gaozhou City	735.60	764.15	102.3	104.0
化州市	Huazhou City	650.15	663.96	101.6	103.3
肇庆市	Zhaoqing				
端州区	Duanzhou District	464.23	478.99	96.7	103.8
鼎湖区	Dinghu District	156.91	163.96	106.3	105.3
高要区	Gaoyao District	542.59	561.45	103.9	104.5
四会市	Sihui City	754.27	759.15	102.6	101.9
广宁县	Guangning County	182.78	189.68	101.1	105.0
德庆县	Deqing County	150.86	153.67	86.7	102.2
封开县	Fengkai County	172.83	180.34	103.8	106.3
怀集县	Huaiji County	297.09	305.26	104.8	104.0
清远市	Qingyuan				
清城区	Qingcheng District	717.90	745.34	101.3	104.8
清新区	Qingxin District	315.39	324.81	101.2	104.0
英德市	Yingde City	405.21	420.47	101.7	104.8
连州市	Lianzhou City	181.30	188.56	101.3	105.3
佛冈县	Fogang County	166.67	171.57	102.0	104.0
阳山县	Yangshan County	140.78	144.42	101.7	103.5
连山县	Lianshan County	49.23	50.94	103.1	104.6
连南县	Liannan County	73.67	74.06	105.2	101.2
潮州市	Chaozhou				
湘桥区	Xiangqiao District	319.84	322.62	102.8	100.6
潮安区	Chaoan District	654.49	672.49	101.6	103.2
饶平县	Raoping County	343.40	361.49	103.9	104.9
揭阳市	Jieyang				
榕城区	Rongcheng District	584.72	596.64	98.7	101.3
揭东区	Jiedong District	498.10	496.79	98.0	101.5
普宁市	Puning City	642.98	670.76	99.6	104.0
揭西县	Jiexi County	260.51	261.70	99.1	102.2
惠来县	Huilai County	290.54	419.13	98.4	157.0
云浮市	Yunfu				
云城区	Yuncheng District	259.25	271.12	102.7	104.7
云安区	Yunan District	135.56	138.35	102.7	103.0
罗定市	Luoding City	322.23	335.03	102.0	105.1
新兴县	Xinxing County	314.67	317.59	101.9	102.1
郁南县	Yunan County	141.79	145.32	103.1	103.5

23−2 各县(市、区)三次产业地区生产总值

Gross Domestic Product of the Three Strata of Industry by County (County-level City and District)

单位：亿元 (100 million yuan)

县(市、区)	County (County-level City and District)	第一产业 Primary Industry 2022	2023	第二产业 Secondary Industry 2022	2023	第三产业 Tertiary Industry 2022	2023
广州市	Guangzhou						
越秀区	Yuexiu District			123.42	137.11	3528.02	3673.13
海珠区	Haizhu District	1.19	1.40	440.68	486.37	2069.87	2232.39
荔湾区	Liwan District	5.37	5.32	343.25	355.25	868.25	917.36
天河区	Tianhe District	2.53	2.77	437.86	470.52	5781.56	6077.98
白云区	Baiyun District	35.22	36.96	552.47	589.33	1906.65	2185.73
黄埔区	Huangpu District	4.92	5.34	2460.02	2325.94	1802.61	1983.90
花都区	Huadu District	52.82	56.59	742.04	697.85	976.57	1047.07
番禺区	Panyu District	36.23	37.67	997.70	1050.83	1677.79	1778.45
南沙区	Nansha District	75.60	69.54	977.93	976.49	1198.95	1277.51
从化区	Conghua District	34.24	34.34	127.21	133.43	247.33	256.71
增城区	Zengcheng District	64.29	67.85	524.46	552.60	735.99	832.01
深圳市	Shenzhen						
福田区	Futian District	1.71	1.76	541.86	567.34	4960.08	5135.45
罗湖区	Luohu District	0.46	0.40	149.34	163.42	2450.47	2644.36
盐田区	Yantian District	0.28	0.34	146.04	149.30	663.32	700.38
南山区	Nanshan District	0.85	1.10	2466.27	2529.67	5686.74	6035.25
宝安区	Baoan District	0.91	0.87	2348.12	2499.35	2337.06	2701.79
龙岗区	Longgang District	2.30	2.26	3406.47	3602.99	1740.24	1878.53
龙华区	Longhua District	0.59	0.62	1429.70	1401.59	1521.63	1608.51
坪山区	Pingshan District	1.23	1.37	783.09	945.68	343.85	382.84
光明区	Guangming District	2.28	2.16	999.86	1089.76	401.09	434.73
珠海市	Zhuhai						
香洲区	Xiangzhou District	1.71	1.77	932.63	977.02	1763.47	1840.35
金湾区	Jinwan District	15.61	16.95	615.36	624.31	236.26	245.82
斗门区	Doumen District	49.56	51.00	250.88	270.78	204.69	205.22
汕头市	Shantou						
金平区	Jinping District	3.08	3.22	239.92	254.79	368.49	379.55
龙湖区	Longhu District	8.45	8.82	215.17	225.81	396.43	410.71
澄海区	Chenghai District	46.32	49.59	274.26	297.62	200.37	210.10
濠江区	Haojiang District	8.58	9.09	103.08	105.87	73.75	72.54
潮阳区	Chaoyang District	35.47	36.26	297.92	310.10	201.69	209.34
潮南区	Chaonan District	22.53	22.95	318.14	321.98	183.83	191.48
南澳县	Nanao County	11.96	12.04	7.37	7.09	17.84	19.37
佛山市	Foshan						
禅城区	Chancheng District	0.64	0.66	790.61	815.55	1483.18	1571.29
南海区	Nanhai District	66.35	68.76	2041.37	2140.08	1653.69	1721.66
顺德区	Shunde District	70.39	73.71	2462.07	2626.24	1611.72	1617.05
高明区	Gaoming District	36.82	38.33	784.76	817.64	222.86	244.53
三水区	Sanshui District	45.36	47.32	1069.53	1114.21	355.66	379.10
韶关市	Shaoguan						
浈江区	Zhengjiang District	8.71	8.71	61.88	61.89	158.54	167.31
武江区	Wujiang District	8.38	8.61	125.66	126.87	176.32	184.58
曲江区	Qujiang District	21.01	22.30	100.48	110.64	72.29	77.24
乐昌市	Lechang City	32.14	34.51	28.44	30.08	77.68	81.44
南雄市	Nanxiong City	38.63	38.97	29.69	29.04	66.05	67.89
仁化县	Renhua County	26.31	28.20	54.03	54.18	43.43	44.48
始兴县	Shixing County	28.34	29.96	29.69	28.95	42.74	44.18
翁源县	Wengyuan County	34.95	36.96	35.12	37.10	62.68	66.05
新丰县	Xinfeng County	17.50	18.82	22.49	23.33	42.07	43.00
乳源县	Ruyuan County	10.95	11.68	62.44	57.09	44.83	46.78

23-2 续表 1 continued

单位：亿元 (100 million yuan)

县(市、区)	County (County-level City and District)	第一产业 Primary Industry 2022	第一产业 Primary Industry 2023	第二产业 Secondary Industry 2022	第二产业 Secondary Industry 2023	第三产业 Tertiary Industry 2022	第三产业 Tertiary Industry 2023
河源市	Heyuan						
源城区	Yuancheng District	3.95	3.59	253.78	260.12	277.71	282.33
东源县	Dongyuan County	30.88	34.12	67.23	70.11	75.24	77.45
和平县	Heping County	27.65	28.63	34.00	36.24	68.11	70.35
龙川县	Longchuan County	32.86	34.16	40.72	44.07	98.86	103.40
紫金县	Zijin County	44.48	47.03	56.75	58.52	89.30	91.90
连平县	Lianping County	22.83	25.10	29.77	30.07	48.26	51.03
梅州市	Meizhou						
梅江区	Meijiang District	9.42	9.54	123.60	131.90	156.06	163.54
梅县区	Meixian District	60.26	63.02	78.59	87.15	100.40	108.31
兴宁市	Xingning City	53.21	55.29	36.84	38.83	112.18	118.94
平远县	Pingyuan County	15.14	15.90	24.29	26.65	47.95	51.17
蕉岭县	Jiaoling County	18.47	18.78	45.65	51.26	42.17	44.33
大埔县	Dabu County	30.52	32.45	18.61	19.82	52.32	54.58
丰顺县	Fengshun County	26.63	27.45	42.63	52.01	50.79	52.96
五华县	Wuhua County	42.63	43.61	38.17	36.49	99.25	104.45
惠州市	Huizhou						
惠城区	Huicheng District	44.88	46.47	967.14	1030.74	937.27	1001.71
惠阳区	Huiyang District	25.40	27.25	1205.00	1226.03	475.44	502.69
惠东县	Huidong County	81.28	87.44	269.99	269.69	382.58	405.00
博罗县	Boluo County	89.37	94.24	443.15	466.46	278.27	278.20
龙门县	Longmen County	38.13	40.67	78.81	77.43	83.58	85.67
汕尾市	Shanwei						
市城区	Urban District	41.41	44.75	126.76	143.55	195.69	206.49
陆丰市	Lufeng City	82.43	84.60	157.36	172.11	177.91	188.54
海丰县	Haifeng County	44.16	45.27	182.98	193.70	189.96	206.08
陆河县	Luhe County	17.73	17.88	44.02	54.53	70.25	73.33
江门市	Jiangmen						
蓬江区	Pengjiang District	8.07	8.03	332.84	345.37	538.01	564.84
江海区	Jianghai District	7.41	8.54	178.28	178.36	114.42	119.39
新会区	Xinhui District	60.74	72.09	471.89	511.27	410.99	427.88
台山市	Taishan City	127.20	116.44	206.69	233.01	180.61	197.95
开平市	Kaiping City	55.25	61.31	227.26	245.01	175.06	194.04
鹤山市	Heshan City	33.77	40.96	249.45	274.00	177.28	187.91
恩平市	Enping City	30.98	39.64	63.61	68.12	124.60	128.09
阳江市	Yangjiang						
江城区	Jiangcheng District	57.54	59.44	215.77	219.02	302.95	314.85
阳东区	Yangdong District	59.52	59.96	182.74	178.51	109.68	111.40
阳春市	Yangchun City	67.44	66.60	104.52	103.54	186.09	192.89
阳西县	Yangxi County	68.43	69.85	85.96	100.94	101.01	104.79

23-2 续表 2 continued

单位：亿元 (100 million yuan)

县(市、区)	County (County-level City and District)	第一产业 Primary Industry 2022	2023	第二产业 Secondary Industry 2022	2023	第三产业 Tertiary Industry 2022	2023
湛江市	Zhanjiang						
赤坎区	Chikan District	1.50	1.14	80.06	82.06	282.43	297.19
霞山区	Xiashan District	2.89	3.07	193.81	199.21	250.34	255.72
麻章区	Mazhang District	53.82	57.40	416.99	415.15	132.02	145.65
坡头区	Potou District	24.37	19.40	280.17	277.15	109.79	101.92
雷州市	Leizhou City	154.08	161.81	44.84	47.72	170.61	176.89
廉江市	Lianjiang County	139.29	141.09	198.23	200.59	204.16	214.08
吴川市	Wuchuan City	39.39	41.49	106.36	105.73	160.84	167.67
遂溪县	Suixi County	152.43	160.00	95.08	86.78	174.12	179.65
徐闻县	Xuwen County	116.34	121.52	38.12	40.22	88.73	93.28
茂名市	Maoming						
茂南区	Maonan District	36.19	38.55	603.19	586.77	516.77	527.23
电白区	Dianbai District	166.21	170.01	290.96	301.61	353.62	368.65
信宜市	Xinyi City	161.69	165.22	85.55	84.04	302.84	317.03
高州市	Gaozhou City	188.14	192.04	188.78	201.44	358.67	370.67
化州市	Huazhou City	155.83	159.46	174.00	171.56	320.32	332.94
肇庆市	Zhaoqing						
端州区	Duanzhou District	0.25	0.26	132.68	133.78	331.29	344.96
鼎湖区	Dinghu District	11.86	12.04	77.39	83.14	67.67	68.78
高要区	Gaoyao District	116.06	121.41	289.25	297.55	137.29	142.49
四会市	Sihui City	72.40	73.65	411.27	402.20	270.60	283.31
广宁县	Guangning County	60.75	62.29	56.43	59.45	65.60	67.94
德庆县	Deqing County	44.20	44.80	43.99	43.39	62.67	65.48
封开县	Fengkai County	61.79	62.69	59.21	63.93	51.82	53.72
怀集县	Huaiji County	119.80	121.79	69.10	71.13	108.19	112.34
清远市	Qingyuan						
清城区	Qingcheng District	30.38	32.12	323.57	342.30	363.94	370.93
清新区	Qingxin District	60.09	61.12	123.88	123.83	131.42	139.86
英德市	Yingde City	89.09	94.98	154.86	159.63	161.26	165.87
连州市	Lianzhou City	51.38	52.33	46.77	49.61	83.14	86.63
佛冈县	Fogang County	25.85	26.49	74.95	76.44	65.87	68.65
阳山县	Yangshan County	50.26	51.38	26.27	26.37	64.25	66.66
连山县	Lianshan County	11.70	11.53	11.63	12.28	25.91	27.12
连南县	Liannan County	13.32	13.09	19.46	18.57	40.88	42.40
潮州市	Chaozhou						
湘桥区	Xiangqiao District	9.87	10.46	93.30	88.36	216.68	223.80
潮安区	Chaoan District	28.99	30.00	414.86	422.17	210.64	220.33
饶平县	Raoping County	85.57	91.27	117.11	123.47	140.72	146.75
揭阳市	Jieyang						
榕城区	Rongcheng District	13.49	13.51	199.00	199.24	372.23	383.89
揭东区	Jiedong District	45.72	46.58	227.05	207.68	225.33	242.53
普宁市	Puning City	47.73	48.66	207.81	201.41	387.43	420.69
揭西县	Jiexi County	53.02	55.16	69.12	62.51	138.37	144.04
惠来县	Huilai County	63.83	66.19	95.34	242.95	131.37	110.00
云浮市	Yunfu						
云城区	Yuncheng District	21.05	21.33	85.97	94.31	152.23	155.48
云安区	Yunan District	18.60	19.01	69.96	69.58	47.01	49.76
罗定市	Luoding City	67.93	68.00	84.93	88.86	169.37	178.17
新兴县	Xinxing County	77.18	79.81	107.07	103.24	130.42	134.55
郁南县	Yunan County	33.50	34.41	31.48	31.29	76.81	79.62

23-3 各县(市、区)三次产业地区生产总值指数

Gross Domestic Product of the Three Industries by County (County-level City and District)

上年=100 (preceding year=100)

县(市、区)	County (County-level City and District)	第一产业 Primary Industry 2022	第一产业 Primary Industry 2023	第二产业 Secondary Industry 2022	第二产业 Secondary Industry 2023	第三产业 Tertiary Industry 2022	第三产业 Tertiary Industry 2023
广州市	Guangzhou						
越秀区	Yuexiu District			89.0	110.8	100.5	104.2
海珠区	Haizhu District	96.0	130.9	102.2	119.9	101.2	106.2
荔湾区	Liwan District	102.8	100.2	101.2	104.9	101.1	104.7
天河区	Tianhe District	106.6	127.6	97.1	108.0	102.8	104.8
白云区	Baiyun District	104.5	106.6	93.5	106.9	98.0	108.4
黄埔区	Huangpu District	106.6	110.1	99.3	98.0	103.0	105.5
花都区	Huadu District	104.7	110.1	94.6	96.4	102.1	105.9
番禺区	Panyu District	93.6	99.0	102.9	106.5	100.7	103.6
南沙区	Nansha District	106.7	98.8	104.3	103.4	104.0	105.2
从化区	Conghua District	100.2	106.9	93.7	106.3	99.8	103.5
增城区	Zengcheng District	99.7	104.3	99.5	106.5	107.5	110.2
深圳市	Shenzhen						
福田区	Futian District	154.7	101.4	102.6	102.9	102.8	102.8
罗湖区	Luohu District	106.7	85.9	86.8	106.1	103.9	107.3
盐田区	Yantian District	167.3	120.0	109.2	104.0	102.9	105.6
南山区	Nanshan District	71.3	134.7	101.0	106.3	104.1	104.7
宝安区	Baoan District	133.0	104.7	103.5	106.8	101.8	110.3
龙岗区	Longgang District	121.8	90.7	102.1	105.5	104.1	107.4
龙华区	Longhua District	94.6	108.4	100.8	98.8	104.9	105.1
坪山区	Pingshan District	107.7	117.9	115.1	122.1	111.6	109.4
光明区	Guangming District	106.3	99.0	105.2	109.5	106.5	107.9
珠海市	Zhuhai						
香洲区	Xiangzhou District	68.4	106.1	103.3	105.6	100.9	103.5
金湾区	Jinwan District	110.4	105.3	106.8	101.6	95.4	102.8
斗门区	Doumen District	107.5	105.0	107.1	109.3	100.3	98.7
汕头市	Shantou						
金平区	Jinping District	106.3	106.6	101.7	106.1	101.4	103.0
龙湖区	Longhu District	101.5	101.5	95.7	106.3	103.9	104.0
澄海区	Chenghai District	105.0	103.7	105.7	107.3	101.6	104.7
濠江区	Haojiang District	106.8	107.5	99.2	104.8	96.5	97.2
潮阳区	Chaoyang District	105.6	102.3	96.4	103.9	102.1	104.8
潮南区	Chaonan District	104.9	104.8	101.7	101.1	103.2	104.4
南澳县	Nanao County	99.2	99.8	105.3	96.3	102.5	108.9
佛山市	Foshan						
禅城区	Chancheng District	105.6	97.7	102.0	106.0	103.7	105.4
南海区	Nanhai District	106.6	104.4	104.1	104.7	101.1	103.9
顺德区	Shunde District	102.0	104.4	101.9	107.1	98.9	100.7
高明区	Gaoming District	115.9	106.0	104.0	106.5	100.1	104.7
三水区	Sanshui District	104.8	104.9	103.2	106.6	99.0	103.1
韶关市	Shaoguan						
浈江区	Zhengjiang District	99.9	104.1	93.4	101.1	102.4	105.7
武江区	Wujiang District	101.1	105.1	101.1	102.5	101.0	105.0
曲江区	Qujiang District	102.1	107.3	80.1	112.4	100.1	107.0
乐昌市	Lechang City	102.0	105.5	97.8	107.0	101.0	105.3
南雄市	Nanxiong City	102.1	102.4	98.9	98.8	101.9	104.1
仁化县	Renhua County	113.0	107.7	114.7	101.8	101.7	102.6
始兴县	Shixing County	106.7	106.9	94.4	98.9	102.2	104.1
翁源县	Wengyuan County	103.0	107.9	97.9	105.5	102.6	104.2
新丰县	Xinfeng County	106.5	105.0	89.0	105.1	101.6	102.6
乳源县	Ruyuan County	115.6	111.4	114.6	94.0	96.1	104.8

23-3 续表 1 continued

上年=100 (preceding year=100)

县(市、区)	County (County-level City and District)	第一产业 Primary Industry 2022	2023	第二产业 Secondary Industry 2022	2023	第三产业 Tertiary Industry 2022	2023
河源市	Heyuan						
源城区	Yuancheng District	100.7	91.7	101.7	104.0	101.3	101.3
东源县	Dongyuan County	105.9	109.9	105.1	105.8	99.9	103.2
和平县	Heping County	103.9	105.4	100.3	107.5	98.8	103.6
龙川县	Longchuan County	97.9	105.4	99.9	109.9	101.3	104.6
紫金县	Zijin County	110.2	105.8	99.7	103.8	96.8	103.2
连平县	Lianping County	104.8	106.6	111.0	100.0	94.3	106.4
梅州市	Meizhou						
梅江区	Meijiang District	106.9	103.9	98.6	108.7	101.5	104.0
梅县区	Meixian District	104.3	105.9	94.9	110.3	102.4	106.4
兴宁市	Xingning City	104.5	106.2	99.5	108.8	100.4	105.3
平远县	Pingyuan County	103.7	106.0	94.9	108.0	102.9	106.1
蕉岭县	Jiaoling County	107.3	106.0	93.3	110.7	104.0	104.9
大埔县	Dabu County	104.4	104.9	89.5	109.5	103.4	104.1
丰顺县	Fengshun County	104.5	105.6	93.1	119.4	104.6	103.8
五华县	Wuhua County	104.5	105.8	96.0	101.6	102.9	104.8
惠州市	Huizhou						
惠城区	Huicheng District	107.9	106.2	103.3	105.9	105.4	108.1
惠阳区	Huiyang District	99.7	107.4	107.3	105.8	100.0	103.0
惠东县	Huidong County	109.4	106.7	101.5	105.7	101.4	103.5
博罗县	Boluo County	105.8	106.5	105.2	107.9	101.0	99.6
龙门县	Longmen County	109.0	106.5	96.9	102.0	112.4	101.4
汕尾市	Shanwei						
市城区	Urban District	110.2	102.8	109.7	108.1	93.5	105.3
陆丰市	Lufeng City	104.6	103.3	91.1	103.6	98.3	104.4
海丰县	Haifeng County	108.0	102.7	97.2	102.3	103.9	105.8
陆河县	Luhe County	104.4	103.1	156.7	120.9	123.0	102.9
江门市	Jiangmen						
蓬江区	Pengjiang District	117.3	105.6	104.1	105.0	104.5	103.6
江海区	Jianghai District	100.9	104.0	98.8	104.5	108.4	102.7
新会区	Xinhui District	98.3	106.4	102.8	109.6	105.1	104.6
台山市	Taishan City	120.5	106.1	105.6	108.1	90.1	104.3
开平市	Kaiping City	104.4	105.9	107.2	106.2	97.7	104.4
鹤山市	Heshan City	98.6	105.1	109.4	109.3	96.8	102.3
恩平市	Enping City	88.6	106.3	107.7	111.3	105.2	103.9
阳江市	Yangjiang						
江城区	Jiangcheng District	100.4	102.4	97.6	104.2	103.8	105.1
阳东区	Yangdong District	101.1	103.7	96.8	99.0	105.6	102.7
阳春市	Yangchun City	106.6	105.0	89.8	100.6	100.9	104.6
阳西县	Yangxi County	99.9	101.1	109.3	113.0	102.8	104.5

23-3 续表 2 continued

上年=100 (preceding year =100)

县(市、区)	County (County-level City and District)	第一产业 Primary Industry 2022	2023	第二产业 Secondary Industry 2022	2023	第三产业 Tertiary Industry 2022	2023
湛江市	Zhanjiang						
赤坎区	Chikan District	98.8	105.1	101.2	100.5	102.2	103.7
霞山区	Xiashan District	86.8	92.3	97.0	100.0	104.7	104.6
麻章区	Mazhang District	105.1	103.5	80.3	99.2	104.9	105.9
坡头区	Potou District	89.8	101.9	109.6	99.8	107.7	108.1
雷州市	Leizhou City	103.3	103.9	108.6	105.6	100.2	102.8
廉江市	Lianjiang County	102.0	103.9	110.6	105.3	95.6	105.4
吴川市	Wuchuan City	110.8	103.3	101.9	99.3	98.6	104.9
遂溪县	Suixi County	108.2	104.2	101.6	90.9	97.9	102.9
徐闻县	Xuwen County	107.0	103.9	169.5	100.6	98.3	104.1
茂名市	Maoming						
茂南区	Maonan District	101.5	105.0	84.7	103.5	110.9	102.7
电白区	Dianbai District	104.3	103.8	103.6	105.3	102.0	103.4
信宜市	Xinyi City	104.6	104.5	96.2	106.1	102.4	103.6
高州市	Gaozhou City	104.8	105.2	102.9	103.5	100.7	103.5
化州市	Huazhou City	106.0	104.7	100.8	101.0	99.8	103.5
肇庆市	Zhaoqing						
端州区	Duanzhou District	105.9	151.6	90.3	101.9	99.3	104.4
鼎湖区	Dinghu District	102.0	99.9	119.5	109.0	95.4	102.1
高要区	Gaoyao District	105.9	104.6	105.3	104.8	99.6	103.7
四会市	Sihui City	101.9	103.8	104.5	99.6	100.2	104.7
广宁县	Guangning County	101.3	105.0	100.8	106.5	101.0	103.7
德庆县	Deqing County	105.1	103.5	63.4	97.3	98.8	104.5
封开县	Fengkai County	101.8	105.3	106.1	109.3	103.9	104.1
怀集县	Huaiji County	105.0	104.5	104.7	103.2	104.7	104.0
清远市	Qingyuan						
清城区	Qingcheng District	111.6	104.2	102.7	107.2	99.3	102.9
清新区	Qingxin District	105.9	104.4	92.7	102.8	107.5	104.8
英德市	Yingde City	110.2	108.5	98.8	105.0	99.9	102.5
连州市	Lianzhou City	103.0	106.2	96.8	107.2	102.9	103.7
佛冈县	Fogang County	110.6	106.4	95.0	105.6	107.0	101.4
阳山县	Yangshan County	101.0	104.2	108.9	101.3	99.8	103.7
连山县	Lianshan County	101.8	103.8	116.6	113.3	98.8	101.1
连南县	Liannan County	108.4	104.1	107.2	96.1	103.1	102.5
潮州市	Chaozhou						
湘桥区	Xiangqiao District	105.1	104.7	104.1	93.9	102.2	103.0
潮安区	Chaoan District	104.5	101.9	99.6	102.8	105.2	104.0
饶平县	Raoping County	106.0	105.9	106.8	105.8	100.6	103.6
揭阳市	Jieyang						
榕城区	Rongcheng District	103.0	102.0	91.5	98.9	103.9	102.8
揭东区	Jiedong District	104.6	104.8	93.2	99.0	101.8	103.2
普宁市	Puning City	105.5	104.7	91.4	103.0	102.7	104.2
揭西县	Jiexi County	107.8	104.8	87.1	96.6	102.8	103.9
惠来县	Huilai County	104.7	104.8	85.9	287.4	104.4	104.5
云浮市	Yunfu						
云城区	Yuncheng District	104.2	105.3	109.4	109.9	99.2	101.7
云安区	Yunan District	104.2	106.5	99.6	100.3	106.9	105.5
罗定市	Luoding City	104.2	105.2	99.4	105.8	102.5	104.7
新兴县	Xinxing County	104.1	105.4	99.9	98.7	102.2	102.7
郁南县	Yunan County	104.2	106.6	99.7	100.7	104.1	103.1

23-4 各县(市、区)人均地区生产总值及指数

Per Capita Gross Domestic Product and Growth Rates by County (County-level City and District)

县(市、区)	County (County-level City and District)	绝对数（元） Absolute Figure (yuan)		指数(上年=100) Index(Preceding year=100)	
		2022	2023	2022	2023
广州市	Guangzhou				
越秀区	Yuexiu District	351523	383228	100.5	109.1
海珠区	Haizhu District	138766	152535	102.0	110.2
荔湾区	Liwan District	108008	113257	106.4	104.6
天河区	Tianhe District	278992	293798	103.0	105.1
白云区	Baiyun District	68095	77001	98.7	108.4
黄埔区	Huangpu District	357162	357527	104.1	100.1
花都区	Huadu District	103729	104895	97.3	101.5
番禺区	Panyu District	96405	101840	98.9	104.5
南沙区	Nansha District	246201	244931	99.6	100.5
从化区	Conghua District	55727	57662	96.6	104.3
增城区	Zengcheng District	86033	92599	101.2	106.5
深圳市	Shenzhen				
福田区	Futian District	357728	375831	104.1	104.2
罗湖区	Luohu District	240076	273623	108.9	113.2
盐田区	Yantian District	379311	401049	104.7	106.1
南山区	Nanshan District	449980	472139	103.1	105.0
宝安区	Baoan District	103810	114196	102.1	107.5
龙岗区	Longgang District	122383	128951	101.8	105.0
龙华区	Longhua District	117487	120227	103.9	102.4
坪山区	Pingshan District	191995	217160	108.7	113.3
光明区	Guangming District	123819	132183	103.4	107.0
珠海市	Zhuhai				
香洲区	Xiangzhou District	192239	199625	101.0	103.5
金湾区	Jinwan District	191619	195055	102.9	101.5
斗门区	Doumen District	82004	85185	103.7	104.0
汕头市	Shantou				
金平区	Jinping District	78852	82441	101.7	104.5
龙湖区	Longhu District	96303	99559	99.8	104.0
澄海区	Chenghai District	59380	63424	103.9	105.8
濠江区	Haojiang District	68606	69253	98.2	101.8
潮阳区	Chaoyang District	32156	33281	98.7	103.8
潮南区	Chaonan District	42271	43083	101.9	102.1
南澳县	Nanao County	57720	60201	101.9	104.7
佛山市	Foshan				
禅城区	Chancheng District	170152	178524	103.1	105.6
南海区	Nanhai District	102014	107238	103.1	105.0
顺德区	Shunde District	127832	133815	101.1	105.1
高明区	Gaoming District	220765	231733	103.0	105.6
三水区	Sanshui District	174319	175012	97.7	101.2
韶关市	Shaoguan				
浈江区	Zhengjiang District	63220	65768	100.1	104.7
武江区	Wujiang District	81317	83314	99.8	103.4
曲江区	Qujiang District	66689	72290	89.5	109.6
乐昌市	Lechang City	36220	38436	101.0	106.2
南雄市	Nanxiong City	38036	38602	101.6	102.9
仁化县	Renhua County	66630	68291	109.3	103.5
始兴县	Shixing County	50793	51987	101.0	103.5
翁源县	Wengyuan County	41083	43386	101.3	105.6
新丰县	Xinfeng County	41922	43586	99.0	104.0
乳源县	Ruyuan County	62787	61205	106.2	99.9

23-4 续表 1 continued

县(市、区)	County (County-level City and District)	绝对数（元） Absolute Figure (yuan) 2022	2023	指数(上年=100) Index(Preceding year=100) 2022	2023
河源市	Heyuan				
源城区	Yuancheng District	75515	76789	101.0	102.2
东源县	Dongyuan County	49226	51482	102.1	105.1
和平县	Heping County	36738	38376	100.4	105.2
龙川县	Longchuan County	29065	30690	100.5	106.2
紫金县	Zijin County	34702	36028	100.6	104.2
连平县	Lianping County	35447	37422	101.2	104.8
梅州市	Meizhou				
梅江区	Meijiang District	66084	69717	100.3	106.0
梅县区	Meixian District	43020	46666	100.5	108.0
兴宁市	Xingning City	26125	27714	101.8	106.9
平远县	Pingyuan County	46461	50373	101.7	107.7
蕉岭县	Jiaoling County	58332	63485	100.7	108.8
大埔县	Dabu County	31105	33198	101.7	106.8
丰顺县	Fengshun County	25001	27583	100.3	109.5
五华县	Wuhua County	19504	19945	101.4	104.2
惠州市	Huizhou				
惠城区	Huicheng District	92949	99070	104.5	107.0
惠阳区	Huiyang District	120703	124158	105.1	104.9
惠东县	Huidong County	72069	74730	102.3	104.5
博罗县	Boluo County	66982	69317	103.8	104.8
龙门县	Longmen County	62858	63878	105.2	102.6
汕尾市	Shanwei				
市城区	Urban District	80262	86834	100.0	105.7
陆丰市	Lufeng City	33684	35905	96.5	103.9
海丰县	Haifeng County	56201	59915	101.0	103.8
陆河县	Luhe County	52970	58439	128.6	108.6
江门市	Jiangmen				
蓬江区	Pengjiang District	101375	105619	103.7	103.9
江海区	Jianghai District	79806	80931	101.0	103.1
新会区	Xinhui District	103344	110967	103.5	107.4
台山市	Taishan City	57037	61104	103.6	107.0
开平市	Kaiping City	61185	67253	103.3	106.0
鹤山市	Heshan City	85350	92823	102.4	105.8
恩平市	Enping City	45374	48972	103.4	106.6
阳江市	Yangjiang				
江城区	Jiangcheng District	70144	72164	100.9	104.4
阳东区	Yangdong District	73070	72579	99.9	101.0
阳春市	Yangchun City	40616	41151	98.7	103.6
阳西县	Yangxi County	58478	63049	103.4	106.0

23-4 续表 2 continued

县(市、区)	County (County-level City and District)	绝对数（元） Absolute Figure (yuan) 2022	2023	指数(上年=100) Index(Preceding year=100) 2022	2023
湛江市	Zhanjiang				
赤坎区	Chikan District	85475	88877	100.6	102.5
霞山区	Xiashan District	67375	68551	100.3	101.9
麻章区	Mazhang District	112512	114386	86.9	100.5
坡头区	Potou District	121290	116225	106.9	102.0
雷州市	Leizhou City	27895	29156	102.3	103.5
廉江市	Lianjiang County	39625	40582	102.2	104.8
吴川市	Wuchuan City	33667	34461	101.0	102.4
遂溪县	Suixi County	50911	51371	102.0	100.5
徐闻县	Xuwen County	38247	39922	109.2	103.0
茂名市	Maoming				
茂南区	Maonan District	109526	108808	95.9	102.8
电白区	Dianbai District	53511	55348	102.6	103.9
信宜市	Xinyi City	53604	54886	101.4	103.7
高州市	Gaozhou City	55379	57561	102.4	104.0
化州市	Huazhou City	49872	50740	101.1	102.9
肇庆市	Zhaoqing				
端州区	Duanzhou District	76340	78795	96.6	103.8
鼎湖区	Dinghu District	73445	75594	104.6	103.7
高要区	Gaoyao District	73032	75741	103.7	104.7
四会市	Sihui City	116562	116662	102.2	101.4
广宁县	Guangning County	45255	47670	102.1	106.5
德庆县	Deqing County	45067	45472	85.9	101.2
封开县	Fengkai County	45796	47415	103.1	105.4
怀集县	Huaiji County	37076	38296	105.3	104.6
清远市	Qingyuan				
清城区	Qingcheng District	63596	65986	101.1	104.8
清新区	Qingxin District	51001	52511	101.0	104.0
英德市	Yingde City	42927	44518	101.5	104.7
连州市	Lianzhou City	47987	49905	101.3	105.2
佛冈县	Fogang County	52661	54184	101.9	104.0
阳山县	Yangshan County	38271	39245	101.6	103.4
连山县	Lianshan County	51577	53314	103.0	104.5
连南县	Liannan County	54386	54640	104.9	101.1
潮州市	Chaozhou				
湘桥区	Xiangqiao District	55389	55821	102.7	100.5
潮安区	Chaoan District	55526	57008	101.5	103.1
饶平县	Raoping County	41931	44175	103.8	105.0
揭阳市	Jieyang				
榕城区	Rongcheng District	62205	63251	98.2	100.9
揭东区	Jiedong District	53145	52907	97.7	101.3
普宁市	Puning City	31815	33049	98.9	103.5
揭西县	Jiexi County	38606	38797	98.9	102.2
惠来县	Huilai County	27607	39637	97.7	156.2
云浮市	Yunfu				
云城区	Yuncheng District	63207	65837	102.5	104.2
云安区	Yunan District	57261	58303	102.4	102.7
罗定市	Luoding City	34180	35541	101.7	105.1
新兴县	Xinxing County	72815	73593	101.7	102.2
郁南县	Yunan County	38004	38935	102.9	103.5

注：本表中，绝对数按当年价格计算，指数按可比价格计算。
Note: In this table, the absolute figures are calculated at current prices, and indices are calculated at comparable prices.

23-5 各县(市、区)农林牧渔业总产值

Gross Output Value of Agriculture and Growth Rates by County (County-level City and District)

县(市、区)	County (County-level City and District)	绝对数（万元） Absolute Figure (10000 yuan)		指数(上年=100) Index(Preceding year=100)	
		2022	2023	2022	2023
广州市	Guangzhou				
越秀区	Yuexiu District				
海珠区	Haizhu District	20798	28282	98.8	136.8
荔湾区	Liwan District	82830	82284	103.0	101.3
天河区	Tianhe District	103492	112084	105.1	108.2
白云区	Baiyun District	682812	721425	104.4	106.9
黄埔区	Huangpu District	95125	96334	107.0	103.9
花都区	Huadu District	926465	1036716	105.9	114.9
番禺区	Panyu District	650739	640489	95.3	98.6
南沙区	Nansha District	1330324	1255184	107.0	95.8
从化区	Conghua District	615819	629625	100.2	107.3
增城区	Zengcheng District	1179282	1225509	99.8	104.6
深圳市	Shenzhen				
福田区	Futian District	44157	45230	106.1	101.9
罗湖区	Luohu District	8459	7372	111.4	74.4
盐田区	Yantian District	5146	6192	262.3	90.8
南山区	Nanshan District	25784	37026	77.1	155.4
宝安区	Baoan District	21473	33739	103.1	304.4
龙岗区	Longgang District	49675	48550	112.1	103.5
龙华区	Longhua District	10123	10534	95.4	106.3
坪山区	Pingshan District	22437	25040	106.2	112.9
光明区	Guangming District	43080	40334	96.8	97.3
珠海市	Zhuhai				
香洲区	Xiangzhou District	65021	79122	99.8	104.9
金湾区	Jinwan District	231526	251219	111.7	103.7
斗门区	Doumen District	917599	967419	105.7	108.7
汕头市	Shantou				
金平区	Jinping District	60639	63075	107.5	106.1
龙湖区	Longhu District	169427	179590	105.1	104.3
澄海区	Chenghai District	902866	970649	105.2	104.6
濠江区	Haojiang District	157950	167351	108.7	107.2
潮阳区	Chaoyang District	623568	644536	108.7	103.5
潮南区	Chaonan District	398312	404395	106.0	104.2
南澳县	Nanao County	236775	241772	100.7	102.0
佛山市	Foshan				
禅城区	Chancheng District	14241	14852	102.0	104.8
南海区	Nanhai District	1259584	1325676	109.1	105.7
顺德区	Shunde District	1340028	1397071	100.5	104.4
高明区	Gaoming District	737042	767914	115.7	107.6
三水区	Sanshui District	943145	986625	103.9	105.8
韶关市	Shaoguan				
浈江区	Zhengjiang District	151187	148163	100.4	104.4
武江区	Wujiang District	143054	140121	102.0	105.1
曲江区	Qujiang District	359711	374648	102.3	106.6
乐昌市	Lechang City	525444	553681	103.5	105.7
南雄市	Nanxiong City	631070	637181	102.6	102.8
仁化县	Renhua County	416771	438666	130.8	108.1
始兴县	Shixing County	443435	466879	108.5	107.2
翁源县	Wengyuan County	615996	668332	103.7	109.2
新丰县	Xinfeng County	289241	330091	105.6	106.5
乳源县	Ruyuan County	177942	174313	118.3	111.3

23-5 续表 1 continued

县(市、区)	County (County-level City and District)	绝对数（万元） Absolute Figure (10000 yuan) 2022	2023	指数(上年=100) Index(Preceding year=100) 2022	2023
河源市	Heyuan				
源城区	Yuancheng District	65661	58262	106.4	90.3
东源县	Dongyuan County	491799	543066	107.4	110.4
和平县	Heping County	430776	446303	102.2	106.3
龙川县	Longchuan County	509657	530504	103.6	105.3
紫金县	Zijin County	689815	720030	105.4	106.5
连平县	Lianping County	349818	386419	105.4	108.5
梅州市	Meizhou				
梅江区	Meijiang District	142427	143523	106.0	103.8
梅县区	Meixian District	947985	979456	103.4	105.5
兴宁市	Xingning City	869357	904405	103.1	106.7
平远县	Pingyuan County	254743	264090	105.1	106.1
蕉岭县	Jiaoling County	297652	300009	107.7	106.7
大埔县	Dabu County	449403	477521	104.6	104.1
丰顺县	Fengshun County	439792	445692	104.1	106.6
五华县	Wuhua County	708005	706347	104.9	106.4
惠州市	Huizhou				
惠城区	Huicheng District	675434	696894	108.6	106.0
惠阳区	Huiyang District	384621	408888	99.6	107.5
惠东县	Huidong County	1257747	1344717	107.5	106.6
博罗县	Boluo County	1421942	1493345	107.6	107.2
龙门县	Longmen County	602754	638940	113.1	106.2
汕尾市	Shanwei				
市城区	Urban District	656257	714050	108.9	105.3
陆丰市	Lufeng City	1377875	1420724	105.0	104.9
海丰县	Haifeng County	764918	784320	105.0	105.3
陆河县	Luhe County	293380	296113	108.0	103.0
江门市	Jiangmen				
蓬江区	Pengjiang District	161354	174805	99.8	108.4
江海区	Jianghai District	128165	137266	100.3	106.0
新会区	Xinhui District	1128277	1223354	106.5	109.1
台山市	Taishan City	2252867	2462227	103.2	106.5
开平市	Kaiping City	1092619	1114120	107.3	106.9
鹤山市	Heshan City	635771	642206	101.0	106.1
恩平市	Enping City	552904	572308	103.1	107.3
阳江市	Yangjiang				
江城区	Jiangcheng District	930471	960473	100.4	102.9
阳东区	Yangdong District	1000475	1018022	101.1	106.1
阳春市	Yangchun City	1188256	1182716	109.4	106.1
阳西县	Yangxi County	1084063	1097920	101.5	101.4

23−5 续表 2 continued

县(市、区)	County (County-level City and District)	绝对数（万元） Absolute Figure (10000 yuan)		指数(上年=100) Index(Preceding year=100)	
		2022	2023	2022	2023
湛江市	Zhanjiang				
赤坎区	Chikan District	23216	17003	109.6	75.8
霞山区	Xiashan District	46361	54475	93.7	108.6
麻章区	Mazhang District	868130	867348	102.3	102.5
坡头区	Potou District	395580	419203	101.4	101.6
雷州市	Leizhou City	2425851	2537196	103.8	102.7
廉江市	Lianjiang County	2287562	2298293	102.8	103.3
吴川市	Wuchuan City	706942	704494	104.2	103.0
遂溪县	Suixi County	2480945	2602987	105.3	104.0
徐闻县	Xuwen County	1806211	1847102	106.0	103.8
茂名市	Maoming				
茂南区	Maonan District	602374	610595	101.9	105.4
电白区	Dianbai District	2766526	2830789	104.4	103.8
信宜市	Xinyi City	2459654	2513441	105.2	103.9
高州市	Gaozhou City	3020354	3065046	104.8	105.4
化州市	Huazhou City	2451331	2510770	106.0	104.7
肇庆市	Zhaoqing				
端州区	Duanzhou District	4019	4078	105.9	103.3
鼎湖区	Dinghu District	243253	250446	103.3	103.0
高要区	Gaoyao District	1806470	1896691	103.6	104.9
四会市	Sihui City	1182059	1207235	103.5	106.3
广宁县	Guangning County	867470	890059	103.6	105.3
德庆县	Deqing County	702527	713211	103.0	101.8
封开县	Fengkai County	997761	1015700	101.6	105.5
怀集县	Huaiji County	1790619	1827975	104.6	104.6
清远市	Qingyuan				
清城区	Qingcheng District	566028	588715	106.7	105.1
清新区	Qingxin District	973175	1015922	101.8	105.1
英德市	Yingde City	1577607	1630197	111.7	108.8
连州市	Lianzhou City	841342	856574	106.7	106.2
佛冈县	Fogang County	401171	431626	109.2	106.9
阳山县	Yangshan County	791633	805783	103.4	104.0
连山县	Lianshan County	175517	174148	102.7	103.9
连南县	Liannan County	197977	204413	103.7	104.0
潮州市	Chaozhou				
湘桥区	Xiangqiao District	155873	164741	111.7	104.9
潮安区	Chaoan District	484629	500315	103.4	102.4
饶平县	Raoping County	1459396	1558323	105.9	106.2
揭阳市	Jieyang				
榕城区	Rongcheng District	214398	213459	99.8	101.9
揭东区	Jiedong District	706573	728794	102.9	105.2
普宁市	Puning City	709331	726873	106.1	104.8
揭西县	Jiexi County	891755	925105	107.2	105.3
惠来县	Huilai County	1021712	1048288	105.0	105.3
云浮市	Yunfu				
云城区	Yuncheng District	330863	334216	100.0	107.7
云安区	Yunan District	288350	293549	104.1	104.0
罗定市	Luoding City	1045061	1043712	104.9	105.5
新兴县	Xinxing County	1385381	1429493	105.4	106.3
郁南县	Yunan County	532232	544664	103.9	107.9

注：本表中，绝对数按当年价格计算，指数按可比价格计算。
Note: In this table, the absolute figures are calculated at current prices, and indices are calculated at comparable prices.

23-6 各县(市、区)粮食产量

Output of Grain by County (County-level City and District)

单位：吨 (ton)

县(市、区)	County (County-level City and District)	粮食 Grain 2022	粮食 Grain 2023	#稻谷 Rice 2022	#稻谷 Rice 2023
广州市	Guangzhou				
越秀区	Yuexiu District				
海珠区	Haizhu District				
荔湾区	Liwan District				
天河区	Tianhe District				
白云区	Baiyun District	3141	3049	2090	2060
黄埔区	Huangpu District	2706	2707	1772	1879
花都区	Huadu District	11206	11156	3668	3855
番禺区	Panyu District	1304	1304	553	532
南沙区	Nansha District	7221	7224	5021	4958
从化区	Conghua District	73218	73224	64900	64774
增城区	Zengcheng District	55044	53256	47874	46189
深圳市	Shenzhen				
福田区	Futian District				
罗湖区	Luohu District				
盐田区	Yantian District				
南山区	Nanshan District				
宝安区	Baoan District				
龙岗区	Longgang District	212	177	58	48
龙华区	Longhua District				
坪山区	Pingshan District				
光明区	Guangming District	940	242	110	103
珠海市	Zhuhai				
香洲区	Xiangzhou District	166	154	47	59
金湾区	Jinwan District	2810	2728	1629	1860
斗门区	Doumen District	26972	26854	24726	24544
汕头市	Shantou				
金平区	Jinping District	10623	10618	10403	10347
龙湖区	Longhu District	20243	20229	15688	15717
澄海区	Chenghai District	91947	92321	72508	72323
濠江区	Haojiang District	15219	15201	8633	8587
潮阳区	Chaoyang District	163382	163356	107894	107411
潮南区	Chaonan District	156976	157001	106765	106588
南澳县	Nanao County	3855	3854	1758	1758
佛山市	Foshan				
禅城区	Chancheng District				
南海区	Nanhai District	5017	6209	3658	4398
顺德区	Shunde District	213	531		
高明区	Gaoming District	32238	30198	27147	24593
三水区	Sanshui District	12040	13839	8278	9777
韶关市	Shaoguan				
浈江区	Zhengjiang District	19913	19596	18413	17143
武江区	Wujiang District	24724	24589	22948	22344
曲江区	Qujiang District	76042	75945	69824	69293
乐昌市	Lechang City	90494	90152	72358	69987
南雄市	Nanxiong City	209679	207697	191783	190536
仁化县	Renhua County	69308	69361	58065	60998
始兴县	Shixing County	74831	74088	68971	66523
翁源县	Wengyuan County	95324	95351	88119	88214
新丰县	Xinfeng County	54690	54482	49456	49421
乳源县	Ruyuan County	44022	43917	36795	35970

23-6 续表 1 continued

单位：吨 (ton)

县(市、区)	County (County-level City and District)	粮食 Grain 2022	粮食 Grain 2023	#稻谷 Rice 2022	#稻谷 Rice 2023
河源市	Heyuan				
源城区	Yuancheng District	11370	11369	10198	9168
东源县	Dongyuan County	154443	154277	147276	147047
和平县	Heping County	118869	118856	113215	113629
龙川县	Longchuan County	239223	239210	227059	226099
紫金县	Zijin County	200643	200392	190966	191614
连平县	Lianping County	90895	90483	86077	84156
梅州市	Meizhou				
梅江区	Meijiang District	23034	21420	17914	16256
梅县区	Meixian District	161811	149103	150524	137265
兴宁市	Xingning City	293531	304506	282978	292028
平远县	Pingyuan County	80819	87321	70097	74166
蕉岭县	Jiaoling County	68008	68043	62643	62585
大埔县	Dabu County	45783	49460	40336	43137
丰顺县	Fengshun County	119304	119042	101877	101781
五华县	Wuhua County	345414	339516	330814	323508
惠州市	Huizhou				
惠城区	Huicheng District	81414	94847	65021	67983
惠阳区	Huiyang District	43003	44496	24476	21613
惠东县	Huidong County	205269	203946	149812	148621
博罗县	Boluo County	161227	160829	127216	125815
龙门县	Longmen County	112814	112521	106665	105895
汕尾市	Shanwei				
市城区	Urban District	25510	25200	22136	21794
陆丰市	Lufeng City	182120	182039	154707	150236
海丰县	Haifeng County	179950	170701	156632	149000
陆河县	Luhe County	57000	57335	50764	50983
江门市	Jiangmen				
蓬江区	Pengjiang District	2331	2347	1258	1264
江海区	Jianghai District	639	659	586	603
新会区	Xinhui District	136350	129714	117462	107480
台山市	Taishan City	404140	404171	384048	383716
开平市	Kaiping City	234877	234937	219289	219082
鹤山市	Heshan City	61280	61715	54191	54862
恩平市	Enping City	150706	155089	144757	143489
阳江市	Yangjiang				
江城区	Jiangcheng District	93002	93196	88755	88780
阳东区	Yangdong District	136966	136608	123753	123269
阳春市	Yangchun City	275747	275835	250912	249363
阳西县	Yangxi County	129595	129709	119710	119511

23-6 续表 2 continued

单位：吨 (ton)

县(市、区)	County (County-level City and District)	粮食 Grain 2022	粮食 Grain 2023	#稻谷 Rice 2022	#稻谷 Rice 2023
湛江市	Zhanjiang				
赤坎区	Chikan District	1913	1901	1661	1446
霞山区	Xiashan District	4626	4209	3673	3195
麻章区	Mazhang District	86511	84605	75239	73570
坡头区	Potou District	65711	66023	56364	56361
雷州市	Leizhou City	391372	384920	342570	334121
廉江市	Lianjiang County	435450	425950	362123	348803
吴川市	Wuchuan City	165619	161917	151602	146161
遂溪县	Suixi County	259217	256368	199753	190663
徐闻县	Xuwen County	136008	133070	77391	74491
茂名市	Maoming				
茂南区	Maonan District	136127	136184	119507	119670
电白区	Dianbai District	299186	299343	266266	267708
信宜市	Xinyi City	344800	344866	259893	259780
高州市	Gaozhou City	405147	405185	386350	384958
化州市	Huazhou City	346463	346475	305712	303244
肇庆市	Zhaoqing				
端州区	Duanzhou District				
鼎湖区	Dinghu District	35713	31803	29858	26032
高要区	Gaoyao District	240599	240119	217754	216952
四会市	Sihui City	122827	120566	92222	89788
广宁县	Guangning County	181273	180914	154143	153701
德庆县	Deqing County	139544	139187	128976	128456
封开县	Fengkai County	218907	218590	195728	195017
怀集县	Huaiji County	294747	294138	269154	268143
清远市	Qingyuan				
清城区	Qingcheng District	69232	69262	65985	65306
清新区	Qingxin District	131120	131148	121984	121815
英德市	Yingde City	192305	192445	169267	169198
连州市	Lianzhou City	109746	109748	94902	94597
佛冈县	Fogang County	57770	57843	55324	55236
阳山县	Yangshan County	101495	101611	69463	69214
连山县	Lianshan County	40745	40748	37889	37769
连南县	Liannan County	33878	33958	21714	21468
潮州市	Chaozhou				
湘桥区	Xiangqiao District	25457	25322	20427	20266
潮安区	Chaoan District	99976	99348	77765	76151
饶平县	Raoping County	152980	151910	128082	126251
揭阳市	Jieyang				
榕城区	Rongcheng District	71942	70263	57011	55513
揭东区	Jiedong District	182283	180477	110878	108471
普宁市	Puning City	197204	196766	133502	133094
揭西县	Jiexi County	177459	174715	120490	117456
惠来县	Huilai County	185287	184825	104155	104111
云浮市	Yunfu				
云城区	Yuncheng District	50776	50133	45990	44977
云安区	Yunan District	70765	70700	55950	55503
罗定市	Luoding City	247945	247934	231528	230825
新兴县	Xinxing County	139900	140013	133176	132947
郁南县	Yunan County	133100	133140	120879	121239

23-7 各县(市、区)糖蔗、园林水果和蔬菜产量

Output of Sugarcane,Fruits and Vegetable by County (County-level City and District)

单位：吨 (ton)

县(市、区)	County (County-level City and District)	糖蔗 Sugarcane 2022	糖蔗 Sugarcane 2023	园林水果 Fruits 2022	园林水果 Fruits 2023	蔬菜 Vegetable 2022	蔬菜 Vegetable 2023
广州市	Guangzhou						
越秀区	Yuexiu District						
海珠区	Haizhu District			3210	5503	13220	7826
荔湾区	Liwan District					2913	2942
天河区	Tianhe District			228	185	6424	6472
白云区	Baiyun District			10987	12637	846669	883959
黄埔区	Huangpu District			17519	20424	55332	54142
花都区	Huadu District			26293	31023	541002	546513
番禺区	Panyu District			7987	8827	181504	173944
南沙区	Nansha District			261774	258618	718948	664917
从化区	Conghua District			137530	143139	321094	322444
增城区	Zengcheng District			353030	364201	1428580	1478121
深圳市	Shenzhen						
福田区	Futian District						
罗湖区	Luohu District			12	157	94	116
盐田区	Yantian District			1	1	2	2
南山区	Nanshan District			4368	6262	133	106
宝安区	Baoan District			1234	1264	25095	25970
龙岗区	Longgang District	361	318	512	307	22830	22485
龙华区	Longhua District			4		8852	8855
坪山区	Pingshan District			429	157	39646	41385
光明区	Guangming District		17	232	3649	40845	39331
珠海市	Zhuhai						
香洲区	Xiangzhou District			3397	2336	4580	3340
金湾区	Jinwan District			77156	63425	46359	45789
斗门区	Doumen District			19523	19141	89085	88401
汕头市	Shantou						
金平区	Jinping District			1084	1175	46738	46954
龙湖区	Longhu District			330	1236	215102	216120
澄海区	Chenghai District			112690	125628	739918	744691
濠江区	Haojiang District			905	895	62310	62370
潮阳区	Chaoyang District			151686	161182	345478	343887
潮南区	Chaonan District			40675	45483	384427	393357
南澳县	Nanao County			5228	5350	12360	12207
佛山市	Foshan						
禅城区	Chancheng District					3344	3432
南海区	Nanhai District			3705	4099	308797	313738
顺德区	Shunde District			6698	6101	76689	72911
高明区	Gaoming District			11856	14337	180911	189799
三水区	Sanshui District			19019	20131	281886	286949
韶关市	Shaoguan						
浈江区	Zhengjiang District			20353	20549	67858	72441
武江区	Wujiang District			12918	13171	90197	91939
曲江区	Qujiang District		7424	39690	37153	110415	112154
乐昌市	Lechang City	20		192216	198212	277689	285504
南雄市	Nanxiong City			63951	69869	253031	256857
仁化县	Renhua County			137006	144251	134714	149614
始兴县	Shixing County	373	338	132068	151252	184525	189032
翁源县	Wengyuan County	24744	25754	57561	60628	131093	136534
新丰县	Xinfeng County	344	336	35578	35174	187138	187587
乳源县	Ruyuan County			23021	22553	62902	65523

23-7 续表 1 continued

单位：吨 (ton)

县(市、区)	County (County-level City and District)	糖蔗 Sugarcane 2022	糖蔗 Sugarcane 2023	园林水果 Fruits 2022	园林水果 Fruits 2023	蔬菜 Vegetable 2022	蔬菜 Vegetable 2023
河源市	Heyuan						
源城区	Yuancheng District			5118	5731	45545	46705
东源县	Dongyuan County	25546	25376	42132	45968	127826	134255
和平县	Heping County			49037	46155	143702	145623
龙川县	Longchuan County			85648	86174	160809	165189
紫金县	Zijin County			160315	161138	235567	237956
连平县	Lianping County			130033	146116	117653	120951
梅州市	Meizhou						
梅江区	Meijiang District			41915	44684	122149	124042
梅县区	Meixian District			836594	886511	519971	539400
兴宁市	Xingning City			178861	203212	874518	905133
平远县	Pingyuan County			94121	87636	74697	78744
蕉岭县	Jiaoling County	2265	717	61334	65024	144163	152692
大埔县	Dabu County			228195	250463	214423	219308
丰顺县	Fengshun County			68339	70724	232890	236692
五华县	Wuhua County			99622	107806	409452	422929
惠州市	Huizhou						
惠城区	Huicheng District	2735	1031	52269	62294	608786	616365
惠阳区	Huiyang District			47869	61552	550982	558850
惠东县	Huidong County			147386	178692	921842	935135
博罗县	Boluo County	45656	45875	259902	284834	1100032	1103020
龙门县	Longmen County	5111	5312	516711	529138	360401	377364
汕尾市	Shanwei						
市城区	Urban District			14519	14637	79644	79638
陆丰市	Lufeng City			148886	162353	749809	781765
海丰县	Haifeng County	5023	5083	77106	81997	553540	583560
陆河县	Luhe County			126776	132533	111865	114606
江门市	Jiangmen						
蓬江区	Pengjiang District		30	3160	3426	80766	80523
江海区	Jianghai District			7114	7431	54274	55173
新会区	Xinhui District	2587	2704	179514	210508	215338	216103
台山市	Taishan City	153		77611	97246	642101	661224
开平市	Kaiping City			57590	59784	441062	466341
鹤山市	Heshan City			22790	26129	324808	320875
恩平市	Enping City	73198	66294	55208	58130	216106	220887
阳江市	Yangjiang						
江城区	Jiangcheng District			17344	29032	99002	99800
阳东区	Yangdong District	3967	3149	70210	73893	222841	228096
阳春市	Yangchun City	8499	8210	284062	299575	447914	468316
阳西县	Yangxi County			47800	49880	213916	216091

23-7 续表 2 continued

单位：吨 (ton)

县(市、区)	County (County-level City and District)	糖蔗 Sugarcane 2022	糖蔗 Sugarcane 2023	园林水果 Fruits 2022	园林水果 Fruits 2023	蔬菜 Vegetable 2022	蔬菜 Vegetable 2023
湛江市	Zhanjiang						
赤坎区	Chikan District			314	278	18497	17028
霞山区	Xiashan District		3	488	558	12269	11661
麻章区	Mazhang District	310607	294995	89034	110288	134612	125452
坡头区	Potou District	16411	15449	20354	22636	107970	112319
雷州市	Leizhou City	4249447	4299693	864445	890304	1040896	1094744
廉江市	Lianjiang County	306156	282769	522964	556851	1119521	1172951
吴川市	Wuchuan City	81442	84184	77072	70306	189783	196342
遂溪县	Suixi County	4228545	4071452	484951	515315	1033314	1075853
徐闻县	Xuwen County	938816	913820	1229940	1242751	882476	882685
茂名市	Maoming						
茂南区	Maonan District	23817	23600	47927	51571	398074	401999
电白区	Dianbai District	5003	5544	442851	444494	1050524	1082329
信宜市	Xinyi City			1255110	1308647	631344	650910
高州市	Gaozhou City	10146	6965	1981291	2094221	1004753	1025419
化州市	Huazhou City	491721	481279	848167	867546	786809	804277
肇庆市	Zhaoqing						
端州区	Duanzhou District			764	791	5102	5212
鼎湖区	Dinghu District			25929	25812	123795	124290
高要区	Gaoyao District			224586	244062	1126697	1163239
四会市	Sihui City			186363	200295	335055	348686
广宁县	Guangning County			181213	185654	284994	304781
德庆县	Deqing County			545199	551145	302325	305737
封开县	Fengkai County	11328	10223	477508	491011	371197	393122
怀集县	Huaiji County	193	174	535393	546531	669564	694841
清远市	Qingyuan						
清城区	Qingcheng District	3345		41153	39396	288365	292782
清新区	Qingxin District			287403	275244	708760	731310
英德市	Yingde City	199815	185792	45806	47367	823625	847875
连州市	Lianzhou City	13		161291	181381	866682	904213
佛冈县	Fogang County			154259	180637	264396	274754
阳山县	Yangshan County	158	45	99211	114352	783424	809589
连山县	Lianshan County			42109	42552	155929	162578
连南县	Liannan County			26606	27084	156592	161960
潮州市	Chaozhou						
湘桥区	Xiangqiao District			85447	86166	72713	73420
潮安区	Chaoan District			47245	41398	177084	170928
饶平县	Raoping County			159529	161575	320160	332397
揭阳市	Jieyang						
榕城区	Rongcheng District			42460	44547	214991	219044
揭东区	Jiedong District			44449	49340	690756	710833
普宁市	Puning City			290778	316931	503286	523468
揭西县	Jiexi County			206355	231349	406562	418709
惠来县	Huilai County			150792	162482	478297	488875
云浮市	Yunfu						
云城区	Yuncheng District			42718	43331	36919	37765
云安区	Yunan District			65120	63456	74668	76965
罗定市	Luoding City			87244	103269	121689	124122
新兴县	Xinxing County			134579	140537	390177	400512
郁南县	Yunan County			198723	211139	39053	40438

23-8 各县(市、区)猪肉产量、禽肉产量
Output of Pork and Output of Meat of Poultry by County (County-level City and District)

单位：万吨 (10000 tons)

县(市、区)	County (County-level City and District)	猪肉产量 Output of Pork		禽肉产量 Output of Meat of Poultry	
		2022	2023	2022	2023
广州市	Guangzhou				
越秀区	Yuexiu District				
海珠区	Haizhu District				
荔湾区	Liwan District				
天河区	Tianhe District				
白云区	Baiyun District	0.39	0.39	0.83	0.09
黄埔区	Huangpu District				
花都区	Huadu District	1.23	0.90	0.60	0.57
番禺区	Panyu District			0.42	0.36
南沙区	Nansha District	0.83	0.96	0.31	0.33
从化区	Conghua District	1.85	2.08	0.79	0.67
增城区	Zengcheng District	0.76	1.00	1.45	0.95
深圳市	Shenzhen				
福田区	Futian District				
罗湖区	Luohu District				
盐田区	Yantian District				
南山区	Nanshan District				
宝安区	Baoan District				
龙岗区	Longgang District				
龙华区	Longhua District				
坪山区	Pingshan District				
光明区	Guangming District			0.02	
珠海市	Zhuhai				
香洲区	Xiangzhou District				
金湾区	Jinwan District			0.09	0.07
斗门区	Doumen District	0.81	0.88	0.12	0.13
汕头市	Shantou				
金平区	Jinping District				
龙湖区	Longhu District	0.02	0.01	0.79	0.80
澄海区	Chenghai District	1.26	1.32	3.55	3.99
濠江区	Haojiang District	0.19	0.18	0.07	0.07
潮阳区	Chaoyang District	1.32	1.40	0.10	0.06
潮南区	Chaonan District	1.69	1.85	0.03	0.01
南澳县	Nanao County	0.07	0.04	0.03	0.02
佛山市	Foshan				
禅城区	Chancheng District				
南海区	Nanhai District	1.26	1.13	0.32	0.23
顺德区	Shunde District	0.83	0.86	0.05	
高明区	Gaoming District	2.12	2.17	2.70	2.64
三水区	Sanshui District	3.71	3.81	6.22	6.56
韶关市	Shaoguan				
浈江区	Zhengjiang District	1.14	1.25	0.07	0.08
武江区	Wujiang District	1.32	1.37	0.14	0.11
曲江区	Qujiang District	3.33	3.23	0.78	0.63
乐昌市	Lechang City	3.42	3.34	0.29	0.33
南雄市	Nanxiong City	3.48	3.16	1.40	1.49
仁化县	Renhua County	1.74	2.33	0.51	0.37
始兴县	Shixing County	1.41	1.69	0.40	0.41
翁源县	Wengyuan County	4.31	5.17	3.09	3.89
新丰县	Xinfeng County	1.33	1.47	1.44	1.57
乳源县	Ruyuan County	1.36	1.53	0.11	0.09

23-8 续表 1 continued

单位：万吨 (10000 tons)

县(市、区)	County (County-level City and District)	猪肉产量 Output of Pork 2022	2023	禽肉产量 Output of Meat of Poultry 2022	2023
河源市	Heyuan				
源城区	Yuancheng District		0.01	0.73	0.51
东源县	Dongyuan County	2.57	3.18	1.65	1.67
和平县	Heping County	1.85	1.97	1.62	1.83
龙川县	Longchuan County	2.61	2.79	1.04	1.13
紫金县	Zijin County	2.05	2.16	1.85	2.01
连平县	Lianping County	1.68	1.71	0.75	1.17
梅州市	Meizhou				
梅江区	Meijiang District	0.34	0.41	0.13	0.13
梅县区	Meixian District	2.49	2.74	1.21	1.30
兴宁市	Xingning City	3.73	4.06	2.25	2.09
平远县	Pingyuan County	1.03	1.13	0.32	0.35
蕉岭县	Jiaoling County	1.32	1.42	0.60	0.72
大埔县	Dabu County	1.49	1.63	0.82	0.85
丰顺县	Fengshun County	1.31	1.42	3.35	3.58
五华县	Wuhua County	4.19	4.51	1.75	1.81
惠州市	Huizhou				
惠城区	Huicheng District	1.67	1.89	0.70	0.79
惠阳区	Huiyang District	0.11	0.13	0.20	0.22
惠东县	Huidong County	4.37	4.63	1.40	1.49
博罗县	Boluo County	3.98	4.02	4.75	5.40
龙门县	Longmen County	1.22	1.18	0.88	1.04
汕尾市	Shanwei				
市城区	Urban District	0.44	0.54	0.25	0.24
陆丰市	Lufeng City	3.98	4.04	1.52	1.63
海丰县	Haifeng County	1.99	2.13	0.93	0.95
陆河县	Luhe County	1.05	1.11	0.43	0.47
江门市	Jiangmen				
蓬江区	Pengjiang District			0.10	0.04
江海区	Jianghai District			0.01	…
新会区	Xinhui District	2.14	2.19	2.73	2.90
台山市	Taishan City	4.19	4.37	2.92	5.63
开平市	Kaiping City	4.05	4.61	7.35	7.52
鹤山市	Heshan City	2.81	2.84	1.76	1.84
恩平市	Enping City	4.40	4.81	1.73	1.65
阳江市	Yangjiang				
江城区	Jiangcheng District	1.63	1.83	0.38	0.45
阳东区	Yangdong District	4.83	5.63	1.31	1.34
阳春市	Yangchun City	11.89	12.61	1.72	1.96
阳西县	Yangxi County	2.96	3.08	1.38	1.75

23-8 续表 2 continued

单位：万吨 (10000 tons)

县(市、区)	County (County-level City and District)	猪肉产量 Output of Pork 2022	猪肉产量 Output of Pork 2023	禽肉产量 Output of Meat of Poultry 2022	禽肉产量 Output of Meat of Poultry 2023
湛江市	Zhanjiang				
赤坎区	Chikan District			0.01	0.02
霞山区	Xiashan District			0.03	0.04
麻章区	Mazhang District	1.61	1.50	0.69	0.62
坡头区	Potou District	1.89	1.53	0.44	0.47
雷州市	Leizhou City	4.59	5.69	1.55	1.60
廉江市	Lianjiang County	11.12	11.28	2.91	3.03
吴川市	Wuchuan City	2.71	3.03	2.53	2.47
遂溪县	Suixi County	8.13	8.62	5.12	5.25
徐闻县	Xuwen County	2.10	3.16	0.59	0.56
茂名市	Maoming				
茂南区	Maonan District	4.96	5.70	4.10	3.03
电白区	Dianbai District	10.14	10.41	4.58	4.23
信宜市	Xinyi City	7.41	7.59	11.39	11.28
高州市	Gaozhou City	11.11	11.48	7.18	6.67
化州市	Huazhou City	13.60	14.03	3.13	3.00
肇庆市	Zhaoqing				
端州区	Duanzhou District				
鼎湖区	Dinghu District		0.02	0.35	0.36
高要区	Gaoyao District	6.03	6.10	6.18	6.95
四会市	Sihui City	3.79	3.77	5.41	5.96
广宁县	Guangning County	4.25	4.39	1.59	1.25
德庆县	Deqing County	0.59	0.61	0.94	0.76
封开县	Fengkai County	2.73	2.84	0.83	0.85
怀集县	Huaiji County	7.72	8.05	2.39	1.76
清远市	Qingyuan				
清城区	Qingcheng District	1.64	1.69	4.83	4.65
清新区	Qingxin District	2.87	3.20	4.32	3.93
英德市	Yingde City	8.99	10.31	3.93	4.87
连州市	Lianzhou City	3.44	3.48	0.88	0.90
佛冈县	Fogang County	1.38	1.55	0.43	0.61
阳山县	Yangshan County	4.02	4.04	2.19	2.22
连山县	Lianshan County	0.68	0.70	0.25	0.23
连南县	Liannan County	0.26	0.28	0.40	0.36
潮州市	Chaozhou				
湘桥区	Xiangqiao District	0.37	0.41	0.34	0.37
潮安区	Chaoan District	0.65	0.77	0.40	0.41
饶平县	Raoping County	2.38	2.34	2.29	2.28
揭阳市	Jieyang				
榕城区	Rongcheng District	0.37	0.36	0.05	0.05
揭东区	Jiedong District	1.65	1.87	0.84	0.83
普宁市	Puning City	2.21	2.35	0.41	0.41
揭西县	Jiexi County	3.20	3.13	1.85	1.83
惠来县	Huilai County	1.97	2.38	1.35	1.52
云浮市	Yunfu				
云城区	Yuncheng District	1.42	1.40	1.86	2.14
云安区	Yunan District	1.18	1.23	0.76	0.77
罗定市	Luoding City	3.32	3.49	2.31	2.61
新兴县	Xinxing County	4.82	5.75	16.03	15.93
郁南县	Yunan County	2.13	2.49	3.09	3.26

23-9 各县(市、区)规模以上工业企业单位数、总产值及利润总额

Number of Industrial Enterprises and Gross Output Value of Industry Enterprises and Total Profits above Designated Size by County (County-level City and District)

县(市、区)	County (County-level City and District)	单位数（个） Number of Enterprises (unit)		总产值(万元) Gross Output Value(10000 yuan)		利润总额（万元） Total Profit(10000 yuan)	
		2022	2023	2022	2023	2022	2023
广州市	Guangzhou						
越秀区	Yuexiu District	14	15	749349	981962	-70444	6781
海珠区	Haizhu District	78	76	8092610	8908110	166596	247403
荔湾区	Liwan District	88	84	3656861	3740420	452943	391207
天河区	Tianhe District	136	134	10576627	11384116	250445	519351
白云区	Baiyun District	1099	1109	11349596	12357028	473730	580139
黄埔区	Huangpu District	1263	1321	89985962	88347348	6992730	5234133
花都区	Huadu District	1154	1154	25450966	23248381	1128040	858342
番禺区	Panyu District	1196	1145	26712636	29628729	1076620	1089064
南沙区	Nansha District	717	704	40152040	40823955	3928110	3699458
从化区	Conghua District	300	295	5025300	5445138	289650	309335
增城区	Zengcheng District	833	836	17533878	18943911	593837	981427
深圳市	Shenzhen						
福田区	Futian District	213	203	18899969	20378576	1037678	1092423
罗湖区	Luohu District	140	138	12618400	14275478	648091	906603
盐田区	Yantian District	89	92	10768623	11807785	272780	366170
南山区	Nanshan District	1012	1074	75788627	78898159	9183491	8638089
宝安区	Baoan District	5113	5361	97234883	98792503	5745153	5647976
龙岗区	Longgang District	2382	2502	100785784	108674183	8697334	13063918
龙华区	Longhua District	2020	1894	64324368	62302115	3067248	3248305
坪山区	Pingshan District	794	835	34666107	47721861	1556854	1569687
光明区	Guangming District	1907	1961	40895195	40819859	1642771	1875487
珠海市	Zhuhai						
香洲区	Xiangzhou District	760	725	22762985	24256883	3908546	3958672
金湾区	Jinwan District	697	707	26611903	26722730	1896642	2108365
斗门区	Doumen District	335	346	9786012	10440420	160096	265692
汕头市	Shantou						
金平区	Jinping District	321	310	4816561	4609534	505486	176131
龙湖区	Longhu District	305	294	4954961	4286508	290937	206868
澄海区	Chenghai District	375	400	3425904	3813543	49875	89639
濠江区	Haojiang District	131	134	2776857	2978561	52468	95908
潮阳区	Chaoyang District	511	513	7684355	6510667	595794	545862
潮南区	Chaonan District	532	568	10324994	7924964	489484	324485
南澳县	Nanao County	6	6	58120	64959	30268	17219
佛山市	Foshan						
禅城区	Chancheng District	627	623	21902425	24070919	950210	1069106
南海区	Nanhai District	4344	4307	74072719	75688583	4787720	3869016
顺德区	Shunde District	3082	3003	100583612	95027941	7944273	7570112
高明区	Gaoming District	662	711	40749915	42865052	4192833	4255263
三水区	Sanshui District	1136	1240	42345485	43824226	2180059	2277539
韶关市	Shaoguan						
浈江区	Zhengjiang District	57	55	1828285	1816767	22857	50086
武江区	Wujiang District	76	72	1707374	1732122	76004	119324
曲江区	Qujiang District	98	104	5772211	6279110	-213338	57759
乐昌市	Lechang City	78	88	619308	707507	-42949	3939
南雄市	Nanxiong City	80	83	769904	807126	-8381	35348
仁化县	Renhua County	37	41	1132471	1251615	155697	87352
始兴县	Shixing County	45	43	811936	804181	-3162	15561
翁源县	Wengyuan County	65	66	952079	1018359	18043	14855
新丰县	Xinfeng County	43	42	543468	542951	-5741	-10478
乳源县	Ruyuan County	62	66	2040999	1793183	210388	98753

23-9 续表 1 continued

县(市、区)	County (County-level City and District)	单位数（个）Number of Enterprises (unit) 2022	2023	总产值(万元) Gross Output Value(10000 yuan) 2022	2023	利润总额（万元）Total Profit(10000 yuan) 2022	2023
河源市	Heyuan						
源城区	Yuancheng District	240	248	8552645	8638683	127697	310164
东源县	Dongyuan County	119	126	1667173	2321573	33522	4463
和平县	Heping County	41	45	650984	674373	94117	56974
龙川县	Longchuan County	70	69	1231206	1440568	50106	48764
紫金县	Zijin County	107	111	1637186	1844845	149893	142211
连平县	Lianping County	50	50	859044	908918	70966	42214
梅州市	Meizhou						
梅江区	Meijiang District	74	77	2796790	3012119	145818	126986
梅县区	Meixian District	110	112	1932497	2187919	68718	74262
兴宁市	Xingning City	88	94	807489	913915	9037	18839
平远县	Pingyuan County	54	52	457285	574527	35755	8490
蕉岭县	Jiaoling County	52	56	795245	753962	-5467	29515
大埔县	Dabu County	44	42	436729	462897	-25361	16237
丰顺县	Fengshun County	71	70	947695	1099643	23323	20355
五华县	Wuhua County	54	54	413046	494985	20877	36433
惠州市	Huizhou						
惠城区	Huicheng District	1420	1457	38618029	39815968	1410981	1241618
惠阳区	Huiyang District	1374	1305	52713820	51069872	858055	1212587
惠东县	Huidong County	383	419	3877087	4362431	261307	337029
博罗县	Boluo County	1104	1191	14573516	15448175	471951	495362
龙门县	Longmen County	84	94	1212106	1172095	41686	86775
汕尾市	Shanwei						
市城区	Urban District	72	78	4902706	4479688	-13113	73912
陆丰市	Lufeng City	97	97	2980821	2392969	102517	159118
海丰县	Haifeng County	119	120	3567640	2544693	3999	46413
陆河县	Luhe County	28	30	1059217	1446590	39686	101342
江门市	Jiangmen						
蓬江区	Pengjiang District	612	640	11999141	12427692	365974	517479
江海区	Jianghai District	450	477	6604854	6688318	337804	243886
新会区	Xinhui District	707	786	14406655	15030578	464737	491915
台山市	Taishan City	311	320	7244873	7505977	84054	256808
开平市	Kaiping City	423	453	5436623	5612079	250934	219296
鹤山市	Heshan City	589	673	8524771	9181860	406222	450030
恩平市	Enping City	172	187	2100117	2315724	26699	50971
阳江市	Yangjiang						
江城区	Jiangcheng District	196	205	14772611	15106927	274894	215805
阳东区	Yangdong District	186	172	3453682	3458749	820043	804128
阳春市	Yangchun City	73	75	2914240	2785979	216486	174282
阳西县	Yangxi County	51	57	2066441	2400790	159155	334774

23−9 续表 2 continued

县(市、区)	County (County-level City and District)	单位数（个） Number of Enterprises (unit)		总产值(万元) Gross Output Value(10000 yuan)		利润总额（万元） Total Profit(10000 yuan)	
		2022	2023	2022	2023	2022	2023
湛江市	Zhanjiang						
赤坎区	Chikan District	31	30	1149511	1230324	-56652	50925
霞山区	Xiashan District	63	65	3558805	3888441	100530	80810
麻章区	Mazhang District	104	104	19777316	18011257	434118	191185
坡头区	Potou District	69	69	3426287	3146917	1375687	1062877
雷州市	Leizhou City	64	65	808255	957774	-41295	61335
廉江市	Lianjiang County	189	199	1585156	1618140	23923	24519
吴川市	Wuchuan City	129	125	942889	982445	23087	-20661
遂溪县	Suixi County	120	127	2130004	1907568	-29465	10632
徐闻县	Xuwen County	46	41	333055	326848	62655	46196
茂名市	Maoming						
茂南区	Maonan District	117	126	17975702	17282774	-30786	467160
电白区	Dianbai District	220	219	3850105	4689871	-4975	152356
信宜市	Xinyi City	51	54	279485	289901	14418	17000
高州市	Gaozhou City	163	168	1462595	1490726	48620	48039
化州市	Huazhou City	123	125	1207836	1092010	20612	14871
肇庆市	Zhaoqing						
端州区	Duanzhou District	137	128	3117007	3098081	113111	190485
鼎湖区	Dinghu District	107	122	2490869	2922698	46996	39225
高要区	Gaoyao District	430	448	11892079	13011420	746843	972614
四会市	Sihui City	610	638	21221504	21544603	472921	688178
广宁县	Guangning County	83	98	2163678	1570816	177006	66425
德庆县	Deqing County	88	89	1193625	1274214	34417	40998
封开县	Fengkai County	41	46	987109	778785	134262	47911
怀集县	Huaiji County	66	65	788266	676671	14777	25011
清远市	Qingyuan						
清城区	Qingcheng District	387	398	14862128	16188913	597671	683228
清新区	Qingxin District	175	178	3960635	4069147	446461	157615
英德市	Yingde City	228	241	4699560	4804497	205222	148261
连州市	Lianzhou City	71	68	1095698	1114261	101088	86679
佛冈县	Fogang County	122	126	3336084	3510699	175766	235775
阳山县	Yangshan County	28	26	227511	234372	20210	23312
连山县	Lianshan County	9	9	65816	92948	1215	6980
连南县	Liannan County	14	13	85131	122091	2109	-9620
潮州市	Chaozhou						
湘桥区	Xiangqiao District	183	185	3302031	2391628	214088	77355
潮安区	Chaoan District	754	722	7584704	7350508	394702	342232
饶平县	Raoping County	141	126	2992551	3048455	216594	229029
揭阳市	Jieyang						
榕城区	Rongcheng District	551	505		6713883	248898	158179
揭东区	Jiedong District	470	425		4138361	439089	195226
普宁市	Puning City	347	358		3579062	166823	108266
揭西县	Jiexi County	112	110		722705	197489	43319
惠来县	Huilai County	92	72		11113593	-252288	221326
云浮市	Yunfu						
云城区	Yuncheng District	99	101	1968932	2532174	-55683	42932
云安区	Yunan District	74	82	1312356	1274474	31425	21264
罗定市	Luoding City	81	80	1421507	1433979	53439	43459
新兴县	Xinxing County	111	114	1944601	1894656	63219	77125
郁南县	Yunan County	61	61	521791	506132	573	7858

23－10 各县(市、区)房地产开发投资及商品房销售面积

Investment in Fixed Assets and Floor Space of Commercial Building Sold by County (County-level City and District)

县(市、区)	County (County-level City and District)	房地产开发投资(万元) Investment in Real Estate Development (10000 yuan)		商品房销售面积(万平方米) Floor Space of Commercial Building Sold (10000 sq.m)	
		2022	2023	2022	2023
广州市	Guangzhou				
越秀区	Yuexiu District	208391	234109	8.18	8.95
海珠区	Haizhu District	2696311	2906264	62.55	89.57
荔湾区	Liwan District	2895261	3574594	64.03	68.56
天河区	Tianhe District	2455399	3367124	92.69	124.23
白云区	Baiyun District	3876970	3747048	73.61	94.99
黄埔区	Huangpu District	5794740	5818007	342.00	358.70
花都区	Huadu District	2222688	1874543	73.96	97.96
番禺区	Panyu District	4145750	4702555	143.43	148.27
南沙区	Nansha District	5863092	3629057	160.92	177.21
从化区	Conghua District	364576	285844	40.42	41.62
增城区	Zengcheng District	4443255	2975328	312.28	194.43
深圳市	Shenzhen				
福田区	Futian District	1970708	1901383	33.60	37.41
罗湖区	Luohu District	2472866	2532316	39.93	59.43
盐田区	Yantian District	697778	799266	28.11	24.07
南山区	Nanshan District	5738093	7248920	131.56	127.91
宝安区	Baoan District	7657201	8933381	106.87	152.71
龙岗区	Longgang District	5396241	5049347	137.21	146.24
龙华区	Longhua District	4623144	4922916	93.13	94.12
坪山区	Pingshan District	2205510	2083264	25.46	31.59
光明区	Guangming District	3846058	4403827	83.25	88.51
珠海市	Zhuhai				
香洲区	Xiangzhou District	4901609	3412531	154.53	144.23
金湾区	Jinwan District	1501234	900748	81.09	52.39
斗门区	Doumen District	1169191	789085	104.02	74.39
汕头市	Shantou				
金平区	Jinping District	484290	480381	56.14	48.67
龙湖区	Longhu District	1598003	1412054	128.11	129.70
澄海区	Chenghai District	507628	298474	49.08	50.41
濠江区	Haojiang District	328460	286821	79.19	33.69
潮阳区	Chaoyang District	623262	428084	57.99	58.40
潮南区	Chaonan District	203951	218569	27.60	33.87
南澳县	Nanao County	32019	56644	4.05	8.27
佛山市	Foshan				
禅城区	Chancheng District	4014813	3472365	260.12	183.01
南海区	Nanhai District	6011905	3749409	491.74	339.70
顺德区	Shunde District	7684628	4666551	404.57	319.73
高明区	Gaoming District	805304	516848	100.67	69.56
三水区	Sanshui District	1048551	365007	139.97	102.78
韶关市	Shaoguan				
浈江区	Zhengjiang District	47446	67164	18.33	10.50
武江区	Wujiang District	366966	336348	90.01	66.78
曲江区	Qujiang District	106382	146796	18.78	19.22
乐昌市	Lechang City	96168	105713	27.49	24.87
南雄市	Nanxiong City	154184	95488	23.01	20.55
仁化县	Renhua County	66589	39202	16.22	9.14
始兴县	Shixing County	33680	67059	9.99	11.47
翁源县	Wengyuan County	118690	101585	18.87	19.46
新丰县	Xinfeng County	108086	105745	16.89	13.45
乳源县	Ruyuan County	37392	22863	9.04	9.49

23-10 续表 1 continued

县(市、区)	County (County-level City and District)	房地产开发投资(万元) Investment in Real Estate Development (10000 yuan)		商品房销售面积(万平方米) Floor Space of Commercial Building Sold (10000 sq.m)	
		2022	2023	2022	2023
河源市	Heyuan				
源城区	Yuancheng District	750134	612881	94.63	75.79
东源县	Dongyuan County	269677	355867	103.21	89.63
和平县	Heping County	150464	68549	18.47	16.67
龙川县	Longchuan County	62024	138044	9.86	12.26
紫金县	Zijin County	132691	130925	24.57	24.19
连平县	Lianping County	36392	18015	6.12	4.53
梅州市	Meizhou				
梅江区	Meijiang District	257197	212532	53.94	54.78
梅县区	Meixian District	198618	141362	44.90	36.23
兴宁市	Xingning City	230659	292150	44.08	56.76
平远县	Pingyuan County	61125	36174	10.43	14.15
蕉岭县	Jiaoling County	56818	47218	13.92	15.37
大埔县	Dabu County	65324	61518	16.31	16.46
丰顺县	Fengshun County	66802	80480	20.94	17.47
五华县	Wuhua County	156734	72865	44.11	30.36
惠州市	Huizhou				
惠城区	Huicheng District	4336360	4518430	555.07	561.51
惠阳区	Huiyang District	3756210	3429819	397.31	295.44
惠东县	Huidong County	1054858	808392	138.90	131.29
博罗县	Boluo County	1554587	1386890	199.91	132.04
龙门县	Longmen County	167808	111090	19.16	18.29
汕尾市	Shanwei				
市城区	Urban District	558180	423948	60.47	53.09
陆丰市	Lufeng City	248114	212332	60.39	49.97
海丰县	Haifeng County	292785	379071	93.17	97.24
陆河县	Luhe County	126344	91741	36.67	30.64
江门市	Jiangmen				
蓬江区	Pengjiang District	1749085	1277810	142.59	142.49
江海区	Jianghai District	397668	262493	69.64	50.52
新会区	Xinhui District	1138055	813122	94.63	96.12
台山市	Taishan City	824600	552478	100.00	113.17
开平市	Kaiping City	458964	438227	53.58	58.57
鹤山市	Heshan City	495340	429462	84.78	63.48
恩平市	Enping City	319335	213539	53.99	58.65
阳江市	Yangjiang				
江城区	Jiangcheng District	312649	319459	74.91	75.96
阳东区	Yangdong District	141795	128085	41.26	27.48
阳春市	Yangchun City	188145	179859	77.40	59.05
阳西县	Yangxi County	127077	143130	47.62	42.88

23−10 续表 2 continued

县(市、区)	County (County-level City and District)	房地产开发投资(万元) Investment in Real Estate Development (10000 yuan)		商品房销售面积(万平方米) Floor Space of Commercial Building Sold (10000 sq.m)	
		2022	2023	2022	2023
湛江市	Zhanjiang				
赤坎区	Chikan District	750830	731962	64.12	77.60
霞山区	Xiashan District	434922	550349	60.88	64.33
麻章区	Mazhang District	213682	182624	25.84	24.65
坡头区	Potou District	350319	394680	34.20	47.15
雷州市	Leizhou City	90423	94843	21.31	17.08
廉江市	Lianjiang County	191639	144320	26.13	23.04
吴川市	Wuchuan City	568262	633629	45.55	50.75
遂溪县	Suixi County	232378	129088	37.62	28.82
徐闻县	Xuwen County	100847	81116	19.73	12.20
茂名市	Maoming				
茂南区	Maonan District	931663	949785	116.19	77.20
电白区	Dianbai District	656196	676273	72.02	81.71
信宜市	Xinyi City	424281	373893	78.70	76.10
高州市	Gaozhou City	463161	334416	73.80	74.88
化州市	Huazhou City	262493	288694	44.80	35.23
肇庆市	Zhaoqing				
端州区	Duanzhou District	503602	430026	88.15	77.46
鼎湖区	Dinghu District	653089	247239	72.27	44.43
高要区	Gaoyao District	334470	341371	51.19	54.34
四会市	Sihui City	977208	657336	120.35	119.25
广宁县	Guangning County	119050	51964	33.58	29.45
德庆县	Deqing County	35068	30539	17.90	18.51
封开县	Fengkai County	86007	82546	13.60	15.79
怀集县	Huaiji County	442286	232743	60.75	51.36
清远市	Qingyuan				
清城区	Qingcheng District	1749927	1655217	260.06	253.08
清新区	Qingxin District	245658	142592	46.48	35.53
英德市	Yingde City	282711	284725	98.89	79.51
连州市	Lianzhou City	114683	114838	20.93	20.09
佛冈县	Fogang County	265297	250072	57.42	42.11
阳山县	Yangshan County	58222	44395	16.11	11.71
连山县	Lianshan County	13872	5580	1.40	0.70
连南县	Liannan County	18365	10308	3.76	2.93
潮州市	Chaozhou				
湘桥区	Xiangqiao District	413693	253016	75.52	69.59
潮安区	Chaoan District	211132	165507	24.10	11.63
饶平县	Raoping County	261582	82676	25.59	35.57
揭阳市	Jieyang				
榕城区	Rongcheng District	480089	361383	46.40	44.56
揭东区	Jiedong District	350152	218597	21.71	22.82
普宁市	Puning City	435672	408373	71.15	69.91
揭西县	Jiexi County	113784	75792	25.11	22.21
惠来县	Huilai County	239327	239923	32.62	34.26
云浮市	Yunfu				
云城区	Yuncheng District	255692	194611	57.17	45.67
云安区	Yunan District	19761	14066	6.40	7.62
罗定市	Luoding City	341482	308435	53.47	62.40
新兴县	Xinxing County	228982	185110	83.21	53.34
郁南县	Yunan County	117212	67550	26.03	26.25

注：湛江含市直数据，深圳含深汕合作区数据，分县区合计小于全市。
Note: Due to the projects that can't be classified by region and the development zone projects, the sum of the counties are less than the city.

23-11 各县(市、区)社会消费品零售总额

Total Retail Sales of Consumer Goods by County (County-level City and District)

单位：万元 (10000 yuan)

县(市、区)	County (County-level City and District)	社会消费品零售总额 Total Retail Sales of Consumer Goods 2022	2023	#商品零售 Retail Sales 2022	2023
广州市	Guangzhou				
越秀区	Yuexiu District	12232127	13295740	10868659	11760106
海珠区	Haizhu District	9589731	9983819	9017880	9226535
荔湾区	Liwan District	6470943	7111532	5598545	6040283
天河区	Tianhe District	20237930	21527863	18410521	19164245
白云区	Baiyun District	10696782	11639873	10031299	10779763
黄埔区	Huangpu District	14281849	15524578	14077754	15221649
花都区	Huadu District	7881521	8512965	7546519	8120634
番禺区	Panyu District	12639796	13179109	11738887	12068714
南沙区	Nansha District	2947894	3324515	2704372	3062645
从化区	Conghua District	1417064	1437863	1298242	1296407
增城区	Zengcheng District	4585896	4588343	4352970	4314367
深圳市	Shenzhen				
福田区	Futian District	22730642	24147909	20474294	20207396
罗湖区	Luohu District	12587077	13917453	11337626	12689597
盐田区	Yantian District	1526520	1658333	1374991	1481392
南山区	Nanshan District	13739930	14812505	12376041	11958797
宝安区	Baoan District	14320670	15483490	12899135	14602886
龙岗区	Longgang District	14876780	15882283	13400043	15129994
龙华区	Longhua District	12636705	13532715	11382327	12647696
坪山区	Pingshan District	1973406	2496732	1777516	2423312
光明区	Guangming District	2376487	2592439	2140586	2463704
珠海市	Zhuhai				
香洲区	Xiangzhou District	9069939	9410379	8335023	8374034
金湾区	Jinwan District	575249	602824	528638	536436
斗门区	Doumen District	801552	776512	736604	690997
汕头市	Shantou				
金平区	Jinping District	5232501	5447631	4662110	4848594
龙湖区	Longhu District	3055229	3114266	2786038	2807508
澄海区	Chenghai District	1794428	1893435	1654346	1746989
濠江区	Haojiang District	481545	500821	445433	462328
潮阳区	Chaoyang District	2169570	2287411	1931241	2033597
潮南区	Chaonan District	1928700	2019290	1710114	1787069
南澳县	Nanao County	188299	199913	156101	165467
佛山市	Foshan				
禅城区	Chancheng District	8195782	8475193	7785246	7988563
南海区	Nanhai District	12217473	12653663	11246137	11553617
顺德区	Shunde District	11954540	12496776	11137306	11558573
高明区	Gaoming District	1306369	1382011	1213306	1273828
三水区	Sanshui District	2261489	2337123	2069274	2122833
韶关市	Shaoguan				
浈江区	Zhengjiang District	1274553	1198422	1209949	1132496
武江区	Wujiang District	780847	816087	725302	752565
曲江区	Qujiang District	384032	417795	347666	377003
乐昌市	Lechang City	559620	593321	510779	540789
南雄市	Nanxiong City	470196	501501	424923	452573
仁化县	Renhua County	257885	271425	233086	244009
始兴县	Shixing County	290018	301668	262030	272124
翁源县	Wengyuan County	427939	447856	387206	404083
新丰县	Xinfeng County	269496	282406	242762	253066
乳源县	Ruyuan County	225147	236999	201776	211467

23-11 续表 1 continued

单位：万元 (10000 yuan)

县(市、区)	County (County-level City and District)	社会消费品零售总额 Total Retail Sales of Consumer Goods		#商品零售 Retail Sales	
		2022	2023	2022	2023
河源市	Heyuan				
源城区	Yuancheng District	1428202	1382208	1325782	1337180
东源县	Dongyuan County	435164	468031	404702	425908
和平县	Heping County	395927	422850	356334	376337
龙川县	Longchuan County	608845	653787	560137	601484
紫金县	Zijin County	558152	573388	516271	471707
连平县	Lianping County	353851	381102	325542	350613
梅州市	Meizhou				
梅江区	Meijiang District	1464667	1511203	1381612	1418703
梅县区	Meixian District	1450515	1557939	1321414	1416777
兴宁市	Xingning City	1031097	1079192	925265	968088
平远县	Pingyuan County	332531	350659	297146	313635
蕉岭县	Jiaoling County	384177	402331	344633	360670
大埔县	Dabu County	479941	507618	429192	453937
丰顺县	Fengshun County	551457	597885	493422	534461
五华县	Wuhua County	873791	941254	781497	841676
惠州市	Huizhou				
惠城区	Huicheng District	9238043	9612747	8480523	8396735
惠阳区	Huiyang District	3012835	3110415	2765783	2716948
惠东县	Huidong County	4230209	4523628	3883332	3951389
博罗县	Boluo County	3312361	3558078	3040747	3107981
龙门县	Longmen County	611771	644082	561606	562606
汕尾市	Shanwei				
市城区	Urban District	1153834	1159048	1007468	995736
陆丰市	Lufeng City	1635820	1696415	1409026	1434151
海丰县	Haifeng County	1577811	1655430	1391724	1440307
陆河县	Luhe County	387836	403630	348866	358755
江门市	Jiangmen				
蓬江区	Pengjiang District	2672093	2720583	2434267	2448524
江海区	Jianghai District	668772	711502	609249	640352
新会区	Xinhui District	3017140	3065964	2748604	2759368
台山市	Taishan City	2301046	2388504	2096245	2149653
开平市	Kaiping City	1858056	1889949	1692682	1700954
鹤山市	Heshan City	1588613	1689794	1447221	1520814
恩平市	Enping City	984735	1012700	897090	911430
阳江市	Yangjiang				
江城区	Jiangcheng District	2238545	2207813	2005586	1952557
阳东区	Yangdong District	699358	706078	626743	624831
阳春市	Yangchun City	1482408	1546200	1321928	1366826
阳西县	Yangxi County	536011	568973	475400	501188

23−11 续表 2 continued

单位：万元 (10000 yuan)

县(市、区)	County (County-level City and District)	社会消费品零售总额 Total Retail Sales of Consumer Goods		#商品零售 Retail Sales	
		2022	2023	2022	2023
湛江市	Zhanjiang				
赤坎区	Chikan District	4290108	4472117	3842785	3980429
霞山区	Xiashan District	3315785	3559452	3069903	3250460
麻章区	Mazhang District	1491433	1596964	1330015	1423282
坡头区	Potou District	436410	469385	342956	366347
雷州市	Leizhou City	1815745	1945787	1606559	1721219
廉江市	Lianjiang County	3113219	3357885	2689514	2898466
吴川市	Wuchuan City	1612093	1737945	1416979	1526764
遂溪县	Suixi County	1445302	1564829	1203167	1303290
徐闻县	Xuwen County	746218	801051	611956	656731
茂名市	Maoming				
茂南区	Maonan District	4830525	5138800	4485772	4680028
电白区	Dianbai District	3138454	3321994	2449139	2561799
信宜市	Xinyi City	2308912	2443684	2105806	2126005
高州市	Gaozhou City	2570851	2719659	2243479	2368331
化州市	Huazhou City	2250182	2375778	1957952	2068229
肇庆市	Zhaoqing				
端州区	Duanzhou District	2829910	2988302	2641551	2761695
鼎湖区	Dinghu District	1068265	1093928	1037230	1059369
高要区	Gaoyao District	889465	955304	798142	852198
四会市	Sihui City	4283078	4515688	4213356	4437222
广宁县	Guangning County	495035	530089	458072	489659
德庆县	Deqing County	517484	555392	477448	511876
封开县	Fengkai County	350320	375358	307398	327808
怀集县	Huaiji County	737104	791956	659165	707619
清远市	Qingyuan				
清城区	Qingcheng District	2824311	2799352	2706333	2611347
清新区	Qingxin District	710081	783294	675717	730688
英德市	Yingde City	985116	1058268	935590	987195
连州市	Lianzhou City	401183	427167	380083	398478
佛冈县	Fogang County	389157	414094	377189	386283
阳山县	Yangshan County	337181	356629	307945	332678
连山县	Lianshan County	54381	56780	50236	52966
连南县	Liannan County	110162	118466	101305	110510
潮州市	Chaozhou				
湘桥区	Xiangqiao District	1411263	1458929	1297320	1329125
潮安区	Chaoan District	2397714	2512695	2222859	2332312
饶平县	Raoping County	1061818	1118057	975414	1027173
揭阳市	Jieyang				
榕城区	Rongcheng District	3097962	3132653	2972089	3000507
揭东区	Jiedong District	2196697	2241990	2107435	2147415
普宁市	Puning City	3439416	3599767	3299650	3447916
揭西县	Jiexi County	910576	930941	873575	891671
惠来县	Huilai County	1037761	1083122	995592	1037432
云浮市	Yunfu				
云城区	Yuncheng District	1184531	1194915	1081727	1107003
云安区	Yunan District	212786	221800	192518	199700
罗定市	Luoding City	1374853	1432213	1268725	1308833
新兴县	Xinxing County	607073	640316	533557	560967
郁南县	Yunan County	462700	485727	423327	437550

23-12 各县(市、区)财政收支
Local Government Budgetary Revenue and Expenditure by County (County-level City and District)

单位：万元 (10000yuan)

县(市、区)	County (County-level City and District)	地方一般公共预算收入 Local Government General Public Budget Revenue		地方一般公共预算支出 Local Government General Public Budget Expenditure	
		2022	2023	2022	2023
广州市	Guangzhou				
越秀区	Yuexiu District	537001	576440	1364528	1375206
海珠区	Haizhu District	691968	599733	1381284	1434394
荔湾区	Liwan District	534341	578939	1172425	1184835
天河区	Tianhe District	813420	827748	1377554	1801944
白云区	Baiyun District	747474	815183	1919114	1722993
黄埔区	Huangpu District	1820952	2081401	3357432	3283819
花都区	Huadu District	757825	884791	1488690	1406183
番禺区	Panyu District	1042625	1184020	1675581	1910381
南沙区	Nansha District	1170157	1256277	2949974	2824973
从化区	Conghua District	272242	287034	889031	889335
增城区	Zengcheng District	968549	995189	1971038	1759229
深圳市	Shenzhen				
福田区	Futian District	1942706	2077852	3104741	2688502
罗湖区	Luohu District	893960	1395035	2051693	1889930
盐田区	Yantian District	329097	367693	702781	614605
南山区	Nanshan District	3616214	3827939	4342423	4315405
宝安区	Baoan District	2991877	3829404	4763327	5206354
龙岗区	Longgang District	2841726	3729464	5083488	5178455
龙华区	Longhua District	1514784	1678435	3312098	3150849
坪山区	Pingshan District	547788	807349	1752557	1603744
光明区	Guangming District	808022	1092076	1788652	2239069
珠海市	Zhuhai				
香洲区	Xiangzhou District	420835	449667	981973	838409
金湾区	Jinwan District	424882	545215	787729	830443
斗门区	Doumen District	230724	314886	734293	692153
汕头市	Shantou				
金平区	Jinping District	85968	104096	303832	319587
龙湖区	Longhu District	152398	146164	336539	283548
澄海区	Chenghai District	141765	165639	460046	422431
濠江区	Haojiang District	42947	66475	206593	209111
潮阳区	Chaoyang District	163077	206118	706067	733748
潮南区	Chaonan District	84137	118706	572874	605122
南澳县	Nanao County	12814	14309	126057	122433
佛山市	Foshan				
禅城区	Chancheng District	1140247	970934	1258454	1150311
南海区	Nanhai District	2584349	2265802	2688591	2819002
顺德区	Shunde District	2656521	2286131	2693925	2659379
高明区	Gaoming District	441900	393483	603835	555535
三水区	Sanshui District	692536	607361	790466	843191
韶关市	Shaoguan				
浈江区	Zhengjiang District	39312	42661	175438	250895
武江区	Wujiang District	37339	46835	166993	174110
曲江区	Qujiang District	77573	82297	266800	253334
乐昌市	Lechang City	84924	98026	397948	391331
南雄市	Nanxiong City	75023	66864	416224	414807
仁化县	Renhua County	44303	49771	267146	292982
始兴县	Shixing County	41556	44060	253740	301606
翁源县	Wengyuan County	67295	64811	331794	350915
新丰县	Xinfeng County	48920	50060	254697	265357
乳源县	Ruyuan County	52416	55177	288312	283440

23-12 续表 1 continued

单位：万元 (10000yuan)

县(市、区)	County (County-level City and District)	地方一般公共预算收入 Local Government General Public Budget Revenue		地方一般公共预算支出 Local Government General Public Budget Expenditure	
		2022	2023	2022	2023
河源市	Heyuan				
源城区	Yuancheng District	107071	82579	284451	271806
东源县	Dongyuan County	126830	138937	555692	547288
和平县	Heping County	41316	46764	376462	373138
龙川县	Longchuan County	65668	79871	679183	638866
紫金县	Zijin County	83948	86878	511955	520249
连平县	Lianping County	46599	57005	347737	357268
梅州市	Meizhou				
梅江区	Meijiang District	59280	75269	274513	294775
梅县区	Meixian District	132291	142497	640055	569305
兴宁市	Xingning City	82562	102917	709259	718854
平远县	Pingyuan County	53478	63847	315987	290841
蕉岭县	Jiaoling County	60415	71095	291224	277364
大埔县	Dabu County	51505	54869	437546	461205
丰顺县	Fengshun County	65581	75643	489975	447159
五华县	Wuhua County	124300	132009	881547	775638
惠州市	Huizhou				
惠城区	Huicheng District	417359	441919	881518	856659
惠阳区	Huiyang District	684057	645599	871009	851106
惠东县	Huidong County	405813	462724	900820	872287
博罗县	Boluo County	662169	776439	1104548	1145320
龙门县	Longmen County	196465	226997	490692	514002
汕尾市	Shanwei				
市城区	Urban District	78483	85022	337969	280399
陆丰市	Lufeng City	114400	132576	945598	910895
海丰县	Haifeng County	135867	156735	695419	606141
陆河县	Luhe County	45746	50736	336836	306576
江门市	Jiangmen				
蓬江区	Pengjiang District	299551	302763	412092	375649
江海区	Jianghai District	142820	149148	241898	219388
新会区	Xinhui District	546809	576972	834111	850868
台山市	Taishan City	355166	384046	834627	839584
开平市	Kaiping City	307742	310319	566454	571388
鹤山市	Heshan City	357292	376968	489526	481153
恩平市	Enping City	134418	139726	410785	411161
阳江市	Yangjiang				
江城区	Jiangcheng District	49811	46320	243343	245870
阳东区	Yangdong District	161129	194048	440924	458264
阳春市	Yangchun City	168865	129145	737612	712564
阳西县	Yangxi County	136050	148908	392631	453884

23-12 续表 2 continued

单位：万元 (10000yuan)

县(市、区)	County (County-level City and District)	地方一般公共预算收入 Local Government General Public Budget Revenue		地方一般公共预算支出 Local Government General Public Budget Expenditure	
		2022	2023	2022	2023
湛江市	Zhanjiang				
赤坎区	Chikan District	29726	39337	140221	139067
霞山区	Xiashan District	65089	67620	175979	193143
麻章区	Mazhang District	66565	60641	158260	166085
坡头区	Potou District	45254	51067	200681	227073
雷州市	Leizhou City	88140	116859	721195	788726
廉江市	Lianjiang County	169956	177870	836460	915522
吴川市	Wuchuan City	88739	95963	527101	513737
遂溪县	Suixi County	57031	107962	530282	510850
徐闻县	Xuwen County	61403	87685	474107	516356
茂名市	Maoming				
茂南区	Maonan District	120630	131609	481962	461622
电白区	Dianbai District	277510	259452	1134482	905845
信宜市	Xinyi City	124548	131418	808506	810479
高州市	Gaozhou City	173743	184866	915259	959050
化州市	Huazhou City	152410	171172	830672	850771
肇庆市	Zhaoqing				
端州区	Duanzhou District	111615	148774	287355	296334
鼎湖区	Dinghu District	81926	107409	155699	176853
高要区	Gaoyao District	281811	339093	539566	553079
四会市	Sihui City	184301	304207	426113	483942
广宁县	Guangning County	79421	84362	347827	355729
德庆县	Deqing County	47975	104043	341811	341016
封开县	Fengkai County	262218	74914	447896	353702
怀集县	Huaiji County	73857	80501	565965	542080
清远市	Qingyuan				
清城区	Qingcheng District	167666	198889	485909	536283
清新区	Qingxin District	170043	161004	527627	513724
英德市	Yingde City	291590	310815	839411	839869
连州市	Lianzhou City	62450	76732	375962	391338
佛冈县	Fogang County	127658	135890	381372	347494
阳山县	Yangshan County	63179	69861	387930	388279
连山县	Lianshan County	24380	24780	192898	188429
连南县	Liannan County	23959	28969	222277	237758
潮州市	Chaozhou				
湘桥区	Xiangqiao District	58181	61620	261034	235715
潮安区	Chaoan District	126791	140791	712828	614989
饶平县	Raoping County	89199	98748	632471	643179
揭阳市	Jieyang				
榕城区	Rongcheng District	55484	89734	317190	318607
揭东区	Jiedong District	64272	68998	515831	437527
普宁市	Puning City	217798	228149	1056892	1051499
揭西县	Jiexi County	37871	46382	603924	561711
惠来县	Huilai County	91725	212769	702791	756463
云浮市	Yunfu				
云城区	Yuncheng District	55638	109152	320717	304862
云安区	Yunan District	215113	126758	351233	273878
罗定市	Luoding City	135479	107119	699692	667686
新兴县	Xinxing County	142906	147493	414519	464142
郁南县	Yunan County	206254	190922	379568	394667

23-13 各县(市、区)城镇居民人均可支配收入

Per Capita Disposable Income of Urban Households by County (County-level City and District)

县(市、区)	County (County-level City and District)	2022 绝对值(元) Value (yuan)	2022 增速(%) Ratio(%)	2023 绝对值(元) Value (yuan)	2023 增速(%) Ratio(%)
广州市	Guangzhou				
越秀区	Yuexiu District	84621	2.7	90376	6.8
海珠区	Haizhu District	78130	2.1	84419	8.0
荔湾区	Liwan District	78133	4.8	83094	6.3
天河区	Tianhe District	93613	4.9	94717	1.2
白云区	Baiyun District	77511	2.6	81805	5.5
黄埔区	Huangpu District	83607	5.2	86784	3.8
花都区	Huadu District	66283	3.0	67774	2.3
番禺区	Panyu District	72541	3.2	76705	5.7
南沙区	Nansha District	64268	4.4	67288	4.7
从化区	Conghua District	51116	3.6	53160	4.0
增城区	Zengcheng District	61164	4.7	64559	5.5
深圳市	Shenzhen				
福田区	Futian District	95729	3.4	101810	6.4
罗湖区	Luohu District	76352	3.3	80799	5.8
盐田区	Yantian District	77604	5.6	83310	7.4
南山区	Nanshan District	95710	5.9	102576	7.2
宝安区	Baoan District	66587	0.2	70008	5.1
龙岗区	Longgang District	61284	1.3	64154	4.7
龙华区	Longhua District	66553	3.4	71168	6.9
坪山区	Pingshan District	66033	2.9	69806	5.7
光明区	Guangming District	63102	5.2	67598	7.1
珠海市	Zhuhai				
香洲区	Xiangzhou District	74353	1.2	76531	2.9
金湾区	Jinwan District	46584	3.1	49052	5.3
斗门区	Doumen District	54721	3.5	57142	4.4
汕头市	Shantou				
金平区	Jinping District	44767	4.2	45993	2.7
龙湖区	Longhu District	47250	5.2	48751	3.2
澄海区	Chenghai District	34436	2.2	35546	3.2
濠江区	Haojiang District	32732	5.0	33825	3.3
潮阳区	Chaoyang District	31365	4.0	31472	0.3
潮南区	Chaonan District	29462	4.3	30262	2.7
南澳县	Nanao County	20064	4.0	21356	6.4
佛山市	Foshan				
禅城区	Chancheng District	62965	4.1	66510	5.6
南海区	Nanhai District	66340	3.9	69592	4.9
顺德区	Shunde District	69981	3.7	73235	4.7
高明区	Gaoming District	46056	4.1	48786	5.9
三水区	Sanshui District	50270	3.9	52864	5.2
韶关市	Shaoguan				
浈江区	Zhengjiang District	45928	2.3	47377	3.2
武江区	Wujiang District	46454	2.9	48150	3.7
曲江区	Qujiang District	37473	2.6	39450	5.3
乐昌市	Lechang City	32860	3.2	34266	4.3
南雄市	Nanxiong City	33890	4.5	35057	3.4
仁化县	Renhua County	34295	2.8	36044	5.1
始兴县	Shixing County	32710	2.6	34229	4.6
翁源县	Wengyuan County	34022	3.5	35446	4.2
新丰县	Xinfeng County	32710	3.0	34060	4.1
乳源县	Ruyuan County	33827	4.3	35579	5.2

23−13 续表 1 continued

县(市、区)	County (County-level City and District)	2022 绝对值(元) Value (yuan)	2022 增速(%) Ratio(%)	2023 绝对值(元) Value (yuan)	2023 增速(%) Ratio(%)
河源市	Heyuan				
源城区	Yuancheng District	36366	1.9	38184	5.0
东源县	Dongyuan County	29052	4.1	30901	6.4
和平县	Heping County	29509	2.4	30917	4.8
龙川县	Longchuan County	27360	3.4	29132	6.5
紫金县	Zijin County	26630	4.0	28285	6.2
连平县	Lianping County	27874	2.5	29425	5.6
梅州市	Meizhou				
梅江区	Meijiang District	42620	4.2	44495	4.4
梅县区	Meixian District	41256	3.6	41627	0.9
兴宁市	Xingning City	31408	3.2	32539	3.6
平远县	Pingyuan County	30991	4.6	31983	3.2
蕉岭县	Jiaoling County	33026	3.7	34578	4.7
大埔县	Dabu County	29047	3.2	29645	2.1
丰顺县	Fengshun County	30383	3.3	30790	1.3
五华县	Wuhua County	26320	4.9	27610	4.9
惠州市	Huizhou				
惠城区	Huicheng District	61603	1.0	63275	2.7
惠阳区	Huiyang District	51297	1.0	53097	3.5
惠东县	Huidong County	35585	3.7	36614	2.9
博罗县	Boluo County	41938	3.9	42691	1.8
龙门县	Longmen County	32625	4.9	33435	2.5
汕尾市	Shanwei				
市城区	Urban District	35494	5.6	37364	5.3
陆丰市	Lufeng City	31922	5.3	33716	5.6
海丰县	Haifeng County	39238	4.7	41170	4.9
陆河县	Luhe County	27710	5.0	29036	4.8
江门市	Jiangmen				
蓬江区	Pengjiang District	55805	4.1	58648	5.1
江海区	Jianghai District	51460	3.9	53965	4.9
新会区	Xinhui District	48229	4.9	50355	4.4
台山市	Taishan City	33721	2.9	36022	6.8
开平市	Kaiping City	36220	3.8	38074	5.1
鹤山市	Heshan City	37959	2.1	40570	6.9
恩平市	Enping City	31250	4.7	33221	6.3
阳江市	Yangjiang				
江城区	Jiangcheng District	39519	4.1	41727	4.3
阳东区	Yangdong District	37489	3.5	37808	0.8
阳春市	Yangchun City	33079	2.9	34189	3.4
阳西县	Yangxi County	30715	2.8	31987	4.1

注：江城区2023年城镇居民人均可支配收入不含海陵区、高新区数据，与2022年数据不可比，增速为可比口径。

Note: The per capita disposable income of urban households in Jiangcheng District in 2023 does not include data from Hailing District and High tech Zone, and is not comparable to the data from 2022. The growth rate is based on a comparable standard.

23−13 续表 2 continued

县(市、区)	County (County-level and District)	2022		2023	
		绝对值(元) Value (yuan)	增速(%) Ratio(%)	绝对值(元) Value (yuan)	增速(%) Ratio(%)
湛江市	Zhanjiang				
赤坎区	Chikan District	43923	3.0	44272	0.8
霞山区	Xiashan District	52010	1.0	52407	0.8
麻章区	Mazhang District	35220	4.7	36799	4.5
坡头区	Potou District	37109	1.5	37972	2.3
雷州市	Leizhou City	27401	3.8	28490	4.0
廉江市	Lianjiang County	32506	3.9	33995	4.6
吴川市	Wuchuan City	30809	4.8	31803	3.2
遂溪县	Suixi County	29517	3.7	30251	2.5
徐闻县	Xuwen County	29531	1.8	30502	3.3
茂名市	Maoming				
茂南区	Maonan District	38036	2.2	38843	2.1
电白区	Dianbai District	32722	2.8	33690	3.0
信宜市	Xinyi City	31842	2.7	32874	3.2
高州市	Gaozhou City	32263	2.4	33307	3.2
化州市	Huazhou City	31504	1.9	32551	3.3
肇庆市	Zhaoqing				
端州区	Duanzhou District	44128	1.2	44852	1.6
鼎湖区	Dinghu District	34384	3.8	36010	4.7
高要区	Gaoyao District	35017	3.5	35402	1.1
四会市	Sihui City	41934	1.1	43159	2.9
广宁县	Guangning County	30370	3.9	31940	5.2
德庆县	Deqing County	30783	2.5	31259	1.5
封开县	Fengkai County	30895	4.1	32371	4.8
怀集县	Huaiji County	35192	3.0	36091	2.6
清远市	Qingyuan				
清城区	Qingcheng District	40842	2.8	42625	4.4
清新区	Qingxin District	36502	2.9	37835	3.7
英德市	Yingde City	33686	2.9	35003	3.9
连州市	Lianzhou City	35574	4.0	36893	3.7
佛冈县	Fogang County	35475	3.2	36718	3.5
阳山县	Yangshan County	33700	2.5	34895	3.5
连山县	Lianshan County	30065	4.2	31146	3.6
连南县	Liannan County	31264	3.8	32194	3.0
潮州市	Chaozhou				
湘桥区	Xiangqiao District	34129	4.8	36031	5.6
潮安区	Chaoan District	27745	4.9	29075	4.8
饶平县	Raoping County	26492	5.1	27952	5.5
揭阳市	Jieyang				
榕城区	Rongcheng District	29881	-0.5	30296	3.6
揭东区	Jiedong District	31758	2.8	33254	4.7
普宁市	Puning City	31700	3.0	33051	4.3
揭西县	Jiexi County	24676	3.4	25228	2.2
惠来县	Huilai County	26364	3.7	27605	4.7
云浮市	Yunfu				
云城区	Yuncheng District	32662	4.3	34234	4.8
云安区	Yunan District	31653	5.5	31917	0.8
罗定市	Luoding City	32073	5.3	33553	4.6
新兴县	Xinxing County	33655	4.3	34587	2.8
郁南县	Yunan County	31264	4.0	32210	3.0

注：2023年，空港经济区并入榕城区，城镇居民人均可支配收入数据与2022年不可比，增速为可比口径。

Nots: In 2023, the Airport Economic Zone was merged into Rongcheng District, and the per capita disposable income data of urban residents is incomparable to 2022, with a growth rate of comparable caliber.

23–14 各县(市、区)农村居民人均可支配收入

Per Capita Disposable Income of Rural Households by County (County-level City and District)

县(市、区)	County (County-level City and District)	2022 绝对值(元) Value (yuan)	2022 增速(%) Ratio (%)	2023 绝对值(元) Value (yuan)	2023 增速(%) Ratio (%)
广州市	Guangzhou				
越秀区	Yuexiu District				
海珠区	Haizhu District				
荔湾区	Liwan District				
天河区	Tianhe District				
白云区	Baiyun District	36356	4.5	39120	7.6
黄埔区	Huangpu District				
花都区	Huadu District	34731	4.8	36537	5.2
番禺区	Panyu District	48696	4.9	51569	5.9
南沙区	Nansha District	42168	5.9	44824	6.3
从化区	Conghua District	27779	5.3	29613	6.6
增城区	Zengcheng District	33835	6.6	36474	7.8
深圳市	Shenzhen				
福田区	Futian District				
罗湖区	Luohu District				
盐田区	Yantian District				
南山区	Nanshan District				
宝安区	Baoan District				
龙岗区	Longgang District				
龙华区	Longhua District				
坪山区	Pingshan District				
光明区	Guangming District				
珠海市	Zhuhai				
香洲区	Xiangzhou District				
金湾区	Jinwan District				
斗门区	Doumen District	35829	4.2	38025	6.1
汕头市	Shantou				
金平区	Jinping District				
龙湖区	Longhu District	27038	7.2		
澄海区	Chenghai District	24162	4.6	25403	5.1
濠江区	Haojiang District	21698	6.2	22818	5.2
潮阳区	Chaoyang District	20482	6.2	21302	4.0
潮南区	Chaonan District	21355	6.3	22445	5.1
南澳县	Nanao County	16802	6.3	18158	8.1
佛山市	Foshan				
禅城区	Chancheng District				
南海区	Nanhai District	45651	4.9	48426	6.1
顺德区	Shunde District				
高明区	Gaoming District	33951	5.1	36320	7.0
三水区	Sanshui District	37635	5.2	40090	6.5
韶关市	Shaoguan				
浈江区	Zhengjiang District	23793	3.4	24995	5.1
武江区	Wujiang District	25175	3.9	26434	5.0
曲江区	Qujiang District	23207	4.0	24541	5.8
乐昌市	Lechang City	20175	4.3	21702	7.6
南雄市	Nanxiong City	20614	5.6	21904	6.3
仁化县	Renhua County	22369	5.4	23620	5.6
始兴县	Shixing County	21239	4.7	22439	5.7
翁源县	Wengyuan County	20330	4.7	21721	6.8
新丰县	Xinfeng County	20165	6.1	21726	7.7
乳源县	Ruyuan County	20149	6.2	21710	7.7

注：1.深圳市因完成城市化，无农村居民相关数据。

2.2023年启用新住户抽样调查样本，龙湖区2023年农村居民样本量不足以发布农村居民人均可支配收入数据。

Note: a)There is on data of Shenzhen city due to its total urbanization.

b)In 2023, a new household sampling survey sample was launched, but the sample size of rural residents in Longhu District in 2023 is insufficient to release data on per capita disposable income of rural residents.

23−14 续表 1 continued

县(市、区)	County (County-level City and District)	2022 绝对值(元) Value (yuan)	2022 增速(%) Ratio(%)	2023 绝对值(元) Value (yuan)	2023 增速(%) Ratio(%)
河源市	Heyuan				
源城区	Yuancheng District	27832	5.2	30016	7.8
东源县	Dongyuan County	20531	5.2	22307	8.7
和平县	Heping County	19845	6.7	21544	8.6
龙川县	Longchuan County	20137	5.0	21928	8.9
紫金县	Zijin County	20660	5.6	22364	8.3
连平县	Lianping County	20141	6.4	21810	8.3
梅州市	Meizhou				
梅江区	Meijiang District	25209	4.3	26444	4.9
梅县区	Meixian District	25468	5.4	27350	7.4
兴宁市	Xingning City	21996	4.4	23934	8.8
平远县	Pingyuan County	22456	5.8	23691	5.5
蕉岭县	Jiaoling County	22257	5.9	24394	9.6
大埔县	Dabu County	18038	4.7	19413	7.6
丰顺县	Fengshun County	18097	4.9	19346	6.9
五华县	Wuhua County	16617	6.0	18245	9.8
惠州市	Huizhou				
惠城区	Huicheng District	29785	3.1	31730	6.5
惠阳区	Huiyang District	31345	2.9	32845	4.8
惠东县	Huidong County	28067	4.7	29380	4.7
博罗县	Boluo County	27987	4.8	29359	4.9
龙门县	Longmen County	27107	5.4	28309	4.4
汕尾市	Shanwei				
市城区	Urban District	22286	6.5	23725	6.5
陆丰市	Lufeng City	21052	7.2	22561	7.2
海丰县	Haifeng County	23588	6.9	25339	7.4
陆河县	Luhe County	16478	5.9	17636	7.0
江门市	Jiangmen				
蓬江区	Pengjiang District				
江海区	Jianghai District				
新会区	Xinhui District	29754	6.9	31921	7.3
台山市	Taishan City	22937	4.3	23172	1.0
开平市	Kaiping City	24195	5.2	25753	6.4
鹤山市	Heshan City	24593	5.0	26442	7.5
恩平市	Enping City	20488	6.4	21896	6.9
阳江市	Yangjiang				
江城区	Jiangcheng District	24836	5.1	29289	6.2
阳东区	Yangdong District	24966	5.6	25500	2.1
阳春市	Yangchun City	21964	5.6	23238	5.8
阳西县	Yangxi County	23928	6.3	25744	7.6

注：江城区2023年农村居民人均可支配收入不含海陵区、高新区数据，与2022年数据不可比，增速为可比口径。

Note: The per capita disposable income of rural residents in Jiangcheng District in 2023 does not include data from Hailing District and High tech Zone, and is not comparable to the data from 2022. The growth rate is based on a comparable standard.

23−14 续表 2 continued

县(市、区)	County (County-level City and District)	2022 绝对值(元) Value (yuan)	2022 增速(%) Ratio(%)	2023 绝对值(元) Value (yuan)	2023 增速(%) Ratio(%)
湛江市	Zhanjiang				
赤坎区	Chikan District				
霞山区	Xiashan District	21372	4.0	21959	2.7
麻章区	Mazhang District	23207	5.6	24613	6.1
坡头区	Potou District	21281	4.0	21984	3.3
雷州市	Leizhou City	17652	5.1	18666	5.7
廉江市	Lianjiang County	23708	5.2	25055	5.7
吴川市	Wuchuan City	25339	5.2	26471	4.5
遂溪县	Suixi County	22602	4.7	23407	3.6
徐闻县	Xuwen County	21818	2.6	22795	4.5
茂名市	Maoming				
茂南区	Maonan District	23051	4.4	24332	5.6
电白区	Dianbai District	22656	4.5	24021	6.0
信宜市	Xinyi City	22404	4.1	23813	6.3
高州市	Gaozhou City	22523	4.0	24150	7.2
化州市	Huazhou City	22529	3.6	23950	6.3
肇庆市	Zhaoqing				
端州区	Duanzhou District				
鼎湖区	Dinghu District	31061	4.1	32545	4.8
高要区	Gaoyao District	27381	4.4	28349	3.5
四会市	Sihui City	30488	2.8	31801	4.3
广宁县	Guangning County	19931	5.8	21224	6.5
德庆县	Deqing County	25154	3.3	25545	1.6
封开县	Fengkai County	19798	6.0	20960	5.9
怀集县	Huaiji County	20824	4.7	21613	3.8
清远市	Qingyuan				
清城区	Qingcheng District	26024	4.7	27826	6.9
清新区	Qingxin District	20867	4.7	22240	6.6
英德市	Yingde City	21230	5.5	22634	6.6
连州市	Lianzhou City	18428	5.9	19553	6.1
佛冈县	Fogang County	20684	5.0	21988	6.3
阳山县	Yangshan County	19131	3.9	20311	6.2
连山县	Lianshan County	17831	6.2	18980	6.4
连南县	Liannan County	18198	5.7	19114	5.0
潮州市	Chaozhou				
湘桥区	Xiangqiao District	22127	5.9	23584	6.6
潮安区	Chaoan District	22097	6.0	23677	7.1
饶平县	Raoping County	19272	6.2	20534	6.5
揭阳市	Jieyang				
榕城区	Rongcheng District				
揭东区	Jiedong District	21768	4.9	22885	5.1
普宁市	Puning City	21307	5.1	22362	5.0
揭西县	Jiexi County	15381	6.6	16075	4.5
惠来县	Huilai County	16931	6.0	17867	5.5
云浮市	Yunfu				
云城区	Yuncheng District	21583	5.6	22660	5.0
云安区	Yunan District	20376	6.3	21426	5.2
罗定市	Luoding City	20197	6.0	21251	5.2
新兴县	Xinxing County	23257	5.8	24665	6.1
郁南县	Yunan County	19656	4.3	20749	5.6

附录

APPENDIX

附　录

简要说明

一、本篇资料包括部分省市社会经济主要指标、中国香港特别行政区、中国澳门特别行政区、中国台湾省主要统计指标及国际主要统计指标。

二、附录 A、附录 B、附录 C 资料来源于国家统计局编辑、中国统计出版社出版的《中国统计摘要》。附录 D 资料来源于国家统计局编辑、中国统计出版社出版的《国际统计年鉴——2023》。

三、一些国际组织及其组成成员：

经济合作与发展组织（经合组织，OECD），成员国有 38 个：澳大利亚、奥地利、比利时、加拿大、智利、捷克、丹麦、爱沙尼亚、芬兰、法国、德国、希腊、匈牙利、冰岛、爱尔兰、以色列、意大利、日本、韩国、拉脱维亚、立陶宛、卢森堡、墨西哥、荷兰、新西兰、挪威、波兰、葡萄牙、斯洛伐克、斯洛文尼亚、西班牙、瑞典、瑞士、土耳其、英国、美国、哥伦比亚、哥斯达黎加。

欧洲联盟（欧盟，EU），成员国有 27 个：法国、德国、意大利、荷兰、比利时、卢森堡、丹麦、爱尔兰、希腊、西班牙、葡萄牙、奥地利、芬兰、瑞典、塞浦路斯、捷克、爱沙尼亚、匈牙利、拉脱维亚、立陶宛、马耳他、波兰、斯洛伐克、斯洛文尼亚、保加利亚、罗马尼亚和克罗地亚。

欧洲货币联盟（欧元区，Euro Area），成员国有 20 个：德国、比利时、奥地利、荷兰、法国、意大利、西班牙、葡萄牙、卢森堡、爱尔兰、芬兰、希腊、斯洛文尼亚、塞浦路斯、马耳他、斯洛伐克、爱沙尼亚、拉脱维亚、立陶宛和克罗地亚。

东南亚国家联盟（东盟，ASEAN），成员国有 10 个：菲律宾、马来西亚、泰国、新加坡、印度尼西亚、文莱（1984 年）、越南（1995 年）、缅甸（1997 年）、老挝（1997 年）和柬埔寨（1999 年）。

北美自由贸易区（NAFTA）：成立于 1994 年 1 月 1 日，成员国有 3 个，加拿大、墨西哥和美国。

西方七国（G7）：包括美国、日本、英国、德国、法国、意大利和加拿大。

四、一些国家(含地区)分类含义：

按收入分组国家：按照世界银行 2021 年分组标准，高收入国家指按图表集法计算的人均国民总收入 13205 美元及以上的国家，中等偏上收入国家指人均国民总收入 4256 美元至 13205 美元的国家，中等偏下收入国家指人均国民总收入 1086 美元至 4255 美元的国家，低收入国家指人均国民总收入 1085 美元及以下的国家。

发达国家或地区与发展中国家或地区：联合国统计司对“发达国家或地区”及“发展中国家或地区”没有一个明确的划分标准。通常是把亚洲的日本、塞浦路斯和以色列，北美的加拿大、美国、百慕大、格陵兰、圣皮埃尔和密克隆，大洋洲的澳大利亚、新西兰、赫德岛和麦克唐纳岛、诺福克岛、科科斯（基林）群岛、圣诞岛，欧洲，都列入发达国家或地区。国际货币基金组织指出“发达经济体”包括 40 个国家或地区，他们是：安道尔、澳大利亚、奥地利、比利时、加拿大、塞浦路斯、捷克、丹麦、爱沙尼亚、芬兰、法国、德国、希腊、中国香港、冰岛、爱尔兰、以色列、意大利、日本、韩国、拉脱维亚、立陶宛、卢森堡、中国澳门、马耳他、荷兰、新西兰、挪威、葡萄牙、波多黎各、圣马力诺、新加坡、斯洛伐克、斯洛文尼亚、西班牙、瑞典、瑞士、中国台湾、英国及美国。其他为新兴市场及发展中经济体。

五、2023 年各省市资料均为快速年报数。

六、本篇资料由广东省统计局综合统计处负责整理、编辑。

Appendix

Brief Introduction

I. The data in this chapter include main social and economic indicators of some provinces and municipalities,main statistical indicators of Hong Kong and Macao Special Administrative Regions and Taiwan Province of the People’s Republic of China, as well as main international statistical indicators.

II. Data in Appendices A, B, C come from China Statistical Abstract compiled by National Bureau of Statistics and published by China Statistics Press. Data in Appendix D come from International Statistical Yearbook compiled by National Bureau of Statistics and published by China Statistics Press.

III. International organizations and their members included are as follows:

Organization for Economic Co-operation and Development (OECD), has 38 members, i.e., Australia，Austria，Belgium， Canada, Chile，Czech Republic，Denmark，Estonia，Finland，France，Germany，Greece，Hungary，Iceland，Ireland，Israel， Italy，Japan，Korea，Latvia，Lithuania，Luxembourg，Mexico，Netherlands，New Zealand，Norway，Poland，Portugal，Slovak Republic，Slovenia，Spain，Sweden，Switzerland，Turkey，United Kingdom，United States，Columbia，Costa Rica.

European Union (EU), it expanded to 27 members, i.e., France, Germany, Italy, Netherlands, Belgium, Luxembourg, Denmark, Ireland, Greece, Spain, Portugal, Austria, Finland, Sweden, Cyprus, the Czech Republic, Estonia, Hungary, Latvia, Lithuania, Malta, Poland, Slovakia , Slovenia, Bulgaria, Romania and Croatia.

European Monetary Union (Euro Area), it has 20 members and member countries are Germany, Belgium, Austria, Netherlands, France, Italy, Spain, Portugal, Luxembourg, Ireland, Finland, Greece, Slovenia, Cyprus, Malta, Slovak, Estonia, Latvia, Lithuania and Croatia.

Association of South East Asian Countries (ASEAN), it has 10 members, i.e., the Philippines, Malaysia, Thailand, Singapore, Indonesia, Brunei Darussalam (1984), Viet Nam (1995), Myanmar (1997), Lao People's Democratic Republic (1997) and Cambodia (1999).

North American Free Trade Area(NAFTA), was founded on January 1, 1994, with members unchanged hitherto, i.e., Canada, Mexico and the United States.

Group 7, includes the United States, Japan, the United Kingdom, Germany, France, Italy and Canada.

IV. Countries (territories) are classified as follows:

Countries by Income Group According to the criteria by the World Bank, countries and territories (referred to as economies) are classified into high income (higher than $13205), higher middle income (between $4256 and $13205), lower middle income (between $1086 and $4255) and low income ($1085 and below) groups by their per capita GNI (calculated by Atlas method)in the year 2021.

Developed and Developing Countries or Areas: There is no established convention for the designation of "developed" and "developing" countries or areas in the United Nations system. In common practice, Japan, Cyprus, Israelin Asia, Canada, the United States, Bermuda, Greenland, Saint Pierre and Miquelon in northern America, Australia, New Zealand, Heard Island and McDonald Islands, Norfolk Island, Cocos (Keeling) Islands, Christmas Island in Oceania, and Europe are considered "developed" regions or areas. Advanced economies in International Monetary Fund (IMF) are composed of 40 countries: Andorra,Australia, Austria, Belgium, Canada, Cyprus, Czech Republic, Denmark, Estonia, Finland, France, Germany, Greece, Hong Kong SAR, Iceland, Ireland, Israel, Italy, Japan, Korea, Latvia, Lithuania, Luxembourg, Macao SAR, Malta, Netherlands, New Zealand, Norway, Portugal, Puerto Rico, San Marino, Singapore, Slovak Republic, Slovenia, Spain, Sweden, Switzerland, Taiwan Province of China, United Kingdom, and United States. Others are emerging market and developing economies.

V. The data of various provinces and municipalities in 2023 all come from flash annual reports.

VI. The data in this chapter are prepared and compiled by the Division of Comprehensive Statistics of Guangdong Provincial Bureau of Statistics.

附录A-1 人口及地区生产总值（2023年）

Population and Gross Domestic Product (2023)

地 区	Province or Municipality	年末常住人口(万人) Year-end Permanent Population (10000 persons)	年末城镇人口比重(%) Proportion of Urban Population (%)	地区生产总值(亿元) Gross Domestic Product (100 million yuan)	第一产业 Primary Industry	第二产业 Secondary Industry	第三产业 Tertiary Industry	地区生产总值比上年增长(%) Increase by (%)	人均地区生产总值(元) Per Capita GDP (yuan)	人均地区生产总值比上年增长(%) Increase by(%)
全 国	**National Total**	**140967**	**66.16**	**1260582.1**	**89755.2**	**482588.5**	**688238.4**	**5.2**	**89358**	**5.4**
北 京	Beijing	2186	87.83	43760.7	105.5	6525.6	37129.6	5.2	200278	5.2
天 津	Tianjing	1364	85.49	16737.3	268.5	5982.6	10486.2	4.3	122752	4.6
河 北	Hebei	7393	62.77	43944.1	4466.2	16435.3	23042.6	5.5	59332	5.8
山 西	Shanxi	3466	64.97	25698.2	1388.9	13329.7	10979.6	5.0	73984	5.2
内蒙古	Nei Monggol	2396	69.58	24627.0	2737.3	11703.6	10186.1	7.3	102677	7.4
辽 宁	Liaoning	4182	73.51	30209.4	2651.0	11734.5	15823.9	5.3	72107	5.9
吉 林	Jilin	2339	64.73	13531.2	1644.8	4585.0	7301.4	6.3	57739	7.1
黑龙江	Heilongjiang	3062	67.11	15883.9	3518.3	4291.3	8074.3	2.6	51563	3.6
上 海	ShangHai	2487	89.46	47218.7	96.1	11613.0	35509.6	5.0	190321	5.0
江 苏	Jiangsu	8526	75.04	128222.2	5075.8	56909.7	66236.7	5.8	150487	5.6
浙 江	Zhejiang	6627	74.23	82553.2	2332.0	33952.7	46268.6	6.0	125043	5.3
安 徽	Anhui	6121	61.51	47050.6	3496.6	18871.8	24682.2	5.8	76830	5.7
福 建	Fujian	4183	71.04	54355.1	3217.7	23966.4	27171.0	4.5	129865	4.5
江 西	Jiangxi	4515	63.13	32200.1	2450.4	13706.5	16043.2	4.1	71216	4.1
山 东	Shandong	10123	65.53	92068.7	6506.2	35987.9	49574.6	6.0	90771	6.2
河 南	Henan	9815	58.08	59132.4	5360.1	22175.3	31597.0	4.1	60073	4.4
湖 北	Hubei	5838	65.47	55803.6	5073.4	20215.5	30514.7	6.0	95538	5.9
湖 南	Hunan	6568	61.16	50012.9	4621.3	18822.8	26568.8	4.6	75938	5.0
广 东	Guangdong	12706	75.42	135673.2	5540.7	54437.3	75695.2	4.8	106985	4.7
广 西	Guangxi	5027	56.78	27202.4	4468.2	8924.1	13810.1	4.1	54005	4.2
海 南	Hainan	1043	62.46	7551.2	1507.4	1448.5	4595.3	9.2	72958	8.0
重 庆	Chongqing	3191	71.67	30145.8	2074.7	11699.1	16372.0	6.1	94147	6.4
四 川	Sichuan	8368	59.49	60132.9	6056.6	21306.7	32769.5	6.0	71835	6.0
贵 州	Guizhou	3865	55.94	20913.3	2894.3	7311.4	10707.5	4.9	54172	4.7
云 南	Yunnan	4673	52.92	30021.1	4206.6	10256.3	15558.2	4.4	64107	4.6
西 藏	Tibet	365	38.88	2392.7	215.0	883.0	1294.7	9.5	65642	9.7
陕 西	Shaanxi	3952	65.16	33786.1	2649.8	16068.9	15067.4	4.3	85448	4.3
甘 肃	Gansu	2465	55.49	11863.8	1641.3	4080.8	6141.8	6.4	47867	6.9
青 海	Qinghai	594	62.80	3799.1	387.0	1612.8	1799.2	5.3	63903	5.3
宁 夏	Ningxia	729	67.31	5315.0	428.1	2487.2	2399.6	6.6	72957	6.3
新 疆	Xinjiang	2598	59.24	19125.9	2742.2	7710.3	8673.4	6.8	73774	6.6

注：地区生产总值为初步核算数。
Note: GDP is the preliminary calculated number.

附录A−2 固定资产投资完成情况（2023年）

Investment in Fixed Assets (2023)

地 区	Province or Municipality	固定资产投资增速（不含农户）(%) Investment in Fixed Assets (excluding farmers) (%)	房地产开发投资额（亿元）Real Estate Development (100 million yuan)	商品房销售额（亿元）Total Sales of Commercial Housing (100 million yuan)	#住宅 Residential Buildings	房屋竣工面积（万平方米）Completion of Commercial Housing Area (10000 sq.m)	商品房销售面积（万平方米）Floor Space of Commercial Buildings Sold (10000 sq.m)
全 国	**National Total**	**3.0**	**110912.9**	**116622.2**	**102989.6**	**99831**	**111735**
北 京	Beijing	4.9	4195.7	4233.2	3809.3	2042	1123
天 津	Tianjing	-16.4	1231.5	1893.4	1810.2	1814	1177
河 北	Hebei	6.3	3093.5	3538.6	3374.1	3421	4323
山 西	Shanxi	-6.6	1751.5	1588.2	1505.1	2345	2353
内蒙古	Nei Monggol	19.8	963.4	993.1	902.8	1217	1512
辽 宁	Liaoning	4.0	1744.7	1557.0	1404.8	2242	2071
吉 林	Jilin	0.3	823.8	730.2	671.9	671	1057
黑龙江	Heilongjiang	-14.8	457.0	554.4	488.5	829	858
上 海	ShangHai	13.8	5885.8	7260.0	6685.2	2096	1808
江 苏	Jiangsu	5.2	11891.3	12682.1	11269.7	8817	11019
浙 江	Zhejiang	6.1	13197.9	11503.8	10147.4	9934	6106
安 徽	Anhui	4.0	4659.4	3872.8	3563.8	5634	4678
福 建	Fujian	2.5	4403.4	4656.7	3811.3	4265	4225
江 西	Jiangxi	-5.9	1580.7	2482.4	2100.7	1935	3433
山 东	Shandong	5.2	8168.9	9541.5	8174.2	8862	11287
河 南	Henan	2.1	4189.4	4546.5	4209.8	6044	6965
湖 北	Hubei	5.0	5409.0	4619.5	3970.5	3779	5265
湖 南	Hunan	-3.1	3833.1	3700.1	3299.7	4274	5637
广 东	Guangdong	2.5	13465.9	15135.5	13005.5	8017	9622
广 西	Guangxi	-15.5	1337.0	1685.6	1438.5	2615	2917
海 南	Hainan	1.1	1170.7	1493.8	1290.3	741	900
重 庆	Chongqing	4.3	2792.4	2475.0	1953.3	3257	3572
四 川	Sichuan	2.4	5320.6	7170.2	6286.1	4118	8006
贵 州	Guizhou	-5.7	1188.3	1251.7	1123.6	1579	2215
云 南	Yunnan	-10.6	2066.6	1702.2	1486.1	3195	2491
西 藏	Tibet	35.1	79.2	66.8	55.4	67	80
陕 西	Shanxi	0.2	2943.3	2973.5	2721.1	2172	2711
甘 肃	Gansu	5.9	1263.1	900.8	845.7	1241	1497
青 海	Qinghai	-7.5	201.4	166.5	154.4	270	236
宁 夏	Ningxia	5.5	436.1	479.4	441.0	1039	690
新 疆	Xinjiang	12.4	1168.5	1167.5	989.7	1298	1903

注：各地固定资产投资不含跨省投资。

Note: Trans-provincial investments are not included in the investment in fixed assets of various province.

附录A-3 居民人均收入与支出(2023年)
Per Capita Income and Expenditure (2023)

单位：元 (yuan)

地区	Province or Municipality	全体居民 All residents		城镇居民 Urban resident		农村居民 Rural resident	
		人均可支配收入 Per Capita Disposable Income	人均消费支出 Per Capita Consumption Expenditure	人均可支配收入 Per Capita Disposable Income	人均消费支出 Per Capita Consumption Expenditure	人均可支配收入 Per Capita Disposable Income	人均消费支出 Per Capita Consumption Expenditure
全国	**National Total**	**39218**	**26796**	**51821**	**32994**	**21691**	**18175**
北京	Beijing	81752	47586	88650	50897	37358	26277
天津	Tianjing	51271	34914	55355	37586	30851	21553
河北	Hebei	32903	22920	43631	27906	20688	17244
山西	Shanxi	30924	19756	41327	24524	17677	13684
内蒙古	Nei Monggol	38130	27025	48676	32249	21221	18650
辽宁	Liaoning	37992	24865	45896	29091	21483	16040
吉林	Jilin	29797	21411	37503	26677	19472	14354
黑龙江	Heilongjiang	29694	22052	36492	25882	19756	16453
上海	ShangHai	84834	52508	89477	54919	42988	30782
江苏	Jiangsu	52674	35491	63211	40461	30488	25029
浙江	Zhejiang	63830	42194	74997	47762	40311	30468
安徽	Anhui	34893	23607	47446	27900	21144	18905
福建	Fujian	45426	31869	56153	37674	26722	21746
江西	Jiangxi	34242	23379	45554	27733	21358	18421
山东	Shandong	39890	24293	51571	30251	23776	16075
河南	Henan	29933	21011	40234	25570	20053	16638
湖北	Hubei	35146	27106	44990	31500	21293	20922
湖南	Hunan	35895	25462	49243	31035	20921	19210
广东	Guangdong	49327	34331	59307	39333	25142	22209
广西	Guangxi	29514	19749	41287	24427	18656	15435
海南	Hainan	33192	23752	42661	28930	20708	16924
重庆	Chongqing	37595	26515	47435	31531	20820	17964
四川	Sichuan	32514	23550	45227	29280	19978	17901
贵州	Guizhou	27098	20161	42772	27693	14817	14260
云南	Yunnan	28421	20995	43563	28338	16361	15147
西藏	Tibet	28983	17220	51900	28858	19924	12619
陕西	Shaanxi	32128	22012	44713	27303	16992	15647
甘肃	Gansu	25011	19013	39833	27044	13131	12575
青海	Qinghai	28587	20327	40408	25373	15614	14790
宁夏	Ningxia	31604	21629	42395	27076	17772	14649
新疆	Xinjiang	28947	19715	40578	26134	17948	13645

附录A-4 居民消费价格指数（2023年）

Consumer Price Indices (2023)

上年=100 (Preceding Year=100)

地 区	Province or Municipality	居民消费价格指数 Consumer Price Index	食品烟酒 Foods, Tobacco and Liquor	衣着 Clothing	居住 Residence	生活用品及服务 Daily Necessities and Services	交通通信 Transportation and Communication	教育文化和娱乐 Education, Culture and Recreation	医疗保健 Health Care	其他用品和服务 Other Articles and Services
全 国	**National Total**	**100.2**	**100.3**	**101.0**	**100.0**	**100.1**	**97.7**	**102.0**	**101.1**	**103.2**
北 京	Beijing	100.4	100.1	100.6	100.3	100.3	98.3	102.8	100.2	104.2
天 津	Tianjing	100.4	100.5	101.0	100.5	100.0	97.2	103.1	100.4	103.6
河 北	Hebei	100.6	100.5	102.3	100.3	100.6	97.6	101.5	103.2	103.2
山 西	Shanxi	99.9	99.8	100.3	100.0	100.3	98.0	100.4	100.9	102.4
内蒙古	Nei Monggol	100.6	100.6	101.2	100.1	100.5	98.0	101.5	103.3	103.5
辽 宁	Liaoning	100.1	100.1	100.5	100.4	100.2	98.1	101.0	100.1	103.1
吉 林	Jilin	99.9	99.3	100.1	100.0	100.2	97.8	101.4	100.7	103.4
黑龙江	Heilongjiang	100.6	100.6	101.7	100.1	100.3	98.1	101.6	102.5	102.8
上 海	ShangHai	100.3	98.8	102.0	100.2	100.4	99.1	103.6	100.2	104.8
江 苏	Jiangsu	100.4	101.0	101.4	100.0	100.6	96.7	101.8	103.2	103.9
浙 江	Zhejiang	100.3	100.6	101.0	99.6	100.4	97.9	102.8	101.0	103.6
安 徽	Anhui	100.2	100.5	101.6	99.7	100.1	97.5	102.0	100.7	103.2
福 建	Fujian	100.0	100.9	100.0	99.8	99.9	96.7	101.6	100.7	103.1
江 西	Jiangxi	100.3	100.4	101.9	100.1	99.8	97.5	102.3	100.7	103.3
山 东	Shandong	100.1	100.3	100.6	100.1	100.0	97.7	102.0	100.2	103.7
河 南	Henan	99.8	99.6	99.8	99.6	99.6	97.9	101.4	100.9	103.2
湖 北	Hubei	100.1	99.9	101.3	100.4	100.2	97.5	101.8	100.5	102.9
湖 南	Hunan	100.2	99.4	101.0	100.4	100.1	98.0	101.6	102.0	103.0
广 东	Guangdong	100.4	101.4	101.8	99.5	99.9	97.7	102.7	100.4	102.3
广 西	Guangxi	99.8	100.0	102.1	99.1	99.0	96.9	101.8	101.5	102.1
海 南	Hainan	100.3	101.3	99.8	99.4	100.2	98.5	101.8	99.8	102.0
重 庆	Chongqing	99.7	98.6	101.0	100.2	99.8	98.8	101.3	100.2	102.4
四 川	Sichuan	100.0	99.8	99.0	100.4	100.0	97.9	102.5	100.6	102.6
贵 州	Guizhou	99.7	99.8	102.0	99.8	100.0	97.3	100.4	100.0	101.9
云 南	Yunnan	100.3	100.9	100.5	100.3	100.2	97.2	102.2	100.7	103.0
西 藏	Tibet	99.9	99.9	100.1	100.2	100.0	98.1	100.6	101.0	103.7
陕 西	Shaanxi	100.1	99.8	100.4	100.4	99.7	97.9	101.0	101.4	103.8
甘 肃	Gansu	100.5	100.3	100.2	99.6	100.0	99.2	101.6	103.5	103.2
青 海	Qinghai	100.5	99.4	100.5	100.1	100.1	99.2	104.2	102.1	103.5
宁 夏	Ningxia	100.4	100.3	100.5	100.6	99.8	98.5	101.7	100.8	104.6
新 疆	Xinjiang	100.0	99.6	102.5	100.0	99.4	98.0	101.0	100.3	104.4

附录A−5 农林牧渔业总产值和增速（2023年）

Gross Output Value of Farming,Forestry,Animal Husbandry and Fishery and Growth Rate (2023)

地 区	Province or Municipality	农林牧渔业总产值（亿元）Gross Output Value of Farming, Forestry, Animal Husbandry and Fishery (100 million yuan)	#农业 Farming	#林业 Forestry	#畜牧业 Animal Husbandry	#渔业 Fishery	农林牧渔业总产值比上年增长(%) Growth Rate in Gross Output Value of Farming, Forestry ,Animal Husbandry and Fishery (%)
全 国	**National Total**	**158507.2**	**87073.4**	**7006.1**	**38964.6**	**16116.2**	**4.2**
北 京	Beijing	252.6	135.6	65.9	42.0	4.0	-4.6
天 津	Tianjing	511.3	269.4	6.0	145.5	71.9	1.3
河 北	Hebei	7770.9	4081.0	259.1	2395.0	351.2	3.0
山 西	Shanxi	2291.7	1332.7	177.4	642.8	9.6	4.0
内蒙古	Nei Monggol	4447.3	2288.0	116.9	1898.7	32.2	5.5
辽 宁	Liaoning	5266.8	2284.5	144.6	1691.5	957.0	4.7
吉 林	Jilin	3128.0	1494.5	70.1	1402.2	65.4	5.0
黑龙江	Heilongjiang	6492.5	4200.4	208.0	1722.9	155.1	2.6
上 海	ShangHai	269.6	145.2	7.2	47.0	52.7	-0.7
江 苏	Jiangsu	8935.5	4844.1	188.4	1230.1	1903.2	3.9
浙 江	Zhejiang	3978.0	1871.9	198.3	393.2	1375.3	4.2
安 徽	Anhui	6247.9	2906.3	479.9	1746.3	689.5	4.4
福 建	Fujian	5729.2	2193.5	454.8	1083.4	1789.6	4.3
江 西	Jiangxi	4198.9	2003.4	399.8	978.3	554.1	4.2
山 东	Shandong	12531.9	6462.4	244.5	2973.7	1807.6	5.1
河 南	Henan	10304.6	6471.2	162.2	2596.0	141.5	2.2
湖 北	Hubei	9106.9	4428.8	356.3	1934.3	1602.0	4.4
湖 南	Hunan	8199.4	4141.5	513.7	2232.1	635.0	3.7
广 东	Guangdong	9202.1	4431.0	562.7	1696.8	2005.3	5.1
广 西	Guangxi	7229.3	4253.5	543.7	1505.3	583.0	4.7
海 南	Hainan	2410.3	1319.7	111.4	334.2	523.0	4.8
重 庆	Chongqing	3154.3	1978.0	188.1	766.6	142.9	4.5
四 川	Sichuan	9977.8	5821.7	481.8	3035.6	359.1	4.0
贵 州	Guizhou	4953.6	3360.3	358.5	907.9	81.2	4.0
云 南	Yunnan	6834.5	4041.8	485.2	1969.3	125.4	4.3
西 藏	Tibet	320.1	132.6	9.5	170.0	0.3	13.1
陕 西	Shaanxi	4724.9	3468.1	96.4	864.4	36.7	4.0
甘 肃	Gansu	2927.7	2001.6	37.3	700.1	1.8	6.1
青 海	Qinghai	575.6	259.3	12.6	290.9	4.3	4.7
宁 夏	Ningxia	885.7	459.5	10.6	358.0	22.8	7.6
新 疆	Xinjiang	5648.3	3991.4	55.6	1210.6	33.6	6.5

注：本表绝对数按当年价格计算，增速按可比价格计算。
Note: the figures in this table are calculated at current prices, the growth rate is calculated at comparable prices.

附录A-6 主要农产品产量（2023年）

Output of Major Agricultural Products (2023)

单位：万吨 (10000 tons)

地 区	Province or Municipality	粮食 Grain	油料 Oil-bearing	糖料 Sugarcane	肉类 Meat	蔬菜 Vegetable	水果 Fruits
全 国	**National Total**	**69541.0**	**3863.7**	**11376.3**	**9748.2**	**82868.1**	**32744.3**
北 京	Beijing	47.8	1.0		4.2	207.5	41.8
天 津	Tianjing	255.7	0.4	…	31.5	253.7	42.3
河 北	Hebei	3809.9	118.3	65.5	495.0	5498.0	1563.2
山 西	Shanxi	1478.1	17.9	0.1	155.0	1065.9	1082.8
内蒙古	Nei Monggol	3957.8	206.2	305.4	291.2	1097.1	213.3
辽 宁	Liaoning	2563.4	128.1	0.9	473.7	2139.7	928.2
吉 林	Jilin	4186.5	88.4	1.6	309.4	540.0	157.2
黑龙江	Heilongjiang	7788.2	16.5	24.6	328.5	870.5	188.9
上 海	ShangHai	101.9	0.6	0.1	12.2	254.8	31.7
江 苏	Jiangsu	3797.7	103.4	5.3	331.7	6135.6	1015.2
浙 江	Zhejiang	638.8	35.6	37.7	119.9	1992.5	733.4
安 徽	Anhui	4150.8	189.0	8.8	497.1	2630.1	828.8
福 建	Fujian	511.0	24.4	28.5	311.4	1804.8	914.3
江 西	Jiangxi	2198.3	148.1	61.4	369.1	1860.9	799.0
山 东	Shandong	5655.3	280.7	…	910.1	9272.4	3208.2
河 南	Henan	6624.3	703.0	8.0	679.1	8045.6	2561.6
湖 北	Hubei	2777.0	394.9	26.5	457.9	4502.7	1191.5
湖 南	Hunan	3068.0	293.1	35.0	582.6	4488.8	1266.1
广 东	Guangdong	1285.2	121.0	1271.1	507.5	4099.3	2127.8
广 西	Guangxi	1395.4	80.8	7223.2	478.9	4425.0	3553.2
海 南	Hainan	147.0	7.9	86.5	76.4	632.9	592.6
重 庆	Chongqing	1095.9	77.5	8.4	215.8	2362.0	645.9
四 川	Sichuan	3593.8	438.6	39.3	697.1	5417.9	1490.4
贵 州	Guizhou	1119.7	111.0	34.7	246.9	3470.0	756.7
云 南	Yunnan	1974.0	68.5	1586.9	536.1	2960.8	1380.9
西 藏	Tibet	108.9	5.0	…	31.3	88.4	3.1
陕 西	Shaanxi	1323.7	60.6	0.3	135.7	2151.2	2335.5
甘 肃	Gansu	1272.9	63.1	16.9	157.4	1822.6	1044.0
青 海	Qinghai	116.2	32.1		41.4	158.5	2.5
宁 夏	Ningxia	378.8	4.6	…	41.4	544.5	310.5
新 疆	Xinjiang	2119.2	43.2	499.9	222.6	2074.2	1733.8

注：水果产量含瓜果产量。
Note:The output of fruits includes melons in this table.

附录A−7　规模以上工业企业主要经济指标（2023年）

Main Economic Indicators of Industrial Enterprises above Designated Size (2023)

单位：亿元　　　　(100 million yuan)

地　区	Province or Municipality	营业收入 Business Revenue	营业成本 Business Cost	利润总额 Total Profit	应收账款 Accounts Receivable	产成品存货 Finished Goods Inventory	资产总计 Total Assets
全　国	**National Total**	**1334390.8**	**1130986.0**	**76858.3**	**237155.1**	**61425.9**	**1673576.9**
北　京	Beijing	27807.9	23453.0	1692.3	6744.4	1339.1	70966.8
天　津	Tianjing	24004.7	20494.7	1443.7	3775.7	933.7	26175.0
河　北	Hebei	51584.8	46254.8	1166.0	7938.7	2008.0	63540.0
山　西	Shanxi	34873.8	28865.9	2823.7	6573.0	1281.8	60004.6
内蒙古	Nei Monggol	28466.0	22632.9	3020.2	3626.7	924.3	46634.2
辽　宁	Liaoning	35677.3	30675.0	1500.9	5327.2	1650.7	44009.7
吉　林	Jilin	14019.0	11975.5	809.1	2039.4	594.3	20150.4
黑龙江	Heilongjiang	11861.0	9918.4	396.2	1823.6	596.6	19756.2
上　海	ShangHai	44960.4	37183.6	2497.8	9654.4	2004.4	56468.5
江　苏	Jiangsu	168354.6	143548.6	9344.4	38440.6	9370.7	186712.1
浙　江	Zhejiang	110954.9	94350.2	5905.6	22946.8	6412.2	137728.0
安　徽	Anhui	50875.0	43969.5	2418.4	10768.8	2267.3	62404.2
福　建	Fujian	56505.5	48987.7	3429.3	6747.6	2301.8	53522.6
江　西	Jiangxi	40922.2	36231.2	2068.0	5676.9	1509.2	36111.4
山　东	Shandong	113496.2	98484.6	5586.1	16029.3	5558.3	128440.2
河　南	Henan	46451.7	41096.5	1764.7	8159.8	1830.2	55334.1
湖　北	Hubei	45935.9	39070.7	2344.8	7015.1	1929.2	56380.8
湖　南	Hunan	39277.8	32271.9	2052.1	5570.3	1329.3	38578.5
广　东	Guangdong	185803.6	155020.6	10575.2	35623.6	8850.9	210715.1
广　西	Guangxi	23275.4	20813.5	706.9	4049.0	1219.9	28584.0
海　南	Hainan	3532.8	2907.1	187.5	490.4	120.6	5223.4
重　庆	Chongqing	26821.8	23147.5	1371.6	4491.9	985.5	27778.7
四　川	Sichuan	49344.7	40136.1	4506.1	8180.5	2161.9	69848.8
贵　州	Guizhou	10085.6	7692.0	1072.7	1928.4	483.3	20252.1
云　南	Yunnan	19568.0	15661.9	1501.9	2220.2	981.3	29151.4
西　藏	Tibet	554.9	409.8	51.3	92.8	19.2	2499.5
陕　西	Shaanxi	28599.6	22024.3	3523.3	4772.6	1122.5	46055.9
甘　肃	Gansu	11122.3	9513.8	514.0	1595.8	413.8	16321.3
青　海	Qinghai	4200.3	3405.2	486.4	754.1	123.3	8402.3
宁　夏	Ningxia	7912.9	6798.2	377.4	1191.2	403.0	13741.4
新　疆	Xinjiang	17540.3	13991.1	1720.7	2906.3	699.7	32085.9

附录A–8 主要工业产品产量（2023年）

Output of Major Industrial Products (2023)

地 区	Province or Municipality	发电量（亿千瓦小时）Generating Capacity (billion kilowatt hours)	生 铁（万吨）Pig Iron (ten thousand tons)	钢 材（万吨）Steels (ten thousand tons)	水 泥（万吨）Cement (ten thousand tons)	农用化肥（万吨）Agricultural Chemical Fertilizer (ten thousand tons)	汽 车（万辆）Car (10000 vehicles)	家用电冰箱（万台）Household Refrigerators (10000 sets)	微型计算机设备（万台）Micro-computers Equipment (10000 units)
全 国	**National Total**	**94564.4**	**87101.3**	**136268.2**	**202293.0**	**5713.6**	**3011.3**	**9632.3**	**33056.9**
北 京	Beijing	471.6		183.7	200.0		100.3		615.8
天 津	Tianjin	837.5	1895.3	5991.9	484.0	61.0	89.5		
河 北	Hebei	4125.9	19530.7	29792.6	9982.0	232.6	84.1		
山 西	Shanxi	4572.8	6015.3	6876.6	4660.6	425.9	10.6		19.5
内蒙古	Nei Monggol	7629.9	2347.9	3385.8	3729.6	466.7	10.6		
辽 宁	Liaoning	2362.9	6948.9	7848.4	3814.0	38.1	94.3	179.2	
吉 林	Jilin	1158.7	1359.9	1588.2	2032.1	19.0	155.9		
黑龙江	Heilongjiang	1327.4	865.7	933.3	1944.7	82.8	9.0		1.0
上 海	ShangHai	1006.6	1460.4	1917.2	441.7	0.8	215.6		1900.9
江 苏	Jiangsu	6390.5	9762.2	16193.9	14280.3	187.1	165.0	1426.7	2762.2
浙 江	Zhejiang	4580.7	873.6	3155.8	12710.8	33.4	152.6	517.5	140.0
安 徽	Anhui	3549.4	3111.2	4164.9	13251.7	215.4	208.8	2946.5	2125.8
福 建	Fujian	3302.5	1486.1	3956.8	8038.7	23.2	33.2		466.1
江 西	Jiangxi	1852.6	2446.7	3646.3	8341.1	91.7	48.0	77.5	2370.8
山 东	Shandong	6508.1	7293.9	10858.5	12894.3	465.8	197.4	962.8	0.6
河 南	Henan	3534.6	2819.1	3400.2	9553.9	432.3	78.3	61.2	165.5
湖 北	Hubei	3206.0	2863.8	3848.6	9892.7	670.9	179.0	612.4	1347.2
湖 南	Hunan	1797.5	2180.8	2890.8	8285.9	58.0	44.7		141.7
广 东	Guangdong	7010.3	2437.6	6319.1	14322.3	10.7	519.2	2169.0	7335.0
广 西	Guangxi	2382.9	3402.1	5200.5	9998.8	27.4	97.5	205.9	173.4
海 南	Hainan	478.9			1545.4	65.5	3.0		
重 庆	Chongqing	1120.2	651.6	2072.2	5477.8	184.2	231.8	150.3	7400.5
四 川	Sichuan	5006.5	1983.6	4045.9	12151.6	316.5	97.5	140.0	5337.8
贵 州	Guizhou	2368.8	390.6	579.9	5883.4	243.6	4.8	161.4	2.8
云 南	Yunnan	4151.0	1472.1	2459.0	9610.5	250.6	1.8		743.7
西 藏	Tibet	163.0			1198.4				
陕 西	Shaanxi	3103.8	1182.8	1629.4	5768.4	155.8	147.0	21.6	2.9
甘 肃	Gansu	2109.0	814.7	1179.4	4125.5	21.0			
青 海	Qinghai	1009.7	67.1	69.7	1192.2	476.8			
宁 夏	Ningxia	2314.3	326.4	582.2	1670.0	73.9			
新 疆	Xinjiang	5130.7	1111.4	1497.3	4810.5	382.6	1.9	0.2	3.6

附录A-9 建筑业主要指标（2023年）
Indicators of Construction Industry (2023)

地 区	Province or Municipality	企业个数（个）Number of Enterprises (unit)	从事建筑业活动的从业人员平均人数（万人）Number of Employed Persons of Construction Enterprises (10000 persons)	建筑业总产值（亿元）Gross Output Value of Construction Enterprises (100 million yuan)	房屋建筑施工面积（万平方米）Construction Area of Housing Construction (10000 square meters)	房屋建筑竣工面积（万平方米）Completion Area of Housing Construction (10000 square meters)	按建筑业总产值计算的劳动生产率（元/人）Labor Productivity Calculated by Gross Output Value of Construction Industry (yuan/person)
全 国	**National Total**	**157929**	**6795.3**	**315911.9**	**1513425.6**	**385587.9**	**464899**
北 京	Beijing	2701	229.3	14272.5	104439.0	13767.0	622369
天 津	Tianjing	3351	77.8	5072.3	17763.4	3754.9	651770
河 北	Hebei	4126	136.4	7261.3	33436.5	7800.0	532247
山 西	Shanxi	3800	134.5	6147.1	22173.4	4205.7	457106
内蒙古	Nei Monggol	1105	29.8	1459.5	6667.9	1271.6	490057
辽 宁	Liaoning	5880	67.9	4326.6	11583.1	3399.3	637236
吉 林	Jilin	2610	43.1	2219.9	5637.8	2052.7	514767
黑龙江	Heilongjiang	2056	38.5	1426.0	3310.1	1216.7	370529
上 海	ShangHai	2429	145.8	10045.8	56244.5	9707.7	688888
江 苏	Jiangsu	14761	1125.7	43140.2	258944.7	73189.8	383245
浙 江	Zhejiang	10854	604.0	24593.5	165952.2	46267.0	407193
安 徽	Anhui	8873	253.1	12466.8	59769.3	15465.6	492507
福 建	Fujian	9269	537.0	17383.4	96623.9	19447.0	323728
江 西	Jiangxi	6877	253.4	10827.8	35467.7	12584.4	427345
山 东	Shandong	12483	352.3	18686.6	97786.7	22676.8	530468
河 南	Henan	10049	281.3	11476.8	59861.0	12653.3	408043
湖 北	Hubei	6888	299.4	21348.2	79153.4	26825.1	713013
湖 南	Hunan	4207	309.0	15176.1	75122.3	25459.6	491169
广 东	Guangdong	11192	451.9	25195.3	103432.0	24153.4	557487
广 西	Guangxi	2853	125.6	5933.1	26725.7	5789.5	472488
海 南	Hainan	392	8.4	494.4	1846.7	1396.0	591615
重 庆	Chongqing	3966	232.0	9709.7	31839.5	11184.2	418542
四 川	Sichuan	9343	432.9	17401.5	62066.7	18265.5	401988
贵 州	Guizhou	2354	83.1	3939.0	14179.3	2452.2	473746
云 南	Yunnan	4612	171.5	7890.9	16324.1	5674.1	460097
西 藏	Tibet	497	5.1	228.9	330.0	241.6	450828
陕 西	Shaanxi	4330	205.5	10340.5	38932.8	7774.8	503140
甘 肃	Gansu	2725	54.4	2686.7	11073.0	2078.2	493772
青 海	Qinghai	620	11.0	614.1	962.9	225.1	558302
宁 夏	Ningxia	768	20.5	741.5	1652.4	678.9	362469
新 疆	Xinjiang	1958	75.2	3405.9	14124.1	3930.1	452815

注：本表为具有资质等级的施工总承包、专业承包建筑业企业(不含劳务分包建筑业企业)数据。

Note: Data in this table refer to construction enterprises with qualification grade of main contractor and professional contractors(not including labor subcontracting construction enterprises).

附录A-10 客运量和旅客周转量（2023年）

Passenger Traffic and Passenger-kilometers (2023)

地 区	Province or Municipality	客运量（万人）Passenger Traffic (10000 Persons)	#铁路 Railways	#公路 Highways	#水运 Waterways	旅客周转量（亿人公里）Passenger-kilometers (100 million kilometers)	#铁路 Railways	#公路 Highways	#水运 Waterways
全 国	**National Total**	**930442**	**385450**	**457264**	**25771**	**28609.7**	**14729.4**	**3517.6**	**53.8**
北 京	Beijing	40885	15165	25720		236.7	163.2	73.5	
天 津	Tianjing	13187	4969	8056	162	226.5	178.8	47.4	0.2
河 北	Hebei	20418	12388	8030		1080.4	1003.9	76.5	
山 西	Shanxi	12379	8514	3659	206	277.5	231.9	45.6	0.1
内蒙古	Nei Monggol	7538	5060	2478		216.5	184.2	32.3	
辽 宁	Liaoning	28002	11187	16285	530	643.5	553.2	86.6	3.8
吉 林	Jilin	14503	5933	8443	127	290.3	225.4	64.8	0.1
黑龙江	Heilongjiang	16265	8161	7872	232	282.5	229.6	52.6	0.3
上 海	ShangHai	19966	13007	6326	633	190.1	119.0	70.2	0.9
江 苏	Jiangsu	73556	31821	38904	2831	1311.0	1052.6	257.3	1.1
浙 江	Zhejiang	51460	26686	19680	5094	923.1	739.3	178.1	5.7
安 徽	Anhui	25898	15191	10484	223	998.7	883.7	114.6	0.3
福 建	Fujian	25584	12471	12024	1089	466.2	378.6	86.6	1.0
江 西	Jiangxi	24638	12702	11708	228	832.7	749.1	83.3	0.3
山 东	Shandong	35997	21003	12442	2552	981.4	810.9	162.1	8.4
河 南	Henan	59098	20224	38583	291	1496.2	1124.6	371.1	0.4
湖 北	Hubei	36512	17042	18753	718	867.3	743.2	120.1	3.9
湖 南	Hunan	46863	17552	27953	1358	1142.4	967.8	172.5	2.1
广 东	Guangdong	70296	36939	30583	2774	1275.8	1014.1	253.1	8.6
广 西	Guangxi	29826	12078	16854	893	636.2	467.5	165.1	3.6
海 南	Hainan	9626	3035	4307	2284	91.4	47.8	39.4	4.2
重 庆	Chongqing	27943	9538	17532	872	381.4	267.3	108.5	5.5
四 川	Sichuan	61012	21927	37977	1108	757.1	529.0	227.0	1.0
贵 州	Guizhou	25122	8067	16709	345	504.0	370.7	132.6	0.6
云 南	Yunnan	23178	9442	13121	616	429.0	294.5	133.5	1.0
西 藏	Tibet	1174	421	753		46.3	22.4	23.9	
陕 西	Shaanxi	24903	12057	12754	92	636.3	528.4	107.7	0.2
甘 肃	Gansu	15729	6200	9371	157	468.5	402.4	66.0	0.2
青 海	Qinghai	2601	1033	1439	129	117.9	86.9	30.8	0.1
宁 夏	Ningxia	3870	1053	2591	226	71.8	43.3	28.4	0.1
新 疆	Xinjiang	20453	4583	15871		422.4	316.2	106.2	
不分地区	Not Classified by Region	61958				10309.0			

注：不分地区合计为民航完成数。

Notes: The total passenger-kilometers not classified by region refers to that completed by civil aviation.

附录A−11 货运量和货物周转量(2023年)

Freight Traffic and Freight Ton_Kilometers (2023)

地 区	Province or Municipality	货运量 (万吨) Freight volume (10000 tons)	#铁路 Railways	#公路 Highways	#水运 Waterways	货物周转量 (亿吨公里) Turnover of goods (100 million tons)	#铁路 Railways	#公路 Highways	#水运 Waterways
全 国	**National Total**	**5570636**	**503535**	**4033681**	**936746**	**247745**	**36460**	**73950**	**129952**
北 京	Beijing	19707	308	19399		1063	806	257	
天 津	Tianjing	56073	11673	33742	10659	2786	567	690	1529
河 北	Hebei	253091	30124	217492	5475	14797	5437	8472	888
山 西	Shanxi	222753	101001	121751	1	6877	3494	3383	…
内蒙古	Nei Monggol	236621	90250	146372		5556	3196	2360	
辽 宁	Liaoning	179704	20073	153305	6325	4686	1197	2869	620
吉 林	Jilin	54410	5376	49034		2013	572	1441	
黑龙江	Heilongjiang	54458	12137	41619	701	1942	1012	891	39
上 海	ShangHai	153213	547	50436	102230	32790	22	895	31872
江 苏	Jiangsu	310363	9315	183485	117563	13232	369	3459	9404
浙 江	Zhejiang	344881	5565	222803	116512	15062	278	3142	11642
安 徽	Anhui	422888	8054	260939	153895	12097	834	3793	7471
福 建	Fujian	178749	5211	110497	63040	12231	215	1319	10697
江 西	Jiangxi	209403	5131	188006	16267	5348	598	4257	493
山 东	Shandong	346633	35842	285567	25224	15043	1869	7999	5175
河 南	Henan	283056	12521	251333	19202	12229	2696	8183	1349
湖 北	Hubei	248947	6159	173045	69743	8593	1172	2424	4997
湖 南	Hunan	228497	5091	200674	22732	3037	1015	1574	447
广 东	Guangdong	371033	12344	252809	105880	29304	371	2850	26083
广 西	Guangxi	228355	11503	172005	44846	5590	772	2000	2817
海 南	Hainan	35987	890	7774	27324	11713	13	45	11655
重 庆	Chongqing	141104	2518	117584	21001	3929	335	1127	2467
四 川	Sichuan	201400	8437	185814	7148	3434	1160	1984	291
贵 州	Guizhou	102678	6503	95909	266	1469	678	784	6
云 南	Yunnan	144427	6226	137540	661	2062	515	1539	8
西 藏	Tibet	5058	104	4954		162	36	125	
陕 西	Shaanxi	180282	46129	134102	51	4478	2548	1930	…
甘 肃	Gansu	79807	9905	69902		4246	2155	2091	
青 海	Qinghai	21605	3622	17983		803	594	210	
宁 夏	Ningxia	54996	9935	45061		947	281	665	
新 疆	Xinjiang	103783	21041	82742		2843	1654	1189	
不分地区	Not Classified by Region	96674				7383			

注：不分地区合计中包括民航、管道等完成数。货运量和货物周转量的全国总计等于分省数与不分地区数据之和。

Notes: The Freight Traffic and freight ton-kilometers not classified by region refer to pipelines ,civil aviation and that completed by companies abroad under the China Ocean Shipping (Group) Company.The Freight Traffic and freight ton-kilometers is equal to the sum of the provinces and the not classified by region .

附录A-12 国内外贸易（2023年）

Retail Trades and Foreign Trades (2023)

地 区	Province or Municipality	社会消费品零售总额（亿元）Total Retail Sales of Social Consumer Goods (100 million yuan)	进出口总额（亿美元）Total Import and Export Volume (100 million dollars)	出口 Export	进口 Import	进出口总额（亿元）Total Import and Export Volume (100 million yuan)	出口 Export	进口 Import
全 国	**National Total**	**471495.2**	**59368.3**	**33800.2**	**25568.0**	**417568.3**	**237725.9**	**179842.4**
北 京	Beijing	14462.7	5187.5	852.7	4334.7	36466.3	6000.1	30466.3
天 津	Tianjing	3820.7	1138.4	516.8	621.6	8004.7	3631.7	4373.0
河 北	Hebei	15040.5	826.6	498.1	328.5	5818.4	3505.5	2312.9
山 西	Shanxi	7981.8	240.4	149.0	91.4	1693.7	1050.3	643.4
内蒙古	Nei Monggol	5374.3	279.1	111.5	167.6	1965.3	785.7	1179.6
辽 宁	Liaoning	10362.1	1089.5	502.8	586.7	7659.6	3535.6	4124.0
吉 林	Jilin	4150.4	238.1	88.9	149.1	1679.1	627.0	1052.1
黑龙江	Heilongjiang	5634.2	423.6	107.9	315.6	2978.3	760.6	2217.7
上 海	ShangHai	18515.5	5990.3	2471.2	3519.1	42121.6	17377.9	24743.7
江 苏	Jiangsu	45547.5	7461.3	4794.4	2666.9	52493.8	33719.1	18774.6
浙 江	Zhejiang	32550.2	6967.8	5073.0	1894.8	48998.0	35665.5	13332.5
安 徽	Anhui	23008.3	1143.9	743.5	400.4	8052.2	5231.2	2821.0
福 建	Fujian	22109.6	2808.1	1672.6	1135.5	19743.5	11766.4	7977.1
江 西	Jiangxi	13659.8	812.4	561.0	251.4	5697.7	3928.5	1769.2
山 东	Shandong	36141.8	4640.6	2761.8	1878.7	32642.6	19430.2	13212.4
河 南	Henan	26004.4	1151.6	750.1	401.5	8107.9	5280.0	2827.9
湖 北	Hubei	24041.9	916.4	616.0	300.4	6449.7	4333.3	2116.4
湖 南	Hunan	20203.3	880.1	572.2	307.9	6175.0	4009.4	2165.6
广 东	Guangdong	47494.9	11802.6	7731.0	4071.6	83040.7	54386.5	28654.2
广 西	Guangxi	8651.6	984.9	515.9	469.1	6936.5	3639.5	3297.0
海 南	Hainan	2511.3	329.2	105.7	223.5	2312.8	742.1	1570.7
重 庆	Chongqing	15130.3	1015.6	680.2	335.3	7137.4	4782.2	2355.2
四 川	Sichuan	26313.4	1361.1	858.1	503.1	9574.9	6033.9	3541.0
贵 州	Guizhou	9011.2	107.9	73.9	34.0	759.8	520.5	239.3
云 南	Yunnan	11560.7	367.7	131.5	236.3	2588.0	926.1	1661.9
西 藏	Tibet	879.8	15.4	13.8	1.6	109.8	98.2	11.5
陕 西	Shaanxi	10759.0	575.4	374.5	200.9	4042.1	2630.9	1411.1
甘 肃	Gansu	4329.7	70.1	17.6	52.4	491.7	123.8	367.9
青 海	Qinghai	987.7	6.9	4.2	2.7	48.7	29.5	19.1
宁 夏	Ningxia	1354.9	29.3	21.4	7.9	205.4	149.8	55.6
新 疆	Xinjiang	3849.7	506.8	428.9	77.8	3573.3	3024.9	548.4

附录B-1 中国香港特别行政区主要社会经济指标
Main Statistical Indicators of Hong Kong Special Administrative Region

指　　标	Item	2000	2010	2020	2022	2023
本地生产总值	**Gross Domestic Product (GDP)**					
按2021年环比物量计算①	At 2021Link Ratios①					
本地生产总值年增长率 (%)	Annual Growth Rate (%)	7.7	6.8	-6.5	-3.7@	3.2@
本地生产总值 (亿港元)	GDP (HKD 100 million)	15596	23245	26941	27624@	28512@
人均本地生产总值 (港元)	Per Capita GDP (HKD)	233993	330921	360124	376038@	378342@
按当年价格计算	At Current Prices					
本地生产总值年增长率 (%)	Annual Growth Rate (%)	4.0	7.1	-5.9	-2.1@	6.5@
本地生产总值 (亿港元)	GDP (HKD 100 million)	13375	17763	26758	28091@	29913@
人均本地生产总值 (港元)	Per Capita GDP (HKD)	200675	252887	357679	382393@	396933@
人口及生命统计	**Population and Vital Events**					
年中人口 (万人)	Mid-year Population (10000 persons)	666.5	702.4	748.1	734.6	753.6
粗出生率 (‰)	Crude Birth Rate (‰)	8.1	12.6	5.8	4.4	4.4#
粗死亡率 (‰)	Crude Death Rate (‰)	5.1	6.0	6.8	8.7	7.2#
劳动、就业	**Labor and Employment**					
劳动人口 (万人)	Labor Force (10000 persons)	337.4	363.1	391.8	377.6	382.2
劳动人口参与率 (%)	Labor Force Participation Rate (%)	61.4	59.6	59.7	58.2	57.3
失业率 (%)	Unemployment Rate (%)	4.9	4.3	5.8	4.3	2.9
政府收支、货币、金融(亿港元)	**Public Accounts, Money and Finance (HKD 100 million)**					
政府收入总额②	Total Government Revenue ②	2251	3765	5642	6222	
政府支出总额②	Total Government Expenditure ②	2329	3014	8160	8105	
货币供应量M3	Money Supply M3	36928	71563	156440	165694	172341
居民消费物价指数③	**Consumer Price Index③**					
(2019年10月至2020年9月=100)	(Oct. 2019 to Sep. 2020 = 100)					
综合消费物价指数	Composite Consumer Price Index	70.9	74.0	99.9	103.3	105.5
工业生产	**Industrial Production**					
工业生产指数④ (2015年=100)	Index of Industrial Production④ (2015=100)		101.9	95.8	101.2	105.0#
工业电力消费量 (万亿焦耳)	Industrial Electricity Consumption (tera joules)	17769	11080	10672	11087	11126
工业煤气消费量 (万亿焦耳)	Industrial Gas Consumption (tera joules)	982	917	1653	1704	1743
运输、旅游	**Transport and Tourism**					
进出香港的货物	Goods in and out of Hong Kong					
总卸下 (万吨)	Total disburden (10000 tons)	13035	17282	18380	12936	12355#
总装上 (万吨)	Total laden (10000 tons)	8692	12882	8900	7601	6923#
集装箱吞吐量⑤ (万标准集装箱单位)	Volume of Containers Handled⑤ (10000 TEUs)	1810	2370	1797	1669	1440
访港旅客⑥ (万人次)	Visitor Arrivals⑥ (10000 person-times)	1306	3603	357	60	3400
酒店入住率 (%)	Hotel Room Occupancy Rate (%)	83	87	46	66	82
对外商品贸易	**External Merchandise Trade**					
港产品出口 (亿港元)	Domestic Exports (HKD 100 million)	1810	695	474	626	656
转口 (亿港元)	Re-exports (HKD 100 million)	13917	29615	38801	44690	41118
进口 (亿港元)	Imports (HKD 100 million)	16580	33648	42698	49275	46450
教育	**Education**					
小学学生人数⑦ (人)	Student Enrolment in Primary Schools⑦ (person)	498175	334415	368255	337549	329780
中学学生人数⑦⑧ (人)	Student Enrolment in Secondary Schools⑦⑧ (person)	490039	486817	343478	333774	341919#

注：本表数据由香港特别行政区政府统计处提供，国家统计局整理编辑。
@数字将于日后进行修订，#为临时数字。
①以环比物量计算的本地生产总值及其组成部分的参照年为2021年。
②财政年度数字。指当年4月1日至第二年3月31日。
③2019年10月起的消费物价指数是根据2019/20年住户开支统计调查所得的开支权数编制。较早的指数则是根据旧的开支权数而经过按比例换算与新基期的指数拼接。
④自2005年统计年度开始，所有工业生产指数均按《香港标准行业分类2.0版》编制。
⑤1998年起，采用一系列新的集装箱吞吐量数字，与1998年以前的数字不可比。
⑥1996年及以后的数字包括澳门访港的非澳门居民旅客人数。
⑦数字包括特殊学校的学生人数。
⑧数字亦包括夜校、技工级课程及毅进文凭课程的学生人数。

Notes: Data in this table are provided by the Census and Statistics Department of the Government of Hong Kong Special Administrative Region, and further prepared and edited by the National Bureau of Statistics.
@Figures are subject to revision as more data become available.
①The chain volume measures of GDP and its components have been re-referenced by 2021.
②Figures are as at end of the financial year. Financial year is from 1 April to 31 March of the next year,unless otherwise specified.
③The CPI from October 2019 is compiled based on the expenditure weights obtained from the 2019 / 20 household expenditure survey. The earlier indices are based on the old expenditure weights and split joint by converted in proportion to the indices of the new base period.
④Since 2005, all indices of industrial production are compiled based on the Hong Kong Standard Industrial Classification (HSIC) Version 2.0.
⑤Since 1998,new figures of container throughput are adopted,and therefore not comparable with the previous years.
⑥Figures of 1996 and after include arrival of non-Macao residents via Macao.
⑦Figures include students enrolled in special schools.
⑧Figures include students enrolled in night schools, technician level courses, and Yi Jin diploma courses.

附录B-2　中国澳门特别行政区主要社会经济指标
Main Statistical Indicators of Macao Special Administrative Region

指　　标	Item	2000	2010	2020	2022	2023
本地生产总值①	**Gross Domestic Product① (GDP)**					
以2021年环比物量计算	At 2021 Link Ratios					
本地生产总值实际增长率（支出法） (%)	Real Growth Rate of GDP by Expenditure	5.7	25.1	-54.3	-21.4	80.5
本地生产总值 (亿澳门元)	GDP (100 million MOP)	1179.5	3434.4	2006.9	1948.6	3518.0
人均本地生产总值(万澳门元)	Per Capita GDP (10000 MOP)	27.4	64.0	29.5	28.7	51.9
按当年价格计算	At Current Prices					
本地生产总值名义增长率（支出法） (%)	Nominal Growth Rate of GDP by Expenditure	3.9	31.1	-54.5	-20.4	92.3
本地生产总值 (亿澳门元)	GDP (100 million MOP)	543.7	2260.0	2024.7	1973.1	3794.8
人均本地生产总值(万澳门元)	Per Capita GDP (10000 MOP)	12.6	42.1	29.7	29.1	55.9
人口及生命统计	**Population and Vital Events**					
年中人口 (万人)	Mid-year Estimates of Population (10000 persons)	43.1	53.7	68.5	67.7	67.9
出生率 (‰)	Crude Birth Rate (‰)	8.9	9.5	8.1	6.4	5.5
死亡率 (‰)	Crude Death Rate (‰)	3.1	3.3	3.3	4.4	4.4
劳动、就业	**Labor**					
劳动人口 (万人)	Labor Force (10000 persons)	20.9	32.4	40.5	37.9	37.5
失业率 (%)	Unemployment Rate (%)	6.8	2.8	2.5	3.7	2.7
对外商品贸易	**External Trade**					
出口 (亿澳门元)	Exports (100 million MOP)	203.8	69.6	108.1	135.2	133.4
本地产品出口 (亿澳门元)	Domestic Exports (100 million MOP)	170.8	23.9	15.6	20.2	15.5
转口 (亿澳门元)	Re-exports (100 million MOP)	33.0	45.7	92.5	115.0	117.9
进口 (亿澳门元)	Imports (100 million MOP)	181.0	441.2	925.6	1398.1	1414.4
工业生产	**Industrial Production**					
工业电力消耗量 (亿千瓦小时)	Industrial Electricity Consumption (100 million kwh)	1.5	1.5	1.4	1.5	1.6
运输、旅游	**Transport and Tourism**					
进出澳门货运车辆数目 (万辆)	Lorries Entering and Departing Macao (10000 times)	45.4	35.8	29.8	34.2	38.3
访澳旅客② (万人次)	Visitor Arrivals② (10000 person-times)	832.3	2496.5	589.7	570.0	2821.3
酒店入住率 (%)	Hotel Room Occupancy Rate (%)	58	80	29	38	82
政府收支、货币、金融	**Government Accounts, Money and Finance**					
政府总收入① (亿澳门元)	Total Government Revenue① (100 million MOP)	153.4	884.9	1016.7	1096.4	949.9
政府总开支① (亿澳门元)	Total Government Expenditure① (100 million MOP)	150.2	383.9	961.3	1021.5	871.6
货币供应（广义货币供应量M2） (亿澳门元)	Money Supply (M2) (100 million MOP)	849.2	2430.5	6923.6	7177.1	7265.8
消费价格指数	**Consumer Price Index**					
(2018年4月至2019年3月=100)	(Apr.2018 to Mar.2019= 100)					
综合消费价格指数	Composite Consumer Price Index	56.90	70.66	102.60	103.70	104.68
教育③	**Education③**					
小学生 (人)	Students in Primary Education (person)	46260	23785	35450	37854	38349
中学生 (人)	Students in Secondary Education (person)	39673	37224	27627	30274	31617
高等教育学生 (人)	Students in Higher Education (person)	9000	25539	39093	49594	55611

注：本表数据由澳门特别行政区政府统计暨普查局提供，国家统计局整理编辑。

①数字在日后得到更多资料时会作出修订。

②自2008年开始，访澳旅客不包括外地雇员及学生等。

③不包括特殊教育学生。第n年的学生人数是指n/n+1学年年底学生人数。2007/2008学年起不包括回归教育学生人数；2010/2011学年起为注册学生人数。

Notes: Data in this table are provided by the Statistics and Census Services of the Government of Macao Special Administrative Region, and further prepared and edited by the National Bureau of Statistics.

①Figures are subject to revision as more data become available.

②Starting from 2008,foreign employees and students are not included in Macao Visitor arrivals.

③Special education students are not included.The number of students in year n refers to the number of students at the end of the n/n+1 academic year. The number of students returning to education will not be included from the 2007/2008 academic year.Starting from the 2010/2011 academic year, statistics only include registered students.

附录C　中国台湾省主要社会经济指标

Main Statistical Indicators of Taiwan Province

指　　标		Item		2000	2010	2020	2022	2023
国民经济核算		**National Accounts**						
本地居民生产总值	(新台币亿元)	Gross National Product	(NT$ 100 million)	104652	144761	204866	233746	242528
本地生产总值	(新台币亿元)	Gross Domestic Product	(NT$ 100 million)	103285	140603	199148	226798	235509
经济增长率	(%)	Economic Growth Rate	(%)	6.3	10.3	3.4	2.6	1.3
人均本地居民生产总值		Per Capita Gross Domestic Product						
新台币元		NT$		471734	625560	868732	1E+06	1037999
美元		USD		15105	19765	29369	33624	33299
居民储蓄总额	(新台币亿元)	Gross Deposits	(NT$ 100 million)	30597	47529	79409	97077	91563
储蓄率	(%)	Deposit Rate		29.2	32.8	38.8	41.5	37.8
人口		**Population**						
户籍登记人口数①	(万人)	Year-end Population①	(10000 persons)	2228	2316	2356	2326	2342
人口自然增加率	(‰)	Natural Population Growth Rate	(‰)	8.08	0.91	-0.34	-2.93	-2.99
人口密度	(人/平方公里)	Population Density	(persons/sq.km)	616	640	651	643	647
劳动、就业		**Labor and Employment**						
劳动力人口	(万人)	Labor Force	(10000 persons)	978	1107	1196	1185	1194
失业率	(%)	Unemployment Rate	(%)	3.0	5.2	3.9	3.7	3.5
工业		**Industry**						
工业生产指数	(2021年=100)	Index of Industrial Production	(2021=100)	38.7	62.3	87.2	98.2	86.1
制造业生产指数	(2021年=100)	Index of Industrial Production	(2021=100)	36.8	60.6	86.5	98.0	85.5
对外贸易		**Foreign Trade**						
贸易额	(亿美元)	Total Value of Imports and Exports	(USD 100 million)					
出口		Exports		1519	2774	3451	4794	4324
进口		Imports		1407	2557	2861	4280	3514
运输、旅游		**Transportation and Tourism**						
铁路客运人数	(亿人次)	Railways	(100 million persons)	4.6	7.8	10.3	8.9	11.3
公路客运人数	(亿人次)	Highways	(100 million persons)	11.5	11.1	10.8	8.4	9.6
航空客运人数	(亿人次)	Airway	(100 million persons)	0.3	0.3	0.1	0.1	0.3
高速公路通行车辆数③	(万辆次)	Vehicles for Motorway Transportation③	(10000 unit-times)	45381	55506	607532	618001	638352
每百人机动车辆数①	(辆)	Vehicles per 100 Persons①	(unit)	76.4	93.8	94.6	98.2	98.8
港埠货物装卸量	(万收费吨)	Inward and Outward Movements Cargo	(10000 tons)	56695	65540	70299	71900	66625
观光	(万人次)	Tourism	(10000 person-times)					
出岛旅客		Outbound Tourists		733	942	234	148	1180
来台湾旅客		Inbound Tourists		262	557	138	90	649
财政、金融		**Public Accounts and Finance**						
赋税实征净额②	(新台币亿元)	Revenue②	(NT$ 100 million)	19298	16222	23987	32479	34562
货币供应量M2①	(新台币亿元)	Money Supply M2①	(NT$ 100 million)	188978	309544	501879	575086	607548
年增长率	(%)	Average Annual Growth Rate	(%)	6.5	5.5	9.4	6.7	5.6
存款①	(新台币亿元)	Deposits①	(NT$ 100 million)	193087	310063	492197	563301	594271
物价年涨跌率	**(%)**	**Price Indices Annual Growth Rate**	**(%)**					
批发		Wholesale Trade Price		1.81	5.46	-7.77	12.42	-1.99
消费者		Consumer Price		1.26	0.97	-0.23	2.95	2.49

注：①年底数。
②为年度资料。
③从2013年12月30日起，国道高速公路由计次收费改为计程电子收费。

Notes: ① Year-end data.
② Annual data.
③Since 30th December 2013, toll for national highway has been charged for mileage instead of charged by the number of times.

附录D-1 部分国家和地区主要经济指标（2022年）

Main Economic Indicators of Some Countries and Territories (2022)

国家和地区	Country or Territory	国内生产总值（亿美元）Gross Domestic Product (USD 100 million)	人均国民总收入（美元）Per Capita Gross National Income (USD)	国内生产总值增长率(%) Growth Rate of GDP (%)	对GDP增长贡献率(%) Contribution Share in GDP Growth (%)		
					第一产业 Primary Industry	第二产业 Secondary Industry	第三产业 Tertiary Industry
世　　界	World	1013257	12869	3.1			
高收入国家	High Income	616675	51451	2.8			
中等收入国家	Middle Income	387810	6266	3.6			
中等偏下收入国家	Lower Middle Income	81715	2527	5.2			
中等偏上收入国家	Upper Middle Income	306095	10549	3.1			
中低收入国家	Low and Middle Income	393098	5682	3.6			
低收入国家	Low Income	5281	723	3.4			
最不发达地区	Least Developed	14271	1234	4.5			
中　　国	China	179632	12850	3.0	10.2	49.7	40.7
巴　　西	Brazil	19201	8140	2.9	-3.1	11.3	84.6
加 拿 大	Canada	21379	52960	3.4	6.1	18.3	75.4
法　　国	France	27791	45290	2.5	0.6	-6.9	101.5
德　　国	Germany	40825	54030	1.8	-1.8	-7.0	98.2
印　　度	India	34166	2390	7.2	6.9	15.0	65.6
印度尼西亚	Indonesia	13191	4580	5.3	5.4	30.1	53.9
意 大 利	Italy	20497	38200	3.7	-0.9	12.1	84.7
日　　本	Japan	42322	42440	1.0	1.3①	66.9①	74.7①
韩　　国	Korea,Rep.	16739	36190	2.6			
马来西亚	Malaysia	4070	11830	8.7		28.6	70.4
墨 西 哥	Mexico	14659	10820	3.9	3.1	30.3	57.7
俄 罗 斯	Russia	22404	12750	-2.1	-11.9	2.4	65.5
新 加 坡	Singapore	4668	67200	3.6			
泰　　国	Thailand	4954	7230	2.6			
英　　国	United Kingdom	30891	49240	4.3	0.5	-2.2	91.1
美　　国	United States	254397	76770	1.9	-3.8①	10.1①	85.9①

注：①2021年数据。
Note:①Data refer to 2021.

附录D-1 续表 continued

国家和地区	Country or Territory	GDP产业构成（%）Structure of GDP by Production Approach (%)			能源生产量（2020年，万吨标准油）Energy Production (2020, 10000 tons of SOE)	能源最终消费量(2020年，万吨标准油) Total Energy Consumption (2020, 10000 tons of SOE)	货物进出口贸易总额（亿美元）Total Merchandise Imports and Exports (USD 100 million)	货物出口总额（亿美元）Merchandise Exports (USD 100 million)	货物进口总额（亿美元）Merchandise Imports (USD 100 million)
		农业增加值占GDP比重 Agriculture	工业增加值占GDP比重 Industry	服务业增加值占GDP比重 Service Industry					
世　界	World	4.3	28.0	63.9①	1467275	1008210	505959	249258	256701
高收入国家	High Income	1.3①	22.4①	70.0①					
中等收入国家	Middle Income	8.8	34.9	52.2					
中等偏下收入国家	Lower Middle Income	15.4	28.8	49.1					
中等偏上收入国家	Upper Middle Income	6.9	36.6	53.0					
中低收入国家	Low and Middle Income	9.0	34.8	52.0					
低收入国家	Low Income	25.0	25.6	33.8					
最不发达地区	Least Developed Countries	18.3	30.6	42.3					
中　国	China	7.3	39.9	52.8	298239	231669	63097	35935	27162
巴　西	Brazil	6.8	20.7	58.9	31440	23239	6264	3341	2922
加拿大	Canada	1.7②	24.1②	67.7②	53912	19113	11810	5991	5819
法　国	France	1.8	17.4	70.3	12715	15094	14361	6179	8183
德　国	Germany	1.1	26.7	62.7	10166	22447	32283	16576	15708
印　度	India	16.6	25.6	48.6	60893	63248	11738	4534	7204
印度尼西亚	Indonesia	12.4	41.4	41.8	44621	15241	5294	2920	2374
意大利	Italy	2.0	23.0	64.8	3417	11779	13463	6570	6893
日　本	Japan	1.0①	28.8①	69.9①	5340	26724	16442	7469	8972
韩　国	Korea,Rep.	1.6	31.8	58.2	5243	18170	14150	6836	7314
马来西亚	Malaysia	8.9	39.2	50.8	9331	5605	6468	3525	2943
墨西哥	Mexico	4.1	32.1	58.8	15387	9858	12045	5782	6263
俄罗斯	Russia	3.9	32.8	54.0	152950	54457	8687	5883	2804
新加坡	Singapore	0.0	24.2	70.9	59	1875	9914	5158	4756
泰　国	Thailand	8.8	35.0	56.2	6125	9441	5903	2871	3032
英　国	United Kingdom	0.7	17.9	71.0	10017	11938	13542	5302	8239
美　国	United States	1.0①	17.9①	77.6①	221433	153973	54401	20643	33758

注：①2021年数据。②2019年数据。
Note:①Data refer to 2021. ②Data refer to 2019.

附录D-2 部分国家和地区国内生产总值

Gross Domestic Product of Some Countries and Territories

单位：亿美元 (USD 100 million)

国家和地区	Country or Territory	2000	2010	2015	2020	2021	2022
世　界	**World**	**338990**	**667071**	**752833**	**852577**	**975297**	**1013257**
高收入国家	High Income	277637	457643	482692	539474	601977	616675
中等收入国家	Middle Income	58302	199707	263064	305784	365289	387810
中等偏下收入国家	Lower Middle Income	13777	45666	57464	66190	75956	81715
中等偏上收入国家	Upper Middle Income	44525	154040	205600	239594	289333	306095
中、低收入国家	Low and Middle Income	60113	205481	267542	310166	369965	393098
低收入国家	Low Income	1868	5942	4507	4380	4650	5281
最不发达地区	Least Developed Countries	2207	7059	9560	11627	12681	14271
中　国	China	12113	60872	110616	146877	178205	179632
中国香港	HongKong SAR,China	1717	2286	3094	3449	3689	3598
中国澳门	Macao SAR,China	68	282	450	253	310	240
阿根廷	Argentina	2842	4236	5947	3857	4879	6311
澳大利亚	Australia	4162	11489	13518	13304	15590	16930
孟加拉国	Bangladesh	534	1153	1951	3739	4163	4602
白俄罗斯	Belarus	127	572	565	614	697	728
巴　西	Brazil	6554	22088	18022	14761	16496	19201
保加利亚	Bulgaria	132	508	508	704	840	903
加拿大	Canada	7448	16173	15565	16476	20015	21379
捷　克	Czech Rep.	618	2091	1880	2460	2818	2905
埃　及	Egypt	998	2190	3294	3838	4247	4767
法　国	France	13656	26452	24392	26474	29594	27791
德　国	Germany	19480	33997	33576	38877	42785	40825
印　度	India	4684	16756	21036	26716	31503	34166
印度尼西亚	Indonesia	1650	7551	8609	10591	11865	13191
伊　朗	Iran	1096	4868	4082	2397	3591	4135
以色列	Israel	1360	2384	3034	4133	4885	5250
意大利	Italy	11467	21361	18366	18975	21554	20497
日　本	Japan	49684	57591	44449	50488	50055	42322
哈萨克斯坦	Kazakhstan	183	1480	1844	1711	1971	2255
韩　国	Korea,Rep.	5762	11437	14660	16443	18184	16739
马来西亚	Malaysia	938	2550	3014	3375	3738	4070
墨西哥	Mexico	7421	11054	12133	11207	13126	14659
蒙　古	Mongolia	11	72	116	133	153	171
缅　甸	Myanmar	89	495	597	790	663	623
荷　兰	Netherlands	4175	8474	7656	9098	10297	10094
新西兰	New Zealand	526	1465	1781	2126	2556	2481
尼日利亚	Nigeria	692	3670	4930	4322	4408	4726
巴基斯坦	Pakistan	995	1967	3000	3004	3485	3747
菲律宾	Philippines	837	2084	3064	3618	3941	4043
波　兰	Poland	1722	4757	4771	5994	6813	6881
罗马尼亚	Romania	373	1700	1779	2514	2858	3007
俄罗斯	Russia	2597	15249	13635	14931	18369	22404
新加坡	Singapore	961	2398	3080	3484	4238	4668
南　非	South Africa	1518	4174	3467	3383	4201	4053
西班牙	Spain	5984	14221	11962	12781	14457	14178
斯里兰卡	Sri Lanka	163	586	851	844	885	744
泰　国	Thailand	1264	3411	4013	5005	5056	4954
土耳其	Turkey	2743	7770	8643	7203	8199	9071
乌克兰	Ukraine	324	1412	910	1566	1998	1605
英　国	United Kingdom	16655	24855	29279	26978	31415	30891
美　国	United States	102509	150490	182060	210605	233151	254397
委内瑞拉	Venezuela	1171	3932				
越　南	Viet Nam	312	1472	2393	3466	3661	4088

附录D-3 部分国家和地区国内生产总值增长率

Growth Rates of GDP of Some Countries and Territories

单位：% (%)

国家和地区	Country or Territory	2000	2010	2015	2020	2021	2022
世　界	**World**	**4.5**	**4.5**	**3.1**	**-3.1**	**6.2**	**3.1**
高收入国家	High Income Countries	4.1	3.0	2.4	-4.2	5.6	2.8
中等收入国家	Middle Income Countries	5.9	7.9	4.5	-1.2	7.3	3.6
中等偏下收入国家	Lower Middle Income Countries	4.4	6.6	5.0	-3.2	6.1	5.2
中等偏上收入国家	Upper Middle Income Countries	6.3	8.3	4.3	-0.7	7.6	3.1
中低收入国家	Low and Middle Income Countries	5.8	7.9	4.4	-1.2	7.2	3.6
低收入国家	Low Income Countries	3.3	6.7	-0.4	0.1	1.8	3.4
最不发达地区	Most Underdeveloped Countries	4.3	6.1	2.7	-0.2	2.6	4.5
中　国	China	8.5	10.6	7.0	2.2	8.4	3.0
中国香港	Hong Kong, China	7.7	6.8	2.4	-6.5	6.4	-3.5
中国澳门	Macao, China	5.7	25.1	-21.5	-54.3	23.5	-21.5
阿根廷	Argentina	-0.8	10.1	2.7	-9.9	10.7	5.0
澳大利亚	Australia	3.9	2.2	2.2	-0.3	2.1	4.3
孟加拉国	Bangladesh	5.3	5.6	6.6	3.4	6.9	7.1
白俄罗斯	Belarus	5.8	7.8	-3.8	-0.7	2.4	-4.7
巴　西	Brazil	4.4	7.5	-3.5	-3.3	5.0	2.9
保加利亚	Bulgaria	4.6	1.6	3.4	-4.0	7.7	3.9
加拿大	Canada	5.2	3.1	0.7	-5.1	5.0	3.4
捷　克	Czech Republi	4.0	2.4	5.4	-5.5	3.6	2.4
埃　及	Egypt	6.4	5.1	4.4	3.6	3.3	6.6
法　国	France	3.9	1.9	1.1	-7.5	6.4	2.5
德　国	Germany	2.9	4.2	1.5	-3.8	3.2	1.8
印　度	India	3.8	8.5	8.0	-5.8	9.1	7.2
印度尼西亚	Indonesia	4.9	6.2	4.9	-2.1	3.7	5.3
伊　朗	Iran	5.8	5.8	-1.4	3.3	4.7	3.8
以色列	Israel	8.7	5.7	2.5	-1.9	8.6	6.8
意大利	Italy	3.8	1.7	0.8	-9.0	8.3	3.7
日　本	Japan	2.8	4.1	1.6	-4.3	2.1	1.0
哈萨克斯坦	Kazakhstan	9.8	7.3	1.2	-2.5	4.3	3.2
韩　国	Korea，Rep.	9.1	6.8	2.8	-0.7	4.3	2.6
马来西亚	Malaysia	8.9	7.4	5.1	-5.5	3.3	8.7
墨西哥	Mexico	5.0	5.0	2.7	-8.7	5.8	3.9
蒙　古	Mongolia	1.1	6.4	2.4	-4.6	1.6	5.0
缅　甸	Myanmar	13.7	9.6	7.0	-9.0	-12.0	4.0
荷　兰	Netherlands	4.2	1.3	2.0	-3.9	6.2	4.3
新西兰	New Zealand	2.9	1.5	3.7	-0.7	5.2	2.9
尼日利亚	Nigeria	5.0	8.0	2.7	-1.8	3.6	3.3
巴基斯坦	Pakistan	4.3	1.5	4.2	-1.3	6.5	4.7
菲律宾	Philippines	4.4	7.3	6.3	-9.5	5.7	7.6
波　兰	Poland	4.6	2.9	4.4	-2.0	6.9	5.3
罗马尼亚	Romania	2.5	-3.9	3.2	-3.7	5.7	4.6
俄罗斯	Russia	10.0	4.5	-2.0	-2.7	5.6	-2.1
新加坡	Singapore	9.0	14.5	3.0	-3.9	8.9	3.6
南　非	South Africa	4.2	3.0	1.3	-6.0	4.7	1.9
西班牙	Spain	5.2	0.2	3.8	-11.2	6.4	5.8
斯里兰卡	Sri Lanka	6.0	8.0	4.2	-4.6	3.5	-7.8
泰　国	Thailand	4.5	7.5	3.1	-6.1	1.5	2.6
土耳其	Turkey	6.9	8.4	6.1	1.9	11.4	5.5
乌克兰	Ukraine	5.9	4.1	-9.8	-3.8	3.4	-29.1
英　国	United Kingdom	4.3	2.2	2.2	-10.4	8.7	4.3
美　国	United States of America	4.1	2.7	2.7	-2.8	5.9	1.9
委内瑞拉	Venezuela	3.7	-1.5				
越　南	Viet Nam	6.8	6.4	7.0	2.9	2.6	8.0

附录D-4 部分国家和地区人均国民总收入

Per Capita Gross National Income of Some Countries and Territories

单位：美元 (USD)

国家和地区	Country or Territory	2000	2010	2015	2020	2021	2022
世 界	**World**	**5521**	**9425**	**10598**	**11057**	**12093**	**12869**
高收入国家	High Income	25378	39259	41712	43946	48348	51451
中等收入国家	Middle Income	1219	3521	4875	5296	5829	6266
中等偏下收入国家	Lower Middle Income	620	1584	2026	2130	2319	2527
中等偏上收入国家	Upper Middle Income	1792	5543	7966	8865	9821	10549
中低收入国家	Low and Middle Income	1156	3301	4484	4824	5296	5682
低收入国家	Low Income	405	1080	738	661	678	723
最不发达地区	Least Developed Countries	304	795	1010	1090	1148	1234
中 国	China	940	4340	7890	10520	11950	12850
中国香港	Hong Kong SAR,China	26930	33620	41180	48550	54370	54370
中国澳门	Macao SAR,China	14580	43710	60760	44420	46350	43680
阿根廷	Argentina	7430	9270	12600	9010	9980	11590
澳大利亚	Australia	21300	46750	60550	53630	57240	60840
孟加拉国	Bangladesh	430	800	1210	2300	2570	2820
白俄罗斯	Belarus	1380	6150	6750	6410	7040	7210
巴 西	Brazil	3910	9610	10160	7910	7850	8140
保加利亚	Bulgaria	1660	7010	7430	9530	11050	13350
加拿大	Canada	22750	44490	47590	43810	48720	52960
捷 克	Czech Rep.	6340	19400	18370	21800	24530	26100
埃 及	Egypt	1370	2250	3160	3010	3520	4100
法 国	France	24990	43970	41130	39250	43810	45290
德 国	Germany	26180	44680	45780	47970	52050	54030
印 度	India	440	1210	1590	1900	2150	2390
印度尼西亚	Indonesia	570	2510	3420	3900	4170	4580
伊 朗	Iran	1770	6110	5480	3270	3510	3980
以色列	Israel	19990	30350	36550	43120	49350	55140
意大利	Italy	21910	37960	33000	32440	36420	38200
日 本	Japan	36810	43910	39380	40870	43450	42440
哈萨克斯坦	Kazakhstan	1270	7440	11380	8710	8880	9620
韩 国	Korea,Rep.	11030	22280	28720	33040	35200	36190
马来西亚	Malaysia	3490	8110	10400	10320	10740	11830
墨西哥	Mexico	6620	9560	10660	8960	9920	10820
蒙 古	Mongolia	460	2010	3850	3720	3730	4260
缅 甸	Myanmar	190	870	1220	1310	1230	1270
荷 兰	Netherlands	28160	53430	49300	50170	58170	60230
新西兰	New Zealand	14070	29670	40660	41590	45770	49090
尼日利亚	Nigeria		2130	2860	2110	2160	2160
巴基斯坦	Pakistan	470	1020	1320	1420	1470	1560
菲律宾	Philippines	1180	2360	3350	3350	3550	3950
波 兰	Poland	4670	12670	13250	15300	16910	18900
罗马尼亚	Romania	1710	8710	9610	12710	14190	15570
俄罗斯	Russia	1710	9980	11780	10750	11760	12750
新加坡	Singapore	23680	44930	53160	55260	63000	67200
南 非	South Africa	3280	6810	6550	6110	6540	6780
西班牙	Spain	15790	31970	28460	27180	30090	32090
斯里兰卡	Sri Lanka	870	2380	3860	3880	4000	3610
泰 国	Thailand	1980	4510	5580	6920	7090	7230
土耳其	Turkey	4260	10380	12080	9160	10010	10640
乌克兰	Ukraine	680	3030	2800	3570	4110	4260
英 国	United Kingdom	29420	41770	44380	38750	45550	49240
美 国	United States	35960	49150	56620	64650	70900	76770
委内瑞拉	Venezuela	4080	11690				
越 南	Viet Nam	380	1370	2480	3450	3590	4010

附录D-5 部分国家和地区人均国内生产总值增长率

Growth Rates of Per Capita GDP of Some Countries and Territories

单位：% (%)

国家和地区	Country or Territory	2000	2010	2015	2020	2021	2022
世　界	**World**	**3.1**	**3.3**	**1.9**	**-4.0**	**5.3**	**2.3**
高收入国家	High Income	3.5	2.4	1.8	-4.6	5.6	2.5
中等收入国家	Middle Income	4.4	6.6	3.2	-2.2	6.4	2.9
中等偏下收入国家	Lower Middle Income	2.4	4.9	3.4	-4.5	4.8	4.1
中等偏上收入国家	Upper Middle Income	5.3	7.5	3.5	-1.2	7.2	2.8
中低收入国家	Low and Middle Income	4.3	6.5	3.0	-2.3	6.1	2.6
低收入国家	Low Income	0.6	3.7	-2.9	-2.7	-0.9	0.7
最不发达地区	Least Developed Countries	1.8	3.6	0.2	-2.6	0.2	2.1
中　国	China	7.6	10.1	6.4	2.0	8.4	3.0
中国香港	Hong Kong SAR,China	6.7	6.0	1.5	-6.2	7.4	-2.6
中国澳门	Macao SAR,China	4.2	21.9	-22.9	-55.2	21.7	-22.4
阿根廷	Argentina	-1.9	9.8	1.6	-10.8	9.7	4.0
澳大利亚	Australia	2.7	0.6	0.7	-1.6	2.0	3.0
孟加拉国	Bangladesh	3.3	4.4	5.3	2.3	5.7	6.0
白俄罗斯	Belarus	6.3	8.0	-4.0	-0.3	3.3	-3.9
巴　西	Brazil	3.0	6.5	-4.4	-3.9	4.4	2.4
保加利亚	Bulgaria	5.1	2.2	4.1	-3.4	8.5	10.6
加拿大	Canada	4.2	2.0	-0.1	-6.1	4.4	1.6
捷　克	Czech Rep.	4.3	2.1	5.2	-5.7	5.4	0.8
埃　及	Egypt	4.2	3.0	2.1	1.8	1.6	4.9
法　国	France	3.2	1.4	0.8	-7.8	6.1	2.1
德　国	Germany	2.8	4.3	0.6	-3.9	3.1	1.1
印　度	India	2.0	7.0	6.7	-6.7	8.2	6.5
印度尼西亚	Indonesia	3.4	4.9	3.7	-2.9	3.0	4.6
伊　朗	Iran	4.1	4.3	-3.6	2.5	4.0	3.0
以色列	Israel	5.8	3.8	0.5	-3.6	6.8	4.8
意大利	Italy	3.7	1.4	0.9	-8.5	8.9	4.1
日　本	Japan	2.6	4.1	1.7	-4.0	2.6	1.5
哈萨克斯坦	Kazakhstan	10.1	5.8	-0.3	-3.8	3.0	-0.1
韩　国	Korea,Rep.	8.2	6.3	2.3	-0.8	4.5	2.8
马来西亚	Malaysia	6.1	5.6	3.5	-6.6	2.1	7.5
墨西哥	Mexico	3.4	3.6	1.5	-9.3	5.2	3.2
蒙　古	Mongolia	0.2	5.0	0.2	-6.4	…	3.5
缅　甸	Myanmar	12.5	8.8	6.1	-9.7	-12.6	3.3
荷　兰	Netherlands	3.5	0.8	1.5	-4.4	5.6	3.3
新西兰	New Zealand	2.3	0.3	1.6	-2.8	4.7	2.6
尼日利亚	Nigeria	2.3	5.1	0.1	-4.2	1.2	0.8
巴基斯坦	Pakistan	1.1	-0.8	2.9	-3.0	4.6	2.7
菲律宾	Philippines	2.1	5.4	4.6	-11.0	4.1	6.0
波　兰	Poland	5.7	3.2	4.5	-1.8	7.4	7.9
罗马尼亚	Romania	2.6	-3.3	3.6	-3.1	6.5	5.0
俄罗斯	Russia	10.5	4.5	-2.2	-2.5	6.0	-2.2
新加坡	Singapore	7.2	12.5	1.8	-3.6	13.5	0.3
南　非	South Africa	3.2	1.8	-0.8	-7.1	3.7	1.1
西班牙	Spain	4.8	-0.3	3.9	-11.6	6.3	5.0
斯里兰卡	Sri Lanka	5.4	7.0	3.7	-5.1	2.4	-7.9
泰　国	Thailand	3.4	6.8	2.6	-6.3	1.3	2.5
土耳其	Turkey	5.4	6.8	4.7	0.9	10.4	4.5
乌克兰	Ukraine	7.0	4.5	-9.4	-3.1	4.4	-17.1
英　国	United Kingdom	3.9	1.4	1.4	-10.7	8.8	4.4
美　国	United States	2.9	1.9	2.0	-3.7	5.8	1.6
委内瑞拉	Venezuela	1.7	-2.8				
越　南	Viet Nam	5.6	5.3	5.9	1.9	1.7	7.2

主要统计指标解释

国民总收入 国内生产总值减去生产税和进口税净额，减去支付给国外的雇员报酬和财产收入，加来自国外的雇员报酬和财产收入（即国内生产总值减去支付给非常住单位的初次收入，加上收到的非常住单位的初次收入）。按市场价格计算国民总收入的另一种方法是各部门所有初次收入的总和。国民总收入即国民生产总值，国民生产总值是以往国民核算中使用的概念。

按购买力平价计算的人均国民总收入 根据购买力平价计算的人均国民总收入。购买力平价国民总收入是用购买力平价比率、以国际元计算的国民总收入。国民总收入中一国际元的购买力等于美国一美元购买力。

香港居民消费价格指数 《香港统计年刊》中称为“消费物价指数”。香港特别行政区政府统计处编制不同的居民消费价格指数数列，以反映消费价格变动对不同开支范围的住户的影响。甲类、乙类及丙类消费价格指数分别根据较低、中等及较高开支范围的住户消费模式编制而成。而综合消费价格指数是根据上述住户的整体开支模式而编制，反映消费价格转变对全体住户的影响。

Explanatory Notes on Main Statistical Indicators

Gross National Income is gross domestic product (GDP) minus net taxes on production and imports, minus remuneration and property income for employees abroad, plus the corresponding items from employees abroad (in other words, GDP minus primary incomes payable to non-resident units plus primary incomes receivable from non-resident units). An alternative approach to measuring GNI at market prices is the sum of gross primary incomes from all sectors. Gross national income is identical to gross national product (GNP), as previously used in national accounts.

Per Capita GNI in PPP is per capita GNI based on purchasing power parity (PPP). PPP GNI is gross national income (GNI) converted to international dollars using purchasing power parity rates. An international dollar has the same purchasing power over GNI as a U.S. dollar has in the United States of America.

Consumer Price Index by Residents in Hong Kong refers to a series of consumer price indices reflected in Hong Kong Annual Digest of Statistics. The series of consumer price indices (CPIs) are compiled by the Census and Statistics Department of Hong Kong Special Administrative Region to reflect the impact of consumer price changes on households in different expenditure ranges. The CPI(A), CPI(B) and CPI(C) are compiled based on the expenditure patterns of households in the relatively low, medium and relatively high expenditure ranges. By aggregating the expenditure patterns of all households covered by the above three indices, a composite CPI is also compiled to reflect the impact of consumer price changes on the household sector as a whole.